ON COOKING

ON COOKING

A TEXTBOOK OF CULINARY FUNDAMENTALS
SECOND CANADIAN EDITION

Sarah R. Labensky
Mississippi University for Women

Alan M. Hause
Fabulous Food Catering

Fred L. Malley
Southern Alberta Institute of Technology

Anthony Bevan
Humber College of Applied Arts and Technology

Settimio Sicoli
Vancouver Community College

With Steven Labensky
Photographs by Richard Embery
Drawings by Stacey Winters Quattrone

Prentice Hall

Toronto

National Library of Canada Cataloguing in Publication Data

Main entry under title:

On cooking : a textbook of culinary fundamentals

2nd Canadian ed.
Includes bibliographical references and index.
ISBN 0-13-062093-9

1. Cookery. I. Labensky, Sarah R.

TX651.O53 2003   641.5   C2001-903646-9

Vice-President, Editorial Director: Michael J. Young
Senior Editor: Sophia Fortier
Senior Developmental Editor: Lise Dupont
Senior Production Editor: Joe Zingrone
Copy Editor: Susan Broadhurst
Proofreaders: Susan Broadhurst and Madeline Koch
Production Manager: Wendy Moran
Page Layout: Debbie Kumpf
Permissions Research: Susan Wallace-Cox
Art Director: Mary Opper
Interior and Cover Design: Sarah Battersby
Cover Image: Premium Stock/Firstlight.ca

3 4 5   06 05 04

Printed and bound in the United States of America.

CONTENTS

PART THREE
COOKING

FOREWORD

Cornelia Volino

Cornelia Volino is a recognized professional chef, educator and culinary consultant. She has worked in various capacities in the hospitality industry — including restaurant management, product distribution and promotion, research and development—and as an associate producer of a television cooking show. She has competed in and judged local and international culinary competitions, and for many years taught culinary arts and coordinated apprenticeship training. Currently, she is a partner of Mediterra, an upscale fish and seafood restaurant, and is establishing an international Internet site to service the hospitality industry. For seven years, Cornelia served on the board of the Escoffier Society of Toronto and is now both the national president of the Canadian Federation of Chefs and Cooks and the continental director of the Americas for the World Association of Cooks Societies.

Canadian culinary educators have long awaited a comprehensive instructional textbook to assist students entering a career in the culinary arts in this country. *On Cooking: A Textbook of Culinary Fundamentals*, Second Canadian Edition, provides a detailed approach to basic cook training in Canada, and introduces the requirements for becoming a great Canadian chef.

In years past, culinary educators in Canada have had to rely on foreign materials that lacked the focus on Canadian techniques, styles, regulations and food products provided in this text. By generating a text that exemplifies Canadian lifestyles and skill sets, the authors are helping to define a culinary culture unique to Canada while ensuring a high standard of learning outcomes.

Culinary students entering the hospitality industry must be equipped to meet the extensive requirements and challenges of their trade. Numerous professional Canadian chefs and their recipes are featured in this text, providing students with the opportunity to explore career paths, food trends and cuisine styles from coast to coast.

This edition of *On Cooking* includes updated meat guidelines reflecting the recent changes in Canadian meat regulations; coverage of emerging technologies and trends, including information on new cooking media (e.g., induction cooking); more detailed content in Chapter 10, "Stocks and Sauces," and Chapter 29, "Pies, Pastries and Cookies"; a more standardized recipe format; and more than 90 new and unique recipes by prominent Canadian chefs.

In addition, the articles and sidebars throughout the book depict a tradition rich in ethnic and cultural influences and provide a foundation in culinary history. This exposure will create an awareness of the expectations and expertise required of an aspiring chef.

In short, this second Canadian edition of *On Cooking* provides a comprehensive framework within which culinary educators can strengthen the skills of tomorrow's cooks and chefs and launch them into careers of culinary excellence. We and generations to come will graciously savour the rewards.

Cornelia Volino
Vancouver

PREFACE

Welcome to the second Canadian edition of *On Cooking: A Textbook of Culinary Fundamentals*. Learning to cook entails much more than simply learning to follow a recipe. Consequently, this is neither a cookbook nor a collection of recipes. It is a carefully designed text intended to teach you the fundamentals of the culinary arts and to prepare you for a rewarding career in the food service industry.

Many chapters have extensive illustrated sections identifying foods and equipment. Throughout the book we emphasize culinary principles, not recipes (although we include more than 500 of them). Whenever possible, we focus on the general procedure, highlighting fundamental principles and skills, whether it be for preparing a yeast bread or grilling a piece of fish. We discuss both the *how* and *why* of cooking. Only then are specific applications and sample recipes given.

Numerous hotel and restaurant chefs throughout Canada have contributed recipes to this book, including some international offerings—usually accompanied by photographs of the dishes as prepared in their kitchens, or of the chefs themselves. These recipes and illustrations allow you to explore the different techniques and presentation styles used by a range of professionals and help to characterize Canadian cuisine.

In order to provide you with a sense of the rich tradition of cookery, informative sidebars on food history, chefs' biographies and other topics are scattered throughout the book. Also included are several short essays by prominent culinarians on topics ranging from tempering chocolate to tasting spicy foods.

We wish you much success in your culinary career and hope this text will continue to inform and inspire you long after graduation.

A Note on the Recipes

Recipes are important and useful as a means of standardizing food preparation and recording information. We include recipes that are primarily designed to reinforce and explain techniques and procedures presented in the text. Many recipe yields are intentionally low in order to be less intimidating to beginning cooks and more useful in small schools and kitchens.

All ingredients are listed in both metric and U.S. measurements. The metric recipes have been written to reinforce the simplicity of the system. Weights for ingredients are used to make food costing easier and to professionalize the recipes. Electronic scales are readily available and inexpensive. U.S. equivalents have been left in volume measures in most cases. Please do not directly compare the metric conversions against U.S. measurements; they are not intended to be identical and adjustments have been made. We strongly recommend that you work only in one system as switching back and forth leads to disappointment in the end product. Each product is unique and there are no magic conversions that work across the spectrum.

Throughout this book, unless otherwise noted, *mirepoix* refers to a preparation of 2 parts onion, 1 part celery and 1 part carrot by weight; *pepper* refers to ground black pepper, preferably freshly ground; *butter* refers to whole, unsalted butter; and *TT* means "to taste."

A nutritional analysis is provided with each recipe. This information is provided as a reference only. There is a 20 percent margin of error, due primarily to choices for specific ingredients and variations in the size of fruits and vegetables. When a recipe offers a choice of ingredients, the first-mentioned ingredient was the one used in the calculations. Ingredients listed as "to taste" (TT) and "as needed" are generally omitted from the analysis. In addition, canola oil and 3.25 percent whole milk are used throughout for "vegetable oil" and "milk," respectively. When the recipe gives a choice of serving or weight, the first mentioned is used.

Recipes marked with the rainbow symbol are considered healthful and may be low in calories, fat, saturated fat and/or sodium; some may also be a good source of vitamins, protein, fibre or calcium. These dishes are not necessarily dietetic; rather, they should be consumed as part of a well-balanced diet.

Detailed procedures for standard techniques (for example, "deglaze the pan" or "monter au beurre") are presented in the text and generally are not repeated in each recipe. No matter how detailed the written recipe, we must assume that you have certain knowledge, skills and judgment.

Variations appear at the end of selected recipes. These give you the opportunity to see how one set of techniques or procedures can be used to prepare different dishes with only minor modifications.

You should also rely upon the knowledge and skill of your instructor or chef for guidance. While some skills and an understanding of theory can be acquired through reading and study, no book can substitute for repeated, hands-on preparation and observation.

Special Features of the Second Canadian Edition

- *Integrated Canadian content throughout the text*. The Second Canadian Edition of *On Cooking* contains Canadian regulations on cuts of meat, grading systems for meat and produce, etc.
- *National Standards* for professional cooks.
- *New recipes by Canadian chefs*. Spotlighting some of the tremendous culinary talent in our country, this collection of contemporary recipes adds a truly Canadian flavour. Accompanied by a photo of the chef and a brief caption describing some of the highlights of his or her career, these recipes will give students a glimpse of the many career paths they can choose from.
- *Updated coverage of emerging technologies and trends throughout the text*.
- *Greater depth in the meat chapters, especially in Chapters 12, "Principles of Meat Cookery," 13, "Beef" and 14, "Veal."*
- *More detail in Chapter 10, "Stocks and Sauces," and Chapter 29, "Pies, Pastries and Cookies."*
- *Clearer differentiation between the basic recipes (see new "Applying the Basics" recipe tabs) and others collected at the end of each chapter.*
- *Improved nutritional analyses*. In keeping with our increasingly health-conscious society, every recipe in the text now has its own nutritional analysis to help readers make informed choices about the foods they prepare.

Supplements

The following ancillary package is available to supplement the text.

- *Instructor's Resource Manual with Test Item File and Transparency Masters*. In addition to handy chapter outlines, lists of key terms, and pertinent discussion questions with answers, this Instructor's Manual contains multiple choice, matching and true–false test questions with an answer key. Test questions are also available in computerized format for easy manipulation.

- *Companion Website.* An online site devoted to *On Cooking* includes an interactive study guide with immediate feedback, over 280 additional recipes, links to other culinary sites, a syllabus builder, tips from the authors, informative supplementary articles on such topics as buffet presentation, and more.
- *Recipe Software on CD-ROM.* This indispensable disk includes all the recipes in the book plus over 280 additional recipes. It automatically generates shopping lists, allowing instructors to customize ingredients, class size and yield. It also allows students and instructors to print out recipes. It includes a link to the text Website.
- *Study Guide.* This Study Guide provides a complete overview of the *On Cooking* text. It includes hundreds of multiple choice, terminology, fill-in-the-blank, short answer, matching, labelling and product identification questions.

Acknowledgments

The authors of the Second Canadian Edition would like to thank a number of people for their invaluable contributions to this edition. At Pearson Education Canada, we have thoroughly enjoyed working with senior acquisitions editor Sophia Fortier, senior developmental editor Lise Dupont, senior production editor Joe Zingrone, and production manager Wendy Moran. Many thanks also to the fine and diligent eye of copy editor Susan Broadhurst.

We are deeply indebted to Howard Selig and Lesleigh Landry for their meticulous work on the nutritional analyses for all of the recipes. In addition, Master pâtissier Hermann Greineder of SAIT proved an invaluable resource on the baking chapters and Gilbert Noussitou of Camosun College provided valuable comments on Chapters 10, "Steaks and Sauces," 12, "Principles of Meat Cookery," 13, "Beef," and 14, "Veal."

We would also like to thank all those who graciously agreed to review the manuscript or who provided feedback throughout the development of the text: Erik Andersen (Camosun College); Kim Coates (Cambrian College); Glen Dahl (Sault College); Jeff Gill (Red River College); Hermann Greineder (Southern Alberta Institute of Technology); Viola Hards (Centennial College); Susan Leswal (Aldergrove Community Secondary School); Steve McCready (New Brunswick Community College); Robert Mitchell (Nova Scotia Community College); Gilbert Noussitou (Camosun College); Mario Ramsay (Algonquin College); John Reimers (Red River College); Stan Townsend (Northern Alberta Institute of Technology); and Ralph Walker (St. Clair College).

This book would not have been possible without the assistance and support of many people who contributed to the first American edition of *On Cooking*. The authors are particularly indebted to Steve Labenksy for his countless hours with a sharp pencil, his comments and criticism and his constant support, as well as to photographer Richard Embery for his talent, professionalism and commitment to quality. The nutritional analyses for the American recipes were prepared by William Miller. Special thanks go to Kristy Riding, Tim Moore and the entire kitchen staff of Continental Catering for their support. Thanks also to Leland Atkinson, Nancy Calomiris, Gaye Ingram, Lisa Kelly, Richard Martinez, Charlotte Morrissey, Ernst Reck, Chantal van de Brug and Stacey Winters Quattrone for their help. We are also grateful to the many chefs, restaurateurs, writers and culinary professionals who provided recipes and essays for this book.

The authors wish to thank the following companies for their generous donations of equipment and supplies: J.A. Henckels Zwillingswerk, Inc., All-Clad Metalcrafters, Inc. and Parrish's Cake Decorating Supplies, Inc. We also wish to thank Shamrock Foods Company, East Coast Seafood of Phoenix Inc., KitchenAid Home Appliances, Taylor Environmental Instruments, Hobart Corporation, Williams-Sonoma, architect Michael Apostolos, and Randy Dougherty of ISF International.

The authors would also like to acknowledge the following reviewers of the Second American Edition for their comments and assistance: George Anbinder (Culinary Arts Department, Newbury College); Neil Becker (New York Restaurant School); Deane Cobber (Columbus State Community College); Linda Cullen (Greater New Bedford Vocational and Technical High School); Albert D'Addario (Newbury College); Janet De Lucia (Cuyahoga Community College); Fred T. Faria (The Hospitality College, Johnson & Wales University); Deborah Foster (Ball State University); Martin Goldman (Mercer County Community College); Joe Harrold (Florida Community College at Jacksonville); Connie Holt (Widener University); William Jarvie (The Hospitality College, Johnson & Wales University); David Kamen (New York Restaurant School); Lisa R. Kennon (Hotel & Restaurant Management, University of North Texas); George Krieger (Baltimore International Culinary College); Lew Lichtman (New York Restaurant School); Deborah K. Lynch (Middlesex County College); John Martin (ATI Career Institute); Fedele Panzarino (New York City Technical College); David F. Schneider (Macomb Community College); Greg Tompkins (California Culinary Academy); Michael Varnava (New York Restaurant School); Michael Vignapiano (New York Restaurant School).

ABOUT THE AUTHORS

Sarah R. Labensky, CCP, is a cookbook author, academic administrator, cooking teacher, working caterer, industry consultant, active community volunteer, and passionate culinary professional. Chef Sarah, as she is affectionately known by her students, is founding director of the Culinary Arts Institute at Mississippi University for Women (. . . and smart men too!). She teaches cooking and management courses, and administers this unique four-year baccalaureate degree program. Prior to joining MUW's faculty, she was a professor of Culinary Arts at Scottsdale Community College (Arizona). Before teaching, Chef Sarah spent many years as a working pastry cook and caterer. She holds a J.D. degree from Vanderbilt University, a B.S. degree *cum laude* in Public Administration from Murray State University (Kentucky), and a Culinary Certificate from Scottsdale Community College (Arizona).

Sarah is co-author of the best-selling culinary textbook, *On Cooking: A Textbook of Culinary Fundamentals*, which was nominated for an IACP/ Julia Child Cookbook award. She also co-authored *Webster's New World Dictionary of Culinary Arts* (Prentice Hall, 1997; 2nd ed., 2000), which was nominated for a James Beard Foundation Book Award, and *Applied Math for Food Service* (Prentice Hall, 1998). She is now series editor for Prentice Hall's culinary arts publications.

Chef Sarah is active in numerous professional organizations. A member of the Board of Directors of the International Association of Culinary Professionals (IACP), she is also a member of The American Culinary Federation, The James Beard Foundation, and Les Dames d'Escoffier. She is a past president of Arizona Women in Food & Wine and served for many years on the board of directors for the Arizona chapter of the American Institute of Wine & Food.

Alan M. "Skip" Hause is the executive chef and owner of What's the Occasion? Catering, Inc. and Fabulous Food in Phoenix, Arizona. His career began in restaurants in the New York area. He excelled and graduated with honours on the dean's list from the Culinary Institute of America. Settling in Phoenix, he worked as the executive chef for a large local catering company. In 1996 he opened his own business with his wife, Chantal.

Active in charity work thought the Southwest, he has supported SOS Taste of the Nation, The Scottsdale Culinary Festival, Tour de Noel, Meals on Wheels at Universal Studios, and Windows of Hope. Chef Hause teaches cooking classes throughout the Phoenix metropolitan area, is actively involved in Careers Through Culinary Arts Program, Inc. (C-CAP), and is an active member of the American Culinary Federation (ACF).

Fred Malley's career includes being an educator, chef, food and beverage manager, caterer, and food stylist. His interest and passion for food began early in life and has continually evolved. He instructs aspiring culinarians at the Southern Alberta Institute of Technology in Calgary and mentors for professional designation. Curriculum development is a particular interest, and he was actively involved in the development of National Occupational Standards for professional cook, line cook, kitchen helper, food and beverage manager, and entry level cook training as a director of the Canadian Tourism Human Resource Council. Fred co-authored "Food Safety and Sanitation" (SAIT), collaborated on "Fundamentals of Canadian Cheeses and Their Uses in Fine Cuisine" (Dairy Farmers of Canada) and provided input into Alberta's Apprentice Cook outline and exams. As a director of the Canadian Federation of Chefs and Cooks, he chaired the Canadian Culinary Institute for five years, the body responsible for professional certification of chefs throughout Canada.

Chef Malley is a certified chef de cuisine (CCC), a DACUM facilitator, and certified for Evolutive Cuisine with Canadian Cheeses (ECCC) with Distinction. Fred is active in the Alberta Culinary Arts Foundation as a director and was a support member for Culinary Team Alberta in 1996. He is a member of Epsilon Pi Tau and holds a degree in Adult Education. His food styling appears internationally for major corporations, and he has ventured into research and development for food companies.

Anthony Bevan, a native of Dublin, Ireland, graduated from the Dublin Institute of Technology's two-year culinary program—one of Europe's top hospitality schools. Upon graduation, he continued his culinary training in Basel, Switzerland. Returning to Ireland, he soon worked his way through the ranks and in a few short years became the youngest executive chef in a high-quality hotel. He led the culinary brigades of other fine hotels and restaurants until finally opening his own leading edge restaurant called "Knocklofty House," in Tipperary, Ireland.

After four successful years at Knocklofty House, Tony moved to Canada and joined the culinary faculty team at Cambrian College, Sudbury. During his tenure at Cambrian (10 years) he became the coordinator for Hospitality Studies, won the "Teaching Excellence Award" and was awarded an Aboriginal name "Gaage Aan Kwod," (meaning "Clear Sky") by members of the Ojibwe First Nation. He played a major role in the establishment of Canada's first fully accredited Aboriginal Culinary Program and Aboriginal Hotel Lodge Management DIP Program for the "Wabnode Institute," programs in which he coordinated and taught. He also led a delegation of Aboriginal community leaders and "Wabnode" culinary students to Ireland, where they participated in an ethno-culinary seminar at the Dublin Institute of Technology and were officially received by the then-president of Ireland, Mary Robinson. He has also been regularly featured on CBC regional radio and written a column for the *Sudbury Star*.

Moving to Toronto in 1997, Tony joined the team at Humber College as a professor in the HRT Alliance culinary program and now enjoys the challenges of being a member of one of Canada's leading edge culinary faculties. In collaboration with seventeen of Toronto's top chefs and with various members of the public and separate school boards, Tony recently developed an exciting initiative called "Chef Alliance" (www.chefalliance.com), whereby high school students have the opportunity to enter into the culinary industry as apprentices while still at school. Tony received the College Innovation of the Year Award from Humber College in 1999 for this achievement. He also devotes his time to creating international work placements for students and graduates of HRT Alliance's culinary programs. As the chair of the Curriculum Advisory Committee for the trade of cook for the Ministry of Training, Colleges and Universities, Tony contributes towards the development of apprenticeship training in Ontario.

Settimio Sicoli graduated from British Columbia's University of Victoria with majors in anthropology and psychology. His culinary journey began when he enrolled in the Professinal Cook Training program at Vancouver Community College. Upon graduation, Settimio served his three-year apprenticeship at Hotel Vancouver, successfully attaining his professional Red Seal designation. He continued his culinary training in Europe, at the Hilton International Hotel in Mainz, Germany. Returning to Canada, he joined the kitchen brigade at the University Club of Vancouver—one of Vancouver's presitigious private business clubs—attaining the position of executive chef.

In March, 1987, Settimio was asked to join the faculty at Vancouver Community College's Culinary Arts Department. During his tenure at the college, Settimio has been instrumental in establishing the first ever Culinary Arts ESL combined skills program and has obtained his Provincial Instuctors Diploma with a post secondary endorsement. He has held the positions of assistant department head and department head of Culinary Arts, and is the former associate dean of the Tourism, Hospitality, and Business Division. He currently instructs various compoments of the Culinary Arts program.

Aside from his instructional responsibilities, Settimio has been active for years in many professional associations. He is past-president and chair of the British Columbia Chefs' Association and is chef director on the Vancouver Branch's Board. He is the CFCC Western Region vice-president of the Canadian Federation of Chefs and Cooks. Settimio is also the founding director of British Columbia's Culinary Arts Foundation; former first vice-president of Canadian Chef Educators; director of both the B.C. Restaurant "FoodService Expo" and Annual Food and Beverage Conference; chairman (since 1994) of the Provincial Cook Training Articulation Committee; and board member of the Trade Advisory Commitee, which reports to the Provincial Cook Training Apprentice Board, now known as the Industry Training Advisory Commission (ITAC).

PART ONE

PROFESSIONALISM

Chefs and cooks must be able to do more than properly prepare and present foods. They must understand traditions and factors influencing change. They are responsible for making sure that the food served is wholesome and safe to eat and that they and those around them work in a safe and efficient manner. Further, chefs and cooks must make sure that the foods they serve are nutritious or at least should offer customers sufficient selection so they can construct a nutritious meal. And, finally, chefs and cooks are responsible for producing food in a cost-effective manner as well as accurately calculating, tracking and controlling the cost of food and labour in the kitchen.

Part One opens with a chapter on professionalism. It traces the history of chefs, cooks and restaurants, discusses the modern food service operation and factors influencing its development and explains what attributes an apprentice cook must have to become a professional chef. The following chapters address food safety and sanitation, nutrition, menu planning and food costing.

CHAPTER 1
PROFESSIONALISM

> *"Cookery is become an art, a noble
> science; cooks are gentlemen."*
> —Robert Burton, British author, 1621

LEARNING OUTCOMES

After studying this chapter you will be
able to:

+ name key historical figures responsible for developing food service
  professionalism
+ discuss the development of the
  modern food service industry
+ explain the organization of classical
  and modern kitchen brigades
+ explain the role of the professional
  chef in modern food service
  operations
+ identify the attributes an apprentice
  or student cook needs to become a
  professional chef

*ubstitute "professionals" for "gentlemen" and Burton's words
are as true today as they were almost four hundred years ago. Like
the fine arts, great cookery requires taste and creativity, an appreciation of beauty and a mastery of technique. Like the sciences, successful cookery demands a certain level of knowledge and an
understanding of basic principles. And, like the "gentlemen" of
Burton's days, today's professional chefs must exercise sound judgment and be committed to achieving excellence in their endeavours.*

*This books helps implement Burton's philosophy. It describes foods
and cooking equipment, explains culinary principles and cooking
techniques and provides recipes utilizing these principles and techniques. This book cannot, however, provide taste, creativity, commitment and judgment. For these we rely upon you.*

CHEFS AND RESTAURANTS

Cooks have produced food in quantity for as long as people have eaten together.
For millennia, chefs have catered to the often elaborate dining needs of the
wealthy and powerful, whether they be Asian, Native Canadian, European or
African. And for centuries, vendors in China, Europe and elsewhere have sold to
the public foods they prepared themselves or bought from others.

But the history of the professional chef is of relatively recent origin. Its cast
is mostly French and it is intertwined with the history of restaurants. For only
with the development of restaurants during the late 18th and early 19th centuries were chefs expected to produce, efficiently and economically, different
dishes at different or the same times for different diners.

The 18th Century—Boulanger's Restaurant

The word "restaurant" is derived from the French word *restaurer* (to restore).
Since the 16th century, the word "restorative" had been used to describe rich
and highly flavoured soups or stews capable of restoring lost strength.
Restoratives, like all other cooked foods offered and purchased outside the
home, were made by guild members. Each guild had a monopoly on preparing certain food items. For example, during the reign of Henri IV of France
(1553–1610), there were separate guilds for *rôtisseurs* (who cooked *la grosse
viande*, the main cuts of meat), *pâtissiers* (who cooked poultry, pies and tarts),
tamisiers (who baked breads), *vinaigriers* (who made sauces and some stews,
including some restoratives), *traiteurs* (who made ragouts) and *porte-chapes*
(caterers who organized feasts and celebrations).

The French claim that the first modern restaurant opened one day in 1765
when a Parisian tavernkeeper, a Monsieur Boulanger, hung a sign advertising
the sale of his special restorative, a dish of sheep feet in white sauce. His establishment closed shortly thereafter as the result of a lawsuit brought by a guild
whose members claimed that Boulanger was infringing on their exclusive right
to sell prepared dishes. Boulanger triumphed in court and later reopened.

Boulanger's establishment differed from the inns and taverns that had existed throughout Europe for centuries. These inns and taverns served foods prepared (usually off-premises) by the appropriate guild. The food—of which there was little choice—was offered by the keeper as incidental to the establishment's primary function: providing sleeping accommodations or drink. Customers were served family-style and ate at communal tables. Boulanger's contribution to the food service industry was to serve a variety of foods prepared on premises to customers whose primary interest was dining.

Several other restaurants opened in Paris during the succeeding decades, including the Grande Taverne de Londres in 1782. Its owner, Antoine Beauvilliers (1754–1817), was the former steward to the Comte de Provence, later King Louis XVIII of France. He advanced the development of the modern restaurant by offering his wealthy patrons a menu listing available dishes during fixed hours. Beauvilliers' impeccably trained wait staff served patrons at small, individual tables in an elegant setting.

The French Revolution (1789–1799) had a significant effect on the budding restaurant industry. Along with the aristocracy, guilds and their monopolies were generally abolished. The revolution also allowed the public access to the skills and creativity of the well-trained, sophisticated chefs who had worked in the aristocracy's private kitchens. Although many of the aristocracy's chefs either left the country or lost their jobs (and, some, their heads), a few opened restaurants catering to the growing urbanized middle class.

The Early 19th Century— *Carême and* Grande Cuisine

As the 19th century progressed, more restaurants opened, serving a greater selection of items and catering to a wider clientele. By mid-century, there were several large, grand restaurants in Paris serving elaborate meals, decidedly reminiscent of the *grande cuisine* (also known as *haute cuisine*) of the aristocracy. **Grande cuisine**, which arguably reached its peak of perfection in the hands of Antonin Carême, was characterized by meals consisting of dozens of courses of elaborately and intricately prepared, presented, garnished and sauced foods. Other restaurateurs blended the techniques and styles of *grande cuisine* with the simpler foods and tastes of the middle class (*cuisine bourgeoisie*) to create a new cuisine simpler than *grande cuisine* but more than mere home cooking.

The Late 19th Century— *Escoffier and* Cuisine Classique

Following the lead set by the French in both culinary style and the restaurant business, restaurants opened in the Americas and throughout Europe during the 19th century. Charles Ranhofer (1836–1899) was the first internationally renowned chef of an American restaurant, Delmonico's in New York City. In 1893 Ranhofer published his "franco-american" encyclopedia of cooking, *The Epicurean*, containing more than 3500 recipes.

One of the finest restaurants outside of France was the dining room at London's Savoy Hotel, opened in 1898 under the directions of Cesar Ritz (1850–1918) and Auguste Escoffier. Escoffier is generally credited with refining the *grande cuisine* of Carême to create *cuisine classique* or **classic cuisine**. By doing so, he brought French cuisine into the 20th century.

✦✦✦

MARIE-ANTOINE (ANTONIN) CARÊME
(1783–1833)

Carême, known as the "cook of kings and the king of cooks," was an acknowledged master of French *grande cuisine*. Abandoned on the streets of Paris as a child, he worked his way from cook's helper in a working-class restaurant to become one of the most prestigious chefs of his (or, arguably, any other) time. During his career he was chef to the famous French diplomat and gourmand Prince de Talleyrand, the Prince Regent of England (who became King George IV), Tsar Alexander I of Russia and Baron de Rothschild, among others.

His stated goal was to achieve "lightness," "grace," "order" and "perspicuity" in the preparation and presentation of food. As a *pâtissier*, he designed and prepared elaborate and elegant pastry and confectionery creations, many of which were based on architectural designs. (He wrote that "the fine arts are five in number, namely: painting, sculpture, poetry, music, architecture—the main branch of which is confectionery.") As a showman, he garnished his dishes with ornamental hatelets (skewers) threaded with colourful ingredients such as crayfish and intricately carved vegetables, and presented his creations on elaborate socles (bases). As a *saucier*, he standardized the use of roux as a thickening agent, perfected recipes and devised a system for classifying sauces. As a *garde-manger*, Carême popularized cold cuisine, emphasizing moulds and aspic dishes. As a culinary professional, he designed kitchen tools, equipment and uniforms.

As an author, he wrote and illustrated important texts on the culinary arts, including *Le Maître d'hotel français* (1822), describing the hundreds of

Photo courtesy of Barbara Wheaton.

dishes he personally created and cooked in the capitals of Europe; *Le Pâtissier royal parisien* (1825), containing fanciful designs for *les pieces montées*, the great decorative centre-pieces that were the crowning glory of grand dinners; and his five-volume masterpiece on the state of his profession, *L'Art de la cuisine au XIXe siècle* (1833), the last two volumes of which were completed after his death by his associate Plumerey. Carême's writings almost single-handedly refined and summarized five hundred years of culinary evolution. But his treatises were not mere cookbooks. Rather, he analyzed cooking, old and new, emphasizing procedure and order and covering every aspect of the art known as *grande cuisine*.

Carême died before the age of 50, burnt out, according to Laurent Tailhade, "by the flame of his genius and the coal of the spits." But this may have been the glory he sought, for he once wrote:

> Imagine yourself in a large kitchen at the moment of a great dinner. … [S]ee twenty chefs coming, going, moving with speed in this cauldron of heat, look at the great mass of charcoal, a cubic metre for the cooking of entrees, and another mass on the ovens for the cooking of soups, sauces, ragouts, for frying and the water baths. Add to that a heap of burning wood in front of which four spits are turning, one which bears a sirloin weighing 45–50 pounds, the other fowl or game. In this furnace everyone moves with speed; not a sound is heard, only the chef has a right to speak, and at the sound of his voice, everyone obeys. Finally, the last straw; for about half an hour, all windows are closed so that the air does not cool the dishes as they are being served. This is the way we spend the best years of our lives. We must obey even when physical strength fails, but it is the burning charcoal that kills us. … [C]harcoal kills us but what does it matter? The shorter the life, the greater the glory.

The 20th Century—Point and Nouvelle Cuisine

This century has witnessed a trend towards lighter, more naturally flavoured and more simply prepared foods. Fernand Point was a master practitioner of this movement. But this master's goal of simplicity and refinement was carried to even greater heights by a generation of chefs Point trained: principally, Paul

AUGUSTE ESCOFFIER
(1846–1935)

Escoffier's brilliant culinary career began at the age of 13 in his uncle's restaurant and continued until his death at the age of 89. Called the "Emperor of the world's kitchens," he is perhaps best known for defining French cuisine and dining during *La Belle Époque* (the "Gay Nineties").

Unlike Carême, Escoffier never worked in an aristocratic household. Rather, he exhibited his culinary skills in the dining rooms of the finest hotels in Europe, including the Place Vendôme in Paris and the Savoy and Carlton Hotels in London.

Escoffier did much to enhance the *grande cuisine* that arguably reached its perfection under Carême. Crediting Carême with providing the foundation for great—that is, French—cooking, Escoffier simplified the profusion of flavours, dishes and garnishes typifying Carême's work. He also streamlined some of Carême's overly elaborate and fussy procedures and classifications. For example, he reduced Carême's elaborate system of classifying sauces into the five families of sauces still recognized today. Escoffier sought simplicity and aimed for the perfect balance of a few superb ingredients. Some consider his refinement of *grande cuisine* to have been so radical as to credit him with the development of a new

cuisine referred to as *cuisine classique* (classic or classical cuisine).

His many writings include *Le Livre des menus* (1912), in which, discussing the principles of a well-planned meal, he analogizes a great dinner to a symphony with contrasting movements that should be appropriate to the occasion, the guests and the season, and *Ma cuisine* (1934), surveying *cuisine bourgeoisie*. But his most important contribution is a culinary treatise intended for the professional chef entitled *Le Guide culinaire* (1903). Still in use today, it is an astounding collection of more than five thousand classic cuisine recipes and garnishes. In it, Escoffier emphasizes the mastery of techniques, the thorough understanding of cooking principles and the appreciation of ingredients: attributes he considered the building blocks professional chefs should use to create great dishes.

Escoffier was honoured as a Chevalier of the French Legion of Honour in 1920 for his work in enhancing the reputation of French cuisine.

Bocuse, Jean and Pierre Troisgros, Alain Chapel, François Bise and Louis Outhier. They, along with Michel Guérard and Roger Vergé, were the pioneers of **nouvelle cuisine** in the early 1970s.

Their culinary philosophy was premised on the rejection of overly rich, needlessly complicated dishes. These chefs emphasized healthful eating. The ingredients must be absolutely fresh and of the highest possible quality; the cooking methods should be simple and direct whenever possible. The

FERNAND POINT
(1897–1955)

A massive man with a monumental personality, Point refined and modernized the classic cuisine of Escoffier. By doing so, he laid the foundations for *nouvelle cuisine*.

Point received his early training in some of the finest hotel-restaurant kitchens in Paris. In 1922 he and his family moved to Vienne, a city in southeast France near Lyon, and opened a restaurant. Two years later his father left the restaurant to Fernand, who renamed it *La Pyramide*. During the succeeding years it became one of the culinary wonders of the world.

Point disdained dominating sauces and distracting accompaniments and garnishes. He believed that each dish should have a single dominant ingredient, flavour or theme; garnishes must be simple and match "like a tie to a suit." Procedure was of great importance. He devoted equal efforts to frying an egg and creating the marjolaine (a light almond and hazelnut spongecake filled with chocolate and praline buttercreams). His goal was to use the finest of raw ingredients to produce perfect food that looked elegant and simple. But simplicity was not easy to achieve. As he once said, "A bearnaise sauce is simply an egg yolk, a shallot, a little tarragon vinegar, and butter, but it takes years of practice for the result to be perfect."

accompaniments and garnishes must be light and must contribute to an overall harmony; the completed plates must be elegantly designed and decorated. Following these guidelines, some traditional cooking methods have been applied to untraditional ingredients, and ingredients have been combined in new and previously unorthodox fashions. For chefs with taste, skill, knowledge and judgment, this works.

INFLUENCES ON MODERN FOOD SERVICE OPERATIONS

From Monsieur Boulanger's humble establishment, a great industry has grown. Today there are more than 60 000 restaurants in Canada, as well as institutional and catering facilities. The dramatic growth and diversification of the food service industry are due in part to the Industrial Revolution and the social and economic changes it wrought, including the introduction of new technologies, foods, concerns and consumers.

New Technologies

Technology has always had a profound effect on cooking. For example, the development of clay and, later, metal vessels that could contain liquids and withstand as well as conduct heat offered prehistoric cooks the opportunity to stew, make soups and porridge, pickle and brine foods and control fermentation. But it was not until the rapid technological advances fostered by the Industrial Revolution that anything approaching the modern kitchen was possible.

One of the most important advancements was the introduction of the cast-iron stove. Prior to the 19th century, most cooking was done on spits or grills or in cauldrons or pots set on or in a wood- or coal-burning hearth. Hearthside cooking did not lend itself well to the simultaneous preparation of many items nor to items requiring constant and delicate attention. With the introduction of cast-iron stoves during the 1800s (first wood- and coal-burning, then, by mid-century, gas and, by the early 20th century, electric), cooks could more comfortably and safely approach the heat source and control its temperatures. They were also able to prepare efficiently and hold for later use or service a multitude of smaller amounts of items requiring different cooking methods or ingredients. This is a necessity at a restaurant simultaneously catering to different diners' demands.

Also of great importance were developments in food preservation and storage techniques. For thousands of years, food had been preserved by sun-drying, salting, smoking, pickling, sugar-curing or fermenting. Although useful, these procedures destroy or distort the appearance and flavour of most foods. By the early 19th century, preserving techniques that had minimal effect on appearance and flavour began to emerge. For example, by 1800 the Frenchman François Appert successfully "canned" foods by subjecting foods stored in sterilized glass jars to very high heat. An early mechanical refrigerator was developed by the mid-1800s; soon reliable iceboxes, refrigerators and, later, freezers were available. During the 20th century, freeze-drying, vacuum-packing and irradiation have become common preservation techniques.

While advancements were being made in preservation and storage techniques, developments in transportation technology were also underway. During the 19th century, steam-powered ships and railroads were able to bring foods quickly to market from distant suppliers. Indeed, by the early 1900s, live

Atlantic oysters were available on the western plains. During the 20th century, temperature-controlled cargo ships, trains, trucks and airplanes all have been used as part of an integrated worldwide food transportation network.

Combined with dependable food preservation and storage techniques, improved transportation networks have freed chefs from seasonal and geographic limitations in their choice of foods and have expanded consumers' culinary horizons.

Engineering advancements also have facilitated or even eliminated much routine kitchen work. Since the start of the Industrial Revolution, chefs have come to rely increasingly on mechanical and motorized food processors, mixers and cutters as well as a wealth of sophisticated kitchen equipment such as high carbon stainless steel knife blades, convection steamers and combitherm ovens.

New Foods

Modern food preservation, storage and transportation techniques have made both fresh and exotic foods regularly available to chefs and consumers. Many of these foods are themselves more wholesome as the result of progress in agriculture and animal husbandry.

Advancements in agriculture such as the switch from organic to chemical fertilizers and the introduction of pesticides and drought- or pest-resistant strains have resulted in increased yields of crops. Traditional hybridization techniques and, more recently, genetic engineering have produced new or improved grains and, for better or for worse, fruits and vegetables that have a longer shelf life and are more amenable to mass-production handling, storage and transportation methods. Organic production is re-emerging in the marketplace in response to consumer demands for more natural foods.

Likewise, advancements in animal husbandry and aquaculture have led to a more reliable supply of leaner, healthier meat, poultry and fish. Moreover, foods found traditionally only in the wild (for example game, wild rice and many mushrooms) are now being raised commercially and are routinely available.

Food preservation and processing techniques have also led to the development of packaged, prepared convenience foods. After careful thought and testing, today's chef can rely on many of these products. Doing so allows greater flexibility and more time to devote to other preparations.

New Concerns

Consumer concerns about nutrition and diet, particularly during the last decade or so, have fuelled changes in the food service industry. Obviously, what we eat affects our health. Adequate amounts of certain nutrients promote good health by preventing deficiencies; good nutrition also helps prevent chronic diseases and increases longevity. Chefs should provide their customers with nutritious foods.

The public has long been concerned about food safety. Federal, provincial and local governments have helped promote food safety by inspecting and grading meats and poultry, regulating label contents for packaged foods and setting sanitation standards. All these standards, especially sanitation standards, affect the way foods are prepared, stored and served.

Concerns about nutrition and food safety have resulted in renewed interest in organically grown fruits and vegetables and free-range-raised animals. Consumers are more aware of additives and preservatives used in commercial food production.

◆◆◆

CULINARY FRENCH

Perhaps one of the most enduring legacies of French chefs and culinarians is the common usage of many French words in today's professional kitchens. Some, like *canapé* and *bain marie*, are simply the name of a food item or piece of equipment of French origin. Others, such as *sauté*, are French verbs with no equally terse and descriptive English counterpart. Still others, for example *julienne*, are not only used as nouns (julienne of carrot), but also as verbs (to julienne a carrot) and adjectives (julienned carrot). Often we forget the origins of these words and spell them without the original accent marks.

Here we list just a few of the more commonly encountered culinary French terms. As you study this book, note how many other words are of French origin.

Bain marie (bane mah-ree)—a hot-water bath for gently cooking foods or keeping cooked foods hot; the container holding the food in the hot-water bath is also referred to as a bain marie.

Brunoise (broo-nwahz)—cube-shaped cuts (1–2 mm × 1–2 mm × 1–2 mm/1/16 inch × 1/16 inch × 1/16 inch) of vegetables or other foods.

Canapé (kahn-ah-pay)—an hors d'oeuvre (another French term, meaning appetizer) usually composed of a small piece of bread or toast topped with a savoury spread and garnish.

Chef (chehf)—literally, "leader" or "chief," the person in charge of a kitchen or department.

Demi-glace (de-me glass)—literally, "half-glaze," a mixture of brown stock and brown sauce reduced by half.

Ganache (gah-nasch)—a rich pastry or candy filling made with chocolate, heavy cream and other flavourings.

Julienne (ju-lee-en)—noun: stick-shaped cuts (1–2 mm × 1–2 mm × 2.5–5 cm/1/16 inch × 1/16 inch × 1–2 inches) of vegetables or other foods; verb: to cut food into the stick-shaped pieces; adjective: stick-shaped.

Mayonnaise (may-o-nayz)—a basic cold emulsion sauce made of egg yolks and oil and seasoned with vinegar, mustard and seasonings.

Mirepoix (meer-pwa)—a mixture of onions, carrots and celery, used to flavour stocks, stews and other dishes.

Mise en place (meez on plahs)—literally, "everything in place," the preparation and assembly of all ingredients and equipment needed before a dish can be cooked.

Purée (pur-ray)—noun: food that is processed by mashing, straining or fine chopping to achieve a smooth pulp; verb: to process food to achieve a smooth pulp.

Rondeau (ron-doe)—a shallow, wide, straight-sided pot with two loop handles.

Roux (roo)—a thickener for sauces made by cooking together equal weights of fat and flour.

Sachet (sa-shay)—or Sachet d'épices (sa-shay day pees), literally "bag of spices," aromatic ingredients such as bay leaf, thyme, cloves, peppercorns and parsley stems, tied in a cheesecloth bag and used to flavour stocks and other dishes.

Sauté (saw-tay)—to cook in an open pan in a small amount of fat at high temperature.

Sous-chef (sue chehf)—literally "under chef," the chef who is second in command of a kitchen.

Vinaigrette (vih-nay-greht)—a temporary emulsion of oil and vinegar seasoned with herbs, spices and other flavourings.

New Consumers

Demographic and social changes have contributed to the diversification of the food service industry by creating or identifying new consumer groups with their own desires or needs. By tailoring their menu, prices and decor accordingly, food service operations cater to consumers defined by age (baby boomers and seniors, in particular), type of household (singles, couples and families), income, education and geography.

Since the previous century, especially in the decades following World War II, there has also been a rapid increase in the number and type of institutions providing food services. These include hospitals, schools, retirement centres, hotels and resorts (which may, in turn, have fine dining, coffee shop, banquet and room service facilities), factories and office complexes. Each of these institutions presents the professional chef with unique challenges, whether they be culinary, dietary or budgetary.

Through travel or exposure to the many books and magazines about food, consumers are becoming better educated and more sophisticated. Educated consumers provide a market for new foods and cuisines as well as an appreciation for a job well done.

Although some consumers may frequent a particular restaurant because its chef or owner is a celebrity or the restaurant is riding high on a crest of fad or fashion, most consumers choose a restaurant—whether it be a fast-food burger place or an elegant fine dining restaurant—because it provides quality food at a cost they are willing to pay. To remain successful, then, the restaurant must carefully balance its commitment to quality with marketplace realities.

THE FOOD SERVICE OPERATION

To function efficiently, a food service operation must be well organized and staffed with appropriate personnel. This staff is traditionally called a **brigade**. Currently we refer to the "team," and sometimes the chef's title is kitchen leader. Although a chef will be most familiar with the back of the house or kitchen brigade, he or she should also understand how the dining room or front of the house operates. Staffing any food service facility ultimately depends on the type and complexity of the menu. (Types and styles of menus are discussed in Chapter 4, Menu Planning and Food Costing.)

The Classic Kitchen Brigade

Escoffier is credited with developing the kitchen brigade system used in large restaurant kitchens. From the chaos and redundancy found in the private kitchens of the aristocracy, he created a distinct hierarchy of responsibilities and functions for commercial food service operations.

At the top is the *chef de cuisine* or *chef*, who is responsible for all kitchen operations, developing menu items and setting the kitchen's tone and tempo.

His or her principal assistant is the *sous-chef* (the under chef or second chef), who is responsible for scheduling personnel and replacing the chef and station chefs as necessary. The *sous-chef* may function as the *aboyeur* (expediter or announcer), who accepts the orders from the dining room, relays them to the various station chefs and then reviews the dishes before service. Point-of-sales systems have modified this practice.

The *chefs de partie* (station chefs) produce the menu items and are under the direct supervision of the chef or *sous-chef.* Previously, whenever a cook needed an item, he or his assistants produced it; thus several cooks could be making the same sauce or basic preparation. Under Escoffier's system, each station chef is assigned a specific task based upon either cooking method and equipment or the category of items to be produced. They include:

♦ The *saucier* (sauté station chef), who holds one of the most demanding jobs in the kitchen, is responsible for all sautéed items and most sauces.

+ The *poissonier* (fish station chef) is responsible for fish and shellfish items and their sauces. This position is occasionally combined with the sauté station.

+ The *grillardin* (grill station chef) is responsible for all grilled items.

+ The *friturier* (fry station chef) is responsible for all fried items.

+ The *rôtisseur* (roast station chef) is responsible for all roasted items and jus or other related sauces. The grill and fry stations are sometimes subsumed into the roast station.

+ The *potager* (soup station chef) is responsible for soups and stocks.

+ The *legumier* (vegetable station chef) is responsible for all vegetable and starch items.

+ The *potager* and *legumier* stations are often combined into a single vegetable station whose chef is known as the *entremetier*. *Entremets* were the courses served after the roast and were usually composed of vegetables, fruits, fritters or sweet items (the sorbet served before the main course in some contemporary restaurants is a vestigial *entremet*).

+ The *garde-manger* (pantry chef) is responsible for buffets and cold food preparations, including salads and salad dressings, cold appetizers, charcuterie items, pâtés, terrines and similar dishes. The *garde-manger* supervises:

    The *boucher* (butcher), who is responsible for butchering meats and poultry (fish and shellfish are usually fabricated by the fish station chef).

    The chefs responsible for hors d'oeuvre and breakfast items.

+ The *tournant*, also known as the roundsman or swing cook, works where needed, often covering for the *chefs des parties'* days off.

+ The *pâtissier* (pastry chef) is responsible for all baked items, including breads, pastries and desserts. Unlike the several station chefs, the *pâtissier* is not necessarily under the *sous-chef*'s direct supervision. The *pâtissier* supervises the following:

    The *boulanger* (bread baker), who makes the breads, rolls and baked dough containers used for other menu items (for example, *bouchées* and *feuilletés*).

    The *confiseur*, who makes candies and petits fours.

    The *glacier*, who makes all chilled and frozen desserts.

    The *décorateur*, who makes showpieces and special cakes.

+ Depending upon the size and needs of any station or area, there are one or more *demi-chefs* (assistants) and *commis* (apprentices) who work with the station chef or pastry chef to learn the area.

The Modern Kitchen Brigade

Today most food service operations utilize a simplified version of Escoffier's kitchen brigade.

The **executive chef**, working chef or kitchen leader is a team player who coordinates kitchen activities and directs the kitchen staff's training and work efforts. Taking into consideration factors such as food costs, food availability and popularity as well as labour costs, kitchen skills and equipment, the executive chef plans menus and creates recipes. He or she sets and enforces nutrition, safety and sanitation standards and participates in (or at least observes) the preparation and presentation of menu items to ensure that quality standards are rigorously and consistently maintained. The chef or kitchen leader may also be responsible for purchasing food items and, often, equipment. In

◆◆◆

THE DINING ROOM

Like the back-of-the-house (i.e., kitchen) staff, the front-of-the-house (i.e., dining room) staff is also organized into a brigade. The dining room brigade is led by the **dining room manager** (French *maître d'hotel* or *maître d'*), who generally trains all service personnel, oversees wine selections and works with the chef to develop the menu. He or she organizes the seating chart and may also seat the guests. Working with this manager are:

The **wine steward** (French *chef de vin* or *sommelier*), who is responsible for the wine service, including purchasing wines, assisting guests in selecting wines and then serving the wines.

The **headwaiter** (French *chef de salle*), who is responsible for service throughout the dining room or a section of it. In smaller operations, his or her role may be assumed by the *maître d'* or a captain.

The **captains** (French *chefs d'étage*), who are responsible for explaining the menu to guests and taking their orders. They are also responsible for any tableside preparations.

The **front waiters** (French *chefs de rang*), who are responsible for ensuring that the tables are set correctly for each course, foods are delivered properly to the right tables and the needs of the guests are met.

The **backwaiters** (French *demi-chefs de rang* or *commis de rang*, also known as dining room attendants or buspersons), who are responsible for clearing plates, refilling water glasses and other general tasks appropriate for new dining room workers.

Whether a restaurant uses this entire array of staff depends upon the nature and size of the restaurant and the type of service provided. With **American service** there is one waiter (also called a server) who takes the order and brings the food to the table. The table is then cleaned by a dining room attendant. With **French service** there are two waiters: a captain and a waiter. The captain takes the order, does the tableside cooking and brings the drinks, appetizers, entrees and desserts to the table. The waiter serves bread and water, clears each course, crumbs the table and serves the coffee. With **Russian service**, the entree, vegetables and potatoes are served from a platter onto a plate by the waiter. With **buffet service**, usually found in specialty restaurants and some institutional settings such as schools and correctional facilities, diners generally serve themselves or are served by workers assigned to specific areas of the buffet. Restaurants offering buffet service generally charge by the meal; if they charge by the dish they are known as cafeterias.

some food service operations, the executive chef may assist in designing the menu, dining room and kitchen. He or she also educates the dining room staff so that they can correctly answer questions about the menu. The chef may also work with food purveyors to learn about new food items and products, as well as with equipment vendors, food stylists, restaurant consultants, public relations specialists, sanitation engineers, nutritionists and dietitians.

The executive chef is assisted by a **sous-chef** or **executive sous-chef**, who participates in, supervises and coordinates the preparation of menu items. His or her primary responsibility is to make sure that the food is prepared, portioned, garnished and presented according to the standards established by the executive chef. The sous-chef may be the cook principally responsible for producing menu items and supervising the kitchen.

Large hotels and conference centres with multiple dining facilities may have several sous-chefs, each responsible for a specific facility or function. There could be, for instance, a restaurant chef and a banquet chef. Sous-chefs report to the executive chef, and each in turn has a brigade/team functioning with him or her.

Like Escoffier's station chefs, **line cooks** (or section cooks) are responsible for preparing menu items according to recipe specifications. Making the most of time, talent, space and equipment, the chef assigns responsibilities to each of the line cooks. Depending upon the size and type of operation, the sauté, broiler, fry, soup and vegetable stations may be combined into one position, as may the pantry, cold foods and salad stations.

The **pastry chef** is responsible for developing recipes for and preparing desserts, pastries, frozen desserts and breads. He or she is usually responsible for purchasing the food items used in the bake shop.

And, as in Escoffier's days, **apprentices** and **kitchen helpers** are assigned where needed in today's kitchens.

New styles of dining have created new positions since Escoffier's days. The most notable is the **line/short-order cook**, who is responsible for quickly preparing foods to order in smaller operations. He or she will work the broiler, deep-fat fryer and griddle as well as make sandwiches and even some sautéed items.

Another is the **institutional cook**, who generally works with large quantities of prepackaged or prepared foods for a captive market such as a school, hospital or prison.

Camp cooks often prepare food in remote locations with limited facilities. They usually work for an industrial catering firm contracting multiple sites. Many sites are very modern and have high standards for food preparation and service.

The Professional Chef

Although there is no one career ladder for producing a good professional chef, we believe that with training, skill, taste, judgment, dedication and pride a student cook or apprentice will develop into a professional chef.

Training

Chefs must be able to identify, purchase, utilize and prepare a wide variety of foods. They should be able to train and supervise a safe, skilled and efficient staff. To do all this successfully, chefs must possess a body of knowledge and understand and apply certain scientific and business principles. Schooling helps. A culinary program—whether at the secondary or post-secondary level—should, at a minimum, provide the student cook with a basic knowledge of foods, food styles and the methods used to prepare foods. Student cooks must be able to apply sanitation, nutrition and business procedures such as food costing. They start their apprenticeship at this time. After approximately three years of work experience and technical training, they take the Journeyperson's exam and Interprovincial Red Seal. This can be followed by achieving Certified Chef de Cuisine (CCC) status.

This book is designed to help you learn these basics. Many chapters have extensive sections identifying foods and equipment. Throughout this book we emphasize culinary principles, not recipes. Whenever possible, whether it be preparing puff pastry or grilling a steak, we focus on the general procedure, highlighting fundamental principles and skills; we discuss both the how and the why of cooking. Only then are specific applications and sample recipes given. We also want you to have a sense of the rich tradition of cookery, so informative sidebars on food history, chef biographies and other topics are scattered throughout the book.

In this way, we follow the trail blazed by Escoffier, who wrote in the introduction to *Le Guide culinaire* that his book is not intended to be a compendium of recipes to be slavishly followed, but rather his treatise should be a tool that leaves his colleagues "free to develop their own methods and follow their own inspiration; ... the art of cooking ... will evolve as a society evolves, ... only basic rules remain unalterable."

As with any profession, an education does not stop at graduation. The acquisition of knowledge continues after the student cook joins the ranks of the employed. He or she should take additional classes on unique or ethnic cuisines, nutrition, business management or specialized skills. Apprentices and professionals should regularly review some of the many periodicals and books devoted to cooking and should travel and try new dishes to broaden their culinary horizons. The professional cook should also become involved in professional organizations in order to meet peers and exchange ideas.

Skill

Culinary schooling alone does not make a student a cook. Nothing but practical, hands-on experience will provide even the most academically gifted student with the skills needed to produce, consistently and efficiently, quality foods or to organize, train, motivate and supervise a staff.

Many food service operations recognize that new workers, even those who have graduated from culinary programs, need time and experience to develop and hone their skills. Therefore, many graduates start at entry-level positions. They should not be discouraged; advancement will come and the training pays off in the long run. Today culinary styles and fashions change frequently. What do not go out of fashion are well-trained, skilled and knowledgeable cooks. They can adapt.

Taste

No matter how knowledgeable or skilled the cook, he or she must be able to produce food that tastes great or the consumer will not return. A cook can only do so if confident about his or her own sense of taste.

Our total perception of taste is a complex combination of smell, taste, sight, sound and texture. All senses are involved in the enjoyment of eating; all must be considered in creating or preparing a dish. The cook should develop a taste memory by sampling foods, both familiar and unfamiliar. He or she should think about what is being tasted, make notes and experiment with flavour combinations and cooking methods. But a cook should not be inventive simply for the sake of invention. Rather, cooks must consider how the flavours, appearances, textures and aromas of various foods will interact to create a total taste experience.

Judgment

Selecting menu items, determining how much of what item to order, deciding whether and how to combine ingredients and approving finished items for service are all matters of judgment. Although knowledge and skill play a role in developing judgment, sound judgment comes only with experience.

Dedication

Becoming a cook is hard work; so is being one. The work is often physically taxing, the hours are usually long and the pace is frequently hectic. Despite these pressures, the cook is expected to efficiently produce consistently fine foods that are properly prepared, seasoned, garnished and presented. To do so, the cook must be dedicated to the job.

The dedicated cook should never falter. The food service industry is competitive and dependent upon the continuing good will of an often fickle public. One bad dish or one off night can result in a disgruntled diner and lost business. The chef should always be mindful of the food prepared and the customer served.

The cook must also be dedicated to co-workers. Virtually all food service operations rely on teamwork to get the job done well. Good teamwork requires dedication to a shared goal as well as a positive attitude. The chef is the individual who provides leadership and mentoring to the team.

Pride

Not only is it important that the job be well done, but the professional cook should also have a sense of pride in doing it well. Pride should also extend to personal appearance and behaviour in and around the kitchen. The professional cook should be well groomed and in uniform when working.

The professional cook's uniform consists of comfortable shoes, trousers (either solid white, solid black, black-and-white checked or black-and-white striped), a white double-breasted jacket, an apron and a neckerchief usually knotted or tied cravat style. The uniform has certain utilitarian aspects: Checked trousers disguise stains; the double-breasted white jacket can be rebuttoned to hide dirt, and the double layer of fabric protects from scalds and burns; the neckerchief absorbs facial perspiration; and the apron protects the uniform and insulates the body. Side towels are useful. This uniform should be worn with pride. Shoes should be polished; trousers and jacket should be pressed.

The crowning element of the uniform is the toque. The toque is the tall white hat worn by cooks and chefs almost everywhere. Although the toque traces its origin to the monasteries of the 6th century, the style worn today was introduced at the end of the 19th century. Most cooks now wear a standard 15- or 24-cm-high (6- or 9-inch) toque, but historically a cook's rank in the kitchen dictated the type of hat worn. Beginners wore flat-topped calottes; cooks with more advanced skills wore low toques and the master chefs wore high toques called *dodin-bouffants*. Culinary lore holds that the toque's pleats—101 in all—represented the 101 ways its wearer could successfully prepare eggs.

Some establishments are switching to other styles of hats. The change is usually part of a marketing plan. In addition, colours and designs have been introduced into uniforms. But functionality must always be kept in mind.

*C*ONCLUSION

The art and science of cookery form a noble profession with a rich history and long traditions. With training, knowledge, skill, taste, judgment, dedication and pride, the student cook or apprentice can become part of this profession. In this book we provide you with the basic knowledge and describe the techniques at which you must become skilled. Dedicate yourself to learning this information and mastering your skills. Once you have done so, take pride in your accomplishments. Good luck.

QUESTIONS FOR DISCUSSION

1. Describe the kitchen brigade system. How does the classic brigade compare with modern teams?
2. What are the roles of a chef, sous-chef and line cook in a modern kitchen?
3. Describe the differences in a meal prepared by Carême and one prepared by Point.
4. List and explain three technological advances affecting food preparation.
5. Discuss the societal changes that have contributed to diversification in the modern food service industry.

WEBLINKS

Canadian Federation of Chefs and Cooks
   www.cfcc.ca

Cuisine Canada
   www.cuisinecanada.ca

National Film Board of Canada: Documentary Films about Food and Food Industries
   www.onf.ca/FMT/E/cate/F/Food_and_Food_Industries.html

Food and Culinary Links for the Culinary Historian
   www.foodbooks.com/foodlink.htm

New York Public Library Culinary History Research Guide
   www.nypl.org/research/chss/grd/resguides/culryla.html

All Things Culinary: Culinary Links on StarChefs
   www.starchefs.com/Links/menu.html

CHAPTER 2
FOOD SAFETY AND SANITATION

━━━━━ ♦♦♦ ━━━━━

LEARNING OUTCOMES

After studying this chapter, you will be able to:

♦ identify the causes of food-borne illnesses
♦ handle foods in a safe manner
♦ take appropriate actions to create and maintain a safe and sanitary working environment

━━━━━━━━━━━━━━━━

*T*he Canadian Food Inspection Agency has overall responsibility for setting and monitoring food safety standards. The industry is assuming more responsibility and accountability for food safety, and the role of health inspectors is evolving. Providing consumers with safe food is the food handler's most important responsibility. Food handlers include anyone coming into contact with food or food preparation equipment. Food handlers are also the primary cause of food-related illnesses.

By understanding how food-borne illnesses are caused and what can be done to prevent them, you will be better able to protect your customers. This chapter is not meant to be a complete discussion of sanitation in food service operations. It should, however, alert you to practices that can result in food-borne illnesses.

Federal, provincial and municipal health, building and other codes are designed in part to ensure that food is handled in a safe and proper manner. Always consult your local health department for information and guidance. Take an approved safe food handling course or upgrade your present certificate. And always be conscious of what you can do to create and maintain a safe product and safe environment for your customers, your fellow employees and yourself.

Sanitation refers to the creation and maintenance of conditions that will control food contamination or food-borne illness. **Contamination** refers to the presence, generally unintended, of harmful organisms or substances. Contaminants can be (1) biological, (2) chemical or (3) physical. When consumed in sufficient quantities, food-borne contaminants can cause illness or injury, long-lasting disease or even death.

Contamination occurs in two ways: direct contamination and cross-contamination. **Direct contamination** is the contamination of raw foods, or the plants or animals from which they come, in their natural settings or habitats. Chemical and biological contaminants such as bacteria and fungi are present in the air, soil and water. So foods can be easily contaminated by their general exposures to the environment: Grains can become contaminated by soil fumigants in the field and shellfish can become contaminated by ingesting toxic marine algae.

Chemicals and microorganisms generally cannot move on their own, however. They need to be transported, an event known as **cross-contamination**. The major cause of cross-contamination is people. Food handlers can transfer biological, chemical and physical contaminants to food while processing, preparing, cooking or serving it. It is therefore necessary to view sanitation as the correction of problems caused by direct contamination and the prevention of cross-contamination during processing and service.

Direct Contamination

Biological Contaminants

Biologically based food-borne illnesses can be caused by several **microorganisms**, primarily bacteria, parasites, viruses and fungi. By understanding how these organisms live and reproduce, you can better understand how to protect food from them.

Bacteria

Bacteria, which are single-celled microorganisms, are the leading cause of food-borne illnesses. See Figure 2.1. Most bacteria reproduce by binary fission: their genetic material is first duplicated and the nucleus then splits, each new nucleus taking some of the cellular material with it. See Figure 2.2. Under favourable conditions each bacterium can divide every 15–30 minutes. Within 12 hours, 1 bacterium can become a colony of 72 billion bacteria, more than enough to cause serious illness.

Some rod-shaped bacteria are capable of forming spores. Spores are thick-walled structures used as protection against a hostile environment. The bacteria essentially hibernate within their spores where they can survive extreme conditions that would otherwise destroy them. When conditions become favourable, the bacteria return to a viable state. This is important in food sanitation because bacterial spores may not be destroyed by heating or sanitizing techniques.

Some bacteria are beneficial, such as those that aid in digesting food or decomposing garbage. Other bacteria spoil food, but without rendering it unfit for human consumption. These bacteria, called **putrefactives**, are not a sanitation concern. (Indeed, in some cultures, they are not even a culinary concern. Cultures differ on what constitutes "bad" meat, for example, and red meat is sometimes hung for a time or "aged" to allow bacteria to tenderize the meat.)

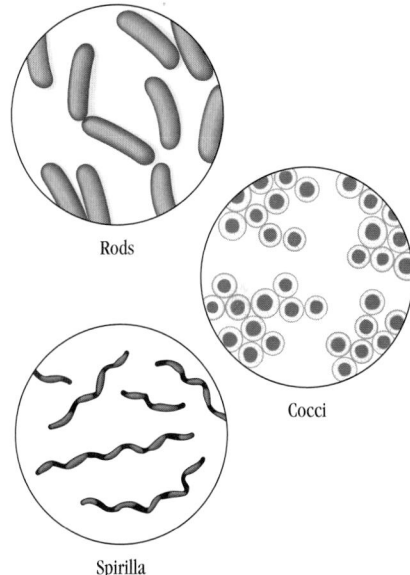

Rods

Cocci

Spirilla

FIGURE 2.1 *Bacteria can be classified by shape: Rods are short, tubular structures; cocci are disks, some of which form clusters; and spirilla are corkscrews.*

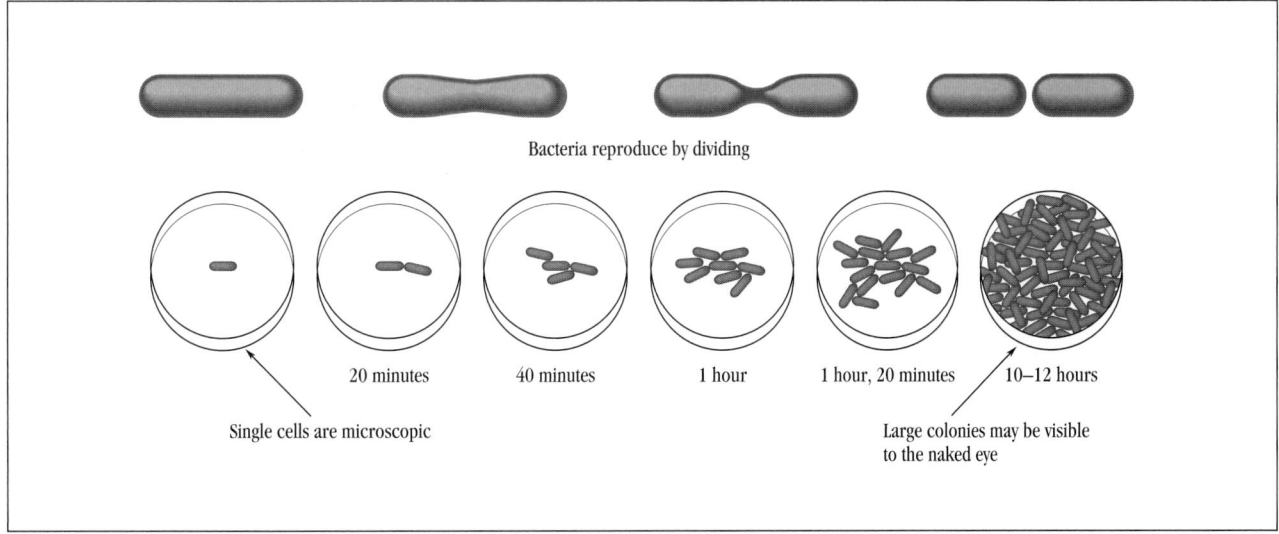

Bacteria reproduce by dividing

20 minutes 40 minutes 1 hour 1 hour, 20 minutes 10–12 hours

Single cells are microscopic

Large colonies may be visible to the naked eye

FIGURE 2.2 *One bacterium divides into 2; the 2 bacteria each divide, creating 4; the 4 become 16 and so on. It takes only a very short time for one bacterium to produce millions more.*

The bacteria that are dangerous when consumed by humans are called **pathogenic**. These are the bacteria that must be destroyed or controlled in a food service operation.

Intoxications and Infections

Depending upon the particular microorganism, pathogenic bacteria can cause illnesses in humans in one of three ways: by intoxication, infection or toxin-mediated infection.

Botulism is a well-known example of an **intoxication**. Certain bacteria produce **toxins**, a byproduct of their life processes. You cannot smell, see or taste toxins. Ingesting these toxin-producing bacteria by themselves does not cause illness. But when their toxins are ingested, the toxins can poison the consumer. Proper food-handling techniques are critical in preventing an intoxication, because even if food is cooked to a sufficiently high temperature to kill all bacteria present, the toxins they leave behind are usually not destroyed.

The second type of bacterial illness is an **infection**. Salmonella is the most well-known example. An infection occurs when live pathogenic bacteria (infectants) are ingested. The bacteria then live in the consumer's intestinal tract. It is the living bacteria, not their waste products, that cause an illness. An infectant must be alive when eaten for it to do any harm. Fortunately, these bacteria can be destroyed by cooking foods to sufficiently high temperatures, usually 74°C (165°F) or higher, and maintaining the temperature for sufficient time.

The third type of bacterial illness has characteristics of both an intoxication and an infection, and is referred to as a **toxin-mediated infection**. Examples are *Clostridium perfringens* and *Escherichia coli 0157:H7*. When these living organisms are ingested they establish colonies in human or animal intestinal tracts where they then produce toxins. These bacteria are particularly dangerous for young children, the elderly, the infirm or immunosuppressed individuals.

Preventing Bacterial Intoxications and Infections

All bacteria, like other living things, need certain conditions in order to complete their life cycles. Like humans, they need food, a comfortable temperature, moisture, the proper pH, the proper atmosphere and time. The best way to prevent bacterial intoxications and infections is to control the factors bacteria need to survive and multiply.

Food Bacteria need food for energy and growth. The foods on which bacteria thrive are referred to as **potentially hazardous foods**. Potentially hazardous foods include those high in protein such as meat, poultry, fish and shellfish. Dairy products, eggs, grains and some vegetables are also sufficiently high in protein to support bacterial growth. These foods and items containing these foods (for example, custard, hollandaise sauce and quiche) must be handled with great care.

Temperature Temperature is the most important factor in the pathogenic bacteria's environment because it is the factor most easily controlled by food service workers. Most microorganisms are destroyed at high temperatures. Freezing slows, but does not stop, growth nor does it destroy bacteria.

Most of the bacteria that cause food-borne illnesses multiply rapidly at temperatures between 16°C and 49°C (60°F–120°F). Therefore, the broad range of temperatures between 4°C and 60°C (40°F–140°F) is referred to as the **temperature danger zone**. See Figure 2.3. By keeping foods out of the temperature danger zone you decrease the bacteria's ability to thrive and reproduce.

This is known as the **time-and-temperature principle**. Potentially hazardous foods should be heated or cooled quickly so that they are within the temperature danger zone as briefly as possible.

To control the growth of any bacteria that may be present, it is important to maintain the internal temperature of food at or above 60°C (140°F), or 4°C (40°F) or below. Simply stated: *Keep hot foods hot, cold foods cold.*

Keep hot foods hot. The high internal temperatures reached during cooking (74°C–100°C/165°F–212°F) kill most of the bacteria that can cause food-borne illnesses. When foods are reheated the internal temperature should reach or exceed 77°C (170°F) for two minutes in order to kill any bacteria that may have grown during storage. Once properly heated, hot foods must be held at temperatures of 60°C (140°F) or above. Foods that are to be displayed or served hot must be heated rapidly to reduce the time within the temperature danger zone. When heating or reheating foods:

◆ Use shallow containers to promote rapid thermalization.
◆ Heat small quantities at a time.
◆ Stir frequently.
◆ Heat foods as close to service time as possible.
◆ Use preheated ingredients whenever possible to prepare hot foods.
◆ Never use a steam table for heating or reheating foods. Bring the food to an appropriate internal temperature (at least 77°C/170°F) for two minutes before placing it in the steam table for holding.

Keep cold foods cold. Foods that are to be displayed, stored or served cold must be cooled rapidly. When cooling foods:

◆ Refrigerate semisolid foods at 4°C (40°F) or below in containers that are less than 5 cm (2 inches) deep. (Increased surface area decreases cooling time.)
◆ Avoid crowding the refrigerator; allow air to circulate around foods.
◆ Vent hot foods in an ice water bath as illustrated in Chapter 10, Stocks and Sauces. Stir frequently.
◆ Use prechilled ingredients, for example mayonnaise, to prepare cold foods.
◆ Store cooked foods above raw foods to prevent cross-contamination.

Keep frozen foods frozen. Freezing at –18°C (0°F) or below essentially stops bacterial growth but will not kill the bacteria. Do not place hot foods in a standard freezer. They will not cool more rapidly and the release of heat can raise the temperature of other foods in the freezer. Only a special blast or shock freezer can be used for chilling hot items. If one is not available, cool hot foods as mentioned above before freezing them. When frozen foods are thawed, bacteria that are present will begin to grow. Therefore,

◆ Never thaw foods at room temperature.
◆ Thaw foods gradually under refrigeration. Place them in a container to prevent cross-contamination from dripping or leaking liquids.
◆ Thaw foods under cold running water if items are wrapped in plastic.
◆ Thaw foods in a microwave *only* if the food will be prepared and served immediately.

Time   When bacteria are moved from one place to another they require time to adjust to new conditions. This resting period, during which very little growth occurs, is known as the **lag phase**. This phase averages two to four hours. It is followed by the **log phase**, a period of accelerated growth, which lasts until the bacteria begin to crowd others within their colony, creating competition for food, space and moisture. This begins the **decline** or **negative**

FIGURE 2.3

◆◆◆

CAUTION

E.coli, Listeria and *C.botulinum* can grow at refrigerator temperatures.

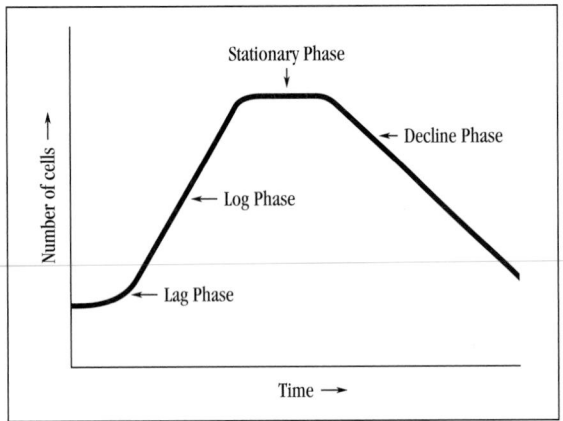

FIGURE 2.4 *Bacterial Growth Curve*

growth phase, during which bacteria die at an accelerated rate. See Figure 2.4.

Because of the lag phase, foods can be in the temperature danger zone for *very short periods* during preparation without an unacceptable increase in bacterial growth. Exposure to the temperature danger zone is cumulative, however, and should not exceed two hours total. The less time food is in the temperature danger zone, the less opportunity bacteria have to multiply.

Moisture   Bacteria need a certain amount of moisture, which is expressed as water activity or A_W. Water itself has an A_W of 1.0. Any food with an A_W of .85 or greater is considered potentially hazardous. See Table 2.1. Bacteria cannot flourish where the A_W is too low, usually below .85. This explains why dry foods such as flour, sugar or crackers are rarely subject to bacterial infestations. A low A_W only halts bacterial growth, however; it does not kill the microorganisms. When a dried food such as beans, eggs or rice is rehydrated, any bacteria present can flourish and the food may become potentially hazardous.

Acid/Alkaline Balance   Bacteria are affected by the **pH** of their environment. See Table 2.2. Although they can survive in a wider range, they prefer a neutral environment with a pH of 6.6 to 7.5. Growth is usually halted if the pH is 4.6 or less. Acidic foods such as lemon juice, tomatoes and vinegar create an unfavourable environment for bacteria. Simply adding an acidic ingredient to foods should not, however, be relied upon to destroy bacteria or preserve foods. The amount of acidity appropriate for flavouring is not sufficient to ensure the destruction of bacteria.

Atmosphere   Bacteria need an appropriate atmosphere. Some bacteria, known as **aerobes**, thrive on oxygen, while others, known as **anaerobes**, do not require the presence of oxygen. Others, known as **facultative**, can adapt and will survive with or without oxygen. Unfortunately, most pathogenic bacteria are facultative. See Table 2.3.

Canning, which creates an anaerobic atmosphere, destroys bacteria that need oxygen. But it also creates a favourable atmosphere for anaerobic and facultative bacteria. A complete vacuum need not be formed for anaerobic bacteria to thrive, however. A tight foil covering, a complete layer of fat, even a well-fitting lid can create an atmosphere sufficiently devoid of oxygen to permit growth of anaerobic bacteria. *Clostridium botulinum* is anaerobic and is one of the most deadly forms of food poisoning.

Parasites

Parasites are tiny organisms that depend on nutrients from a living host to complete their life cycle. Meat animals, fish, shellfish and humans can all play host to parasites. Several types of very small parasitic worms can enter an animal through contaminated feed, then settle in the host's intestinal tract or muscles, where they grow and reproduce. The ones most commonly found in foods are *trichinella spiralis* and *anisakis*.

TABLE 2.1	WATER ACTIVITY OF COMMON FOODS
0.0	
.1	
.2	
.3	
.4	
.5	dried pasta
.6	
.7	flour, dry milk
.75	jam, jelly, crisp cooked bacon
.8	
.85	MINIMUM FOR BACTERIAL GROWTH
.9	raw bacon
.95	soft cheese
.98	poultry and meat
1.0	distilled water

TABLE 2.2   pH OF COMMON FOODS

	0	
	1.0	
A	2.0	limes, lemons
C	3.0	commercial mayonnaise
I	4.0	orange juice
D	4.6	bananas
	5.0	most vegetables (5.0 to 7.0)
	6.4	chicken and fresh meats
NEUTRAL	7.0	distilled water, fish
	8.0	crackers
A	8.5	baking soda in water
L	9.0	
K	10.0	
A	11.0	
L	12.0	household ammonia
I	13.0	
	14.0	

TABLE 2.3   CHARACTERISTICS OF BACTERIAL ILLNESSES

Common Name	Organism Name	Form	Sources	Prevention
Staph	Staphylococcus aureus	Toxin	Starchy foods, cold meats, bakery items, custards, milk products, humans with infected wounds or sores	Wash hands and utensils before use; exclude unhealthy food handlers; avoid having foods at room temperature
Perfringens or CP	Clostridium perfringens	Cells and toxin	Reheated meats, sauces, stews, casseroles	Keep cooked foods at an internal temperature of 60°C (140°F) or higher; reheat leftovers to internal temperature of 75°C (170°F) or higher
Botulism	Clostridium botulinum	Toxin, cells, spores	Cooked foods held for an extended time at warm temperatures with limited oxygen; rice, potatoes, smoked fish, canned vegetables	Keep internal temperature of cooked foods above 60°C (140°F) or below 4°C (40°F); reheat leftovers thoroughly; discard swollen cans
Salmonella	Salmonella	Cells	Poultry, eggs, milk, meats, fecal contamination	Thoroughly cook all meat, poultry, fish and eggs; avoid cross-contamination with raw foods; maintain good personal hygiene
Strep	Streptococcus	Cells	Infected food handlers	Do not allow employees to work if ill; protect foods from customers' coughs and sneezes
E. coli or 0157	Escherichia coli 0157:H7 (enteropathogenic strains)	Cells and toxins	Any food, especially raw milk, raw vegetables, raw or rare beef (especially ground), humans (fecal)	Thoroughly cook or reheat items
Listeria	Listeria monocytogenes	Cells	Milk products, deli meats, humans	Avoid raw milk and cheese made from unpasteurized milk; keep storage areas clean

Trichinosis is caused by eating undercooked game or pork infected with trichina larvae. Trichinosis has been virtually eradicated by grain-feeding hogs and testing them before slaughter. Traditionally it was thought that pork must be cooked to internal temperatures of 77°C (170°F) or higher to eradicate the larvae. This generally resulted in a dry, tough product. Scientists have now determined that trichina larvae are killed if held at 58°C (137°F) for 10 seconds. The Canadian Food Inspection Agency currently recommends cooking pork products to an internal temperature of 66°C (150°F). All commercially packaged cured or smoked pork products must be heated to an internal temperature of 68°C (155°F) during processing.

Anisakiasis is another illness caused by parasitic roundworms. Anisakis worms reside in the organs of fish, especially bottom feeders or those taken from contaminated waters. Raw or undercooked fish is most often implicated in anisakiasis. Fish should be thoroughly cleaned immediately after being caught so that the parasites do not have an opportunity to spread. Cooking to a minimum internal temperature of 63°C (145°F) for at least 15 seconds or freezing at –20°C (–4°F) for 7 days is recommended, as they can survive even highly acidic marinades.

Cyclospora infections are caused by a single-celled parasite found in water or food contaminated by infected feces. Produce from undeveloped countries is a common source of cyclospora parasites, as is untreated water. Avoiding such products is the best prevention method.

Viruses

Other biologically based food-borne illnesses such as hepatitis A and Norwalk virus are caused by viruses. Viruses are the smallest known form of life. They invade the living cells of a host, take over those cells' genetic material, and cause the cells to produce more viruses.

Viruses do not require a host to survive, however. They can survive—but not multiply—while lying on any food or food contact surface. Unlike bacteria, viruses can be present on any food, not just a potentially hazardous food. The food or food contact surface simply becomes a means of transportation between hosts.

Unlike bacteria, viruses are not affected by the water activity, pH or oxygen content of their environment. Some, however, can be destroyed by temperatures higher than 85°C (185°F) for one minute. Basically, the only way to prevent food-borne viral illnesses is to prevent contamination in the first place.

Hepatitis A often enters the food supply through shellfish harvested from sewage-polluted waters. The virus is carried by humans, some of whom may never know they are infected, and is transmitted by poor personal hygiene and cross-contamination. The actual source of contamination may be hard to establish, though, because it may take months for symptoms to appear.

The **Norwalk virus** is spread almost entirely by poor personal hygiene among infected food handlers. The virus is found in human feces, contaminated water or vegetables fertilized by manure. The virus can be destroyed by high cooking temperatures but not by sanitizing solutions or freezing. In fact, Norwalk virus has even been found in ice cubes.

Foods most likely to transmit viral diseases are those that are not heated after handling. These include salads, sandwiches, milk, baked products, uncooked fish and shellfish and sliced meats. The best techniques for avoiding viral food-borne illnesses are to observe good personal hygiene habits, avoid cross-contamination and use only foods obtained from reputable sources.

Fungi

Fungi are a large group of plants ranging from single-celled organisms to giant mushrooms. Fungi are everywhere: in the soil, air and water. Poisonous mushrooms, a type of fungus, can cause illness or death if consumed. The most common fungi, however, are moulds and yeasts.

Moulds

Moulds are algae-like fungi that form long filaments or strands. These filaments often extend into the air, appearing as cottony or velvety masses on food. Large colonies of mould are easily visible to the naked eye. Although many food moulds are not dangerous, and some are even very beneficial, rare types known as mycotoxicoses do form toxins that have been linked to foodborne illnesses. For the most part, however, moulds only affect the appearance and flavour of foods. They cause discolouration, odours and off-flavours.

Unlike bacteria, moulds can grow on almost any food at almost any temperature, moist or dry, acidic or alkaline. Mould cells can be destroyed by heating to 60°C (140°F) for 10 minutes. Their toxins are heat resistant, however, and are not destroyed by normal cooking methods. Therefore, foods that develop mould should be discarded and any container or storage area cleaned and sanitized. The roots can grow 2.5 cm (1 inch) into the host product.

Yeasts

Yeasts require water and carbohydrates (sugar or starch) for survival. As the organisms consume carbohydrates they expel alcohol and carbon dioxide gas through a process known as **fermentation**. Fermentation is of great benefit in making bread and alcoholic beverages.

Although naturally occurring yeasts have not been proven to be harmful to humans, they can cause foods to spoil, developing off-flavours, odours and discolouration. Yeasts are killed at temperatures of 58°C (136°F) or above.

Chemical Contaminants

The contamination of foods by a wide variety of chemicals is a very real and serious danger, one about which the public has shown a strong interest. Chemical contamination is usually inadvertent and invisible, making it extremely difficult to detect. The only way to avoid such hazards is for everyone working in a food service operation to follow proper procedures when handling foods or chemicals.

Chemical hazards include contamination with (1) the residual chemicals used in growing the food supply, (2) food service chemicals and cleaners and (3) toxic metals.

Residual Chemicals

Chemicals such as antibiotics, fertilizers, insecticides and herbicides have brought about great progress in controlling plant, animal and human diseases, permitting greater food yields and stimulating animal growth. The benefits derived from these chemicals, however, must be contrasted with the adverse effects on humans when chemicals are used indiscriminately or improperly.

The danger of these chemicals lies in the possible contamination of human foods, which occurs when chemical residues remain after the intended goal is achieved. Fruits and vegetables must be washed and peeled properly to reduce the risk of consuming residual chemicals.

Food Service Chemicals and Cleaners

A more common contamination problem involves the common chemicals found in most every food service operation. Cleaners, polishes, pesticides and abrasives are often poisonous to humans. Illness and even death can result from foods contaminated by such common items as bug spray, drain cleaner, oven cleaner or silver polish. These chemicals pose a hazard if used or stored near food supplies. Even improperly washing or rinsing dishes and utensils leaves a soap residue, which is then transmitted via food to anyone using the item.

To avoid food service chemical contamination, make sure all cleaning chemicals are clearly labelled and stored well away from food preparation and storage areas. Always use these products as directed by the manufacturer; never reuse a chemical container or package. Follow WHMIS guidelines.

Toxic Metals

Another type of chemical contamination occurs when metals such as lead, mercury, copper, zinc and antimony are dispersed in food or water. For example:

◆ Metals can accumulate in fish and shellfish living in polluted waters or in plants grown in soil contaminated by the metals.
◆ Using an acidic food such as tomatoes or wine in a zinc (galvanized) or unlined copper container causes metal ions to be released into the food.
◆ Antimony is used in bonding enamelware; it can be released into food when the enamel is chipped or cracked, so great care must be taken when using enamelware (terrines).
◆ Lead enters the water supply from lead pipes and solder and is found in the glaze on some imported ceramic items.

Consuming any of these metals can cause poisoning.

To prevent metal contamination, use only approved food service equipment and utensils and re-tin copper cookware as needed. Never serve fish or shell-fish that was illegally harvested or obtained from uninspected sources.

Physical Contaminants

Physical contaminants include foreign objects that find their way into foods by mistake. Examples include metal shavings created by a worn can opener, pieces of glass from a broken container, hair, lubricants and dirt. Physical contaminants may be created by intentional tampering, but they are most likely the result of poor safety and sanitation practices or a lack of training.

CROSS-CONTAMINATION

Generally, microorganisms and other contaminants cannot move by themselves. Rather, they are carried to foods and food contact surfaces by humans, rodents or insects. This transfer is referred to as cross-contamination.

Cross-contamination is the process by which one item, such as your fingers or a cutting board, becomes contaminated and then contaminates another food or tool. For example, a chef's knife and cutting board are used in fabricating a potentially hazardous food such as a chicken. In this case, the chicken had been directly contaminated with salmonella at the hatchery. If the knife and board are not cleaned *and sanitized* properly, anything that touches them can also become contaminated. So, even though cooking the chicken to an appropriate internal temperature may destroy the salmonella in the chicken, the uncooked salad greens cut on the same cutting board or with the same knife can contain live bacteria. Health regulations require separate cutting boards for raw and cooked products.

Cross-contamination can occur with bacteria or other microorganisms, chemicals, dirt and debris. Side towels are an especially common source of cross-contamination. If a cook uses a side towel to wipe a spill off the floor, then uses that same towel to dry his hands after visiting the restroom, he has recontaminated his hands with whatever bacteria or dirt was on the floor. Cross-contamination also occurs when raw foods come in contact with cooked foods. Never store cooked food below raw food in a refrigerator, and never return cooked food to the container that held the raw food. Cross-contamination can also occur easily from smoking, drinking or eating, unless hands are properly washed after each of these activities.

Reducing Cross-Contamination

Cross-contamination can be reduced or even prevented by (1) personal cleanliness, (2) dish and equipment cleanliness and (3) pest control.

Personal Cleanliness

To produce clean, sanitary food, all food handlers must maintain high standards of personal cleanliness and hygiene. This begins with good grooming.

Humans provide the ideal environment for the growth of microorganisms. Everyone harbours bacteria in the nose and mouth. These bacteria are easily spread by sneezing or coughing, by not disposing of tissues properly and by not washing hands frequently and properly. Touching your body, then touching food or utensils transfers bacteria. Human waste carries many dangerous microorganisms, so it is especially important to wash your hands thoroughly *for at least 30 seconds* after visiting the toilet. An employee who is ill should not be allowed in the operation.

Current research shows that the human immunodeficiency virus (HIV), the causative agent of AIDS, is not spread by food. According to the Canadian Food Inspection Agency (*Meat Manual of Procedures*, Ch. 1, section 1.5.2, AIDS in Food Processing Establishments, 1990), HIV will *not* survive in food. Even if contamination does occur in a food processing establishment—which is unlikely—there is no risk to the general public. Government departments and agencies enforce strict standards for the sanitary production, preparation and handling of food. These standards of good personal hygiene and workplace sanitation were not developed in response to AIDS, but have been in effect in one form or another for many years.

There have been no documented or suspected cases of transmission of HIV through food. As a result, there is no medical or public health reason to restrict an HIV-infected person from working in food production, preparation or handling establishments, unless the individual has another illness for which any worker would be restricted.

There are several things you can do to decrease the risk of an illness being spread by poor personal hygiene:

✦ Wash your hands frequently and thoroughly. Gloves are not a substitute for proper hand washing and may create a false sense of security.

◆ Keep your fingernails short, clean and neat. Do not bite your nails or wear nail polish.

◆ Keep any cut or wound antiseptically bandaged. An injured hand should also be covered with a disposable glove.

◆ Bathe daily, or more often if required.

◆ Keep your hair clean and restrained.

◆ Wear work clothes that are clean and neat. Avoid wearing jewellery or watches.

◆ Do not eat, drink, smoke or chew gum in food preparation areas.

Dish and Equipment Cleanliness

One of the primary requirements for any food service facility is cleanability. But there is an important difference between clean and sanitary. **Clean** means that the item has no visible soil on it. **Sanitary** means that harmful substances are reduced to safe levels. Thus, something may be clean without being sanitary; the visible dirt can be removed, but disease-causing microorganisms can remain.

The cleaning of dishes, pots, pans and utensils in a food service operation involves both removing soil and sanitizing. Soil can be removed manually or by machine. Sanitizing can be accomplished with heat or chemical disinfectants.

Procedures for manually washing, rinsing and sanitizing dishes and equipment generally follow the three-compartment sink setup shown in Figure 2.5. The dish/pot washer must:

1. Scrape and pre-rinse the item to remove soil. Cutlery must be presoaked in a mild detergent solution.
2. Wash the item in the first sink compartment at a temperature not lower than 45°C (113°F) using an approved detergent. A brush or cloth may be used to remove any remaining soil.
3. Rinse the item in the second sink compartment using clear, hot water of at least 45°C (113°F).
4. Sanitize the item in the third sink compartment by either:
   a. immersing it in 77°C (170°F) water for at least two minutes, or
   b. immersing it in an approved chemical sanitizing solution according to the manufacturer's directions. Use test strips to verify adequate concentrations. Note: A basket or rack must be used for immersion and a test thermometer must be available.
5. Empty, clean and refill each sink compartment as necessary and check the water temperature regularly.

◆◆◆

CHEMICAL SANITIZERS

At a temperature of 45°C (113°F) and for at least two minutes, utensils may be sanitized with solutions containing at least:

1. 100 mg of available chlorine per litre,
2. 25 mg of available iodine per litre, and
3. 200 mg of quaternary ammonium compound per litre.

FIGURE 2.5 *The Three-Compartment Sink* *Procedure—scrape, pre-rinse, wash, rinse, sanitize and air-dry each item.*

Food service items, dishes, silverware and utensils should always be allowed to air-dry, as towel-drying may recontaminate them.

Machine-washing dishes or utensils follows a similar procedure. The dishwasher should first scrape and rinse items as needed, then load the items into dishwasher racks so that the spray of water will reach all surfaces. The machine cleans the items with a detergent in wash water of at least 60°C (140°F) for hot-temperature machines, then sanitizes them with either a hot-water rinse (at least 82°C/180°F) for 30 seconds or a suitable time-temperature combination or chemical disinfectant. When the machine cycle is complete, items should be inspected for residual soil, allowed to air-dry and stored in a clean area.

Work tables and stationary equipment must also be cleaned and sanitized properly. Equipment and surfaces, including floors, walls and work tables, should be easily exposed for inspection and cleaning and should be constructed so that soil can be removed effectively and efficiently with normal cleaning procedures. A thorough cleaning schedule should be implemented and closely monitored to prevent problems from developing.

The following points are important to the safety and cleanliness of any food service facility:

◆ Equipment should be disassembled for cleaning; any immersible pieces should be cleaned and sanitized like other items.
◆ All work tables or other food contact surfaces should be cleaned with detergent, then sanitized with a clean cloth dipped in a sanitizing solution. An acceptable sanitizing solution is made by combining 4.5 L (1 gallon) of lukewarm water with 15 mL (1 Tbsp.) of chlorine bleach. This solution must be replaced every two hours. Other chemical sanitizers should be prepared and used according to health department and manufacturer's directions.
◆ Surfaces, especially work surfaces with which food may come in contact, should be smooth and free of cracks, crevices or seams in which soil and microorganisms can hide.
◆ Floors should be nonabsorbent and should not become slippery when wet.
◆ Walls and ceilings should be smooth and light-coloured so that soil is easier to see.
◆ Light should be ample and well located throughout food preparation and storage areas. All light bulbs should be covered with a sleeve or globe to protect surroundings from shattered glass.

The design of a kitchen can also affect food safety and sanitation. Food preparation equipment should be arranged in such a way as to decrease the chances of cross-contamination. The work flow should eliminate crisscrossing and backtracking. Employees should be able to reach storage, refrigeration and cleanup areas easily. Dish- and pot-washing areas and garbage facilities should be kept as far from food preparation and storage areas as possible. Cleaning supplies and other chemicals should be stored away from foods.

In most communities, the design of a food service facility is controlled in part by public health regulations. The local health and building codes should be consulted when planning any construction or remodelling, or when purchasing and installing new equipment.

Pest Control

Food can be contaminated by insects (e.g., roaches and flies) and rodents (e.g., mice and rats). These pests carry many harmful bacteria on their bodies and defecate frequently, thus contaminating any surface with which they come in contact. An insect or rodent infestation is usually considered a serious health risk and should be dealt with immediately and thoroughly. Pests must be controlled by (1) building them out of the facility, (2) creating an environment in which they cannot find food, water or shelter and (3) relying on professional extermination.

The best defence against pests is to prevent infestations in the first place by building them out. Any crack—no matter how small—in door frames, walls or window sills should be repaired immediately and all drains, pipes and vents should be well sealed. Inspect all deliveries thoroughly and reject any packages or containers found to contain evidence of pests.

Flies are a perfect method of transportation for bacteria because they feed and breed on human waste and garbage. Use screens or "fly fans" (also known as air curtains) to keep them out in the first place. Control of garbage is also essential because moist, warm, decaying organic material attracts flies and provides favourable conditions for eggs to hatch and larvae to grow.

Pest control also requires creating an inhospitable environment for pests. Store all food and supplies at least 15 cm (6 inches) off the floor and 5 cm (2 inches) away from walls. Rotate stock often to disrupt nesting places and breeding habits. Provide good ventilation in storerooms to remove humidity, airborne contaminants, grease and fumes. Do not allow water to stand in drains, sinks or buckets, as cockroaches are attracted to moisture. Clean up spills and crumbs immediately and completely to reduce their food supply.

Despite your best efforts to build pests out and maintain proper housekeeping standards, it is still important to watch for the presence of pests. For example, cockroaches leave a strong, oily odour and feces that look like large grains of pepper. Cockroaches prefer to search for food and water in the dark, so seeing any cockroach on the move in the daylight is an indication of a large infestation.

Rodents (mice and rats) tend to hide during the day, so an infestation may be rather serious before any creature is actually seen. Rodent droppings, which are shiny black to brownish grey, may be evident, however. Rodent nests made from scraps of paper, hair or other soft materials may be spotted.

Should an infestation occur, consult a licensed pest control operator immediately. With early detection and proper treatment, infestations can be eliminated. Be very careful in attempting to use pesticides or insecticides yourself. These chemicals are toxic to humans as well as to pests. Great care must be used to prevent contaminating food or exposing workers or customers to the chemicals.

HACCP SYSTEMS

Now that you understand what contaminants are and how they can be destroyed or controlled, it is necessary to put this information into practice during day-to-day operations. Although local health departments inspect all food service facilities on a regular basis, continual self-inspection and control are essential for maintaining sanitary conditions.

Hazard Analysis Critical Control Points (HACCP) continues to be an effective and efficient method for managing and maintaining sanitary conditions in all types of food service operations. Developed by Pillsbury in 1971 for NASA to ensure food safety for astronauts, HACCP—and a similar system adopted by the National Restaurant Association known as Sanitary Assessment of the Food Environment/S.A.F.E.—is a rigorous system of self-inspection. It focuses on the

---

✦✦✦
CANADIAN
FOOD INSPECTION AGENCY

While the safety of agri-food products produced in Canada is the ultimate responsibility of the food industry, the role of the Canadian Food Inspection Agency's (CFIA's) food inspection programs is to ensure that in federally registered establishments, appropriate steps are taken by industry to produce a safe product for consumers.

The Food Safety Enhancement Program, established in 1996, is designed to encourage the adoption of Hazard Analysis Critical Control Points (HACCP) principles. HACCP has been recognized internationally as a logical tool towards a more modern, scientifically based inspection system. The key element of a HACCP-based system is its preventive nature and the exercising of control throughout the manufacturing process, at critical steps called critical control points. By doing so, defects that could affect the safety of the food being processed can be readily detected and corrected at these points before the product is completely processed and packaged.

Source: Adapted from Canadian Food Inspection Agency, *Food Safety Enhancement Program (FSEP) Manual*, Chapter 1 (www.inspection.gc.ca/english/toce.shtml, Aug. 8, 2001).

TABLE 2.4   HACCP ANALYSIS—THE FLOW OF FOOD

Control Point	Hazard	Critical Action
Menu and recipes	Potentially hazardous foods; human hands involved in food preparation	Plan physical work flow; train employees; buy from approved sources
Receiving	Contaminated or spoiled goods	Inspect and reject delivery if necessary
Storage	Cross-contamination to and from other foods; bacterial growth; spoilage	Maintain proper temperatures; rotate stock; discard if necessary
Preparation	Cross-contamination; bacterial growth	Wash hands and utensils; avoid temperature danger zone
Cooking	Bacterial survival; physical or chemical contamination	Cook to proper temperatures
Holding and service	Contamination; bacterial growth	Use clean equipment; maintain proper temperatures
Cooling leftovers	Bacterial survival and growth	Cool rapidly, cover and refrigerate
Reheating	Bacterial survival and growth	Heat rapidly to 75°C (170°F); maintain temperatures; do not mix old and new products

flow of food through the food service facility, from the decision to include an item on the menu through service to the consumer.

A HACCP critical control point is any step during the processing of a food when a mistake can result in the transmission, growth or survival of pathogenic bacteria. At each of these steps there is some hazard of contamination. The HACCP process begins by identifying the steps and evaluating the type and severity of hazard that can occur. It then identifies what actions can be taken to reduce or prevent each risk of hazard. See Table 2.4. The activities that present the highest risk of hazard should be monitored most closely. For example, a cook's failure to wash his hands before handling cooked food presents a greater risk of hazard than does a dirty floor. In other words, hazards must be prioritized and correction of critical concerns should take priority. See Figure 2.6.

Whatever system is followed, however, all personnel must be constantly aware of and responsive to problems and potential problems associated with the safety of the food they are serving. Accurate record keeping is a requirement of an effective HACCP program.

THE SAFE WORKER

Kitchens are filled with objects that can cut, burn, break, crush or sprain the human body. The best way to prevent work-related injuries is through proper training, adherence to good work habits and careful supervision.

FIGURE 2.6 *An HACCP System Flowchart*

The federal government enacted legislation designed to reduce hazards in the work area, thereby reducing accidents. The Occupational Health and Safety Act (OHSA) covers a broad range of safety matters. Employers who fail to follow its rules can incur financial penalties. Unfortunately, human error is the leading cause of accidents, and no amount of legislation can protect someone who doesn't work in a safe manner.

Safe behaviour on the job reflects pride, professionalism and consideration for fellow workers. The following list should alert you to conditions and activities aimed at preventing accidents and injuries:

◆ Clean up spills as soon as they occur.
◆ Learn to operate equipment properly; always use guards and safety devices.
◆ Wear clothing that fits properly; avoid wearing jewellery, which may get caught in equipment.
◆ Use knives and other equipment for their intended purpose only.
◆ Walk, do not run.
◆ Keep exits, aisles and stairs clear and unobstructed.
◆ Always assume a pot or pan is hot; handle with dry towels.
◆ Position pot and pan handles out of the aisles so they do not get bumped.
◆ Get help or use a cart when lifting or moving heavy objects.
◆ Avoid back injury by lifting with your leg muscles; stoop, do not bend, when lifting.
◆ Use a well-placed ladder or stool for climbing; do not use a chair, box, drawer or shelf.
◆ Keep breakable items away from food storage or production areas.
◆ Warn people when you must walk behind them, especially when carrying a hot pan.

Some accidents will inevitably occur, and it is important to act appropriately in the event of an injury or emergency. This may mean calling for help or providing first aid. Every food service operation should be equipped with a complete first-aid kit. Municipal regulations may specify the exact contents of the kit. Be sure that the kit is conveniently located and well stocked at all times.

The Canadian Red Cross, St. John Ambulance and other agencies offer approved training in first aid, cardiopulmonary resuscitation (CPR) and the Heimlich manoeuvre used for victims of choking. All employees should be trained in basic emergency procedures. A list of emergency telephone numbers should be posted by each telephone.

*C*ONCLUSION

All food service workers are responsible for supplying food that is safe to eat. Microorganisms that cause food-borne illnesses are found in all types of food; they can be destroyed or their growth can be severely limited by proper food handling procedures. By learning about food contaminants, how they are spread and how they can be prevented or controlled, you can help ensure customer safety. You are also responsible for your own physical safety as well as that of your customers and fellow workers. Maintaining sanitary and safe facilities and high standards of personal hygiene is a necessary part of this responsibility.

QUESTIONS FOR DISCUSSION

1. Foods can be contaminated in several ways. Explain the differences between biological, chemical and physical contamination. Give an example of each.

2. Under what conditions will bacteria thrive? Explain what you can do to alter these conditions.

3. What is the temperature danger zone? What is its significance in food preparation?

4. Explain how improper or inadequate pest control can lead to food-borne illnesses.

5. Define the letters HACCP. How is this system used in a typical food service facility?

WEBLINKS

Canadian Food Inspection Agency/Agence canadienne d'inspection
   des aliments
   www.cfia-acia.agr.ca

Health Canada: Food Quality and Safety Programs
   www.hc-sc.gc.ca/datahpsb/npu/agr1.htm

Agriculture and Agri-Food Canada: HACCP Implementation Manual
   www.inspection.gc.ca/english/ppc/psps/haccp/haccpe.shtml

Centers for Disease Control and Prevention: Division of Bacterial and Mycotic
   Diseases: Foodborn Diseases
   www.cdc.gov/ncidod/dbmd/foodborn.htm

Foodnet: Food Safety
   foodnet.fic.ca/page4.html

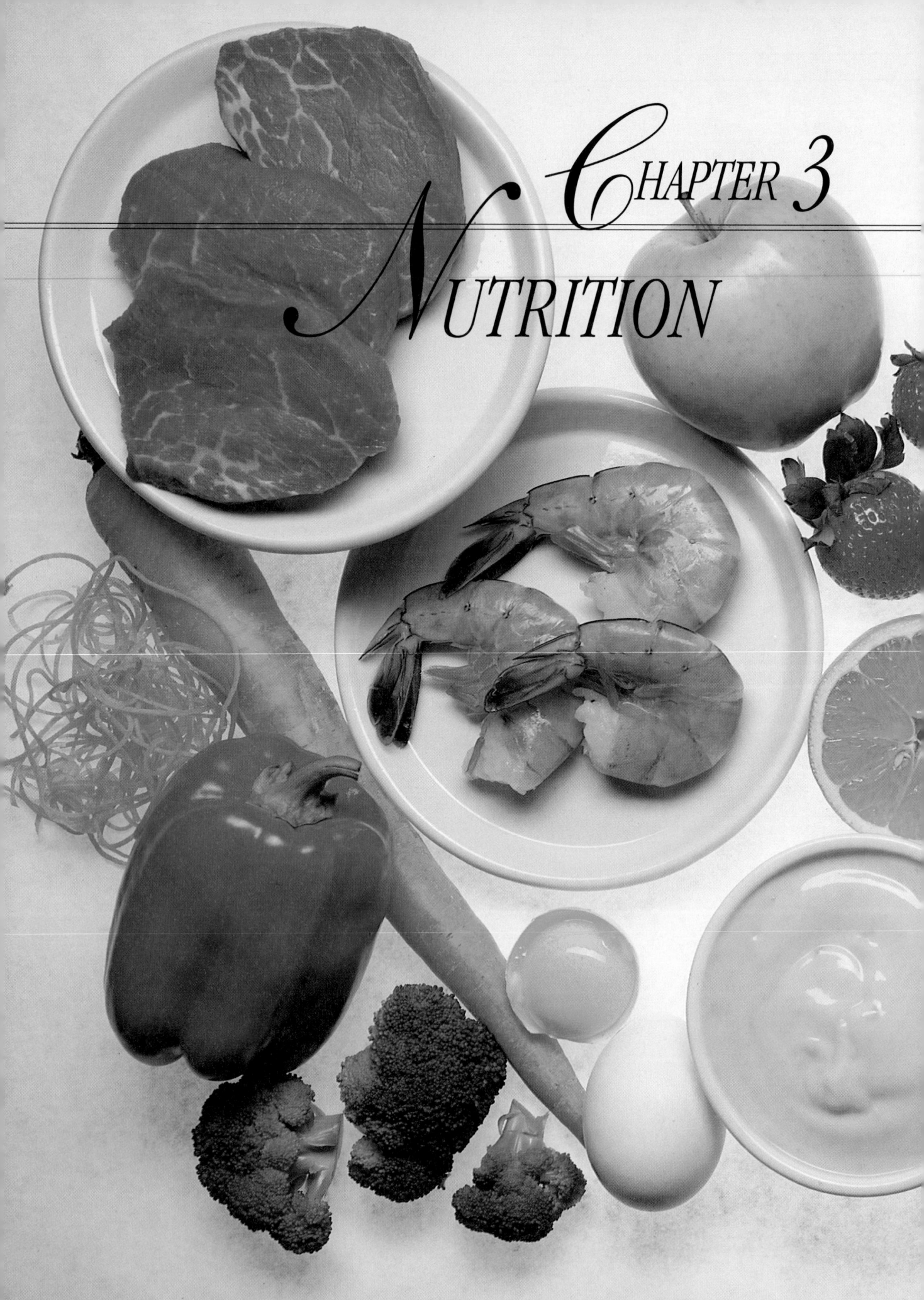

CHAPTER 3
NUTRITION

After studying this chapter you will be able to:

+ identify categories of nutrients and explain their importance in a balanced diet
+ explain the evolution of Canada's Food Guide and its significance in planning nutritious menus
+ describe the effects storage and preparation techniques have on various foods' nutritional values
+ identify the use of ingredient substitutes and alternatives
+ understand product nutrition labels
+ provide diners with nutritious foods

ince the days of prehistoric hunters and gatherers, people have understood that some animals and plants are good to eat and others are not. For thousands of years, cultures worldwide have attributed medicinal or beneficial effects to certain foods, particularly plants, and have recognized that foods that would otherwise be fine to eat may be unhealthy if improperly prepared or stored.

But it was not until the past few decades that people have become increasingly concerned about understanding how all foods affect their health and what foods can and should be consumed in order to promote good health. These concerns comprise the study of nutrition.

This chapter cannot provide an in-depth study of the nutritional sciences. Rather, it sets forth basic information about nutrients, food additives, and ingredient substitutes and alternatives. It also provides guidelines for reading package labels and preparing nutritious meals.

Detailed nutritional information about many specific foods is found throughout the book. All recipes are accompanied by a nutritional analysis; recipes for dishes particularly low in calories, fat or sodium are marked with a 🌿.

Nutrition is the science that studies nutrients, (chemical) substances found in food that nourish the body by promoting growth, maintenance and repair and by facilitating body functions. Some nutrients also provide energy.

The six categories of nutrients are carbohydrates, fats, proteins, vitamins, minerals and water. **Essential nutrients** are those that must be provided by food because the body does not produce them in sufficient quantities or cannot make them at all. (See Table 3.1.) Some nutritional components are considered nonessential because healthy, well-nourished bodies can make them in sufficient quantities to satisfy their needs.

Our bodies depend upon the various nutrients for different purposes and require different amounts of each depending on age, sex and health. In addition, some nutrients depend on one another for proper functioning. For example, calcium and vitamin D work together in the body: Vitamin D promotes the absorption of the calcium that the body utilizes for proper bone growth. Because foods differ with regard to their nutritional content, it is important to eat a variety of foods in order to achieve a proper nutritional balance.

TABLE 3.1   ESSENTIAL NUTRIENTS

Essential nutrients are those that must be provided because the human body does not produce them in sufficient quantities. They are:

Energy Nutrients	Carbohydrates
	Fats (linoleic and linolenic acids)
	Proteins (the amino acids: histidine, isoleucine, leucine, lysine, methionine, phenylalanine, threonine, tryptophan and valine)
Water	
Vitamins	Thiamin, riboflavin, niacin, pantothenic acid, biotin, vitamin B_6, vitamin B_{12}, folate, vitamin C, vitamin A, vitamin D, vitamin E and vitamin K
Minerals	Calcium, chloride, magnesium, phosphorus, potassium, sodium, sulphur, selenium, zinc, chromium, copper, fluoride, iodide, iron, manganese and molybdenum

ESSENTIAL NUTRIENTS

Three of the essential nutrients provide calories or energy. Sometimes referred to as macronutrients, they are carbohydrates, fats and proteins.

A **calorie** (abbreviated *kcal*) is the way we describe the amount of energy in food. The number of calories in a food is measured by a device called a calorimeter, which burns the food and measures the heat the food gives off. From that measurement, an estimate for how the food would be burned in the body is calculated. The results of the calculation are the calorie designations assigned to the energy nutrients.

One gram of pure fat supplies 9 kcal; one gram of pure carbohydrate supplies 4 kcal, as does one gram of pure protein. Most foods are a combination of carbohydrates, proteins and fats; their kcal content may not be easily determined unless we know how much of each nutrient the food contains.

Vitamins and minerals are essential nutrients and must be provided through the diet because the body cannot manufacture them in quantities adequate to ensure good health. They have no calories. Because they are needed in smaller amounts than the other nutrients, they are sometimes referred to as micronutrients.

Carbohydrates

Carbohydrates are composed of carbon, hydrogen and oxygen and are found exclusively in plant foods and milk sugars. **Simple carbohydrates** include monosaccharides (single sugars) and disaccharides (double sugars). See Table 3.2. Simple carbohydrates are found in the naturally occurring sugars in fruit, vegetables and milk, as well as in sweeteners such as honey, corn syrup and table sugar. **Complex carbohydrates** are composed of long chains of the monosaccharide glucose. Starch is a complex carbohydrate. Complex carbohydrates are found in vegetables, fruits and cereal grains such as wheat, barley and oats. The body digests (or breaks down) these sugars and starches into glucose. Glucose, also known as blood sugar, is a very important source of energy for the body.

Another complex carbohydrate is fibre. Fibre is a unique carbohydrate because humans cannot digest it, so they do not derive calories from it. **Dietary fibre**, which generally comes from the seeds and cell walls of fruits, vegetables and cereal grains, plays an important role in health. Because the body cannot digest dietary fibre, it passes through the digestive system almost completely unchanged. This helps keep the digestive tract running smoothly. Fibre increases fecal bulk, which encourages proper elimination of waste products from the large intestines and helps avoid some forms of gastrointestinal distress. Some forms of fibre also reduce serum cholesterol.

TABLE 3.2	SUGARS
Monosaccharides	Disaccharides
Glucose (blood sugar)	Lactose (milk sugar)
Fructose (fruit sugar)	Maltose (malt sugar)
Galactose (part of milk sugar)	Sucrose (table sugar)

Fats

Fats, like carbohydrates, are composed of carbon, hydrogen and oxygen. The differences between carbohydrates and fats are the number and arrangement of the carbon, hydrogen and oxygen atoms. Fats are found in both animal and plant foods, although fruits contain very little fat. Fats provide calories, help carry fat-soluble vitamins and give food a creamy, pleasant mouthfeel.

Depending upon their structure, the fats in foods can be classified as saturated, monounsaturated or polyunsaturated. Most foods contain a combination of the three, although one kind may predominate. If saturated fat is the most abundant kind (as in the fat surrounding muscle meats), we describe the food as being saturated even though it contains a mixture of all three fats.

Saturated fats are found mainly in animal products such as milk, eggs and meats, as well as in tropical oils such as coconut and palm. Monounsaturated fats come primarily from plants and plant foods such as avocados and olives and the oils made from them. Polyunsaturated fats come from plants (soy and corn, for example) and fish.

Vegetable oils like canola and olive are high in monounsaturated fat. Cottonseed, sunflower, corn and safflower oils are high in polyunsaturated fat. All oils, however, are a combination of the three kinds of fat.

Saturated fats such as butter, lard and other animal fats are usually solid at room temperature. Monounsaturated and polyunsaturated fats are usually liquid at room temperature. Hydrogenation is a process by which a liquid fat is made more solid (or saturated) by the addition of hydrogen atoms. Hydrogenation increases the percentage of saturated fatty acids, resulting in a more solid product (such as margarine made from a polyunsaturated oil like corn oil). It also reduces the tendency to rancidity so shelf life is increased.

The body has more difficulty breaking down saturated fats than it does monounsaturated and polyunsaturated fats. Research suggests that high-fat diets, especially diets high in saturated fat, may be linked to heart disease, obesity and certain forms of cancer. Saturated fats are also linked to high levels of blood cholesterol, which are associated with arteriosclerosis (hardening of the arteries). Although the liver can produce all the cholesterol the body needs, additional cholesterol is often provided in the diet. Dietary cholesterol is found only in foods of animal origin. Meats, poultry, fish, shellfish, eggs and dairy products are all sources of dietary cholesterol. Fruits, vegetables and grains are cholesterol free.

Proteins

Proteins are found in both animal and plant foods. They differ from carbohydrates and fats in that they contain nitrogen as well as carbon, hydrogen and oxygen. Protein chains are composed of amino acids, the building blocks of protein. There are 20 amino acids, 9 of which are essential. People who eat a varied diet with adequate calories and protein can easily get all of the essential amino acids. The specific combination of amino acids gives each protein its unique characteristics and properties.

Proteins are necessary for manufacturing, maintaining and repairing body tissues. They are essential for the periodic replacement of the outer layer of skin as well as for blood clotting and scar tissue formation. Hair and nails, which provide a protective cover for the body, are composed of proteins.

Another important function of protein is the regulation of body processes. Proteins regulate the balance of water, acids and bases and move nutrients in and out of cells. Proteins contribute to the immune system by producing antibodies, which are necessary for combatting diseases. Proteins also form the enzymes that act as catalysts for body functions and the hormones that help direct body processes.

Water

The human body is approximately 60% water. Water is necessary for transporting nutrients and wastes throughout the body. It cushions the cells, lubricates the joints, maintains stable body temperatures and assists waste elimination. It also promotes functioning of the nervous system and muscles.

Although the principal sources of water are beverages, water is also the predominant nutrient by weight in most foods. Some foods such as tomatoes, oranges, watermelon and iceberg lettuce are particularly high in water. Others such as dried fruits, nuts and seeds are lower. Water is also formed by the body when other nutrients are metabolized.

The average adult should consume at least 8 to 10 glasses (2L or 64 fl. oz.) of water a day to ensure adequate intake. People who perspire a lot should drink more water to replace body water lost through sweat.

Vitamins

Vitamins are vital dietary substances needed to regulate **metabolism** and for normal growth and body functions. They are essential and noncaloric, needed in the body in small amounts.

There are 13 vitamins. Table 3.3 lists them, their principal functions in the human body, the foods that contain high concentrations of these nutrients and some of the preparation and storage techniques that help retain the maximum amount of the various vitamins in their food sources.

Vitamins are divided into two categories: fat soluble and water soluble. The fat-soluble vitamins are A, D, E and K and are found in foods containing fat. Excess supplies of these vitamins may be stored in fatty tissues and the liver. Water-soluble vitamins are vitamin C and the B-complex vitamins, including thiamin (B_1), riboflavin (B_2), niacin (B_3), cyano-cobalamin (B_{12}), pyridoxine (B_6), pantothenic acid, biotin and folate. Vitamins B_1 and B_2 are commonly referred to by their names, thiamin and riboflavin, respectively; whereas, cobalamin and pyridoxine are commonly referred to by their letter designations, B_{12} and B_6, respectively. Water-soluble vitamins are not stored to the extent that fat-soluble vitamins are, and excesses may be excreted in the urine. Because of these differences, deficiencies in water-soluble vitamins usually develop more rapidly.

Virtually all foods contain some vitamins. Many factors contribute to a particular food's vitamin concentration: an animal's feed; the manner by which the produce is harvested, stored or processed; even the type of soil, sunlight, rainfall and temperature have significant effects on a food's vitamin content. For example, tomatoes have a higher concentration of vitamin C when picked ripe from the vine rather than when picked green. Also, different varieties of fruits and vegetables have different vitamin contents. A Wegener apple, for example, has 19 mg of vitamin C while a Red Delicious has only 6 mg.

You can control vitamin concentration and retention through careful food preparation:

1. Prepare vegetables as close to service time as possible; vegetables cut long before service lose more vitamins than those cut immediately before cooking.

2. Whether a vegetable is boiled, steamed or microwaved also determines the amount of vitamins it retains. Because the B-complex vitamins and vitamin C are water soluble, they are easily leached (washed out) or destroyed by food processing and preparation techniques involving high temperatures and water. Steaming and microwaving help retain nutrients (when steaming, keep the water level below the vegetables). But microwave cooking is best because it cooks vegetables with minimal water in less time.

3. In general, roasting and grilling meats, poultry, fish and shellfish preserve more vitamins than stewing and braising. The temperatures to which foods are cooked and length of time they are cooked may affect vitamin retention as well.

4. Storage affects vitamin concentrations. For example, long exposure to air may destroy vitamin C. Using airtight containers prevents some of this loss. Riboflavin is sensitive to light, so milk products (which are good sources of riboflavin) should be stored in opaque containers.

TABLE 3.3   VITAMINS: THEIR FUNCTIONS, SOURCES AND TECHNIQUES FOR RETAINING MAXIMUM NUTRIENT CONTENT

Vitamin	Functions in the Human Body	Sources	Techniques for Nutrient Retention
Vitamin A	Keeps the skin healthy; protects eyes; protects mouth and nose linings; supports immune functioning	Deep yellow and orange vegetables, leafy green vegetables, deep orange fruits, egg yolks, liver, fortified milk	Serve fruits and vegetables raw or lightly cooked; store vegetables covered and refrigerated; steam vegetables; roast or broil meats
Vitamin D	Helps body absorb calcium; regulates calcium and phosphorus in the bones; assists bone mineralization	Fortified milk, butter, some fish oils, eggs yolks (exposure to sunlight produces vitamin D in the body)	It is stable under heat and insoluble in water, therefore it is unaffected by cooking
Vitamin E	Antioxidant; protects membranes and cell walls	Vegetable oils, whole grains, dark leafy vegetables, wheat germ, nuts, seeds, whole grains	Use whole grain flours; store foods in airtight containers; avoid exposing the food to light and air
Vitamin K	Assists blood-clotting proteins	Liver, dark green leafy vegetables (bacteria in the intestinal tract also produce some vitamin K)	Steam or microwave vegetables; do not overcook meats
Vitamin C (Ascorbic acid)	Supports immune system functioning; repairs connective tissues; promotes healing; assists amino acid metabolism	Citrus fruits, green vegetables, strawberries, cantaloupes, tomatoes, broccoli, potatoes	Serve fruits and vegetables raw; steam or microwave vegetables
Thiamin (Vitamin B_1)	Assists energy metabolism; supports nervous system functioning	Meats (especially pork), legumes, whole grains	Use enriched or whole grain pasta or rice; do not wash whole grains before cooking or rinse afterwards; steam or microwave vegetables; roast meats at moderate temperatures; cook meats only until done
Riboflavin (Vitamin B_2)	Assists energy metabolism	Milk, cheese, yogurt, fish, enriched grain breads and cereals, dark green leafy vegetables	Store foods in opaque containers; roast or broil meats or poultry
Niacin (Vitamin B_3)	Promotes normal digestion; supports nervous system functioning; assists energy metabolism	Meats, poultry, fish, dark green leafy vegetables, whole grain or enriched breads and cereals, nuts	Steam or microwave vegetables; roast or broil beef, veal, lamb and poultry (pork retains about the same amount of niacin regardless of cooking method)
Vitamin B_6	Necessary for protein metabolism and red blood cell formation	Meats, fish, poultry, shellfish, whole grains, dark green vegetables, potatoes, liver	Serve vegetables raw; cook foods in a minimum amount of water and for the shortest possible time; roast or broil meats and fish
Vitamin B_{12}	Helps produce red blood cells; assists metabolism	Animal foods only, particularly milk, eggs, poultry and fish	Roast or broil meats, poultry and fish
Folate	Necessary for protein metabolism and red blood cell formation	Orange juice, dark green leafy vegetables, organ meats, legumes, seeds	Serve vegetables raw; steam or microwave vegetables; store vegetables covered and refrigerated
Biotin	Coenzyme in energy metabolism, glycogen synthesis and fat metabolism	Widespread in foods	
Pantothenic acid	Coenzyme in energy metabolism	Widespread in foods	

Minerals

Minerals cannot be manufactured by the body. They are obtained by eating plants that have drawn minerals from the ground or the flesh of animals that have eaten such plants.

Minerals are a critical component in hard and soft tissues (e.g., the calcium, magnesium and phosphorus present in bones and teeth). Minerals also regulate certain necessary body functions. For example, nerve impulses are transmitted through an exchange of sodium and potassium ions in the nerve cells.

Minerals are divided into two categories: trace minerals and major minerals. Trace minerals such as iron are needed in only very small amounts. Major minerals such as calcium are needed in relatively larger quantities. Table 3.4 lists

TABLE 3.4 MINERALS: THEIR FUNCTIONS AND SOURCES

Mineral	Functions in the Human Body	Sources
Major Minerals		
Calcium	Helps build bones and teeth; helps blood clot; promotes muscle and nerve functions	Dairy products, canned salmon and sardines, broccoli, kale, tofu, turnips
Magnesium	Muscle entraction; assists energy metabolism; bone formation	Green leafy vegetables, whole grains, legumes, fish, shellfish, cocoa
Phosphorus	Helps build bones and teeth; assists energy metabolism; formation of DNA	All animal tissues, milk, legumes, nuts
Potassium	Maintains electrolyte and fluid balance; promotes normal body functions; assists protein metabolism	Meats, poultry, fish, fruits (especially bananas, oranges and cantaloupes), legumes, vegetables
Sodium	Maintains normal fluid balance; necessary for nerve impulse transmission	Salt, soy sauce, processed foods, MSG
Chloride	With sodium, involved in fluid balance; component of stomach acid	Salt, soy sauce, meats, milk, processed foods
Sulphur	A component of some proteins, insulin and the vitamins biotin and thiamin	All protein-containing foods
Trace Minerals		
Iron	Part of hemoglobin (the red substance in blood that carries oxygen); prevents anemia	Liver, meats, shellfish, enriched breads and cereals, legumes
Zinc	A component of insulin; enhances healing; a component of many enzymes; involved in taste perception; bone formation	Protein foods, whole grain breads and cereals, fish, shellfish, poultry, vegetables
Selenium	Antioxidant	Fish, shellfish, meats, eggs, grains (depends on soil conditions)
Iodine	Component of thyroid hormone	Iodized salt, fish, shellfish, bread, plants grown in iodine-rich soil
Copper	Facilitates iron absorption; part of enzymes	Meats, fish, shellfish, nuts, seeds
Fluoride	Necessary for bone and teeth formation; helps teeth resist tooth decay	Fluoridated drinking water, fish, shellfish
Chromium	Insulin cofactor	Liver, whole grains, brewer's yeast, nuts, oils
Molybdenum	Cofactor in metabolism	Legumes, cereals
Manganese	Cofactor in metabolism	Whole grains, nuts, organ meats
Cobalt	Component of vitamin B_{12} (cobalamin)	

some minerals, their principal functions in the human body and the foods that contain high concentrations of these nutrients.

As with vitamins, food processing and preparation can reduce a food's mineral content. Soaking or cooking in large amounts of water can leach out small quantities of water-soluble minerals. Processing or refining grains, such as the wheat used to make white flour, also removes minerals.

EATING FOR HEALTH

It is generally recognized that a balanced diet is an important component of a healthy lifestyle. Eating well and exercising can contribute to a longer, healthier life.

Health Organization Recommendations

Planning a diet to enhance health is made simpler by diet and exercise recommendations from organizations such as the Canadian Heart Association and the Canadian Cancer Society. Both stress the importance of controlling the amount of fat in the diet and consuming in greater quantities plant foods such as vegetables, fruits and whole grains.

Another useful planning tool is *Canada's Food Guide to Healthy Eating*, published by Health Canada. The Food Guide recommends moderating the consumption of fats, cholesterol, sugar, salt and alcohol while increasing the consumption of grains, fruits and vegetables. Variety, energy, balance and moderation are the three central principles. Although some details of this guide are unique to Canada, the basic healthy eating principles that it promotes are much the same as the Food Pyramid used in the U.S. and the food guides of other international societies. By illustrating what foods are important and recommending a range of servings, they eliminate the guesswork of eating nutritiously.

The goal of healthy eating is to promote the shift from the traditional Canadian diet that is based heavily on protein-rich, higher-fat foods to one that includes more complex carbohydrates, fibre, key vitamins and minerals. This shift is presented visually in the Food Guide by the rainbow design illustrated in Figure 3.1. The larger outside arcs encourage eating proportionally more grain products, vegetables and fruits; the smaller inside arcs represent the smaller amounts required of milk and meat products. See Figure 3.2.

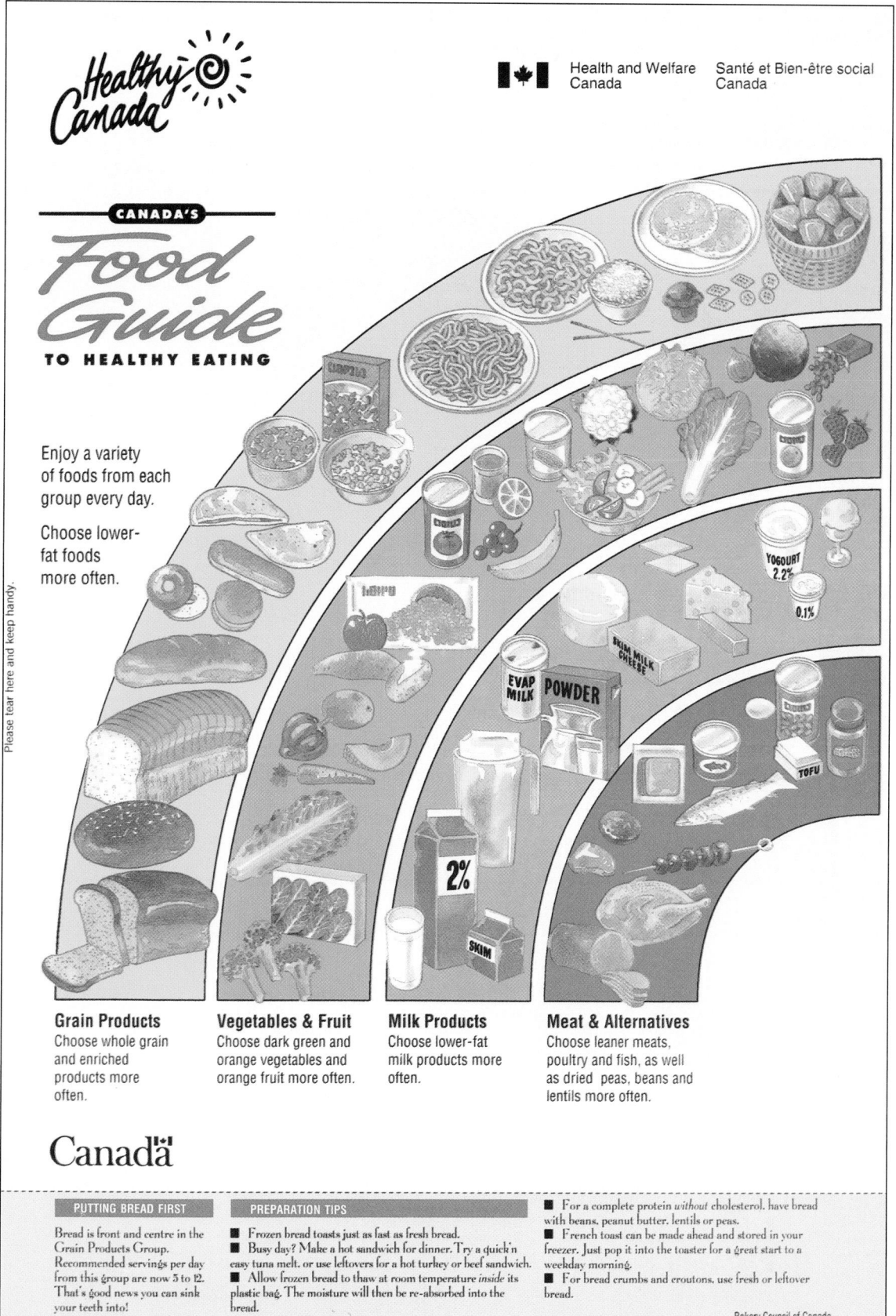

Health and Welfare Canada

Santé et Bien-être social Canada

Healthy Canada

CANADA'S Food Guide
TO HEALTHY EATING

Enjoy a variety of foods from each group every day.

Choose lower-fat foods more often.

Please tear here and keep handy.

Grain Products
Choose whole grain and enriched products more often.

Vegetables & Fruit
Choose dark green and orange vegetables and orange fruit more often.

Milk Products
Choose lower-fat milk products more often.

Meat & Alternatives
Choose leaner meats, poultry and fish, as well as dried peas, beans and lentils more often.

Canada

PUTTING BREAD FIRST

Bread is front and centre in the Grain Products Group. Recommended servings per day from this group are now 5 to 12. That's good news you can sink your teeth into!

PREPARATION TIPS

■ Frozen bread toasts just as fast as fresh bread.
■ Busy day? Make a hot sandwich for dinner. Try a quick'n easy tuna melt, or use leftovers for a hot turkey or beef sandwich.
■ Allow frozen bread to thaw at room temperature *inside* its plastic bag. The moisture will then be re-absorbed into the bread.

■ For a complete protein *without* cholesterol, have bread with beans, peanut butter, lentils or peas.
■ French toast can be made ahead and stored in your freezer. Just pop it into the toaster for a great start to a weekday morning.
■ For bread crumbs and croutons, use fresh or leftover bread.

Bakery Council of Canada

FIGURE 3.1   *Canada's Food Guide to Healthy Eating*
Source: Minister of Supply and Services Canada 1992, Cat. No. H39-252/1992E.

Different People Need Different Amounts of Food

The amount of food you need every day from the 4 food groups and other foods depends on your age, body size, activity level, whether you are male or female and if you are pregnant or breast-feeding. That's why the Food Guide gives a lower and higher number of servings for each food group. For example, young children can choose the lower number of servings, while male teenagers can go to the higher number. Most other people can choose servings somewhere in between.

Grain Products
5-12
SERVINGS PER DAY

Vegetables & Fruit
5-10
SERVINGS PER DAY

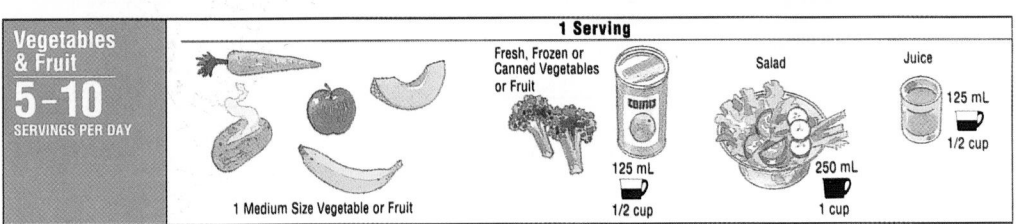

Milk Products
SERVINGS PER DAY
Children 4–9 years: 2–3
Youth 10–16 years: 3–4
Adults: 2–4
Pregnant & Breast-feeding
Women: 3–4

Other Foods

Taste and enjoyment can also come from other foods and beverages that are not part of the 4 food groups. Some of these foods are higher in fat or Calories, so use these foods in moderation.

Meat & Alternatives
2-3
SERVINGS PER DAY

Enjoy eating well, being active and feeling good about yourself. That's VITALITÉ

GOOD NEWS

Now more than ever, you can enjoy a lot more bread in all its different shapes and textures each and every day.

NUTRITION TIPS

■ All bread is low in fat. One slice (one serving from the Grain Products group) averages just 75 calories.
■ Fibre is great for people who want to eat less. Bread's fibre helps satisfy your hunger without adding many extra calories.

■ When you have a sandwich, the bread provides you with 9 essential nutrients: thiamin, riboflavin, niacin, folacin, pantothenic acid, phosphorus, magnesium, iron and zinc.
■ All white flour in Canada is enriched. So *all* bread contains B vitamins and iron.

Bakery Council of Canada

FIGURE 3.2   *Servings and Selections from Canada's Food Guide to Healthy Eating*
Source: *Canada's Food Guide to Healthy Eating*, Minister of Supply and Services Canada 1992, Cat. No. H39-252/1992E.

INGREDIENT SUBSTITUTES AND ALTERNATIVES

More and more people are becoming health-conscious consumers. Many are trying to cut down on foods high in salt, fat, added sugar and cholesterol. To a degree, people can accomplish their goals—and cooks can assist them—by turning to ingredient substitutes and alternatives where possible.

Here we use the term **ingredient substitute** to mean the replacement of one ingredient with another of presumably similar—although not necessarily identical—flavour, texture, appearance and other characteristics. The substitute may be more nutritious, however. So, someone who is avoiding fats can use reduced fat or nonfat sour cream in place of regular sour cream when baking quick breads. The differences in flavour, texture, appearance and baking quality should be minimal.

We use the term **ingredient alternative** to mean the replacement of one ingredient with another of different flavour, texture, appearance or other characteristic, but one that will not compromise—although it may change—the flavour of the dish. As with the ingredient substitute, the ingredient alternative may be more nutritious. Lemon juice and herbs, for instance, can be used as flavouring alternatives to salt; a salsa of fresh vegetables can replace a cream-based sauce. The dishes will not taste the same, but they will still taste good.

In attempting to modify a recipe, the cook should first identify the ingredient(s) and/or cooking method(s) that may need to be changed. He or she can then use the following principles—reduce, replace or eliminate—to make a dish healthier:

1. Reduce the amounts of the ingredient(s); or
2. Replace the ingredient(s) with a substitute that will do the least to change the flavour and appearance of the dish; or
3. Eliminate the ingredient(s).

Salt Substitutes and Alternatives

A concern in the Canadian diet is excessive sodium (salt). Research has linked excessive amounts of sodium to hypertension (high blood pressure), heart and kidney diseases and strokes.

Cooks can contribute to a more healthful diet by decreasing the amount of salt and other high-sodium products such as soy sauce. Salt substitutes, which contain potassium chloride instead of sodium chloride, are available. "Lite" salt has a portion of the sodium content replaced by potassium but still contains some real salt for a truer flavour.

In addition, pepper, lemon, herbs, spices, fruits and flavoured vinegars can be used as salt alternatives to heighten flavour.

Sugar Substitutes

Saccharin, the oldest artificial sugar substitute, has been used for nearly a century. A petroleum derivative, it has no calories and tastes 300 times sweeter than table sugar. Saccharin has a bitter aftertaste, however, and many people find it unpalatable. Along with its sweetness come health concerns: some studies have linked saccharin with tumours in rats.

Aspartame (also known as Nutrasweet®), approved in Canada in 1982, is composed of the amino acids aspartic acid and phenylalanine. Unlike saccharin, aspartame does not have an aftertaste. It is 180 times sweeter than table sugar. It is now widely used in soft drinks, frozen yogurts, fruit spreads, candies and similar products. Aspartame breaks down when heated, so it cannot be used in cooked foods. According to the Health Protection Branch of Health Canada, aspartame is a safe substitute for sugar, although it is a risk for those people with the rare disorder phenylketonuria (PKU), who cannot metabolize the phenylalanine in aspartame. Appropriate warnings are printed on all aspartame-sweetened foods. It is not recommended for pregnant women.

Another sugar substitute is acesulfame K or acesulfame potassium (also known as Sunnette®), which is the most recent artificial sweetener to come on the market. The body cannot metabolize acesulfame K, so it passes through the digestive system unchanged. Like aspartame, it has no aftertaste. Acesulfame K is used in chewing gum, dry beverage mixes, instant coffees and teas, gelatins and nondairy creamers. It is more stable than aspartame, so it can be used in baking.

Sucralose (also known as Splenda®) is a noncaloric sugar substitute approved by the Health Protection Branch in 1991. Made from processed sugar, its tightly bound chlorine atoms pass through the body quickly without being broken down. Sucralose has a clean, sugar-like taste and no aftertaste. Because it remains stable in any temperature and storage conditions, it can be used in beverages, canning, baking and cooking.

Fat Substitutes and Alternatives

Several types of fat substitutes are available; they are either synthetic or derived from naturally occurring food substances. Two of the more recent products are Olestra® and Simplesse®.

Olestra is made of sucrose and vegetable oil. The two are bonded together and the final product consists of molecules too large to be digested. Because it cannot be digested, Olestra does not add any calories. Currently, Olestra is used in snack foods such as potato chips. It may become a useful substitute for fats in baking or cooking, but health concerns have kept it from being widely available. Approval is pending in Canada.

Simplesse is a fat substitute used in frozen desserts such as ice creams and yogurt. Simplesse, made from egg whites or milk proteins, has a rich, creamy texture similar to fat but is fat free. Products made with Simplesse are not usually fat free, however, because other fat-containing ingredients are added.

Caprenin and salarim are fat substitutes used in the candy industry and are not available for home or restaurant use.

Other Ingredient Substitutes and Alternatives

There are many other ingredient substitutes, some of which are identified in Table 3.5. Often ingredient substitutes and alternatives have a dramatic impact on the nutritional values of a completed dish. For example, in Figures 3.3A and B we list the ingredients for a sheet pan of traditional fudge brownies and one made with ingredient substitutes. Note the differences, especially in the values for fat and cholesterol.

Ingredient substitutes and, especially, ingredient alternatives change the nutritional values of a dish; they may also change its flavour, texture or appearance. Sometimes these changes will be acceptable; sometimes they will not. Because some ingredient substitutes and alternatives result in unsatisfactory flavours, textures or appearance, many recipes may not be suitable for substitution or alteration. Prepare a test batch first if you are unsure.

TABLE 3.5 INGREDIENT SUBSTITUTES

For	Use
Bacon	Well-cooked, drained bacon or soy-based bacon
Butter	Powdered butter granules plus liquid (either skim milk or water) or butter-flavoured oil sprays
Chocolate	Cocoa (vegetable oil may be added as needed)
Cream cheese	Reduced-fat cream cheese or fat-free cream cheese
Emulsified salad dressing	Start with a base of reduced-fat or nonfat yogurt, sour cream or mayonnaise, then thin with skim milk; or use a slurry-thickened broth or juice as the oil and add vinegar and other seasonings; or blend silken tofu with other ingredients for a creamy dressing
Light cream	Equal portions of 1% milk and skim evaporated milk
Mayonnaise	Reduced-fat mayonnaise (it can be mixed with reduced-fat or nonfat sour cream)
Sour cream	Reduced-fat or nonfat sour cream; drained reduced-fat or nonfat plain yogurt without gelatin
Whipped cream	Whipped chilled evaporated skim milk; the milk and beaters need to be very cold (needs to be stabilized)

TRADITIONAL FUDGE BROWNIES

Yield: 88 5-cm (2-inch) Squares

Unsweetened chocolate	1 kg	2 lb.
Butter	1 kg	2 lb.
Eggs	22	22
Sugar	2.9 kg	5 lb. 12 oz.
Vanilla extract	60 mL	2 fl. oz.
All-purpose flour	750 g	1 lb. 10 oz.
Pecan pieces	500 g	1 lb.

Nutritional values per 5-cm (2-inch) square:

Calories	343
Total carbohydrates	41 g
Total fat	17 g
Protein	4 g
Saturated fat	9 g
Sodium	16 mg
Cholesterol	70 mg
Vitamin C	0

FIGURE 3.3A

CALORIE-REDUCED BROWNIES

Yield: 88 5-cm (2-inch) Squares

Unsweetened chocolate	125 g	4 oz.
Cake flour	500 g	1 lb.
Cocoa powder	275 g	9 oz.
Salt substitute	10 g	2 tsp.
Egg whites	12	12
Whole eggs	10	10
Granulated sugar	1 kg	2 lb. 2 oz.
Corn syrup	1 kg	2 lb.
Unsweetened applesauce	725 mL	1-1/2 pt.
Canola oil	200 mL	7 fl. oz.
Vanilla extract	30 mL	2 Tbsp.

Nutritional values per 5-cm (2-inch) square:

Calories	150
Total carbohydrates	26 g
Total fat	5 g
Protein	2 g
Saturated fat	0.8 g
Sodium	82 mg
Cholesterol	19 mg
Vitamin C	4 mg

FIGURE 3.3B

Great strides in agriculture have been made during the past two centuries. Pesticides, fungicides and herbicides now eliminate or control pests that once would have devoured, ruined or choked crops. Chemical fertilizers increase yields of many of the world's staples. But not everyone has greeted these developments with open arms.

During the past few decades, scientific and medical investigators have documented, or at least suggested, health risks associated with certain synthetic pesticides, fertilizers and other products. These findings have led to a renewed interest in a back-to-the-basics approach to farming: organic farming. Specialty farms, orchards and even wineries now offer organically grown products (or, in the case of wineries, wines made from organically grown grapes). These products come with few, if any, intentional additives and should be free of any incidental additives. Proponents argue that these products are better for consumers and better for the health of the farm workers.

The National Standard of Canada for Organic Agriculture was introduced in 1999. There are still some provincial variances but in order to market a product as organic the following requirements must be met: no use of antibiotic drugs in livestock feed; no use of chemical fertilizers or fertilizers that contain industrial or human waste; no use of synthetic pesticides; no use of genetically modified materials in seed for crops or in livestock feed; livestock must be grown in humane conditions (free range); and manure must be composted before use. Farms must be inspected annually for compliance and labelling claims are monitored by the Canadian Food Inspection Agency. There are numerous certifying bodies and the chef needs to be aware of the standards adhered to when sourcing organic products.

Package Labelling

To ensure that consumers have accurate information about packaged foods, the Consumer Packaging and Labelling Act and the Food and Drug Regulations require that most food products be clearly labelled. The language that may be used on these labels is closely regulated; even the minimum type size of the information is specified. The *Guide to Food Labelling and Advertising*, published by the Canadian Food Inspection Agency (1996), spells out requirements and is the source of most of the information that follows.

Mandatory Information

With few exceptions (such as one-bite confections sold individually), prepackaged products must be labelled. The label must include the common name of the product (e.g., "orange juice from concentrate," "mixed vegetables"), the net quantity, the name and address of the manufacturer or dealer and a list of ingredients, in descending order of proportion by weight in the food. Certain ingredients used in small amounts, such as seasonings, vitamins, minerals and additives, may be given in any order at the end of the list. Most products with a durable life of less than 90 days must have a "best before" date. The net quantity must be given in metric measures—grams or millilitres—and may also be given in imperial or U.S. measures such as ounces or fluid ounces. If the package suggests a natural flavour (e.g., a picture of an apple) but an artificial flavour is used, this information must be given next to the image. In most cases, mandatory information must be shown in both French and English.

Nutritional Information

A breakdown of nutritional content is not required. However, if it is given, it must follow specific formats set out in the *Guidelines on Nutrition Labelling* (Health Canada, 1996) and the Food and Drug Regulations and must not be misleading or deceptive. Nutrition labelling must be given in both official languages. A serving size must be given in grams or millilitres, and a household measure (e.g., 1 cup) should be used as well.

Nutrient information must include a "core list": energy (in both calories and kilojoules), and protein, fat and carbohydrates (in grams). Other information is optional. If one fat component (e.g., monounsaturates) is given, the other three components (polyunsaturates, saturates, cholesterol) must be given as well. If vitamins and minerals are listed, they must be given as a percentage of recommended daily intake. The United States' "Nutrition Facts" information is not permitted on foods sold in Canada, since the two countries use different methods of calculating nutrient values. Canadian regulations are pending (2002).

Nutritional Claims

Many products carry nutrient claims, such as "a good source of...," "low in...," "sugar-free" or "low calorie." Such terms have specific definitions that must be used accurately. A food may not be listed as a source of a nutrient, for example, unless it contains at least 5% of the recommended daily intake for that nutrient. Standards for foods described as "a good source of" or "high in" a nutrient are specific to each nutrient. Figure 3.4 shows a label giving nutrient information and making appropriate nutrient claims.

This food may be labelled "fat free" although it does contain a small amount of fat, because that amount is nutritionally insignificant: less than 0.5 grams of fat per serving and per reference amount.

Similar food products now list similar portion sizes, making nutritional comparison easier. The serving-size declaration must include the word "serving," must be given in grams or millilitres, and should also include a common or household measure.

If either sodium or potassium is listed, both must be stated.

Canadian Diabetes Association food choice values may be given, and are helpful for diabetics planning meals; the Canadian Celiac Association's gluten-free symbol is also allowed when applicable. Other endorsements may not be allowed, especially if they suggest a food may prevent disease.

No individual food may be called "essential" but nutrients assigned recommended daily intakes (RDI or RNI, recommended nutrient intake) may be. A food may not be called a "source" of a nutrient unless it contains at least 5% of the RDI.

Macronutrients are listed in grams; micronutrients are given as a percentage of RNI. RNI are usually for adult males and may be misleading for children or pregnant or lactating women.

The ingredient list, and most other mandatory information, must be shown in both English and French. In general, ingredients must be listed in descending order of proportion by weight in the food. Exceptions include spices, natural and artificial flavours, additives, vitamins and minerals, which may be shown at the end of the ingredient list in any order.

- Fat Free
- No Artifical Flavours or Colours
- No Preservatives

- Sans Matières grasses
- Sans Arôme ou Colorant Artificiels
- Sans Agent de Conservation

Nutrition Information | Information Nutritionnelle

Per 30 g serving cereal (250 mL, 1 cup) Par portion de 30 g de céréale (250 mL, 1 tasse)		Per 30 g serving cereal with 125 mL partly skimmed milk (2%) Par portion de 30 g de céréale avec 125 mL de lait partiellement écrémé (2%)	
Energy	115 Cal 470 kJ	180 Cal 740 kJ	Énergie
Protein	2.2 g	6.5 g	Protéines
Fat	0.1 g	2.6 g	Matières Grasses
Carbohydrate	26 g	32 g	Glucides
Sugars	3.2 g	9.4 g	Sucres
Starch	22 g	22 g	Amidon
Dietary Fibre	0.5 g	0.5 g	Fibres Alimentaires
Sodium	245 mg	310 mg	Sodium
Potassium	30 mg	230 mg	Potassium

% of Recommended Daily Intake			% de l'apport quotidien recommandé
Vitamin A	0%	7%	Vitamine A
Vitamin D	0%	23%	Vitamine D
Vitamin B1	46%	50%	Vitamine B1
Vitamin B2	1%	14%	Vitamine B2
Niacin	8%	13%	Niacine
Vitamin B6	10%	13%	Vitamine B6
Folacin	8%	11%	Folacine
Vitamin B12	0%	25%	Vitamine B12
Pantothenate	7%	13%	Pantothénate
Calcium	0%	15%	Calcium
Phosphorus	3%	14%	Phosphore
Magnesium	4%	11%	Magnésium
Iron	28%	29%	Fer
Zinc	12%	18%	Zinc

Canadian Diabetes Association Food Choice Value: 30 g (250 mL, 1 cup) cereal.
Le système des choix d'aliments de l'Association canadienne du diabète: 30 g (250 mL, 1 tasse) céréale = 1½ • choice/choix

Ingredients/Ingrédients
Corn, Rice, Sugar, Salt, Fancy Molasses, Barley Malt Syrup, Baking Soda, Colour, Vitamins (Thiamin Hydrochloride, Niacinamide, Pyridoxine Hydrochloride, Folic Acid, d-Calcium Pantothenate), Minerals (Iron, Zinc Oxide).
May Contain Traces of Soybeans.
Maïs, Riz, Sucre, Sel, Mélasse Qualité Fantaisie, Sirop d'orge Malté, Bicarbonate de Sodium, Colorant, Vitamines (Chlorhydrate de Thiamine, Niacinamide, Chlorhydrate de Pyridoxine, Acide Folique, d-Pantothénate de Calcium), Minéraux (Fer, Oxyde de Zinc). **Peut Contenir des Traces de Graines de Soja.**

FIGURE 3.4   *A Product Label Showing Nutritional Information in Approved Format*

As consumers express increasing concern about fat consumption, the term "fat free" has become particularly important. In 1997, Health Canada relaxed the definition of "fat free" to include foods that contain nutritionally insignificant amounts of fat: less than 0.5 grams of fat in a serving, and in a "reference amount" defined by regulation as the amount a person would typically consume at one time. The new definition matches U.S. and international standards.

Health Claims

Beyond simply making a claim about content, manufacturers sometimes want to claim certain benefits for a food. The language of health claims, too, is tightly regulated. For example, a food may be described as "wholesome" but should not be described as "healthy" where the word may suggest that simply eating the food will bring health. Manufacturers must not claim that a specific food may prevent a disease. Claims must be based on *Nutrition Recommendations for Canadians* or *Canada's Food Guide to Healthy Eating*, and must be substantiated by nutrient information. For example, it would be acceptable to claim: "Consuming a variety of fibre-containing foods is part of a healthy diet; this product is high in fibre." The package would then have to give the fibre content, which would have to meet criteria for "high." Table 3.6 shows the health claims that may be made for specific nutrients.

TABLE 3.6 ACCEPTABLE BIOLOGICAL ROLE CLAIMS FOR NUTRIENTS

Protein	Helps build and repair body tissues Helps build antibodies
Fat	Supplies energy Aids in the absorption of fat-soluble vitamins
Carbohydrate	Supplies energy Assists in the utilization of fats
Vitamin A	Aids normal bone and tooth development Aids in the development and maintenance of night vision Aids in maintaining the health of the skin and membranes
Vitamin D	Factor in the formation and maintenance of bones and teeth Enhances calcium and phosphorus absorption and utilization
Vitamin E	Protects the fat in body tissues from oxidation
Vitamin C	Factor in the development and maintenance of bones, cartilage, teeth and gums
Thiamine (Vitamin B_1)	Releases energy from carbohydrate Aids normal growth
Riboflavin (Vitamin B_2)	Factor in energy metabolism and tissue formation
Niacin	Aids in normal growth and development Factor in energy metabolism and tissue formation
Vitamin B_6	Factor in energy metabolism and tissue formation
Folacin	Aids in red blood cell formation
Vitamin B_{12}	Aids in red blood cell formation
Pantothenic acid	Factor in energy metabolism and tissue formation
Calcium	Aids in the formation and maintenance of bones and teeth
Phosphorus	Aids in the formation and maintenance of bones and teeth
Magnesium	Factor in energy metabolism, tissue formation and bone development
Iron	Factor in red blood cell formation
Zinc	Factor in energy metabolism and tissue formation
Iodine	Factor in the normal function of the thyroid gland

Source: *Guide to Food Labelling and Advertising*. Section 7.5.2, Specific Claims, Canadian Food Inspection Agency, 3/01/92, www.cfia-acia.agr.ca.

Nutritional Labelling for Restaurant Menus

Restaurants are not required to give nutritional information on menu items. If they do, the information must be accurate and meet the same standards as packaging material. Some restaurateurs like to use a heart symbol or claim that particular menu items are "heart smart choices." Such claims may be prohibited because they suggest that the food will prevent disease. However, a check mark may be used to identify menu items as healthy choices if it is part of a clearly identified nutrition information program.

CONSUMER CONCERNS ABOUT FOOD AND NUTRITION

Many food ingredients have been linked to medical conditions. Some of the links are tenuous at best; others may be well supported by research. Nutrition is a science and new information about the relationship of food to health and disease is always emerging.

Canadians have voiced concerns about the possible links of certain fats and dietary cholesterol to heart disease; they want to know if sugar intake is related to obesity, diabetes and heart disease.

Some people are concerned that pesticide residues in produce may be dangerous and they will seek out restaurants that serve organically grown produce. Some people are curious about the alleged medicinal or health benefits of foods. Others have metabolic or digestive conditions that make it difficult or even dangerous for them to eat specific ingredients. Because of these concerns, patrons may request that their meals be prepared in special ways or that ingredients be deleted from or added to a dish.

The tremendous public interest in nutrition presents a special challenge to chefs. They should be able to prepare and serve food that meets the high standards for health demanded by some patrons, while maintaining the flavour and appearance important to everyone.

Nutrition and the Chef

Canada's Food Guide to Healthy Eating was designed to guide food consumption for a more healthful life. It presents a plan for a balanced diet. Chefs can use it to plan balanced menus as well. As the Food Guide suggests, chefs do not need to use only meat as the centre of the plate presentation. It demands that a variety of breads, pasta and grains be included on the menu along with an interesting selection of vegetable dishes. And it cautions against the use of too much fat and sugar. The rainbow symbol is used to identify healthful food offerings (Figure 3.5).

FIGURE 3.5   *The Symbol for a Healthful Recipe*

Although not every food service operation can (or should) be devoted to "health food," to the extent appropriate, you should offer healthful dining alternatives. Your ability to do so depends, of course, upon your facility. Chefs at hospitals, prisons and schools have much greater control over the foods they offer. Therefore, they have a far greater opportunity and responsibility to provide selections for a well-balanced diet. Chefs at most restaurants, however, do not have such captive audiences. But that does not mean that you can shirk your responsibilities.

You assist customers when you:

1. Use proper purchasing and storage techniques in order to preserve nutrients.
2. Offer a variety of foods from each arc of the Food Guide rainbow so that customers have a choice.
3. Offer entrees that emphasize plant instead of animal foods.
4. Offer dishes that are considerate of special dietary needs such as low fat or low salt.
5. Use cooking procedures that preserve rather than destroy nutrients.
6. Use cooking procedures that minimize the use of added fat (e.g., stocks, sauces and soups can be cooled and the congealed fats removed; foods can be browned in the oven instead of being sautéed in hot fat).
7. Use equipment that minimizes the use of added fat (e.g., nonstick pans).
8. Train the wait staff to respond properly to nutritional questions diners may have about menu items.
9. Use ingredient alternatives or substitutes where appropriate. If a dish does not lend itself to ingredient alternatives or substitutes, consider creating a new dish that replaces less nutritious traditional foods or preparations with more nutritious ones. For example, instead of serving a sauce made with butter, flour and cream, you can reduce an appropriately seasoned wine, stock or juice and then thicken it with fruit or vegetable purées or starches.

♦♦♦

THE CUSTOMERS WHO COUNT

I have spent 19 years of my professional life in the "fine dining" or "gourmet" field. As of the date of this publication, I will have completed more than 20 years in transition to what I now call a "Minimax" lifestyle.

Minimax is not the opposite of fine "gourmet dining." As a culinary philosophy it has its place about midway. Minimax is a constructed word that can be understood internationally. Mini refers to minimum, in this case to risks encountered by unwise or excessive consumption of food. Max, on the other hand, refers to maximum possible enhancement of food, using natural aromas, colours and textures rather than the classic Western dependence on salts, fats and sugars.

Your future customers will be involved in a struggle when they read your menu. With their subjective right brains, they will be remembering former meals with enormous relish. With their objective left brains, they will apply what they know about fat, calories and sodium. Without some help they will either be confused, perplexed, rebellious or guilty.

Somehow then, you, who will make up the educated centre of the restaurant business of the future, will have to address the needs of those who want to make changes and still celebrate a night out at a comforting restaurant.

My suggestion is that you devise recipes that avoid fat as a primary source of calories for at least two appetizers, two entrées and one dessert. I would simply describe these on the menu for what they contain and not call them "low-fat" or "diet" or, for that matter, by any special name (even Minimax!). I would then present a small, very attractive, folded menu card with a phrase such as "For Our Customers Who Count" on the outside, and then simply list the nutritional benefits from the low-fat specials in an attractive, easy-to-read manner.

If your management chooses to establish such a menu, it will be extremely important that you weigh each dish correctly and have it analyzed by an approved nutrition system.

The reason for accuracy is that some, if not most, of the "customers who count" do so for very critical reasons. To give someone an oversized portion of meat with a great sauce that far exceeds, say, 30% calories from fat is actually highly irresponsible and may even attract possible litigation in the future.

When you reduce fat in a classical dish, there will be a reduction in flavour, since "fat carries flavour." By drawing attention away from the taste change and enhancing the sense of smell (aroma), sight (colour and presentation) and touch (texture), you can actually improve the finished dish.

I have found that the fusion idea has helped make this a reality. Fusion is simply merging seasonings from one culture with those from another. In this way it helps to see Northern European specialties that use abundant dairy products as "velvet memories," and North African and Asian seasonings as "future bright notes."

It is then possible to consider a modification to, say, sauce hollandaise by lowering the fat and adding a good Asian fish sauce to which shreds of mint and flecks of red pepper are added to spike interest with aroma, colour and texture.

Whatever you choose to do, let me give you this last word of encouragement. Study hard, read the classics and see the future through them. If you've ever skipped smooth stones on flat water you'll know that the first bounce really matters. If your attitude to very rich classics is negative and condemning, then what you try to achieve will certainly fail to go the distance.

Therefore, don't condemn anyone's work. Aim to please today's customer with all the skills that our exciting profession has developed for thousands of years.

You have my very best wishes for a most successful career. Now go skip your stone…for your customers' sakes!

GRAHAM KERR, author, chef and host of
THE GALLOPING GOURMET
and GRAHAM KERR'S KITCHEN,
seen on PBS-TV and The Discovery Channel

The nutrient information provided here is for reference only. There is a 20% margin of error, due primarily to choices for specific ingredients and variations in the size of fruits and vegetables. Preparation techniques and serving sizes may also significantly alter the values of many nutrients. When a recipe offers a choice of ingredients, the first-mentioned ingredient was the one used in the calculations. Ingredients listed as "to taste" (TT) and "as needed" were omitted from the analysis. In addition, olive oil and 3% whole milk were used throughout for "vegetable oil" and "milk," respectively. When given a choice of serving size or weight, the first mentioned was used.

CONCLUSION

A basic understanding and appreciation of nutrition are important for both the consumer and those who prepare the foods consumed.

What you serve is important. Carbohydrates, proteins, fats, water, vitamins and minerals, in varying amounts, are all necessary for good health. *Canada's Food Guide to Healthy Eating* can guide selections to create and maintain a healthful diet.

How foods are prepared is also important. Remember that some cooking and storage techniques preserve nutrients; others do not. In addition, by substituting or modifying ingredients and preparation methods, many dishes can be made more nutritious.

$\mathcal{Q}$UESTIONS FOR DISCUSSION

1. Identify the six categories of nutrients and list two sources for each.
2. What are the differences between saturated fats and unsaturated fats? Identify two sources for each.
3. List four things you can do to reduce the loss of minerals and vitamins when storing or preparing foods.
4. Describe *Canada's Food Guide to Healthy Eating*. Explain how a chef can use it to plan well-balanced meals and how a consumer can use it to establish a healthful diet. What other diet planning tools can be used along with the Food Guide?
5. Create two menus for a Thanksgiving dinner, both nutritionally balanced, but one high in calories, fat and so on, and the other including the traditional foods but reduced in fat, calories, cholesterol and sodium.

$\mathcal{W}$EBLINKS

Canada Food Guide
www.hc-sc.gc.ca/hppb/nutrition/pube/foodguid/food1.htm
National Institute of Nutrition
www.nin.ca
Jean Fremont's (Simon Fraser University Professor)
Nutrition and Food on the Web—Finding the Right Stuff
www.sfu.ca/~jfremont
International Union of Nutritional Sciences
www.monash.edu.au/IUNS
Food Science and Nutrition Resources
www.uwstout.edu/lib/subjects/foodsc.htm
Foods and Nutrition Solutions
www.ag.uiuc.edu/~robsond/solutions/nutrition.html
Journal of Nutrition in Recipe and Menu Development
bubl.ac.uk/journals/agr/jniramd/

CHAPTER 4

MENU PLANNING AND FOOD COSTING

━━━━━ ◆◆◆ ━━━━━

LEARNING OUTCOMES

After studying this chapter you will be able to:

◆ identify the different types and styles of menus

◆ explain the purpose of standardized recipes

◆ calculate the cost per portion for recipes

◆ convert recipe yield amounts

◆ determine menu prices and calculate food cost percentages

◆ control food costs

━━━━━━━━━━━━━━━━━

oday's professional cook must master more than the basics of béchamel, butchering and bread baking. You must be equally skilled in the business of food services. This means knowing what products cost and how much an operation should charge for its menu items.

Although computers are almost as common in kitchens as whisks, no machine can ever replace a cook's hands-on ability to apply food cost controls. Accurate measurements, portion control and proper food handling directly affect the food service operation's bottom line. In addition, cooks must, at the very least, be able to conduct yield tests, calculate recipe costs and use food cost percentages.

This chapter first introduces you to various types and styles of menus. It then explains a standardized recipe format and presents the basics of food cost controls as well as information on measurements and techniques for changing or converting recipe yields. It then describes methods for determining unit and recipe costs, including calculations for raw yield tests. It concludes with a discussion of the methods for pricing menus and controlling food costs. This chapter does not attempt to cover menu design, accounting principles or computer applications. It will, however, provide a foundation of practical techniques to be used by anyone with common sense and a calculator.

THE MENU

Whether it lists ethnic dishes, hamburgers, just desserts or classic cuisine, and whether the prices range from inexpensive to exorbitant, the menu is the soul of every food service operation. Its purposes are to identify for the consumer the foods and beverages the operation offers, to create consumer enthusiasm and to increase sales. When combined with excellent food and great service, a well-planned menu helps ensure success.

Most menus offer consumers sufficient selections to build an entire meal. A typical Canadian or American main meal consists of three courses. The first course may be a hot or cold appetizer, soup or salad. The second course is the **entree** or main dish, usually meat, poultry, fish or shellfish accompanied by a vegetable and starch. The third course is dessert, either a sweet preparation or fruit and cheese. For a more formal meal, there may be a progression of first courses, including a hot or cold appetizer and soup, as well as a fish course served before the main dish (which, in this case, would not be fish). For some meals sorbet or granité may follow the fish course as a palate cleanser. Occasionally, a light salad will be presented as a palate cleanser after the main dish and before dessert, cheese and friandises.

Types of Menus

Menus are classified according to the regularity with which the foods are offered:

1. **Static menu**—All patrons are offered the same foods every day. Once a static menu is developed and established, it rarely changes. Static menus are typically found in fast-food operations, ethnic restaurants, steakhouses and the like.

   Static menus can also be used in institutional settings. For example, a static menu at an elementary school could offer students, along with a vegetable and dessert, the same luncheon choices every school day: a cheeseburger, fish sticks, chicken tacos, pizza wedges or a sandwich.

2. **Cycle menu**—A cycle menu is developed for a set time period; at the end of that period it repeats itself (i.e., on a seven-day cycle, the same menu is used every Monday). Some cycle menus are written on a seasonal basis, with a new menu for each season to take advantage of product availability. Cycle menus are used commonly in schools, hospitals and other institutions. Although cycle menus may be repetitious, the repetition is not necessarily noticeable to diners because of the length of the cycles.

3. **Market menu**—A market menu is based upon product availability during a specific time period; it is written to use foods when they are in peak season or readily available. Market menus are becoming increasingly popular with chefs (and consumers) as they challenge the chef's ingenuity in using fresh, seasonal products. Market menus are short-lived, however, because of limited product availability and perishability. In fact, they often change daily.

4. **Hybrid menu**—A hybrid menu combines a static menu with a cycle menu or a market menu of specials.

Food service operations may have separate menus for breakfast, lunch or dinner. If all three meals are available all day and are listed on the same menu, the menu is often called a California menu; California menus are typically found in 24-hour restaurants. Depending on the food service operation's objectives, separate specialty menus for drinks, hors d'oeuvre, desserts, brunch or afternoon tea, for example, are used.

Regardless of whether the menu is static, cycle, market or hybrid, it can offer consumers the opportunity to purchase their selections à la carte, semi à la carte, table d'hôte or some combination of the three.

1. **À la carte**—Every food and beverage item is priced and ordered separately.

2. **Semi à la carte**—With this popular menu style, some food items (particularly appetizers and desserts) are priced and ordered separately, while the entree is accompanied by and priced to include other items, such as a salad, starch or vegetable.

3. **Table d'hôte** or **prix fixe**—This menu offers a complete meal at a set price. (The term *table d'hôte* is French for "host's table" and is derived from the innkeeper's practice of seating all guests at a large communal table and serving them all the same meal.) A table d'hôte meal can range from very elegant to a diner's blue-plate special.

Many menus combine à la carte, semi à la carte and table d'hôte choices. For example, appetizers, salads and desserts may be available à la carte; entrees may be offered semi à la carte (they come with a salad, starch and vegetable), while the daily special is a complete (table d'hôte or prix fixe) meal.

Menu Language

The menu is the principal way in which the food service operation, including the chef, communicates with the consumer. A well-designed menu often reflects the input of design, marketing, art and other consultants as well as the chef and management. The type of folds, cover, artwork, layout, typefaces, colours and paper are all important considerations. But the most important consideration is the language.

The menu should list the foods offered. It may include descriptions such as the preparation method, essential ingredients and service method as well as the quality, cut and quantity of product. For example, the menu can list "Striploin Steak" or "Mesquite Grilled 250 g Certified Canadian Angus Beef Striploin Steak."

Federal laws require that certain menu language be accurate. Areas of particular concern include statements about quantity, quality, grade and freshness as well as dietary and nutritional claims. Accurate references to an item's source are also important. If brand names are used, those brands must be served. If the restaurant claims to be serving "Fresh Dover Sole," it must be just that, not frozen sole from New England. (On the other hand, like French or Russian dressing, "English mint sauce" is a generic name for a style of food, so using that geographical adjective is appropriate even if the mint sauce is not made in England.) A reference to "our own fresh-baked" desserts means that the restaurant regularly bakes the desserts on premises, serves them soon after baking and does not substitute commercially prepared or frozen goods.

STANDARDIZED RECIPES

Menu writing and **recipe** development are mutually dependent activities. Once the menu is created, standardized recipes should be prepared for each item. A **standardized recipe** is one that will produce a known quality and quantity of food for a specific operation. It specifies (1) the type and amount of each ingredient, (2) the preparation and cooking procedures and (3) the yield and portion size.

Standardized recipes may be found in books or provided by manufacturers, but usually they are recipes customized to your operation—cooking time, temperature and utensils should be based on the equipment actually available. Yield should be adjusted to an amount appropriate for your operation. A recipe must be tested repeatedly and adjusted to fit your facility and your needs before it can be considered standardized.

Standardized recipes are a tool for the chef and management. The written forms assist with training cooks, educating service staff and controlling financial matters. They also help ensure that the customer will receive a consistent quality and quantity of product. Accurate recipe costing and menu pricing depend on having and using standardized recipes.

Although formats differ, a standardized recipe form, such as that reproduced in Figure 4.1, will usually include:

+ Name of product
+ Yield
+ Portion size
+ Presentation and garnish
+ Ingredient quality and quantity
+ Preparation procedures
+ Cooking time and temperature
+ Holding procedures

STANDARD RECIPE CARD FOR ITEM:					DATE REVISED					
QUANTITY PRODUCED					RECIPE FILE NO.					
PORTION SIZE					RESTAURANT					
NO. OF PORTIONS PRODUCED					SALES PRICE					

INGREDIENTS	QTY/ WEIGHT	PURCH UNIT	DATE: UNIT COST	TOTAL	DATE: UNIT COST	TOTAL	DATE: UNIT COST	TOTAL	PREPARATION PROCEDURE
TOTAL COST									
COST PER PORTION									
COST % PER PORTION									

FIGURE 4.1 *Standardized Recipe Form*

The form may also include information on costing and a photograph of the finished dish. Each form should be complete, consistent and simple to read and follow. The forms should be stored in a readily accessible place. Index cards, notebook binders or a computerized database may be used, depending on the size and complexity of the operation.

MEASUREMENTS AND CONVERSIONS

Measurement Formats

Accurate measurements are among the most important aspects of food production. Ingredients and portions must be measured correctly to ensure consistent product quality. In other words, the cook must be able to prepare a recipe the same way each time, and portion sizes must be the same from one order to the next.

In a kitchen, measurements may be made in three ways: weight, volume and count.

Weight refers to the mass or heaviness of a substance. It is expressed in terms such as kilograms, grams, ounces and pounds. Weight may be used to measure liquid or dry ingredients (for example, 800 g of eggs for a bread recipe) and portions (for example, 85 g of sliced turkey for a sandwich). As weight is generally the most accurate form of measurement, portion scales or balance scales are commonly used in kitchens.

Volume refers to the space occupied by a substance. This is mathematically expressed as *height* × *width* × *length*. It is expressed in terms such as millilitres, litres, cups, quarts, gallons, teaspoons, fluid ounces and bushels. Volume is most commonly used to measure liquids. It may also be used for dry ingredients when the amount is too small to be weighed accurately (for example, 1 mL/1/4 tsp. of salt). Although measuring by volume is somewhat less accurate than measuring by weight, volume measurements are generally quicker to do.

Frequently, mistakes are made in food preparation by cooks who assume wrongly that weight and volume are equal. Do not be fooled—250 mL of solid food does not always equal 250 g. While it is true that 1 standard cup contains 8 *fluid* ounces, it is not true that the contents of that standard cup will *weigh* 8 ounces. For example, the weight of 1 cup of diced apples will vary depending on the size of the apple pieces. Errors are commonly made in the bakeshop by cooks who assume that 8 ounces of flour is the same as 1 cup of flour. In fact, 225 mL (1 cup) of flour may weigh from 100 to 140 g (3 1/2–5 oz.) depending on types and conditions.

It is not unusual to see both weight and volume measurements used in a single recipe. When a recipe ingredient is expressed in weight, weigh it. When it is expressed as a volume, measure it. Like most rules, however, this one has exceptions. The weight and volume of water is the same. For this ingredient you may use whichever measurement is most convenient.

Count refers to the number of individual items. Count is used in recipes (for example, 4 eggs) and in portion control (for example, 2 fish fillets or 1 ear of corn). Count is also commonly used in purchasing to indicate the size of the individual items. For example, a "96 count" case of lemons means that an 18 kg (40 lb.) case contains 96 individual lemons; a "115 count" case means that the same 18 kg (40 lb.) case contains 115 individual lemons. So, each lemon in the 96-count case is larger than those in the 115-count case. Shrimp is another item commonly sold by count. Depending on the size of the individual pieces, 450 g (1 lb.) of shrimp may contain from 8 to several hundred shrimp. When placing an order, the chef must specify the desired count. For example, when ordering 450 g (1 lb.) of 21–25-count shrimp the chef expects to receive not less than 21 nor more than 25 shrimps.

Measurement Systems

The measurement formats of weight, volume and count are used in the imperial, U.S. and metric measurement systems. Because each of these systems is uses in modern food service operations, you should be able to prepare recipes written in any of the three.

The **imperial system** originated in Great Britain and a few other countries. It uses pounds and ounces for weight, and pints and fluid ounces for volume.

The **U.S. system** is the most difficult system to understand. It uses pounds for weight and cups for volume.

The **metric system**, used in Canada, is the most commonly used system in the world. Developed in France during the late 18th century, it was intended to fill the need for a mathematically rational and uniform system of measurement.

◆◆◆

END OF AN ERA

The imperial system is rapidly disappearing. The UK has officially gone metric. In the modern world, global trade requires a standard system and so too will the U.S. system slowly disappear. Export products routinely list metric and U.S. equivalents.

✦✦✦

FANNIE MERRITT FARMER
(1857–1915)

Fannie Farmer is more than the name on a cookbook. She was an early, vigorous and influential proponent of scientific cooking, nutrition and academic training for culinary professionals.

At the age of 30, Farmer enrolled in the Boston Cooking School. The school's curriculum was not designed to graduate chefs, but rather to produce cooking teachers. After graduating from the two-year course, Farmer stayed on, first as assistant principal and then as principal.

During her years there (and, indeed, for the rest of her career), she was obsessed with accurate measurements. She waged a campaign to eliminate measurements such as a "wine glass" of liquid, a "handful" of flour, a chunk of butter the "size of an egg" or a "heaping spoonful" of salt. For, as she once wrote, "correct measurements are absolutely necessary to insure the best results." Farmer also sought to replace the European system of measuring ingredients by weight with, for her, a more scientific measurement system based on volume and level measures (e.g., a level tablespoon). To a great degree, she succeeded.

Her writings reflect her concern for accurate measurements. Her first book, *The Boston Cooking School Cookbook* (1896), includes clearly written recipes with precise measurements. Later editions add recipe yields, oven temperatures and baking times.

After leaving the Boston Cooking School, she opened "Miss Farmer's School of Cookery." The curriculum listed 60 lessons divided into 6 courses. The first course covered the basics: laying a fire and using a gas stove; making breads, eggs, soups, potatoes and coffee. The second and third courses emphasized more advanced cooking. Pastry, desserts and salads were taught during the fourth course; presentation and service were taught during the fifth course. Quite progressively for the time, her sixth course taught cooking for nurses and emphasized nutrition and the dietary needs of the sick and elderly. (This may have reflected Farmer's personal interests, for she was partially disabled and in poor health from time to time.)

Farmer wrote other cookbooks, including *Food and Cookery for the Sick and Convalescent* (1904) and *A New Book of Cookery* (first published in 1912 and republished in several revised versions). Her writings never address the joys of cooking and eating; rather, they reflect a scientific approach to cooking and rely on clearly written, accurately measured recipes for good, solid food.

The metric system is a decimal system in which the gram, litre and metre are the basic units of weight, volume and length, respectively. Larger or smaller units of weight, volume and length are formed by adding a prefix to the words *gram*, *litre* or *metre*. Some of the more commonly used prefixes in food service operations are deca- (10), hecto- (100), kilo- (1000), deci- (1/10), centi- (1/100) and milli- (1/1000). Thus, a kilogram is 1000 grams; a decametre is 10 metres; a millilitre is 1/1000 of a litre. Because the metric system is based on multiples of 10, it is extremely easy to increase or decrease recipe amounts.

The most important thing for a cook to know about the metric system is that *you do not need to convert between the metric system and the U.S. or imperial system in recipe preparation*. If a recipe is written in metric units, use

TABLE 4.1   COMMON ABBREVIATIONS AND CONVERSIONS

teaspoon	=	tsp.
tablespoon	=	Tbsp.
cup	=	c.
pint	=	pt.
quart	=	qt.
gram	=	g
millilitre	=	mL
litre	=	L
ounce	=	oz.
fluid ounce	=	fl. oz.
pound	=	lb.
kilogram	=	kg
dash	=	1/8 teaspoon
3 teaspoons	=	1 tablespoon
2 tablespoons	=	1 fl. oz.
4 tablespoons	=	1/4 cup (2 fl. oz.)
5-1/3 tablespoons	=	1/3 cup (2-2/3 fl. oz.)
16 tablespoons	=	1 cup (8 fl. oz.)
2 cups	=	1 pint (16 fl. oz.)
2 pints	=	1 quart (32 fl. oz.)
4 quarts	=	1 gallon (128 fl. oz.)*
2 gallons	=	1 peck
4 pecks	=	1 bushel
1 gram	=	0.035 ounce (1/30 oz.)
1 ounce	=	28.35 grams
454 grams	=	1 pound
2.2 pounds	=	1 kilogram (1000 grams)
1 teaspoon	=	5 millilitres
1 tablespoon	=	15 millilitres
1 cup	=	0.24 litres (for practical purposes, 250 mL)

*Note that the gallon measurements in this book are based on the U.S. gallon—128 fl. oz.

metric measuring equipment; if it is written in U.S. units, use U.S. measuring equipment. Most modern measuring equipment is calibrated in both U.S. and metric increments. The need to convert amounts will arise only if the proper equipment is unavailable.

Converting Grams and Ounces

As you can see from Table 4.1, 1 ounce equals 28.35 grams. So, *to convert ounces to grams, multiply the number of ounces by 28* (rounded for convenience).

8 ounces × 28 = 224 grams (225 g for practical use)

And *to convert grams to ounces, divide the number of grams by 28.*

224 ÷ 28 = 8 ounces

To help you develop a framework for judging conversions, remember that:

- a kilogram is about 2.2 pounds
- a gram is about 1/30 ounce
- a pound is about 450 grams
- a litre is slightly more than a quart
- a centimetre is slightly less than 1/2 inch
- 0° Celsius is the freezing point of water (32°F)
- 100° Celsius is the boiling point of water (212°F) at sea level

These approximations are not a substitute for accurate conversions, however. Appendix I contains additional information on equivalents and metric conversions. There is no substitute for knowing this information. In fact, it should become second nature to you. Try to avoid converting recipes, especially for baking and pastry. The results may be substandard. Remember that most recipes are based on proportions of ingredients.

RECIPE CONVERSIONS

Whether 6 servings or 60, every recipe is designed to produce or **yield** a specific amount of product. A recipe's yield may be expressed in *volume*, *weight* or *servings* (for example, 1 litre of sauce; 4 kg of bread dough; 8 100-mL servings). If the expected yield does not meet your needs, you must convert (i.e., increase or decrease) the ingredient amounts. Recipe conversion is sometimes complicated by *portion size conversions*. For example, it may be necessary to convert a recipe that initially produces 24 250-mL servings of soup into a recipe that produces 62 180-mL servings.

It is just as easy to change yields by uneven amounts as it is to double or halve recipes. The mathematical principle is the same: *Each ingredient is multiplied by a* **conversion factor**. Do not take shortcuts by estimating recipe amounts or conversion factors. Inaccurate conversions lead to inedible foods, embarrassing shortages or wasteful excesses. Take the time to learn and apply proper conversion techniques. Most recipes can be doubled or halved without too much quality being lost. Seasonings may need further adjustments when doing larger conversion factors.

Converting Total Yield

When portion size is unimportant or remains the same, recipe yield is converted by a simple two-step process:

STEP 1: Divide the desired (new) yield by the recipe (old) yield to obtain the conversion factor (C.F.).

$$\text{new yield} \div \text{old yield} = \text{conversion factor}$$

$$\frac{N}{O} = \text{C.F.}$$

STEP 2: Multiply each ingredient quantity by the conversion factor to obtain the new quantity.

$$\text{old quantity} \times \text{conversion factor} = \text{new quantity}$$

$$\begin{array}{r} \text{Old Quantity} \\ \underline{\times \ \text{C.F.}} \\ \text{New Quantity} \end{array}$$

Example 4.1

You need to convert a recipe for cauliflower soup. The present recipe yields 6 L; you need to make only 3 L.

First, determine the conversion factor:

$$3 \text{ L} \div 6 \text{ L} = 0.50$$

Second, the conversion factor is applied to each ingredient in the soup recipe:

CAULIFLOWER SOUP

	old quantity	×	C.F.	=	new quantity
Cauliflower, chopped	2.5 kg	×	0.5	=	1.25 kg (or 1250 g)
Celery stalks	4	×	0.5	=	2
Onion	1	×	0.5	=	1/2
Chicken stock	2 L	×	0.5	=	1 L
Heavy cream	1300 mL	×	0.5	=	650 mL

Converting Portion Size

A few additional steps are necessary to convert recipes when portion sizes must also be changed.

STEP 1: Determine the total yield of the existing recipe by multiplying the number of portions by the portion size.

$$\text{original portions} \times \text{original portion size} = \text{total (old) yield}$$

$$\begin{array}{r} \text{Number of Portions} \\ \underline{\times \ \text{Portion Size}} \\ \text{Yield} \end{array}$$

STEP 2: Determine the total yield desired by multiplying the new number of portions by the new portion size.

$$\text{desired portions} \times \text{desired portion size} = \text{total (new) yield}$$

STEP 3: Obtain the conversion factor as described above.

$$\text{total (new) yield} \div \text{total (old) yield} = \text{conversion factor}$$

$$\frac{\text{New Yield}}{\text{Old Yield}} = \text{C.F.}$$

STEP 4: Multiply each ingredient quantity by the conversion factor.

$$\text{old quantity} \times \text{conversion factor} = \text{new quantity}$$

Example 4.2

Returning to the cauliflower soup: The original recipe produced 6 L or 48 servings of 125 mL. Now you need 72 servings of 180 mL.

STEP 1: Total original yield is $48 \times 125 = 6000$ mL

STEP 2: Total desired yield is $72 \times 180 = 12\,960$ mL

STEP 3: Conversion factor is calculated by dividing total new yield by total old yield:

$$12\,960 \div 6000 = 2.25$$

STEP 4: Old ingredient quantities are multiplied by conversion factor to determine new quantities:

CAULIFLOWER SOUP

	old quantity	×	C.F.	=	new quantity
Cauliflower, chopped	2.5 kg	×	2.25	=	5.625 kg
Celery stalks	4	×	2.25	=	9
Onion	1	×	2.25	=	2.25
Chicken stock	2 L	×	2.25	=	4.5 L
Heavy cream	1300 mL	×	2.25	=	2.925 L

Additional Conversion Problems

When making very large recipe changes—for example, from 5 to 50 portions or 600 to 36 portions—you may encounter additional problems. The mathematical conversions described above do not take into account changes in equipment, evaporation rates, unforeseen recipe errors or cooking times. Chefs learn to use their judgment, knowledge of cooking principles and skills to compensate for these factors.

Equipment

When you change the size of a recipe, you must often change the equipment used as well. Problems arise, however, when the production techniques previously used no longer work with the new quantity of ingredients. For example, if you normally make a muffin recipe in small quantities by hand and you increase the recipe size, it may be necessary to prepare the batter in a mixer. But if mixing time remains the same, the batter may become over-mixed, resulting in poor-quality muffins. Trying to prepare a small amount of product in equipment that is too large for the task can also affect its quality.

Evaporation

Equipment changes can also affect product quality because of changes in evaporation rates. Increasing a soup recipe may require substituting a tilt skillet for a saucepan. But because a tilt skillet provides more surface area for evaporation than does a saucepan, reduction time must be decreased to prevent overthickening the soup. The increased evaporation caused by an increased surface area may also alter the strength of the seasonings.

Recipe Errors

A recipe may contain errors in ingredients or techniques that are not obvious when it is prepared in small quantities. When increased, however, small mistakes often become big (and obvious) ones, and the final product suffers.

The only solution is to test recipes carefully and rely on your knowledge of cooking principles to compensate for unexpected problems.

Time

Do not multiply time specifications given in a recipe by the conversion factor used with the recipe's ingredients. *All things being equal, cooking time will not change* when recipe size changes. For example, a muffin requires the same amount of baking time whether you prepare 1 dozen or 14 dozen. Cooking time will be affected, however, by changes in evaporation rate or heat conduction caused by equipment changes. *Mixing time* may change when recipe size is changed. Different equipment may perform mixing tasks more or less efficiently than previously used equipment. Again, rely on experience and good judgment or ask your supervisor.

CALCULATING UNIT COSTS AND RECIPE COSTS

Unit Costs

Food service operations purchase most foods from suppliers in bulk or wholesale packages. For example, canned goods are purchased by the case; produce by the flat, case or lug; and flour and sugar by 10- or 20-kg bags. Even fish and meats are often purchased in large cuts, not individual serving-sized portions. The purchased amount is rarely used for a single recipe, however. It must be broken down into smaller units such as kilograms, litres, grams or millilitres.

In order to allocate the proper ingredient costs to the recipe being prepared, it is necessary to convert **as-purchased costs or prices** to **unit costs or prices**. To find the unit cost (i.e., the cost of a particular unit, say a single egg) in a package containing multiple units (e.g., a 30-dozen case), divide the as-purchased cost (A.P. cost) of the package by the number of units in the package.

A.P. cost ÷ number of units = cost per unit

$$\frac{\text{A.P. \$}}{\text{\# of Units}} = \text{\$ Per Unit}$$

Example 4.3

A case of #10 (2.84 L) cans contains 6 individual cans. If a case of tomato paste costs $23.50, then each can costs $3.92.

$$\$23.50 \div 6 = \$3.92$$

If your recipe uses less than the total can, you must continue dividing the cost of the can until you arrive at the appropriate unit amount. Continuing with the tomato paste example, if you need only 0.225 L, or 225 mL (1 cup), find out how much 1 litre costs by dividing the cost per item by the volume.

$$\$3.92 \div 2.84 \text{ L} = \$1.380 \text{ per L}$$

To calculate how much 225 mL costs, multiply this figure by the desired unit amount (0.225 L):

$$1.380 \times 0.225 = 0.3105 \text{ (to 4 decimal places)}$$

The whole operation can be expressed by the formula

$$\frac{\text{cost per item (\$3.92)} \times \text{unit required (0.225 L, or 1 cup)}}{\text{unit size (2.84 L)}} = \$0.31$$

◆◆◆

When calculating unit costs, it is vital that the unit size and the unit required be expressed in the same measurement unit. For example, if the can is measured in fluid ounces, then the unit required must also be in fluid ounces. In the example opposite, if the volume remains the same but the can size is 28 ounces, and you want to know how much a cup costs, you need to recalculate cost based on the new A.P. cost. Costing problems arise when products are purchased by weight and recipes are expressed by volume. Water is the only substance with a one to one relationship of volume and weight (1 mL = 1 g).

RECIPE COSTING FORM

Menu Item _Maple Glazed Carrots_   Date _May 2002_

| Ingredient | Quantity | COST | | | TOTAL COST |
		As Purchased	Yield %	Edible Portion	
Carrots	2.2 kg	16.35/22.68 kg	85	.848/kg	1.866
Butter	125 g	3.10/454 g	100	6.828/kg	.854
Salt	10 g	6.25/20 kg	100	.3125/kg	.003
Pepper	1.5 g	8.73/540 g	100	.0162/kg	.025
Maple Syrup	125 mL	9.60/1 L	100	9.60/L	1.20
Parsley, chop.	20 g	0.31/150 g bunch	50	.0042/g	.083

TOTAL COST OF RECIPE $ _4.04_

Total Yield _2 kg_   Size of Portion _100 g_

Cost per Portion _.202_

Desired
Food Cost Percentage _28%_   Suggested Selling Price _.73_

FIGURE 4.2   _Recipe Costing Form_

Recipe Costs

With a typical recipe, you calculate the **total recipe cost** with the following two-step procedure:

STEP 1: Determine the cost for the given quantity of each recipe ingredient with the unit costing procedures described above.

STEP 2: Add all of the ingredient costs together to obtain the total recipe cost.

The total recipe cost can then be broken down into the **cost per portion**, which is the most useful figure for food cost controls. To arrive at cost per portion, divide the total recipe cost by the total number of servings or portions produced by that recipe.

$$\frac{\text{Recipe \$}}{\text{\# Portions}} = \text{\$ per portion}$$

total recipe cost ÷ number of portions = cost per portion

The Recipe Costing Form shown in Figure 4.2 is useful for organizing recipe costing information. It provides space for listing each ingredient, the quantity of each ingredient needed, the cost of each unit and the total cost for the ingredient. Total yield, portion size and cost per portion are listed at the bottom of the form. Note that there is no space for recipe procedures, as these are irrelevant in recipe costing.

YIELD TESTS

Computing the cost of recipe ingredients is a simple matter if the foods are used the way they are received and there is no waste or trim. This is rarely the case, however. The amount of a food item as purchased (A.P.) and the amount of the **edible portion (E.P.)** of that same item may vary considerably, particularly with meats and fresh produce. In this context, yield is the usable or edible quantity remaining after processing the as-purchased quantity of the food item. That is, yield refers to the amount of usable lettuce after the case of iceberg is cleaned, or the amount of meat that is served after trimming. The **yield factor or percentage** is the ratio of the usable quantity to the purchased quantity. It is always less than 100% and may be calculated in dollars or weight/volume amounts.

Because purchase specifications and fabrication techniques vary from operation to operation, there are no precise, standard yield amounts. Each kitchen must determine its own yield factors. Yield tests must be conducted on A.P. items as they are received from purveyors. To be effective, several tests must be conducted and the results averaged to arrive at a specific operation's yield factor for that item.

The method of calculating yield varies depending on whether the item's trim is all waste (for example, vegetable peelings) or whether the trim creates usable or saleable byproducts (for example, meat and poultry).

Raw Yield Tests without Byproducts

The simplest yield test procedure is for items that have no usable or saleable byproducts. These items include most produce as well as some fish and shellfish. Unless these items are ready to serve *as received* from the purveyor, trimming is required and some trim is waste. For example, 450 g of apples may yield only 360 g of flesh after peeling and coring. If the recipe requires 450 g of peeled, cored apples, the chef must start with more than 450 g of A.P. apples. In order to determine accurate costs for such items, the trim loss must be taken into account. Even seedless grapes do not have a 100% yield factor. The weight of stems and bad grapes must be calculated and deducted from the A.P. weight to determine the correct price per 450 g of servable fruit.

There are three steps for calculating yield when all trim is waste:

STEP 1: Calculate the total weight of the trim produced from the specified A.P. quantity. This is known as **trim loss**.

STEP 2: Subtract the trim loss from the A.P. weight to arrive at the total yield weight.

STEP 3: Divide the yield weight by the A.P. weight to determine the yield factor.

Example 4.4

Nine hundred grams of fresh garlic generate 126 g of trim loss. Therefore, the yield weight is 774 g and the yield factor is 86% or 0.86:

$$900 \text{ g} - 126 \text{ g} = 774 \text{ g}$$

$$774 \div 900 = 0.86 = 86\%$$

Remember, subtract trim loss from A.P. weight, then divide yield weight by A.P. weight to arrive at the yield percentage. Note that the yield factor will always be some number less than 1, and the yield percentage will always be less than 100%.

TABLE 4.2   COMMON PRODUCE YIELD FACTORS

Produce	Yield Factor (%)	Produce	Yield Factor (%)	Produce	Yield Factor (%)
Apples	75	Grapefruit	45	Peaches	75
Apricots	94	Grapes	90	Pears	75
Artichokes	48	Kiwi	80	Peppers	82
Avocados	75	Leeks	50	Pineapple	50
Bananas	70	Lemons	45	Plums	75
Berries	95	Lettuce	75	Potatoes	80
Broccoli	70	Limes	45	Radishes	90
Cabbage	79	Melons	55	Rhubarb	85
Carrots	78	Mushrooms	90	Scallions	65
Cauliflower	55	Nectarines	86	Spinach	60
Celery	75	Okra	82	Squash, summer	90
Cherries	82	Onions	90	Squash, winter	70
Corn, cob	28	Oranges	60	Tomatoes	90
Cucumbers	95	Papayas	65	Turnips	75
Eggplant	85	Parsley	85	Watercress	90
Garlic	88	Pea pods	90	Watermelon	45

Because each operation has its own standards for cleaning and trimming raw products, yield factors should be customized. Lists of common yield factors are available, however, as an indication of industry norms. Some of these are included in Table 4.2.

Applying Yield Factors

Now that you understand what yield factors are and how to calculate them, we look at how they are used in costing recipes. First, yield factors are used for accurate recipe costing.

Example 4.5

Carrots cost $6.50 per 10-kg bag and have a yield factor of 78%. In other words, 22% of that 10-kg bag is waste. The price should be recalculated to account for that waste; that is, the A.P. (as purchased) unit cost must be converted to an E.P. (edible portion) unit cost. This is done by dividing A.P. cost by the yield percentage.

$$\text{A.P. cost (\$)} \div \text{yield percentage} = \text{E.P. cost (\$)}$$

$$0.65/\text{kg} \ (6.50 \div 10) \div 0.78 = 0.84/\text{kg}$$

Thus, the carrots have an E.P. unit cost of $0.84 per kilogram (as compared with an A.P. price of $0.65 per kilogram). Note that E.P. cost is always greater than A.P. cost. When costing a recipe, you should use the $0.84-per-kilogram price as the accurate ingredient cost.

Second, yield factors are necessary for accurate purchasing. Most recipes list ingredients in E.P. quantities. Therefore, the chef must consider waste or trim amounts when ordering these items. If only the amounts listed in the recipe are ordered and then the item requires trimming, the number of portions (or recipe yield) will be less than the desired amount.

Example 4.6

A recipe requires 12 kg of shredded cabbage. The yield factor for cabbage is 79%. Therefore, 12 kg is 79% of the A.P. quantity. Divide the amount needed by the yield factor to determine the minimum A.P. quantity.

$$\text{E.P. quantity} \div \text{yield percentage} = \text{A.P. quantity}$$

$$12 \text{ kg} \div 0.79 = 15.19 \text{ kg}$$

It will take 15.2 kg of cabbage to provide the 12 kg of shredded cabbage. (This figure will be increased to an even amount for purchasing because yield factors are, at best, only an estimate.) Note that the A.P. figure must always be greater than the E.P. figure in this formula.

FOOD COST

Perhaps no other cost is emphasized as much by food service managers as **food cost**. Food cost refers to the cost of all foods used in the fabrication of menu items. This figure is also known as the **cost of goods sold** or **raw food cost** ("raw" is a bit misleading as food cost includes precooked and packaged foods as well as uncooked foods).

Food costs are calculated in two ways: (1) as a total cost of all foods used during a given time period, and (2) as a cost of one particular portion or menu item. Total cost is used as a general guideline for budgeting and menu planning. The portion or item cost is used to calculate menu prices; it helps the chef stay within cost limitations.

Cost of Goods Sold

The "goods" sold by a food service operation are, of course, the foods used in producing menu items. Before you can calculate cost of goods sold you must take a physical inventory of all foodstuffs on hand. **Inventory** should be taken periodically: at the end of each week, month, quarter or other accounting period. Taking inventory requires listing and counting all foods in the kitchen, storerooms and refrigerators. The quantities are then *extended;* that is, multiplied by the unit cost. The extended prices are then added to calculate the total inventory value.

Whether prepared foods or open containers are included in the inventory depends on the operation. Often small quantities of prepared foods or open containers are not inventoried on the theory that a certain amount of such items is always on hand, the value of which is minimal but fairly consistent from one accounting period to the next.

To properly calculate the cost of goods sold you must conduct an inventory at the beginning and end of the desired period and maintain records of all purchases during the period. The time period covered by this calculation could be any duration: week, month, quarter or year. After the total value of the inventory for both the beginning and the end of the period has been established, cost of goods sold is calculated as follows:

	Value of food inventory at beginning of period
PLUS	Food purchased during period
MINUS	Inventory at end of period
MINUS	Staff meals, promotions, write-offs and returns
	Cost of food sold

Example 4.7 (Simplified)

The total value of food in inventory on December 1 is $7600. The restaurant purchases $2300 worth of food during December and the inventory on January 1 is worth $5600. The cost of goods sold during the month of December is $4300 (in other words, the food produced during the month of December cost $4300):

$$(7600 + 2300) - 5600 = 4300$$

Once management knows the cost of goods sold, it can compare this figure with the dollar value of sales for the same period. This comparison gives management an indicator of performance for that period compared to budget.

Food Cost Percentages

The **food cost percentage** is the ratio of costs to sales. It shows what each dollar of sales costs. For example, a 35% food cost means that $0.35 of each dollar received went to pay for the foods the operation used. Food cost percentage is determined by dividing food cost by sales.

$$\text{food cost} \div \text{sales} = \text{food cost percentage}$$

Example 4.8

Refer back to Example 4.7 and assume that sales for December totalled $10 750. The food cost percentage for the month would be 40%:

$$4300 \div 10\ 750 = 0.40 = 40\%$$

By itself a single food cost percentage is meaningless. To be useful, it should be compared with the food cost percentages for other months of the same year or the same month in previous years. It is also helpful to know the food cost percentages for other similarly situated food service operations.

Food cost percentages can also be calculated on individual menu items. If the food items in a sliced turkey sandwich cost $2.80 and the sandwich sells for $5.25, the food cost percentage is 53% (2.80 divided by 5.25). Many operations would find this unacceptably high. To reduce the percentage and increase gross profits, the operation must either increase the selling price or decrease the ingredient costs.

Changing menu price, raw food cost or portion size will change the food cost percentage. If the food cost percentage is too high, the gross profit (contribution margin) will be insufficient to cover operating expenses. If the percentage is too low, customers may feel they are not getting their money's worth and take their business elsewhere. Setting an appropriate percentage requires sound judgment, knowledge of the competition and accurate cost information. Periodic evaluations are necessary to ensure that the desired objective is actually maintained.

ESTABLISHING MENU PRICES

After determining the cost of food items, you can calculate menu prices. A few of the many methods for setting menu prices are explained below. Some techniques are highly structured and closely related to food costs; others are unstructured and unrelated to actual food costs. As a practical matter, no one method is right for every operation and a combination of methods may provide the best pricing information.

Cost-Based Pricing

Food Cost Percentage Pricing

For this technique, you must first determine the food cost percentage desired for the particular facility. After calculating each item's raw food cost you determine the selling price with the following formula:

$$\text{cost per portion} \div \text{food cost percentage} = \text{selling price}$$

Example 4.9

If the raw food cost for 1 sandwich is $1.70 and the desired food cost percentage is 23%, the selling price must be at least $7.39:

$$1.70 \div 0.23 = 7.391$$

In this situation, 23% of the sales price for each item will go to cover the raw food cost for that item. The higher the food cost percentage, the lower the portion of the sales price available for labour, fixed expenses, overhead or profit. Determining the appropriate food cost percentage for the facility is critical to the successful use of this method.

Factor Pricing

A variation on food cost percentage pricing is factor pricing. First, you take the desired food cost percentage and divide it into 100 to arrive at a cost factor. The cost of each item is then multiplied by the cost factor to arrive at the menu price. Using the previous example, the factor is 4.35 ($100 \div 23 = 4.35$), and the menu price for a $1.70 item is $7.39 ($1.70 \times 4.35 = 7.39$).

Both food cost percentage and factor pricings are fast and easy to use. But these methods are sometimes unreliable because they assume that other costs associated with preparing food stay the same for each menu item. These systems wrongly assume that the costs for labour, energy and overhead are the same for a rack of lamb entree and a seafood salad. These methods may be fine-tuned somewhat by adjusting the desired food cost percentage according to the type of food or menu category. Appetizers may be assigned a lower food cost percentage than, say, desserts or side dishes.

Prime Cost Pricing

The food service industry uses a figure known as **prime cost** to refer to the total of raw food cost plus direct labour. Direct labour is the labour actually required for an item's preparation. If, for example, food cost is $2.10 and direct labour is $1.50, then prime cost is $3.60. As with the food cost percentage example above, the prime cost percentage can be divided into the prime cost amount to determine menu price.

Example 4.10

The raw food cost for a rack of lamb is $7.50; it takes a cook a total of 9 minutes to clean and trim it for service. If that cook is paid $8.50 per hour, the direct labour cost is $1.26 ($8.50 per hour = 0.14 per minute; $0.14 \times 9 = $1.26).

The prime cost of the rack of lamb is $8.76 ($7.50 + 1.26). The selling price is then determined by dividing prime cost by the desired prime cost percentage. If management decided that the desired prime cost percentage is 48%, then the rack of lamb should be priced at $18.25 ($8.76 \div 0.48 = 18.25$).

Perceived Value Pricing

This is a rather backwards way of setting prices based on what a customer will perceive as an appropriate price. First determine what the market price is for the same or a similar item. Then calculate what you can serve for that price. Assume, for example,

1. the market price for a complete fried chicken dinner is $9.95,
2. the desired profit is 7% of sales,
3. overhead expenses are 27% of sales, and
4. labour is approximately 23% of sales.

Subtract the total of these items (57%) from the $9.95 selling price and you find that your total food cost for the fried chicken dinner must not be more than $4.28. This technique requires a thorough knowledge of the market and good historical information on labour and overhead costs. With the necessary information, you can determine how much to spend on raw product for each menu item and still make the desired profit.

Noncost-Based Pricing

Noncost-based pricing techniques rely on nonmonetary factors to set menu prices. Traditional prices in the area for the same or similar items may affect an operation's ability to set prices. This is particularly true for special or loss-leader items such as 99-cent jumbo sodas or $2.99 breakfast specials.

While the competition's prices are an important consideration, you should not simply copy them. Your competition's costs are not your costs no matter how similar the final food items appear. If you must charge higher prices than your competition, seek out some way to differentiate your product or service.

Virtually all food service operations are seeking to charge the highest price possible without a loss of sales. The customer's perception of value is therefore critical. The menu can be used as a tool for educating customers. Descriptive language or an explanation of unique or special dishes can be included. Customers who understand the value of service, atmosphere, out-of-season foods and specialty products will tolerate higher prices for those items.

Psychological Impact of Pricing

Regardless of how you arrive at a menu price, you may wish to round the figure up or down for psychological impact. It is human nature to perceive some prices as higher or lower than they actually are. For example, using a 9 or 5 as the last digit in a price creates the impression of a discount; prices ending in a 9 or 5 appeal to price-conscious customers. Prices ending in a 0 are perceived as more expensive and higher quality and so are often used on fine-dining menus.

The number of digits in a price is also important: $9.95 seems much less expensive than $10.25. Likewise, the first numeral in a price affects perception. When changing menu prices, an increase from $5.95 to $6.45 is seen as greater than an increase from $6.25 to $6.75, although both are 50-cent increases.

Patrons do not like to see a large spread in menu prices. It may make them think something is wrong with one of the items or may cause confusion. For example, a lobster dinner for $34.50 may be a reasonable price, but it may be inappropriate on a menu where all other items are less than $15.00. In general, the highest price should not be more than double the lowest price within the same food category. If the least expensive appetizer is $6.00, then the most expensive appetizer should not exceed $12.00.

Establishing menu prices is one of the most difficult yet important things a chef or manager can do to affect the facility's success. No one method is best for all operations, so careful study of several approaches is recommended.

CONTROLLING FOOD COSTS

Many things affect food costs in any given operation; most can be controlled by the chef or manager. These controls do not require mathematical calculations or formulas, just basic management skills and a good dose of common sense. The following factors all have an impact on the operation's bottom line:

+ menu
+ purchasing/ordering
+ receiving
+ storing
+ issuing
+ kitchen procedures
    establishing standard portions
    waste
+ sales and service

Chefs tend to focus their control efforts in the area of kitchen preparation. While this may seem logical, it is not adequate. A good chef will be involved in all aspects of the operation to help prevent problems from arising or to correct those that may occur.

Menu

A profitable menu is based upon many variables including customer desires, physical space and equipment, ingredient availability, cost of goods sold, employee skills and competition. All management personnel, including the chef, should be consulted when planning the menu. Menu changes, while possibly desirable, must be executed with as much care as the original design.

Purchasing/Ordering

Purchasing techniques have a direct impact on cost controls. On the one hand, **parstock** must be adequate for efficient operations; on the other hand, too much inventory wastes space and resources and may spoil. Generally, inventory should turn over on a regular basis. Approximately two and a half times per month ensures good cash flow and should minimize spoilage. Each operation must establish appropriate inventory and purchasing levels. Before any items are ordered, purchasing specifications should be established and communicated to potential purveyors. Specifications should precisely describe the item, including grade, quality, packaging and unit size. Each operation should design its own form to best meet its specific needs. A sample specification form is shown in Figure 4.3. This information can be used to obtain price quotes from several purveyors. Update these quotes periodically to ensure that you are getting the best value for your money.

Menu Item: *Beef Striploin (220–300 g)*

Product: *Angus Beef Striploin, fresh*   Date: *May 2002*

Grade/Quality: *AAA, Certified Canadian Angus, 21 days age*

Weight/Size: *10/12; OXI Trim*   Product Code:
                                        CMC #180

Packaging: *Vacuum*

Delivery Conditions: *Refrigerated truck; 0–4° C*
                     Product to be 4° C or less
Comments:
Open boxes to verify product, weight and condition
(i.e., no broken bags/leakers)

Figure 4.3   *Specification Form*

Receiving

Whether goods are received by a full-time clerk, as they are in a large hotel, or by the chef or kitchen manager, certain standards should be observed. The person signing for merchandise should first confirm that the items were actually ordered. Second, determine whether the items listed on the invoice are the ones being delivered and that the price and quantity listed are accurate. Third, the items, especially meats and produce, should be checked for quality, freshness, temperature and weight. Established purchase specifications should be readily available.

Storing

Proper storage of foodstuffs is crucial in order to prevent spoilage, pilferage and waste. Stock must be rotated so that the older items are used first. Such a system for rotating stock is referred to as **FIFO: First In, First Out**. Storage areas should be well ventilated and lit to prevent infestation and mould. High-cost items and liquor are often locked up separately from standard groceries.

Issuing

It may be necessary, particularly in larger operations, to limit storeroom access to specific personnel. Maintaining ongoing inventory records or parstock sheets helps the ordering process. Controlling issuances eliminates waste caused by multiple opened containers and ensures proper stock rotation.

Kitchen Procedures: Establishing Standard Portions

Standardizing portions is essential to controlling food costs. Unless portion quantity is uniform, it will be impossible to compute portion costs accurately. Portion discrepancies can also confuse or mislead customers.

Actual portion sizes depend on the food service operation itself, the menu, the prices and the customers' desires. Some items are generally purchased preportioned for convenience (for example, steaks are sold in uniform cuts, baking potatoes are available in uniform sizes, butter comes in preportioned pats and bread comes sliced for service). Other items must be portioned by the establishment prior to service. Special equipment makes consistent portioning easy. There are machines to slice meats, cutting guides for cakes and pies and portion scales for weighing quantities. Standardized portion scoops and ladles are indispensable for serving vegetables, soups, stews, salads and similar foods. Many of these items are discussed and illustrated in Chapter 5, Tools and Equipment.

Once acceptable portion sizes are established, employees must be properly trained to present them. If each employee of a sandwich shop prepared sandwiches the way he or she would like to eat them, customers would probably never receive the same sandwich twice. Customers may become confused and decide not to risk a repeat visit. Obviously, carelessness in portioning can also drastically affect food cost.

Kitchen Procedures: Waste

The chef must also control waste from overproduction or failure to use leftovers. With an adequate sales history, the chef can accurately estimate the quantity of food to prepare for each week, day or meal. If the menu is designed properly, the chef can also use leftovers and trim from product fabrication. The less waste generated in food preparation, the lower the overall food cost will be. A periodic inspection of waste receptacles allows for monitoring of waste or carelessness. Checking refrigerators regularly helps to ensure efficient product use and handling.

Sales and Service

An improperly trained sales staff can undo even the most rigorous of food cost controls. Front-of-the-house personnel are, after all, ultimately responsible for the sales portion of the food cost equation. Proper training is once again critical. Prices charged must be accurate and complete. Poor service can lead to the need to serve for free ("comp") an excessive amount of food. Dropped or spilled foods do not generate revenues. It is important to record these items for tracking purposes.

ONCLUSION

No food service operation can become successful based on the chef's cooking ability alone. A well-designed, enticing and accurately priced menu is also necessary. By following a standardized recipe you should be able to repeatedly produce a known quality and quantity of food for your specific food service operation. Based upon the regularity with which you offer these foods, your menu can be classified as static, cycle, market or hybrid. You can offer your menu items either à la carte, semi à la carte or table d'hôte.

You must be able to understand and apply proper techniques for converting recipes, food costing, menu pricing and loss control. Although computers are useful and are becoming more common in kitchens, no machine can substitute for a chef's watchful eye and hands-on controls.

QUESTIONS FOR DISCUSSION

1. Describe the four types of menus. Can each type of menu offer foods à la carte, semi à la carte and/or table d'hôte? Explain your answer.

2. Discuss three factors in food preparation that affect successful recipe size changes.

3. Why is it important to calculate the portion cost of a recipe in professional food service operations? Why is the full recipe cost inadequate?

4. List several factors that might cause one operation's yield factor for lettuce to be higher than another operation's. Explain why standardized yield factor lists are unreliable.

5. How is food cost percentage calculated? How can this figure be used (or misused) to evaluate the success of an operation?

6. Discuss three psychological factors used in setting menu prices.

WEBLINKS

Labensky: Applied Math for Food Service
 www.prenticehall.ca/allbooks/ect_0138492174.html

Food Service Resource List: Meal Planning/Preparation
 www.nal.usda.gov/fnic/service/foodmp1.htm

Food Service Resource List: Cost Control
 www.nal.usda.gov/fnic/service/foodcc1.htm

Meals for You: Choose recipes and meal plans by ingredient or nutritional content
 www.mealsforyou.com

Foodwine.com: An Electronic Gourmet Guide, updated daily
 www.globalgourmet.com

PART TWO

PREPARATION

Mise en place *is the essence of preparation. Although it means "everything in its place," the term connotes more than merely having all ingredients and tools on hand and being ready to begin preparing a dish.*
Rather, it suggests that the chef can identify, appreciate and understand how the necessary tools and equipment work, how the foods are cut and what the basic flavouring ingredients and staples are.

To assist you in preparing to cook, Part Two presents information about the tools and equipment routinely found in professional kitchens, then discusses how a professional kitchen is organized. There is a chapter on knife skills as well as chapters on kitchen staples (herbs and spices, condiments, oils, vinegars, nuts, coffee and tea) and eggs and dairy products (including milk, cream, cultured milk products and cheese).

Understanding this information is critical before successful cooking can begin.

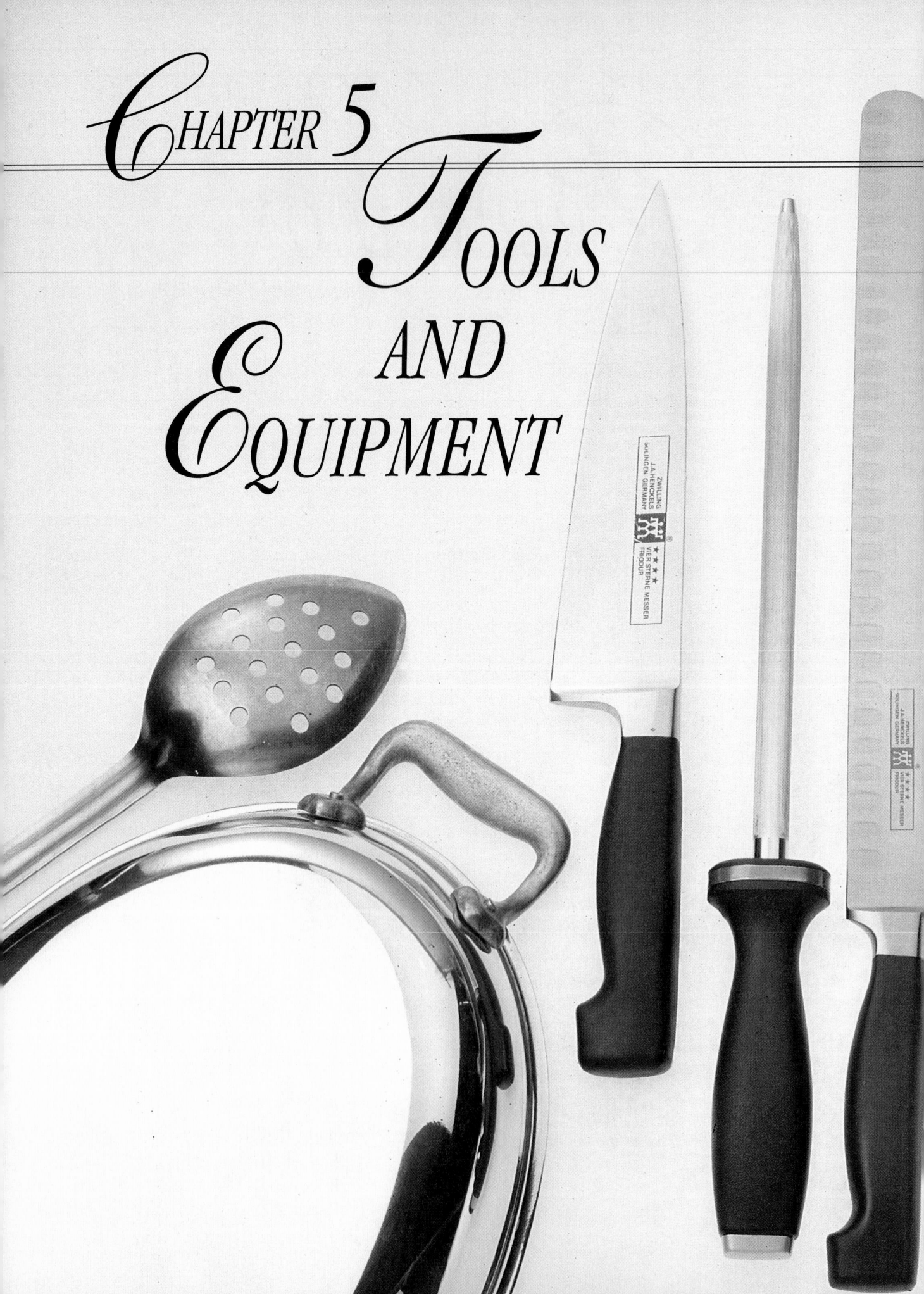

CHAPTER 5 TOOLS AND EQUIPMENT

LEARNING OUTCOMES

After studying this chapter you will be able to:

+ recognize a variety of professional kitchen tools and equipment
+ select and care for knives properly
+ understand how a professional kitchen is organized

Having the proper tools and equipment for a particular task may mean the difference between a job well done and one done carelessly, incorrectly or even dangerously. This chapter introduces some of the tools and equipment typically used in a professional kitchen. Items are divided into categories according to their function: hand tools, knives, measuring and portioning devices, cookware, strainers and sieves, processing equipment, storage containers, heavy equipment, buffet equipment and safety equipment.

A wide variety of specialized tools and equipment is available to today's chef. Breading machines, mandolines and food processors are designed to speed production by reducing handwork. Other devices—for instance, a duck press or a couscousière—are used only for unique tasks in preparing a few menu items. Much of this specialized equipment is quite expensive and found only in food manufacturing operations or specialized kitchens; a discussion of it is beyond the scope of this chapter. Brief descriptions of some of these specialized devices are, however, found in the Glossary. Baking pans and tools are discussed in Chapter 26, Principles of the Bakeshop.

This chapter is illustrated with generic drawings because manufacturers' designs differ. We end this chapter with a discussion of how a professional kitchen should be designed and organized.

Before using any equipment, study the operator's manual or have someone experienced with the particular item instruct you on proper procedures for its use and cleaning. And remember, always practise safety.

STANDARDS FOR TOOLS AND EQUIPMENT

Well-designed tools and equipment have characteristics that are beneficial to the overall efficiency and safety of the operation.

1. Equipment must be easily cleaned.
2. All food contact surfaces must be nontoxic (under intended end-use conditions), nonabsorbent, corrosion resistant and nonreactive.
3. All food contact surfaces must be smooth, that is, free of pits, cracks, crevices, ledges, rivet heads and bolts.

4. Internal corners and edges must be rounded and smooth; external corners and angles must be smooth and sealed.

5. Coating materials must be nontoxic and easily cleaned; coatings must resist chipping and cracking.

6. Waste and waste liquids must be easily removed.

SELECTING TOOLS AND EQUIPMENT

In general, only commercial food service tools and equipment should be used in a professional kitchen. Household tools and appliances may not withstand the rigours of a professional kitchen. Look for tools that are well constructed. For example, joints should be welded, not bonded with solder; handles should be comfortable, with rounded borders; plastic and rubber parts should be seamless.

Before purchasing or leasing any particular piece of equipment you should evaluate several factors:

1. Is this equipment necessary for producing menu items?

2. Will this equipment perform the job required in the space available?

3. Is this equipment the most economical for the operation's specific needs?

4. Is this equipment easy to clean, maintain and repair?

HAND TOOLS

Hand tools are designed to aid in cutting, shaping, moving or combining foods. They have few, if any, moving parts. Knives, discussed separately below, are the most important hand tools. Others are metal or rubber spatulas, spoons, whisks, tongs and specialized cutters. In addition to the items shown in Figure 5.1, many hand tools designed for specific tasks, such as pressing tortillas or pitting cherries, are available. Sturdiness, durability and safety are the watchwords when selecting hand tools. Choose tools that can withstand the heavy use of a professional kitchen and those that are easily cleaned.

KNIVES

Knives are the most important items in your tool kit. With a sharp knife, the skilled cook can accomplish a number of tasks more quickly and efficiently than any machine. Good-quality knives are expensive but will last for many years with proper care. Select easily sharpened, well-constructed knives that are comfortable and balanced in your hand. Knife construction and commonly used knives are discussed here; knife safety and care as well as cutting techniques are discussed in Chapter 6, Knife Skills.

Vegetable Peeler

Melon Ball Cutter
(The smaller end is also known as a Parisian Scoop)

Zester

Perforated, Plain and Slotted Spoons

Straight Tongs

Balloon and French Whisks

Table-Mounted Can Opener

Rubber Spatula

Chef's Fork

Meat Mallet

Grill Spatula

Palette Knife (Straight or Cake Spatula)

FIGURE 5.1

Knife Construction

A good knife begins with a single piece of metal, stamped, cut or—best of all—forged and tempered into a blade of the desired shape. The metals generally used for knife blades are:

1. **Carbon steel**—An alloy of carbon and iron, it was traditionally used for blades because it is soft enough to be sharpened easily. It corrodes and discolours easily, however, especially when used with acidic foods. It is not recommended for food service applications.

2. **Stainless steel**—It will not rust, corrode or discolour and is extremely durable. But a stainless steel blade is much more difficult to sharpen than a

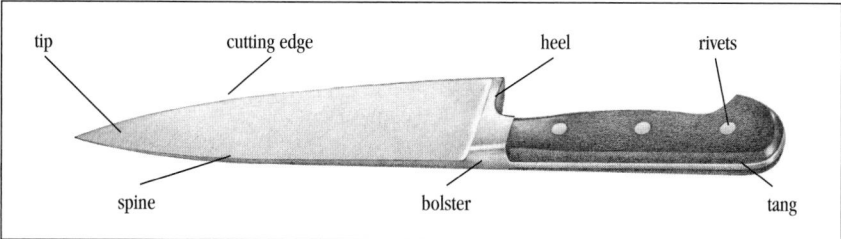

FIGURE 5.2

carbon steel one, although once an edge is established it lasts longer than the edge on a carbon steel blade.

3. **High carbon stainless steel**—An alloy combining the best features of carbon steel and stainless steel, it neither corrodes nor discolours and can be sharpened almost as easily as carbon steel. It is now the most frequently used metal for blades.

A portion of the blade, known as the tang, fits inside the handle. See Figure 5.2. The best knives are constructed with a full tang running the length of the handle; they also have a bolster where the blade meets the handle (the bolster is part of the blade, not a separate collar). Less expensive knives may have a 3/4-length tang or a thin "rattail" tang. Neither provide as much support, durability or balance as a full tang.

Knife handles are often made of composite plastic materials. Moulded polypropylene handles are permanently bonded to a tang without seams or rivets. Any handle should be shaped for comfort and ground smooth to eliminate crevices where bacteria can grow.

Knife Shapes and Sharpening Equipment

You will collect many knives during your career, many with specialized functions not described here. This list includes only the most basic knives and sharpening equipment. Knives and equipment described below are illustrated in Figure 5.3.

French or Chef's Knife

An all-purpose knife used for chopping, slicing and mincing. Its rigid 20- to 35-cm-long (8- to 14-inch) blade is wide at the heel and tapers to a point at the tip.

Utility Knife

An all-purpose knife used for cutting fruits and vegetables and carving poultry. Its rigid 15- to 20-cm-long (6- to 8-inch) blade is shaped like a chef's knife but narrower.

Boning Knife

A smaller knife with a thin blade used to separate meat from bone. The blade is usually 12.5 to 17.5 cm (5 to 7 inches) long and may be flexible or rigid.

Paring Knife

A short knife used for detail work or cutting fruits and vegetables. The rigid blade is from 5 to 10 cm (2 to 4 inches) long. A **turning knife** is similar to a paring knife but with a curved blade; it is used for shaping curved surfaces or turning vegetables.

Paring Knife

Rigid Boning Knife

Utility Knife

Cleaver

Serrated Slicer

French or Chef's Knife

Oyster Knife

Flexible Slicer

Butcher Knife

Clam Knife

Three-Sided Sharpening Stone

Steel

FIGURE 5.3

Cleaver

The large, heavy rectangular blade of this knife is used for chopping or cutting through bones.

Slicer

A knife with a long, thin blade used primarily for slicing cooked meat. The tip may be round or pointed and the blade may be flexible or rigid. A similar knife with a serrated edge is used for slicing bread or pastry items.

Butcher Knife

Sometimes known as a **scimitar** because the rigid blade curves up in a 25-degree angle at the tip, this knife is used for fabricating raw meat and is available with 15- to 35-cm (6- to 14-inch) blades.

Oyster and Clam Knives

The short, rigid blades of these knives are used to open oyster and clam shells. The tips are blunt; only the clam knife has a sharp edge.

Sharpening Stone

Also known as a **whetstone**, a sharpening stone is used to put an edge on a dull blade.

Steel

A steel is used to hone or straighten a blade immediately after and between sharpenings.

MEASURING AND PORTIONING DEVICES

Recipe ingredients must be measured precisely, especially in the bakeshop, and foods should be measured when served to control portion size and cost. The devices used to measure and portion foods are, for the most part, hand tools designed to make food preparation and service easier and more precise. The accuracy they afford prevents the cost of mistakes made when accurate measurements are ignored.

Measurements may be based upon weight (e.g., grams, ounces, pounds) or volume (e.g., millilitres, litres, quarts). Therefore it is necessary to have available several measuring devices, including liquid and dry measuring cups and a variety of scales. Thermometers and timers are also measuring devices and are discussed here (see Figure 5.4 for illustrations). When purchasing measuring devices look for quality construction and accurate markings.

> ◆◆◆
> ### MEASURING PRECISELY
>
> Although many measuring devices are routinely used in kitchens, the most precise way to measure is by weight. Volume measures appear in this text for the convenience of the user.

Scales

Scales are necessary to determine the weight of an ingredient or a portion of food (for example, the sliced meat for a sandwich). Portion scales use a spring mechanism, round dial and single flat tray. They are available calibrated in grams, ounces or pounds. Electronic scales also use a spring mechanism but provide digital readouts. They are often required by law where foods are priced for sale by weight. Balance scales (also known as baker's scales) use a two-tray and free-weights counterbalance system. A balance scale allows more weight to be measured at one time because it is not limited by spring capacity. Any scale must be properly used and maintained to provide an accurate reading.

TABLE 5.1   PORTION SCOOP CAPACITIES

Scoop Number	Volume		Approximate Weight*	
	Metric	U.S.	Metric	U.S.
6	160 mL	2/3 c.	160 g	5 oz.
8	120 mL	1/2 c.	120 g	4 oz.
10	90 mL	3 fl. oz.	85–100 g	3 to 3-1/2 oz.
12	80 mL	1/3 c.	75–85 g	2-1/2 to 3 oz.
16	60 mL	1/4 c.	60 g	2 oz.
20	45 mL	1-1/2 fl. oz.	50 g	1-3/4 oz.
24	40 mL	1-1/3 fl. oz.	40 g	1-1/3 oz.
30	30 mL	1 fl. oz.	30 g	1 oz.
40	24 mL	0.8 fl. oz.	23 g	0.8 oz.
60	15 mL	1/2 fl. oz.	15 g	1/2 oz.

*Weights are approximate because they vary by food. Verify weights by scale to ensure accurate portion sizes.

Volume Measures

Ingredients may be measured by volume using measuring spoons and measuring cups. Measuring spoons sold as a set usually include 2-, 5- and 15-mL units (or the U.S. equivalent). Liquid measuring cups are available in capacities from 100 mL to 1 L. They have a lip or pour spout above the top line of measurement to prevent spills. Measuring cups for dry ingredients are usually sold in sets of 60-, 75-, 125- and 250-mL units. They do not have pour spouts, so the top of the cup is level with the top measurement specified. Glass measuring cups are not recommended because they can break. Avoid using bent or dented measuring cups as the damage may distort the measurement capacity.

Ladles

Long-handled ladles are useful for portioning liquids such as stocks, sauces and soups. The capacity, in millilitres or ounces, is stamped on the handle.

Portion Scoops

Portion scoops (also known as dishers) resemble ice cream scoops. They come in a range of standardized sizes and have a lever-operated blade for releasing their contents. Scoops are useful for portioning salads, vegetables, muffin batters or other soft foods. A number, stamped on either the handle or the release mechanism, indicates the number of level scoopfuls per U.S. quart. The higher the scoop number, the smaller the scoop's capacity. Metric scoops are also available. See Table 5.1 for scoop capacities.

Thermometers

Various types of thermometers are used in the kitchen.

Stem-type thermometers, including instant-read models, measure the temperature of a food. The thermometer is inserted into foods to obtain temperature readings between –18°C (0°F) and 104°C (220°F). Temperatures are shown on either a dial noted by an arrow or a digital readout. An instant-read thermometer is a small stem-type model, designed to be carried in a pocket and used to provide quick temperature readings. An instant-read thermometer

---

♦♦♦

HOW TO CALIBRATE A STEM-TYPE THERMOMETER

All stem-type thermometers should be calibrated at least weekly as well as whenever they are dropped. To calibrate a stem-type thermometer, fill a glass with shaved ice, then add water. Place the thermometer in the ice slush and wait until the temperature reading stabilizes. Following the manufacturer's directions, adjust the thermometer's calibration nut until the temperature reads 0°C (32°F). Check the calibration by returning the thermometer to the slush.

should not be left in foods that are cooking because doing so damages the thermometer.

Candy and fat thermometers measure temperatures up to 200°C (400°F) using mercury in a column of glass. A back clip attaches to the pan, keeping the chef's hands free. Be careful not to subject glass thermometers to quick temperature changes or the glass may shatter.

Because proper temperatures must be maintained for holding and storing foods, oven and refrigerator thermometers are also useful. Select thermometers with easy-to-read dials or column divisions.

Timers

Portable kitchen timers are useful for any busy cook. Small digital timers can be carried in a pocket; some even time three functions at once. Select a timer with a loud alarm signal and long timing capability.

Measuring Spoons

Liquid Measuring Cup

Dry Measuring Cups

Portion Scoop

Portion Scale

Instant-Read Thermometer

Candy Thermometer

Ladles

Baker's Scale

FIGURE 5.4

COOKWARE

Cookware includes the sauté pans and stockpots used on the stove top as well as the roasting pans, hotel pans and specialty moulds used inside the oven. Cookware should be selected for its size, shape, ability to conduct heat evenly and overall quality of construction.

Metals and Heat Conduction

Cookware that fails to distribute heat evenly may cause hot spots that burn foods. Because different metals conduct heat at different rates, and thicker layers of metal conduct heat more evenly than thinner ones, the most important considerations when choosing cookware are the type and thickness (known as the *gauge*) of the material used. No one cookware or material suits every process or need, however; always select the most appropriate material for the task at hand.

Copper

Copper is an excellent conductor: it heats rapidly and evenly and cools quickly. Indeed, unlined copper pots are unsurpassed for cooking sugar and fruit mixtures. But copper cookware is extremely expensive. It also requires a great deal of care and is often quite heavy. Moreover, because copper may react with some foods, copper cookware usually has a tin lining, which is soft and easily scratched. Because of these problems, copper is now often sandwiched between layers of stainless steel or aluminum in the bottom of pots and pans.

Aluminum

Aluminum is the metal used most commonly in commercial utensils. It is lightweight and, after copper, conducts heat best. Aluminum is a soft metal, though, so it should be treated with care to avoid dents. Do not use aluminum containers for storage or for cooking acidic foods because the metal reacts chemically with many foods. Light-coloured foods, such as soups or sauces, may be discoloured when cooked in aluminum, especially if stirred with a metal whisk or spoon.

Anodized aluminum has a hard, dark, corrosion-resistant surface that helps prevent sticking and discolouration.

Stainless Steel

Although stainless steel conducts and retains heat poorly, it is a hard, durable metal particularly useful for holding foods and for low-temperature cooking where hot spots and scorching are not problems. Stainless steel pots and pans are available with aluminum or copper bonded to the bottom or with an aluminum-layered core. Although expensive, such cookware combines the rapid, uniform heat conductivity of copper and aluminum with the strength, durability and nonreactivity of stainless steel. Stainless steel is also ideal for storage containers because it does not react with foods.

Cast Iron

Cast-iron cookware distributes heat evenly and holds high temperatures well. It is often used in griddles and large skillets. Although relatively inexpensive, cast iron is extremely heavy and brittle. It must be kept properly conditioned and dry to prevent rust and pitting.

Glass

Glass retains heat well but conducts it poorly. It does not react with foods. Tempered glass is suitable for microwave cooking provided it does not have any metal band or decoration. Commercial operations rarely use glass cookware because of the danger of breakage.

Ceramics

Ceramics, including earthenware, porcelain and stoneware, are used primarily for baking dishes, casseroles and baking stones because they conduct heat uniformly and retain temperatures well. Ceramics are nonreactive, inexpensive and generally suitable for use in a microwave oven (provided there is no metal in the glaze). Ceramics are easily chipped or cracked, however, and should not be used over a direct flame. Also, quick temperature changes may cause the cookware to crack or shatter.

Plastic

Plastic containers are frequently used in commercial kitchens for food storage or service, but they cannot be used for heating or cooking except in a microwave oven. Plastic microwave cookware is made of phenolic resin. It is easy to clean, relatively inexpensive and rigidly shaped, but its glasslike structure is brittle and it can crack or shatter.

Enamelware

Pans lined with enamel should not be used for cooking; in many areas, their use in commercial kitchens is prohibited by law. The enamel can chip or crack easily, providing good places for bacteria to grow. Also, the chemicals used to bond the enamel to the cookware can cause food poisoning if ingested.

♦♦♦

ROMAN POTS, SOUTHERN STILLS AND CRAFT FAIRS

Lead is poisonous. Ingesting it can cause severe gastrointestinal pains, anemia and central nervous system disorders including intelligence and memory deficits and behavioural changes.

The unwitting and dangerous consumption of lead is not limited to children eating peeling paint chips. Some historians suggest that the use of lead cookware and lead-lined storage vessels and water pipes may have caused pervasive lead poisoning among the elite of the Roman Empire and thus contributed to the Empire's decline. There is also ample evidence that from ancient times until just a few hundred years ago, wine was heated in lead vessels to sweeten it. This had a disastrous effect on the drinker and, for several centuries in countries throughout Europe, on the wine purveyor as well. The former could be poisoned and the latter could be punished by death for selling adulterated wine. More recently it was found that much of the moonshine whisky produced in the American South contained lead in potentially toxic ranges. The source was determined to be the lead solder used in homemade stills, some of which even included old lead-containing car radiators as condensers.

Although commercially available cookware will not contain lead, be careful of imported pottery and those lovely hand-thrown pots found at craft fairs—there could be lead in the glaze.

Nonstick Coatings

Without affecting a metal's ability to conduct heat, a polymer (plastic) known as polytetrafluoroethylene (PTFE) and marketed under the trade names Teflon® and Silverstone® may be applied to many types of cookware. It provides a slippery, nonreactive finish that prevents food from sticking and allows the use of less fat in cooking. Cookware with nonstick coatings requires a great deal of care, however, as the coatings can scratch, chip and blister. Do not use metal spoons or spatulas in cookware with nonstick coatings and do not use intense heat.

Common Cookware

Pots

Pots are large round vessels with straight sides and two loop handles. Available in a range of sizes based on volume, they are used on the stove top for making stocks or soups, or for boiling or simmering foods, particularly where rapid evaporation is not desired. Flat or fitted lids are available. See Figure 5.5 for illustrations of pots and other common cookware.

Pans

Pans are round vessels with one long handle and straight or sloped sides. They are usually smaller and shallower than pots. Pans are available in a range of diameters and are used for general stove-top cooking, especially sautéing, frying or reducing liquids rapidly.

Woks

Originally used to prepare Asian foods, woks are now found in many professional kitchens. Their round bottoms and curved sides diffuse heat and make it easy to toss or stir contents. Their large domed lids retain heat for steaming vegetables. Woks are useful for quickly sautéing strips of meat, simmering a whole fish or deep-frying appetizers. Stove-top woks range in diameter from 30 to 75 cm (12 to 30 inches); larger built-in gas or electric models are also available.

Hotel Pans

Hotel pans (also known as steam-table pans) are rectangular stainless steel pans designed to hold food for service in steam tables. Hotel pans may also be used for baking, roasting or poaching inside an oven. Perforated pans useful for draining, steaming or icing down foods are also available. The standard full-size pan is 30 by 50 cm (12 by 20 inches), with pans one-half, one-third, one-sixth and other fractions of this size available. Hotel-pan depth is standardized at 5 cm (2 inches) (referred to as a "200 pan"), 10, 15 and 20 cm (4, 6 and 8 inches).

Moulds

Pâté moulds are available in several shapes and sizes, and are usually made from tinned steel. Those with hinged sides, whether smooth or patterned, are more properly referred to as *pâté en croûte* moulds. The hinged sides make it easier to remove the baked pâté. Terrine moulds are traditionally lidded earthenware or enamelled cast-iron containers used for baking forcemeat mixtures. They may be round, oval or rectangular. Timbale moulds are small (about 75 to 120 mL/4 oz.) metal or ceramic containers used for moulding aspic or baking individual portions of mousse, custard or vegetables. They may be round or oval and their slightly flared sides allow the contents to release cleanly when inverted.

Stockpot with Spigot

Sauce Pot

Sautoir (Straight Sides)

Saucepan

Cast-Iron Skillet (Griswold)

Sauteuse (Sloped Sides)

Rondeau/Brazier

Wok

Pâté en Croûte Mould

Timbales

Hotel Pans

FIGURE 5.5

STRAINERS AND SIEVES

Strainers and sieves are used primarily to aerate and remove impurities from dry ingredients and drain or purée cooked foods. Strainers, colanders, drum sieves, conical strainers and etâmines are nonmechanical devices with a stainless steel mesh or screen through which food passes. The size of the mesh or screen varies from extremely fine to several millimetres wide; select the fineness best suited for the task at hand. See Figure 5.6.

Etâmine

Round Mesh Strainer (Sieve)

Conical Strainer (Chinois)

Colander

Flour Sifter

Drum Sieve (Tamis)

Food Mill

Skimmer

Spider

FIGURE 5.6

Conical Strainer (Chinois) and Etâmine

Both the etâmine and the conical strainer are cone-shaped metal strainers. The conical shape allows liquids to filter through small openings. An etâmine is made from a very fine mesh, while a conical strainer has a perforated metal body. Both are used for straining stocks and sauces, with the etâmine being particularly useful for consommé. A conical strainer can also be used with a pestle to purée soft foods.

Skimmer and Spider

Both the skimmer and spider are long-handled tools used to remove foods or impurities from liquids. The flat, perforated disk of a skimmer is used for skimming stocks or removing foods from soups or stocks. The spider has a finer mesh disk, which makes it better for retrieving items from hot fat. Wooden-handled spiders are available but are less sturdy and harder to clean than all-metal designs.

Cheesecloth

Cheesecloth is a loosely woven cotton gauze used for straining stocks and sauces and wrapping poultry or fish for poaching. Cheesecloth is also indispensable for making sachets. Always rinse cheesecloth thoroughly before use; this removes lint and prevents the cheesecloth from absorbing other liquids.

Food Mill

A food mill purées and strains food at the same time. Food is placed in the hopper and a hand-crank mechanism turns a blade in the hopper against a perforated disk, forcing the food through the disk. Most models have interchangeable disks with various-sized holes. Choose a mill that can be taken apart easily for cleaning.

Flour Sifter

A sifter is used for aerating, blending and removing impurities from dry ingredients such as flour, cocoa and leavening agents. The 2 L (8-cup) hand-crank sifter shown in Figure 5.6 uses 4 curved rods to brush the contents through a curved mesh screen. The sifter should have a medium-fine screen and a comfortable handle.

PROCESSING EQUIPMENT

Processing equipment includes both electrical and nonelectrical devices used to chop, purée, slice, grind or mix foods. See Figure 5.7. Before using any such equipment, be sure to review its operating procedures and ask for assistance if necessary. Always turn the equipment off and disconnect the power before disassembling, cleaning or moving the appliance. Any problems or malfunctions should be reported to your supervisor immediately. *Never place your hand into any machinery when the power is on. Processing equipment is powerful and can cause serious injury.*

Slicer

An electric slicer is used to cut meat, bread, cheese or raw vegetables into uniform slices. It has a circular blade that rotates at high speed. Food is placed in a carrier, then passed (manually or by an electric motor) against the blade.

Slice thickness is determined by the distance between the blade and the carrier. Because of the speed with which the blade rotates, foods can be cut into extremely thin slices very quickly. An electric slicer is convenient for preparing moderate to large quantities of food, but the time required to disassemble and clean the equipment makes it impractical when slicing only a few items.

Mandoline

A mandoline is a manually operated slicer made of stainless steel with adjustable slicing blades. It is also used to make julienne and waffle-cut slices. Its narrow, rectangular body sits on the work counter at a 45-degree angle. Foods are passed against a blade to obtain uniform slices. It is useful for slicing small quantities of fruits or vegetables when using a large electric slicer would be unwarranted. To avoid injury, always use a hand guard or steel glove when using a mandoline.

Food Chopper or Buffalo Chopper

This chopper is used to process moderate to large quantities of food to a uniform size, such as chopping onions or grinding bread for crumbs. The food is placed in a large bowl rotating beneath a hood where curved blades chop it. The size of the cut depends on how long the food is left in the machine. Buffalo choppers are available in floor or tabletop models. The motor can usually be fitted with a variety of other tools such as a meat grinder or a slicer/shredder, making it even more useful.

Food Processor

A food processor has a motor housing with a removable bowl and S-shaped blade. It is used, for example, to purée cooked foods, chop nuts, prepare compound butters and emulsify sauces. Special disks can be added that slice, shred or julienne foods. Bowl capacity and motor power vary; select a model large enough for your most common tasks.

Blender

Though similar in principle to a food processor, a blender has a tall, narrow food container and a four-pronged blade. Its design is better for processing liquids or liquefying foods quickly. A blender is used to prepare smooth drinks, purée soups and sauces, blend batters and chop ice. A **vertical cutter/mixer** (VCM) operates like a very large, powerful blender. A VCM is usually floor-mounted and has a capacity of 55 to 300 L (15–80 gallons). Motorized blender blades at the end of a shaft are available for blending products in large containers.

Mixer

A vertical mixer is indispensable in the bakeshop and most kitchens. The U-shaped arms hold a metal mixing bowl in place; the selected mixing attachment fits onto the rotating head. The three common mixing attachments are the whip (used for whipping eggs or cream), the paddle (used for general mixing) and the dough hook (used for kneading bread). Most mixers have several operating speeds. Bench models range in capacity from 4.5 to 20 L (4.5 to 20 qt.), while floor mixers can hold as much as 140 L (140 qt.). Some mixers can be fitted with shredder/slicers, meat grinders, juicers or power strainers, making the equipment more versatile.

Juicer

Two types of juicers are available: reamers and extractors. Reamers, also known as citrus juicers, remove juice from citrus fruits. They can be manual or

Meat Slicer

Buffalo Chopper with Slicer and Meat Grinder Attachments

Mandoline

Heavy-Duty Blender

Food Processor

25-L Mixer and Attachments

Citrus Juicer

FIGURE 5.7

electric. Manual models use a lever arm to squeeze the fruit with increased pressure. They are most often used to prepare small to moderate amounts of juice for cooking or beverages. Juice extractors are electrical devices that create juice by liquefying raw fruits, vegetables and herbs. They use centrifugal force to filter out fibre and pulp.

STORAGE CONTAINERS

FIGURE 5.8

Proper storage containers are necessary for keeping leftovers, overproduction and opened packages of food safe for consumption. Proper storage can also reduce the costs incurred by waste or spoilage.

While stainless steel pans such as hotel pans are suitable and useful for some items, the expense of stainless steel and the lack of airtight lids makes these pans impractical for general storage purposes. Aluminum containers are not recommended because the metal can react with even mildly acidic items. Glass containers are generally not allowed in commercial kitchens because of the hazards of broken glass. The most useful storage containers are those made of high-density plastic (such as polyethylene and polypropylene).

Storage containers must have well-fitting lids and should be available in a variety of sizes, including some that are small enough to hold even minimal quantities of food without allowing too much exposure to oxygen. Round and square plastic containers are widely available. Flat, snap-on lids allow containers to be stacked for more efficient storage. Containers may be clear or opaque white, which helps protect light-sensitive foods. Larger containers may be fitted with handles and spigots, making them especially suited for storing stock. Some storage containers are marked with graduated measurements, so content quantity can be determined at a glance. See Figure 5.8.

Large quantities of dry ingredients, such as flour, sugar and rice, can be stored in rolling bins. The bins should be seamless with rounded corners for easy cleaning. They should have well-fitting but easy-to-open lids and should move easily on well-balanced casters.

HEAVY EQUIPMENT

Heavy equipment includes the gas-, electric- or steam-operated appliances used for cooking, reheating or holding foods. Heavy equipment also includes dishwashers and refrigeration units. Heavy equipment should be installed in a fixed location determined by the kitchen's traffic flow and space limitations.

Heavy equipment may be purchased or leased new or used. Used equipment is most often purchased in an effort to save money. While the initial cost is generally less for used equipment, the buyer should also consider the lack of a manufacturer's warranty or dealership guarantee and how the equipment was maintained by the prior owner. Functional used equipment is satisfactory for back-of-the-house areas, but it is usually better to purchase new equipment if it will be visible to the customer. Leasing equipment may be appropriate for some operations. The cost of leasing is less than purchasing and, if something goes wrong with the equipment, the operator is generally not responsible for repairs or service charges.

Stove Tops

Stove tops or ranges are often the most important cooking equipment in the kitchen. They have one or more burners powered by gas or electricity. The

FIGURE 5.9 *Gas burner and flat top range with dual ovens and an overhead broiler (salamander).*

burners may be open or covered with a cast-iron or steel plate. Open burners supply quick, direct heat that is easy to regulate. A steel plate, known as a **flat top**, supplies even but less intense heat. Although it takes longer to heat than a burner, the flat top supports heavier weights and makes a larger area available for cooking. Many stoves include both flat tops and open burner arrangements. See Figure 5.9.

Griddles are similar to flat tops except they are made of a thinner metal plate. Foods are usually cooked directly on the griddle's surface, not in pots or pans which can nick or scratch the surface. (A griddle is illustrated in Figure 5.10.) The surface should be properly cleaned and conditioned after each use. Griddles are popular for short-order and fast-food-type operations.

Ovens

An oven is an enclosed space where food is cooked by being surrounded with hot, dry air. Conventional ovens are often located beneath the stove top. They have a heating element located at the unit's bottom or floor, and pans are placed on wire racks inside the oven's cavity. (See Figure 5.9.) Conventional ovens may also be separate, free-standing units or decks stacked one on top of the other. In stack ovens, pans are placed directly on the deck or floor and not on wire racks.

Convection ovens use internal fans to circulate the hot air. This tends to cook foods more quickly and evenly. Convection ovens are almost always

Griddle

Steam Kettle

Deep Fryer

Stack Oven

Overhead Broiler

Tilting Skillet

Gas Grill

Convection Steamer

FIGURE 5.10

free-standing units, powered either by gas or electricity. Because convection ovens cook foods more quickly, temperatures may need to be reduced by 10°C to 20°C (25°F to 50°F) from those recommended for conventional ovens.

Combitherm ovens are very versatile. They can function as a low-pressure steamer, convection oven or a combination of the two. The programmable features allow for performing complex cooking procedures to achieve superior end products.

Microwave Ovens

Microwave ovens are electrically powered ovens used to cook or reheat foods. They are available in a range of sizes and power settings. Microwave ovens will not brown foods unless fitted with special browning elements. Microwave cooking is discussed in more detail in Chapter 9, Principles of Cooking.

Broilers and Grills

Broilers and grills are generally used to prepare meats, fish and poultry. For a grill, the heat source is beneath the rack on which the food is placed. For a broiler, the heat source is above the food. Most broilers are gas powered; grills may be gas or electric or may burn wood or charcoal. A **salamander** is a small overhead broiler primarily used to finish or top-brown foods. (See Figure 5.9.) A **rotisserie** is similar to a broiler except that the food is placed on a revolving spit in front of the heat source. The unit may be open or enclosed like an oven; it is most often used for cooking poultry or meats.

Tilting Skillets

Tilting skillets are large, free-standing, flat-bottomed pans about 15 cm (6 inches) deep with an internal heating element below the pan's bottom. They are usually made of stainless steel with a cover, and have a hand-crank mechanism that turns or tilts the pan to pour out the contents. Tilting skillets can be used as stockpots, braziers, fry pans, griddles or steam tables, making them one of the most versatile of modern commercial appliances.

Steam Kettles

Steam kettles (also known as steam-jacketed kettles) are similar to stockpots except they are heated from the bottom and sides by steam circulating between layers of stainless steel. The steam may be generated internally or from an outside source. Because steam heats the kettle's sides, foods cook more quickly and evenly than they would in a pot sitting on the stove top. Steam kettles are most often used for making sauces, soups, custards or stock. Steam kettles are available in a range of sizes, from a 9-L (2-gallon) tabletop model to a 450-L (100-gallon) floor model. Some models have a tilting mechanism that allows the contents to be poured out; others have a spigot near the bottom through which liquids can be drained.

Steamers

Pressure and convection steamers are used to cook foods rapidly and evenly, using direct contact with steam. Pressure steamers heat water above the boiling point in sealed compartments; the high temperature and sealed compartment increase the internal pressure in a range of 1.8 to 6.8 kg (4 to 15 lb.) per square inch. The increased pressure and temperature cook the foods rapidly. Convection steamers generate steam in an internal boiler, then release it over the foods in a cooking chamber. Both types of steamer are ideal for cooking vegetables with a minimal loss of flavour or nutrients.

Deep Fryers

Deep fryers are used only to fry foods in hot fat. The fryers may be either gas or electric and should have thermostatic controls to maintain the fat at a preset temperature. Frying procedures are discussed in Chapter 21, Deep-Fat Frying.

Refrigerators

Proper refrigeration space is an essential component of any kitchen. Many foods must be stored at low temperatures to maintain quality and safety. Most

---

◆◆◆

INDUCTION— THE NEWEST HEAT SOURCE

Induction cooking uses a special induction coil placed below the stove top's surface in combination with specially designed cookware made of cast iron or magnetic stainless steel. The coil generates a magnetic current so that the cookware is heated rapidly with magnetic friction. Heat energy is then transferred from the cookware to the food by conduction. The cooking surface, which is made of a solid ceramic material, remains cool. Only the cookware and its contents get hot.

Induction cooking is a relatively new process, more popular in Europe than in Canada. But it is gaining acceptance in professional kitchens because of the speed with which foods can be heated and the ease of cleanup. It is often used on buffet action stations to prepare quick-cooking items such as omelettes and stir-fries.

=== ◆◆◆ ===
BUFFET EQUIPMENT

Food service operations that prepare buffets or cater off-premise events need specialized equipment to ensure that food is handled safely and efficiently and displayed appropriately. Proper temperatures must be maintained during transportation, display and service.

Insulated carriers hold food at a consistent temperature for a period of time. They are designed to hold hotel pans or sheet pans and are available with wheels for easy movement. Some are available with a spigot for serving hot or cold beverages. Any carrier should be easy to clean and a convenient size for the space available and the type of operation.

Temperature remains a concern when arranging food on a buffet table. Chafing dishes are commonly used for keeping hot foods hot during service. Chafing dishes are designed so that cans of solid fuel can be placed under a deep hotel pan of hot water. Like a bain marie, the hot water helps maintain the temperature of food placed in a second hotel pan suspended over the first. Chafing dishes, however, should never be used to heat food. Chafing dishes are available in several sizes and shapes, but the most convenient are those based on the size of a standard hotel pan. Round, deep chafing dishes are useful for serving soups or sauces. Exteriors can be plain or ornate, and made of silver, copper or stainless steel.

Roast beef, turkey, ham or other large cuts of meat are sometimes carved on a buffet in front of guests. Heat lamps can be used to keep these foods warm. Heat lamps are also useful for maintaining the temperature of pizza or fried foods, which might become soggy if held in a chafing dish.

Pastries, breads and cold foods can be arranged on a variety of platters, trays, baskets and serving pieces, depending on the size and style of the buffet. Some of the most elegant and traditional serving pieces are flat display mirrors. These may be plastic or glass and are available in a wide variety of shapes and sizes. The edges should be sealed in an easy-to-clean plastic to prevent chipping.

Although many of these items can be rented, operations that serve buffets on a regular basis may prefer to invest in their own transportation and serving equipment.

commercial refrigeration is of two types: walk-in units and reach-in or upright units.

A walk-in is a large, room-sized box capable of holding hundreds of kilograms of food on adjustable shelves. A separate freezer walk-in may be positioned nearby or even inside a refrigerated walk-in.

Reach-ins may be individual units or parts of a bank of units, each with shelves approximately the size of a full sheet pan. Reach-in refrigerators and freezers are usually located throughout the kitchen to provide quick access to foods. Small units may also be placed beneath the work counters. Freezers and refrigerators are available in a wide range of sizes and door designs to suit any operation.

Other forms of commercial refrigeration include chilled drawers located beneath a work area that are just large enough to accommodate a hotel pan, and display cases used to show foods to the customer.

Dishwashers

Mechanical dishwashers are available to wash, rinse and sanitize dishware, glassware, cookware and utensils. Small models clean one rack of items at a time, while larger models can handle several racks simultaneously on a conveyor belt system. Sanitizing may be accomplished with either extremely hot water (82°C/180°F) or with chemicals automatically dispensed during the final rinse cycle. Any dishwashing area should be carefully organized for efficient use of equipment and employees and to prevent recontamination of clean items.

SAFETY EQUIPMENT

There are certain items that are critical to the well-being of a food service operation although they are not used in food preparation. These are safety devices, many of which are required by provincial or local law. Failing to include safety equipment in a kitchen or failing to maintain it properly endangers workers and customers.

Fire Extinguishers

Fire extinguishers are canisters of foam, dry chemicals (such as sodium bicarbonate or potassium bicarbonate) or pressurized water used to extinguish small fires. They must be placed within sight of and easily reached from the work areas in which fires are more likely to occur. Different classes of extinguishers use different chemicals to fight different types of fire. The appropriate class must be used for the specific fire. See Table 5.2. Fire extinguishers must be recharged and checked from time to time. Be sure they have not been discharged, tampered with or otherwise damaged.

TABLE 5.2	FIRE EXTINGUISHERS	
Class	Symbol	Use
Class A	▲	Fires involving wood, paper, cloth or plastic
Class B	■	Fires involving oil, grease or flammable chemicals
Class C	●	Fires involving electrical equipment or wiring

Combination extinguishers—AB, BC and ABC—are also available.

Ventilation Systems

Ventilation systems (also called ventilation hoods) are commonly installed over cooking equipment to remove vapours, heat and smoke. Most systems include fire extinguishing agents or sprinklers. A properly operating hood makes the kitchen more comfortable for the staff and reduces the danger of fire. The system must be designed, installed and inspected by professionals, then cleaned and maintained regularly. A return or makeup air system is installed to ensure air quality and good circulation.

First-Aid Kits

First-aid supplies should be stored in a clearly marked box, conspicuously located near food preparation areas. Occupational Health and Safety guidelines may specify the kit's exact contents. Generally, they should include a first-aid manual, bandages, gauze dressings, adhesive tape, antiseptics, scissors, cold packs and other supplies. The kit should be checked regularly and items replaced as needed. In addition, cards with emergency telephone numbers should be placed inside the first-aid kit and near a telephone. Emergency response procedures must be communicated to staff and a copy of them must be available for quick reference.

THE PROFESSIONAL KITCHEN

The kitchen is the heart of the food service operation. There, food and other items are received, stored, prepared and plated for service; dining room staff places orders, retrieves foods ready for service and returns dirty service items; dishes and other wares are cleaned and stored; and the chef conducts business. But commercial space is expensive, and most food service operators recognize that the greater the number of customers served, the greater the revenues. Often this translates into a large dining area and small kitchen and storage facilities. Therefore, when designing a kitchen, it is important to use the space wisely so that each of its functions can be accomplished efficiently.

Regardless of the kitchen's size, its design begins with a consideration of the tasks to be performed. Analyzing the menu identifies these tasks. A restaurant featuring steaks and chops, for example, will need areas to fabricate and grill meats. If it relies on commercially prepared desserts and breads, it will not need a bakeshop but will still need space to hold and plate baked goods.

Once all food preparation tasks are identified, a work area for each particular task is designated. These work areas are called **work stations**. At a steak restaurant, an important work station is the broiler. If the restaurant serves fried foods, it will also need a fry station. The size and design of each work station is determined by the volume of food the operation intends to produce.

Usually work stations using the same or similar equipment for related tasks are grouped together into **work sections**. See Table 5.3. (Note that work stations correspond to the kitchen brigade system discussed in Chapter 1, Professionalism.) For example, in a typical

TABLE 5.3	WORK SECTIONS AND THEIR STATIONS
Sections	Stations
Hot-foods section	Broiler station Fry station Griddle station Sauté/sauce station Holding
Garde-manger section	Salad greens cleaning Salad preparation Cold-foods preparation Sandwich station Showpiece preparation
Bakery section	Mixing station Dough holding and proofing Dough rolling and forming Baking and cooling Dessert preparation* Frozen dessert preparation* Plating desserts*
Banquet section	Steam cooking Dry heat cooking (roasting, broiling) Holding and plating
Short-order section	Griddle station Fry station Broiler station
Beverage section	Hot-beverage station Cold-beverage station Alcoholic beverage station

*These stations are sometimes found in the *garde-manger* section.

♦♦♦

ALEXIS SOYER
(1809–1858)

Alexis Soyer
Photo courtesy of Barbara Wheaton.

The father of the contemporary celebrity chef was Alexis Soyer, a Frenchman whose tragically short working life was spent mostly in London. He was a flamboyant, talented and egocentric showman. He was also a renowned chef, restaurateur, social activist, author, purveyor of prepared foods and inventor.

In 1831 Soyer left his thriving catering business and restaurant in Paris for London. (A scandal was rumoured to be behind his sudden departure.) There he quickly established a reputation as a talented chef in the latest French fashion. By 1838 he was employed at a gentlemen's club called the Reform. Able to assist in planning the club's new kitchen facility, Soyer installed the most modern equipment: gas ovens with temperature controls, a steam-driven mechanical spit and a storage locker cooled by running water. From this modern kitchen he produced his signature dish: lamb chops Reform.

The Reform was founded by members of the Liberal Party, a political party interested in social reform. Their chef soon joined the party

"The Kitchen Department of the Reform Club" (1841). "To show them at one glance," wrote the *Spectator*, "the partition walls are cut away, and a bird's eye view is given of the several kitchens, larders, sculleries, and batterie de cuisine; the different functionaries are at their posts, and the accomplished chef, Monsieur Soyer, is in the act of pointing out to a favoured visitor the various contrivances suggested by his ingenuity and experience."

◆◆◆

ranks. He developed recipes for inexpensive, nutritious soups for the working class and in 1847 went to Ireland and opened soup kitchens to feed those who were starving as a result of the Potato Famine.

His most important writings reflect his interests in good food for the masses. The intended audience for *The Modern Housewife* (1849) was the middle class; the growing urban working class was the intended audience for his second book, *A Schilling Cookery for the People* (1855).

In 1851 Soyer opened his own lavishly decorated and expensively equipped restaurant called the Gastronomic Symposium of All Nations. It closed shortly thereafter, in part because of Soyer's debts, in part because he lost his operating licence as a result of the rowdiness in the restaurant's American-style bar, at which customers were publicly served cocktails for the first time in London.

In addition to cooking and writing, Soyer created and marketed several prepared food items: Soyer's Sauce, Soyer's Nectar and Soyer's Relish. He was also fascinated with kitchen gadgets and invented several, including a sink stopper, jelly mould, egg cooker and coffeepot. The most notable, however, was a portable "Magic Stove" weighing less than 2 kg (4 lb.), similar to a modern chafing dish. Soyer's final triumph was in the Crimean War (1854–1857). He developed army rations, reorganized field and hospital kitchens and introduced one of his last inventions, the campaign stove. Portable, efficient and requiring little fuel, it was used by the British army for the next 90 years.

(a)

Stainless Steel Hood

1 Convection Oven
2 Under-Counter Freezer Unit
3 Griddle Top
4 Cheese Melter
5 6-Burner Top/Oven Below
6 Salamander
7 Under-Counter Refrigerator
8 Broiler Top
9 Stainless Steel Work Table with Open Shelves
10 Deep-Fat Fryers
11 Stainless Steel Overshelves

12 Steam Table with Open Shelves Below
13 Stainless Steel Dual Shelf with Top Heat Rod
14 Under-Counter Freezer with Work Surface
15 Conveyor Toaster
16 Bain Marie with Under-Counter Refrigerator
17 Microwave Table with Shelf
18 Microwave
19 Reach-In Refrigerator Unit

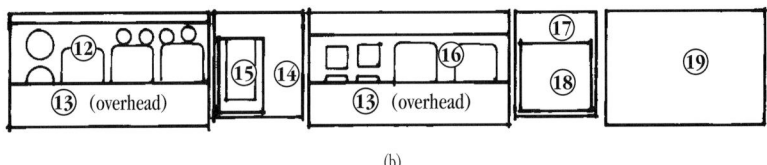

(b)

FIGURE 5.11   *Typical Hot-Foods Section Floor Plan*

full-service restaurant, there will be a single hot-foods section. It can consist of broiler, fry, griddle, sauté and sauce stations. Both advance preparation and last-minute cooking may be performed in the hot-foods section. The principal cooking equipment (a range, broiler, deep-fat fryer, oven, griddle, etc.) will be arranged in a line under a ventilation hood. A typical plan for this hot-foods section is shown in Figure 5.11. Although each work station within the hot-foods section may be staffed by a different line cook, the proximity of the stations allows one line cook to cover more than one station if the kitchen is short-handed or when business is slow.

Merely considering the plan of the work station or section is not enough, however. When designing the work area, you must also consider the elevation. That is, a kitchen designer not only examines what equipment should be placed next to the other (for example, the range next to the deep-fat fryer), but also what equipment and storage facilities can be placed beneath or on top of the other. For example, in a bakeshop, rolling storage carts for flour and sugar or an under-the-counter refrigerator for eggs and dairy products may be located beneath the work surface, while mixing bowls and dry ingredients are stored on shelves above. Figure 5.12 illustrates the elevation for the hot-foods section whose plan is shown in Figure 5.11. Ideally, each station should be designed so that the cook takes no more than three steps in any direction to perform all assigned station tasks.

In addition to the work sections where the menu items are produced, a typical restaurant kitchen includes areas dedicated to:

1. *Receiving and storing foods and other items.* There should be separate freezer, refrigerator and dry-goods storage facilities. Each should have proper

Stainless Steel Hood

(a)

1   Convection Oven
2   Under-Counter Freezer Unit
3   Griddle Top
4   Cheese Melter
5   6-Burner Top/Oven Below
6   Salamander
7   Under-Counter Refrigerator
8   Broiler Top
9   Stainless Steel Work Table with Open Shelves
10 Deep-Fat Fryers
11 Stainless Steel Overshelves

12 Steam Table with Open Shelves Below
13 Stainless Steel Dual Shelf with Top Heat Rod
14 Under-Counter Freezer with Work Surface
15 Conveyor Toaster
16 Bain Marie with Under-Counter Refrigerator
17 Microwave Table with Shelf
18 Microwave
19 Reach-In Refrigerator Unit

(b)

FIGURE 5.12   *Typical Hot-Foods Section Elevation*

temperature, humidity and light controls in order to maintain the stored items properly and safely. Depending upon the operation's size and the work stations' specific needs, there can be either a central storage area or each station or section can maintain its own storage facilities. Typically, however, there is a combination of central and section storage. For example, up to 45 kg (100 lb.) of flour and sugar can be stored in rolling bins under a work table in the bakeshop, while several hundreds of kilograms or pounds more remain in a central dry goods area. Similarly, one box of salt can be stored near the hot line for immediate use, while the remainder of the case is stored in a central dry goods area. Additional storage space will be needed for cleaning and paper supplies, dishes and other service ware. *Never store cleaning supplies and other chemicals with foods.*

FIGURE 5.13   *Diagram of Kitchen*

2. *Washing dishes and other equipment.* These dish- and equipment-washing facilities should have their own sinks. Food-preparation and hand-washing sinks should be separate.

3. *Employee use.* Restrooms, locker facilities and an office are also found in most food service facilities.

The guiding principle behind a good kitchen design is to maximize the flow of goods and staff from one area to the next and within each area itself. Maximizing flow creates an efficient work environment and helps reduce preparation and service time.

Figure 5.13 shows the several sections of a professional kitchen. It includes an area for front-of-the-house staff to circulate, drop off orders, retrieve finished dishes and return dirty dishes. The design allows for the flow of foods from receiving to storage, to food preparation areas, to holding and service areas and then to the dining room as well as the flow of dirty dishes from the dining room back into the kitchen. The work sections are arranged to take advantage of shared equipment. For instance, by placing the bakeshop next to the hot-foods section, they can share ovens. The *garde-manger* and dessert sections, both of which rely on refrigerated foods, are conveniently located near the walk-in refrigerator and freezer area. The beverage station is located near the dining room entrance so that food servers do not have to walk through food preparation areas to fill beverage orders. The office is next to receiving so that the chef can easily check and receive orders. The central storage areas are easily accessible to the receiving area as well as to the food production areas, while the cleaning-supply storage is near the dishwashing area. In general, the design eliminates the need for staff from one work station or section to cross through another station or section.

Governmental building, health, fire and safety codes will dictate, to a degree, certain aspects of a professional kitchen's design. But to make the most of these spaces, the well-designed kitchen should reflect a sound understanding of the tasks to be performed and the equipment necessary to perform them. Hiring a professional kitchen designer is a good investment when building or retrofitting a food service facility.

CONCLUSION

There are hundreds of tools and pieces of equipment that can help you prepare, cook, store and present food. Every year, manufacturers offer new or improved items. Throughout your career you will use many of them. Select those that are well constructed, durable and best suited for the task at hand. Then use them in a safe and efficient manner.

The way in which equipment is arranged and stored in a kitchen is also important. Good kitchen design emphasizes the efficient flow of goods and staff from one work section to another as well as within each work section or station.

QUESTIONS FOR DISCUSSION

1. What six characteristics should be considered in the selection of tools and equipment?
2. List the parts of a chef's knife and describe the knife's construction.
3. List six materials used to make commercial cookware and describe the advantages and disadvantages of each.
4. Describe six pieces of equipment that can be used to slice or chop foods.
5. List three classes of fire extinguishers. For each one, describe its designating symbol and identify the type or types of fire it should be used to extinguish.
6. Explain the relationship between work sections and work stations and the kitchen brigade system discussed in Chapter 1, Professionalism.

WEBLINKS

Health Canada: Cookware Safety
 www.hc-sc.gc.ca/main/hc/web/datapcb/communc/home/pubs/cooke.htm

InterTrade Systems—Foodservice Products and Services
 www.itrade.net/

Cookware Manufacturers Association
 www.cookware.org

North American Association of Food Equipment Manufacturers
 www.nafem.org

The Food Resource: Pictures of Culinary Equipment
 www.orst.edu/food-resource/misc/equip.html

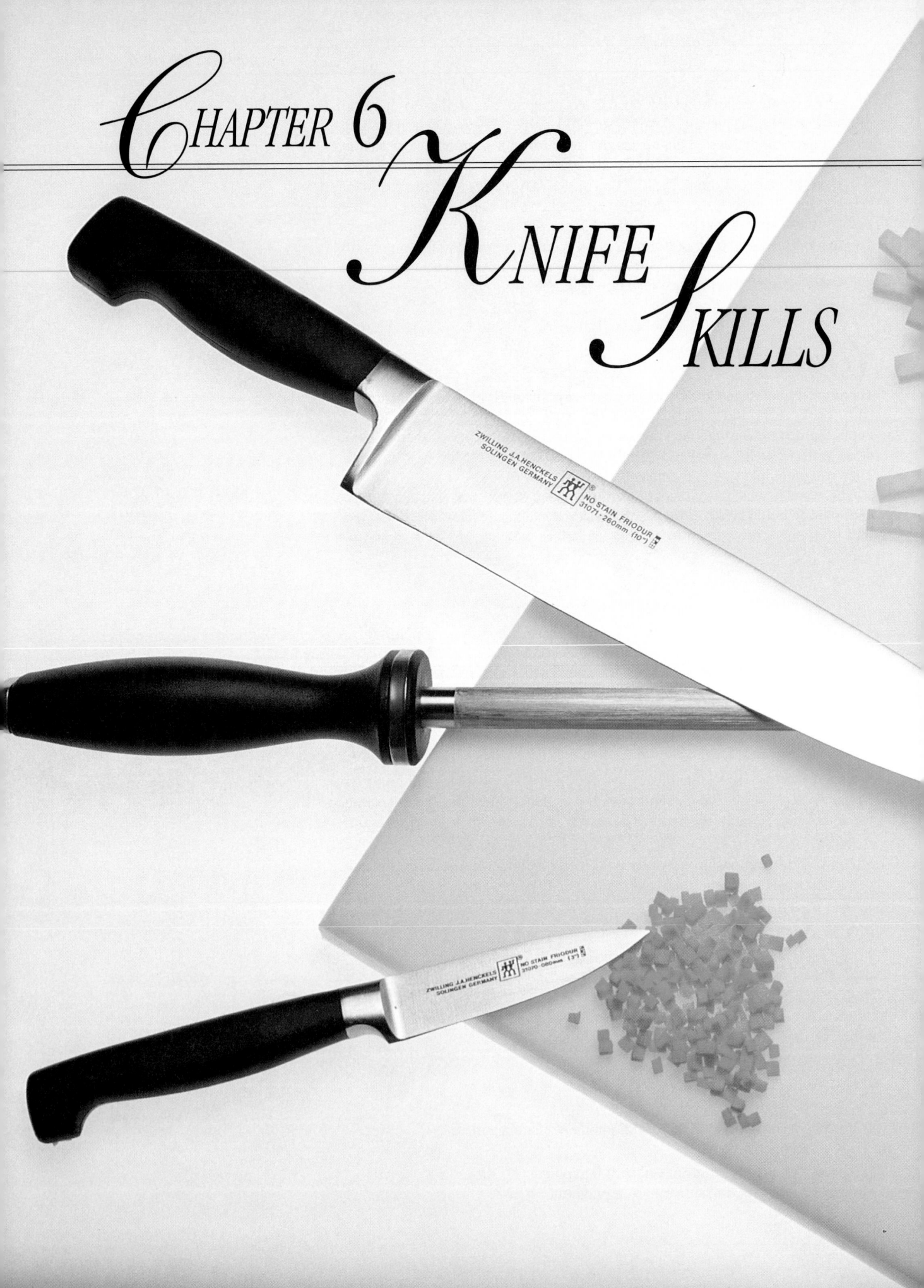

CHAPTER 6 KNIFE SKILLS

LEARNING OUTCOMES

After studying this chapter you will be able to:

◆ care for knives properly
◆ use knives safely and properly
◆ cut foods into a variety of classic shapes

Every professional must become skilled in the use of certain tools. The professional cook is no exception. One of the most important tools the apprentice cook must master is the knife. Good knife skills are critical to a cook's success because the knife is the most commonly used tool in the kitchen. Every cook spends countless hours slicing, dicing, mincing and chopping. Learning to perform these tasks safely and efficiently is an essential part of your training.

At first, professional knives may feel large and awkward and the techniques discussed below may not seem all that efficient. But as you become familiar with knives and practise your knife skills, using knives correctly will become second nature.

Knives are identified in Chapter 5, Tools and Equipment. Here we show how they are used to cut vegetables. The techniques presented, however, can be used for most any food that holds its shape when cut. Knife skills for butchering and fabricating meat, poultry, fish and shellfish are discussed in Chapters 12, Principles of Meat Cookery, through 19, Fish and Shellfish.

A note about language: Many of the classic cuts are known by their French names: julienne, *for example. Although these words are nouns and entered the English language as nouns (e.g.,* a julienne *of carrot), they are also used as verbs (to* julienne *a carrot) and adjectives (*julienned *carrots).*

USING YOUR KNIFE SAFELY

The first rule of knife safety is to *think about what you are doing*. Other basic rules of knife safety are:

1. Use the correct knife for the task at hand.
2. Always cut away from yourself.
3. Always cut on a cutting board. Do not cut on glass, marble or metal.
4. Keep knives sharp; a dull knife is more dangerous than a sharp one.
5. When carrying a knife, hold it point down, parallel to and close to your leg as you walk.
6. A falling knife has no handle. Do not attempt to catch a falling knife; step back and allow it to fall.
7. Never leave a knife in a sink of water; anyone reaching into the sink could be injured or the knife could be dented by pots or other utensils.

CARING FOR YOUR KNIFE

Knife Sharpening

A sharpening stone called a **whetstone** is used to put an edge on a dull knife blade. To use a whetstone, place the heel of the blade against the whetstone at a 20-degree angle. Keeping that angle, press down on the blade while pushing it away from you in one long arc, as if to slice off a thin piece of the stone. The entire length of the blade should come in contact with the stone during each sweep. Repeat the procedure on both sides of the blade until sufficiently sharp. With a triple-faced stone, such as that shown to the right, you progress from the coarsest to the finest surface. Any whetstone can be moistened with either water or mineral oil, but not both. Do not use vegetable oil on a whetstone as it will soon become rancid and gummy.

A **steel** does not sharpen a knife. Instead, it is used to hone or straighten the blade immediately after and between sharpenings. To use a steel, place the blade against the steel at a 20-degree angle. Then draw the blade along the entire length of the steel. Repeat the technique several times on each side of the blade.

A final note on knife care: Do not wash knives in commercial dishwashers. The heat and harsh chemicals can damage the edge and the handle. The blade can also be damaged if it knocks against cookware or utensils. In addition, the knife could injure an unsuspecting worker. Always wash and dry your knives by hand immediately after each use.

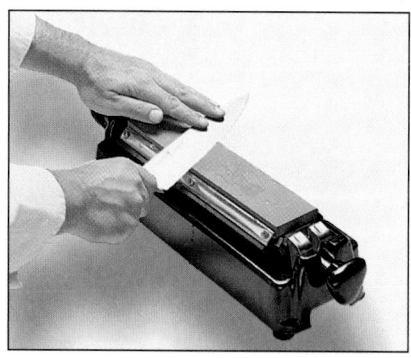

When sharpening a knife against a three-sided whetstone, go from the coarsest to the finest surface.

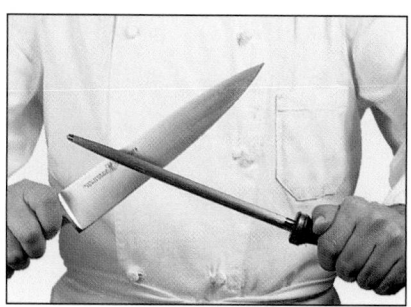

Honing a knife against a steel straightens the blade between sharpenings.

GRIPPING YOUR KNIFE

There are several ways to grip a knife. Use the grip that is most comfortable for you or the one dictated by the job at hand. Whichever grip you use should be firm but not so tight that your hand becomes tired. Gripping styles are shown below.

The most common grip: Hold the handle with three fingers while gripping the blade between the thumb and index finger.

A variation on the most common grip: Grip the handle with four fingers and place the thumb on the front of the handle.

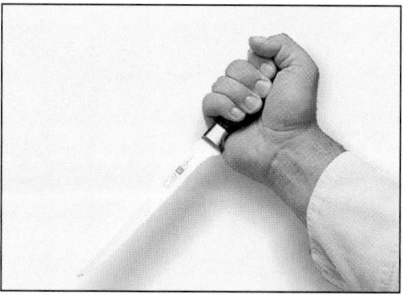

The underhand grip for a rigid boning knife: Grip the handle in a fist with four fingers and thumb. This grip allows you to use the knife tip to cut around joints and separate flesh from bone when boning meat and poultry.

CONTROLLING YOUR KNIFE

To safely produce even cuts, you must control (or guide) your knife with one hand and hold the item being cut with the other. Always allow the blade's sharp edge to do the cutting. Never force the blade through the item being cut. Smooth, even strokes should be used. Using a dull knife or excessive force with any knife produces, at best, poor results and, at worst, a significant safety risk. Cutting without using your hand as a guide may also be dangerous. Two safe cutting methods that produce good results are shown below.

Method A

1. Keep your fingertips curled back, then grip the item being cut with three fingertips and your thumb. Hold the knife in the other hand. While keeping the knife's tip on the cutting board, lift the heel of the knife.

2. Use the second joint of your index finger as a guide and cut a slice using a smooth, even, downward stroke. Adjust the position of the guiding finger after each slice to produce slices of equal size. After a few cuts, slide your fingertips and thumb down the length of the item and continue slicing. For this slicing technique, the knife's tip acts as the fulcrum.

Method B

1. Grip the item as described above. Using the second joint of your index finger as a guide, lift the knife's tip and slice by drawing the knife slightly back toward you and down through the item, cutting the item to the desired thickness.

2. The motion of the knife should come almost entirely from the wrist, not the elbow. Allow the weight of the knife to do most of the work; very little downward pressure needs to be applied to the knife. For this slicing technique, your wrist should act as the fulcrum.

CUTTING WITH YOUR KNIFE

A knife is used to shape and reduce an item's size. Uniformity of size and shape ensures even cooking and enhances the appearance of the finished product. Items are shaped by slicing, chopping, dicing, mincing or by other special cutting techniques.

Slicing

To slice is to cut an item into relatively broad, thin pieces. Slices may be either the finished cut or the first step in producing other cuts. Slicing is typically used to create three specialty cuts: the chiffonade, rondelle and diagonal. Slicing skills are also used to produce oblique or roll cuts and lozenges.

A **chiffonade** is a preparation of finely sliced or shredded leafy vegetables used as a garnish or a base under cold presentations. As shown here, slicing spinach *en chiffonade* is a relatively simple process.

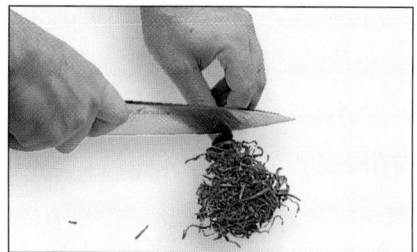

1. Wash and destem the leaves as necessary. Stack several leaves on top of each other and roll them tightly like a cigar.

2. Make fine slices across the leaves while holding the leaf roll tightly.

As seen below, **rondelles** or **rounds** are easily made disk-shaped slices of cylindrical vegetables or fruits.

Peel the item (if desired) and place it on a cutting board. Make even slices perpendicular to the item being cut.

Diagonals are elongated or oval-shaped slices of cylindrical vegetables or fruits. They are produced with a cut similar to that used to cut rondelles except that the knife is held at an angle to the item being cut.

Peel the item (if desired) and place it on a cutting board. Position the knife at the desired angle to the item being cut and slice it evenly.

Oblique or **roll-cut** items are small pieces with two angle-cut sides. This relatively simple cut is most often used on carrots and parsnips.

Lozenges are diamond-shaped cuts prepared from firm vegetables such as carrots, turnips, rutabagas and potatoes.

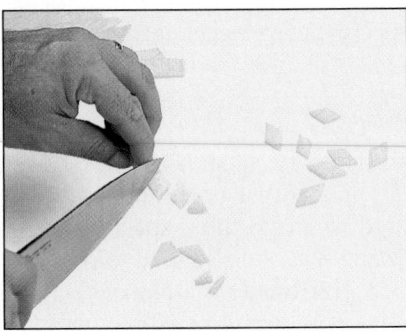

1. Slice the item into long slices of the desired thickness. Then cut the slices into strips of the desired width.

2. Cut the strips at an angle to produce diamond shapes.

Horizontal Slicing

To horizontal slice is to **butterfly** or cut a **pocket** into meats, poultry or fish. It is also a method of cutting used to thinly slice soft vegetables.

1. With your hand opened and your fingers arched upward, hold the item to be cut firmly in the centre of your palm.

2. Holding the knife parallel to the table, slice a pocket to the desired depth or cut through the item completely.

Chopping

To chop is to cut an item into small pieces where uniformity of size and shape is neither necessary (for example, coarsely chopped onions for a *mirepoix* that will be removed from the stock before service) nor feasible (for example, parsley).

Coarse Chopping

Coarse chopping does not mean carelessly hacking up food. Rather, the procedure is identical to that used for slicing but without the emphasis on uniformity. Coarsely chopped pieces should measure approximately 2 cm × 2 cm × 2 cm (3/4 inch × 3/4 inch × 3/4 inch).

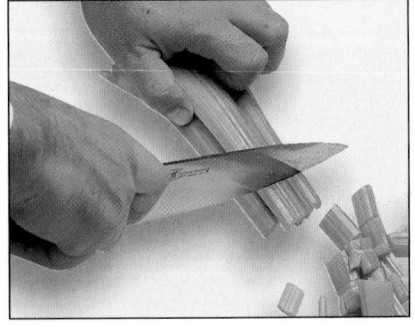

Grip the knife as for slicing. Hold the item being chopped with your other hand. It may not be necessary to use your finger as a guide because uniformity is not crucial.

Chopping Parsley and Similar Foods

Parsley can be cut very coarsely or very finely. As shown below, it is easy to chop parsley and similar foods properly regardless of the desired fineness.

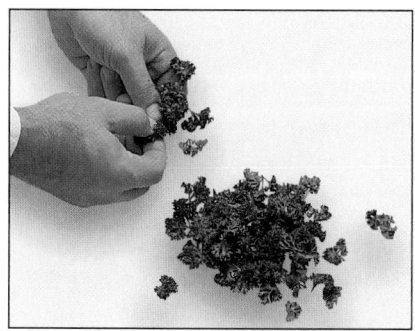

1. Wash the parsley in cold water; drain well. Remove the parsley sprigs from the stems.

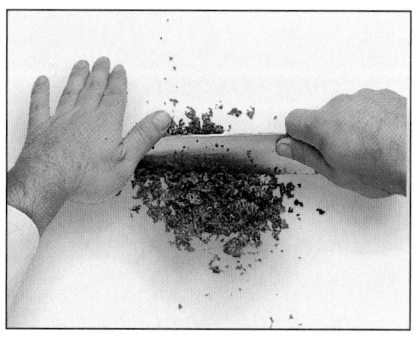

2. Grip the knife in one hand. With the other hand spread flat, hold the knife's tip on the cutting board. Keeping the knife's tip on the board, chop the parsley sprigs by rocking the curved blade of the knife up and down while moving the knife back and forth over the parsley.

3. Place the chopped parsley in a clean kitchen towel or a double layer of cheesecloth. Rinse it under cold water and squeeze out as much water as possible. The chopped parsley should be dry and fluffy.

Chopping Garlic

A daily chore in many food service facilities, peeling and chopping garlic is a simple job made easy with the procedure shown here.

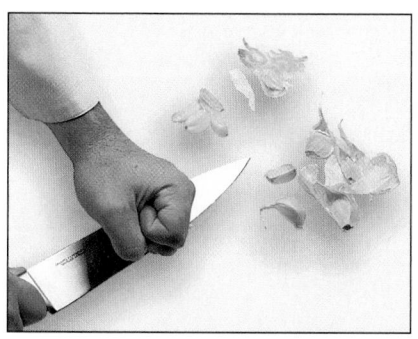

1. Break the head of garlic into individual cloves with your hands. Lightly crush the cloves using the flat edge of a chef's knife or a mallet. They will break open and the peel can be separated easily from the garlic flesh.

2. With a flat hand, hold the knife's tip on the cutting board. Using a rocking motion, chop the garlic cloves to the desired size. Garlic is usually chopped very finely.

3. Garlic paste can be made by first finely chopping the garlic and then turning the knife on an angle and repeatedly dragging the edge of the knife along the cutting board, mashing the garlic.

Cutting Sticks and Dicing

To dice is to cut an item into cubes. Before an item can be diced, it must first be cut into certain-sized sticks. These techniques are most often used when uniformity of size and shape are important (for example, julienned carrots for a salad or brunoised vegetables for a garnish).

The dicing technique is typically used to create the classic cuts known as brunoise, small dice, medium dice, large dice and paysanne. Although most cooks have some notion of what size and shape "small diced" potatoes or julienne carrots may be, there are size ranges and specific shapes for these cuts. Exact size will depend on the use or look desired.

Julienne—a stick-shaped item with dimensions of 1–2 mm × 1–2 mm × 2.5–4 cm (1/16 inch × 1/16 inch × 1–2 inches).

Allumette—a stick-shaped item, originally pertaining to potatoes only, with dimensions of 3 mm × 3 mm × 5–6 cm (1/8 inch × 1/8 inch × 2 to 2-1/2 inches).

Batonnet—a stick-shaped item with dimensions of 6 mm × 6 mm × 5–6 cm (1/4 inch × 1/4 inch × 2 to 2-1/2 inches).

Small dice—a cube-shaped item with dimensions of 3 mm × 3 mm × 3 mm (1/8 inch × 1/8 inch × 1/8 inch).

Brunoise—a cube-shaped item with dimensions of 1–2 mm × 1–2 mm × 1–2 mm (1/16 inch × 1/16 inch × 1/16 inch).

Medium dice (macedoine)—a cube-shaped item with dimensions of 6 mm × 6 mm × 6 mm (1/4 inch × 1/4 inch × 1/4 inch).

Large dice (mirepoix)—a cube-shaped item with dimensions of 12 mm × 12 mm × 12 mm (1/2 inch × 1/2 inch × 1/2 inch).

Paysanne—a flat, rectangular or triangular-shaped item with dimensions of 12 mm × 12 mm × 3 mm thick (1/2 inch × 1/2 inch × 1/8 inch).

Cutting Julienne, Allumette and Batonnet

Julienne, allumette and batonnet are matchstick-shaped cuts prepared using the same procedure as cutting sticks for dicing.

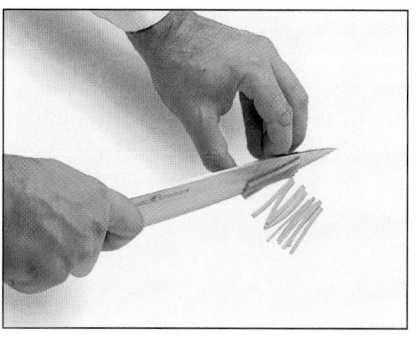

1. Peel the item (if desired) and square off the sides. Trim the item so that the slices cut from it will be the proper length. Cut even slices of the desired thickness, 1–2 mm (1/16 inch) for julienne, 3 mm (1/8 inch) for allumette or 6 mm (1/4 inch) for batonnet.

2. Stack the slices and cut them evenly into sticks (also referred to as "planks") that are the same thickness as the slices.

Cutting Brunoise and Small, Medium and Large Dice

Brunoise as well as small, medium and large dice are made by first cutting the item into sticks following the procedure for cutting julienne, allumette or batonnet, then making cuts perpendicular to the length of the sticks to produce small cubes. Making a 1–2 mm (1/6-inch) cut perpendicular to the length of a julienne produces a brunoise. Making a 3-mm (1/8-inch) cut perpendicular to the length of a batonnet produces a small dice. A 6-mm (1/4-inch) cut from a 6-mm (1/4-inch) baton produces a medium dice and a 12-mm (1/2-inch) cut from a 12-mm (1/2-inch) baton produces a large dice.

Julienne, allumette, batonnet, and baton sticks and the large, medium, small and brunoise dices cut from them.

Cutting Paysanne

Paysanne is a classic vegetable cut for garnishing soups and other dishes. It resembles a 12-mm (1/2-inch) dice that has been cut in thin slices. It is produced by following the procedures for dicing, but in the final step the 12-mm × 12-mm (1/2-inch × 1/2-inch) sticks are cut into slices 3 mm (1/8 inch) thick.

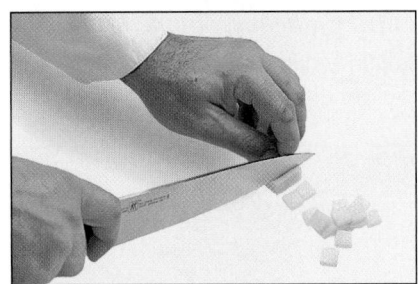

Cutting paysanne from a 12-mm × 12-mm (1/2-inch × 1/2-inch) stick.

Dicing an Onion

Onions are easily peeled and diced to any size desired using the procedure shown here.

1. Use a paring knife to remove the stem end. Trim the root end but leave it nearly intact (this helps prevent the onion from falling apart while being diced). Peel away the outer skin; be careful not to remove and waste too much onion.

2. Cut the onion in half through the stem and root. Place the cut side down on the cutting board.

3. Cut parallel slices of the desired thickness vertically through the onion from the root towards the stem end without cutting completely through the root end.

4. Make a single horizontal cut on a small onion or two horizontal cuts on a large onion through the width of the onion, again without cutting through the root end.

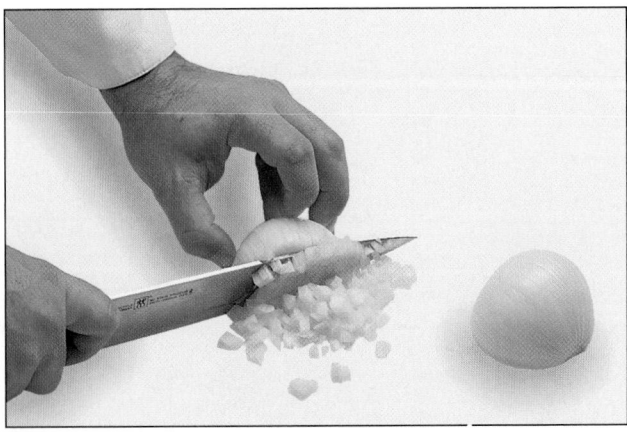

5. Turn the onion and cut slices perpendicular to the previous slices to produce diced onion.

Mincing

To mince is to cut an item into very small pieces. The terms "finely chopped" and "minced" are often used interchangeably and are most often used when referring to garlic, shallots, herbs and other foods that do not have to be uniform in shape.

Mincing Shallots

The procedure for mincing shallots is shown here.

1. Peel and dice the shallots, following the procedure for peeling and dicing an onion.

2. With a flat hand, hold the knife's tip on the cutting board. Using a rocking motion, mince the shallots with the heel of the knife.

Turning (Shaping)

Turning (*tourner,* "to turn" in French) is a cutting technique that results in a football-shaped finished product traditionally with seven equal sides and blunt ends. The size of the finished product may vary, the most common being 5 cm (2 inches) long. Some products are partially turned or shaped to achieve a better yield or for variety. Turned vegetables are generally associated with finer dining establishments. Due to higher labour and food cost, the practice is not prevalent. This is a more complicated procedure than other cuts and takes considerable practice to produce good results.

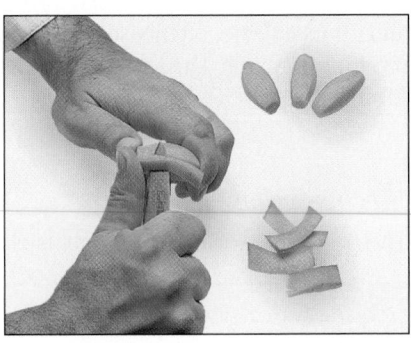

1. Cut the item being "turned" into pieces 5 cm × 2–2.5 cm (2 inches × 3/4 to 1 inch). Each piece should have flat ends. (Potatoes, turnips and beets may be cut into as many as 6 or 8 pieces; carrots can simply be cut into 5-cm/2-inch lengths.) Peeling is optional because in most cases the item's entire surface area is trimmed away.

2. Holding the item between the thumb and forefinger, use a turning knife or a paring knife to cut 7 curved sides on the item, creating a flat-ended, football-shaped product.

Using a Mandoline

The mandoline is a nonmechanical cutting tool. It does the jobs that can be done with a chef's knife, such as producing very thinly sliced apples or large quantities of julienned vegetables, quickly, easily and very accurately. It can also make cuts such as a ridged slice or **gaufrette** that cannot be done with a conventional chef's knife.

When using the mandoline always use the guard or a steel-mesh glove to protect your hand.

1. To use the mandoline, position the legs and set the blade to the desired shape and thickness.

2. Slide the guard into place.

3. To slice, slide the item against the blade with a single, smooth stroke.

4. To cut gaufrette, select the ridged blade and set it to the desired thickness. Make the first slice, turn the item 60 degrees to 90 degrees and make the second slice. Turn the item back to the original position and make another slice, and so on.

CONCLUSION

Although many slicing and dicing machines are available, none can ever completely replace a skilled chef with a sharp knife. As an apprentice, becoming efficient with your knives should be a high priority. Possessing good knife skills allows you to produce more attractive products in a safe and efficient manner. You will use the classic cuts and techniques outlined in this chapter throughout your career. You should memorize the procedures and practise them often. And remember, a dull or carelessly handled knife is dangerous.

QUESTIONS FOR DISCUSSION

1. Explain the step-by-step procedures for sharpening a knife using a three-sided whetstone.
2. What is the purpose of a steel?
3. Why is it necessary to cut vegetables into uniform shapes and sizes?
4. Describe the following cutting procedures: slicing, chopping and dicing.
5. Identify the dimensions of the following cuts: julienne, batonnet, brunoise, small dice, medium dice, large dice and paysanne.
6. Describe the procedure for making turned or shaped vegetables.
7. Describe three preparations for which a mandoline would be useful.

WEBLINKS

Sharpen Your Knife Skills
   www.extrahelp.com/extrahelp/nightknife.html
Better Homes and Gardens: Keeping Knives Sharp
   www.bhglive.com/survival/cookhelpers/knifshar.htm
General Housewares: Caring for Your Cutlery
   www.ghw.com/carving_tools/knife_care/knife_care.phtml
How to Dice an Onion
   www.eatingwell.com/recipes/abc/step/onion/

CHAPTER 7

KITCHEN STAPLES

LEARNING OUTCOMES

After studying this chapter you will be able to:

◆ recognize and use a variety of herbs, spices, nuts, oils, vinegars and condiments
◆ prepare a bouquet garni, sachet or oignon piquet
◆ prepare and serve quality coffees and teas

*C*ertain foods are used in almost all stations of the kitchen with such regularity that they have become known as **staples**. Included are many of the processed, packaged items we often take for granted: salt, pepper, flour, sugar, oil and flavourings. There is, however, no single list of staples. Each food service operation will have its own list depending on the menu and the cooking methods used.

This chapter identifies and discusses selected herbs and spices, salt, nuts, oils, vinegars and condiments as well as two popular beverages, coffee and tea. We provide identifying characteristics for some of the more common staples and set forth standards of quality and usage. Other staples, such as flour and sugar, are covered in Chapter 26, Principles of the Bakeshop.

HERBS AND SPICES

Herbs and spices are the kitchen staples used as **flavourings**. **Herbs** refer to the large group of **aromatic** plants whose leaves, stems or flowers are used to add flavours to other foods. Most herbs are available fresh or dried. Because drying alters their flavours and aromas, fresh herbs are generally preferred and should be used if possible. **Spices** are strongly flavoured or aromatic portions of plants used as flavourings, **condiments** or aromatics. Spices are the bark, roots, seeds, buds or berries of plants, most of which grow naturally only in tropical climates. Spices are almost always used in their dried form, rarely fresh, and can usually be purchased whole or ground. Some plants—dill, for example—can be used as both an herb (its leaves) and a spice (its seeds).

Herbs

Basil (Fr. *basilique*) is considered one of the great culinary herbs. It is available in a variety of "flavours"—cinnamon, garlic, lemon, even chocolate—but the most common is sweet basil. **Sweet basil** has light green, tender leaves and small white flowers. Its flavour is strong, warm and slightly peppery, with a hint of cloves. Basil is used in Mediterranean cuisines and has a special affinity for garlic and tomatoes. When purchasing fresh basil, look for bright green leaves; avoid flower buds and wilted or rust-coloured leaves. Dried sweet basil is readily available, but has a decidedly weaker flavour.

Basil

Opal basil is named for its vivid purple colour. It has a tougher, crinkled leaf and a medium-strong flavour. Opal basil may be substituted for sweet basil in cooking and its appearance makes it a distinctive garnish.

Opal basil

Bay (Fr. *laurier*), also known as sweet laurel, is a small tree from Asia that produces tough, glossy leaves with a sweet balsamic aroma and peppery flavour. Bay symbolized wisdom and glory in ancient Rome; the leaves were

Bay leaves

used to form crowns or "laurels" worn by emperors and victorious athletes. In cooking, dried bay leaves are often preferred over the more bitter fresh leaves. Essential in French cuisine, bay leaves are part of the traditional bouquet garni and court bouillon. Whole dried leaves are usually added to a dish at the start of cooking, then removed when sufficient flavour has been extracted.

Chervil

Chervil (Fr. *cerfeuil)*, also known as sweet cicely, is native to Russia and the Middle East. Its lacy, fernlike leaves are similar to parsley and can be used as a garnish. Chervil's flavour is delicate, similar to parsley but with the distinctive aroma of anise. It should not be heated for long periods. Chervil is commonly used in French cuisine and is one of the traditional *fines herbes.*

Chives (Fr. *ciboulette*) are perhaps the most delicate and sophisticated members of the onion family. Their hollow, thin grass-green stems grow in clumps and produce round, pale purple flowers, which are used as a garnish. Chives may be purchased dried, quick-frozen or fresh. They have a mild onion flavour and bright green colour. Chives complement eggs, poultry, potatoes, fish and shellfish. They should not be cooked for long periods or at high temperatures. Chives make an excellent garnish when snipped with scissors or carefully chopped and sprinkled over finished soups or sauces.

Chives

Garlic chives, also known as Chinese chives, actually belong to another plant species. They have flat, solid (not hollow) stems and a mild garlic flavour. They may be used in place of regular chives if their garlic flavour is desired.

Garlic chives

Cilantro is the green leafy portion of the plant that yields seeds known as coriander. The flavours of the two portions of this plant are very different and cannot be substituted for each other.

Cilantro, also known as Chinese parsley, is sharp and tangy with a strong aroma and an almost citrus flavour. It is widely used in Asian, Mexican and South American cuisines, especially in salads and sauces. It should not be subjected to heat and cilantro's flavour is completely destroyed by drying. Do not use yellow or discoloured leaves or the tough stems.

Cilantro

Dill (Fr. *aneth*), a member of the parsley family, has tiny, aromatic, yellow flowers and feathery, delicate blue-green leaves. The leaves taste like parsley, but sharper, with a touch of anise. Dill seeds are flat, oval and brown, with a bitter flavour similar to caraway. Both the seeds and the leaves of the dill plant are used in cooking. Dill is commonly used in Scandinavian and Central European cuisines, particularly with fish and potatoes. Both leaves and seeds are used in pickling and sour dishes. Dill leaves are available fresh or dried but lose their aroma and

Dill

Epazote

Lemon grass

Oregano

flavour during cooking, so add them only after the dish is removed from the heat. Dill seeds are available whole or ground and are used in fish dishes, pickles and breads.

Epazote, also known as wormseed or stinkweed, grows wild throughout the Americas. It has a strong aroma similar to kerosene and a wild flavour. Fresh epazote is used in salads and as a flavouring in Mexican and Southwestern cuisines. It is often cooked with beans to reduce their gaseousness. Dried epazote is brewed to make a beverage.

Fine herbs (Fr. *fines herbes*) are a combination of parsley, tarragon, chervil and chives widely used in French cuisine. The mixture is available dried or you can create your own from fresh ingredients.

Lavender is an evergreen with thin leaves and tall stems bearing spikes of tiny purple flowers. Although lavender is known primarily for its aroma, which is widely used in perfumes, soaps and cosmetics, the flowers are also used as a flavouring, particularly in Middle Eastern and Provençale cuisines. These flowers have a sweet, lemony flavour and can be crystallized and used as a garnish. Lavender is also used in jams and preserves and to flavour teas and tisanes.

Lavender

Lemon grass, also known as citronella grass, is a tropical grass with the strong aroma and taste of lemon. It is similar to scallions in appearance but with a woody texture. Only the lower base and white leaf stalks are used. Available fresh or quick-frozen, lemon grass is widely used in Indonesian and Southeast Asian cuisines.

Marjoram (Fr. *marjolaine*), also known as sweet marjoram, is a flowering herb native to the Mediterranean and used since ancient times. Its flavour is similar to thyme but sweeter; it also has a stronger aroma. Marjoram is now used in many European cuisines. Although it is available fresh, marjoram is one of the few herbs whose flavour increases when dried. Wild marjoram is more commonly known as oregano.

Mint (Fr. *menthe*), a large family of herbs, includes many species and flavours (even chocolate). **Spearmint** is the most common garden and commercial variety. It has soft, bright green leaves and a tart aroma and flavour. Mint does not blend well with other herbs, so its use is confined to specific dishes, usually fruits or fatty meats such as lamb. Mint has an affinity for chocolate. It can also be brewed into a beverage or used as a garnish. **Peppermint** has thin, stiff, pointed leaves and a sharper menthol flavour and aroma. Fresh peppermint is used less often in cooking or as a garnish than spearmint, but peppermint oil is a common flavouring in sweets and candies.

Spearmint

Peppermint

Oregano (Fr. *origan*), also known as wild marjoram, is a pungent, peppery herb used in Mediterranean cuisines, particularly Greek and Italian, as well as in Mexican cuisine. It is a classic complement to tomatoes. Oregano's thin, woody stalks bear clumps of tiny, dark green leaves, which are available dried and crushed.

Marjoram

Parsley (Fr. *persil)* is probably the best-known and most widely used herb in the world. It grows in almost all climates and is available in many varieties, all of which are rich in vitamins and minerals. The most common type in North America and Northern Europe is **curly parsley**. It has small curly leaves and a bright green colour. Its flavour is tangy and clean. Other cuisines use a variety sometimes known as **Italian parsley**, which has flat leaves, a darker colour and coarser flavour. Curly parsley is a ubiquitous garnish; both types can be used in virtually any food except sweets. Parsley stalks have a stronger flavour than the leaves and are part of the standard bouquet garni. Chopped parsley forms the basis of many fine herb blends.

Parsley

Italian Parsley

Rosemary (Fr. *romarin)* is an evergreen bush that grows wild in warm, dry climates worldwide. It has stiff, needlelike leaves; some varieties bear pale blue flowers. It is highly aromatic, with a slight odour of camphor or pine. Rosemary is best used fresh. When dried, it loses flavour and its leaves become very hard and unpleasant to chew. Whole rosemary stems may be added to a dish such as a stew and then removed when enough flavour has been imparted. They may also be added to a bouquet garni. Rosemary has a great affinity for roasted and grilled meats, especially lamb.

Rosemary

Sage (Fr. *sauge)* was used as a medicine for centuries before it entered the kitchen as a culinary herb. Culinary sage has narrow, fuzzy, grey-green leaves and blue flowers. Its flavour is strong and balsamic, with notes of camphor. Sage is used in poultry dishes, with fatty meats or brewed as a beverage. Sage's strong flavour does not blend well with other herbs. It dries well and is available in whole or chopped leaves or rubbed (coarsely ground).

Sage

Savory (Fr. *sariette)*, also known as summer savory, has been used since ancient times. Its leaves are small and narrow and it has a sharp, bitter flavour, vaguely like thyme. It dries well and is used in bean dishes, sausages and herb mixtures.

Tarragon (Fr. *estragon)*, another of the great culinary herbs, is native to Siberia. It is a bushy plant with long, narrow, dark green leaves and tiny grey flowers. Tarragon goes well with fish and tomatoes and is essential in many French dishes such as béarnaise sauce and fine herb blends. Its flavour is strong and diffuses quickly through foods. It is available dried, but drying may cause haylike flavours to develop.

Savory

Tarragon

Thyme (Fr. *thym)* has been popular since 3500 B.C., when Egyptians used it as a medicine and for embalming. Thyme is a small, bushy plant with woody stems, tiny green-grey leaves and purple flowers. Its flavour is strong but refined, with notes of sage. Thyme dries well and complements virtually all types of meat, poultry, fish, shellfish and vegetables. It is often included in a bouquet garni or added to stocks.

Thyme

Spices

Allspice

Allspice, also known as Jamaican pepper, is the dried berry of a tree that flourishes in Jamaica, and one of the few spices still grown exclusively in the New World. Allspice is available whole; in berries that look like large, rough, brown peppercorns; or ground. Ground allspice is not a mixture of spices, although it does taste like a blend of cinnamon, cloves and nutmeg. Allspice is now used throughout the world, in everything from cakes to curries, and is often included in peppercorn blends.

Anise seeds

Anise (Fr. *anis*) is native to the eastern Mediterranean, where it was widely used by ancient civilizations. Today, it is grown commercially in warm climates throughout India, North Africa and southern Europe. The tiny, grey-green egg-shaped seeds have a distinctively strong, sweet flavour, similar to licorice and fennel. When anise seeds turn brown they are stale and should be discarded. Anise is used in pastries as well as fish, shellfish and vegetable dishes, and is commonly used in alcoholic beverages (e.g., Pernod and ouzo). The green leaves of the anise plant are occasionally used fresh as a herb or in salads.

Star anise, also known as Chinese anise, is the dried, star-shaped fruit of a Chinese magnolia tree. Although botanically unrelated, its flavour is similar to anise seeds but more bitter and pungent. It is an essential flavour in many Chinese dishes and one of the components of five-spice powder.

Capers

Capers (Fr. *capres*) come from a small bush that grows wild throughout the Mediterranean basin. Its unopened flower buds have been pickled and used as a condiment for thousands of years. Fresh capers are not used, as the sharp, salty-sour flavour develops only after curing in strongly salted white vinegar. The finest capers are the smallest, known as *nonpareils*, which are produced in France's Provence region. Capers are used in a variety of sauces (tartare, remoulade) and are excellent with fish and game. Capers will keep for long periods if moistened by their original liquid. Do not add or substitute vinegar, however, as this causes the capers to spoil.

♦♦♦

A PINCH OF HISTORY

Spices have been used for many purposes for thousands of years. Egyptian papyri dating back to 2800 B.C. identify several spices native to the Middle and Far East that were used by the ruling and priestly classes for therapeutic, cosmetic, medicinal, ritualistic and culinary purposes.

By A.D. 300 the Romans were regularly importing spices for use as perfumes, medicines, preservatives and ingredients from China and India via long, difficult caravan journeys over sea and land. Spices were extremely expensive and unavailable to all but the wealthiest citizens.

After Rome fell in the second half of the 5th century A.D., much of the overland route through southern Europe became prey to bandits; and after Constantinople fell in 1453, the spice routes through the Middle East were controlled by the Ottoman Turks. Spice costs soared and economies based upon the spice trade, such as that of Venice, were at risk.

By then highly spiced food had become the norm, especially in wealthier households. So, in part to maintain their culinary norm, the Europeans set out to break the Ottoman Turk monopoly. These efforts led to Columbus's discovery of the Americas and Vasco de Gama's discovery of a sea route to India. Although the New World contained none of the spices for which Columbus was searching, it provided many previously unknown foods and flavourings that changed European tables forever, including chiles, vanilla, tomatoes, potatoes and chocolate.

Formation of the Dutch East India Company in 1602 marked the start of the Dutch colonial empire and made spices widely available to the growing European middle classes. The transplantation and cultivation of spice plants eventually weakened the once-powerful trading empires until, by the 19th century, no European country could monopolize trade. Prices fell dramatically.

Caraway is perhaps the world's oldest spice. Its use has been traced to the Stone Age and seeds have been found in ancient Egyptian tombs. The caraway plant grows wild in Europe and temperate regions of Asia. It produces a small, crescent-shaped brown seed with the peppery flavour of rye. Seeds may be purchased whole or ground. (The leaves have a mild, bland flavour and are rarely used in cooking.) Caraway is a very European flavour, used extensively in German and Austrian dishes, particularly breads, meats and cabbage. It is also used in cheeses and to flavour the liqueur kummel.

Caraway seeds

Cardamom is one of the most expensive spices, second only to saffron in cost. Its seeds are encased in 6-mm-long (1/4-inch) light green or brown pods. Cardamom is highly aromatic. Its flavour, lemony with notes of camphor, is quite strong and is used in both sweet and savoury dishes. Cardamom is widely used in Indian and Middle Eastern cuisines, where it is also used to flavour coffee. Scandinavians use cardamom to flavour breads and pastries. Ground cardamom loses its flavour rapidly and is easily adulterated, so it is best to purchase whole seeds and grind your own as needed.

Cardamom seeds

Chiles, including paprika, chile peppers, bell peppers and cayenne, are members of the *capsicum* plant family. Although cultivated for thousands of years in the West Indies and Americas, capsicum peppers were unknown in the Old World prior to Spanish explorations during the 15th century. Capsicum peppers come in all shapes and sizes, with a wide range of flavours, from sweet to extremely hot. Some capsicums are used as a vegetable, while others are dried, ground and used as a spice. Fresh chiles and bell peppers are discussed in Chapter 22, Vegetables. Capsicums are botanically unrelated to *piper nigrum*, the black peppercorns discussed below.

For our purposes, chile *refers to the plant,* chili *refers to the stewlike dish containing chiles and* chilli *refers to the commercial spice powder.*

Cayenne, sometimes simply labelled "red pepper," is ground from a blend of several particularly hot types of dried red chile peppers. Its flavour is extremely hot and pungent; it has a bright orange-red colour and fine texture.

Paprika, also known as Hungarian pepper, is a bright red powder ground from particular varieties of red-ripened and dried chiles. The flavour ranges from sweet to pungent; the aroma is distinctive and strong. It is essential to many Spanish and eastern European dishes. Mild paprika is meant to be used in generous quantities and may be sprinkled on prepared foods as a garnish.

Cayenne pepper

Paprika

Chilli powder

Crushed chiles

Chilli powders are made from a wide variety of dried chile peppers, ranging from sweet and mild to extremely hot and pungent. The finest pure chile powders come from dried chiles that are simply roasted, ground and sieved. Commercial chilli powder, an American invention, is actually a combination of spices—oregano, cumin, garlic and other flavourings—intended for use in Mexican dishes. Each brand is different and should be sampled before using.

Crushed chiles, also known as chile flakes, are blended from dried, coarsely crushed chiles. They are quite hot and are used in sauces and meat dishes.

Cinnamon (Fr. *cannelle*) and its cousin **cassia** are among the oldest known spices: cinnamon's use is recorded in China as early as 2500 B.C. and Asia still produces most of these products. Both cinnamon and cassia come from the bark of small evergreen trees, peeled from branches in thin layers and dried in the sun. High-quality cinnamon should be pale brown and thin, rolled up like paper into sticks known as quills. Cassia is coarser and has a stronger, less subtle flavour than cinnamon. Consequently, it is cheaper than true cinnamon. Cinnamon is usually purchased ground because it is difficult to grind. Cinnamon sticks are used when long cooking times can be allowed in order to extract the flavour (for example, in stews or curries). Cinnamon's flavour is most often associated with pastries and sweets, but has a great affinity for lamb and spicy dishes. Labelling laws do not require that packages distinguish

Ground cinnamon and cinnamon sticks

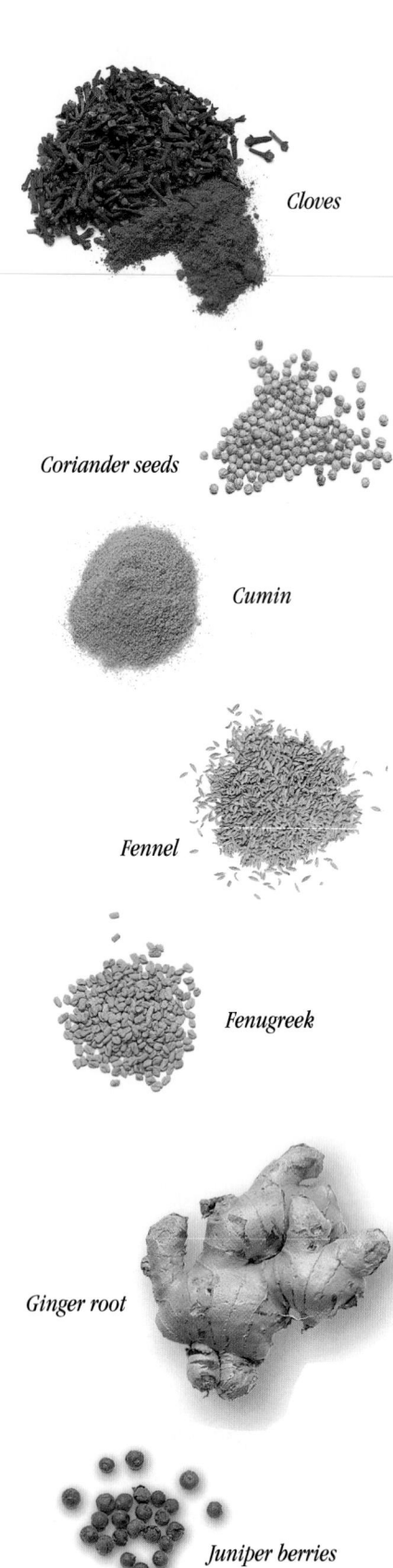

Cloves

Coriander seeds

Cumin

Fennel

Fenugreek

Ginger root

Juniper berries

between cassia and cinnamon, so most of what is sold as cinnamon in North America is actually cassia, blended for consistent flavour and aroma.

Cloves (Fr. *clous girofle*) are the unopened buds of evergreen trees that flourish in muggy tropical regions. When dried, whole cloves have hard, sharp prongs that can be used to push them into other foods, such as onions or fruit, in order to provide flavour. Cloves are extremely pungent, with a sweet, astringent aroma. A small amount provides a great deal of flavour. Cloves are used in desserts and meat dishes, preserves and liqueurs. They may be purchased whole or ground.

Coriander seeds come from the cilantro plant. They are round and beige, with a distinctive sweet, spicy flavour and strong aroma. Unlike other plants in which the seeds and the leaves carry the same flavour and aroma, coriander and cilantro are distinct. Coriander seeds are available whole or ground and are frequently used in Indian cuisine and pickling mixtures.

Cumin is the seed of a small delicate plant of the parsley family that grows in North Africa and the Middle East. The small seeds are available whole or ground and look (but do not taste) like caraway seeds. Cumin has a powerful earthy flavour and tends to dominate any dish in which it is included. It is used in Indian, Middle Eastern and Mexican cuisines, in sausages and a few cheeses.

Fennel (Fr. *fenouil*) is a perennial plant with feathery leaves and tiny flowers long cultivated in India and China as a medicine and cure for witchcraft. Its seeds are greenish brown with prominent ridges and short, hairlike fibres. Their taste and aroma are similar to anise, though not as sweet. Whole seeds are widely used in Italian stews and sausages; Central European cuisines use fennel with fish, pork, pickles and vegetables. Ground seeds can also be used in breads, cakes and cookies. The same plant produces a bulbous stalk used as a vegetable.

Fenugreek (Fr. *fenugrec*), grown in Mediterranean countries since ancient times, is a small, beanlike plant with a tiny flower. The seeds, available whole or ground, are pebble-shaped and transfer their pale orange colour to the foods with which they are cooked. Their flavour is bittersweet, like burnt sugar with a bitter aftertaste. Fenugreek is a staple in Indian cuisine, especially curries and chutneys.

Ginger (Fr. *gingembre*) is a well-known spice obtained from the root of a tall, flowering tropical plant. Fresh ginger root is known as a "hand" because it looks vaguely like a group of knobby fingers. It has greyish-tan skin and a pale yellow, fibrous interior. Fresh ginger should be plump and firm with smooth skin. It should keep for about a month under refrigeration. Its flavour is fiery but sweet, with notes of lemon and rosemary. Fresh ginger is widely available and is used in Indian and Asian cuisines. It has a special affinity for chicken, beef and curries. Ginger is also available peeled and pickled in vinegar, candied in sugar or preserved in alcohol or syrup. Dried, ground ginger is a fine yellow powder widely used in pastries. Its flavour is spicier and not as sweet as fresh ginger.

Juniper is an evergreen bush grown throughout the northern hemisphere. It produces round purple berries with a sweet flavour similar to pine. Juniper berries are used for flavouring gin and other alcoholic beverages, and are crushed and incorporated in game dishes, particularly venison and wild boar.

Mustard seeds (Fr. *moutarde*), available in black, brown and yellow, come from three different plants in the cabbage family. Mustard seeds are small, hard spheres with a bitter flavour. The seeds have no aroma, but their flavour is sharp and fiery hot. Yellow seeds have the mildest and black seeds the strongest flavour. All are sold whole and can be crushed for cooking. Mustard seeds are a standard component of pickling spices and are processed and blended for pre-pared mustards, which are discussed below. Ground or dry mustard is a bright yellow powder made from a blend of ground seeds, wheat flour and turmeric.

Mustard seeds

Ground mustard

Nutmeg (Fr. *muscade*) and **mace** come from the yellow plumlike fruit of a large tropical evergreen. These fruits are dried and opened to reveal the seed known as nutmeg. The seed is surrounded by a bright red lacy coating or aril; the aril is the spice mace. Whole nutmegs are oval and look rather like a piece of smooth wood. The flavour and aroma of nutmeg are strong and sweet, and a small quantity provides a great deal of flavour. Nutmeg should be grated directly into a dish as needed; once grated, flavour loss is rapid. Nutmeg is used in many European cuisines, mainly in pastries and sweets, but is also important in meat and savoury dishes.

Mace is an expensive spice, with a flavour similar to nutmeg but more refined. It is almost always purchased ground and retains its flavour longer than other ground spices. Mace is used primarily in pastry items.

Mace (left) and whole and ground nutmeg (right)

Peppercorns (Fr. *poivre*) are the berries of a vine plant (*piper nigrum*) native to tropical Asia. Peppercorns should not be confused with the chile (capsicum) peppers discussed above. Peppercorns vary in size, colour, pungency and flavour. Many of these differences are the result of variations in climate and grow-ing conditions. Good-quality pepper is expensive and should be purchased whole and ground fresh in a peppermill as needed. Whole peppercorns will last indefinitely if kept dry. They should be stored well covered in a cool, dark place.

Black and **white peppercorns** are produced from the same plant, but are picked and processed differently. For black peppercorns, the berries are picked when green and simply dried whole in the sun. Black pepper has a warm, pungent flavour and aroma. Tellicherry peppercorns from the southwest coast of India are generally considered the finest black peppercorns in the world and are priced accordingly.

For white peppercorns, the berries are allowed to ripen until they turn red. The ripened berries are allowed to ferment, then the outer layer of skin is washed off. Nowadays, white pepper may be produced by mechanically removing the outer skin from black peppercorns. This is not true white pep-per, and the resulting product should be labelled "decorticated." White pepper has less aroma than black pepper but is useful in white sauces or where the appearance of black speckles is undesirable.

Black pepper (left) and white pepper (right)

Green peppercorns are unripened berries that are either freeze-dried or pickled in brine or vinegar. Pickled green peppercorns are soft, with a fresh, sour flavour similar to capers. They are excellent in spiced butters and sauces or with fish.

Pink peppercorns are actually the berries of a South American tree, not a vine pepper plant. Pink peppercorns are available dried or pickled in vinegar. Although attractive, their flavour is bitter and pinelike, with less spiciness than true pepper. Pink peppercorns are no longer available in some areas because of reported toxic side effects.

Poppy seeds (Fr. *pavot*) are the ripened seeds of the opium poppy, which flourishes in the Middle East and India. (When ripe, the seeds do not contain any of the medicinal alkaloids found elsewhere in the plant.) The tiny blue-grey seeds are round and hard with a sweet, nutty flavour. Poppy seeds are used in pastries and breads.

Poppy seeds

Saffron

Sesame seeds

Turmeric

Saffron (Fr. *safran*) comes from the dried stigmas of the saffron crocus. Each flower bears only three threadlike stigmas, and each must be picked by hand. It takes about 250 000 flowers to produce 450 g (1 lb.) of saffron, making it the most expensive spice in the world. Beware of bargains; there is no such thing as cheap saffron. Luckily, a tiny pinch is enough to colour and flavour a large quantity of food. Good saffron should be a brilliant orange colour, not yellow, with a strong aroma and a bitter, honeylike taste. Saffron produces a yellow dye that diffuses through any warm liquid. Valencia or Spanish saffron is considered the finest. It is commonly used with fish and shellfish (a necessity for bouillabaisse) and rice dishes such as paella and risotto. When using saffron threads, first crush them gently, then soak them in some hot liquid from the recipe. Powdered saffron is less expensive but more easily adulterated. It may be added directly to the other ingredients when cooking.

Sesame seeds, also known as benne seeds, are native to India. They are small, flat ovals, with a creamy white colour. Their taste is nutty and earthy, with a pronounced aroma when roasted or ground into a paste (known as tahini). Sesame seeds are the source of sesame oil, which has a mild, nutty flavour and does not go rancid easily. Sesame seeds are roasted and used in or as a garnish for breads and meat dishes. They are popular in Indian and Asian cuisines, with a black variety of seeds most popular as a Japanese condiment.

Turmeric, also known as Indian saffron, is produced from the roots of a flowering tropical plant related to ginger. Unlike ginger, fresh turmeric is not used in cooking. It is only available dried and usually ground. Turmeric is renowned for its vibrant yellow colour and is used as a food colouring and dye. Turmeric's flavour is distinctive and strong; it should not be substituted for saffron. Turmeric is a traditional ingredient in Indian curries, to which it imparts colour as well as flavour.

Spice Blends

Many countries and cuisines have created recognizable combinations of spice flavours that are found in a variety of dishes. Although many of these blends are available ready-prepared for convenience, most can be mixed by the chef as needed. A few of the more common spice blends are described here.

Chinese five-spice powder is a combination of equal parts finely ground Szechuan pepper, star anise, cloves, cinnamon and fennel seeds. This blend is widely used in Chinese and some Vietnamese foods and is excellent with pork and in pâtés.

Curry powder is a European invention that probably took its name from the Tamil word *kari*, meaning a sauce. Created by 19th-century Britons returning from colonial India, it was meant to be the complete spicing for a "curry" dish. There are as many different formulas for curry powder as there are manufacturers, some mild and sweet (Bombay or Chinese style), others hot and pungent (Madras style). Typical ingredients in curry powder are black pepper, cinnamon, cloves, coriander, cumin, ginger, mace and turmeric. Curry pastes are widely available; they are fried spices mixed with oil, onions, garlic and other flavourings.

Pickling spice

Pickling spice, as with other blends, varies by manufacturer. Most pickling spice blends are based on black peppercorns and red chiles, with some or all of the following added: allspice, cloves, ginger, mustard seeds, coriander seeds, bay leaves and dill. These blends are useful in making cucumber or vegetable pickles as well as in stews and soups.

Quatre-épices, literally "four spices" in French, is a peppery mixture of black peppercorns with lesser amounts of nutmeg, cloves and dried ginger. Sometimes cinnamon or allspice is included. Quatre-épices is used in charcuterie and long-simmered stews.

Using Herbs and Spices

Herbs and spices are a simple, inexpensive way to bring individuality and variety to foods. Their proper use leads to better-flavoured and distinctively different dishes. They add neither fat nor sodium and virtually no calories to foods; most contain only 3 to 10 calories per 5 mL (1 tsp.). Table 7.1 lists just a few uses for some of the more common herbs and spices.

Although the flavours and aromas of fresh herbs are generally preferred, dried herbs are widely used because they are readily available and convenient. Purchase only the amount of dried herbs that can be used within a short time. If stored in a closed container in a cool, dry place, dried herbs should last for two to three months.

Use less dried herbs than you would fresh herbs. The loss of moisture strengthens and concentrates the flavour in dried herbs. In general, you should use only one-half to one-third as much dried herb as fresh in any given recipe. For example, if a recipe calls for 15 mL/10 g (1 Tbsp.) of fresh basil, you should substitute only 5 mL/3 g (1 tsp.) of dried basil. You can usually add more later if necessary.

Spices are often available whole or ground. Once ground, they lose their flavours rapidly, however. Whole spices should keep their flavours for many months if stored in airtight containers in a cool, dry place away from direct light. Stale spices lose their spicy aroma and develop a bitter or musty aftertaste. Discard them.

Because ground spices release their flavours quickly, they should be added to cooked dishes near the end of the cooking period. In uncooked dishes that call for ground spices (for example, salad dressings), the mixture should be allowed to stand for several hours to develop good flavour.

While some combinations are timeless—rosemary with lamb, dill with salmon, nutmeg with spinach, caraway with rye bread—less common pairings can be equally delicious and far more exciting. A chef must be willing and able to experiment with new flavours. But first you must be familiar with the distinctive flavour and aroma of the herb or spice. Then you can experiment, always bearing in mind the following guidelines:

- ✦ Flavourings should not hide the taste or aroma of the primary ingredient;
- ✦ Flavourings should be combined in balance, so as not to overwhelm the palate; and
- ✦ Flavourings should not be used to disguise poor quality or poorly prepared products.

Even when following a well-tested recipe, the quantity of flavourings may need to be adjusted because of changes in brands or the condition of the ingredients. A cook should strive to develop his or her palate to recognize and correct subtle variances as necessary.

TABLE 7.1   USES FOR SOME COMMON HERBS AND SPICES

Flavouring	Form	Suggested Uses
Allspice	Whole or ground	Fruits, relishes, braised meats
Anise	Whole or ground	Asian cuisines, pastries, breads, cheeses
Basil	Fresh or dried	Tomatoes, salads, eggs, fish, chicken, lamb, cheeses
Caraway	Whole or ground	Rye bread, cabbage, beans, pork, beef, veal
Chervil	Fresh or dried	Chicken, fish, eggs, salads, soups, vegetables
Chives	Fresh or dried	Eggs, fish, chicken, soups, potatoes, cheeses
Cilantro	Fresh leaves	Salsa, salads, Mexican cuisine, fish, shellfish, chicken
Cloves	Whole or ground	Marinades, baked goods, braised meats, pickles, fruits, beverages, stocks
Cumin	Whole or ground	Chili, sausages, stews, eggs
Dill	Fresh or dried leaves; whole seeds	Leaves or seeds in soups, salads, fish, shellfish, vegetables, breads; seeds in pickles, potatoes, vegetables
Fennel	Whole seeds	Sausages, stews, sauces, pickling, lamb, eggs
Ginger	Fresh root or powder	Asian, Caribbean and Indian cuisines, pastries, curries, stews, meats
Marjoram	Fresh or dried	Sausages, pâtés, meats, poultry, stews, green vegetables, tomatoes, game
Nutmeg	Ground	Curries, relishes, rice, eggs, beverages
Rosemary	Fresh or dried	Lamb, veal, beef, poultry, game, marinades, stews
Saffron	Threads or ground	Rice, breads, potatoes, soups, stews, chicken, fish, shellfish
Sage	Fresh or dried	Poultry, charcuterie, pork, stuffings, pasta, beans, tomatoes
Tarragon	Fresh or dried	Chicken, fish, eggs, salad dressings, sauces, tomatoes
Thyme	Fresh or dried	Fish, chicken, meats, stews, charcuterie, soups, tomatoes
Turmeric	Ground	Curries, relishes, rice, eggs, breads

Bouquet Garni and Sachet

The *bouquet garni* and the *sachet* are used to introduce flavourings, seasonings and aromatics into stocks, sauces, soups and stews.

A **bouquet garni**, shown in Figure 7.1, is a selection of herbs (usually fresh) and vegetables tied into a bundle with twine. The twine makes it easy to remove the bouquet when sufficient flavour has been extracted. A standard bouquet garni consists of parsley stems, celery, thyme, leeks and carrots.

FIGURE 7.1 *Bouquet Garni*

FIGURE 7.2 *Sachet*

A **sachet** (also known as a *sachet d'épices*), shown in Figure 7.2, is made by tying seasonings together in cheesecloth. A standard sachet consists of peppercorns, bay leaves, parsley stems, thyme, cloves and, optionally, garlic. The exact quantity of these ingredients is determined by the amount of liquid the sachet is meant to flavour.

Bouquets garni and sachets are used to add flavours in such a way that the ingredients can be easily removed from a dish when the flavours have been extracted. A similar technique, although less commonly used, is an **oignon piqué**, or studded onion. To prepare an oignon piqué, peel the onion and trim off the root end. Attach one or two dried bay leaves to the onion using whole cloves as pins. The oignon piqué is then simmered in milk or stock to extract flavours.

SALT

Salt (Fr. *sel*) is the most basic seasoning and its use is universal. It preserves foods, heightens their flavours and provides the distinctive taste of saltiness. The presence of salt can be tasted easily but not smelled. Temperature affects saltiness. The cooler a food, the saltier it tastes, so it is best to undersalt hot foods that will be chilled prior to service (chilled soups, for example).

Culinary or **table salt** is sodium chloride (NaCl), one of the minerals essential to human life. Salt contains no calories, proteins, fats or carbohydrates. It is available from several sources, each with its own flavour and degree of saltiness.

Rock salt, mined from underground deposits, is available in both edible and nonedible forms. It is used for home freezing.

Common kitchen or table salt is produced by pumping water through underground salt deposits, then bringing the brine to the surface to evaporate, leaving behind crystals. Chemicals are usually added to prevent table salt from absorbing moisture and thus keep it free-flowing. Iodized salt is commonly used in North America. The iodine has no effect on the salt's flavour or use; it is simply added to provide an easily available source of iodine, an important nutrient, to a large number of people.

Sea salt is obtained, not surprisingly, by evaporating sea water and purifying the crystals left behind. Many chefs consider its flavour stronger or purer than mined salt.

Rock salt

Fleur de sel

♦♦♦

ABOUT FLAVORS

Flavor is to food what hue is to color. It is what timbre is to music. Flavor is adjective; food is noun. Each ingredient has its own particular character, which is altered by every other ingredient it encounters. A secret ingredient is one that mysteriously improves the flavor of a dish without calling attention to itself. It is either undetectable or extremely subtle, but its presence is crucial because the dish would not be nearly as good without it.

Primary flavors are those that are obvious, such as the flavors of chicken and tarragon in a chicken tarragon, shrimp and garlic in a shrimp scampi, or beef and red wine in a beef *à la Bourguignon*. Secret ingredients belong to the realm of secondary flavors. However obvious it is that you need tarragon to prepare a chicken tarragon, you would not achieve the most interesting result using *only* tarragon. Tarragon, in this case, needs secondary ingredients—a hint of celery seed and anise—to make it taste more like quintessential tarragon and at the same time more than tarragon. In

this way, primary flavors often depend on secret ingredients to make them more interesting and complex. Using only one herb or spice to achieve a certain taste usually results in a lackluster dish—each mouthful tastes the same. Whether they function in a primary or secondary way, flavors combine in only three different ways: They marry, oppose, or juxtapose.

When flavors marry, they combine to form one taste. Some secondary flavors marry with primary ones to create a new flavor greater than the sum of its parts, and often two flavors can do the job better than one. It may sound like an eccentric combination, but vanilla marries with the flavor of lobster, making it taste more like the essence of lobster than lobster does on its own. And when ginger and molasses marry, they create a flavor superior to either alone.

Opposite flavors can highlight or cancel each other; they can cut or balance each other. Sweet/sour, sweet/salty, sweet/hot, salty/sour, and salty/tart are all opposites. Salt and sugar

are so opposed, in fact, that when used in equal amounts they cancel each other entirely. Sweet relish helps to cancel the salty flavor of hot dogs. Chinese sauces usually contain some sugar to help balance the saltiness of soy sauce.

Because flavors are sensed on different parts of the tongue and palate, and because they are tasted at different times, we can juxtapose them, using flavors side by side or in layers. The layering of flavors makes the food we taste more interesting because each mouthful is different.

Knowing how to combine many flavors and aromas to achieve a simple and pure result (and knowing when not to combine flavors) will make you a better, more confident cook. Good cooks over the centuries have known these things intuitively—but they've had neither the huge variety of ingredients nor the knowledge of world cuisines that we have today.

from SECRET INGREDIENTS
by CHEF MICHAEL ROBERTS

♦♦♦

RECIPES FOR ETHNIC CUISINES

In *Ethnic Cuisine: The Flavor Principle Cookbook*, Elisabeth Rozin writes: "Every culture tends to combine a small number of flavoring ingredients so frequently and so consistently that they become definitive of that particular cuisine" (p. xiv). She calls these defining flavours "flavor principles" and notes that they are "designed to abstract what is absolutely fundamental about a cuisine and thus, to serve as a guide in cooking and developing new recipes" (p. xvii). She identifies the following "flavor principles":

Central Asia: cinnamon, fruit and nuts

China: generally—soy sauce, rice wine and ginger root

    Northern China (Mandarin/Peking)—miso and/or garlic and/or sesame

Western China (Szechuan)—sweet, sour and hot

Southern China (Canton)—black beans, garlic

Eastern Europe (Jewish): onion and chicken fat

Eastern and Northern Europe: sour cream and dill or paprika or allspice or caraway

France: generally—olive oil, garlic and basil *or* wine and herb *or* butter and/or sour cream and/or cheese plus wine and/or stock

    Southern France—olive oil, garlic, parsley and/or anchovy plus tomato as a variation

    Provence—olive oil, thyme, rosemary, marjoram, sage plus tomato as a variation

    Normandy—apple, cider, Calvados

Greece: tomato, cinnamon or olive oil, lemon, oregano

India: Northern—cumin, ginger, garlic

    Southern—mustard seed, coconut, tamarind, chile

Italy: generally—olive oil, garlic, basil

    Northern Italy—wine vinegar, garlic

    Southern Italy—olive oil, garlic, parsley and/or anchovy plus tomato as a variation

Japan: soy sauce, sake, sugar

Mexico: generally—tomato and chile *or* lime and chile

    Yucatan—sour orange, garlic, achiote

North Africa: cumin, coriander, cinnamon, ginger, onion and/or tomato and/or fruit

Spain: olive oil, garlic, nut or olive oil, onion, pepper, tomato

Thailand: fish sauce, curry, chile

West Africa: tomato, peanut, chile

Kosher salt has large, irregular crystals and is used in the "koshering" or curing of meats. It is purified rock salt that contains no iodine or additives. It can be substituted for common kitchen salt.

Because it is nonorganic, salt keeps indefinitely. It will, however, absorb moisture from the atmosphere, which prevents it from flowing properly. Salt is a powerful preservative; its presence stops or greatly slows down the growth of many undesirable organisms. Salt is used to preserve meats, vegetables and fish. It is also used to develop desirable flavours in bacon, ham, cheeses and fish products as well as pickled vegetables.

Kosher salt

NUTS

A **nut** (Fr. *noix*) is the edible single-seed kernel of a fruit surrounded by a hard shell. A hazelnut is an example of a true nut. The term is used more generally, however, to refer to any seed or fruit with an edible kernel in a hard shell. Walnuts and peanuts are examples of non-nut "nuts" (peanuts are legumes that grow underground; walnuts have two kernels). Nuts are a good source of protein and B vitamins but are high in fat. (Table 7.2 on page 141 provides a nutrition comparison.) Their high fat content makes them especially susceptible to rancidity and odour absorption. Nuts should be stored in nonmetal, airtight containers in a cool, dark place. Most nuts may be kept frozen for up to one year.

Nuts are used in foods to provide texture and flavour. They are often roasted in a low (135°C/275°F) oven before use to heighten their flavour. Allowing roasted nuts to cool to room temperature before grinding prevents them from releasing too much oil.

Almonds (Fr. *amande*) are the seeds of a plumlike fruit. Native to western India, the almond was first cultivated by the ancient Greeks. It is now a major commercial crop in California. Almonds are available whole, sliced, slivered or ground. Blanched almonds have had their brown, textured skins removed; natural almonds retain their skins. Unless the brown colour of natural almond skin is undesirable, the two types can be used interchangeably in recipes. Almonds are frequently used in pastries and candies and are the main ingredient in marzipan.

Almonds

Cashews, native to the Amazon, are now cultivated in India and east Africa. The cashew nut is actually the seed of a plant related to poison ivy. Because of toxins in the shell, cashews are always sold shelled. They are expensive and have a strong flavour. Cashews are used in some Asian cuisines and make a wonderful addition to cookies and candies.

Cashews

Chestnuts (Fr. *marrons*) are true nuts that must be cooked before using. Available steamed, dried, boiled or roasted, they are often sold as a canned purée, with or without added sugar. Candied or glazed chestnuts are also available. Most chestnuts are grown in Europe, primarily Italy, but new varieties are beginning to flourish in North America. Their distinctive flavour is found in many sweet dishes and pastries. Because of their high starch content, chestnuts are also used in soups and sauces and may be served as a side dish.

Coconuts (Fr. *noix de coco*) are the seeds from one of the largest of all fruits. They grow on the tropical coconut palm tree. The nut is a dark brown oval, covered with coarse fibres. The shell is thick and hard; inside is a layer of white, moist flesh. The interior also contains a clear liquid known as coconut water. (This is not the same as coconut milk or coconut cream, both of which are prepared from the flesh.) Coconut has a mild aroma, a sweet,

Chestnuts

Coconuts

Hazelnuts

Macadamias

Peanuts

Pecans

Pine Nuts

Pistachios

nutty flavour and a crunchy, chewy texture. Fresh coconuts are readily available but require some effort to use. Coconut flesh is available shredded or flaked, with or without added sugar. Coconut is most often used in pastries and candies and is also an important ingredient in Indian and Caribbean cuisines. A good fresh coconut should feel heavy; you should be able to hear the coconut water sloshing around inside. Avoid cracked, moist or mouldy coconuts.

Hazelnuts (Fr. *noisette*) are true nuts that grow wild in the northeast and upper midwest of the United States. The cultivated form, known as a **filbert**, is native to temperate regions throughout the northern hemisphere. A bit larger than the hazelnut, it has a weaker flavour than its wild cousin. Both nuts look like smooth brown marbles. Filberts are more abundant, so are generally less expensive. Hazelnuts are often ground for use in cakes or pastries. Their distinctive flavour goes well with chocolate and coffee.

To remove the hazelnut's bitter skin, roast whole nuts in a 135°C (275°F) oven for 12 to 15 minutes. They should give off a good aroma and just begin to darken. While still hot, rub the nuts in a dry towel or against a mesh sifter to remove the skin.

Macadamias, although commercially significant in Hawaii, are actually native to Australia. This small round nut is creamy white with a sweet, rich taste and high fat content. Its shell is extremely hard and must be removed by machine, so the macadamia is always sold out of the shell. Its flavour blends well with fruits, coconut and white and dark chocolate.

Peanuts (Fr. *arachide*), also known as groundnuts, are actually legumes that grow underground. The peanut is native to South America; it made its way into North America via Africa and the slave trade. Peanuts are a good source of protein and fat and became an important source of food and oil during World War II. They may be eaten raw or roasted and are available shelled or unshelled, with or without their thin red skins. Peanuts are used in Asian cuisines and are ubiquitous ground with a bit of oil into peanut butter.

Pecans (Fr. *noix de pacane*), native to the Mississippi River Valley, are perhaps the most popular nuts in America. Their flavour is rich and mapley and appears most often in breads, sweets and pastries. They are available whole in the shell or in various standard sizes and grades of pieces.

Pine nuts (Fr. *pignon*), also known as piñon nuts and pignole, are the seeds of several species of pine tree. The small, creamy white, teardrop-shaped nuts are commonly used in dishes from Spain, Italy and the American Southwest. They are rarely chopped or ground due to their small size, and will only need roasting if being used in a dish that will not receive further cooking. Pine nuts are used in breads, pastries and salads and are essential to classic pesto sauce.

Pistachios (Fr. *pistaches*) are native to central Asia, where they have been cultivated for more than 3000 years. California now produces most of the pistachios marketed in this country. Pistachios are unique for the green colour of their meat. When ripe, the shell opens naturally at one end, aptly referred to as "smiling," which makes shelling the nuts quite easy. Red pistachios are dyed,

TABLE 7.2 NUTRITIONAL VALUES OF COMMON NUTS

Per 28 g (1 oz.) Serving	Calories	Protein (g)	Carbohydrates (g)	Total Fat (g)	Saturated Fat (g)	Sodium (mg)
Almonds, whole kernels	167	5.7	5.8	14.8	1.4	3
Cashews, dry roasted	163	4.4	9.3	13.2	2.6	4
Chestnuts, roasted and peeled	70	0.9	15.0	0.6	0.1	1
Filberts, blanched	191	3.6	4.5	19.1	1.4	1
Macadamias	199	2.4	3.9	20.9	3.1	1
Peanuts, raw	159	7.2	4.5	13.8	1.9	5
Pecans	190	2.2	5.2	19.2	1.5	trace
Walnuts, English	182	4.1	5.2	17.6	1.6	3

The Corinne T. Netzer Encyclopedia of Food Values 1992

not natural. Pistachios are sold whole, shelled or unshelled, and are used in pastries and meat dishes, particularly pâtés. They should be peeled after shelling by soaking them briefly in hot water and rubbing them with a towel.

Walnuts (Fr. *noix*), relatives of the pecan, are native to Asia, Europe and North America. The black walnut, native to Appalachia, has a dark brown meat and strong flavour. The English walnut, now grown primarily in California, has a milder flavour, is easier to shell and is less expensive. Walnuts are more popular than pecans outside the United States. They are used in baked goods and are pressed for oil.

English walnuts

OILS

Oils (Fr. *huile*) are a type of fat that remains liquid at room temperature. Cooking oils are refined from various seeds, plants and vegetables. (Other fats, such as butter and margarine, are discussed in Chapter 8, Eggs and Dairy Products; animal and solid fats are discussed in Chapter 26, Principles of the Bakeshop.)

When purchasing oils you should consider their use, smoke point, flavour and cost. Fats, including oils and **shortenings**, are manufactured for specific purposes such as deep-fat frying, cake-baking, salad dressings and sautéing. Most food service operations purchase different ones for each of these needs.

Fats break down at different temperatures. The temperature at which a given fat begins to break down and smoke is known as its **smoke point** (see Table 7.3). Choose fats with higher smoke points for high temperature cooking such as deep-fat frying and sautéing. If a fat with a low smoke point is used for high temperature cooking, it may break down, burn and impart undesirable flavours.

The flavour and cost of each oil must also be considered. For example, both corn oil and walnut oil may be used in a salad dressing. Their selection may depend on balancing cost (corn oil is less expensive) against flavour (walnut oil has a stronger, more distinctive flavour).

When fats spoil they are said to go **rancid**. Rancidity is a chemical change caused by exposure to air, light or heat. It results in objectionable flavours and odours. Different fats turn rancid at different rates, but all fats benefit from refrigerated storage away from moisture, light and air. (Some oils are packaged in coloured glass containers because certain tints of green and yellow block

Canola oil

Hazelnut oil

Extra virgin olive oil

the damaging light rays that can cause an oil to go rancid.) Oils may become thick and cloudy under refrigeration. This is not a cause for concern. The oils will return to their clear, liquid states at room temperature. Stored fats should also be covered to prevent the absorption of odours.

Vegetable oils are extracted from a variety of plants, including corn, cottonseed, peanuts and soybeans, by pressure or chemical solvents. The oil is then refined and cleaned to remove unwanted colours, odours or flavours. Vegetable oils are virtually odourless and have a neutral flavour. Because they contain no animal products they are cholesterol-free. If a commercial product contains only one type of oil it is labelled "pure" (as in "pure corn oil"). Products labelled "vegetable oil" are blended from several sources. Products labelled "salad oil" are highly refined blends of vegetable oil.

Canola oil is processed from rapeseeds. Its popularity is growing rapidly because it contains no cholesterol and has a high percentage of monounsaturated fat. Canola oil is useful for frying and general cooking because it has no flavour and a high smoke point.

Nut oils are extracted from a variety of nuts and are almost always packaged as a "pure" product, never blended. A nut oil should have the strong flavour and aroma of the nut from which it was processed. Popular examples are walnut and hazelnut oils. These oils are used to give flavour to salad dressings, marinades and other dishes. But heat diminishes their flavour, so nut oils are not recommended for frying or baking. Nut oils tend to go rancid quickly and therefore are usually packaged in small containers.

Olive oil (Fr. *huile d'olive*) is the only oil that is extracted from a fruit rather than a seed, nut or grain. Olive oil is produced primarily in Spain, Italy, France, Greece and North Africa; California produces a relatively minor amount of olive oil. Like wine, olive oils vary in colour and flavour according to the variety of tree, the ripeness of the olives, the type of soil, the climate and the producer's preferences. Colours range from dark green to almost clear, depending on the ripeness of the olives at the time of pressing and the amount of subsequent refining. Colour is not a good indication of flavour, however. Flavour is ultimately a matter of personal preference. A stronger-flavoured oil may be desired for some foods, while a milder oil is better for others. Good olive oil should be thicker than refined vegetable oils, but not so thick that it has a fatty texture.

The label designations—extra virgin, virgin and pure—refer to the acidity of the oil (a low acid content is preferable) and the extent of processing used to extract the oil. The first cold-pressing of the olives results in virgin oil. (The designation "virgin" is used only when the oil is 100% unadulterated olive oil, unheated and without any chemical processing.) Virgin oil may still vary in quality depending on its acidity level. Extra virgin oil is virgin oil with an acidity level of not more than 1%; virgin oil may have an acidity level of up to 3%. Pure olive oil is processed from the pulp left after the first pressing using heat and chemicals. Pure oil is lighter in flavour and less expensive than virgin oil.

Flavoured oils, also known as **infused oils**, are an interesting and increasingly popular condiment. These oils may be used as a cooking medium or flavouring accent in marinades, dressings, sauces or other dishes. Flavours include basil and other herbs, garlic, citrus and spice. Flavoured oils are generally prepared with olive oil for additional flavour or canola oil, both considered more healthful than other fats.

Top-quality commercially flavoured oils are prepared by extracting aromatic oils from the flavouring ingredients and then emulsifying them with a high-grade oil; any impurities are then removed by placing the oil in a centrifuge.

◆◆◆

THE OLIVE

Olives are the fruit of a tree native to the Mediterranean area. Green olives are those harvested unripened; black olives are fully ripened. The raw fruit is inedibly bitter and must be washed, soaked and pickled before eating. Green olives should have a smooth, tight skin. Ripe olives will be glossy but softer, with a slightly wrinkled skin. Many varieties and flavours are available, from the tiny black Niçoise to the large purplish Kalamata. Olives are packaged in a range of sizes, from medium (the smallest) to jumbo (the largest). (Colossal and super colossal olives are actually smaller than jumbos.) Pitted olives are also available. The cavity may be filled with strips of pimento, jalapeño pepper, almonds or other foods for flavour and appearance.

Olives are used as a finger food for snacks or hors d'oeuvre, or added to salads or pasta. They may even be cooked in breads, soups, sauces, stews or casseroles. A paste made of minced ripe olives, known as tapenade, is used as a dip or condiment.

TABLE 7.3   THE SMOKE POINT AND NUTRITIONAL VALUES OF COMMON FATS

Per 28 g (1 oz.) Serving	Smoke Point	Calories	Total Fat (g)	Saturated Fat (g)
Olive oil	225°C/437°F	251	28.4	3.8
Peanut oil	218°C/425°F	251	28.4	4.8
Lard*	188°C/370°F	230	25.6	10.0
Canola oil	218°C/425°F	251	28.4	2.0
Walnut oil	163–204°C/ 325–400°F	240	28.0	4.0
Butter, clarified**	204°C/400°F	248	28.2	17.6
Whole butter, unsalted*	127°C/260°F	200	22.8	14.2

The Corinne T. Netzer Encyclopedia of Food Values 1992

*discussed in Chapter 26

**discussed in Chapter 8

Jumbo Spanish olives

Ripe California olives

Kalamata olives

Nicoise olives

Using the aromatic oils of the flavouring ingredients yields a more intense flavour than merely steeping the same ingredients in the oil. Flavoured oils should be stored as you would any other high-quality oil.

VINEGARS

Vinegar (Fr. *vinaigre*) is a thin, sour liquid used for thousands of years as a preservative, cooking ingredient, condiment and cleaning solution. Vinegar is obtained through the fermentation of wine or other alcoholic liquid. Bacteria attack the alcohol in the solution, turning it into acetic acid. No alcohol will remain when the transformation is complete. The quality of vinegar depends upon the quality of the wine or other liquid on which it is based. Vinegar flavours are as varied as the liquids from which they are made.

Vinegars should be clear and clean looking, never cloudy or muddy. Commercial vinegars are pasteurized, so an unopened bottle should last indefinitely in a cool, dark place. Once opened, vinegars should last about three months if tightly capped. Any sediment that develops can be strained out; if mould develops, discard the vinegar.

Wine vinegars are as old as wine itself. They may be made from white or red wine, sherry or even champagne, and should bear the colour and flavour hallmarks of the wine used. Wine vinegars are preferred in French and Mediterranean cuisines.

Malt vinegar is produced from malted barley. Its slightly sweet, mild flavour is used as a condiment, especially with fried foods.

Distilled vinegar, made from grain alcohol, is completely clear with a stronger vinegary flavour and higher acid content than other vinegars. It is preferred for pickling and preserving.

Cider vinegar is produced from unpasteurized apple juice or cider. It is pale brown in colour with a mild acidity and fruity aroma. Cider vinegar is particularly popular in North America.

Rice vinegar is a clear, slightly sweet product brewed from rice wine. Its flavour is clean and elegant, making it useful in a variety of dishes.

Flavoured vinegars are simply traditional vinegars in which herbs, spices, fruits or other foods are steeped to infuse their flavours. They are easily produced from commercial wine or distilled vinegars, using any herb, spice or fruit desired.

Balsamic vinegar, raspberry vinegar and cider vinegar

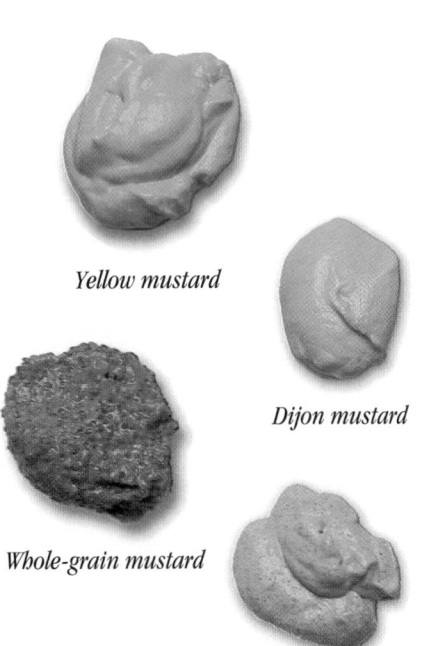

Yellow mustard

Dijon mustard

Whole-grain mustard

Brown mustard

The use of flavoured vinegars is extremely popular but definitely not new. Clove, raspberry and fennel vinegars were sold on the streets of Paris during the 13th century. Making fruit-flavoured vinegars was also one of the responsibilities of North American housewives during the 18th and 19th centuries.

Balsamic vinegar (It. *aceto Balsamico)* is newly popular in North America, though it has been produced in Italy for more than 800 years. To produce balsamic vinegar, red wine vinegar is aged in a succession of wooden barrels made from a variety of woods—oak, cherry, locust, ash, mulberry and juniper—for at least 4, but sometimes up to 50, years. The resulting liquid is dark reddish-brown and sweet. Balsamic has a high acid level, but the sweetness covers the tart flavour, making it very mellow. True balsamic is extremely expensive because of the long aging process and the small quantities available. Most of the commercial products imported from Italy are now made by a quick caramelization and flavouring process. Balsamic is excellent as a condiment or seasoning and has a remarkable affinity for tomatoes and strawberries.

CONDIMENTS

Strictly speaking, a condiment is any food added to a dish for flavour, including herbs, spices and vinegars. Today, however, *condiments* more often refer to cooked or prepared flavourings, such as prepared mustards, relishes, bottled sauces and pickles. Several frequently used condiments are discussed here. These staples may be used to alter or enhance the flavour of a dish during cooking or added to a completed dish at the table by the consumer.

Prepared mustard is a mixture of crushed mustard seeds, vinegar or wine and salt or spices. It can be flavoured in many ways—with herbs, onions, peppers and even citrus zest. It can be a smooth paste or coarse and chunky, depending on how finely the seeds are ground and whether the skins are strained out. Prepared mustard gets its tangy taste from an essential oil that forms only when the seeds are crushed and mixed with water. Prepared mustard can be used as a condiment, particularly with meat and charcuterie items, or as a flavouring ingredient in sauces, stews and marinades.

Dijon mustard takes its name from a town and the surrounding region in France that prepares about half of the world's mustard. French mustard labelled "Dijon" must, by law, be produced only in that region. Dijon and Dijon-style mustards are smooth with a rich, complex flavour. Western Canada grows the largest percentage of the world's mustard seed.

English and Chinese mustards are made from mustard flour and cool water. They are extremely hot and powerful. American or "ballpark" mustard is mild and vinegary with a bright yellow colour.

Mustard never really spoils, its flavour just fades away. Because of its high acid content, mustard does not turn rancid, but it will oxidize and develop a dark surface crust. Once opened, mustard should be kept well covered and refrigerated.

Soy sauce is a thin, dark brown liquid fermented from cooked soybeans, wheat and salt. Available in several flavours and strengths, it is ubiquitous in most Asian cuisines. Light soy sauce is thin, with a light brown colour and a very salty flavour. Dark soy sauce is thicker and dark brown, with a sweet, less salty flavour. Necessary for preparing many Asian dishes, soy sauce is also used in marinades and sauces and as an all-purpose condiment. Other soy-based condiments include tamari, teriyaki sauce and fermented bean paste (miso).

Ketchup (also known as catsup) originated in Pakistan and referred to any salty extract from fish, fruits or vegetables. Prepared tomato ketchup, as we know it, is really a syrupy sauce, created in America and used worldwide as a

---

Even the most sophisticated food service operation occasionally uses prepared condiments or flavourings. The products described here are widely used and available from grocery stores or wholesale purveyors. Some are brand-name items that have become almost synonymous with the product itself; others are available from several manufacturers.

Barbecue sauce—Like ketchup, commercial barbecue sauce is a mixture of tomatoes, vinegar and spices; it tends to be hotter and sweeter than ketchup, however. Commercial barbecue sauce is used primarily for marinating or basting meat, poultry or fish. A tremendous variety of barbecue sauces is available, with various flavours, textures and aromas. Sample several before selecting the most appropriate for your specific needs.

Fish sauce—Fish sauce is a thin, dark brown liquid made from anchovy extract and salt. It is the quintessential Thai seasoning, but is used throughout Southeast Asia. It is extremely salty with a powerful aroma. There is no substitute; only a small amount is necessary for most dishes.

Hoisin—Hoisin sauce is a dark, thick, salty-sweet sauce made from fermented soybeans, vinegar, garlic and caramel. It is used in Chinese dishes or served as a dipping sauce.

Old Bay® seasoning—Old Bay® is a dry spice blend containing celery salt, dry mustard, paprika and other flavourings. It is widely used in shellfish preparations, especially boiled shrimp and crab.

Oyster sauce—Oyster sauce is a thick, dark sauce made from oyster extract. It has a salty-sweet flavour and rich aroma. Oyster sauce is often used with stir-fried meats and poultry.

Pickapeppa® sauce—Pickapeppa® sauce is a dark, thick, sweet-hot blend of tomatoes, onions, sugar, vinegar, mango, raisins, tamarinds and spices. Produced in Jamaica, it is used as a condiment for meat, game or fish and as a seasoning in sauces, soups and dressings.

Tabasco® sauce—Tabasco® sauce is a thin, bright red liquid blended from vinegar, chiles and salt. Its fiery flavour is widely used in sauces, soups and prepared dishes; it is a popular condiment for Mexican, southern and southwestern cuisines. Tabasco® sauce has been produced in Louisiana since 1868. Other "Louisiana-style" hot sauces (those containing only peppers, vinegar and salt) may be substituted.

Worcestershire sauce—Worcestershire sauce is a thin, dark brown liquid made from malt vinegar, tamarind, molasses and spices. It is used as a condiment for beef and as a seasoning in sauces, soups, stews and prepared dishes. Its flavour should be rich and full, but not salty.

---

flavouring ingredient or condiment. It is bright red and thick, with a tangy, sweet-sour flavour. Ketchup, with its high sugar content, can be stored either in the refrigerator or at room temperature; it should keep well for up to four months after opening. Ketchup does not turn rancid or develop mould but it will darken and lose flavour as it ages.

COFFEES AND TEAS

Coffee and tea are the staples of most beverage menus. Despite the relatively low price, a quality cup of coffee or tea can be extremely important to a customer's impression of your food service operation. A cup of coffee is often either the very first or the very last item consumed by a customer. Tea, whether iced or hot, is often consumed throughout the meal. Consequently, it is important that you learn to prepare and serve these beverages properly.

Coffee

Coffee (Fr. *café)* begins as the fruit of a small tree growing in tropical and subtropical regions throughout the world. The fruit, referred to as a cherry, is bright red with translucent flesh surrounding two flat-sided seeds. These seeds are the coffee beans. When ripe, the cherries are harvested by hand, then cleaned, fermented and hulled, leaving the green coffee beans. The beans are then roasted, blended, ground and brewed. Note that any coffee bean can be roasted to any degree of darkness, ground to any degree of fineness and brewed by any number of methods.

Only two species of coffee bean are routinely used: *arabica* and *robusta.* Arabica beans are the most important commercially and the ones from which the finest coffees are produced. Robusta beans do not produce as flavourful a drink as arabica. Nevertheless, robusta beans are becoming increasingly significant commercially, due in part to the fact that robusta trees are heartier and more fertile than arabica trees.

The conditions in which the beans are grown have almost as much effect on the final product as subsequent roasting, grinding and brewing. Because coffee takes much of its flavour and character from the soil, sunlight and air, the beans' origin is critical to the product's final quality. Each valley and mountain produces coffee distinct from all others, so geographic names are used to identify the beans regardless of whether they are from arabica or robusta trees. Thus, purveyors may offer beans known as Colombian, Chanchamayo (from Peru), Kilimanjaro (from Tanzania), Blue Mountain (from Jamaica), Java, Sumatra or Kona (from Hawaii), to name a few.

While many so-called gourmet coffees are made from a single type of bean, nearly all coffee sold in Canada and the United States is a blend of various qualities and types of bean.

Roasting Coffee

Roasting releases and enhances the flavours in coffee. It also darkens the beans and brings natural oils to the surface. Traditionally, almost everyone roasted their own coffee beans because all coffee beans were sold green. Today, however, roasting is left to experts who possess the necessary equipment.

It is important to recognize and understand some of the standard descriptions used for various types of roasting. No single international organization controls the naming of roasted coffee, however, so a coffee roaster may refer to products by any name. The following descriptions are based on the most common terminology.

Green coffee beans

City-roast beans

French-roast beans

+ **City roast:** Also called American or brown roast, city roast is the most widely used coffee style in the United States. City roast produces a beverage that may lack brilliance or be a bit flat, yet it is the roast most North Americans assume they prefer because it is the roast most often used in grocery store blends.
+ **Brazilian roast:** Somewhat darker than a city roast, Brazilian roast should begin to show a hint of dark-roast flavour. The beans should show a trace of oil. In this context, the word "Brazilian" has no relationship to coffee grown in Brazil.
+ **Viennese roast:** Also called medium-dark roast, Viennese roast generally falls somewhere between a standard city roast and French roast.
+ **French roast:** French roast, also called New Orleans or dark roast, approaches espresso in flavour without sacrificing smoothness. The beans should be the colour of semi-sweet chocolate, with apparent oiliness on the surface.
+ **Espresso roast:** Espresso roast, also called Italian roast, is the darkest of all. The beans are roasted until they are virtually burnt. The beans should be black with a shiny, oily surface.

Grinding Coffee

Unlike roasting, which is best left to the experts, the grinding of coffee beans is best left to the consumer or food service operation. Whole coffee beans stay fresh longer than ground coffee. Ground coffee kept in an airtight container away from heat and light will stay fresh for three or four days. Whole beans will stay fresh for a few weeks and may be kept frozen for several months, as long as they are dry and protected from other flavours. Frozen coffee beans do not need to be thawed before grinding and brewing. Do not refrigerate coffee.

The fineness of the grind depends entirely on the type of coffee maker being used. The grind determines the length of time it takes to achieve the optimum (19%) extraction from the beans. The proper grind is simply whatever grind allows this to happen in the time it takes a specific coffee maker to complete its brewing cycle. Follow the directions for your coffee maker or ask your specialty coffee purveyor for guidance.

Brewing Coffee

Coffee is brewed by one of two methods: decoction or infusion. **Decoction** means boiling a substance until its flavour is removed. Boiling is the oldest method of making coffee, but is no longer used except in preparing extremely strong Turkish coffee. **Infusion** refers to the extraction of flavours at temperatures below boiling. Infusion techniques include steeping (mixing hot water with ground coffee), filtering (slowly pouring hot water over ground coffee held in a disposable cloth or paper filter) and dripping (pouring hot water over ground coffee and allowing the liquid to run through a strainer). Percolating is undesirable as the continuous boiling ruins the coffee's flavour.

The secrets to brewing a good cup of coffee are knowing the exact proportion of coffee to water as well as the length of time to maintain contact between the two. The best results are nearly always achieved by using 2 level tablespoons of ground coffee per 3/4 measuring cup (175 mL, or 6 oz.) of water. (A standard cup of coffee is three-quarters the size of a standard 250-mL/8-oz. measuring cup; 450 g or about 1 lb. of coffee yields approximately 80 level tablespoons or enough for 40 "cups" of coffee.) An Approved Coffee Measure (ACM) was developed by the Coffee Brewing Institute to measure 2 level tablespoons accurately. ACM scoops are readily available and are often included with retail coffee packages.

Premeasured packages of ground coffee are generally used with commercial brewing equipment. These packages are available in a range of sizes for making single pots or large urns of coffee of varying strengths.

If stronger coffee is desired, use more coffee per cup of water, not a longer brewing time. For weaker coffee, prepare regular-strength coffee and dilute it with hot water. Never reuse coffee grounds.

Coffeepots and carafes should be cleaned well with hot water between each use; coffee makers should be disassembled and cleaned according to the manufacturer's directions. Unless properly cleaned, oils from coffee form a film on the inside of the maker and pots, imparting a rancid or stale flavour to each subsequent batch.

Finally, coffee should be served as soon as it is brewed. Oxidation takes a toll on the aroma and flavour, which soon become flat and eventually bitter. Coffee may be held for a short time on the coffee maker's hot plate at temperatures of 85°C to 88°C (185°F to 190°F). A better holding method, however, is to immediately pour freshly brewed coffee into a thermal carafe. Never attempt to reheat cold coffee, as drastic temperature shifts destroy flavour.

Tasting Coffee

Coffee can be judged on four characteristics: aroma, acidity, body and flavour.

As a general rule, coffee will taste the way it smells. Some coffees, particularly Colombian, are more fragrant than others, however.

Acidity, also called wininess, refers to the tartness of the coffee. Acidity is a desirable characteristic that indicates snap, life or thinness. Kenyan and Guatemalan are examples of particularly acidic coffees.

Body refers to the feeling of heaviness or thickness that coffee provides on the palate. Sumatran is generally the heaviest, with Mexican and Venezuelan being the lightest.

◆◆◆

DON'T WRECK THE ENDING

Lots of time and thought are spent on selecting the wines to accompany the various savory courses of a meal, but too often at the sweet course the dessert wine finds itself up against its worst enemy: chocolate. A good sauterne, or a good-quality dessert wine of almost any kind, works best with a fruit tart or with noncitrus sorbets accompanied by "dry cookie-like things," to use Richard Olney's phrase. Chocolate, whether in the form of pastry or confection, belongs with coffee, whose aromatic bitterness is a perfect foil for it.

RICHARD H. GRAFF
Chairman, CHALONE WINE GROUP

Flavour, of course, is the most ambiguous as well as the most important characteristic. Terms such as mellow, harsh, grassy or earthy are used to describe the rather subjective characteristic of flavour.

Serving Coffee

Coffee may be served unadorned, unsweetened and black (without milk or cream). The customer then adds the desired amount of sugar and milk. Other coffee beverages are made with specific additions and provide value-added menu alternatives. The most common ways of serving coffee are described here.

Espresso

Cappuccino

Caffè latte

- ✦ **Espresso:** Espresso (Sp. *café expreso*) refers to a unique brewing method in which hot water is forced through finely ground and packed coffee under high pressure. Properly made, it will be strong, rich and smooth, not bitter or acidic. Espresso is usually made with beans that have been roasted very dark, but any type of bean may be used. A single serving of espresso uses about 7 g (1/4 oz.) of coffee to 45 mL (1-1/2 oz.) of water. Americans tend to prefer a larger portion, known as *espresso lungo*, made with 60 to 90 mL (2 to 3 oz.) of water.
- ✦ **Espresso machiatto:** Espresso "marked" with a tiny portion of steamed milk.
- ✦ **Cappuccino:** One-third espresso, one-third steamed milk and one-third foamed milk; the total serving is still rather small, about 120 to 180 mL (4 to 6 oz.).
- ✦ **Caffè latte:** One-third espresso, two-thirds steamed milk without foam; usually served in a tall glass.
- ✦ **Café au lait:** The French version of the Italian *caffè latte*, café au lait (or *café crème*) is made with strong coffee instead of espresso and hot, not steamed, milk. It is traditionally served in a handleless bowl.
- ✦ **Caffè mocha:** One-third espresso, two-thirds steamed milk, flavoured with chocolate syrup; usually topped with whipped cream and chocolate shavings or cocoa.
- ✦ **Flavoured coffees:** Dried, ground chicory root has long been added to coffee, particularly by the French, who enjoy its bitter flavour. Toasted barley, dried figs and spices have also been used by various cultures for years. Coffees flavoured with vanilla, chocolate, liqueurs, spices and nuts have recently become popular in the Americas. These flavours are added to roasted coffee beans by tumbling the beans with special flavouring oils. The results are strongly aromatic flavours such as vanilla hazelnut, chocolate raspberry or maple walnut.

Decaffeinated Coffee

Caffeine is an alkaloid found in coffee beans (as well as in tea leaves and cocoa beans). It is a stimulant that can improve alertness or reduce fatigue. In excess, however, caffeine can cause some people to suffer palpitations or insomnia. Regular filtered coffee contains from 85 to 100 milligrams of caffeine per cup. Robusta beans contain more caffeine than the better-quality arabica beans. Decaffeinated coffee (with 97% or more of the caffeine removed) is designed to meet consumer desires for a caffeine-free product.

Tea

Tea (Fr. *thé*) is the name given to the leaves of *Camellia sinensis*, a tree or shrub that grows at high altitudes in damp tropical regions. Although tea comes from only one species of plant, there are three general types of tea—

✦✦✦
COFFEE'S OTHER USES

In addition to its use as a beverage, coffee is frequently an ingredient in mixed drinks such as Irish coffee (with whisky and cream) or café brulot (with orange, cloves and brandy). Coffee is also used in stews, sauces and pan gravy. It may be added to breads, such as rye and pumpernickel, cakes, custards, ice creams, dessert sauces and frostings. The flavour of coffee has a strong affinity for chocolate, nuts and rum.

◆◆◆
A CUP OF COFFEE HISTORY

Some anthropologists suggest that coffee was initially consumed by central African warriors in the form of a paste made from mashed coffee beans and animal fat rolled into balls. Eaten before battle, the animal fat and bean protein provided nourishment; the caffeine provided a stimulant.

A hot coffee drink may first have been consumed sometime during the 9th century A.D. in Persia. Made by a decoction of ripe beans, the drink was probably very thick and acrid. Nevertheless, by the year 1000, the elite of the Arab world were regularly drinking a decoction of dried coffee beans. The beans were harvested in Abyssinia (Ethiopia) and brought to market by Egyptian merchants. Within a century or so, *kahwa* became immensely popular with members of all strata of Arab society. Coffeehouses

opened throughout the Levant, catering to customers who sipped the thick, brown brew while discussing affairs of heart and state.

Although European travellers to the Ottoman Empire had tasted coffee, and a few Arab or Turkish merchants living in Marseilles offered their guests a chance to sample the rare drink, coffee did not become popular in Europe until the 17th century. Its popularity is due in great part to Suleiman Aga, the Grand Panjandrum of the Ottoman Empire. In 1669 he arrived at the court of King Louis XIV of France as ambassador, bringing with him many exotic treasures, including *caffe*. Offered at his opulent parties, *caffe* soon became the drink of choice for the French aristocracy.

Coffee became popular in Vienna as a fortune of war. By 1683 the Turks were at the gates

of Vienna. A decisive battle was fought and the Turks fled, leaving behind stores of gold, equipment, supplies and a barely known provision—green coffee beans. One of the victorious leaders, Franz George Kolschitzky, recognized the treasure, took it as his own and soon opened the first coffeehouse in Vienna, The Blue Bottle.

Despite its growing popularity, coffee was exorbitantly expensive, in part, the result of the Sultan's monopoly on coffee beans. His agents, principally in Marseilles, controlled the sale of beans. But the monopoly was not to survive. By the end of the 17th century, the Dutch had stolen coffee plants from Arabia and began cultivating them in Java. By the early 18th century, the French had transported seedlings to the West Indies; from there coffee plantations spread throughout the New World.

◆◆◆
A CUP OF TEA HISTORY

Some believe that the Chinese Emperor Shen Nung discovered tea drinking in 2737 B.C. Legend holds that the Emperor was boiling his drinking water beneath a tree when some leaves fell into the pot. Enchanted by the drink, he began to cultivate the plant. Whether myth or truth, it is known that a hot drink made from powdered dried tea leaves whipped into hot water was regularly consumed in China sometime after the 4th century. Later, decoctions of tea leaves (as well as rice, spices and nuts) became popular. But it was not until the Ming dynasty (A.D. 1368–1644) that infusions of tea leaves became commonplace.

By the 9th century, tea drinking had spread to Japan. In both Chinese and Japanese cultures, tea drinking developed into a ritual. For the Chinese, a cup of tea became the mirror of the soul. For the Japanese, it was the drink of immortality.

Tea was first transported from China to Europe by Dutch merchants during the early 1600s. By mid-century, it was introduced into England. In 1669 the East India Company was granted a charter by Queen Elizabeth I to import tea, a monopoly it held until 1833. To ensure a steady supply, the English surreptitiously procured plants from China and started plantations throughout the Indian subcontinent, as did the Dutch.

Tea drinking became fashionable in England, at least in court circles, through Charles II (raised in exile at The Hague in Holland, he reigned from 1660 until 1685) and his Portuguese wife, Catherine of Braganza. Queen Anne of England (reigned 1702–1714) introduced several concepts that eventually became part of the English tea custom. For example, she substituted tea for ale at breakfast

and began using large silver pots instead of tiny china pots.

The social custom of afternoon tea began in the late 1700s, thanks to Anna, Duchess of Bedford. Historians attribute to her the late afternoon ritual of snacking on sandwiches and pastries accompanied by tea. She began the practice in order to quell her hunger pangs between breakfast and dinner (which was typically served at 9:30 or 10:00 P.M.).

Eventually two distinct types of teatime evolved. Low tea was aristocratic in origin and consisted of a snack of pastries and sandwiches, with tea, served in the late afternoon as a prelude to the evening meal. High tea was bourgeois in origin, consisting of leftovers from the typically large middle-class lunch, such as cold meats, bread and cheeses. High tea became a substitute for the evening meal.

black, green and oolong. The differences among the three are the result of the manner in which the leaves are treated after picking.

Black tea is amber-brown and strongly flavoured. Its colour and flavour result from fermenting the leaves. Black tea leaves are named or graded by leaf size. Because larger leaves brew more slowly than smaller ones, teas are sorted by leaf size for efficient brewing. *Souchong* denotes large leaves, *pekoe* denotes medium-sized leaves and *orange pekoe* denotes the smallest whole leaves. (Note that *orange pekoe* does not refer to any type of orange flavour.) Broken tea, graded as either broken orange pekoe or broken pekoe, is

Fruit tea

Gunpowder

Darjeeling

✦✦✦
TEA FLAVOURS

The following descriptions apply to some of the teas frequently available through wholesalers or gourmet suppliers. Taste several different ones to find the best for your purposes. Remember that the same tea from different blenders or distributors may taste different, and that different flavours will be more or less appropriate for different times of the day. You may wish to offer your patrons a selection of flavours.

Assam—rich black tea with a reddish colour from Northern India. It is valued by connoisseurs, especially for breakfast.

Ceylon—a full-flavoured black tea with a golden colour and delicate fragrance. Ideal for serving iced, it does not become cloudy when cold.

Darjeeling—the champagne of teas, it is a full-bodied, black tea with muscat flavour from the foothills of the Himalayas.

Earl Grey—a blend of black teas, usually including Darjeeling, flavoured with oil of bergamot. A popular choice for afternoon tea.

English Breakfast—English blend of Indian and Sri Lankan black teas; it is full-bodied and robust, with a rich colour.

Gunpowder—Green Chinese tea with a tightly curled leaf and grey-green colour. It has a pungent flavour and a light straw colour. It is often served after the evening meal.

Keemum—a mellow black Chinese tea with a strong aroma. It is less astringent than other teas and is delicious iced.

Lapsang Souchong—a large-leafed (souchong) tea from the Lapsang district of China. It has a distinctive tarry, smoky flavour and aroma, appropriate for afternoon tea or dinner.

Formosa Oolong—a unique and expensive large-leafed oolong tea with the flavour of ripe peaches. It is appropriate for breakfast or afternoon tea.

---

smaller, resulting in a darker, stronger brew. Broken tea is most often used in tea bags. These grades apply to both Chinese and Indian black teas.

Green tea is yellowish-green in colour with a bitter flavour. Leaves used for green tea are not fermented. Chinese green tea leaves are also graded according to leaf size and age. The finest green tea is Gunpowder, followed by Imperial and Hyson.

Oolong tea is partially fermented to combine the characteristics of black and green teas. Oolong is popular in China and Japan, often flavoured with jasmine flowers. Oolong tea leaves are also graded by size and age.

As with coffee, tea takes much of its flavour from the geographic conditions in which it is grown. Teas are named for their place of origin, for example, Darjeeling, Ceylon (now Sri Lanka) or Assam. Many popular and commercially available teas are actually blends of leaves from various sources. Blended and unblended teas may also be flavoured with oils, dried fruit, spices, flowers or herbs.

Brewing Tea

Tea may be brewed by the cup or the pot. In either case, it is important to use the following procedure.

1. Always begin with clean equipment and freshly drawn cold water. Water that has been sitting in a kettle or hot water tank contains less air and will taste flat or stale.

2. Warm the teapot by rinsing it out with hot water. This begins to relax the tea leaves and ensures that the water will stay hot when it comes in contact with the tea.

3. Place 5 mL (1 tsp.) of loose tea or one tea bag per 3/4 cup (180 mL/6 oz.) of water capacity in the warmed teapot.

4. As soon as the water comes to a boil, pour the appropriate amount over the tea. Do not allow the water to continue boiling as this removes the oxygen, leaving a flat taste. The water should be at a full boil when it comes in contact with the tea so that the tea leaves will uncurl and release their flavour.

5. Replace the lid of the teapot and allow the tea to infuse for three to five minutes. Time the brew. Colour is not a reliable indication of brewing time: Tea leaves release colour before flavour and different types of tea will be different colours when properly brewed.

6. Remove the tea bags or loose tea from the water when brewing is complete. This can be accomplished easily if the teapot is fitted with a removable leaf basket or if a tea bag or a perforated tea ball is used. Otherwise, decant the tea through a strainer into a second warmed teapot.

7. Serve immediately, accompanied with sugar, lemon, milk (not cream) and honey as desired. Dilute the tea with hot water if necessary.

8. Do not reuse tea leaves. Four hundred and fifty grams (1 lb.) of tea yields 200 cups, making it the most inexpensive beverage after tap water.

For iced tea, prepare regular brewed tea using 50% more tea. Then pour into a pitcher or glass filled with ice. The stronger brew will hold its flavour better as the ice melts. Sweeten with simple syrup as desired.

Serving Tea

Black and oolong tea may be served hot or cold, but green tea is best served hot. Black tea is served with milk or lemon and sugar; green and oolong tea are most often served plain. Adding milk to hot tea is a British preference (not normally followed in Europe or Asia) and reduces the astringency of the tea. Iced tea, an American invention, may be served plain or sweetened, and is often garnished with lemon, orange or fresh mint.

CONCLUSION

Kitchen staples include fresh and dried herbs, spices, salt, nuts, oils, vinegars, condiments, coffees and teas. You must be able to recognize, purchase, store and use many of these staples.

The only way to determine which brand or type of staple is best for your particular needs is to taste, smell, sample and use a variety of those available. Cost, convenience and storage factors must also be considered. By maintaining a supply of seasonings, flavourings, condiments and other staples you will be able to create new dishes or enhance standard ones at a moment's notice.

QUESTIONS FOR DISCUSSION

1. What is a staple? Does every kitchen keep the same staples on hand? Explain your answer.
2. What are the differences between an herb and a spice? Give an example of a plant that is used as both an herb and a spice.
3. If a recipe calls for a fresh herb and you have only the dried herb, what do you do? Explain your answer.
4. What is the difference between a sachet and a bouquet garni? Identify the ingredients in a standard sachet and a standard bouquet garni.
5. Discuss the importance of using proper preparation and service techniques for coffee and tea. How can these beverages be used to improve or enhance your food service operation?

WEBLINKS

Flavouring the World: The FAQ about Spices
  www.open.hr/space/herbs/culinary/spices.htm
Frequently Asked Questions about Coffee and Caffeine
  www.cs.unb.ca/~alopez-o/caffaq.html
The U.K. Tea Council Online
  www.tea.co.uk
Culinary Herb FAQ
  ibiblio.org/herbmed/faqs/culi-cont.html
The Curry House: International Curry Recipes and Other Information
  www.curryhousehouse.co.uk

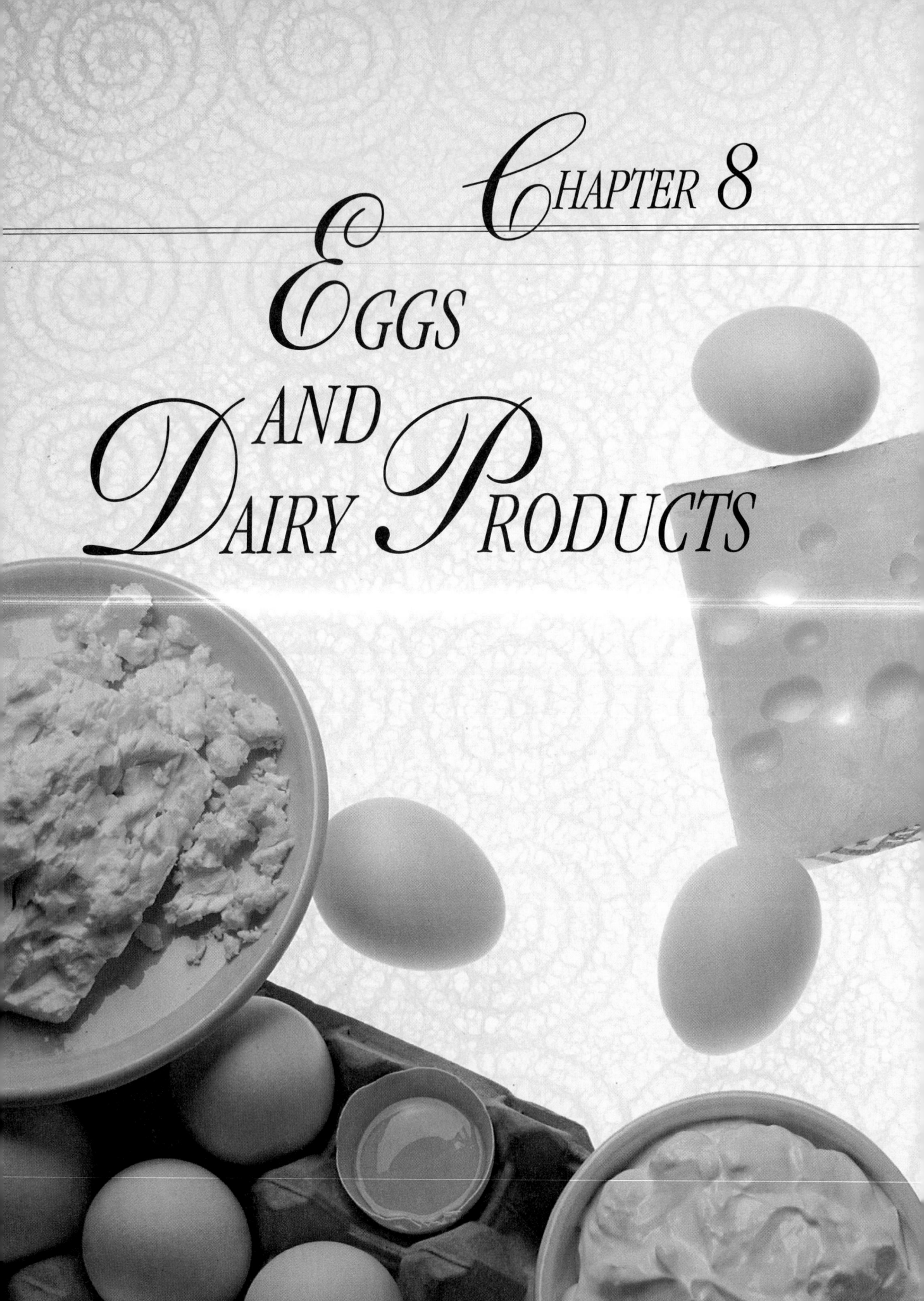

CHAPTER 8

EGGS
AND
DAIRY PRODUCTS

◆◆◆

LEARNING OUTCOMES

After studying this chapter you will be able to:

◆ describe the composition of eggs
◆ purchase and store eggs properly
◆ prepare whipped egg whites
◆ identify, store and use a variety of milk-based products
◆ explain how to clarify butter
◆ identify, store and serve a variety of fine cheeses

*E*ggs and milk are unique in that they, along with seeds, are the only foods that are truly designed to support life: Eggs support chick embryos; milk supports calves. Thus they are among the most nutritious of foods. Eggs as well as milk and milk-based products (known collectively as dairy products) are also extremely versatile. They are used throughout the kitchen, either served alone or as ingredients in everything from soups and sauces to breads and pastries. High quality and freshness are critical for their proper use. Learn to select the finest products, whether they are eggs, whole milk, butter or Brie, and handle them with care.

EGGS

Nature designed eggs to be the food source for developing chicks. Eggs, particularly chicken eggs, are also an excellent food for humans because of their high protein content, low cost and ready availability. Quail eggs are also used in food service operations. Duck and goose eggs are too fatty to be useful, however.

Eggs can be cooked in a variety of ways, some of which are described in Chapter 32, Breakfast and Brunch. Eggs are also incorporated into other dishes to provide texture, structure, flavour, moisture and nutrition.

Composition

The primary parts of an egg are the shell, yolk and albumen. See Figure 8.1.

The **shell**, composed of calcium carbonate, is the outermost covering of the egg. It prevents microbes from entering and moisture from escaping, and protects the egg during handling and transport. Shell colour is determined by the breed of the hen; for chickens it can range from bright white to brown. Shell colour has no effect on quality, flavour or nutrition.

The **yolk** is the yellow portion of the egg. It constitutes just over one-third of the egg and contains three-fourths of the calories, most of the minerals and

Figure 8.1 *An Egg*

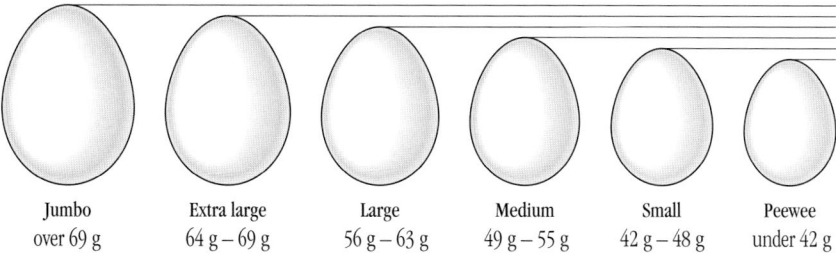

| Jumbo | Extra large | Large | Medium | Small | Peewee |
| over 69 g | 64 g – 69 g | 56 g – 63 g | 49 g – 55 g | 42 g – 48 g | under 42 g |

FIGURE 8.2 *Egg Sizes*

vitamins and all of the fat. The yolk also contains lecithin, the compound responsible for emulsification in products such as hollandaise sauce and mayonnaise. Egg yolk solidifies (coagulates) at temperatures between 65°C and 70°C (149°F and 158°F). Although the colour of a yolk may vary depending on the hen's feed, colour does not affect quality or nutritional content.

The **albumen** is the clear portion of the egg and is often referred to as the **egg white**. It constitutes about two-thirds of the egg and contains more than half of the protein and riboflavin. Egg white coagulates, becoming firm and opaque, at temperatures between 62°C and 65°C (144°F and 149°F).

An often misunderstood portion of the egg is the **chalazae cords**. These thick, twisted strands of egg white anchor the yolk in place. They are neither imperfections nor embryos. The more prominent the chalazae, the fresher the egg. Chalazae do not interfere with cooking or with whipping egg whites.

Eggs are sold in jumbo, extra large, large, medium, small and peewee sizes, as determined by weight per dozen. See Figure 8.2. Food service operations generally use medium eggs due to cost, except for breakfast cookery.

When separating eggs into whites and yolks, there is a range of weight for each component. Generally, medium eggs will have 30 g of albumen and 24 g of yolk. Large eggs will have approximately 34 g of albumen and 27 g of yolk.

Grading

Eggs are graded by the Canadian Food Inspection Agency (CFIA) (Egg and Egg Products Division). The grade A, B or C is given an egg based upon interior and exterior quality, not size. The qualities for each grade are described in Table 8.1. Grade has no effect on nutritional values.

Storage

Egg quality is quickly diminished by improper handling. Eggs should be stored at temperatures below 4°C (40°F) and at a relative humidity of 70–80%. Eggs

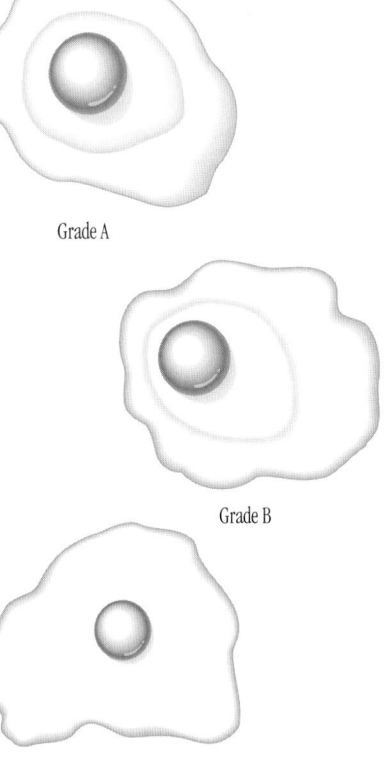

Grade A

Grade B

Grade C

TABLE 8.1   EGG GRADES

	Grade A	Grade B	Grade C
Albumen	Firm	Watery	Thin and watery
Yolk	Round, well centred	Slightly flattened	Loose
Shell	Clean, no cracks, normal shape	No cracks, but rough texture	May be cracked
Use	Sold at retail markets for household use	Used for commercial baking or further processing	Not sold to consumers; sold to commercial processors for further processing

will age more during one day at room temperature than they will during one week under proper refrigeration. As eggs age, the white becomes thinner and the yolk becomes flatter. While this will change the appearance of poached or fried eggs, age has little effect on nutrition or behaviour during cooking procedures. Older eggs, however, should be used for hard-boiling, as the shells are easier to remove than those of fresh eggs.

Cartons of fresh, uncooked eggs will keep for at least four to five weeks beyond the pack date if properly refrigerated. Hard-boiled eggs left in their shells and refrigerated should be used within one week.

Store eggs away from strongly flavoured foods to reduce odour absorption. Rotate egg stock to maintain freshness. Do not use dirty, cracked or broken eggs as they may contain bacteria or other contaminants. Frozen eggs should be thawed in the refrigerator and used only in dishes that will be thoroughly cooked, such as baked products.

Sanitation

Eggs are a potentially hazardous food. Rich in protein, they are an excellent breeding ground for bacteria. Salmonella is of particular concern with eggs and egg products because this bacteria is commonly found in a chicken's intestinal tract. Although shells are cleaned at packing houses, some bacteria may remain. Therefore, to prevent contamination, it is best to avoid mixing a shell with the liquid egg.

Inadequately cooking or improperly storing eggs may lead to food-borne illnesses. **Pasteurization** is achieved when the whole egg stays at a temperature of 60°C (140°F) for 3.5 minutes. Hold egg dishes below 4°C (40°F) or above 63°C (145°F). Never leave an egg dish at room temperature for more than one hour, including preparation and service time. Never reuse a container after it has held raw eggs without thoroughly cleaning and sanitizing it. Do not use your fingers to separate eggs.

Whipped Egg Whites

Egg whites are often whipped into a foam that is then incorporated into cakes, custards, soufflés, pancakes or other products. The air beaten into the egg foam gives products lightness and assists with leavening. Egg whites are usually whipped to a soft peak or stiff stage.

Basic Procedure for Whipping Egg Whites

1. Use fresh egg whites that are completely free of egg yolk or other impurities. Warm the egg whites to room temperature before whipping; this causes a better foam to form.
2. Use a clean bowl and whisk. Even a tiny amount of fat can prevent the egg whites from foaming properly.
3. Whip the whites on medium speed until very foamy, then add salt or cream of tartar as directed.
4. Continue whipping until soft peaks form, then gradually add granulated sugar (or hot syrup, if preparing meringues) as directed.
5. Whip until stiff peaks form. Properly whipped egg whites should be moist and shiny; over-whipping will make the egg whites appear dry and spongy or curdled.
6. Use the whipped egg whites immediately. If liquid begins to separate from the whipped egg whites, discard them; they cannot be rewhipped successfully.

Egg whites whipped to soft peaks.

Egg whites whipped to stiff peaks.

Spongy, over-whipped egg whites.

Egg Products

Food service operations often want the convenience of buying eggs out of the shell in the exact form needed: whole eggs, yolks only or whites only. These processed items are called *egg products* and are subject to strict pasteurization standards and CFIA inspections. Egg products can be frozen, refrigerated or dried. Precooked, preportioned and blended egg products are also available.

Egg Substitutes

Concerns about the cholesterol content of eggs have increased the popularity of egg substitutes. There are two general types of substitute. The first is a complete substitute made from soy or milk proteins. It should not be used in recipes where eggs are required for thickening. The second substitute contains real albumen, but the egg yolk has been replaced with vegetable or milk products. Egg substitutes have a different flavour than real eggs, but may be useful for persons on a restricted diet.

Nutrition

Eggs contain vitamins A, D, E and K and the B-complex vitamins. They are rich in minerals but also in cholesterol. The nutritional values of an egg are listed in Table 8.2. Eggs are a good source of protein.

TABLE 8.2	NUTRITIONAL VALUES OF EGGS					
	Energy	Protein	Total Fat	Saturated Fat	Carbohydrates	Cholesterol
One large egg contains	75 calories	6 g	5 g	1.5 g	0.5 g	215 mg
Canadian Egg Marketing Agency						

DAIRY PRODUCTS

Dairy products include cow's milk and foods produced from cow's milk such as butter, yogurt, sour cream and cheese. The milk of other mammals, namely goats, sheep and buffaloes, is also made into cheeses that are used in commercial food service operations. Regulations affecting dairy products are

═══════ ✦✦✦ ═══════

PERFECT FOOD?

Humans are the only mammal to regularly consume another mammal's milk. There is growing debate as to the prudence of this practice. The prevalence of lactose intolerance is now more widely documented, as well as intolerance to soy products, a widely accepted substitute. There may be an ethnocultural link to these conditions. It has also been suggested that although we regularly enjoy global access to almost any fruit or vegetable, our bodies may not be able to take full advantage of the nutrients due to inherited predispositions to certain foods. For example, those of northern European heritage may only derive sensory pleasure from a pineapple, as their bodies do not have the full capability to process the food completely. Likewise, Asians tend to have an intolerance for lactose and alcohol. Further research will help to clarify the situation and help us to understand how to best fuel our bodies.

both federal and provincial, although they are being standardized under the Canadian Food Inspection Agency.

Milk

Milk is not only a popular beverage, but is also used in the preparation of many dishes. It provides texture, flavour, colour and nutritional value for cooked or baked items. Indeed, milk is considered one of the most nutritious foods available, providing proteins, vitamins and minerals (particularly calcium). But milk is also highly perishable and is an excellent bacterial breeding ground. Care must be exercised in the handling and storage of milk and other dairy products.

Whole milk—that is, milk as it comes from the cow—is composed primarily of water (about 88%). It contains not less than 3.25% milkfat and at least 8% other milk solids (proteins, milk sugar [lactose] and minerals).

Fresh whole milk is not available raw, but must be processed as described below.

Processing Techniques

Pasteurization

By law, all milk must be pasteurized prior to retail sale. Pasteurization is the process of heating milk to a sufficiently high temperature for a sufficient length of time to destroy pathogenic bacteria. This typically requires holding milk at a temperature of 72°C (161°F) for 16 seconds. Pasteurization also destroys enzymes that cause spoilage thus increasing shelf life. Milk's nutritional value is not significantly affected by pasteurization.

Ultra-Pasteurization

Ultra-pasteurization is a process in which milk is heated to a very high temperature (135°C/275°F) for a very short time (2 to 4 seconds) in order to destroy virtually all bacteria. Ultra-pasteurization is most often used with whipping cream and individual creamers. Although the process may reduce cream's whipping properties, it extends its shelf life dramatically.

Ultra-High-Temperature Processing

Ultra-high-temperature processing (UHT) is a form of ultra-pasteurization in which milk is held at a temperature of 138°–150°C (280°–300°F) for 2 to 6 seconds. It is then packed in sterile containers under sterile conditions and aseptically sealed to prevent bacteria from entering the container. Unopened UHT milk can be stored without refrigeration for at least three months. Although UHT milk can be stored unrefrigerated, it should be chilled before serving and stored like fresh milk once opened. UHT processing may give milk a slightly cooked taste but it has no significant effect on milk's nutritional value. It has long been available in Europe and Canada.

Homogenization

Homogenization is a process in which the fat globules in whole milk are reduced in size and permanently dispersed throughout the liquid. This prevents the fat from clumping together and rising to the surface as a layer of cream. Although homogenization is not required, milk sold commercially is generally homogenized because it ensures a uniform consistency, a whiter colour and a richer taste.

Certification

Certification is a method of controlling the quality of milk by controlling the condition of the animals from which milk is obtained. Certification is not a true processing technique; rather it requires frequent veterinary examinations of the cows and health department inspections of the dairy farm, the equipment and the employees who handle milk. Pasteurization has replaced the need for certification, but milk from certified herds is still available in a few areas.

Milkfat Removal

Whole milk can also be processed in a centrifuge to remove all or a portion of the milkfat, resulting in **lowfat milk** or partly **skim milk**.

Partly skim milk is whole milk from which sufficient milkfat has been removed to produce a liquid with 2% to 3.2% milkfat. (All lowfat milks must still contain at least 8% milk solids.) Vitamin A is added to lowfat milk to replace that removed along with the milkfat. It will be labelled with the fat content.

Skim milk, also referred to as lowfat milk, has had as much milkfat removed as possible. The fat content must be not more than 1%. Skim milk must also contain at least 8% milk solids and be fortified with vitamin A.

Storage

Fluid milk should be kept refrigerated at or below 4°C (40°F). Its shelf life is reduced by half for every five-degree rise in temperature above 4°C (40°F). Keep milk containers closed to prevent absorption of odours and flavours. Freezing is not recommended.

Concentrated Milks

Concentrated or condensed milk products are produced by using a vacuum to remove all or part of the water from whole milk. The resulting products have a high concentration of milkfat and milk solids and an extended shelf life.

Evaporated milk is produced by removing approximately 60% of the water from whole, homogenized milk. Evaporated milk must contain at least 7.5% milkfat and 25% milk solids. Vitamins may be added as required. The concentrated liquid is canned and heat-sterilized. This results in a cooked flavour and darker colour. Evaporated skim milk has a milkfat content of not more than 0.3% and less than 17% milk solids other than fat. A can of evaporated milk requires no refrigeration until opened, although the can should be stored in a cool place. Evaporated milk can be reconstituted with an equal amount of water and used like whole milk for cooking or drinking.

Sweetened condensed milk is similar to evaporated milk in that 60% of the water has been removed. But unlike evaporated milk, sweetened condensed milk contains sweeteners and a minimum of 8% milkfat. Sweetened condensed milk is also canned; the canning process darkens the colour and adds a caramel flavour. Sweetened condensed milk cannot be substituted for whole milk or evaporated milk because of its sugar content. Its distinctive flavour is most often found in desserts and confections.

Dry milk powder is made by removing virtually all of the moisture from pasteurized milk. It is a graded product. The moisture content will vary depending on the process used. Milk powder graded as Canada #1 has less than 4% moisture and 1.2% milkfat; Canada #2 has less than 1.29% milkfat and 5% moisture by weight. Dry whole milk contains a minimum of 2.6% milkfat.

◆◆◆
IMITATION AND ARTIFICIAL
DAIRY PRODUCTS

Coffee whiteners, imitation sour cream, whipped topping mixes and some whipped toppings in pressurized cans are made from nondairy products. These products usually consist of corn syrup, emulsifiers, vegetable fats, colouring agents and artificial flavours. These products are generally less expensive and have a longer shelf life than the real dairy products they replace, but their flavours are no match. Imitation and artificial products may be useful, however, for persons with allergies or on a restricted diet. If you choose to use these products you cannot claim to be using real dairy products on menus or labels. Mislabelling or misrepresenting products is unethical and illegal.

Nonfat milk powder is made from skim milk and must contain less than 1.2% milkfat by weight. Both types of dry milk are usually fortified with vitamins A and D.

The lack of moisture prevents the growth of microorganisms and allows dry whole and nonfat milk powders to be stored for extended periods without refrigeration. However, because of its high milkfat content, dried whole milk can turn rancid if not stored in a cool place. Either type of dry milk can be reconstituted with water and used like fresh milk. Milk powder may also be added to foods directly, with additional liquid included in the recipe. This procedure is typical in bread making and does not alter the function of the milk or the flavour in the finished product.

Cream

Cream is a rich, liquid milk product containing at least 18% milkfat. It must be pasteurized or ultra-pasteurized and may be homogenized. Cream has a slight yellow or ivory colour and is more viscous than milk. It is used throughout the kitchen to give flavour and body to sauces, soups and desserts. Whipping cream, containing not less than 30% milkfat, can be whipped into a stiff foam and used in pastries and desserts. Cream is marketed in several forms with different fat contents, as described below.

Table cream is a mixture of whole milk and cream containing not less than 18% milkfat. It is often served with cereal or coffee, but does not contain enough fat to whip into a foam.

Half-and-half, light cream or **coffee cream** are all products with more than 10% but less than 18% milkfat. These products are often used in baked goods or soups as well as with coffee, fruit and cereal.

Whipping cream ranges from 30% to 35% milkfat. It is generally used for thickening and enriching sauces and making ice cream. It can be whipped into a foam and used as a dessert topping or folded into custards or mousses to add flavour and lightness.

Storage

Ultra-pasteurized cream will keep for six to eight weeks if refrigerated. Unwhipped cream should not be frozen. Whipped, sweetened cream can be frozen, tightly covered, for up to three months, then slowly thawed in the refrigerator. Keep cream away from strong odours and bright lights, as they can adversely affect its flavour.

Cultured Dairy Products

Cultured dairy products such as yogurt, buttermilk and sour cream are produced by adding specific bacterial cultures to fluid dairy products. The bacteria convert the milk sugar lactose into lactic acid, giving these products their body and tangy, unique flavours. The acid content also retards the growth of undesirable microorganisms; thus cultured products have been used for centuries to preserve milk.

Buttermilk originally referred to the liquid remaining after cream was churned into butter. Today buttermilk is produced by adding a culture (*Streptococcus lactis*) to fresh, pasteurized skim or lowfat milk. This results in a tart milk with a thick texture. Buttermilk is most often used as a beverage or in baked goods.

Sour cream is produced by adding the same culture to pasteurized, homogenized light cream. The resulting product is a white, tangy gel used as a condiment or to give baked goods a distinctive flavour. Sour cream must have the milkfat content clearly labelled.

Crème fraîche is a cultured cream popular in French cuisine. Although thinner and richer than sour cream, it has a similar tart, tangy flavour. It is used extensively in soups and sauces, especially with poultry, rabbit and lamb dishes. It is easily prepared from the following recipe.

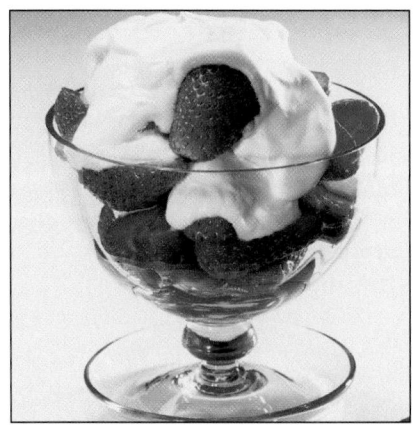

Crème fraîche

Applying the Basics

RECIPE 8.1

CRÈME FRAÎCHE

Yield: 500 mL (2 cups)

Whipping cream	500 mL	16 fl. oz.
Buttermilk, with active cultures	30 mL	1 fl. oz.

1. Heat the cream (preferably not ultra-pasteurized) to about 43°C (100°F).
2. Remove the cream from the heat and stir in the buttermilk.
3. Allow the mixture to stand in a warm place, loosely covered, until it thickens, approximately 12–36 hours.
4. Chill thoroughly before using. Crème fraîche will keep for up to 10 days in the refrigerator.

RECIPE 8.1

Approximate values per 30 g (1 oz.) serving:

Calories	90
Total fat	10 g
Saturated fat	6 g
Cholesterol	35 mg
Sodium	10 mg
Total carbohydrates	1 g
Protein	1 g

Yogurt is a thick, tart, custardlike product made from milk (either whole, lowfat or nonfat) cultured with *Lactobacillus bulgaricus* and *Streptococcus thermophilus*. Though touted as a health or diet food, yogurt contains the same amount of milkfat as the milk from which it is made. Yogurt may also contain a variety of sweeteners, flavourings and fruits. Yogurt is generally eaten as is, but may be used in baked products, salad dressings and frozen desserts. It is used in many Middle Eastern cuisines.

Storage

Cultured products should be kept refrigerated at 4°C (40°F) or below. Under proper conditions sour cream will last up to four weeks, yogurt up to three weeks and buttermilk up to two weeks. Freezing is not recommended for these products, but dishes prepared with cultured products generally can be frozen.

Butter

Butter is a fatty substance produced by agitating or churning cream. Its flavour is unequalled in sauces, breads and pastries. Butter contains at least 80% milkfat, not more than 20% moisture. It may or may not contain added salt. Butter is firm when chilled and soft at room temperature. It melts into a liquid at approximately 38°C (98°F) and reaches the smoke point at 127°C (260°F).

Government grading of dairy products, including butter, is mandatory as described in the Canada Agricultural Products Act—Dairy Products Regulations. The three grades of dairy products have grade names of **Canada 1**, **Canada 2** and **Canada 3**. The Canada grade label on the butter package assures the consumer that the butter meets federal standards for the grade indicated.

GHEE

Ghee is an Indian version of clarified butter originally made from water buffalo milk. It has a long shelf life, a high smoke point and a nutty caramel-like flavour. Ghee flavoured with ginger, peppercorns or cumin is also available.

♦ Canada 1: Butter of superior quality, with fresh, sweet flavour and aroma, a smooth creamy texture and good spreadability.
♦ Canada 2: Butter of very good quality, with pleasing flavour and fairly smooth texture.
♦ Canada 3: A processing grade used only for dairy products packed in bulk.

Salted butter is butter with up to 2.5% salt added. This not only changes the butter's flavour, but also extends its keeping qualities. When using salted butter in cooking or baking, the salt content must be considered in the total recipe.

Whipped butter is made by incorporating air into the butter. This increases its volume and spreadability, but also increases the speed at which the butter will become rancid. Because of the change in density, whipped butter should not be substituted in recipes calling for regular butter.

Storage

Butter should be well wrapped and stored at temperatures between 0°C and 2°C (32°F and 35°F). Unsalted butter is best kept frozen until needed. If well wrapped, frozen butter will keep for up to nine months at a temperature of –18°C (0°F).

Clarified Butter

Unsalted whole butter is approximately 80% fat. Although whole butter can be used for cooking or sauce making, sometimes a more stable and consistent product will be achieved by using butter that has had the water and milk solids removed by a process called clarification. It can be purchased commercially.

Skimming milk solids from the surface of melted butter.

Ladling the butterfat into a clean pan.

Basic Procedure for Clarifying Butter

1. Slowly warm the butter in a saucepan over low heat without boiling or agitation. As the butter melts, the milk solids rise to the top as a foam and the water sinks to the bottom.
2. When the butter is completely melted, skim just the milk solids from the top. Simmer until the oil clears.
3. When all the milk solids have been removed, ladle the butterfat into a clean saucepan, being careful to leave the water in the bottom of the pan.
4. The clarified butter is now ready to use. Four hundred and fifty-four grams (1 lb.) of whole salted butter will yield approximately 340 g (12 oz.) of clarified butter (a yield of 75%).

Clarified butter will keep for extended periods in either the freezer or refrigerator.

Margarine

Margarine is not a dairy product but is included in this section because it is so frequently substituted for butter in cooking, baking and table service. Margarine is manufactured from vegetable or animal fats or a combination of such fats. Flavourings, colourings, emulsifiers, preservatives and vitamins are added, and the mixture is firmed or solidified by exposure to hydrogen gas at very high temperatures, a process known as hydrogenation. Generally, the firmer the margarine the greater the degree of hydrogenation and the longer its shelf life. Like butter, margarine is approximately 80% fat and 20% moisture. But even the finest margarine cannot match the flavour of butter.

===
◆◆◆
===

MARGARINE:
FROM LABORATORY BENCH TO DINNER TABLE

Margarine was invented by a French chemist in 1869 after Napoleon III offered a prize for the development of a synthetic edible fat. Originally produced from animal fat and milk, margarine is now made almost exclusively from vegetable fats.

In *On Food and Cooking, The Science and Lore of the Kitchen*, Harold McGee recounts the history of margarine. He explains that margarine caught on quickly in Europe and America, with large-scale production underway by 1880. But the American dairy industry and the U.S. government put up fierce resistance. First, margarine was defined as a harmful drug and its sale restricted. Then it was heavily taxed; stores had to be licensed to sell it and, like alcohol and tobacco, it was bootlegged. The U.S. government refused to purchase it for use by the armed forces. And, in an attempt to hold it to its true colours, some states did not allow margarine to be dyed yellow (animal fats and vegetable oils are much paler than butter); the dye was sold separately and mixed in by the consumer. World War II, which brought butter rationing, probably did the most to establish margarine's respectability. But it was not until 1967 that yellow margarine could be sold in Wisconsin.

Today North Americans consume nearly three times as much margarine as butter. Both price and the concern about heart disease are responsible for this differential. Current research indicates that hydrogenated fats are potentially a greater health risk, however.

===

Margarine packaged in tubs is softer and more spreadable than solid products and generally contains more water and air. Indeed, diet margarine is approximately 50% water. Because of their decreased density, these soft products should not be substituted for regular butter or margarine in cooking or baking.

Specially formulated and blended margarine or shortening are available for commercial use in making puff pastry, croissant doughs, frostings and the like.

Nutrition

Dairy products are naturally high in vitamins, minerals and protein. Often liquid products such as milk are fortified with additional vitamins and minerals. Their fat content varies depending upon the amount of milkfat left after processing. Specific nutritional values for selected dairy products are found in Table 8.3.

TABLE 8.3   NUTRITIONAL VALUES OF DAIRY PRODUCTS

Per 250-mL serving (except *15 mL)	Energy (Kcal)	Protein (g)	Carbohydrates (g)	Fat (g)	Cholesterol (mg)	Sodium (mg)
Whole milk (≥3.25% MF)	159	9	12	9	35	126
Skim milk (0.1% MF)	90	9	13	tr	5	133
Buttermilk (0.8% MF)	105	9	12	2	9	272
Heavy whipping cream (35% MF)*	49	tr	tr	5	19	5
Half-and-half (10% MF)*	18	tr	1	2	5	6
Sour cream (14% MF)*	23	tr	1	2	6	6

Reproduced with permission from *Nutrient Value of Some Foods,* Health Canada Web site, 1999, Communications Canada, 2002.

Natural Cheeses

Cheese (Fr. *fromage*; It. *fromaggio*) is one of the oldest and most widely used foods known. It is served alone or as a principal ingredient in or an accompaniment to countless dishes. Cheese is commonly used in commercial kitchens, appearing in everything from breakfast to snacks to desserts.

Literally hundreds of natural cheeses are produced worldwide. Although their shapes, ages and flavours vary according to local preferences and traditions, all natural cheeses are produced in the same basic fashion as has been used for centuries. Each starts with a mammal's milk; cows, goats and sheep are the most commonly used. The milk proteins (known as *casein*) are coagulated with the addition of an enzyme, usually rennet, which is found in calves' stomachs. As the milk coagulates, it separates into solid curds and liquid whey. After draining off the whey, either the curds are made into fresh cheese, such as ricotta or cottage cheese, or the curds are further processed by cutting, kneading and cooking. The resulting substance, known as "green cheese," is packed into moulds to drain. Salt or special bacteria may be added to the moulded cheeses, which are then allowed to age or ripen under controlled conditions to develop the desired texture, colour and flavour.

Cheeses are a product of their environment, which is why most fine cheeses cannot be reproduced outside their native locale. The breed and feed of the milk animal, the wild spores and moulds in the air and even the wind currents in a storage area can affect the manner in which a cheese develops. (Roquefort, for example, develops its distinctive flavour from aging in particular caves filled with crosscurrents of cool, moist air.) Canada has a thriving cheese industry and produces world-class products. They are unsurpassed in quality; Canada has among the strictest standards in the world.

Some cheeses develop a natural rind or surface because of the application of bacteria (bloomy rind) or by repeated washing with brine (washed rind). Most natural rinds may be eaten if desired. Other cheeses are coated with an inedible wax rind to prevent moisture loss. Fresh cheeses have no rind whatsoever.

Moisture and fat contents are good indicators of a cheese's texture and shelf life. The higher the moisture content, the softer the product and the more perishable it will be. Low-moisture cheeses may be used for grating and will keep for several weeks if properly stored. (Reduced water activity levels prohibit bacterial growth.) Fat content ranges from low fat (less than 20% fat) to double cream (at least 60% fat) and triple cream (at least 72% fat). Cheeses with a high fat content will be creamier and have a richer taste and texture than low-fat products.

Most cheeses contain high percentages of fat and protein. Cheese is also rich in calcium, phosphorus and vitamin A. As animal products, natural cheeses contain cholesterol. Today, many low-fat, even nonfat, processed cheeses are available. Sodium has also been reduced or eliminated from some modern products. See Table 8.4.

Cheese Varieties

Cheeses can be classified by country of origin, ripening method, fat content or texture. Here we classify fine cheeses by texture; the Dairy Bureau of Canada recognizes six categories: fresh or unripened, soft, semi-soft, firm and hard. A separate section on goat's milk and other cheeses is also included.

Fresh or Unripened Cheeses

Fresh cheeses are uncooked and unripened. Referred to as *fromage blanc* or *fromage frais* in French, they are generally mild and creamy with a tart tanginess. They should not taste acidic or bitter. Fresh cheeses have a moisture content of 40% to 80% and are highly perishable.

Cream cheese is soft cow's milk cheese containing a minimum of 30% fat. It is available in various-sized solid white blocks or whipped and flavoured. It is used throughout the kitchen in baking, dips, dressings and confections and is popular as a spread for bagels or toast.

✦✦✦
MAKING MOZZARELLA

In Italy, mozzarella is made every day; it is meant to be consumed just as often. Before there was refrigeration, the balls of mozzarella were stored in well water to keep them cool, which is where the tradition originated of storing fresh mozzarella in liquid.

Once the milk is coagulated and the curds are cut, the mass is slowly stirred to enhance the whey's expulsion. A few hours later, when the curds are mature, they are removed from the whey, chopped or shredded and then mixed with hot water.

To test the exact amount of maturity, a handful of curds is dipped into a bucket of hot water for 10 seconds. When the curds are removed, they should be kneaded briefly and then, holding the mass with two hands, it should be pulled and stretched out to determine its maturity. When it is exactly ready to be strung it can be stretched as thin and opaque as tissue paper. At this point, small amounts of curd are dumped into a small vat and stirred with hot water using a paddle. This is known as "stringing" the cheese because as the curds are mixed with the water they begin to melt somewhat and become stringy. The more the cheese is stirred the longer the strings are stretched. Eventually all the strings come together to make a large mass of satiny-smooth cheese. In Italian the word *filare* means "to string"; therefore, all cheeses that are strung are members of the *pasta filata* family.

When stringing is complete the cheese is ready to be shaped and hand-formed into balls. The balls are tossed immediately into vats of cool water so they will maintain the desired shapes. When cool, the balls are immersed in brine solution and then wrapped in parchment paper.

PAULA LAMBERT, *owner*
MOZZARELLA COMPANY, *Dallas, Texas*

TABLE 8.4 NUTRITIONAL VALUES OF COMMON CHEESES

Per 50 g serving (except *)	Energy (Kcal)	Protein (g)	Carbohydrates (g)	Fat (g)	Cholesterol (mg)	Sodium (mg)
Blue	177	11	1	14	38	698
Cheddar	201	13	1	17	53	310
Cottage* (2% MF, 125 mL)	107	16	4	2	10	483
Cream	175	4	1	17	55	148
Feta	136	7	2	11	46	577
Mozzarella, part skim	140	14	2	9	27	254
Swiss	188	14	2	14	46	130
Processed cheddar* (regular slice)	117	7	1	10	29	443

Reproduced with permission from *Nutrient Value of Some Foods* (Health Canada Web site, 1999, Communications Canada, 2002.

Mascarpone is a soft cow's milk cheese originally from Italy's Lombard region. It contains 70% to 75% fat and is extremely smooth and creamy. Mascarpone is highly perishable and is available in bulk or in 250- or 500-g (8- or 16-oz.) tubs. Its pale ivory colour and rich, sweet flavour are useful in both sweet and savoury sauces as well as desserts. It is also eaten plain, with fresh fruit, or spread on bread and sprinkled with cocoa or sugar.

Ricotta is a soft cheese of Italian origin, similar to cottage cheese, made from the whey left when other cow's milk cheeses are produced. It contains from zero to 10% fat. It is white or ivory in colour and creamy in texture, with a small grain and mellow, sometimes slightly tart, flavour. Ricotta is an important ingredient in many pasta dishes and desserts.

Soft Cheeses

Soft cheeses are characterized by their bloomy rinds and creamy centres. They are among the most delicious and popular of cheeses. They ripen quickly and are at their peak for only a few days, sometimes less. Canadian soft cheeses are not cooked or pressed. Moisture content ranges from 50% to 60%.

Bel paese is a 20th-century Italian creation made from cow's milk and containing approximately 50% fat. It is mild and creamy with a fruity flavour. The inside is yellowish and the outside is brown or grey. Bel paese is excellent for snacking and melts easily.

Brie is a surface-ripened cheese of French origin made with whole cow's milk and containing a minimum of 23% milkfat. Brie is made in round, flat disks weighing 1 or 2 kg (2 or 4 lb.); it is coated with a bloomy white rind. At the peak of ripeness it is creamy and rich, with a texture that oozes. Some Bries are called double or triple cream. Selecting a properly ripened Brie is a matter of judgment and experience. Select a cheese that is bulging a bit inside its rind; there should be just the beginning of brown colouring on the rind. If underripe, Brie will be bland with a hard, chalky core. Once the cheese is cut it will not ripen any further. If overripe, Brie will have a brownish rind that may be gummy or sagging and will smell strongly of ammonia. The rind is edible. The classic after-dinner cheese, Brie is also used in soups, sauces and hors d'oeuvre. Canada produces many fine Bries, particularly in Alberta and Quebec.

Brie

Boursin is a triple-cream cow's milk cheese from France containing approximately 75% fat. Boursin is usually flavoured with peppers, herbs or garlic. It is rindless, with a smooth, creamy texture, and is packed in small, foil-wrapped cylinders. Boursin is a good breakfast cheese and a welcome addition to any cheese board. It is also a popular filling for baked chicken.

Camembert is a surface-ripened cheese originating in France and containing a minimum of 22% fat. Camembert is firmer than Brie, but milder. It is shaped in small round or oval disks and is coated with a white bloomy rind. Selecting a properly ripened Camembert is similar to selecting a Brie, but Camembert will become overripe and ammoniated even more quickly than Brie. Camembert is an excellent dessert or after-dinner cheese and goes particularly well with fruit. Like Brie, double and triple cream varieties, as well as blue-veined varieties, are available.

Semi-soft Cheeses

This large category is separated into groups based on the ripening method. Moisture content ranges between 40% and 60%, while fat content is between 10% and 30%.

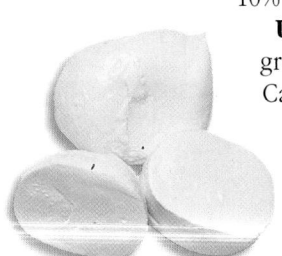

Mozzarella

Unripened: Pasta filata or stretched curd cheeses make up most of this group. Many of these cheeses are of Italian origin but are produced in Canada. Mozzarella is the most prevalent type and is used extensively in pizza and pasta dishes. It has a smooth, elastic character and mild flavour. Fresh mozzarella is known as bocconcini and comes packed in brine. Mild and delicate, it goes well with ripe tomatoes, virgin olive oil and a little fresh basil. Scamorza, Trecce and Fior di Latte are other types; some of these unripened cheeses are smoked or aged for flavour.

Interior Ripened: These cheeses have usually been pressed, cooked and ripened. The rind may be washed if it is firm enough as it forms. Most of these cheeses are mild and supple in texture. Havarti, with its small holes and mild flavour, may be enhanced with spices. Danish in origin, it has a creamy texture. Monterey Jack is a widely used variety that originated in the United States. It comes in blocks and is mild on its own, but it is often flavoured with chiles and other seasonings. Saint Paulin and Munster are two other interior-ripened cheeses.

Oka

Surface Ripened: These cheeses ripen from the surface to the centre. They are turned, washed and kept in cold rooms. Some have a pungent smell and flavour. Oka, Canada's most famous and true cheese, is of this type. Oka has its origins with Trappist monks in France who produced Port Salut. The conditions in Quebec produced Oka instead. Only in recent years has the original production facility become commercial. The pale yellow to red rind containing a pale yellow interior has delighted connoisseurs the world over with its mellow, buttery, nutty flavour.

Feta

Feta is a semi-soft Greek or Italian product originally made from sheep's and/or goat's milk. Cow's milk fetas are common, too. It is a white, flaky cheese that is pickled (but not ripened) and stored in brine water, giving it a shelf life of four to six weeks. Its flavour becomes sharper and saltier with age. Feta is good for snacks and salads and melts easily for sauces and fillings. Limburger and Stella Alpine are other examples of this cheese type.

Havarti is a cow's milk monastery-style cheese from Denmark containing 45% to 60% fat. Havarti is also known as **Danish Tilsit** or by the brand name **Dofino**. Pale yellow with many small, irregular holes, it is sold in small rounds, rectangular blocks or loaves. Havarti has a mild flavour and creamy texture. It is often flavoured with dill, caraway seeds or peppers. Havarti is very popular for snacking and on sandwiches.

Port Salut is a monastery cow's milk product from France containing approximately 50% fat. Port Salut is smooth, rich and savoury. It is shaped in thick wheels with a dense, pale yellow interior and an edible, bright orange rind. The Danish version is known as **Esrom**. Canada's most famous cheese, Oka, has its origins in Port Salut. Oka is produced in Quebec and has a worldwide reputation.

Havarti

Firm Cheeses

Firm cheeses are the largest Canadian cheese category. Some are close-textured and crumbly, like cheddar; others are dense, holey cheeses like Swiss Emmenthaler. All firm cheeses are interior ripened. Their moisture content ranges from 35% to 52%. Interior ripening is a common characteristic.

Cheddars are produced in both North America and Great Britain. Cheddar is a cow's milk cheese made primarily in the northern United States and most of Canada, containing a minimum of 31% fat. The best cheddars are non-coloured and aged two to five years. Hand-turned cheddars are now a rarity. Cheddars have a dense, crumbly texture and may be white or coloured orange with vegetable dyes, depending on local preference. "Marble" cheddar is popular in western Canada. Flavours range from mild to very sharp, depending on the age of the cheese. **Colby** and **brick** are similar to cheddars. Cheddars are sold in a variety of shapes and sizes, often coated with wax. Good-quality cheddars are welcome additions to any cheese board, while those of lesser quality are better reserved for cooking and sandwiches. **English cheddar** is a variety of cow's milk cheese produced in Great Britain containing approximately 45% fat. Perhaps the most imitated cheese in the world, true English cheddar is available in Canada. Canadian cheese manufacturers have enhanced the original English recipe and Canadian cheddar has become famous the world over. It is a moist yet sliceable cheese, aged at least six months. It is a most versatile cheese, ideal for any time of day and with nearly any meal. It is used in numerous ways for both desserts and in cooking.

Cheddar—Wisconsin Sharp, Vermont Cabot, Canadian Black Diamond

Emmenthaler (Swiss) is a cow's milk cheese of Swiss origin containing approximately 45% fat. Emmenthaler is the original Swiss cheese; it accounts for over half of Switzerland's cheese production. It is mellow, rich and nutty with a natural rind and a light yellow interior full of large holes. It is ripened in three stages with the aid of fermenting bacteria. The holes or "eyes" are caused by CO_2 gases expanding inside the cheese during fermentation. Authentic Emmenthaler is sold in 90-kg (200-lb.) wheels with the word "Switzerland" stamped on the rind like the spokes of a wheel. Emmenthaler is popular for sandwiches,

Emmenthaler (Swiss)

snacks and after dinner with fruit and nuts. **Gruyère** is used for **fondue** and quiche.

Gouda is a Dutch cheese containing approximately 48% fat. Gouda is sold in various-sized wheels covered with red or yellow wax. The cheese is yellow with a few small holes and a mild, buttery flavour. Gouda may be sold soon after production or it may be aged for several months, resulting in a firmer, more flavourful cheese. Gouda is widely popular for snacking.

Fontina is a cow's milk cheese from Italy's Piedmont region containing approximately 45% fat. The original, known as **fontina Val D'Aosta**, has a dark gold, crusty rind; the pale gold, dense interior has a few small holes. It is nutty and rich. The original must have a purple trademark stamped on the rind. Other fontinas (known as **fontal** or **fontinella**) are produced in Denmark, France, Sweden, North America and other regions of Italy. They tend to be softer, with less depth of flavour, and may have a rubbery texture. Fontina is a good after-dinner cheese; it also works well as a stuffing ingredient.

Jarlsberg is a Swiss-type cow's milk cheese from Norway containing approximately 45% fat. Jarlsberg closely resembles Swiss Emmenthaler in both taste and appearance. It is mild with a delicate, sweet taste and large holes. Jarlsberg has a pale yellow interior; it is coated with yellow wax and sold in huge wheels. It has a long shelf life and is popular for sandwiches, snacks and in cooking.

Other Canadian-produced cheeses in this category include Camosun, Edam, Fruilano, New Bra and Saint André.

Hard Cheeses

Hard cheeses are not simply cheeses that have been allowed to dry out. Rather, they are carefully aged for extended periods of time and have a moisture content from 5% to 30%. Hard cheeses are most often used for grating; the best flavour will come from cheeses grated as needed. Even the finest hard cheeses begin to lose their flavour within hours of grating. The most famous and popular of the hard cheeses are those from Italy, where they are known as *grana*. Hard cheeses can be served as a table cheese or garnish.

Asiago is a cow's milk cheese containing approximately 30% fat. After only one year of aging, Asiago is sharp and nutty with a cheddarlike texture. If aged for two years or more, Asiago becomes dry, brittle and suitable for grating. Either version should be an even white to pale yellow in colour with no dark spots, cracks or strong aromas. It is sold in small wheels and keeps for long periods if well wrapped. Asiago melts easily and is often used in cooking.

Asiago

Parmigiano-Reggiano (Parmesan) is a cow's milk cheese made exclusively in the region near Parma, Italy, containing from 32% to 35% fat. Parmigiano-Reggiano is one of the world's oldest and most widely copied cheeses. Used primarily for grating and cooking, it is rich, spicy and sharp with a golden interior and a hard oily rind. It should not be overly salty or bitter. Reggiano, as it is known, is produced only from mid-April to mid-November. It is shaped into huge wheels of about 36 kg (80 lb.) each, with the name stencilled repeatedly around the rind. Parmesan is produced in the United States, Argentina and elsewhere, but none can match the distinctive flavour of freshly grated Reggiano. Domestically produced Parmesan is widely available in Canada, grated, shredded or in block form. Premium products are now on the market.

Parmigiano-Reggiano (Parmesan)

Pecorino Romano is a sheep's milk cheese from central and southern Italy containing approximately 35%

fat. Romano is very brittle and sharper than other grating cheeses, with a "sheepy" tang. Its light, grainy interior is whiter than Parmesan or Asiago. It is packed in large cylinders with a yellow rind. Romano is often substituted for, or combined with, Parmesan in cooking but it is also good eaten with olives, sausages and red wine.

Provolone is a cow's milk cheese originating in southern Italy containing a minimum of 24% fat. Provolone *dolce*, aged only two months, is mild, with a smooth texture. Provolone *piccante*, aged up to six months, is stronger, with a white-yellow fibrous interior. Smoked provolone is also popular, especially for snacking. Provolone is shaped in various ways, from huge salamis to plump spheres to tiny piglets shaped by hand. It is excellent in sandwiches and for cooking, and is often used for melting and in pizza and pasta dishes.

Other Types of Cheeses

Gorgonzola is a blue-veined cow's milk cheese from Italy containing 48% fat. Gorgonzola has a white or ivory interior with bluish-green veins. It is creamier than Stilton or Roquefort, with a somewhat more pungent, spicy, earthy flavour. White Gorgonzola has no veins but a similar flavour, while aged Gorgonzola is drier and crumbly with a very strong, sharp flavour. The milder Gorgonzolas are excellent with fresh peaches or pears or crumbled in a salad. Gorgonzola is also used in sauces and in the *torta con basilico*, a cake-like cheese loaf composed of layers of cheese, fresh basil and pine nuts.

Gorgonzola

Roquefort is a blue-veined sheep's milk cheese from France containing approximately 45% fat. One of the oldest cheeses, Roquefort is intensely pungent with a rich, salty flavour and strong aroma. It is a white paste with veins of blue mould and a thin natural rind shaped into thick, foil-wrapped cylinders. Roquefort is always aged for at least three months in the limestone caves of Mount Combalou. Since 1926 no producer outside this region can legally use the name Roquefort or even "Roquefort-style." Roquefort is an excellent choice for serving before or after dinner and is, of course, essential for Roquefort dressing. Ermite is an excellent Canadian cheese produced in the Roquefort style.

Stilton is a blue-veined cow's milk cheese from Great Britain containing 45% fat. Stilton is one of the oldest and grandest cheeses in the world. It has a white or pale yellow interior with evenly spaced blue veins. Stilton's distinctive flavour is pungent, rich and tangy, combining the best of blues and cheddars. It is aged in cool ripening rooms for four to six months to develop the blue veining; it is then sold in tall cylinders with a crusty, edible rind. Stilton should be wrapped in a cloth dampened with salt water and stored at cool temperatures, but not refrigerated. It is best served alone, with plain crackers, dried fruit or vintage port.

Stilton

Goat's Milk Cheeses

Because of their increasing popularity, cheeses made from goat's milk deserve a few words of their own. Although goats give less milk than cows, their milk is higher in fat and protein and richer and more concentrated in flavour. Cheeses made with goat's milk have a sharp, tangy flavour. They may range in texture from very soft and fresh to very hard, depending on age.

Chèvre (French for "goat") refers to small, soft, creamy cheeses produced in a variety of shapes: cones, disks, pyramids or logs. Chèvres are often coated with ash, herbs or seasonings. They are excellent for cooking and complement a wide variety of flavours. Unfortunately, they have a short shelf life, perhaps only two weeks. Cheese labelled *pure chèvre* must be made with 100% goat's milk, while others may be a mixture of cow's and goat's milk.

Goat's milk cheeses

Canada's Natricia, Woolwich and Tournevent dairies produce excellent chèvre cheeses. French brands include Bucheron, Chevrotin and Montrachet.

Processed Cheeses

Pasteurized processed cheese is made from a combination of aged and green cheeses that are mixed with emulsifiers and flavourings, pasteurized and poured into moulds to solidify. Manufacturers can thus produce cheeses with consistent textures and flavours. Processed cheeses are commonly used in food service operations because they are less expensive than natural cheeses. And, because they will not age or ripen, their shelf life is greatly extended. Nutritionally, processed cheeses generally contain less protein, calcium and vitamin A and more sodium than natural cheeses.

Processed cheese food contains less natural cheese (but at least 51% by weight) and more moisture than regular processed cheese. Often vegetable oils and milk solids are added, making cheese food soft and spreadable.

Cold pack is a processed cheese product made primarily of old cheddar; it is not heated in processing. Sugars are usually added to mellow the flavour.

Imitation cheese is usually manufactured with dairy byproducts and soy products mixed with emulsifiers, colourings and flavouring agents and enzymes. Although considerably less expensive than natural cheese, imitation cheese tends to be dense and rubbery, with little flavour other than that of salt.

Serving Cheeses

Cheeses may be served at any time of day. In Northern Europe they are common for breakfast; in Great Britain they are a staple at lunch. Cheeses are widely used for sandwiches, snacks and cooking in Canada, and they are often served following the entree or instead of dessert at formal dinners.

◆◆◆

CANADIAN CHEESE HISTORY

Some of the milk from cows arriving with Cartier in 1541 was likely made into cheese. The first North American dairy farm was the Champlain farm at Cap Tourmente in 1629. Nova Scotia's export of six tons of cheese in 1764 was the first documented production.

Originally produced from ewe's milk and coloured with marigolds, cheddar is a widely produced cheese in Canada, although it is made from cow's milk now. Black Diamond cheddar was the result of the wax coating protecting the cheese reacting with the mould it was transported in and turning black.

Some of Canada's finest cheeses are based on monastery production methods the monks brought with them from Europe. Oka is the most famous and is regarded as a true Canadian cheese.

Fine cheeses are now produced throughout Canada. They include Sir Laurier d'Artabaska, Miranda, Clos St. Ambroise, Migneron, Laracam, Cantonnier and Bénédictin, to name a few.

Cheese board set for service

◆◆◆

WINE AND CHEESE: CLASSIC COMBINATIONS

Some cheeses are delicious with beers or ales. Others are best with strong coffee or apple cider, and nothing accompanies a cheddar cheese sandwich as well as ice-cold milk. For most cheeses, however, the ultimate partner is wine. Wine and cheese bring out the best in each other. The proteins and fats in cheeses take the edge off harsh or acidic wines, while the tannins and acids in wines bring out the creamy richness of cheeses.

Because of their natural affinity, certain pairings are universal favourites: Stilton with port, Camembert with Bordeaux, Roquefort with Sauternes and English cheddar with Burgundy. Although taste preferences are an individual matter, cheese–wine marriages follow two schools of thought: Either pair likes or pair opposites.

Pairing like with like is simple: Cheeses are often best served with wines produced in the same region. For example, a white burgundy would be an excellent choice for cheeses from Burgundy such as Montrachet; and goat cheeses from the Rhone Valley go well with wines of that region. Hearty Italian wines such as Chianti, Barolo and Valpolicella are delicious with Italian cheese—Gorgonzola, provolone, taleggio. And a dry, aged Monterey Jack is perhaps the perfect mate for California zinfandel.

Opposites do attract, however. Sweet wines such as Sauternes and Gewürztraminer go well with sharp, tangy blues, especially Roquefort. And light, sparkling wines such as Champagne or Spanish Cava are a nice complement to rich, creamy cheeses such as Brie and Camembert.

The flavour and texture of natural cheeses are best at room temperature. So, except for fresh cheeses, all cheeses should be removed from the refrigerator 30 minutes to an hour before service to allow them to come to room temperature. Fresh cheeses, such as cottage and cream, should be eaten chilled.

Any selection of fine cheeses should include a variety of flavours and textures: from mild to sharp, from soft to creamy to firm. Use a variety of shapes and colours for visual appeal. Do not precut the cheeses as this only causes them to become dry. Provide an adequate supply of serving knives so that stronger-flavoured cheeses will not combine with and overpower milder ones. Fine cheeses are best appreciated with plain bread and crackers, as salted or seasoned crackers can mask the cheese's flavour. Noncitrus fruits are also a nice accompaniment. Carefully pairing cheeses and wines can lead to a wonderful taste experience.

Storage

Most cheeses are best kept refrigerated, well wrapped to keep odours out and moisture in. Firm and hard cheeses can be kept for several weeks; fresh cheeses will spoil in 7 to 10 days because of their high moisture content. Some cheeses that have become hard or dry may still be grated for cooking or baking. Freezing is possible but not recommended because it changes the cheese's texture, making it mealy or tough. Shock-freezing produces the best results due to the small size of the moisture crystals.

CONCLUSION

Eggs and dairy products are versatile foods used throughout the kitchen. They may be served as is or incorporated into many dishes, including soups, sauces, entrees, breads and desserts. Fine natural cheeses are useful in prepared dishes but are most important for buffets, as the cheese course during a meal or whenever cheese is the primary ingredient or dominant flavour. Eggs and dairy products spoil easily and must be handled and stored properly.

◆◆◆

COOKING WITH CHEESE

The Dairy Bureau of Canada promotes a concept of Evolutive Cuisine. It allows the chef creativity in blending techniques and nontraditional ingredients with original presentations and decorating practices. The objective is to preserve and enhance flavours while maintaining nutritional soundness. Effectively cooking with cheese is a part of this concept.

We need to remember that cheese is a living organism. Each type of cheese has characteristics that must be considered. These include fat content, moisture content, pH level, buffering capacity, thickening power and the reactions of proteins and minerals to other ingredients or heat. When creating or adapting a recipe, all of these factors must be considered. For example, if low-fat mascarpone is used to make a butterscotch sauce, you must add more fat (butter) for the sauce to have the right characteristics. To use a snow goat cheese to liaise a jus-based sauce, the alcohol in the wine must be evaporated and the reduction removed from the fire before the room temperature cheese is whisked in. Whipping cream may have to be added to a purée soup to buffer the liquid to achieve successful incorporation of the cheese.

For detailed information, *Fundamentals of Canadian Cheeses and Their Use in Fine Cuisine* is an excellent resource.

$\mathcal{Q}$UESTIONS FOR DISCUSSION

1. Explain the criteria used in grading eggs. Why might you prefer to use eggs with lower grades?
2. What are the differences between egg products and egg substitutes?
3. What is milkfat and how is it used in classifying milk-based products?
4. If a recipe calls for whole milk and you have only dried milk, what do you do? Explain your answer.
5. What is clarified butter and when is it used? Describe the procedure for clarifying butter.
6. The texture and shelf life of cheese depend on what two factors?
7. Cheeses are categorized as fresh, soft, semi-soft, firm and hard. Give two examples of each and explain how they are generally used.

$\mathcal{W}$EBLINKS

Canadian Egg Marketing Agency
  www.canadaegg.ca
Dairy Farmers of Canada
  www.dairyfarmers.org
Canadian Food Inspection Agency/Agence canadienne
  d'inspection des aliments
  www.cfia-acia.agr.ca
Egg Nutrition Center
  www.enc-online.org
CheeseNet
  cheesenet.wgx.com

PART THREE
COOKING

Learning to cook is not simply a matter of following recipes. You must understand and appreciate why and how chemical and physical reactions occur in foods, why foods respond to heat the way they do and which foods respond best to particular cooking techniques. You must also be able to identify the foods being used.

The following chapters present this information; each chapter is devoted to a specific category of food. A chapter on deep-fat frying is included in this section because the principles and techniques discussed there apply to a wide variety of foods. A chapter on the specialized subject of charcuterie is also included, as its study forms part of any well-rounded culinary education.

CHAPTER 9
PRINCIPLES OF COOKING

LEARNING OUTCOMES

After studying this chapter you will be able to:

◆ explain how heat is transferred to foods through conduction, convection and radiation
◆ recognize how heat affects foods
◆ identify the procedures for using various cooking methods

ooking can be defined as the transfer of energy from a heat source to a food. This energy alters the food's molecular structure, changing its texture, flavour, aroma and appearance. But why is food cooked at all? The obvious answer is that cooking makes food taste better. Cooking also destroys undesirable microorganisms and makes foods easier to ingest and digest.

To cook foods successfully, you must first understand the ways in which heat is transferred: conduction, convection and radiation. You should also understand what the application of heat does to the proteins, sugars, starches, water and fats in foods.

Perhaps most importantly, you must understand the cooking methods used to transfer heat: broiling, grilling, roasting and baking, sautéing, pan-frying, deep-fat frying, poaching, simmering, boiling, steaming, braising and stewing. Each method is used for many types of food, so you will be applying one or more of them every time you cook. The cooking method you select gives the finished product a specific texture, appearance, aroma and flavour. A thorough understanding of the basic procedures involved in each cooking method helps you produce consistent, high-quality products.

This chapter discusses each of the cooking methods in general terms without applying them to any specific food. These methods will be discussed again in more detail as they are used in the following chapters.

HEAT TRANSFER

Heat is a type of energy. When a substance gets hot, its molecules have absorbed energy, which causes the molecules to vibrate rapidly, expand and bounce off one another. As the molecules move, they collide with nearby molecules, causing a transfer of heat energy. The faster the molecules within a substance move, the higher its temperature. This is true whether the substance is air, water, an aluminum pot or a sirloin steak.

Heat energy may be transferred *to* foods via conduction, convection or radiation. See Figure 9.1. Heat then travels *through* foods by conduction. Only heat is transferred—cold is simply the absence of heat, so cold cannot be transferred from one substance to another.

Conduction

Conduction is the most straightforward means of heat transfer. It is simply the movement of heat from one item to another through direct contact. For example, when the flame of a gas burner touches the bottom of a sauté pan, heat is conducted to the pan. The metal of the pan then conducts heat to the surface of the food lying in that pan.

Some materials conduct heat better than others. Water is a better conductor of heat than air. This explains why a potato cooks much faster in boiling water than in an oven, and why you cannot place your hand in boiling water at a

Conduction

Convection

Infrared Radiation

Microwave Radiation

FIGURE 9.1 *Arrows indicate heat patterns during conduction, convection and radiation.*

temperature of 100°C (212°F), but can place your hand, at least very briefly, into a 200°C (400°F) oven. Generally, metals are good conductors (as discussed in Chapter 5, Tools and Equipment, copper and aluminum are the best conductors), while liquids and gases are poor conductors.

Conduction is a relatively slow method of heat transfer because there must be physical contact to transfer energy from one molecule to adjacent molecules. Consider what happens when a metal spoon is placed in a pot of simmering soup. At first the spoon handle remains cool. Gradually, however, heat travels up the handle, making it warmer and warmer, until it becomes too hot to touch.

Conduction is important in all cooking methods because it is responsible for the movement of heat from the surface of a food to its interior. As the molecules near the food's exterior gather energy, they move more and more rapidly. As they move, they conduct heat to the molecules nearby, thus transferring heat *through* the food (from the exterior of the item to the interior).

In conventional heating methods (nonmicrowave), the heat source causes food molecules to react largely from the surface inward, so that layers of molecules heat in succession. This produces a range of temperatures within the food, which means that the outside can brown and form a crust long before the interior is noticeably warmer. That is why a steak can be fully cooked on the outside but still rare on the inside.

Convection

Convection refers to the transfer of heat through a fluid, which may be liquid or gas. Convection is actually a combination of conduction and a mixing in which molecules in a fluid (whether air, water or fat) move from a warmer area to a cooler one. There are two types of convection: natural and mechanical.

Natural convection occurs because of the tendency of warm liquids and gases to rise while cooler ones fall. This causes a constant natural circulation of heat. For example, when a pot of stock is placed over a gas burner, the molecules at the bottom of the pot are warmed. These molecules rise while cooler, heavier molecules sink. Upon reaching the pot's bottom, the cooler molecules are warmed and begin to rise. This ongoing cycle creates currents within the stock, and these currents distribute the heat throughout the stock.

Mechanical convection relies on fans or stirring to circulate heat more quickly and evenly. This explains why foods heat faster and more evenly when stirred. Convection ovens are equipped with fans to increase the circulation of air currents, thus speeding up the cooking process. But even conventional ovens (that is, not convection ovens) rely on the natural circulation patterns of heated air to transfer heat energy to items being baked or roasted.

Radiation

Unlike conduction and convection, **radiation** does not require physical contact between the heat source and the food being cooked. Instead, energy is transferred by waves of heat or light striking the food. Two kinds of radiant heat are used in the kitchen: infrared and microwave.

Infrared cooking uses an electric or ceramic element heated to such a high temperature that it gives off waves of radiant heat that cook the food. Radiant heat waves travel at the speed of light in any direction (unlike convection heat, which only rises) until they are absorbed by a food. Infrared cooking is commonly used with toasters and broilers. The glowing coals of a fire are another example of radiant heat.

Microwave cooking relies on radiation generated by a special oven to penetrate the food, where it agitates water molecules, creating friction and heat. This energy then spreads throughout the food by conduction (and by convection in liquids). Microwave cooking is much faster than other methods because energy penetrates the food up to a depth of several centimetres, setting all water molecules in motion at the same time. Heat is generated quickly and uniformly throughout the food. Microwave cooking does not brown foods, however, and often gives meats a dry, mushy texture, making microwave ovens an unacceptable replacement for traditional ovens.

Because microwave radiation affects only water molecules, a completely waterless material (such as a plate) will not get hot. Any warmth felt in a plate used when microwaving food results from heat being conducted from the food to the plate.

Microwave cooking requires the use of certain types of utensils, usually heat-resistant glass or microwaveable plastic. Even heat-resistant glass can shatter, however, and it is not recommended for professional use. The aluminum utensils most common in professional kitchens cannot be used because metal deflects microwaves and this can damage the oven. Pure stainless steel is microwave safe.

♦♦♦

INDUCTION— THE NEWEST HEAT SOURCE

Induction cooking uses a special induction coil placed below the stove top's surface in combination with specially designed cookware made of cast iron or magnetic stainless steel. The coil generates a magnetic current so that the cookware is heated rapidly with magnetic friction. Heat energy is then transferred from the cookware to the food by conduction. The cooking surface, which is made of a solid ceramic material, remains cool. Only the cookware and its contents get hot.

Induction cooking is a relatively new process, more popular in Europe than North America. However, it is gaining acceptance in professional kitchens because of the speed with which foods can be heated and the ease of cleanup. It is widely used for buffet action stations.

THE EFFECTS OF HEAT

Foods are composed of proteins, carbohydrates (starches and sugars), water and fats, plus small amounts of minerals and vitamins. Changes in shape, texture, colour and flavour of foods may occur when heat is applied to each of these nutrients. By understanding these changes and learning to control them, you will be able to prepare foods with the characteristics desired. Although volumes are written on these subjects, it is sufficient for you to know the following processes as you begin your study of cooking.

Proteins Coagulate

The proper term for the cooking of proteins is **coagulation**. Proteins are large, complex molecules found in every living cell, plant as well as animal. Coagulation refers to the irreversible transformation of proteins from a liquid or semiliquid state to a solid state. As proteins cook they lose moisture, shrink and become firm. Common examples of coagulation are the firming of meat fibres during cooking, egg whites changing from a clear liquid to a white solid when heated and the setting of the structure of wheat proteins (known as gluten) in bread during baking. Most proteins complete coagulation at 71°C to 85°C (160°F–185°F).

Starches Gelatinize

Gelatinization is the proper term for the cooking of starches. Starches are complex carbohydrates present in plants and grains such as potatoes, wheat, rice and corn. When a mixture of starch and liquid is heated, remarkable changes occur. The starch granules absorb water, causing them to swell, soften and clarify slightly. The liquid visibly thickens because of the water being absorbed into the starch granules and the granules themselves swelling to occupy more space.

Gelatinization occurs gradually over a range of temperatures—66°C to 100°C (150°F–212°F)—depending on the type of starch used. Starch gelatinization affects not only sauces or liquids to which starches are added for the express purpose of thickening, but also any mixture of starch and liquid that is heated. For example, the flour (a starch) in cake batter gelatinizes by absorbing the water from eggs, milk or other ingredients as the batter bakes. This causes part of the firming and drying associated with baked goods.

Sugars Caramelize

The process of cooking sugars is properly known as **caramelization**. Sugars are simple carbohydrates used by all plants and animals to store energy. As sugars cook they gradually turn brown and change flavour. Caramelized sugar is used in many sauces, candies and desserts. But caramelized sugar is also partly responsible for the flavour and colour of bread crusts and the browning of meats and vegetables. In fact, it is the process of caramelization that is responsible for most flavours we associate with cooking.

Sucrose (common table sugar) begins to brown at about 170°C (338°F). The naturally occurring sugars in other foods such as maltose, lactose and fructose also caramelize, but at varying temperatures. Because high temperatures are required for browning (i.e., caramelizing), most foods will brown only on the outside and only through the application of dry heat. Because water cannot be heated above 100°C (212°F), foods cooked with moist-heat methods do not get hot enough to caramelize. Foods cooked with dry-heat methods, including those using fats, will reach the high temperatures at which browning occurs.

Water Evaporates

All foods contain some water. Some foods, especially eggs, milk and leafy vegetables, are almost entirely water. Even as much as 75% of raw meat is water.

As the internal temperature of a food increases, water molecules move faster and faster until the water turns to a gas (steam) and vaporizes. This **evaporation** of water is responsible for the drying of foods during cooking.

Fats Melt

Fat is an energy source for the plant or animal in which it is stored. Fats are smooth, greasy substances that do not dissolve in water. Their texture varies from very firm to liquid. Oils are simply fats that remain liquid at room temperature. Fats **melt** when heated; that is, they gradually soften, then liquefy. Fats will not evaporate. Most fats can be heated to very high temperatures without burning, so they can be used as a cooking medium to brown foods.

COOKING METHODS

Foods can be cooked in air, fat, water or steam. These are collectively known as **cooking media**. There are two general types of cooking methods: dry heat and moist heat.

Dry-heat cooking methods are those using air or fat. They are broiling, grilling, roasting and baking, sautéing, pan-frying and deep-fat frying. Foods cooked using dry-heat cooking methods have a rich flavour caused by browning.

Moist-heat cooking methods are those using water or steam. They are poaching, simmering, boiling and steaming. Moist-heat cooking methods are used to emphasize the natural flavours of food.

Other cooking methods employ a combination of dry- and moist-heat cooking methods. The two most significant of these **combination cooking methods** are braising and stewing. See Table 9.1.

TABLE 9.1   COOKING METHODS

Method	Medium	Equipment
Dry-Heat Cooking Methods		
Broiling	Air	Overhead broiler, salamander, rotisserie
Grilling	Air	Grill
Roasting	Air	Oven
Baking	Air	Oven
Sautéing	Fat	Stove
Pan-frying	Fat	Stove, tilt skillet
Deep-fat frying	Fat	Deep-fat fryer
Moist-Heat Cooking Methods		
Poaching	Water or other liquid	Stove, oven, steam-jacketed kettle, tilt skillet
Simmering	Water or other liquid	Stove, steam-jacketed kettle, tilt skillet
Boiling	Water or other liquid	Stove, steam-jacketed kettle, tilt skillet
Steaming	Steam	Stove, convection steamer
Combination Cooking Methods		
Braising	Fat then liquid	Stove (and oven), tilt skillet
Stewing	Fat then liquid	Stove (and oven), tilt skillet

Each of these cooking methods can be applied to a wide variety of foods—meats, fish, vegetables and even pastries. Here, we discuss only the general characteristics of these cooking methods. Detailed procedures for applying these methods to specific foods are found in subsequent chapters.

Dry-Heat Cooking Methods

Cooking by dry heat is the process of applying heat either directly, by subjecting the food to the heat of a flame, or indirectly, by surrounding the food with heated air or heated fat.

Broiling

Broiling uses radiant heat from an overhead source to cook foods. The temperature at the heat source can be as high as 1100°C (2000°F). The food to be broiled is placed on a preheated metal grate. Radiant heat from overhead cooks the food, while the hot grate below marks it with attractive crosshatch marks.

Delicate foods that may be damaged by being placed directly on a metal grate or foods on which crosshatch marks are not desirable may be placed on a preheated heat-proof platter then placed under the broiler. Cooking will take place through indirect heat from the preheated platter as well as from the direct heat from the broiler's overhead heat source.

Grilling

Although similar to broiling, grilling uses a heat source located beneath the cooking surface. Grills may be electric or gas or they can burn wood or charcoal, which will add a smoky flavour to the food. Specific woods such as mesquite, hickory or vine clippings can be used to create special flavours. Grilled foods are often identified by crosshatch markings. The illustrations below show the traditionally accepted procedure for positioning foods on the grill to create these markings.

1. Decide which side of the grilled food will be presented face up to the customer. Place the food on the hot grill with this side facing down. If the item is oblong, place it at a 45-degree angle to the bars on the cooking grate. Cook long enough for the food to develop dark charred lines where it touches the grate.

2. Rotate the food 90 degrees and allow it to cook long enough for the grates to char it to the same extent as in step 1. (See sidebar "Grilled Meats—Theory and Practice.")

3. Turn the food over and finish cooking it. It is usually unnecessary to create the crosshatch markings on the reverse side, as this will not be seen by the customer.

Roasting and Baking

Roasting and baking are the processes of surrounding a food with dry, heated air in a closed environment. The term *roasting* is usually applied to meats and poultry, while *baking* is used when referring to fish, fruits, vegetables, starches, breads or pastry items. Heat is transferred by convection to the food's surface, and then penetrates the food by conduction. The surface dehydrates and the food browns from caramelization, completing the cooking process.

Sautéing

Sautéing is a dry-heat cooking method that uses conduction to transfer heat from a hot sauté pan to food with the aid of a small amount of fat. Heat then penetrates the food through conduction. High temperatures are used to sauté, and the foods are usually cut into small pieces to promote even cooking.

To sauté foods properly, begin by heating a sauté pan on the stove top, then add a small amount of fat. The fat should just cover the bottom of the pan. Heat the fat or oil to the point where it just begins to smoke. The food to be cooked should be as dry as possible when it is added to the pan to promote browning and to prevent excessive spattering. Place the food in the pan in a single layer. The heat should be adjusted so the food cooks thoroughly; it should not be so hot that the outside of the food burns before the inside is cooked. The food should be turned or tossed periodically to develop the proper colour. Larger items should be turned using tongs without piercing the surface. Smaller items are often turned by using the sauteuse's sloped sides to flip them back on top of themselves. When tossing sautéed foods, keep the pan in contact with the heat source as much as possible to prevent it from cooling. Sautéing sometimes includes the preparation of a sauce directly in the pan after the main item has been removed.

Stir-frying is a variation of sautéing. A wok is used instead of a sauté pan; the curved sides and rounded bottom of the wok diffuse heat and facilitate tossing and stirring. Otherwise, stir-frying procedures are the same as those outlined for sautéing and will not be discussed separately here.

Pan-Frying

Pan-frying shares similarities with both sautéing and deep-fat frying. It is a dry-heat cooking method in which heat is transferred by conduction from the pan to the food, using a moderate amount of fat. Heat is also transferred to the food from the hot fat by convection. Foods to be pan-fried are usually coated in breading. This forms a seal that keeps the food moist and prevents the hot fat from penetrating the food, causing it to become greasy.

To pan-fry foods properly, first heat the fat in a sauté pan. Use enough fat so that the food being cooked is immersed one-third to one-half in the fat. The fat should be at a temperature somewhat lower than that used in sautéing; it should not smoke but should be hot enough so that when the food is added it crackles and spatters from the rapid vaporization of moisture. If the temperature is too low, the food will absorb excessive amounts of fat; if it is too high, the food will burn on the outside before the interior is fully cooked. When the food is properly browned on one side, turn it without piercing it, using tongs. Always turn the food away from you to prevent being burned by any fat that may splash. When the food is fully cooked, remove it from the pan, drain it on absorbent paper and serve it immediately.

Deep-Fat Frying

Deep-fat frying is a dry-heat cooking method that uses convection to transfer heat to food submerged in hot fat. Heat then penetrates the food, cooking the interior through conduction. Foods to be deep-fat fried are usually first coated in batter or breading. This preserves moisture and prevents the food from absorbing excessive quantities of fat. Deep-fat fried foods should cook thoroughly while developing an attractive deep golden-brown colour. Foods to be deep-fat fried should be of a size and shape that allows them to float freely in the fat.

Today most deep-fat frying is done in specially designed commercial fryers. These fryers have built-in thermostats, making temperature control more precise. To deep-fat fry food, first heat the fat or oil to temperatures between 160°C and 190°C (325°F and 375°F). Slowly place the food in the fat, where it should float freely. Use tongs to turn it if necessary. When the food is done, remove it from the fat, drain it on absorbent paper and serve it immediately.

Moist-Heat Cooking Methods

Cooking with moist heat is the process of applying heat to food by submerging it directly into a hot liquid or by exposing it to steam. See Table 9.2.

Poaching

Poaching is a moist-heat cooking method that uses convection to transfer heat from a liquid to a food. For poaching, the food is submerged in a liquid held at temperatures between 71°C and 82°C (160°F and 180°F). The surface of the liquid should show only slight movement, but no bubbles.

The flavour of the poaching liquid strongly affects the ultimate flavour of the finished product, so stock, court bouillon or broth is generally used. Poaching is most often associated with foods that do not require lengthy cooking to tenderize them, such as eggs or fish.

To poach food, first bring the poaching liquid to a boil in a suitably shaped cooking vessel. Add the food to be poached either by placing it directly into the liquid or by lowering it into the liquid using a specially designed rack. Adjust the heat as necessary to maintain the desired temperature throughout the cooking process. Do not allow the liquid to reach a boil, as the agitation will cause meats to become tough and stringy and will destroy tender foods such as fresh fruit or fish. For partially submerged foods, a cartouche is used to trap the steam. The liquid used to poach food is sometimes used to make an accompanying sauce.

Simmering

Simmering is another moist-heat cooking method that uses convection to transfer heat from a liquid to a food. For simmering, the food is submerged in a liquid held at temperatures between 85°C and 96°C (185°F and 205°F). Because simmering temperatures are slightly higher than those used for poaching, there should be more action on the liquid's surface, with a few air bubbles breaking through.

As with poaching, the liquid used for simmering has a great effect on the food's flavour. Be sure to use a well-flavoured stock or broth and to add mirepoix, herbs and seasonings as needed. Simmered foods should be moist and very tender.

Boiling

Boiling is another moist-heat cooking method that uses the process of convection to transfer heat from a liquid to a food. Boiling uses large amounts of rapidly bubbling liquid to cook foods. The turbulent waters and the relatively high temperatures cook foods more quickly than do poaching or simmering. Few foods, however, are cooked by true boiling. Most "boiled" meats are actually simmered. Even "hard-boiled" eggs are really only simmered. Starches such as pasta and potatoes are among the only types of food that are truly boiled.

TABLE 9.2   MOIST-HEAT COOKING METHODS

Method	Liquid's Temperature	Liquid's Condition	Uses
Poaching	71°C–82°C 160°F–180°F	Liquid moves slightly but no bubbles	Eggs, fish, fruits
Simmering	85°C–96°C 185°F–205°F	Small bubbles break through the liquid's surface	Meats, stews, chicken
Boiling	100°C (sea level) 212°F	Large bubbles and rapid movement	Vegetables, pasta
Steaming	100°C or higher 212°F or higher	Food is in contact only with the steam generated by a boiling liquid	Vegetables, fish, shellfish

Under normal atmospheric pressure at sea level, water boils at 100°C (212°F). The addition of other ingredients or a change in atmospheric pressure can change the boiling point, however. As altitude increases, the boiling point decreases because of the drop in atmospheric pressure. For every 305 m (1000 feet) above sea level, the boiling point of water drops 1°C (2°F). In the city of Calgary at 1100 m, for example, water boils at 97°C (206°F). Because the boiling temperature is lower it will take longer to cook foods in Calgary than in, for example, Montreal.

The addition of alcohol also lowers the boiling point of water because alcohol boils at about 80°C (175°F). In contrast, the addition of salt, sugar or other substances raises the boiling point slightly. This means that foods cooked in salted water cook faster because the boiling point is one or two degrees higher than normal.

Steaming

Steaming is a moist-heat cooking method that uses the process of convection to transfer heat from the steam to the food being cooked. The food to be steamed is placed in a basket or rack above a boiling liquid. The food should not touch the liquid; it should be positioned so that the steam can circulate around it. A lid should be placed on the steaming pot to trap the steam and also create a slight pressure within the pot, which speeds the cooking process. The liquid used to steam the food is sometimes used to make a sauce served with the item.

Another type of steaming uses a low pressure convection steamer. Convection steamers use steam to cook food very quickly in an enclosed chamber. Convection steamer cooking does not result in a flavoured liquid that can be used to make a sauce. High pressure steamers are also available.

Combination Cooking Methods

Some cooking methods employ both dry-heat and moist-heat cooking techniques. The two principal combination methods are braising and stewing. In both methods the first step is usually to brown the main item using dry heat. The second step is to complete cooking by simmering the food in a liquid. Combination methods are good for less tender but flavourful cuts of meat.

Braising

Braised foods benefit from the best qualities of both dry- and moist-heat cooking methods. Foods to be braised are usually large pieces that are first browned in a small amount of fat at high temperatures. As with sautéing, heat is transferred from the pan to the food mainly by the process of conduction. Vegetables and seasonings are added and enough sauce or liquid is added to come one-third to one-half up the item being cooked. The pan is covered and the heat is reduced. The food is cooked at low heat, using a combination of simmering and steaming to transfer heat from the liquid (conduction) and the air (convection) to the food. This can be done on the stove top or in the oven. A long, slow cooking period helps tenderize the main item. Braised foods are usually served with a sauce made from the cooking liquid.

Stewing

Stewing also uses a combination of dry- and moist-heat cooking methods. Stewing is most often associated with smaller pieces of food that are first cooked either by browning them in a small amount of fat or oil or by **blanching** them in a liquid. Cooking is then finished in a liquid or sauce. Stewed foods have enough liquid added to cover them completely and are simmered at a constant temperature until tender. Cooking time is generally shorter for stewing than for braising because the main items are smaller.

$\mathcal{C}$ONCLUSION

Cooking is the transfer of heat energy to foods by conduction, convection or radiation. Cooking changes the molecular structure of certain nutrients. When heat is applied, proteins coagulate, starches gelatinize, sugars caramelize, fats melt and water evaporates. Foods can be cooked using a variety of methods. Some use dry heat: broiling, grilling, roasting and baking, sautéing, pan-frying and deep-fat frying. Others use moist heat: poaching, simmering, boiling and steaming. Still others use a combination of the two: braising and stewing. The method used affects the texture, appearance and flavour of the cooked foods. You must understand these principles in order to ensure that foods are properly cooked.

$\mathcal{Q}$UESTIONS FOR DISCUSSION

1. Describe the differences between conduction and convection. Identify four cooking methods that rely on both conduction and convection to heat foods. Explain your choices.
2. Identify two cooking methods that rely on infrared heat. What is the principal difference between these methods?
3. At the same temperature, will a food cook faster in a convection oven or a conventional oven? Explain your answer.
4. Describe the process of caramelization and its significance in food preparation. Will a braised food have a caramelized surface? Explain your answer.
5. Describe the process of coagulation and its significance in food preparation. Will a pure fat coagulate if heated? Explain your answer.
6. Describe the process of gelatinization and its significance in food preparation. Will a pure fat gelatinize? Explain your answer.

$\mathcal{W}$EBLINKS

National Food Safety Database: Microwave Cooking Do's and Don'ts
    www.foodsafety.org/nc/nc191.htm

Induction Cooking
    www.ripples.co.uk/induct.html

National Food Safety Database: Commercial Broilers
    www.foodsafety.org/eh/eh399.htm

Food Irradiation
    www.physics.isu.edu/radinf/food.htm

CHAPTER 10
STOCKS AND SAUCES

━━━ ◆◆◆ ━━━
LEARNING OUTCOMES

After studying this chapter you will be able to:

◆ prepare a variety of stocks
◆ caramelize bones and mirepoix
◆ deglaze a pan
◆ reduce a stock to a glaze
◆ cook a roux and incorporate it with a liquid
◆ use a liaison
◆ prepare beurre blanc or beurre rouge
◆ make pan gravy and coulis
◆ prepare salsa and relish
◆ recognize and classify sauces
◆ prepare a variety of classic and modern sauces

A stock *is a flavoured liquid; a good stock is the key to a great soup, sauce or braised dish. The French appropriately call a stock* fond *("base"), as stocks are the basis for many classic and modern dishes.*

A **sauce** *is a thickened liquid used to flavour and enhance other foods. A good sauce adds flavour, moisture, richness and visual appeal. A sauce should complement food; it should never disguise it. A sauce can be hot or cold, sweet or savoury, smooth or chunky.*

Although the thought of preparing stocks and sauces may be intimidating, the procedures are really quite simple. Carefully follow the basic procedures outlined in this chapter, use high-quality ingredients and, with practice and experience, you will soon be producing fine stocks and sauces.

This chapter addresses hot sauces as well as coulis, salsas and relishes. Cold sauces, generally based on mayonnaise, are discussed in Chapter 24, Salads and Salad Dressings; dessert sauces are discussed in Chapter 31, Custards, Creams, Frozen Desserts and Dessert Sauces.

STOCKS

All standard stocks are made from a combination of bones (protein-based stock only), vegetables, seasonings and liquids. Although they are all different, all quality stocks share four common important characteristics regardless of the type:

◆ Body: Body is obtained from the dissolution of certain proteins (collagens) in protein-based stocks. Note: Vegetable stocks do not use bones and, as such, tend to have less body than regular stocks.

◆ Flavour: Flavour results from the use of flavouring vegetables (mirepoix), spices and herbs (sachet) or herbs and vegetables (bouquet garni). The browning of bones and mirepoix for brown stocks also has a beneficial effect on flavour. Note: Burning the bones or mirepoix will impart an unpleasant, bitter flavour.

◆ Clarity: Clarity is achieved by removing impurities (scum) through blanching and refreshing the bones at the beginning of the cooking process and/or continually removing scum from the top of the stock. Adhere to these critical rules for clear stock production:
  1. Use only cold water.
  2. Never cover a stock with a lid during cooking.
  3. Always cook a stock at a simmer, not a boil.
  4. Never stir a stock.

◆ Colour: Many ingredients, such as carrots or leeks, may impart colour in a white stock. Overuse of such ingredients may have a negative impact on the colour of the finished product, making it too green or orange. With a brown stock, colour is achieved through browning bones and mirepoix, plus adding tomoto purée.

There are several types of stocks:

A **white stock** is made by simmering chicken, veal or beef bones in water with vegetables and seasonings. The stock remains relatively colourless during the cooking process, as long as colourless vegetables are used.

A **brown stock** is made from chicken, veal, beef or game bones and vegetables, all of which are browned before being simmered in water with seasonings. The stock has a rich, dark brown colour.

A **fish stock** is made by sweating aromatic vegetables, adding white, lean fish bones, water and seasonings, then simmering for 20 to 45 minutes. When making a **fumet**, dry white wine and sometimes a little lemon juice is used as part of the liquid.

A **court bouillon** is made by simmering vegetables and seasonings in water and an acidic liquid such as vinegar or wine. It is used to poach fish, shellfish or vegetables.

A **vegetable stock**, made without meat products, is made with vegetables or parts of vegetables that do not contain excessive amounts of the following:

✦ starches—they make the stock cloudy

✦ chlorophyll—the green pigment of vegetables turns grey when cooked for a long time

✦ anthocyanins—the water-soluable pigment in vegetables such as beets and red cabbage adds a strong, undesirable colour to the stock

✦ strong flavours (such as cabbage, cauliflower, etc.)

Ingredients

The basic ingredients of most stocks are bones, a vegetable mixture known as a **mirepoix**, seasonings and water.

Bones

Bones are the most important ingredient for producing a good protein-based stock. Bones add flavour, body and colour. Traditionally, the kitchen or butcher shop saved the day's bones to make stock. However, because many meats and poultry items are now purchased previously cut or portioned, food service operations often purchase bones specifically for stock making.

Different bones release their flavour at different rates. Even though the bones are cut into 8- to 10-cm (3- to 4-inch) pieces, a stock made entirely of beef and/or veal bones requires 6 to 8 hours of cooking time, while a stock made entirely from chicken bones requires only 2 to 3 hours.

Beef and Veal Bones

The best bones for beef and veal stock are from younger animals. They contain a higher percentage of **cartilage** and other **connective tissue** than do bones from more mature animals. Connective tissue has a high **collagen** content. Through the cooking process, the collagen is converted into **gelatin** and water. The gelatin adds richness and body to the finished stock.

The best beef and veal bones are knuckles and shank bones, as they have a high collagen content. Beef and veal bones should be cut with a meat saw into small pieces, approximately 8 to 10 cm (3 to 4 inches) long, so that they can release as much flavour and collagen as possible while the stock cooks.

Chicken Bones

The best bones for chicken stock are from the neck and back. If a whole chicken carcass is used, it can be cut up for easier handling.

BROTH

Bones are used to produce stock. When bones are substituted with meat, or bones containing a lot of meat, the resulting liquid is called a broth (see Chapter 11, Soups, for more on broths).

Fish Bones

The best bones for fish stock are from lean fish such as sole, halibut, cod or turbot. Bones from fatty fish (e.g., salmon, tuna and swordfish) do not produce good stock because of their high fat content and distinctive flavours. However, if such bones are used, the resulting stock takes on the name of the fish bones that were used (i.e., salmon stock, tuna stock, etc.). The entire fish carcass can be used, but it should be cut up with a cleaver or heavy knife for easy handling and even extraction of flavours. After cutting, the pieces should be rinsed in cold water to remove blood, loose scales and other impurities.

Other Bones

Lamb, turkey, game and ham bones can also be used for white or brown stocks. While mixing bones is generally acceptable, be careful of blending strongly flavoured bones, such as those from lamb or game, with beef, veal or chicken bones. The former's strong flavours may not be appropriate or desirable in the finished product.

Mirepoix

A French classical flavouring agent made of "flavouring vegetables" is used to lay down a base flavour in stocks, soups, sauces, stews, braised dishes and pot roasts. The original mirepoix was composed of carrots, onions, celery, lardons, sprig of thyme and bay leaves. For dietary reasons, many chefs often omit the lardons.

In many cases the mirepoix is removed before finishing or is puréed and mixed into the final product—for example, with puréed soups. For these reasons mirepoix does not have to be a precise cut. The length of cooking time dictates the size of the cut. Lengthy cooking requires large cuts while shorter times demand smaller cuts. The usual ratio is 2 parts onion to 1 part each of celery and carrot. See Figure 10.1. To introduce colour and flavour, the mirepoix is browned either by sautéing or roasting it in the oven. The dry heat caramelizes the carbohydrates in the vegetables. For a white finished product, a white mirepoix is used, made up of rough-cut onion, celery, white of leek and mushrooms.

FIGURE 10.1   *Mirepoix Ingredients*

Flavouring Vegetables

Not all vegetables are suitable for laying a foundation of flavour, for some have overpowering flavours, such as turnip, fennel, peppers, etc. Others will impart a bitter flavour, like cabbage, and some will affect colour—beets, for example. Certain root vegetables, such as potatoes, will release starch, which clouds the final product. The following vegetables are suitable to use as flavouring vegetables: carrots, celery, celeriac, mushrooms, garlic, leeks, onions, shallots and tomatoes.

Seasonings

Principal stock seasonings are peppercorns, bay leaves, thyme, parsley stems and, optionally, garlic. These seasonings generally can be left whole. A stock is cooked long enough for all their flavours to be extracted so there is no reason to chop or grind them. Seasonings generally are added to the stock at the start of cooking. Some chefs do not add seasonings to beef or veal stock until midway through the cooking process, however, because of the extended cooking times. Seasonings can be added as a spice bag (sachet d'épices) or a bouquet garni.

Salt, an otherwise important seasoning, is not added to stock. Because a stock has a variety of uses, it is impossible for the chef to know how much salt to add when preparing it. If, for example, the stock was seasoned to taste with salt, the chef could not reduce it later; salt is not lost through reduction and the concentrated product would taste too salty. Similarly, seasoning the stock to taste with salt could prevent the chef from adding other ingredients that are high in salt when finishing a recipe. Unlike many seasonings whose flavours must be incorporated into a product through lengthy cooking periods, salt can be added at any time during the cooking process with the same effect.

Principles of Stock Making

The following principles apply to all stocks. You should follow them in order to achieve the highest quality stock possible. See Figure 10.2.

A. Start the Stock in Cold Water

The ingredients should always be covered with cold water. When bones are covered with cold water, impurities are drawn out and dissolve. As the water heats, the impurities coagulate and rise to the surface, where they can be removed easily by skimming. If the bones were covered with hot water, the impurities would coagulate more quickly and remain dispersed in the stock without rising to the top, making the stock cloudy.

If the water level falls below the bones during cooking, add water to cover them. Flavour and gelatin cannot be extracted from bones that are not under water, and bones exposed to the air will darken and discolour a white stock.

B. Simmer the Stock Gently

The stock should be brought to a boil and then reduced to a simmer, a temperature of approximately 85°C (185°F). While simmering, the ingredients release their flavours into the liquid. If kept at a simmer, the liquid will remain clear as it reduces and a stock develops (see sidebar for recommended cooking times).

Never boil a stock for any length of time. Rapid boiling of a stock, even for a few minutes, causes impurities and fats to blend with the liquid, making it cloudy. Never cover a stock with a lid.

C. Skim the Stock Frequently

A stock should be skimmed often to remove the impurities that rise to the surface during cooking. If they are not removed, they may make the stock cloudy.

D. Add Mirepoix, Herbs and Spices

Some chefs add the mirepoix, herbs and spices at the beginning of the cooking process, but, since the main reason for adding mirepoix, herbs and spices is to flavour the stock, many chefs prefer to add all flavourings 2 to 3 hours before the end of the cooking time, or long enough to release the flavours. This method also allows for skimming without removing the flavourings that are floating on the surface of the stock.

E. Strain the Stock Carefully

Once a stock finishes cooking, the liquid must be separated from the bones, vegetables and other solid ingredients. In order to keep the liquid clear, it is important not to disturb the solid ingredients when removing the liquid. This is easily accomplished if the stock is cooked in a steam kettle or stockpot with a spigot at the bottom.

◆◆◆
STANDARD RATIO OF INGREDIENTS

A generally accepted ratio of ingredients for a given amount of water is 50% bones (by weight) and 10% mirepoix (by weight). For example, to produce 20 litres of finished stock, one would need 10 kilograms of bones and 2 kilograms of mirepoix.

Start the stock in cold water.
Simmer the stock gently.
Skim the stock frequently.
Add mirepoix, herbs and spices.
Strain the stock carefully.
Cool the stock quickly.
Store the stock properly.
Degrease the stock.

FIGURE 10.2 *Principles of Stock Making*

◆◆◆
RECOMMENDED COOKING TIMES

White Stocks
◆ Chicken (poultry): 2–3 hours
◆ Veal, beef: 4–6 hours

Brown Stocks
◆ Chicken (poultry): 2–3 hours
◆ Veal, beef: 4–6 hours

Fish Stocks: 30–40 minutes

Vegetable Stocks: 30–40 minutes

Some chefs still prefer to cook meat stocks longer, particularly if the bone pieces are large.

FIGURE 10.3   *Venting a Stockpot*

If the stock is cooked in a standard stockpot, to strain it:

1. Skim as much fat and as many impurities from the surface as possible before removing the stockpot from the heat. Note: Some chefs prefer to leave some fat in the stock as it rises to the top and solidifies to form a seal when the stock is cooled. It is then easily removed as a solid block before the stock is used (see Figure 10.4).
2. After removing the pot from the heat, carefully ladle the stock from the pot without stirring it.
3. Strain the stock through a conical strainer lined with several layers of cheescloth.

F. Cool the Stock Quickly

Most stocks are prepared in large quantities, cooled and held for later use. Great care must be taken when cooling a stock to prevent food-borne illnesses or souring. A stock can be cooled quickly and safely with the following procedure:

1. Keep the stock in a nonreactive metal container. A plastic container insulates the stock and delays cooling.
2. Vent the stockpot in an empty sink by placing it on blocks or a rack. This allows water to circulate on all sides and below the pot when the sink is filled with water. See Figure 10.3 above.
3. Install an overflow pipe in the drain and fill the sink with cold water or a combination of cold water and ice. Make sure that the weight of the stockpot is adequate to keep it from tipping over.
4. Let cold water run into the sink and drain out the overflow pipe. Stir the stock frequently to facilitate even, quick cooling.

G. Store the Stock Properly

Once the stock is cooled, transfer it to a sanitized covered container (either food-grade plastic or nonreactive metal) and store it in the refrigerator. Stocks can be stored for up to one week under refrigeration or frozen for several months. Refrigerated stocks should be reheated after 4 or 5 days and simmered for 20 minutes. This will extend their shelf life by reducing bacterial counts. Chill quickly before storing again.

H. Degrease the Stock

Degreasing a stock is simple: When a stock is refrigerated, fat rises to its surface, hardens and is easily lifted or scraped away before the stock is reheated. See Figure 10.4.

White Stock

A white stock may be made from beef, veal or chicken bones. The finished stock should have a good flavour, good clarity, high gelatin content and little or no colour. Veal bones are preferred usually, but any combination of beef, veal or chicken bones may be used.

FIGURE 10.4 *Lifting Fat from the Surface of a Cold Stock*

Blanching and Refreshing Bones

Chefs disagree on whether the bones for a white stock should be blanched and refreshed to remove impurities. Some chefs argue that the process keeps the stock as clear and colourless as possible; others argue that blanching and refreshing removes flavour, and advocate the continual removal of impurities from the stock.

Basic Procedure for Blanching and Refreshing Bones

If you choose to blanch the bones:

1. Wash the cut-up bones; place them in a stockpot and cover them with cold water.
2. Bring the water to a boil over high heat.
3. As soon as the water boils, skim the rising impurities. Drain the water from the bones and discard it. Rinse the bones.
4. Refill the pot with cold water and proceed with the stock recipe.

Applying the Basics

RECIPE 10.1

WHITE STOCK

Yield: 10 L (2 gal.)

Bones: veal, chicken or beef	5 kg	10 lb.
Cold water	14 L	3 gal.
Mirepoix	1 kg	2 lb.
Sachet:		
Bay leaves	2	2
Dried thyme	0.25 g	1/2 tsp.
Peppercorns, crushed	0.25 g	1/2 tsp.
Parsley stems	8	8

1. Cut the washed bones into pieces approximately 8–10 cm (3–4 inches) long.
2. Place the bones in a stockpot and cover them with cold water. If blanching, bring the water to a boil, skimming off the scum that rises to the surface. Drain off the water and the impurities. Rinse the bones, then add the 14 L (3 gal.) of cold water and bring to a boil. Reduce to a simmer.
3. If not blanching the bones, bring the cold water to a boil. Reduce to a simmer and skim the scum that forms.
4. Add the mirepoix and sachet to the simmering stock.

RECIPE 10.1

Approximate values per 250 mL serving:

Calories	32
Total fat	1.8 g
Saturated fat	0.6 g
Cholesterol	0.9 mg
Sodium	18 mg
Total carbohydrates	3.8 g
Protein	0.2 g

5. Continue simmering and skimming the stock for 4–6 hours. (If only chicken bones are used, simmer for 2–3 hours.)
6. Strain, cool and refrigerate.

Brown Stock

A brown stock is made from chicken, veal, beef or game bones. The finished stock should have a good flavour, rich dark brown colour and high gelatin content. Many chefs believe that a brown stock made from veal bones is superior.

The primary differences between a brown stock and a white stock are that for a brown stock, the bones and mirepoix are caramelized before being simmered and a tomato product is added. These extra steps provide the finished stock with a rich dark colour and a more intense flavour.

Caramelizing

Caramelization refers to the process of browning the carbohydrates (sugars) and amino acids (present in proteins) found on the surface of most foods. This gives the stock its characteristic flavour and colour. Do not burn the bones or mirepoix, as this will impart a bitter flavour.

Basic Procedure for Caramelizing Bones

For caramelizing, do not wash or blanch the bones, as this retards browning. To caramelize:

1. Place the cut-up bones in a roasting pan one layer deep. It is better to roast several pans of bones than to overfill one pan.
2. Roast the bones in a hot oven (190°C/375°F) until brown. Stirring occasionally, brown the bones thoroughly but do not allow them to burn.
3. Transfer the roasted bones from the pan to the stockpot.

Deglazing the Pan

After the bones are caramelized, the excess fat should be removed and reserved for future use. The caramelized and coagulated proteins remaining in the roasting pan are very flavourful. To utilize them, you **deglaze** the pan.

Basic Procedure for Deglazing the Pan

1. Place the pan on the stove top over medium heat and add enough water to cover the bottom of the pan approximately 1 cm (1/2 inch) deep.
2. Stir and scrape the pan bottom to dissolve and remove all of the caramelized materials while the water heats.
3. Pour the deglazing liquid (also known as the deglazing liquor) over the bones in the stockpot.

Basic Procedure for Caramelizing Mirepoix

1. Add a little of the reserved fat from the roasted bones to the roasting pan after it has been deglazed. (Or use a sautoir large enough to contain all of the mirepoix comfortably.)
2. Sauté the mirepoix, browning all of the vegetables well and evenly without burning them. Alternatively, this may be done in an oven.
3. Add the caramelized mirepoix to the stockpot.

REMOUILLAGE

French for "rewetting," a stock produced by reusing the bones left from making another stock. After draining the original stock from the stockpot, add fresh mirepoix, a new sachet and enough water to cover the bones and mirepoix and a second stock can be made. A remouillage is treated like the original stock; allow it to simmer for 3–4 hours before straining. A remouillage will not be as clear, as flavourful or have as much body as the original stock. It is often used to make braised or stewed products or in place of water when making stocks.

Most any tomato product can be used in a brown stock: fresh tomatoes, canned whole tomatoes, crushed tomatoes, tomato purée or paste. If using a concentrated tomato product such as purée or paste, use approximately half or one-third the amount by weight of fresh or canned tomatoes. The tomato product should be added to the stockpot when the mirepoix is added.

Applying the Basics

RECIPE 10.2

BROWN STOCK

Yield: 10 L (2 gal.)

Bones: veal or beef, cut in 8–10 cm (3–4 in.) pieces	5 kg	10 lb.
Cold water	14 L	3 gal.
Mirepoix	1 kg	2 lb.
Tomato paste	250 mL	8 fl. oz.
Sachet:		
Bay leaves	2	2
Dried thyme	0.25 g	1/2 tsp.
Peppercorns, crushed	0.25 g	1/2 tsp.
Garlic cloves, crushed	10 g	3
Parsley stems	12	12

1. Place the bones in a roasting pan, one layer deep, and brown in a 190°C (375°F) oven. Turn the bones occasionally to brown them evenly.
2. Remove the bones and place them in a stockpot. Pour off the fat from the roasting pan and reserve it.
3. Deglaze the roasting pan with part of the cold water.
4. Add the deglazing liquor and the rest of the cold water to the bones, covering them completely. Bring to a boil and reduce to a simmer.
5. Add a portion of the reserved fat to the roasting pan and sauté the mirepoix until evenly browned. Then add it to the simmering stock.
6. Add the tomato paste and sachet to the stock and continue to simmer for 4–6 hours, skimming as necessary.
7. Strain, cool and refrigerate.

◆◆◆
FRENCH TERMINOLOGY

White Stocks
Chicken: Fond de volaille
Veal: Fond de veau
Beef: Fond de boeuf
Vegetable: Fond de legumes

Brown Stocks
Chicken: Fond de volaille brun
Veal: Fond de veau brun
Beef: Fond de boeuf brun
Game: Fond de gibier

RECIPE 10.2

Approximate values per 250 mL serving:

Calories	36
Total fat	1.8 g
Saturated fat	0.6 g
Cholesterol	0.9 mg
Sodium	52 mg
Total carbohydrates	4.6 g
Protein	0.3 g

1. Caramelize the bones.

2. Deglaze the pan with water.

3. Caramelize the mirepoix.

4. Add the proper amount of water.

Fish Stock and Fish Fumet

A fish stock and fish fumet are similar and can be used interchangeably in most recipes. Both are clear with a pronounced fish flavour and very light body. A fumet, however, is more strongly flavoured and aromatic. An essence results from reducing a fumet by half.

The fish bones and crustacean shells used to make a fish stock or fumet should be washed but never blanched because blanching removes too much flavour. Because of the size and structure of fish bones and crustacean shells, stocks and fumets made from them require much less cooking time than other stocks; 30 to 45 minutes is usually sufficient to extract full flavour. Mirepoix or other vegetables should be cut small so that all of their flavours can be extracted during the shorter cooking time.

The procedure for making a fish stock is very similar to that for making a white stock.

Applying the Basics

RECIPE 10.3

FISH STOCK

Yield: 8 L (2 gal.)

White mirepoix, small dice	300 g	8 oz.
Mushroom trimmings	50 g	2 oz.
Clarified butter	50 g	2 oz.
Fish bones or crustacean shells	4.5 kg	10 lb.
Water	9 L	9 qt.
Sachet:		
Bay leaves	1	1
Dried thyme	0.25 g	1/2 tsp.
Peppercorns, crushed	0.25 g	1/4 tsp.
Parsley stems	6	6

1. Sweat mirepoix and mushrooms in butter for 1 minute.

2. Combine all ingredients except the sachet in a stockpot.

3. Bring to a simmer and skim impurities as necessary.

4. Add the sachet and simmer for 30–45 minutes.

5. Strain, cool and refrigerate.

RECIPE 10.3

Approximate values per 250 mL serving:

Calories	40
Total fat	4 g
Saturated fat	2.1 g
Cholesterol	12 mg
Sodium	166 mg
Total carbohydrates	0.8 g
Protein	0.1 g

A fish stock is sometimes used to make fish fumet; if so, the resulting product is very strongly flavoured. A fish fumet is also flavoured with white wine and lemon juice. When making a fumet, **sweat** the bones and vegetables before adding the cooking liquid and seasonings.

Applying the Basics

FISH FUMET

Yield: 8 L (2 gal.)

Clarified butter	50 g	2 oz.
White mirepoix, small dice	450 g	1 lb.
Parsley stems	12	12
Mushroom trimmings	75 g	3 oz.
Fresh thyme	2 sprigs	2 sprigs
Fish bones	4.5 kg	10 lb.
Dry white wine	750 mL	1-1/4 pint
Lemon juice (optional)	60 mL	2 fl. oz.
Fish stock	8 L	8 qt.
Lemon slices (optional)	2–3	2–3

1. Melt the butter in a stockpot.
2. Add the mirepoix, parsley stems, mushrooms and thyme and sweat 1 minute. Add fish bones. Cover the pot and sweat the bones on low heat. Do not stir.
3. Sprinkle the bones with the white wine and lemon juice (if using).
4. Add the fish stock and lemon slices (if using). Bring to a simmer and cook approximately 30–40 minutes, skimming frequently.
5. Strain, cool and refrigerate.

RECIPE 10.4

Approximate values per 250 mL serving:

Calories	25
Total fat	2.4 g
Saturated fat	1.1 g
Cholesterol	8.1 mg
Sodium	157 mg
Total carbohydrates	0.7 g
Protein	0.1 g

1. Sweat the mirepoix, parsley stems, mushrooms, thyme and fish bones.

2. Add cold stock and simmer.

Vegetable Stock

A good vegetable stock should be clear and light-coloured. Because no animal products are used, it has no gelatin content. A vegetable stock can be used instead of a meat-based stock in most recipes. This substitution is useful when preparing vegetarian dishes or as a lighter, more healthful alternative when preparing sauces and soups. Although many combinations of vegetables can be used for stock making, more variety is not always better. Sometimes a vegetable stock made with one or two vegetables that complement the finished dish particularly well will produce better results than a stock made with too many vegetables.

RECIPE 10.5

Approximate values per 250 mL serving:

Calories	43
Total fat	3.5 g
Saturated fat	0.3 g
Cholesterol	0 mg
Sodium	19 mg
Total carbohydrates	2.5 g
Protein	0.3 g

━━━━ ◆◆◆ ━━━━

COMMERCIAL BASES

Commercially produced flavour (or convenience) bases are widely used in food service operations. They are powdered or dehydrated flavourings added to water to create stocks or, when used in smaller amounts, to enhance the flavour of sauces and soups. Although inferior to well-made stocks, flavour bases do reduce the labour involved in the production of stocks, sauces and soups. Used properly, they also ensure a consistent product. Because bases do not contain gelatin, stocks and sauces made from them do not benefit from reduction.

Bases vary greatly in quality and price. Sodium (salt) is the main ingredient in most bases. Better bases are made primarily of meat, poultry or fish extracts. Combinations of sugars and specific amino acids can be heated to create flavour enhancers and substitutes. To judge the quality of a flavour base, prepare it according to package directions and compare the flavour to that of a well-made stock. Bases can be improved by adding a mirepoix, standard sachet and a few appropriate bones to the mixture, then simmering for one or two hours. It can then be strained, stored and used like a regular stock.

Although convenience bases are widely used in the industry, it is important to remember that only high-quality bases/extracts are an acceptable substitute for well-made stocks..

Applying the Basics

VEGETABLE STOCK

Yield: 4 L (1 gal.)

Vegetable oil	60 mL	2 fl. oz.
Mirepoix, small dice	600 g	1 lb. 4 oz.
Leek, whites and greens, chopped	125 g	4 oz.
Garlic cloves, chopped	4	4
Fennel, small dice	100 g	4 oz.
Tomato, diced	90 g	3 oz.
Water	4.5 L	4-1/2 qt.
Sachet:		
Bay leaf	1	1
Dried thyme	0.25 g	1/2 tsp.
Peppercorns, crushed	0.25 g	1/4 tsp.
Parsley stems	8	8

1. Heat the oil. Add the vegetables and sweat for 10 minutes.

2. Add the water and sachet.

3. Bring the mixture to a boil, reduce to a simmer and cook for 30–40 minutes.

4. Strain, cool and refrigerate.

Court Bouillon

A court bouillon (acidic cooking liquid), while not actually a stock, is prepared in much the same manner as stocks so it is included here. A court bouillon (French for "short broth") is a flavoured liquid, usually water and wine or vinegar, in which vegetables and seasonings have been simmered to impart their flavours and aromas.

Court bouillon is most commonly used to poach foods such as fish and shellfish. Recipes vary depending upon the foods to be poached. Although a court bouillon can be made in advance and refrigerated for later use, its simplicity lends itself to fresh preparation whenever needed.

Applying the Basics

COURT BOUILLON

Yield: 4 L (1 gal.)

Water	4.5 L	5 qt.
White wine vinegar	180 mL	6 fl. oz.
Lemon juice	60 mL	2 fl. oz.
Salt	10 g	1/4 oz.
Mirepoix	700 g	1 lb. 8 oz.
Peppercorns, crushed	15 g	1/2 oz.
Bay leaves	3	3
Dried thyme	0.25 g	1/2 tsp.
Parsley stems	8	8

1. Combine all ingredients and bring to a boil.
2. Reduce to a simmer and cook for 45 minutes.
3. Strain and use immediately or cool and refrigerate.

NOTE: This recipe can be used for poaching almost any fish, but it is particularly well suited to salmon, trout or shellfish. When poaching shellfish, replace the water and vinegar with equal parts white wine and water (nage).

Glaze

A glaze is the reduction and concentration of a stock. Four litres (1 gallon) of stock produces only 250–500 mL (8–16 fl. oz.) of glaze. *Glace de viande* is made from brown stock, reduced until it becomes dark and syrupy. *Glace de volaille* is made from chicken stock and *glace de poisson* from fish stock.

Glazes are added to soups or sauces to increase and intensify flavours. They are also used as a source of intense flavouring for several of the derivative sauces discussed below. In many contemporary kitchens, glazes are used in place of traditional basic sauces such as demi-glace and veloutés.

Basic Procedure for Reducing a Stock to a Glaze

1. Simmer the stock over very low heat. Be careful not to let it burn and skim it often.
2. As it reduces and the volume decreases, transfer the liquid into progressively smaller saucepans. Strain the liquid each time it is transferred into a smaller saucepan.
3. Strain it a final time, cool and refrigerate. A properly made glaze will keep for several months under refrigeration.

See Table 10.1 for troubleshooting tips for stocks.

TABLE 10.1   TROUBLESHOOTING CHART FOR STOCKS

Problem	Reason	Solution
Cloudy	Impurities	Start stock in cold water
	Stock boiled during cooking	Strain through layers of cheesecloth
Lack of flavour	Not cooked long enough	Increase cooking time
	Inadequate seasoning	Add more flavouring ingredients
	Improper ratio of bones to water	Add more bones
		Reduce liquid
Lack of colour	Improperly caramelized bones and mirepoix	Caramelize bones and mirepoix until darker
	Not cooked long enough	Cook longer
Lack of body	Wrong bones used	Use bones with a higher content of connective tissue
	Insufficient reduction	Cook longer
	Improper ratio of bones to water	Add more bones
Too salty	Commercial base used	Change base or make own
	Salt added during cooking	stock; do not salt stock

◆◆◆

BASIC SAUCES

Béchamel

Fish velouté

Chicken velouté

Veal velouté

Espagnole—demi-glace

Tomato sauce

Hollandaise sauce

SAUCES

With a few exceptions, a sauce is a liquid plus thickening agent plus seasonings. Any cook can produce fine sauces by learning to:

1. Make good stocks;
2. Use thickening agents and/or techniques properly to achieve the desired texture, flavour and appearance; and
3. Use seasonings properly to achieve the desired flavours.

Classic hot sauces are divided into two groups: **basic** (mother or leading sauces) (Fr. *sauce mère*) and **derivative** (small or compound sauces). The five classic basic sauces are béchamel, velouté, espagnole (brown), tomato and hollandaise. Except for hollandaise, basic sauces are rarely served as is; more often they are used to create the many derivative sauces.

Not all sauces fall into the traditional classifications, however. Some sauces use purées of fruits or vegetables as their base; they are known as **coulis**. Others, such as **beurre blanc** (French for "white butter") and **beurre rouge** ("red butter"), are based on an acidic reduction in which whole butter is incorporated. **Flavoured butters**, **salsas**, **relishes**, **coulis** and **pan gravy** are also used as sauces in modern food service operations.

Thickening Agents

Although there are exceptions, most sauces are thickened by the gelatinization of starches. As discussed in Chapter 9, Principles of Cooking, gelatinization is the process by which starch granules absorb moisture when placed in a liquid and heated. As the moisture is absorbed, the product thickens. Starches generally used to thicken sauces are flour, cornstarch, arrowroot and modified starches. Gelatinization may sound easy, but it takes practice to produce a good sauce that

+ is clean, free of lumps and other impurities,
+ has a good flavour that is not pasty or floury,
+ has a consistency that will coat the back of a spoon (the French call this *nappé*), has a smooth texture, and
+ will not separate or break when the sauce is held hot or reduced.

Roux

Roux is the traditional means used to thicken sauces. It is a combination of equal parts, by weight, of flour and fat, cooked together to form a paste. Cooking the flour in fat coats the starch granules with the fat and prevents them from lumping together or forming lumps when introduced into a liquid. In some production kitchens, large amounts of roux are prepared and held for use as needed. Smaller operations may make roux as required for each recipe.

There are three types of roux, as shown in Figure 10.5:

1. **White roux**—It is cooked only briefly and should be removed from the heat as soon as it develops a frothy, bubbly appearance. It is used in white sauces, such as béchamel, or in dishes where little or no colour is desired.
2. **Blond roux**—Cooked slightly longer than white roux, blond roux should begin to take on a little colour as the flour caramelizes. It is used in ivory-coloured sauces, such as velouté, or where a richer flavour is desired.

FIGURE 10.5   *White, Blond and Brown Roux*

♦♦♦
A SAUCY HISTORY

The word "sauce" is derived from the Latin word *salus*, meaning "salted." This derivation is appropriate. For millennia, salt has been the basic condiment for enhancing and/or disguising the flavour of many foods. Over the centuries, sauces have also been used for these purposes.

Cooks of ancient Rome flavoured many dishes with *garum*, a golden-coloured sauce made from fermented fish entrails combined with brine, condiments, water and wine or vinegar. They also used a sauce referred to as a "single," made from oil, wine and brine. When boiled with herbs and saffron it became a "double" sauce. To this the Byzantines later added pepper, cloves, cinnamon, cardamom and coriander or spikenard (a fragrant ointment made from grains).

During the Middle Ages chefs (and their employers) were fond of either very spicy or sweet-and-sour sauces. A typical sauce for roasted meat consisted of powdered cinnamon, mustard, red wine and a sweetener such as honey. It was thickened, if at all, with bits of stale or grilled bread. Other sauces were based on verjuice, prepared from the juice of unripe grapes or crabapples. To it were added other fruit juices, honey, flower petals and herbs or spices. Indeed, most medieval sauces were heavily spiced. Perhaps this was done to showcase the host's wealth, perhaps to hide the taste of salt-cured or less-than-fresh meats.

Guillaume Tirel (c. 1312–1395), who called himself **Taillevent**, was the master chef for Charles V of France. Around 1375 Taillevent wrote *Le Viandier*, the oldest-known French cookbook. The cooking style he describes relies heavily on pounding, puréeing and spicing most foods so that the finished dish bears little resemblance in shape, texture or taste to the original ingredients. Included in his methods

for what can only be described as ways of masking poor-quality ingredients are 17 sauces. Among them is a recipe for a *cameline* sauce. It is made from grilled bread soaked in wine; the wine-soaked bread is then drained, squeeze-dried and ground with cinnamon, ginger, pepper, cloves and nutmeg; this mixture is then diluted with vinegar. There is also a recipe for a sauce called *taillemaslée*, made of fried onions, verjuice, vinegar and mustard. (Appropriately, on his grave marker Taillevent is dressed as a sergeant-at-arms whose shield is decorated with three cooking pots.)

Recipes for some sauces of the Renaissance, such as *poivrade* or *Robert*, are recognizable today. Most sauces enjoyed in Renaissance-era Italy and France consisted of some combination of concentrated cooking juices, wines, herbs and spices (especially pepper), sometimes thickened with bread. Sweet, fruit-based sauces were also popular. Most importantly for the development of modern cuisine, however, was the growing use of sauces based on broths

thickened with cream, butter and egg yolks and flavoured with herbs and spices.

Although he died in relative obscurity, many now consider **François Pierre de La Varenne** (1618–1678) to be one of the founding fathers of French cuisine. His treatises, especially *Le Cuisinier français* (1651), detail the early development, methods and manners of French cuisine. His analysis and recipes mark a departure from medieval cookery and a French cuisine heavily influenced by Italian traditions. His writings were uniquely modern in that he included recipes for new foods (especially fruits and vegetables native to the Americas or the Far East) and for indigenous foods (such as saltwater fish) that were gradually becoming more popular. La Varenne is credited with introducing roux as a thickening agent for sauces, especially velouté sauces. He emphasized the importance of properly prepared *fonds* and the reduction of cooking juices to concentrate flavours. He also popularized the use of bouquets garni to flavour stocks and sauces.

Sometime during the early 18th century, the chef to the French Duc de Levis-Mirepoix pioneered the use of onions, celery and carrots to enhance the flavour and aroma of stocks. The mixture, named for the chef's employer, soon became the standard way of enriching stocks. An enriched stock greatly improves the quality of the sauces derived from it.

During the early 19th century, **Antonin Carême** developed the modern system for classifying hundreds of sauces. It is unknown how many sauces Carême actually invented himself, but he wrote treatises containing the theories and recipes for many of the sauces still used today. Carême's extravagant lists of sauces were reduced and simplified by chefs later in the 19th century, most notably by **Auguste Escoffier**.

---

3. **Brown roux**—It is cooked until it develops a darker colour and a nutty aroma and flavour. Brown roux is used in brown sauces and dishes where a dark colour is desired. It is important to remember that cooking a starch before adding a liquid breaks down the starch granules and prevents gelatinization from occurring. Therefore, because brown roux is cooked longer than white roux, more brown roux is required to thicken a given quantity of liquid.

Cook the roux.

Basic Procedure for Making Roux

Whether it will be white, blond or brown, the procedure for making roux is the same:

1. Using a heavy saucepan to prevent scorching, heat the clarified butter or other fat.
2. Add all of the flour and stir to form a paste. Although all-purpose flour can be used, it is better to use cake or pastry flour because it contains a higher percentage of starch. See Table 10.2. Do not use high-gluten flour because of its lower starch content. (Flours are discussed in Chapter 26, Principles of the Bakeshop.)
3. Cook the paste over medium heat until the desired colour is achieved. It should have the consistency of wet cement. Stir the roux often to avoid burning. Burnt roux will not thicken a liquid; it will simply add dark specks and an undesirable flavour.

The temperature and amount of roux being prepared determine the exact length of cooking time. Generally, however, a white roux needs to cook for only a few minutes, long enough to minimize the raw flour taste. Blond roux is cooked longer, until the paste begins to change to a slightly darker colour. Brown roux requires a much longer cooking time to develop its characteristic colour and aroma. A good roux will be stiff, not runny or pourable.

General Rule:

(a)

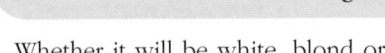

Warm stock

Hot roux

(b)

Warm roux

Hot stock

Incorporating Roux into a Liquid

There are two ways to incorporate roux into a liquid without causing lumps:

1. Warm or cold stock can be added to the hot roux while stirring vigorously with a whisk or wooden spoon.
2. Room-temperature roux can be added to a hot stock while stirring vigorously with a whisk.

When the roux and the liquid are completely incorporated and the sauce begins to boil, it is necessary to cook the sauce for a period of time to remove any raw flour taste that may remain. Most cooks feel a minimum of 20 minutes is necessary.

NOTE: Avoid using aluminum pots when using a whisk to incorporate a roux. Aluminum is a relatively soft metal and the whisk will scrape particles of aluminum into the sauce causing discolouration and off-flavour.

TABLE 10.2   PROPORTIONS OF ROUX TO LIQUID

Flour	+	Butter	=	Roux	+	Liquid	=	Sauce
200 g/6 oz.	+	200 g/6 oz.	=	400 g/12 oz.	+	4 L/1 gal.	=	light
250 g/8 oz.	+	250 g/8 oz.	=	500 g/1 lb.	+	4 L/1 gal.	=	medium
375 g/12 oz.	+	375 g/12 oz.	=	750 g/24 oz.	+	4 L/1 gal.	=	heavy

VARIABLES: The starch content of a flour determines its thickening power. Cake flour, being lowest in protein and highest in starch, has more thickening power than bread flour, which is high in protein and low in starch. In addition, a dark roux has less thickening power than a lighter one, so more will be needed to thicken an equal amount of liquid.

Guidelines for Using Roux

1. Avoid using aluminum pots. The scraping action of the whisk will turn light sauces grey and will impart a metallic flavour.
2. Use sufficiently heavy pots to prevent sauces from scorching or burning during extended cooking times.
3. Avoid extreme temperatures. Roux should be no colder than room temperature so that the fat is not fully solidified. Extremely hot roux is dangerous and can spatter when combined with a liquid. Stocks should not be ice cold when combined with roux; the roux will become very cold and the solidified pieces may be very difficult to work out with a whisk.
4. Avoid overthickening. Roux does not completely thicken a sauce until the sauce is at the simmering point; the thickening action continues for several minutes while the sauce simmers. If a sauce is to cook for a long time, it will also be thickened by reduction.

Cornstarch

Cornstarch, a very fine white powder, is a pure starch derived from various species of corn. It is used widely as a thickening agent for hot and cold sauces and is especially popular in Asian cuisines for thickening sauces and soups. Liquids thickened with cornstarch have a glossy sheen that may or may not be desirable and will gel when cooled.

One unit of cornstarch thickens about twice as much liquid as an equal unit of flour. Sauces thickened with cornstarch are less stable than those thickened with a flour-based agent because cornstarch breaks down (the starch molecules burst) and loses its thickening power after prolonged heating. Products thickened with regular cornstarch should not be reheated or frozen.

Incorporating Cornstarch

Cornstarch must be mixed with a cool liquid before it is introduced into a hot one. The cool liquid separates the granules of starch and allows them to begin absorbing liquid without lumping. A solution of starch and cool liquid is called a **slurry**.

The starch slurry is added to a hot liquid while stirring continuously to prevent lumping. Although the gelatinization point differs depending on the starch used, most starches begin to gelatinize at 60°C (140°F), while complete gelatinization occurs at, or just below, the simmering point. Simmer for 2 to 3 minutes.

Modified Starches

These starches have been treated chemically to modify one or more of their physical or chemical properties. Because these starches are much more stable, especially at high temperatures and at freezing temperatures, they are typically used in commercially processed foods and in foods destined for the freezer. This category also includes natural starches, such as waxy maize (corn) or waxy rice starch, which contain predominently amylopectin.

Pre-gelatinized Starches

These starches have been fully gelatinized and dried by the manufacturer before sale in a powdered form. They can be manufactured from either a native starch or a modified starch. Pre-gelatinized starches develop viscosity when dispersed in cold or warm liquid without the need for further heating, making them good candidates for thickening liquids that may lose colour or flavour during cooking (e.g., fruit juices).

◆◆◆
WHITE WASH

When using flour as a thickener, it can also be mixed with water instead of fat. The resulting solution is known as white wash and it is incorporated into a hot liquid in the same manner as cornstarch. Note that white wash is not a preferred thickening method because it weakens the flavour of the finished product.

◆◆◆
STARCHES

Other starches used to thicken liquids include potato starch, tapioca, rice flour, instant wheat flour and sweet rice. Each imparts a unique flavour and texture to the sauce. Generally, you cannot substitute one starch for another without field-testing first.

Arrowroot is a superior starch for sauce thickening. Unlike most other starches, it cooks out clear and shiny and is fully cooked out below the simmering point.

Waxy maize is a type of cornstarch that can be frozen and reheated without breaking down. It is also more acid-tolerant than regular cornstarch.

Arrowroot

Arrowroot, derived from the roots of several tropical plants, is similar in texture, appearance and thickening power to cornstarch and is used in exactly the same manner. Although it is slightly more expensive, arrowroot does not break down as quickly as cornstarch and it produces a clearer finished product.

Beurre Manié

Beurre manié is a combination of equal amounts, by volume, of flour and soft whole butter. The flour and butter are kneaded together until smooth. The mixture is then formed into pea-sized balls and whisked into a simmering sauce. Beurre manié is used for quick thickening or adjusting at the end of the cooking process. The butter also adds shine and flavour to the sauce as it melts.

Liaison

Unlike the thickeners described above, a liaison does not thicken a sauce through gelatinization. A liaison is a mixture of egg yolks and heavy (whipping) cream, which adds richness and smoothness with minimal thickening. Special care must be taken to prevent the yolks from coagulating when they are added to a hot liquid because this could curdle the sauce. The ratio is generally 3 yolks to 200 mL (6 fl. oz.) cream.

1. Add hot liquid to the egg yolks and cream mixture.

2. Add the tempered egg yolks and cream mixture to the hot liquid.

Basic Procedure for Using a Liaison

1. Whisk together one part egg yolk and three parts 35% whipping cream. Combining the yolk with cream raises the temperature at which the yolk's proteins coagulate, making it easier to incorporate them into a sauce without lumping or curdling.

2. **Temper** the egg yolk mixture by slowly adding a small amount of the hot liquid while stirring continuously.

3. When enough of the hot liquid has been added to the egg yolk mixture to warm it thoroughly, begin adding the warmed egg yolk mixture to the remaining hot liquid. Be sure to stir the mixture carefully to prevent the yolk from overcooking or lumping. Plain egg yolks fully coagulate at temperatures between 65°C and 70°C (149°F and 158°F). Mixing them with cream raises the temperatures at which they coagulate to approximately 82°C–85°C (180°F–185°F). Temperatures over 85°C (185°F) will cause the yolks to curdle. Liaison is preferably added to a sauce (or soup) just before service. However, it is sometimes necessary to hold the item for a while before service. In this case, great care must be taken to hold the sauce above 60°C (140°F) for food safety and sanitation reasons, yet below 85°C (185°F) to prevent curdling.

Finishing Techniques

Reduction

As sauces cook, moisture is released in the form of steam (evaporates). As steam escapes, the remaining ingredients concentrate, thickening the sauce and strengthening the flavours. This process, known as **reduction**, is commonly used to thicken sauces that require no starches or other flavour-altering ingredients. Sauces are often finished by allowing them to reduce until the desired consistency is reached.

Straining

Smoothness is important to the success of most sauces. They can be strained through either a conical strainer lined with several layers of cheesecloth or a fine mesh etâmine. As discussed below, often vegetables, herbs, spices and other seasonings are added to a sauce for flavour. Straining removes these ingredients as well as any undesirable lumps remaining in the sauce after the desired flavour and consistency have been reached.

Monter au Beurre

Monter au beurre is the process of swirling or whisking whole butter into a sauce to give it shine, flavour and richness. Compound or flavoured butters, discussed on page 219, can be used in place of whole butter to add specific flavours. Monter au beurre is widely used to enrich and finish derivative sauces.

TABLE 10.3	SAUCE FAMILIES	
Liquid	Thickener	Basic Sauce
Milk	Roux—white	Béchamel
White stock	Roux	Velouté
Veal stock	— blonde	Veal velouté
Chicken stock	— blonde	Chicken velouté
Fish stock	— white	Fish velouté
Brown stock	Roux—brown	Espagnole (brown sauce)
Tomato	Roux optional	Tomato sauce
Butter	Egg yolks	Hollandaise

Sauce Families

Basic (leading or mother) **sauces** are the foundation for the entire classic repertoire of hot sauces. The five basic sauces—béchamel, velouté, espagnole (also known as brown), tomato and hollandaise—can be seasoned and garnished to create a wide variety of derivative or compound sauces. The five basic sauces are distinguished principally by the liquids and thickeners used to create them. See Table 10.3.

    Derivative (small or compound) **sauces** are grouped together into families based on their basic sauce. Some derivative sauces have a variety of uses; others are traditional accompaniments for specific foods. A derivative sauce may be named for its ingredients, place of origin or creator. Although there are numerous classic derivative sauces, we have included only a few of the more popular ones following each of the basic sauce recipes.

The Béchamel Family

Named for its creator, Louis de Béchamel (1630–1703), steward to Louis XIV of France, béchamel sauce is the easiest basic sauce to prepare. Traditionally it was made by adding heavy cream to a thick veal velouté. Although some chefs still believe a béchamel should contain veal stock, today the sauce is almost always made by thickening scalded milk with a white roux and adding seasonings. It is used for vegetable, egg, gratin dishes and pasta dishes.

QUALITY STANDARD

A properly made béchamel is rich, creamy and absolutely smooth with no hint of graininess. The flavours of the onion and clove used to season it should be apparent but not overwhelm the sauce's clean, milky taste. The sauce should be the colour of heavy cream and have a deep lustre. It should be thick enough to coat foods lightly but should not taste like the roux used to thicken it.

Applying the Basics

BÉCHAMEL

Yield: 4 L (1 gal.)

Oignon piqué (studded onion)	150 g	5-1/2 oz.
Milk	4 L	1 gal.
Flour	250 g	8 oz.
Clarified butter	250 g	8 oz.
Salt and white pepper	TT	TT
Nutmeg	TT	TT

RECIPE 10.7

Approximate values per 100 mL serving:

Calories	142
Total fat	9.7 g
Saturated fat	6 g
Cholesterol	30 mg
Sodium	148 mg
Total carbohydrates	9.6 g
Protein	4.1 g

1. Add the oignon piqué to the milk in a heavy saucepan and simmer for 20 minutes to infuse the flavours.

2. In a separate stainless steel pot, make a white roux with the flour and butter.

3. Remove the oignon piqué from the milk. Gradually add the hot milk to the roux while stirring constantly with a whisk to prevent lumps. Bring to a boil.

4. Reduce the sauce to a simmer, add the seasonings and continue cooking for 20–30 minutes.

5. Strain the sauce through a conical strainer lined with cheesecloth. Melted butter can be carefully ladled over the surface of the sauce to prevent a skin from forming. Hold for service or cool in a water bath.

Béchamel Sauce Derivatives

With a good béchamel, producing the derivative sauces in its family is quite simple. The quantities indicated below are for 1 L (1 quart) of béchamel. The final step for each recipe is to season to taste with salt and pepper.

Anchovy/Anchois   Add to béchamel 25 g (1 oz.) anchovy purée.

Cheddar   Add to béchamel 250 g (8 oz.) grated old or medium cheddar cheese, a dash of Tabasco sauce and 15 mL (1 Tbsp.) dry mustard.

Cream Sauce   Add to béchamel 250–350 mL (8–12 oz.) scalded cream and a few drops of lemon juice.

Egg/aux Oeufs (Écossaise)   Add to béchamel 6 chopped hard-boiled eggs.

Mornay   Add to béchamel 125 g (4 oz.) grated Gruyère cheese and 25 g (1 oz.) grated Parmesan cheese. Thin as desired with scalded cream. Remove the sauce from the heat and swirl in 60 g (2 oz.) whole butter.

Mustard/Moutard   Add to béchamel 15 g (2 Tbsp.) dry mustard or 30 g (1 oz.) Dijon or English mustard.

Nantua   Add to béchamel 125 mL (4 fl. oz.) heavy cream and 175 g (6 oz.) crayfish butter (see page 220). Add paprika to achieve the desired colour. Garnish the finished sauce with diced crayfish meat.

Parsley/Persil   Add to béchamel 30 g (1 oz.) chopped parsley.

Soubise (modern)   Sweat 250 g (8 oz.) diced, blanched onion in 25 g (1 oz.) butter. Add béchamel, 250 mL (8 fl. oz.) cream and 5 g (1 tsp.) sugar and simmer until the onions are fully cooked. Strain through a fine etâmine.

The Velouté Family

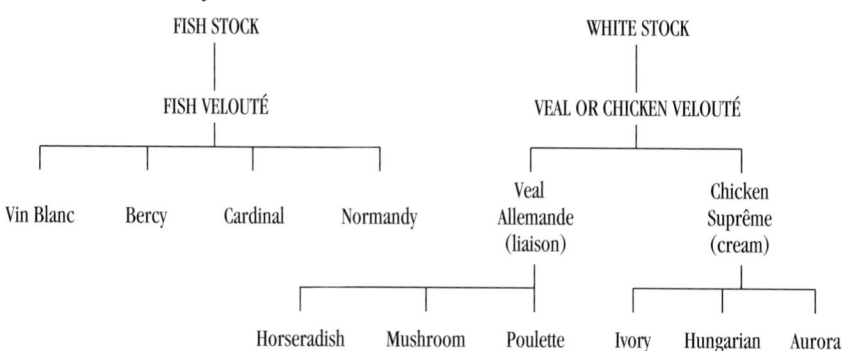

Velouté sauces are made by thickening a white stock or fish stock with roux. The white stock can be made from veal or chicken bones. A fish velouté sauce, made from fish stock, is used to create a few derivative sauces. A velouté sauce made from veal or chicken stock is usually used to make one of two intermediary sauces—allemande and suprême—from which many sauces are derived. Allemande sauce is made by adding lemon juice, veal stock and mushrooms to a veal velouté and finishing it with a liaison. Suprême sauce is made by reducing cream and chicken stock in a chicken velouté. See Table 10.4.

QUALITY STANDARD

A properly made velouté should be rich, smooth and lump-free. If made from chicken or fish stock, it should taste of chicken or fish. A velouté made from veal stock should have a more neutral flavour. The sauce should be ivory-coloured, with a deep lustre. It should be thick enough to cling to foods without tasting like the roux used to thicken it.

Applying the Basics

RECIPE 10.8

VELOUTÉ

Yield: 4 L (1 gal.)

Clarified butter	250 g	8 oz.
Flour	250–300 g	8–10 oz.
Chicken, veal or fish stock, warm	5 L	5 qt.
Salt and white pepper (optional)*	TT	TT

1. Melt the butter in a heavy saucepan. Add the flour and cook to make a blond or white roux.
2. Gradually add the warm stock to the roux, stirring constantly with a whisk or wooden spoon to prevent lumps. Bring to a boil and reduce to a simmer.
3. Simmer and reduce to 4 L (1 gal.), approximately 30 minutes.
4. Strain through a conical strainer lined with cheesecloth.
5. Melted butter may be carefully ladled over the surface of the sauce to prevent a skin from forming. Hold for service or cool in a water bath.

*Seasonings are optional; their use depends upon the seasonings in the stock and the sauce's intended use.

RECIPE 10.8

Approximate values per 100 mL serving:

Calories	109
Total fat	8 g
Saturated fat	4.4 g
Cholesterol	17 mg
Sodium	18 mg
Total carbohydrates	8.5 g
Protein	0.8 g

TABLE 10.4   VELOUTÉ SAUCES

Fish stock	+	Roux	=	Velouté				
Chicken stock	+	Roux	=	Velouté	+	Cream and mushroom	=	Suprême
Chicken stock	+	Roux	=	Velouté	+	Wine and paprika	=	Hongroise
Veal stock	+	Roux	=	Velouté	+	Liaison and lemon and veal stock reduction	=	Allemande

Fish Velouté Sauce Derivatives

A few derivative sauces can be made from fish velouté. The quantities given are for 1 L (1 quart) fish velouté sauce. The final step for each recipe is to season to taste with salt and pepper.

Bercy   Sauté 60 g (2 oz.) finely diced shallots in butter. Then add 250 mL (8 fl. oz.) dry white wine and 250 mL (8 fl. oz.) fish stock. Reduce this mixture by one-third and add the fish velouté and 300 mL (10 fl. oz.) of cream and reduce to 1 L (1 qt.). Finish with 100 g (3 oz.) butter and garnish with 30 g (3 Tbsp.) chopped parsley and 25–50 mL (1–2 fl. oz.) lemon juice.

Cardinal   Add 250 mL (8 fl. oz.) fish fumet to 500 mL (1 pint) fish velouté and 500 mL (1 pint) béchamel. Reduce this mixture by half and add 500 mL (1 pint) heavy cream and a dash of cayenne pepper. Bring to a boil and swirl in 45 g (1-1/2 oz.) lobster butter (see page 220) and 30 mL (1 fl. oz.) brandy. Garnish with chopped lobster coral at service time.

Normandy   Add 125 g (4 oz.) mushroom trimmings, 125 mL (4 fl. oz.) shellfish liquor (oyster, clam, mussel) and 250 mL (8 fl. oz.) fish stock plus 10 mL (2 tsp.) lemon juice to 1 L (1 qt.) fish velouté. Reduce by one-third and finish with a 3–egg yolk and 250-mL (8 fl. oz.) cream liaison. Strain through a fine etâmine.

Applying the Basics

RECIPE 10.9

ALLEMANDE SAUCE

Yield: 1 L. (1 qt.)

Veal velouté	750 mL	24 fl. oz.
Veal stock	750 mL	24 fl. oz.
Mushrooms, chopped	60 g	2 oz.
Peppercorns, crushed	5 g	1 tsp.
Bay leaf	1	1
Salt and cayenne pepper	TT	TT
Lemon juice	30 mL	1 fl. oz.
Cream, 35%	250 mL	8 fl. oz.
Egg yolks	3	3

1. Combine velouté, stock, mushrooms, peppercorns and bay leaf.
2. Simmer to reduce liquid to 1 L (1 qt.).
3. Season with salt, cayenne and lemon juice.
4. Incorporate cream and egg yolk liaison.
5. Strain and do not allow to boil.

RECIPE 10.9

Approximate values per 100 mL serving:

Calories	53
Total fat	4.5 g
Saturated fat	2.5 g
Cholesterol	28 mg
Sodium	159 mg
Total carbohydrates	2.6 g
Protein	0.6 g

Allemande Sauce Derivatives

Several derivative sauces are easily produced from an allemande sauce made with a veal velouté. The quantities given are for 1 L (1 qt.) allemande. The final step for each recipe is to season to taste with salt and pepper.

Horseradish　Add to allemande 125 mL (4 fl. oz.) 40% cream and 5 g (1 tsp.) dry mustard. Just before service add 60 g (2 oz.) freshly grated horseradish. The horseradish should not be cooked with the sauce.

Mushroom　Sauté 125 g (4 oz.) sliced mushrooms in 15 g (1/2 oz.) butter; add 25 mL (1 fl. oz.) white wine. Then add the allemande to the mushrooms. Do not strain. Garnish with 25 g (1 oz.) each chopped parsley and chives.

Poulette　Sauté 250 g (8 oz.) sliced mushrooms and 15 g (1/2 oz.) diced shallots in 30 g (1 oz.) butter. Add to the allemande; then simmer and strain. Finish with 15 mL (1 Tbsp.) lemon juice and 15 g (1 Tbsp.) chopped parsley.

Applying the Basics

RECIPE 10.10

SUPRÊME SAUCE

Yield: 2 L (2 qt.)

Chicken velouté sauce	2 L	2 qt.
Chicken stock	600 mL	24 fl. oz.
Mushroom trimmings	250 g	8 oz.
Cream, 35%	500 mL	16 fl. oz.
Salt and white pepper	TT	TT

1. Simmer the velouté sauce, stock and mushroom trimmings until reduced to 2 L (2 qt.).
2. Stir in the cream and return to a simmer.
3. Adjust the seasonings.
4. Strain through a conical strainer lined with cheesecloth.

RECIPE 10.10

Approximate values per 100 mL serving:

Calories	319
Total fat	26 g
Saturated fat	15 g
Cholesterol	68 mg
Sodium	341 mg
Total carbohydrates	19 g
Protein	2.2 g

Suprême Sauce Derivatives

The following derivative sauces are easily made from suprême sauce. The quantities given are for 1 L (1 qt.) suprême sauce. The final step for each recipe is to season to taste with salt and pepper.

Aurora　Add 350 mL (12 fl. oz.) tomato sauce and 175 mL (6 fl. oz.) 35% cream. Simmer for 5 minutes, strain and mount with 250 g (8 oz.) butter.

Hungarian　Sweat 90 g (3 oz.) diced onion in 60 g (2 oz.) butter. Add 15 g (1 Tbsp.) paprika and sweat. Add 250 mL (8 fl. oz.) white wine and reduce. Stir in the suprême sauce. Cook for 2–3 minutes, strain and finish with 250 mL (8 fl. oz.) cream.

Ivory　Add to suprême 90 g (3 oz.) glace de volaille.

The Espagnole (Brown Sauce) Family

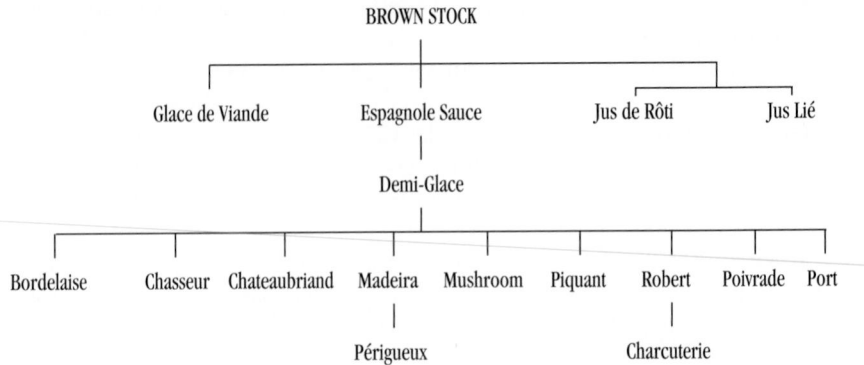

The basic sauce of the espagnole or brown sauce family is full bodied and rich. It is made from brown stock to which brown roux, mirepoix and tomato purée are added. Most often this sauce is used to produce demi-glace. Brown stock is also used to make jus lié. Demi-glace is used to create the derivative sauces of the espagnole family.

Applying the Basics

RECIPE 10.11

ESPAGNOLE (BROWN SAUCE)

Yield: 4 L (1 gal.)

Mirepoix, medium dice	500 g	1 lb.
Fat or clarified butter	200 g	7 oz.
Flour	250 g	8 oz.
Tomato purée	250 mL	8 oz.
Brown stock	5 L	5 qt.
Sachet:		
Bay leaf	1	1
Dried thyme	2 g	1/2 tsp.
Peppercorns, crushed	2 g	1/2 tsp.
Parsley stems	8	8

RECIPE 10.11

Approximate values per 100 mL serving:

Calories	106
Total fat	6.8 g
Saturated fat	3.7 g
Cholesterol	14 mg
Sodium	79 mg
Total carbohydrates	10 g
Protein	1.1 g

1. Sauté the mirepoix in fat until well caramelized.
2. Add the flour and cook to make a brown roux.
3. Add the tomato purée. Stir to break up any lumps of roux. Add brown stock. Bring to a boil; reduce to a simmer.
4. Add the sachet.
5. Simmer for approximately 1–1.5 hours, allowing the sauce to reduce. Skim the surface as needed to remove impurities.
6. Strain the sauce through a conical strainer lined with several layers of cheesecloth. Cool in a water bath or hold for service.

Demi-Glace

Brown stock is used to make the espagnole or brown sauce described above. Espagnole sauce can then be made into demi-glace, which in turn is used to make the derivative sauces of the espagnole family. Demi-glace is half brown sauce and half brown stock, reduced by half. It is usually finished with a small amount of madeira or sherry wine. Because demi-glace creates a richer, more flavourful base, it produces finer derivative sauces than those made directly from a brown sauce.

QUALITY STANDARD

A properly made demi-glace is rich, smooth and lump-free. Its prominent roasted flavour comes from the bones used for the brown stock. There should be no taste of roux. The caramelized bones and mirepoix as well as the tomato product contribute to its glossy dark brown, almost chocolate, colour. It should be barely thick enough to cling to food without being pasty or heavy.

Applying the Basics

RECIPE 10.12

DEMI-GLACE

Yield: 1 L (1 qt.)

Brown stock	1 L	1 qt.
Espagnole (brown sauce)	1 L	1 qt.

1. Combine the stock and sauce in a saucepan over medium heat.
2. Simmer until the mixture is reduced by half (i.e., a yield of 1 L or 1 quart).
3. Strain and cool in a water bath.

RECIPE 10.12

Approximate values per 50 mL serving:

Calories	69
Total fat	4.1 g
Saturated fat	2.1 g
Cholesterol	7.2 mg
Sodium	74 mg
Total carbohydrates	7.3 g
Protein	0.8 g

Espagnole (Brown) Sauce Derivatives

Demi-glace is used to produce many derivative sauces. The quantities given are for 1 L (1 qt.) demi-glace. The final step for each recipe is to season to taste with salt and pepper.

Bordelaise   Sweat 100 g (3-1/2 oz.) chopped shallots, 1 bay leaf, 1 sprig of thyme and 5 g (1 tsp.) cracked peppercorns and add 500 mL (16 fl. oz.) dry red wine. Reduce by three-fourths, then add demi-glace and simmer for 15 minutes. Strain through a fine etâmine. Finish with 60 g (2 oz.) meat glaze, mount with 100 g (3-1/2 oz.) butter and garnish with sliced, poached beef marrow.

Chasseur (Hunter's Sauce)   Sweat 30 g (1 oz.) diced shallots and 250 g (8 oz.) sliced mushrooms in butter. Add 250 mL (8 fl. oz.) white wine and 30 mL (1 fl. oz.) brandy and reduce by half. Add demi-glace and 250 g (8 oz.) tomato concasser and simmer 5 minutes. Finish with 30 g (1 oz.) meat glaze and 7 g (1/2 Tbsp.) each parsley and chives, chopped.

Chateaubriand   Sweat 125 g (4 oz.) each sliced shallots and mushrooms in butter. Add 1 sprig of thyme, 2 bay leaves and 500 mL (16 fl. oz.) white wine. Reduce by two-thirds. Add demi-glace and reduce by half. Strain. Mount with 350 g (12 oz.) parsley butter and finish with 30 g (1 oz.) fresh chopped tarragon.

Madeira or Port   Bring demi-glace to a boil, reduce slightly. Then add 125 mL (4 fl. oz.) madeira wine or port. Mount with 60 g (2 oz.) butter.

Mushroom   Sweat 50 g (2 oz.) shallots and 500 g (16 oz.) sliced mushrooms in 50 g (2 oz.) butter. Add 150 mL (5 fl. oz.) red, white or madeira wine. Reduce liquid by two-thirds. Add demi-glace and reduce to desired consistency.

Périgueux   Add finely diced truffles to madeira sauce. *Périgourdine* sauce is the same, except that the truffles are cut into relatively thick slices.

Piquante   Sweat 125 g (4 oz.) shallot and add 300 mL (10 fl. oz.) each white wine and white wine vinegar and 5 g (2 tsp.) cracked peppercorns. Reduce the mixture by three-quarters. Then add demi-glace and simmer for 10 minutes. Strain. Add 125 g (4 oz.) diced cornichons, 60 g (2 oz.) capers, 5 g (1/2 Tbsp.) fresh tarragon, 5 g (1/2 Tbsp.) fresh parsley and 5 g (1/2 Tbsp.) fresh chervil. Do not strain.

Poivrade   Sweat 350 g (12 oz.) mirepoix in 30 g (2 Tbsp.) butter. Add 2 bay leaves, a sprig of thyme, 4 parsley stems and 1 crushed garlic clove. Then add 500 mL (16 fl. oz.) white wine and 125 mL (4 fl. oz.) white wine vinegar. (Red wine vinegar and red wine are also often used.) Reduce by half, add demi-glace and reduce to 1 L (1 qt.). Then add 20 crushed peppercorns and 50 g (2 oz.) meat glaze and simmer for 5 more minutes. Strain through a fine etâmine and mount with up to 60 g (2 oz.) butter.

Robert   Sauté 125 g (4 oz.) chopped onion in 30 g (1 oz.) butter. Add 250 mL (8 fl. oz.) dry white wine and reduce by two-thirds. Add demi-glace and simmer for 10 minutes. Strain and then add 10 g (2 tsp.) dry mustard dissolved in wine and 60 g (2 oz.) meat glaze. If the finished Robert sauce is garnished with sliced sour pickles, preferably cornichons, it is known as *charcuterie sauce*.

◆◆◆

POIVRADE FOR GAME

Poivrade is also the name given a flavourful sauce traditionally made with game stock and seasoned with peppercorns. It is used for the wonderful *Sauce Grand Veneur*, one of the most complex derivative sauces in the classic repertoire. For *Grand Veneur*, game stock is flavoured with demi-glace and finished with cream and currant jelly. The sweetness balances the strong flavour of the game meats.

The Tomato Sauce Family

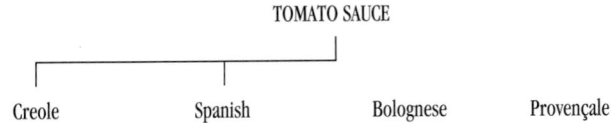

Classic tomato sauce is made from tomatoes, vegetables, seasonings and white stock and thickened with a blond or brown roux. In today's kitchens, however, most tomato sauces are not thickened with roux. Rather, they are tomatoes, herbs, spices, vegetables and other flavouring ingredients simmered together and puréed.

QUALITY STANDARD

A properly made tomato sauce is thick, rich and full-flavoured. Because it is a puréed sauce, its texture is somewhat coarser than other basic sauces, but it should still be smooth. The vegetables and other seasonings should add flavour, but none should be pronounced. Tomato sauce should not be bitter, acidic or overly sweet. It should be deep red and thick enough to cling to foods.

Applying the Basics

RECIPE 10.13

BASIC TOMATO SAUCE

Yield: 2 L (2 qt.)

Carrot, cut in small dice	50 g	2 oz.
Celery, cut in small dice	50 g	2 oz.
Onion, cut in small dice	50 g	2 oz.
Garlic cloves, chopped or crushed	15 g	4
Olive oil	90–120 mL	3–4 fl. oz.
Tomato paste	500 g	1 lb.
White stock	2 L	2 qt.
Sugar	5 g	1 tsp.
Sachet:		
Bay leaf	1/2	1/2
Sage	0.25 g	1/4 tsp.
Thyme	0.5 g	1/2 tsp.
Rosemary	0.5 g	1/2 tsp.
Peppercorns	8	8
Fennel seeds, crushed (optional)	0.25 g	1/4 tsp.

1. Sweat the vegetables in the oil (to sweat an ingredient is to sauté it on medium heat, stirring regularly without letting it colour).

2. Add tomato paste and sweat for 2 minutes.

3. Add the remaining ingredients and simmer gently for about 1 hour.

4. Adjust the seasoning and press the sauce through a food mill, if desired, or blend in a food processor to purée.

VARIATION: Reduce the olive oil by half and sweat 100 g (4 oz.) of finely chopped bacon before adding vegetables.

Tomato Sauce Derivatives or Variations

The following derivative sauces are made by adding the listed ingredients to 1 L (1 quart) tomato sauce. The final step for each recipe is to season to taste with salt and pepper.

Bolognese This sauce is not a derivative of tomato sauce. Sweat 100 g (3-1/2 oz.) diced onion and 1 clove crushed garlic in 30 mL (1 fl. oz.) olive oil. Add 500 g (16 oz.) ground veal or beef and 200 g (6 oz.) diced pancetta (optional) and sauté until meat browns lightly. Add tomato sauce, 5 g (2 tsp.) fresh basil, chopped, and 10 g (2 tsp.) fresh oregano leaves and 25 g (1/3 cup) chopped Italian parsley. Simmer. Adjust seasoning to taste. Often used with pasta dishes as garnish or to prepare lasagne. **Yield:** 1.8 L (60 fl. oz.).

Creole Sauté 175 g (6 oz.) finely diced onion, 125 g (4 oz.) thinly sliced celery and 5 g (1 tsp.) garlic in 30 mL (1 fl. oz.) olive oil. Add tomato sauce, a bay leaf and a pinch of thyme; simmer for 15 minutes. Then add 125 g (4 oz.) finely diced green pepper, 100 g (3-1/2 oz.) diced okra, 100 g (3-1/2 oz.) sliced green olives and a dash of hot pepper sauce; simmer for 15 minutes longer. Remove bay leaf.

Spanish Sauté 150 g (5-1/2 oz.) sliced onions with 100 g (3-1/2 oz.) thinly sliced celery, 150 g (5-1/2 oz.) sliced sweet peppers, and 5 g (1 clove) of garlic

◆◆◆

USE OF CRUSHED VS. PURÉED TOMATOES

Depending on whether you use crushed or puréed tomatoes, the simmering time and the amount of stock will vary.

RECIPE 10.13

Approximate values per 100 mL serving:

Calories	92
Total fat	5.7 g
Saturated fat	1 g
Cholesterol	0.7 mg
Sodium	215 mg
Total carbohydrates	8.9 g
Protein	1.2 g

in 50 mL (2 fl. oz.) olive oil. Finish with 125 g (4 oz.) sliced mushrooms, sweated, and 125 g (4 oz.) **tomato concassée**. Season with chiles, salt and pepper to taste.

Provençale This sauce is not a derivative of tomato sauce. A simple version is 500 g (1 lb.) **tomato concassée** sautéed in 100 mL (4 fl. oz.) olive oil, flavoured with 5 g (1 clove) garlic, diced, and 50 g (2 oz.) chopped shallots. Season with salt and pepper and a pinch of sugar. Finish with 15 g (1/2 oz.) chopped fines herbes. It goes well with light-flavoured fish, meats, or vegetables.

The Hollandaise Family

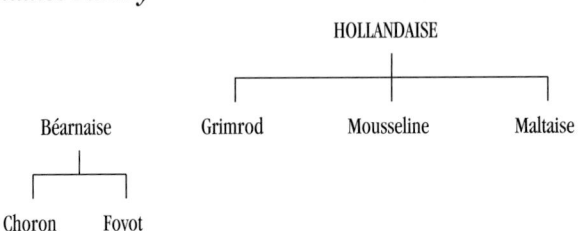

Hollandaise and the derivative sauces made from it are **emulsified** sauces. Egg yolks, which contain large amounts of lecithin, a natural emulsifier, are used to emulsify warm butter and a small amount of water, lemon juice or vinegar. By vigorously whipping the egg yolks with the liquid over heat to form a soft foam, then folding in the warm butter, the lecithin coats the individual oil droplets and holds them in suspension in the liquid.

QUALITY STANDARD

A properly made hollandaise is smooth, buttery, pale lemon-yellow–coloured and very rich, but light in texture. It is lump-free and should not exhibit any signs of separation. The buttery flavour should dominate but not mask the flavours of the egg, lemon and vinegar. The sauce should be frothy and light, not heavy like a mayonnaise. It should be able to be glazed under a salamander or broiler without breaking.

Temperatures and Food Safety Concerns

Temperatures play an important role in the proper production of a hollandaise sauce. As the egg yolks and liquid are whisked together, they are cooked over a bain marie until they thicken to the consistency of slightly whipped cream (ribbon stage). Do not overheat this mixture, because even slightly cooked eggs lose their ability to emulsify. The clarified butter used to make the sauce should be warm but not so hot as to cook the egg yolks further. Although hollandaise sauce can be made from whole butter, a more stable and consistent product will be achieved by using butter that has had the water and milk solids removed through clarification. (Clarification is described in Chapter 8, Eggs and Dairy Products.)

Emulsified butter sauces containing eggs are unique in that they must be held at the specific temperatures most conducive to bacterial growth: 4°C–60°C (40°F–140°F). If the sauce is heated above 65°C (150°F), the eggs will cook and the sauce will break and become grainy. If the sauce temperature falls below 7°C (45°F), the butter will solidify, making the sauce unusable. In order to minimize the risk of food-borne illnesses while maintaining the integrity of the sauce:

1. Always use clean, sanitized utensils.
2. Schedule sauce production as close to the time of service as possible. Never hold hollandaise-based sauces more than 20–30 minutes.
3. Make small batches of sauce.
4. Never mix an old batch of sauce with a new one.
5. Use pasteurized yolks, if available.

With practice, classic hollandaise can be produced quickly and efficiently. Nevertheless, a recipe for blender hollandaise is included for those operations with a need for this technique. In addition, many operations no longer make classic hollandaise due to health concerns or municipal regulations. These companies use a starch-based mixture that imitates hollandaise.

♦♦♦
NOTE

The right proportion of water and fat (butter) is critical to a light and stable emulsion. It is not the acid that creates the emulsion, just the liquid. The acid provides flavour.

Applying the Basics

RECIPE 10.14

HOLLANDAISE

Yield: 750 mL (24 fl. oz.)

Black peppercorns, crushed	18	18
White wine vinegar	90 mL	3 fl. oz.
Lemon juice	30 mL	1 fl. oz.
Water	60 mL	2 fl. oz.
Egg yolks, pasteurized	6	6
Butter, clarified, warm	450 g	1 lb.
Lemon juice	TT	TT
Salt and white pepper	TT	TT
Cayenne pepper	TT	TT

1. Combine the peppercorns, vinegar, lemon juice and water in a small saucepan and reduce by one-half.
2. Place the egg yolks in a stainless steel bowl. Strain the acidic reduction through a conical strainer and add to the egg yolks. There should be 15 mL (1/2 oz.) of moisture (reduction) per egg yolk.
3. Place the bowl over a double boiler, whipping the mixture continuously with a wire whip. As the yolks cook, the mixture will thicken. When the mixture is thick enough to leave a trail across the surface when the whip is drawn away, remove the bowl from the double boiler. Do not overcook the egg yolks.

RECIPE 10.14

Approximate values per 50 mL serving:

Calories	395
Total fat	43 g
Saturated fat	26 g
Cholesterol	221 mg
Sodium	41 mg
Total carbohydrates	0.4 g
Protein	1.7 g

1. Combine the egg yolks with the acidic reduction in a stainless steel bowl.

2. Whip the mixture over a double boiler until it is thick enough to leave a trail when the whip is removed.

3. Using a kitchen towel and sauce pot to firmly hold the bowl containing the yolks, add the butter slowly while whipping continuously.

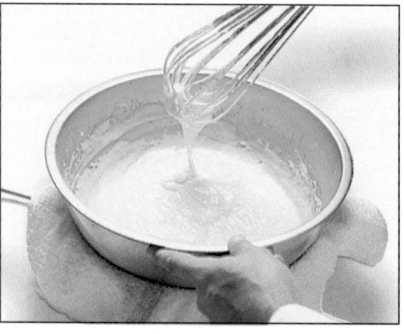

4. Hollandaise at the proper consistency.

4. Begin to add the warm clarified butter to the egg yolk mixture a little at a time, while constantly whipping the mixture to form an emulsion. Once the emulsion is started, the butter may be added more quickly. Continue until all the butter is incorporated.

5. Adjust the acidity of the sauce with a little lemon juice, if needed. Adjust the seasonings with salt, white pepper and cayenne pepper.

6. Strain the sauce through cheesecloth if necessary and hold for service in a warm (not simmering) bain marie.

Applying the Basics

RECIPE 10.15

HOLLANDAISE, BLENDER METHOD

Yield: 1 L (1 qt.)

Egg yolks	9	9
Water, warm	90 mL	3 fl. oz.
Lemon juice	30 mL	1 fl. oz.
Cayenne pepper	TT	TT
Salt	5 g	1 tsp.
White pepper	0.25 g	1/4 tsp.
Tabasco sauce	TT	TT
Whole butter	750 g	24 oz.

RECIPE 10.15

Approximate values per 50 mL serving:

Calories	305
Total fat	33 g
Saturated fat	20 g
Cholesterol	178 mg
Sodium	106 mg
Total carbohydrates	0.3 g
Protein	1.6 g

1. Place the egg yolks, water, lemon juice, cayenne pepper, salt, white pepper and Tabasco sauce in the bowl of the blender. Cover and blend on high speed for approximately 5 seconds.

2. Heat the butter to approximately 80°C (175°F). This allows the butter to cook the yolks as it is added to them.

3. Turn the blender on and immediately begin to add the butter in a steady stream. Incorporate all of the butter in 20–30 seconds. Adjust the seasonings.

4. If any lumps are present, strain the sauce through cheesecloth. Transfer the sauce to a stainless steel container and adjust the seasonings. Hold for service in a bain marie, remembering the sanitation precautions discussed previously.

Procedure for Rescuing a Broken Hollandaise

Occasionally a hollandaise will break or separate and appear thin, grainy or even lumpy. A sauce breaks when the emulsion has not formed or the emulsified butter, eggs and liquid have separated. There are several reasons why this may happen: The temperature of the eggs or butter may have been too high or too low; the butter may have been added too quickly; the egg yolks may have been overcooked; too much butter may have been added or the sauce may not have been whipped vigorously enough to start or may have been over-whipped.

Broken hollandaise can often be rescued and re-emulsified. To do so, you must first determine the cause of the problem.

Feel the bowl in which the sauce was prepared to determine if it is too hot or too cold. If the bowl is too hot, allow the sauce to cool. If it is too cold, reheat the sauce over a double boiler before attempting to rescue it.

For 1 L (1 qt.) of broken sauce, place 15 mL (1 Tbsp.) of water in a clean stainless steel bowl and slowly beat in the broken sauce. If the problem seems to be that the eggs were overcooked or too much butter was added, add a yolk to the water before incorporating the broken sauce.

Hollandaise Sauce Derivatives

The following derivative sauces are easily made by adding the listed ingredients to 750 mL (24 fl. oz.) of hollandaise. The final step for each recipe is to season to taste with salt and pepper. Béarnaise is presented here as a derivative sauce as that is now general practice, although some chefs consider it a basic sauce since it has a unique tarragon flavour added to the reduction.

Béarnaise   Combine 25 g (1 oz.) chopped shallots, 10 g (1/3 oz.) chopped fresh tarragon, 5 g (1/4 oz.) chopped fresh chervil and 1 g (1 tsp.) crushed peppercorns with 100 mL (3 fl. oz.) white wine vinegar and 25 mL (1 fl. oz.) water. Reduce to 90 mL (3 fl. oz.). Add this reduction to the egg yolks and proceed with the hollandaise recipe. Strain the finished sauce and season to taste with salt and cayenne pepper. Garnish with additional chopped fresh tarragon.

Choron   Stir 60 g (2 oz.) tomato purée into a béarnaise.

Foyot   Add to béarnaise 75 g (2-1/2 oz.) melted glace de viande.

Grimrod   Infuse a hollandaise sauce reduction with saffron.

Maltaise   Add to hollandaise 50 mL (1-1/2 fl. oz.) blood orange juice and 5 g (2 tsp.) finely grated blood orange zest. Regular oranges may be used for this sauce.

Mousseline (Chantilly Sauce)   Whip 125 mL (4 fl. oz.) 35% cream until stiff. Fold it into the hollandaise just before service. It is usually glazed under a broiler or salamander.

Beurre Blanc and Beurre Rouge

Beurre blanc and beurre rouge are emulsified butter sauces made without egg yolks. The small amounts of lecithin and other emulsifiers naturally found in butter are used to form an oil-in-liquid emulsion. Although similar to hollandaise in concept, beurre blancs are a class in themselves. They are not classified as either basic or compound sauces. Beurre blancs are thinner and lighter than hollandaise and béarnaise. They should be smooth and slightly thicker than heavy cream.

Beurre blanc and beurre rouge are made from three main ingredients: shallots, white (Fr. *blanc*) wine or red (Fr. *rouge*) wine and whole butter (not clarified). The shallots and wine provide flavour, while the butter becomes the sauce. A good beurre blanc or beurre rouge is rich and buttery, with a light, acidic flavour that responds well to other seasonings and flavourings, thereby lending itself to the addition of herbs, spices and vegetable purées to complement the dish with which it is served. Its pale colour changes depending upon the flavourings added. It should be light and airy yet still liquid, while thick enough to cling to food.

Basic Procedure for Making Beurre Blanc or Beurre Rouge

1. Use a nonaluminum pan to prevent discolouring the sauce. Do not use a thin-walled or nonstick pan, as heat is not evenly distributed in a thin-walled pan and a nonstick pan makes it difficult for an emulsion to set.

2. Over medium heat, reduce the wine, shallots and herbs or other seasonings, if used, until au sec (i.e., nearly dry). Some cooks add a small amount of 40% cream at this point and reduce the mixture. Although not necessary, the added cream helps stabilize the finished sauce.

3. Whisk in cold butter a small amount at a time. The butter should be well chilled, as this allows the butterfat, water and milk solids to be gradually incorporated into the sauce as the butter melts and the mixture is whisked.

4. When all of the butter is incorporated, strain and hold the sauce in a bain marie.

Temperature

Do not let the sauce become too hot. At 58°C (136°F) some of the emulsifying proteins begin to break down and release the butterfat they hold in emulsion. Extended periods at temperatures over 58°C (136°F) will cause the sauce to separate. If the sauce separates, it can be corrected by cooling to approximately 43°C–49°C (110°F–120°F) and whisking to reincorporate the butterfat.

If the sauce is allowed to cool below 30°C (85°F), the butterfat will solidify. If the sauce is reheated it will separate into butterfat and water; whisking will not re-emulsify it. Cold beurre blanc can be used as a soft, flavoured butter, however, simply by whisking it at room temperature until it smooths out to the consistency of mayonnaise.

Applying the Basics

RECIPE 10.16

CLASSIC BEURRE BLANC

Yield: 1 L (1 qt.)

White wine	30 mL	1 fl. oz.
White wine vinegar	125 mL	4 fl. oz.
Salt	7 g	1-1/2 tsp.
White pepper	0.5 g	1/2 tsp.
Shallots, minced	30 g	1 oz.
Whole butter, chilled	1 kg	2 lb.

1. Combine the white wine, white wine vinegar, salt, white pepper and shallots in a small saucepan. Reduce the mixture until approximately 30 mL (2 Tbsp.) of liquid remain. If more liquid than that is allowed to remain, the resulting sauce will be too thin. For a thicker sauce, reduce the mixture au sec.

2. Cut the butter into pieces approximately 30 g (1 oz.) in weight. Over low heat, whisk in the butter a few pieces at a time, using the chilled butter to keep the sauce between 43°C and 49°C (100°F and 120°F).

RECIPE 10.16

Approximate values per 50 mL serving:

Calories	372
Total fat	41 g
Saturated fat	25 g
Cholesterol	109 mg
Sodium	142 mg
Total carbohydrates	0.3 g
Protein	0.5 g

1. Reduce the shallots and wine *au sec*.

2. Whisk in the cold butter a little at a time.

3. Strain the sauce.

3. Once all of the butter has been incorporated, remove the saucepan from the heat. Strain through a conical strainer and hold the sauce between 38°C and 54°C (100°F and 130°F) for service.

VARIATIONS: *Lemon-Dill*—Heat 30 mL (2 Tbsp.) lemon juice and whisk it into the beurre blanc. Stir in 10 g (1/3 oz.) chopped fresh dill.

Pink Peppercorn—Add 10 g (1/3 oz.) coarsely crushed pink peppercorns to the shallot-wine reduction when making beurre rouge. Garnish the finished sauce with whole pink peppercorns.

Applying the Basics

RECIPE 10.17

"MY" BEURRE BLANC SAUCE
Chef Marcel Kretz, CM
Retired

Yield: 625 mL (24 fl. oz.)

Dry shallots, chopped	50 g	2
White wine	250 mL	8 fl. oz.
Fish stock	250 mL	8 fl. oz.
Fresh tarragon leaves	5 g	1 tsp.
Parsley sprigs, chopped	5 g	2–3
White pepper, crushed	TT	TT
Cream, 35%	500 mL	18 fl. oz.
Unsalted butter, cubed	280 g	9 oz.
Salt	TT	TT
Lemon juice, if desired	TT	TT

1. Sauté the shallots lightly; deglaze with the white wine and fish stock.

2. Add the tarragon, parsley sprigs, crushed pepper and reduce the mixture by half. Add the cream and reduce by half again.

3. Decrease the heat and add the cubed butter piece by piece, whipping constantly, until the sauce is smooth.

4. Check and adjust the seasoning. Pass the sauce through a fine sieve.

5. Keep the sauce at a low heat in a double boiler. It will keep fairly well for a full-service period.

Serve with poached fish or seafood.

VARIATIONS: Clear chicken stock can be used instead of fish stock. It can be served with fowl or vegetable flan or mousse.

Marcel Kretz
Born, raised and trained in France, Marcel has had an illustrious, award-winning career in Europe and Canada. He is credited with launching the movement to emphasize Quebec products in top Quebec restaurants, and in 1998 became the first chef ever to receive the Order of Canada.

RECIPE 10.17

Approximate values per 50 mL serving:

Calories	329
Total fat	35 g
Saturated fat	22 g
Cholesterol	110 mg
Sodium	98 mg
Total carbohydrates	2.2 g
Protein	1.2 g

Compound Butters

A compound butter is made by incorporating various seasonings into softened whole butter. These butters, also known as *beurres composés*, give flavour and colour to derivative sauces or may be served as sauces or condiments in their own right. For example, a slice of maître d'hôtel butter (parsley butter) is often placed on a grilled steak or piece of fish at the time of service. The butter quickly melts, creating a sauce for the beef or fish.

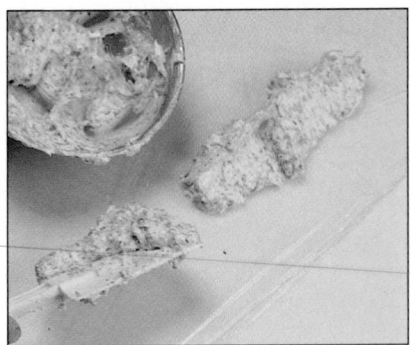

1. Place the compound butter on the plastic wrap.

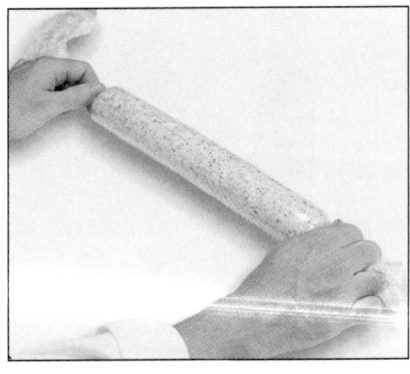

2. Roll the butter in the plastic wrap to form a cylinder.

Butter and flavouring ingredients can be combined in a blender, food processor or mixer. Using parchment paper or plastic wrap, the butter is then rolled into a cylinder, chilled and sliced as needed. Or it can be piped into rosettes and refrigerated until firm. Most compound butters will keep for two to three days in the refrigerator, or they can be frozen for longer storage.

Recipes for Compound Butters

For each of the following butters, add the listed ingredients to 450 g (1 lb.) of softened, unsalted butter. The compound butter should then be seasoned with salt and pepper to taste.

Basil Butter Mince 50 g (2 oz.) basil, 50 g (2 oz.) shallots and add to butter with 10 mL (2 tsp.) lemon juice.

Herb Butter Add to the butter up to 150 g (5 oz.) of mixed chopped fresh herbs such as parsley, dill, chives, tarragon or chervil.

Lobster or Crayfish Butter Grind 250 g (8 oz.) cooked lobster or crayfish meat, shells and/or coral with 450 g (1 lb.) butter. Place in a saucepan and clarify. Strain the butter through a fine conical strainer lined with cheesecloth. Refrigerate, then remove the butterfat when firm.

Maître d'Hôtel Mix into the butter 8 g (1/4 oz.) finely chopped parsley, 45 mL (3 Tbsp.) lemon juice and a dash of white pepper.

Montpelier Blanch 30 g (1 oz.) parsley, 30 g (1 oz.) chervil, 30 g (1 oz.) watercress and 30 g (1 oz.) tarragon in boiling water. Refresh thoroughly. Mince 2 hard-boiled egg yolks, 8 g (2) garlic cloves and 30 g (2) gherkin pickles. Blend everything into the butter.

Red Pepper Butter Purée 250 g (8 oz.) roasted, peeled red bell peppers until liquid, cool, then add to the butter.

Shallot Butter Blanch 250 g (8 oz.) of peeled shallots in boiling water. Dry and finely dice them and when cool, mix with the butter.

Jus and Pan Gravy

Drippings in roasting pans are used to make a number of sauces to be served with the roasted meat. They are lighter in texture and body than a demi-glace but have the distinctive flavour of the caramelized drippings. The term *lié* appears when the liquid is thickened with a starch. Pan gravy is roux thickened.

Jus de Rôti and Jus A mirepoix is roasted with the drippings and the pan is deglazed with brown stock and a little wine if desired. The fat is removed after simmering and skimming. Always strain the jus. Traditionally, with larger roasts, additional small cut bones were added to the mirepoix to enhance flavour. Tomato purée may be added to boost flavour and colour.

Jus lié Jus thickened with arrowroot, cornstarch or modified starch. Fond lié refers to a reduced, thickened stock.

Pan Gravy Flour is added to the roasting fat and reduced drippings to make a roux. Stock is then added to make the gravy. The final product should have the characteristics of a good brown sauce with a meatier, richer flavour from the drippings.

Basic Procedure for Making Pan Gravy

1. Remove the cooked meat or poultry from the roasting pan.
2. If mirepoix was not added during the roasting process, add it to the pan containing the drippings and fat.
3. Place the roasting pan on the stove top and clarify the fat by cooking off any remaining moisture.
4. Pour off the fat, reserving it to make the roux.
5. Deglaze the pan using an appropriate stock. The deglazing liquid may be transferred to a saucepan for easier handling or the gravy may be finished directly in the roasting pan.
6. Add enough stock or water to the deglazing liquid to yield the proper amount of finished gravy.
7. Determine the amount of roux needed to thicken the liquid and prepare it in a separate pan, using a portion of the reserved fat.
8. Add the roux to the liquid and bring the mixture to a simmer. Simmer until the mirepoix is well cooked, the flavour is extracted and the flour taste is cooked out.
9. Strain the gravy and adjust the seasonings.

QUALITY STANDARD

A properly made jus lié or pan gravy is very rich and smooth. It shares many flavour characteristics with demi-glace. Its colour should be dark brown and glossy from the concentrated gelatin content. Its consistency is somewhat lighter than demi-glace, but it should still cling lightly to foods.

Coulis

The term *coulis* refers to a sauce made from a purée of vegetables or fruit thinned down to sauce consistency. A vegetable coulis can be served either as a hot or cold accompaniment to various food preparations. It is often made from a single vegetable base (popular examples include broccoli, tomatoes and sweet red peppers) cooked with flavouring ingredients such as onions, garlic, shallots, herbs and spices and then puréed. An appropriate liquid (stock, water or cream) may be added to thin the purée if necessary. Vegetable coulis are often prepared with very little fat and served as a healthy alternative to a heavier, classic sauce.

A fruit coulis, often made from fresh or frozen berries, is generally used as a dessert sauce. It is usually as simple as puréed fruit thinned to the desired consistency with sugar syrup and strained. (If heated and thickened with starches, it becomes a fruit sauce.)

Typically, both vegetable and fruit coulis have a texture similar to that of thin tomato sauce. Their textures can range from smooth to slightly grainy. The flavour and colour of a coulis should be that of the main ingredient. Herbs, spices and other flavouring ingredients should only complement and not dominate the coulis.

◆◆◆

COULIS AND PURÉES: IS THERE A DIFFERENCE?

A coulis and a purée are two different things! A coulis should be as smooth as possible, thus the name coulis, which refers to what runs off the strainer. A puréed fruit or vegetable differs from a coulis in that a purée is generally thicker and coarser than a coulis.

Basic Procedure for Making Coulis

Here, we include a procedure for making a vegetable coulis. Procedures for making fruit coulis are included as recipes in Chapter 31, Custards, Creams, Frozen Desserts and Dessert Sauces.

1. Cook the main ingredient and any additional flavouring ingredients with an appropriate liquid.
2. Purée the main ingredient and flavouring ingredients in a food mill, blender or food processor.
3. Combine the purée with the appropriate liquid and simmer to blend the flavours.
4. Pass the purée through a sieve.
5. Thin and season the coulis as desired.

Applying the Basics

RECIPE 10.18

RED PEPPER COULIS

Yield: 1 L (1 qt.)

Vegetable or olive oil	30 mL	1 fl. oz.
Garlic, chopped	15 g	1/2 oz.
Onion, small dice	90 g	3 oz.
Red bell pepper, medium dice	1.25 kg	3 lb.
White wine	250 mL	8 fl. oz.
Chicken stock	450 mL	1 pt.
Salt and pepper	TT	TT

1. Heat the oil and sauté the garlic and onion until translucent, without browning.
2. Add the red pepper and sauté until tender.
3. Deglaze the pan with the white wine.
4. Add the chicken stock, bring to a simmer and cook for 15 minutes. Season with salt and pepper.
5. Purée in a blender or food processor and strain through a sieve.
6. Adjust the consistency and seasonings and hold for service.

RECIPE 10.18

Approximate values per 50 mL serving:

Calories	42
Total fat	1.9 g
Saturated fat	0.2 g
Cholesterol	0.2 mg
Sodium	296 mg
Total carbohydrates	5.5 g
Protein	0.7 g

CONTEMPORARY SAUCES

Modern chefs and menu writers are relying less on traditional sauces and more on salsas, relishes, juices, broths, essences and infused oils in their work. Unlike classic sauces, these modern accompaniments do not rely on meat-based stocks and starch thickeners, but rather on fresh vegetables, vegetable juices, aromatic broths and intensely flavoured oils. The names for these sauces are not codified, as are those in the classic sauce repertoire. Chefs apply various terms freely, using whatever name best fits the dish and the overall menu. Most of these contemporary sauces can be prepared more quickly than their classic counterparts, and the use of fresh fruits and vegetables enhances the healthfulness of the dish. These so-called modern sauces may have a lighter body and less fat than classic sauces, but they are still derived from classical culinary techniques and principles. The sauces should be appropriate in flavour, texture and appearance and should complement, not overwhelm, the food they accompany.

Vegetable Juice Sauces

Juice extractors make it possible to prepare juice from fresh, uncooked vegetables such as carrots, beets and spinach. Thinner and smoother than a purée, vegetable juice can be heated, reduced, flavoured and enriched with butter to create colourful, intensely flavoured sauces. Cream or stock can be added to finish the sauce. Sauces made from vegetable juices are sometimes referred to as an **essence** or **tea** on menus.

Juice from a single type of vegetable provides the purest, most pronounced flavour, but two or more vegetables sometimes can be combined successfully. Care must be taken, however, when mixing too many flavours and colours. Also, flavours and colours may change or react during the cooling process. Be careful of mixing too many flavours and colours in the juice, however. Juiced vegetable sauces are particularly appropriate with pasta, shellfish and poultry, and can be useful in vegetarian cuisine or as a healthier alternative to classic sauces.

Basic Procedure for Making a Vegetable Juice Sauce

1. Wash and peel vegetables as needed.
2. Process the vegetables through a juice extractor.
3. Place the juice in a saucepan and add stock, lemon juice, herbs or other flavourings as desired.
4. Bring the sauce to a simmer and reduce as necessary.
5. Strain the sauce through a fine etâmine.
6. Adjust the seasonings and whisk in whole butter to finish, if desired.

Broth

Broth, which also appears on menus as **tea**, **essence** or **nage**, is very similar to court bouillon (see page 198) but without the extra acidity. These thin, flavourful liquids are generally served in a pool beneath the main food. The broth should not be so abundant as to turn an entree into a soup, but it should provide moisture and flavour. The essence, broth or nage is often made by simply reducing and straining the liquid in which the main food was cooked. Alternatively, a specifically flavoured stock, tomato, for example, can be prepared, then clarified like consommé to create a broth or essence to accompany an appetizer or entree.

Applying the Basics

RECIPE 10.19

PIQUANTE LEMON GRASS BOUILLON

JAMIE KENNEDY
Jamie Kennedy's Seasons *(Vancouver: Whitecap Books Ltd., 2000)*

Yield: 900 mL (30 fl. oz.)

Tomato consommé (see sidebar)	1 L	34 fl. oz.
Lemon grass, chopped	1 stalk	1 stalk
Green chiles, split lengthwise	2	2

1. Bring consommé to a simmer.
2. Add lemon grass and chiles and simmer 30 minutes to infuse. Strain through a fine sieve. Reserve.

NOTE: Jamie serves this with seared grouper marinated with lemon grass. Garnish is baked, diced sweet potato and leek combined with fresh, diced tomato.

◆◆◆
JAMIE KENNEDY'S
TOMATO CONSOMMÉ

2 kg ripe tomatoes
3 cloves garlic
1 leek, washed
2 celery stalks
12 basil leaves
5 mL nutmeg
4 egg whites
Salt and pepper

Coarsely chop the vegetables and herbs. Pulse 5 seconds in food processor. Transfer to heavy-bottomed pot and add remaining ingredients. Bring quickly to a boil. When raft forms, reduce heat and simmer 2 hours. Strain through cheesecloth. If not used immediately, freeze. Yield: 1.5 L.

—from *Jamie Kennedy's Seasons* (Vancouver: Whitecap Books Ltd., 2000).

Jamie Kennedy
Jamie Kennedy has been one of Canada's pre-eminent chefs for two decades. He continues to amaze and delight diners who have followed his career from Scaramouche to Palmerston, to his current location, JK at the Museum, in Toronto's Royal Ontario Museum.

RECIPE 10.19

Approximate values per 125 mL serving:

Calories	69
Total fat	0.9 g
Saturated fat	0.2 g
Cholesterol	0 mg
Sodium	292 mg
Total carbohydrates	13 g
Protein	2.2 g

✦✦✦
FLAVOUR UNITS FOR 250 mL (8 FL. OZ.) OIL

Nuts	75 g	2-1/2 oz.
Chile peppers (seedless)	15 g	1/2 oz.
Garlic	20 g	5 cloves
Citrus zest	40 g	1-1/4 oz.
Shallots	25 g	1 oz.
Herbs	30 g	1 oz.
Ginger root	25 g	1 oz.
Dried mushrooms	15 g	1/2 oz.
Peppercorns	10 each	10 each

Source: Adapted from Producers of Canadian Canola, "Canola Cooks."

Flavoured Oil

Small amounts of intensely flavoured oils can be used to dress or garnish a variety of dishes. Salads, soups, vegetable and starch dishes, as well as entrees, can be enhanced with a drizzle of colourful, appropriately flavoured oil. Because such small quantities are used, these oils provide flavour and moisture without adding too many calories or fat.

Unless the flavouring ingredient goes especially well with olive oil (for example, basil), select a high-quality but neutral oil such as sunflower, safflower or canola. The Producers of Canadian Canola have CFIA approval for the following method of preparing a flavoured oil. No deviations from the procedure are acceptable due to the risk of botulism toxin developing. It is important that all moisture be evaporated. The more flavour units in the oil, the longer it will take to process.

Basic Procedure for Making a Flavoured Oil

Use either a 500 mL (18 fl. oz.) tempered glass measure or a 796 mL (27 fl. oz.) tin can that has been thoroughly washed, label removed.

1. Heat oil and flavouring ingredients in a 150°C (300°F) oven until the oil reaches a temperature of 120°C (250°F).
2. Remove from oven and cool on a rack for 30 minutes.
3. Strain the oil though a coffee filter pre-soaked with plain canola oil.
4. Store flavoured oil in a covered clean glass jar in a refrigerator. Use within 1 month.

Heating times: 1 unit—1 hr. 20 mins.; 2 units—1 hr. 40 mins.; 3 units—2 hr.; 4 units—2 hr. 20 mins.; 5 units—2 hr. 40 mins.; 6 units—3 hr.

Applying the Basics

RECIPE 10.20

ROSEMARY ORANGE OIL

Yield: 225 mL (8 oz.)

Canola oil	250 mL	8 fl. oz.
Orange zest	60 g	2 oz.
Rosemary	15 g	1/2 oz.

1. Preheat oven to 150°C (300°F).
2. Place all ingredients in a 500 mL (16 fl. oz.) tempered glass container.
3. Heat oil for 1 hour 40 minutes (2 units) to an internal temperature of 120°C (250°F).
4. Allow oil to cool for 30 minutes.
5. Strain into a glass jar, seal and store, refrigerated, for up to 1 month.

RECIPE 10.20

Approximate values per 15 mL serving:

Calories	126
Total fat	14 g
Saturated fat	1 g
Cholesterol	0 mg
Sodium	0 mg
Total carbohydrates	0 g
Protein	0 g

Salsa, Relish and Chutneys

Salsa (Spanish for sauce) is most commonly known as a chunky mixture of raw tomato, other vegetables, chiles and cilantro, eaten with chips or ladled over Mexican foods. **Relish** is most commonly known as a sweet green condiment spooned on a hot dog. **Chutneys** are known as a condiment served with curries. However, salsas, relishes and chutneys can be used as sauces with many meat, poultry, fish, shellfish or vegetable dishes. They can include many different fruits and vegetables such as oranges, pineapple, papaya, black beans, jicama and tomatillos.

Although not members of any classic sauce family, salsas and relishes are condiments currently enjoying great popularity because of their intense fresh flavours, ease of preparation, and low fat and calorie content. Salsas and relishes are often a riot of colours, textures and flavours, simultaneously cool and hot, spicy and sweet.

Basic Procedure for Making a Salsa

1. Cut or chop the ingredients.
2. Precook and chill items as directed in the recipe.
3. Toss all ingredients together and refrigerate, allowing the flavours to combine for at least 30 minutes before service.

Basic Procedure for Making a Relish

1. Clean, peel, trim and cut ingredients to desired size.
2. Precook, blanch or sauté items as directed in the recipe.
3. Combine all ingredients with the vinegar and sugar.
4. Cook gently until soft.

Applying the Basics

RECIPE 10.21

TOMATO SALSA (PICO DE GALLO)

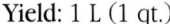

Yield: 1 L (1 qt.)

Tomatoes, seeded, small dice	750 g	5
Green onions, sliced	1 bunch	1 bunch
Garlic cloves, minced	15 g	3
Cilantro, chopped	60 g	1/2 bunch
Jalapeño peppers, chopped fine	3	3
Lemon juice	60 mL	2 fl. oz.
Cumin, ground	1 g	1/2 tsp.
Salt and pepper	TT	TT

Combine all ingredients and gently toss. Adjust seasonings and refrigerate.

RECIPE 10.21

Approximate values per 50 mL serving:

Calories	12
Total fat	0.1 g
Saturated fat	0 g
Cholesterol	0 mg
Sodium	101 mg
Total carbohydrates	2.4 g
Protein	0.4 g

USING SAUCES

Although many classic sauces were designed for or intended to be used with specific dishes, modern chefs often mix and match sauces with foods in unique or nontraditional ways. Nonclassic sauces, such as salsa or relish, may be prepared in a range of flavours using a wide variety of ingredients.

The uses shown in Table 10.5 for classic and nonclassic sauces are just suggestions. Most sauces can be used in many different dishes. It depends on your taste, creativity and judgment.

TABLE 10.5   USING SAUCES

Sauce	Qualities	Derivative Sauces or Flavourings	Use
Béchamel	Smooth, rich and creamy; no graininess; cream-coloured with rich sheen	Cheddar Cream sauce Mornay Nantua Soubise	Vegetables, pasta Vegetables, pasta, eggs, fish Fish, shellfish, poultry, vegetables Fish, shellfish Veal, pork, eggs

Velouté	Smooth and rich; ivory-coloured; good flavour of the stock used; not pasty or heavy	Fish velouté
		  Bercy
		  Cardinal
		  Normandy
		Allemande (veal)
		  Horseradish
		  Mushroom
		  Poulette
		Suprême (chicken)
		  Aurora
		  Hungarian
		  Ivory
			
			Poached fish
			Lobster, white fish, crab, eggs
			Delicate white fish, oysters
			
			Roast beef, corned beef, baked ham
			Sautéed poultry, white meats
			Vegetables, sweetbreads
			
			Eggs, chicken, sweetbreads
			Eggs, chicken, chops, sweetbreads
			Eggs, braised poultry

Espagnole	Smooth and rich; dark brown colour; good meat flavour	Bordelaise Chasseur Chateaubriand Chevreuil Madeira/Port Mushroom Périgueux/Périgourdine Piquant Poivrade Robert	Sautéed or grilled meats Sautéed or grilled meats and poultry Broiled meats Roasted meats and game Grilled or roasted meats and game, ham Sautéed or grilled meats and poultry Sautéed poultry, grilled meats and game, sweetbreads Pork Grilled or roasted meats, game Pork
Tomato	Thick and rich; slightly grainy; full-flavoured	Tomato Bolognese Creole Provençale Spanish	Meats, poultry, vegetables, pasta and for making small sauces Pasta Fish, eggs, chicken Pasta, grilled or sautéed poultry and white meats Eggs, fish
Hollandaise/ Béarnaise	Smooth and rich; buttery flavour; light and slightly frothy; pale yellow colour; no signs of separating	Grimrod Maltaise Mousseline Choron Foyot	Grilled meats and fish Eggs, poached fish Poached fish, eggs, vegetables Grilled or sautéed meats and fish Grilled meats and fish
Beurre blanc and beurre rouge	Rich and buttery; thinner than hollandaise; light and airy; pale-coloured	Wide variety of seasonings and flavourings may be used	Steamed, grilled or poached fish; chicken or vegetables
Compound butter	Flavour ingredients should be evenly distributed	Wide variety of seasonings and flavourings may be used	Grilled meats, poultry and fish; finishing sauces, condiment, spread
Jus de rôti, Jus lié, Pan gravy	Smooth; deep rich colour; meaty flavour	Made from pan drippings	Roasted meats and poultry
Coulis	Rich colour; moderately thin, grainy texture; strongly flavoured	Made with a wide variety of vegetables or fruits	Vegetables, grilled or poached meats, poultry and fish
Salsa and relish	Chunky; bright colours; not watery	Made with a wide variety of vegetables, fruits and seasonings	Meats, fish, vegetables and poultry; used as a sauce or condiment

CONCLUSION

In *Le Guide culinaire*, Auguste Escoffier wrote, "Indeed, stock is everything in cooking. . . . Without it, nothing can be done. If one's stock is good, what remains of the work is easy; if, on the other hand, it is bad or merely mediocre, it is quite hopeless to expect anything approaching a satisfactory result." Because stocks and the sauces made from them are still the basis for much of contemporary cuisine, Escoffier's words are as true today as when he wrote them.

Both the classic basic sauces and the derivative sauces made from them as well as sauces such as beurre blanc and beurre rouge, coulis, salsas and relishes that are not based on classic recipes all share two goals: to complement the foods with which they are served and to neither mask nor disguise poorly prepared foods. With practice and care (and the right ingredients), you will be able to make great sauces.

QUESTIONS FOR DISCUSSION

1. Why are the bones of younger animals preferred for making stocks?
2. Why should a stock made from beef or veal bones cook longer than a stock made from fish bones? What is the result if a stock does not cook long enough?
3. What can cause a stock to become cloudy? How can you prevent this from happening?
4. List three differences in the production of a white stock and a brown stock.
5. List the five classic basic sauces and explain how they are used to prepare derivative sauces.
6. Why is demi-glace preferred when making brown sauces? Is jus lié different from classic demi-glace? Can they be used interchangeably?
7. Why are temperatures important when making hollandaise sauce? What precautions must be taken when holding hollandaise for service?
8. Compare a beurre blanc and a hollandaise sauce. How are they similar? How are they different?
9. How are compound butters used in making sauces? What are the ingredients for a traditional maître d'hôtel butter?
10. What are the differences between a salsa, chutney and relish? Can these items be used in place of classic sauces? Explain your answer.

ADDITIONAL SAUCE RECIPES

RECIPE 10.22

MUSHROOM TARTS WITH GARLIC CREAM

NOTE: *This dish appears in the chapter opening photograph.*

CITRUS, LOS ANGELES, CA
Chef Michel Richard

Yield: 6 Servings

RECIPE 10.22

Approximate values per serving:

Calories	670
Total fat	54 g
Saturated fat	25 g
Cholesterol	120 mg
Sodium	1172 mg
Total carbohydrates	37 g
Protein	9 g

GARLIC CREAM

Garlic cloves, peeled	100 g	30
Cream, 35%	500 mL	1 pt.
Salt and pepper	TT	TT

1. Place the garlic in a saucepan. Cover with 8 cm (3 inches) of cold water and bring to a boil. Drain and rinse with cold water. Repeat the process two more times. Then thinly slice the garlic and return it to the saucepan.
2. Add cream. Bring to a boil. Reduce the heat and simmer gently until reduced by half or to a thick, saucelike consistency, stirring occasionally.
3. Season with salt and pepper.

PUFF PASTRY

Puff pastry	250 g	8 oz.

1. Line a large baking sheet with parchment paper. Roll the pastry into a 25 cm x 22.5 cm (10 inch x 9 inch) rectangle on a lightly floured surface.
2. Cut into six 7.5 cm x 12.5 cm (3 inch x 5 inch) squares using a fluted pastry cutter. Transfer to a baking sheet and dock the dough with a fork.
3. Cover and refrigerate at least 1 hour before baking.
4. Bake at 180°C (350°F) until puffed, browned and baked through, approximately 30 minutes.

MUSHROOMS

Fresh shiitake mushrooms	750–1000 g	1-1/2–2 lb.
Olive oil	30 mL	2 Tbsp.
Salt and pepper	TT	TT

1. Trim the stems of the mushrooms. Heat a sauté pan over medium-high heat and film with oil. Add the mushrooms and cook until lightly brown and tender, approximately 5 minutes, stirring frequently.
2. Season with salt and pepper.
3. To serve the tart, slice each piece of puff pastry in half horizontally, using a serrated knife. Arrange on 6 plates.
4. Rewarm the garlic cream and mushrooms. Spoon cream onto the bottom of each piece of pastry. Overlap the mushrooms on top of cream, alternating light and dark pieces. Set the top pieces of pastry at an angle over the mushrooms so the filling is visible.
5. Serve with poivrade or Robert sauce (see page 212) and garnish with a herb sprig, if desired.

◆◆◆

RECIPE 10.23

DUXELLE SAUCE

Yield: 750 mL (1-1/2 pt.)

Mushrooms, chopped fine	250 g	8 oz.
Shallots, chopped fine	90 g	3 oz.
Clarified butter	30 mL	1 fl. oz.
Olive oil	30 mL	1 fl. oz.
Dry white wine	350 mL	12 fl. oz.
Demi-glace	500 mL	1 pt.
Cream, 35%	60 mL	2 fl. oz.
Salt and pepper	TT	TT
Parsley, chopped fine	15 mL	1 Tbsp.

1. Sauté the mushrooms and the shallots in the butter and oil. The mushrooms will release their liquid and darken. Cook until completely dry.
2. Deglaze with the white wine and reduce by two-thirds.
3. Add the demi-glace. Bring to a boil, then simmer for 5 minutes.
4. Stir in the cream. Adjust seasonings. Garnish with parsley.

RECIPE 10.23

Approximate values per 50 mL serving:

Calories	102
Total fat	7.9 g
Saturated fat	3.6 g
Cholesterol	15 mg
Sodium	174 mg
Total carbohydrates	6.6 g
Protein	1.2 g

◆◆◆

RECIPE 10.24

BARBECUE SAUCE

Yield: 1 L (1 qt.)

Onion, brunoise	50 g	2 oz.
Garlic, chopped	30 g	1 oz.
Vegetable oil	125 mL	4 fl. oz.
Cider vinegar	125 mL	4 fl. oz.
Molasses	125 mL	4 fl. oz.
Honey	125 g	4 oz.
Beer	125 mL	4 fl. oz.
Lemon juice	30 mL	1 oz.
Ketchup	1 L	32 fl. oz.
Dry mustard	15 g	1/2 oz.
Worcestershire sauce	30 mL	2 Tbsp.
Salt and pepper	TT	TT
Chilli powder	5 g	1 Tbsp.

1. Sweat the onion and garlic in the oil until tender.
2. Combine the remaining ingredients and simmer for 30 minutes.

NOTE: Spices, herbs and other flavourings may be incorporated.

RECIPE 10.24

Approximate values per 50 mL serving:

Calories	170
Total fat	6.3 g
Saturated fat	0.5 g
Cholesterol	0 mg
Sodium	735 mg
Total carbohydrates	27 g
Protein	1.2 g

Simon Smotkowicz, CCC

Simon has been a member and a leader of award-winning Canadian culinary teams for many years, most recently managing Team Canada to a world championship in Glasgow in 1997 and 2001. In 1995 he was elected Chef of the Year for the Western Region by his peers in the CFCC.

RECIPE 10.25

Approximate values per 50 mL serving:

Calories	144
Total fat	11 g
Saturated fat	1.5 g
Cholesterol	0 mg
Sodium	239 mg
Total carbohydrates	9.1 g
Protein	2.1 g

◆◆◆

RECIPE 10.25

PINE NUT AND PISTACHIO RELISH

SHAW CONFERENCE CENTRE, EDMONTON, AB
Executive Chef Simon Smotkowicz, CCC

Yield: 1.5 L (1-1/2 qt.)

Large eggplant, peeled and finely chopped	1	1
Salt	TT	TT
Virgin olive oil	225 mL	8 fl. oz.
Spanish onion, finely chopped	200 g	6-1/2 oz.
Garlic cloves, peeled and minced	15 g	1/2 oz.
Tomatoes, peeled, seeded and diced	800 g	28 oz.
Fresh basil, minced	2 g	1 Tbsp.
Fresh oregano, minced	2 g	1 Tbsp.
Fresh thyme, minced	0.5 g	1/2 tsp.
Celery stalks, trimmed and finely chopped	200 g	7 oz.
Green olives, pitted and finely chopped	175 g	6 oz.
Pine nuts, toasted	100 g	4 oz.
Green pistachio nuts, unsalted, shelled	100 g	4 oz.
Red wine vinegar	125 mL	4 fl. oz.
Brown sugar	125 g	4-1/2 oz.
Cracked black pepper	TT	TT

1. Put the chopped eggplant in a colander and sprinkle it lightly with salt. Set aside and allow to sweat for 20–30 minutes.
2. Heat 50 mL (2 fl. oz.) olive oil in a large skillet over medium-high heat.
3. Add the onion and garlic and sauté until translucent. Add the tomatoes, basil, oregano and thyme and sauté for 4 minutes. Add the chopped celery and olives and sauté for a further 3 minutes.
4. Thoroughly rinse the salt from the eggplant under cold running water and dry on paper towels. In a separate pan, with the pine nuts and pistachios, sauté the eggplant in the remaining olive oil for 3 minutes.
5. Remove the pan from the heat and combine the eggplant mixture with the tomato mixture and allow to cool.
6. Mix vinegar and sugar until dissolved and add to the eggplant-tomato relish. Adjust seasoning to taste and serve warm or at room temperature.

◆◆◆

RECIPE 10.26

TOMATO ANCHOVY SAUCE

HALIFAX, NS
Chef Michael Smith

Yield: 750 mL (1-1/2 pt.)

Ripe tomatoes, chopped	600 g	20 oz.
Anchovies	50 g	2 oz.
Lemons, zested and juiced	2	2
Extra virgin olive oil	125 mL	4 fl. oz.
Dijon mustard	15 g	1 Tbsp.
Tabasco sauce	dash	dash

Michael Smith

Chef Michael Smith has dedicated his career to furthering the ideals of Canadian Cuisine. He hosts Food Network Canada's "Chef at Large" and frequently crisscrosses the country leading cooking classes. His company "Chef Michael's Flavours" brings the flavours of the Maritimes to the world.

1. Place all ingredients in a high-speed blender and process until smooth.

2. Strain the purée through a fine mesh strainer. Chill and reserve.

NOTE: Michael comments—Only use ripe tomatoes or make something else. It's great served warm with grilled fish or cold with smoked salmon. To preserve the tomato flavours, only heat when needed.

◆ ◆ ◆

RECIPE 10.27

PESTO SAUCE

Yield: 900 g (1-1/2 pt.)

Olive oil	350 mL	12 fl. oz.
Pine nuts	100 g	3 oz.
Fresh basil leaves	200 g	6 oz.
Garlic, chopped	15 g	1 Tbsp.
Parmesan cheese, grated	125 g	4 oz.
Romano cheese, grated	125 g	4 oz.
Salt and pepper	TT	TT

1. Place one-third of the olive oil in a blender or food processor and add all the remaining ingredients.

2. Blend or process until smooth. Add the remaining olive oil and blend for a few seconds to incorporate.

VARIATION: *Walnut Pesto*—Substitute walnuts for pine nuts in the above recipe.

◆ ◆ ◆

RECIPE 10.28

OXTAIL JUS*

HALIFAX, NS
Chef Michael Smith

Yield: 1.25 L (40 fl. oz.)

Butter	60 g	4 oz.
Onions, sliced	1.8 kg	4 lb.
Garlic, fine mince	10 g	4 cloves
Oxtail broth	1 L	32 fl. oz.
Red wine vinegar	5 mL	1 tsp.
Salt and pepper	TT	TT

1. Over medium heat, melt butter, add onions and begin cooking. Once the moisture has evaporated and the sugars begin to caramelize, lower the heat. Stir continuously and as the onions caramelize, gradually lower the heat. Stir continuously so the fonds do not burn.

2. When the onions are an even, deep golden-brown colour, stir in the garlic and cook for a few minutes until the garlic is fully aromatized.

3. Place onions in a blender with 250 mL (8 fl. oz.) of the broth and purée. Strain the purée into a clean pot and add remaining broth. Simmer to release the air and strain again through a fine mesh sieve.

4. Balance the flavours by adding the vinegar and adjust seasoning with salt and pepper.

*This recipe relies on a vegetable puree to lightly thicken the sauce instead of a traditional roux or cornstarch.

RECIPE 10.26

Approximate values per 100 mL serving:

Calories	186
Total fat	17 g
Saturated fat	2.4 g
Cholesterol	5.7 mg
Sodium	302 mg
Total carbohydrates	5.4 g
Protein	2.9 g

RECIPE 10.27

Approximate values per 50 mL serving:

Calories	312
Total fat	30 g
Saturated fat	6.4 g
Cholesterol	15 mg
Sodium	334 mg
Total carbohydrates	2.5 g
Protein	8.1 g

Michael Smith

Chef Michael Smith has dedicated his career to furthering the ideals of Canadian Cuisine. He hosts Food Network Canada's "Chef at Large" and frequently crisscrosses the country leading cooking classes. His company "Chef Michael's Flavours" brings the flavours of the Maritimes to the world.

RECIPE 10.28

Approximate values per 100 mL serving:

Calories	93
Total fat	5.4 g
Saturated fat	2.9 g
Cholesterol	12 mg
Sodium	199 mg
Total carbohydrates	9.9 g
Protein	1.2 g

WEBLINKS

Canada Info
   www.canolainfo.org

Searchable Online Archives of Recipes: Sauce Recipes
   www.recipesource.com

Amy Gale's rec.food.recipes archive: Sauces and Marinade Recipes
   www.cs.cmu.edu/~mjw/recipes/sauces/index.html

Culinaria Online: Collected Recipes—Sauces
   www.culinaria.com/collectedRecipes/sauces.html

Recipes
   recipes.alastra.com/sauces

Salsa
   recipes.alastra.com/salsa

CHAPTER 11
SOUPS

◆◆◆

LEARNING OUTCOMES

After studying this chapter you will be able to:

◆ prepare a variety of clear and thick soups, including broths and bouillons, consommés, cream soups, purée soups, bisques and chowders
◆ garnish and serve soups appropriately

*M*any classic soups are successfully prepared only if recipes are followed strictly. The successful preparation of other soups depends upon the mastery of specialized techniques. But where classic recipes need neither be followed nor special techniques employed, perhaps no other area of the kitchen allows the cook to use his or her imagination and creativity as much as the soup station.

The variety of ingredients, seasonings and garnishes that can be used for soups is virtually endless, provided you understand the basic procedures for making different kinds of soup. Great soups can be made using the finest and most expensive ingredients or leftovers from the previous evening's dinner service and trimmings from the day's production.

This chapter extends to soups the skills and knowledge learned in Chapter 10, Stocks and Sauces. In Chapter 10 we discussed making stocks, thickening liquids, using a liaison and skimming impurities, techniques that apply to soup making as well. Here we discuss techniques such as clarifying consommés and thickening soups with vegetable purées. This chapter also covers cream soups, cold soups and guidelines for garnishing and serving a variety of soups.

Most soups can be classified by cooking technique and appearance as either clear or thick.

Clear soups include **broths** and **bouillons** made from meat, poultry, game, fish or vegetables as well as **consommés**, which are stocks or broths clarified to remove impurities.

Thickened soups include cream soups and purée soups. The most common **cream soups** are those made from vegetables cooked in a liquid that is thickened with a starch and puréed; cream is then incorporated to add richness and flavour. **Purée soups** are generally made from starchy vegetables or legumes. After the main ingredient is simmered in a liquid, the mixture—or a portion of it—is puréed. Velouté soups are basically cream soups with the addition of a liaison.

Some soups (notably **bisques** and **chowders** as well as **cold soups** such as gazpacho and fruit soup) are generally regarded as thick soups. They use special preparation methods or a combination of the methods mentioned above.

QUALITY STANDARD

A soup's quality is determined by its flavour, appearance and texture. A good soup should be full flavoured, with no off or sour tastes. Flavours from each of the soup's ingredients should blend and complement, with no one flavour overpowering another. Consommés should be crystal clear. The vegetables in vegetable soups should be brightly coloured, not grey. Garnishes should be attractive and uniform in size and shape. The soup's texture should be very precise. If it is supposed to be smooth, then it should be very smooth and lump-free. If the soft and crisp textures of certain ingredients are supposed to contrast, the soup should not be overcooked, as this causes all the ingredients to become mushy and soft.

Garnishing is an important consideration when preparing soups. When applied to soups, the word *garnish* has two meanings. The first is the one more typically associated with the word. It refers to foods added to the soup as decoration—for example, a broccoli floret floated on a bowl of cream of broccoli soup. The second refers to foods that may serve not only as decorations but also as critical components of the final product—for example, noodles in a bowl of chicken noodle soup. In this context, the noodles are not ingredients because they are not used to make the chicken soup. Rather they are added to chicken soup to create a different dish. These additional items are still referred to as garnishes, however.

CLEAR SOUPS

All clear soups start as broth or as stock. Broths may be served as finished items, used as the base for other soups or refined (clarified) into consommés.

Broths and Bouillons

The techniques for making stocks, discussed in Chapter 10, are identical to those used for making broths and bouillons. Like stocks, broths are prepared by simmering flavouring ingredients in a liquid for long periods of time. Broths and stocks differ, however, in two ways. First, broths are made with meat instead of just bones. Second, broths (often with a garnish) can be served as finished dishes, while stocks are generally used to prepare other items.

Broths are made from meat, poultry, fish or vegetables cooked in a liquid. An especially full-flavoured broth results when a stock and not just water is used as the liquid. Cuts of meat from the shank, neck or shoulder result in more flavourful broths, as will the flesh of mature poultry. Proper temperature, skimming and straining help produce well-flavoured, clear broths.

Basic Procedure for Preparing Broths

1. Truss or cut the main ingredient.
2. Brown the meat; brown or sweat the mirepoix or vegetables as necessary.
3. Place the main ingredient and mirepoix or vegetables in an appropriate stockpot and add enough cold water or stock to cover. Add a bouquet garni or sachet d'épices if desired.
4. Bring the liquid slowly to a boil; reduce to a simmer and cook, skimming occasionally, until the main ingredient is tender and the flavour is fully developed.
5. Carefully strain the broth through a conical strainer lined with cheesecloth; avoid disturbing the flavouring ingredients in order to preserve the broth's clarity.
6. Cool and store following the procedures for cooling stocks. Or bring to a boil, garnish as desired and hold for service.

♦♦♦

ESCOFFIER'S CLASSIFICATION OF SOUPS

In his 1903 culinary treatise *Le Guide culinaire*, Auguste Escoffier recognized many more categories of soups than we do today. They include:

Clear soups, which are always "clear consommés with a slight garnish in keeping with the nature of the consommé."

Purées, which are made from starchy vegetables and are thickened with rice, potato or soft bread crumbs.

Cullises, which use poultry, game or fish for a base and are thickened with rice, lentils, espagnole sauce or bread soaked in boiling salted water.

Bisques, which use shellfish cooked with a mirepoix as a base and are thickened with rice.

Veloutés, which use velouté sauce as a base and are finished with a liaison of egg yolks and cream.

Cream soups, which use béchamel sauce as a base and are finished with heavy cream.

Special soups, which are those that do not follow the procedures for veloutés or creams.

Vegetable soups, which are usually *paysanne* or peasant-type and "do not demand very great precision in the apportionment of the vegetables of which they are composed, but they need great care and attention, notwithstanding."

Foreign soups, "which have a foreign origin whose use, although it may not be general, is yet sufficiently common."

Because of changes in consumer health consciousness and kitchen operations, many of the distinctions between Escoffier's classic soups have now become blurred and, in some cases, eliminated. As discussed in this chapter, for example, clear consommés and vegetable soups are now made with stocks or broths; most cream soups use velouté as a base and are finished with milk or cream rather than a liaison. But not everything has changed: The procedures for making purées and bisques are essentially the same today as they were when Escoffier haunted the great kitchens of Europe.

Applying the Basics

RECIPE 11.1

BEEF BROTH

Yield: 4 L (4 qt.)

Beef shank, neck or shoulder cut in 5-cm-thick (2-inch) pieces	2.25 kg	5 lb.
Vegetable oil	125 mL	4 fl. oz.
Beef stock	4 L	1 gal.
Mirepoix	500 g	1 lb.
Turnip, medium dice	125 g	4 oz.
Leeks, medium dice	125 g	4 oz.
Tomato, seeded and diced	125 g	4 oz.
Sachet:		
Bay leaf	1	1
Dried thyme	0.25 g	1/4 tsp.
Peppercorns, crushed	0.5 g	1/2 tsp.
Parsley stems	8	8
Garlic cloves, crushed	1	1
Salt	TT	TT

1. Brown the meat in 60 mL (2 fl. oz.) of oil, then place it in a stockpot. Add the stock and bring to a simmer. Simmer gently for 2 hours, skimming the surface as necessary.

2. After the meat has simmered for 2 hours, caramelize the mirepoix in the remaining oil and add it to the liquid. Add the turnip, leeks, tomato and sachet.

3. Simmer until full flavour has developed, approximately 1 hour. Skim the surface as necessary.

4. Carefully strain the broth through cheesecloth and season to taste. Cool and refrigerate.

RECIPE 11.1

Approximate values per 175 mL serving:

Calories	59
Total fat	5.2 g
Saturated fat	0.4 g
Cholesterol	0 mg
Sodium	97 mg
Total carbohydrates	2 g
Protein	1 g

Broth-Based Soups

Broths are often used as bases for such familiar soups as vegetable, chicken noodle or beef barley.

Transforming a broth into a broth-based vegetable soup, for example, is quite simple. Although a broth may be served with a vegetable (or meat) garnish, a broth-based vegetable soup is a soup in which the vegetables (and meats) are cooked directly in the broth, adding flavour, body and texture to the finished product. Any number of vegetables can be used to make a vegetable soup; it could be a single vegetable as in onion soup or a dozen different vegetables for a hearty minestrone. Making a mixed vegetable soup allows the cook to use his or her imagination and whatever produce may be on hand.

When making broth-based vegetable soups, each ingredient must be added at the proper time so that all ingredients are cooked when the soup is finished. The ingredients must cook long enough to add their flavours and soften sufficiently but not so long that they lose their identity and become too soft or mushy.

Because broth-based vegetable soups are made by simmering ingredients directly in the broth, they are generally not as clear as plain broths. But appearance is still important. So, when cutting ingredients for the soup, pay particular attention that the pieces are uniform and visually appealing. Small dice, julienne, batonnet or paysanne cuts are recommended.

Basic Procedure for Preparing Broth-based vegetable soups

1. Sweat long-cooking vegetables in butter or fat.
2. Add the appropriate stock or broth and bring to a simmer.
3. Add seasonings such as bay leaves, dried thyme, crushed peppercorns, parsley stems and garlic, in a sachet, allowing enough time for the seasonings to fully flavour the soup.
4. Add additional ingredients according to their cooking times.
5. Simmer the soup to blend all the flavours.
6. If the soup is not going to be served immediately, cool and refrigerate it.
7. Just before service add any garnishes that were prepared separately or do not require cooking.

Applying the Basics

RECIPE 11.2

CHICKEN NOODLE SOUP

Yield: 6 L (6 qt.)

Chicken	2–2.5 kg	1
Water	6 L	6 qt.
Mirepoix	500 g	1 lb.
Vegetable oil	25 mL	1 fl. oz.
Carrot, julienne	350 g	12 oz.
Celery, julienne	250 g	8 oz.
Leek, julienne	450 g	16 oz.
Turnip, white, julienne	125 g	4 oz.
Sachet	1	1
Noodles, broken, 2.5 cm (1 inch)	250 g	7 oz.
Salt and pepper	TT	TT
Parsley, chopped	garnish	garnish

1. Cook fowl in water and mirepoix for 4 hours. Reserve stock; chill chicken if necessary. Dice or pull meat.
2. Sweat julienned vegetables in oil until transluscent.
3. Add stock and simmer with sachet 15 minutes.
4. Meanwhile, cook noodles in boiling, salted water until al dente. Drain and rinse well.
5. Add noodles and chicken meat to soup, simmer 5 minutes and adjust seasoning. Finish with chopped parsley.

RECIPE 11.2

Approximate values per 175 mL serving:

Calories	113
Total fat	4.9 g
Saturated fat	1.1 g
Cholesterol	23 mg
Sodium	389 mg
Total carbohydrates	11 g
Protein	6.1 g

Consommés

A consommé is a stock or broth that has been clarified to remove impurities so that it is crystal clear. Traditionally, all clear broths were referred to as consommés; a clear broth further refined using the process described below was referred to as a double consommé. The term *double consommé* is still used occasionally to describe any strongly flavoured consommé.

QUALITY STANDARD

Well-prepared consommés should be rich in the flavour of the main ingredient. Beef and game consommés should be dark in colour; consommés made from

1. Combine the ingredients for the clearmeat: chill for 3-4 hours.

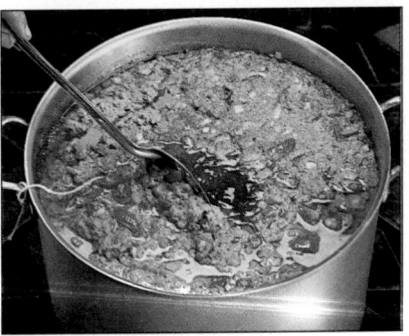

2. Make a hole in the raft to allow the liquid to bubble through.

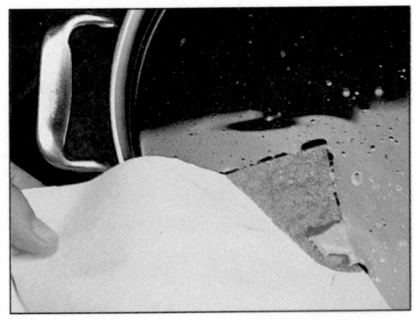

3. Degrease the consommé with a paper towel.

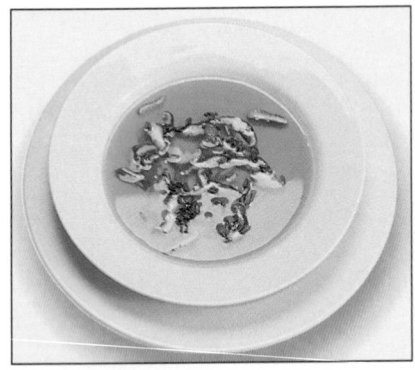

4. The finished consommé.

poultry should have a golden to light amber colour. They should have substantial body as a result of their high gelatin content, and all consommés should be perfectly clear with no trace of fat.

Because a consommé is a refined broth, it is absolutely essential that the broth or stock used be of the highest quality. Although the clarification process adds some flavour to the consommé, the finished consommé will be only as good as the stock or broth from which it was made.

The Clarification Process

To make a consommé, you clarify a stock or broth. The stock or broth to be clarified must be cold and grease-free. To clarify, the cold degreased stock or broth is combined with a mixture known as a **clearmeat** or **clarification**. A clearmeat is a mixture of egg whites; ground meat, poultry or fish; mirepoix, herbs and spices; and an acidic product, usually tomatoes, lemon juice or wine. (An **onion brûlé** is also often added to help flavour and colour the consommé as a remedial action.)

The stock or broth and clearmeat are then slowly brought to a simmer. As the albumen in the egg whites and meat begins to coagulate, it traps impurities suspended in the liquid. As coagulation continues, the albumen-containing items combine with the other clearmeat ingredients and rise to the liquid's surface, forming a **raft**. As the mixture simmers, the raft ingredients release their flavours, further enriching the consommé.

After simmering, the consommé is carefully strained through several layers of cheesecloth to remove any trace of impurities. It is then completely degreased, either by cooling and refrigerating, then removing the solidified fat, or by carefully ladling the fat from the surface. The result is a rich, flavourful, crystal-clear consommé.

Basic Procedure for Making Consommés

1. In a suitable heavy-bottomed stockpot (one with a spigot makes it much easier to strain the consommé when it is finished), combine the ground meat, lightly beaten egg white and other clearmeat ingredients.

2. Add the cold stock or broth and stir to combine with the clearmeat ingredients.

3. Over medium heat, slowly bring the mixture to a simmer, stirring occasionally.

4. As the raft forms, make a hole in its centre so that the liquid can bubble through, cooking the raft completely and extracting as much flavour as possible from the raft ingredients.

5. Simmer the consommé until full flavour develops, approximately 1 to 1.5 hours.

6. Carefully strain the consommé through several layers of cheesecloth and degrease completely.

7. If the consommé will not be used immediately, it should be cooled and refrigerated, following the procedures for cooling stocks discussed in Chapter 10. When the consommé is completely cold, remove any remaining fat that solidified on its surface.

8. If, after reheating the consommé, small dots of fat appear on the surface, they can be removed by blotting with a small piece of paper towel.

Applying the Basics

RECIPE 11.3

BEEF CONSOMMÉ

Yield: 4 L (4 qt.)

Egg whites	350 g	12
Ground beef, lean, preferably shank, neck or shoulder	1 kg	2 lb.
Mirepoix	450 g	1 lb.
Tomato, seeded and diced	350 g	12 oz.
Brown beef stock or broth, cold	5 L	5 qt.
Onion brûlé (optional)	2 halves	2 halves
Sachet:		
Bay leaves	2	2
Dried thyme	1 g	1/2 tsp.
Peppercorns, crushed	1 g	1/2 tsp.
Parsley stems	8	8
Cloves, whole	2	2
Salt	TT	TT

1. Whip the egg whites until slightly frothy.
2. Combine the egg whites, beef, mirepoix and tomatoes in an appropriate stockpot.
3. Add the cold beef stock or broth; mix well and add the onion brûlé and sachet.
4. Bring the mixture to a simmer over moderate heat, stirring occasionally. Stop stirring when the raft begins to form.
5. Break a hole in the centre of the raft to allow the consommé to bubble through.
6. Simmer until full flavour develops, approximately 1.5 hours.
7. Strain through several layers of cheesecloth, degrease and adjust the seasonings. Cool and refrigerate or hold for service.

Correcting a Poorly Clarified Consommé

A clarification may fail for a variety of reasons. For example, if the consommé is allowed to boil or if it is stirred after the raft has formed, a cloudy consommé can result. If the consommé is insufficiently clear, a second clarification can be performed using the following procedure. This second clarification should be performed only once, however, and only if absolutely necessary, because the eggs not only remove impurities but also some of the consommé's flavour and richness.

1. Thoroughly chill and degrease the consommé.
2. Lightly beat one egg white per litre (quart) of consommé and combine with the cold consommé.
3. Slowly bring the consommé to a simmer, stirring occasionally. Stop stirring when the egg whites begin to coagulate.
4. When the egg whites are completely coagulated, carefully strain the consommé.

◆◆◆

CLASSIC CONSOMMÉS

Beef Consommé

Brunoise—brunoise of leeks, carrots, turnip, celery, peas and chervil.

Célestine—julienne of savory crepe, traditionally thickened with tapioca.

Julienne—julienne of leeks, carrots, turnips, celery, cabbage, sorrel and chervil.

Chicken Consommé

Caroline—royale, rice and chervil.

Mimosa—sieved white and yolk of hard-boiled egg.

Fish Consommé

George Sand—white fish and crayfish quenelles, morels, carp soft roe on croutons made from French stick bread.

Game Consommé

Saint-Hubert—white wine, game and lentil royale, julienne of game.

RECIPE 11.3

Approximate values per 175 mL serving:

Calories	62
Total fat	3.1 g
Saturated fat	1.0 g
Cholesterol	1.5 mg
Sodium	259 mg
Total carbohydrates	8.0 g
Protein	0.6 g

THICK SOUPS

There are two kinds of thick soups: cream velouté-based soups and purée soups. In general, cream velouté-based soups are thickened with a roux or other starch, while purée soups rely on a purée of the main ingredient for thickening. But in certain ways the two soups are very similar: Some purée soups are finished with cream or partially thickened with a roux or other starch.

Cream Soups

Most cream soups are made by simmering the main flavouring ingredient (for example, broccoli for cream of broccoli soup) in a white stock or thin velouté sauce to which seasonings have been added. The mixture is then puréed and strained. After the consistency has been adjusted, the soup is finished by adding cream. In classic cuisine, thin béchamel sauce is often used as the base for cream soups and can be substituted for velouté in many cream soup recipes, if desired.

Both hard vegetables (e.g., celery and squash) and soft or leafy vegetables (e.g., spinach, corn, broccoli and asparagus) are used for cream soups. Hard vegetables are generally sweated in butter without browning before the liquid is added. Soft and leafy vegetables are generally added to the soup after the liquid is brought to a boil. Because cream soups are puréed, it is important to cook the flavouring ingredients until they are soft and can be passed through a food mill easily.

All cream soups are finished with milk or cream. Using milk thins the soup while adding richness; using the same amount of cream adds much more richness without the same thinning effect. Cold milk and cream curdle easily if added directly to a hot or acidic soup, but there are several steps that can be taken to prevent curdling:

1. Never add cold milk or cream to hot soup. Bring the milk or cream to a simmer before adding it to the soup. Or, temper the milk or cream by gradually adding some hot soup to it and then incorporating the warmed mixture into the rest of the soup.
2. If possible, add the milk or cream to the soup just before service.
3. Do not boil the soup after the milk or cream has been added.
4. The presence of roux or other starch helps prevent curdling. Therefore, béchamel or cream sauce is often used instead of milk or cream to finish cream soups.

(Recall from Chapter 10 that a béchamel sauce is made by thickening milk with a roux, and a cream sauce is made by adding cream to a béchamel sauce.)

Basic Procedure for Making Cream Soups

1. In a soup pot, sweat hard vegetables such as squash, onions, carrots and celery in oil or butter without browning.
2. In order to thicken the soup:
   (a) add flour and cook to make a blond roux, then add the cooking liquid (i.e., the stock), or
   (b) add the stock to the vegetables, bring the stock to a simmer and add a blond roux that was prepared separately, or
   (c) add a thin velouté or béchamel sauce to the vegetables.
3. Bring to a boil and reduce to a simmer.

4. Add any soft vegetables such as broccoli or asparagus, and a sachet or bouquet garni as desired.

5. Simmer the soup, skimming occasionally, until the vegetables are very tender.

6. Purée the soup by passing it through a food mill, blender, food processor or vertical chopper mixer (VCM) and strain through a conical strainer. If the soup is too thick, adjust the consistency by adding boiling white stock.

7. Finish the soup by adding hot milk or cream or a thin béchamel or cream sauce. Adjust the seasonings and serve.

Applying the Basics

RECIPE 11.4

CREAM OF BROCCOLI SOUP

Yield: 6 L (6 qt.)

Onion, medium dice	350 g	12 oz.
Celery, medium dice	90 g	3 oz.
Broccoli stalks, chopped	1.25 kg	3 lb.
Whole butter	90 g	3 oz.
Chicken velouté sauce, hot	4 L	4 qt.
Chicken stock, hot	approx. 2 L	approx. 2 qt.
Cream, 35%, hot	700 mL	24 fl. oz.
Salt and white pepper	TT	TT
Broccoli florets, blanched	250 g	8 oz.

1. Sweat the onions, celery and broccoli in the butter, without browning, until they are nearly tender.

2. Add the velouté sauce. Bring to a simmer and cook until the vegetables are tender, approximately 15 minutes. Skim the surface periodically.

3. Purée the soup, then strain it through a fine conical strainer or etâmine.

4. Return the soup to the stove and thin it to the correct consistency with the hot chicken stock.

5. Bring the soup to a simmer and add the hot cream. Season to taste with salt and white pepper.

6. Garnish with blanched broccoli florets just before service.

VARIATIONS: To make cream of asparagus, cauliflower, corn, pea or spinach soup, substitute an equal amount of the chosen vegetable for the broccoli. If using fresh spinach, precook the leaves slightly before proceeding with the recipe.

Purée Soups

Purée soups are hearty soups made by cooking starchy vegetables or legumes in a stock or broth, then puréeing all or a portion of them to thicken the soup. Purée soups are similar to cream soups in that they both consist of a main ingredient that is first cooked in a liquid, then puréed. The primary difference is that unlike cream soups, which are thickened with starch, purée soups generally do not use additional starch for thickening. Rather, purée soups depend on the starch content of the main ingredient for thickening. Also, purée soups are generally coarser than cream soups and are typically not strained after puréeing. When finishing purée soups with cream, follow the guidelines discussed above for adding cream to cream soups.

♦♦♦
CLASSIC CREAM SOUPS

Crème Dubarry—Cauliflower
Crème de Céleri—Celery
Crème de Tomates—Tomato
Crème Solférino—Tomato and potato
Crème Portugaise—Tomato and rice
Crème Palestine—Artichoke
Crème Soubise—White onion
Crème de Poireaux—Leek

♦♦♦
CLASSIC VELOUTÉ SOUPS

Velouté Agnès Sorel—Chicken velouté with mushrooms, julienne of mushrooms, white of chicken, ox tongue and liaison.

Bagration-Maigre—Fish velouté flavoured with mushrooms, julienne of sole, quenelles of white fish and crayfish, crayfish and liaison.

RECIPE 11.4

Approximate values per 175 mL serving:

Calories	256
Total fat	20 g
Saturated fat	12 g
Cholesterol	54 mg
Sodium	280 mg
Total carbohydrates	16 g
Protein	3 g

♦♦♦
CLASSIC PURÉE SOUPS

Potage St. Germain—Green pea
Potage Crècy—Carrot
Potage Soissonnaise—Haricot bean
Potage Bonne Femme—Potato and leek
Potage Freneuse—Turnip
Potage Cressonière—Potato and watercress

Purée soups can be made with dried or fresh beans such as peas, lentils and navy beans, or with any number of vegetables including cauliflower, celery root, turnips and potatoes. Diced potatoes or rice are often used to help thicken vegetable purée soups.

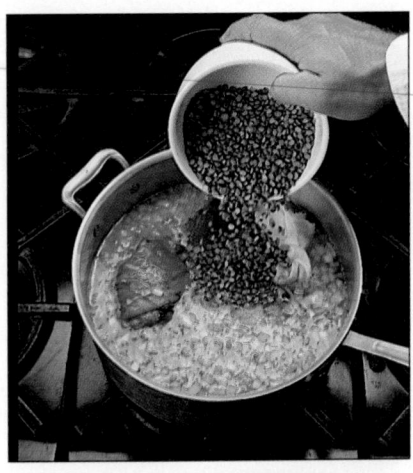

Basic Procedure for Making Purée Soups

1. Sweat the mirepoix in butter without browning.
2. Add the cooking liquid.
3. Add the main ingredients and a sachet or bouquet garni.
4. Bring to a boil, reduce to a simmer and cook until all the ingredients are soft enough to purée easily. Remove and discard the sachet or bouquet garni.
5. Reserve a portion of the liquid to adjust the soup's consistency. Purée the rest of the soup by passing it through a food mill, food processor, blender or VCM.
6. Add enough of the reserved liquid to bring the soup to the correct consistency. If the soup is still too thick, add hot stock as needed.
7. Return the soup to a simmer and adjust the seasonings.
8. Add hot cream to the soup if desired.

Applying the Basics

RECIPE 11.5

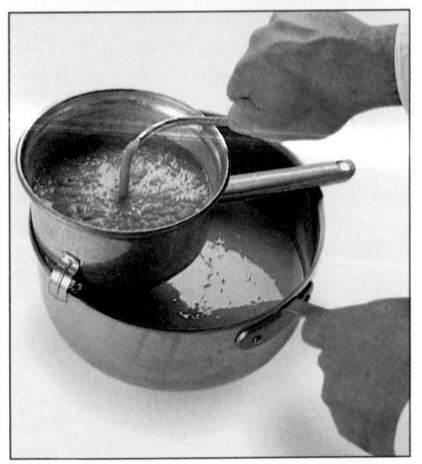

Split pea soup

PURÉE OF SPLIT PEA SOUP

Yield: 4 L (4 qt.)

Split peas, washed and soaked	800 g	1 lb. 12 oz.
Bacon, diced	100 g	3 oz.
Mirepoix, medium dice	500 g	1 lb.
Garlic cloves, chopped	10 g	2
White stock	3 L	3 qt.
Ham hocks or meaty ham bones	700 g	1-1/2 lb.
Sachet:		
Bay leaves	2	2
Dried thyme	0.25 g	1/2 tsp.
Peppercorns, crushed	0.5 g	1/2 tsp.
Salt and pepper	TT	TT
Croutons, sautéed in butter	as needed for garnish	

1. Soak peas in water overnight.
2. In a stockpot, render the bacon by cooking it slowly and allowing it to release its fat; sweat the mirepoix and garlic in the fat without browning them.
3. Add the white stock, drained peas, ham hocks or bones and sachet. Bring to a boil, reduce to a simmer and cook until the peas are soft, approximately 1–1.5 hours.
4. Remove the sachet and ham hocks or bones. Pass the soup through a food mill and return it to the stockpot.
5. Remove the meat from the hocks or bones. Cut the meat into a medium dice and add it to the soup.
6. Bring the soup to a simmer and, if necessary, adjust the consistency by adding hot stock. Adjust the seasonings with salt and pepper and serve, garnished with croutons.

VARIATIONS: White beans, yellow peas, and other dried beans or lentils can be soaked overnight in water and used instead of split peas.

RECIPE 11.5

Approximate values per 175 mL serving:

Calories	266
Total fat	10 g
Saturated fat	3.7 g
Cholesterol	26 mg
Sodium	272 mg
Total carbohydrates	29 g
Protein	15 g

Adjusting the Consistency of Thick Soups

Cream and purée soups tend to thicken when made in advance and refrigerated. To dilute a portion being reheated, add a small amount of stock, broth, water or milk.

If the soup is too thin, additional roux, beurre manié or cornstarch mixed with cool stock can be used to thicken it. If additional starch is added to thicken the soup, it should be used sparingly and the soup should be simmered a few minutes to cook out the starchy flavour. A liaison of egg yolks and heavy cream can be used to finish cream soups when added richness is also desired. Remember, the soup must not boil after the liaison is added or it may curdle.

OTHER SOUPS

Several popular types of soup do not fit the descriptions of or follow the procedures for clear or thick soups. Soups such as bisques and chowders as well as many cold soups use special methods or a combination of the methods used for clear and thick soups.

Bisques

Traditional bisques are shellfish (crustaceans) soups thickened with cooked rice. Today bisques are prepared using a combination of the cream and purée soup procedures. They are generally made from shrimp, lobster or crayfish and are thickened with a roux instead of rice for better stability and consistency.

Much of a bisque's flavour comes from crustacean shells, which are simmered in the cooking liquid, puréed (along with the mirepoix), returned to the cooking liquid and strained after further cooking. Puréeing the shells and returning them to the soup also adds the thickness and grainy texture associated with bisques, although this is rarely done today.

Bisques are enriched with cream, following the procedures for cream soups, and can be finished with butter for additional richness. The garnish should be diced flesh from the appropriate shellfish.

Basic Procedure for Making Bisques

1. Caramelize the mirepoix and main flavouring ingredient in fat.
2. Add paprika and a tomato product and deglaze with wine.
3. Add the cooking liquid (stock or velouté).
4. Incorporate roux if needed.
5. Simmer, skimming as needed.
6. Strain the soup, reserving the solids and liquid. Optional: Purée the solids in a food chopper or processor and return them to the liquid. Return to a simmer.
7. Strain the soup through a fine etâmine or a conical strainer lined with cheesecloth.
8. Return the soup to a simmer and finish with hot cream.

To add even more richness to the bisque, monter au beurre with whole butter or a compound butter such as shrimp or lobster butter just before the soup is served. Also, if desired, add 100 mL (4 fl. oz.) of sherry to each 4 L (1 gallon) of soup just before service.

◆◆◆
CROUTONS

A crouton is simply a piece of bread that is toasted, sautéed or dried. Two types are often used.

The more familiar ones are small seasoned cubes of bread that are baked or toasted and sprinkled over soups or salads.

A more classic variety is made by sautéing slices of bread in clarified butter or olive oil until brown and crisp. The bread may be rough slices from a baguette or cut into shapes (such as hearts, diamonds or circles) from larger slices. Sautéed croutons have two advantages over the toasted variety: They stay crisp longer after coming in contact with moist foods, and they gain flavour from the butter or olive oil in which they are cooked. Sautéed croutons can be used to decorate the border of a serving dish, as a base for canapés, a garnish for soups, an accompaniment to spreads or caviar or a base under some meat and game dishes. Dry toasted croutons may be referred to as sippets.

Shrimp bisque

SHRIMP BISQUE

Yield: 4 L (4 qt.)

Mirepoix, small dice	350 g	12 oz.
Shrimp shells and/or lobster or crayfish shells and bodies, crushed	1 kg	2 lb.
Clarified butter	175 g	6 oz.
Garlic cloves, chopped	2	2
Paprika	30 g	1 oz.
Tomato paste	50 g	2 oz.
Brandy	125 mL	4 fl. oz.
Dry sherry wine	350 mL	12 fl. oz.
Fish stock	3 L	3 qt.
Fish velouté (made with shrimp stock)	2 L	2 qt.
Sachet:		
Bay leaf	2	2
Dried thyme	1 g	1/2 tsp.
Peppercorns, crushed	1 g	1/2 tsp.
Cream, 35%, hot	500 mL	16 fl. oz.
Salt	TT	TT
Cayenne pepper	TT	TT
Shrimps, peeled and deveined	400 g	12 oz.

1. Caramelize the mirepoix and shrimp shells in the butter.

2. Add the garlic, paprika and tomato paste and sauté lightly.

3. Add the brandy and flambé.

4. Add the sherry wine. Deglaze and reduce the liquid by half.

5. Add the stock, velouté and sachet and simmer for approximately 1 hour, skimming occasionally.

6. Strain and press the mixture through a medium conical strainer to extract as much liquid as possible.

7. Strain the bisque through a fine etâmine lined with cheesecloth.

8. Return the bisque to a simmer and add the hot cream.

9. Season to taste with salt and cayenne pepper.

10. Cook the shrimps and slice or dice them as desired. Garnish each portion of soup with cooked shrimp.

RECIPE 11.6

Approximate values per 175 mL serving:

Calories	279
Total fat	25 g
Saturated fat	15 g
Cholesterol	91 mg
Sodium	320 mg
Total carbohydrates	9.6 g
Protein	3.8 g

Chowders

Although chowders are usually associated with the Eastern Seaboard, where fish and clams are plentiful, they are of French origin. Undoubtedly the word *chowder* is derived from the Breton phrase *faire chaudière*, which means to make a fish stew in a cauldron. The procedure was probably brought to Nova Scotia by French settlers and later introduced into New England.

Chowders are hearty soups with chunks of the main ingredients (including, virtually always, diced potatoes) and garnishes. With some exceptions (notably, Manhattan clam chowder), chowders contain milk or cream. Although there are thin chowders, most chowders are thickened with roux. The procedures for making chowders are similar to those for making cream soups except that chowders are not puréed and strained before the cream is added.

Basic Procedure for Making Chowders

1. Render finely diced salt pork over medium heat.
2. Sweat mirepoix in the rendered pork.
3. Add flour to make a roux.
4. Add the liquid.
5. Add the seasoning and flavouring ingredients according to their cooking times.
6. Simmer, skimming as needed.
7. Add milk or cream.

Applying the Basics

RECIPE 11.7

NEW-ENGLAND–STYLE CLAM CHOWDER

Yield: 3.5 L (3-1/2 qt.)

Salt pork/bacon, diced	250 g	8 oz.
Butter	50 g	2 oz.
Onions, jardinière	100 g	3-1/2 oz.
Celery, jardinière	200 g	7 oz.
Flour, pastry	200 g	7 oz.
Fish stock, warm	1.5 L	60 fl. oz.
Clam nectar	600 mL	20 fl. oz.
Sachet	1	1
Potatoes, diced	125 g	4 oz.
Baby clams, tinned*	700 mL	28 fl. oz.
Cream, 35%	250 mL	8 fl. oz.
Salt and pepper	TT	TT

1. Render salt pork/bacon with butter.
2. Sweat vegetables until transluscent.
3. Add flour and cook roux to white/blond stage.
4. Whisk in heated fish stock until smooth.
5. Stir in clam nectar, add sachet and simmer 15 minutes.
6. Add potatoes and simmer until tender.
7. Stir in baby clams and juice.
8. Return to simmer, add cream and adjust seasoning.

NOTE: Some chefs add red or green peppers or carrots. Corn is a popular addition in western Canada.

*If using fresh clams for the chowder, wash and steam approximately 15 L (1/2 bushel) of chowder clams in a small amount of water to yield 1.25 L (1-1/4 qt.) of clam meat. Chop the clams. Strain the liquid through several layers of cheesecloth to remove any sand that may be present. Continue with the recipe, starting at step 1.

RECIPE 11.7

Approximate values per 225 mL serving:

Calories	306
Total fat	24 g
Saturated fat	11 g
Cholesterol	78 mg
Sodium	782 mg
Total carbohydrates	14 g
Protein	8.4 g

Cold Soups

Cold soups can be as simple as a chilled version of a cream soup or as unique as a cold fruit soup blended with yogurt. Other than the fact that they are cold, cold soups are difficult to classify because many of them use unique or combination preparation methods. Regardless, they are divided here into two categories: those that require cooking and those that do not.

Cooked Cold Soups

Many cold soups are simply chilled versions of hot soups. For example, Consommé Madrilène and Consommé Portugaise are prepared hot and served cold. Vichyssoise, probably the most popular of all cold soups, is a cold version of purée of potato-leek soup. When serving a hot soup cold, there are several considerations:

1. If the soup is to be creamed, add the cream at the last minute. Although curdling is not as much of a problem as it is with hot soups, adding the cream at the last minute helps extend the soup's shelf life.

2. Cold soups should have a thinner consistency than hot soups. To achieve the proper consistency, use less starch if starch is used as the thickener, or use a higher ratio of liquid to main ingredient if the soup is thickened by puréeing. Consistency should be checked and adjusted at service time.

3. Cold dulls the sense of taste, so cold soups require more seasoning than hot ones. Taste the soup just before service and adjust the seasonings as needed.

4. Always serve cold soups as cold as possible.

Applying the Basics

RECIPE 11.8

VICHYSSOISE (COLD POTATO-LEEK SOUP)

Yield: 2 L (2 qt.)

Leek, white part only	500 g	1 lb.
Whole butter	125 g	4 oz.
Potato, large dice	500 g	1 lb.
Chicken stock	1.75 L	60 fl. oz.
Salt and white pepper	TT	TT
Cream, 35%	350 mL	12 fl. oz.
Chives, snipped	as needed	as needed

1. Split the leeks lengthwise and wash well to remove all sand and grit. Slice them thinly.

2. Sweat the leeks in the butter without browning them.

3. Add the potatoes and chicken stock, season with salt and pepper and bring to a simmer.

4. Simmer until the leeks and potatoes are very tender, approximately 45 minutes.

5. Purée the soup in a food processor, blender or food mill; strain through a fine sieve.

6. Chill the soup well.

7. At service time, incorporate the cream and adjust the seasonings. Serve in chilled bowls, garnished with snipped chives.

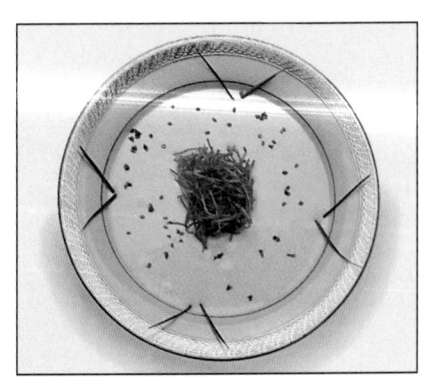

Vichyssoise

RECIPE 11.8

Approximate values per 150 mL serving:

Calories	256
Total fat	20 g
Saturated fat	12 g
Cholesterol	59 mg
Sodium	416 mg
Total carbohydrates	17 g
Protein	2 g

Many cooked cold soups use fruit juice (typically apple, grape or orange) as a base and are thickened with cornstarch or arrowroot as well as with puréed fruit. For additional flavour, wine is sometimes used in lieu of a portion of the fruit juice. Cinnamon, ginger and other spices that complement fruit are commonly added, as is lemon or lime juice, which adds acidity as well as flavour. Crème fraîche, yogurt or sour cream can be used as an ingredient or garnish to add richness.

Applying the Basics

CHILLED CHERRY SOUP

Yield: 4 qt. (4 L)

Cherries, pitted	2.25 kg	5 lb.
Apple juice	approx. 2 L	approx. 2 qt.
Sachet:		
Cinnamon sticks	2	2
Cloves, whole	4	4
Honey	175 g	6 oz.
Cornstarch	30 g	1 oz.
Lemon juice	TT	TT
Dry champagne or sparkling wine, chilled	250 mL	8 fl. oz.
Crème fraîche	as needed for garnish	
Toasted almonds, slivered	as needed for garnish	

1. Combine the cherries, apple juice, sachet and honey. Bring to a simmer and cook for 30 minutes. Remove the sachet.
2. Dilute the cornstarch with a small amount of cold apple juice. Add it to the soup for thickening. Simmer the soup for 10 minutes to cook out the starchy taste.
3. Purée the soup in a food processor or blender and strain if desired.
4. Chill the soup thoroughly.
5. At service, adjust the seasoning with the lemon juice. Stir in the champagne or sparkling wine and serve garnished with crème fraîche and toasted, slivered almonds.

NOTE: If using tinned cherries, replace the apple juice with the cherry juice.

Approximate values per 150 mL serving:

Calories	132
Total fat	2.5 g
Saturated fat	0.8 g
Cholesterol	4.1 mg
Sodium	8.6 mg
Total carbohydrates	26 g
Protein	1.4 g

Uncooked Cold Soups

Some cold soups are not cooked at all. Rather they rely only on puréed fruits or vegetables for thickness, body and flavour. Cold stock is sometimes used to adjust the soup's consistency. Dairy products such as cream, sour cream or crème fraîche are sometimes added to enrich and flavour the soup.

Because uncooked cold soups are never heated, enzymes and bacteria are not destroyed and the soup can spoil quickly. When preparing uncooked cold soups, always prepare small batches as close to service time as possible.

Applying the Basics

GAZPACHO

Yield: 3 L (3 qt.)

Roma tomato, peeled and diced	500 g	1 lb.
Onion, medium dice	125 g	4 oz.
Green pepper, medium dice	50 g	2 oz.
Red pepper, medium dice	50 g	2 oz.
Cucumber, peeled, seeded, medium dice	250 g	8 oz.
Garlic, minced	15 g	1/2 oz.

Gazpacho

Continued

Red wine vinegar	50 mL	1-1/2 fl. oz.
Lemon juice	30 mL	1 fl. oz.
Olive oil	50 mL	2 fl. oz.
Salt and pepper	TT	TT
Cayenne pepper	TT	TT
Fresh bread crumbs (optional)	50 g	2 oz.
Tomato or V-8 juice	1.5 L	1-1/2 qt.
White stock	as needed	as needed
Garnish:		
Tomato, peeled, seeded, small dice	125 g	4 oz.
Red pepper, small dice	60 g	2 oz.
Green pepper, small dice	60 g	2 oz.
Yellow pepper, small dice	60 g	2 oz.
Cucumber, peeled, seeded, small dice	60 g	2 oz.
Green onion, sliced fine	30 g	1 oz.
Croutons	as needed	as needed

1. Combine and purée all ingredients except the tomato juice, stock and garnish in a VCM, food processor or blender.
2. Stir in the tomato juice.
3. Adjust the consistency with stock.
4. Stir in the vegetable garnishes and adjust the seasonings.
5. Serve in chilled cups or bowls garnished with croutons.

RECIPE 11.10

Approximate values per 150 mL serving:

Calories	56
Total fat	2.5 g
Saturated fat	0.3 g
Cholesterol	0 mg
Sodium	476 mg
Total carbohydrates	7.1 g
Protein	1.2 g

GARNISHING SOUPS

Garnishes can range from a simple sprinkle of chopped parsley on a bowl of cream soup to tiny profiteroles stuffed with foie gras adorning a crystal-clear bowl of consommé. Some soups are so full of attractive, flavourful and colourful foods that are integral parts of the soup (for example, vegetables and chicken in chicken vegetable soup) that no additional garnishes (as either decoration or component) are necessary. In others, the garnish determines the type of soup. For example, a beef broth garnished with cooked barley and diced beef becomes beef barley soup. See Table 11.1.

Guidelines for Garnishing Soups

Although some soups (particularly consommés) have traditional garnishes, many soups depend on the chef's imagination and the kitchen's inventory for the finishing garnish. The only rules are:

1. The garnish should be attractive and not hang over the spoon.
2. The meats and vegetables used should be neatly cut into an appropriate and uniform shape and size. This is particularly important when garnishing a clear soup such as a consommé, as the consommé's clarity highlights the precise (or imprecise) cuts.
3. The garnish's texture and flavour should complement the soup.
4. Starches and vegetables used as garnishes should be cooked separately, reheated and placed in the soup bowl before the hot soup is added. If they are cooked in the soup, they may cloud or thicken the soup or alter its flavour, texture and seasoning.

TABLE 11.1   SOUPS, THEIR THICKENING AGENTS AND FINISHES

Category	Type	Thickening Agent or Method	Finish
Clear soups	Broths	None	Assorted garnishes
	Consommés	Usually none	Assorted garnishes
Thick soups	Cream soups	Roux and/or puréeing	Assorted garnishes, cream or béchamel sauce
	Purée soups	Puréeing	Assorted garnishes; cream is optional
Other soups	Bisques	Roux or rice and puréeing	Garnish of main ingredient, cream and/or butter
	Chowders	Roux	Cream
Cold soups	Cooked cold soups	Roux, arrowroot, cornstarch, puréeing, sour cream, yogurt	Assorted garnishes, cream, crème fraîche or sour cream
	Uncooked cold soups	Puréeing	Assorted garnishes, cream, crème fraîche or sour cream

5. Garnishes should be cooked just until done; meat and poultry should be tender but not falling apart, vegetables should be firm but not mushy and pasta and rice should maintain their identity. These types of garnishes are usually held on the side and added to the hot soup at the last minute to prevent overcooking.

Garnishing Suggestions

◆ Clear soups—any combination of julienne cuts of the same meat, poultry, fish or vegetable that provides the dominant flavour in the stock or broth, vegetables (cut uniformly into any shape), pasta (flat, small tortellini or tiny ravioli), gnocchi, quenelles, barley, spaetzle, white or wild rice, croutons, crepes, tortillas, or won tons.

◆ Cream soups, hot or cold—toasted slivered almonds, sour cream or crème fraîche, croutons, grated cheese or puff pastry fleurons; cream vegetable soups are usually garnished with slices or florets of the main ingredient.

◆ Purée soups—julienne cuts of poultry or ham, sliced sausage, croutons, grated cheese, bacon bits.

◆ Any soup—finely chopped fresh herbs, snipped chives, edible flower blossoms or petals, parsley or watercress.

SOUP SERVICE

Preparing Soups in Advance

Most soups can be made ahead of time and reheated as needed for service. To preserve freshness and quality, small batches of soup should be heated as needed throughout the meal service.

Clear soups are quite easy to reheat because there is little danger of scorching. If garnishes are already added to a clear soup, care should be taken not to overcook the garnishes when reheating the soup. All traces of fat should be removed from a consommé's surface before reheating.

Thick soups present more of a challenge. To increase shelf life and reduce the risk of spoilage, cool and refrigerate a thick soup when it is still a base (that is, before it is finished with milk or cream). When needed, carefully reheat the soup base just before service using a heavy-gauge pot over low heat. Stir often to prevent scorching and to rethermalize the soup more quickly. Then finish the soup (following the guidelines noted above) with boiling milk or cream, a light béchamel sauce or a liaison and adjust the seasonings. Always taste the soup after reheating and adjust the seasonings as needed.

Temperatures

The rule is simple: Serve hot soup hot and cold soup cold. Hot clear soups should be served near boiling. Hot cream soups should be served at slightly lower temperatures; 90°C–93°C (190°F–200°F) is acceptable. Cold soups should be served at a temperature of 4°C (40°F) or below. Preheating or chilling service bowls is required.

Conclusion

Soup, often served as the first course, may determine the success or failure of an entire meal. Although a wide variety of ingredients can be used to make both clear and thick soups, including trimmings and leftovers, poor-quality ingredients make poor-quality soups. By using, adapting and combining the basic techniques described in this chapter with different ingredients, you can create an infinite number of new and appetizing hot or cold soups. But exercise good judgment when combining flavours and techniques; they should blend well and complement each other. Moreover, any garnishes that are added should contribute to the appearance and character of the finished soup. And remember, always serve hot soups hot and cold soups cold.

Questions for Discussion

1. What are the differences between a stock and a broth?
2. What are the differences between a beef consommé and a beef-based broth? How are they similar?
3. What are the differences between a cream soup and a purée soup? How are they similar?
4. Create a recipe for chicken consommé.
5. Discuss several techniques for serving soup. What can be done to ensure that soups are served at the correct temperature?
6. Explain how and why soups are garnished. Why is it sometimes said that the noodles in a chicken noodle soup are actually a garnish?

ADDITIONAL SOUP RECIPES

RECIPE 11.11 (ABORIGINAL)

BUTTERNUT SQUASH AND MAPLE SOUP

SCHOOL OF HOSPITALITY, RECREATION, AND TOURISM, HUMBER COLLEGE, TORONTO, ON
Chef Anthony Bevan, CCC

Yield: 10–12 Servings

Butternut squash	1.5 kg	3 lb.
Onion	500 g	1 lb.
Grated ginger	25 g	2 Tbsp.
Walnut oil	100 mL	6 Tbsp.
White stock (white venison stock makes an excellent base)	3.5 L	6 pt.
Maple syrup	TT	TT
Salt (optional)	TT	TT
Chiffonade of fresh mint	as needed for garnish	

1. Peel the squash. Remove the seeds and toast them in a hot oven.
2. Rough-cut the squash and onion into mirepoix.
3. Sweat the squash, onion and ginger in the walnut oil.
4. Add the stock and bring to a boil, then simmer for 40 minutes.
5. Purée the soup and strain it into a clean pot.
6. Season with the maple syrup to taste. (Although not traditional, salt may be added to taste.)
7. When serving, sprinkle the soup with the toasted seeds and mint.

Anthony Bevan, CCC
Anthony is a native of Ireland, where he was Executive Chef at several five-star restaurants and chef-owner of Knocklofty House in Tipperary. He arrived in Canada in 1987 and played a major role in the development of Canada's first aboriginal culinary program. He currently teaches at Humber College.

RECIPE 11.11

Approximate values per 250 mL serving:

Calories	303
Total fat	15 g
Saturated fat	2.6 g
Cholesterol	2.5 mg
Sodium	58 mg
Total carbohydrates	39 g
Protein	3.0 g

◆ ◆ ◆

RECIPE 11.12

THAI MUSHROOM AND COCONUT SOUP

STAGE WEST HOTEL, TORONTO, ON
Executive Chef Rudolph Fischbacher

Yield: 650 mL (24 fl. oz.)

Coconut milk	500 mL	16 fl. oz.
Ginger, minced	20 g	3/4 oz.
Garlic, puréed	5 g	2 cloves
Lemon grass, chopped	1 stalk	1 stalk
Kaffir leaves	4	4
Brown sugar	15 g	1 Tbsp.
Crushed chile/Sambal olek	2 g	1/2 tsp.
Cilantro root, chopped	10 g	2 tsp.
Mushroom caps, sliced	250 g	9 oz.
Salt and pepper	TT	TT
Lime juice, fresh	125 mL	4-1/2 fl. oz.
Cilantro leaves, chiffonade	1/2 bunch	1/2 bunch

Continued

Rudi Fischbacher
Rudi trained in his native Austria and worked in Switzerland, Sweden, Spain and Germany before coming to Canada. Currently he is the Executive Chef and Food and Beverage Manager at the Stage West Hotel. He and his staff of 50 provide services for dinner theatre, banquets, the restaurant, lounge, patio and in-room dining.

1. Place first 8 ingredients in a sauce pot and bring to a boil. Simmer 5 minutes.
2. Strain and add mushrooms. Simmer 5–10 minutes. Adjust seasoning.
3. Add lime juice and cilantro just before serving.

✦✦✦

RECIPE 11.13

VICHYSSOISE OF OYSTERS WITH CAVIAR CHANTILLY

MUSTARD GRILLE, MISSISSAUGA, ON
Executive Chef Anthony Borgo

Yield: 4 Servings

Leeks, julienned	500 g	1 lb.
Onions, julienned	250 g	8 oz.
Butter	100 g	3 oz.
Potato, finely sliced	250 g	8 oz.
Fish stock, boiling	600 mL	20 fl. oz.
Cream, 35%	250 mL	8 fl. oz.
Salt and white pepper	TT	TT
Caviar Chantilly:		
Cream, 35%	125 mL	4 fl. oz.
Iranian caviar	15 g	1 Tbsp.
Chives, finely chopped	5 g	4 tsp.
Oysters, freshly shucked	8	8
Chervil sprigs	4	4

1. Clean the leeks, making sure to use only the white part of the stalks. Slice the leeks and onions very thin.
2. Sweat the leeks and onions in the butter until they are soft, but without colouring them. Then add the finely sliced raw potato and the boiling stock and cook over a high heat for 6 minutes.
3. Add the cream and cook for a further 2 minutes. Purée, then pass through a fine sieve. Season to taste.
4. Prepare the caviar Chantilly by whipping the cream and folding in the caviar and finely chopped chives. To serve, place 2 of the freshly shucked oysters into each bowl. Add the hot soup. Garnish with a quenelle of the caviar/chive cream and a sprig of fresh chervil. Serve immediately.

✦✦✦

RECIPE 11.14

MOROCCAN HARIRA (LAMB, CHICKEN AND LENTIL SOUP)

Yield: 4 L (4 qt.)

Olive oil	150 mL	5 fl. oz.
Stewing lamb, cubed	1.25 kg	2 lb. 8 oz.
Chicken pieces	1.5 kg	3–4 lb.
Garlic cloves, puréed	20 g	5
Onion, chopped fine	1 kg	2 lb.

RECIPE 11.12

Approximate values per 175 mL serving:

Calories	308
Total fat	26 g
Saturated fat	23 g
Cholesterol	0 mg
Sodium	218 mg
Total carbohydrates	14 g
Protein	4.4 g

Anthony Borgo
Since graduating in 1991, Anthony has gained a wealth of international experience working in Ireland, England, Switzerland, Japan and Canada and has risen through the ranks in the kitchen to the position of Executive Chef.

RECIPE 11.13

Approximate values per 250 mL serving:

Calories	781
Total fat	61 g
Saturated fat	36 g
Cholesterol	264 mg
Sodium	1016 mg
Total carbohydrates	42 g
Protein	16 g

Chickpeas, canned	250 g	8 oz.
Chicken stock	5 L	5 qt.
Turmeric	3 g	1-1/2 tsp.
Ginger, ground	2.5 g	1-1/2 tsp.
Coriander	2.5 g	1-1/2 tsp.
Cinnamon	2.5 g	1-1/2 tsp.
Tomatoes, canned, chopped	1.25 kg	2 lb. 8 oz.
Lentils, washed	250 g	8 oz.
Rice	125 g	4 oz.
Salt and pepper	TT	TT
Parsley, chopped	50 g	5 Tbsp.
Whole eggs, beaten	5	5
Lemon juice	75 mL	5 Tbsp.

1. Heat the oil in a large, heavy sauté pan. Lightly brown the lamb, then transfer it to a large saucepot. Repeat for the chicken, garlic and onion.

2. Add the chickpeas, stock, spices, tomatoes and lentils. Cover and simmer for 40 minutes.

3. Add the rice and simmer 20 minutes longer.

4. Remove the chicken pieces from the soup. Skin them and remove the meat from the bones. Dice the meat and return it to the soup.

5. Adjust the seasonings, add the parsley and return to a simmer.

6. Immediately before service, whisk the eggs and lemon juice together. Then slowly pour them into the soup, stirring to create strands of egg throughout the soup.

7. Serve in heated bowls with lemon wedges and harissa (recipe follows) on the side.

HARISSA

Yield: 85 g (6 Tbsp.)

Dried chile peppers, crushed	6 g	1 Tbsp.
Cayenne pepper	8 g	1 Tbsp.
Cumin, ground	5 g	2 tsp.
Caraway seeds	3 g	2 tsp.
Garlic cloves	6 g	2
Olive oil	50 mL	3 Tbsp.
Salt	5 g	1 tsp.

1. Grind the spices and garlic together in a mortar and pestle, blender or spice grinder.

2. Heat the oil. Stir in the spices and salt and cook over a low flame, stirring constantly, for 3 minutes.

◆◆◆

RECIPE 11.15

FRENCH ONION SOUP

Yield: 5 L (5 qt.)

Yellow onion, thinly sliced	3 kg	6-1/2 lb.
Garlic	10 g	2 cloves
Olive oil	25 mL	1 fl. oz.
Red wine	100 mL	3 fl. oz.
Brown stock	4.5 L	4-1/2 qt.

Continued

RECIPE 11.14

Approximate values per 250 mL serving:

Calories	541
Total fat	25 g
Saturated fat	6.1 g
Cholesterol	172 mg
Sodium	540 mg
Total carbohydrates	38 g
Protein	41 g

Harissa—Approximate values per 5 mL serving:

Calories	29
Total fat	2.8 g
Saturated fat	0.4 g
Cholesterol	0 mg
Sodium	109 mg
Total carbohydrates	0.7 g
Protein	0.2 g

Fresh thyme leaves	10 g	4 tsp.
Salt and pepper	TT	TT
Toasted French bread slices	as needed for garnish	
Gruyère cheese, grated	as needed for garnish	

1. Sauté the onions and garlic in the olive oil over low heat. Carefully caramelize them thoroughly without burning.
2. Deglaze the pan with the red wine. Cook au sec. The onions will be a very dark, even brown.
3. Add the brown stock and thyme.
4. Bring to a simmer and cook 20 minutes to develop flavour. Adjust the seasonings.
5. Serve in warm bowls. Top each portion with a slice of toasted French bread and a thick layer of cheese. Place under the broiler or salamander until the cheese is melted and lightly browned.

VARIATION: Cook 50 g (2 oz.) flour with the cooked onions and moisten with stock. The soup will have rustic quality with more body. This soup may be made with chicken/veal stock or half beef and chicken stock. White wine or sherry may be used. Some chefs use basil or marjoram.

♦♦♦

RECIPE 11.16

MINESTRONE

Minestrone is a rich vegetable soup of Italian heritage. Northern Italian versions are made with beef stock, butter, rice and ribbon-shaped pasta. Southern Italian versions contain tomatoes, garlic, olive oil and tube-shaped pasta. The vegetables should be fresh and varied. Substitute or change those listed as necessary to reflect the season.

Yield: 4 L (4 qt.)

Dry white beans	150 g	5 oz.
Olive oil	25 mL	1 Tbsp.
Onion, paysanne	125 g	4 oz.
Garlic cloves, minced	5 g	1
Celery, paysanne	150 g	6 oz.
Carrot, paysanne	125 g	4 oz.
Zucchini, diced	250 g	8 oz.
Green beans, cut in 1.25-cm (1/2-inch) pieces	150 g	5 oz.
Cabbage, diced	250 g	8 oz.
White stock	2.5 L	2-1/2 qt.
Tomato, concassée	250 g	8 oz.
Tomato paste, low-sodium	30 g	1 oz.
Orzo pasta, cooked	75 g	3 oz.
Fresh oregano, chopped	8 g	2 tsp.
Fresh basil, chopped	10 g	1 Tbsp.
Fresh chervil, chopped	3 g	1 tsp.
Fresh parsley, chopped	20 g	2 Tbsp.
Salt and pepper	TT	TT
Parmesan cheese, grated (optional)	as needed for garnish	

1. Soak the beans in cold water overnight, then drain.
2. Cover the beans with water and simmer until tender, about 40 minutes.

RECIPE 11.15

Approximate values per 175 mL serving:

Calories	131
Total fat	5.7 g
Saturated fat	2.2 g
Cholesterol	9 mg
Sodium	309 mg
Total carbohydrates	16 g
Protein	3.9 g

Minestrone

RECIPE 11.16

Approximate values per 250 mL serving:

Calories	127
Total fat	4.0 g
Saturated fat	0.9 g
Cholesterol	1.1 mg
Sodium	406 mg
Total carbohydrates	19 g
Protein	3.7 g

3. Sauté the onions in the oil. Add garlic, celery and carrot and cook for 3 minutes.

4. Add the remaining vegetables, one type at a time, cooking each briefly.

5. Add the stock, tomatoes and tomato paste. Simmer for 45 minutes.

6. Add the drained beans and orzo.

7. Stir in the chopped herbs and season to taste with salt and pepper.

8. Bring the soup to a simmer and simmer 15 minutes. Serve in warm bowls, garnished with Parmesan cheese.

NOTE: If substituting dry herbs, use one-third the amount.

✦✦✦

RECIPE 11.17 (ABORIGINAL)

IROQUOIS FISH SOUP

SCHOOL OF HOSPITALITY, RECREATION, AND TOURISM, HUMBER COLLEGE, Toronto, ON
Chef Anthony Bevan, CCC

Anthony Bevan, CCC
Anthony is a native of Ireland, where he was Executive Chef at several five-star restaurants and chef-owner of Knocklofty House in Tipperary. He arrived in Canada in 1987 and played a major role in the development of Canada's first aboriginal culinary program. He currently teaches at Humber College.

Yield: 14 Portions

Onion, finely diced	175 g	6 oz.
Ginger root, grated	10 g	1 Tbsp.
Sunflower oil	45 mL	3 Tbsp.
Garlic clove, puréed	10 g	3
Mushrooms, fresh, sliced (chanterelle, oyster, shiitake and/or morel)	900 g	2 lb.
Fish stock	3.5 L	120 fl. oz.
Lima beans (fresh or frozen)	350 g	12 oz.
Sweet corn kernels, dried	175 g	6 oz.
Wild bergamot, chopped (or fresh oregano)	10 g	2 Tbsp.
Freshwater fish fillets (trout, pickerel, perch, white fish and/or bass), cut into 2.25-cm (1-inch) squares	2.25 kg	5 lb.
Fresh dillweed	as needed for garnish	

1. Sweat the onion and ginger in the sunflower oil.

2. Add the garlic and mushrooms.

3. Add the fish stock, lima beans and corn kernels, bring to a boil and simmer for 40 minutes.

4. Add the chopped bergamot or oregano and simmer for 5 minutes.

5. Add fish and simmer for 5 minutes.

6. Serve garnished with a feather of dillweed.

RECIPE 11.17

Approximate values per 400 mL serving:

Calories	463
Total fat	19 g
Saturated fat	4.4 g
Cholesterol	104 mg
Sodium	276 mg
Total carbohydrates	31 g
Protein	42 g

NOTE: Traditionally, aboriginal people would use wild ginger root instead of oriental ginger; wild leek instead of onions; and wild garlic in place of garlic cloves. Water would have been the liquid used, but a good fish stock lays down an excellent foundational flavour. Salt was not a part of the North American diet until the Europeans arrived; the most common seasoning used was maple sugar.

Dried Sweet Corn Kernels: Among the Iroquois, corn is held in high esteem. As one of "The Three Sisters" (corn, beans and squash), it is considered important for spiritual and physical well-being. To preserve the sweet corn, the aboriginal people dried the kernels. In the modern kitchen the same results

Continued

may be achieved by removing the sweet corn kernels from the cob. Spread the kernels on a baking sheet and place in an oven at 82°C (180°F). Stir the kernels from time to time. Leave them in the oven until the corn is very hard but not burned. This may take in excess of 3 hours. Store the dried kernels in an airtight container, where they can be stored indefinitely.

◆◆◆

RECIPE 11.18

CHOWDER OF WILD MUSHROOMS WITH WILD RICE, BEANS AND FIREWEED HONEY

FAIRMONT CHÂTEAU LAKE LOUISE, LAKE LOUISE, AB
Director, Food and Beverage, David MacGillivray

David MacGillivray

From the time he was 15 years old, working in a restaurant in Picton, Ontario, David knew he wanted to be a chef. He quickly became renowned in Canada, particularly for his work in the Edith Cavell Dining Room at Jasper Park Lodge. He is now the Director of Food and Beverage at the luxurious Château Lake Louise.

Yield: 10 Servings

Butter	100 g	4 oz.
Garlic cloves, chopped	2	2
Shallots, medium, small dice	100 g	4
Flour	100 g	4 oz.
Chicken stock	2 L	70 fl. oz.
Dried porcini mushroom powder	30 g	1 oz.
Canola oil	125 mL	5 fl. oz.
Oyster mushrooms, sliced	100 g	4 oz.
Shiitake mushrooms, sliced	100 g	4 oz.
Chanterelle mushrooms, sliced	100 g	4 oz.
Dried morel mushrooms, soaked in water and sliced when soft	75 g	3 oz.
White wine	250 mL	8 fl. oz.
Wild rice, cooked	75 g (uncooked weight)	3 oz. (uncooked weight)
Black beans, cooked	75 g (uncooked weight)	3 oz. (uncooked weight)
White beans, cooked	75 g (uncooked weight)	3 oz. (uncooked weight)
Potato, peeled, diced and cooked	150 g	6 oz.
Fireweed honey	50 mL	2 fl. oz.
Fresh rosemary, chopped	30 g	4 Tbsp.
Heavy cream	500 mL	20 fl. oz.
Salt and cracked pepper	TT	TT

1. Melt the butter in a heavy-bottomed soup pot, over medium heat.

2. Add the garlic and shallots and cook until translucent, approximately 3–5 minutes.

3. Add the flour and incorporate it thoroughly to make a roux. Stir the roux constantly to avoid burning. The roux should cook for 3–5 minutes over medium heat.

4. In a separate pot, bring the chicken stock to a boil. Once the roux is cooked, add the stock to the roux. Whisk continuously to prevent any flour clots from developing.

5. Reduce the heat to medium-low, add the dried mushroom powder to the soup and let it simmer.

6. In a large frying pan over high heat, heat the canola oil and sauté the oyster mushrooms, shiitake mushrooms and chanterelles, stirring frequently.

RECIPE 11.18

Approximate values per 300 mL serving:

Calories	614
Total fat	42 g
Saturated fat	19 g
Cholesterol	92 mg
Sodium	533 mg
Total carbohydrates	48 g
Protein	11 g

7. Drain the excess oil from the pan and add the morels. Add white wine to deglaze the pan. Cook for 2–3 minutes over medium-high heat.

8. Add the mushrooms and wine mixture to the soup base. Let the soup simmer for 45 minutes, then add the rice, beans and potatoes.

9. Add the honey, rosemary and cream. Continue to cook for 15 minutes. Season with salt and pepper.

10. Serve in a large soup tureen or in individual bowls.

◆◆◆

RECIPE 11.19

CELERY AND QUEBEC BLUE CHEESE (BÉNÉDICTIN) SOUP

SOUTHERN ALBERTA INSTITUTE OF TECHNOLOGY, CALGARY, AB
Chef Instructor Simon Dunn, CCC

Yield: 3 L (3 qt.)

Butter	100 g	3-1/2 oz.
Flour	125 g	4 oz.
Chicken stock, warm	3 L	3 qt.
Celery, macedoine	1 kg	2 lb.
Onion, macedoine	500 g	1 lb.
Butter	250 g	8 oz.
Cream, 35%	150 mL	6 fl. oz.
Salt and white pepper	TT	TT
Bénédictin, crumbled	200 g	7 oz.

1. Prepare a blond roux.
2. Add warm chicken stock to make a velouté.
3. Sweat celery and onion in butter until tender. Add to velouté. Simmer for 10 minutes.
4. Blend in cream and adjust seasoning with salt and pepper.
5. Finish with crumbled Bénédictin (or substitute Stilton) or half the amount of Ermite.

◆◆◆

RECIPE 11.20

PRAIRIE BLACK BEAN SOUP WITH CILANTRO SOUR CREAM

HARDWARE GRILL, EDMONTON, AB
Chef/Owner Larry Stewart, CCC

Yield: 5 L (5 qt.)

Dried black beans, washed	500 g	1 lb.
Chicken stock	4 L	4 qt.
Double-smoked bacon, diced	250 g	8 oz.
Onion, jardinière	175 g	6 oz.
Carrot, jardinière	175 g	6 oz.
Celery, jardinière	175 g	6 oz.

Continued

Photo by George Webber, SAIT.

Simon Dunn, CCC
Born and classically trained in Great Britain, Simon was most recently the Executive Chef at The Inn on Lake Bonavista, which was ranked as one of the top 100 restaurants in Canada for the duration of his tenure. Simon cooked for members of the British Royal family during his career in the Royal Air Force and is currently a chef instructor at S.A.I.T.

RECIPE 11.19

Approximate values per 175 mL serving:

Calories	321
Total fat	26 g
Saturated fat	15 g
Cholesterol	67 mg
Sodium	531 mg
Total carbohydrates	17 g
Protein	4.8 g

Larry Stewart, CCC
Run by Larry since its opening in 1996, the Hardware Grill recently received a two-star rating, making it one of only 57 restaurants nationwide to have earned this ranking for food, wine and service. As the owner, Larry is also proud of the fact that his restaurant is listed in Where to Eat in Canada for the fourth consecutive year.

RECIPE 11.20

Approximate values per 175 mL serving:

Calories	182
Total fat	9.3 g
Saturated fat	3.7 g
Cholesterol	12 mg
Sodium	249 mg
Total carbohydrates	19 g
Protein	5.5 g

Garlic, minced	30 g	1-1/2 Tbsp.
Cumin, ground	2 g	1 tsp.
Chili powder	25 g	3 Tbsp.
Cayenne pepper	0.25 g	1/3 tsp.
Salt	10 g	2 tsp.
Black pepper	2.5 g	1 tsp.

1. Combine the beans and stock and bring to a simmer, covered, for 2 hours.
2. Remove half of the beans from the pot with a slotted spoon. Purée in a food processor and return to the pot.
3. Add the remaining ingredients and simmer, covered, for 1 hour.
4. Serve in warmed bowls garnished with dollops of cilantro sour cream.

CILANTRO SOUR CREAM

Yield: 400 mL (14 fl. oz.)

Sour cream	250 mL	8 oz
Cilantro, chopped	1 bunch	1 bunch
Lime juice	30 mL	1 fl. oz
Roma tomato, diced	100 g	3 oz.

Combine all ingredients.

◆◆◆

RECIPE 11.21

ROASTED CORN CHOWDER

Yield: 3.25 L (3-1/4 qt.)

Corn, unshucked	8 ears	8 ears
Butter	25 g	1 oz.
Leek, sliced	125 g	4 oz.
Celery, small dice	150 g	5 oz.
Onion, diced, 0.5 cm (1/4 inch)	500 g	16 oz.
Red peppers, diced, 0.5 cm (1/4 inch)	150 g	5 oz.
Green peppers, diced, 0.5 cm (1/4 inch)	150 g	5 oz.
Béchamel, thin	1.5 L	3 pt.
Potato, diced, 1 cm (1/2 inch)	900 g	2 lb.
Fresh thyme	3 g	1 tsp.
Cream, 35%, warm	300 mL	10 fl. oz.
Salt and black pepper	TT	TT
Tabasco sauce	TT	TT
Parsley, chopped fine	as needed for garnish	

RECIPE 11.21

Approximate values per 200 mL serving:

Calories	295
Total fat	15 g
Saturated fat	9.0 g
Cholesterol	48 mg
Sodium	499 mg
Total carbohydrates	34 g
Protein	6.1 g

1. Roast the ears of corn, in their husks, in a 200°C (400°F) oven for 45 minutes. Cool, shuck the corn and cut off the kernels.
2. Sweat the vegetables in butter.
3. Add the béchamel and bring to a simmer.
4. Add the corn kernels. Simmer 20 minutes and add potato and thyme and simmer until tender.
5. Add the warm cream; adjust the seasonings with salt, pepper and Tabasco sauce.
6. Serve in warm bowls garnished with chopped parsley.

✦✦✦

RECIPE 11.22

MELON SOUP WITH CRISP PANCETTA, ARUGALA AND BORAGE

LA CHAUMIÈRE, CALGARY, AB
Chef/Co-Owner Robert Matthews

Yield: 10 Servings

Ingredient	Metric	Imperial
Watermelon, skinless, seeded	1 kg	2-1/4 lb.
Salt and white pepper	TT	TT
Mint leaves, fine dice	10 g	1 Tbsp.
Lemon juice	50 mL	3 Tbsp.
Arugala leaves, stalk removed	10	10
Borage leaves, core spine removed	10	10
Cantaloupe, balls	10	10
Muskmelon, balls	10	10
Honeydew, balls	10	10
Port wine	20 mL	4 tsp.
Pancetta, crisp	50 g	1-1/2 oz.
Borage blossoms	30	30

1. Purée watermelon until smooth. Pass through sieve.
2. Season melon with salt, pepper, mint and lemon juice. Chill until very cold.
3. Cut arugala and borage leaves into fine chiffonade.
4. Marinate melon balls in port.
5. To serve, ladle soup into rimmed soup plates. Set a complement of 3 melon balls in each place. Set chiffonade in centre. Sprinkle with pancetta and borage blossoms.

Robert Matthews

The year Bob began his professional chef training was also the year he represented Canada on the Men's Olympic Cycling Team —20 years later, he's an Olympic competitor in the culinary arena! After completing the Professional Cooking Program at the Southern Alberta Institute of Technology, Bob worked in Canada and abroad until finally becoming Personal Chef to the Canadian Ambassador for Japan, a position he held for five years. He returned to Canada in 1999 and became chef/co-owner of the highly regarded La Chaumière.

RECIPE 11.22

Approximate values per 125 mL soup serving with 30 g melon balls:

Calories	85
Total fat	3 g
Saturated fat	1 g
Cholesterol	4.3 mg
Sodium	670 mg
Total carbohydrates	12 g
Protein	2.6 g

✦✦✦

RECIPE 11.23

CREAM OF FENNEL AND GRUYÈRE SOUP SCENTED WITH SHERRY

FAIRMONT SOUTHAMPTON PRINCESS, BERMUDA
Executive Chef David Garcelon, CCC

Yield: 5 L (5 qt.)

Ingredient	Metric	Imperial
Butter	375 g	12 oz.
Fennel, sliced	750 g	1 lb. 8 oz.
Onion, diced	375 g	12 oz.
Flour	375 g	12 oz.
Chicken stock, warm	4 L	4 qt.
Cream, 35%	1 L	1 qt.
Salt and pepper	TT	TT
Fennel, julienned	300 g	10 oz.
Gruyère, grated	450 g	1 lb.
Sherry	125 mL	4 fl. oz.

David Garcelon, CCC

A graduate of the Culinary Institute of Canada, David worked in Vancouver and Toronto before becoming Executive Chef at both Fairmont's Jasper Park Lodge and Delta's Lodge at Kananaskis. He recently traded in his skis for sandals and snorkel gear to become Executive Chef in Bermuda.

Continued

RECIPE 11.23

Approximate values per
150 mL serving:

Calories	338
Total fat	27 g
Saturated fat	16 g
Cholesterol	83 mg
Sodium	362 mg
Total carbohydrates	17 g
Protein	6.7 g

1. Melt butter in pot. Sweat fennel and onions.
2. Add flour and cook out roux.
3. Add warm stock, stirring constantly. Bring to a boil and simmer until vegetables are tender.
4. Purée soup in a food processor.
5. Add cream, seasoning and julienne of fennel.
6. Whisk in the cheese and finish with sherry.
7. Serve immediately.

$\mathcal{W}$EBLINKS

Food Institute of Canada: Soup Recipes
  foodnet.fic.ca/recipes/soups.html

Searchable Archive of Recipes: Soup Recipes
  SOAR.Berkeley.EDU/recipes/soups/

Cool No-Cook Summer Soups
  www.vegkitchen.com/coolsoups.html

In the Kitchen with Chef Tell: Soup Recipes
  www.mbctv.com/cheftell/soup.html

Soups
  www.cs.umd.edu/users/kandogan/FTA/TurkishCuisine/soups.html

Soups 2
  recipes.alastra.com/soups

CHAPTER 12

PRINCIPLES OF MEAT COOKERY

LEARNING OUTCOMES

After studying this chapter you will be able to:

+ identify the structure and composition of meats
+ explain meat inspection and grading practices
+ purchase meats appropriate for your needs
+ store meats properly
+ prepare meats for cooking
+ apply various cooking methods to meats: broiling or grilling, roasting, sautéeing, pan-frying, simmering, braising, stewing
+ carve a beef hip or leg of lamb

eats—beef, veal, lamb and pork—often consume the largest portion of your food purchasing dollar. In this chapter we discuss how to protect your investment. You will learn how to determine the quality of meat, how to purchase meat in the form that best suits your needs and how to store it. We also discuss several of the dry-heat, moist-heat and combination cooking methods introduced in Chapter 9, Principles of Cooking, and how they can best be used so that a finished meat item is appealing to both the eye and palate. Although each of the cooking methods is illustrated with a single beef, veal, lamb or pork recipe, the analysis is intended to apply to all meats.

In Chapters 13 through 16 you will learn about the specific cuts of beef, veal, lamb and pork typically used in food service operations, as well as some basic butchering procedures. Recipes using these cuts and applying the various cooking methods are included at the end of each of those chapters.

MUSCLE COMPOSITION

The carcasses of cattle, sheep, hogs and furred game animals consist mainly of edible lean muscular tissue, fat, connective tissue and bones. They are divided into large cuts called **primals**. Primal cuts are rarely cooked; rather, they are usually broken down to **subprimal cuts** which, in turn, can be cooked as is or used to produce **fabricated cuts**. For example, the beef primal known as a short loin can be divided into subprimals including the strip loin. The strip loin can be fabricated into other cuts including strip loin steaks. The primals, subprimals and fabricated cuts of beef, veal, lamb and pork are discussed in Chapters 13 through 16, respectively; game is discussed in Chapter 18.

Muscle tissue gives meat its characteristic appearance; the amount of connective tissue determines the meat's tenderness. Beef muscle tissue is approximately 72% water, 20% protein, 7% fat and 1% minerals. A single muscle is composed of many bundles of muscle cells or fibres held together by connective tissue. (See Figures 12.1 and 12.2.) The thickness of the cells, the size of the cell bundles and the connective tissues holding them together form the grain of the meat and determine the meat's texture. When the fibre bundles are small, the meat has a fine grain and texture. Grain also refers to the direction in which the muscle fibres travel. When an animal fattens, some of the water and proteins in the lean muscle tissue are replaced with fat, which appears as **marbling**.

Connective tissue forms the walls of the long muscle cells and binds them into bundles. It surrounds the muscle as a membrane and also appears as the tendons and ligaments that attach the muscles to the bone. Most connective tissue is composed of either **collagen** or **elastin**. Collagen breaks down into water-soluble gelatin when cooked using moist heat. Elastin, on the other hand, will not break down under normal cooking conditions. Because elastin remains stringy and tough, tendons and ligaments should be trimmed away before meat is cooked.

FIGURE 12.1 *Muscle Tissue*

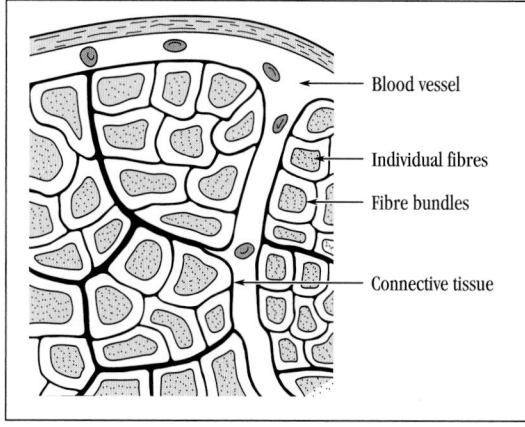

FIGURE 12.2 *Crosscut of a Bundle of Muscle Fibres*

Connective tissue develops primarily in the frequently used muscles. Therefore, cuts of meat from the shoulder (also known as the chuck), which the animal uses constantly, tend to be less tender than those from the back (also known as the loin), which are used less frequently. As an animal ages, the collagen present within the muscles becomes more resistant to breaking down through moist-heat cooking. Therefore, the meat of an older animal tends to be less tender than that of a younger one.

Nutrition

Although nutritional content of beef, veal, pork and lamb differs, generally, all are high in protein, saturated fats and cholesterol. Consumed in moderate quantities, however, meat can be part of a healthful diet.

Inspection and Grading of Meats

Inspection

All meat produced for public consumption in Canada is subject to health inspection under the supervision of the Canadian Food Inspection Agency. Inspections ensure that products are processed under strict sanitary guidelines and are wholesome and fit for human consumption. Inspections do not indicate a meat's quality or tenderness. Whole carcasses of beef, pork, lamb and veal are labelled with a round stamp, which also identifies the processing facility. See Figure 12.3. The stamp shown in Figure 12.3 is also used for fabricated or processed meats and is found on either the product or its packaging. Imported products must also be inspected. The revised Canada Food Inspection System (CFIS) was implemented in 1998.

FIGURE 12.3 *Canada Meat Inspection Stamp*

Grading

Canadian grading provides a voluntary, uniform system by which producers, distributors and consumers can measure differences in the quality of meats and make price/quality comparisons. There are two parts to this grading system: quality grades and yield assessments. (See Figures 12.4 and 12.5.)

FIGURE 12.4   *Grade Stamp for Canada AAA Beef*

FIGURE 12.5   *Yield Stamp*

Quality grades, provided and paid for by the industry, group meats of similar quality, yield and value.

Grading takes into account five factors:

1. The animal's age determined by the degree of bone ossification.
2. The colour of the meat.
3. The conformation of the muscling.
4. The fat colour.
5. The sex of the animal.

For beef, the intramuscular fat or marbling is taken into account also. It is assessed on the rib eye at the quarter break. For example, beef graded A or better must have at least "traces to slight" marbling and "good with some deficiency to excellent" muscling.

A Computer Vision System (CVS) uses cameras to assist in carcass sorting. The rib-eye camera takes a digitized picture of the rib eye. The computer software analyzes the marbling and could assist in grade assignment. The second camera takes a picture of the whole carcass and combines the information with the rib-eye scan. A yield score is calculated that provides an estimate of saleable yield. Testing has shown the computer-generated yield score to be twice as accurate as the yield ruler. A grader still assesses the final grade. Processors are using the CVS to differentiate the sub-levels within Prime and AAA.

Carcass pasteurization is performed in large processing plants. The process involves three steps: removing water left on the carcass surface by the final wash, exposing the carcass to a hot-water or steam blanket and quickly chilling the carcass surface with a cold-water shower. A special chamber is used for the process.

Beef: Canada has a well-defined beef grading system with A or higher being the best. The main grades are Canada Prime, AAA, AA, A, B1, B2, B3, B4, D and E grades. Approximately 82% (1999) of Canadian beef production is A grade or higher, and Canada Prime represents 1% of production. Systems are being developed to reward producers of higher grade meat.

Veal: There are currently 10 grades of veal in Canada with A1, A2, A3 and A4 being the highest. Criteria include muscle conformation, flesh colour and fat deposits. Grading is carried out for the producer but consumers generally purchase based on colour (white to pink). Grading does not differentiate between milk- and grain-fed animals except in Quebec, where "milk-fed" is a regulated term. For menu terminology, the term "veal" is generally used, but if you specify "milk-fed" then you must have invoices to support your claim. "Baby beef" is not a recognized term, although "calf" is often used to describe veal liver. Graded carcasses are grade stamped. The minimum weight for a hide-off carcass is 80 kg (176 lb.) and the maximum is 160 kg (352 lb.). An ungraded veal carcass may weigh up to 180 kg (396 lb.) hide-off. The animal is generally a minimum of two weeks old.

Pork: Pork grading is mainly done for the hog producer and for export. Domestic consumption does not show a grade stamp. The producer is paid according to the fat-to-lean ratio and most pork is trimmed at the plant. Of the 12 grades, Canada Yield Class is the most desirable. The carcass weighs 40 kg (88 lb.) or more and the yield percentage, by probe, of lean to fat on the loin meat must be between 54.7% and 64.3% or higher.

Sheep: Most sheep are marketed as spring lamb or genuine spring lamb. Older sheep are generally processed into value-added products. Spring lamb is 5–12 months old and weighs 13.5–29.5 kg (30–65 lb.). The fat will be white and the flesh dark pink. The following characteristics are assessed and scored on a matrix grading: the appearance of the break joint, the yield, the fat level, the muscling, the colour of the pectoral muscle and the colour of the fat. For example, muscling is rated on a scale of 1 to 5 with M5 being the highest. Grading is done primarily for the producer as most lamb is sold ungraded.

AGING MEATS

When animals are slaughtered their muscles are soft and flabby. Within 6 to 24 hours rigor mortis sets in, causing the muscles to contract and stiffen. Rigor mortis dissipates within 48 to 72 hours under refrigerated conditions. All meats should be allowed to rest, or age, long enough for rigor mortis to dissipate completely. Meats that have not been aged long enough for rigor mortis to dissipate, or that have been frozen during this period, are known as "green meats." They will be very tough and flavourless when cooked. Current research verifies that aging contributes to the tenderness of beef. Little benefit is realized past 14 days. Marbling accounts for less than 5% of tenderness.

Typically, initial aging takes place while the meat is being transported from the slaughterhouse to the supplier or food service operation. Beef and lamb are sometimes aged for longer periods to increase their tenderness and flavour characteristics. Pork is not aged further because its high fat content turns rancid easily, and veal does not have enough fat to protect it during an extended aging period.

Wet Aging

Today, most pre-portioned or precut meats are packaged and shipped in vacuum-sealed plastic packages, for example, Cryovac®. Wet aging is the process of storing vacuum-packaged meats under refrigeration for up to 6 weeks. This allows natural enzymes and microorganisms time to break down connective tissue, which tenderizes and flavours the meat. As this chemical process takes place, the meat develops a slight off odour that is released when the package is opened and dissipates in a few minutes. Bag aging generally results in a yield loss of only 1–2%, significantly lower than dry (air) aging. A liquid called purge will be in the bag. Beef generally has the greatest capacity for aging. Exercise caution with the length of time. Most other meats must be used within a shorter time frame. Commercially vacuum-packaged and chilled pork, for example, has a shelf life of about 21 days.

Dry Aging

Dry aging is the process of hanging fresh meats in an environment of controlled temperature, humidity and air flow for up to four weeks. This allows enzymes and microorganisms to break down connective tissues. Dry aging is actually the beginning of the natural decomposition process. Dry aged meats can lose from 5% to 20% of their weight through moisture evaporation. Moisture loss combined with additional trimming can substantially increase the cost of dry aged meats. Dry aged meats are generally available only through smaller distributors and specialty butchers.

Irradiation

This process is pending (2001) approval for use in Canada. Other countries are irradiating meats and produce to increase shelf life by inhibiting the growth of some bacteria by altering the water activity (A_W) of the product. Changing the molecular structure of the water restricts microbial growth.

PURCHASING AND STORING MEATS

Several factors determine the cuts of meat your food service operation should use:

1. Menu—The menu identifies the types of cooking methods used. If meats are to be broiled, grilled, roasted, sautéed or fried, more tender cuts should be used. If they are to be stewed or braised, cuts with more connective tissue can be used to produce flavourful dishes.
2. Menu price—Cost constraints may prevent an operation from using the best quality meats available. Generally, the more tender the meat, the more expensive it is. But the most expensive cuts are not always the best choice for a particular cooking method. For example, a beef tenderloin is one of the most expensive cuts of beef. Although excellent grilled, it will not necessarily produce a better braised dish than the less tender chuck.
3. Quality—Often, several cuts of meat can be used for a specific dish, so each food service operation should develop its own quality specifications.

Purchasing Meats

Once you have identified the cuts of meat your operation needs, you must determine the forms in which they will be bought. Meats are purchased in a variety of forms: whole, sides, quarters, primal cuts or portion cuts (known as portion control or PC) ready to cook and serve. You should consider the following when deciding how to purchase meats:

1. Employee skills—Do your employees have the skills necessary to reduce large pieces of meat to the desired cuts?
2. Menu—Can you use the variety of bones, meat and trimmings that result from fabricating large cuts into individual portions?
3. Storage—Do you have ample refrigeration and freezer space so that you can be flexible in the way you purchase your meats?
4. Cost—Considering labour costs and trim usage, is it more economical to buy larger cuts of meat or PC units?

CMC/IMPS

The Canadian Meat Council (CMC) publishes full-colour manuals that name and number cuts of meat. The United States Department of Agriculture (USDA) publishes Institutional Meat Purchasing Specifications (IMPS). The CMC/IMPS system is a widely accepted and useful tool in preventing miscommunications between purchasers and purveyors. Meats are indexed by a numerical system: Beef cuts are designated by the 100 series, lamb by the 200 series, veal by the 300 series, pork by the 400 series, and portion cuts by the 1000 series. Commonly used cuts of beef, veal, lamb and pork and their CMC/IMPS numbers, as well as applicable cooking methods and serving suggestions, are discussed in Chapters 13 through 16. However, there are numbering differences in some cases and it is important to communicate clearly with your supplier to ensure the correct product is ordered and received.

Storing Meats

Meat products are highly perishable, so temperature control is the most important thing to remember when storing meats. Fresh meats should be stored at temperatures of –1°C to +2°C (30°F–35°F). Vacuum-packed meats should be left in their packaging until they are needed. Under proper refrigeration, vacuum-packed meats with unbroken seals have a shelf life of three to four weeks. If the seal is broken, shelf life is reduced to only a few days. Meats that are not vacuum packed should be loosely wrapped or wrapped in air-permeable paper. Do not wrap meats tightly in plastic wrap, as this creates a good breeding ground for bacteria and will significantly shorten a meat's shelf life. Store meats on trays and away from other foods to prevent cross-contamination.

Meats freeze at about –2°C (28°F). When freezing meats, the faster the better. Slow freezing produces large ice crystals that tend to rupture the muscle tissues, allowing water and nutrients to drip out when the meat is thawed. Most commercially packaged meats are frozen by blast freezing, which quickly cools by blasting –40°C (–40°F) air across the meat.

The ideal temperature for maintaining frozen meat is –45°C (–50°F). Frozen meat should not be maintained at any temperature warmer than –18°C (0°F). Moisture- and vapourproof packaging will help prevent **freezer burn**. The length of frozen storage life varies with the species and type of meat. As a general rule, properly handled meats can be frozen for up to six months. Frozen meats should only be thawed at refrigerator temperatures, not at room temperature or in warm water.

PREPARING MEATS

Certain procedures are often applied to meats before cooking to add flavour and/or moisture, or to enhance tenderness. These include marinating, barding, larding, jacquarding, tumbling and needling.

Marinating—Wet and Dry

Wet marinating is the process of soaking meat in a seasoned liquid to flavour and tenderize it. Marinades can be simple blends (herbs, seasonings and oil) or a complicated cooked recipe (red wine, fruit and other ingredients). Mild marinades should be used on more delicate meats, such as veal. Game and beef require strongly flavoured marinades. In wine-based marinades, white

◆◆◆

JACQUARDING, TUMBLING AND NEEDLING

Jacquarding—a process of piercing muscle tissue with needles to tenderize.

Tumbling—a process in which solid muscle meat is tumbled with crushed ice and/or a seasoned liquid until the meat absorbs a prescribed percentage of its weight in liquid. An emulsifier may be added or a vacuum used to promote faster, more complete absorption. The tumbling "releases" the protein and allows the liquid to emulsify with the fat in the muscle fibres. There are strict regulations governing the types of meats that may be tumbled (or pumped) and the allowable levels of moisture added. Sold as "seasoned" product or "water added."

Needling—a process in which a solution is injected into the muscle to provide moisture and flavour. Products are referred to as marinated or enhanced. The moisture retention must be declared.

Barding a Pheasant

Larding Meat

wine is usually used for white meats and red wine for red meats. Not only does the wine add a distinctive flavour, the acids in it help break down connective tissues and tenderize the meat.

Veal and pork generally require less time to marinate than game, beef and lamb. Smaller pieces of meat take less time than larger pieces. When marinating meat, be sure to cover it completely and keep it refrigerated. Stir or turn the meat frequently to ensure that the marinade penetrates evenly.

Dry marinating generally involves rubbing herbs and spices into the surface of the meat, fish, poultry or game. Dry rubs may have sugar and salt in them as well, although both may draw moisture out of the product. Depending on the concentrations of salts and the use of nitrates and nitrites, dry marinating can become a form of curing. The product may be placed on a rack and sometimes is pressed as it undergoes the marinating process.

Barding

Barding is the process of covering the surface of meat or poultry with thin slices of pork backfat or bacon and tying them in place with butcher's twine. Barded meat or poultry is usually roasted. As the item cooks, the backfat continuously bastes it, protecting the meat from drying and enhancing moistness. A drawback to barding is that the backfat prevents the meat or poultry from developing the crusty exterior associated with roasting.

Larding

Larding is the process of inserting small strips of pork fat into meat with a larding needle to imitate marbling. Larded meat is usually cooked by braising. During cooking, the added fat melts and coats the meat fibres contributing to moistness. Although once popular, larding is rarely used today because advances in feeding practices and selective breeding produce better marbled meats.

APPLYING VARIOUS COOKING METHODS

Dry-Heat Cooking Methods

Dry-heat cooking methods subject food directly to the heat of a flame (broiling and grilling), hot air (roasting) or heated fat (sautéing and pan-frying). These cooking methods firm proteins without significant breakdown of connective tissue. They are not recommended for less tender cuts or those high in connective tissue.

Broiling and Grilling

To serve a good-quality broiled or grilled product you must start with good-quality meat. The broiling or grilling process adds flavour; additional flavours are derived from seasonings. The broiler or grill should brown and sear the meat for flavour and appearance. The grill should leave distinctive crosshatch marks on the meat's surface.

Selecting Meats to Broil or Grill

Only the most tender cuts should be broiled or grilled because the high heat and short cooking times do not tenderize. Intramuscular fat adds flavour as the meat cooks, so the meat should be well marbled. Some external fat is also beneficial. Too much fat, however, will cause the broiler or grill to flare up, burning or discolouring the meat and adding objectionable flavours. Silverskin (elastin) toughens when meat is broiled or grilled. Trim away as much of it as possible.

Cooking Temperatures

Red meats should be cooked at sufficiently high temperatures to caramelize their surface, making them more attractive and flavourful. At the same time, the broiler or grill cannot be too hot or the meat's exterior will burn before the interior is cooked.

Because veal and pork are normally cooked to higher internal temperatures than beef and lamb, they should be cooked at slightly lower temperatures so the exterior is a deep golden colour while the interior is cooked to the desired doneness, but still moist.

Seasoning Meats to Be Broiled or Grilled

Meats that have not been marinated should be well seasoned with salt and pepper just before being placed on the broiler or grill. If they are seasoned and allowed to rest, the salt will dissolve and draw out moisture, making it difficult to brown the meat properly. Some chefs feel that broiled or grilled meats should be seasoned on the cooked surface only. Pork and veal, which have a tendency to dry out when cooked, should be basted with seasoned butter or oil during cooking to help keep them moist. Meats can be glazed or basted with sauces or marinade liquids as they cook, but observe food safety guidelines and excercise caution with high-sugar products that may burn.

Degrees of Doneness

Consumers request and expect meats to be properly cooked to specific degrees of doneness. It is your responsibility to understand and comply with these requests. Meats can be cooked very rare (or bleu), rare, medium rare, medium, medium well or well done. Figure 12.6 shows the proper colour for these different degrees of doneness. This guide can be used for red meats cooked by any method.

Larger cuts of meat, such as a chateaubriand or thick chops, are often started on the broiler or grill to develop colour and flavour and then finished in a low heat oven to ensure complete, even cooking.

Determining Doneness

Broiling or grilling meat to the proper degree of doneness is an art. Larger pieces of meat will take longer to cook than smaller ones, but how quickly a piece of meat cooks is determined by many other factors: the temperature of the broiler or grill, the temperature of the piece of meat when placed on the broiler or grill, the type of meat and the thickness of the cut. Because of these variables, timing alone is not a useful tool in determining doneness.

A thermometer is the most reliable method of determining doneness; however, its use is not very practical or accurate with cuts such as steaks. Cutting a steak to observe the colour is not acceptable to the customer. The most used method of determining doneness is by pressing the piece of meat with tongs and gauging the amount of resistance it yields. Very rare (bleu) meat will offer almost no resistance and will feel almost the same as raw meat. Meat cooked rare will feel spongy and offer slight resistance to pressure. Meat cooked medium will feel slightly firm and springy to the touch. Meat cooked well done will feel quite firm and will spring back quickly when pressed. See Table 12.1.

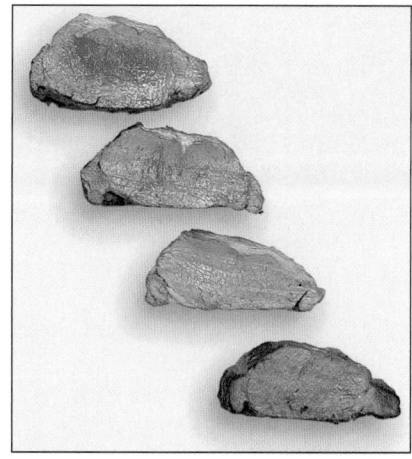

FIGURE 12.6 *Degrees of Doneness Beef roasted rare, medium rare, medium and medium well.*

1. Brush the lamb chops with oil.

2. Place the lamb chops on the grill.

3. Rotate the lamb chops 90 degrees to create crosshatch marks.

4. Turn the chops over to finish them on the other side.

TABLE 12.1   DETERMINING DONENESS OF BEEF STEAK

Degree of Doneness	Colour	Degree of Resistance
Very rare (bleu)	Very red and raw-looking centre (the centre is cool to the touch)	Almost no resistance
Rare	Large deep red centre	Spongy; very slight resistance
Medium rare	Bright red centre	Some resistance; slightly springy
Medium	Rosy pink to red centre	Slightly firm; springy
Medium well	Very little pink at the centre, almost brown throughout	Firm; springy
Well done	No red	Quite firm; springs back quickly when pressed

Accompaniments to Broiled and Grilled Meats

Because a broiler or grill cannot be deglazed to form the base for a sauce, compound butters or sauces such as béarnaise are often served with broiled or grilled meats. Brown sauces such as bordelaise, chasseur, périgueux or brown mushroom sauce also complement many broiled or grilled items. Additional sauce suggestions are found in Table 10.5.

Basic Procedure for Broiling or Grilling Meats

1. Heat the broiler or grill.

2. Use a wire brush to remove any charred or burnt particles that may be stuck to the broiler or grill grate. The grate can be wiped with a lightly oiled towel to remove any remaining particles and help season it.

3. Prepare the item to be broiled or grilled by trimming off excess fat and connective tissue and marinating or seasoning as desired. The meat may be brushed lightly with oil to help keep it from sticking to the grate, but excess fat will cause flare-ups.

4. Place the item in the broiler or on the grill. Following the example in Chapter 9, turn the meat to produce the attractive crosshatch marks associated with grilling. Use tongs to turn or flip the meat without piercing the surface in order to prevent valuable juices from escaping.

5. Cook the meat to the desired doneness while developing the proper surface colour. To do so, adjust the position of the meat on the broiler or grill or adjust the distance between the grate and heat source.

Applying the Basics

RECIPE 12.1

GRILLED LAMB CHOPS WITH HERB BUTTER

Yield: 2 Servings

Lamb chops, loin or rib, approx. 2.5 cm (1 inch) thick	6	6
Salt and pepper	TT	TT
Oil	as needed	as needed
Herb butter	6 thin slices or	6 small rosettes

1. Preheat the grill for 15 minutes or until the grate is sufficiently heated.
2. Season the lamb chops with salt and pepper; lightly brush with oil.
3. Place the lamb chops on the grill, turning as necessary to produce the proper crosshatching. Cook to the desired doneness.
4. Remove the lamb chops from the grill and place a slice or rosette of herb butter on each chop.
5. Serve immediately as the herb butter melts. The plate can be placed under the broiler for a few seconds to help melt the herb butter.

RECIPE 12.1

Approximate values per serving:

Calories	524
Total fat	44 g
Saturated fat	20 g
Cholesterol	161 mg
Sodium	368 mg
Total carbohydrates	0.1 g
Protein	32 g

Roasting

Properly roasted meats should be tender, juicy and evenly cooked to the appropriate degree of doneness. They should have a pleasant appearance when whole as well as when sliced and plated.

Seasoning Meats to Be Roasted

Seasonings are especially important with smaller roasts and roasts with little or no fat covering. With these roasts, some of the seasonings penetrate the meat while the remainder help create the highly seasoned crust associated with a good roast. A large roast with heavy fat covering (for example, a ponderosa hip or prime rib) does not benefit from being seasoned on the surface because the seasonings will not penetrate the fat layer, which is trimmed away before service.

When practical, a roast with excess fat should be trimmed, leaving just a thin fat layer so that the roast bastes itself while cooking. A lean roast can be barded or larded before cooking to add richness and moisture. Lamb legs are sometimes studded with garlic cloves by piercing the meat with a paring knife and then pressing slivers of raw garlic into the holes.

A roast is sometimes cooked on a bed of mirepoix, or mirepoix is added to the roasting pan as the roast cooks. The mirepoix raises the roast off the bottom of the roasting pan, preventing the bottom from overcooking. This mirepoix, however, does not add any flavour to the roast. Rather, it combines with the drippings to add flavour to the jus, sauce or gravy that is made with them.

Cooking Temperatures

Small roasts such as a rack of lamb or a beef tenderloin should be seared first to caramelize the surface and then roasted at 135°C–165°C (275°F–325°F) to ensure a tender, juicy product with a higher yield.

Traditionally, large roasts were started at high temperatures to sear the meat and seal in the juices; they were then finished at lower temperatures. Studies have proven, however, that roasts cooked at constant, low temperatures provide a juicier product with better yield and less shrinkage. Temperatures between 120°C and 135°C (250°F and 275°F) are ideal for large roasts. These temperatures will result in an evenly cooked centre portion.

Determining Doneness

The doneness of small roasts such as a rack of lamb is determined in much the same way as with broiled or grilled meats. With experience, the cook develops a sense of timing as well as a feel for gauging the amount of resistance by touching the meat. These techniques, however, are not infallible, especially with large roasts.

Although timing is useful as a general guide for planning purposes, there are too many variables for it to be relied upon exclusively. As a guideline, roasts will require 30 to 50 minutes per kilogram (15–20 minutes per pound), depending on the desired doneness, type and size of roast and internal temperature of the cut.

◆◆◆

MORE ABOUT ROASTING

Because roasting is a dry-heat cooking method, the best results come from using tender, well-marbled cuts from the rib, loin or leg. Larger or less tender cuts benefit from low-temperature roasting for longer times. This promotes moisture retention (better yield and flavour) and tenderness if the item is not cooked to medium-well or well done.

◆◆◆

THE CHALLENGE

Selecting the best oven temperature for a roast requires considering several factors. The size of the roast, degree of marbling, shape, equipment and time available all play a role. Too high a heat will result in a drier, lower yield, less tender product. Too low a temperature may not allow for browning or melting of the marbled fat or hydrolyzing of the collagen. Generally, large cuts are cooked with low heat for longer times and smaller cuts on higher heat for shorter times.

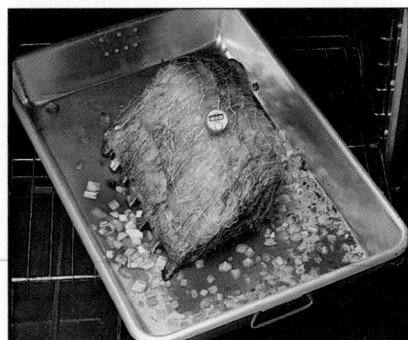

FIGURE 12.7 *The Proper Placement of an Instant-Read Thermometer*

TABLE 12.2

Degree of Doneness	Internal Temperature After Carryover
Very rare (Bleu)	52–54°C 125–130°F
Rare	55–60°C 130–140°F
Medium	60–65°C 140–150°F
Well done	65–75°C 150–165°F

The best way to determine the doneness of a large roast is to use an instant-read thermometer as shown in Figure 12.7. The thermometer is inserted into the centre or thickest part of the roast and away from any bones. The proper finished temperatures for roasted meats are listed in Table 12.2.

Carryover Cooking and Resting

Cooking does not stop the moment a roast is removed from the oven. Through conduction, the heat applied to the outside of the roast continues to penetrate, cooking the centre for several more minutes. Indeed, the internal temperature of a small roast can rise by as much as 3°C–6°C (5°F–10°F) after being removed from the oven. With a larger roast, such as a 20-kg (50-lb.) beef hip, it can rise by as much as 11°C (20°F). Therefore, remove roasted meats before they reach the desired degree of doneness and allow carryover cooking to complete the cooking process. The temperatures listed in Table 12.2 are internal temperatures after allowing for carryover cooking.

As meat cooks, its juices flow towards the centre. If the roast is carved immediately after it is removed from the oven, its juices would run from the meat, causing it to lose its colour and become dry. Letting the meat rest before slicing allows the juices to redistribute themselves evenly throughout the roast, so the roast will retain more juices when carved. Small roasts, like a rack of lamb, need to rest only 5–10 minutes; larger roasts such as a hip of beef require as much as an hour.

Accompaniments to Roasted Meats

Roasts may be served with a sauce based on their natural juices (called *au jus*), as described in Recipe 12.2, Roast Prime Rib of Beef Au Jus, or with a pan gravy made with drippings from the roast. Additional sauce suggestions are found in Table 10.5.

Basic Procedure for Roasting Meats

1. Trim excess fat, tendons and silverskin from the meat. Leave only a thin fat covering, if possible, so the roast bastes itself as it cooks.
2. Season the roast as appropriate and place it in a roasting pan. The roast may be placed on a bed of mirepoix or on a rack.
3. Roast the meat, uncovered, at the desired temperature (the larger the roast, the lower the temperature), usually 120°C–165°C (250°F–325°F).
4. If a jus or pan gravy is desired and a mirepoix was not added at the start of cooking, it may be added 30–45 minutes before the roast is done, thus allowing it to caramelize while the roast finishes cooking.
5. Cook to the desired temperature.
6. Remove the roast from the oven, allowing carryover cooking to raise the internal temperature to the desired degree of doneness. Allow the roast to rest before slicing or carving it. As the roast rests, prepare the jus, sauce or pan gravy.

RECIPE 12.2

Approximate values per serving:

Calories	551
Total fat	37 g
Saturated fat	16 g
Cholesterol	148 mg
Sodium	504 mg
Total carbohydrates	4.4 g
Protein	50 g

Applying the Basics

RECIPE 12.2

ROAST PRIME RIB OF BEEF AU JUS

Yield: 18 250-g (8-oz.) boneless servings

| Beef rib, cover off, CMC#109D, approx. 7.5 kg (16 lb.) | 1 | 1 |

Salt and pepper	TT	TT
Garlic, chopped	TT	TT
Mirepoix	500 g	1 lb.
Brown stock	2 L	2 qt.

1. Season the roast with the salt, pepper and chopped garlic. Place the roast in an appropriate-sized roasting pan. Roast at 120°C–135°C (250°F–275°F).

2. Add the mirepoix to the pan approximately 1 hour before the roast is finished cooking. Continue cooking until the internal temperature reaches 52°C (125°F), approximately 4–4.5 hours. Carryover cooking will raise the internal temperature of the roast to approximately 60°C (140°F).

3. Remove the roast from the pan and allow it to rest in a warm place for 30 minutes.

4. Drain the excess fat from the roasting pan, reserving the mirepoix and any drippings in the roasting pan.

5. Caramelize the mirepoix on the stove top; allow the liquids to evaporate, leaving only brown drippings in the pan.

6. Deglaze the pan with brown stock. Stir to loosen all the drippings.

7. Simmer the jus, reducing it slightly and allowing the mirepoix to release its flavour; season with salt and pepper if necessary.

8. Strain the jus through a conical strainer lined with cheesecloth. Skim any remaining fat from the surface with a ladle.

9. Trim and slice the roast as described opposite and serve with approximately 30–60 mL (1–2 fl. oz.) jus per person.

1. Drain off the excess fat.

2. Caramelize the mirepoix.

3. Deglaze the pan with brown stock.

4. Simmer the jus, reducing it slightly and allowing the mirepoix to release its flavours.

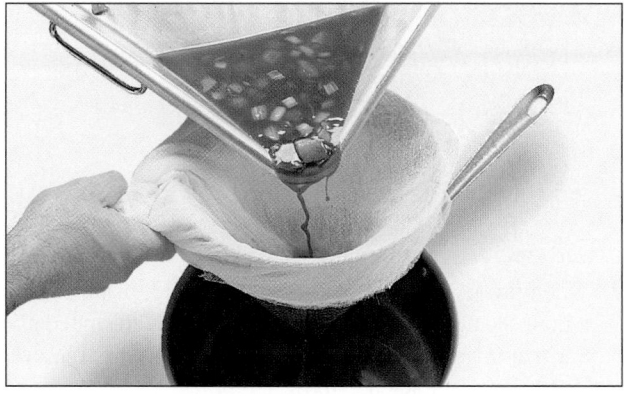

5. Strain the jus through a conical strainer and cheesecloth.

Carving Roasts

All the efforts that went into selecting and cooking a perfect roast will be wasted if the roast is not carved properly. Roasts are always carved against the grain; carving with the grain produces long stringy, tough slices. Cutting across the muscle fibres produces a more attractive and tender portion. Portions may be cut in a single thick slice, as with Roast Prime Rib of Beef, or in many thin slices. The photographs following illustrate several different carving procedures.

Carving Prime Rib (Roast Ready, Cap On CMC#109)

1. Remove the netting, cap fat and chine bones.

2. Trim the excess fat from the eye muscle.

3. Slice the rib in long, smooth strokes, the first cut (end cut) without a rib bone, the second cut with a rib bone, and so on.

Carving Prime Rib on the Slicer

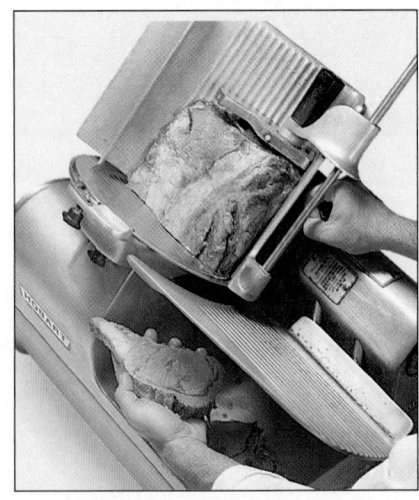

1. When producing large quantities of prime rib, it is often more practical to slice it on a slicing machine. Following the steps illustrated above, remove the netting, cap fat and chine bone; trim excess fat from the eye muscle. Then use a long slicer, completely remove the rib eye from the rib bones, being careful to stay as close as possible to the bones to avoid wasting any meat.

2. After placing the rib on the slicing machine, set the machine to the desired thickness. The blade will have to be adjusted often because a roast's shape fluctuates.

Carving a Beef Hip

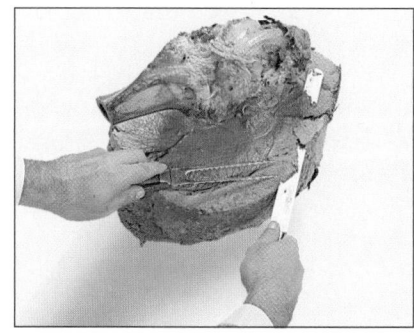

1. After setting the roast on the cutting board with the exposed femur bone (large end of the roast) down and the tibia (shank bone) or "handle" up, trim the excess exterior fat to expose the lean meat.

2. Begin slicing with a horizontal cut towards the shank bone, then make vertical cuts to release the slices of beef.

3. Keep the exposed surface as level as possible. Continue carving, turning the roast as necessary to access all sides.

Carving a Leg of Lamb

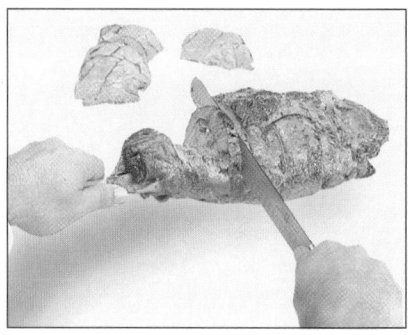

1. Hold the shank bone firmly, cut towards the bone.

2. Cut parallel to the shank bone to remove the slices.

3. Rotate the leg as needed to access the meat on all sides.

Sautéing

Sautéing is a dry-heat cooking method using high heat and selected for smaller cuts in which heat is conducted by a small amount of fat. Sautéed meats should be tender (a reflection of the quality of the raw product), of good colour (determined by proper cooking temperatures) and have a good overall flavour. Any accompanying sauce should be well seasoned and complement the meat without overpowering it.

Selecting Meats to Sauté

As with broiling, grilling and roasting, you should use tender meats of the highest quality in order to produce good results when sautéing. The cuts should be uniform in size and shape to promote even cooking.

Seasoning Meats to Be Sautéed

The meat can be marinated or simply seasoned with salt and pepper. If marinated, the meat must be patted dry before cooking to ensure proper browning. Some meats are dusted with flour before cooking to help dry the surface and promote even browning. It may provide some thickening of the sauce. The sauces that almost always accompany sautéed meats provide much of the flavour.

Determining Doneness

As with broiled and grilled meats, the doneness of sautéed meats is determined by touch and timing. Red meats should be well browned; veal and pork should be somewhat lighter.

Accompaniments to Sautéed Meats

Sauces served with sautéed meats are usually made directly in the sauté pan, utilizing the **fond**. They often incorporate a previously thickened sauce. Additional sauce suggestions for sautéed meats are found in Table 10.5.

Basic Procedure for Sautéing Meats

1. Heat a sauté pan and add enough oil or clarified butter just to cover the bottom. The pan should be large enough to hold the meat in a single layer. A pan that is too large may cause the fat or meat to burn.
2. Cut the meat into **cutlets**, **escallopes**, **émincés**, **medallions**, **mignonnettes**, **noisettes**, **chops** or small even-sized pieces. Season the meat and dredge in flour if desired.
3. Add the meat to the sauté pan in a single layer. Do not crowd the pan.
4. Adjust the temperature so that the meat's exterior browns properly without burning and the interior cooks. The heat should be high enough to complete the cooking process before the meat begins to stew in its own juices.
5. Small items may be tossed using the sauté pan's sloped sides to flip them back on top of themselves. Do not toss the meat more than necessary, however. The pan should remain in contact with the heat source as much as possible to maintain proper temperatures. Larger items should be turned using tongs or a kitchen fork. Avoid splashing hot fat.
6. Transfer the meat to another pan and proceed with preparing the sauce and/or garnish; combine the meat with the sauce and finish cooking.

Basic Procedure for Making a Sauce in the Sauté Pan

1. If a sauce is to be made in the sauté pan, hold the meat in a warm spot while preparing the sauce. When the meat is removed from the pan, leave a small amount of fat as well as the fond. If there is excessive fat, degrease the pan, leaving just enough to cover its bottom. Add ingredients such as garlic, shallots and mushrooms that will be used as garnishes and sauce flavourings; sauté them.
2. Deglaze the pan with wine or stock. Scrape the pan, loosening the fond and allowing it to dissolve in the liquid. Reduce the deglazing liquid by approximately three-quarters.
3. Add fond lié (or demi-glace) or stock to the pan. Cook and reduce the sauce to the desired consistency. Other sauces may be used.
4. Add any ingredients that do not require cooking such as herbs and spices. Adjust the seasonings with salt and pepper.
5. For service, the meat may be returned to the pan for a moment to reheat it and coat it with the finished sauce. The meat should remain in the sauce just long enough to reheat. Do not attempt to cook the meat in the sauce.

Applying the Basics

RECIPE 12.3

SAUTÉED VEAL SCALLOPINI WITH WHITE WINE LEMON SAUCE

Yield: 6 180-g (6-oz.) Servings

Veal scallopini, 90 g (3 oz.) each	12	12
Clarified butter	60 g	2 fl. oz.
Flour	120 g	4 oz.
Salt and pepper	TT	TT
Shallots, chopped	20 g	2 Tbsp.
White wine	175 mL	6 fl. oz.
Lemon juice	50 mL	2 fl. oz.
Brown veal stock	125 mL	4 fl. oz.
Unsalted butter*	50 g	2 oz.
Lemon wedges	12	12

1. Pound the scallopini to a uniform thickness, as described in Chapter 14, Veal.
2. Heat a sauté pan and add the clarified butter.
3. Dredge the scallopini in seasoned flour and add to the pan in a single layer. Sauté on each side for 1–2 minutes. As the first scallopini are done, remove them to a warm platter and sauté the remaining scallopini.
4. Add the chopped shallots to the pan and sauté.
5. Deglaze the pan with the white wine and lemon juice.
6. Add the brown veal stock and reduce by half.
7. Swirl in the unsalted butter (monter au beurre).
8. Adjust the seasonings with salt and pepper.
9. Serve 2 scallopini per person with approximately 30 mL (1 fl. oz.) of sauce. Garnish with lemon wedges.

*The sauce may be modified to reduce the amount of butter. In Step 7, thicken the sauce with arrowroot or cornstarch and finish with 10 g (2 tsp.) butter.

Pan-Frying

Pan-frying is generally selected for larger cuts and uses more fat and lower heat than sautéing to conduct heat. Pan-fried meats should be tender (a reflection of the quality of the raw product), of good colour (determined by proper cooking temperatures) and with a good overall flavour. Meats to be pan-fried are

---

◆◆◆
SCALLOPINI SAUCE

The sauce for the scallopini can be easily adapted to produce a wide variety of dishes. Omit the wine and lemon and try tomato sauce, zingara, marsala or mushroom sauce. Add a vegetable or fruit garnish or fresh herbs or a bit of cream.

RECIPE 12.3

Approximate values per serving:

Calories	665
Total fat	49 g
Saturated fat	19 g
Cholesterol	165 mg
Sodium	1180 mg
Total carbohydrates	20 g
Protein	36 g

---

1. Add the veal cutlets to the pan. Note the relationship of scallopini to pan size.

2. Add the chopped shallots to the pan and sauté them.

3. Deglaze the pan with white wine and lemon juice.

4. Add the brown veal stock and reduce by half.

5. Swirl in the butter and adjust the seasonings.

usually breaded. In addition to providing flavour, breading seals the meat. The breading should be free from breaks, thus preventing the fat from coming into direct contact with the meat or collecting in a pocket formed between the meat and the breading. Pan-fried items should be golden in colour and the breading should not be soggy.

Selecting Meats to Pan-Fry

As with other dry-heat cooking methods, tender meats of high quality should be used because the meat will not be tenderized by the cooking process. Meats that are pan-fried are often cut into cutlets or escallops and may be delicate, pounded or jacquarded to tenderize.

Seasoning Meats to Be Pan-Fried

Pan-fried meats are usually seasoned lightly with salt and pepper either by applying them directly to the meat or adding them to the flour used in the breading procedure.

Determining Doneness

The most accurate way to determine the doneness of a pan-fried item is by timing. The touch method is difficult to use because of the large amounts of hot fat. It also may not be as accurate as with broiled or grilled meats because pan-fried meats are often quite thin.

Accompaniments to Pan-Fried Meats

Any sauce served with pan-fried meats is usually made separately because there is often no fond (drippings) created during the pan-frying process. Sauce suggestions are listed in Table 10.5.

Basic Procedure for Pan-Frying Meats

1. Slice the meat into cutlets and pound, if required, as described in Chapter 14, Veal.

2. Bread the meat using the standard breading procedure detailed in Chapter 21, Deep-Fat Frying.

3. Heat a moderate amount of fat or oil in a heavy pan. The temperature should be slightly lower than that used to sauté so that the breading will be nicely browned when the item is fully cooked.

4. Place the meat in the pan, being careful not to splash the hot oil. The meat should be immersed one-third. Fry until golden brown. Turn and brown the other side. Ideally, pan-fried meats should be fully cooked when they are well browned on both sides.

5. Remove the meat from the pan; drain it on absorbent paper before serving.

Applying the Basics

RECIPE 12.4

BREADED PORK CUTLETS

Yield: 10 125-g (4-oz.) Servings

Pork cutlet, 125 g (4 oz.) each	10	10
Salt and pepper	TT	TT
Standard breading:	as needed	as needed
Flour		
Eggs		
Milk		
Bread crumbs		
Vegetable oil	as needed	as needed
Butter (optional)	175 g	6 oz.
Lemon wedges	20	20

1. Using a mallet, pound the cutlets to an even thickness, approximately 0.5 cm (1/4 inch). Season the cutlets with salt and pepper.
2. Bread the cutlets using the standard breading procedure described in Chapter 21, Deep-Fat Frying.
3. Heat a heavy pan to moderate heat; add approximately 0.25 cm (1/8 inch) of oil.
4. Add the cutlets in a single layer. Do not crowd the pan. Brown on one side, then the other. Total cooking time should be approximately 4 minutes.
5. Remove the cutlets and drain on absorbent paper.
6. Melt the butter in a small pan until it foams.
7. Place one cutlet on each plate and pour approximately 15 mL (1/2 fl. oz.) butter over each portion. Garnish with lemon wedges.

NOTE: Chops, plain or stuffed, use this method, as does Cordon Bleu.

Moist-Heat Cooking Methods

Moist-heat cooking methods subject food to heat and moisture. Moist heat is often, but not always, used to tenderize tougher cuts of meat through long, slow cooking. Simmering is the only moist-heat cooking method discussed here as it is the one most frequently used with meat. Poaching is covered in fish, poultry and egg cooking.

RECIPE 12.4

Approximate values per serving:

Calories	444
Total fat	24 g
Saturated fat	6.8 g
Cholesterol	155 mg
Sodium	590 mg
Total carbohydrates	19 g
Protein	38 g

1. Add the breaded cutlets to the hot pan. Note the amount of oil in the pan.

2. Turn the cutlets to brown on the second side.

3. Melt the butter in a separate pan until it foams.

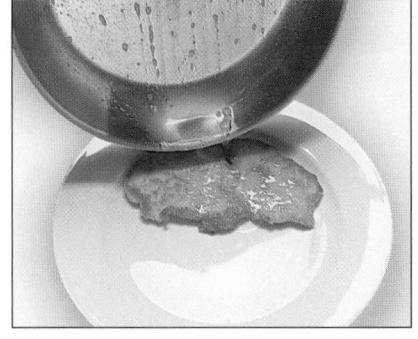

4. Pour the butter over the cutlet.

Simmering

Simmering is usually associated with specific tougher cuts of meat that need to be tenderized through long, slow, moist cooking. Quality simmered meats are moist and have good flavour and texture. The flavour is determined by the cooking liquid; the texture and moistness are a result of proper cooking temperatures and time.

Selecting Meats to Simmer

Meats such as fresh or corned beef brisket, fresh or cured hams and tongue are often simmered. Beef briskets and tongues, pork butts and hams are often simmered whole. The recipe name usually says "boiled."

Seasoning Meats to Be Simmered

If the meat to be simmered was cured and/or smoked (as with cured hams, ham hocks, smoked pork butt, corned beef or pickled tongue), the cooking liquid will not be used to make a sauce but should be seasoned with herbs and spices. Indeed, simmering cured meats helps leach out some of the excess salt, making the finished dish more palatable.

Cooking Temperatures

Moist-heat cooking methods generally use lower temperatures than dry-heat cooking methods. Meats are normally simmered at temperatures between 82°C and 93°C (180°F and 200°F). In larger food service operations, meats such as hams and corned beef are cooked at temperatures as low as 65°C (150°F) for up to 12 hours. Although lower cooking temperatures result in less shrinkage and a more moist and tender finished product, long cooking times may not always be practical, cost efficient or healthy.

Determining Doneness

Tougher cuts are almost always cooked well done, which is determined by tenderness. The size and quality of the raw product determines the cooking time. Undercooked meats will be tough and chewy. Overcooked meats will be stringy and may even fall apart.

To test large cuts of meat for doneness, a kitchen fork should be inserted into the meat and the meat should slide easily off the fork. Smaller pieces of meat should be tender to the bite or easily cut with a table fork.

Accompaniments to Simmered Meats

Simmered meats are often served with boiled or steamed vegetables, for example, corned beef and cabbage. Pickled meats are often served with mustard or horseradish sauce on the side or perhaps a cider raisin sauce.

Basic Procedure for Simmering Meats

1. Cut, trim or tie the meat according to the recipe.
2. Bring an adequate amount of liquid to a boil. There should be enough liquid to cover the meat completely. Too much liquid will leach off much of the meat's flavour; too little will leave a portion of the meat exposed, preventing it from cooking. Because the dish's final flavour is determined by the flavour of the liquid, use plenty of mirepoix, flavourings and seasonings.
3. When simmering smoked or cured items, start them in cold water. This helps draw off some of the strong pickled or smoked flavours.
4. Add the meat to the liquid.

5. Reduce the heat to the desired temperature and cook until the meat is tender. Do not allow the cooking liquid to boil. Boiling results in a tough or over-cooked and stringy product. If the simmered meat is to be served cold, a moister and juicier product can be achieved by removing the pot from the stove before the meat is fully cooked. The meat and the liquid can be cooled in a water bath like that for a stock, as described in Chapter 10, Stocks and Sauces. This allows the residual heat in the cooking liquid to finish cooking the meat.

Applying the Basics

RECIPE 12.5

NEW ENGLAND BOILED DINNER

Yield: 12 180-g (6-oz.) Servings

Corned beef brisket, 3.6 kg (8 lb.)	1	1
White stock	as needed	as needed
Sachet:		
Bay leaves	2	2
Dried thyme	0.25 g	1/2 tsp.
Peppercorns, cracked	0.5 g	1/2 tsp.
Parsley stems	10	10
Mustard seeds	10 g	1 Tbsp.
Cinnamon sticks	10 g	2
Allspice berries (whole)	4	4
Baby red beets	24	24
Baby turnips	24	24
Baby carrots	24	24
Brussels sprouts	24	24
Pearl onions	24	24
Potatoes, Red Bliss	24	24
Salt and pepper	TT	TT

1. Place the beef in a pot and add enough stock to cover it. Add the sachet, bring to a boil and reduce to a simmer.

2. Simmer until the beef is tender, approximately 3 hours. Remove the beef and hold in a hotel pan in a small amount of the cooking liquid.

3. Peel or prepare the vegetables and potatoes as needed and cook separately in a portion of the cooking liquid.

4. Carve the beef and serve with 2 of each of the vegetables and horseradish sauce (see page 209).

RECIPE 12.5

Approximate values per serving:

Calories	673
Total fat	45 g
Saturated fat	14 g
Cholesterol	162 mg
Sodium	426 mg
Total carbohydrates	20 g
Protein	47 g

1. Place the corned beef and sachet in an appropriate pot and cover with stock.

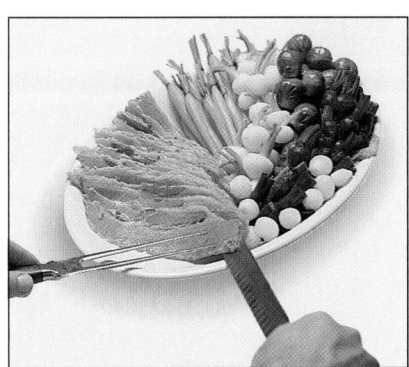

2. Carve the beef and present it with the vegetable garnish.

Combination Cooking Methods

Braising and stewing are referred to as combination cooking methods because both dry heat and moist heat are used to achieve the desired results.

Braising

Braised meats are first browned and then cooked in a liquid that serves as a sauce for the meat. A well-prepared braised dish has the rich flavour of the meat in the sauce and the moisture and flavour of the sauce in the meat. It should be fork tender but not falling apart. The meat should have an attractive colour from the initial browning and final glazing.

Selecting Meats to Braise

Braising can be used for tender cuts (such as those from the loin or rib) or tougher cuts (such as those from the chuck or shank). Any meat to be braised should be well marbled with ample fat content to produce a moist finished product.

If tender cuts such as veal chops or pork chops are braised, the finished dish has a uniquely different flavour and texture than if they were cooked by a dry-heat method. Tender cuts require shorter cooking times than tougher cuts because lengthy cooking is not needed to break down connective tissue.

More often, braising is used with tougher cuts that are tenderized by the long, moist cooking process. Cuts from the chuck, outside round and shank are popular choices, as they are very flavourful and contain relatively large amounts of collagen, which adds richness to the finished product.

Large pieces of meat can be braised, then carved like a roast (pot roast). Portion control cuts and diced meats can also be braised.

Seasoning Meats to Be Braised

The overall flavour of a braised dish is largely the result of using quality cooking liquids and the mirepoix, herbs, spices and other ingredients that flavour the meat as it cooks. Braised meats can be marinated before they are cooked to help tenderize them and add flavour. The marinade may be incorporated into the braising liquid. Salt and pepper may be added to the flour if the meat is dredged before it is browned, or the meat may be seasoned directly (although the salt may draw out moisture and inhibit browning).

As a general rule, flavouring and seasoning ingredients, including tomato products, are added at the start of simmering to ensure even flavour penetration during cooking. Care must be taken not to overseason too early, as the sauce will reduce during cooking.

Cooking Temperatures

Braised meats are usually browned before simmering. As a general rule, smaller cuts are floured before browning; larger cuts are not. Flouring dries the surface of the meat, promotes even browning and provides some thickening to the sauce that accompanies the meat. Whether floured or not, the meat is browned in fat. After browning, white meats should be golden to amber in colour; red meats should be dark brown. Do not brown the meat too quickly at too high a temperature, as it is important to develop a well-caramelized surface. The caramelized surface adds colour and flavour to the final product.

The meat and the braising liquid are brought to a simmer over direct heat and the pot is covered. Cooking can be finished in the oven or on the stove top. The oven provides gentle, even heat without the risk of scorching. If the braise is finished on the stove top, proper temperatures must be maintained carefully throughout the cooking process and great care must be taken to prevent scorching or burning. Lower temperatures and longer cooking times result in more even cooking and thorough penetration of the cooking liquid, providing a more flavourful final product.

Finishing Braised Meats

Near the end of the cooking process, the lid may be removed from oven-braised meats. Finishing braised meats without a cover serves two purposes. First, the meat can be glazed by basting it often. (As the basting liquid evaporates, the meat is browned and a strongly flavoured glaze is formed.) Second, removing the lid allows the cooking liquid to reduce, thickening it and concentrating its flavours for use as a sauce.

Determining Doneness

Braised meats are done when they are tender. A fork inserted into the meat should meet little resistance. Properly braised meats should remain intact and not fall apart when handled gently.

Braised meats that fall apart or are stringy are overcooked. If the finished product is tough, it was probably undercooked or cooked at too high a temperature. If the entire dish lacks flavour, the meat may not have been properly browned or the cooking liquid may have been poorly seasoned.

Accompaniments to Braised Meats

Large braised items are often served like roasts. They are carved across the grain in thin slices and served with their sauce. Vegetables can be cooked with the braised meat, cooked separately and added when the main item has finished cooking or added at service. If the vegetables are cooked with the main item, they should be added at intervals based on their individual cooking times to prevent overcooking.

Basic Procedure for Braising Meats

The liquid used for braising is usually thickened in one of three ways:

1. With a roux added at the start of the cooking process; the roux thickens the sauce as the meat cooks.
2. Prethickened before the meat is added.
3. Thickened after the meat is cooked either by puréeing the mirepoix or by using roux, arrowroot or cornstarch.

The procedure for braising meats includes variations for whichever thickening method is selected.

1. Heat a small amount of oil in a heavy pan.
2. Dredge the meat to be braised in seasoned flour, if desired, and add it to the oil.
3. Brown the meat well on all sides and remove from the pan.
4. Add a mirepoix to the pan and caramelize it well. If using roux, it should be added at this time.
5. Add the appropriate stock or sauce so that when the meat is returned to the pan it will be approximately one-third immersed.
6. Add aromatics and seasonings.
7. Return the meat to the sauce. Tightly cover the pot and bring it to a simmer. Cook slowly either on the stove top or by placing the covered pot directly in an oven at 120°C–150°C (250°F–300°F).
8. Cook the item, basting or turning it often so that all sides of the meat benefit from the moisture and flavour of the sauce.
9. When the meat is done, remove it from the pan and hold it in a warm place while the sauce is finished.
10. The sauce may be reduced on the stove top to intensify its flavours. If the meat was braised in a stock, the stock may be thickened using a roux, arrowroot or cornstarch. Strain the sauce or, if desired, purée the mirepoix and other ingredients and return them to the sauce. Adjust the sauce's consistency as desired.

PARADOX

Cooking any meat to achieve optimum palatability is a challenge. The product's characteristics and the customer's desires must be brought together. Longer cooking times, often associated with less tender cuts, usually means the product will be well done. Well-done meat becomes dry and stringy. The hydrolyzed collagen (gelatin) ends up in the sauce as does any fat. The cook must find a balance in controlling the cooking process to achieve the best results despite the chemistry. Careful thought must go into planning the menu, purchasing the appropriate product and applying the best cooking method to ensure customer satisfaction. Always analyze a recipe thoroughly and, if necessary, adapt the ingredients or method to have the chemistry working for you. Even very tender, well-marbled cuts can be ruined by applying inappropriate methodologies. Tenderloin can be tough!

David MacGillivray

From the time he was 15 years old, working in a restaurant in Picton, Ontario, David knew he wanted to be a chef. He quickly became renowned in Canada, particularly for his work in the Edith Cavell Dining Room at Jasper Park Lodge. He is now the Director of Food and Beverage at the luxurious Château Lake Louise.

Applying the Basics

RECIPE 12.6

ALBERTA BEEF CHEEKS WITH ROOT VEGETABLES, BABY ONIONS AND WILD MUSHROOMS, BRAISED IN A STONE CHURCH BACO NOIR SAUCE

FAIRMONT CHÂTEAU LAKE LOUISE, LAKE LOUISE, AB
Director, Food and Beverage, David MacGillivray

NOTE: You can use beef stewing meat as a substitute for the cheeks if they are unavailable or not to your liking.

Yield: 6 Servings

Canola oil	50 mL	2 fl. oz.
Beef cheeks (trimmed of excess fat)	2 kg	4.5 lb.
Salt and pepper	TT	TT
Onion, peeled and chopped	300 g	1
Carrot, peeled and chopped	75 g	1
Celery stalk, chopped	75 g	1
Garlic cloves, minced	25 g	6
Stone Church Baco Noir	500 mL	18 fl. oz.
Bay leaves	2	2
Brown stock	3 L	100 fl. oz.
Canola oil	50 mL	2 fl. oz.
Carrots, medium, peeled and large dice	150 g	2
Purple-top turnip, peeled, large dice	150 g	1
Parsnip, medium, peeled, large dice	150 g	2
Fresh baby onions, large, cippoline if available	350 g	8–10
Chanterelles	50 g	2 oz.
Lobster mushrooms	50 g	2 oz.
Portobello mushrooms	75 g	2-1/2 oz.
Stone Church Baco Noir	250 mL	9 fl. oz.
Roasted garlic	50 g	2 oz.
Salt and coarsely ground black pepper	TT	TT
Butter	100 g	3-1/2 oz.

1. In a heavy-bottomed pot, heat canola oil, season the cheeks with salt and pepper and brown evenly and thoroughly.
2. Remove the cheeks from the pot and add the vegetables and garlic and sauté until tender.
3. Add red wine and bay leaves and deglaze the pan. Return the cheeks to the pan and add the stock.
4. Cover with a lid and place in an oven at 180°C (275°F). Cook the cheeks for 4–5 hours, checking occasionally.
5. Remove the pan from the oven. Take the cheeks out of the broth and set aside. Strain the broth through a fine etâmine and set aside for finishing.
6. To finish the dish, in a heavy-bottomed saucepan, heat 50 mL (2 fl. oz.) canola oil and sauté the root vegetables, onions and mushrooms, approximately 5 minutes.

7. Add the remaining 250 mL (9 fl. oz.) wine from the bottle, and the poaching stock.

8. Cook the vegetables, mushrooms and the stock over medium heat for approximately 30 minutes, or until tender.

9. Add the beef cheeks to the broth to bring them back to temperature.

10. Remove the cheeks and slice them; place them on a serving platter.

11. Remove the vegetables and surround the cheeks with them. Cover and keep warm in a low oven.

12. Bring the stock to a boil and add the roasted garlic. Reduce heat to medium and cook for 15 minutes. Remove from the heat and adjust the seasoning with salt and pepper. Whisk in the butter at the last minute and ladle over the beef cheeks and vegetables.

13. Serve the cheeks on a large earthenware platter with a big bowl of creamy mashed potatoes and warm bread for sopping up the sauce.

Stewing

Stewing is a combination cooking method. In many ways, the procedures for stewing and braising are identical, although stewing is usually associated with smaller or bite-sized pieces of meat.

There are two main types of stews: brown stews and white stews.

When making **brown stews**, the meat is first browned in fat; then a cooking liquid is added. The initial browning adds flavour and colour to the finished product. The same characteristics apply to a good brown stew that apply to a good braised dish: It should be fork tender and have an attractive colour and rich flavour.

There are two types of **white stews**: **fricassees**, in which the meat is first cooked in a small amount of fat without colouring, then combined with a cooking liquid; and **blanquettes**, in which the meat is first blanched, then rinsed and added to a cooking liquid. White stew should have the same flavour and texture characteristics as a brown stew, but should be white or ivory in colour.

Vegetables to garnish stews are cut uniformly and attractively, as they are left in the dish for service. Flavourings such as a bouquet garni or sachet can easily be removed.

Selecting Meats to Stew

Stewing uses moist heat to tenderize meat just as braising does, therefore many of the same cuts can be used. Meats that are to be stewed should be trimmed of excess fat and connective tissue and cut uniformly into 2.5- to 5-cm (1- to 2-inch) cubes.

Seasoning Meats to Be Stewed

Stews, like braised meats, get much of their flavour from their cooking liquid. A stew's seasoning and overall flavour are a direct result of the quality of the cooking liquid and the vegetables, herbs, spices and other ingredients added during cooking.

Cooking Temperatures

Meats for brown stews are first cooked at high temperatures over direct heat until well browned. Meats for fricassees are first sautéed at low temperatures so they do not develop colour.

RECIPE 12.6

Approximate values per serving:

Calories	943
Total fat	59 g
Saturated fat	20 g
Cholesterol	241 mg
Sodium	1167 mg
Total carbohydrates	35 g
Protein	68 g

◆◆◆

STEW TERMINOLOGY

Ragout—A general term that refers to white or brown stews in which the meat is cooked by dry heat before liquid is added. In French, *ragoût* means "to bring back the taste."

Fricassee—A white ragout usually made from white meat or small game, seared without browning and garnished with small onions and mushrooms.

Navarin—A brown ragout generally made with lamb, root vegetables, onions and peas.

Blanquette—A white stew in which the meat is first blanched, then added to a stock or sauce to complete the cooking and tenderizing process. Blanquettes are finished with a liaison of egg yolks and heavy cream.

Chili con carne—A ragout of ground or diced meat cooked with onions, chile peppers, cumin and other spices. Despite the objections of purists, chili sometimes contains beans.

Paprikash—A Hungarian stew thickened with onions, flavoured with paprika and garnished with potatoes. Pörkölt is braised and has more paprika and less liquid. Gulyás (goulash) is more like a soup.

Once the cooking liquid has been added and the moist-heat cooking process has begun, do not allow the stew to boil. Stews benefit from low-temperature cooking. If practical, stews can be covered and finished in the oven.

Determining Doneness

Stewed meats are done when they are fork tender. Test them by removing a piece of meat to a plate and cutting it with a fork. Any vegetables that are cooked with the meat should be added at the proper times so that they and the meat are completely cooked at the same time.

Accompaniments to Stewed Meats

Stews are often complete meals in themselves, containing meat, vegetables and starches in one dish. Stews that do not contain a starch are often served with pasta, rice, boiled potatoes or dumplings.

Basic Procedure for Stewing Meats—Brown Stews

Red meats, lamb or game are used in brown stews. The procedure for making a brown stew is very similar to braising.

1. Trim the meat of excess fat and silverskin and cut into 2.5- to 5-cm (1- to 2-inch) pieces.
2. Dredge the meat in flour if desired. Heat an appropriate-sized pan and add enough oil to cover the bottom. Cook the meat in the oil, browning it well on all sides. Onions and garlic can be added at this time and browned.
3. Add flour to the meat and fat and cook to make a brown roux.
4. Gradually add the liquid to the roux, stirring to prevent lumps. Bring the stew to a boil and reduce to a simmer.
5. Add a tomato product and a sachet or a bouquet garni. Cover and place in the oven or continue to simmer on the stove top until the meat is tender. Add other ingredients such as vegetables or potatoes at the proper time so that they will be done when the meat is tender.
6. When the meat is tender, remove the sachet or bouquet garni. The meat may be strained out and the sauce thickened with roux, cornstarch or arrowroot or reduced to concentrate its flavours.
7. If not added during the cooking process, vegetables and other garnishes may be cooked separately and added to the finished stew.

1. Brown the beef.

2. Sauté the garlic and onions until slightly browned.

Applying the Basics

RECIPE 12.7

Brown Beef Stew

Yield: 8 250-mL (8-fl. oz.) Servings

Oil	60 mL	2 fl. oz.
Beef chuck or shank, trimmed and cut into 3.5-cm (1-1/2-in.) cubes	2 kg	4 lb. 8 oz.
Salt	10 g	2 tsp.
Pepper	0.5 g	1/2 tsp.
Onion, small dice	300 g	10 oz.
Garlic clove, chopped	5 g	1
Red wine	250 mL	8 fl. oz.
Brown stock	1 L	1 qt.
Tomato purée	125 mL	4 fl. oz.

Sachet:

Bay leaves	2	2
Dried thyme	0.25 g	1/2 tsp.
Peppercorns, crushed	0.5 g	1/2 tsp.
Parsley stems	10	10

1. Heat a heavy pot until very hot and add the oil.
2. Season the beef and add it to the pot, browning it well on all sides. Do not overcrowd the pot. If necessary, cook the beef in several batches.
3. Add the onion and garlic and sauté until the onion is slightly browned.
4. Add the red wine and brown stock.
5. Add the tomato purée and the sachet.
6. Bring to a simmer and cook until the beef is tender, approximately 1.5–2 hours.
7. Degrease the stew by skimming off the fat.
8. Optional: Remove the cooked beef from the sauce, strain the sauce and thicken slightly with a starch product. Return the beef to the sauce.

VARIATION: Vegetables such as mushrooms, turnips, carrots, celery and pearl onions can be cooked separately and added to the stew as garnish.

Basic Procedure for Stewing Meats—Braised White Stews (Fricassees)

The procedure for making fricassees is similar to the procedure for brown stews. The primary difference is that the meat is sautéed but not allowed to brown. The braised white stew (fricassee) procedure outlined below is the basis for Recipe 14.12, Veal Fricassee.

1. Trim meat of excess fat and silverskin and cut into 2.5- to 5-cm (1- to 2-inch) pieces.
2. Heat an appropriate-sized pan and add enough oil to cover the bottom. Add the meat (and often an onion) to the pan and cook without browning.
3. Sprinkle the meat (and onion) with flour and cook to make a blond roux.
4. Gradually add the liquid, stirring to prevent lumps. Bring the stew to a boil and reduce to a simmer.
5. Add a bouquet garni and seasonings. Cover the stew and place in the oven or continue to simmer on the stove top, being careful not to burn or scorch the stew.
6. Continue to cook until the meat is tender. If the sauce is too thin, remove the meat from the sauce and hold the meat in a warm place. Reduce the sauce to the proper consistency on the stove top or thicken it by adding a small amount of blond roux, cornstarch or arrowroot.

Basic Procedure for Stewing Meats—Simmered White Stews (Blanquettes)

Unlike fricassees, blanquettes contain meat that is blanched, not sautéed. (Because the meat is cooked only by moist heat and never by dry heat, the blanquette cooking process is not a true combination cooking method; nevertheless, because of its striking similarities to stewing, it is included here.) The most common blanquette is made with veal and is known as blanquette de veau, but any white meat or lamb can be prepared in this manner using a variety of garnishes.

RECIPE 12.7

Approximate values per serving:

Calories	682
Total fat	50 g
Saturated fat	17 g
Cholesterol	172 mg
Sodium	710 mg
Total carbohydrates	10 g
Protein	48 g

3. Add the red wine and beef stock.

4. Add the tomato purée and sachet.

5. Degrease the stew.

1. Trim meat of excess fat and silverskin and cut into 2.5- to 5-cm (1- to 2-inch) pieces.
2. Blanch the cubed meat by placing the meat in an appropriate pot, covering with cool water, adding salt and bringing it rapidly to a boil. Drain the water. Rinse the meat to remove any impurities.
3. Return the meat to the pot and add enough stock to cover. Add a bouquet garni, salt and pepper. Simmer until the meat is tender, approximately 1 to 1.5 hours.
4. Strain the meat from the stock. Discard the bouquet garni. Bring the stock to a boil, thicken it with a blond roux and simmer for 15 minutes.
5. Return the meat to the thickened stock and heat to just under 85°C (185°F). Remove from the heat and add the egg yolk and cream liaison just before service. Do not boil or the egg yolks will curdle.
6. If any vegetables are to be added they should be cooked separately and added to the thickened stock with the meat.
7. Adjust the seasoning with a few drops of lemon juice, nutmeg or salt and pepper as needed.

Conclusion

Because meat may account for the largest portion of your food-cost dollar, it should be purchased carefully, stored properly and fabricated appropriately. The various cuts and flavours of meat (beef, veal, lamb and pork) can be successfully broiled, grilled, roasted, sautéed, pan-fried, simmered, braised or stewed, provided you follow a few simple procedures and learn which cuts respond best to the various cooking methods.

Questions for Discussion

1. Explain the difference between primals, subprimals and fabricated cuts of meat. Why is it important to be skilled in meat fabrication?
2. What is connective tissue composed of and where is it found? What happens to connective tissues at normal cooking temperatures?
3. Discuss the government's role in regulating the marketing and sale of meat.
4. Explain why meats are subject to a health inspection. What is the purpose of grading carcass meat?
5. At what temperature should fresh meat be stored? At what temperature should frozen meat be stored?
6. Would it be better to grill or braise a piece of meat that contains a great deal of connective tissue? Explain your answer.
7. List three ways to improve the cooking qualities of lean meats. What techniques can be used to compensate for the lack of fat?
8. Describe the similarities between sautéing meats and pan-frying them. Describe the differences.
9. Describe the similarities between braising meats and stewing them. Describe the differences.

WEBLINKS

Meat Cuts and Grading
   www.aps.uoguelph.ca/~swatland/ch3_0.htm

Beef Information Centre
   www.cattlemen.bc.ca/bic.htm

Alberta Pork Producers
   www.albertapork.com

Ontario Veal Association
   www.ontarioveal.on.ca

ABC's of Meat Cooking
   www.tasteofamerica.com/abc/abc_meat.html

CHAPTER 13
BEEF

LEARNING OUTCOMES

After studying this chapter you will be able to:

✦ identify the primal, subprimal and fabricated cuts of beef
✦ perform basic butchering procedures: cut stew, cut a strip loin, trim and cut a tenderloin, butterfly
✦ apply appropriate cooking methods to several common cuts of beef

*B*eef is the meat of domesticated cattle. Most of the beef Canadians eat comes from steers or heifers specifically raised for beef. Although Canadians are consuming less beef today than we once did, we still consume far more beef than any other meat. The beef we are eating is safe and healthy due to stringent regulations governing production, processing and importation.

PRIMAL AND SUBPRIMAL CUTS OF BEEF

After the steer or heifer is slaughtered, it is cut into four pieces (called quarters) for easy handling. This is done by first splitting the carcass down the backbone into two bilateral halves. Each half is divided into the forequarter (the front portion) and hindquarter (the rear portion) by cutting along the natural curvature between the twelfth and thirteenth ribs. The quartered carcass is then further reduced into the primal cuts and the subprimal and fabricated cuts.

The primal cuts of beef are the square chuck, point brisket and shank, rib, plate, short loin, sirloin, flank and hip. Figure 13.1 shows the relationship between a steer's bone structure and the primal cuts. Figure 13.2 shows the primal cuts of beef and their location on the carcass. Table 13.1 (page 302) identifies common beef cuts and suggests preparation methods. An entire beef carcass can range in weight from 225 kg to more than 360 kg (500–800 lb.).

Frontquarter

Square Chuck

The primal chuck is the animal's shoulder; it accounts for approximately 28% of carcass weight. It contains a portion of the backbone (which, in turn, consists of feather, finger and chine bones), five rib bones and portions of the blade and arm bones.

Because an animal constantly uses its shoulder muscles, chuck contains a high percentage of connective tissue and is quite tough. This tough cut of beef, however, is one of the most flavourful.

The primal chuck is used less frequently than other primal cuts in food service operations. If cooked whole, the chuck is difficult to cut or carve because of the large number of bones and relatively small muscle groups that travel in different directions.

The primal chuck produces several subprimal or fabricated cuts: shoulder clod, chuck roll, chuck tender, stew meat and ground chuck. Because the meat is tougher, the fabricated cuts usually benefit from moist-heat cooking or combination cooking methods such as stewing and braising.

Point Brisket and Shank

The brisket and shank are located beneath the primal chuck on the front half of the carcass. Together, they form a single primal that accounts for approximately 8% of the carcass weight. This primal consists of the animal's breast (the brisket), which contains ribs and breast bone, and its arm (the foreshank), which contains only the shank bone.

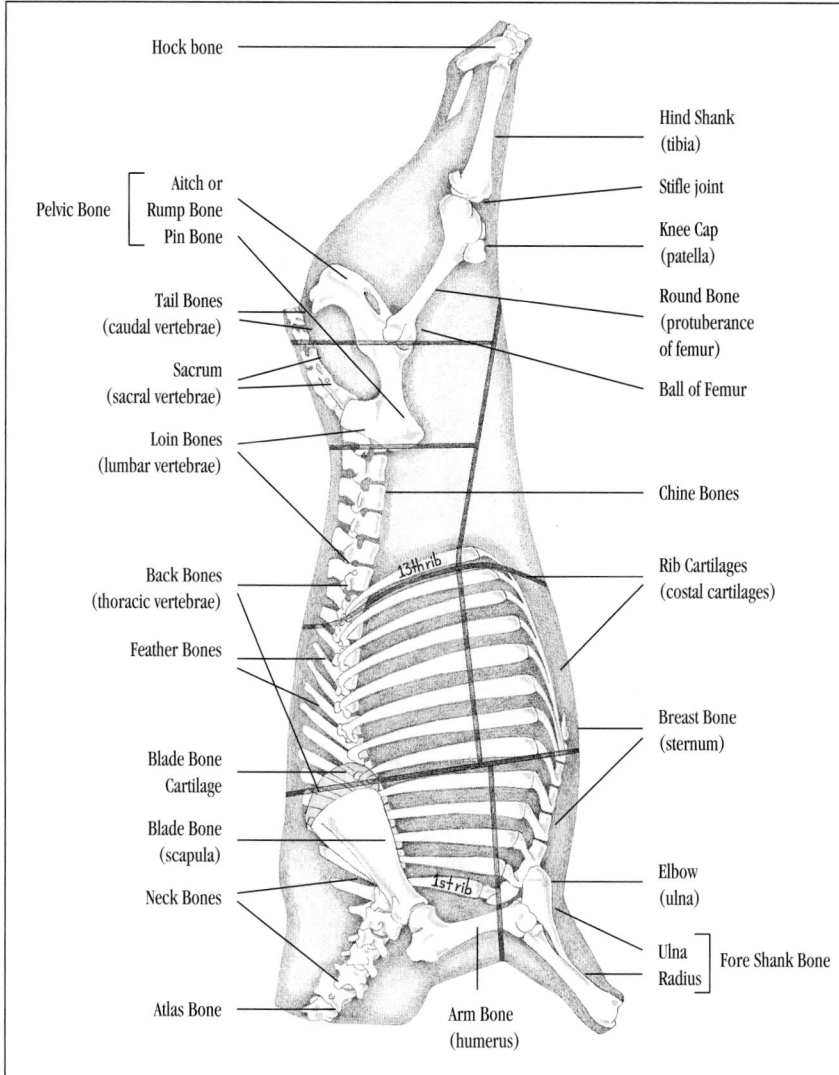

FIGURE 13.1   *The Skeletal Structure of a Steer*

SMALLER CARCASSES

Pressure and demand by restaurants is causing renewed interest in smaller carcasses. Thicker steaks can be cut from lighter animals and still meet portion standards. A premium price is being paid to acquire smaller muscles. However, the efficiencies and yields achieved from larger carcasses dictates that they will remain a strong market presence. New ways of fabricating and preparing the larger muscles will have to be found.

◆◆◆

BSE (MAD COW DISEASE)

Bovine Spongiform Encephalopathy (BSE) has caused global concerns over the safety of beef for human consumption. Canada has regulations in place to restrict the importation of live animals. The feeding of sheep- or cattle-based protein to cattle is banned. Canada has not imported meat or bone meal from the UK since 1982. Only four other countries are considered BSE free by the CFIA (January 2001). To further ensure a safe food supply, the Canadian Cattle Identification Program was introduced on January 2001. Canadian cattle are identified by a unique number on an ear tag.

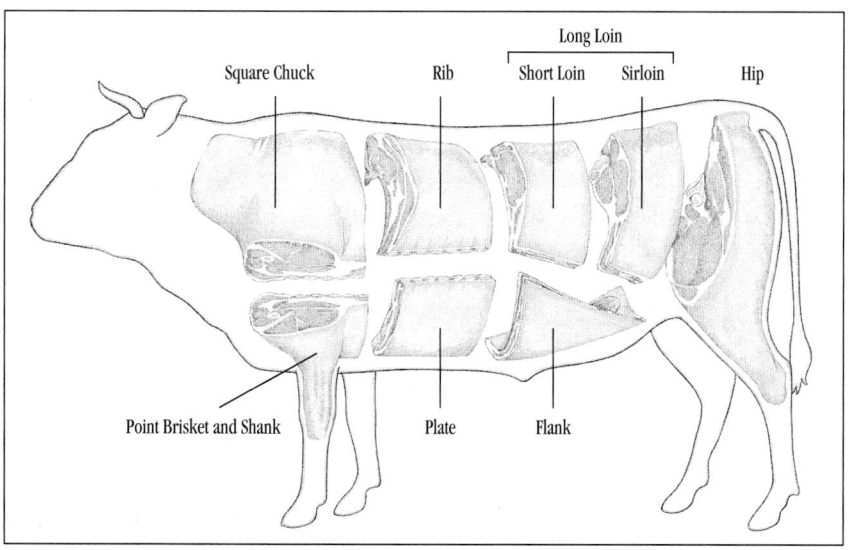

FIGURE 13.2   *The Primal Cuts of Beef*

The ribs and breast bone are always removed from the brisket before cooking. The boneless brisket is very tough and contains a substantial percentage of fat, both intermuscular and subcutaneous. It is well suited for moist-heat and combination cooking methods such as simmering or braising. It is often pickled or corned to produce corned beef brisket, or cured and peppered to make pastrami.

Beef foreshanks are very flavourful and high in collagen. Because collagen converts to gelatin when cooked using moist heat, foreshanks are excellent for making soups and stocks. Ground shank meat is often used to help clarify and flavour consommés because of its rich flavour and high collagen content.

Rib

The primal beef rib accounts for approximately 10% of carcass weight. It consists of ribs 6 through 12 as well as a portion of the backbone.

This primal is best known for yielding roast prime rib of beef. Prime rib is not named after the quality grade Canada Prime. Rather, its name reflects the fact that it constitutes the majority of the primal cut. The eye meat of the rib (the centre muscle portion) is not a well-exercised muscle and therefore is quite tender. It also contains large amounts of marbling compared to the rest of the carcass and produces rich, full-flavoured roasts and steaks. Although roasting the eye muscle on the rib bones produces a moister roast, the eye meat can be removed to produce a boneless rib eye roast or cut into rib eye steaks. The rib bones that are separated from the rib eye meat are quite meaty and flavourful and can be served as barbecued beef back ribs. The ends of the rib bones that are trimmed off the primal rib to produce the rib roast are known as beef short ribs.

Beef Rib Eye Roll Steak,
CMC#1112

Beef Rib, FCO, Roast Ready,
Cover Off, Short Cut.
CMC#109D

Plate

The plate is located directly below the primal rib on a side of beef; it accounts for only a small portion of the overall weight of the carcass, approximately 9%. The plate contains rib bones and cartilage and produces the meaty plate short ribs and skirt steak.

Short ribs are meaty, yet high in connective tissue, and are best when braised. Skirt steak is often marinated and grilled as fajitas. Other, less meaty portions of the plate are trimmed and ground.

Skirt Steak,
Inner,
CMC#121D

Hindquarter

Short Loin

The short loin is the anterior (front) portion of the beef loin. It is located just behind the rib and becomes the first primal cut of the hindquarter when the side of beef is divided into a forequarter and hindquarter. It accounts for approximately 8% of carcass weight.

The short loin contains a single rib, the thirteenth, and a portion of the backbone. With careful butchering, this small primal can yield several subprimal and fabricated cuts, all of which are among the most tender, popular and expensive cuts of beef.

The loin eye muscle, a continuation of the rib eye muscle, runs along the top of the T-shaped bones that form the backbone. Beneath the loin eye muscle on the other side of the backbone is the tenderloin, the most tender cut of all.

When the short loin is cut in cross sections with the bone in, it produces—starting with the rib end of the short loin—club steaks (which do not contain any tenderloin), T-bone steaks (which contain only a small portion of tenderloin) and porterhouse steaks (which are cut from the sirloin end of the short loin and contain a large portion of tenderloin).

The whole tenderloin also can be removed and cut into chateaubriand, filet mignon and tournedos. A portion of the tenderloin is located in the sirloin portion of the loin. When the entire beef loin is divided into the primal short loin and primal sirloin, the large end of the tenderloin (the butt tenderloin) is separated from the remainder of the tenderloin and remains in the sirloin; the smaller end of the tenderloin (the short tenderloin) remains in the short loin. If the tenderloin is to be kept whole, it must be removed before the short loin and sirloin are separated. The loin eye meat can be removed from the bones, producing a boneless strip loin, which is very tender and can be roasted or cut into boneless strip loin steaks.

Beef Loin
T-bone Steak, CMC#1173A

Beef Loin,
Strip Loin,
Short Cut, Boneless,
CMC#180

Beef Loin, Full Tenderloin,
Side Muscle Off, Defatted,
CMC#189C

Sirloin

The sirloin is located in the hindquarter, between the short loin and the round. It accounts for approximately 7% of carcass weight and contains part of the backbone as well as a portion of the hip bone.

The sirloin produces bone-in or boneless roasts and steaks that are flavourful and tender. With the exception of the tenderloin portion, however, these subprimals and fabricated cuts are not as tender as those from the strip loin. Innovative cuts from the sirloin include the Flap, Ball Tip, Tri Tip, Tenderloin Roll and Top Cap muscle.

Beef Loin,
Top Sirloin Butt,
CMC#184

Beef Loin,
Top Sirloin Butt Steak,
Centre Cut, Boneless, CMC#1184B

Flank

The flank is located directly beneath the loin, posterior to (behind) the plate. It accounts for approximately 6% of carcass weight. The flank contains no bones.

Although quite flavourful, it is tough meat with a good deal of fat and connective tissue. Flank meat is usually trimmed and ground, with the exception of the flank steak, which can be stuffed, rolled and braised or marinated and grilled to become a London Broil.

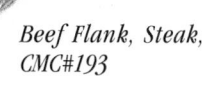

Beef Flank, Steak,
CMC#193

Hip

The primal hip is very large, weighing as much as 90 kg (200 lb.) and accounting for approximately 24% of carcass weight. It is the hind leg of the animal and contains the round, aitch, shank and tail bones.

Meat from the hip is flavourful and fairly tender. The hip yields a wide variety of subprimal and fabricated cuts: the inside round, outside round flat, eye of round (the outside round flat and the eye of round together are called the bottom round), knuckle and shank. See Figure 13.3. Steaks cut from the hip

Beef Round
Beef Top Round
Inside, CMC#168

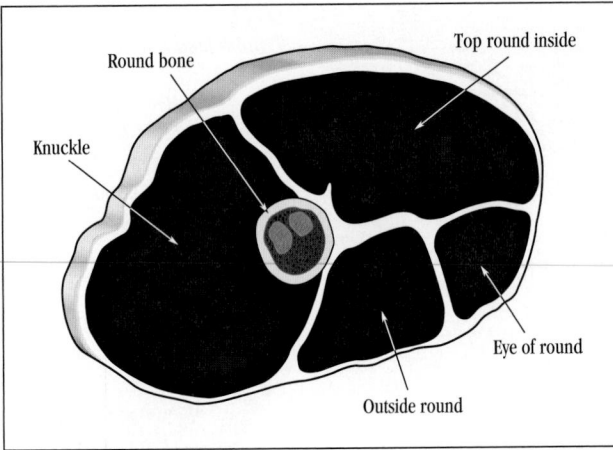

FIGURE 13.3   *Cross Cut of Muscles in a Whole Hip*

*Beef Round, Rump
and Shank Partially Removed, Handle On
(Ponderosa Hip), CMC#164A*

are tougher, but because they have large muscles and limited intermuscular fat, the top round and knuckle make good roasts. The outside round is best when braised. The hindshank is prepared in the same fashion as the foreshank.

Organ Meats

Several beef organ meats are used in food service operations. This group of products is known as **offal**. It includes the heart, kidney, tongue, tripe (stomach lining) and oxtail. They are thoroughly cleaned but have stronger flavours and are tough. Soaking in cold water with a little salt helps draw out impurities. Offal benefit from moist-heat cooking and are often used in soup, stew or braised dishes. Tongue may be pickled and used for garnishing pâtés. Kidney, after blanching several times, is used for steak and kidney pies. Beef liver is used, but calves liver is the most popular.

BUTCHERING PROCEDURES

Although most food service operations buy their beef previously cut and portioned, cooks should be able to fabricate some cuts of beef and perform basic butchering tasks.

Basic Procedure for Cutting a Strip Loin Steak from a Boneless Strip Loin

1. Square up the strip loin by trimming off the lip so it extends 2.5 to 5 cm (1 to 2 inches) from the eye muscle.

2. Turn the strip over and trim off any fat or connective tissue.

3. Turn the strip back over and trim the fat covering to a uniform thickness of 0.5 cm (1/4 inch).

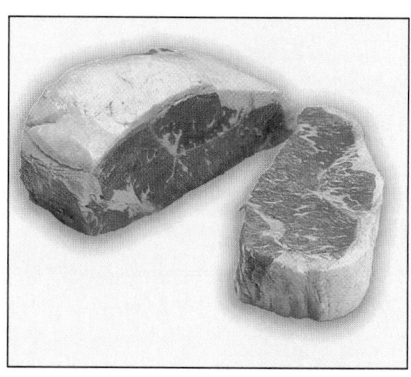

4. Cut the steaks to the thickness or weight desired.

5. The eye meat of steaks located on the sirloin end of the strip is divided by a strip of connective tissue. Steaks cut from this area are called vein steaks and are inferior to steaks cut from the rib end of the strip.

Basic Procedure for Trimming a Full Beef Tenderloin and Cutting It into Chateaubriand, Filet Mignon and Tender Tips

1. Cut and pull the excess fat from the entire tenderloin to expose the meat.

2. Remove the chain muscle from the side of the tenderloin. (Although it contains much connective tissue, the chain muscle may be trimmed and the meat used as tenderloin trimmings in various dishes.)

3. Trim away all the fat and silverskin. Do so by loosening a small piece of silverskin, then, holding the loosened silverskin tightly with one hand, cut it away in long strips, angling the knife up towards the silverskin slightly so that only the silverskin is removed and no meat is wasted.

4. Cut the tenderloin as desired into (left to right) tenderloin tips, filet mignon, filet steak/tournedos, chateaubriand.

Basic Procedure for Butterflying Meats

Many cuts of boneless meats such as tenderloin and boneless loin steaks can be butterflied to create a thinner cut that has a greater surface area and cooks more quickly.

1. Make the first cut nearly all the way through the meat, keeping it attached by leaving approximately 0.5 cm (1/4 inch) uncut.

2. Make a second cut, this time cutting all the way through, completely removing the steak from the tenderloin. Flatten the meat to achieve uniform thickness.

TABLE 13.1   USING COMMON CUTS OF BEEF

Primal	Subprimal or Fabricated Cut	CMC	Cooking Methods	Serving Suggestions
Square Chuck	Chuck roll tied	116A	Combination (braise; stew)	Pot roast; beef stew
	Stew meat	135A	Combination (stew)	Beef stew
	Ground beef	136	Dry heat (broil or grill; roast) Combination (braise; stew)	Hamburgers; meatloaf Chili con carne; beef stews
Point Brisket and Shank	Brisket	120	Moist heat (simmer)	Corned beef; New England boiled dinner
			Combination (braise)	Pot roast
	Shank	117	Combination (braise)	Shredded beef for tamales or hash
Rib	Roast ready cap on	109	Dry heat (roast)	Roast prime rib
	Rib eye steak	1112	Dry heat (roast)	Rib eye steak
Plate	Skirt steak	121D	Dry heat (broil or grill)	Fajitas
	Short ribs	123A	Combination (braise)	Braised short ribs
Short Loin	Porterhouse or T-bone steaks	1173 1173A	Dry heat (broil or grill)	Steaks
	Strip loin	180	Dry heat (broil or grill; roast; sauté)	Strip loin steak; minute steak entrecôtes bordelaise
	Tenderloin	189	Dry heat (broil or grill; roast)	Tournedos Rossini; beef Wellington
Flank	Flank steak	193	Dry heat (broil or grill) Combination (braise)	London broil; stir-fry Braised stuffed flank steak
Hip	Ponderosa hip	164A	Dry heat (roast)	Roast beef
	Inside round	168	Dry heat (roast) Combination (braise)	Roast beef Braised beef roulade

CONCLUSION

Antonin Carême once said that "beef is the soul of cooking." It is also the most popular meat consumed in Canada and undoubtedly will play an important role on almost any menu. Beef's assertive flavour stands up well to a wide array of sauces and seasonings.

Prefabricated products are readily available. In fact, voluntary package-labelling conventions adopted by the beef industry in 1998 (such as "grilling steak" instead of just "steak") will make it easier for consumers to know how to cook the various cuts available at the meat counter. Performing basic fabrication procedures in restaurant kitchens is becoming a rarity. Each primal and subprimal cut has its own distinct characteristics. The primal rib, short loin and sirloin produce the most popular and most expensive cuts of beef. Once the beef is properly fabricated, choose the appropriate dry-heat, moist-heat or combination cooking method for that cut.

QUESTIONS FOR DISCUSSION

1. List each beef primal cut and describe its location on the carcass. For each primal cut, identify two subprimal or fabricated cuts taken from it.
2. Would it be better to use the chuck for grilling or stewing? Explain your answer.
3. Which fabricated cuts contain a portion of the tenderloin? What cooking methods are best suited for these cuts? Explain your answer.
4. Name four cuts that can be produced from a whole beef tenderloin. Describe a preparation procedure for each cut.
5. Most steaks are cut from the hindquarter. What popular steak is cut from the forequarter, and why is it tender when other cuts from the forequarter are relatively tough?

ADDITIONAL BEEF RECIPES

RECIPE 13.1

BEEF TENDERLOIN WITH TWO-COLOURED POTATO RÖSTI, WILD MUSHROOM AND BABY ONION RAGOUT

HILTON HOTEL, Toronto, ON
Executive Chef John Cirillo, CCC

Yield: 4 Servings   **Method:** Pan-roasting

John Cirillo, CCC
A Toronto native, John has spent more than half his life doing what he loves best: practicing the art of cooking. It is a passion that seized him early in his life and led him to the Culinary Program at George Brown College (Toronto). His apprenticeship at the Hilton Toronto Airport was so positive that he has been in Hilton hotel kitchens, in Canada and abroad, ever since!

Beef tenderloin, each 175 g (6 oz.)	4	4
Red wine	50 mL	2 fl. oz.
Wild mushroom ragout (recipe follows)	350 mL	12 fl. oz.
Cream, 35%	250 mL	8 fl. oz.
Veal demi-glace	350 mL	12 fl. oz.
Salt and pepper	TT	TT
Rösti (white and sweet potato)	4	4
Lemon zest	pinch	pinch
Herb sprig garnish	as needed	as needed

Continued

RECIPE 13.1

Approximate values per serving:

Calories	1057
Total fat	85 g
Saturated fat	42 g
Cholesterol	280 mg
Sodium	801 mg
Total carbohydrates	30 g
Protein	43 g

1. Sear tenderloin in sauté pan and transfer to a 175°C (350°F) oven and cook to desired doneness. Keep meat warm.
2. In same pan, deglaze with red wine and add mushroom ragout, cream and demi-glace. Reduce to thicken and adjust seasoning.
3. Place rösti on plate with vegetable garnish of choice, set tenderloin and top with ragout.
4. Garnish with lemon zest and herb spring.

WILD MUSHROOM RAGOUT

Butter	125 g	4 oz.
Olive oil	50 mL	2 fl. oz.
Shallots, diced	10 g	1 Tbsp.
Garlic purée	3 g	1/2 tsp.
Wild mushrooms	250 g	8 oz.
Pearl onions	125 g	4 oz.
Red wine	125 mL	4 fl. oz.
Balsamic vinegar	30 mL	1 fl. oz.
Fine herbs, fresh	5 g	1 tsp.
Lemon zest	pinch	pinch

1. Sauté shallots, garlic, mushrooms and onions in butter and oil until browned.
2. Add wine and vinegar and reduce au sec.
3. Add herbs and lemon zest. Cool and reserve.

Guy Blain

♦♦♦

RECIPE 13.2

BEEF MEDALLIONS WITH BRIE AND NUTS

RESTAURANT LE BALUCHON, SAINT-PAULIN, QC
Chef Guy Blain

Yield: 4 Portions   **Method:** Pan-Frying

Beef strip loin	500 g	1 lb.
Salt and pepper	TT	TT
Oil	as needed	as needed
Brie	80 g	3 oz.
Walnuts	50 g	2 oz.
Sauce Bordelaise	200 mL	6 fl. oz.

1. Portion the meat into 4 medallions.
2. Season with salt and pepper.
3. Pan-fry in oil to desired degree of doneness.
4. Top with brie and walnuts.
5. Nappé with sauce.

RECIPE 13.2

Approximate values per serving:

Calories	541
Total fat	44 g
Saturated fat	18 g
Cholesterol	108 mg
Sodium	695 mg
Total carbohydrates	6.3 g
Protein	30 g

♦♦♦

RECIPE 13.3

BEEF STROGANOFF

Yield: 8 250-g (8-oz.) Servings   **Method:** Sautéing

Tenderloin tips, émincé	1 kg	2 lb.
Clarified butter	45 mL	1-1/2 oz.

Onion, small dice or julienne	125 g	4 oz.
Paprika	30 g	5 Tbsp.
Mushrooms, sliced	450 g	1 lb.
Red wine	125 mL	4 fl. oz.
Demi-glace	300 mL	10 fl. oz.
Sour cream	250 mL	8 fl. oz.
Cornichons, julienne	150 g	1 cup
Fresh parsley, chopped	10 g	1 Tbsp.
Salt and pepper	TT	TT
Egg noodles, cooked	700 g	24 oz.

RECIPE 13.3

Approximate values per serving:

Calories	671
Total fat	27 g
Saturated fat	12 g
Cholesterol	182 mg
Sodium	630 mg
Total carbohydrates	67 g
Protein	40 g

1. Sauté the tenderloin tips in the butter, searing on all sides. Remove the meat and set aside.

2. Add the onion to the pan and sauté lightly then add paprika and sweat. Add the mushrooms and sauté until soft.

3. Deglaze with red wine.

4. Add the demi-glace. Bring to a boil, reduce to a simmer and cook 5 minutes.

5. Add the sour cream, pickle and any meat juices that accumulated while holding the meat.

6. Return the meat to the sauce to reheat. Stir in the parsley. Adjust the seasonings and serve over egg noodles.

❖ ❖ ❖

RECIPE 13.4

SEARED BEEF TOURNEDOS IN MUSHROOM BROTH

DONOVANS RESTAURANT, INVERCARGILL, NEW ZEALAND
Chef/Owner Graham Hawkes

Yield: 6 Servings   **Method:** Grilling

Beef tenderloin, each 150 g (5 oz.)	6	6
Black pepper, fresh ground	TT	TT
Sea salt	TT	TT
Barley, roasted (recipe follows)	600 g	24 oz.
Pumpkin, diced (recipe follows)	240 g	8 oz.
Mushrooms, assorted (recipe follows)	420 g	1 lb.
Enoki mushrooms, seared	1 pkg.	1 pkg.
Mushroom broth (recipe follows)	500 mL	16 fl. oz.
Thyme	6 sprigs	6 sprigs
Tomato concasser	120 g	4 oz.
Olive oil	as needed	as needed

1. Season and grill tournedos to medium-rare.

2. Divide barley among 6 rimmed soup plates. Scatter pumpkin and mound the mushrooms. Place the meat, ladle mushroom broth around the steak and garnish with mushrooms, thyme and tomato concasser.

BARLEY

Pearl barley	225 g	7 oz.
Water	600 mL	22 fl. oz.

1. Roast barley in a hot oven for about 10 minutes or until lightly browned.

2. Put in saucepan with water and simmer until tender.

Graham Hawkes
Following the completion of a six-year apprenticeship, Graham travelled to Australia and then on to New Zealand, where he was Executive Chef in one of the country's largest function-facilitated hotels. In 1992, Graham purchased Donovans Restaurant, Southlands. When he is not involved assisting various industry bodies, you will find him behind the stove at Donovans, an award-winning restaurant.

RECIPE 13.4

Approximate values per serving:

Calories	463
Total fat	15 g
Saturated fat	4.7 g
Cholesterol	84 mg
Sodium	450 mg
Total carbohydrates	45 g
Protein	37 g

Continued

PUMPKIN

Pumpkin, diced	300 g	12 oz.
Olive oil	as needed	as needed

. Sauté pumpkin in oil until browned and transfer to a 160°C (300°F) oven and roast until tender, approximately 10–15 minutes.

MUSHROOMS

Mushroom medley:		
brown, oyster, shiitake	800 g	1 lb. 12 oz.
Fresh thyme leaves	2 g	1 tsp.
Garlic, chopped	5 g	1 clove
Sea salt and pepper	TT	TT

1. Place all ingredients in a roasting pan, add a bit of water, cover and bake in a hot oven until tender, 200°C (400°F) for 30 minutes.
2. Strain liquid into mushroom broth and reserve mushrooms.

MUSHROOM BROTH

Button mushrooms	1 kg	2 lb.
Light beef or veal stock	600 mL	20 fl. oz.
Thyme	1 sprig	1 sprig
Garlic, minced	1 clove	1 clove

1. Bring stock and mushrooms to a boil and simmer to reduce by 3/4. Strain the liquid and discard the mushrooms. Add mushroom medley liquor.
2. Add thyme and garlic to broth, return to boil and set aside.

◆◆◆

RECIPE 13.5

PEPPER STEAK

Yield: 2 Servings   **Method:** Sautéing

Boneless strip steaks,		
each approx. (250 g) 8 oz.	2	2
Salt, kosher	TT	TT
Peppercorns, cracked	25 g	2 Tbsp.
Clarified butter	25 mL	1 fl. oz.
Cognac	25 mL	1 fl. oz.
Cream, 35%	125 mL	4 fl. oz.
Meat glaze	25 mL	1 fl. oz.
Whole butter	50 g	2 oz.

RECIPE 13.5

Approximate values per serving:

Calories	939
Total fat	75 g
Saturated fat	41 g
Cholesterol	309 mg
Sodium	749 mg
Total carbohydrates	10 g
Protein	56 g

1. Season the steaks with salt. Spread the peppercorns in a hotel pan and press the steaks into them, lightly coating each side.
2. Sauté the steaks in the clarified butter over high heat for 2–3 minutes on each side.
3. Remove the pan from the heat. Pour the cognac over the steaks, return the pan to the heat and flambé. When the flames subside, remove the steaks from the pan and keep them warm on a plate.
4. Add the cream and meat glaze to the pan. Bring to a boil and reduce for 2 minutes over high heat; monter au beurre. Pour this sauce over the steaks and serve immediately.

♦♦♦

RECIPE 13.6

GRILLED BEEF FLANK STEAK WITH SHALLOT TOMATO BUTTER

TEATRO RESTAURANT, CALGARY, AB
Executive Chef Michael Allemeier, CCC

Yield: 6 Portions		**Method:** Grilling
Beef flank steaks, each 175 g (6 oz.)	6	6
Paprika	35 g	6 Tbsp.
Fresh thyme, coarsely chopped	50 g	1/2 cup
Black pepper, fresh ground	7 g	1 Tbsp.
Canola oil	500 mL	16 fl. oz.

1. Mix paprika, thyme and pepper together and rub into the flank steaks.
2. Place steaks in a sealable container, add the canola oil and mix gently. Refrigerate, covered, for 3–6 days.
3. Preheat the grill or broiler on high heat. Remove steaks from fridge, drain and allow to come to room temperature (30 minutes).
4. Sear the steaks for 3–4 minutes per side, keeping them rare.
5. Rest steaks for 5–10 minutes and carve thinly across the grain.

SHALLOT TOMATO BUTTER

Tomato concassée	1 kg	2 lb.
Olive oil	50 mL	1-1/2 fl. oz.
Butter	225 g	1/2 lb.
Shallots, fine dice	125 g	4 oz.

1. Stew the tomatoes in olive oil until au sec. Cool.
2. Place tomatoes and butter in food processor and purée. Fold in shallots.
3. Roll or pipe, then chill.

♦♦♦

RECIPE 13.7

HUNGARIAN-STYLE BEEF GOULASH (PÖRKÖLT)

Yield: 15 250-g (8-oz.) Servings		**Method:** Stewing
Onion, fine dice	1.25 kg	2 lb. 12 oz.
Lard or vegetable oil	250 mL	8 fl. oz.
Hungarian paprika	120 g	1 cup
Beef stewing meat, cut in 2.5-cm (1-inch) cubes	2.25 kg	5 lb.
Salt	15 g	1 Tbsp.
White stock	2–3 L	2–3 qt.
Garlic, chopped	100 g	1/2 cup
Caraway seeds, crushed	3 g	1 tsp.
Red wine	250 mL	8 fl. oz.
Double-smoked bacon, 1-cm (1/2-inch) cubes	500 g	1 lb.
Red pepper, diced	350 g	12 oz.
Tomato concassée	500 g	1 lb.
Pepper	TT	TT

Continued

1. Sauté the onion in the lard or oil until wilted.
2. Reduce the heat and add the paprika. Fry until fragrant.
3. Add the meat and salt, browning the meat while stirring it. Brown the meat well.
4. Moisten the meat with 1.5 L (1-1/2 qt.) of stock and then add the garlic, caraway seeds and wine. The meat should be just covered. Cover the pot and simmer. Stir occasionally. Add more liquid only if needed.
5. When the meat begins to soften (1 hour), add the bacon, red pepper, and tomato concasser. Simmer until the meat is tender (30–45 minutes).
6. Adjust seasoning with salt and pepper.

◆◆◆

RECIPE 13.8

BEEF BOURGUIGNON

Yield: 10 250-g (8-oz.) Servings   **Method:** Stewing

Marinade:		
Garlic cloves, crushed	10 g	3
Onions, sliced	400 g	3
Carrots, sliced	150 g	2
Parsley stalks	10	10
Bouquet garni:		
Carrot stick, 10 cm (4 inches)	1	1
Leek, split, 10-cm (4-inch) piece	1	1
Fresh thyme	1 sprig	1 sprig
Bay leaf	1	1
Peppercorns, crushed	2 g	10
Salt	5 g	1 tsp.
Dry red wine, preferably Burgundy	750 mL	26 fl. oz.
Beef chuck, cubed for stew	2 kg	4 lb.
Vegetable oil	60 mL	2 fl. oz.
Flour	15 g	2 Tbsp.
Tomato paste	15 mL	1 Tbsp.
Tomatoes, quartered, seeded	4	4
Brown stock	500 mL	1 pt.
Mushrooms, quartered	500 g	1 lb.
Unsalted butter	50 g	1-1/2 oz.
Lardons of lean double smoked bacon	250 g	8 oz.
Pearl onions, boiled and peeled	30	30
Salt and pepper	TT	TT

1. Combine the garlic, onions, carrots, parsley, bouquet garni, peppercorns, salt and wine to make a marinade.
2. Marinate the meat for several hours under refrigeration.
3. Remove and drain the meat. Reserve the marinade.
4. Dry the beef and sauté it in the oil until well browned. Do this in several batches if necessary.
5. Return all the meat to the pot. Sprinkle with flour and cook to make a blond roux.
6. Stir in the tomato paste and cook for 5 minutes.
7. Add the reserved marinade, tomatoes and brown stock. Cook in a 180°C (350°F) oven until the meat is tender, approximately 2.5 hours.

8. Remove the meat from the sauce. Strain the sauce through a conical strainer, pressing to extract all of the liquid. Discard the solids. Return the liquid and beef to the pot.

9. Sauté the mushrooms in the butter and add them to the meat and sauce. Lightly sauté the lardons and add to stew. Add the onions and adjust the seasonings. Simmer for 10 minutes to blend the flavours.

◆◆◆

RECIPE 13.9

CHILI CON CARNE

Yield: 3 L (3 qt.)   **Method:** Braising

Onion, medium dice	500 g	1 lb.
Vegetable oil	15 mL	1 Tbsp.
Garlic, chopped	15 g	1/2 oz.
Ground beef or 1-cm (1/2-inch) diced round	1.25 kg	2 lb. 8 oz.
Tomato, crushed	1 kg	2 lb.
Tomato, diced	1.75 kg	4 lb.
Tomato paste	125 mL	4 fl. oz.
Brown stock	500 mL	1 pt.
Chilli powder	30 g	1 oz.
Cumin	5 g	2 tsp.
Sambal olek	15 mL	1 Tbsp.
Oregano leaves	1 g	1 tsp.
Bay leaves	3	3
Salt and pepper	TT	TT

RECIPE 13.9

Approximate values per serving:

Calories	405
Total fat	25 g
Saturated fat	9.1 g
Cholesterol	78 mg
Sodium	847 mg
Total carbohydrates	22 g
Protein	23 g

1. Sauté the onion in the oil until tender. Add the garlic and sauté 1 minute.

2. Add the beef and brown, stirring occasionally. Drain off the excess fat.

3. Add the remaining ingredients, bring to a simmer, cover and cook for 1 hour or until meat is tender.

4. Remove the bay leaves and adjust the seasonings and consistency (corn-meal will add body).

NOTE: Purists will argue that beans should not be in chili con carne. If you must, add 1 kg (2 lb.) cooked kidney or pinto beans.

 EBLINKS

Beef Information Centre (Mississauga)
   www.beefinfo.org/

Beef Information Centre (Vancouver)
   www.cattlemen.bc.ca/bic.htm

Canada Beef Export Federation
   www.cbef.com/

Food Institute of Canada's FoodNet: Beef Recipes, Section 1
   foodnet.fic.ca/recipes/beef1.html

Food Institute of Canada's FoodNet: Beef Recipes, Section 2
   foodnet.fic.ca/recipes/beef2.html

Searchable Online Archive of Recipes: Beef Recipes
   SOAR.berkeley.edu/recipes/meat/beef/

CHAPTER 14 VEAL

After studying this chapter you will be able to:

+ identify the primal, subprimal and fabricated cuts of veal
+ perform basic butchering procedures: boning a leg of veal, cutting and pounding cutlets, cutting émincé, boning a veal loin, tying meats, cleaning and pressing sweetbreads, cleaning calves' liver, cleaning veal kidneys
+ apply appropriate cooking methods to several common cuts of veal

FORMULA-FED VEAL VERSUS FREE-RANGE VEAL

Much of the veal produced today is known as formula-fed veal. Formula-fed calves are fed only nutrient-rich liquids; they are tethered in pens only slightly larger than their bodies to restrict their movements. Preventing the calves from eating grasses and other foods containing iron keeps their flesh white; restricting movement keeps their muscles from toughening. In recent years controversy and allegations of cruelty have arisen concerning these methods.

An alternative to formula-fed veal is free-range veal. Free-range veal is produced from calves that are allowed to roam freely and eat grasses and other natural foods. Because they consume feed containing iron, their flesh is a reddish pink and has a substantially different flavour than meat from formula-fed calves of the same age.

Opinions differ on which has the better flavour. Some chefs prefer the consistently mild, sweet taste of formula-fed veal. Others prefer the more substantial flavour of free-range veal. The two are interchangeable in recipes.

ows must calve before they begin to give milk. Bull calves are the basis of today's veal industry. Veal is the meat of youthful bovine carcasses weighing less than 160 kg hide off. Quebec and Ontario produce 97% of the veal in Canada. Veal is lighter in colour than beef, has a more delicate flavour and is generally more tender. Veal has a firm texture, light pink colour and very little fat. As soon as a calf starts eating solid food, the iron in the food begins to turn the young animal's meat red. Grain-fed veal tends to be a deeper red, with some marbling and external fat.

Veal's low fat content makes it a popular meat, especially among those looking for an alternative to beef. Its delicate flavour is complemented by both classic and modern sauces.

PRIMAL AND SUBPRIMAL CUTS OF VEAL

The veal carcass is split down the backbone into two bilateral halves or sides. Each side is separated into five primal cuts: the shoulder, the foreshank and breast (attached), the rib, the loin and the leg. Occasionally, through special order, some other cuts are available.

Figure 14.1 shows the relationship between the animal's bone structure and the primal cuts. As with all meats, it is important to know the location of bones when cutting or working with veal. This makes meat fabrication and carving easier and aids in identifying cuts. Figure 14.2 shows the primal cuts of veal and their location. A graded veal carcass will also indicate the meat colour. Smaller muscles are available through imports. Table 14.1 (page 321) identifies common cuts of veal and suggests preparation methods.

Front/Shoulder

The veal shoulder accounts for 21% of carcass weight. It contains four rib bones (as opposed to five in the beef chuck) and portions of the backbone, blade and arm bones.

The backbone, blade and arm bones are sometimes removed and the meat roasted or stuffed and braised. Although shoulder chops and steaks can be fabricated, they are inferior to the chops cut from more tender areas such as the loin or rib. Often the shoulder meat is ground or cubed for stew. Because of the relatively large amount of connective tissue it contains, meat from the shoulder is best braised or stewed.

Foreshank and Breast

The foreshank and breast are located beneath the shoulder and part of the rib section on the front half of the carcass. The shank is generally purchased separately as is the breast. Combined, they account for approximately 16% of carcass weight. This section contains rib bones and rib cartilage, breast bones and shank bones. Because the calf is slaughtered young, many of the breast bones are cartilaginous rather than bony.

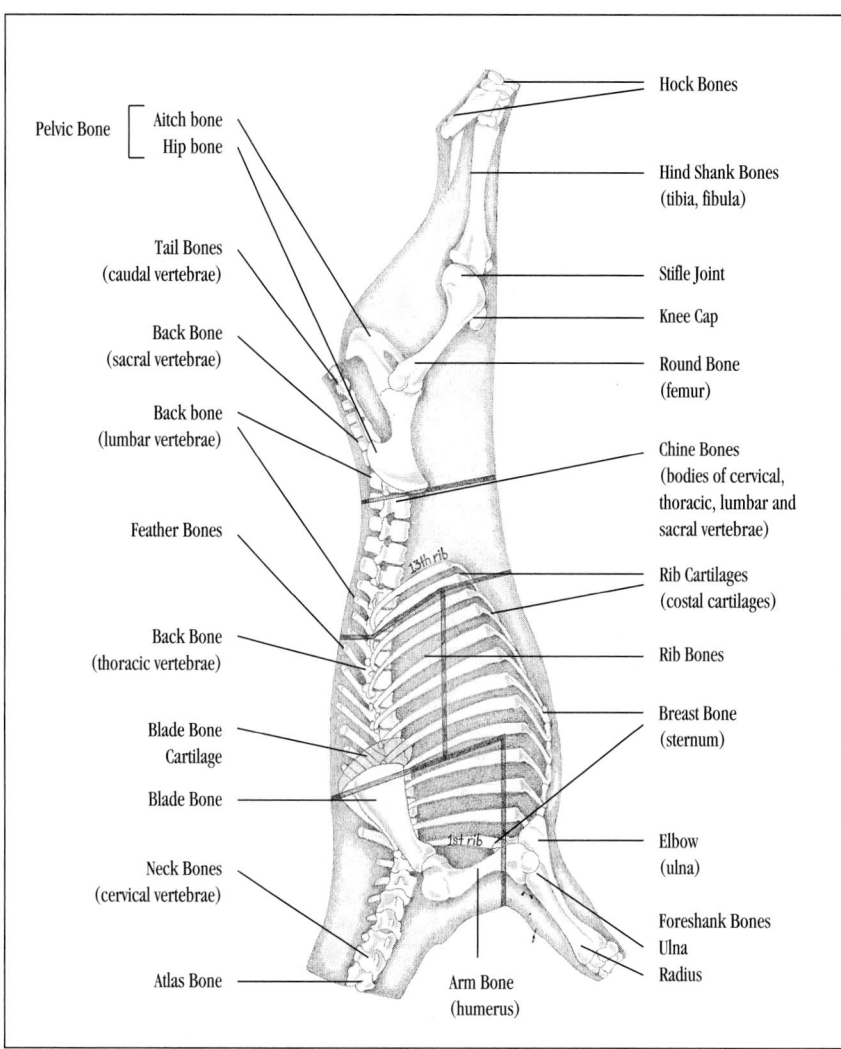

FIGURE 14.1   *The Skeletal Structure of a Veal Carcass*

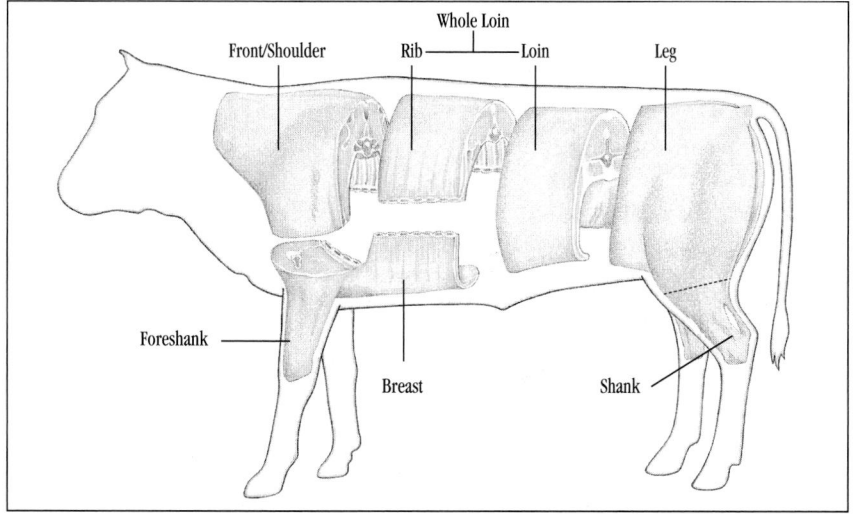

FIGURE 14.2   *The Primal Cuts of Veal*

This cartilage, as well as the connective tissue present in the breast, breaks down during long moist cooking, thus making the breast a flavourful choice for braising. Veal breast can also be cubed for stews such as veal fricassee and veal blanquette, rolled and stuffed, or trimmed and ground.

The foreshank is also very flavourful but tough. It can be braised whole or sliced perpendicular to the shank bone and braised to produce osso buco.

Whole Loin

The primal whole loin contains the ribs and loin sections of the carcass. When purchased whole, it is often fabricated into chops, although it may be boned for roasting or preparing loin cutlets.

Veal Rib, Split, CMC#305

Rib

The rib, also known as a veal rack, is a very tender, relatively small cut accounting for approximately 9% of carcass weight. It is relatively expensive. The double rack (or hotel rack) consists of both racks, each with seven rib bones and a portion of the backbone. It is a special order.

Veal hotel racks can be roasted either whole or split into two ribs. Veal ribs can be boned out to produce a veal rib eye. More often, veal ribs are trimmed and cut into chops, which can also be bone-in or boneless, to be grilled, sautéed or braised.

Loin

The veal loin is posterior to the primal rib, contains two ribs (numbers 12 and 13) and accounts for approximately 10% of carcass weight. The loin consists of the loin eye muscle on top of the chine bones and the tenderloin on the interior.

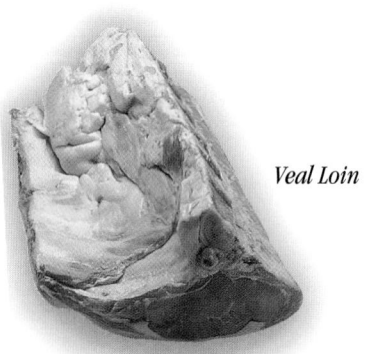

Veal Loin

The veal loin is very tender and the tenderloin is, without a doubt, the most tender cut of veal. If the veal loin is separated from the primal leg before the tenderloin is removed, the tenderloin will be cut into two pieces. The small portion (short tenderloin) remains in the loin and the large portion (butt tenderloin) remains in the sirloin portion of the primal leg. The tenderloin is sometimes removed and cut into medallions. The veal loin is often cut into chops, bone-in or boneless. It is usually cooked using dry heat such as broiling, grilling, roasting or sautéing.

Boneless Strip Loin

Loin Chops

Leg

The primal veal leg consists of both the sirloin and the leg. Together they account for approximately 42% of carcass weight. The primal leg is separated from the loin by a cut perpendicular to the backbone immediately anterior to the hip bone, and it contains portions of the backbone, tail bone, hip bone, aitch bone, round bone and hind shank.

Veal Leg, CMC#334

Although it is tender enough to be roasted whole, the veal leg is typically fabricated into cutlets. To fabricate this cut, the leg is first broken down into its major muscles: the top round, eye of round, knuckle, sirloin, bottom round (which includes the sirloin) and butt tenderloin. Each of these muscles can be reduced to cutlets by trimming all fat and visible connective tissue and slicing against the grain to the desired thickness. The cutlets may be pounded carefully to tenderize them further and to prevent them from curling when cooked.

The hindshank is somewhat meatier than the foreshank but both are prepared and cooked in the same manner.

Because the veal carcass is small enough to be handled easily, it is sometimes purchased in forms larger than the primal cuts described above. Depending on employee skill, available equipment and storage space and an ability to utilize fully all the cuts and trimmings that fabricating meat produces, you may want to special order veal in one of the following forms:

Top Round

♦ *Foresaddle:* The anterior portion of the carcass after it is severed from the hindsaddle by a cut following the natural curvature between the eleventh and twelfth ribs. It contains the primal shoulder, foreshank and breast, and rib.

♦ *Hindsaddle:* The posterior portion of the carcass after it is severed from the foresaddle. It contains the primal loin and leg.

♦ *Back:* The trimmed rib and loin sections in one piece. The back is particularly useful for producing large quantities of veal chops.

♦ *Veal side:* One bilateral half of the carcass, produced by cutting lengthwise through the backbone.

Hindshank Cut for Osso Buco

Organ Meats

Several veal organ meats are used in food service operations.

Sweetbreads

Sweetbreads are the thymus glands of veal and lamb. As an animal ages, its thymus gland shrinks; therefore sweetbreads are not available from older cattle or sheep. Veal sweetbreads are much more popular than lamb sweetbreads in this country. Good-quality sweetbreads should be plump and firm, with the exterior membrane intact. Delicately flavoured and tender, they can be prepared by almost any cooking method. Clarify with your purveyor that you are purchasing veal and not beef sweetbreads.

Sweetbreads

Veal (Calves') Liver

Veal liver is much more popular than beef liver because of its tenderness and mild flavour. Good-quality calves' liver should be firm and moist, with a shiny appearance and without any off-odour. It is most often sliced and sautéed or broiled and served with a sauce.

Calves' Liver

Kidneys

Kidneys

Kidneys are more popular in other parts of the world than in Canada. Good-quality kidneys should be plump, firm and encased in a shiny membrane. Properly prepared kidneys have a rich, yet mild flavour and firm texture; they are best prepared by dry-heat cooking methods and are sometimes used in stew or steak and kidney pie.

BUTCHERING PROCEDURES

Some food service operations purchase veal in primal or other large cuts and fabricate it in-house to their own specifications. There are several important veal fabrication and butchering techniques you should master.

Basic Procedure for Boning a Leg of Veal

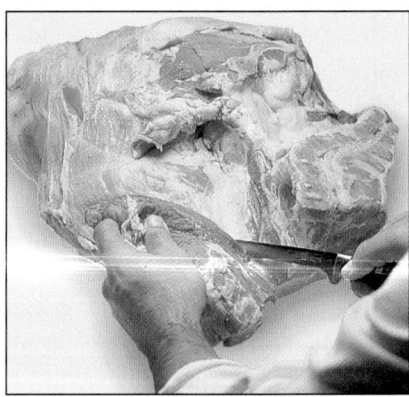

1. Remove the shank by cutting through the knee joint. Remove the excess fat and flank meat.

2. Remove the butt tenderloin from the inside of the pelvic bone.

3. Remove the pelvic bone by carefully cutting around the bone, separating it from the meat. Continue until the bone is completely freed from the meat.

4. With the inside of the leg up, remove the inside (top) round by cutting along the natural seam.

5. Remove the shank meat. (It is the round piece of meat lying between the eye of round and the bone, on the shank end of the leg.)

6. Remove the round bone and the knuckle together by cutting around the bone and through the natural seams separating the knuckle from the other muscles. Separate the knuckle meat from the bone.

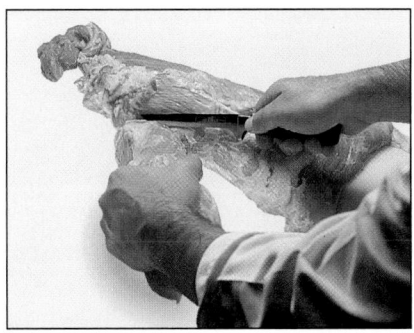

7. Remove the sirloin tip.

8. Remove the eye of round from the outside (bottom) round.

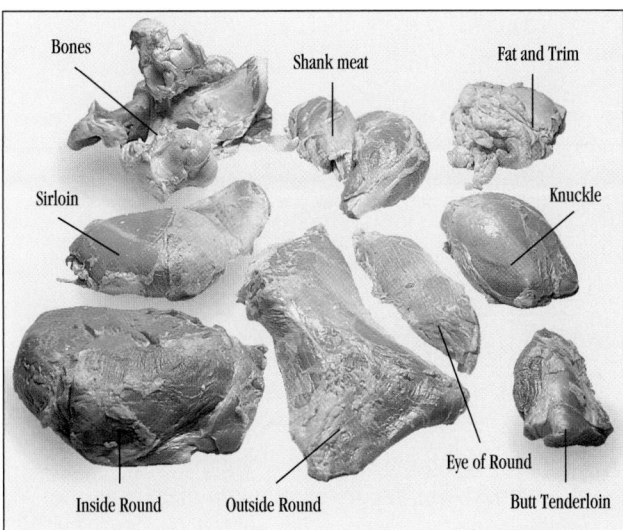

9. The completely boned-out veal leg, producing an inside round, eye of round, knuckle, shank meat, butt tenderloin, sirloin, outside round, bones and trimmings.

❖❖❖

MENU TERMINOLOGY

Generally, if the word "veal" is used, there is not a problem with misrepresentation. However, a qualifier such as "milk-fed" must be supported by invoices to prove that is what is being served. A restaurant could face fraud charges. In Quebec, "grain-fed" is legally recognized, but this is not the case elsewhere in Canada. The CFIA does not recognize the term "baby beef." Technically, "calves'" liver should be called veal liver but the term currently enjoys general usage acceptance.

Basic Procedure for Cutting and Pounding Cutlets

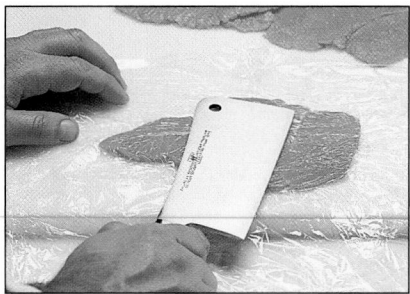

1. Veal cutlets are cut from relatively large pieces of veal (here, a portion of the inside round). All fat and silverskin must be trimmed. Going against the grain, cut slices approximately 0.5 cm (1/4 inch) thick; cut on the bias to produce larger pieces.

2. Place the cutlets between two pieces of plastic wrap and pound lightly to flatten and tenderize the meat. Be careful not to tear or pound holes in the meat.

Basic Procedure for Cutting Émincé

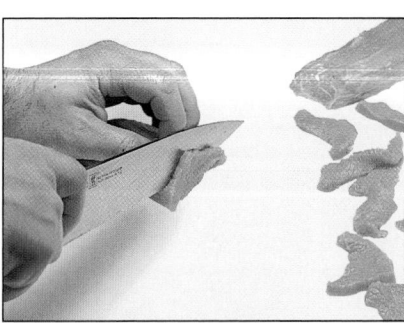

1. Émincé is cut from relatively small, lean pieces of meat. Here veal is cut across the grain into small, thin slices.

Basic Procedure for Boning a Veal Loin and Cutting It into Boneless Veal Sirloin Chops

1. Remove the tenderloin in a single piece from the inside of the loin by following the vertebrae and cutting completely around the tenderloin.

2. From the backbone side, cut along the natural curve of the backbone, separating the loin meat from the backbone.

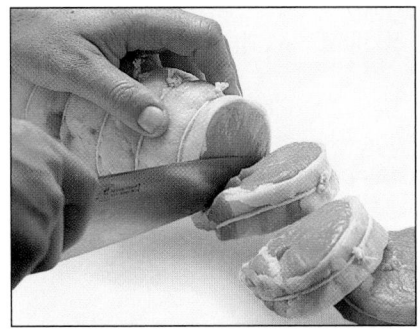

3. Trim any excess fat from the loin, and trim the flank to create a 7.5-cm (3-inch) lip. Tightly roll up the loin with the flank on the outside.

4. Tie the loin, using the procedure described below, at 2.5-cm (1-inch) intervals. Cut between the pieces of twine for individual boneless sirloin chops.

Basic Procedure for Tying (Trussing) Meats

Here we apply the tying procedure to a boneless veal loin; the same procedure can be used on any type of meat.

1. Cut a piece of string long enough to wrap completely around the loin. Holding one end between the thumb and forefinger, pass the other end around it and cross the strings. Loop the loose end of the string around your finger.

2. Wrap the string around itself and pass the loose end back through the hole (slip knot).

3. Pull to tighten the knot. Adjust the string so it is snug against the meat.

4. Loop one end of the string around your thumb and forefinger. Reach through with your thumb and forefinger and pull the other string back through the loop. Pull both strings to tighten the knot, thus preventing the first knot from loosening (half hitch). Trim the ends of the strings.

5. Continue in this fashion until the entire loin is tied. The strings should be tied at even intervals, just snug enough to hold the shape of the loin; they should not dig into or cut the meat.

Basic Procedure for Cleaning and Pressing Sweetbreads

Before fabrication, you should submerge the sweetbreads in cold water with a little salt and cover and place them in the refrigerator overnight to draw out any blood; then blanch them in a court bouillon for 5 minutes.

1. Remove the sweetbreads from the poaching liquid and allow them to cool.

2. Using your hands, pull off any sinew or membranes that may be present on the surface of the sweetbreads.

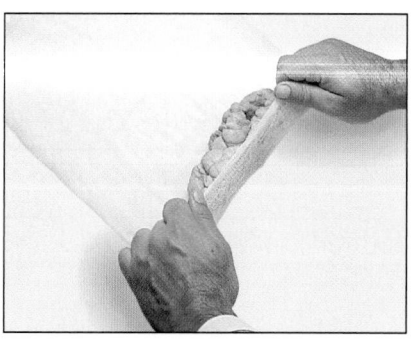

3. Wrap the sweetbreads in cheese-cloth.

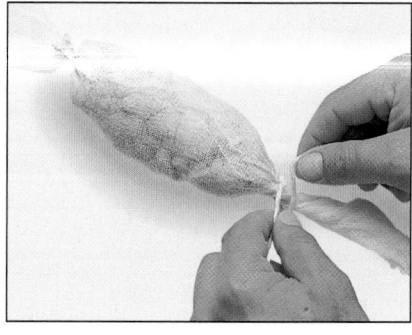

4. Tie the ends with butcher's twine.

5. Place the wrapped sweetbreads in a half hotel pan or similar container.

6. Place another half hotel pan on top of the sweetbreads; place a weight in the pan to press the sweetbreads. Pressing sweetbreads in this manner improves their texture.

Basic Procedure for Cleaning Calves' Liver

1. Trim the large sinew and outer membrane from the bottom of the liver.

2. Turn the liver over and peel the membrane off with your hands.

3. The liver can be cut into thick or thin slices as needed.

TABLE 14.1   USING COMMON CUTS OF VEAL

Primal	Subprimal or Fabricated Cut	CMC	Cooking Methods	Serving Suggestions
Front/ Shoulder	Cubed veal		Combination (stew)	Blanquette or fricassee
	Ground veal	396	Dry heat (broil or grill) Combination (braise)	Veal patties; pojarski Stuffing; meatballs
Foreshank and breast	Foreshank	312	Combination (braise)	Osso buco
	Breast	313	Combination (braise)	Stuffed veal breast
Rib	Rack	305	Dry heat (broil or grill; roast)	Grilled veal chop; roast veal with porcini mushrooms
	Rib chops	1306	Dry heat (broil or grill) Combination (braise)	Grilled veal chop Braised veal chop with risotto
	Rib eye	307	Dry heat (broil or grill; roast) Combination (braise)	Broiled veal rib eye with chipotle sauce; roasted veal rib eye marchand de vin Braised rib eye
Loin	Veal loin	331	Dry heat (broil or grill; roast; sauté)	Roasted veal loin with wild mushrooms; Sautéed veal medallions with green peppercorn sauce
	Loin chops	1332	Dry heat (broil or grill; sauté) Combination (braise)	Broiled or sautéed veal chops with mushroom sauce Braised veal chops Lyonnaise
	Striploin, boneless	334	Dry heat (broil or grill; roast; sauté)	Roasted veal loin sauce poulette
	Veal tenderloin	345	Dry heat (broil or grill; roast; sauté)	Grilled tenderloin; roasted tenderloin; sautéed tenderloin with garlic and herbs
Leg	Leg	334	Dry heat (roast; sauté) Combination (stew)	Veal scallopini Blanquette
	Inside round	349	Dry heat (roast; sauté)	Veal marsala
	Outside round	350	Dry heat (sauté) Combination (braise)	Sautéed cutlets with Calvados Stuffed veal cutlets
	Hindshank	337	Moist heat (simmer)	Veal broth
	Centre cut	1337	Combination (braise)	Osso buco
Offal	Sweetbreads	3722	Dry heat (pan-fry; sauté) Combination (braise)	Sautéed sweetbreads beurre noisette Braised sweetbreads Madeira
	Calves' liver	3724	Dry heat (broil or grill; sauté)	Broiled or sautéed calves' liver with onion and bacon
	Kidneys		Combination (braise)	Kidney pie
	Tails			Soup and stock

Basic Procedure for Cleaning Veal Kidneys

1. Split the kidneys lengthwise, exposing the fat and sinew.

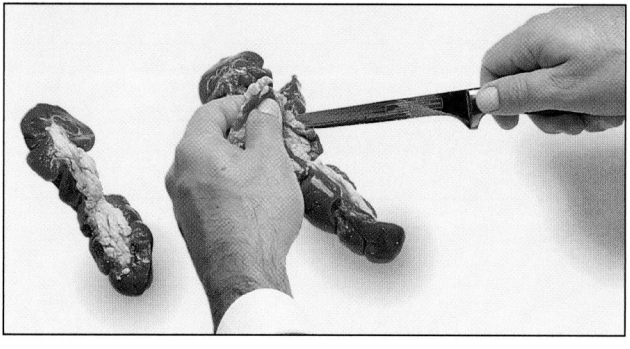

2. With a sharp knife, trim away the fat and sinew. The kidney is now ready for cooking.

CONCLUSION

Although veal may not be as popular as beef or pork, it is versatile, easy to cook and adds variety to menus. Veal is much more delicately flavoured than beef, with a finer texture and lighter colour. Its flavour blends well with a variety of sauces and other ingredients without overpowering them. Veal can be cooked by almost any dry-heat, moist-heat or combination cooking method.

Veal quality varies greatly among purveyors. Purchase only from reputable companies to be sure you are receiving a consistently high-quality product. Because veal carcasses are relatively small, they are sometimes purchased as primal cuts for your further fabrication.

QUESTIONS FOR DISCUSSION

1. Compare and contrast the appearance and flavour of beef and veal.
2. What are the differences between formula-fed veal and free-range veal?
3. Describe two differences between a beef carcass and a veal carcass.
4. List each veal primal and describe its location on the carcass. For each primal, identify two subprimals or fabricated cuts taken from it.
5. Would it be better to use a veal loin for grilling or braising? Explain your answer.
6. What are veal sweetbreads? Describe how sweetbreads should be prepared for cooking.

DDITIONAL VEAL RECIPES

RECIPE 14.1

MIGNONS OF VEAL ON SPINACH WITH CRAYFISH

WESTIN PRINCE HOTEL, TORONTO, ON
Executive Chef Hans U. Herzig

Yield: 10 Portions
(each with 3 mignons of veal and 8 crayfish tails)

Method: Sautéing

Hans U. Herzig
Hans was born in Switzerland, trained in Europe, and came to Canada to work at the Windsor Arms in Toronto. Among the highlights of his career, he was captain of the Canadian team that won 10 gold medals in the 1988 World Culinary Olympics.

Crayfish tails	80	80
Fish stock	500 mL	18 fl. oz.
Cream, 35%	500 mL	18 fl. oz.
White wine	200 mL	7 fl. oz.
Saffron	TT	TT
Salt and black pepper	TT	TT
Potatoes	250 g	8–10 oz.
Wild rice	50 g	2 oz.
Egg yolks	3	3
Butter	150 g	5 oz.
Nutmeg	TT	TT
Fresh spinach leaves	500 g	1 lb.
Shallots	15 g	1/2 oz.
Tomatoes	6	6
Chervil	TT	TT
Black trumpet mushrooms	50 g	2 oz.
Trimmed veal tenderloin, cut into 30 slices	1 kg	2.2 lb.

1. Boil the crayfish. Remove the tails and peel them.
2. Reduce fish stock to half, add three-quarters of the cream and simmer slowly for about 30 minutes until sauce is reduced by half.
3. Add white wine. Add saffron, salt and pepper to taste. Add the remaining cream and reduce until the sauce is of a consistency to coat the back of a spoon.
4. Boil the potatoes and rice them.
5. Cook the wild rice for about 45 minutes. Add the rice to the potatoes along with egg yolks and a little of the butter. Mix together well and season with salt and a dash of nutmeg.
6. With two spoons, form quenelles (see Chapter 20, page 517) and poach them in either lightly salted water or chicken stock filling the pan to a depth of about 5 cm (2 in.).
7. Blanch the spinach and allow to cool. Sauté in remaining butter with the shallots.
8. Fillet the tomatoes and quickly sauté them with a little chopped chervil and the black trumpet mushrooms.
9. Season veal mignons with salt and pepper and sauté.
10. Put a ladle of sauce on a serving plate and put some spinach in the centre. Place 3 mignons on top and garnish with the sautéed tomatoes, chervil and mushrooms.
11. Place 4 wild rice quenelles on the plate and arrange the preheated crayfish tails, each garnished with a chervil leaf.

RECIPE 14.1

Approximate values per serving:

Calories	592
Total fat	44 g
Saturated fat	25 g
Cholesterol	323 mg
Sodium	537 mg
Total carbohydrates	16 g
Protein	33 g

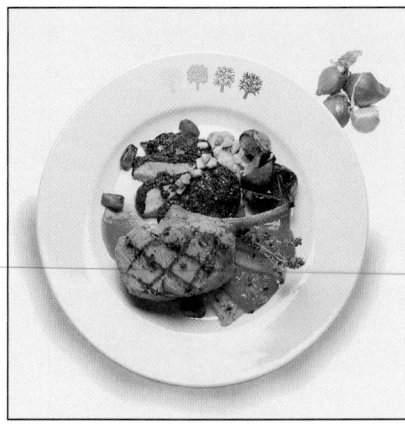

◆◆◆

RECIPE 14.2

ROSEMARY-ROASTED VEAL CHOPS WITH PORCINI MUSHROOMS

THE FOUR SEASONS, NEW YORK, NY
Chef Christian Albin

Yield: 4 350-g (12-oz.) Servings   **Method:** Roasting

Veal chops, each 350 g (12 oz.)	4	4
Salt and pepper	TT	TT
Fresh rosemary	4 sprigs	4 sprigs
Flour	as needed	as needed
Paprika	TT	TT
Clarified butter	125 mL	4 fl. oz.
White wine	125 mL	4 fl. oz.
Brown veal stock	450 mL	16 fl. oz.
Unsalted butter	50 g	2 oz.

1. Season the veal chops with salt and pepper. Press a rosemary sprig onto one side of each chop. Mix the flour and paprika and dredge the chops (both sides) in this mixture.
2. Heat the clarified butter in a sauté pan. Place the chops in the pan, rosemary side down. Roast in a preheated 190°C (375°F) oven for 7 minutes. Turn the chops carefully to keep the rosemary sprigs intact. Roast for 5–6 minutes more. Remove the chops and keep warm.
3. To make the sauce, degrease the pan and deglaze with the white wine. Add the veal stock and any juices that have accumulated under the chops. Simmer to reduce to 250 mL (8 fl. oz.). Monter au beurre, strain and adjust the seasonings.
4. Serve the chops with grilled porcini mushrooms.

◆◆◆

RECIPE 14.3

ROAST VEAL LOIN

Yield: 6 180-g (6-oz.) Servings   **Method:** Roasting

Boneless veal loin roast, 1.5 kg (3 lb.)	1	1
Salt and pepper	TT	TT
Onions, chopped medium	350 g	2
Carrots, chopped medium	150 g	2
Garlic cloves, chopped	15 g	4
Fresh thyme	3 sprigs	3 sprigs
Bay leaves	2	2
Jus lié	500 mL	1 pt.

1. Tie the veal loin roast with butcher's twine. Sear quickly to colour.
2. Season the meat with salt and pepper and place it in a roasting pan. Scatter the onions, carrots, garlic, thyme and bay leaves around it.
3. Roast at 120°C (250°F) for approximately 65 minutes (internal temperature of 50°C/150°F).
4. Remove the meat from the roasting pan and cut away the twine. Hold in a warm place for service.

RECIPE 14.2

Approximate values per serving:

Calories	621
Total fat	45 g
Saturated fat	24 g
Cholesterol	238 mg
Sodium	728 mg
Total carbohydrates	9.9 g
Protein	44 g

RECIPE 14.3

Approximate values per serving:

Calories	399
Total fat	23 g
Saturated fat	9.7 g
Cholesterol	183 mg
Sodium	500 mg
Total carbohydrates	4.1 g
Protein	44 g

5. Deglaze the roasting pan with the jus lié. Strain the vegetables and liquid through a conical strainer into a small saucepan. Discard the solids.

6. Bring the sauce to a boil and skim as much fat as possible from the surface. Season with salt and pepper. Carve the veal. Spoon a portion of the sauce over the veal; serve the remainder on the side.

VARIATION: Instead of searing the raw meat, once the roast has rested, pan-fry quickly in herb butter before carving.

❖❖❖

RECIPE 14.4

SAUTÉED VEAL CUTLETS WITH CALVADOS

Yield: 6 170-g (6-oz.) Servings　　　　　　**Method:** Sautéing

Mushrooms, sliced	350 g	12 oz.
Clarified butter	125 mL	4 fl. oz.
Golden Delicious apples	3	3
Veal cutlets, pounded, each 170 g (6 oz.)	6	6
Salt and pepper	TT	TT
Shallots, minced	50 g	2
Calvados	50 mL	2 fl. oz.
Crème fraîche	250 mL	8 fl. oz.
Fresh parsley, chopped	10 g	1 Tbsp.

1. Sauté the mushrooms in a portion of the clarified butter until dry. Remove and reserve.

2. Peel and core the apples. Cut each into 12 wedges.

3. Sauté the apple wedges in a portion of the clarified butter until slightly browned and tender. Remove and reserve.

4. Season the veal cutlets with salt and pepper. Sauté in the remaining clarified butter. (This may be done in two or three batches.) Remove and reserve.

5. Add the shallots to the pan and sauté without browning.

6. Deglaze with the Calvados. Flambé the Calvados.

7. Add the sautéed mushrooms and crème fraîche. Bring to a boil and reduce until it thickens slightly.

8. Return the cutlets to the pan to reheat. Serve each cutlet with sauce, garnished with six apple slices and chopped parsley.

RECIPE 14.4

Approximate values per serving:

Calories	691
Total fat	51 g
Saturated fat	26 g
Cholesterol	239 mg
Sodium	457 mg
Total carbohydrates	15 g
Protein	43 g

❖❖❖

RECIPE 14.5

SAUTÉED CALVES' LIVER WITH ONIONS

Yield: 10 175-g (6-oz.) Servings　　　　　　**Method:** Sautéing

Onion, julienned	750 g	1 lb. 8 oz.
Clarified butter	100 mL	3 fl. oz.
Salt and pepper	TT	TT
White wine	250 mL	8 fl. oz.
Fresh parsley, chopped	10 g	1 Tbsp.
Calves' liver, 175-g (6-oz.) slices	10	10
Flour	as needed	as needed

RECIPE 14.5

Approximate values per serving:

Calories	292
Total fat	12 g
Saturated fat	2.7 g
Cholesterol	641 mg
Sodium	544 mg
Total carbohydrates	11 g
Protein	35 g

Continued

1. Sauté the onion in 30 mL (1 fl. oz.) of butter until golden-brown. Season with salt and pepper.

2. Add the white wine, cover and braise until the onions are tender, approximately 10 minutes. Stir in the chopped parsley.

3. Dredge the liver in flour seasoned with salt and pepper.

4. In a separate pan, sauté the liver in the remaining clarified butter until done. The liver should be slightly pink in the middle.

5. Serve the liver with a portion of the onion and its cooking liquid.

◆◆◆

RECIPE 14.6

VEAL MARENGO

Yield: 6 300-g (10-oz.) Servings   **Method:** Braising

Lean boneless veal, cut in 5-cm (2-in.) cubes	1.25 kg	2 lb. 8 oz.
Salt and pepper	TT	TT
Flour for dredging the veal	as needed	as needed
Vegetable oil	50 mL	1-1/2 fl. oz.
Clarified butter	100 mL	3 fl. oz.
Onion, sliced fine	350 g	12 oz.
Carrot, sliced fine	300 g	10 oz.
Garlic cloves, crushed	10 g	2
Flour	20 g	2 Tbsp.
Tomato paste	30 mL	1 fl. oz.
Dry white wine	175 mL	6 fl. oz.
Brown veal stock	500 mL	16 fl. oz.
Bouquet garni:		
Carrot stick, 10 cm (4 in.)	1	1
Leek, split, 10-cm (4-in.) piece	1	1
Fresh thyme	1 sprig	1 sprig
Bay leaf	1	1
Mushrooms, washed and quartered	250 g	8 oz.
Tomato, diced	500 g	1 lb.
Pearl onions, boiled and peeled	350 g	24

1. Season the veal cubes with salt and pepper and dredge in flour.

2. Sauté the veal in 30 mL (1 fl. oz.) of oil and 30 g (1 oz.) of butter, browning well on all sides. Remove the meat and set aside.

3. Add 50 g (1-1/2 oz.) of butter and sauté the onion, carrot and garlic without colouring. Sprinkle with the 20 g (2 Tbsp.) flour and cook to make a blond roux. Stir in the tomato paste and return the veal to the pan.

4. Add the wine, stock and bouquet garni to the pan; bring to a boil. Cover and braise until the meat is tender, approximately 1.5 hours.

5. Sauté the mushrooms until dry in 15 mL (1 Tbsp.) of oil and 20 g (1/2 oz.) of butter without browning. Add the tomato to the pan and sauté over high heat for 3 minutes. Season with salt and pepper. Remove from the heat and reserve.

6. When the veal is tender, remove it from the pan with a slotted spoon and set aside. Strain the sauce.

7. Return the veal to the sauce along with the mushrooms, tomato and pearl onions. Bring to a boil and simmer for 5 minutes. Adjust the seasonings.

RECIPE 14.6

Approximate values per serving:

Calories	619
Total fat	31 g
Saturated fat	13 g
Cholesterol	218 mg
Sodium	928 mg
Total carbohydrates	37 g
Protein	48 g

RECIPE 14.7

CALVES' SWEETBREAD PICATTA AND DUCK FOIE GRAS WITH CARAMELIZED PEAR AND SQUASH

CASINO DE HULL, HULL, QC
Executive Chef François Hanchay

François Hanchay
François trained from a very young age in the kitchens of Plat d'Argent. After working in various hotels and restaurants across Quebec, and completing a two-year stint as executive sous-chef at Casino de Montréal, he joined the team at Casino de Hull in 1995. In 2000, he was awarded the Trophée du Président by the Canadian Federation of Chefs and Cooks for his involvement, behaviour and contribution to the profession.

Yield: 4 Servings		**Method:** Poaching and Sautéing
Calves' sweetbreads	500 g	1 lb.
Foie gras	200 g	7 oz.
Veal stock	400 mL	14 fl. oz.
Liquorice powder	1 g	1/2 tsp.
Butter	50 g	1-1/2 oz.
Sugar	50 g	1-1/2 oz.
Pear, diced	125 g	4 oz.
Butternut squash, diced	125 g	4 oz.
Flour	30 g	1 oz.
Salt and pepper	TT	TT
Butter	75 g	3 oz.
Spinach	1/2 bunch	1/2 bunch
Dried pear	4 slices	4 slices
Chives	8 stems	8 stems

1. Soak sweetbreads in water in the refrigerator overnight.

2. Prepare a court bouillon without vinegar or lemon. Poach the sweetbreads on low temperature until firm. Remove from court bouillon, cool and clean membranes. Slice into picatta (serving portions) and chill.

3. Slice foie gras into 4 portions and chill.

4. Prepare liquorice sauce from veal stock and liquorice powder. Mount with 50 g (2 oz.) butter at service time.

5. Divide the butter and sugar between 2 sauté pans. Add the pear to one and squash to the other. Sauté until they are caramelized. Reserve.

6. For service, lightly flour and season the picatta and foie gras. Brown in sauté pan in butter. Sauté spinach leaves in butter to wilt.

7. Place spinach in centre of 4 plates. Arrange the sweetbreads and place a slice of foie gras. Garnish with caramelized pears and squash.

8. Ribbon liquorice sauce around the plate, decorate with dried pear pieces and chive tied in knot. Serve hot.

RECIPE 14.7

Approximate values per serving:

Calories	684
Total fat	44 g
Saturated fat	24 g
Cholesterol	727 mg
Sodium	897 mg
Total carbohydrates	39 g
Protein	33 g

RECIPE 14.8

VEAL ÉMINCÉ ZURICH STYLE

Yield: 8 Servings		**Method:** Sautéing
Veal émincé	1 kg	2 lb. 4 oz.
Salt and pepper	TT	TT
Flour	as needed	as needed
Clarified butter	125 mL	4 fl. oz.
Shallots, diced	20 g	3/4 oz.
Field mushrooms, sliced	350 g	12 oz.

RECIPE 14.8

Approximate values per serving:

Calories	357
Total fat	21 g
Saturated fat	12 g
Cholesterol	155 mg
Sodium	371 mg
Total carbohydrates	9.9 g
Protein	32 g

Continued

Porcini mushrooms, sliced	100 g	3 oz.
Brandy	25 mL	1 fl. oz.
White wine	125 mL	4 fl. oz.
Veal demi-glace	250 mL	8 fl. oz.
Cream, 35%	150 mL	5 fl. oz.

1. Dry veal with paper towelling. Season with salt and pepper. Lightly dust with flour.
2. In a hot sauteuse, heat clarified butter and sear veal quickly and reserve. Pour off excess oil.
3. Add shallots and mushrooms to pan. Sauté until almost dry. Flame with brandy and deglaze with wine.
4. Add demi-glace and cream to pan and reduce by one-third. Return veal and any juices to pan and heat thoroughly. Adjust seasonings.
5. Serve with spaetzle, noodles or rösti.

Settimio Sicoli

Settimio served his apprenticeship at Hotel Vancouver, then added to his culinary training overseas, at the Hilton International Hotel in Mainz, Germany. Upon returning home in 1981, Settimio joined the kitchen brigade of the University Club of Vancouver attaining the position of Executive Chef, until he was asked to join the Culinary Arts Department at Vancouver Community College in 1987.

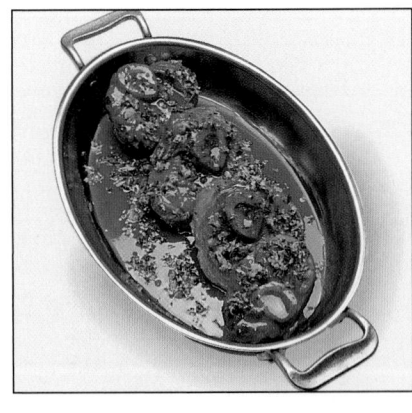

♦♦♦

RECIPE 14.9

OSSO BUCO

VANCOUVER COMMUNITY COLLEGE, Vancouver, BC
Chef Instructor Settimio Sicoli

Yield: 4 Servings   **Method:** Braising

Veal shank, cut in 2.5-cm (1-in.) pieces	8–12 pieces	8–12 pieces
Salt and pepper	TT	TT
Flour	125 g	4 oz.
Olive oil	60 mL	2 fl. oz.
Garlic clove, minced	5 g	1
Carrot, diced	125 g	4 oz.
Lemon zest	15 g	1/2 oz.
White wine	250 mL	8 fl. oz.
Brown veal stock	1 L	1 qt.
Tomato purée	30 mL	2 Tbsp.
Tomato concassée	200 g	7 oz.
Gremolada:		
Garlic clove, chopped fine	5 g	1
Lemon zest	15 g	1
Fresh Italian parsley, chopped	15 g	1-1/2 Tbsp.

1. Season the veal with salt and pepper and dredge the pieces in flour. Sauté them in olive oil until brown on both sides.
2. Add the garlic and carrot and sauté lightly.
3. Add the lemon zest, wine, stock and tomato purée and concassée. Bring to a boil and reduce to a simmer. Braise on the stove top or in a 160°C (325°F) oven until the meat is tender but not falling from the bone, approximately 40–60 minutes.
4. Remove the veal shanks, reserve, keeping warm, and reduce the sauce until thick. Adjust the seasonings.
5. At service time, transfer the meat to a serving platter and ladle the sauce over it. Combine the gremolada ingredients and sprinkle over the meat and sauce. Allow two large or three smaller pieces per person.

VARIATION: *Osso Buco Milanese*—Add two minced anchovy fillets to gremolada and serve with saffron rice.

RECIPE 14.9

Approximate values per serving:

Calories	515
Total fat	23 g
Saturated fat	4.7 g
Cholesterol	120 mg
Sodium	772 mg
Total carbohydrates	42 g
Protein	35 g

◆◆◆

RECIPE 14.10

STUFFED BREAST OF VEAL

Yield: 12 250-g (8-oz.) Servings   **Method:** Braising

Stuffing (forcemeat):		
Onion, small dice	250 g	8 oz.
Garlic, chopped	10 g	2 tsp.
Whole butter	25 g	1 oz.
Ground veal	500 g	1 lb.
Fresh bread crumbs	125 g	4 oz.
Nutmeg	0.5 g	1/4 tsp.
Salt and pepper	TT	TT
Eggs, beaten	2	2
Mushrooms, sliced	500 g	1 lb.
Clarified butter	50 mL	2 fl. oz.
Spinach leaves, stemmed and washed	125 g	4 oz.
Veal breast, approx. 3.6 kg (8 lb.)	1	1
Mirepoix, large dice	500 g	1 lb.
White wine	250 mL	8 fl. oz.
Brown veal stock	1.5 L	1-1/2 qt.
Garlic, chopped	5 g	1 tsp.
Bouquet garni:		
Carrot stick, 10 cm (4 inches)	1	1
Leek, split, 10-cm (4-inch) piece	1	1
Fresh thyme	1 sprig	1 sprig
Bay leaf	2	2

1. To make the stuffing, sauté the onion and garlic in the butter until tender. Cool. Combine with the remaining stuffing ingredients and mix well.

2. Sauté the mushrooms in 25 mL (1 fl. oz.) of the clarified butter and cool.

3. Blanch the spinach and cool.

4. Bone the veal breast. Reserve the bones.

5. Butterfly the veal breast and open it into a large rectangular shape.

6. Spread the stuffing over the breast; leave a 2.5-cm (1-inch) border around the edges.

7. Open the spinach leaves and carefully lay them on top of the stuffing. Sprinkle the mushrooms on top of the spinach leaves.

8. Roll the breast up in a cylindrical shape so the spinach leaves form a spiral in the centre. Tie with butcher's twine.

9. Brown the breast in the remaining clarified butter.

10. Remove the breast and pour off all but 25 mL (1 fl. oz.) of the fat. Add the mirepoix to the pan and sauté.

11. Add the reserved veal bones and place the veal breast on top of the bones.

12. Add the wine, stock, garlic and bouquet garni.

13. Cover and braise the breast until tender, approximately 2.5 hours.

14. Remove the breast from the pan and remove the twine. Skim any fat from the sauce.

15. Reduce the sauce and, if desired, thicken it slightly with a small amount of starch. Strain it through a fine conical strainer and adjust the seasonings.

16. Slice the veal breast and serve with the sauce.

RECIPE 14.10

Approximate values per serving:

Calories	626
Total fat	42 g
Saturated fat	18 g
Cholesterol	232 mg
Sodium	494 mg
Total carbohydrates	14 g
Protein	48 g

❖❖❖

RECIPE 14.11

VEAL MARSALA

Yield: 6 160-g (6-oz.) Servings   **Method:** Sautéing

Veal cutlets, pounded, each 80 g (3 oz.)	12	12
Salt and pepper	TT	TT
Flour	approx. 60 g	approx. 2 oz.
Clarified butter	60 mL	2 fl. oz.
Olive oil	60 mL	2 fl. oz.
Dry marsala	175 mL	6 fl. oz.
Brown veal stock	125 mL	4 fl. oz.
Whole butter	50 g	1-1/2 oz.

RECIPE 14.11

Approximate values per serving:

Calories	582
Total fat	42 g
Saturated fat	18 g
Cholesterol	182 mg
Sodium	506 mg
Total carbohydrates	12 g
Protein	39 g

1. Season the cutlets with salt and pepper. Dredge in flour and sauté the cutlets in a mixture of the clarified butter and oil, a few at a time, until all are cooked.
2. Remove the cutlets and set aside. Degrease the pan and deglaze with marsala. Add the stock and reduce until it begins to thicken.
3. Return the cutlets to the sauce to reheat. Remove the cutlets to plates or a serving platter.
4. Reduce the sauce until it becomes syrupy; adjust the seasonings. Monter au beurre and spoon the sauce over the veal.

❖❖❖

RECIPE 14.12

VEAL FRICASSEE

Yield: 16 250-g (8-oz.) Servings   **Method:** Stewing

Veal stewing meat, cut in 5-cm (2-inch) cubes	3.5 kg	8 lb.
Salt and white pepper	TT	TT
Butter	175 g	6 oz.
Onion, small dice	350 g	12 oz.
Garlic, chopped	5 g	1 tsp.
Flour	175 g	6 oz.
White wine	125 mL	4 fl. oz.
White stock	3 L	3 qt.
Bouquet garni:		
Carrot stick, 10 cm (4 inches)	1	1
Leek, split, 10-cm (4-inch) piece	1	1
Fresh thyme	1 sprig	1 sprig
Bay leaf	1	1
Cream, 35%, hot	500 mL	16 fl. oz.

RECIPE 14.12

Approximate values per serving:

Calories	564
Total fat	36 g
Saturated fat	18 g
Cholesterol	246 mg
Sodium	477 mg
Total carbohydrates	17 g
Protein	43 g

1. Season the veal with salt and pepper and sauté in the butter without browning, approximately 2 minutes.
2. Add the onion and garlic and sauté without colouring, approximately 2 minutes.
3. Add the flour and cook to make a blond roux, approximately 3 minutes.
4. Add the white wine and white stock, stir well to remove any lumps of roux and bring to a simmer. Add the bouquet garni, cover and braise until the veal is tender, approximately 30 minutes.

5. Remove the veal from the sauce and reserve. Strain the sauce through a fine conical strainer and return it to the pan. Degrease the sauce.

6. Add the heavy cream to the sauce. Reduce slightly to thicken if necessary. Return the veal to the sauce and adjust the seasonings.

7. Serve the fricassee with rice pilaf.

 EBLINKS

Food Institute of Canada: Veal Recipes
    foodnet.fic.ca/recipes/veal.html

Ontario Veal Association
    www.ontarioveal.on.ca

Steak Central: Choosing the Best Veal
    www.bestbeef.com/bestbeef/choosing_best/ChooseTheBest.html

CHAPTER 15
LAMB

LEARNING OUTCOMES

After studying this chapter you will be able to:

+ identify the primal, subprimal and fabricated cuts of lamb
+ perform basic butchering procedures: frenching a rack of lamb, trimming and boning a lamb leg, boning a lamb loin, cutting lamb noisettes
+ apply appropriate cooking methods to several common cuts of lamb

Lamb is the meat of sheep slaughtered under the age of one year. Meat from sheep slaughtered after that age is called yearling or mutton. Spring lamb is young lamb that has not been fed grass. Because lamb is slaughtered at an early age, it is quite tender and can be prepared by almost any cooking method.

Lamb has a special and distinctive flavour. It goes well with boldly flavoured sauces and accompaniments.

PRIMAL AND SUBPRIMAL CUTS OF LAMB

After the young sheep is slaughtered, it is usually reduced to the primal cuts: front/shoulder, breast, rack, loin and leg. Like veal, these primals are crosscut sections and contain both bilateral halves (for example, the primal leg contains both hind legs). Generally the pieces are sold separately. Lamb primals are not classified into a forequarter and hindquarter like beef, or a foresaddle and hindsaddle like veal.

Figure 15.1 shows the relationship between the lamb's bone structure and the primal cuts. As with all meats, it is important to know the location of bones when cutting or working with lamb. This makes meat fabrication and carving easier and aids in identifying cuts. Figure 15.2 shows the primal cuts of lamb and their location on the carcass. A lamb carcass generally weighs between 13 and 30 kg (30 and 65 lb.). Table 15.1 (see page 340) lists uses for common cuts of lamb.

Front/Shoulder

The primal lamb front is a relatively large cut accounting for approximately 45% of carcass weight. The front contains the shoulder, which consists of four rib bones, the arm, blade and neck bones as well as many small, tough muscles whose grains travel in different directions. The breast and shank are also part of the front.

All the bone and muscle groups make it difficult to cook and carve a whole shoulder. It may be boned and rolled with or without stuffing. Cubing for stew is a common application. Although the shanks are excellent braised, they are often made into mince along with the breast.

Flank

Located below the whole loin, the primal flank is a small part of the carcass and is not generally marketed as is. It is ground for patties or shepherd's pie.

Whole Loin

The primal whole loin accounts for approximately 21% of carcass weight. It can be purchased as a saddle, but is usually broken down into racks and loins.

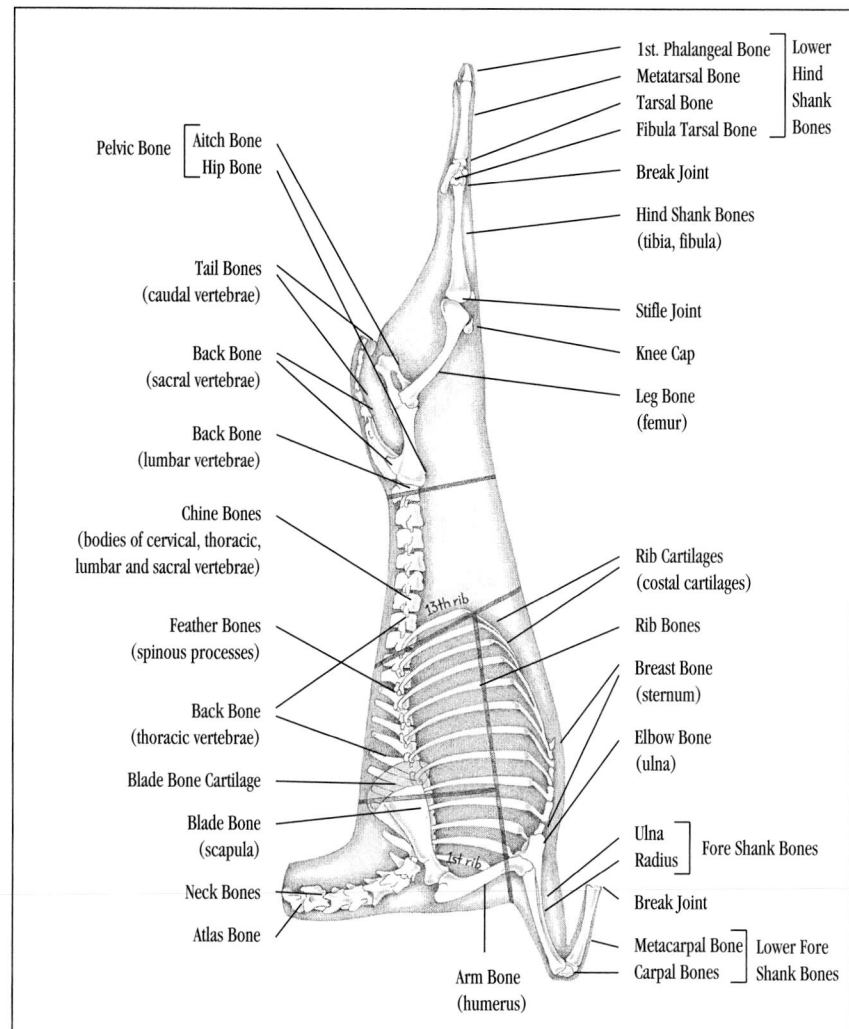

FIGURE 15.1 *The Skeletal Structure of a Lamb*

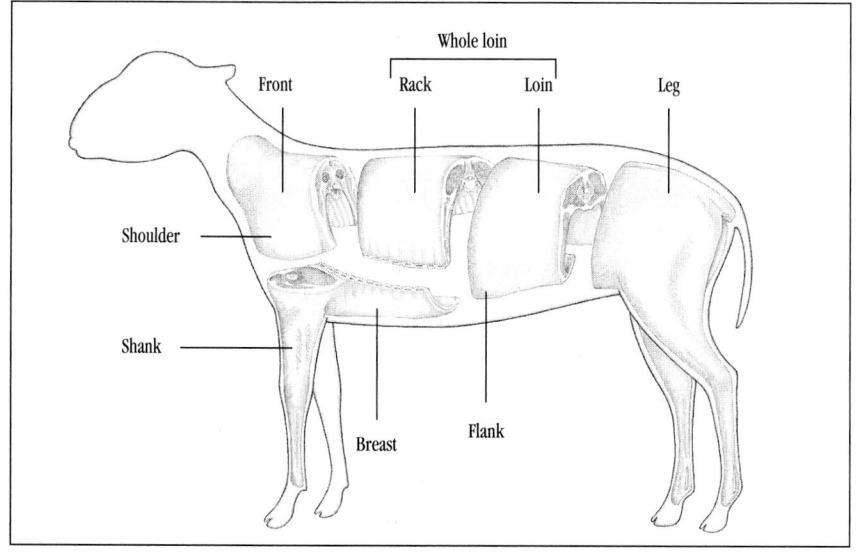

FIGURE 15.2 *The Primal Cuts of Lamb*

Rack

The lamb rack is also known as the hotel rack. It is located between the front and loin. Containing eight ribs and portions of the backbone, it accounts for approximately 8% of carcass weight.

The rack is valued for its tender rib eye muscle. The hotel rack is usually split in half and trimmed so that each set of ribs can be easily cut into chops. The split racks can then be grilled, broiled or roasted as racks or cut into single or double rib chops before cooking.

Lamb Rack

Frenched Lamb Rack

Loin

The loin is located between the rib and leg. It contains rib number 13 and portions of the backbone as well as the loin eye muscle and tenderloin. It accounts for approximately 13% of carcass weight.

The loin meat is very tender and is invariably cooked using a dry-heat method such as broiling, grilling or roasting. The loin may be boned to produce boneless roasts or chops or cut into chops with the bone in. The loin eye may be removed and cut into medallions or noisettes.

Lamb Loin Trimmed

Leg

The primal legs are a large section accounting for approximately 34% of carcass weight. They are the posterior portion of the carcass, separated from the loin by a straight cut anterior to the hip bone cartilage. As with veal, the cut of meat that would be the sirloin on a beef carcass is separated from the lamb loin by this cut and becomes part of the primal leg. The lamb leg contains several bones: the backbone, tail, hip, aitch, round and shank bones.

The primal leg is rarely used as is. More often it is partially or fully boned. Lamb legs are quite tender—the sirloin end more so than the shank end—and are well suited to a variety of cooking methods. A bone-in leg is often roasted for buffet service or braised with vegetables or beans for a hearty dish. Steaks can also be cut from the bone-in leg, with the sirloin end producing the most tender cuts. A boneless leg can be tied and roasted, with or without stuffing, or trimmed and cut into kebabs. The shank end can be diced for stew or ground for patties.

Lamb Leg

Because lamb carcasses are so easily handled, purveyors often sell them whole or cut in a variety of ways to better meet their customers' needs. As well as whole carcass, primal and fabricated cuts, lamb can be purchased in the following forms (by special order):

✦ *Foresaddle:* The anterior portion of the carcass after it is severed from the hindsaddle by a cut following the natural curvature between the twelfth and thirteenth ribs. It contains the primal shoulder, breast and foreshank and rack.

Boned, Rolled and Netted Leg of Lamb

✦ *Hindsaddle:* The posterior portion of the carcass after it is severed from the foresaddle. It contains the primal loin and leg together with the kidneys.

◆ *Saddle:* The trimmed rack and loin sections in one piece. The back is particularly useful for producing large quantities of lamb chops.

BUTCHERING PROCEDURES

Lamb is unique among the common meat animals in that it is small enough to be handled easily in its carcass form. Thus, food service operations sometimes purchase lamb whole and fabricate the desired cuts themselves. This is practical if the operation has the necessary employee skills, equipment and storage space, as well as a need for all the various cuts and trimmings butchering a whole carcass produces. A few important lamb fabrication and butchering techniques follow.

Basic Procedure for Frenching a Rack of Lamb

1. With a meat saw, trim the ribs to approximately 7.5 cm (3 inches), measuring from the rib eye on each side of the rack.

2. Turn the rack over and cut down both sides of the feather bones, completely separating the meat from the bone.

3. Turn the rack back over. Using a meat saw, cut between the ribs and the chine bone at a 45-degree angle, exposing the lean meat between the ribs and the vertebral junctures.

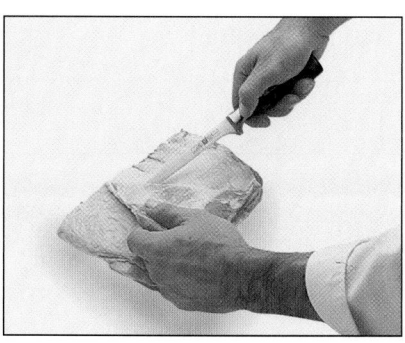

4. By pulling and cutting along the natural seam, remove the thick layers of fat and the meat between them from the rack's surface.

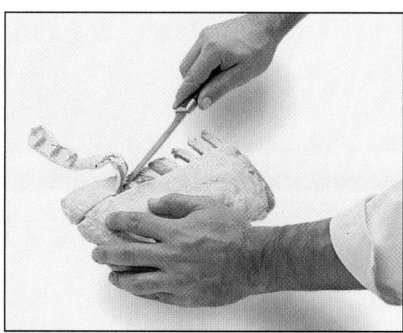

5. Make an even cut through the fat, perpendicular to the ribs, 2.5 cm (1 inch) from the rib eye. Trim away all meat and fat from the rib ends. The ribs should be completely clean.

6. Trim away the fat covering. Leave either a thin layer to protect the meat during cooking or trim the fat away completely to produce a very lean rack. The rack can also be cut into chops.

Basic Procedure for Trimming and Boning a Lamb Leg for Roasting or Grilling

1. With the tip of the knife, trim around the pelvic bone; stay close to the bone to avoid wasting any meat. Cut the sinew inside the socket and remove the bone.

2. Trim away most of the exterior fat.

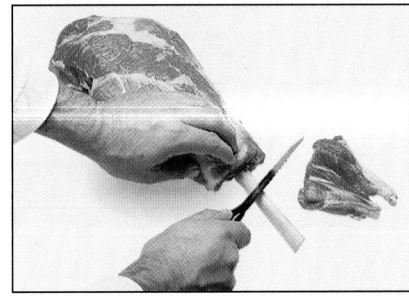

3. Cut off the shank portion completely and scrape the bone clean. This makes a handle to hold while carving the lamb.

4. Fold the flap of the sirloin over on top of the ball of the leg bone and tie with butcher's twine. This helps the leg cook evenly.

Basic Procedure for Boning a Lamb Loin for Roasting

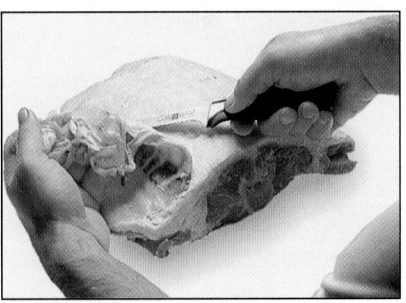

1. Start with a trimmed lamb loin (double). With the skin side up, trim the thin layer of connective tissue called the fell from the loin's surface.

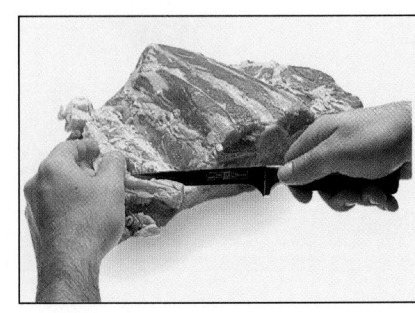

2. Turn the loin over and trim the fat from around the tenderloins.

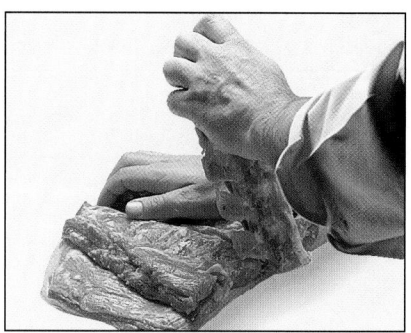

3. Starting in the middle of the back-bone, cut between the tenderloin and the vertebrae, separating them but leaving the tenderloin attached to the flank. Continue until you reach the end of the ver-tebrae. Repeat on the other side.

4. Slide the knife under the vertebrae and rib and cut back all the way to the backbone, separating the eye muscle from the vertebrae.

5. Pull the backbone out with your hands, keeping the loins intact.

6. Turn the loins over and trim the sur-face fat to 0.6 cm (1/4 inch).

7. Roll the flank flaps under from each side.

8. Tie the roast with butcher's twine at even intervals.

Basic Procedure for Cutting Lamb Noisettes from a Loin

1. Remove the loin eye muscle by cutting down along the backbone and along the vertebrae. Trim the eye muscle, leaving a thin layer of fat if desired.

2. Cut the eye meat into noisettes of the desired thickness.

TABLE 15.1 USING COMMON CUTS OF LAMB

Primal	Subprimal or Fabricated Cut	IMPS	Cooking Methods	Serving Suggestions
Shoulder/ Front	Shoulder lamb chop	1207	Dry heat (broil or grill)	Broiled or grilled lamb chops
	Diced lamb	1295	Combination (stew)	Lamb stew; lamb curry
	Ground lamb	1296	Dry heat (broil or grill; sauté)	Patties
Breast	Breast	209	Combination (braise)	Lamb breast stuffed with mushrooms
Hotel Rack	Lamb rack	204	Dry heat (broil or grill; roast; sauté)	Roast rack of lamb with garlic and rosemary
	Frenched lamb rack	204C	Dry heat (broil or grill; roast; sauté)	Broiled lamb with mustard and hazelnut crust
Loin	Lamb loin trimmed	232	Dry heat (broil or grill; roast; sauté)	Noisettes of lamb with roasted garlic sauce
	Loin chops	1232	Dry heat (broil or grill; sauté)	Broiled loin chops with herb butter
Leg	Lamb leg	233A	Dry heat (broil or grill; roast)	Kebabs; roast leg of lamb
	Boned, rolled, tied leg of lamb	233B	Dry heat (roast)	Roast leg of lamb

CONCLUSION

Even though lamb accounts for a small percentage of the meat consumed in this country, many people who do not prepare lamb at home will order it at a restaurant. Because lamb is slaughtered under the age of one year, its meat is tender and it can be prepared by almost any cooking method. Its distinctive flavour allows you to offer bold, robust sauces and accompaniments that might mask the flavours of other meats.

QUESTIONS FOR DISCUSSION

1. Describe the basic differences between a lamb carcass and a beef carcass.
2. List each lamb primal and describe its location on the carcass. Identify two subprimals or fabricated cuts taken from each primal.
3. Which cooking methods are most appropriate for a breast of lamb? Explain your answer.
4. Describe the procedure for preparing a frenched rack of lamb from a primal hotel rack.
5. What is the best way to purchase lamb for a food service operation that cuts its own meat and uses large quantities of lamb chops? Explain your answer.

*A*DDITIONAL *L*AMB *R*ECIPES

RECIPE 15.1

*R*OAST *R*ACK OF *L*AMB WITH *M*INT AND *C*ELERIAC *S*AUCE

BISHOP'S RESTAURANT, VANCOUVER, BC
Executive Chef Dennis Green

Yield: 4 125-g (4-oz.) Servings   **Method:** Roasting

Lamb racks, cleaned and frenched, each 1 kg (2 lb.)	2	2
Salt and pepper	TT	TT
Fresh white bread cubes, crusts removed	150 g	2 cups
Fresh mint, chopped	20 g	2 Tbsp.
Fresh parsley, chopped	20 g	2 Tbsp.
Fresh chives, chopped	15 g	2 Tbsp.
Dijon mustard	30 mL	2 Tbsp.
Potato and Celeriac Purée (recipe follows)	as needed	as needed
Mint and Celeriac Sauce (recipe follows)	as needed	as needed
Fresh mint sprigs	2	2

Dennis Green
Dennis was raised in Vancouver and started cooking when he was 17. He served his apprenticeship at a small bistro named the Avenue Grill near his high school. He joined Bishop's in 1993 and has been the Executive Chef there since 1997.

1. Season the lamb racks with salt and pepper and sear on both sides.
2. Transfer the lamb to a roasting pan and roast in a 130°C (250°F) oven until medium rare, approximately 35–40 minutes.
3. Meanwhile, combine the bread cubes and the herbs in a food processor and process until well blended. Set aside.
4. Remove the lamb from the roasting pan and smear with the mustard. Coat the racks with the bread crumb mixture.
5. Allow the lamb to rest for 10 minutes before carving.
6. Serve with Potato and Celeriac Purée and Mint and Celeriac Sauce. Garnish with fresh mint.

RECIPE 15.1

Approximate values per serving:

Calories	764
Total fat	40 g
Saturated fat	20 g
Cholesterol	214 mg
Sodium	1202 mg
Total carbohydrates	53 g
Protein	48 g

POTATO AND CELERIAC PURÉE

Yield: 8 120-g (4-oz.) Servings

Potatoes, peeled and cut into pieces	750 g	1 lb. 8 oz.
Celeriac (celery root), peeled and cut into 2.5-cm (1-inch) pieces	250 g	8 oz.
Cream, 35%	250 mL	8 fl. oz.
Butter	30 mL	2 Tbsp.
Salt and pepper	TT	TT

1. Combine the potatoes and celeriac in a saucepan and cover with water. Bring to a boil, reduce the heat and simmer until tender, approximately 30 minutes.
2. Strain. Mash the potatoes and celeriac using a food mill or potato ricer.
3. Heat the cream and the butter just to a boil. Add to the hot potato mixture. Using an electric mixer fitted with the whip attachment, whip the purée until fluffy. Season to taste with salt and pepper.

Potato and Celeriac Purée—
Approximate values per serving:

Calories	231
Total fat	15 g
Saturated fat	9.1 g
Cholesterol	51 mg
Sodium	321 mg
Total carbohydrates	21 g
Protein	3.1 g

Continued

MINT AND CELERIAC SAUCE

Yield: 500 mL (16 fl. oz.)

Butter	30 g	2 Tbsp.
Shallots, chopped fine	125 g	4 oz.
Garlic, minced	10 g	2 cloves
Celeriac (celery root), peeled and chopped	125 g	4 oz.
Red wine vinegar	30 mL	1 fl. oz.
Port	125 mL	4 oz.
Fresh mint, chopped	100 mL	1/2 cup
Demi-glace	500 mL	16 fl. oz.

Mint and Celeriac Sauce—
Approximate values per
50 mL serving:

Calories	110
Total fat	6.7 g
Saturated fat	3.6 g
Cholesterol	14 mg
Sodium	102 mg
Total carbohydrates	11 g
Protein	1.4 g

1. Melt the butter in a saucepan. Add the shallots, garlic and celeriac and sauté until tender but not brown.

2. Add the vinegar and reduce au sec.

3. Add the port and mint and reduce by half.

4. Add the demi-glace and simmer for 30 minutes. Strain and keep warm for service. The sauce can be made up to 1 day in advance and refrigerated, then reheated as needed.

◆◆◆

RECIPE 15.2

SHISH KEBAB

Yield: 10 225-g (7-1/2-oz.) Servings   **Method:** Grilling or Broiling

Marinade:		
Onion, small dice	350 g	12 oz.
Garlic, chopped	30 g	1 oz.
Lemon juice	125 mL	4 fl. oz.
Pepper	3 g	1 tsp.
Fresh oregano, chopped	5 g	2 tsp.
Olive oil	250 mL	8 fl. oz.
Cumin, ground	5 g	2 tsp.
Coriander, ground	6 g	1 Tbsp.
Fresh mint, chopped	8 g	2 tsp.
Lamb leg or shoulder, boneless, trimmed		
and cut in 5-cm (2-inch) cubes	2.2 kg	5 lb.
Salt	TT	TT

RECIPE 15.2

Approximate values per serving:

Calories	554
Total fat	38 g
Saturated fat	8.7 g
Cholesterol	152 mg
Sodium	332 mg
Total carbohydrates	6 g
Protein	47 g

1. Combine the marinade ingredients and add the lamb. Marinate for 2 hours.

2. Place 3–4 cubes of lamb on each of 10 skewers. Season with salt. Grill or broil to the desired doneness. Serve with rice pilaf.

◆◆◆

RECIPE 15.3

ROAST LEG OF LAMB

Yield: 12 Servings, each 150–180 g (5–6 oz.)   **Method:** Roasting

Leg of lamb, 2.7–3.6 kg (6–8 lb.)	1	1
Garlic, chopped	15 g	1 Tbsp.
Dijon mustard	30 mL	2 Tbsp.
Salt and pepper	TT	TT

Garlic heads	12	12
Fresh thyme	1 sprig	1 sprig
Fresh rosemary	1 sprig	1 sprig
Water	250 mL	8 fl. oz.
Chicken glaze	60 g	2 oz.

1. Bone and trim the leg of lamb, removing most of the fat; leave the shank bone intact.

2. Rub the leg with the chopped garlic and tie with twine.

3. Brush the lamb with Dijon mustard and season with salt and pepper.

4. Transfer the lamb to a roasting pan. Surround it with the garlic heads, thyme and rosemary. Roast at 135°C (275°F) for approximately 2–2.5 hours (internal temperature of 60–65°C/145°F), turning the leg 3–4 times. When the lamb is done, remove it and the garlic from the pan and set aside.

5. To make the sauce, add the water and chicken glaze to the pan and bring to a boil. Simmer 5 minutes and strain.

6. Cut the bottoms off the garlic heads. Serve 1 head with each lamb portion and top each serving with 15 mL (1 Tbsp.) of sauce.

RECIPE 15.3

Approximate values per serving:

Calories	385
Total fat	27 g
Saturated fat	14 g
Cholesterol	132 mg
Sodium	312 mg
Total carbohydrates	3.4 g
Protein	32 g

--- ♦♦♦ ---

RECIPE 15.4

STUFFED LEG OF LAMB

Yield: 12 Servings, each 275–300 g (9–10 oz.)   **Method:** Roasting

Bacon, fine dice	100 g	3 oz.
Fennel, fine dice	300 g	1 bulb
Garlic cloves, chopped fine	10 g	2
Wild mushrooms such as shiitake, chanterelles or porcini, chopped	350 g	12 oz.
Parsley, chopped	20 g	2 Tbsp.
Fresh thyme	1 g	1/2 tsp.
Fresh rosemary	2 g	1/2 tsp.
Salt and pepper	TT	TT
Dry white wine	250 mL	8 fl. oz.
Fresh bread crumbs	100 g	3 oz.
Lamb leg, 2.7–3.6 kg (6–8 lb.)	1	1
Mirepoix	500 g	1 lb.

1. To make the stuffing, sauté the bacon until crisp. Add the fennel and sauté lightly.

2. Add the garlic and sauté. Add the mushrooms, parsley, thyme, rosemary, salt and pepper and sauté an additional 2 minutes.

3. Deglaze with white wine and reduce by three-quarters. Remove from the heat.

4. Stir in the bread crumbs.

5. Completely bone out the leg, following the natural seams in the meat. Cut off the shank meat for use in another recipe. Fill the cavity left by the bone with stuffing.

6. Season the lamb with salt and pepper. Close the leg around the stuffing and seal the opening by tying with butcher's twine.

7. Place the stuffed leg in a roasting pan on a bed of mirepoix.

8. Roast at 135°C (275°F) until medium rare, approximately 2 hours. Serve au jus or with a pan gravy.

--- ♦♦♦ ---

VARIATION

A lamb shoulder can be boned, stuffed and rolled. Braise it with a small amount of liquid. Try an onion stuffing.

RECIPE 15.4

Approximate values per serving:

Calories	278
Total fat	13 g
Saturated fat	5.1 g
Cholesterol	112 mg
Sodium	340 mg
Total carbohydrates	8.3 g
Protein	32 g

Reto Aeschlimann, CCC

Born, raised and trained in Switzerland, Reto had an illustrious career in Spain, Ecuador, Canada, Korea and China before returning to Canada in 1998. He became a Certified Chef de Cuisine in 2001 and has won several awards, including a silver at the 1993 Salon Culinaire Mondial, in Basel, Switzerland, with the Ecuadorian Team, which he selected and trained. Great Events Corp. is located at the Spruce Meadows equestrian facility in Calgary.

RECIPE 15.5

Approximate values per serving, including Tomato Chutney:

Calories	809
Total fat	29 g
Saturated fat	6.4 g
Cholesterol	228 mg
Sodium	1098 mg
Total carbohydrates	103 g
Protein	34 g

Tomato Chutney—Approximate values per 60 mL serving:

Calories	136
Total fat	7.1 g
Saturated fat	1 g
Cholesterol	0 mg
Sodium	104 mg
Total carbohydrates	17 g
Protein	0.9 g

◆◆◆

RECIPE 15.5

RACK OF LAMB IN A CRISPY POTATO CRUST WITH FRESH TOMATO CHUTNEY

GREAT EVENTS GROUP CORP., CALGARY, AB

Executive Chef Reto Aeschlimann, CCC

Yield: 4 Servings		**Method:** Deep-Frying/Bake
Potatoes, shredded or julienned	1.25 kg	2 lb. 12 oz.
Onion, finely chopped	125 g	4 oz.
Flour	90 g	3 oz.
Eggs, beaten	3	3
Salt and pepper	TT	TT
Nutmeg, ground	2 g	3/4 tsp.
Lamb racks, frenched	2 kg	2-1/4 lb.
Flour	as needed	as needed
Lamb jus	400 mL	14 fl. oz.

1. Prepare potato crust mixture by combining potatoes, onion, flour (90 g/ 3 oz.), eggs and seasonings.
2. Trim silverskin from the loin muscle, season with salt and pepper and dredge in flour.
3. Firmly press the potato mixture evenly around the loin muscle, leaving the bones exposed.
4. Carefully place the racks in a deep fat fryer basket. Lower the racks into the hot fat and cook to golden colour. Place lamb racks on a tray and finish in a 140°C (275°F) oven.
5. Allow lamb to rest. Carve onto a plate, place jus and garnish with vegetables and tomato chutney.

TOMATO CHUTNEY

Olive oil	30 mL	1 fl. oz.
Onions, diced	100 g	3 oz.
White wine vinegar	15 mL	1 Tbsp.
Tomato concassée	250 g	8 oz.
Honey	60 g	2 fl. oz.
Salt and pepper	TT	TT

1. Sauté onions in olive oil until translucent. Deglaze with vinegar.
2. Add tomatoes and honey and simmer to desired consistency. Adjust seasoning.

◆◆◆

RECIPE 15.6

SEARED FIVE SPICE LAMB LOIN WITH ROASTED PEANUT PASTE

DONOVANS RESTAURANT, INVERCARGILL, NEW ZEALAND
Chef/Owner Graham Hawkes

Yield: 6 Servings   **Method:** Sautéing

Hoisin sauce	225 mL	8 fl. oz.
Green onion, chopped	1	1
Soy sauce	30 mL	2 Tbsp.
Dry sherry	225 mL	8 fl. oz.
Garlic, crushed	5 g	1 large clove
Five spice powder	10 g	1 Tbsp.
Fresh ginger, grated	15 g	1 Tbsp.
Lamb loin, fully trimmed	900 g	2 lb.
Roasted peanuts	100 g	3 oz.
Sambal olek	15 g	1 Tbsp.
Garlic	10 g	3 cloves
Sugar	25 g	1-1/2 Tbsp.
Ketchup	30 mL	2 Tbsp.
Oyster sauce	50 mL	3 Tbsp.
Lemon juice	30 mL	1 fl. oz.
Cooked rice	100 g	1/2 cup
Miso paste	75 g	5 Tbsp.
Stock or water	75 mL	5 Tbsp.

Graham Hawkes
Following the completion of a six-year apprenticeship, Graham travelled to Australia and then on to New Zealand, where he was Executive Chef in one of the country's largest function-facilitated hotels. In 1992, Graham purchased Donovans Restaurant, Southlands. When he is not involved assisting various industry bodies, you will find him behind the stove at Donovans, an award-winning restaurant.

1. Combine hoisin, green onion, soy, sherry, garlic, five spice powder and ginger in saucepan and simmer for 15 minutes. Cool. Pour marinade over lamb and refrigerate for 6 hours.

2. Combine peanuts, sambal olek, garlic and sugar in food processor and purée until smooth. Add ketchup, oyster sauce, lemon juice, rice and miso and purée until smooth. Adjust consistency with stock.

3. Remove lamb from marinade 30 minutes before cooking and pat dry.

4. Heat a small amount of oil in a heavy pan until very hot and sear lamb on all sides until well browned but still pink inside. Let rest 6 minutes.

5. To serve, spoon some warm peanut sauce into centre of plate, unmould a timbale of jasmine rice on sauce and arrange slices of lamb loin resting against the rice. Finish with sautéed mushrooms and chives. Drizzle a little hoisin sauce overtop.

RECIPE 15.6

Approximate values per serving:

Calories	415
Total fat	19 g
Saturated fat	5.2 g
Cholesterol	128 mg
Sodium	1111 mg
Total carbohydrates	21 g
Protein	40 g

Simon Dunn, CCC

Born and classically trained in Great Britain, Simon was most recently the Executive Chef at The Inn on Lake Bonavista, which was ranked as one of the top 100 restaurants in Canada for the duration of his tenure. Simon cooked for members of the British Royal family during his career in the Royal Air Force and is currently a chef instructor at S.A.I.T.

RECIPE 15.7

Approximate values per serving:

Calories	424
Total fat	32 g
Saturated fat	8.5 g
Cholesterol	64 mg
Sodium	381 mg
Total carbohydrates	17 g
Protein	17 g

♦♦♦

RECIPE 15.7

LAMB ROGAN JOSH

SOUTHERN ALBERTA INSTITUTE OF TECHNOLOGY, CALGARY, AB
Chef Instructor Simon Dunn, CCC

Yield: 350 g (12 oz.)   **Method:** Stewing

Onion, brunoise	175 g	6 oz.
Vegetable oil	50 mL	1-1/2 fl. oz.
Lamb shoulder, diced	200 g	7 oz.
Garlic, crushed	5 g	1 clove
Ginger, grated	10 g	1 Tbsp.
Red chile, minced	1	1
Tomato paste	5 mL	1 tsp.
Black pepper	3 g	1 tsp.
Stock or water	500 mL	16 fl. oz.
Whole cloves	2	2
Cinnamon stick	1/2	1/2
Tomato, diced	150 g	5 oz.
Salt	TT	TT
Yogurt	30 mL	1 fl. oz.

1. Brown onions in hot oil and remove from pan. Add lamb and brown on high heat.
2. Add garlic, ginger, chile, tomato paste and pepper. Return onions and stir well.
3. Add stock, cloves and cinnamon stick and stew until very tender.
4. Add fresh tomato and adjust seasoning. Finish with yogurt.

♦♦♦

RECIPE 15.8

ROAST RACK OF LAMB WITH CRISP POTATO AND VEGETABLE NAPOLEON AND KALAMATA OLIVE BUTTER

WILDWOOD RESTAURANT GROUP, CALGARY, AB
Executive Chef Michael Noble

Yield: 4 Servings   **Method:** Roasting

Vegetable Napoleon:		
Red pepper, seeded, cut into sections and grilled	175 g	1
Red onion, cut into pieces and grilled	300 g	1
Zucchini, sliced 1 cm (1/2 inch) thick and grilled	1/2	1/2
Japanese eggplant, sliced 1 cm (1/2 inch) thick and grilled	1/2	1/2
Salt and ground black pepper	TT	TT
Fresh basil, chopped	TT	TT

Michael Noble

Michael was fated to become a chef after cooking a successful Belgian waffle in a high school economics class! He began his apprenticeship in Vancouver, though he also gained valuable European experience in the early stages of his career. In 1996, Michael opened Vancouver's Diva at the Met and, within a year, it was propelled into the culinary spotlight, winning awards from Gourmet Magazine, Vancouver Magazine, and GQ. One of Canada's leading chefs, Michael achieved Canada's highest standing ever at the Bocuse d'Or World Cuisine championship in Lyons in 1995 and 1997.

Potato Pancakes:

Potatoes (about 2: see weight), grated coarse, water squeezed out	350 g	12 oz.
Salt and white pepper	TT	TT
Egg white	1	1
Parsley, chopped	10 g	1 Tbsp.
Clarified butter	as needed	as needed

Kalamata Olive Butter:

Kalamata olives, pits removed and cut into strips	50 g	2 oz.
Shallot, chopped	25 g	1
Lemon juice	50 mL	1 lemon
Sherry vinegar	15 mL	1 Tbsp.
Cream, 35%	150 mL	6 fl. oz.
Butter, cut into cubes	40 g	1-1/2 oz.
Salt and pepper	TT	TT
Parsley, chopped	as needed	as needed

Lamb Rack:

Lamb racks, bones frenched, 900 g (2 lb.) before cleaning	2	2
Salt and ground black pepper	TT	TT
Dijon mustard mix, grainy	30 g	1 oz.
Herbed bread crumbs	as needed	as needed

1. Grill all the vegetables and let cool. Cut into dice, combine in a bowl and season. Add the chopped basil. Set aside.

2. Heat a heavy skillet over moderate heat. Place the grated potato in a bowl. Season it with salt and pepper and mix in the egg white and chopped parsley by hand. Divide the potato mixture into small pancakes (you'll need 12 pancakes for 4 servings).

3. In a hot skillet cook the pancakes in the clarified butter until brown on one side, flip them over and cook on the other side. Remove them from the pan and drain on a paper towel. Set them aside.

4. To assemble the Napoleon, alternate layers of potato pancake and vegetable mix to create a tower assembly. Set aside and leave at room temperature.

5. To make the Kalamata Olive Butter, sauté the olives and shallot together briefly. Add the lemon juice and sherry vinegar and reduce slightly. Add the cream and reduce to a sauce consistency. Whisk in the butter, piece by piece. Season with salt and pepper, stir in the parsley and set aside in a warm (but not hot) location.

6. To assemble the dish, sear the seasoned rack of lamb in a skillet. Roast it at 180°C (350°F), until desired doneness is reached (12–15 minutes). Let it rest in a warm place for at least 15 minutes. Brush on the Dijon mustard mix and sprinkle with the bread crumbs, then gratinée under the broiler. Cut the rack into single bones and arrange each on the plate with the warm Vegetable Napoleon, some fine beans, the Kalamata Olive Butter and a little of the lamb jus.

RECIPE 15.8

Approximate values per serving:

Calories	732
Total fat	52 g
Saturated fat	29 g
Cholesterol	185 mg
Sodium	1504 mg
Total carbohydrates	42 g
Protein	24 g

Carol Paradis

Born in Mont Joli, Québec, Carol began his culinary career doing research on Canadian cooking for a Québec culinary museum. Having taught at the Wolfgang Puck Cooking School and the French Culinary Institute in New York, Carol spent the last two years as Chef-Proprietor of Bistro du Lapin Agile, in Sutton, Québec. Currently, he works as a chef-consultant doing things like functioning as the Executive Chef at the 2001 Tennis Masters Series and the 2001 International Meeting of Airports.

RECIPE 15.9

Approximate values per serving:

Calories	512
Total fat	32 g
Saturated fat	14 g
Cholesterol	157 mg
Sodium	529 mg
Total carbohydrates	14 g
Protein	42 g

♦♦♦

RECIPE 15.9

BRAISED LAMB SHANKS WITH ROSEMARY JUS

BISTRO DU LAPIN AGILE, Sutton, PQ
Executive Chef Carol Paradis

Yield: 4–6 Portions   **Method:** Braising

Lamb shanks	6–8	6–8
Lamb broth	700 mL	24 fl. oz.
Red wine	250 mL	8 fl. oz.
Bay leaves	6	6
Roasted garlic	10 g	4 cloves
Onion, brunoise	100 g	3 oz.
Fresh rosemary	50 g	2 oz.
Fresh marjoram	10 g	1/2 oz.
Black pepper, crushed	TT	TT
Salt	TT	TT

1. Sear lamb shanks on all sides until golden brown, about 2 minutes in a braiser.
2. Place all other ingredients into pan and bring to a simmer. Cover and place in oven.
3. Cook for approximately 2 hours at 160°C (350°F) until lamb is tender.
4. Strain jus and serve lamb in a rimmed plate with garlic mashed potatoes or polenta and the jus.

♦♦♦

RECIPE 15.10

CUMIN CORIANDER CRUSTED LAMB LOIN, BASIL MASCARPONE AND CHÈVRE, TRUFFLED LAMB JUS

THE FAIRMONT PALLISER, Calgary, AB
Executive Chef Takashi Ito, CCC

Yield: 2 150-g (5-1/2-oz.) Portions   **Method:** Pan-frying

Lamb loin, cleaned	300 g	10 oz.
Salt and pepper	TT	TT
Mascarpone cheese	40 g	1-1/2 oz.
Chèvre cheese	40 g	1-1/2 oz.
Fresh basil, chopped	2 g	1/2 tsp.
Black pepper, coarsely ground	pinch	pinch
Lamb Spice:		
Cumin, ground	7 g	1 Tbsp.
Fennel, ground	3 g	1-1/2 tsp.
Coriander, ground	3 g	1-1/2 tsp.
Chilli powder	3 g	1-1/2 tsp.
Garlic, minced	10 g	2 cloves

Takashi Ito, CCC

Takashi has been a Certified Chef de Cuisine since 1992, and has won several medals in competition, including the gold at the 1993 Grand Salon Culinaire in Vancouver. He is particularly notable for his skill and creativity in carving ice-sculptures, for which he has also won numerous awards.

Orange zest	5 g	1 strip
Rosemary, finely chopped	5 g	1-1/2 tsp.
Sauce:		
Lamb glaze	60 mL	2 fl. oz.
Truffle oil	5 mL	1 tsp.

1. Combine spice mix.
2. Season lamb with salt and pepper and rub spice mix on lamb.
3. Pan-fry loins to desired doneness.
4. Combine mascarpone, chèvre, basil and pepper. Pipe onto 2 plates.
5. Slice lamb and arrange on cheese.
6. Combine sauce ingredients and drizzle sauce on plate.

✦✦✦

RECIPE 15.11

IRISH LAMB STEW

Yield: 12 250-g (8-oz.) Servings   **Method:** Stewing

Lamb shoulder, in 4-cm (1-1/2-inch) cubes	1.75 kg	4 lb.
White stock	1.5 L	3 pt.
Sachet:		
Bay leaf	1	1
Dried thyme	0.5 g	1/2 tsp.
Peppercorns, crushed	1 g	1/2 tsp.
Parsley stems	10	10
Garlic cloves, crushed	15 g	4
Onion, sliced	500 g	1 lb.
Leek, sliced	250 g	8 oz.
Potato, peeled, large dice	700 g	1 lb. 8 oz.
Salt and white pepper	TT	TT
Carrots, turned or baton	20	20
Turnips, turned or baton	20	20
Potatoes, turned or baton	20	20
Pearl onions, peeled	20	20
Parsley, chopped, fresh	15 g	1 Tbsp.

1. Combine the lamb, stock, sachet, onion, leeks and potato. Season with salt and white pepper. Bring to a simmer and skim the surface. Simmer the stew on the stove or cover and cook in the oven at 180°C (350°F) until the lamb is tender, approximately 1 hour.
2. Degrease the stew; remove and discard the sachet.
3. Remove the pieces of potato and purée them in a food mill or ricer. Use the potato purée to thicken the stew to the desired consistency.
4. Simmer the stew for 10 minutes to blend the flavours.
5. Cook the turned or baton vegetables, potatoes and pearl onions separately. At service, heat the vegetable garnishes and add to each portion of stew.
6. Garnish with chopped parsley and serve.

❖❖❖

RECIPE 15.12

NAVARIN OF LAMB

Yield: 10 300-g (10-oz.) Servings   **Method**: Stewing

Lean lamb shoulder, large dice	1.5 kg	3 lb.
Olive oil	50 mL	3 Tbsp.
Sugar	15 g	1 Tbsp.
Salt and pepper	TT	TT
Flour	25 g	3 Tbsp.
White stock	1 L	1 qt.
White wine	125 mL	4 fl. oz.
Tomato concassée	250 g	8 oz.
Bouquet garni:		
Carrot stick, 10 cm (4 inches)	1	1
Leek, split, 10-cm (4-inch) piece	1	1
Fresh thyme	1 sprig	1 sprig
Bay leaf	1	1
Potato, peeled, medium dice	700 g	1 lb. 8 oz.
Carrot, medium dice	450 g	1 lb.
White turnip, peeled, medium dice	450 g	1 lb.
Pearl onions, peeled	12	12
Green peas, fresh	175 g	6 oz.

1. In a brazier, brown the meat in the olive oil.
2. Sprinkle the meat with the sugar and season with salt and pepper.
3. Add the flour and cook to make a blond roux.
4. Add the stock and wine. Add the tomatoes and bouquet garni; bring to a boil. Cover and cook in the oven at 190°C (375°F) until the meat is almost tender, approximately 1–1.5 hours.
5. Remove the meat and hold in a warm place. Strain the sauce and skim off any excess fat.
6. Combine the sauce, meat, potato, carrot, turnip and onions. Cover and cook until the vegetables are almost tender, approximately 25 minutes.
7. Add the peas and cook for 10 minutes more.
8. Serve in an individual casserole (cocotte) with accompaniments on the side.

RECIPE 15.12

Approximate values per serving:

Calories	519
Total fat	23 g
Saturated fat	7.1 g
Cholesterol	144 mg
Sodium	197 mg
Total carbohydrates	32 g
Protein	46 g

◆◆◆

RECIPE 15.13

NOISETTES OF LAMB WITH GARLIC SAUCE

RECIPE 15.13

Approximate values per serving:

Calories	371
Total fat	23 g
Saturated fat	5.6 g
Cholesterol	103 mg
Sodium	201 mg
Total carbohydrates	13 g
Protein	28 g

Yield: 4 Servings   **Method:** Sautéing

Lamb noisettes, each 60–90 g (2–3 oz.)	8	8
Salt and pepper	TT	TT
Fresh thyme	5 mL	1 tsp.
Garlic heads	3	3
Rosemary, fresh	1 sprig	1 sprig
Olive oil	60 mL	2 fl. oz.
Red wine	125 mL	4 fl. oz.
Jus lié	500 mL	16 fl. oz.

1. Season the noisettes with salt, pepper and thyme.

2. Break the garlic into cloves. Cook the cloves with the rosemary in 30 mL (1 fl. oz.) of oil over low heat until they are very soft, approximately 10 minutes.

3. Deglaze with the wine. Add the jus lié; simmer and reduce by half.

4. Strain the sauce through an etâmine, pushing to extract some of the garlic. Return the sauce to the saucepan and adjust the consistency and seasonings.

5. Sauté the noisettes to the desired degree of doneness in the remaining oil; serve with the sauce.

WEBLINKS

Lamb Informational Resources
   www.orst.edu/instruct/nfm433/p/stu/rl/info/p3_index.html
American Sheep Industry Association: Lamb Information
   www.sheepusa.org/resource/materials.htm#Lamb

CHAPTER 16
PORK

LEARNING OUTCOMES

After studying this chapter you will be able to:

✦ identify the primal, subprimal and fabricated cuts of pork
✦ perform basic meat-cutting procedures: boning a pork loin, tying a pork roast, cutting a chop from a loin, cutting a pocket in a pork chop, trimming a pork tenderloin
✦ apply appropriate cooking methods to several common cuts of pork

ork is the meat of hogs usually butchered before they are one year old. With the exception of beef, Canadians consume more pork than any other meat. World pork consumption constitutes more than 70% of all meats eaten. The pork we eat is leaner and healthier than it once was because of advances in animal husbandry.

Because hogs are butchered at a young age, their meat is generally very tender and has a delicate flavour. It is well suited to a variety of cooking methods. A great deal of the pork marketed in North America is cured to produce products such as smoked hams and smoked bacon. Cured pork products are discussed in Chapter 20, Charcuterie.

PRIMAL AND SUBPRIMAL CUTS OF PORK

After a hog is slaughtered, it is generally split down the backbone, dividing the carcass into bilateral halves. Like the beef carcass, each side of the hog carcass is then further broken down into the primal cuts: shoulder, butt, belly, loin and fresh leg.

Hogs are bred specifically to produce long loins: The loin contains the highest-quality meat and is the most expensive cut of pork. Pork is unique in that the ribs and loin are considered a single primal cut. They are not separated into two different primals as are the ribs and loin of beef, veal and lamb.

Figure 16.1 shows the relationship between the hog's bone structure and the primal cuts. As with all meats, it is important to know the location of bones when cutting or working with pork. This makes meat fabrication and carving easier and aids in identifying cuts. Figure 16.2 shows the primal cuts of pork and their location on the carcass. Table 16.1 (page 361) identifies common cuts of pork and suggests preparation methods. A hog carcass generally weighs in a range of 55 to 95 kg (120 to 210 lb.).

Shoulder

Picnic Shoulder

The picnic is the lower portion of the hog's foreleg; it accounts for approximately 20% of carcass weight. The shoulder contains the arm and shank bones and has a relatively high ratio of bone to lean meat.

Because all pork comes from hogs slaughtered at a young age, the shoulder is tender enough to be cooked by any method. It is, however, one of the toughest cuts of pork. It is available smoked or fresh. The shoulder is fairly inexpensive and, when purchased fresh, it can be cut into shoulder steaks or boned and cut for stir-fry or stew.

The foreshank is called the shoulder hock and is almost always smoked. Shoulder hocks are often simmered for long periods in soups, stews and braised dishes to add flavour and richness.

Shoulder Butt

The butt is a square cut located just above the picnic shoulder. It accounts for approximately 7% of carcass weight.

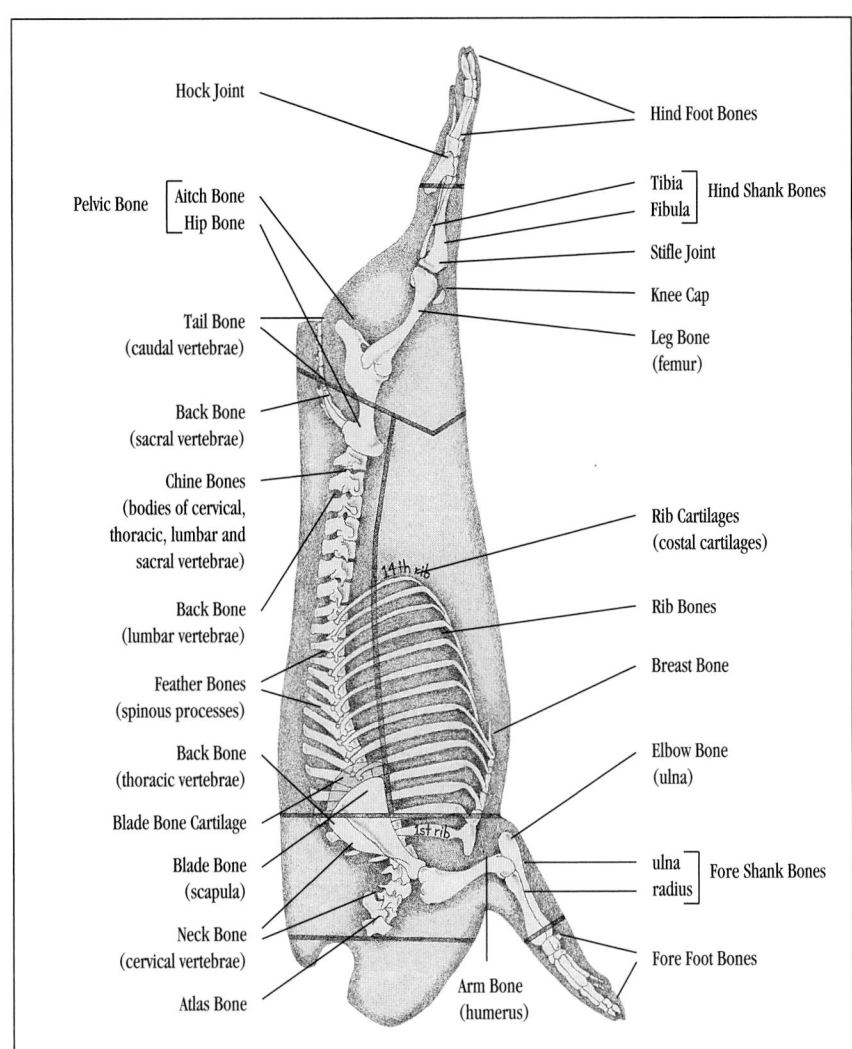

FIGURE 16.1   *The Skeletal Structure of a Hog*

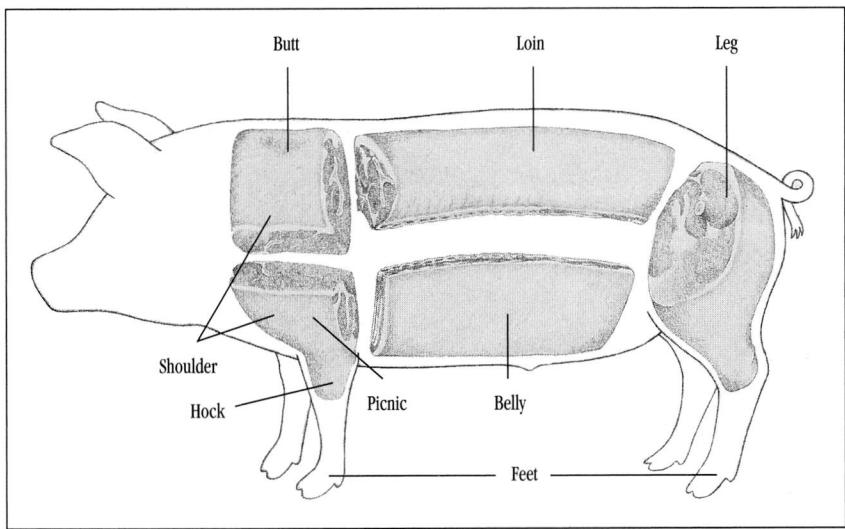

FIGURE 16.2   *The Primal Cuts of Pork*

The shoulder butt is very meaty and tender, with a good percentage of lean meat to fat. Containing only a small portion of the blade bone, the butt is a good choice when a recipe calls for a solid piece of lean pork. The fresh shoulder butt is sometimes cut into steaks or chops to be broiled or sautéed. When the butt is smoked, it is usually boneless and called a cottage ham.

Shoulder Butt

Belly

The primal pork belly is located below the loin. Accounting for approximately 16% of carcass weight, it is very fatty with only streaks of lean meat. It contains the spareribs, which are always separated from the rest of the belly before cooking.

Spareribs usually are sold fresh but can also be smoked. Long, slow cooking and a dry rub spice mixture yield tender, flavourful ribs. Radiant-heat slow cooker–type ovens are very effective for cooking these cuts. The remainder of the pork belly is nearly always cured and smoked to produce side bacon.

Pork Side Spareribs

Loin

The loin is cut from directly behind the shoulder butt and includes the entire rib section as well as the loin and a portion of the sirloin area. The primal loin accounts for approximately 20% of carcass weight. It contains a portion of the blade bone on the shoulder end, a portion of the hip bone on the leg end, all of the ribs and most of the backbone.

The primal pork loin is the only primal cut of pork not typically smoked or cured. Most of the loin is a single, very tender eye muscle. It is quite lean but contains enough intramuscular and subcutaneous fat to make it an excellent choice for a moist-heat cooking method such as braising. Or it can be prepared with dry-heat cooking methods such as roasting or sautéing. The loin also contains the pork tenderloin, located on the inside of the rib bones on the sirloin end of the loin. The tenderloin is the

Pork Loin

Pork Tenderloin

Pork Backribs

Pork Loin Chops

♦♦♦

HOGS:
A SOURCE FOR SLOGANS

Hogs were first brought to Florida by Spanish explorers in 1539, and they thrived in this heavenly new environment. The British shipped hogs to the colonies and as early as 1639 Virginia's colonists were supplying England with ham and bacon. During colonial days, pork was packed in barrels for shipment, giving rise to the term "meat packing."

During the War of 1812, the United States government shipped pork to American soldiers. It was packed in barrels stamped with the letters "US" and the name of the meat packer, Sam Wilson. The soldiers referred to the meat as "Uncle Sam's meat," thus giving birth to the national government's nickname, Uncle Sam.

most tender cut of pork; it is very versatile and can be trimmed, cut into medallions and sautéed or the whole tenderloin can be roasted or braised. The most popular cut from the loin is the pork chop. Chops can be cut from the entire loin, the choicest being centre-cut chops from the primal loin after the blade bone and sirloin portions at the front and rear of the loin are removed. The pork loin can be purchased boneless or boned and tied as a roast. A boneless pork loin is smoked to produce Canadian back bacon. The rib bones, when trimmed from the loin, can be served as barbecued pork backribs.

Although not actually part of the primal loin, backfat is the thick layer of fat—sometimes more than 2.5 cm (1 inch) thick—between the skin and the lean eye muscle. It has a variety of uses in the kitchen, especially in the preparation of charcuterie items.

Fresh Leg

The primal fresh leg is the hog's hind leg. It is a rather large cut accounting for approximately 24% of carcass weight. The leg contains the aitch, leg and hind shank bones. Like the legs of other meat animals, it contains large muscles with relatively small amounts of connective tissue.

Like many other cuts of pork, legs are often cured and smoked. But fresh legs also produce great roasts. When boned and seamed like veal, cutlets and kebobs can be fabricated. When cured and smoked, hams are available in a variety of styles; they can be purchased bone-in, shankless or boneless, partially or fully cooked. Fully cooked hams are also available canned. There is a specific ham for nearly every use and desired degree of convenience. The shank portion of the leg is called the leg shank. It is used in the same manner as the shoulder hock.

Fresh Leg

FABRICATING PROCEDURES

Other than suckling pigs (which are very young, small whole pigs used for roasting or barbecuing), pork products generally are not purchased in forms larger than the primal cuts described previously. There are a few important pork fabrication techniques that you should master, however.

Basic Procedure for Boning a Pork Loin

1. Starting on the sirloin end of a full pork loin, remove the tenderloin in one piece by making smooth cuts against the inside of the rib bones. Pull gently on the tenderloin as you cut.

2. Turn the loin over and cut between the ribs and the eye meat. Continue separating the meat from the bones, following the contours of the bones, until the loin is completely separated from the bones.

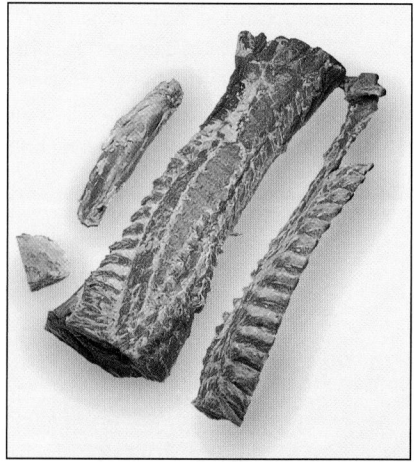

4. The fully boned loin will consist of (from left to right) the tenderloin, boneless loin and loin bones.

3. Trim around the blade bone on the shoulder end of the loin and remove it.

Basic Procedure for Tying a Boneless Pork Roast with the Half-Hitch Method

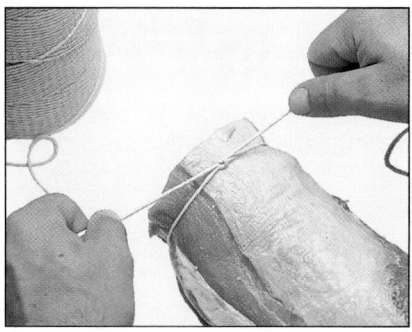

1. Wrap the loose end of the string around the pork loin and tie it with a double knot.

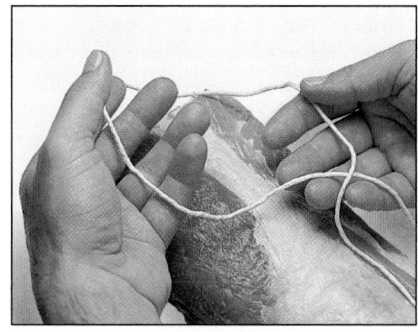

2. Make a loop and slide it down over the roast to approximately 2.5 cm (1 inch) from the first knot.

3. Make another loop and slide it down. Continue in this fashion until the whole roast has been tied.

4. Turn the roast over and cut the string, leaving enough to wrap lengthwise around the roast to the original knot.

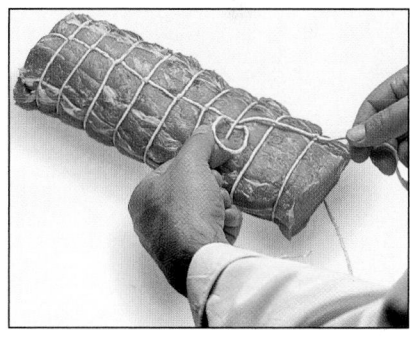

5. Wrap the string around the end of the roast, then around the string that formed the last loop. Continue in this fashion for the length of the roast, pulling the string tight after wrapping it around each loop.

6. Turn the roast back over. Wrap the string around the front end of the roast and secure it to the first loop at the point where you tied the first knot.

7. The finished roast. Note the even intervals at which the strings are tied. They should be just snug enough to hold the shape of the roast; they should not dig in or cut the meat.

Basic Procedure for Cutting a Chop from a Pork Loin

Centre-cut pork chops can be cut from the centre portion of a bone-in pork loin without the aid of a saw by using a boning knife and a heavy cleaver. Trim the excess fat from the loin, leaving a 0.5-cm (1/4-inch) layer to protect the meat during cooking.

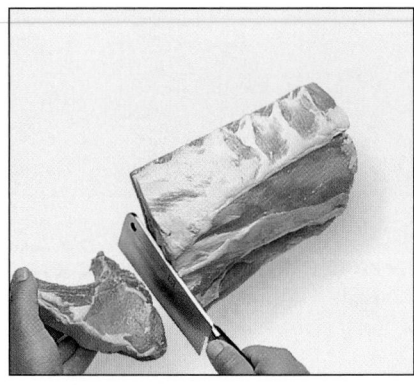

1. Cut through the meat with the knife.

2. Use the cleaver to chop through the chine bone.

3. To produce a cleaner chop, trim the meat from the end of the rib bone. Then, with the boning knife, separate the loin meat from the chine bones and separate the chine bone from the rib with the cleaver.

Basic Procedure for Cutting a Pocket in a Pork Chop

To make a pocket in a pork chop for stuffing, start with a thick chop or a double rib chop. Cut the pocket deep enough to hold ample stuffing, but be careful not to puncture either side of the chop.

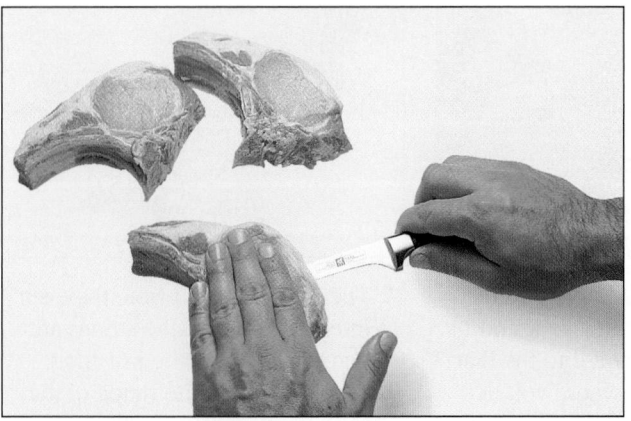

Use the tip of a boning knife to cut a pocket.

TABLE 16.1   USING COMMON CUTS OF PORK

Primal	Subprimal or Fabricated Cut	CMC/ Export	Cooking Methods	Serving Suggestions
Shoulder	Shoulder picnic	C311	Dry (baked)	Smoked shoulder picnic
	Shoulder butt	C320	Dry heat (broil or grill; sauté) Moist heat (simmer)	Broiled shoulder butt steaks Choucroûte
Belly	Bacon –fresh	C400	Dry heat (sauté) Moist heat (simmer) Combination (braise)	Breakfast meat Seasoning Seasoning
	Side spareribs	C500/502	Dry heat (low temperature)	Barbecued spareribs
Loin	Pork loin –boneless Pork tenderloin Pork backribs Pork loin chops	C200 C201 C227 C505	Dry heat (roast) Combination (braise) Dry heat (broil or grill; sauté; roast) Combination (steam then grill) Dry heat (broil or grill) Combination (braise)	Roast pork Braised pork chops Roast pork tenderloin Barbecued backribs Broiled loin chop with mushroom sauce Braised loin chop with leeks and fennel
Fresh leg	Fresh leg	C100/101	Dry heat (roast)	Roast pork with apricots and almonds

Basic Procedure for Trimming a Pork Tenderloin

As with a beef tenderloin, the pork tenderloin must be trimmed of all fat and silverskin. Follow the procedures outlined in Chapter 13, Beef, for trimming a beef tenderloin.

Use a boning knife to remove the silverskin from a pork tenderloin. Keep the silverskin tight and maintain a slight upward pressure on the knife to trim only the silverskin.

 ONCLUSION

Pork can be enjoyed cured, processed or fresh. The mild flavour of fresh pork blends well with many different seasonings, making it a popular menu item. It is naturally tender and can be prepared by almost any dry-heat, moist-heat or combination cooking method. Properly fabricated and prepared, it is a nutritious, healthy meat.

*Q*UESTIONS FOR *D*ISCUSSION

1. List each pork primal cut and describe its location on the carcass. Identify two subprimals or fabricated cuts taken from each primal.
2. What is unique about the primal pork loin as compared to the beef or veal loin?
3. Are backfat and bacon taken from the same primal? How are they different?
4. What is the only primal cut of pork that is not typically smoked or cured? How is it best cooked? Explain your answer.

*A*DDITIONAL PORK RECIPES

◆◆◆ COOKING CANADIAN PORK

Cooking pork to well done is not necessary or recommended in Canada. Trichinosis has virtually been eradicated in domestic pork and there has not been a reported case in more than three decades. Wild game is still a concern, however.

Today's leaner pork benefits greatly in palatability and yield through low-temperature cooking and cooking to medium doneness. Tougher cuts will require more cooking to achieve tenderness, although they are usually braised or stewed anyway.

RECIPE 16.1

Approximate values per serving:

Calories	736
Total fat	48 g
Saturated fat	17 g
Cholesterol	175 mg
Sodium	787 mg
Total carbohydrates	38 g
Protein	38 g

RECIPE 16.1

*B*ARBECUED *R*IBS

NOTE: *This dish appears in the Chapter Opening photograph.*

Yield: 8 Servings (approx. 4 ribs each)　　　　　　　　　　**Method:** Baking

Salt	30 g	2 Tbsp.
Black pepper, ground	8 g	1 Tbsp.
Crushed red pepper flakes	6 g	1 Tbsp.
Pork backribs, 1.3–1.8 kg (3–4 lb.) slab	2	2
Cider vinegar	175 mL	6 fl. oz.
Water	300 mL	10-1/2 fl. oz.
Sauce:		
Onion, chopped coarse	150 g	5 oz.
Garlic cloves	10 g	3
Green bell pepper, chopped coarse	125 g	4 oz.
Plum tomatoes, canned	500 mL	16 fl. oz.
Vegetable oil	30 mL	2 Tbsp.
Red Devil or other hot sauce	250 mL	8 fl. oz.
Brown sugar	250 g	10 oz.
Lemon juice	50 mL	2 fl. oz.

1. Combine the salt, pepper and red pepper flakes. Rub this mixture over both sides of the ribs, coating them well.
2. Place the ribs in a nonreactive pan and add the vinegar and water. Cover and refrigerate several hours or overnight.
3. Drain the ribs, turn the presentation side up and bake in a 120°C (250°F) oven for 2–2.5 hours or until tender.
4. Prepare the sauce by puréeing the onion, garlic, green pepper and tomatoes in a food processor or blender. Sweat this mixture in a nonreactive saucepan in the vegetable oil and add the remaining sauce ingredients.
6. Simmer the sauce over low heat until it thickens, approximately 15–20 minutes.
7. Brush the ribs with the sauce and return to a hot oven for 15 minutes to glaze the ribs. Serve additional sauce on the side. Serve with Creamy Coleslaw, Recipe 24.32, and Baked Beans, Recipe 22.5.

❖❖❖

RECIPE 16.2

GRILLED MEDALLIONS OF PORK ON A CORNCAKE WITH WHISKY APPLE BUTTER

CHEF LELAND ATKINSON, WASHINGTON, D.C.

Yield: 4 Servings   Method: Grilling

Loin medallions, 90 g (3 oz.) each	8	8
Salt and pepper	TT	TT
Lemon juice	30 mL	1 fl. oz.
Garlic, minced	5 g	1 tsp.
Jalapeño, minced	5 g	1 tsp.
Corncakes (recipe follows)	4	4
Whisky Apple Butter (recipe follows)	as needed	as needed
Fresh cilantro	as needed	as needed

1. Season the pork with salt and pepper and marinate it in the lemon juice, garlic and jalapeño for 2–4 hours.

2. Grill the medallions until done, approximately 4–5 minutes per side.

3. Place the corncakes on four warm plates, top them with a dollop of warm Whisky Apple Butter and two pork medallions. Garnish with fresh cilantro and serve.

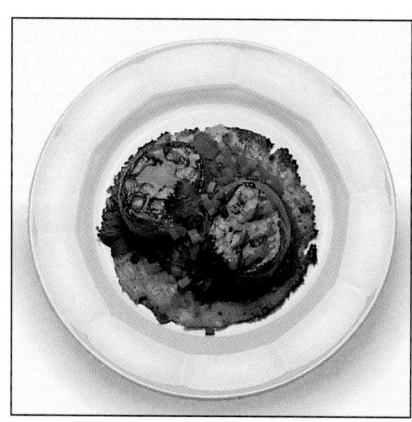

RECIPE 16.2

Approximate values per serving:

Calories	680
Total fat	36 g
Saturated fat	13 g
Cholesterol	272 mg
Sodium	701 mg
Total carbohydrates	49 g
Protein	40 g

CORNCAKES

Yield: 4 150-g (5-oz.) cakes

Green onion, sliced	20 g	2 Tbsp.
Red bell pepper, small dice	20 g	2 Tbsp.
Jalapeño, minced	1	1
Olive oil	30 mL	1 fl. oz.
Fresh corn kernels	250 g	8 oz.
Milk	100 mL	3 fl. oz.
Flour	30 g	4 Tbsp.
Cornmeal	50 g	4 Tbsp.
Eggs	2	2
Egg yolk	1	1
Fresh cilantro, chopped	4 g	1 tsp.
Salt and pepper	TT	TT
Clarified butter or canola oil	as needed	as needed

Corncakes—
Approximate values per serving:

Calories	308
Total fat	17 g
Saturated fat	5.4 g
Cholesterol	174 mg
Sodium	251 mg
Total carbohydrates	30 g
Protein	8.7 g

1. Sauté the onion, bell pepper and jalapeño in the olive oil. Drain and cool to room temperature.

2. In a food processor, blend the corn kernels with a little milk until the mixture is not quite smooth.

3. Remove the corn mixture to a bowl and stir in the remaining milk and the flour and cornmeal.

4. Beat the eggs with the yolk; add the pepper mixture to them. Add the cilantro and combine this mixture with the corn mixture. Season with salt and pepper.

5. Heat a portion of the clarified butter or oil in a sauté pan or on a griddle. Add 150 g (5 oz.) of the batter to form 12-cm (5-inch) pancakes; lightly brown them on each side.

WHISKY APPLE BUTTER

Yield: 700 mL (24 oz.)

Onion, chopped fine	125 g	4 oz.
Sugar	60 g	2 oz.
Cider vinegar	30 mL	1 fl. oz.
Granny Smith apples, peeled and chopped coarse	3	3
Rye whisky	175 mL	6 fl. oz.
Demi-glace	250 mL	8 fl. oz.
Cinnamon, ground	3 g	2 tsp.
Cloves, ground	1 pinch	1 pinch
Whole butter	15 g	1 Tbsp.
Salt and pepper	TT	TT

Whisky Apple Butter—Approximate values per 75 mL serving:

Calories	109
Total fat	3.8 g
Saturated fat	2.0 g
Cholesterol	7.6 mg
Sodium	91 mg
Total carbohydrates	18 g
Protein	0.6 g

1. Combine the onion, sugar and vinegar; simmer for 5 minutes.
2. Add the apples, whisky, demi-glace and spices. Simmer until the apples are completely tender.
3. Purée the mixture in a blender or food processor.
4. Strain and monter au beurre. Adjust the seasonings and keep warm for service.

✦✦✦

RECIPE 16.3

CHINESE BARBECUED PORK

Yield: 6 Servings   **Method:** Roasting

Pork loin	1 kg	2 lb.
Salt	5 g	1 tsp.
Garlic, chopped	15 g	3 cloves
Ginger, grated	10 g	1 Tbsp.
Spring onion, chopped	1	1
Light soy sauce	50 mL	2 fl. oz.
Sugar	50 g	2 oz.
Five spice power	4 g	1 tsp.
Chinese wine or sherry	50 mL	2 fl. oz.
Red colour	3 drops	3 drops
Honey	75 g	2-1/2 oz.

RECIPE 16.3

Approximate values per serving:

Calories	378
Total fat	19 g
Saturated fat	6.7 g
Cholesterol	103 mg
Sodium	906 mg
Total carbohydrates	20 g
Protein	34 g

1. Cut loin lengthwise into 2.5-cm (1-inch) strips.
2. Combine all remaining ingredients and coat pork strips. Marinate 30 minutes.
3. Place a wire rack over a roasting pan half filled with water.
4. Place pork strips on rack and roast for 20 minutes in a 200°C (400°F) oven.
5. Turn strips over and brush with a bit of honey and any remaining marinade.
6. Cook a further 10–15 minutes.

✦✦✦

RECIPE 16.4

PORK LOIN WITH APRICOTS

Yield: 6 200-g (7-oz.) Servings   **Method:** Roasting

Boneless pork loin roast, 1.5 kg (3 lb.)	1	1
Salt and pepper	TT	TT
Apricots, pitted, or other dry fruit	350 g	12 oz.

Carrot, chopped coarse	100 g	3 oz.
Onion, chopped coarse	175 g	6 oz.
Vegetable oil	15 mL	1 Tbsp.
Clarified butter	15 mL	1 Tbsp.
Fresh rosemary	3 g	1 tsp.
Fresh thyme	2 g	1 tsp.
Bay leaf, crushed	1	1
Garlic cloves	10 g	2
Apple juice	250 mL	8 fl. oz.
White stock	250 mL	8 fl. oz.
Sugar	60 g	2 oz.
Vinegar	60 mL	2 fl. oz.

1. Trim and butterfly the pork loin; reserve the trimmings. (To butterfly the loin, slice it partway through the centre and open it like a book, then flatten it into a rectangular shape.) Season with salt and pepper.

2. Reserve 12 apricots and arrange the remaining apricots along the length of the loin. Roll up the loin and tie with butcher's twine.

3. Brown the pork roll and pork trimmings, carrot and onion in the oil and butter.

4. Add the herbs and garlic and roast the pork on the bed of trimmings and vegetables at 135°C (275°F), basting frequently with the fat that accumulates in the pan, until an internal temperature of 60°C (110°F), approximately 60 minutes.

5. Poach the reserved apricots in the apple juice until plump; set aside.

6. Remove the roast from the pan and keep it warm. Degrease the pan and deglaze with white stock. Simmer for 15 minutes, then strain.

7. Combine the sugar and vinegar in a saucepan. Bring to a boil and cook without stirring until the mixture turns a caramel colour. Immediately remove it from the heat and add the juices from the roasting pan. When the sputtering stops, return the pan to the heat and skim any fat from the surface; keep the sauce warm over low heat.

8. Drain the apricots. Remove the twine from the roast. Slice and serve the meat with the sauce and apricots.

VARIATION: Use dried prunes, apples or cranberries instead of apricots.

RECIPE 16.4

Approximate values per serving:

Calories	711
Total fat	27 g
Saturated fat	10 g
Cholesterol	132 mg
Sodium	313 mg
Total carbohydrates	70 g
Protein	47 g

♦♦♦

RECIPE 16.5

MAPLE BAKED HAM

Yield: 25 175-g (6-oz.) Servings   **Method:** Roasting

Ham, fully cooked, bone in, 5.4–6.3 kg (12–14 lb.)	1	1
Brown or maple sugar	175 g	6 oz.
Cloves, ground	1 g	1/2 tsp.
Crushed pineapple, with juice	500 g	16 oz.
Maple syrup	250 mL	8 fl. oz.
Orange marmalade	250 g	8 oz.

1. Peel the rind from the ham and trim the exterior fat to an even thickness of 0.5 cm (1/4 inch). Score the fat surface decoratively.

2. Combine the sugar and cloves and pat this mixture evenly over the top of the ham. Roast the coated ham at 135°C (275°F) for 1 hour.

3. Combine the pineapple, maple syrup and marmalade in a saucepan over medium heat.

RECIPE 16.5

Approximate values per serving:

Calories	370
Total fat	14 g
Saturated fat	5 g
Cholesterol	94 mg
Sodium	2411 mg
Total carbohydrates	25 g
Protein	36 g

Continued

4. Brush some of the sauce over the ham and cook until heated through, basting frequently, approximately 2 hours.

5. Remove the ham from the roasting pan. Keep it warm and allow it to rest 30 minutes before carving.

RECIPE 16.6

GRILLED PORK TENDERLOIN WITH CASCABEL CHILE AND HONEY GLAZE

VINCENT ON CAMELBACK, PHOENIX, AZ
Chef Vincent Guerithault

RECIPE 16.6

Approximate values per serving:

Calories	466
Total fat	10 g
Saturated fat	2.9 g
Cholesterol	119 mg
Sodium	447 mg
Total carbohydrates	51 g
Protein	43 g

Yield: 6 175-g (6-oz.) Servings   **Method:** Grilling

Pork tenderloins, each approx. 400 g (14 oz.)	3	3
Olive oil	15 mL	1 Tbsp.
Salt	5 g	1 tsp.
Black pepper, coarsely ground	5 g	2 tsp.
Cascabel Chile and Honey Glaze (recipe follows)		

1. Rub the tenderloins with oil and season with salt and pepper.

2. Grill the tenderloins on all sides, a total of approximately 5 minutes. Brush with the Cascabel Chile and Honey Glaze and cook an additional 2 minutes on each side.

3. Remove the pork from the grill and allow it to rest for 5 minutes before slicing.

4. Slice each tenderloin on the bias into 12 slices. Drizzle the remaining Cascabel Chile and Honey Glaze over the sliced pork.

CASCABEL CHILE AND HONEY GLAZE

Yield: 350 g (12 oz.)

Cascabel Chile and Honey Glaze—Approximate values per 30 g serving:

Calories	104
Total fat	0.3 g
Saturated fat	0.1 g
Cholesterol	0.1 mg
Sodium	20 mg
Total carbohydrates	25 g
Protein	0.3 g

Cascabel chiles (if not available, substitute 2 jalapeños)	4	4
Honey	350 g	12 oz.
Chicken stock	125 mL	4 fl. oz.
Tomato purée	45 mL	3 Tbsp.
Paprika	2.5 g	1 tsp.
Cumin, ground	2.5 g	1 tsp.

1. Soften the cascabel chiles by soaking them in warm water for approximately 2 hours.

2. Combine all ingredients in a saucepan and simmer over medium heat for approximately 10 minutes.

3. Remove from the heat and purée in a blender.

RECIPE 16.7

STUFFED PORK CHOPS

Yield: 10 Servings   **Method:** Braising

Thick-cut pork chops, each approx. 225 g (8 oz.)	10	10

Celery, small dice	100 g	3 oz.
Onion, small dice	150 g	5 oz.
Apple, small dice	50 g	2 oz.
Whole butter, melted	175 g	6 oz.
Fresh bread cubes, 1.2 cm (1/2 inch)	225 g	8 oz.
Parsley, chopped	10 g	1 Tbsp.
Sage, fresh, chopped	5 g	2 tsp.
Salt and pepper	TT	TT
Lemon juice and zest	1/2 lemon	1/2 lemon
White stock	approx. 150 mL	approx. 5 fl. oz.
Canola oil	50 mL	2 fl. oz.
Demi-glace	1 L	1 qt.

1. Cut pockets in the chops.

2. Sauté the celery, onion and apple in 60 g (2 oz.) of butter until tender.

3. Combine the celery, onion, apple and remaining butter with the bread cubes, parsley, sage, salt and pepper, lemon juice and zest. Add enough stock to moisten the dressing.

4. Stuff the mixture into each of the pork chops. Seal the pockets with toothpicks and tie with butcher's twine.

5. In a brazier, brown the stuffed chops well on each side in the canola oil.

6. Add the demi-glace. Bring to a simmer, cover and place in a 165°C (325°F) oven. Cook until tender, approximately 45 minutes.

7. Remove the chops from the pan. Degrease the sauce and reduce to the desired consistency. Strain the sauce and adjust the seasonings.

◆ ◆ ◆

RECIPE 16.8

SMOKED LOIN OF PORK, HAZELNUT AND MAPLE SYRUP CRUST, APPLE CIDER SAUCE

ST. PIUS X SCHOOL, MONTREAL, QC
Chef Otto R. Daniels, Jr., CCC

Yield: 20 Servings   **Method:** Hot-smoking

Pork loin, boneless centre cut	4 kg	10 lb.
Sesame oil	200 mL	7 fl. oz.
Salt and pepper	TT	TT
Maple syrup	300 mL	10 fl. oz.
Dijon mustard	175 mL	6 fl. oz.
Hazelnuts, finely chopped	250 g	2 cups
Maple or apple wood chips	as needed	as needed
Rougemont sparkling apple cider	50 mL	2 fl. oz.
Demi-glace	1 L	1 qt.
Gorgonzola cheese, grated	175 g	6 oz.
Cream, 15%	100 mL	3 fl. oz.
Chives, finely chopped	30 g	1 oz.

1. Sear the pork loin in the sesame oil to a light golden-brown colour. Season with salt and pepper.

2. Combine the maple syrup and mustard and coat the loin with this mixture. Coat the loin with the hazelnuts, fat side up.

3. Place the pork in a roasting pan. Hot smoke in a smoker oven at 150°C (300°F) to an internal temperature of 65°C (150°F).

Continued

Otto R. Daniels, Jr.
Currently a teacher of professional cooking and coach/coordinator of culinary competitions, Otto is also studying for his Bachelor of Education degree. He has personally won medals and trophies in numerous competitions, and under his tutelage the St. Pius X team won four consecutive provincial championships from 1994 to 1997.

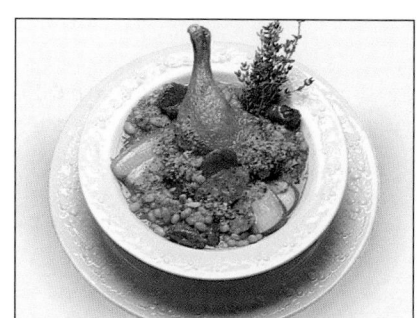

RECIPE 16.7

Approximate values per serving:

Calories	661
Total fat	53 g
Saturated fat	22 g
Cholesterol	147 mg
Sodium	440 mg
Total carbohydrates	16 g
Protein	30 g

RECIPE 16.8

Approximate values per serving:

Calories	639
Total fat	43 g
Saturated fat	13 g
Cholesterol	117 mg
Sodium	464 mg
Total carbohydrates	24 g
Protein	39 g

4. Remove from oven and place loin in a separate pan. Keep warm.

5. Deglaze the roasting pan with the cider and add the demi-glace, cheese and cream. Reduce the sauce to a coating consistency.

6. Strain sauce through a fine strainer and garnish with chives.

7. Adjust seasoning and add cider if consistency is too thick.

◆◆◆

RECIPE 16.9

CASSOULET

CALGARY, AB
Chef dee Hobsbawn-Smith

dee Hobsbawn-Smith

dee—a Calgary-based professional chef, caterer, culinary educator and author—has been delighting Calgary diners and readers since 1983. She studied cooking at Vancouver Vocational Institute, completed her Red Seal in Calgary, and studied with eminent chef and educator Madeleine Kamman in Annecy, France. Since selling her restaurant, Foodsmith, in 1994, dee has turned to food writing and now has three cookbooks and many magazine articles and columns under her belt.

◆◆◆

ABOUT CASSOULET

Cassoulet originates in the south of France. The beans are the common ingredient along with a meat stew and duck confit. The contents vary widely, with lamb often used. The recipe presented here is a more straightforward method with a twist. One could add some fresh tomato concassée as a garnish. The baked crust is not here, but a crusty bread on the side and a simple salad will round out the meal.

RECIPE 16.9

Approximate values per serving:

Calories	749
Total fat	25 g
Saturated fat	8.1 g
Cholesterol	85 mg
Sodium	853 mg
Total carbohydrates	88 g
Protein	43 g

Yield: 8 Servings　　　　　　　　　　　　**Method**: Stewing

Ingredient		
Great northern beans	750 g	3 cups
Onion, large dice	350 g	12 oz.
Leeks, large dice	350 g	12 oz.
Carrots, large dice	200 g	7 oz.
Celery rib, large dice	175 g	6 oz.
Garlic, sliced	30 g	8 cloves
Olive oil	15 mL	1 fl. oz.
Leek and cabbage sausage (or other)	2 links	2 links
Bay leaves	2	2
Fresh rosemary	2–3 sprigs	2–3 sprigs
Fresh thyme	4–5 sprigs	4–5 sprigs
Sage, fresh	2–3 sprigs	2–3 sprigs
Oregano, dry	0.5 g	1 tsp.
Basil, dry	0.5 g	1 tsp.
Star anise	1–2	1–2
Cinnamon stick	5 g	1/2 stick
Lemon zest	10 g	1 Tbsp.
Black peppercorns, cracked	8 g	1 Tbsp.
Allspice berries	2 g	1/2 tsp.
Cloves, whole	5	5
Red wine	250 mL	8 fl. oz.
Pomegranate molasses	125 mL	4 fl. oz.
Duck legs	1 kg	4–6
Pork hocks	1 kg	2
Brown chicken or beef stock	2 L	2 qt.
Herb-infused wine vinegar	25 mL	1 fl. oz.
Kosher salt and pepper	TT	TT

1. Soak beans in 3 times as much water overnight.

2. In heavy-bottomed brazier, cook the onion, leeks, carrots, celery and garlic in the olive oil. Add small amounts of water to prevent burning. When tender, allow liquid to evaporate and brown the vegetables.

3. Add the sausage, herbs and spices, wine, molasses, beans, duck legs, pork hocks and stock. Stir well, bring to a boil, cover tightly and continue to cook in a 190°C (375°F) oven for approximately 3 hours. The flavour will be mellowed and the beans tender.

4. Skim any fat from the surface, add the vinegar and adjust seasoning.

5. Skin the pork hocks and shred the meat.

6. Serve generous portions with the duck leg, sausage and shredded pork arranged attractively.

◆◆◆

RECIPE 16.10

PORK TENDERLOIN MEDALLIONS WITH SHIITAKE MUSHROOMS, GOAT CHEESE AND PORT WINE

SOUTHERN ALBERTA INSTITUTE OF TECHNOLOGY, CALGARY, AB
Chef Instructor Colin Maxwell, CCC

Yield: 4 150-g (5-oz.) Servings   **Method:** Sautéing

Pork tenderloin medallions, each 75 g (2-1/2 oz.)	8	8
Clarified butter	30 mL	2 Tbsp.
Shallots, chopped	5 g	2 tsp.
Garlic, chopped	3 g	1 tsp.
Ginger, chopped	3 g	1 tsp.
Shiitake mushrooms, sliced	125 g	8
Brandy	25 mL	1 fl. oz.
Port wine	100 mL	3 fl. oz.
Demi-glace	175 mL	6 fl. oz.
Cream, 35%	175 mL	6 fl. oz.
Goat cheese slices, unripened, each 15 g (1/2 oz.)	8	8

Colin Maxwell, CCC
Currently an Instructor at SAIT, Colin had much of his training in England. He came to Canada in 1979 and quickly became the Executive Sous Chef at the Chateau Airport Hotel, where he helped run the Flight Kitchen. He was a member of Team Calgary in the 1987 World Culinary Arts Show in Vancouver, and sat on the Red Seal Exam Revision Committee in 1998.

1. Sauté the pork in clarified butter, cooking to medium. Remove from pan and keep warm.
2. Sweat shallots, garlic and ginger in the same pan for about 1 minute or until soft. Add mushrooms and cook 1 more minute.
3. Flame with brandy. Add port wine and reduce liquid by half.
4. Add demi-glace and cream. Simmer until sauce thickens.
5. Place goat cheese on medallions and warm under salamander. (Do not cook cheese.)
6. Arrange the pork on the serving plate with garnishes and coat the meat with sauce.

RECIPE 16.10

Approximate values per serving:

Calories	554
Total fat	38 g
Saturated fat	22 g
Cholesterol	186 mg
Sodium	247 mg
Total carbohydrates	13 g
Protein	40 g

◆◆◆

RECIPE 16.11

PAPAYA MARINATED PORK

SOUTHERN ALBERTA INSTITUTE OF TECHNOLOGY, CALGARY, AB
Chef Instructor J. Otto Daniels, CCC

Yield: 6 Servings   **Method:** Sautéing

Papaya Marinade:		
Pineapple juice	150 mL	5 fl. oz.
Soy sauce	50 mL	1-1/2 fl. oz.
Garlic, fine chopped	25 g	3/4 oz.
Ginger, fine chopped	25 g	3/4 oz.
Papaya, fine chopped	50 g	1-1/2 oz.
Lemon juice	25 mL	3/4 fl. oz.
Cayenne pepper	0.25 g	1/2 tsp.
Honey	100 g	3 oz.
Pork tenderloin	875 g	1 lb. 12 oz.
Papaya, whole, cut into 12 pieces	2	2

J. Otto Daniels, CCC
Originally trained in Hungary, Otto is a Master Chef in both France and Italy, as well as a Certified Chef de Cuisine in Canada. He was a coach/advisor for the Canadian national culinary team and recently ventured to Japan to help market products for Export and Agriculture Canada.

Continued

Vegetable oil	60 mL	2 fl. oz.
Spring vegetable greens	300 g	10 oz.
Salt and pepper	TT	TT
Caramelized Ginger Vinaigrette (recipe follows)	TT	TT

1. Mix the marinade ingredients together.
2. Put the pork tenderloin in 300 mL (10 fl. oz.) of the marinade and leave in refrigerator for 24 hours.
3. Slice the tenderloin into six medallions, each about 1 cm (1/2 inch) thick.
4. Place the papaya sections in a pan in a 180°C (350°F) oven for 2 minutes.
5. In half the vegetable oil, sear the pork medallions for about 1 minute on each side. The pork will be medium (slightly pink) but the carryover cooking will finish it.
6. In the remaining vegetable oil, stir-fry the spring greens just to wilt. Season to taste.
7. Serve each pork medallion on a bed of the wilted spring greens with two papaya sections. Drizzle equal portions of the vinaigrette over each serving.

CARAMELIZED GINGER VINAIGRETTE

Granulated sugar	125 g	4 oz.
Rice wine vinegar	250 mL	8 fl. oz.
Ginger, julienned	75 g	2-1/2 oz.
Salt and pepper	TT	TT

1. Place the sugar in a stainless steel pot on the stove to caramelize (be careful not to burn the sugar).
2. Add the vinegar to the caramelized sugar and liquefy completely.
3. Add ginger to liquid and simmer 2 minutes. Season with salt and pepper.

◆◆◆

RECIPE 16.12

SMOKED WILD BOAR WITH APPLE AND CRANBERRY SAUCE

TORONTO, ON
Chef David Jones

Yield: 6 Servings		**Method:** Roasting/Smoking
Wild boar, saddle	3 kg	6-1/2 lb.
Brine for Smoking Wild Game (recipe follows)		
Hickory, apple and maple wood chips, for smoking		
Sauce:		
Dried cranberries	75 g	2-1/2 oz.
Apple cider	125 mL	4 fl. oz.
Shallots, minced	100 g	3 whole
Cider vinegar	25 mL	5 tsp.
White wine, dry	125 mL	4 fl. oz.
Maple syrup	50 mL	3 Tbsp.
Veal stock	500 mL	16 fl. oz.
Lemon juice, fresh	10 mL	2 tsp.

RECIPE 16.11

Approximate values per serving:

Calories	423
Total fat	15 g
Saturated fat	2.5 g
Cholesterol	95 mg
Sodium	418 mg
Total carbohydrates	39 g
Protein	33 g

Caramelized Ginger Vinaigrette— Approximate values per 40 mL serving:

Calories	94
Total fat	0.1 g
Saturated fat	0 g
Cholesterol	0 mg
Sodium	52 mg
Total carbohydrates	23 g
Protein	0.2 g

David Jones

David was born in Wales and trained in Canada. His career has been varied, from running hotel kitchens to developing a property in a Cree community on the shores of James Bay, to providing training to the U.S. Navy in Hong Kong, Hawaii and California. David has instructed in the culinary programs at Humber College and is currently with the Toronto District School Board.

Dijon mustard	3 mL	1/2 tsp.
Unsalted butter	30 g	1 oz.
Salt and freshly ground black pepper	TT	TT

1. Marinate the refrigerated boar in the brine for at least 2 days prior to smoking.

2. Soak the wood chips in water for at least 30 minutes prior to using. Drain well.

3. Hot-smoke the boar for 1.5–2 hours, replenishing the wood as required.

4. To prepare the sauce, soak the cranberries in cider for 45 minutes. Sweat shallots in a small amount of butter.

5. Add all the remaining ingredients except mustard, butter and salt and pepper.

6. Reduce sauce to the desired consistency, then add mustard.

7. Monter au beurre. Adjust seasoning with salt and pepper.

8. Allow boar to rest a few moments before slicing; serve with the sauce.

NOTE: The basic brine can be supplemented with some crushed juniper berries, cloves and orange zest.

RECIPE 16.12

Approximate values per serving:

Calories	499
Total fat	15 g
Saturated fat	5.8 g
Cholesterol	185 mg
Sodium	1860 mg
Total carbohydrates	27 g
Protein	64 g

BRINE FOR SMOKING WILD GAME

Yield: 1.5 L (48 fl. oz.)

Cider vinegar	500 mL	16 fl. oz.
Water	1 L	1 qt.
Salt, non-iodized	250 g	8 oz.
Black peppercorns, cracked	10 g	1 Tbsp.
Brown sugar	100 g	3 oz.
Mace	0.75 g	1/2 tsp.
Parsley, chopped	3 g	1 tsp.
Onions, chopped	700 g	2 medium
Carrot, sliced	75 g	1 medium
Red wine, dry	250 mL	8 fl. oz.

1. Bring all ingredients except wine to a boil. Simmer for 30 minutes.

2. Strain and add wine. Chill.

◆◆◆
SMOKING WILD GAME

1. Pour brine over meat and refrigerate for 3–4 days, stirring often.

2. Remove meat from marinade and air dry.

3. Smoke meat for 2–5 hours, depending on thickness of meat.

4. Finish meat on broiler or in oven.

WEBLINKS

Consumer Information—Ontario Pork
  www.porkpeople.com/storage.html

Canada Pork International
  www.cfta.ca/cpi/cpi.html

Canadian Pork Council: Pork Nutrition
  www.cpc-ccp.com/nutrition.html

U.S. National Pork Producers Council
  www.nppc.org

CHAPTER 17 POULTRY

*P*oultry is the collective term for domesticated birds bred for eating. They include chickens, ducks, geese, guineas, pigeons and turkeys. (Game birds such as pheasant, quail and partridge are described in Chapter 18, Game.) Poultry is generally the least expensive and most versatile of all main dish foods. It can be cooked by almost any method and its mild flavour goes well with a wide variety of sauces and accompaniments.

In this chapter we discuss the different kinds and classes of poultry and how to choose those that best suit your needs. You will learn how to store poultry properly to prevent food-borne illnesses and spoilage; how to process birds to produce the specific cuts you need and how to apply a variety of cooking methods properly.

Many of the cooking methods discussed here have been applied previously to meats. Although there are similarities with these methods, there are also many distinct differences. As you study this chapter, review the corresponding cooking methods for meats and note the similarities and differences.

MUSCLE COMPOSITION

The muscle tissue of poultry is similar to that of mammals in that it contains approximately 72% water, 20% protein, 7% fat and 1% minerals; it consists of bundles of muscle cells or fibres held together by connective tissue. Unlike red meat, poultry does not contain the intramuscular fat known as marbling. Instead, a bird stores fat in its skin, abdominal cavity and the fat pad near its tail. Poultry fat is softer and has a lower melting point than other animal fats. It is easily rendered during cooking.

As with red meats, poultry muscles that are used more often tend to be tougher than those used less frequently. Also, the muscles of an older bird

FREE-RANGE CHICKENS

Chicken has become increasingly popular in recent years, in part because it is inexpensive, versatile and considered healthier than meat. Indeed, more than 10 million chickens are processed weekly in this country. To meet an ever-increasing demand, chickens are raised indoors in huge chicken houses that may contain as many as 20,000 birds. They are fed a specially formulated mixture composed primarily of corn and soybean meal. Animal protein, vitamins, minerals and small amounts of antibiotics are added to produce quick-growing, healthy birds.

Many consumers feel that chickens raised this way do not have the flavour of chickens

that are allowed to move freely and forage for food. Some consumers are concerned about the residual effects of the vitamins, minerals and antibiotics added to the chicken feed. To meet the demand for chickens raised the "old-fashioned way," some farmers raise (and many fine establishments offer) free-range chickens.

Although the CFIA has not standardized regulations for free-range chicken, generally the term *free-range* applies to birds that are allowed unlimited access to the area outside the chicken house. Often they are raised without antibiotics, fed a vegetarian diet (no animal fat or byproducts), processed without the use of preservatives

and raised under more humane growing methods than conventionally grown birds. Most free-range chickens are marketed at 9–10 weeks old and weigh 2 to 2.5 kg (4-1/2 to 5 lb.)—considerably more mature and heavier than conventional broilers. They are generally sold with heads and feet intact and are more expensive than conventionally raised chickens.

Many consumers (in both the dining room and the kitchen) feel that free-range chicken is superior in flavour and quality. Others find no perceptible differences. As a consumer you will have to decide whether any difference is worth the added expense.

tend to be tougher than those of a younger one. Because the majority of poultry is marketed at a young age, however, it is generally very tender.

The breast and wing flesh of chickens and turkeys is lighter in colour than the flesh of their thighs and legs. This colour difference is due to a higher concentration of the protein myoglobin in the thigh and leg muscles. Myoglobin is the protein that stores oxygen for the muscle tissues to use. More active muscles require more myoglobin and tend to be darker than less active ones. Because chickens and turkeys generally do not fly, their breast and wing muscles contain little myoglobin and are therefore a light colour. Birds that do fly have only dark meat. Dark meat also contains more fat and connective tissue than light meat, and its cooking time is longer.

Skin colour may vary from white to golden yellow, depending on what the bird was fed. Such colour differences are not an indication of overall quality.

Cornish Game Hen

IDENTIFYING POULTRY

Agriculture Canada recognizes nine categories or **kinds** of birds: chicken, duck, goose, pheasant, quail, ostrich, guinea, pigeon and turkey. Each poultry kind is divided into **classes** based predominantly on the bird's age and tenderness. The sex of young birds is not significant for culinary purposes. It does matter, however, with older birds: Older male birds are tough and stringy and have less flavour than older female birds. Tables 17.1 through 17.6 list identifying characteristics and suggested cooking methods for each of the various kinds and classes of poultry.

Chicken Broiler/ Fryer

Chicken

Chicken (Fr. *poulet*) is the most popular and widely eaten poultry in the world. It contains both light and dark meat and has relatively little fat. A young, tender chicken can be cooked by almost any method; an older bird is best stewed or braised. Chicken is extremely versatile and may be flavoured, stuffed, basted or garnished with almost anything. Chicken is inexpensive and readily available, fresh or frozen, in a variety of forms.

Capon

TABLE 17.1   CHICKEN CLASSES

Class	Description	Age	Weight	Cooking Method
Game hen	Young or immature progeny of Cornish chickens or of a Cornish chicken and a White Rock chicken; very flavourful	5–6 weeks	300–450 g (8 oz.–1 lb.)	Split and broil or grill; roast
Broiler/fryer	Young with soft, smooth-textured skin; relatively lean; flexible breastbone	6–8 weeks	up to 2 kg (4 lb.)	Any cooking method; very versatile
Roaster	Young with tender meat and smooth-textured skin; breastbone is less flexible than broiler's	8–9 weeks	2 kg (4 lb.) and over	Any cooking method
Capon	Surgically castrated male; tender meat with soft, smooth-textured skin; bred for well-flavoured meat; contains a high proportion of light to dark meat and a relatively high fat content	4–6 months	2–4 kg (6–10 lb.)	Roast
Fowl	Mature female; flavourful but less tender meat; nonflexible breastbone	Over 7 months	1 kg (2 lb.) and over	Stew or braise

TABLE 17.2   DUCK CLASSES

Class	Description	Age	Weight	Cooking Method
Young	Young bird with tender meat; rich flavour; easily dented windpipe	16 weeks or less	2–2.5 kg (4–6 lb.)	Roast
Mature	Old bird with tough flesh; hard bill and windpipe	6 months or older	2–2.5 kg (4–6 lb.)	Braise

Young Duckling

Duck

The duck (Fr. *canard*) used most often in commercial food service operations is a young duckling. It contains only dark meat and large amounts of fat. In order to make the fatty skin palatable, it is important to render as much fat as possible. Duck has a high percentage of bone and fat to meat; for example, a 2-kg (4-lb.) duck will serve only two people, while a 2-kg (4-lb.) roasting chicken will serve four people.

Goose

A goose (Fr. *oie*) contains only dark meat and has very fatty skin. It is usually roasted at high temperatures to render the fat. Roasted goose is popular at holidays and is often served with an acidic fruit-based sauce to offset the fattiness.

Young Goose

TABLE 17.3   GOOSE CLASSES

Class	Description	Age	Weight	Cooking Method
Young	Rich, tender dark meat with large amounts of fat; easily dented windpipe	6 months or less	2.5–5.5 kg (6–12 lb.)	Roast at high temperature to start, accompany with acidic sauces
Mature	Tough flesh and hard windpipe	Over 6 months	4.5–7 kg (10–16 lb.)	Braise or stew

Young Guinea

Guinea

A guinea or guinea fowl (Fr. *pintade*) is the domesticated descendant of a game bird. It has both light and dark meat and a flavour similar to pheasant. Guinea is tender enough to sauté. Because it contains little fat, a guinea is usually barded prior to roasting. Guinea, which is relatively expensive, is not as popular here as it is in Europe.

TABLE 17.4 GUINEA CLASSES

Class	Description	Age	Weight	Cooking Method
Young	Tender meat; flexible breastbone	3 months	0.3–0.7 kg (12 oz.–1 lb. 8 oz.)	Bard and roast; sauté
Mature	Tough flesh; hard breastbone	Over 3 months	0.5–1 kg (1–2 lb.)	Braise or stew

TABLE 17.5 PIGEON CLASSES

Class	Description	Age	Weight	Cooking Method
Squab	Immature pigeon; very tender, dark flesh and a small amount of fat	4 weeks	0.3–0.7 kg (12 oz.–1 lb. 8 oz.)	Broil, roast or sauté
Pigeon	Mature bird; coarse skin and tough flesh	Over 4 weeks	0.5–1 kg (1–2 lb.)	Braise or stew

Pigeon

The young pigeon (Fr. *pigeon*) used in commercial food service operations is referred to as squab. Its meat is dark, tender and well suited for broiling, sautéing or roasting. Squab has very little fat and benefits from barding.

Squab

Turkey

Turkey

Turkey (Fr. *dinde*) is the second most popular poultry kind in Canada. It has both light and dark meat and a relatively small amount of fat. Younger turkey is economical and can be prepared in almost any manner.

TABLE 17.6 TURKEY CLASSES

Class	Age	Weight	Cooking Method
Young	24 weeks	7–12 kg (16–30 lb.) and under	Roast or cut into cutlets and sauté or pan–fry
Mature	24+ weeks	12+ kg (30+ lb.)	Roast or stew

Livers, Gizzards, Hearts and Necks

Livers, gizzards, hearts and necks are commonly referred to as **giblets**. Although most poultry kinds are sold with giblets, chickens can be purchased with or without them, depending on your needs.

Giblets can be used in a variety of ways. Gizzards (a bird's second stomach), hearts and necks are most often used to make giblet gravy or to fortify a stock. Necks are very flavourful and can be added to stocks for flavour and richness. Livers are not added to stocks, however, because of their strong flavour.

Chicken livers are often used in pâtés, sautéed or broiled with bacon and served as an appetizer.

Foie Gras

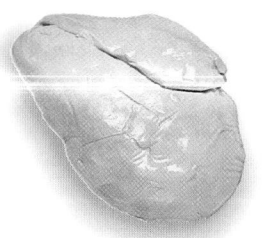

Duck Foie Gras

Foie gras is the enlarged liver of a duck or goose. Considered a delicacy since Roman times, it is now produced in many parts of the world. Foie gras is produced by methodically fattening the birds by force-feeding them specially prepared corn while limiting their activity. Fresh foie gras consists of two lobes that must be separated, split and deveined. Good foie gras will be smooth, round and putty-coloured. It should not be yellow or grainy. Goose foie gras is lighter in colour and more delicate in flavour than that of duck. Duck foie gras has a deeper, winey flavour and is far more common than goose foie gras. Fresh foie gras can be grilled, roasted, sautéed or made into pâtés or terrines. No matter which cooking method is used, care must be taken not to overcook the liver. Foie gras is so high in fat that overcooking will result in the liver actually melting away. Most foie gras used in this country is pasteurized or canned. Canned foie gras may consist of solid liver or small pieces of liver compacted to form a block. Canned foie gras mousse is also available. Truffles are a natural accompaniment to foie gras and are used in many tinned preparations. Fresh foie gras is available from Quebec.

Ratites

Ratites are a family of flightless, bird-like animals with small wings and flat breastbones. They include the ostrich, emu and rhea. These exotic animals are farm raised and the meat is commercially available, but much of their value is in their hides, which are tanned for leather. Butchering them is specialized due to their unique bone and muscle structure.

Ratite meat, which is classified as red meat, is a dark cherry-red colour with a flavour similar to beef, but a little sweeter. Low in fat and calories, it is considered one of the healthiest red meats to eat. Most ratite meat is from animals slaughtered at 10–13 months of age. It is generally cut from the back, which contains a cut called tenderloin, the thigh (also known as the fan) and the leg. Market forms include steaks, filets, medallions, roasts, émincé, cubes or ground. A product called FIBREMIX is used by some processors to prepare consistently sized steaks.

Ratite meat is often prepared like veal or wild game. The more tender cuts can be marinated and then cooked by dry-heat cooking methods, especially broiling, grilling, pan-frying and sautéing. Because this meat has little fat, care

TABLE 17.7   NUTRITIONAL VALUES OF POULTRY

For 28 g (1 oz.) uncooked poultry with skin	Kcal	Protein (g)	Total fat (g)	Saturated fat (g)	Cholesterol (mg)	Sodium (mg)
Chicken, breast	49	5.9	2.6	0.8	18	18
Chicken, thigh	60	4.9	4.3	1.2	24	22
Duck	115	3.3	11.2	3.7	22	18
Goose	105	4.5	9.5	2.8	23	21
Squab	83	5.2	6.7	2.4	mq*	mq*
Turkey, breast	45	6.2	2.0	0.5	18	17
Turkey, leg	41	5.5	1.9	0.6	20	21

The Corinne T. Netzer Encyclopedia of Food Values, 1992
*mq = measurable quantity, but data are unavailable

must be taken to avoid overcooking; these products are usually served rare to medium. Tougher cuts, such as those from the leg, are best ground or prepared with combination cooking methods. The meat lends itself well to charcuterie preparations and makes a fine dry cured and smoked product.

NUTRITION

Poultry is an economical source of high-quality protein. Poultry's nutritional value is similar to other meats, except that skinless chicken and turkey breast meat is lower in fat and higher in niacin than other lean meats. (See Table 17.7.) Generally, dark meat contains more niacin and riboflavin than white meat.

◆◆◆

The Ostrich News in 1995 reported the following nutritional values per 28 g (1 oz.):

	Ostrich	Emu
Protein	6.3 g	6.6 g
Calories	28.0 g	30.0 g
Cholesterol	18.1 mg	16.3 mg
Fat	0.28 g	0.48 g
Saturated fat	0.07 g	0.17 g
Sodium	18.0 mg	17.0 mg
Calcium	0.5 mg	0.3 mg
Iron	2.3 mg	1.4 mg

INSPECTION AND GRADING OF POULTRY

Inspection

All poultry produced for public consumption in Canada is subject to health inspection. Inspections ensure that products are processed under strict sanitary guidelines and are wholesome and fit for human consumption. Inspections do not indicate a product's quality or tenderness.

Grading

Grading poultry is voluntary. Birds are graded according to their overall quality with the grade (Canada A, B, utility or C) shown on the packaging. (See Figures 17.1 and 17.2.)

According to Agriculture Canada, Grade A poultry is free from deformities, with thick flesh and a well-developed fat layer; it is free of pinfeathers, cuts or tears and broken bones; the carcass is free from discolouration and, if it is frozen, free from defects that occur during handling or storage. Nearly all poultry used in wholesale and retail outlets is Grade A or utility. Grade B and C birds are used primarily for processed poultry products. In addition, poultry may be sold as "ungraded."

FIGURE 17.1 *Grade Stamp for Utility Grade*

FIGURE 17.2 *Grade Stamp for Canada Grade A Poultry*

Quality grades have no bearing on the product's tenderness or flavour. A bird's tenderness is usually indicated by its class (for example, a "young turkey" is younger and more tender than a yearling). Its grade (Canada A, B, utility or C) within each class is determined by its overall quality.

PURCHASING AND STORING POULTRY

Purchasing Poultry

Poultry can be purchased in many forms: fresh or frozen, whole or cut up, bone-in or boneless, portion controlled (PC), individually quick frozen (IQF), tumbled or ground. Chicken and turkey are also widely used in prepared and convenience items and are available fully cooked and vacuum-wrapped or boned and canned. Although purchasing poultry in a ready-to-use form is convenient, it is not always necessary: Poultry products are easy to fabricate and portion. Whole fresh poultry is also less expensive than precut or frozen products.

As with meats, you should consider your menu, labour costs, storage facilities and employee skills when deciding whether to purchase whole fresh poultry or some other form.

Storing Poultry

Poultry is highly perishable and particularly susceptible to contamination by salmonella bacteria. It is critical that poultry be stored at the correct temperatures.

Fresh chickens and other small birds can be stored on ice or at 0–2°C (32–34°F) for up to two days; larger birds can be stored up to four days at these temperatures. Frozen poultry should be kept at –18°C (0°F) or below (the colder the better) and can be held for up to six months. It should be thawed gradually under refrigeration, allowing two days for chickens and up to four days for larger birds. Never attempt to cook poultry that is still partially frozen: It will be impossible to cook the product evenly and the areas that were still frozen may not reach the temperatures necessary to destroy harmful bacteria. Never partially cook poultry one day and finish cooking it later: Bacteria are more likely to grow under such conditions and result in food poisoning. Poultry should be rinsed in clear, running water before processing.

Sanitation and Cross-Contamination

Review the information in Chapter 2, Food Safety and Sanitation, before butchering any poultry. Be sure that all work surfaces, cutting boards, knives, hands and other equipment used to prepare poultry products are clean and sanitary. Be careful that juices and trimmings from poultry do not come in contact with other foods. Anything coming in contact with raw poultry should be cleaned and sanitized with a chlorine solution of 200 ppm before it comes in contact with any other food. Cooked foods should never be placed in containers that were used to hold the raw product. Kitchen towels that are used to handle poultry or clean up after butchering should be sanitized before being reused to prevent cross-contamination.

FABRICATING PROCEDURES

Poultry is easier to fabricate than meats and is often processed on-site. You should be able to perform the following commonly encountered procedures.

Because the different kinds of poultry are similar in structure, these procedures apply to a variety of birds.

Basic Procedure for Cutting a Bird in Half

Often the first step in preparing poultry is to cut the bird in half. Broiler and fryer chickens are often split to make two portions. This procedure removes the backbone and breast bone (also known as the keel bone) for a neat finished product.

1. Square up the bird by placing it on its back and pressing on the legs and breast to create a more uniform appearance.

2. Place the bird on its breast and hold the tail tightly with the thumb and forefinger of one hand. Using a rigid boning knife and in a single swift movement, cut alongside the backbone from the bird's tail to neck.

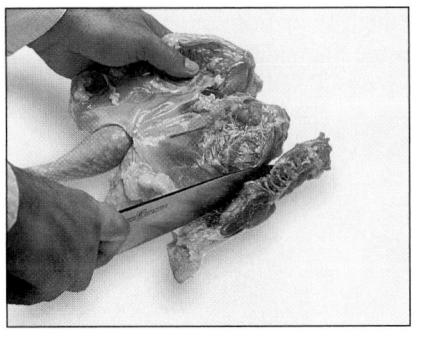

3. Lay the bird flat on the cutting board and remove the backbone by cutting through the ribs connecting it to the breast.

4. Bend the bird back, breaking the breast bone free.

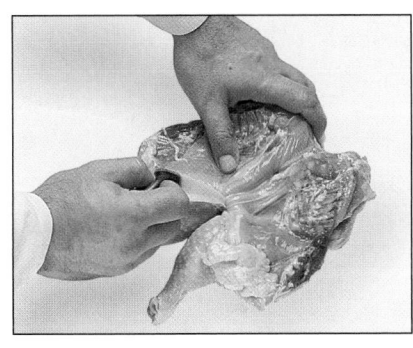

5. Run your fingers along the bone to separate the breast meat from it; pull the bone completely free. Be sure to remove the flexible cartilage completely.

6. Cut through the skin to separate the bird into two halves. The halves are ready to be cooked; for a more attractive presentation, follow steps 7 and 8.

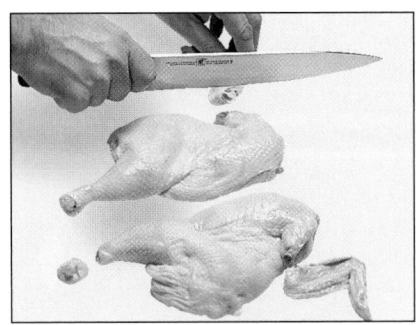

7. Trim off the wing tips and the ends of the leg bone.

8. Make a slit in the skin below the leg and tuck the leg bone into the slit.

Basic Procedure for Cutting a Bird into Pieces

This is one of the most common butchering procedures. It is also very simple once you understand the bird's structure and are able to find each of its joints.

1. Remove the leg by pulling the leg and thigh away from the breast and cutting through the skin and flesh towards the thigh joint.

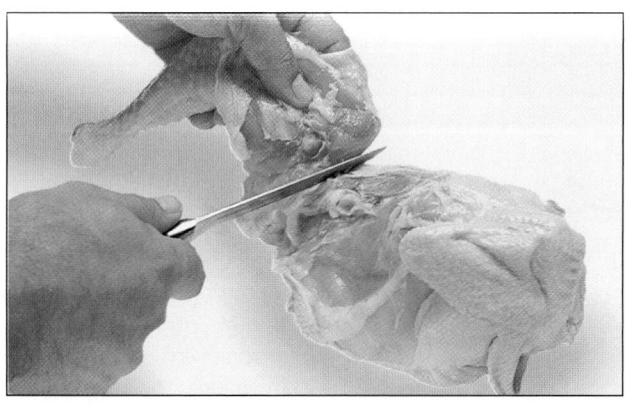

2. Cut down to the thigh joint, twist the leg to break the joint and cut the thigh and leg from the carcass. Be careful to trim around the oyster meat (the tender morsel of meat located next to the backbone); leave it attached to the thigh. Repeat with the other leg.

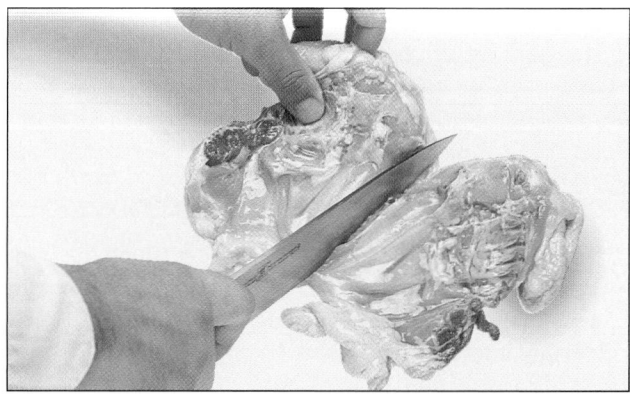

3. To split the breast, follow steps 2 through 6 for cutting a bird in half. Cut the breast into two halves.

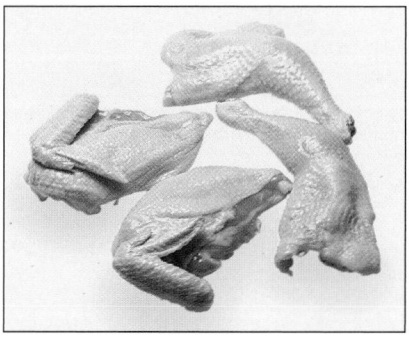

4. The bird is now cut into four pieces.

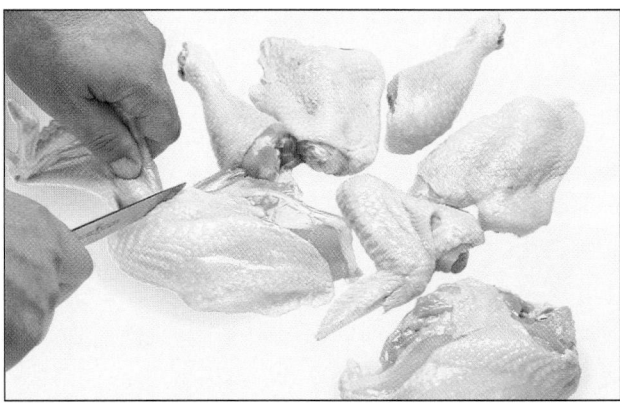

5. To cut the bird into six pieces, separate the thigh from the leg by making a cut guided by the line of fat on the inside of the thigh and leg.

6. To cut the bird into eight pieces, separate the wing from the breast by cutting through the joint, or split the breast, leaving a portion of the breast meat attached to the wing.

Basic Procedure for Preparing a Boneless Breast

A boneless chicken breast is one of the most versatile and popular poultry cuts. It can be broiled, grilled, baked, sautéed, pan-fried or poached. Boneless turkey breast can be roasted or sliced and sautéed in a manner similar to veal. The skin can be removed or left intact.

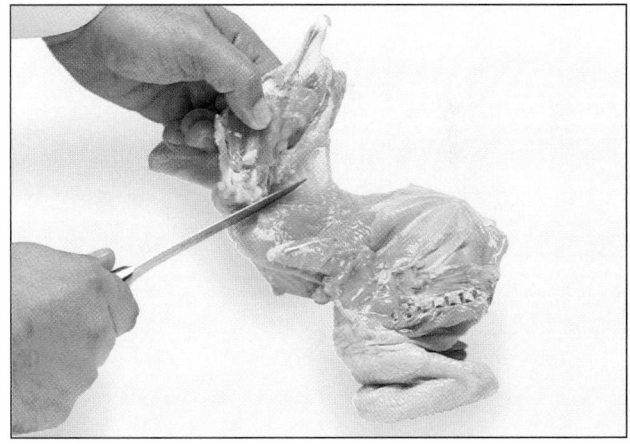

1. Remove the keel bone from the bone-in breast, following steps 4, 5 and 6 for cutting a bird in half.

2. With the chicken breast lying skin side down, separate the rib bones, wing and wishbone from the breast. Leave the two tender pieces of meat known as the tenderloins attached to the breast. Repeat the procedure on the other side, being sure to remove the small wishbone pieces from the front of the breast.

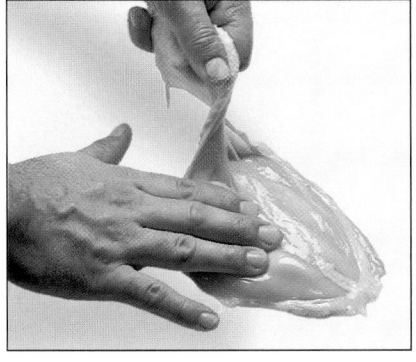

3. The skin may be left intact or removed to produce a skinless boneless breast, which can then be split into single breasts.

Basic Procedure for Preparing a Suprême or Frenched Breast

A chicken suprême or frenched breast is half of a boneless chicken breast with the first wing bone attached. The tip of the wing bone is removed, yielding a neat and attractive portion that can be prepared by a variety of cooking methods. The skin can be left on or removed.

1. Remove the legs from a chicken following steps 1 and 2 for cutting a bird into pieces. Place the bird on its back. Locate the wishbone, trim around it and remove it.

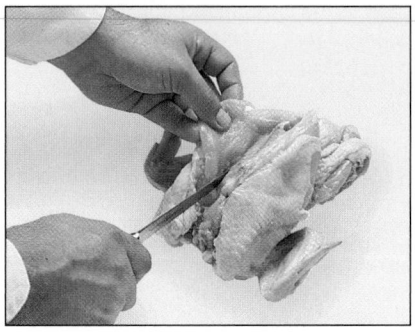

2. Cut along one side of the breast bone, separating the meat from the bone.

3. Following the natural curvature of the ribs, continue cutting to remove the meat from the bones.

4. When you reach the wing joint, cut through the joint, keeping the wing attached to the breast portion. Cut the breast free from the carcass.

5. Make a cut on the back of the joint between the first and second wing bones.

6. Break the joint and pull the meat and skin back to expose a clean bone. Trim the wing bone.

7. The suprême can be prepared skin-on or skinless.

Basic Procedure for Boning a Chicken Leg

Chicken breasts are usually more popular than legs and thighs. There are, however, uses for boneless, skinless leg and thigh meat; they can be stuffed for ballotines or cut for stir-fry or cutlets, for example.

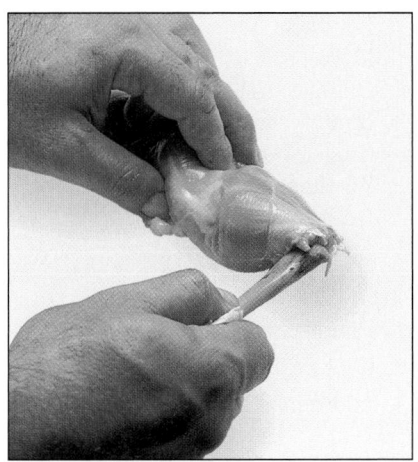

1. Carefully cut through the skin, meat and tendons at the base of the leg. Be sure to cut through completely to the bone.

2. Pull the skin off the leg with your hands, then break the joint between the leg and thigh. Twist and pull out the leg bone.

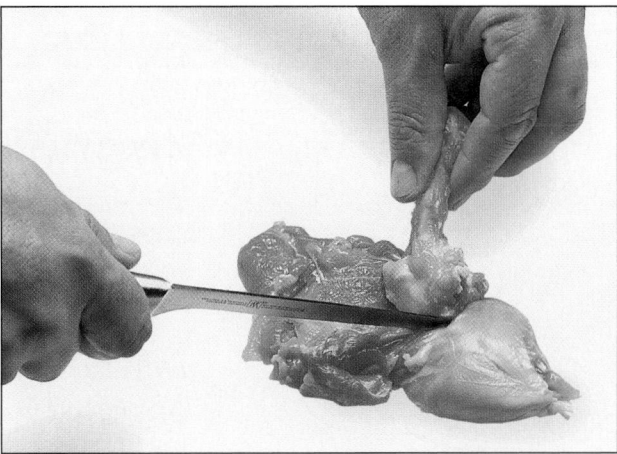

3. Working from the inside of the thigh, cut along both sides of the thigh bone, separating it from the meat.

4. Cut around the cartilage at the joint between the leg and thigh and remove the thigh bone and cartilage.

MARINATING POULTRY

Most poultry is quite mild in flavour, so a marinade is often used to add flavour and moisture, especially to poultry that will be broiled or grilled. Barbecued chicken is one of the simplest and best-known forms of marinated poultry. Poultry is often marinated in a mixture of white wine or lemon juice, oil, pepper, herbs and spices, such as that given in Recipe 17.1 or buttermilk.

Applying the Basics

APPLE CITRUS MARINADE

Yield: 2.5 L (2–1/2 qt.)

Apple juice	1 L	1 qt.
Brown sugar	225 g	1/2 lb.
Kosher salt	300 g	11 oz.
Oranges, sliced	12	12
Lemon, sliced	1	1
Ginger, fresh, sliced	50 g	2 oz.
Whole cloves	8	8
Bay leaves	3	3
Garlic, chopped	15 g	1/2 oz.
Water, cold	1.5 L	1-1/2 qt.

1. Dissolve sugar and salt in apple juice by boiling. Skim any foam.

2. Cool mixture.

3. Add remaining ingredients.

Poultry absorbs flavours quickly, so if pieces are left too long in an acidic marinade they may take on undesirable flavours. Two hours is often sufficient, with smaller pieces requiring less time in the marinade than larger ones.

If the marinade contains oil, drain it well to avoid flare-up when the item is placed on the broiler or grill. Use a clean paper towel to wipe excess moisture from the poultry's surface so that it browns more easily. The marinade can be used to baste the item during cooking, but leftover marinade should not be served uncooked or reused because of the danger of bacterial contamination from the raw poultry.

APPLYING VARIOUS COOKING METHODS

The principles of cooking discussed in Chapter 9 and applied to meats in earlier chapters also apply to poultry. Dry-heat methods are appropriate for young, tender birds. Moist-heat methods should be used with older, less-tender products.

Dry-Heat Cooking Methods

Cooking poultry with dry-heat methods—broiling and grilling, roasting, sautéing, pan-frying and deep-fat frying—presents some unique challenges. Large birds such as turkeys benefit from low-heat cooking but are better when served with the crispy skin gained through higher temperatures. Duck and goose skin contains a great deal of fat that must be rendered during the cooking process. Small birds such as squab must be cooked at sufficiently high temperatures to crisp their skins but can be easily overcooked. Boneless chicken breasts, particularly flavourful and popular when broiled or grilled, are easily overcooked and become dry because they do not contain bones to help retain moisture during cooking. Proper application of the following dry-heat cooking methods will help meet these challenges and ensure a good-quality finished product.

Broiling and Grilling

Broiled and grilled poultry should have a well-browned surface and can show crosshatched grill marks. It should be moist, tender and juicy throughout. It may be seasoned to enhance its natural flavours or marinated or basted with any number of flavoured butters or sauces.

Selecting Poultry to Broil or Grill

Smaller birds such as Cornish hens, chickens and squab are especially well suited for broiling or grilling. Whole birds should be split or cut into smaller pieces before cooking; their joints may be broken so that they lie flat. Quail and other small birds can be skewered before being broiled to help them cook evenly and retain their shape. Be especially careful when cooking breast portions or boneless pieces: The direct heat of the broiler or grill can overcook the item very quickly.

Seasoning Poultry to Be Broiled or Grilled

Poultry is fairly neutral in flavour and responds well to marinating. Poultry may also be basted periodically during the cooking process with flavoured butter, oil or barbecue sauce. At the very least, broiled or grilled poultry should be well seasoned with salt and pepper just before cooking.

Determining Doneness

With the exception of duck breasts and squab, which are sometimes left pink, broiled or grilled poultry is always cooked well done. This makes the poultry particularly susceptible to becoming dry and tough because it contains little fat and is cooked at very high temperatures. Particular care must be taken to ensure that the item does not become overcooked.

Four methods are used to determine the doneness of broiled or grilled poultry:

1. *Touch*—When the item is done it will have a firm texture, resist pressure and spring back quickly when pressed with tongs.
2. *Temperature*—Use an instant-read thermometer to determine the item's internal temperature. This may be difficult, however, because of the item's size and the heat from the broiler or grill. Insert the thermometer in the thickest part of the item away from any bones. It should read 74–77°C (165–170°F) at the coolest point. The higher temperature (77°C/170°F) is recommended for safety; if the product is large and stuffed, the temperature should be 85°C (185°F) to ensure the stuffing is thoroughly cooked.
3. *Looseness of the joints*—When bone-in poultry is done, the leg will begin to move freely in its socket.
4. *Colour of the juices*—Poultry is done when its juices run clear or show just a trace of pink. This degree of doneness is known in French as **à point**.

Accompaniments to Broiled and Grilled Poultry

If the item was basted with a herb butter it can be served with additional butter; if the item was basted with barbecue sauce, it should be served with the same sauce. Be careful, however, that any marinade or sauce that came in contact with the raw poultry is not served unless it is cooked thoroughly to destroy harmful bacteria. Additional sauce suggestions are found in Table 10.5.

Broiled or grilled poultry is very versatile and goes well with almost any side dish. Seasoned and grilled vegetables are a natural accompaniment, and deep-fat-fried potatoes are commonly served.

Basic Procedure for Broiling or Grilling Poultry

As with meats, broiled or grilled poultry can be prepared by placing it directly on the grate. Poultry is also often broiled using a rotisserie.

1. Heat the broiler or grill.
2. Use a wire brush to remove any charred or burnt particles that may be stuck to the broiler or grill grate. The grate can be wiped with a lightly oiled towel to remove any remaining particles and help season it.

3. Prepare the item to be broiled or grilled by marinating or seasoning as desired; it may be brushed lightly with oil to keep it from sticking to the grate.

4. Place the item on the grate, presentation side (skin side) down. Following the example in Chapter 9, turn the item to produce the attractive crosshatch marks associated with broiling or grilling. Baste the item often. Use tongs to turn or flip the item without piercing the surface so that valuable juices do not escape.

5. Develop the proper surface colour while cooking the item until it is done *à point*. To do so, adjust the position of the item on the broiler or grill or adjust the distance between the grate and heat source. Large pieces and bone-in pieces that are difficult to cook completely on the broiler or grill can be finished in the oven.

A commonly used procedure to cook a large volume of poultry is to place the seasoned items in a broiler pan or other shallow pan and then place the pan directly under the broiler. Baste the items periodically, turning them once when they are halfway done. Items begun this way can be easily finished by transferring the entire pan to the oven.

1. Marinate the squab in apple citrus marinade.

2. Dry the squab with paper towels.

3. Brush the squab with the melted basil butter.

4. Grill the squab.

5. Serve the squab with a slice of basil butter.

Applying the Basics

RECIPE 17.2

GRILLED SQUAB WITH BASIL BUTTER

Yield: 4 Servings

Squab, whole	4	4
Fresh basil leaves	16	16
Apple Citrus Marinade (Recipe 17.1)	500 mL	16 fl. oz.
Salt and pepper	TT	TT
Basil butter	160 g	6 oz.

1. Remove the backbone and breast bone from each squab. The birds will lie flat and remain in one piece.

2. Make a slit below each leg and tuck the leg bone into the slit.

3. Carefully slide two basil leaves under the skin over each breast to cover the meat.

4. Marinate the squab in the apple citrus marinade for 1–2 hours.

5. Heat and prepare the grill.

6. Remove the squab from the marinade and pat dry with paper towelling. Season with salt and pepper.

7. Melt approximately 120 g (4 oz.) of the basil butter, leaving enough for eight thin slices to be served with the finished dish.

8. Brush the squab with basil butter and place it skin side down on the grill. Grill the squab, turning once and basting periodically with the melted basil butter. Finish in the oven if necessary.

9. Serve the squab with a slice of basil butter melting over each breast.

RECIPE 17.2

Approximate values per serving:

Calories	1554
Total fat	130 g
Saturated fat	52 g
Cholesterol	490 mg
Sodium	3318 mg
Total carbohydrates	12 g
Protein	84 g

Roasting

Properly roasted (or baked) poultry is attractively browned on the surface and tender and juicy throughout. Proper cooking temperatures ensure a crisp exterior and juicy interior. Most roasted poultry is cooked until the juices run clear. Squab and duck breasts are an exception: They are often served medium rare or pink.

Selecting Poultry to Roast

Almost every kind of poultry is suitable for roasting, but younger birds produce a more tender finished product. Because of variations in fat content, different kinds of poultry require different roasting temperatures and procedures.

Basic Procedure for Trussing Poultry

Trussing is tying a bird into a more compact shape with string or butcher's twine. This allows the bird to cook more evenly, helps the bird retain moisture and improves the appearance of the finished product. There are many methods for trussing poultry, some of which require a special tool called a trussing needle. Here we show a simple method using butcher's twine.

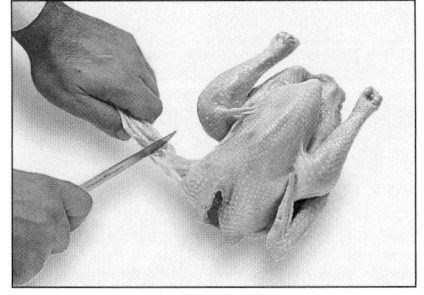

1. Square up the bird by pressing it firmly with both hands. Tuck the first joint of the wing behind the back or trim off the first and second joints as shown.

2. Cut a piece of butcher's twine approximately three times the bird's length. With the breast up and the neck towards you, pass the twine under the bird approximately 2.5 cm (1 inch) in front of the tail.

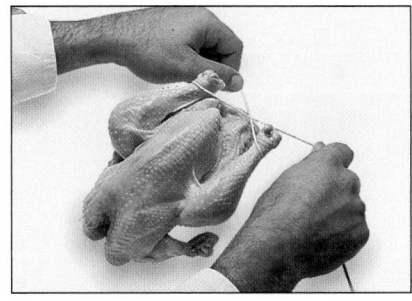

3. Bring the twine up around the legs and cross the ends, creating an X between the legs. Pass the ends of the twine below the legs.

4. Pull the ends of the twine tightly across the leg and thigh joint and across the wing if the first and second joint were trimmed off or just above the wings if they are intact.

5. Pull the string tight and tie it securely just above the neck.

6. Two examples of properly trussed birds: one with the wings intact and one with the first and second wing joints removed.

Seasoning Poultry to Be Roasted

Although the mild flavour of most poultry is enhanced by a wide variety of herbs and spices, roasted poultry is often only lightly seasoned with salt and pepper. Poultry that is roasted at high temperatures should never be seasoned with herbs on its surface because the high cooking temperatures will burn them. If herbs or additional spices are used they should be stuffed into the cavity. A mirepoix or a bouquet garni may also be added to the cavity for additional flavour. The cavities of dark-meated birds such as ducks and geese are often stuffed with fresh or dried fruits.

Cooking Temperatures

Small birds such as squab and Cornish game hens should be roasted at the relatively high temperatures of 190–200°C (375–400°F). These temperatures help produce crisp, well-coloured skins without overcooking the flesh. Chickens are best roasted at temperatures between 180°C and 190°C (350°F and 375°F). This temperature range allows the skin to crisp and the flesh to cook without causing the bird to stew in its own juices. Large birds such as capons and turkeys are started at high temperatures of 200–220°C (400–425°F) to brown the skin, then finished at lower temperatures of 135–160°C (275–325°F) to promote even cooking and produce a moister product. Ducks and geese, which are very high in fat, must be roasted at the high temperatures of 190–220°C (375–425°F) to render as much fat from the skin as possible. Duck and goose skin is often pricked before roasting so the rendered fat can escape; this helps to create crispy skin.

Barding Poultry to Be Roasted

Guineas, squabs or any skinless birds without an adequate fat covering to protect them from drying out during roasting can be barded. Bard the bird by covering its entire surface with thin slices of pork backfat, securing them with butcher's twine. See page 272.

Basting Roasted Poultry

With the exception of fatty birds such as ducks and geese, all poultry items should be basted while they roast to help retain moisture. To baste a bird, spoon or ladle the fat that collects in the bottom of the roasting pan over the bird at 15-to-20-minute intervals. Lean birds that are not barded will not produce enough fat for basting and may be brushed with butter in the same manner.

Determining Doneness

Four methods are used to determine the doneness of roasted poultry. It is best to use a combination of these methods.

1. *Temperature*—Test the internal temperature of the bird with an instant-read thermometer. The thermometer should be inserted in the bird's thigh, which is the last part to become fully cooked. It should not touch the bone and should read a minimum of 74°C (165°F). To ensure a safer product, it is recommended that poultry be cooked to 77°C (170°F) and as high as 85°C (185°F) for stuffed birds. This method works best with large birds such as capons and turkeys. Large birds are subject to some degree of carryover cooking. This is not as much of a concern with poultry as it is with meat because large birds are always cooked well done.
2. *Looseness of the joints*—The thigh and leg will begin to move freely in their sockets when the bird is done.

TABLE 17.8   GENERAL ROASTING TEMPERATURES AND TIMES

Poultry Kind or Class	Cooking Temperatures		Minutes	
Capons	180–190°C	350–375°F	35–40 min. per kg	18–20 min. per lb.
Chickens	190–200°C	375–400°F	30–35 min. per kg	15–18 min. per lb.
Ducks and geese	190–220°C	375–425°F	25–30 min. per kg	12–15 min. per lb.
Game hens	190–200°C	375–400°F	45–60 min. total	
Guineas	190–200°C	375–400°F	35–40 min. per kg	18–20 min. per lb.
Squab	200°C	400°F	30–40 min. total	
Turkeys (large)	160°C	325°F	25–30 min. per kg	12–15 min. per lb.

3. *Colour of juices*—This method is used with birds that are not stuffed. Use a kitchen fork to tilt the bird, allowing some of the juices that have collected in the cavity to run out. Clear juices may indicate that the bird is done. If the juices are cloudy or pink, the bird is undercooked.

4. *Time*—Because there are so many variables, timing alone is less reliable than other methods. It is useful, however, for planning production when large quantities are roasted and as a general guideline when used with other methods. Table 17.8 gives some general timing guidelines for roasting several kinds of poultry.

Accompaniments to Roasted Poultry

The most common accompaniments to roasted poultry are bread stuffing and gravy. Large birds, such as capons and turkeys, produce adequate drippings for making sauce or pan gravy. Small birds, such as squab and Cornish game hens, are often stuffed with wild rice or other ingredients and served with a sauce that is made separately.

Ducks and geese are complemented by stuffings containing rice, fruits, berries and nuts. They are very fatty and if stuffed, they should be roasted on a rack or mirepoix bed to ensure that the fat that collects in the pan during roasting does not penetrate the cavity, making the stuffing greasy. Ducks and geese are often served with a citrus- or fruit-based sauce. Its high acid content complements these rich, fatty birds.

Basic Procedure for Stuffing Poultry

Small birds such as Cornish game hens, small chickens and squab can be stuffed successfully. Stuffing larger birds, especially for volume production, is impractical and can be dangerous for the following reasons:

1. *Safety*—Stuffing is a good bacterial breeding ground and because it is difficult to control temperatures inside a stuffed bird, there is a risk of foodborne illness.

2. *Practicality*—Stuffing poultry is labour intensive.

3. *Quality*—Stuffed poultry must be cooked longer to cook the stuffing properly; this may cause the meat to be overcooked, becoming dry and tough.

When stuffing any bird, use the following guidelines.

1. Always be aware of temperatures when mixing the raw ingredients. All ingredients should be cold when they are mixed together, and the mixture's temperature should never be allowed to rise above 4°C (40°F).

2. Stuff the bird as close to roasting time as possible.
3. The neck and main body cavities should be loosely stuffed. The stuffing will expand during cooking.
4. After the cavities are filled, their openings should be secured with skewers and butcher's twine or by trussing.
5. After cooking, remove the stuffing from the bird and store separately.

Basic Procedure for Roasting Poultry

1. Season, bard, stuff and/or truss the bird as desired.
2. Place the bird in a roasting pan. It may be placed on a rack or mirepoix bed to prevent scorching and promote even cooking.
3. Roast uncovered, basting every 15 minutes.
4. Allow the bird to rest before carving to allow even distribution of juices. As the bird rests, prepare the pan gravy or sauce.

Applying the Basics

RECIPE 17.3

ROAST TURKEY WITH CHESTNUT DRESSING AND GIBLET GRAVY

Yield: 16 Servings: each 120 g (4 oz.) turkey, 90 g (3 oz.) dressing, 120 mL (4 fl. oz.) gravy

Young turkey, 5.5–6.5 kg (12–15 lb.) with giblets	1	1
Salt and pepper	TT	TT
Mirepoix	600 g	21 oz.
Onion, small dice	250 g	8 oz.
Celery, small dice	175 g	6 oz.
Whole butter	125 g	4 oz.
Fresh bread cubes	1 kg	2 lb.
Eggs, beaten	2	2
Fresh parsley, chopped	10 g	1 Tbsp.
Chicken stock	2 L	2-1/4 qt.
Chestnuts, cooked and peeled, chopped coarse	250 g	8 oz.
Pastry flour	90 g	3 oz.

1. Place the turkey in the roasting pan.

2. Add the mirepoix to the roasting pan.

1. Remove the giblets from the turkey's cavity and set aside. Season the turkey inside and out with salt and pepper. Truss the turkey.
2. Place the turkey in a roasting pan. Roast at 200°C (400°F) for 30 minutes. Reduce the temperature to 160°C (325°F) and continue cooking the turkey to an internal temperature of 77°C (170°F), approximately 2.5–3 hours. Baste the turkey often during cooking. Approximately 45 minutes before the turkey is done, add the mirepoix to the roasting pan. If the turkey begins to overbrown, cover it loosely with aluminum foil.
3. To make the dressing, sauté the diced onion and celery in the butter until tender.
4. In a large bowl, toss together the bread cubes, salt, pepper, eggs, parsley, sautéed onions and celery, 125 mL (4 fl. oz.) of chicken stock and the chestnuts.

5. Place the dressing in a buttered hotel pan and cover with aluminum foil or buttered parchment paper. Bake at 175°C (350°F) to an internal temperature of 65°C (150°F), approximately 45 minutes.

6. As the turkey roasts, simmer the giblets (neck, heart and gizzard) in 1 L (1 qt.) of the chicken stock until tender, approximately 1.5 hours.

7. When the turkey is done, remove it from the roasting pan and set aside to rest. Degrease the roasting pan, reserving 90 g (3 oz.) of the fat to make a roux.

8. Place the roasting pan on the stove top and brown the mirepoix.

9. Deglaze the pan with a small amount of chicken stock. Transfer the mirepoix and stock to a saucepot and add the remaining stock and the broth from the giblets. Bring to a simmer and degrease.

10. Make a blond roux with the reserved fat and the flour. Add the roux to the liquid, whisking well to prevent lumps. Simmer 15 minutes. Strain the gravy through a conical strainer lined with cheesecloth.

11. Remove the meat from the turkey neck. Trim the gizzard. Finely chop the neck meat, heart and gizzard and add to the gravy. Adjust the seasonings.

12. Carve the turkey and serve with a portion of chestnut dressing and giblet gravy.

RECIPE 17.3

Approximate values per serving:

Calories	651
Total fat	31 g
Saturated fat	10 g
Cholesterol	171 mg
Sodium	691 mg
Total carbohydrates	48 g
Protein	45 g

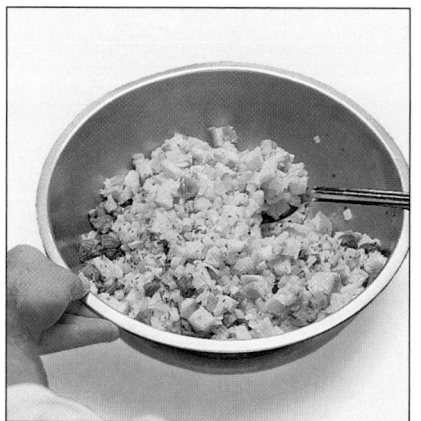

3. Toss the dressing ingredients together.

4. Brown the mirepoix.

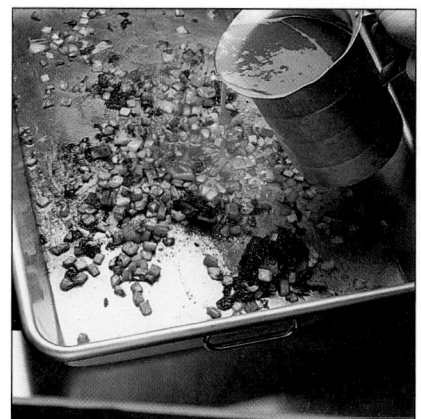

5. Deglaze the roasting pan.

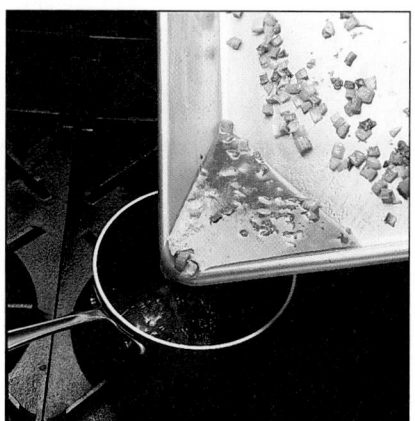

6. Transfer the mirepoix and stock to a saucepot.

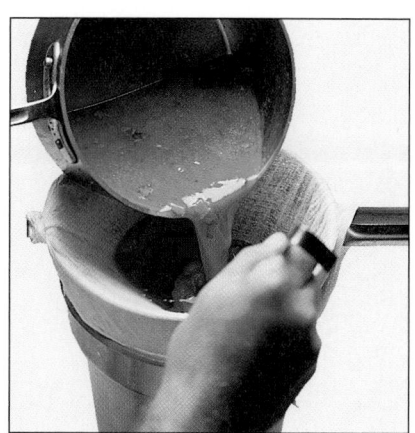

7. Strain the gravy through a conical strainer and cheesecloth.

Carving Roasted Poultry

Poultry can be carved in the kitchen, at tableside or on a buffet in a variety of manners. The carving methods described below produce slices of both light and dark meat.

Basic Procedure for Carving a Turkey, Capon or Other Large Bird

1. After roasting, allow the turkey to stand for 20 minutes so the juices can redistribute themselves. Holding the turkey firmly with a carving fork, pry a leg outward and locate the joint. Remove the leg and thigh in one piece by cutting through the joint with the tip of a knife.

2. Repeat the procedure on the other side. Once both legs and thighs have been removed, slice the meat from the thigh by holding the leg firmly with one hand and slicing parallel to the bone.

3. Separate the thigh from the leg bone by cutting through the joint. Slice the meat from the leg by cutting parallel to the bone.

4. Cut along the breastbone, following the natural curvature of the bones to separate the breast meat from the ribs.

5. Remove an entire half breast and slice it on the cutting board as shown. Cut on an angle to produce larger slices.

6. Alternatively, the breast can be carved on the bird. Make a horizontal cut just above the wing in towards the rib bones.

7. Slice the breast meat as shown.

Basic Procedure for Carving a Chicken or Other Small Bird

1. After allowing the chicken to rest for 15 minutes so the juices can redistribute themselves, cut through the skin between the leg and breast.

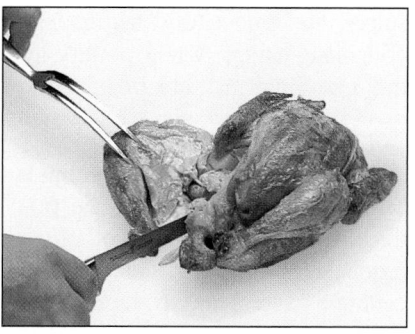

2. Use a kitchen fork to pry the leg and thigh away from the breast. Locate the thigh's ball joint and cut through it with the knife tip, separating it completely from the rest of the chicken. Be sure to cut around the delicate oyster meat, leaving it attached to the thigh.

3. With the knife tip, cut through the skin and meat on one side of the breast bone. Cut and pull the meat away from the bones with the knife.

4. Cut through the wing joint, separating the breast and wing from the carcass. Repeat this procedure on the other side of the bird.

5. The chicken is now quartered.

6. To cut it into eight pieces, separate the wings from the breasts and the thighs from the legs.

Sautéing

Sautéed poultry should be tender and juicy, its flavour developed by proper browning. Additional flavours come from a sauce made by deglazing the pan, usually with wine, and adding garnishes, seasonings and liquids. Stir-frying is a popular method of sautéing poultry; boneless pieces are cut into strips and quickly cooked with assorted vegetables and flavourings.

Selecting Poultry to Sauté

Most poultry is quite tender and well suited for sautéing. Although small birds such as squab can be sautéed bone-in, large pieces and bone-in cuts from larger birds should not be sautéed. Boneless breasts, suprêmes, and cutlets are the most common and practical cuts for sautéing. Because they are high in fat, boneless duck breasts can be sautéed without additional fat.

Seasoning Poultry to Be Sautéed

Poultry has a delicate flavour that is enhanced by a wide variety of herbs, spices, condiments and marinades. Flavour combinations are limited only by your imagination. When poultry items are dusted with flour before sautéing, the seasonings may first be added to the flour.

Cooking Temperatures

The sauté pan and the cooking fat must be hot before the poultry is added. The temperature at which the poultry is then sautéed is determined by its thickness and the desired colour of the finished product. A thin, boneless slice requires relatively high temperatures so that its surface is browned before the centre is overcooked. A thicker cut such as a suprême requires lower temperatures so that neither its surface nor the fond are burned before the item is fully cooked. Adjust the temperature throughout the cooking process to achieve the desired results, never letting the pan become too cool.

If the pan is overcrowded or otherwise allowed to cool, the poultry will cook in its own juices and absorb oil from the pan, resulting in a poor-quality product.

Determining Doneness

Thin cuts of poultry cook very quickly, so timing is a useful practice; it is less useful with thicker cuts. Experienced cooks can tell the doneness of an item by judging the temperature of the sauté pan and the colour of the item being cooked.

A more practical method is to press the item with tongs and judge the resistance. Very undercooked poultry will offer little resistance and feel mushy. Slightly underdone poultry will feel spongy and will not spring back when the tongs are removed. Properly cooked poultry will feel firm to the touch and will spring back when the tongs are removed. Overcooked poultry will feel very firm, almost hard, and will spring back quickly.

Accompaniments to Sautéed Poultry

Sautéed poultry is usually served with a sauce made directly in the pan in which the item was cooked. The sauce uses the fond for added flavour. A wide variety of ingredients, including garlic, onions, shallots, mushrooms and tomatoes, are commonly added to the pan as well as wine and stock. Table 10.5 suggests several sauces for sautéed poultry.

Sautéed items are often served with a starch such as pasta, rice or potatoes.

Basic Procedure for Sautéing Poultry

1. Heat a sauté pan and add enough fat or oil just to cover the bottom.
2. Add the poultry item, presentation side down, and cook until browned.
3. Turn the item, using tongs or by tossing the item back upon itself using the pan's sloped sides.
4. Larger items can be finished in an oven. Either place the sauté pan in the oven or transfer the poultry to another pan. The latter procedure allows a sauce to be made in the original pan as the poultry cooks in the oven. Reserve smaller pieces that are thoroughly cooked in a holding cabinet so that the pan can be used for making the sauce.

Basic Procedure for Making a Sauce in the Sauté Pan

1. Pour off any excess fat or oil from the sauté pan, leaving enough to sauté the sauce ingredients.
2. Add ingredients such as garlic, shallots and mushrooms that will be used as garnishes and sauce flavourings; sauté them.

3. Deglaze the pan with wine, stock or other liquids. Scrape the pan, loosening the fond and allowing it to dissolve in the liquid. Reduce the liquid.
4. Add any ingredients that do not require long cooking times such as herbs and spices. Adjust the sauce's consistency and seasonings.
5. For service, the poultry can be returned to the pan for a moment to reheat it and coat it with the sauce. The poultry should remain in the sauce just long enough to reheat. Do not attempt to cook the poultry in the sauce.
6. Serve the poultry with the accompanying sauce.

1. Sauté the breasts in butter.

Applying the Basics

RECIPE 17.4

CHICKEN SAUTÉ WITH ONIONS, GARLIC AND BASIL

Yield: 6 175-g (6-oz.) Servings

Chicken breasts, boneless, skinless, each approx. 175 g (6 oz.)	6	6
Salt and pepper	TT	TT
Flour	as needed	as needed
Clarified butter	30 mL	1 fl. oz.
Onion, small dice	60 g	2 oz.
Garlic cloves, chopped	25 g	6
Dry white wine	125 mL	4 fl. oz.
Lemon juice	15 mL	1 Tbsp.
Tomato concassée	175 g	6 oz.
Chicken stock	125 mL	4 fl. oz.
Fresh basil leaves, chiffonade	6	6

2. The fond left in the pan after sautéing the chicken.

1. Season the chicken with salt and pepper; dredge in flour.
2. Sauté the breasts in the butter, browning them and cooking *à point*. Reserve in a holding cabinet.
3. Add the onion and garlic to the fond and butter in the pan; sauté until the onion is translucent.
4. Deglaze the pan with the white wine and lemon juice.
5. Add the tomato and the chicken stock. Sauté to combine the flavours; reduce the sauce to the desired consistency.
6. Add the basil to the sauce and return the chicken breasts for reheating. Adjust the seasonings and serve 1 breast per serving with a portion of the sauce.

3. Sauté the onions and garlic.

4. Deglaze the pan with white wine and lemon juice.

RECIPE 17.4

Approximate values per serving:

Calories	271
Total fat	7.6 g
Saturated fat	3.8 g
Cholesterol	114 mg
Sodium	450 mg
Total carbohydrates	8.7 g
Protein	42 g

5. Add the tomatoes and chicken stock and simmer to combine the flavours.

6. Return the chicken to the pan to reheat.

Pan-Frying

Pan-fried poultry should be juicy. Its coating or batter should be crispy, golden-brown, not excessively oily and free from any breaks that allow fat to penetrate. Both the poultry and the coating should be well seasoned.

Selecting Poultry to Pan-Fry

The most common pan-fried poultry is fried chicken. Young tender birds cut into small pieces produce the best results. Other cuts commonly pan-fried are boneless portions such as chicken breasts and turkey cutlets.

Seasoning Poultry to Be Pan-Fried

Pan-fried poultry is usually floured, breaded or battered before cooking. (Breadings and batters are discussed in Chapter 21, Deep-Fat Frying). Typically, the seasonings are added to the flour, breading or batter before the poultry item is coated. Seasonings can be a blend of any number of dried herbs and spices, but often only salt and pepper are required because the poultry will be served with a sauce or other accompaniments for additional flavours.

Cooking Temperatures

The fat should always be hot before the poultry is added. The temperature at which it is cooked is determined by the length of time required to cook it thoroughly. Pan-frying generally requires slightly lower temperatures than those used for sautéing. Within this range, thinner items require higher temperatures to produce good colour in a relatively short time. Thicker items and those containing bones require lower cooking temperatures and longer cooking times.

Determining Doneness

Even the largest pan-fried items may be too small to be accurately tested with an instant-read thermometer, so timing and experience are the best tools to determine doneness. Thin cutlets cook very quickly, so it is relatively easy to judge their doneness. On the other hand, fried chicken can take as long as 30–45 minutes to cook, requiring skill and experience to determine doneness.

Accompaniments to Pan-Fried Poultry

Because pan-frying does not produce fond or drippings that can be used to make a sauce, pan-fried poultry is usually served with lemon wedges, a vegetable garnish or a separately made sauce. Fried chicken is an exception; it is sometimes served with a country gravy made by degreasing the pan, making a roux with a portion of the fat and adding milk and seasonings.

Basic Procedure for Pan-Frying Poultry

1. Heat enough fat in a heavy sauté pan to immerse the item to be cooked one-quarter to halfway. The fat should be at approximately 160°C (325°F).
2. Add the floured, breaded or battered item to the hot fat, being careful not to splash. The fat must be hot enough to sizzle and bubble when the item is added.
3. Turn the item when the first side is the proper colour; it should be half cooked at this point. Larger items may need to be turned more than once to brown them properly on all sides.
4. Remove the browned poultry from the pan and drain it on absorbent paper.

Applying the Basics

RECIPE 17.5

PAN-FRIED CHICKEN WITH PAN GRAVY

Yield: 8 2-piece Servings

Frying chickens, each 1.1–1.4 kg (2 lb. 8 oz.–3 lb.), cut in 8 pieces	2	2
Salt and pepper	TT	TT
Garlic powder	10 g	2 tsp.
Onion powder	6 g	2 tsp.
Dried oregano	0.5 g	1 tsp.
Dried basil	1 g	1 tsp.
Flour	275 g	9-1/2 oz.
Buttermilk	250 mL	8 fl. oz.
Oil	as needed	as needed
Onion, small dice	125 g	4 oz.
Chicken stock	750 mL	1-1/2 pt.

1. Season the chicken with salt and pepper.
2. Add the herbs and spices to 250 g (8 oz.) of the flour.
3. Dip the chicken pieces in the buttermilk.
4. Dredge the chicken in the seasoned flour.
5. Pan-fry the chicken in 1 cm (1/2 inch) of oil until done, approximately 40 minutes, turning so it cooks evenly. Reduce the heat as necessary to prevent the chicken from becoming too dark. Or remove the chicken when well browned, drain it and finish cooking it in the oven.
6. To make the pan gravy, pour off all but 50 mL (1-1/2 fl. oz.) of oil from the pan, carefully reserving the fond.
7. Add the diced onions and sauté until translucent.
8. Add 50 g (1-1/2 oz.) of flour and cook to make a blond roux.
9. Whisk in the stock and simmer approximately 15 minutes.
10. Strain through cheesecloth and adjust the seasonings.
11. Serve 1/4 chicken (2 pieces) per person with 125 mL (4 fl. oz.) gravy.

RECIPE 17.5

Approximate values per serving:

Calories	536
Total fat	32 g
Saturated fat	6.7 g
Cholesterol	92 mg
Sodium	642 mg
Total carbohydrates	34 g
Protein	28 g

1. Dip the chicken pieces in the buttermilk.

2. Dredge the chicken in the flour mixture.

3. Add the chicken to the oil. The bubbling fat indicates the proper cooking temperature.

4. Turn the chicken so it cooks evenly.

5. Sauté the diced onions until translucent.

6. Add the liquid to the roux.

Moist-Heat Cooking Methods

The moist-heat cooking methods most often used with poultry are poaching and simmering. Poaching is used to cook tender birds for short periods of time. Simmering is used to cook older, tougher birds for longer periods to tenderize them. Poaching and simmering are similar procedures, the principal differences being the temperature of the cooking liquid and the length of cooking time.

Poaching and Simmering

Poached or simmered poultry should be moist, tender and delicately flavoured. Although cooked in stock, overcooking will cause the poultry to be dry and tough. During cooking, some of the poultry's flavour is transferred to the cooking liquid, which can be used to make a sauce for the finished product.

Selecting Poultry to Poach or Simmer

Young birds are best suited for poaching; boneless chicken pieces are the most commonly used parts. Older, tougher birds are usually simmered. Duck and geese are rarely poached or simmered because of their high fat content.

Seasoning Poultry to Be Poached or Simmered

When poaching poultry it is especially important to use a well-seasoned and highly flavoured liquid in order to infuse as much flavour as possible into the item being cooked. Either strong stock with a sachet or a mixture of stock or water and white wine with a bouquet garni or oignon piqué produces good results. The poultry should be completely covered with liquid so that it cooks evenly. However, if too much liquid is used and it is not strongly flavoured, flavours may be leached out of the poultry, resulting in a bland finished product.

Poultry is often simmered in water instead of stock. A sachet and a generous mirepoix should be added to help flavour it. Typically, simmering birds results in a strong broth that may be used to complete the recipe or reserved for other uses.

Cooking Temperatures

For best results, poultry should be poached at low temperatures, between 75°C and 80°C (165°F and 175°F). Cooking poultry to the proper doneness at these temperatures produces a product that is moist and tender.

Simmering is done at slightly higher temperatures, between 85°C (185°F) and just below the boiling point. When simmering, do not allow the liquid to boil, as this may result in a dry, tough and stringy finished product.

Determining Doneness

Poached poultry, whether whole or boneless, is cooked just until done. An instant-read thermometer inserted in the thigh or thicker part of the bird should read 77°C (170°F). Any juices that run from the bird should be clear.

Simmered poultry is usually cooked for longer periods to allow the moist heat to tenderize the meat. A chicken that weighs 1.5 kg (3 lb. 8 oz.), for example, may take 2.5 hours to cook, depending on its age.

Accompaniments to Poached and Simmered Poultry

Poached or simmered poultry can be served hot or cold. The meat from these birds can be served cold in salads, hot in casseroles or used in any dish that calls for cooked poultry.

Poached items are typically served with a flavoured mayonnaise or a sauce made from the reduced poaching liquid, such as sauce suprême. Poultry is also often poached as a means of producing a low-calorie dish. If so, a vegetable coulis makes a good sauce or the poultry can be served with a portion of its cooking liquid and a vegetable garnish.

Simmered poultry to be served cold will be more moist and flavourful if it is cooled in its cooking liquid. To do so, remove the pot containing the bird and the cooking liquid from the heat when the bird is still slightly undercooked. Cool the meat and broth in a water bath following the procedures in Chapter 10, Stocks and Sauces. Once cooled, remove the meat and wipe off any congealed broth before proceeding with the recipe.

Basic Procedure for Poaching or Simmering Poultry

1. Cut or truss the item to be cooked as directed in the recipe.
2. Prepare the cooking liquid and bring it to a simmer. Submerge the poultry in the cooking liquid, or arrange the items to be poached in an appropriate pan and add the poaching liquid to the pan.
3. Poach or simmer the item to the desired doneness in the oven or on the stove top. Maintain the proper cooking temperature throughout the process.
4. Remove the item and hold it for service in a portion of the cooking liquid or, using an ice bath, cool the item in its cooking liquid.
5. The cooking liquid may be used to prepare an accompanying sauce or reserved for use in other dishes.

Applying the Basics

RECIPE 17.6

POACHED BREAST OF CHICKEN WITH TARRAGON SAUCE

Yield: 8 175-g (6-oz.) Servings

Chicken breasts, boneless, skinless, each approx. 175 g (6 oz.) each	8	8
Whole butter	45 g	1-1/2 oz.
Salt and white pepper	TT	TT
White wine, warm	125 mL	4 fl. oz.
Chicken stock	500 mL	16 fl. oz.
Bay leaf	1	1
Dried thyme	0.25 g	1/4 tsp.
Dried tarragon	0.5 g	1 tsp.
Flour, pastry	30 g	1 oz.
Cream, 35%	125 mL	4 fl. oz.
Fresh tarragon sprigs	as needed	as needed

1. Trim any rib meat and fat from the breasts.
2. Select a pan that will just hold the breasts when they are placed close together. Rub the pan with approximately 15 g (1/2 oz.) of butter.

Continued

3. Season the chicken breasts with salt and pepper and arrange them in the buttered pan, presentation side up.

4. Add the preheated white wine, stock, bay leaf, thyme and dried tarragon.

5. Cut and butter a piece of parchment paper and cover the chicken breasts.

6. Bring the liquid to a simmer and reduce the temperature to poach the chicken.

7. Make a blond roux with 30 g (1 oz.) of butter and 30 g (1 oz.) of flour; set aside to cool.

8. When the breasts are done, remove them from the liquid. Thicken the liquid with the roux. Add the cream. Simmer and reduce to the desired consistency.

9. Strain the sauce through cheesecloth and adjust the seasonings.

10. Serve each breast napped with approximately 60 mL (2 fl. oz.) of sauce; garnish each portion with a sprig of fresh tarragon.

RECIPE 17.6

Approximate values per serving:

Calories	383
Total fat	14 g
Saturated fat	7 g
Cholesterol	163 mg
Sodium	583 mg
Total carbohydrates	4 g
Protein	54 g

1. Arrange the breasts in an appropriate pan.

2. Add the white wine, chicken stock and seasonings to the pan.

3. Cover the breasts with a piece of buttered parchment paper.

4. Add the cream to the thickened sauce.

5. Plate the poached chicken breast.

Combination Cooking Methods

Braising and stewing use both dry and moist heat to produce a moist, flavourful product. One difference between braising and stewing when applied to meats is the size of the cut being cooked: Large cuts of meat are braised; smaller ones are stewed. Because most poultry is relatively small, this distinction does not readily apply in poultry cookery; therefore, the two cooking methods are discussed together here.

Braising and Stewing

Braised or stewed poultry should be moist and fork tender. The poultry is always served with the liquid in which it was cooked. Ducks and geese are braised or stewed in much the same way as red meats. Chicken cacciatore, coq au vin and chicken fricassee are examples of braised or stewed chicken dishes.

Selecting Poultry to Braise or Stew

Braising and stewing, being slow, moist cooking processes, are often thought of as means to tenderize tough meats. Although they can be used to tenderize older, tougher birds, these cooking methods are more often selected as a way to add moisture and flavour to poultry that is inherently tender, such as young ducks and chickens. Typically, the birds are disjointed and cooked bone-in, just until done, so that they retain their juiciness.

Seasoning Poultry to Be Braised or Stewed

Braised or stewed items obtain much of their flavour from the cooking liquid and other ingredients added during the cooking process. The main item and the cooking liquid should be well seasoned. If other seasonings such as a studded onion, sachet, bouquet garni or dried herbs and spices are required, they should be added at the beginning of the cooking process rather than at the end. This allows the flavours to blend and penetrate the larger pieces of poultry. If the poultry is dredged in flour prior to browning, seasonings may be added directly to the flour. As with all dishes using combination cooking methods, the finished dish should have the flavour of the poultry in the sauce and the moisture and flavour of the sauce in the poultry.

Cooking Temperatures

Some recipes, such as chicken cacciatore and coq au vin, require the main item to be thoroughly browned during the initial stages; others, such as chicken fricassee, do not. In either case, after the addition of the liquid it is important to maintain a slow simmer rather than a rapid boil. This can be done on the stove top or in the oven. Low temperatures control the cooking and produce a tender, juicy finished product.

Determining Doneness

Tenderness is the key to determining doneness. It can be determined by inserting a kitchen fork into the poultry. There should be little resistance and the poultry should freely fall off the fork. The pieces should retain their shape, however; if they fall apart they are overdone. Small boneless pieces can be tested by cutting into them with a fork.

Accompaniments to Braised or Stewed Poultry

All braises and stews are cooked in a liquid that results in a sauce or broth served as part of the finished dish. Rice, pasta or boiled potatoes are natural accompaniments to almost any braised or stewed dish, as are steamed vegetables.

Basic Procedure for Braising or Stewing Poultry

1. Sear the main item in butter or oil, developing colour as desired.
2. Add vegetables and other ingredients as called for in the recipe and sauté.
3. Add the appropriate liquid.

♦♦♦
"ALTERNATIVE METHOD"

Some chefs prefer to thicken the braising/stewing liquid after the product is cooked. You have more control of the consistency of the sauce and more choices of thickening agents. You may also add flour at the end of step 2 to prepare a roux.

4. Cover and simmer on the stove top or in the oven until done.
5. Add seasonings and garnishes at the appropriate times during the cooking process.
6. If the dish requires a thickened sauce, pour off two-thirds of the liquid into another pot. Thicken this liquid with an appropriate starch product, simmer to cook starch, strain and recombine with other ingredients.
7. Finish the dish by adding cream or a liaison, if needed, or by adjusting its consistency. Adjust the seasonings.
8. Serve a portion of the main item with the sauce and appropriate garnish.

Applying the Basics

RECIPE 17.7

CHICKEN FRICASSEE

Yield: 8 2-piece Servings

Frying chickens, each 1.1–1.4 kg (2 lb. 8 oz.–3 lb.), cut into 8 pieces	2	2
Salt and white pepper	TT	TT
Clarified butter	90 mL	3 fl. oz.
Onion, medium dice	300 g	10 oz.
Flour (see "Alternative Method" sidebar)	90 g	3 oz.
Dry white wine	250 mL	8 fl. oz.
Chicken stock	1 L	1 qt.
Sachet:		
Bay leaf	1	1
Dry thyme	0.5 g	1/2 tsp.
Peppercorns, cracked	1 g	1/2 tsp.
Parsley stems	8	8
Garlic clove, crushed	5 g	1
Cream, 35%	250 mL	8 fl. oz.
Nutmeg	TT	TT

1. Season the chicken with salt and white pepper.
2. Sauté the chicken in the butter without browning. Add the onions and continue to sauté until they are translucent.
3. Sprinkle the flour over the chicken and onions and stir to make a roux. Cook the roux for 2 minutes without browning. (Alternative step.)
4. Deglaze the pan with white wine. Add the chicken stock and sachet; season with salt. Cover the pot and simmer until done, approximately 30–45 minutes.

1. Sauté the chicken and onions in butter.

2. Sprinkle the flour over the chicken.

3. Deglaze the pan with white wine.

4. Remove the chicken from the pot.

5. Strain the sauce through cheese-cloth.

6. Return the chicken to the sauce to reheat it for service.

5. Remove the chicken from the pot and reserve in a holding cabinet. Strain the sauce through cheesecloth and return it to a clean pan.

6. Add the cream and bring the sauce to a simmer. Add the nutmeg and adjust the seasonings. Return the chicken to the sauce to reheat it for service.

RECIPE 17.7

Approximate values per serving:

Calories	541
Total fat	41 g
Saturated fat	19 g
Cholesterol	159 mg
Sodium	635 mg
Total carbohydrates	18 g
Protein	25 g

CONCLUSION

The renowned French gastronome and author Jean-Anthelme Brillat-Savarin (1755–1826) once observed that "poultry is for the cook what canvas is for the painter." He meant, of course, that poultry, including chicken, duck, goose, guinea, pigeon and turkey, are wonderfully versatile foods that can be cooked by almost any method and with almost any seasonings, and can be served with many accompaniments and garnishes.

QUESTIONS FOR DISCUSSION

1. List the nine categories or kinds of poultry recognized by Agriculture Canada. How are these categories then divided into classes?
2. How should fresh poultry be stored? Discuss several procedures that should be followed carefully when working with poultry to prevent cross-contamination.
3. What is a suprême? Describe the step-by-step procedure for preparing a chicken suprême.
4. What is trussing? Why is this technique used with poultry?
5. Which poultry items are best suited for broiling or grilling? Explain your answer.
6. Describe the characteristics of properly roasted poultry. Which classes of poultry are recommended for roasting?
7. What is foie gras? Why must you be extremely careful when cooking foie gras?

ADDITIONAL POULTRY RECIPES

RECIPE 17.8

ROAST DUCK WITH RÖSTI POTATOES

NOTE: This dish appears in the Chapter Opening photograph

THE FOUR SEASONS, NEW YORK, NY
Chef Christian Albin

Yield: 4 Servings   **Method:** Roasting

Ducks, each 2 kg (4-1/2 lb.)	2	2
Marinade:		
Fresh ginger, peeled and sliced thin	30 g	1 oz.
Garlic cloves, unpeeled and halved	10 g	2
Orange zest, julienne	25 g	2-1/2 Tbsp.
Coriander seeds, crushed	4 g	2 tsp.
Black peppercorns	5 g	1-1/2 tsp.
Soy sauce	250 mL	8 fl. oz.
Honey	40 g	2 Tbsp.
Water	3 L	3 qt.
Jasmine tea leaves, loose	60 mL	4 Tbsp.
Szechuan pepper	8 g	1 Tbsp.
Sugared Orange Zest and		
Orange Sauce (recipe follows)	as needed	as needed
Rösti Potatoes (Recipe 23.14)		

1. Cut the wings off the ducks at the second joint and reserve. Remove the fat from the ducks' cavities.
2. Place the ducks on a rack in the refrigerator, breast sides up, a few centimetres (an inch) apart. Air must circulate around the ducks so that the skin will dry. Leave the birds for 3 days.
3. Combine all of the marinade ingredients and refrigerate for 3 days, stirring daily.
4. Prick the duck skin with a knife point, except for the skin on the breast. Avoid touching or pressing on the breasts, as this will leave dark spots after roasting.
5. Place the ducks on a rack over a shallow pan. Strain the marinade and brush it liberally over the entire surface of both ducks. Spoon the remaining marinade into the ducks' cavities.
6. Let the ducks dry, breast side up, on the rack for 15 minutes. Scrape any marinade drippings from the pan into the cavities.
7. Adjust the oven racks so that one is at the lowest level and the other is directly above the first.
8. Place water in a roasting pan and add the tea leaves. Place the pan on the lower rack of a 180°C (350°F) oven.
9. Position the ducks on the higher oven rack directly over the roasting pan (the ducks should not be touching). Roast undisturbed for 1-1/2 hours.
10. Remove the ducks from the oven. Drain and reserve the juices that have accumulated in the cavity.
11. Sprinkle the ducks with the Szechuan pepper; allow them to rest, then carve.
12. To serve, spoon a layer of Sugared Orange Zest and Orange Sauce over the bottom of a warmed serving platter.

RECIPE 17.8

Approximate values per serving, not including rösti potatoes or orange sauce:

Calories	1385
Total fat	114 g
Saturated fat	39 g
Cholesterol	339 mg
Sodium	2364 mg
Total carbohydrates	8.7 g
Protein	81 g

13. Arrange a pair of drumsticks, wing bones and thighs at each end of the platter. Place the breast in the centre and garnish with orange segments. Sprinkle with the Sugared Orange Zest. Serve the duck with Rösti Potatoes (Recipe 23.14) and the remaining Orange Sauce on the side.

SUGARED ORANGE ZEST AND ORANGE SAUCE

Yield: 350 mL (12 fl. oz.)

Oranges	2	2
Sugar	90 g	3 oz.
Water	250 mL	8 fl. oz.
Granulated sugar	as needed	as needed
Grand Marnier	30 mL	2 Tbsp.
Currant jelly	30 mL	2 Tbsp.
Basic Duck Sauce, hot (recipe follows)	350 mL	12 fl. oz.
Lightly salted butter	30 g	2 Tbsp.
Kosher salt and black pepper	TT	TT

1. Remove the zest from the oranges and julienne. Blanch for 3 minutes in boiling water; drain.
2. Squeeze the oranges and boil the juice until reduced by one-quarter.
3. Place 90 g (3 oz.) of sugar and the water in a saucepan and bring to a boil. Add the julienned zest. Boil until the syrup begins to caramelize, turning light brown.
4. Have a bowl ready with a layer of granulated sugar. Remove the zest from the syrup and toss it in the sugar until the zest is completely coated. Set the zest aside to cool.
5. Continue cooking the syrup until it becomes a dark caramel colour. Stir in the Grand Marnier, currant jelly and reduced orange juice. Whisk until smooth.
6. Pour in the Basic Duck Sauce and whisk until smooth. Cook for a few minutes to thicken slightly. Monter au beurre and season with salt and pepper.

Sugared Orange Zest and Orange Sauce—Approximate values per 60 mL serving:

Calories	306
Total fat	15 g
Saturated fat	5.8 g
Cholesterol	20 mg
Sodium	935 mg
Total carbohydrates	40 g
Protein	2.8 g

BASIC DUCK SAUCE

Yield: 700 mL (1-1/2 pt.)

Vegetable oil	15 mL	1 Tbsp.
Necks and wing tips from 2 ducks		
Celery, chopped	100 g	3 oz.
Carrot, chopped	100 g	3 oz.
Onion, chopped	175 g	6 oz.
Bay leaf	1	1
Mushrooms, large, halved	75 g	3
Garlic cloves	15 g	4
Black pepper, crushed	8 g	1 Tbsp.
Whole cloves	6	6
Tomato purée	30 mL	2 Tbsp.
Flour	15 g	2 Tbsp.
Dry red wine	250 mL	8 fl. oz.
Brown veal stock	900 mL	32 fl. oz.
Cavity juices reserved from 2 roasted ducks		

1. Heat the oven to 200°C (400°F).
2. Heat the oil in a large sauté pan. Add the duck pieces and sauté until they are well caramelized. Place the pan in the oven and roast the duck pieces for 25 minutes at 180°C (350°F), stirring occasionally.

Continued

Basic Duck Sauce—Approximate values per 50 mL serving:

Calories	123
Total fat	9.3 g
Saturated fat	2.8 g
Cholesterol	7.8 mg
Sodium	649 mg
Total carbohydrates	8 g
Protein	1.9 g

3. Add the celery, carrot, onion, bay leaf, mushrooms, garlic, pepper and cloves. Roast for 5 minutes.

4. Place the sauté pan on the stove top and add the tomato purée. Sprinkle the flour over the mixture and stir.

5. Add the red wine and brown stock. Stir; bring to a boil. Reduce the heat and simmer until reduced by half.

6. Stir in the cavity juices and cook for 10 minutes more.

7. Strain the sauce through a conical strainer into a saucepan. Press a ladle against the solids to remove as much liquid as possible.

8. Degrease the sauce and reduce until thick.

◆◆◆

RECIPE 17.9

ROAST CORNISH GAME HEN WITH WILD RICE STUFFING

Yield: 12 Servings   **Method:** Roasting

Onion, fine dice	100 g	3 oz.
Mushrooms, chopped	175 g	6 oz.
Whole butter, melted	175 g	6 oz.
Cooked wild rice	350 g	1-1/2 cups
Dried thyme, crushed	0.5 g	1/2 tsp.
Dried marjoram, crushed	0.5 g	1/2 tsp.
Salt and pepper	TT	TT
Cornish game hens, boned	6	6

1. Sauté the onion and mushrooms in 60 g (2 oz.) of melted butter until tender. Cool.

2. Stir in the rice and herbs and season to taste with salt and pepper.

3. Stuff the cavity of each hen loosely with the rice mixture. Shape the hen, secure with a strip of buttered parchment and place in a roasting pan.

4. Brush the hens with the remaining butter and season with salt and pepper. Roast at 200°C (400°F) for 15 minutes.

5. Reduce the oven temperature to 150°C (300°F) and roast until the juices run clear, approximately 30 minutes. Baste 2–3 times with melted butter.

6. Serve the hens with a pan gravy or a sauce made separately, such as mushroom sauce.

NOTE: A mixture of white and wild rice also works well. If only Cornish chickens are available, use half a bird per serving.

RECIPE 17.9

Approximate values per serving:

Calories	1249
Total fat	93 g
Saturated fat	34 g
Cholesterol	560 mg
Sodium	1132 mg
Total carbohydrates	15 g
Protein	88 g

◆◆◆

RECIPE 17.10

COQ AU VIN

Yield: 8 2-piece Servings   **Method:** Braising

Chickens, each 1–1.4 kg (2–3 lb.)	2	2
Flour for dredging	as needed	as needed
Salt and pepper	TT	TT
Clarified butter	60 mL	2 fl. oz.
Brandy	125 mL	4 fl. oz.
Bouquet garni:		
Carrot stick, 10 cm (4 inches)	1	1
Leek, split, 10-cm (4-inch) piece	1	1
Fresh thyme	1 sprig	1 sprig
Bay leaf	1	1

Garlic cloves, peeled and crushed	25 g	6
Red wine	750 mL	26 fl. oz.
Chicken stock	250 mL	8 fl. oz.
Bacon lardons, double smoked	125 g	4 oz.
Pearl onions, peeled	18	18
Mushroom caps, medium, quartered	10	10
Beurre manié	as needed	as needed
Large triangular croutons	8	8

1. Cut each chicken into eight pieces and dredge in flour seasoned with salt and pepper.
2. Heat the clarified butter in a braising pan; brown the chicken.
3. Add the brandy and ignite. When the flame dies, add the bouquet garni, garlic, red wine and chicken stock. Bring to a boil, then reduce to a simmer.
4. Cover the pan and simmer until the chicken is tender, approximately 40 minutes.
5. In a separate pan, sauté the bacon until the fat begins to render. Add the onions and sauté until they begin to brown. Cook the bacon and onions covered, over low heat, until the onions are tender. Add the mushroom caps and cook them until tender.
6. Remove the chicken from the pan and adjust the sauce's consistency with the beurre manié. Strain the sauce through a conical strainer and adjust the seasonings.
7. Spoon the bacon, onions and mushrooms onto a serving platter, place the chicken over them and ladle the sauce over the finished dish. Serve with triangular croutons.

RECIPE 17.10

Approximate values per serving:

Calories	568
Total fat	40 g
Saturated fat	17 g
Cholesterol	128 mg
Sodium	830 mg
Total carbohydrates	26 g
Protein	26 g

◆◆◆

RECIPE 17.11

CHICKEN CACCIATORE

Yield: 8 2-piece Servings   **Method:** Braising

Frying chickens, each 1.1–1.4 kg		
(2 lb. 8 oz.–3 lb.)	2	2
Flour	60 g	2 oz.
Salt and pepper	TT	TT
Olive oil	60 mL	2 fl. oz.
Onion, medium dice	125 g	4 oz.
Garlic cloves, chopped	15 g	3
Mushrooms, sliced	250 g	8 oz.
Dried thyme	0.25 g	1/4 tsp.
White wine	50 mL	2 fl. oz.
Brandy	30 mL	1 fl. oz.
Demi-glace, veal or chicken	450 mL	16 fl. oz.
Tomato concassée	350 g	12 oz.

1. Cut each chicken into eight pieces and dredge in flour seasoned with salt and pepper.
2. Heat the oil in a heavy brazier and brown the chicken well. Remove the chicken from the pan. Degrease the pan, leaving 15 mL (1 Tbsp.) of fat.
3. Add the onion and garlic and sauté lightly. Add the mushrooms and thyme and continue sautéing until the mushrooms are tender.
4. Deglaze the pan with the white wine and brandy. Add the demi-glace and tomato.
5. Return the chicken to the pan and season with salt and pepper. Cover and cook until the chicken is done, approximately 30 minutes.
6. Serve two pieces of chicken with a portion of sauce.

RECIPE 17.11

Approximate values per serving:

Calories	446
Total fat	30 g
Saturated fat	8.4 g
Cholesterol	98 mg
Sodium	642 mg
Total carbohydrates	19 g
Protein	25 g

Dave Ryan

Canadian born and bred, Dave is one of the only chefs in Canada to win seven provincial culinary competition trophies in just four years. He has won more than 24 medals at competitions in Canada and the U.S., and in 1996 took home a gold medal from the World Culinary Olympics in Berlin. He was Executive Chef at Lake Okanagan Resort in British Columbia before joining the Hospitality Department at Vancouver Community College.

♦♦♦

RECIPE 17.12

CHICKEN MALIBU

VANCOUVER COMMUNITY COLLEGE, VANCOUVER, BC
Chef Instructor Dave Ryan

Yield: 10 Servings

Method: Roasting

Ingredient	Metric	US
Crab meat, fairly dry	300 g	10 oz.
Eggs	2 medium	2 medium
Cream, 35%	125 mL	4 fl. oz.
Fresh white bread, crust removed and processed fine	4 slices	4 slices
Chives, chopped	25 g	3 Tbsp.
Salt and pepper	TT	TT
Chicken breasts, boneless, skinless, each 150 g (5 oz.)	10	10
Butter Sauce:		
Butter	10 g	2 tsp.
Shallots, minced	50 g	2
Bay leaf	1	1
Okanagan Muller Thurgau	250 mL	1 cup
Cream, 35%	375 mL	1-1/2 cup
Butter, chilled, cubed	125 g	1/4 lb.
Lemon juice	10 mL	2 tsp.
Salt and pepper	TT	TT
Chives, chopped	5	5
Canola oil	as needed	as needed
Melon balls: honey dew, cantaloupe, watermelon	3–6 pieces per serving	
Malibu rum	75 mL	2-1/2 fl. oz.

1. For filling, in a chilled bowl, mix together crab meat, eggs, cream, fresh bread, chives and salt and pepper. Reserve in refrigerator.

2. Cut pocket in chicken breasts or butterfly open.

3. Place one-tenth of the crab filling in each chicken breast. Shape the breasts.

4. To make the butter sauce, place 5 g (1 tsp.) of butter in a frying pan over low heat. Add shallots and sauté gently. Add bay leaf, then wine and reduce by half, then add cream and reduce by half again. Lower heat and whisk in the cubed butter, a little at a time. Squeeze in lemon juice and season to taste. Add chives and remove bay leaf. Keep the sauce warm.

5. Oil and season chicken breasts, then mark service side on grill. Place them in pan and finish in oven. Remove the breasts from pan. Reserve in a warm spot. Add a touch of butter to pan and sauté the melon balls lightly; deglaze with Malibu rum and flame off alcohol. Add butter sauce to the melon and rum mixture and pour it generously over sliced chicken breast.

RECIPE 17.12

Approximate values per serving:

Calories	566
Total fat	38 g
Saturated fat	20 g
Cholesterol	244 mg
Sodium	639 mg
Total carbohydrates	11 g
Protein	45 g

♦♦♦

RECIPE 17.13

CHICKEN YAKITORI

Yield: 8 Servings

Method: Grilling

Ingredient	Metric	US
Soy sauce	250 mL	8 fl. oz.
Mirin	250 mL	8 fl. oz.

Granulated sugar	25 g	1 oz.
Ginger, grated	10 g	2 tsp.
Garlic, chopped	15 g	3
Chicken breasts, boneless	1 kg	2 lb.
Cornstarch	10 g	1 Tbsp.
Green onions, sliced	50 g	2
Sesame seeds	15 g	1 Tbsp.

1. Combine the soy sauce, mirin, sugar, ginger and garlic. Reserve 250 mL (8 fl. oz.) of the mixture. Marinate chicken for 30 minutes.

2. Grill chicken over hot charcoal until done. Brush the chicken with soy sauce mixture, basting regularly.

3. To make the sauce, combine 60 mL (2 fl. oz.) of the soy sauce mixture with the cornstarch. Bring the remainder of the mixture to a boil in a small saucepan and stir in the cornstarch slurry. Stirring constantly, continue boiling until the sauce thickens. Simmer 1 minute. Add green onions.

4. Serve with short-grain white rice and garnish with sesame seeds.

◆ ◆ ◆

RECIPE 17.14

CHICKEN AND SNOW PEAS IN BLACK BEAN SAUCE

Yield: 8 Servings   **Method:** Stir-frying

Chicken breasts, boneless, skinless	1 kg	2 lb.
Egg white	1	1
Chinese rice wine	175 mL	6 fl. oz.
Cornstarch	15 g	2 Tbsp.
Soy sauce	50 mL	2 fl. oz.
Onions, small	175 g	2
Peanut or canola oil	125 mL	4 fl. oz.
Garlic, minced	15 g	1 Tbsp.
Fresh ginger, minced	10 g	2 tsp.
Fermented black beans, mashed	50 g	3 Tbsp.
Snow peas, fresh	125 g	4 oz.

1. Slice the chicken into thin strips, approximately 4 cm × 0.6 cm (1-1/2 inches × 1/4 inches).

2. Combine the egg white, 60 mL (2 fl. oz.) of the wine and 8 g (1 Tbsp.) of the cornstarch. Add the chicken, coat evenly and refrigerate for two hours.

3. For the sauce, mix the soy sauce and the remaining wine and cornstarch.

4. Quarter the onions and separate the layers.

5. In a wok, stir-fry the chicken in 90 mL (3 fl. oz.) of oil. Remove and set aside.

6. If necessary, add all of the remaining oil and stir-fry the garlic and ginger for 10 seconds. Add the onions and mashed beans and stir-fry for 30 seconds. Add the snow peas and cook for 1 minute.

7. Return the chicken to the wok, add the sauce mixture and stir-fry until hot and the sauce has thickened.

8. Serve immediately with short-grain white rice.

VARIATION: Add 60 g (2 oz.) sliced mushrooms and reduce the amount of snow peas by half or substitute broccoli.

RECIPE 17.13

Approximate values per serving:

Calories	293
Total fat	13 g
Saturated fat	3.5 g
Cholesterol	80 mg
Sodium	1678 mg
Total carbohydrates	14 g
Protein	30 g

RECIPE 17.14

Approximate values per serving:

Calories	426
Total fat	22 g
Saturated fat	3.8 g
Cholesterol	97 mg
Sodium	688 mg
Total carbohydrates	13 g
Protein	44 g

♦♦♦

RECIPE 17.15

CHICKEN CURRY

Yield: 4 Servings   **Method**: Stir-frying

Onion, brunoise	250 g	8 oz.
Garlic, finely chopped	10 g	2 tsp.
Ghee (or clarified butter)	30 mL	2 Tbsp.
Fresh ginger, grated	60 g	2 oz.
Turmeric	5 g	1-1/2 tsp.
Coriander seeds, ground	3 g	1-1/2 tsp.
Cumin seeds, ground	2 g	1 tsp.
Cayenne pepper	2 g	1 tsp.
Fenugreek, ground	2 g	1/2 tsp.
Coconut milk	575 mL	20 fl. oz.
Roasting chicken, 1.3 kg (3 lb.), cut into eight pieces	1	1
Salt	5 g	1 tsp.
Jalapeño, split and seeded	1	1
Lemon juice	30 mL	1 fl. oz.

RECIPE 17.15

Approximate values per serving:

Calories	706
Total fat	58 g
Saturated fat	36 g
Cholesterol	123 mg
Sodium	608 mg
Total carbohydrates	15 g
Protein	31 g

1. Fry the onion and garlic in the ghee until the onions are pale golden and the oil "returns" to the pan.
2. To make the wet masala, mix the ginger, turmeric, coriander, cumin, cayenne pepper and fenugreek; add just enough of the coconut milk to form a paste.
3. Add the wet masala to the onion and fry for 8 minutes, or until the mixture is fragrant.
4. Add the chicken pieces and cook, turning them frequently, for 6–8 minutes.
5. Add the remaining coconut milk, salt and jalapeño. Bring to a boil, cover and reduce to a simmer. Cook until the chicken is done, approximately 45 minutes.
6. Just before service, stir in the lemon juice and adjust the seasonings. Serve with rice and a chutney or sambals.

♦♦♦

RECIPE 17.16

CHICKEN FILLED WITH SPINACH AND CRABMEAT, LOBSTER AND CAPER SAUCE

CALGARY, AB
Restituto Mendoza

Yield: 4 Portions   **Method**: Pan-roasting/Baking

Fresh spinach	350 g	12 oz.
Béchamel sauce	100 mL	6 Tbsp.
Regianno cheese, grated	30 g	3 Tbsp.
Fresh garlic, minced	5 g	1 tsp.
Fresh basil, minced	5 g	1 tsp.
Crabmeat	200 g	7 oz.
Egg yolk	1	1
Salt and pepper	TT	TT
Chicken breasts, each 175 g (6 oz.)	4	4
Butter	20 g	4 tsp.
Lobster and Caper Sauce (recipe follows)		

Restituto Mendoza

Born in the Philippines, Resi began his culinary career at the age of 19. Training with distinguished European chefs, he completed his apprenticeship in the Philippines and then eventually moved to Canada in 1983. Career highlights include functioning as Executive Chef for five years at the International Hotel in Calgary and Executive Chef at the Calgary Heritage Pointe Golf and Country Club for six years. Resi has been a Culinary Team Canada chef member since 1996, and, in 1999, was chosen as Chef of the Year by the Calgary Branch of the CFCC.

1. Lay the spinach leaves flat on a perforated pan. Steam them until they are just wilted, then chill in fridge.

2. Combine the béchamel, cheese, garlic, basil, crabmeat and egg yolk in a mixing bowl. Season with salt and pepper.

3. Lay the chicken breasts on the cutting board, skin side down, remove the tenderloin and flatten separately. Cover the breasts with plastic and lightly flatten them with a mallet.

4. Lay the spinach over each chicken breast, one leaf thick, leaving 6 mm (1/4 inch) of meat uncovered around the edges.

5. Divide the crab mixture evenly among the breasts, placing a tube shape down the centre of each breast. Then put the tenderloin on top of the crab.

6. Roll each breast into a tight, fat tube and place on a buttered sheet pan, seam side down.

7. Brush the top of each tube with butter, season with salt and pepper and roast at 190°C (375°F) until they reach the internal temperature of 63°C (145°F), approximately 15–20 minutes.

8. At service time, pour the sauce on the bottom of each plate, slice the breast and arrange on the sauce. Garnish as desired.

LOBSTER AND CAPER SAUCE

Fresh shallots, chopped	25 g	2 Tbsp.
Butter, softened	15 g	1 Tbsp.
Fresh ginger, minced	20 g	4 tsp.
Fresh garlic, chopped	5 g	1 tsp.
Capers	15 g	4 tsp.
White wine	175 mL	6 fl. oz.
Lobster stock	400 mL	14 fl. oz.
Lemon juice, freshly squeezed	10 mL	2 tsp.
Cream, 35%	175 mL	6 fl. oz.
Salt and pepper	TT	TT
Butter, softened	100 g	6-1/2 Tbsp.

1. Sauté the shallots, ginger, garlic and capers in butter.

2. Add the white wine, lobster stock and lemon juice. Bring to a boil and reduce to 250 mL (8 fl. oz.).

3. Add the cream and reduce by half or until thick. Adjust seasoning.

4. Whisk in the butter (monter au beurre).

◆ ◆ ◆

RECIPE 17.17

CHICKEN BREAST STUFFED WITH SMOKED SCALLOPS, FENNEL TOMATO BASIL CREAM SAUCE

SOUTHERN ALBERTA INSTITUTE OF TECHNOLOGY, CALGARY, AB
Chef Instructor Colin Maxwell, CCC

Yield: 4 Portions   **Method:** Smoking and Pan-roasting

Wood chips		
Scallops	250 g	8
Salt and black pepper	TT	TT
Lemon juice	30 mL	1 fl. oz.

Continued

RECIPE 17.16

Approximate values per serving:

Calories	492
Total fat	27 g
Saturated fat	10 g
Cholesterol	211 mg
Sodium	918 mg
Total carbohydrates	6.5 g
Protein	52 g

Lobster and Caper Sauce—Approximate values per serving (1 portion/60 mL):

Calories	98
Total fat	9.5 g
Saturated fat	5.8 g
Cholesterol	29 mg
Sodium	118 mg
Total carbohydrates	1.2 g
Protein	0.7 g

Colin Maxwell, CCC
Currently an Instructor at SAIT, Colin had much of his training in England. He came to Canada in 1979, and quickly became the Executive Sous Chef at the Chateau Airport Hotel, where he helped run the Flight Kitchen. He was a member of Team Calgary in the 1987 World Culinary Arts Show in Vancouver, and sat on the Red Seal Exam Revision Committee in 1998.

Chicken breasts, frenched, skin on,		
each 175 g (6 oz.)	4	4
Flour	as needed	as needed
Vegetable oil	30 mL	1 fl. oz.
Butter	30 g	1 oz.
Fennel Tomato Basil Cream Sauce (recipe follows)		

1. Place wood chips in a pan, cover with foil poked with holes and place on a heat source.
2. Season scallops with salt, pepper and lemon juice on a perforated tray and place above the smoke from the wood chips. Lightly smoke each side for about 5 minutes.
3. Trim the chicken breasts neatly and cut a deep pocket in the thick end by the bone.
4. Once the scallops are cooled, insert two scallops into the pocket in each chicken breast.
5. Season the chicken with salt and pepper and lightly dust with flour. Sear the chicken in a pan with oil and butter. Finish cooking the breasts in a 150°C (300°F) oven to an internal temperature of 77°C (140°F).
6. When the chicken is finished, squeeze some lemon juice on it, cut on the bias to reveal the scallops inside and serve with Fennel Tomato Basil Cream Sauce.

FENNEL TOMATO BASIL CREAM SAUCE

Fennel, thin slices, roughly chopped	350 g	2 bulbs
Shallots, diced	15 g	4 tsp.
Garlic, diced	10 g	2 tsp.
Butter	50 g	2 oz.
Vermouth	200 mL	7 fl. oz.
Roma tomatoes, peeled, seeded, chopped	250 g	8 oz.
Pernod	60 mL	2 fl. oz.
Cream, 35%	500 mL	16 fl. oz.
Salt and white pepper	TT	TT
Worcestershire sauce	TT	TT
Tabasco sauce	TT	TT
Lemon juice	1 lemon	1 lemon
Basil, shredded	100 g	1 cup

1. In a braising pot, sweat the fennel, shallots and garlic in butter.
2. Add the vermouth and reduce a small amount.
3. Add the tomatoes and blend the sauce until desired smoothness.
4. Add the Pernod and cream and reduce to desired consistency.
5. Season with salt, white pepper, Worcestershire sauce, Tabasco sauce and lemon juice.
6. Add the basil.

◆ ◆ ◆

RECIPE 17.18

CINNAMON SMOKED BREAST OF DUCK WITH HUCKLEBERRY VERJUS BROWN BUTTER

WILDWOOD RESTAURANT GROUP, CALGARY, AB
Executive Chef Michael Noble

Yield: 4 Appetizers   **Method:** Smoking/Sautéing

Duck breast, each 175–200 g (6–7 oz.)	2	2
Grapeseed oil	10 mL	2 tsp.

RECIPE 17.17

Approximate values per serving, not including fennel sauce:

Calories	341
Total fat	20 g
Saturated fat	6.1 g
Cholesterol	108 mg
Sodium	565 mg
Total carbohydrates	5.3 g
Protein	35 g

Fennel Tomato Basil Cream Sauce—Approximate values per 85 mL serving:

Calories	213
Total fat	19 g
Saturated fat	12 g
Cholesterol	67 mg
Sodium	232 mg
Total carbohydrates	8.7 g
Protein	1.8 g

RECIPE 17.18

Approximate values per serving:

Calories	499
Total fat	43 g
Saturated fat	21 g
Cholesterol	139 mg
Sodium	531 mg
Total carbohydrates	11 g
Protein	17 g

Fresh thyme, picked	5 g	2 tsp.
Cinnamon, ground	1 g	1/2 tsp.
Ground black pepper	TT	TT
Sea salt	TT	TT
Sauce:		
Red verjus	125 mL	4 fl. oz.
Brown duck stock	500 mL	16 fl. oz.
Butter, unsalted	125 g	4 oz.
Huckleberries	50 g	1/4 cup
Raspberry vinegar	10 mL	2 tsp.
Leek, brunoise, sautéed	20 g	2 Tbsp.
Tarragon, fine chop	2 g	1/2 tsp.
Sea salt and black pepper	TT	TT

1. Trim excess fat from duck breast and score the skin. Marinate overnight in oil, thyme, cinnamon and pepper.

2. Remove breasts from marinade, dry and cold smoke for approximately 30 minutes. Season the breasts with sea salt and sauté skin side down over moderate heat, draining fat until skin is crispy. Turn the breast and cook until medium. Let duck rest for 10 minutes.

3. To make the sauce, reduce the verjus by two-thirds and reserve.

4. Reduce the duck stock in the same pan until syrupy. Reserve.

5. Preheat a wide saucepan and add the butter. Cook until the milk solids begin to brown and transfer the browned butter to another warm pan. Add the verjus reduction, duck glace, huckleberries and raspberry vinegar and warm. Add the sautéed leek and tarragon. Season to taste with salt and pepper. Sauce should look separated.

6. To serve, slice the duck thinly and arrange on plates with arugala or mizuna. Spoon some sauce beside the duck.

◆◆◆

Michael Noble

Michael was fated to become a chef after cooking a successful Belgian waffle in a high school economics class! He began his apprenticeship in Vancouver, though he also gained valuable European experience in the early stages of his career. In 1996, Michael opened Vancouver's Diva at the Met and, within a year, it was propelled into the culinary spotlight, winning awards from Gourmet Magazine, Vancouver Magazine, *and* GQ. *One of Canada's leading chefs, Michael achieved Canada's highest standing ever at the Bocuse d'Or World Cuisine championship in Lyons in 1995 and 1997.*

RECIPE 17.19

EVANTAIL OF SEMI-SMOKED BROME LAKE DUCKLING WITH BLUEBERRY CRANBERRY CHUTNEY

FAIRMONT QUEEN ELIZABETH HOTEL, MONTREAL, QC
Executive Chef Alain Pignard

Yield: 75 Canapés   **Method:** Hot-smoking

Small Brome Lake duck breasts,		
boneless, skinless	12	12
Red wine	1.5 L	1.5 qt.
Maple syrup	500 mL	16 fl. oz.
Chutney:		
Honey	350 g	8 oz.
Brown sugar	175 g	6 oz.
Balsamic vinegar	250 mL	8 fl. oz.
Cranberries	1 kg	2 lb.
Blueberries	1 kg	2 lb.
Demi-glace	500 mL	16 fl. oz.
Taro root	1	1
Chervil	1/2 bunch	1/2 bunch

1. Remove half the fat from the duck breasts.

2. Marinate in red wine and maple syrup for 6 hours.

RECIPE 17.19	
Approximate values per serving:	
Calories	73
Total fat	1.4 g
Saturated fat	0.5 g
Cholesterol	12 mg
Sodium	20 mg
Total carbohydrates	12 g
Protein	3.2 g

Continued

3. Smoke for 30 minutes. Keep medium-rare. Cool.

4. To prepare chutney, caramelize the honey and brown sugar with a bit of water. Deglaze with balsamic vinegar, then add the berries and demi-glace. Bring to a simmer. Chill.

5. Cut taro root into thin chips with a slicer or mandolin. Shape with a cutter into 4-cm (1-1/2-inch) rounds. Deep-fry to crisp. Reserve.

6. To serve, slice breast thinly and garnish with room-temperature chutney, taro chips and chervil sprigs.

◆◆◆

RECIPE 17.20

TURKEY SCALLOPINI WITH CAPERS AND LEMON

Yield: 4 Servings   **Method:** Sautéing

Turkey breast, cut into 3-mm (1/8-inch) scallopini, each 90 g (3 oz.)	8	8
Salt and white pepper	TT	TT
Flour	as needed	as needed
Clarified butter	60 mL	2 fl. oz.
Dry white wine	125 mL	4 fl. oz.
Fresh lemon juice	60 mL	2 fl. oz.
Capers	30 g	3 Tbsp.

1. Gently pound each turkey slice with a meat mallet. Season with salt and pepper and dredge in flour.

2. Sauté the turkey in the clarified butter until golden-brown. Remove and hold in a warm place.

3. Deglaze the pan with the wine, then add the lemon juice and capers. Return the turkey to the pan to coat with the sauce and reheat.

4. Serve two slices with a portion of the sauce for each serving.

RECIPE 17.20

Approximate values per serving:

Calories	349
Total fat	14 g
Saturated fat	8.5 g
Cholesterol	163 mg
Sodium	693 mg
Total carbohydrates	7.7 g
Protein	48 g

◆◆◆

RECIPE 17.21

OSTRICH STEAK MANDELLA

HRT ALLIANCE, HUMBER COLLEGE, Toronto, ON
Chef Instructor Robert McCann, CCC

Yield: 4 Portions   **Method:** Pan-frying

Sunflower oil	30 mL	1 fl. oz.
Ostrich, sliced into thin steaks	500 g	1 lb.
Onion, fine chop	125 g	4 oz.
Fennel, fine chop	125 g	4 oz.
Full-bodied red wine	300 mL	10 fl. oz.
Brown game stock	300 mL	10 fl. oz.
Tomato purée	5 mL	1 tsp.
Lovage (to flavour stock and for garnish)	8 leaves	8 leaves
Brown roux (to thicken sauce)	30 g	1 oz.
Ground mace	pinch	pinch
Ground cinnamon	pinch	pinch
Mushrooms, turned	4	4
Mushroom stalks, diced	10 g	1 Tbsp.

Robert McCann, CCC
Bob is a fellow of the Epicurean World Master Chefs Society and vice-chair of the Canadian chapter. In addition to instructing at Humber College, he judges international competitions.

Salt and pepper	TT	TT
Cherries, pitted	8	8
Chives, with buds on	4 strands	4 strands
Button onions, cooked	8	8

RECIPE 17.21

Approximate values per serving:

Calories	318
Total fat	14 g
Saturated fat	4 g
Cholesterol	100 mg
Sodium	570 mg
Total carbohydrates	18 g
Protein	30 g

1. In a fry pan, heat oil and fry meat for 4 minutes until brown. Remove.

2. Add onion and fennel and fry for 4 minutes.

3. Discard surplus oil and add wine, stock, tomato purée and four lovage leaves.

4. Simmer for 8 minutes and thicken with roux, then boil for four minutes and strain.

5. Return strained liquid to a boil and add spices, turned mushrooms and diced mushrooms and season.

6. Return meat to sauce and serve.

7. Use the cherries, lovage, chives and button onions to garnish the plate.

WEBLINKS

Canadian Turkey Marketing Agency
www.canadianturkey.ca/

Chicken Farmers of Canada: Cooking Chicken
www.chicken.ca/www.htm

U.S. National Turkey Federation: Turkey Cooking Information
www.turkeyfed.org/consumer/cookinfo.html

Carving a Turkey
www.learn2.com/04/0441/0441.html

CHAPTER 18
GAME

LEARNING OUTCOMES

After studying this chapter you will be able to:

♦ identify a variety of game
♦ explain game inspection practices
♦ explain how to disjoint a rabbit
♦ purchase game appropriate for your needs
♦ store game properly
♦ prepare game for cooking
♦ apply various cooking methods to game

ame (Fr. gibier*) are animals hunted for sport or food. Traditionally, game supplies depended upon the season and the hunter's success. But game's increasing popularity in food service operations has led to farm-raising techniques. As a result, pheasant, quail, deer, rabbit and other animals, although still considered game, are now ranch-raised and commercially available throughout the year.*

The life of game creatures is reflected in their flesh's appearance, aroma, flavour and texture. Generally, game flesh has a dark colour and a strong but not unpleasant aroma. It has a robust flavour, less fat than other meats or poultry, and is more compact, becoming quite tough in older animals.

Selecting the best cooking methods for game depends on the animal's age and the particular cut of flesh. Younger animals will, of course, be more tender than older ones. Flesh from the loin or less-used muscles will also be tender and therefore can be prepared with dry-heat cooking methods. Flesh from much-used muscles, such as the leg and shoulder, will be tougher and should be prepared with combination cooking methods. Less-tender cuts can also be used in sausages, pâtés and forcemeats as discussed in Chapter 20, Charcuterie.

IDENTIFYING GAME

Furred or Ground Game

Furred game includes large animals such as deer, moose, bear, wild boar and elk as well as smaller animals such as rabbit, squirrel, raccoon and opossum. Although each of these animals (and many others) is hunted for sport and food, only bison, deer, elk and rabbit are widely available to food service operations. Limited supplies of wild reindeer, caribou and musk ox are available. Table 18.1 lists uses for furred game.

Large game animals are rarely sold whole or in primal cuts. Instead, the meat is available precut into subprimals or portions. So, except for those that are used for rabbits, this chapter does not provide breaking techniques.

Antelope

The blackbuck antelope, about half the size of a large deer, is ranch-raised in the United States. Although it has almost no body fat, the meat retains a high amount of moisture. The meat is fine-grained, with a flavour that is only slightly stronger than deer meat (venison). It should be fabricated and cooked in a manner similar to venison.

TABLE 18.1   USING FURRED GAME

Animal	Commonly Purchased Cuts	Cooking Methods	Suggested Use
Antelope	Purchased and prepared in the same manner as deer		
Bison	Purchased and prepared in the same manner as lean beef		
Deer	Loin	Dry heat (roast; sauté; grill)	Sautéed medallions; whole roast loin; grilled steaks
	Leg	Combination (braise; stew)	Marinate and braise; pot roast with cranberries; chili; sausage; forcemeat
	Rack	Dry heat (roast; grill)	Grilled chops
Rabbit	Full carcass	Dry heat (sauté; pan-fry; roast; grill) Combination (braise; stew)	Pan-fried rabbit with cream gravy Braised rabbit with mushrooms
Wild Boar	Loin	Dry heat (roast)	Roast loin with mustard crust
	Chops	Combination (braise)	Marinate and braise; stew with red wine and sour cream; sausage; forcemeat

Bison

Once found in huge herds roaming the plains, bison were hunted into near extinction during the 19th century. Bison now live on reservations or ranches, where they are raised like beef cattle. Wood Buffalo National Park on the Alberta–Nunavut border is home to the largest herd of free-roaming bison. Bison meat is juicy and flavourful and may be prepared in the same manner as lean beef.

Deer

The deer family includes elk, moose, reindeer, red-tailed deer, white-tailed deer (Fr. *chevreuil*) and mule deer. Meat from any of these animals is known as venison (Fr. *venaisan*). Farm-raised venison, particularly from the Scottish red deer bred in New Zealand, Canada and the United States, is commercially available all year. Venison is typically dark red with a mild aroma. It is leaner than other meats, having almost no intramuscular fat or marbling.

The most popular commercial venison cuts are the loin, leg and rack. The loin is tender enough to roast, sauté or grill to medium rare. It can be left attached along the backbone to form a cut known as the saddle. The leg is often marinated in red wine and prepared with combination cooking methods. Other cuts can also be stewed or braised or used in sausages and pâtés. Butchering procedures for venison are similar to those for lamb discussed in Chapter 15.

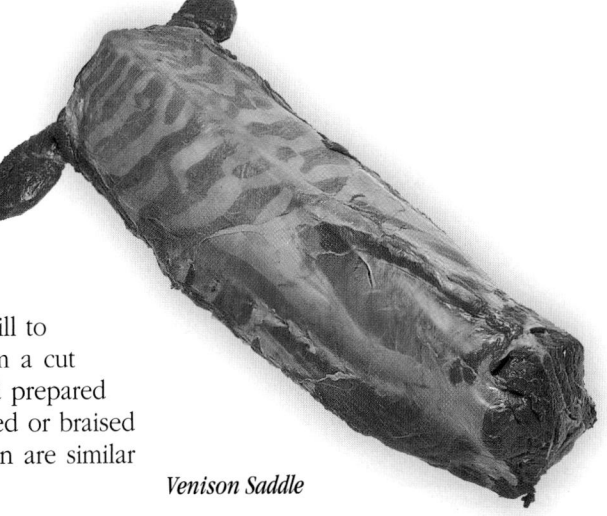

Venison Saddle

Rabbit

Rabbits (Fr. *lapin*) are small burrowing animals that have long been raised for food. Rabbit has mild, lean and relatively tender flesh. Its taste and texture are similar to chicken. Ranch-raised rabbit is available all year, either whole or cut, fresh or frozen. The average weight of a whole dressed rabbit is 1.2–1.4 kg (2 lb. 8 oz.–3 lb.). Young rabbit can be roasted, pan-fried, stewed or braised and is popular in rustic "country-style" dishes, especially casseroles and pâtés.

Basic Procedure for Disjointing a Rabbit

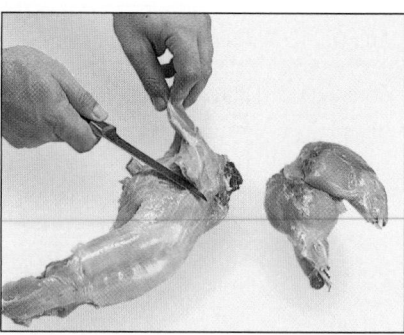

1. Place the rabbit on its back. Remove the hind legs by cutting close to the backbone and through the joint on each side. Each thigh and leg can be separated by cutting through the joint.

2. Remove the forelegs by cutting beneath the shoulder blades.

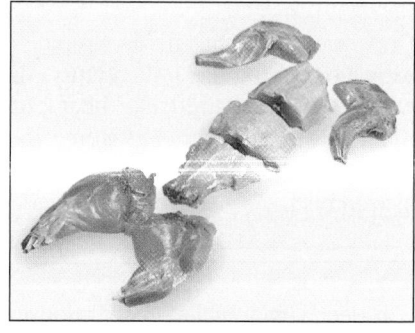

3. Cut through the breast bone and spread open the rib cage. Using a boning knife, separate the flesh from the rib bones and remove the bones.

4. Cut through the backbone to divide the loin into the desired number of pieces.

5. The cut-up rabbit: hind legs, thighs, loin in three pieces, forelegs.

Wild Boar

A close relative of the domesticated hog, wild boar (Fr. *sanglier*) is leaner, with a stronger flavour. Though plentiful in Europe and parts of America, wild boar is available only during autumn. A limited supply of farm-raised boar is available all year, however.

Baby boar (under six months old) is considered a delicacy, but mature animals (one to two years old) have the best flavour. The meat is most often roasted, and may be used in sausages or terrines. Boar can often be substituted in recipes for venison or pork.

Boar Saddle

Feathered or Winged Game

Feathered game includes upland birds such as wild turkeys, pheasants, quails, doves and woodcocks; songbirds such as larks; and waterfowl such as wild geese and ducks. Wild birds cannot be sold in Canada but may be prepared in some private clubs. An ever-increasing number of these birds such as Muscovy duck are being farm-raised to meet increased consumer demand, however.

Game birds are available whole or precut into pieces, fresh or frozen. Butchering techniques will not be shown in this chapter as they are the same as those for domesticated poultry discussed in Chapter 17.

Because game birds tend to have less fat than other poultry, they are often barded with fat and cooked to medium rare. If cooked well done they become dry and stringy.

Partridge

The Hungarian and chukar partridges (Fr. *perdrix*) of Europe were introduced into the United States and Canada during the 19th century. Now found principally in the prairie and western mountain regions, partridges are widely raised on game preserves and farms, producing a good commercial supply.

Chukar Partridge

Their flavour is less delicate than pheasant and the meat tends to be tougher. Partridge may be roasted or cut into pieces and sautéed or braised. Each bird weighs about 450 g (1 lb.) dressed.

Pheasant

Pheasant

The most popular of game birds, the pheasant (Fr. *faisan*) was introduced into Europe from Asia during the Middle Ages. Its mild flavour is excellent for roasting, stewing or braising. The hen is smaller and more tender than the cock. Stock made from the carcass is often used for consommé or sauce.

Farm-raised birds are available fresh or frozen. A dressed bird weighs about 680 g–1 kg (1 lb. 8 oz.–2 lb.) and serves two to four people.

Quail

Quail

The quail (Fr. *caille*) is a migratory game bird related to the pheasant. The more popular European and Californian species are farm-raised and available all year.

Quail are rather small, with only about 30–60 g (1–2 oz.) of breast meat each. Quail may be grilled (especially on skewers), roasted, broiled or sautéed and are often boned and served whole with a stuffing of forcemeat or rice. Because they are so lean, roasted quail benefit from barding.

NUTRITION

Even ranch-raised game animals live in the wild and are generally more active and less well fed than domesticated animals. This lifestyle produces animals whose meat has less fat than domesticated animals. Most game is also lower in cholesterol and has approximately one-third fewer calories than beef. Game is also generally high in protein and minerals. Compare Table 18.2 with Table 17.7 (Poultry).

INSPECTION OF GAME

The Canada Food Inspection Agency and most provinces restrict the sale of wild game. Truly wild game may be served only by those who hunt and share their kill or where a special import permit is obtained, again for private consumption. Special care must be taken to avoid cross-contamination.

TABLE 18.2   NUTRITIONAL VALUES OF GAME

For 28 g (1 oz.) Uncooked Lean Meat	Kcal	Protein (g)	Total Fat (g)	Saturated Fat (g)	Cholesterol (mg)	Sodium (mg)
Beefalo	41	6.6	1.4	0.6	13	22
Bison (American buffalo)	31	6.1	0.5	0.2	18	15
Deer (venison)	34	6.5	0.7	0.3	24	15
Rabbit	39	5.7	1.6	0.5	16	12
Wild boar	35	6.1	1.0	0.3	mq*	mq
Pheasant	51	6.4	2.6	0.8	mq	11
Quail	54	5.6	3.4	1.0	mq	15

The Corinne T. Netzer Encyclopedia of Food Values, 1992
mq* = measurable quantity but data are unavailable

Domestic Game

For resale, mandatory federal and provincial inspections for caribou, reindeer and farm- or ranch-raised game are conducted for wholesomeness. Generally, however, game is processed under the same federal inspection requirements as domesticated meats and poultry. Also, unlike meat and poultry from domesticated animals, game is not graded for quality except for bison.

Imported Game

The Canada Food Inspection Agency accepts game only from countries that have an approved inspection system. The plant processing the meat must also be an approved source. Exotic species may be subject to controls related to handling and cooking after they arrive in Canada.

PURCHASING AND STORING GAME

Purchasing Game

Furred game meats are available fresh, usually in vacuum-sealed packaging, or frozen. Game birds are available cleaned and boned, fresh or frozen. Use the same criteria to determine the freshness of game as you would for any other meat or poultry: The flesh should be firm, without slime or an off-odour.

Fresh game is sometimes **hung** before cutting to allow the meat to mature or age. During hanging, carbohydrates (glycogen) stored in muscle tissues are converted to lactic acid. This process tenderizes the flesh and strengthens its flavour. But hanging is not necessary, especially if you object to "gamy" flavours. Commercially sold game is generally fully aged and ready to use when delivered. It does not need nor will it benefit from hanging.

Storing Game

As with any fresh or frozen meat, game should be well wrapped and stored under refrigeration at temperatures below 4°C (40°F). Because the flesh is generally dry and lean, frozen game should be used within four months. Thaw frozen game slowly under refrigeration to prevent moisture loss.

MARINATING FURRED GAME

Tradition calls for marinating game, particularly furred game, in strong mixtures of red wine, herbs and spices. Commercially raised game does not necessarily have to be marinated. Modern animal husbandry techniques used at game ranches assure the cook of receiving meat from young, tender animals. Farm-raised game animals also have a naturally milder flavour than their truly wild cousins.

For those preferring the flavours imparted by traditional marinades, the following red wine marinade is included. After the meat is removed, the marinade may be added to the cooking liquid or reduced and used in a sauce. Do not serve uncooked marinade.

◆◆◆
HOW TO HANG GAME

The following information may be useful if you find yourself with a need to hang freshly killed game. Most game should be eviscerated (drawn or gutted) as soon as possible, then suspended by either the hind legs or the head in a dry, well-ventilated place. Because the fur or feathers help prevent bacterial contamination, they should be left intact during hanging; game should be skinned or plucked just before butchering. The length of time necessary for hanging depends on the species and age of the animal. Two days may be sufficient for a rabbit, while up to three weeks may be necessary for a deer or boar. Hanging is generally complete when the first whiff of odour is detected (although traditionalists prefer pheasant to be hung until extremely ripe).

WILD GAME—
DELICIOUS, NUTRITIOUS AND AVAILABLE

Wild game is now widely available for use in restaurants and at home. The best of wild game provides a safe, delicious and nutritious dining experience.

In almost all states, our native game animals are protected from harvesting for commercial purposes. It is a violation of state wildlife laws to kill and sell the meat from native species such as the whitetail deer, mule deer, pronghorn antelope, etc. These laws were written when only native game was present in America. Since then, a growing number of non-native species of deer and antelope have been introduced to ranches in America and this has made it possible to harvest deer and antelope legally for meat production.

Oddly enough, however, meats such as antelope, venison, rabbit, and most other game meats are not subject to inspection under federal and most state meat inspection regulations. This is not because the authorities do not believe the meat should be inspected. When the meat inspection laws were written, these meats were not legally available and therefore were not included in the Federal Meat Act. County and city health codes, however, do require that any meat served to the public must be from "an approved source" which is interpreted as "inspected." Therefore, any game meat served in a restaurant should be certified as inspected by either state or federal meat inspection authorities.

Game meat is available from farmed (domesticated) deer and from free-ranging (ranched) deer and antelope. Most farmed deer are taken to a fixed conventional slaughterhouse where they are slaughtered and processed in the same way as cattle, sheep, and goats. Ranched deer can be properly harvested only by an elaborate procedure which involves taking a mobile slaughter facility and meat inspector to the field where the animals are killed by shooting them with a high powered rifle under the supervision of the meat inspector. The carcass is then processed inside the mobile facility to avoid any contamination of the meat. This field harvesting eliminates any stress which might occur in transport of farmed deer to the slaughterhouse.

Farmed deer tend to be relatively more uniform in size and flavor. Free-ranging deer and antelope produce meat of more complex flavor due to the variety of their diet. The difference is somewhat like the difference in cultivated mushrooms and wild mushrooms, or pen-raised chickens compared with free-range chickens. Meat from free-range animals is more expensive due to higher labour and inspection costs.

Meat from both deer and antelope can be legally labelled "venison." All venison is relatively lean when compared with conventional red meats and requires special attention when cooking to avoid drying out the meat and toughening it. Tender cuts should be cooked as little as possible (rare to medium rare) to retain the maximum amount of moisture. Quick sautéing, grilling or roasting to retain a medium rare centre is most satisfactory for tender cuts such as the loin, tenderloin, and leg.

Braising is the most effective method for cooking the less tender cuts such as the shoulder, ribs and shanks. Beef broth or red wine are good liquids for braising. The toughest cut of meat will be very satisfactorily tenderized if braised for a sufficient period of time (which may be as long as two or three hours). When properly cooked, these cuts can surpass the more tender cuts in flavor.

MIKE HUGHES,
Broken Arrow Ranch, Ingram, Texas

Applying the Basics   RECIPE 18.1

RED-WINE GAME MARINADE

Yield: 1.5 L (1-1/2 qt.)

Carrot, chopped fine	75 g	2 oz.
Onion, chopped fine	75 g	2 oz.
Garlic, minced	15 g	1 Tbsp.
Dried thyme	0.25 g	1 tsp.
Bay leaves	2	2
Juniper berries, whole	5 g	2 tsp.
Peppercorns, whole	10 g	1 Tbsp.
Sage, ground	0.25 g	1/2 tsp.
Red wine	1 L	1 qt.
Red wine vinegar	125 mL	4 fl. oz.

1. Combine all ingredients in a noncorrosive container.
2. Place the meat in the marinade and marinate for the desired time. Tender, farm-raised game may need only 30 minutes; older, wild animals may need 1–2 days.

CONCLUSION

Game is becoming increasingly popular because of consumer desires for leaner, healthier meats. Only inspected, farm-raised game can be used in food service operations. Luckily, many popular game items are now farm-raised, government-inspected and readily available. Generally, game flesh has a dark colour, a strong but not unpleasant aroma and a robust flavour. You should butcher, prepare and cook game according to the comparable guidelines for other meats and poultry.

QUESTIONS FOR DISCUSSION

1. Explain the differences between truly wild game and ranch-raised game.
2. What is hanging? Is it necessary for modern food service operations to hang game?
3. Which cuts of furred game are best suited to dry-heat cooking methods? Which are best for combination cooking methods?
4. Can game birds be purchased whole? How are they fabricated?
5. What degree of doneness is best suited for game birds? Explain your answer.

ADDITIONAL GAME RECIPES

RECIPE 18.2

WILD RABBIT AND CHANTERELLE POTAGE

THE FAIRMONT NEWFOUNDLAND, St. John's, NF
Executive Chef William McIlroy

William McIlroy
With a career that spans close to 15 years and three different countries, William has a colourful culinary background that has taken him across the globe, working, studying and teaching in a variety of locations. His greatest memory as a chef dates back to 1993 when he planned a banquet for 300 for the presidents of Ecuador and Peru. The evening's purpose was to begin the peace process between the two feuding countries.

Yield: 12–15 Servings　　　　　　　　**Method:** Stewing

Wild rabbit meat, boneless, no fat, 6-mm (1/4-inch) dice	500 g	1 lb.
Oil	as needed	as needed
Chanterelles, cleaned, 6-mm (1/4-inch) dice	500 g	1 lb.
Butter, unsalted	80 g	3 oz.
Shallots, fine dice	100 g	3-1/2 oz.
Celery, fine dice	100 g	3-1/2 oz.
Leek, white, fine dice	100 g	3-1/2 oz.
Flour	80 g	3 oz.
Brown rabbit stock, warm	2 L	2 qt.
Fresh sage, fine chop	1.5 g	1/2 tsp.
Fresh thyme, fine chop	1.5 g	1/2 tsp.
Dry sherry	50 mL	1-1/2 fl. oz.
Cream, 35%, lightly whipped	200 mL	7 fl. oz.
Salt and pepper	TT	TT

Continued

1. Season the rabbit meat and sear in a very hot pot in a little oil. Reserve the meat.
2. Add a little more oil and sauté the chanterelles. Reserve.
3. Reduce the heat to medium, add the butter and sweat the shallots, celery and leek.
4. Add the flour and cook out the roux for 4-6 minutes. Let cool slightly.
5. Incorporate the warm rabbit stock into the roux in batches, stirring constantly to a smooth consistency. Bring to a boil.
6. Add the rabbit meat and chanterelles and simmer for 45 minutes.
7. Five minutes before service, add the herbs, sherry and cream. Bring back to a boil and adjust seasoning.

RECIPE 18.2

Approximate values per serving:

Calories	269
Total fat	17 g
Saturated fat	8.4 g
Cholesterol	72 mg
Sodium	382 mg
Total carbohydrates	16 g
Protein	13 g

◆◆◆

RECIPE 18.3

RED WINE BRAISED VENISON SHANKS

CAFÉ BRIO, VICTORIA, BC
Chef Jeff Keenliside

Yield: 6 Servings   **Method:** Braising

Venison shanks, each 300–450 g (10–16 oz.)	6	6
Cabernet sauvignon	750 mL	26 fl. oz.
Lemon, thinly sliced	1	1
Fresh rosemary	2 sprigs	2 sprigs
Fresh thyme	2 sprigs	2 sprigs
Bay leaves	2	2
Garlic, sliced	15 g	4 cloves
Salt and pepper	TT	TT
Canola oil	50 mL	3 Tbsp.
Mirepoix	250 g	8 oz.
Brown game or veal stock, hot	1 L	1 qt.
Butter, unsalted	30 g	2 Tbsp.

1. Marinate the shanks in the wine, lemon, herbs and garlic overnight.
2. Remove shanks from marinade and pat dry. Reserve all.
3. Season the shanks and sear in half the oil over medium-high heat until brown. Reserve shanks.
4. Pour off any oil in the pan and sauté the mirepoix until soft. Add the marinade, bring to a boil and reduce by half. Add the hot stock and shanks. Bring to a simmer.
5. Cover the pan and place in a 160°C (325°F) oven for 2.5–3 hours.
6. Carefully remove the shanks. Bring to a simmer.
7. Nappé the shanks with a little sauce and glaze in a hot oven.
8. Monter au beurre the remaining sauce.
9. Serve with polenta and braised kale.

Jeff Keenliside
Though born in Halifax, Jeff was raised on the West Coast. He began his apprenticeship at Aerie Resort and finished it at Café Brio, which specializes in West Coast contemporary food with a Tuscan hint. While working at Brio, Jeff was awarded Apprentice of the Year and was chosen to compete in the Vancouver Island Apprentice Black Box competition.

RECIPE 18.3

Approximate values per serving:

Calories	409
Total fat	25 g
Saturated fat	6.6 g
Cholesterol	134 mg
Sodium	350 mg
Total carbohydrates	12 g
Protein	34 g

+ + +

RECIPE 18.4

Achiote-Basted Rack of Venison with Smoked Corn Pudding

NOTE: *This dish appears in the Chapter Opening photograph.*

THE BOULDERS RESORT, CAREFREE, AZ
Corporate Executive Chef Charles Wiley

Yield: 4 Servings   **Method:** Grilling

Venison chops, each 180 g (6 oz.)	4	4
Achiote Paste (recipe follows)	120 mL	1/2 cup
Kosher salt	TT	TT
Pepper	TT	TT
Olive oil	5 mL	1 tsp.
Shiitake mushroom caps	125 g	8
Haricots verts, blanched and shocked	24	24
Roma tomatoes, quartered	2	2
Smoked Corn Pudding (recipe follows)	500 mL	2 cups
Barley Risotto (recipe follows)	4 servings	4 servings
Venison Red Wine Jus (recipe follows)	125 mL	4 fl. oz.

1. Prepare a mesquite or gas grill. Brush the chops with Achiote Paste and season with salt and pepper. Grill to medium rare, brushing with additional Achiote Paste. Remove the chops from the grill, cover loosely and keep warm.

2. Heat the oil in a small sauté pan and add the mushrooms. Cook for 2–3 minutes over medium heat. Add the haricots verts and tomatoes; season with salt and pepper. Cook for an additional 2–3 minutes; remove from the heat.

3. Spoon 120 mL (1/2 cup) of the Smoked Corn Pudding in the centre of a warm dinner plate. Spoon one-fourth of the haricot vert mixture on top of the pudding. Cut each chop in thirds and arrange the pieces around the pudding. Top with Barley Risotto and pour 30 mL (1 fl. oz.) of Venison Red Wine Jus around the venison. Serve immediately.

ACHIOTE PASTE

Yield: 120 mL (1/2 cup)

Ancho chiles	3	3
Garlic clove	5 g	1
Allspice	0.5 g	1/4 tsp.
Cumin seeds, toasted and ground	1.25 g	1/2 tsp.
Annato (achiote) seeds	4 g	1 tsp.
Olive oil	5 mL	1 tsp.
White wine vinegar	30 mL	2 Tbsp.
Orange juice	60 mL	1/4 cup
Kosher salt	3 g	1/2 tsp.

1. Toast the ancho chiles in a skillet over medium heat for 2 minutes, or until they release some oil and have a toasted aroma. Let cool slightly, then core, seed and tear into strips.

2. Place the ancho strips in a blender with the remaining ingredients and purée until smooth.

RECIPE 18.4

Approximate values per serving including achiote paste, smoked corn pudding, barley risotto and venison red wine jus:

Calories	914
Total fat	42 g
Saturated fat	18 g
Cholesterol	345 mg
Sodium	1750 mg
Total carbohydrates	79 g
Protein	55 g

Achiote Paste—Approximate values per 30 mL serving:

Calories	66
Total fat	2.3 g
Saturated fat	0.3 g
Cholesterol	0 mg
Sodium	301 mg
Total carbohydrates	9.5 g
Protein	1.9 g

Smoked Corn Pudding—
Approximate values per serving:

Calories	343
Total fat	19 g
Saturated fat	10 g
Cholesterol	204 mg
Sodium	711 mg
Total carbohydrates	31 g
Protein	12 g

SMOKED CORN PUDDING

Yield: 500 mL (2 cups)

Whole butter	50 g	3 Tbsp.
Milk	500 mL	1 pt.
Yellow cornmeal	80 g	1/2 cup
Kosher salt	TT	TT
Pepper	TT	TT
Corn, lightly smoked, kernels removed	2 ears	2 ears
Onion, chopped	25 g	3 Tbsp.
Eggs, separated	3	3

1. Coat a 20-cm (8-inch) square pan with 15 g (1 Tbsp.) of butter.
2. In a medium saucepan, bring the milk to a boil. Lower the heat and gradually whisk in the cornmeal. Cook over low heat for 10 minutes, stirring with a wooden spoon.
3. Add the salt, pepper, corn, onion and remaining butter; cook for an additional 3 minutes. Remove from the heat and add the egg yolks one at a time, beating well with a wooden spoon after each addition.
4. Add a pinch of salt to the egg whites and beat with a fine whisk until stiff. Fold the whipped egg whites into the cornmeal mixture, one-half at a time. Pour into the buttered pan and bake at 175°C (350°F) until golden-brown, approximately 30 minutes.

BARLEY RISOTTO

Yield: 4 Servings

Barley Risotto—
Approximate values per serving:

Calories	200
Total fat	7 g
Saturated fat	4 g
Cholesterol	18 mg
Sodium	368 mg
Total carbohydrates	28 g
Protein	6.3 g

Barley	125 g	1/2 cup
Water	500 mL	1 pt.
Whole butter	15 g	1 Tbsp.
Garlic cloves, chopped	15 g	4
Chicken stock	250 mL	1 cup
Green onions or chives, sliced	25 g	3 Tbsp.
Asiago, grated	40 g	1/4 cup
Kosher salt	TT	TT
Pepper	TT	TT

1. Cook the barley in the water until barely done; strain.
2. Melt the butter in a large saucepan over medium heat. Add the garlic and cook until fragrant, approximately 2 minutes. Add the barley and stir with a wooden spoon to coat completely with the butter.
3. Increase the heat and add 125 mL (1/2 cup) of the chicken stock. Stir until all the stock is absorbed, then add the remaining stock. Cook until almost all of the stock is absorbed and remove from heat.
4. Stir in the green onions and cheese, and season to taste with salt and pepper.

VENISON RED WINE JUS

Yield: 500 mL (1 pt.)

Venison Red Wine Jus—
Approximate values per
30 mL serving:

Calories	34
Total fat	1.7 g
Saturated fat	0.6 g
Cholesterol	1.4 mg
Sodium	27 mg
Total carbohydrates	4.1 g
Protein	0.5 g

Bacon, chopped	25 g	2 Tbsp.
Shallots, chopped	50 g	2
Carrots, chopped	100 g	1/2 cup
Garlic, chopped	10 g	2 tsp.
Celery, chopped	75 g	1 rib
Onion, chopped	75 g	1/2 cup
Red wine	500 mL	1 pt.
Venison or venison/veal stock	1 L	1 qt.

1. In a medium saucepan, render the bacon over low heat. Add the shallots, carrot, garlic, celery and onion, cook until tender.

2. Add the red wine and reduce to a syrup.

3. Add the stock and reduce by two-thirds. Pass through a fine strainer and check the consistency. Return to the saucepan and reduce further if necessary.

◆◆◆

RECIPE 18.5

CARIBOU SERVED IN PUFF PASTRY WITH BROAD BEANS AND WILD MUSHROOMS

INSTITUT DE TOURISME ET D'HÔTELLERIE DU QUÉBEC, Montréal, QC
Professeur Jean-Claude Belmont

Yield: 4 Servings   **Method:** Roasting

Sauce:		
Dry shallots, minced	200 g	6
Sweet butter	15 g	1 Tbsp.
Red wine	200 mL	7 fl. oz.
Caribou Alcool, 94%	100 mL	3-1/2 fl. oz.
Caribou brown stock	500 mL	16 fl. oz.
Salt and pepper	TT	TT
Fresh thyme	1 sprig	1 sprig
Garnish:		
Small pearl onions	50 g	2 oz.
Sweet butter	15 g	1 Tbsp.
Morels	50 g	1 oz.
Chanterelles	50 g	1 oz.
Button mushrooms	150 g	3 oz.
Broad beans	200 g	7 oz.
Caribou loin, trimmed	450 g	1 lb.
Oil, salt and pepper	TT	TT
Puff pastry	400 g	14 oz.

Jean-Claude Belmont
Jean-Claude trained in France and worked in some of the most famous hotels in the world before settling in Canada. He now trains students for regional and international competitions. His Quebec Regional Junior Team won the gold medal and the prestigious Joseph Dobler Cup in Berlin in 1996. He is a dedicated promoter of regional foods.

1. To make the sauce, sweat the shallots in butter.

2. Add red wine and Alcool and reduce by one-half.

3. Add stock and seasonings and reduce by one-half.

4. Monter au beurre, strain and reserve.

5. To make the garnish, blanch the onions and drain well.

6. Sauté the onions with all the mushrooms in the butter.

7. Season to taste and keep hot.

8. Blanch the broad beans in salted water and keep warm.

9. Sear the trimmed, seasoned caribou loin in oil.

10. Finish in oven (140°C/275°F), until rare. Let rest 20 minutes.

11. Roll puff pastry and cut into four 13-cm (5-inch) rounds. Let rest 15 minutes, then bake at 190°C (375°F) for 20 minutes.

12. Split the puff pastry into two (top and bottom).

13. Put the bottom on a plate, then add a layer of loin slices. Cover with a layer of sauce (30 mL/2 Tbsp.) and a few beans. Put the top into place.

14. To garnish, drizzle the sauce around the puff pasty. Add a few more beans and sprinkle with chopped herbs.

RECIPE 18.5

Approximate values per serving:

Calories	895
Total fat	51 g
Saturated fat	16 g
Cholesterol	111 mg
Sodium	893 mg
Total carbohydrates	69 g
Protein	40 g

Mikael Volke, CCC

Mikael began cooking in 1986 at the Malborough Inn in Calgary and went on to study at the Southern Alberta Institute of Technology. He worked in restaurants in Calgary and Switzerland before settling in at the Falkridge Corporate Retreat.

RECIPE 18.6

Approximate values per serving (not including polenta):

Calories	136
Total fat	6.6 g
Saturated fat	1.1 g
Cholesterol	43 mg
Sodium	500 mg
Total carbohydrates	5.1 g
Protein	14 g

Soft Oka and Wild Forest Mushroom Polenta— Approximate values per serving:

Calories	290
Total fat	12 g
Saturated fat	4.9 g
Cholesterol	19 mg
Sodium	216 mg
Total carbohydrates	37 g
Protein	8.6 g

✦✦✦

RECIPE 18.6

ROULADE OF BISON, FIRE-ROASTED PEPPERS ON A SOFT OKA AND WILD FOREST MUSHROOM POLENTA

FALKRIDGE CORPORATE RETREAT, CALGARY, AB
Executive Chef Mikael Volke, CCC

Yield: 4 Appetizer Portions   **Method:** Braising

Red pepper, roasted	175 g	1
Bison, round or sirloin slices, each 30 g (1 oz.)	8	8
Dijon mustard	30 mL	1 fl. oz.
Salt and pepper	TT	TT
Fennel, ground	pinch	pinch
Coriander, ground	pinch	pinch
Vegetable oil	15 mL	1 tsp.
Brown beef stock	200 mL	7 fl. oz.
Soft Oka and Wild Forest Mushroom Polenta (recipe follows)		

1. Cut pepper into 5-mm (1/4-inch) strips.
2. Lay out roulades, brush with mustard and season with salt, pepper and spices.
3. Place two pepper strips at one end of each roulade and roll up into cylinders. Secure with toothpicks.
4. Brown roulades in hot skillet with oil.
5. Add stock and braise in a 180°C (375°F) oven for 8–10 minutes.
6. To serve, remove toothpicks, slice on a bias and arrange on polenta. Drizzle pan juices.

SOFT OKA AND WILD FOREST MUSHROOM POLENTA

Shallots, chopped	50 g	2 oz.
Vegetable oil	10 mL	2 tsp.
Wild mushrooms, chopped	60 g	2 oz.
Chicken stock	1 L	1 qt.
Cornmeal	125 g	4 oz.
Oka cheese	75 g	2-1/2 oz.

1. Sweat shallots in oil until translucent, then add mushrooms and cook until tender.
2. Add stock, bring to rolling boil and stir in cornmeal. Simmer 15–20 minutes.
3. Stir in cheese and reserve.

✦✦✦

RECIPE 18.7

GUINEA FOWL BASQUAISE

WORLD TRADE AND CONVENTION CENTRE, HALIFAX, NS
Executive Chef Christophe Luzeux, CCC

Yield: 4 Servings   **Method:** Braising

Guinea fowl breasts, each 160 g (6 oz.)	4	4
Butter	50 g	1-1/2 oz.
Premium cured ham, diced (0.5 cm/1/4 inch)	300 g	10 oz.

Christophe Luzeux, CCC

Christophe comes from Marcq-en-Baroeul in the north of France and was a graduate student of Lycée Michel Servet in Lille, France. Afterwards,

Onions, julienned	350 g	12 oz.
Peppers, red, green and yellow, julienned (0.5 cm/1/4 inch)	500 g	3
Hot pepper, small	1	1
Tomato concassée	750 g	1-1/2 lb.
White wine	250 mL	8 fl. oz.
Cognac	125 mL	4 fl. oz.
Salt and pepper	TT	TT
Parsley, freshly chopped	TT	TT

1. Sear the breasts in butter for 3 minutes on each side. Remove and reserve.

2. Sauté the ham for 1 minute in the same pot. Remove and reserve.

3. Sauté the onions and peppers in the same pot for 8 minutes. Add the tomato, wine and cognac. Simmer for 15 minutes.

4. Add the guinea fowl and ham and simmer another 10 minutes. Season with salt and pepper.

5. Garnish with freshly chopped parsley for service.

be boned bis skills in several of France's top establishments. His more recent culinary achievements include winning silver in the Individual Competition in the 2000 Culinary Team Canada Competition and functioning as the captain of Team Nova Scotia, when it won silver in both 1998 and 1999.

RECIPE 18.7

Approximate values per serving:

Calories	627
Total fat	31 g
Saturated fat	12 g
Cholesterol	203 mg
Sodium	1529 mg
Total carbohydrates	28 g
Protein	59 g

❖❖❖

RECIPE 18.8

BISON MEDALLIONS ON ROASTED PARSNIP AND ONION BREAD AND BUTTER PUDDING, ESPRESSO JUS

SOUTHERN ALBERTA INSTITUTE OF TECHNOLOGY, Calgary, AB
Chef Instructors Georg Windisch, CCC, and Simon Dunn, CCC

Yield: 1 Serving **Method:** Pan-frying

Pudding (4–6 portions):

Parsnips, roasted	125 g	2
Red onion, roasted	125 g	1/2
Eggs, medium	5	5
Cream, 35%	200 mL	7 fl. oz.
Milk	200 mL	7 fl. oz.
Brioche, buttered	6 slices	6 slices

Sauce:

Shallots, brunoise	50 g	2 oz.
Clarified butter	5 mL	1 tsp.
Espresso	5 mL	1 tsp.
Merlot	50 mL	2 fl. oz.
Game stock	100 mL	3 fl. oz.
Bison tenderloin medallions, each 60 g (2 oz.)	2	2
Kosher salt	TT	TT
Crushed black pepper	TT	TT
Clarified butter	10 mL	2 tsp.
Butter, unsalted	10 g	2 tsp.

Garnish: parsnip chips, deep-fried sage leaves, onion straw

1. To make the pudding, season and roast the parsnips and onion until caramelized, purée and cool.

2. Whisk eggs, cream and milk together, strain and incorporate the parsnip-onion purée.

Georg Windisch, CCC and Simon Dunn, CCC

Georg was born and professionally trained in Austria and has extensive work experience in the botel industry in Europe, Australia, Asia and Canada. Before starting his own company and joining S.A.I.T., be was the Executive Chef at the Pan Pacific Hotel in Singapore. Simon was born and classically trained in Great Britain. Most recently, be was the Executive Chef at the renowned Inn on Lake Bonavista.

RECIPE 18.8

Approximate values per serving, including 1/6th of pudding:

Calories	922
Total fat	66 g
Saturated fat	30 g
Cholesterol	384 mg
Sodium	825 mg
Total carbohydrates	44 g
Protein	38 g

Continued

3. Layer the buttered brioche in a well-buttered pan and add the custard.

4. Bake at 175°C (350°F) until top is golden and crisp and custard is set, approximately 25 minutes.

5. To make the sauce, caramelize the shallots in 5 mL (1 tsp.) clarified butter, add the espresso and reduce on low heat.

6. Deglaze with merlot and reduce by one-third. Add the stock and reduce to 75 mL (2-1/2 fl. oz.).

7. Season the bison with salt and pepper. Sear in 10 mL (2 tsp.) clarified butter on high heat to develop colour and flavour. Do not cook past medium-rare. Reserve meat.

8. Deglaze the meat pan with the sauce, whisk in the unsalted butter (mount) and adjust seasoning.

9. Place a wedge of pudding in centre of plate, arrange medallions and drizzle sauce.

10. Garnish with parsnip chips, deep-fried sage leaves and onion straw.

Tony Murakami

Tony started out in Tokyo and then came to Canada, where he worked his way up to executive chef and joined the St. Charles Country Club. Tony is a Certified Master Chef, and highlights of his career include nine gold medals and four grand golds in international competition. He has been recognized by the federal and Manitoba governments for his work.

RECIPE 18.9

Approximate values per serving:

Calories	550
Total fat	50 g
Saturated fat	12 g
Cholesterol	77 mg
Sodium	373 mg
Total carbohydrates	8.9 g
Protein	16 g

◆◆◆

RECIPE 18.9

ROASTED PHEASANT
WITH PRAIRIE BABY LETTUCE LEAVES, WALNUT OIL AND BALSAMIC VINAIGRETTE

ST. CHARLES COUNTRY CLUB, WINNIPEG, MB
Executive Chef Tony Murakami

Yield: 10 Servings   **Method:** Roasting

Whole pheasant, each 1.2–1.5 kg (2-1/2–3-1/2 lb.)	3	3
Butter, unsalted, room temperature	375 g	14 oz.
Salt and pepper	TT	TT
White wine, dry	350 mL	12 fl. oz.
Mirepoix	400 g	3-1/2 cups
Juniper berries	10 g	1 Tbsp.
Mignonette (coarsely ground black pepper)	3 g	1 tsp.
Pheasant or chicken stock	350 mL	12 fl. oz.
Gin	5 mL	1 tsp.
Walnut Oil and Balsamic Vinaigrette:		
Dijon mustard	15 mL	1 Tbsp.
Walnut oil	350 mL	12 fl. oz.
Balsamic vinegar	100 mL	3-1/2 fl. oz.
Shallots, finely chopped	20 g	2 Tbsp.
Dry red chile pepper, crushed	0.5 g	1 tsp.
Salt and pepper	TT	TT
Salad:		
Assortment of baby lettuce leaves, spinach leaves or other leaves	10 portions, each 75 g	10 portions, each 1 cup

Potato chips (small-sized		
baker chipped as garnish)	30 pieces	30 pieces
Tomato petals, skinless	30 pieces	30 pieces

1. Brush pheasant all over with butter and salt and pepper to season. Roast at 200°C (400°F) for 10 minutes. Reduce heat to 150°C (300°F) for 15–20 minutes. Next, pour the white wine over the bird. Take the pheasant out of the oven and let rest for 15 minutes.

2. Sauté the mirepoix until brown. Bone the pheasant and reserve the bones and skin. Set it aside and keep it warm.

3. In a heavy stainless steel pan over medium heat, add pheasant skin, bone, mirepoix, juniper berries, mignonette and anything from the roasting pan. Add stock. Simmer for 20 minutes and skim the fat.

4. Strain the stock and reduce by half or to a syrupy consistency. Add the gin.

5. Make the vinaigrette dressing. Whip the ingredients except salt and pepper with the reduction of the stock. Add salt and pepper to taste.

6. Wash the salad leaves and spin dry. Toss the salad leaves with the vinaigrette. Arrange the greens on a chilled plate, then arrange thinly sliced pheasant on the plate with small potato chips and tomato petals. To make the tomato petals, peel the tomatoes then cut them into quarters or sixths. Seed them and cut away interior flesh to produce a petal- or leaf-like shape.

❖❖❖

RECIPE 18.10

VENISON LOIN IN WILD RICE MANTLE

CULINARY TEAM ALBERTA, CALGARY, AB
Chef Fred Zimmermann, CCC, retired

Yield: 4–6 Servings   **Method:** Roasting

Venison loin, trimmed, silverskin removed	600–800 g	1-1/4–1-3/4 lb.
Salt and pepper	TT	TT
Vegetable oil or butter	30 mL	1 fl. oz.
Pork shoulder, fine grind	150 g	5 oz.
Shallots, diced	50 g	2 oz.
Garlic	5 g	1 clove
Nutmeg or mace	pinch	pinch
Cloves, ground	pinch	pinch
Allspice	pinch	pinch
Egg	1	1
Raw wild rice, cooked	100 g	3 oz.

1. Season and sear the venison loin in a hot skillet and cool.

2. In a food processor, place pork, shallots, garlic, nutmeg, cloves, allspice, egg, salt and pepper and process for 1 minute.

3. Place forcemeat in a bowl and mix in wild rice.

4. Coat the venison loin evenly with the wild rice forcemeat, roll in plastic wrap and then in foil.

5. Bake in a 140°C (285°F) oven for 45–55 minutes to an internal temperature of 55°C (130°F) for medium-rare to medium.

6. Remove from oven and let rest 30 minutes.

7. Unwrap and pan-fry evenly in oil to brown the mantle. Let rest again for a few minutes before carving.

Fred Zimmermann, CCC
A patriarch among Canadian chefs, Fred has over 35 years of experience in the foodservice industry. Having completed his culinary apprenticeship in his native Switzerland, he went on to cook in many of Canada's finest hotels before his 23-year career as Executive Chef at the Westin Calgary. Fred is now retired but still involved in competition, both as participant and international judge. The latter represents a high commendation from Fred's international peers of his professional credentials, knowledge, expertise and accomplishments.

RECIPE 18.10

Approximate values per serving:

Calories	432
Total fat	16 g
Saturated fat	3.4 g
Cholesterol	206 mg
Sodium	416 mg
Total carbohydrates	24 g
Protein	48 g

Dennis Green

Dennis was raised in Vancouver and started cooking when he was 17. He served his apprenticeship at a small bistro named the Avenue Grill near his high school. He joined Bishop's in 1993 and has been the Executive Chef there since 1997.

◆ ◆ ◆

RECIPE 18.11

GRILLED QUAIL WITH ROASTED CORN AND SQUASH CURRY, PEAR BLACKBERRY COMPOTE

BISHOP'S RESTAURANT, VANCOUVER, BC
Executive Chef Dennis Green

Yield: 8 Servings   **Method:** Grilling

Orange zest and juice	1	1
Vegetable oil	60 mL	2 fl. oz.
Thyme, fresh	10 g	1 Tbsp.
Quail, semi-boneless	8	8
Roasted Corn and Squash Curry:		
Corn	4 ears	4 ears
Onion, diced medium	160 g	5 oz.
Green zucchini, diced medium	175 g	6 oz.
Yellow zucchini, diced medium	175 g	6 oz.
Acorn squash, diced medium	175 g	6 oz.
Olive oil	30 mL	1 fl. oz.
Curry powder	3 g	1 tsp.
Cumin	3 g	1 tsp.
Paprika	3 g	1 tsp.
Dry sherry	125 mL	4 fl. oz.
Coconut milk	400 mL	1 tin
Cream, 35%	125 mL	4 fl. oz.
Salt and pepper	TT	TT
Pear Blackberry Compote (recipe follows)		
Salt and pepper	TT	TT

1. Whisk orange zest, juice, oil and thyme together and pour over quail. Marinate in refrigerator for 1 hour.
2. Peel and rinse corn cobs and dry-roast in a nonstick or grill pan. Cut kernels from cobs and set aside.
3. Sauté onion and squash in olive oil until translucent.
4. Add spices and corn, sweat and then deglaze pan with sherry. Cook until squash is tender.
5. Add coconut milk and cream, simmer to reduce slightly and thicken. Correct seasoning and reserve.
6. Remove quail from marinade, season with salt and pepper and grill for 5 minutes on each side over medium heat.
7. Spoon curried vegetables on plate and place quail and compote.

RECIPE 18.11

Approximate values per serving (not including compote):

Calories	551
Total fat	39 g
Saturated fat	18 g
Cholesterol	136 mg
Sodium	491 mg
Total carbohydrates	17 g
Protein	33 g

PEAR BLACKBERRY COMPOTE

Sweet onion, diced	80 g	3 oz.
Sugar	125 g	4 oz.
Rice vinegar	250 mL	8 fl. oz.
Ginger, grated	5 g	1 tsp.
Garlic, minced	8 g	2 cloves
Pears, peeled and diced	1 kg	2 lb.
Blackberries	200 g	7 oz.
Thyme, chopped	10 g	1 Tbsp.

Pear Blackberry Compote—
Approximate values
per 85 mL serving:

Calories	114
Total fat	0.4 g
Saturated fat	0 g
Cholesterol	0 mg
Sodium	1.9 mg
Total carbohydrates	27 g
Protein	0.7 g

1. Combine onion, sugar, vinegar, ginger and garlic in a pot. Bring to a boil.

2. Add pears, blackberries and thyme. Simmer until tender.

3. Cool and serve at room temperature.

EBLINKS

Wild Game Recipes
    diver.ocean.washington.edu/peterl/recipes/recipemain.html
B&E Ranches and North Country Bison: Bison Cooking Tips
    www.ncbison.com/cooking_tips.html
National Food Safety Database: Preservation of Game Meats
    www.foodsafety.org/sd/sd019.htm

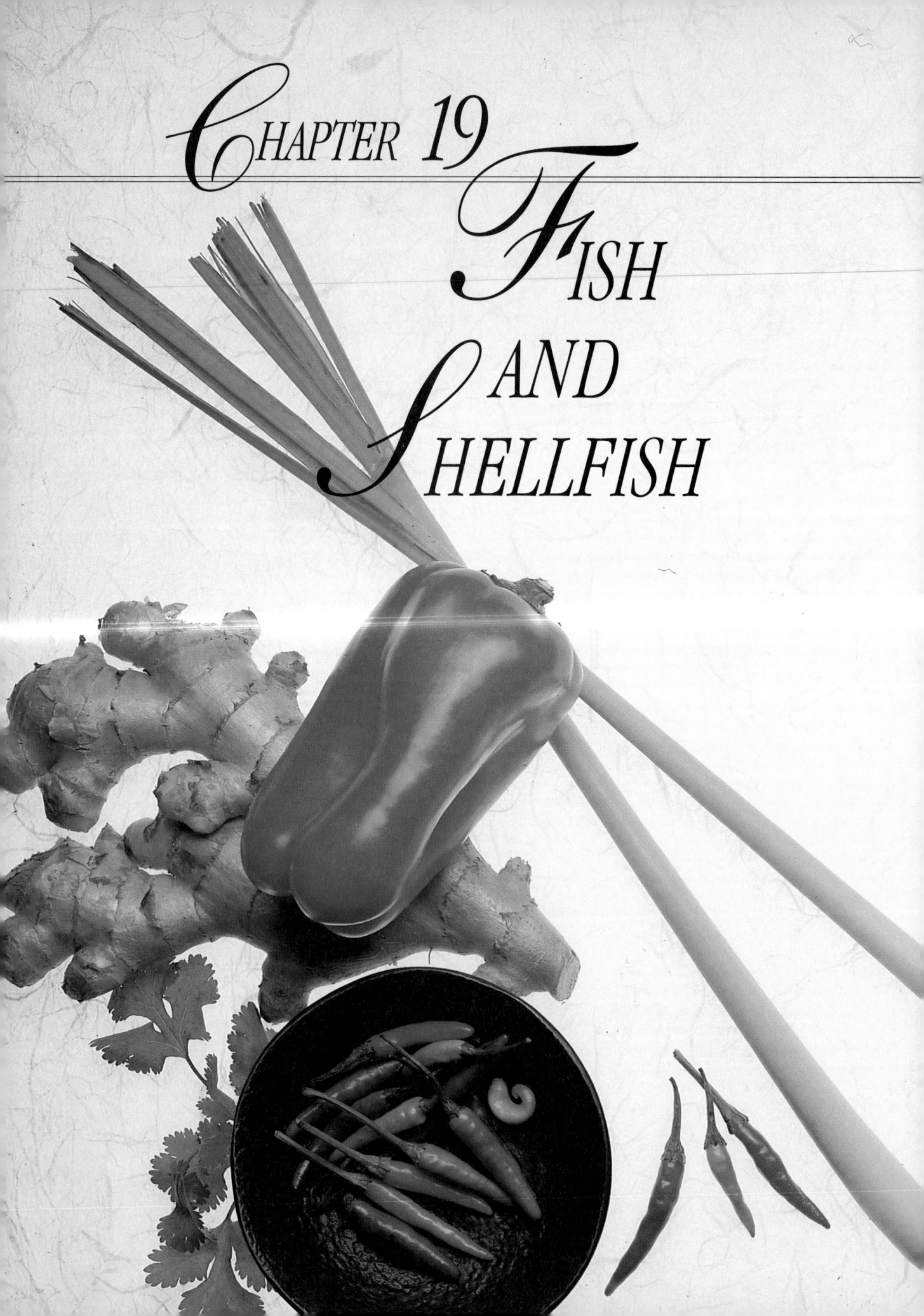

CHAPTER 19
FISH AND SHELLFISH

◆◆◆

LEARNING OUTCOMES

After studying this chapter you will be able to:

◆ describe the structure and composition of fish and shellfish
◆ identify a variety of fish and shellfish
◆ purchase fish and shellfish appropriate for your needs
◆ store fish and shellfish properly
◆ prepare fish and shellfish for cooking: scale fish; pan-dress flatfish; fillet round fish and flatfish; skin Dover sole and fish fillets; pull pin bones from salmon fillets; cut a fillet; cut steaks; peel, devein and butterfly shrimp; prepare live lobster for broiling or sautéing; remove cooked lobster meat from the shell; open clams and oysters; clean and debeard mussels
◆ apply various cooking methods to fish and shellfish: broiling and grilling, baking, sautéing, panfrying, steaming, submersion and shallow poaching, simmering

ish are aquatic vertebrates with fins for swimming and gills for breathing. Of the more than 30 000 species known, most live in the seas and oceans; freshwater species are far less numerous. Shellfish are aquatic invertebrates with shells or carapaces. They are found in both fresh and salt water.

Always an important food source, fish and shellfish have become increasingly popular in recent years, due in part to demands from health-conscious consumers. Because of increased demand and improved preservation and transportation techniques, good-quality fish and shellfish, once found only along seacoasts and lakes, are now readily available to almost every food service operation.

Many fish and shellfish species are very expensive; all are highly perishable. Because their cooking times are generally shorter and their flavours more delicate than meat or poultry, special attention must be given to fish and shellfish to prevent spoilage and to produce high-quality finished products.

In this chapter you will learn how to identify a large assortment of fish and shellfish as well as how to properly purchase and store them, fabricate or prepare them for cooking and cook them by a variety of dry-heat and moist-heat cooking methods. This chapter presents many of the cooking methods applied to meats and poultry in the previous chapters. Review the corresponding procedures for meats and poultry and note the similarities and differences.

STRUCTURE AND MUSCLE COMPOSITION

The fish and shellfish used in food service operations can be divided into three categories: fish, mollusks and crustaceans.

Fish (Fr. *poisson*) include both fresh- and saltwater varieties. They have fins and an internal skeleton of bone and cartilage. Based upon shape and skeletal structure, fish can be divided into two groups: round fish and flatfish. **Round fish** swim in a vertical position and have eyes on both sides of their heads. Their bodies may be truly round, oval or compressed. (See Figure 19.1.) **Flatfish** have asymmetrical, compressed bodies, swim in a horizontal position and have both eyes on top of their heads. Flatfish are bottom dwellers; most are found in deep ocean waters around the world. The skin on top of their bodies is dark, to camouflage them from predators, and can change colour according to their surroundings. Their scales are small and their dorsal and anal fins run the length of their bodies. (See Figure 19.2.)

Mollusks (Fr. *mollusque*) are shellfish characterized by soft, unsegmented bodies with no internal skeleton. Most mollusks have hard outer shells. Single-shelled mollusks such as abalone are known as **univalves**. Those with two shells, such as clams, oysters and mussels, are known as **bivalves**. Squid and octopus, which are known as **cephalopods**, do not have a hard outer shell. Rather, they have a single thin internal shell called a *pen* or *cuttlebone*.

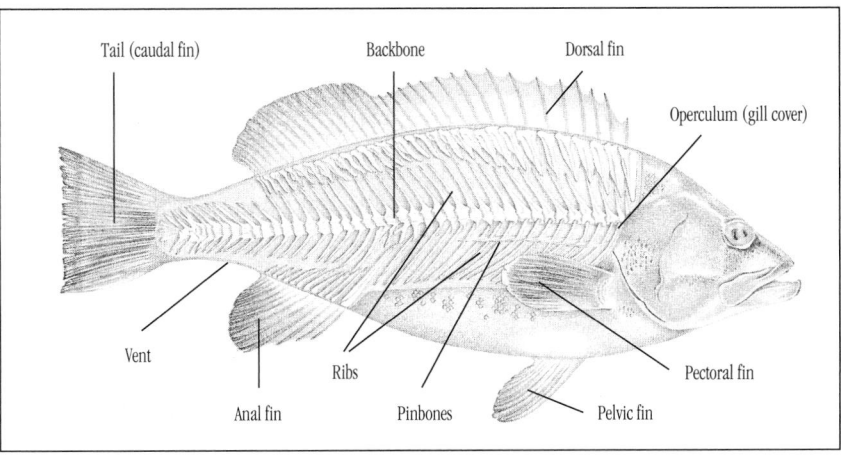

FIGURE 19.1   *Bone Structure of a Round Fish*

Crustaceans (Fr. *crustacé*) are also shellfish. They have a hard outer skeleton or shell and jointed appendages. Crustaceans include lobsters, crabs and shrimp.

The flesh of fish and shellfish consists primarily of water, protein, fat and minerals. Fish flesh is composed of short muscle fibres separated by delicate sheets of connective tissue. Fish, as well as most shellfish, are naturally tender, so the purpose of cooking is to firm proteins and enhance flavour. The absence of the oxygen-carrying protein myoglobin makes fish flesh very light or white in colour. (The orange colour of salmon and some trout comes from pigments found in their food.) Compared to meats, fish do not contain large amounts of intermuscular fat. But the amount of fat a fish does contain affects the way it responds to cooking. Fish containing a relatively large amount of fat, such as salmon and mackerel, are known as fatty or oily fish. Fish such as cod and haddock contain very little fat and are referred to as lean fish. Shellfish are also very lean.

SEAFOOD

"Seafood" means different things to different people. For some, the term applies just to shellfish or to shellfish and other small edible marine creatures. For others it is limited to saltwater shellfish or to saltwater shellfish and fish. For yet others, it refers to all fish and shellfish, both freshwater and saltwater. Because of the term's vagueness, it is not used here.

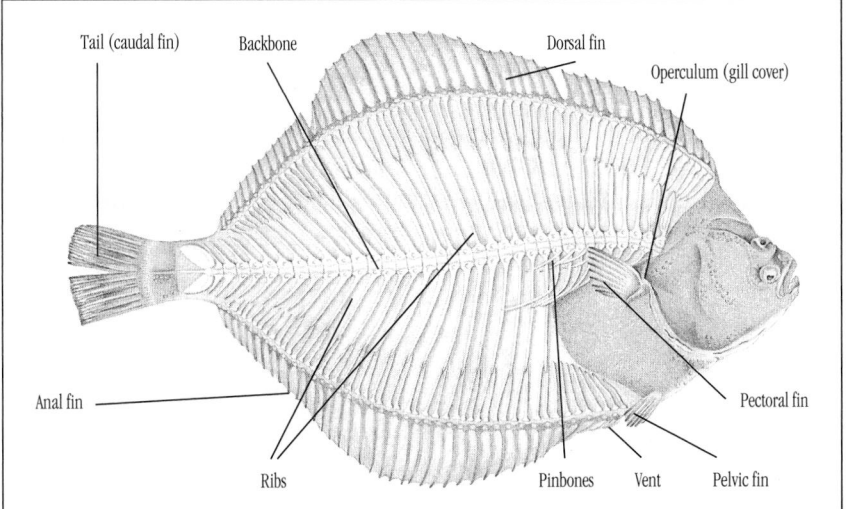

FIGURE 19.2   *Bone Structure of a Flatfish*

IDENTIFYING FISH AND SHELLFISH

Identifying fish and shellfish properly can be difficult because of the vast number of similar-appearing fish and shellfish that are separate species within each family. Adding confusion are the various colloquial names given to the same fish or the same name given to different fish in different localities. Fish with an unappealing name may also be given a catchier name or the name of a similar but more popular item for marketing purposes. Moreover, some species are referred to by a foreign name, especially on menus.

The Canadian Food Inspection Agency publishes regulations concerning acceptable nomenclature for fish and fish products.

Fish

Round Fish

Bass (Fr. *bar*) commonly refers to a number of unrelated fish. The better-known freshwater bass varieties (largemouth, smallmouth, redeye and black) are actually members of the sunfish family. They are lean and delicate but, as game, not commercially available in Canada. The saltwater bass varieties (black sea bass and striped bass) are popular commercial items.

Black Sea Bass

Black sea bass are sometimes referred to as rock sea bass. They have a lean, firm white flesh with a mild flavour and flaky texture. They usually weigh 675 g–1.3 kg (1-1/2–3 lb.) and are most prevalent in the Atlantic Ocean between New York and North Carolina. Black sea bass can be prepared by almost any cooking method and are often served whole in Chinese and Italian cuisines.

Striped Bass

Striped bass, often erroneously referred to as rockfish, are ocean fish that depend on freshwater rivers to reproduce. True striped bass cannot be marketed because pollution and overfishing have damaged the supply. A hybrid of striped bass and either white bass or white perch is being **aquafarmed** for commercial use, however. It is this hybrid that food service operations receive as striped bass. Whole fish weigh 450 g–2.2 kg (1–5 lb.). Striped bass have a rich, sweet flavour and firm texture. They can be steamed, baked, poached or broiled.

Catfish are scaleless freshwater fish common in southern lakes and rivers and now aquafarmed extensively. Aquafarm raising eliminates the "muddy" taste once associated with catfish and ensures a year-round supply. The flesh is pure white with a moderate fat content, a mild, sweet flavour and firm texture. Channel catfish are the most important commercially. They usually weigh

Catfish

675 g–2.2 kg (1-1/2–5 lb.). The smaller of these fish are known as **fiddlers**; they are often deep-fat fried and served whole. Catfish may be prepared by almost any cooking method, but are especially well suited to frying.

Arctic char are a type of salmon found in the far northern rivers. Brook trout and lake trout are also chars. It is lean and pink fleshed. Wild char is available fresh only in August, September, March and April. It is being farm raised.

The **cod** (Fr. *cabillaud*) family includes Atlantic and Pacific cod as well as pollock, haddock, whiting and hake. Cod have a mild, delicate flavour and lean, firm white flesh that flakes apart easily. Cod can be prepared by most

♦♦♦

SURIMI

Surimi is made from a highly processed fish paste coloured, flavoured and shaped to resemble shrimp, lobster, crab or other shellfish. Most surimi is based on Alaskan pollock, but some blends include varying amounts of real crab, shrimp or other items. Available chilled or frozen, surimi is already fully cooked and ready to add to salads, pasta, sauces or other dishes. Surimi is very low in fat and relatively high in protein. Because of processing techniques, however, it has more sodium and fewer vitamins and minerals than the real fish or shellfish it replaces. North Americans now consume more than 45 million kilograms (100 million pounds) of surimi each year and its popularity continues to grow. The Canadian Food Inspection Agency requires that all surimi products be labelled "imitation."

cooking methods, although grilling is not recommended because the flesh is too flaky.

Atlantic cod are the best-selling fish in the Americas. They are available fresh, whole or drawn, or cut into fillets or steaks. They are also available frozen and are often used for precooked or prebreaded sticks or portions. Smoked cod and salt cod are also available. Although cod may reach 90 kg (200 lb.), most market cod weigh 4.5 kg (10 lb.) or less. **Scrod** is a marketing term for cod weighing less than 1.1 kg (2-1/2 lb.).

Haddock, the second most commercially important fish, look like thin, small Atlantic cod and weigh about 900 g–2.3 kg (2–5 lb.). They have a stronger flavour and more delicate texture than Atlantic cod. They are available smoked.

Atlantic Cod

Pacific cod, also known as grey cod, are found in the northern Pacific Ocean and are not as abundant as their Atlantic cousins. Pacific cod are most often available frozen; they should be labelled "true cod" to distinguish them from rock cod and black cod (sable fish), which are unrelated.

Pollock, also known as Boston bluefish or blue cod, are plentiful in the northern Atlantic and Pacific Oceans. Their flesh is grey-pink when raw, turning white when cooked. Pollock are often frozen at sea, then reprocessed into surimi. They can also be salted or smoked.

Pollock

Eels (Fr. *anguille*) are long, snakelike freshwater fish with dorsal and anal fins running the length of their bodies. (The conger eel is from a different family and has little culinary significance.) North American and European eels are available live, whole, gutted or as fillets. Eels have a high fat content and firm flesh; they are sweet and mildly flavoured. Their tough skin should be removed before cooking. Eels may be steamed, baked, fried or used in stews. Baby eels are a springtime delicacy, especially in Spain, where they are pan-fried in olive oil and garlic with hot red peppers. Smoked eels are also available.

Eel

The **grouper** family includes almost 400 varieties found in temperate waters worldwide. The more common Atlantic Ocean varieties are the yellowfin grouper, black grouper, red grouper and gag; the Pacific Ocean varieties are the sea bass (also known as jewfish and different from the black sea bass) and spotted cabrilla. Although some species can reach 360 kg (800 lb.) or more, most commercial varieties are sold in the 2.2–9 kg (5–20 lb.) range. They have lean white flesh with a mild to sweet flavour and very firm texture. Their skin, which is tough and strongly flavoured, is generally removed before cooking. Grouper fillets may be baked, deep-fat fried, broiled or grilled.

Grouper

Herring (Fr. *hareng*) are long, silvery-blue fish found in both the northern Atlantic and Pacific Oceans. Their strongly flavoured flesh has a moderate to high fat content. Whole herring weigh up to 225 g (8 oz.). Fresh herring may be butterflied or filleted and roasted, broiled or grilled. But because herring are very soft and tend to spoil quickly, they are rarely available fresh. More often, they are smoked (known as kippers) or pickled in brine.

Sardines (Fr. *sardine*) are young, small herring with fatty, oily flesh that has a flaky texture. Sardines are usually sold canned, whole or as skinned and boned fillets, or fried or smoked and packed in oil or sauce. Sardines are used primarily for sandwiches and salads.

John Dory, also known as St. Peter's fish, have a distinctive round, black spot with a yellow halo on each side of the body. Their flesh is white, firm and finely flaked. They may be filleted and prepared like flounder and are a classic bouillabaisse ingredient.

John Dory

Mackerel

Mackerel (Fr. *maquereau*) of culinary importance include king and Spanish mackerel as well as tuna and wahoo, which are discussed separately later. The species known as Atlantic and Pacific mackerel are not generally used for food because of their small size and high fat content. Mackerel flesh has a high fat content, grey to pink colouring, a mild flavour and flaky texture. The flesh becomes firm and off-white when cooked. Mackerel are best broiled, grilled, smoked or baked.

Mahi-mahi is the more commonly used name for dolphin or dolphinfish; this Hawaiian name is used to distinguish them from the marine mammal of the same name. (Dolphins and porpoises are marine mammals.) Also known by their Spanish name, *dorado*, mahi-mahi are brilliantly coloured fish found in tropical seas. Mahi-mahi weigh about 6.6 kg (15 lb.) and are sold whole or as fillets. Their flesh is off-white to pink, lean and firm with a sweet flavour. Mahi-mahi can be broiled, grilled or baked. The meat may become dry when cooked, however, so sauce or marinade is recommended.

Mahi-mahi

Monkfish are also known as angler fish, goosefish, rape and lotte. These extraordinarily ugly fish are rarely seen whole, for the large head is usually discarded before reaching market. Only the tail is edible; it is available in fillets, fresh or frozen. The scaleless skin must be removed. The flesh is lean, pearly white and very firm. Its texture and flavour have earned monkfish the nickname of "poor man's lobster." Monkfish absorb flavours easily and are baked, steamed, fried, grilled or broiled. They are also used for stews and soups.

Orange roughy are caught in the South Pacific off the coasts of New Zealand and Australia. They have bright orange skin and firm, pearly-white flesh with a low fat content and extremely bland flavour. Fresh-frozen fillets are widely available year round. Orange roughy are almost always marketed as skinless, boneless frozen fillets, averaging 170–225 g (6–8 oz.) each. They can be broiled, steamed, grilled or prepared in the same manner as cod.

Red snapper is also known as the American or northern red snapper. Although there are many members of the snapper family, only one is the true red snapper. Red-skinned rockfish are often mislabelled as the more popular red snapper or Pacific snapper, a practice that is currently legal only in California. True red snapper has lean, pink flesh that becomes white when cooked; it

Red Snapper

is sweet-flavoured and flaky. They are sold whole or as fillets with the skin left on for identification. Red snapper may reach 15 kg (35 lb.), but most are marketed at only 1.8–2.7 kg (4–6 lb.) or as 450 g–1.3 kg (1–3 lb.) fillets. Red snapper can be prepared using almost any cooking method. The head and bones are excellent for stock.

Salmon (Fr. *saumon*) flourish in both the northern Atlantic and Pacific oceans, returning to the freshwater rivers and streams of their birth to spawn. Salmon flesh gets its distinctive pink-red colour from fat-soluble carotenoids found in the crustaceans on which the fish feed. Salmon is the most popular fish in Canada. It is high in omega-3 fatty acids.

Atlantic salmon is the most important commercially, accounting for one-quarter of all salmon produced worldwide. Extensive aquafarms in Norway, Canada and Scotland produce a steady supply of Atlantic salmon. For marketing purposes, the fish's point of origin is often added to the name (for example, Norwegian, Scottish or Shetland Atlantic salmon). Atlantic salmon have a rich pink colour and moist flesh. Their average weight is from 1.8–5.4 kg (4–12 lb.). Wild Atlantic salmon are almost never available.

Atlantic Salmon

Chinook or **king salmon** from the Pacific are also highly desirable. They average 2.2–13 kg (5–30 lb.) and have red-orange flesh with a high fat content and rich flavour. Like other salmon, their flesh separates into large flakes when cooked. Chinooks are often marketed by the name of the river from which they are harvested (for example, Columbia, Yukon or Copper Chinook salmon). They are distinguished by the black interior of their mouth.

Chinook or King Salmon

Coho or **silver** salmon have pinkish flesh and are available fresh or frozen, wild or from aquafarms. Wild coho average 1.3–5.4 kg (3–12 lb.), while aqua-farmed coho are much smaller, usually less than 450 g (1 lb.).

Other varieties, such as chum, sockeye, red, blueback and pink salmon, are usually canned but may be available fresh or frozen.

Salmon can be prepared by many cooking methods: broiling, grilling, poaching, steaming or baking. Frying is not recommended, however, because of their high fat content. Salmon fillets are often cured or smoked. **Gravlax** is salmon that has been cured for one to three days with salt, sugar and dill. **Lox** is salmon that is cured in a salted brine and then typically cold-smoked. **Nova** is used in the eastern U.S. to refer to a less-salty, cold-smoked salmon.

Mini Coho Salmon

Blacktip Shark

Sharks provide delicious eating, despite their less-than-appealing appearance and vicious reputation. Mako and blue sharks are the most desirable, with mako often being sold as swordfish. Sand shark, sharpnose, blacktip, angel and thresher are also available commercially. Most sharks have lean flesh with a mild flavour and firm texture. The flesh is white with tinges of pink or red when raw, turning off-white when cooked. Makos weigh 13–110 kg (30–250 lb.); other species may reach as much as 450 kg (1000 lb.). All sharks have cartilaginous skeletons and no bones; therefore, they are not actually fish, but rather marine invertebrates. Sharks are usually cut into loins or wheels, then into steaks or cubes. They can be broiled, grilled, baked or fried. An ammonia smell indicates that the shark was not properly treated when caught. Do not buy or eat it.

Swordfish take their name from the long, swordlike bill extending from their upper jaw. These game fish average about 110 kg (250 lb.). Their flesh is lean and sweet with a very firm, meatlike texture; it may be grey, pink or off-white when raw, becoming white when cooked. Swordfish are available cut into wheels or portioned into steaks for grilling or broiling. Swordfish are becoming endangered.

Swordfish Wheel

Tilapia

Tilapia is the name given to several species of freshwater, aquafarm-raised fish bred worldwide. They grow quickly in warm water, reaching about 1.3 kg (3 lb.); they are available whole or filleted, fresh or frozen. The flesh is similar to catfish—lean, white and sweet, with a firm texture. Tilapia are sometimes marketed as cherry snapper or sunshine snapper, even though they are not members of the snapper family.

Trout (Fr. *truite*) are members of the *Salmonidae* family. Most of the freshwater trout commercially available are aquafarm-raised rainbow trout, although brown trout and brook trout are also being aquafarmed. Some trout species spend part of their lives at sea, returning to fresh water to spawn. On the west coast, these are called salmon trout or steelhead. Trout have a low to moderate fat content, a flaky texture and a delicate flavour that can be easily overwhelmed by strong sauces. The flesh may be white, orange or pink. Trout are usually marketed at 225–280 g (8–10 oz.) each, just right for an individual portion. Lake trout are not aquafarmed but are appearing on specialty menus, when available, as a cured and smoked product. Trout can be baked, pan-fried, smoked or steamed.

Red Mountain Trout

Rainbow Trout

Tuna (Fr. *thon*) varieties include the bluefin, yellowfin, bonito, bigeye and blackfin. Ahi is the popular market name for either yellowfin or bigeye tuna. All are members of the mackerel family and are found in tropical and subtropical waters around the world. Tuna are large fish, weighing up to several hundred pounds each. Bluefin, the finest and most desirable for sashimi, are becoming very scarce because of overfishing. Regular canned tuna is usually prepared from yellowfin or skipjack; canned white tuna is prepared from albacore, also known as longfin tuna. Pacific tuna that is frozen at sea to preserve its freshness is referred to as clipper fish. Any of these species may be found fresh or frozen, however. Tuna is usually cut into four boneless loins for market. The loins are then cut into steaks, cubes or chunks. The flesh has a low to moderate fat content (a higher fat content is preferred for sashimi) and a deep red colour. The dark, reddish-brown muscle that runs along the lateral line is very fatty and can be removed. Tuna flesh turns light grey when cooked and is very firm, with a mild flavour. Tuna work well for grilling or broiling and may be marinated or brushed with seasoned oil during cooking. Tuna are often prepared medium rare to prevent dryness.

Yellowfin Tuna

Wahoo, also known as ono, are found throughout tropical and subtropical waters, but are particularly associated with Hawaii (*ono* even means "good to eat" in Hawaiian). They are actually a type of mackerel and are cooked like any other mackerel.

Wahoo

Whitefish species inhabit the freshwater lakes and streams of North America. Lake whitefish, the most important commercially, are related to salmon. They are marketed at up to 3.2 kg (7 lb.) and are available whole or filleted. The flesh is firm and white, with a moderate amount of fat and a sweet flavour. Whitefish may be baked, broiled, grilled or smoked and are often used in processed fish products. They are the source for golden caviar.

Whitefish

Flatfish

Flounder (Fr. *flet*) have lean, firm flesh that is pearly or pinkish-white with a sweet, mild flavour. Although they are easily boned, most are deheaded and gutted at sea and sold as fresh or frozen fillets. These fillets are very thin and can dry out or spoil easily, so extra care should be taken in handling, preparing and storing them. Recipes that preserve moisture work best with flounder; poaching, steaming or frying are recommended. Many types of flounder are marketed as sole, perhaps in an attempt to cash in on the popularity of true sole. The Canadian Federal Fisheries permits this practice. (See Table 19.1.)

English sole are actually flounder caught off the west coast of Canada and the United States. They are usually marketed simply as "fillet of sole." They are a plentiful species of fair to average quality.

Petrale sole, another west coast flounder, are generally considered the finest of the domestic "soles." They are most often available as fillets, which tend to be thicker and firmer than other sole fillets.

English Sole

Petrale Sole

TABLE 19.1　　FLOUNDER (ALSO KNOWN AS SOLE)	
Atlantic Ocean	Pacific Ocean
Blackback/winter flounder/lemon sole	Arrowtooth
Fluke/summer flounder	Petrale sole
Starry flounder	Rex sole
Yellowtail	English sole
Windowpane flounder	Rock sole
Grey sole/witch flounder	Sand sole
	Yellowfin sole
	Domestic Dover sole/Pacific flounder
	Butter sole

Lemon Sole

Alaskan Halibut

True Dover Sole

Turbot

Domestic Dover sole are also Pacific flounder. They are not as delicate or flavourful as other species of sole or flounder. Moreover, they are often afflicted with a parasite that causes the meat to have a slimy, gelatinous texture. Domestic Dover sole are not recommended if other sole or flounder are available.

Lemon sole are the most abundant and popular east coast flounder. They are also known as blackback or winter flounder (during the winter they migrate close to shore from the deeper, colder waters). They average 900 g (2 lb.) in weight.

Halibut are among the largest flatfish; they often weigh up to 135 kg (300 lb.). The Canadian Federal Fisheries recognizes only two halibut species: Atlantic (eastern) and Pacific (northern, Alaskan, western) halibut. Both have lean, firm flesh that is snow-white with a sweet, mild flavour. California halibut, which are actually flounder, are similar in taste and texture but average only 5.4 kg (12 lb.) each. Halibut may be cut into boneless steaks or skewered on brochettes. The flesh, which dries out easily, can be poached, baked, grilled or broiled and is good with a variety of sauces.

Sole (Fr. *sole*) are probably the most flavourful and finely textured flatfish. Indeed, because of the connotations of quality associated with the name, "sole" is widely used for many species that are not members of the sole (*Soleidae*) family. Even though the Canadian Federal Fisheries allows many species of flatfish to be called "sole" for marketing purposes, no true sole is commercially harvested in North American waters. Any flatfish harvested in North American waters and marketed as sole is actually flounder.

True **Dover sole**, a staple of classic cuisine, are a lean fish with pearly-white flesh and a delicate flavour that can stand up to a variety of sauces and seasonings. They are a member of the *Soleidae* family and come only from the waters off the coasts of England, Africa and Europe. They are imported into this country as fresh or frozen fillets and whole fish.

Turbot are a Pacific flatfish of no great culinary distinction. In Europe, however, the species known as turbot (Fr. *turbot*) are large diamond-shaped fish highly prized for their delicate flavour and firm, white flesh. While turbot and brill are separate species, turbot are also marketed as brill. Japanese markets sell brill for fine dining.

Mollusks

Univalves

Univalves are mollusks with a single shell in which the soft-bodied animal resides. They are actually marine snails with a single foot, used to attach the creature to fixed objects such as rocks.

Abalone have brownish-grey, ear-shaped shells. They are harvested in California, but California law does not permit canning abalone or shipping it out of state. Some frozen abalone is available from Mexico; canned abalone is imported from Japan. Abalone are lean with a sweet, delicate flavour similar to that of clams. They are too tough to eat unless tenderized with a mallet or rolling pin. They may then be eaten raw or prepared seviche-style. Great care must be taken when grilling or sautéing abalone as the meat becomes very tough when overcooked.

Conch are found in warm waters off the Florida Keys and in the Caribbean. The beautiful peachy-pink shell of the queen conch is prized by beachcombers. Conch meat is lean, smooth and very firm with a sweet-smoky flavour and chewy texture. It can be sliced and pounded to tenderize it, eaten raw with lime juice, or slow-cooked whole.

Bivalves

Bivalves are mollusks with two bilateral shells attached by a central hinge.

Clams (Fr. *clovisses*) are harvested along both the east and west coasts, with Atlantic clams being more significant commercially. Atlantic Coast clams include hard-shell, soft-shell and surf clams. Clams are available all year, either live in the shell or fresh-shucked (meat removed from the shell). Canned clams, whether minced, chopped or whole, are also available.

Atlantic hard-shell clams or **quahogs** have hard, blue-grey shells. Their chewy meat is not as sweet as other clam meat. Quahogs have different names, depending upon their size. **Littlenecks** are generally under 5 cm (2 inches) across the shell and usually are served on the half shell or steamed. They are the most expensive clams. **Cherrystones** are generally under 7.5 cm (3 inches) across the shell and are sometimes eaten raw but are more often cooked. **Topnecks** are usually cooked and are often served as stuffed clams. **Chowders**, the largest quahogs, are always eaten cooked, especially minced for chowder or soup.

Soft-shell clams, also known as Ipswich, steamer and long-necked clams, have thin, brittle shells that do not completely close because of the clam's protruding black-tipped siphon. Their meat is tender and sweet. They are sometimes fried but are more often served steamed.

Surf clams are deep-water clams that reach sizes of 20 cm (8 inches) across. They are most often cut into strips for frying or are minced, chopped, processed and canned.

Pacific clams are generally too tough to eat raw. The most common is the **Manila clam**, which was introduced along the Pacific Coast during the 1930s. Resembling a quahog with a ridged shell, it can be served steamed or on the half shell. **Geoducks** are the largest Pacific clam, sometimes weighing up to 4.5 kg (10 pounds) each. They look like huge soft-shell clams with a large, protruding siphon. Their tender, rich bodies and briny flavour are popular in Asian cuisines.

A freshwater **Red River clam** is commercially available in Canada.

> ### ♦♦♦
> ### SNAILS
>
> Although snails (more politely known by their French name, *escargots*) are univalve land animals, they share many characteristics with their marine cousins. They can be poached in court bouillon or removed from their shells and boiled or baked briefly with a seasoned butter or sauce. They should be firm but tender; overcooking makes snails tough and chewy. The most popular varieties are the large white Burgundy snail and the small garden variety called *petit gris*. Fresh snails are available from snail ranches through specialty suppliers. The great majority of snails, however, are purchased canned; most canned snails are produced in France or Taiwan.

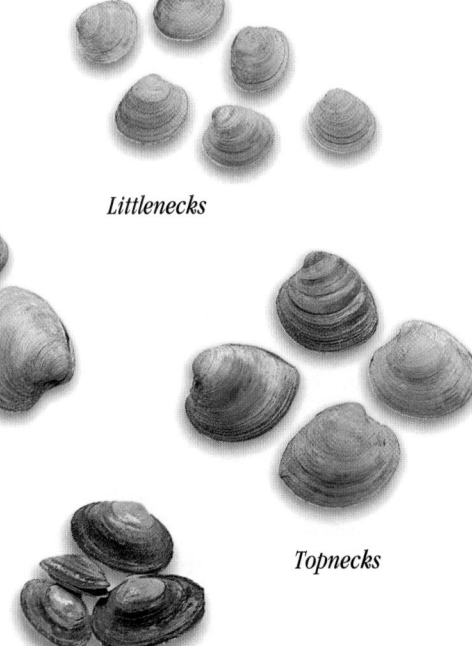

Littlenecks

Cherrystones

Topnecks

Soft-shell Clams

Manila Clams

Cockles

Cockles are small bivalves, about 2.5 cm (1 inch) long, with ridged shells. They are more popular in Europe than in North America and are sometimes used in dishes such as paella and fish soups or stews.

Mussels (Fr. *moule*) are found in waters worldwide. They are excellent steamed in wine or seasoned broth and can be fried or used in soups or pasta dishes.

Blue mussels are the most common edible mussel. They are found in the wild along the Atlantic Coast and are aquafarmed on both coasts. Their meat is plump and sweet with a firm, muscular texture. The orangish-yellow meat of cultivated mussels tends to be much larger than that of wild mussels and therefore worth the added cost. Blue mussels are sold live in the shell and average from 10 to 20 per pound. Although available all year, the best-quality blue mussels are harvested during the winter months.

Blue Mussels

Greenshell (or greenlip) **mussels** from New Zealand and Thailand are much larger than blue mussels, averaging 8 to 12 mussels per 500 g (1 lb.). Their shells are paler grey, with a distinctive bright-green edge.

Greenshell Mussels

Oysters (Fr. *huître*) have a rough grey shell; their soft, grey, briny flesh can be eaten raw or cooked. Most oysters available in this country are commercially grown and sold either live in the shell or shucked. Oysters are excellent live, eaten directly from the shell. They can also be steamed or baked in the shell or shucked and fried, sautéed or added to stews or chowders. There are four main domestic species.

Bluepoint Oysters

Atlantic oysters, also called American or Eastern oysters, have darker, flatter shells than other oysters. Malpeque oysters from Prince Edward Island are considered the finest.

European flat oysters are often incorrectly called Belon (true Belon oysters live only in the Belon river of France); they are very round and flat and look like giant brownish-green Olympias.

Olympias are the only oysters native to the Pacific Coast; they are tiny (about the size of a loonie).

Gulf Oysters

European Flat Oysters

Olympias

Pacific oysters, also called Japanese oysters, are aquafarmed along the Pacific Coast; they have curly, thick striated shells and silvery-grey to gold to almost-white meat.

Although it may seem like there are hundreds of oyster species on the market, there are only two that are commercially significant: the Atlantic oyster and the Pacific oyster. These two species yield dozens of different varieties, however, depending on their origin. For example, Atlantic oysters may be referred to as bluepoints, Malpeque, Florida Gulf, Long Island and so on, while Pacific oysters include Penn Cove Select, Westcott Bay, Hamma-hamma and Kumamoto, among others. An oyster's flavour reflects the minerals, nutrients and salts in its water and mud bed, so a Bristol from Maine and an Apalachicola from Florida will taste very different, even though they are the same Atlantic species. Oysters are at their prime in the winter months, particularly from Christmas to Easter.

Hamma-hamma Oysters

Scallops contain an edible white adductor muscle that holds together the fan-shaped shells. Because they die quickly, they are almost always shucked and cleaned on-board ship. The sea scallop and the bay scallop, both cold-water varieties, and the calico scallop, a warm-water variety, are the most important commercially. Sea scallops are the largest, with an average count of 20 to 30 per pound. Larger sea scallops are also available. Bay scallops average 70 to 90 per pound; calico scallops average 70 to 110 per pound. Fresh or frozen shucked, cleaned scallops are the most common market form, but live scallops in the shell and shucked scallops with roe attached (very popular in Europe) are also available. Scallops are sweet, with a tender texture. Raw scallops should be a translucent ivory colour, nonsymmetrically round and should feel springy. They can be steamed, broiled, grilled, fried, sautéed or baked. When overcooked, however, scallops quickly become chewy and dry. Only absolutely fresh scallops should be eaten raw.

Sea Scallops

Cephalopods

Cephalopods are marine mollusks with distinct heads, well-developed eyes, a number of arms that attach to the head near the mouth and a saclike fin-bearing mantle. They do not have an outer shell; instead, there is a thin internal shell called a *pen* or *cuttlebone*.

Octopus is generally quite tough and requires mechanical tenderization or long, moist-heat cooking to make it palatable. Most octopus is imported from Portugal, though fresh ones are available on the east coast during the winter. Octopus is sold by the kilogram or pound, fresh or frozen, usually whole. Octopus skin is grey when raw, turning purple when cooked. The interior flesh is white, lean, firm and flavourful.

Squid, known by their Italian name, *calamari*, are becoming increasingly popular in this country. Similar to octopus but much smaller, they are harvested along both North and South American coasts and elsewhere around the world (the finest are the east coast loligo or winter squid). They range in size from an average of 8 to 10 per pound to the giant South American squid that is sold as tenderized steaks. The squid's tentacles, mantle (body tube) and fins are edible. Squid meat is white to ivory in colour, turning darker with age. It is moderately lean, slightly sweet, firm and tender, but it toughens quickly if overcooked. Squid are available either fresh, or frozen and packed in blocks. The ink is used for making black noodles.

Squid

Crustaceans

Crustaceans are found in both fresh and salt water. They have a hard outer shell and jointed appendages, and they breathe through gills.

Crayfish (Fr. *écrevisse*), generally called *crayfish* in the North and *crawfish* or *crawdad* in the South, are freshwater creatures that look like miniature lobsters. They are harvested from the wild or aquafarmed in Louisiana and the Pacific Northwest. They are from 8 to 17.5 cm (3-1/2 to 7 inches) in length when marketed and may be purchased live or precooked and frozen. The lean meat, found mostly in the tail, is sweet and tender. Crayfish can be boiled whole and served hot or cold. The tail meat can be deep-fat fried or used in soups, bisques or sauces. Crayfish are a staple of Cajun cuisine, often used in gumbo, étouffée and jambalaya. Whole crayfish become brilliant red when cooked and may be used as a garnish. Caribbean crayfish tails are often erroneously sold on menus as lobster tails. They are also found in Europe and especially Australia. Sizes range from 100 g (3-1/2 oz.) to 4.5 kg (10 lb.) for the Tasmanian crayfish.

Crabs (Fr. *crabe*) are found along the North American coasts in great numbers and are shipped throughout the world in fresh, frozen and canned forms. Crab meat varies in flavour and texture and can be used in a range of prepared dishes, from chowders to curries to casseroles. Crabs purchased live should last up to five days; dead crabs should not be used.

King crabs are very large crabs (usually around 4.5 kg or 10 lb.) caught in the very cold waters of the North Pacific. Their meat is very sweet and snow-white. King crabs are always sold frozen, usually in the shell. In-shell forms include sections or clusters, legs and claws or split legs. The meat is also available in "fancy" packs of whole leg and body meat, or shredded and minced pieces. It is becoming rarer.

Dungeness crabs are found along the west coast. They weigh 675 g–1.8 kg (1-1/2–4 lb.) and have delicate, sweet meat. They are sold live, precooked and frozen, or as picked meat, usually in 2.2-kg (5-lb.) vacuum-packed cans.

Dungeness Crab

Blue crabs are found along the entire eastern seaboard and account for approximately 50% of the total weight of all crab species harvested in the United States. Their meat is rich and sweet. Blue crabs are available as hard-shell or soft-shell. Hard-shell crabs are sold live, precooked and frozen, or as picked meat. Soft-shell crabs are those harvested within six hours after molting and are available live (generally only from May 15 to September 15) or frozen. They are often steamed and served whole. Soft-shells can be sautéed, fried, broiled or added to soups or stews. Blue crabs are sold by size, with an average diameter of 10–18 cm (4–7 inches).

Soft-shell Crabs

Blue Crab

Snow or **spider crabs** are an abundant species, most often used as a substitute for the scarcer and more expensive king crab. They are harvested from Alaskan and British Columbian waters and along the eastern coast of Canada. Snow crab is sold precooked, usually frozen. The meat can be used in soups, salads, omelettes or other prepared dishes. Legs are often served cold as an appetizer.

Stone crabs are generally available only as cooked claws, either fresh or frozen (the claws cannot be frozen raw because the meat sticks to the shell). In stone-crab fishery only the claw is harvested. After the claw is removed, the crab is returned to the water, where in about 18 months it regenerates a new claw. Claws average 75–165 g (2-1/2–5-1/2 oz.) each. The meat is firm, with a sweet taste similar to lobster. Cracked claws are served hot or cold, usually with cocktail sauce, lemon butter or other accompaniments.

Lobsters have brown to blue-black outer shells and firm, white meat with a rich, sweet flavour. Lobster shells turn red when cooked. They are usually poached, steamed, simmered, baked or grilled, and can be served hot or cold. Picked meat can be used in prepared dishes, soups or sautés. Lobsters must be kept alive until just before cooking. Dead lobsters should not be used. The Atlantic, also known as clawed lobster, and the spiny lobster are the most commonly marketed species. The coral (eggs) are a prized delicacy.

Atlantic Lobster

Atlantic lobsters have edible meat in both their tails and claws; they are considered superior in flavour to all other lobsters. They come from the cold waters along the northeast coast and are most often sold live. Atlantic lobsters may be purchased by weight (i.e., 1-1/4 pound [525 g], 1-1/2 pound [650 g] or 2 pounds [900 g] each), or as chix (i.e., less than 1 pound [450 g]). (See sidebar on page 451.) Lobsters may also be purchased as culls (lobsters with only one claw) or bullets (lobsters with no claws). They are available frozen or as cooked, picked meat.

Figure 19.3 shows a cross-section of an Atlantic lobster and identifies the stomach, tomalley (the olive-green liver) and coral (the roe). The stomach is not eaten; the tomalley and coral are very flavourful and are often used in the preparation of sauces and other items.

Spiny lobsters have very small claws and are valuable only for their meaty tails, which are notched with short spines. Nearly all spiny lobsters marketed in this country are sold as frozen tails, often identified as rock lobster. Harvested in many parts of the world, those found off Florida, Brazil and in the Caribbean are marketed as warm-water tails; those found off South Africa, Australia and New Zealand are called cold-water tails. Cold-water spiny tails are considered superior to their warm-water cousins.

Slipper lobster, lobsterette and **squat lobster** are all clawless species found in tropical, subtropical and temperate waters worldwide. Although popular in some countries, their flavour is inferior to both Atlantic and spiny lobsters.

Shrimp (Fr. *crevette*) are found worldwide and are widely popular. Gulf whites, pinks, browns and black tigers are just a few of the dozens of shrimp varieties used in food service operations. Although fresh, head-on shrimp are available, the most common form is raw, head-off (also called green headless) shrimp with the shell on. Most shrimp are deheaded and frozen at sea to preserve freshness. Shrimp are available in many forms: raw, peeled and deveined; cooked, peeled and deveined; individually quick frozen; as well as in a variety of processed, breaded or canned products. Shrimp are graded by size, which can range from 400 per pound (450 g) (titi) to 8 per pound (450 g) (extra-colossal), and are sold in counts per pound. For example, shrimp marketed as "21–26 count" means that there is an average of 21 to 26 shrimp per pound; shrimp marketed as "U-10" means that there are under 10 shrimp per pound.

Prawn is often used interchangeably with the word "shrimp" in English-speaking countries. Although it is perhaps more accurate to refer to freshwater species as prawns and marine species as shrimp, in commercial practice prawn refers to any large shrimp. Equally confusing, *scampi* is the Italian name for the Dublin Bay prawn (which is actually a species of miniature lobster), but in this country *scampi* often refers to shrimp sautéed in garlic butter. The CFIA recognizes "shrimp" as the proper nomenclature for menu writing. **Langoustine** are small North Atlantic (Norway) lobsters.

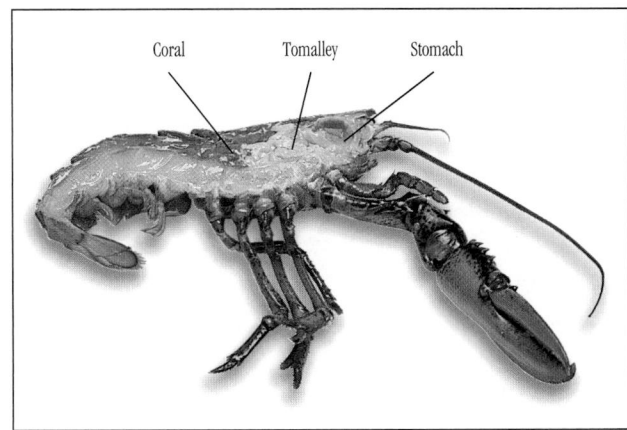

Coral   Tomalley   Stomach

FIGURE 19.3

Shrimp

Green Headless Shrimp

NUTRITION

Fish and shellfish are low in calories, fat and sodium, and are high in vitamins A, B and D and protein. (See Table 19.2.) Fish and shellfish are also high in minerals, especially calcium (particularly in canned fish with edible bones), phosphorus, potassium and iron (especially mollusks). Fish are high in a

TABLE 19.2   NUTRITIONAL VALUES OF FISH AND SHELLFISH

Per 28 g (1 oz.) Raw	Kcal	Protein (g)	Total Fat (g)	Saturated Fat (g)	Cholesterol (mg)	Sodium (mg)
Abalone	30	4.8	0.2	<0.1	24	85
Clam, mixed species	21	3.6	0.3	<0.1	10	16
Cod, Atlantic	23	5.0	0.2	<0.1	12	15
Crab, Alaska king	24	5.2	0.2	mq*	12	237
Flatfish	26	5.3	0.3	0.1	14	23
Lobster	26	5.3	0.3	mq	27	mq
Oyster, eastern	20	2.0	0.7	0.2	16	32
Salmon	40	5.6	1.8	0.3	16	113
Sea bass	27	5.2	0.6	0.1	12	19
Shrimp, mixed species	30	5.7	0.5	0.1	43	42
Surimi	28	4.3	0.3	mq	9	41
Tuna, yellowfin	31	6.6	0.3	0.1	13	10
Whitefish	38	5.4	1.7	0.3	17	14

The Corinne T. Netzer Encyclopedia of Food Values 1992
*mq = measurable quantity, but data are unavailable

group of polyunsaturated fatty acids called omega-3, which may help combat high blood cholesterol levels and aid in preventing some heart disease. Shellfish are not as high in cholesterol as was once thought. Crustaceans are higher in cholesterol than mollusks, but both have considerably lower levels than red meat or eggs.

The cooking methods used for fish and shellfish also contribute to their healthfulness. The most commonly used cooking methods—broiling, grilling, poaching and steaming—add little or no fat.

FIGURE 19.4   *CFIA Mark and Statements*

INSPECTION AND GRADING OF FISH AND SHELLFISH

Inspection

It is necessary to purchase fish and shellfish from approved sources only. The approval-granting agency is the Canadian Food Inspection Agency. For an operation to be an approved facility under federal regulations, it must demonstrate a Quality Management Program, which consists of a prerequisite program for the physical plant and an adherence to Hazardous Analysis Critical Control Point (HACCP) principles. Verify the presence of a tag or stamp illustrated in Figure 19.4. In addition, there are guidelines for product quality, record keeping and a recall process.

Grading

No grading protocol for fish exists in Canada, so a buyer must rely on the integrity of the supplier. Ask the supplier if they are inspected and if they are an approved facility. The assurance of quality for yourself and the customer is well worth the extra you may pay for a superior, safe and wholesome product.

PURCHASING AND STORING FISH AND SHELLFISH

Determining Freshness

Because fish and shellfish are highly perishable, an inspection stamp does not necessarily ensure top quality. A few hours at the wrong temperature or a couple of days in the refrigerator can turn high-quality fish or shellfish into garbage. It is important that you be able to determine for yourself the freshness and quality of the fish and shellfish you purchase or use. Freshness should be checked before purchasing and again just before cooking.

Freshness can be determined by:

1. *Smell*—Smell is by far the easiest way to determine freshness. Fresh fish should have a slight sea smell or no odour at all. Any off-odours or ammonia odours are a sure sign of aged or improperly handled fish.

2. *Eyes*—The eyes should be clear and full. Sunken eyes mean that the fish is drying out and is probably not fresh.

3. *Gills*—The gills should be intact and bright red. Brown gills are a sign of age.

4. *Texture*—Generally, the flesh of fresh fish should be firm. Mushy flesh or flesh that does not spring back when pressed with a finger is a sign of poor quality or age.

5. *Fins and scales*—Fins and scales should be moist and full without excessive drying on the outer edges. Dry fins or scales are a sign of age; damaged fins or scales may be a sign of mishandling.

6. *Appearance*—Fish cuts should be moist and glistening, without bruises or dark spots. Edges should not be brown or dry.

7. *Movement*—Shellfish should be purchased alive and should show movement. Lobsters and other crustaceans should be active. Clams, mussels and oysters that are partially opened should snap shut when tapped with a finger. (Exceptions are geoduck, razor and steamer clams whose siphons protrude, preventing the shell from closing completely.) Ones that do not close are dead and should not be used. Avoid mollusks with broken shells or heavy shells that might be filled with mud or sand.

Purchasing Fish and Shellfish

Fish are available from wholesalers in a variety of market forms (see Figure 19.5):

+ **Whole** or **round**—as caught, intact.
+ **Drawn**—viscera (internal organs) are removed; most whole fish are purchased this way.
+ **Dressed**—viscera, gills, fins and scales are removed.
+ **Pan-dressed**—viscera and gills are removed; fish is scaled and fins and tail are trimmed. The head is usually removed, although small fish, such as trout, may be pan-dressed with the head still attached. Pan-dressed fish are then pan-fried.
+ **Butterflied**—a pan-dressed fish, boned and opened flat like a book. The two sides remain attached by the back or belly skin.
+ **Fillet**—the side of a fish removed intact, boneless or semi-boneless, with or without skin.

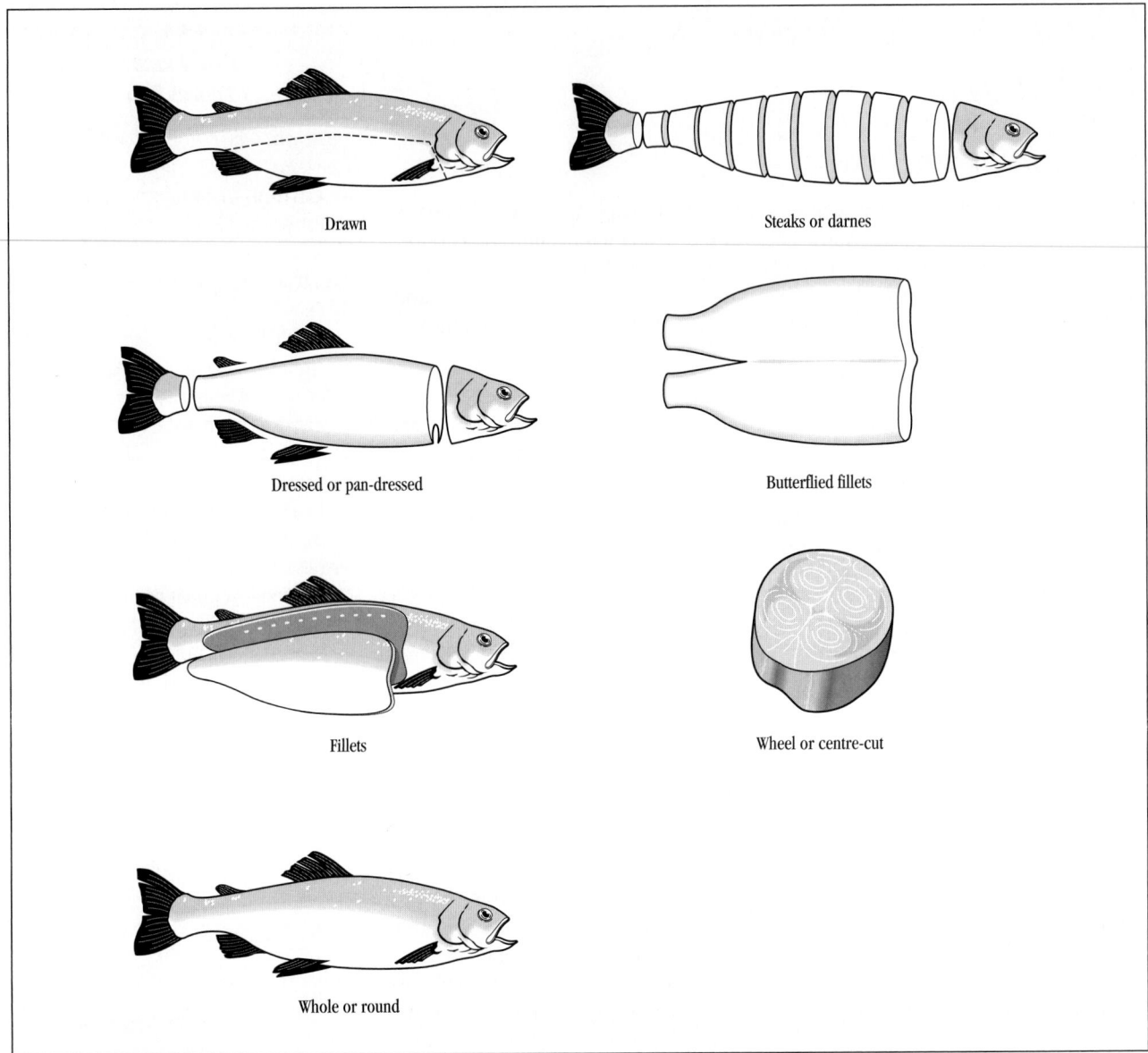

Drawn

Steaks or darnes

Dressed or pan-dressed

Butterflied fillets

Fillets

Wheel or centre-cut

Whole or round

FIGURE 19.5 *Market Forms*

- ✦ **Steak or darne**—cross-section slice, with a small section of backbone attached; usually prepared from large round fish.
- ✦ **Wheel** or **centre-cut**—used for swordfish and sharks, which are cut into large boneless pieces from which steaks are then cut.

You should purchase fish in the market forms most practical for your operation. Although fish fabrication is a relatively simple chore requiring little specialized equipment, before you decide to cut your own fish you should consider

1. the food service operation's ability to utilize the bones and trim that cutting whole fish produces,
2. the employees' ability to fabricate fillets, steaks or portions as needed,
3. the storage facilities, and
4. the product's intended use.

Most shellfish can be purchased live in the shell, shucked (the meat removed from the shell) or processed. Both live and shucked shellfish are usually purchased by counts (i.e., the number per volume). For example, standard live Eastern oysters are packed 200–250 (the count) per bushel (the unit of volume: approximately 35 L); standard Eastern oyster meats are packed 350 per gallon. Crustaceans are sometimes packed by size based on the number of pieces per pound; for example, crab legs or shrimp are often sold in counts per pound. Or they are sold either by grades based on size (whole crabs) or by weight (lobsters).

Storing Fish and Shellfish

The most important concern when storing fish and shellfish is temperature. All fresh fish should be stored at temperatures between -1°C and 1°C (30°F and 34°F). Fish stored in a refrigerator at 4°C (40°F) will have approximately half the shelf life of fish stored at 0°C (32°F).

Most fish are shipped on ice and should be stored on ice in the refrigerator immediately upon receipt. Whole fish should be layered directly in crushed or shaved ice in a perforated pan so that the melted ice water drains away. If crushed or shaved ice is not available, cubed ice may be used provided it is put in plastic bags and gently placed on top of the fish to prevent bruising and denting. Fabricated and portioned fish may be wrapped in moisture-proof packaging before icing to prevent the ice and water from damaging the exposed flesh. Fish stored on ice should be drained and re-iced daily.

Fresh scallops, fish fillets that are purchased in plastic trays, and oyster and clam meats should be set on or packed in ice. Do not let the scallops, fillets or meats come in direct contact with the ice.

Clams, mussels and oysters should be stored at 4°C (40°F), at high humidity and left in the boxes or net bags in which they were shipped. Under ideal conditions, shellfish can be kept alive for up to one week. Never store live shellfish in plastic bags and do not ice them.

If a saltwater tank is not available, live lobsters, crabs and other crustaceans should be kept in boxes with seaweed or damp newspaper to keep them moist. Most crustaceans circulate salt water over their gills; icing them or placing them in fresh water will kill them. Lobsters and crabs will live for several days under ideal conditions.

Like most frozen foods, frozen fish should be kept at temperatures of -18°C (0°F) or colder. Colder temperatures greatly increase shelf life. Frozen fish should be thawed in the refrigerator; once thawed, they should be treated like fresh fish.

◆◆◆
STORING OYSTERS

Fresh oysters in the shell will keep for up to three weeks at a temperature of 2°C (36°F). Store flat side up, layered between wet cloths. Oysters must be shucked in order to freeze them.

FABRICATING PROCEDURES

As discussed, fish and shellfish can be purchased in many forms. Here we demonstrate several procedures for cutting, cleaning and otherwise fabricating or preparing fish and shellfish for cooking and service.

Basic Procedure for Scaling Fish

This procedure is used to remove the scales from fish that will be cooked with the skin on.

Place the fish on a work surface or in a large sink. Grip the fish by the tail and, working from the tail towards the head, scrape the scales off with a fish scaler or the back of a knife. Be careful not to damage the flesh by pushing too hard. Turn the fish over and remove the scales from the other side. Rinse the fish under cold water.

Basic Procedure for Pan-Dressing Flatfish

1. Scale the flatfish. Place the fish on a cutting board and remove the head by making a V-shaped cut around it with a chef's knife. Pull the head away and remove the viscera.

2. Rinse the fish under cold water, removing all traces of blood and viscera from the cavity.

3. Using a pair of kitchen shears, trim off the tail and all of the fins.

Basic Procedure for Filleting Round Fish

Round fish produce two fillets, one from either side.

1. Using a chef's knife, cut down to the backbone just behind the gills. Do not remove the head.

2. Turn the knife towards the tail; using smooth strokes, cut from head to tail parallel to the backbone. The knife should bump against the backbone so that no flesh is wasted; you will feel the knife cutting through the small pin bones. Cut the fillet completely free from the bones. Repeat on the other side.

3. Trim the rib bones from the fillet with a flexible filleting knife.

4. The finished fillet. (Pin bones still must be removed.)

Basic Procedure for Filleting Flatfish

Flatfish produce four fillets: two large bilateral fillets from the top and two smaller bilateral fillets from the bottom. If the fish fillets are going to be

cooked with the skin on, the fish should be scaled before cooking (it is easier to scale the fish before it is filleted). If the skin is going to be removed
before cooking, it is not necessary to scale the fish.

1. With the dark side of the fish facing up, cut along the backbone
from head to tail with the tip of a
flexible filleting knife.

2. Turn the knife and, using smooth
strokes, cut between the flesh and
the rib bones, keeping the flexible
blade against the bone. Cut the fillet completely free from the fish.
Remove the second fillet, following the same procedure.

3. Turn the fish over and remove the
fillets from the bottom half of the
fish, following the same procedure.

Basic Procedure for Skinning Dover Sole

Dover sole is unique in that its skin can be pulled from the whole fish by following this procedure. The flesh of other small flatfish such as flounder,
petrale sole and other types of domestic sole is more delicate; pulling the
skin away from the whole fish could damage the flesh. These fish should be
skinned using a filleting knife after they are filleted.

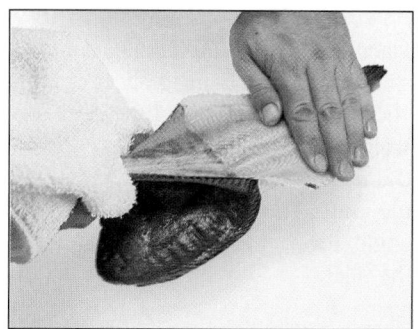

Make a shallow cut in the flesh perpendicular to the length of the fish,
just in front of the tail and with the
knife angled towards the head of the
fish. Using a clean towel, grip the
skin and pull it towards the head of
the fish. The skin should come off
cleanly, in one piece, leaving the
flesh intact.

Basic Procedure for Skinning Fish Fillets

Here we use a salmon fillet to demonstrate the procedure for skinning fish fillets. Use the same procedure to
skin all types of fish fillets.

Place the fillet on a cutting board with the skin side
down. Starting at the tail, use a meat slicer or a chef's
knife to cut between the flesh and skin. Angle the knife
down towards the skin, grip the skin tightly with one
hand and use a sawing motion to cut the skin cleanly
away from the flesh. Keep the skin taut.

Basic Procedure for Pulling Pin Bones from a Salmon Fillet

Round fish fillets contain a row of intramuscular bones running the length of the fillet. Known as pin bones, they are usually cut out with a knife to produce boneless fillets. In the case of salmon, they can be removed with salmon tweezers or small needle-nose pliers.

Place the fillet (either skinless or not) on the cutting board, skin side down. Starting at the front or head end of the fillet, use your fingertips to locate the bones and pull them out one by one with the pliers. Pull at an angle so as not to tear the flesh.

Basic Procedure for Cutting a Fillet

A **fillet** is a boneless cut from a large flat or round fish. Usually cut on an angle, fillets or escallopes look larger and increase plate coverage.

Place the fillet on the cutting board, skin side down. Using a slicer or chef's knife, cut slices of the desired weight. The fillet can be cut to the desired size by adjusting the angle of the knife. The more shallow the angle, the greater the surface area of the fillet.

Basic Procedure for Cutting Steaks from Salmon and Similarly Sized Round Fish

Steaks, or darnes, are produced from salmon and similarly sized round fish by simply making crosscuts of the whole fish. First scale, gut and remove the fins from the fish. Then:

Using a chef's knife, cut through the fish, slicing steaks of the desired thickness. The steaks will contain some bones that are not necessarily removed.

Basic Procedure for Peeling and Deveining Shrimp

Peeling and deveining shrimp is a simple procedure done in most commercial kitchens. The tail portion of the shell is often left on the peeled shrimp to give it an attractive appearance or make it easier to eat. This procedure can be used on both cooked and uncooked shrimp.

1. Grip the shrimp's tail between your thumb and forefinger. Use your other thumb and forefinger to grip the legs and the edge of the shell.

2. Pull the legs and shell away from the flesh, leaving the tail and first joint of the shell in place if desired.

3. Place the shrimp on a cutting board and use a paring knife to make a shallow cut down the back of the shrimp, exposing the digestive tract or "vein."

4. Pull out the vein while rinsing the shrimp under cold water. If the tail is left on, remove the sharp spike.

Basic Procedure for Butterflying Shrimp

Butterflying raw shrimp improves their appearance and increases their surface area for even cooking. To butterfly shrimp, first peel them using the procedure outlined above, then:

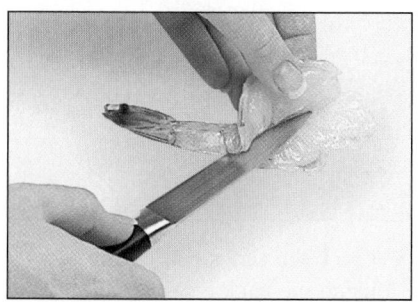

Instead of making a shallow cut to expose the vein, make a deeper cut that nearly slices the shrimp into two bilateral halves. Pull out the vein while rinsing the shrimp under cold water.

♦♦♦

SHRIMP FOR SUSHI AND BARBECUE

To keep the shrimp straight during cooking, insert a skewer or heavy toothpick just under the shell, along the back of the shrimp. This will prevent the shrimp from curling up.

Basic Procedure for Preparing Live Lobster for Broiling

A whole lobster can be cooked by plunging it into boiling water or court bouillon. If the lobster is to be broiled, it must be split lengthwise before cooking.

1. Place the live lobster on its back on a cutting board and pierce its head with the point of a chef's knife. Then, in one smooth stroke, bring the knife down and cut through the body and tail without splitting it completely in half.

2. Use your hands to crack the lobster's back so that it lies flat. Crack the claws with the back of a chef's knife.

3. Cut through the tail and curl each half of the tail to the side. Remove and discard the stomach and brain. The tomalley (the olive-green liver) and, if present, the coral (the roe) may be removed and saved for a sauce or other preparation.

Basic Procedure for Preparing Live Lobster for Sautéing

A whole lobster may also be cut into smaller pieces for sautéing or other preparations.

1. Use the point of a chef's knife to pierce the lobster's head.

2. Cut off the claws and arms.

3. Cut the tail into cross sections.

4. Split the head and thorax in half. The tomalley and coral (if present) may be removed and saved for further use. The head and legs may be added to the recipe for flavour, but there is very little meat in them. However, they are excellent for bisques.

5. Crack the claws with a firm blow, using the back of a chef's knife.

Basic Procedure for Removing Cooked Lobster Meat from the Shell

Many recipes call for cooked lobster meat. Cook the lobster by plunging it into a boiling court bouillon and simmering for 6–8 minutes per 500 g (1 lb.). Remove the lobster and allow it to cool until it can be easily handled. Then:

1. Pull the claws and large legs away from the body. Break the claw away from the leg. Split the legs with a chef's knife and remove the meat, using your fingers or a pick.

2. Carefully crack the claw with a mallet or the back of a chef's knife without damaging the meat. Pull out the claw meat in one piece.

3. Pull the lobster's tail away from its body and use kitchen shears to trim away the soft membrane on the underside of the tail.

4. Pull the meat out of the shell in one piece.

Basic Procedure for Opening Clams

Opening raw clams efficiently requires practice. Like all mollusks, clams should be cleaned under cold running water with a brush to remove all mud, silt and sand that may be stuck to their shells. A knife may be more easily inserted into a clam if the clam is washed and allowed to relax in the refrigerator for at least one hour before it is opened.

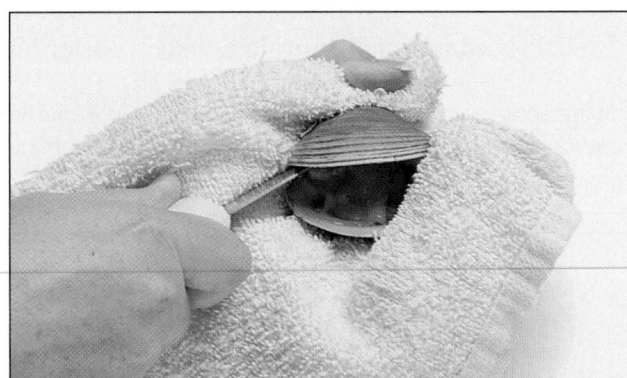

1. Hold the clam firmly in a folded towel in the palm of your hand; the notch in the edge of the shell should be towards your thumb. With the fingers of the same hand, squeeze and pull the blade of the clam knife between the clamshells. Do not push on the knife handle with your other hand; you will not be able to control the knife if it slips and you can cut yourself.

2. Pull the knife between the shells until it cuts the muscle. Twist the knife to pry the shells apart. Slide the knife tip along the top shell and cut through the muscle. Twist the top shell, breaking it free at the hinge; discard it.

3. Use the knife tip to release the clam from the bottom shell.

Basic Procedure for Opening Oysters

1. Clean the oyster by brushing it under running water.

2. Hold the cleaned oyster firmly in a folded towel in the palm of your hand. Insert the tip of an oyster knife in the hinge and use a twisting motion to pop the hinge apart. Do not use too much forward pressure on the knife; it can slip and you could stab yourself.

3. Slide the knife along the top of the shell to release the oyster from the shell (sever adductor muscle). Discard the top shell. Do not lose any of the juices. Reserve, strain and serve with the oysters on the half shell.

4. Use the knife tip to release the oyster from the bottom shell.

Basic Procedure for Cleaning and Debearding Mussels

Mussels are not normally eaten raw. Before cooking, a clump of dark threads called the beard must be removed. Because this could kill the mussel, cleaning and debearding must be done as close to cooking time as possible.

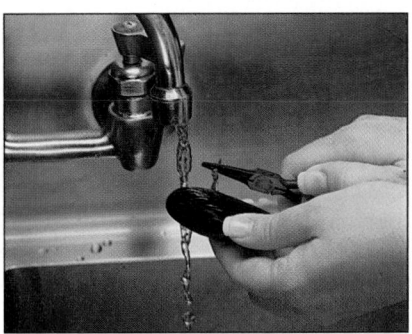

1. Clean the mussel with a brush under cold running water to remove sand and grit.

2. Pull the beard away from the mussel with your fingers or a small pair of pliers.

APPLYING VARIOUS COOKING METHODS

Fish and shellfish can be prepared by the dry-heat cooking methods of broiling and grilling, roasting (baking), sautéing, pan-frying and deep-fat frying, as well as the moist-heat cooking methods of steaming, poaching and simmering. Other than deep-fat frying, which is discussed in Chapter 21, these cooking methods are discussed below.

Determining Doneness

Unlike most meats and poultry, nearly all fish and shellfish are inherently tender and should be cooked just until done. Indeed, overcooking is the most common mistake made when preparing fish and shellfish. The Canadian Department of Fisheries recommends that all fish be cooked 10 minutes for every 2.5 cm (1 inch) of thickness, regardless of cooking method. Although this may be a good general policy, variables such as the type and the form of fish and the exact cooking method used suggest that one or more of the following methods of determining doneness are more appropriate for professional food service operations.

1. *Translucent flesh becomes opaque*—The raw flesh of most fish and shellfish appears somewhat translucent. As the proteins coagulate during cooking, the flesh becomes opaque.
2. *Flesh becomes firm*—The flesh of most fish and shellfish firms as it cooks. Doneness can be tested by judging the resistance of the flesh when pressed with tongs. Raw or undercooked fish or shellfish will be mushy and soft. As the fish cooks, the flesh offers more resistance and springs back quickly.
3. *Flesh separates from the bones easily*—The flesh of raw fish remains firmly attached to the bones. As the fish cooks, the flesh and bones separate easily.
4. *Flesh begins to flake*—Fish flesh consists of short muscle fibres separated by thin connective tissue. As the fish cooks, the connective tissue breaks down

and the groups of muscle fibres begin to flake; that is, they separate from one another. Fish is done when the flesh *begins* to flake. If the flesh flakes easily the fish will be overdone and dry.

Remember, fish and shellfish are subject to carryover cooking. Because they cook quickly and at low temperatures, it is better to undercook the item and allow carryover cooking or residual heat to finish the cooking process. Cook to an internal temperature of 57°C (135°F).

Dry-Heat Cooking Methods

Dry-heat cooking methods are those that do not require additional moisture at any time during the cooking process. The dry-heat cooking methods used with fish and shellfish are broiling and grilling, roasting (usually referred to as baking when used with fish and shellfish), sautéing, pan-frying and deep-fat frying.

Broiling and Grilling

After brushing with flavoured (infused) oil or butter, fish can be grilled directly on the grate or placed on a heated platter under the broiler. Broiled or grilled fish should have a lightly browned surface and a slightly smoky flavour as a result of the intense radiant heat of the broiler or grill. The interior should be moist and juicy. Broiled or grilled shellfish meat should be moist and tender with only slight colouration from the grill or broiler.

Selecting Fish and Shellfish to Broil or Grill

Nearly all types of fish and shellfish can be successfully broiled or grilled. Salmon, trout, swordfish and other oily fish are especially well suited to grilling, as are lean fish such as bass and snapper. Fillets of lean flatfish with delicate textures, such as flounder and sole, are better broiled. They should be placed on a preheated broiling (sizzler) platter before being placed under the broiler.

Oysters and clams are often broiled on the half shell with flavoured butters, bread crumbs or other garnishes and served sizzling hot. Squid can be stuffed, secured with a toothpick and broiled or grilled. Brushed with butter, split lobsters, king crabs and snow crabs are often broiled or grilled. Whole lobsters can be split and broiled or grilled, or their tails can be removed, split and cooked separately. Large crab legs can also be split and broiled or grilled. Shrimp and scallops are often marinated and broiled in flavoured butters or grilled on skewers for easy handling.

Seasoning Fish and Shellfish to Be Broiled or Grilled

All fish should be brushed lightly with butter or oil before being placed on the grill or under the broiler. The butter or oil prevents sticking and helps leaner fish retain moisture. For most fish, a simple seasoning of salt and pepper suffices. But most fish do respond well to marinades, especially those made with white wine and lemon juice. Because most fish are delicately flavoured, they should be marinated for only a brief period of time. (Even marinated fish should be brushed with butter or oil before cooking.) Herbs should be avoided because they will burn from the intense heat of the broiler or grill.

Clams, oysters and other shellfish that are stuffed or cooked with butters, vegetables, bacon or other accompaniments or garnishes gain flavour from these ingredients. Be careful, however, not to overpower the delicate flavours of the shellfish with the addition of too many strong flavourings.

Accompaniments to Broiled and Grilled Fish and Shellfish

Broiled fish and shellfish are served with sauces made separately. Butter sauces such as a beurre blanc are popular, as the richness of the sauce complements the lean fish. Vegetable coulis are a good choice for a healthier, lower-fat accompaniment. Additional sauce suggestions are found in Table 10.5.

If the item is cooked on a broiler platter with a seasoned butter, it is often served with that butter. Lemon or lime wedges are the traditional accompaniment to any broiled or grilled fish.

Almost any side dish goes well with broiled or grilled fish or shellfish. Fried or boiled potatoes, pasta and rice are all good choices. Grilled vegetables are a natural choice.

Basic Procedure for Broiling or Grilling Fish and Shellfish

All fish is delicate and must be carefully handled to achieve an attractive finished product. When broiling whole fish or fillets with their skin still on, score the skin by making several diagonal slashes approximately 5 mm (1/4 inch) deep at even intervals. This prevents the fish from curling during cooking, promotes even cooking and creates a more attractive finished product. Be especially careful not to overcook the item. It should be served as hot as possible as soon as it is removed from the broiler or grill.

1. Heat the broiler or grill.
2. Use a wire brush to remove any charred or burnt particles that may be stuck to the broiler or grill grate. The grate can be wiped with a lightly oiled towel to remove any remaining particles and help season it.
3. Prepare the item to be broiled or grilled. For example, cut the fish into steaks or fillets of even thickness; split the lobster; peel and/or skewer the shrimp. Season or marinate the item as desired. Brush the item with oil or butter.
4. Place the item (presentation side down) on a grill. If using a broiler, place the item directly on the grate or on a preheated broiler platter. Tender fish are usually broiled presentation side up on a broiler platter.
5. If practical, turn the item to produce the attractive crosshatch marks associated with grilling that are discussed in Chapter 9, Principles of Cooking. Items less than 12 mm (1/2 inch) thick cooked on a preheated broiler platter do not have to be turned over.
6. Cook the item to the desired doneness and serve immediately.

Applying the Basics

RECIPE 19.1

BROILED BLACK SEA BASS WITH HERB BUTTER AND SAUTÉED LEEKS

Yield: 1 Serving

Black sea bass fillet, skin on, approx. 200 g (7 oz.)	1	1
Salt and pepper	TT	TT
Whole butter, melted	as needed	as needed
Leek, julienned	1	1
Lemon juice	10 mL	2 tsp.
Herb butter (p. 220)	30 g	1 oz.

RECIPE 19.1

Approximate values per serving:

Calories	541
Total fat	31 g
Saturated fat	16.5 g
Cholesterol	272 mg
Sodium	684 mg
Total carbohydrates	18.5 g
Protein	48 g

1. Score the skin of the bass with three diagonal cuts approximately 5 mm (1/4 inch) deep.

2. Season the bass fillet with salt and pepper and brush with melted butter.

3. Place the fillet on a preheated broiler platter, skin side up, and place under the broiler.

4. Blanch the julienned leeks in boiling water until nearly tender.

5. Drain the leeks and sauté them in 15 mL (2 Tbsp.) of whole butter until tender. Add the lemon juice; season with salt and pepper.

6. Remove the fish from the broiler when done. Top with the herb butter and serve on a bed of sautéed leeks.

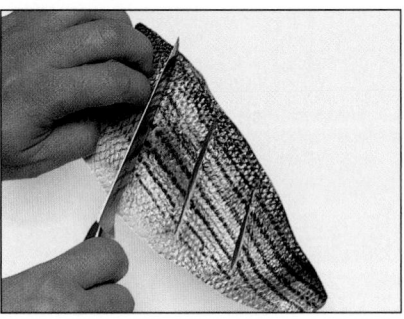

1. Score the skin of the fish.

2. Place the fish on a broiler platter, under the broiler.

3. Serve the fish on a bed of sautéed leeks.

Baking

The terms *baking* and *roasting* are used interchangeably when applied to fish and shellfish. One disadvantage of baking fish is that the short baking time does not allow the surface of the fish to caramelize. To help correct this problem, fish can be browned in a sauté pan with a small amount of butter to achieve the added flavour and appearance of a browned surface, and then finished in an oven.

Selecting Fish and Shellfish to Bake

Fatty fish produce the best baked fish. Fish fillets and steaks are the best market forms to bake, as they cook quickly and evenly and are easily portioned. Although lean fish can be baked, it tends to become dry, and must be basted often.

Seasoning Fish and Shellfish to Be Baked

The most popular seasonings for baked fish are lemon, butter, salt and pepper. Fish can also be marinated before baking for added flavour. But baked fish usually depend on the accompanying sauce for much of their flavour.

Shellfish are often stuffed or mixed with other ingredients before baking. For example, raw oysters on the half shell can be topped with spinach, watercress and Pernod (oysters Rockefeller) and baked. Shrimp are often butterflied, stuffed and baked; lobsters are split, stuffed and baked. Many food service operations remove clams from their shells; mix them with bread crumbs, seasonings or other ingredients; refill the shells and bake the mixture.

Accompaniments to Baked Fish and Shellfish

Baked fish is often served with a flavourful sauce such as a Creole sauce (p. 213) or a beurre blanc (Recipe 10.16). Additional sauce suggestions are found in Table 10.5. Almost any type of rice, pasta or potato is a good accompaniment, as is any variety of sautéed vegetable.

Basic Procedure for Baking Fish and Shellfish

1. Portion the fish and arrange on a well-oiled or buttered pan, presentation side up.
2. Season as desired and brush the surface of the fish or shellfish generously with melted butter; add garnishes or flavourings as desired or directed in the recipe. Sear, if desired, to develop colour.
3. Place the pan in a preheated oven at approximately 65°C (150°F).
4. Baste periodically during the cooking process (more often if the fish is lean). Remove from the oven when the fish is slightly underdone.

Applying the Basics

RECIPE 19.2

BAKED RED SNAPPER WITH STAR FRUIT CHUTNEY

Yield: 4 Servings

Red snapper fillets, 175 g (6 oz.) each	4	4
Salt and white pepper	TT	TT
Whole butter, melted	60 g	2 oz.
Mint leaves, chopped	10 g	1 Tbsp.
Garlic, minced	5 g	1 tsp.
Tomato concassée	125 g	4 oz.
White wine	60 mL	2 fl. oz.
Lemon juice	60 mL	2 fl. oz.
Star Fruit Chutney (recipe follows)	350 g	12 oz.

1. Place the snapper on a buttered baking pan. Season the fillets with salt and white pepper; brush with butter.
2. Combine the mint, garlic and tomatoes and spoon on top of each portion of the fish.
3. Add the white wine and lemon juice to the pan.
4. Bake at 65°C (150°F), basting once halfway through the cooking process, until done, approximately 25 minutes.
5. Serve each portion on a bed of 90 g (3 oz.) of Star Fruit Chutney.

RECIPE 19.2

Approximate values per serving:

Calories	1315
Total fat	15 g
Saturated fat	8 g
Cholesterol	98 mg
Sodium	872 mg
Total carbohydrates	135 g
Protein	42 g

1. Brush the fillets with butter.

2. Top each portion with mint, garlic and tomato concassée.

3. The finished fish.

STAR FRUIT CHUTNEY

Yield: 900 g (2 lb.)

Limes	3	3
Fresh ginger, julienned	125 g	4 oz.
Sugar	100 g	3 oz.
Apples, peeled, medium dice	2	2
Golden raisins	60 g	2 oz.
Dark raisins	60 g	2 oz.
Star fruit, medium dice	700 g	1-1/2 lb.
Cider vinegar	15 mL	1 Tbsp.
Salt and pepper	TT	TT
Cayenne pepper	TT	TT

1. Zest two limes.
2. Squeeze the limes to make 120 mL (4 fl. oz.) of juice.
3. Combine the lime juice, zest, ginger and sugar. Bring to a boil and simmer until the sugar is caramelized.
4. Add the apples and raisins; simmer until the apples are soft but not mushy.
5. Add the star fruit and bring back to a boil. Remove from heat. Add the vinegar. Season to taste with salt, pepper and cayenne pepper.

Star Fruit Chutney—
Approximate values
per 60 g (2 oz.) serving:

Calories	85
Total fat	0 g
Saturated fat	0 g
Cholesterol	0 mg
Sodium	66 mg
Total carbohydrates	22 g
Protein	1 g

Sautéing

Sautéing is a very popular cooking method for fish and shellfish. It lightly caramelizes the food's surface, giving it additional flavour. Typically, other ingredients such as garlic, onions, vegetables, wine and lemon juice are added to the fond to make a sauce.

Selecting Fish and Shellfish to Sauté

Both fatty and lean fish may be sautéed. Flatfish are sometimes dressed and sautéed whole, as are small round fish such as trout. Larger fish such as salmon can be cut into steaks or filleted and cut into fillets. The portions should be relatively uniform in size and thickness and fairly thin to promote even cooking. Although clams, mussels and oysters are not often sautéed, scallops and crustaceans are popular sauté items.

Seasoning Fish and Shellfish to Be Sautéed

Many types of fish—especially sole, flounder and other delicate, lean fish fillets—are often dredged in flour before sautéing. Seasoned butter is used to sauté some items, such as scampi-style shrimp. These items derive their flavour from the butter; additional seasonings should not be necessary.

Cooking Temperatures

The sauté pan and cooking fat must be hot before the fish or shellfish are added. Do not add too much fish or shellfish to the pan at one time or the pan and fat will cool, letting the foods simmer in their own juices. Thin slices and small pieces of fish and shellfish require a short cooking time, so use high temperatures in order to caramelize their surfaces without overcooking. Large, thick pieces of fish or shellfish being cooked in the shell may require slightly lower cooking temperatures to ensure that they are cooked without over-browning their surfaces.

Accompaniments to Sautéed Fish and Shellfish

Sautéed fish and shellfish are nearly always served with a sauce made directly in the sauté pan. This sauce may be as simple as browned butter (beurre noisette) or a complicated sauce flavoured with the fond. In some cases, seasoned butter is used to sauté the fish or shellfish and the butter is then served with the main item. See Table 10.5 for additional sauce suggestions.

Mildly flavoured rice and pasta are good choices to serve with sautéed fish or shellfish.

Basic Procedure for Sautéing Fish and Shellfish

1. Cut or portion the fish or shellfish.
2. Season the item and dredge in seasoned flour if desired.
3. Heat a suitable sauté pan over moderate heat; add enough oil or clarified butter to cover the bottom to a depth of about 3 mm (1/8 inch).
4. Add the fish or shellfish to the pan (fish should be placed presentation side down); cook until done, turning once halfway through the cooking process. Add other foods as called for in the recipe.
5. Remove the fish or shellfish. If a sauce is to be made in the sauté pan, follow the procedures discussed in Chapter 17, Poultry.

Applying the Basics

RECIPE 19.3

SAUTÉED HALIBUT
WITH THREE-COLOUR PEPPERS AND SPANISH OLIVES

Yield: 4 Servings

Ingredient		
Halibut fillets, 175 g (6 oz.) each	4	4
Salt and pepper	TT	TT
Olive oil	60 mL	2 fl. oz.
Onion, sliced	100 g	3 oz.
Garlic, minced	10 g	2 tsp.
Green bell pepper, julienned	100 g	3 oz.
Red bell pepper, julienned	100 g	3 oz.
Yellow bell pepper, julienned	100 g	3 oz.
Tomato, peeled and diced	250 g	8 oz.
Spanish olives, pitted and quartered	60 g	2 oz.
Fresh thyme, chopped	8 g	2 tsp.
Lemon juice	60 mL	2 fl. oz.
Fish stock	60 mL	2 fl. oz.

1. Season the fillets with salt and pepper.
2. Heat a sauté pan and add the olive oil.
3. Sauté the halibut, turning once. Remove and reserve in a warm place.
4. Add the onion and garlic to the same pan and sauté for approximately 1 minute. Add the peppers and sauté for 1–2 minutes more.
5. Add the tomato, olives and thyme; sauté briefly.
6. Add the lemon juice and deglaze the pan. Add the fish stock, simmer for 2 minutes to blend the flavours and adjust the seasonings.
7. Return the fish to the pan to reheat. Serve each fish fillet on a bed of vegetables with sauce and an appropriate garnish.

RECIPE 19.3

Approximate values per serving:

Calories	442
Total fat	21 g
Saturated fat	3 g
Cholesterol	72 mg
Sodium	775 mg
Total carbohydrates	13.5 g
Protein	49 g

1. Sauté the halibut fillets.

2. Sauté the onion, garlic and peppers.

3. Add the fish stock.

4. Return the fish to the pan to reheat.

Pan-Frying

Pan-frying is very similar to sautéing, but it uses more fat to cook the main item. Pan-fried fish is always coated with flour, batter or breading to help seal the surface and prevent the flesh from coming in direct contact with the cooking fat. Properly prepared pan-fried fish and shellfish should be moist and tender with a crisp surface. If battered or breaded, the coating should be intact with no breaks.

Selecting Fish and Shellfish to Pan-Fry

Both fatty and lean fish may be pan-fried. Trout and other small fish are ideal for pan-frying, as are portioned fillets of lean fish such as halibut. Pan-fried fish and shellfish should be uniform in size and relatively thin so they cook quickly and evenly.

Seasoning Fish and Shellfish to Be Pan-Fried

Although fish and shellfish can be marinated or seasoned directly, it is more common to season the flour, batter or breading that will coat them. Batters, for example, can contain cheese, and breadings can contain nuts and other ingredients to add different flavours to the fish or shellfish. Review the battering and breading procedures discussed in Chapter 21, Deep-Fat Frying. Additional seasonings come from sauces and other accompaniments served with the pan-fried fish or shellfish.

Cooking Temperatures

The fat should always be hot before the fish or shellfish are added. Breaded or battered fish fillets cook very quickly, and the fat should be hot enough to brown the coating without overcooking the interior. Whole pan-fried fish take longer to cook and therefore require a slightly lower cooking temperature so the surface does not become too dark before the interior is cooked. Oven finishing may be necessary.

Accompaniments to Pan-Fried Fish and Shellfish

Lemon or lime wedges are the classic accompaniment to pan-fried fish and shellfish. Sauces that accompany pan-fried items are made separately. Mayonnaise-based sauces such as tartar sauce (Recipe 24.19) and rémoulade sauce are especially popular; rich wine-based sauces should be avoided. Vegetable coulis, such as tomato, also complement many pan-fried items. Additional sauce suggestions are found in Table 10.5.

Basic Procedure for Pan-Frying Fish and Shellfish

1. Heat enough clarified butter or oil in a heavy sauté pan to immerse one-third to one-half of the item. The fat temperature should be between 165°C and 180°C (325°F and 350°F).
2. Add the floured, breaded or battered item to the pan, being careful not to splash the hot fat. Cook until done, turning once halfway through the cooking process.
3. Remove the food and drain on absorbent paper.
4. Serve it promptly with an appropriate sauce.

Applying the Basics

RECIPE 19.4

BLUE CRAB CAKES WITH FRESH SALSA

Yield: 15 60-g (2-oz.) Cakes

Blue crab meat	450 g	1 lb.
Cream, 35%	175 mL	6 fl. oz.
Red bell pepper, small dice	60 g	2 oz.
Green bell pepper, small dice	60 g	2 oz.
Clarified butter	as needed	as needed
Green onions, sliced	1 bunch	1 bunch
Fresh bread crumbs	175 g	6 oz.
Salt and pepper	TT	TT
Dijon mustard	15 mL	1 Tbsp.
Worcestershire sauce	TT	TT
Tabasco sauce	TT	TT
Egg, slightly beaten	1	1
Tomato Salsa (Recipe 10.21)	500 mL	1 pt.

RECIPE 19.4

Approximate values per 60 g (2 oz.) serving:

Calories	124
Total fat	6 g
Saturated fat	3 g
Cholesterol	59 mg
Sodium	305 mg
Total carbohydrates	10 g
Protein	8 g

1. Carefully pick through the crab meat, removing any pieces of shell. Keep the lumps of crab meat as large as possible.
2. Place the cream in a saucepan and bring to a boil. Reduce by approximately one-half. Chill the cream well.
3. Sauté the red and green bell peppers in a small amount of clarified butter until tender.
4. Combine the crab meat, reduced cream, peppers, green onions and approximately 90 g (3 oz.) of the bread crumbs along with the salt, pepper, Dijon mustard, Worcestershire sauce, Tabasco sauce and egg. Mix to combine all ingredients, trying to keep the lumps of crab meat intact.

Continued

1. Mix all ingredients for the crab cakes.

2. Form the crab cakes.

3. Pan-fry the crab cakes.

5. Using a mould, form the crab mixture into cakes of the desired size.
6. Place the remaining bread crumbs in an appropriately sized hotel pan. Place the crab cakes, a few at a time, in the hotel pan and cover with the bread crumbs. To help them adhere, press the crumbs lightly into the cakes.
7. Heat a sauté pan over moderate heat and add enough clarified butter to cover the bottom approximately 0.5 cm (1/4 inch) deep.
8. Add the crab cakes to the pan and cook until done, turning once when the first side is nicely browned. Remove and drain on absorbent paper.
9. Serve the crab cakes with fresh Tomato Salsa.

Moist-Heat Cooking Methods

Fish and shellfish lend themselves well to moist-heat cooking methods, especially steaming, poaching and simmering. Steaming best preserves the food's natural flavours and cooks without adding fat. Poaching is also popular, especially for fish. Poached fish can be served hot or cold, whole or as steaks, fillets or portions. Boiling, which usually means simmering, is most often associated with crustaceans.

Steaming

Steaming is a very natural way to cook fish and shellfish without adding fats. Fish are steamed by suspending them over a small amount of boiling liquid in a covered pan. The steam trapped in the pan gently cooks the food while preserving its natural flavours and most nutrients. The liquid used to steam fish and shellfish can be water or a court bouillon with herbs, spices, aromatics or wine added to infuse the item with the additional flavours. Mussels and clams can be steamed by placing them directly in a pan, adding a small amount of wine or other liquid and covering them. Their shells will hold them above the liquid as they cook. Fish and shellfish can also be steamed by wrapping them in parchment paper together with herbs, vegetables, butters or sauces as accompaniments and baking them in a hot oven. This method of steaming is called **en papillote**.

Steamed fish and shellfish should be moist and tender. They should have clean and delicate flavours. Any accompaniments or sauces should complement the main item without masking its flavour. Fish and shellfish cooked en papillote should be served piping hot so that the aromatic steam trapped by the paper escapes as the paper is cut open tableside.

Selecting Fish and Shellfish to Steam
Mollusks (e.g., clams and mussels), fatty fish (e.g., salmon and sea bass) and lean fish (e.g., sole) all produce good results when steamed. The portions should be of uniform thickness and no more than 2.5 cm (1 inch) thick to promote even cooking.

Seasoning Fish and Shellfish to Be Steamed
Steamed fish and shellfish rely heavily on their natural flavours and often require very little seasoning. Nevertheless, salt, pepper, herbs and spices can be applied directly to the raw food before steaming. Flavoured liquids used to steam fish and shellfish will contribute additional flavours. If the liquid is served with the fish or shellfish as a broth or used to make a sauce to accompany the item, it is especially important that the liquid be well seasoned. Lemons, limes and other fruits or vegetables can also be cooked with the fish or shellfish to add flavours. Clams and mussels often do not require additional salt, as the liquor released when they open during cooking is sufficiently salty.

Accompaniments to Steamed Fish and Shellfish

Steamed fish and shellfish are popular partly because they are low in fat. In keeping with this perception, a low-fat or nonfat sauce or a simple squeeze of lemon and steamed fresh vegetables are good accompaniments. If fat is not a concern, then an emulsified butter sauce such as beurre blanc (Recipe 10.16) or hollandaise (Recipe 10.14) may be a good choice. Table 10.5 lists several sauce suggestions.

Classic New England steamed clams are served with a portion of the steaming liquid; steamed mussels are served with a sauce that is created from the wine and other ingredients used to steam them.

Basic Procedure for Steaming Fish and Shellfish

1. Portion the fish to an appropriate size. Clean the shellfish.
2. Prepare the cooking liquid. Add seasoning and flavouring ingredients as desired and bring to a boil.
3. Place the fish or shellfish in the steamer on a rack or in a perforated pan and cover tightly.
4. Steam the fish or shellfish until done.
5. Serve the fish or shellfish immediately with the steaming liquid or an appropriate sauce.

1. Place the fish in the steamer.

Applying the Basics

RECIPE 19.5

STEAMED SALMON WITH LEMON AND OLIVE OIL

Yield: 1 Serving

Lemon zest, blanched	10 g	1 Tbsp.
Lemon juice	30 mL	2 Tbsp.
Salt and pepper	TT	TT
Virgin olive oil	30 mL	2 Tbsp.
White wine	250 mL	8 fl. oz.
Bay leaf	1	1
Leek, chopped	60 g	2 oz.
Fresh thyme	1 sprig	1 sprig
Peppercorns, cracked	3 g	1 tsp.
Salmon fillet or steak, approx. 175 g (6 oz.)	1	1

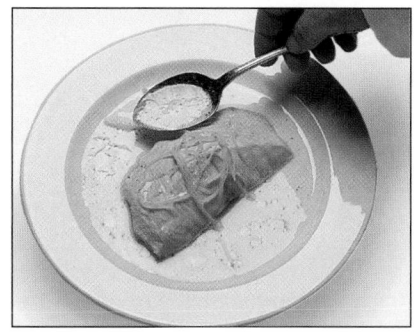

2. Spoon the dressing over the fish.

1. To make the dressing, combine the lemon zest, lemon juice, salt and pepper. Whisk in the olive oil.
2. Combine the wine, bay leaf, leek, thyme and peppercorns in the bottom of a steamer.
3. Season the salmon with salt and pepper and place it in the steamer basket.
4. Cover the steamer and bring the liquid to a boil. Cook the fish until done, approximately 4–6 minutes.
5. Plate the salmon and spoon the dressing over it.

RECIPE 19.5

Approximate values per serving:

Calories	791
Total fat	42 g
Saturated fat	6 g
Cholesterol	124 mg
Sodium	361 mg
Total carbohydrates	17 g
Protein	46 g

Applying the Basics

RED SNAPPER EN PAPILLOTE

Yield: 6 Servings

Clarified butter	as needed	as needed
Leek, julienned	100 g	3 oz.
Fennel, julienned	125 g	4 oz.
Carrot, julienned	100 g	3 oz.
Celery, julienned	100 g	3 oz.
Red bell pepper, julienned	100 g	3 oz.
Red snapper fillets, skin on, 175 g (6 oz.) each	6	6
Salt and pepper	TT	TT
Basil Butter (p. 220)	250 g	9 oz.

1. Cut six heart-shaped pieces of parchment paper large enough to contain the fish and vegetables when folded in half.
2. Brush each piece of parchment paper with clarified butter.
3. Toss the vegetables together. Place one-sixth of the vegetables on half of each piece of the buttered parchment paper.
4. Place one portion of red snapper on each portion of vegetables, skin side up; season with salt and pepper.
5. Top each portion of fish with 40 g (1-1/2 oz.) of basil butter.

Approximate values per serving:

Calories	504
Total fat	36 g
Saturated fat	22 g
Cholesterol	156 mg
Sodium	718 mg
Total carbohydrates	7 g
Protein	37.9 g

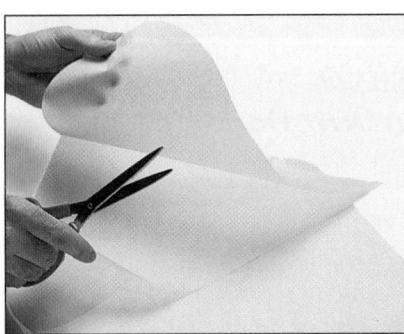

1. Cut heart-shaped pieces of parchment paper.

2. Place the vegetables, red snapper and basil butter on the parchment paper.

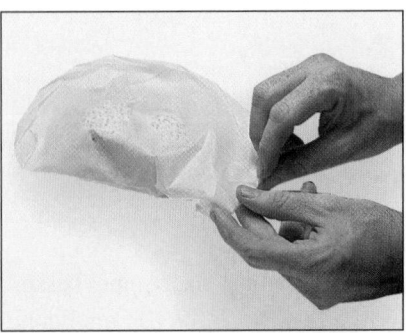

3. Crimp the edge of the parchment paper to seal it.

4. The finished papillotes.

6. Fold each piece of paper over and crimp the edges to seal it.

7. Place the envelopes (papillotes) on sheet pans and bake in a preheated oven at 230°C (450°F) for 8–10 minutes.

8. When baked, the parchment paper should puff up and brown. Remove from the oven and serve immediately. The envelope should be carefully cut open tableside to allow the aromatic steam to escape.

Poaching

Poaching is a versatile and popular method for cooking fish. Shellfish are rarely poached, however. The exception is squid, which can be quickly poached and chilled for use in salads and other preparations.

There are two distinct poaching methods.

The first is the **submersion method**, in which the fish is completely covered with a liquid, usually a court bouillon, fish stock or fish fumet. It is cooked until just done. The poached fish is then served (either hot or cold) with a sauce sometimes made from a portion of the cooking liquid but more often made separately. Whole fish (wrapped in cheesecloth to preserve its shape during cooking), fillets and steaks can all be cooked by submersion poaching.

The second method, called **shallow poaching**, combines poaching and steaming to achieve the desired results. The main item, usually a fillet or steak, is placed on a bed of aromatic vegetables in enough liquid to immerse half of the item. The liquid, called a **cuisson**, is brought to a simmer on the stove top. The pan is then covered with a piece of buttered parchment paper (cartouche) or a lid, and cooking is completed either on the stove top or in the oven. Shallow-poached fish is usually served with a sauce made with the reduced cooking liquid. (Sometimes the main item is sautéed lightly before the cooking liquid is added. If so, the cooking method is more accurately braising, as both dry- and moist-heat cooking methods are used.)

Selecting Fish to Poach

Lean white fish such as turbot, bass and sole are excellent for poaching. Some fatty fish such as salmon and trout are also excellent choices.

Seasoning Fish to Be Poached

Fish poached by either submersion or shallow poaching gain all of their seasonings from the liquid in which they are cooked and the sauce with which they are served. Therefore, it is very important to use a properly prepared court bouillon, fish fumet or a good-quality fish stock well seasoned with vegetables such as shallots, onions or fennel as well as ample herbs, spices and other seasonings. Many poached fish recipes call for wine. When using wine either in the cooking liquid or sauce, be sure to choose a wine of good quality. Most fish are very delicately flavoured, and using poor-quality wine might ruin an otherwise excellent dish. Citrus, especially lemon, is always a popular seasoning; lemon juice or zest may be added to the poaching liquid, the sauce or the finished dish.

Accompaniments to Poached Fish

Poached fish cooked by submersion go well with rich sauces like hollandaise and beurre blanc. If fat is a concern, a better choice may be a vegetable coulis (for example, broccoli or red pepper). Cold poached fish are commonly served with mayonnaise-based sauces such as sauce vert or rémoulade. Shallow-poached fish are served with sauces such as a white wine sauce or beurre blanc made from a reduction of the liquids in which the fish were poached. See Table 10.5 for additional sauce suggestions.

Poached fish are often served with rice or pasta and steamed or boiled vegetables.

Basic Procedure for Submersion Poaching

1. Prepare the cooking liquid. Whole fish should be started in a cold liquid; gradually increasing the liquid's temperature helps preserve the appearance of the fish. Portioned fish should be started in a simmering liquid to preserve their flavour and more accurately estimate cooking time.
2. Use a rack to lower the fish into the cooking liquid. Be sure the fish is completely submerged.
3. Poach the fish at 80–85°C (175–185°F) until done.
4. Remove the fish from the poaching liquid, moisten with a portion of the liquid and hold in a warm place for service. Or remove the fish from the poaching liquid, cover it to prevent drying and allow it to cool, then refrigerate.
5. Serve the poached fish with an appropriate sauce.

Applying the Basics

RECIPE 19.7

WHOLE POACHED SALMON

Yield: 18–20 Servings

Salmon, drawn, 1.8–2.2 kg (4–5 lb.)	1	1
Court bouillon	as needed	as needed

1. Place the fish on a lightly oiled rack or screen and secure with butcher's twine.
2. Place the rack or screen in a pot and cover with cold court bouillon.
3. Bring the court bouillon to a simmer over moderate heat. Reduce the heat and poach the fish at 80–85°C (175–180°F) until done, approximately 30–45 minutes.
4. If the fish is to be served hot, remove it from the court bouillon, draining well, and serve immediately with an appropriate garnish. If it is to be served cold, remove it from the court bouillon, draining well, cool and refrigerate for several hours before decorating and garnishing as desired.

RECIPE 19.7

Approximate values per serving:

Calories	144
Total fat	5 g
Saturated fat	1 g
Cholesterol	65 mg
Sodium	293 mg
Total carbohydrates	0 g
Protein	24 g

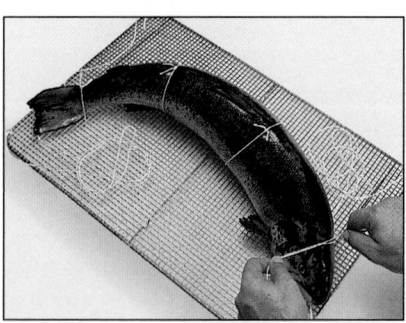

1. Arrange the whole fish on a rack.

2. Prepare the court bouillon.

3. Remove and drain the fish. Serve immediately or chill.

Basic Procedure for Shallow Poaching

1. Butter a sauteuse and add aromatic vegetables as directed in the recipe.
2. Add the fish to the pan.
3. Add the cooking liquid to the pan.
4. Cover the pan with buttered parchment paper (cartouche) or a lid.
5. Bring the liquid to a simmer and cook the fish on the stove top or in the oven until done.
6. Remove the fish from the pan, moisten with a portion of the liquid and hold in a warm place for service.
7. Reduce the cuisson and finish the sauce as directed in the recipe.
8. Serve the poached fish with the sauce.

1. Arrange the sole on the bed of shallots and mushrooms.

Applying the Basics

RECIPE 19.8

FILLETS OF SOLE BONNE FEMME

Yield: 2 Servings

Sole fillets, approx. 75 g (2-1/2 oz.) each	4	4
Salt and pepper	TT	TT
Whole butter	10 g	2 tsp.
Shallots, minced	5 g	1 tsp.
Mushrooms, sliced	125 g	4 oz.
White wine	100 mL	3 fl. oz.
Fish stock	100 mL	3 fl. oz.
Fish velouté	125 mL	4 fl. oz.
Lemon juice	TT	TT
Parsley, chopped	3 g	1 tsp.

1. Season the sole with salt and pepper. Shape into rolls (paupiettes), skin side in, starting at the head end.
2. Melt the butter in a sauté pan. Add the shallots and mushrooms and arrange the sole paupiettes over them. Add the wine and fish stock.
3. Bring the liquid to a simmer. Cover the fish with buttered parchment paper and cook on the stove top or in a 175°C (350°F) oven until done, approximately 5–8 minutes.
4. Remove the sole and reserve in a warm place.
5. Reduce the cuisson until approximately 30 mL (1 fl. oz.) remains. Add the velouté. Add lemon juice to taste and adjust the seasonings. Serve the sauce with the fish, sprinkled with chopped parsley.

2. Cover the fish with buttered parchment paper after the liquid is added.

3. Add the velouté to the cuisson.

RECIPE 19.8

Approximate values per serving:

Calories	283
Total fat	9.5 g
Saturated fat	5 g
Cholesterol	93 mg
Sodium	867 mg
Total carbohydrates	8 g
Protein	33 g

Simmering

"Boiled" lobster, crab and shrimp are not actually boiled; rather, they are cooked whole in their shells by simmering. Although they are not as delicate as some fish, these crustaceans can become tough and are easily overcooked if the cooking liquid is allowed to boil.

Selecting Shellfish to Simmer

Lobsters, crabs and shrimp are commonly cooked by simmering. Their hard shells protect their delicate flesh during the cooking process.

Seasoning Shellfish to Be Simmered

The shellfish being simmered are not seasoned. Rather, they gain flavour by being cooked in a seasoned or flavoured liquid, typically salted water or court bouillon. A sachet of pickling spice or Old Bay Seasoning® is sometimes used for additional flavour.

Determining Doneness

Timing is the best method for determining the doneness of simmered shellfish. This varies depending on the size of the shellfish and how quickly the liquid returns to a simmer after the shellfish are added. Shrimp cook in as little as 3–5 minutes, crabs cook in 5–10 minutes and it can take as little as 6–8 minutes for a 450 g (1 lb.) lobster to cook and 15–20 minutes for a 1.1 kg (2-1/2 lb.) lobster.

Accompaniments to Simmered Shellfish

The standard accompaniments to simmered shellfish are lemon wedges and melted butter. If the shellfish is being eaten cold, there are a variety of flavourful cold sauces to select from. Nearly any type of vegetable or starch goes well with simmered shellfish, and salad preparations are popular as well as freshly baked breads.

Basic Procedure for Simmering Shellfish

1. Bring court bouillon or water to a boil.
2. Add the shellfish to the liquid. Bring the liquid back to a boil and reduce to a simmer. (Whenever an item is added to boiling water, it lowers the water's temperature. The greater the amount of water, however, the faster it will return to a boil. So, to accelerate the time within which the water returns to a boil after the shellfish are added, use as much water as possible.)
3. Cook until done.
4. Remove the shellfish from the liquid and serve immediately. Or cool by plunging them in ice water if they are to be eaten cold.

Applying the Basics

RECIPE 19.9

BOILED LOBSTER

Yield: 1 Serving

Lobster, 675 g (1 lb. 8 oz.)	1	1
Boiling salted water	8 L	2 gal.
Lemon wedges	4	4
Whole butter, melted	60 mL	2 fl. oz.

RECIPE 19.9

Approximate values per serving:

Calories	1095
Total fat	51 g
Saturated fat	30 g
Cholesterol	612 mg
Sodium	3279 mg
Total carbohydrates	20 g
Protein	140 g

1. Drop the lobster into the boiling water. Bring the water back to a boil, reduce to a simmer and cook the lobster until done, approximately 12 minutes.
2. Remove the lobster from the pot, drain and serve immediately with lemon wedges and melted butter on the side.
3. If the lobster is to be eaten cold, plunge it into a sink of ice water to stop the cooking process. When cool enough to handle, remove the meat from the shell following the procedures discussed earlier.

Combination Cooking Methods

Combination cooking methods are used with meats, game and poultry in part to tenderize them. Because fish and shellfish are inherently tender, they do not necessarily benefit from such procedures. As noted above in the section on shallow poaching, fish can, on occasion, be lightly sautéed or browned and then poached. Although this procedure is a combination cooking method, it is used to enhance flavours and not to tenderize the product.

You may encounter fish or shellfish recipes with the word "braised" or "stew" in the title. Note, however, that these recipes rarely follow the traditional combination cooking methods discussed in this book.

CONCLUSION

In part because of consumers' increased health awareness, more and more food service operations are expanding their selections of fish and shellfish. Their task is aided by the tremendous variety of high-quality fish and shellfish now available. A variety of dry-heat and moist-heat cooking methods can be used with these products and a variety of sauces and accompaniments can be served with them. Regardless of how they are served, care and attention are required in order to select, store and avoid overcooking fish and shellfish.

QUESTIONS FOR DISCUSSION

1. Discuss six techniques for determining the freshness of fish and shellfish.
2. What are the physical differences between a flatfish and a round fish? How do fabrication techniques vary for these fish?
3. List four market forms for fish and discuss several factors that may determine the form most appropriate for an operation to purchase.
4. List the three categories of mollusks and give an example of a commonly used food from each category.
5. Discuss four methods for determining the doneness of fish or shellfish. Why is it important not to overcook fish and shellfish?
6. Explain the differences between shallow poaching and submersion poaching. Why is poaching a commonly used method for preparing fish and shellfish?
7. Why are combination cooking methods rarely used with fish and shellfish? Why is boiling rarely used?

ADDITIONAL FISH AND SHELLFISH RECIPES

RECIPE 19.10

SEA BASS WITH THAI CURRY SAUCE AND WOK VEGETABLES

NOTE: This dish appears in the Chapter Opening photograph.

FLYING FISH, SEATTLE, WA
Chef-Owner Christine Keff

Yield: 6 Servings   **Method:** Sautéing

Chilean sea bass fillets, each 150 g (5 oz.)	6	6
Salt and pepper	TT	TT
Peanut oil	15 mL	1 Tbsp.
Wok Vegetables (recipe follows)		
Thai Curry Sauce (recipe follows)		
Fried beet frizzles (for garnish)	as needed	as needed

1. Salt and pepper both sides of the sea bass and set aside. In a large sauté pan, heat the oil over medium-high heat.
2. Gently place the sea bass fillets into the hot pan and cook to desired doneness, turning once.
3. Serve the fish over a bed of Wok Vegetables and drizzle with the Thai Curry Sauce. Top the fish with a mound of fried beet frizzles.

WOK VEGETABLES

Yield: 6 Servings

Green or Napa cabbage	1/2 head	1/2 head
Zucchini	200 g	1
Yellow squash	200 g	1
Peanut oil	15 mL	1 Tbsp.
Fresh ginger root, peeled, chopped fine	2.5-cm knob	1-in. knob
Garlic, chopped fine	10 g	2 cloves
Cilantro, destemmed and chopped coarse	25 g	2 oz.
Peanuts, roasted, unsalted, chopped	25 g	2 Tbsp.
Sesame oil	15 mL	1 Tbsp.
Sesame seeds	2 g	1 tsp.
Soy sauce	30 mL	2 Tbsp.
Fresh lime juice	30 mL	2 Tbsp.
Mirin	30 mL	2 Tbsp.
Rice wine vinegar	30 mL	2 Tbsp.
Salt and pepper	TT	TT

1. Core the cabbage and cut into a rough julienne.
2. Grate the outside of the zucchini and the yellow squash, discarding the inner seeds.
3. Heat the peanut oil in a wok or large skillet over high heat. Add the ginger, garlic, cabbage, squashes, cilantro, peanuts, sesame oil and sesame seeds. Cook, tossing frequently, until the vegetables begin to wilt.
4. Deglaze the pan with soy sauce, lime juice, mirin and vinegar. Season to taste with salt and pepper.

RECIPE 19.10

Approximate values per serving:

Calories	290
Total fat	13 g
Saturated fat	4 g
Cholesterol	60 mg
Sodium	617 mg
Total carbohydrates	13 g
Protein	31 g

Wok Vegetables—
Approximate values per 175 g
(6 oz.) serving:

Calories	114
Total fat	7 g
Saturated fat	1 g
Cholesterol	0 mg
Sodium	443 mg
Total carbohydrates	12 g
Protein	3 g

Claims—low saturated fat; no cholesterol; good source of fibre

THAI CURRY SAUCE

Yield: 6 Servings

Peanut oil	as needed	as needed
Curry Paste (recipe follows)	50 mL	3 Tbsp.
Chicken stock	175 mL	6 fl. oz.
Coconut milk	125 mL	4 fl. oz.

1. Heat a small sauté pan and lightly coat it with peanut oil. Add the Curry Paste and sauté briefly.
2. Add the chicken stock and reduce by half.
3. Add the coconut milk and simmer until the sauce is thick enough to coat a spoon.

Thai Curry Sauce—Approximate values per 30 g (1 oz.) serving:

Calories	35
Total fat	3 g
Saturated fat	2.5 g
Cholesterol	0 mg
Sodium	75 mg
Total carbohydrates	1 g
Protein	1 g

CURRY PASTE

Yield: 250 g (8 oz.)

Fresh galangal, peeled	30 g	1 oz.
Fresh ginger root, peeled	30 g	1 oz.
Fresh turmeric, peeled	30 g	1 oz.
Shallots, peeled	60 g	2 oz.
Garlic, peeled	25 g	6 cloves
Fresh cilantro	15 g	1/2 oz.
Juice of 1/2 lime		
Dried Thai chile, soaked in water to soften	1	1
Peanut oil	as needed	as needed

1. Combine all ingredients except the oil in a food processor and grind.
2. Add just enough peanut oil to make a paste. Continue to process until the paste is smooth.

Curry Paste—Approximate values per 30 g (1 oz.) serving:

Calories	30
Total fat	1 g
Saturated fat	0 g
Cholesterol	0 mg
Sodium	15 mg
Total carbohydrates	5 g
Protein	0 g

✦✦✦

RECIPE 19.11

SEA BASS IN BANANA LEAF WITH AROMATICS

NORTH 44)° RESTAURANT, TORONTO, ON
Chef/Owner Mark McEwan

Yield: 2 Servings   **Method:** Baking

Dry Rub:

Coriander seeds, toasted and crushed	4.5 g	1 Tbsp.
Cracked black pepper	3 g	1 tsp.
Lemon zest	3 g	1 tsp.
Orange zest	3 g	1 tsp.
Thyme leaves	2 g	1 tsp.
Cumin	pinch	pinch
Curry powder	pinch	pinch
Salt	pinch	pinch
Chilean sea bass, each 150 g (5 oz.)	2	2
Banana leaves, each 30 cm (12 inches) square	4	4

Mark McEwan
Mark studied at George Brown College, where he completed two internships and won the Red Seal Award for scholarship. He went on to land a plum apprenticeship at Switzerland's prestigious Grande National Hotel Commis de Cuisine. Highlights of Mark's career include working at the renowned Sutton Place Hotel, where he cooked for Pope John Paul II in 1984; going on to become Chef there at the tender age of 25 (the youngest in Canada to hold that position); co-owning and working at Pronto Ristorante, for years Toronto's most prestigious restaurant; and, most recently, running the infamous North 44)° restaurant.

Continued

Hearts of palm or leek hearts, steamed tender and cooled	4	4
Pearl onions, peeled, blanched, oven-roasted	12	12
Sugar beets, blanched, peeled, cut in half	4	4
Coriander	3 sprigs	3 sprigs
Chiles, halved and seeded	2	2
Ginger, slivered	25 g	2 Tbsp.
Lemon grass, lightly pulverized	2 strands	2 strands
Chervil	4 sprigs	4 sprigs
Salt	pinch	pinch
Coriander oil	30 mL	2 Tbsp.

1. Combine all dry rub ingredients and rub on top of sea bass pieces to form crust.
2. Sear fish spice side down until lightly charred, then sear bottom; remove from pan and cool. Fish should be medium-rare.
3. Put banana leaves on table one on top of another, at opposing angles but centred.
4. Place palm hearts (or leeks) on bottom with pearl onions, sugar beets and sea bass on top.
5. Place herbs, ginger, lemon grass and chervil over top of fish. Add pinch of salt and 15 mL (1 Tbsp.) coriander oil on each fish.
6. Fold the top leaf first, then the second leaf to create a neat, airtight package. Tie with string.
7. Place in 180°C (375°F) oven for 15–18 minutes (until they reach an internal temperature of 60°C/140°F).
8. Place on plate, cut and remove strings. Serve with basmati rice.

◆◆◆

RECIPE 19.12

LENTIL CRUSTED TIGER COD WITH CASSOULET

METROPOLITAN HOTEL, DIVA AT THE MET, Vancouver, BC
Executive Chef Christopher Mills, CCC

Yield: 3 175-g (6-oz.) Portions   **Method:** Stewing and Pan-frying

CASSOULET

Double-smoked bacon, finely chopped	125 g	1/4 lb.
Unsalted butter	15 g	1 Tbsp.
Small onion, finely chopped	100 g	1
Garlic, finely minced	5 g	1 clove
Small leek, white part only, washed, brunoise	50 g	1
Small carrot, brunoise	50 g	1
Salt and white pepper	TT	TT
French green lentils, organic	175 g	6 oz.
Hearty chicken stock	500 mL	16 fl. oz.

Christopher Mills, CCC
Born in Montreal and raised on Vancouver's North Shore, Chris's first culinary inspiration came to him in high school. He began his apprenticeship in 1991 at the Chateau Whistler Resort, and, in only 10 years, rose through the ranks to the position of Executive Chef at the Metropolitan Hotel. He participates in culinary competition, and, having secured gold medals from Team B.C., the Vancouver Culinary Salon, and the Pierre Dubrulle "Rising Star" competition, represented Canada in 2001 and the Bocuse d'Or World Culinary Championship.

Bouquet garni	1	1
Rich demi-glace (reduced veal stock)	60 mL	2 fl. oz.
Cream, 35%	60 mL	2 fl. oz.
Fresh chopped parsley and thyme to finish		

1. In a heavy-based saucepan over low heat, cook the bacon with 15 mL (1 Tbsp.) of water to slowly render it. Add the butter, onion, and garlic to the pan and continue cooking for a few minutes. Add the leek and carrot, cooking a few minutes longer. Adjust seasoning.

2. Once the vegetables are softened, stir in the lentils and add the chicken stock and bouquet garni. Adjust seasoning. Bring the cassoulet to a slow simmer. Cook for 10 minutes and add the demi-glace and cream. Cook for 5–10 minutes. Once the lentils have absorbed most of the liquid and the consistency is similar to stew, the dish is almost finished. Remove the bouquet garni, stir in the fresh chopped herbs and adjust the final seasoning and consistency. Cassoulet can now be served or is even better cooled and heated gently later.

COD

Fresh tiger or rock cod fillets, scaled	500 g	1 lb.
Salt and white pepper	TT	TT
Red lentils, ground fine in a spice mill, sifted	125 g	4 oz.
Vegetable oil	30 mL	2 Tbsp.

1. Season cod with salt and white pepper, then roll the fillets in the ground red lentils, pressing them into the lentil powder until well coated.

2. In a heavy-based saucepan over medium heat, pan-fry the fish in the vegetable oil until lentils form a crust and lightly brown. Serve on 125 g (4 oz.) of cassoulet.

RECIPE 19.12

Cassoulet—
Approximate values per serving:

Calories	439
Total fat	16 g
Saturated fat	8.5 g
Cholesterol	61 mg
Sodium	1437 mg
Total carbohydrates	43 g
Protein	32 g

Cod—
Approximate values per serving:

Calories	305
Total fat	11 g
Saturated fat	1 g
Cholesterol	92 mg
Sodium	386 mg
Total carbohydrates	8 g
Protein	42 g

❖❖❖

RECIPE 19.13

FUTABA-CRUSTED AHI TUNA IN GREEN TEA BROTH

LA CHAUMIÈRE, CALGARY, AB
Chef/Co-Owner Robert Matthews

Yield: 10 Servings **Method:** Sautéing

Red lentils	200 g	7 oz.
Green lentils	200 g	7 oz.
Fish stock	1 L	1 qt.
Cippolini onions	10	10
Garlic	8 g	2 cloves
Salt and pepper	TT	TT
Green tea powder	150 g	5 oz.
Ahi tuna steaks, each 120 g (4 oz.)	10	10
Futaba seasoning	200 g	7 oz.
Tea konnyaku	1 pkg	1 pkg
Asparagus spears	40	40
Bok choy, small	10	10

Robert Matthews

The year Bob began his professional chef training was also the year he represented Canada on the Men's Olympic Cycling Team—twenty years later, he's an Olympic competitor in the culinary arena! After completing the Professional Cooking Program at the Southern Alberta Institute of Technology, Bob worked in Canada and abroad until finally becoming Personal Chef to the Canadian Ambassador for Japan, a position he held for five years. He returned to Canada in 1999 and became chef/co-owner of the highly regarded La Chaumière.

Continued

Sesame oil	100 mL	3-1/2 fl. oz.
Okra	20	20
Shizo	50 g	1-1/2 oz.

1. Soak lentils separately for 1 hour.
2. Boil separately in fish stock until soft. Remove and reserve.
3. Simmer onions in milk until soft, scoop out centres and dice.
4. Sauté diced onion with garlic. Add lentils, season with salt and pepper and fill onion cavities.
5. Bake in a slow oven (145°C/275°F) for 20 minutes.
6. Bring water to 98°C (200°F) and pour over green tea powder.
7. In a hot pan, sauté tuna coated with futaba seasoning until medium-rare. Cut tuna on bias.
8. Prepare julienned noodles of konnyaku, and blanch in hot water to warm.
9. Wash and prepare asparagus and bok choy, then blanch in boiling, salted water.
10. Stir-fry lightly in sesame oil. Season lightly with salt and pepper.
11. Blanch okra until tender.
12. Sauté with sesame oil. Season with shizo.
13. Set onion filled with lentils in pre-warmed bowl and surround with warm konnyaku.
14. Arrange asparagus, bok choy and okra around onion and top with sliced tuna.
15. Finish with green tea broth.

RECIPE 19.13

Approximate values per serving:

Calories	398
Total fat	12 g
Saturated fat	2 g
Cholesterol	72 mg
Sodium	744 mg
Total carbohydrates	28.5 g
Protein	45 g

Michael Noble

Michael was fated to become a chef after cooking a successful Belgian waffle in a high school economics class! He began his apprenticeship in Vancouver, though he also gained valuable European experience in the early stages of his career. In 1996, Michael opened Vancouver's Diva at the Met and, within a year, it was propelled into the culinary spotlight, winning awards from Gourmet Magazine, Vancouver Magazine, and GQ. One of Canada's leading chefs, Michael achieved Canada's highest standing ever at the Bocuse d'Or World Cuisine championship in Lyons in 1995 and 1997.

◆◆◆

RECIPE 19.14

POTATO-CRUSTED SMOKED BLACK COD WITH TOMATO CHUTNEY AND SCALLION OIL

WILDWOOD RESTAURANT GROUP, CALGARY, AB
Excutive Chef Michael Noble

Yield: 4 Servings   **Method:** Sautéing

Scallion Oil:

Green onion, green part only, minced	1 bunch	1 bunch
Olive oil, extra virgin	200 mL	7 fl. oz.
Ground white pepper	TT	TT
Rice wine vinegar	15 mL	1 Tbsp.
Smoked black cod fillets, each 60 g (2 oz.)	4	4
Ground black pepper	TT	TT
Baking potato	250 g	1
Egg white	1	1
Chives, chopped	2 g	1 tsp.
Salt	TT	TT
Flour for dredging	as needed	as needed
Olive oil	as needed	as needed

Tomato Chutney:

Shallot, minced	50 g	1
Red pepper, diced fine	10 g	2 tsp.
Olive oil	25 mL	2 Tbsp.
Raspberry vinegar	50 mL	2 fl. oz.
Sugar	50 g	2 oz.
Tomato concassée	250 g	8 oz.
Salt and ground black pepper	TT	TT
Pea shoots	as garnish	as garnish

1. To make the Scallion Oil, place the minced green onion, olive oil and white pepper in a bowl. Let the mixture stand in a refrigerator for 12–24 hours. Purée it in a blender with the rice wine vinegar.

2. Season the cod portions with the ground black pepper. Sear quickly over a hot grill or in a hot pan and let cool. Grate the potato on a coarse grater. Squeeze out the excess water without rinsing. Place the potato in a bowl. Add egg white, chives and salt. Dredge the cod lightly with flour, pat a little of the potato mixture onto the fish and sauté each piece carefully in olive oil over medium heat until golden-brown and cooked through. Drain on paper towel.

3. To make the Tomato Chutney, sweat the shallot and red pepper in the olive oil. Add the vinegar and sugar and reduce by three-quarters. Add the tomato concassée and continue cooking slowly for approximately 20 minutes, or until the liquid has evaporated and the chutney is deep red in colour. Season with salt and pepper. Set aside.

4. Toss some pea shoots in olive oil. Place on a plate and then top them with the black cod. Put some Tomato Chutney on the cod, then drizzle some Scallion Oil on the plate and serve.

RECIPE 19.14

Approximate values per serving,
with garnishes:

Calories	230
Total fat	11 g
Saturated fat	2 g
Cholesterol	46 mg
Sodium	1177 mg
Total carbohydrates	15 g
Protein	17 g

✦✦✦

RECIPE 19.15

TERIYAKI SALMON WITH PINEAPPLE PAPAYA SALSA

Yield: 4 Servings   **Method:** Grilling

Soy sauce	250 mL	8 fl. oz.
Garlic, crushed	5 g	1 tsp.
Ginger, minced	5 g	1 tsp.
Brown sugar	60 g	2 oz.
Sake	125 mL	4 fl. oz.
Salmon filets, each 120 g (4 oz.)	4	4
Vegetable oil	as needed	as needed
Pineapple Papaya Salsa (Recipe 25.9)	450 g	16 oz.

1. To make the marinade, combine the soy sauce, garlic, ginger, brown sugar and sake.

2. Marinate the salmon filets in the marinade for 15 minutes.

3. Remove the salmon from the marinade and pat dry. Brush the filets with vegetable oil and broil or grill until done.

4. Serve the salmon on a bed of warmed Pineapple Papaya Salsa.

RECIPE 19.15

Approximate values per serving:

Calories	230
Total fat	9 g
Saturated fat	2 g
Cholesterol	65 mg
Sodium	3651 mg
Total carbohydrates	28 g
Protein	35 g

John-Carlo Felicella

John-Carlo was born in Vancouver and trained in the Culinary Arts Program at Vancouver Community College. After working as Executive Chef at two well-known golf country clubs in British Columbia, he ventured into private business and opened his own restaurant, La Toque Blanche, in West Vancouver. In 1999, he also decided to become an instructor at Vancouver Community College, because a key priority for him is the education of young chefs.

RECIPE 19.16

Approximate values per serving:

Calories	568
Total fat	30 g
Saturated fat	15 g
Cholesterol	98 mg
Sodium	727 mg
Total carbohydrates	63 g
Protein	15 g

◆◆◆

RECIPE 19.16

SCALLOP CONFIT, LEMON PRESERVE RAVIOLI AND CANDIED PARSNIP PURÉE

VANCOUVER COMMUNITY COLLEGE, VANCOUVER, BC
Chef John-Carlo Felicella

Yield: 1 serving   **Method:** Sautéing

Scallops, 10–20 count, cleaned	4	4
Salt and cracked pepper	TT	TT
Butter, unsalted	15 g	3 tsp.
Lemon Preserve Ravioli (recipe follows)	1 piece	1 piece
Candied Parsnip Purée (recipe follows)	85 g	3 oz.
Asparagus, peeled	4	4
Chive oil	drizzle	drizzle
Chervil	2 sprigs	2 sprigs

1. Season scallops and sear in 10 g (2 tsp.) lightly browned butter until medium-rare.
2. Blanch ravioli in salted, simmering water.
3. Bring parsnip purée to heat by putting a small amount of cream in the pan to start.
4. Blanch asparagus in salted, simmering water for a few seconds and toss in 5 g (1 tsp.) butter.
5. Put parsnip purée in middle of hot plate.
6. Put asparagus on purée and ravioli on asparagus.
7. Gently put the medium-rare scallops on ravioli.
8. Drizzle with chive oil and garnish with chervil.

LEMON PRESERVE RAVIOLI

Yield: approx. 400 g (14 oz.)

Large white onion	120 g	4 oz.
Medium red onion	120 g	4 oz.
Leeks, trimmed and washed	120 g	4 oz.
Shallots	120 g	4 oz.
Garlic, minced	20 g	1-1/2 Tbsp.
Olive oil	45 mL	1-1/2 Tbsp.
Cream, 35%	500 mL	16 fl. oz.
Candied lemon, fine chop	40 g	1-1/2 oz.
Juice of 1 lemon		
Salt and pepper	TT	TT
Pasta dough	500 g	20 oz.

1. Finely dice the onions, leeks and shallots and slowly caramelize with the garlic in olive oil for approximately 30 minutes.
2. Add cream and reduce to a thick consistency.
3. Add candied lemon and lemon juice and season with salt and pepper. Cool.
4. Cut 7-cm (2-1/2-inch) rounds of pasta dough. Reserve half the rounds for tops.
5. Egg wash the bottoms and place 15–20 g (1 Tbsp.) onion mixture in centre of each round.
6. Place another round on top and press the edges of ravioli to seal.
7. Cook to order in boiling water.

Lemon Preserve Ravioli—
Approximate values per ravioli:

Calories	148
Total fat	11 g
Saturated fat	6 g
Cholesterol	40 mg
Sodium	131 mg
Total carbohydrates	10 g
Protein	2 g

CANDIED PARSNIP PURÉE

Water	2 L	2 qt.
Sugar	500 g	16 oz.
Parsnips, peeled and chopped	500 g	16 oz.
Cream, 35%	50 mL	2 fl. oz.
Chicken stock	50 mL	2 fl. oz.

1. Bring water and sugar to a boil, then add parsnip and simmer until parsnips are very soft. Drain and purée in a robocoup until smooth.

2. When ready to serve, heat purée over medium-low heat until very hot. Adjust consistency with cream and stock.

Candied Parsnip Purée—
Approximate values
per 85 g serving:

Calories	206
Total fat	2 g
Saturated fat	1 g
Cholesterol	5 mg
Sodium	25 mg
Total carbohydrates	49 g
Protein	1 g

♦♦♦

RECIPE 19.17

SALMON IN RICE PAPER WITH A FRESH HERB MOSAIC AND SOY BEURRE BLANC

CHEF LELAND ATKINSON, WASHINGTON, DC

Yield: 4 Servings   **Method:** Sautéing

Salmon fillet portions, each 175 g (6 oz.)	4	4
Salt and pepper	TT	TT
Extra virgin olive oil	30 mL	2 Tbsp.
Rice vinegar	30 mL	2 Tbsp.
Rice paper circles,		
20 cm (8 inches) in diameter	4	4
Fresh basil	4 leaves	4 leaves
Fresh dill	4 sprigs	4 sprigs
Fresh cilantro	4 leaves	4 leaves
Soy Beurre Blanc (recipe follows)	200 mL	8 fl. oz.

1. Season the skin side of the salmon with salt and pepper; drizzle with the olive oil and vinegar.

2. Soak the rice paper in warm water, one sheet at a time, for 30 seconds.

3. Transfer each paper to a work surface and let it stand until pliable.

4. Arrange a portion of the fresh herbs in a mosaic pattern in the centre of the rice paper.

5. Place the salmon flesh side down, centred over the mosaic.

6. Tightly fold in all four sides of the rice paper to enclose the fish.

7. Sauté the salmon, presentation (flesh) side down first, in olive oil until the rice paper is golden-brown. Use caution, as the rice paper browns quickly.

8. Transfer the fish to a 180°C (350°F) oven and cook for 2–3 minutes. Do not overcook.

9. Ladle the Soy Beurre Blanc onto four warm plates and centre the fish on it.

RECIPE 19.17

Approximate values per serving:

Calories	400
Total fat	22 g
Saturated fat	5 g
Cholesterol	105 mg
Sodium	690 mg
Total carbohydrates	3 g
Protein	17 g

SOY BEURRE BLANC

Yield: 350 mL (12 fl. oz.)

Shallots, chopped	30 g	1 oz.
Clarified butter	15 mL	1 Tbsp.
White wine	250 mL	8 fl. oz.
Fresh thyme	1 sprig	1 sprig
Bay leaf	1	1

Continued

Fresh ginger, peeled, chopped	30 g	1 oz.
Cream, 35%	250 mL	8 fl. oz.
Champagne vinegar	5 mL	1 tsp.
Butter, room temperature	125 g	4 oz.
Soy sauce	10 mL	2 tsp.
Fresh lemon juice	15 mL	1 Tbsp.

Soy Beurre Blanc—
Approximate values per serving:

Calories	150
Total fat	16 g
Saturated fat	10 g
Cholesterol	50 mg
Sodium	140 mg
Total carbohydrates	1 g
Protein	1 g

1. Sweat the shallots in clarified butter.
2. Add the wine, thyme, bay leaf and ginger. Simmer slowly, reduce au sec.
3. Add the cream and reduce until slightly thick.
4. Add the vinegar and whisk in the room-temperature butter.
5. Add the soy sauce and fresh lemon juice and strain.
6. Hold the sauce warm and tightly covered until service.

❖❖❖

RECIPE 19.18

RED SNAPPER VERACRUZ

Yield: 4 Servings   **Method:** Sautéing

Red snapper fillets, skinless, each 175 g (6 oz.)	4	4
Salt and pepper	TT	TT
Flour	as needed	as needed
Olive oil	60 mL	2 fl. oz.
Onion, medium dice	175 g	6 oz.
Garlic cloves, minced	15 g	4
Lemon juice	30 mL	1 fl. oz.
Fish or chicken stock	250 mL	8 fl. oz.
Jalapeño, seeded, small dice	1	1
Tomato concassée	650 g	1 lb. 8 oz.
Pimento-stuffed green olives, quartered	150 g	20
Sugar	5 g	1 tsp.
Cinnamon stick	5 g	1
Dried thyme	0.5 g	1/2 tsp.
Dried marjoram	0.5 g	1/2 tsp
Capers	25 g	2 Tbsp.
Fresh cilantro for garnish	as needed	as needed

RECIPE 19.18

Approximate values per serving:

Calories	570
Total fat	22 g
Saturated fat	3 g
Cholesterol	80 mg
Sodium	1820 mg
Total carbohydrates	41 g
Protein	51 g

1. Season the fillets with salt and pepper and dredge in flour. Sauté the fillets in olive oil until done. Remove and reserve in a warm place.
2. Add the onions and garlic to the pan and sauté until tender. Deglaze the pan with the lemon juice and add the stock, jalapeño, tomatoes, olives, sugar, cinnamon stick, thyme and marjoram.
3. Simmer 10 minutes. Remove the cinnamon stick and add the capers. Season with salt and pepper to taste.
4. Return the fish to the pan to reheat. Serve on warm plates garnished with fresh cilantro.

VARIATIONS: Substitute bass or halibut fillets for the red snapper.

◆◆◆

RECIPE 19.19
POACHED FISH STEAKS

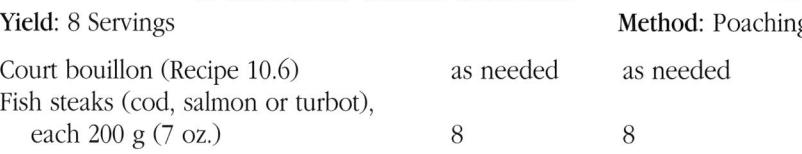

Yield: 8 Servings　　　　　　　　　　**Method**: Poaching

Court bouillon (Recipe 10.6)	as needed	as needed
Fish steaks (cod, salmon or turbot), each 200 g (7 oz.)	8	8

1. Bring the court bouillon to a boil.
2. Arrange the steaks on a rack and lower into the court bouillon.
3. Reduce the heat and poach the fish until done, approximately 5–10 minutes.
4. Remove the fish and drain well. Remove the skin or bones, if necessary. Serve with lemon wedges and an appropriate sauce, such as hollandaise, mousseline or beurre noisette.

◆◆◆

RECIPE 19.20
OLIVE OIL POACHED SALMON WITH OSCIETRA CAVIAR

FOUR SEASONS HOTEL, Toronto, ON
Executive Chef Robert Sulatycky

Yield: 4 Servings　　　　　　　　　　**Method**: Poaching

Olive oil	2 L	2 qt.
Shallots, peeled and sliced	60 g	2 oz.
Fresh basil, bruised	50 g	1-1/2 oz.
Bouquet garni tied with leek to include thyme, parsley, fresh laurel leaf	1	1
Cracked white pepper	10 g	1 Tbsp.
Sea salt	TT	TT
Boneless darnes of Atlantic salmon, each 175 g (6 oz.)	4	4
Freshly ground white pepper	TT	TT
Fresh lemon (for juice)	2 pieces	2 pieces
Oscietra caviar	25 g	1 oz.
Beurre blanc	175 mL	6 fl. oz.
Fleur de sel, French	TT	TT
Sprigs of chervil for garnish		

1. Preheat oven to 63°C (170°F). Place olive oil in an ovenproof dish and add the shallots, basil, bouquet garni, cracked white pepper and 30 g (1 oz.) of sea salt. Place in the low oven and allow the oil to "steep" for up to 2 hours.
2. Season the salmon with sea salt and ground white pepper. Drizzle with lemon juice and place in the oil. Ensure that the oil fully covers the salmon. Poach the salmon in the oil in the oven for approximately 20–25 minutes or until the internal temperature of the salmon reaches 60°C (140°F). When the salmon is done, it will have the appearance of being medium-rare to medium from top to bottom. Remove the container from the oven but leave the salmon in the oil.
3. Stir the caviar into the beurre blanc.
4. Remove the salmon from the oil and drain on paper towel. Remove the skin from each darne.

Continued

Robert Sulatycky

Robert's professional training comes from having worked at top haute cuisine establishments in London and Paris, but he credits the simple cooking methods of his grandmother (now 98), who was an accredited cook all her life, as having inspired his culinary passion. Robert's food stylings have been showcased in the namesake Absolut Vodka print ads, his titled "Absolut Sulatycky" (Fall 1998). In 2000, he not only became the first Canadian chef to receive the coveted Robert Mondavi Culinary Award of Excellence, but he was also handpicked by the producers of The Great Canadian Food Show for an episode that explored the question "What makes a great chef great?"

5. Drizzle more lemon juice on the salmon and sprinkle with fleur de sel. Serve with the caviar sauce and garnish with chervil. Appropriate vegetables would be baby fennel or celery étuvée or asparagus.

✦✦✦

RECIPE 19.21

WICKANINNISH POTLACHE

WICKANINNISH INN AND POINTE RESTAURANT, TOFINO, BC
Chef de Cuisine Jim Garraway

Jim Garraway
Canadian-born and trained, Jim has been cooking since he learned to operate a stove, delighting in preparing lunches for his schoolmates at the age of 14. After training at Vancouver Community College and working at Château Whistler, he joined the Wickaninnish Inn's opening team in 1996 and became chef there in 1999. Jim also co-direct's the Inn's well-established apprenticeship program.

RECIPE 19.21

Approximate values per serving:

Calories	582
Total fat	31 g
Saturated fat	5 g
Cholesterol	118 mg
Sodium	310 mg
Total carbohydrates	23 g
Protein	48 g

Yield: 4 Servings

Method: Stewing and Steaming

Onion, diced	175 g	6 oz.
Fennel, diced	175 g	6 oz.
Carrots, diced	150 g	5 oz.
Olive oil	90 mL	3 fl. oz.
Tomatoes, whole, tinned, chopped	800 mL	28 fl. oz.
Tomato paste	30 mL	1 fl. oz.
Herbs, chopped (cilantro, thyme, basil)	30 g	1 oz.
Halibut, 2 cm (1 inch) dice	250 g	8 oz.
Salmon, 2 cm (1 inch) dice	250 g	8 oz.
Shrimp, 26–30 peeled, deveined	8	8
Scallops	8	8
Mussels, cleaned, bearded	12	12
Clams, manilla, cleaned	12	12
Crab legs, Dungeness	4	4
White wine	125 mL	4 fl. oz.

1. Sweat vegetables in oil. Add tomatoes with liquid, tomato paste and herbs. Simmer for 25 minutes. Reserve.
2. To serve, add fish, shrimp and scallops to tomato stew, simmer 5 minutes.
3. Steam mussels, clams and crab legs in white wine.
4. Ladle fish stew into bowls and garnish with shellfish.

✦✦✦

RECIPE 19.22

STEAMED BLACK BASS WITH SANSHO PEPPER

THE FOUR SEASONS, NEW YORK, NY
Chef Christian Albin

Yield: 6 Servings

Method: Steaming

Black bass fillets, skin on, each approx. 150 g (5 oz.)	6	6
Leek, large, cleaned and cut into strips	1	1
Sansho pepper* and sea salt	TT	TT
Lime	1	1
Lemon	1	1
Olive oil	45 mL	3 Tbsp.
Pommeray mustard	5 mL	1 tsp.
Salt and pepper	TT	TT

1. Place the fish fillets, skin side up, and the leek in a steamer basket. Season with Sansho pepper and sea salt. Steam for approximately 5 minutes.

2. To make the vinaigrette, zest and juice the lime and lemon. Blanch the zests in water. Drain and mix the zests and juices with the olive oil and Pommeray mustard; season to taste with salt and pepper.

3. Plate the fish fillets and garnish with the leeks. Drizzle the vinaigrette over the fish and leeks.

* Sansho pepper (a slightly spicy Japanese seasoning) can be bought in specialty stores.

RECIPE 19.22

Approximate values per serving:

Calories	267
Total fat	11.5 g
Saturated fat	2 g
Cholesterol	154 mg
Sodium	148 mg
Total carbohydrates	6 g
Protein	35 g

◆◆◆

RECIPE 19.23

LIGHTLY GRILLED RED TUNA WITH EGGPLANT COMPOTE AND TOMATO SALPICON WITH CILANTRO

NUANCES, CASINO DE MONTRÉAL, MONTREAL, QC
Chef exécutif, Jean-Pierre Curtat

Yield: 4 Servings   **Method:** Grilling

Tuna, sushi grade	360 g	12 oz.
Diced tuna	200 g	7 oz.
Olive oil	50 mL	2 Tbsp.
Lemon juice	25 mL	1 Tbsp.
Eggplant Compote (recipe follows)	320 g	11 oz.
Tomato Salpicon with Cilantro (recipe follows)		
Balsamic vinegar, reduced	50 mL	2 fl. oz.
Herbs of choice for garnish		

1. Cut the tuna in a rectangular shape and use the trimmings to make the diced tuna.

2. Marinate the diced tuna briefly in a mix of olive oil and lemon juice.

3. Sear the tuna on all sides and bake for 2–3 minutes in a 200°C (400°F) oven. Slice.

4. Heat the Eggplant Compote and place it in an emporte-pièce (ring form) with the marinated diced tuna.

5. Garnish the top in a circle with grilled fish slices.

6. Remove the ring.

7. Place the Tomato Salpicon with Cilantro on top. Lightly pour the reduced balsamic vinegar over top and garnish the centre with herbs.

EGGPLANT COMPOTE

Eggplants, large	2	2
Red bell peppers, roasted	450 g	3
Shallot, chiselled	250 g	8 oz.
Garlic, chopped	50 g	2 oz.
Olive oil	150 mL	5 fl. oz.
Mushrooms, diced	250 g	8 oz.
Crushed tomato	250 g	8 oz.
Anchovy fillets	25 g	10
Tahini (sesame paste)	60 g	2-1/2 oz.
Salt and pepper	TT	TT

1. Bake the eggplants and save the flesh.

2. Peel roasted red peppers and chop the flesh roughly.

Jean-Pierre Curtat
Jean-Pierre completed his culinary studies at l'Institut de tourisme et d'hôtellerie du Québec. Over the years that followed, he apprenticed in various Canadian hotels and restaurants and then dished up culinary delights in Parisian restaurants. He has functioned as Executive Chef of all of the casino's kitchens since 1993, the year the casino opened.

RECIPE 19.23

Approximate values per serving:

Calories	942
Total fat	61 g
Saturated fat	9 g
Cholesterol	29 mg
Sodium	598 mg
Total carbohydrates	52.5 g
Protein	53.5 g

Eggplant Compote—
Approximate values per serving:

Calories	578
Total fat	43 g
Saturated fat	6 g
Cholesterol	4 mg
Sodium	280 mg
Total carbohydrates	45.5 g
Protein	11.5 g

Continued

Tomato Salpicon with Cilantro—
Approximate values per serving:

Calories	77
Total fat	6 g
Saturated fat	1 g
Cholesterol	0 mg
Sodium	248 mg
Total carbohydrates	6 g
Protein	1 g

Gilbert Noussitou, CCC

A graduate of École Hôtelière des Pyrénées, in Toulouse, France, Gilbert has been practicing his trade for 28 years in some of the finest establishments of France, England and Canada. His varied experience includes owning a restaurant, a catering company, and a consulting firm, as well as winning many national and international awards. He currently teaches the Cook Apprenticeship Program at Camosun.

RECIPE 19.24

Approximate values per 60 g (2 oz.) serving:

Calories	208
Total fat	17 g
Saturated fat	6 g
Cholesterol	130 mg
Sodium	824 mg
Total carbohydrates	8 g
Protein	8 g

RECIPE 19.25

Approximate values per serving:

Calories	450
Total fat	18 g
Saturated fat	9 g
Cholesterol	310 mg
Sodium	970 mg
Total carbohydrates	4 g
Protein	69 g

3. Slowly cook the shallot and garlic in the olive oil.

4. Fry the mushrooms gently. Chop the eggplants and add to pan. Reduce to dry well.

5. Add the chopped red pepper, tomato, anchovy fillets and tahini. Cook for 5 minutes and adjust the seasoning with salt and pepper.

TOMATO SALPICON WITH CILANTRO

Tomatoes, medium	4	4
Coriander, chopped	20 g	2 Tbsp.
Olive oil	25 mL	1 Tbsp.
Salt and pepper	TT	TT

1. Blanch the tomatoes and remove the pulp.

2. Roughly cut the pulp.

3. Add the chopped coriander, olive oil, salt and pepper.

✦✦✦

RECIPE 19.24

CORN FLAN AND SMOKED SALMON WITH CHIVE OIL

CAMOSUN COLLEGE, VICTORIA, BC
Chef Instructor Gilbert Noussitou, CCC

Yield: 9 60-g (2-oz.) Servings   **Method:** Baking

Corn kernels	300 g	10 oz.
Cream, 35%	200 mL	7 fl. oz.
Eggs	2	2
Egg yolks	2	2
Salt	TT	TT
Lemon juice	10 mL	2 tsp.
Mustard powder	8 g	2 tsp.
Chile oil	TT	TT
Smoked salmon, thinly sliced	225 g	8 oz.
Chives	as needed	as needed
Fried parsley	as needed	as needed
Potato tuiles	as needed	as needed
Chive oil	50 mL	1-1/2 fl. oz.

1. Simmer corn and cream for 3 minutes. Purée and pass through a fine sieve.

2. Whisk eggs and yolks together and whisk in corn purée. Season with salt, lemon juice, mustard and chile oil.

3. Divide the mixture among nine buttered ramekins. Bake in a bain marie in a 150°C (300°F) oven for approximately 45 minutes or until set.

4. Allow to cool slightly before unmoulding.

5. Place warm flan on plate, arrange smoked salmon attractively and garnish with chives, parsley and tuiles. Drizzle with chive oil.

✦✦✦

RECIPE 19.25

PAUPIETTES OF SOLE WITH MOUSSELINE OF SHRIMP

Yield: 6 Servings   **Method:** Poaching

Shrimp meat	350 g	12 oz.
Egg white	1	1

Cream, 35%	175 mL	6 fl. oz.
Salt and white pepper	TT	TT
Lemon sole fillets, skinless, each 125 g (4 oz.)	12	12
Whole butter	as needed	as needed
Shallots, chopped	50 g	2 oz.
Parsley, chopped	20 g	2 Tbsp.
White vermouth	175 mL	6 fl. oz.
Shrimp stock	350 mL	12 fl. oz.
Beurre manié	approx. 45 g	approx. 1-1/2 oz.

1. Flatten the fillets slightly with a mallet.

1. Purée the raw shrimp meat in a food processor.

2. Add the egg white and pulse to incorporate.

3. Slowly add 60 mL (2 fl. oz.) of the cream to the shrimp while pulsing the processor. Season the mousseline with salt and white pepper.

4. Place the sole fillets skin side up on a cutting board and flatten lightly with a mallet.

5. Spread each fillet with a portion of the mousseline. Roll up the fillets, starting with the thickest part and finishing with the tail portion.

2. Spread the fillets with the prepared mousseline.

6. Butter a sauteuse and sprinkle with the chopped shallots and parsley.

7. Place the sole paupiettes in the sauteuse and add the vermouth and shrimp stock.

8. Bring the liquid to a boil, cover with a piece of buttered parchment paper and place in a 180°C (350°F) oven. Poach until nearly done.

9. Remove the sole from the sauteuse and reserve in a warm place.

10. Return the sauteuse to the heat and reduce the cuisson slightly.

11. Thicken the cuisson to the desired consistency with the beurre manié.

12. Add the remaining cream, bring the sauce to a boil and strain through a fine etâmine. Adjust the seasonings.

13. Serve two paupiettes per portion in a pool of sauce.

3. Roll the paupiettes.

◆◆◆

RECIPE 19.26

PAN-SEARED SCALLOPS AND RAGOUT OF SUMMER VEGETABLES IN A PHYLLO FRYING PAN WITH MINTED ORANGE SAUCE

SHAW CONFERENCE CENTRE, EDMONTON, AB
Executive Chef Simon Smotkowicz, CCC

Simon Smotkowicz, CCC
Simon has been a member and a leader of award-winning Canadian culinary teams for many years, most recently managing Team Canada to a world championship in Glasgow in 1997 and 2001. In 1995 he was elected Chef of the Year for the Western Region by his peers in the CFCC.

Yield: 4 Servings   **Method:** Pan-frying

Phyllo pastry	8 sheets plus 2 sheets cut in half horizontally	8 sheets plus 2 sheets cut in half horizontally
Butter, unsalted clarified	150 g	5-1/2 oz.
Fish stock	125 mL	1/2 cup
Juice from 3 oranges	250 mL	8 fl. oz.
Juice from 1/2 lemon	25 mL	1 fl. oz.
Bay leaf	1	1

Continued

Mint stalks, chopped	20 g	2 Tbsp.
Cream, 35%	250 mL	1 cup
Butter, unsalted, cold	25 g	1 oz.
Champagne vinegar	15 mL	1 Tbsp.
Salt and pepper	TT	TT
Asparagus spears	4	4
Yellow bell pepper, julienned	175 g	1
Tomato, peeled, seeded and diced	125 g	1
Butter	5 g	1 tsp.
Scallops, fresh	8 large	8 large
Olive oil	5 mL	1 tsp.
Mint leaves, julienned	10 g	1 Tbsp.

1. To make phyllo frying pans, brush one whole phyllo sheet with butter and fold in half. Lay it in a small iron frying pan; mould it to the shape of the pan and trim off the excess. Butter a half sheet, roll it up to make a handle and lay it partly in the pan but with 8 cm (3 inches) extending up the real pan handle. To secure the handle, cover the pan area with another folded sheet. Trim this to shape and prick it all over with a fork. Brush once more with butter.

2. Bake in the iron pan for about 12 minutes, or until crisp and brown, at 190°C (375°F).

3. Repeat three times with remaining dough to make four frying pans.

4. In saucepan, mix the fish stock, fruit juices, bay leaf and mint stalks. Bring to a boil, lower heat and reduce by two-thirds. Strain, add cream and simmer for 5 minutes.

5. With a wire whip, incorporate butter in small pieces. Do not let the mixture simmer.

6. Add the champagne vinegar, then season to taste with salt and pepper and reserve.

7. Quickly blanch vegetables in boiling, salted water. Strain, add butter, season and keep warm.

8. Season scallops and sear in very hot pan in olive oil. Serve immediately in a phyllo frying pan with vegetables and orange-minted sauce. Garnish with the mint leaves.

RECIPE 19.26

Approximate values per serving:

Calories	821
Total fat	70 g
Saturated fat	41 g
Cholesterol	211 mg
Sodium	491 mg
Total carbohydrates	34 g
Protein	16 g

◆◆◆

RECIPE 19.27

PAELLA

CHEF LELAND ATKINSON, WASHINGTON, DC

Yield: 4 Servings   **Method:** Braising

Chicken thighs	4	4
Salt and pepper	TT	TT
Olive oil	60 mL	2 fl. oz.
Onion, medium dice	60 g	2 oz.
Garlic, chopped	15 g	1 Tbsp.
Red bell pepper, medium dice	75 g	3 oz.
Green bell pepper, medium dice	50 g	2 oz.
Rice, long grain	350 g	12 oz.

Saffron	1 g	pinch
Chicken stock, well seasoned, hot	750 mL	26 fl. oz.
Chorizo, cooked, sliced	125 g	4 oz.
Clams, scrubbed	12	12
Shrimp, 16–20 count	12	12
Lobster (600 g/21 oz.), cut up	1	1
Mussels, bearded and scrubbed	12	12

1. Season the chicken with salt and pepper. Pan-fry it in the olive oil, browning it well. Cook until done, approximately 20 minutes. Remove the chicken and reserve.
2. Add the onion, garlic and peppers to the pan and sauté until tender.
3. Add the rice and sauté until it turns translucent.
4. Add the saffron to the chicken stock. Stir the chicken stock into the rice and bring to a boil.
5. Add the sliced chorizo and clams to the pan. Cover and place in a 190°C (375°F) oven for 20 minutes.
6. Add the raw shrimp and lobster, and the cooked chicken to the pan. Cover and cook for an additional 15 minutes.
7. Add the mussels to the pan and cook until the shrimp and lobster are done, the chicken is hot and all the shellfish are opened, approximately 5 minutes.

RECIPE 19.27

Approximate values per serving:

Calories	930
Total fat	41 g
Saturated fat	10 g
Cholesterol	650 mg
Sodium	2050 mg
Total carbohydrates	31 g
Protein	110 g

❖ ❖ ❖

RECIPE 19.28

CLAMS CASINO

Yield: 36 Clams   **Method:** Baking

Bacon, diced	100 g	4 slices
Onion, minced	30 g	1 oz.
Red bell pepper, minced	30 g	1 oz.
Green bell pepper, minced	30 g	1 oz.
Whole butter	180 g	6 oz.
Lemon juice	15 mL	1 Tbsp.
Worcestershire sauce	10 mL	2 tsp.
Tabasco sauce	TT	TT
Clams, scrubbed	36	36
Fresh bread crumbs	60 g	2 oz.

1. Fry the bacon until well done. Drain the fat, reserving 30 mL (2 Tbsp.).
2. Sauté the onion and peppers in the bacon fat until tender; remove from the heat and cool.
3. Combine 120 g (4 oz.) of the butter, lemon juice, Worcestershire sauce, Tabasco sauce, bacon pieces and sautéed vegetables and chill.
4. Open the clams, leaving the loosened meat in the bottom shell. Top each clam with 5 mL (1 tsp.) of the vegetable-butter-bacon mixture.
5. Melt the remaining butter in a sauté pan and toss the bread crumbs in the butter. Top each clam with a portion of the bread crumbs.
6. Bake at 200°C (400°F) until light brown and bubbling, approximately 10 minutes. Serve immediately.

RECIPE 19.28

Approximate values per serving:

Calories	55
Total fat	4.5 g
Saturated fat	3 g
Cholesterol	16 mg
Sodium	107 mg
Total carbohydrates	2 g
Protein	2 g

♦♦♦

RECIPE 19.29

OYSTERS ROCKEFELLER

Yield: 1 Serving   **Method:** Poaching

Oysters	6	6
White wine	30 mL	1 fl. oz.
Garlic, finely chopped	15 g	1 Tbsp.
Onion, finely chopped	15 g	1 Tbsp.
Butter	10 g	2 tsp.
Spinach, blanched	125 g	4 oz.
Nutmeg, salt and ground white pepper	TT	TT
Pernod	10 mL	2 tsp.
Rock salt	100 g	4 oz.
Cream, 35%	20 mL	1 fl. oz.
Mornay sauce (p. 206)	125 mL	4 fl. oz.
Bread crumbs	5 g	1 Tbsp.
Parmesan cheese	10 g	1 Tbsp.

1. Shuck the oysters; poach the shucked oysters in their own juices with the white wine.
2. Sauté the garlic and onion in butter, add the spinach, season with nutmeg, salt and pepper and flavour with the Pernod.
3. Heat the cleaned shell bottoms on rock salt for 30 seconds under a broiler or for 1 minute in a hot oven.
4. Stuff the shells with the spinach and top each shell with a poached oyster. Keep them hot.
5. Add the cream to the poaching liquid and reduce by half. Add the mornay sauce to heat up.
6. Top the oyster and spinach with mornay sauce. Sprinkle with a mixture of bread crumbs and Parmesan cheese and gratinée or brown in the oven.

RECIPE 19.29

Approximate values per serving:

Calories	570
Total fat	39 g
Saturated fat	24 g
Cholesterol	151 mg
Sodium	406 mg
Total carbohydrates	30 g
Protein	18 g

♦♦♦

RECIPE 19.30

PAUPIETTES OF ARCTIC CHAR WITH WHITE WINE SABAYON

WESTIN PRINCE HOTEL, TORONTO, ON
Executive Chef Hans U. Herzig

Yield: 10 Servings   **Method:** Baking

Fillets of Arctic char, each 70–80 g (2-1/2—2-3/4 oz.)	20	20
Salt and pepper	TT	TT
Bok choy, greens only, blanched	2 large heads	2 large heads
Butter	100 g	3-1/2 oz.
Shallots, finely diced	2	2
White wine	300 mL	10 fl. oz.
Fish stock	500 mL	18 fl. oz.
Roma tomatoes, medium, peeled and cored	10	10

Hans U. Herzig

Hans was born in Switzerland and trained in Europe; he came to Canada to work at the Windsor Arms in Toronto. Among the highlights of his career, he was captain of the Canadian team that won 10 gold medals at the 1988 World Culinary Olympics.

Asparagus spears, peeled and blanched, approximately 7–8 cm (3 inches) long	70	70
Yukon Gold potatoes, 5-mm (1/4-inches) thick slices, blanched	70	70
Egg yolks	5	5

1. Lay out the fish fillets, season lightly with salt and pepper and top with bok choy greens cut into size of fillets.

2. Roll fillets with greens on the inside and fasten with skewers.

3. Butter the baking dish, add paupiettes, sprinkle with shallots, 200 mL (6 fl. oz.) of the wine and 450 mL (16 fl. oz.) of the fish stock and season. Cover with buttered parchment paper and bake at 190°C (375°F) for 10–12 minutes, until firm.

4. Cut tomatoes into large square fillets, season lightly with salt and pepper and sauté. Simmer asparagus and sliced potatoes in water or stock until heated through.

5. To make the sabayon, put the egg yolks into a stainless steel bowl. Add the remaining wine, the remaining fish stock and a pinch of salt and pepper. Whisk vigorously over simmering water until thick.

6. Arrange two paupiettes on a plate and place the sliced potatoes around them. Coat the paupiettes with sabayon and garnish with tomato and the asparagus spears.

◆◆◆

RECIPE 19.31

STEAMED SCALLOPS WITH GINGER, BASIL AND ORANGE

VINCENT ON CAMELBACK, PHOENIX, AZ
Chef Vincent Guerithault

Yield: 1 Serving **Method:** Steaming

Oranges	2	2
Lime	1	1
Flour tortilla, 20 cm (8 inches)	1	1
Scallops, large	150 g	3
Ginger, grated	5 g	1 tsp.
Carrot, julienned	60 g	2 oz.
Celery, julienned	30 g	1 oz.
Tomato, small dice	25 g	2 Tbsp.
Fresh basil, chopped	10 g	1 Tbsp.
Olive oil	15 mL	1 Tbsp.
Salt and pepper	TT	TT
White wine	250 mL	8 fl. oz.
Shallot, chopped	5 g	1 tsp.

1. Zest half an orange and then cut the oranges in 1-cm (1/2-inch) slices. Peel the lime and cut into 5-mm (1/4-inch) slices.

2. Line a small bamboo steamer with the flour tortilla.

3. Place the scallops on top of the tortilla. Add the orange zest, ginger, carrot, celery, tomato, basil, olive oil, two slices of lime and a dash of salt and pepper. Cover.

4. Place the white wine, chopped shallots, orange slices and remaining lime slices in the bottom of the steamer pan. Steam the scallops over the seasoned wine until done, approximately 5 minutes.

RECIPE 19.30

Approximate values per serving, with sabayon:

Calories	616
Total fat	25 g
Saturated fat	6 g
Cholesterol	129 mg
Sodium	597 mg
Total carbohydrates	53 g
Protein	42 g

RECIPE 19.31

Approximate values per serving:

Calories	604
Total fat	17 g
Saturated fat	2 g
Cholesterol	15 mg
Sodium	498 mg
Total carbohydrates	66 g
Protein	14.5 g

James Olberg

James was born and trained near Toronto, and he completed his apprenticeship at the King Edward Hotel. His career continued at places such as the Sutton Place Hotel, the Four Seasons Hotel, the Metropolitan Hotel, and the Delawanna Inn. In 2001, he joined the award-winning Crowne Plaza Hotel Georgia.

◆◆◆

RECIPE 19.32
TEA-SMOKED ATLANTIC SALMON FILLETS ON LOBSTER EMULSION

CROWNE PLAZA HOTEL GEORGIA, VANCOUVER, BC
Executive Chef James Olberg

Yield: 4 Servings   **Method:** Pan-smoking/Baking

Marinade:		
Sesame oil	250 mL	8 fl. oz.
Soy sauce	20 mL	4 tsp.
Olive oil	250 mL	8 fl. oz.
White wine	125 mL	4 fl. oz.
Garlic, chopped	30 g	1 oz.
Rosemary, chopped	30 g	1 oz.
Black peppercorns, cracked	15 g	1/2 oz.
Atlantic salmon fillets, each 175 g (6 oz.)	4	4
Smoking Ingredients:		
Wood chips	500 g	1 lb.
Wood dust	250 g	8 oz.
Earl Grey tea	3 bags	3 bags
Salt and white pepper	TT	TT
Lobster Emulsion:		
Lobster fumé	500 mL	16 fl. oz.
Shallots, fine chop	60 g	2 oz.
Butter	125 g	4 oz.
Tarragon, chopped	30 g	1 oz.
Salt and white pepper	TT	TT

1. Combine marinade ingredients and let sit for 1 hour.

2. Immerse salmon fillets in marinade for 5 minutes. Remove and blot dry with paper towels. Place in a perforated pan and cover with plastic wrap.

3. Place smoking ingredients in a deeper pan that fits outside the perforated pan. Set salmon pan on top.

4. Heat pans over open flame until smoke is visible. Remove from heat and let smoke for 10 minutes.

5. Season salmon with salt and pepper and sear in a hot pan to colour. Finish in oven.

6. Reduce lobster fumé and shallots to 175 mL (6 fl. oz.). Whisk in butter and tarragon. Adjust seasoning.

7. Serve salmon on truffled mashed potatoes with baby vegetables. Drizzle with lobster emulsion.

RECIPE 19.32

Approximate values per serving:

Calories	903
Total fat	71 g
Saturated fat	22 g
Cholesterol	193 mg
Sodium	1321 mg
Total carbohydrates	17 g
Protein	51 g

◆◆◆

RECIPE 19.33
SHELLFISH BOUILLABAISSE WITH GINGER AIOLI

SHAW CONFERENCE CENTRE, EDMONTON, AB
Executive Chef Simon Smotkowicz, CCC

Yield: 4 Servings   **Method:** Sautéing

Butter, unsalted	50 g	4 Tbsp.
Carrots, medium, peeled and diced	75 g	1

Celery, stalks, peeled and diced	150 g	2
Fennel bulb, cored and diced	150 g	1
Onion, medium, peeled and diced	150 g	1
Ginger root, peeled and minced	40 g	1/4 cup
Clams	12	12
Mussels, cleaned and debearded	12	12
Fish stock	175 mL	6 fl. oz.
Butter, unsalted	60 g	4 Tbsp.
Prawns, shelled	8	8
Lobsters, split lengthwise	2	2
Salt and pepper	TT	TT
Scallops	8	8
White wine	125 mL	4 fl. oz.
Ground ginger	10 g	3 tsp.
Vegetable Broth (recipe follows)	1.25 L	40 fl. oz.
Saffron	pinch	pinch
Butter, unsalted, room temperature	40 g	3 Tbsp.
Ginger Aioli (recipe follows)		

Simon Smotkowicz, CCC
Simon has been a member and a leader of award-winning Canadian culinary teams for many years, most recently managing Team Canada to a world championship in Glasgow in 1997 and 2001. In 1995 he was elected Chef of the Year for the Western Region by his peers in the CFCC.

1. In a large saucepan, heat the butter over medium-high heat, add the vegetables and ginger and sauté until softened.

2. Remove from the pan and set aside. Add the clams, mussels and stock, cover the pan and simmer until the shellfish are just opened. Remove the shellfish from the pan and set aside.

3. In the same pan, heat the butter. Season the prawns and lobsters with salt and pepper and place in the pan. Sauté until pink, remove from the pan and set aside. Season the scallops with salt and pepper, add to the pan and sauté until golden-brown. Remove from the pan and set aside.

4. In the same pan, combine the wine, ginger, Vegetable Broth and saffron and reduce by half. Whisk in the butter and season. Remove from the heat and keep warm.

5. To serve, arrange the vegetables and shellfish in individual bowls, pour the reduced and seasoned broth on top, and spoon the Ginger Aioli over the bouillabaisse as desired.

RECIPE 19.33

Approximate values per serving:

Calories	962
Total fat	74 g
Saturated fat	26 g
Cholesterol	263 mg
Sodium	1824 mg
Total carbohydrates	18 g
Protein	40 g

VEGETABLE BROTH

Yield: 1.25 L (40 fl. oz.)

White wine	250 mL	8 fl. oz.
Carrot, medium, peeled and chopped	75 g	1
Onion, medium, peeled and chopped	150 g	1
Celery stalk, chopped	75 g	1
Tomato, medium, peeled and chopped	150 g	1
Ginger root, peeled and chopped	30 g	3 Tbsp.
Water	1.8 L	64 fl. oz.
Saffron	pinch	pinch
Bouquet garni (celery, bay leaf, thyme and cloves)	1	1

1. Put the wine in a large saucepan, add the vegetables, ginger, water, saffron and bouquet garni and bring to a boil.

2. Reduce the heat and simmer for 20 minutes or until reduced by approximately one-third. Remove from the heat, strain and reserve.

Vegetable Broth—Approximate values per serving:

Calories	38
Total fat	0 g
Saturated fat	0 g
Cholesterol	0 mg
Sodium	17 mg
Total carbohydrates	0.5 g
Protein	0 g

GINGER AIOLI

Yield: 180 mL (6 fl. oz.)

Ginger root, peeled and chopped	10 g	2 tsp.
Garlic clove	5 g	1
White wine	30 mL	1 fl. oz.
Saffron	pinch	pinch
Egg yolk, small	1	1
Olive oil	175 mL	6 fl. oz.
Salt and pepper	TT	TT

1. In a small sauté pan, combine the ginger, garlic, wine and saffron. Bring the mixture to a boil, and reduce until nearly all of the liquid has evaporated.

2. Remove the reduction to the bowl of a food processor fitted with a metal blade and purée the mixture. While processing, incorporate the egg yolk and add the oil in a steady stream until the mixture is emulsified.

3. Season with salt and pepper, remove to another bowl and set aside in the refrigerator.

◆◆◆

RECIPE 19.34

MUSSEL SOUP

THOMAS HANEY SECONDARY SCHOOL, Vancouver, BC
Chef Instructor Pierre Dubrulle

Pierre Dubrulle

Born in France, into a family of restaurateurs, Pierre apprenticed in Lille. Soon afterwards, he was drafted into the French army, where he cooked breakfast, lunch and dinner for 2000 men per day for 18 months. Pierre came to Canada in 1966 and worked in a variety of top-notch dining establishments before owning and operating his own delicatessens and restaurants. He founded The Pierre Dubrulle Culinary School in 1983, and, in 1992, joined Thomas Haney Secondary School as a chef instructor.

Yield: 4 Servings | | **Method:** Simmering

Fresh shell mussels	675 g	1-1/2 lb.
Dry white wine	125 mL	4 fl. oz.
Fish stock	1.5 L	1.5 qt.
Roux, white	100 g	3-1/2 oz.
White pepper, freshly ground	TT	TT
Saffron threads	1 g	1 tsp.
Cream, 35%	250 mL	8 fl. oz.
Carrot, julienned, blanched	125 g	1/2 cup
Leek, julienned, blanched	100 g	1/2 cup
Pernod	5 mL	1 tsp.
Baguette, toasted	1	1
Parmesan cheese, freshly grated	75 g	1/2 cup
Chopped parsley		

1. Wash, clean and debeard mussels.

2. Cook mussels in the white wine in a sauce pot with a tight lid until all the mussels open. Remove mussels and cool. Strain and reserve liquid.

3. Remove mussels from shell and reserve mussels.

4. Reduce stock and cooking liquid by one-third and thicken reduced liquid with roux to achieve a light coating consistency. Simmer to cook out roux. Season with pepper and saffron.

5. Add cream, boil and strain into clean pot. Keep warm. Add carrot and leek.

6. Warm mussels and place in soup bowls. Pour hot soup over mussels. Sprinkle with Pernod. Place baguette slices, sprinkle with cheese and parsley.

◆◆◆

RECIPE 19.35

GINGER MAPLE MARINATED TROUT

FAIRMONT CHÂTEAU LAURIER, Ottawa, ON
Executive Chef Marcel Mundel

Yield: 750 g (1 lb. 10 oz.)   **Method:** Marinating

Rainbow trout fillets	900 g	2 lb.
Maple sugar	175 g	1 cup
Coarse salt	100 g	1/2 cup
Ginger, grated	25 g	2 Tbsp.
Sève d'érable	25 mL	2 Tbsp.
Gingered Mayonnaise:		
Dijon mustard	25 mL	2 Tbsp.
Maple syrup	25 mL	2 Tbsp.
Mayonnaise	500 mL	16 fl. oz.
Ginger, grated	15 g	1 Tbsp.
Lemon juice	15 mL	1 Tbsp.
Salt and pepper	TT	TT

1. Scale and remove pin bones from trout fillets.
2. Place half the trout, skin side down, in a glass or nonreactive pan.
3. Mix the maple sugar, salt and ginger together and spread half on the fillets.
4. Press the remaining trout fillets on top of the first layer, skin side up. Sprinkle with remaining spice mix and sève d'érable liquor.
5. Cover with plastic wrap, weighted down evenly, and refrigerate for 24 hours.
6. Mix together all ingredients for gingered mayonnaise.
7. To serve, scrape excess marinade off fish and slice thinly. Serve with gingered mayonnaise.

Marcel Mundel
Marcel's passion for cooking was inspired at an early age by his mother's talent for cordon bleu. Having grown up on the streets of Strasbourg with a refined taste for European cuisine, he began his training under Alsation Chefs. Nourished by the principles of culinary excellence, Marcel immigrated to Canada in 1981, climbed the culinary ladder in grand-scale hotels, and is now proudly stationed at the Château Laurier, where he cooks for politicians, heads of state and other prestigious guests.

RECIPE 19.35

*Approximate values
per 125 g serving:*

Calories	865
Total fat	58 g
Saturated fat	7 g
Cholesterol	131 mg
Sodium	3974 mg
Total carbohydrates	31.5 g
Protein	32 g

◆◆◆

RECIPE 19.36

CRAYFISH ETOUFFÉE

Yield: 4 Servings   **Method:** Simmering

Lard	125 g	4 oz.
Flour	125 g	4 oz.
Onion, chopped fine	250 g	1 medium
Celery stalk, chopped fine	75 g	1
Green bell pepper, chopped	100 g	1/2
Garlic cloves, minced	10 g	2
Shrimp broth or clam juice	150 mL	5 fl. oz.
Tomato paste	15 mL	1 Tbsp.
Salt	5 g	1 tsp.
Cayenne	0.5 g	1/4 tsp.
Black pepper	0.5 g	1/4 tsp.
Dried thyme	0.25 g	1/4 tsp.
Crayfish tails, peeled	500 g	1 lb.

Continued

Green onions, sliced	4	4
Flat leaf parsley, minced	20 g	2 Tbsp.
White rice, cooked	1 L	1 qt.

1. Heat the lard in a large sauté pan. Whisk in the flour and cook, stirring constantly, to make a medium-dark roux.
2. Add the onion, celery, green bell pepper and garlic and sauté over medium-low heat until the vegetables are wilted, approximately 5 minutes.
3. Slowly add the shrimp broth or clam juice and bring to a boil. Reduce the heat to a simmer and add the tomato paste and the spices. Simmer for 15 minutes to thicken.
4. Add the crayfish tails and simmer for approximately 10 minutes. Add the green onions and parsley and adjust the seasonings. Serve over cooked rice.

✦✦✦

RECIPE 19.37

SEVICHE

SASKATOON, SK

Chef/Consultant David Powell, CCC

Yield: 1 kg (2-1/4 lb.)   **Method:** Marinating

Raw scallops	600 g	1 lb. 4 oz.
Fresh lime juice	175 mL	6 fl. oz.
Scallion, bias cut	1	1
Serrano pepper, minced	1	1
Red onion, fine dice	75 g	2-1/2 oz.
Fresh cilantro, minced	10 g	1 Tbsp.
Olive oil	30 mL	2 Tbsp.
Tomato, peeled, seeded, diced	250 g	9 oz.
Garlic, chopped	8 g	2 tsp.
Salt and pepper	TT	TT

1. Slice the scallops evenly. Place in a nonreactive container and add the lime juice. Cover and marinate in the refrigerator for 4 hours.
2. Toss in the remaining ingredients and season to taste with salt and pepper. Chill thoroughly and serve as a salad, cocktail or canape.
3. If the seviche is going to be held for more than 2 hours, drain the liquid and refrigerate separately. The reserved liquid can then be tossed with the other ingredients at service time.

RECIPE 19.36

Approximate values per serving:

Calories	880
Total fat	32 g
Saturated fat	4 g
Cholesterol	130 mg
Sodium	1154 mg
Total carbohydrates	107 g
Protein	40 g

RECIPE 19.37

Approximate values per 120 g (4 oz.) serving:

Calories	120
Total fat	4.5 g
Saturated fat	0.5 g
Cholesterol	30 mg
Sodium	250 mg
Total carbohydrates	5 g
Protein	13 g

EBLINKS

Preparation of Fish
  www.cyberus.ca/~lapointefish/prepaton.html

Lobster Direct (Nova Scotia)
  www.novaweb.ca/lobster/index.html

British Columbia Salmon Marketing Council
  bcsalmon.ca

Seafood Facts Sheet
  www.fl-seafood.com/Promo_Marketing/factshts.html

Catering UK: Seafood
  www.catering-uk.co.uk/catering-uk/features/jul-feature.html

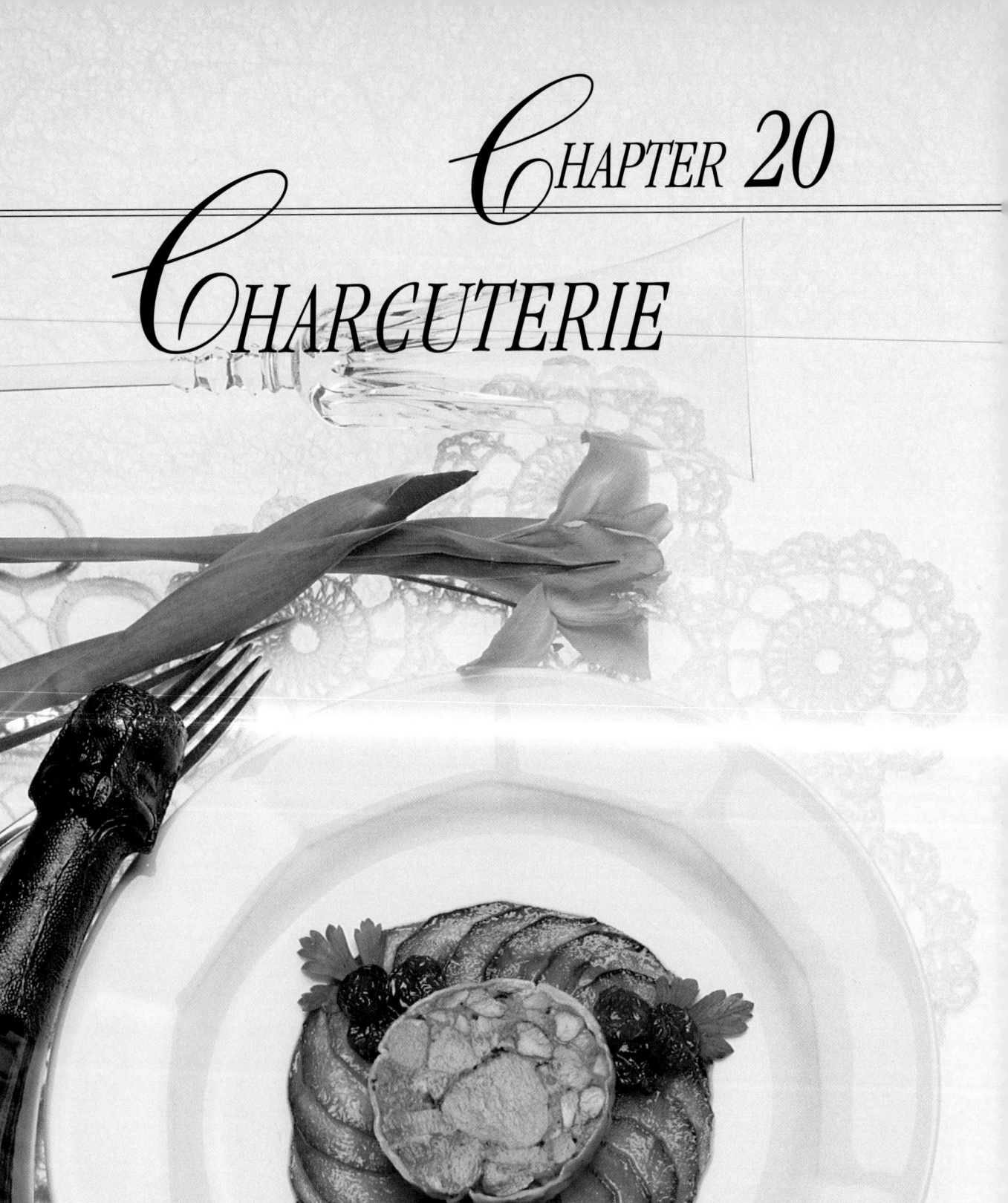

CHAPTER 20
CHARCUTERIE

◆◆◆

LEARNING OUTCOMES

After studying this chapter you will be able to:

◆ prepare a variety of forcemeats: country-style, basic, mousseline, quenelles

◆ assemble and cook a variety of pâtés, terrines and sausages: prepare a terrine, an aspic-jelly-coated chilled mousse, assemble and bake pâtés en croûte, glaze pâté slices with aspic jelly, prepare a poultry galantine, make sausages

◆ explain the proper methods for brining, curing and smoking meats and fish

◆ identify several cured pork products

T

raditionally, charcuterie was limited to the production of pork-based pâtés, terrines and galantines. Over the years, however, it has come to include similar products made with game, poultry, fish, shellfish and even vegetables. Many of these are discussed here.

Charcuterie is an art and science in itself. This chapter is not intended to be a complete guide to the charcutier's art. Instead, we focus on procedures for making common charcuterie items that can be prepared easily in most kitchens. We also discuss the preparation of sausages as well as curing methods, including salt curing, brining, and both cold and hot smoking. The chapter ends with information about several cured pork products.

FORCEMEATS AND THEIR USES

A **forcemeat** is a preparation made from uncooked ground meats, poultry, fish or shellfish, seasoned, then emulsified with fat. Forcemeats are the primary ingredient used to make pâtés, terrines, galantines and sausages.

The word *forcemeat* is derived from the French word *farce*, meaning stuffing. Depending on the preparation method, a forcemeat can be very smooth and velvety, well textured and coarse, or anything in between. Regardless of its intended use, it has a glossy appearance when raw and will slice cleanly when cooked. A properly emulsified forcemeat provides a rich taste and a comforting texture on the palate.

Forcemeats are emulsified products. Emulsification is the process of binding two ingredients that ordinarily would not combine. (Emulsified sauces are discussed in Chapter 10, Stocks and Sauces; emulsified salad dressings are discussed in Chapter 24, Salads and Salad Dressings.) The proteins present in the meat, poultry, fish and shellfish combine easily with both fat and liquids. In forcemeats, these proteins act as a stabilizer that allows the fat and liquids, which ordinarily would not combine, to bind. When improperly emulsified forcemeats are cooked, they lose their fat, shrink, and become dry and grainy. To ensure proper emulsification of a forcemeat:

1. the ratio of fat to other ingredients must be precise,

2. temperatures must be maintained below 4°C (40°F), and

3. the ingredients must be mixed properly.

Forcemeat Ingredients

Forcemeats are usually meat, poultry, fish or shellfish combined with binders, seasonings and sometimes garnishes. Selections from each of these basic categories are used to make an array of forcemeats. All ingredients must be of the finest quality and added in just the right proportions.

Meats

The **dominant meat** is the meat that gives the forcemeat its name and essential flavour. The dominant meat does not have to be beef, veal, lamb, pork or game. It can be poultry, fish or shellfish. When preparing meats, poultry or fish for forcemeat, it is important to trim all silverskin, gristle and small bones so that the meat will be more easily ground and will produce a smoother finished product.

Many forcemeats contain some pork. Pork adds moisture and smoothness to the forcemeat. Without it, poultry-based forcemeats tend to be rubbery, while venison and other game-based forcemeats tend to be dry. The traditional ratio is one part pork to two parts dominant meat.

Many forcemeats also contain some liver. Pork liver is commonly used, as is chicken liver. Liver contributes flavour as well as binding to the forcemeat. For a finer texture, grind the livers and then force them through a drum sieve before incorporating them into the forcemeat.

Fats

Here, **fat** refers to a separate ingredient, not the fat in the dominant meat or pork, both of which should be quite lean in order to ensure the correct ratio of fat to meat. Usually pork backfat or heavy cream is used to add moisture and richness to the forcemeat. Because fat carries flavour, it also promotes the proper infusion of flavours and smoke.

Binders

There are two principal types of binders: panadas and eggs.

A **panada** is something other than fat that is added to a forcemeat to enhance smoothness (especially in fish mousselines, which tend to be slightly grainy in texture), to aid emulsification (especially in vegetable terrines, where the protein levels are insufficient to bind on their own) or both (for example, in liver mousses). It should not make up more than 20% of the forcemeat's total weight. Usually a panada is nothing more than crustless white bread soaked in milk or, more traditionally, a heavy béchamel or rice.

Eggs or egg whites are used as a binding agent in some styles of forcemeat. If used in forcemeats that have a large ratio of liver or liquids, they also add texture. The proteins in the meat, fish or poultry are the primary binder.

Seasonings

Forcemeats are seasoned with salt, curing salt, marinades and various herbs and spices.

Salt not only adds flavour to a forcemeat but also aids in the emulsification of the meat and fat. As with other foods, a forcemeat that lacks salt will taste flat and may not bind properly.

Curing salt is a mixture of salt and sodium nitrite. Sodium nitrite controls spoilage by inhibiting bacterial growth. Equally important, curing salt preserves the rosy pink colours of some forcemeats that might otherwise oxidize to an unappetizing grey. Although currently regarded as substantially safer than the previously used potassium nitrate (saltpetre), some studies suggest that sodium nitrite is a carcinogen. For a typical consumer, however, the amount of sodium nitrite consumed from cured meats should not pose a substantial health threat.

Traditionally, ingredients for forcemeats were marinated for long periods of time, sometimes days, before grinding. The trend today is for shorter marinating times so that the true flavours of the main ingredients shine through. Both classic and contemporary marinades include herbs, citrus zest, spices and liquors, all of which lend flavour, character and nuance to the forcemeat.

Pâté spice is a mixture of several spices and herbs that can be premixed and used as needed.

Applying the Basics

PÂTÉ SPICE

Yield: 220 g (7-2/3 oz.)

Cloves	30 g	1 oz.
Dried ginger	30 g	1 oz.
Nutmeg	30 g	1 oz.
Paprika	30 g	1 oz.
Dried basil	20 g	2/3 oz.
Black pepper	20 g	2/3 oz.
White pepper	20 g	2/3 oz.
Bay leaf	10 g	1/3 oz.
Dried thyme	30 g	1 oz.
Dried marjoram	10 g	1/3 oz.

Grind all ingredients in a spice grinder. Pass through a sieve to remove any large pieces.

NOTE: Either use this mixture as is, or mix 30 g (1 oz.) (or any amount desired) with 450 g (1 lb.) of salt. The salt and spice mixture can then be used to season forcemeats; 10 g (1/3 oz.) per 450 g (1 lb.) of forcemeat usually suffices for most pâtés.

A forcemeat's seasoning and texture can be tested by cooking a small portion before the entire forcemeat is cooked. (Unlike sauces, stews and other dishes, you cannot taste and adjust a forcemeat's flavouring during the cooking process.) A small portion of a hearty forcemeat can be sautéed; a small portion of a more delicate forcemeat should be poached for 3–5 minutes. When cooked, the forcemeat should hold its shape and be slightly firm but not rubbery. If it is too firm, add a little cream.

Garnishes

Forcemeat garnishes are meats, fat, vegetables or other foods added in limited quantities to provide contrasting flavours and textures and to improve appearance. The garnishes are usually diced, chopped or more coarsely ground than the dominant meat. Common garnishes include pistachio nuts, diced backfat, truffles or truffle peelings, and diced ham or tongue.

Equipment for Preparing Forcemeats

To prepare forcemeats properly you should have a food chopper or food processor and a heavy-duty drum sieve with a metal band. You will also need a standard meat grinder or meat-grinding attachment with various-size grinding plates (see Figure 20.1).

FIGURE 20.1 *A blade and assorted plates for a standard grinder.*

Preparing Forcemeats

The three common forcemeat preparations are **country-style**, **basic (or straight)** and **mousseline**. Each can be produced easily in a typical food service operation. Other types of forcemeat preparations such as the emulsified mixture used to make hot dogs and bratwurst are not commonly encountered in food service operations and are discussed in the sidebar.

When preparing any forcemeat certain guidelines must be followed:

1. Forcemeat preparations include raw meats, liver, eggs and dairy products. If improperly handled, these potentially hazardous foods create a good environment for the growth of microorganisms. To avoid the risk of food-borne illness, temperatures must be carefully controlled and all cutting boards and food contact surfaces must be as sanitary as possible at all times.

2. To ensure a proper emulsification, the forcemeat must be kept cold—below 4°C (40°F)—at all times. Refrigerate all moist ingredients and keep forcemeats in progress in an ice bath. Chilling or freezing the metal grinder and food processor parts helps keep the ingredients as cold as possible.

3. Cut all foods into convenient sizes that fit easily into grinder openings. Do not overstuff grinders or overfill food processors. When grinding items twice, always begin with a larger plate, followed by a medium or small plate. For exceptional smoothness, press the forcemeat through a sieve after grinding to remove any lumps or pieces of membrane.

Country-Style Forcemeats

A traditional country-style forcemeat is heavily seasoned with onions, garlic, pepper, juniper berries and bay leaves. It is the simplest of the forcemeats to prepare and yields the heartiest and most distinctive pâtés and sausages.

The dominant meat for a country-style forcemeat is usually ground once through the grinder's large plate, then ground again through the medium plate. This produces the characteristic coarse texture. As with most forcemeats, the dominant meat for a country-style forcemeat is usually marinated and seasoned prior to grinding and then mixed with some liver.

Basic Procedure for Preparing a Country-Style Forcemeat

1. Chill all ingredients and equipment thoroughly. Throughout preparation they should remain at temperatures below 4°C (40°F).
2. Cut all meats into an appropriate size for grinding.
3. Marinate, under refrigeration, the dominant meat and pork with the desired herbs, spices and liquors.
4. If using liver, grind it and force it through a sieve.
5. Cut the backfat into an appropriate size and freeze.
6. Prepare an ice bath for the forcemeat. Then grind the dominant meat, pork and fat as directed in the recipe, usually once through the grinder's largest plate and a second time through the medium plate.
7. If using liver, eggs, panada or garnishes, fold them in by hand with a spoon or spatula, remembering to keep the forcemeat over an ice bath at all times.
8. Cook a small portion of the forcemeat; adjust the seasonings and texture as appropriate.
9. Refrigerate the forcemeat until needed.

✦✦✦
OTHER FORCEMEATS

The 5/4/3 forcemeat contains 5 parts meat, 4 parts fat and 3 parts ice. It is finely ground and blended to produce an emulsion. Sausages, often smoked, are the most common use. Gratin-style forcemeats contain meat or liver that has been sautéed before grinding. Their flavour and texture are very palatable. Forcemeats based on rice or bread are most often used in hot kitchen applications, but any of the forcemeats may be used as a stuffing mixture. Low-temperature cooking is required to avoid a tough, grainy filling when cooked.

Applying the Basics

COUNTRY-STYLE FORCEMEAT

Yield: 1.1 kg (2.5 lb.)

Lean pork, diced	450 g	1 lb.
Pâté spice	3 g	1 Tbsp.
Salt	7 g	1-1/2 tsp.
Pepper	TT	TT
Brandy	30 mL	1 fl. oz.
Pork liver, cleaned and diced	225 g	8 oz.
Backfat, diced	175 g	6 oz.
Double smoked bacon, diced	60 g	2 oz.
Shallots, small dice	45 g	1-1/2 oz.
Garlic, minced	5 g	1-1/2 tsp.
Fresh parsley, chopped	20 g	1-1/2 Tbsp.
Eggs	3	3

1. Combine the diced pork with the pâté spice, salt, pepper and brandy; marinate under refrigeration for several hours.
2. Grind the liver and force it through a drum sieve. Reserve.
3. Grind the marinated pork and backfat through the grinder's large plate.
4. Grind half the pork, backfat and bacon a second time through the medium plate along with the shallots, garlic and parsley.
5. Working over an ice bath, combine the coarse and medium ground pork with the liver and eggs.
6. Cook and taste a small portion of the forcemeat and adjust the seasonings as necessary.

The forcemeat is now ready to use as desired in the preparation of pâtés, terrines, galantines and sausages.

RECIPE 20.2

Approximate values
per 85 g serving:

Calories	247
Total fat	21 g
Saturated fat	7.4 g
Cholesterol	134 mg
Sodium	292 mg
Total carbohydrates	1.5 g
Protein	13 g

1. Marinate the meat with herbs and spices.

2. Press the ground liver through a sieve.

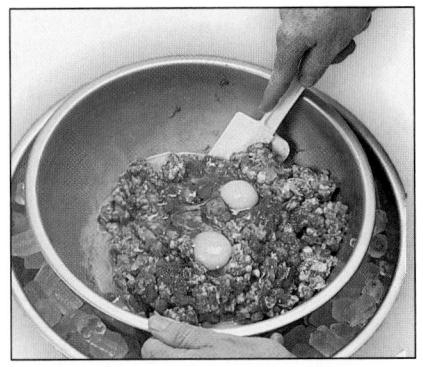

3. Grind half the meat a second time.

4. Incorporate the liver and eggs into the ground mixture over an ice bath to keep the forcemeat cold.

Basic Forcemeats

Smoother and more refined than a country-style forcemeat, a basic or straight forcemeat is probably the most versatile of all. It should be well seasoned, but the seasonings should not mask the dominant meat's flavour. Examples of basic forcemeats are most game pâtés and terrines as well as traditional pâtés en croûte.

A basic forcemeat is made by grinding the meat and fat separately—the meat twice and the fat once. The fat is then worked into the meat, either by hand or in a food processor or chopper. A quicker method involves grinding the fat and meat together and then blending them in a food processor. Whichever method is used, some recipes call for the incorporation of crushed ice to minimize friction, reduce temperature and add moisture.

Basic Procedure for Preparing a Basic Forcemeat

1. Chill all ingredients and equipment thoroughly. Throughout preparation they should remain at temperatures below 4°C (40°F).

2. Cut all meats into an appropriate size for grinding.

3. Marinate, under refrigeration, the dominant meat and pork with the desired herbs, spices and liquors.

4. If using liver, grind it and force it through a sieve.

5. Cut the backfat into an appropriate size and freeze.

6. Grind the meats twice, once through the grinder's large plate and then through the medium plate; hold on an ice bath.

7. Grind the chilled or frozen fat once through the medium plate and add it to the meat mixture.

8. Work the fat into the meat over an ice bath or in a well-chilled food processor or chopping machine.

9. Over an ice bath, add any required eggs, panada and/or garnishes and work them into the mixture.

10. Cook a small portion of the forcemeat in stock or water; adjust the seasonings and texture as appropriate.

11. Refrigerate the forcemeat until needed.

An alternative method for preparing a basic forcemeat replaces steps 6 to 9 with the following procedures:

6A. Grind the meats and fats together twice.

7A. Place them in a food processor or chopper and blend until smooth.

8A. Add any required eggs or panada while the machine is running and blend them in with the meat and fat.

9A. Remove the forcemeat from the machine and, working over an ice bath, fold in any garnishes by hand (use a spatula).

Whichever method is used, a particularly warm kitchen or a lengthy running time in the food processor or chopping machine may necessitate the addition of small quantities of crushed ice to emulsify the forcemeat properly. Add the ice bit by bit while the machine is running.

Applying the Basics

RECIPE 20.3

BASIC FORCEMEAT

Yield: 1.35 kg (3 lb.)

Ingredient	Metric	Imperial
Veal liver	125 g	4 oz.
Shallots	40 g	1-1/2 oz.
Butter	30 g	1 oz.
Veal, diced	250 g	8 oz.
Lean pork, diced	250 g	8 oz.
Double smoked bacon	200 g	7 oz.
Brandy	30 mL	1 fl. oz.
Madeira	30 mL	1 fl. oz.
Pâté spice	3 g	1 tsp.
Salt	7 g	1-1/2 tsp.

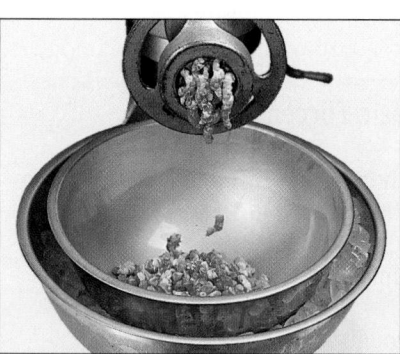

1. Grind the meat through the chilled grinder.

2. Combine the fat with the meat in the food processor.

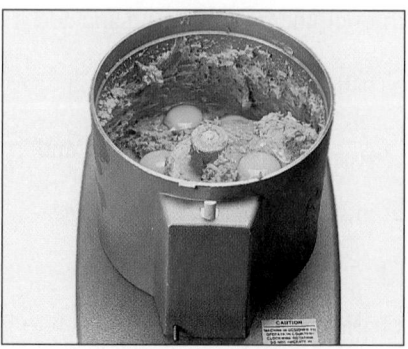

3. Add the eggs and cream to the meat.

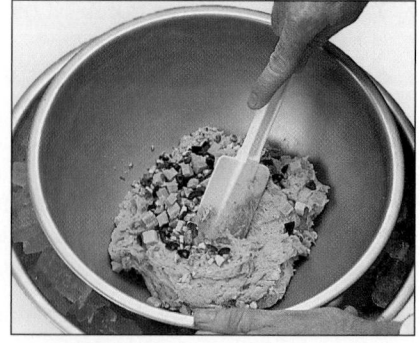

4. Fold the garnishes into the forcemeat.

◆◆◆
ABOUT ENHANCEMENTS

The basic forcemeat recipe in Recipe 20.3 has some enhancements. This one is particularly suited for a House Pâté en Croute. Replace the veal with game if desired. The garnish can be varied, including using backfat-wrapped tenderloin strips, dried fruit or peppercorns.

Cream, 35%	175 mL	6 fl. oz.
Egg	1	1
Ham, medium dice	80 g	3 oz.
Backfat, diced	80 g	3 oz.
Pistachio nuts, peeled	60 g	2 oz.
Black olives, chopped coarse	60 g	2 oz.

1. Sauté liver and shallots in butter. Cool.
2. Combine the veal, pork, bacon, liver and shallots with the brandy, Madeira, pâté spice, and salt; marinate under refrigeration for several hours.
3. Grind the meats through the grinder's large plate and again through the small plate.
4. Place the meat mixture in the bowl of a food processor and pulse until it is emulsified.
5. Work in the cream and egg until the forcemeat is smooth and well emulsified. Do not overprocess the forcemeat.
6. Fold in the ham, backfat, pistachio nuts and olives.
7. Cook a small portion of the forcemeat by poaching or sautéing it. Taste and adjust the seasonings as necessary.

The forcemeat is now ready to use as desired in the preparation of pâtés, terrines, galantines or sausages.

RECIPE 20.3

Approximate values
per 85 g serving:

Calories	263
Total fat	23 g
Saturated fat	9.2 g
Cholesterol	93 mg
Sodium	406 mg
Total carbohydrates	3 g
Protein	11 g

Mousseline Forcemeats

A properly made mousseline forcemeat is light, airy and delicately flavoured. It is most often made with fish or shellfish but sometimes with veal, pork, feathered game or poultry. (A mousseline forcemeat is not the same as a mousse, which usually contains gelatin and is discussed on page 520.)

A mousseline forcemeat is prepared by processing ground meats and cream in a food processor; often egg whites are added to lighten and enrich the mixture. The ratio of fish to eggs to cream is very important. Too many egg whites and the mousseline will be rubbery; too few and it may not bind together. If too much cream is added, the mousseline will be too soft or will fall apart during cooking.

A mousseline forcemeat can be served hot or cold. It can be used to make fish sausages and a variety of timbales and terrines. Or it can be used to make quenelles, which are discussed on page 517. A shrimp mousseline is used with the Paupiettes of Sole, Recipe 19.25.

◆◆◆

COLD, COLD, COLD

Working ground meat or fish with salt helps to extract the proteins needed for binding. The amount of heavy cream a forcemeat can hold in emulsion varies with the freshness of the meat or fish used and how cold the cream and forcemeat are. When incorporating them, do not add the cream too quickly. A temperature of 0–1°C (32–34°F) is recommended.

Basic Procedure for Preparing a Mousseline Forcemeat

1. Chill all ingredients and equipment thoroughly. Throughout preparation they should remain at temperatures below 4°C (40°F).
2. Cut all meats into an appropriate size for processing.
3. Grind the meat in a cold food processor until smooth. Do not overprocess.
4. Add eggs and pulse until just blended.
5. Add cream and seasonings in a steady stream while the machine is running. Stop the machine and scrape down the sides of the bowl once or twice during the processing. Do not run the machine any longer than necessary to achieve a smooth forcemeat.
6. If desired, pass the forcemeat through a drum sieve to remove any sinew or bits of bone.

7. Over an ice bath, fold in any garnishes by hand.

8. Poach a small amount of the mousseline in stock or water. Taste and adjust the seasonings and texture as necessary.

9. Refrigerate until ready for use.

Applying the Basics

RECIPE 20.4

MOUSSELINE FORCEMEAT

Yield: 1.8 kg (4 lb.)

Fish, scallops, skinless chicken breast or lean veal (fresh)	900 g	2 lb.
Salt	15 g	1 Tbsp.
Egg whites	4	4
White pepper	TT	TT
Nutmeg	TT	TT
Cayenne pepper	TT	TT
Cream, 35%, very cold	up to 900 mL	up to 1 qt.

1. Grind the chilled dominant fish or meat through a large plate.

2. Process the meat and salt in a food processor until smooth.

3. Add the egg whites one at a time and pulse the processor until they are incorporated.

4. Scrape down the sides of the processor's bowl and add the spices.

5. With the machine running, add the cream in a slow steady stream. Check the consistency; you may not use all the cream.

6. Scrape down the bowl again and process the mousseline until it is smooth and well mixed. Do not overprocess.

7. Remove the mousseline from the machine and hold in an ice bath. If additional smoothness is desired, force the mousseline through a drum sieve in small batches using a plastic scraper or rubber spatula.

8. Cook a small portion of the forcemeat. Taste and adjust the seasonings and texture as necessary.

The forcemeat is now ready to use as desired in the preparation of pâtés, terrines, galantines or sausages. If frozen fish is used, less cream will be needed and you may have to add some fine white fresh bread to make a panada.

RECIPE 20.4

Approximate values per 85 g serving:

Calories	186
Total fat	16 g
Saturated fat	10 g
Cholesterol	78 mg
Sodium	327 mg
Total carbohydrates	1.3 g
Protein	9.2 g

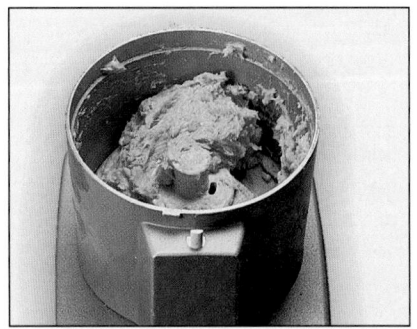

1. Process the ground meat and salt in a cold food processor just until smooth.

2. Add the egg whites and pulse until blended.

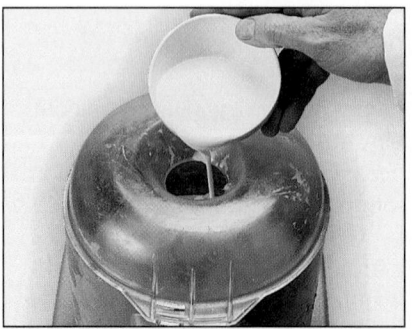

3. Add the cream in a steady stream while the machine runs.

4. Press the forcemeat through a drum sieve to ensure a smooth finished product.

Quenelles

Quenelles are small oblong-shaped portions of a mousseline forcemeat poached in an appropriately flavoured stock. Quenelles are a traditional garnish for many soups and a popular appetizer usually accompanied by a tomato coulis or a fish velouté-based sauce such as sauce nantua. The technique used for making and poaching quenelles is also used for testing the seasoning and consistency of a mousseline forcemeat.

Basic Procedure for Preparing Quenelles

1. Prepare a mousseline forcemeat.
2. Bring an appropriately flavoured poaching liquid to a simmer.
3. Use two spoons to form the forcemeat into oblong-shaped dumplings. For small quenelles use small spoons; for larger quenelles use larger spoons.
4. Poach the quenelles until done. Test by breaking one in half to check the centre's doneness.
5. Small soup-garnish-sized quenelles can be chilled in ice water, drained and held for service. Reheat them in a small amount of stock before garnishing the soup.

Form the quenelles using two spoons; poach gently until done.

USING FORCEMEATS

Forcemeats are used as basic components in the preparation of other foods, including terrines, pâtés, galantines and sausages. Many are used in the hot kitchen as stuffings. Aspic jelly is also an important component of these products.

Terrines, Pâtés and Galantines

Traditionally, a **pâté** was a fine savoury meat filling wrapped in pastry, baked and served hot or cold. A **terrine** was considered more basic, consisting of coarsely ground and highly seasoned meats baked in a waterbath in an earthenware mould and generally served cold. (The mould is also called a terrine, derived from the French word *terre*, meaning earth.) Pâtés baked in pastry are called **pâtés en croûte**. Many types of pâté are baked in loaf-type pans, without a crust, which according to tradition would make them terrines. Today, the terms *pâté* and *terrine* are used almost interchangeably. **Galantines** are made from forcemeats of poultry, fish, game or suckling pig wrapped in the skin of the bird or animal and poached in an appropriate stock, or wrapped in plastic wrap and poached or steamed.

♦♦♦

ASPIC JELLY

Aspic jelly is a savoury jelly produced by increasing the gelatin content of a strong stock and then clarifying the stock following the process for preparing consommé discussed in Chapter 11, Soups. Brown stock produces an amber aspic jelly; white stock produces a light aspic jelly.

Although gelatin is a natural ingredient present in all good stocks, its concentration level is not normally high enough to produce a firm aspic jelly. Additional gelatin is usually added to the stock in order to assist gelling (setting). This can be done in two ways. The first is to produce a stock with an extremely high gelatin content by using gelatinous meats and bones such as calves' feet, pigs' ears and pork skin; the second is to add plain gelatin to a finished stock. An easier method of preparing aspic jelly is to add gelatin directly to a flavourful finished consommé.

Aspic jelly has many applications throughout the kitchen. In addition to adding flavour and shine, a coating of aspic jelly prevents displayed foods from drying out and inhibits the oxidation of sliced red meats. Aspic jelly is often lightly flavoured with liquors such as Madeira and cut into decorative garnishes for both plated presentations and buffet displays. It is also used to bind savoury mousses, glaze slices of pâté and coat moulded mousse. Aspic jelly is funnelled into cooked pâtés en croûte to fill the gaps created when the forcemeat shrinks during the cooking process. Aspic jelly is also the basis of aspic moulds or terrines (often simply called *aspics*), in which layers of cooked meats or vegetables are bound together and held in place by the aspic jelly. Many of these uses are discussed below.

The gelatin content of aspic jelly varies depending upon its intended use. (See Table 20.1.) Verify the bloom strength of the gelatin by testing a small batch. Aspic jelly to be used only on a display can have a very high gelatin content for easier handling. Aspic jelly to be eaten should be fairly firm when cold, gelled at room temperature but tender enough to melt quickly in the mouth when eaten. To test the gelatin content of a liquid pour 5 mL (1 tsp.) onto a plate and refrigerate the plate for a few minutes. If the liquid does not gel firmly, additional gelatin can be softened in a small amount of cool liquid then added to the hot liquid.

TABLE 20.1   GELATIN CONCENTRATIONS

Type of Gel	Amount of Gelatin per 1 L (1 qt.) of Liquid	Typical Use
Soft	50 g (2 oz.)	Edible glazes for sliced meats, pâtés.
Firm	80–100 g (3–4 oz.)	Complete linings, heavily garnished fillings for terrine (aspic) moulds.
Very firm	100–250 g (4–10 oz.)	Nonedible purposes such as coating nonedible centrepieces or trays for presentations. Humidity and water purity are factors.

Terrines, pâtés and galantines are often made with forcemeats layered with garnishes to produce a decorative or mosaic effect when sliced. A wide variety of foods can be used as garnishes including strips of ham, backfat or tongue; mushrooms or other vegetables; truffles and pistachio nuts. Garnishes should always be cooked before they are added to the pâté, terrine or galantine or they will shrink during cooking, creating air pockets.

Pâté Pans, Moulds and Terrines

Pâté pans, moulds and terrines come in a variety of shapes and sizes. Pâtés that are not baked in a crust can be prepared in standard metal loaf pans of any shape, although rectangular ones make portioning the cooked pâté much easier. For pâté en croûte, the best pans are collapsible or hinged, thin-metal ones. They make it easier to remove the pâté after baking. Collapsible and hinged pans come in various shapes and sizes from small plain rectangles to large intricately fluted ovals. Traditional earthenware moulds and terrines as well as ones made from enamel, metal, glass or even plastic are available. Most terrines are rectangular or oval in shape. Several of these pans are illustrated in Chapter 5, Tools and Equipment.

Terrines

Terrines are forcemeats baked in a mould without a crust. The mould can be the traditional earthenware dish or some other appropriate metal, enamel or glass mould. Any type of forcemeat can be used to make a terrine. The terrine can be as simple as a baking dish filled with a forcemeat and baked until done. A more attractive terrine can be constructed by layering the forcemeat with garnishes to create a mosaic effect when sliced. A terrine can even be layered with different forcemeats; for example, a pink salmon mousseline may be layered with a white pike mousseline.

1. Line a mould with thin slices of backfat.

Basic Procedure for Preparing a Terrine

1. Prepare the desired forcemeat and garnishes and keep refrigerated until needed.
2. Line a mould with thin slices of backfat, blanched leafy vegetables or other appropriate liner. (Some chefs claim that the backfat keeps the terrine moist during cooking; most modern chefs do not agree but nevertheless use it for aesthetic purposes.) The lining should overlap slightly, completely covering the inside of the mould and extending over the edge of the mould by approximately 2.5 cm (1 inch). Alternatively, line the mould with plastic wrap.
3. Fill the terrine with the forcemeat and garnishes, being careful not to create air pockets. Tap the mould several times on a solid work surface to remove any air pockets.
4. Fold the liner or plastic wrap over the forcemeat and, if necessary, use additional pieces to completely cover its surface.
5. If desired, garnish the top of the terrine with herbs that were used in the preparation of the forcemeat.
6. Cover the terrine with its lid or aluminum foil and bake in a water bath in a 180°C (350°F) oven. Regulate the oven temperature so the water stays between 77°C and 82°C (170°F and 180°F).
7. Cook the terrine to an internal temperature of 60°C (140°F) for meat-based forcemeats or 55°C (130°F) for fish- or vegetable-based forcemeats.
8. Remove the terrine from the oven and allow it to cool slightly. If desired, pour off any fat and liquid from around the terrine and cover it with cool liquid aspic jelly.

2. Fill the terrine with the forcemeat and garnish.

3. Decorate the top of the terrine with herbs and place the terrine in a water bath.

Several types of terrines are not made from traditional forcemeats; many others are not made from forcemeats at all. But all are nonetheless called terrines because they are moulded or cooked in the earthenware mould called a terrine. These include liver (and foie gras) terrines, vegetable terrines, brawns or aspic terrines, mousses, rillettes and confits.

Liver terrines are popular and easy to make. Puréed poultry, pork or veal livers are mixed with eggs, seasonings and a panada of cream and bread, then baked in a backfat or bacon-lined terrine. Although most livers purée easily in a food processor, a smoother finished product is achieved if the livers are forced through a drum sieve after or in lieu of puréeing them in the processor.

Foie gras terrines are made with fattened geese or duck livers called foie gras. Foie gras is unique, even among other poultry livers, in that it consists almost entirely of fat. (See Chapter 17.) It requires special attention during cooking; if it is cooked improperly or too long it turns into a puddle of very expensive fat.

Vegetable terrines can be made with a relatively low fat content and are becoming increasingly popular. Beautiful vegetable terrines are made by lining

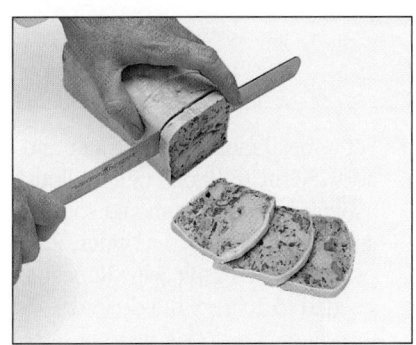

4. Slice the finished terrine.

a terrine with a blanched leafy vegetable such as spinach, then alternating layers of two or three separately prepared vegetable fillings to create contrasting colours and flavours. A different style of vegetable terrine is made by suspending brightly coloured vegetables in a mousseline forcemeat to create a mosaic pattern when sliced.

Brawns or **aspic terrines** are made by simmering gelatinous cuts of meat (most notably, pigs' feet and head, including the tongue) in a rich stock with wine and flavourings. The stock is enriched with gelatin and flavour from the meat, creating an unclarified aspic jelly. The meat is then pulled from the bone, diced and packed into the terrine mould. The stock is reduced to concentrate its gelatin content, strained through cheesecloth and poured over the meat in the terrine. After the terrine has set, it is removed from the mould and sliced for service. The finished product is a rustic and flavourful dish.

A more elegant-appearing brawn is made by lining a terrine mould with aspic jelly, arranging a layer of garnish (for example, sliced meats, vegetables or low-acid fruits) along the mould's bottom, adding aspic jelly to cover the garnish and repeating the procedure until the mould is full.

A **mousse** can be sweet or savoury. Sweet mousses are described in Chapter 31, Custards, Creams, Frozen Desserts and Dessert Sauces. A savoury mousse—which is not a mousseline forcemeat—is made from fully cooked meats, poultry, game, fish, shellfish or vegetables that are puréed and combined with a béchamel or other appropriate sauce, bound with gelatin and lightened with whipped cream. A mousse can be moulded in a decorated, aspic-jelly-coated mould such as that described immediately below, or it can be formed in moulds lined with plastic wrap, which is peeled off after the mousse is unmoulded. A small mousse can be served as an individual portion; a larger moulded mousse can be displayed on a buffet.

Basic Procedure for Preparing an Aspic-Jelly-Coated Chilled Mousse

A mould can be lined with aspic jelly, then decorated and filled with cold mousse. The aspic-jelly-coated mousse is then unmoulded for an attractive presentation.

1. Set a metal mould in ice water and add 250 mL (8 fl. oz.) of cool liquid aspic jelly. Swirl the mould so the aspic jelly adheres to all sides. Pour out the excess aspic jelly. Repeat as needed to achieve the desired thickness; 6 mm (1/4 inch) or less is usually sufficient.

2. Garnish the mould by dipping pieces of vegetable or other foods in the liquid aspic jelly and placing them carefully inside the aspic-jelly-coated mould. The mould can now be filled with a cold filling such as a mousse.

3. Refrigerate the mould until it is well chilled. Unmould the aspic by dipping the mould in warm water, then inverting and tapping the mould on a plate.

Rillettes and **confits** are actually preserved meats. Rillettes are prepared by seasoning and slow-cooking pork or fatty poultry such as duck or goose in generous amounts of their own fat until the meat falls off the bone. The warm meat is mashed and combined with a portion of the cooking fat. The mixture is then packed into a crock or terrine and rendered fat is strained over the top to seal it. Rillettes are eaten cold as a spread accompanied by bread or toast.

Confit is prepared in a similar manner except before cooking the meat or poultry is often lightly salt-cured to draw out some moisture. The confit is then cooked until very tender but not falling apart. Confits are generally served hot. Like rillettes, confits can be preserved by sealing them with a layer of strained rendered fat. Properly prepared and sealed rillettes and confits will keep for several weeks under refrigeration.

Although it is sometimes incorrectly called chicken liver pâté, **chopped chicken liver** is prepared in a similar fashion to a rillette. Chopped chicken liver, however, will not have the keeping qualities of traditional rillettes or confits because it is not normally sealed in a crock or terrine with rendered fat. It should be eaten within a day or two of its preparation.

Pâté en Croûte

Considered by some to be the pinnacle of the charcutier's art, pâtés en croûte are forcemeats baked in a crust. The forcemeat can be country-style, basic or mousseline, but a basic forcemeat is most commonly used. Although pâtés en croûte can be baked without using a mould, a mould helps produce a more attractive finished product.

Pâté Dough (Pâte au Pâté)

The crust surrounding a baking forcemeat must be durable enough to hold in the juices produced as the pâté bakes and to withstand the long baking process. Unfortunately, some of the more durable crusts are tough and unpleasant to eat.

The goal is to achieve a balance so that the crust will hold the juices of the baking pâté and still be relatively pleasant to the palate. Some pâtés, especially more delicate ones such as fish mousselines, can be wrapped in brioche dough (Recipe 28.16).

Applying the Basics

RECIPE 20.5

PÂTÉ DOUGH

SOUTHERN ALBERTA INSTITUTE OF TECHNOLOGY, CALGARY, AB
Chef Instructor Gerd Steinmeyer, CCC

Yield: 1.4 kg (3 lb. 3 oz.), enough for 2 pâtés

Flour, all-purpose	800 g	28-1/2 oz.
Salt	20 g	4 tsp.
Butter, soft	225 g	8 oz.
Water, lukewarm	225–250 mL	8–9 fl. oz.
Eggs, medium	3	3

1. Place the flour and salt in the bowl of a food processor with dough hook in place.
2. Combine the butter, 225 mL (8 fl. oz.) of water and eggs; add them to the flour and salt mixture.
3. Mix until smooth and the dough forms a ball (2–3 minutes). Add more water if needed to make a pliable dough. Refrigerate. The dough will be easier to work with if allowed to rest for at least 1 hour.

◆◆◆
PÂTÉ DOUGH

Pâté dough needs to be pliable yet firm enough to handle. The water amount will vary depending on the humidity where you work. Dried herbs (5–10 mL) may be added to the dough.

Gerd Steinmeyer, CCC
Gerd was born in West Germany and apprenticed at the Hotel School Siegen there. Two highlights of his long and varied career in Alberta include having functioned as Executive Chef to the official German Delegation at the 1988 XV Olympic Winter Games and having successfully coached umpteen young culinarians for local and international culinary competitions. Over the last 10 years, many of his student teams were awarded Best Apprentice Team, Most Outstanding Single Apprentice and/or Top Entry.

RECIPE 20.5

Approximate values per 30 g serving:

Calories	100
Total fat	4.4 g
Saturated fat	2.6 g
Cholesterol	23 mg
Sodium	213 mg
Total carbohydrates	13 g
Protein	2.2 g

Basic Procedure for Assembling and Baking Pâté en Croûte

After preparing a forcemeat and pastry dough, all that remains is to assemble and bake the pâté en croûte. The amount of pastry dough and forcemeat needed is determined by the size of the mould or pan chosen.

1. Prepare the pâté dough and the forcemeat, keeping the forcemeat refrigerated until needed.
2. Roll out the dough into a rectangular shape 3 mm (1/8 inch) thick.
3. Using the pâté mould as a pattern, determine how much dough is needed to line its inside; allow enough dough along each side of the mould's length to cover the top when folded over. Mark the dough. Cut the dough slightly larger than the marked lines. Cut a second rectangular piece of dough that is slightly larger than the top of the mould; it will be used as a lid.
4. Lightly butter the inside of the mould.
5. Lightly dust the large rectangle of dough with flour, fold it over and transfer it to the mould.
6. Use your thumbs and a dough ball made from dough trimmings to form the dough neatly into the corners of the mould. Continue until the dough is of even thickness on all sides and in the corners.
7. Trim the dough, leaving 2 cm (3/4 inch) on the ends and enough dough to cover the top along the sides.
8. Line the mould with thin slices of backfat or ham, allowing 2 cm (3/4 inch) extra around the top of the mould, or as directed in the recipe. This layer helps protect the pastry crust from coming in contact with the moist forcemeat, which would make it soggy.
9. Fill the lined mould with the forcemeat to 1 cm (1/2 inch) below the top of the mould, pressing it well into the corners to avoid air pockets. Layer and garnish as appropriate.
10. Fold the backfat or ham over the top of the forcemeat, using additional pieces if necessary to cover its entire surface. Fold the pastry over the forcemeat.
11. Brush the exposed surface of the pastry with egg wash; carefully cap with the top piece of dough. Press the overlapping dough down inside the sides of the mould with a small spatula.
12. Using round cutters, cut one or two holes in the top to allow steam to escape during cooking. Egg-wash the surface. Place a doughnut-shaped piece of dough around each of the holes. Egg-wash the decorations.

1. Cut the dough into a large rectangle.

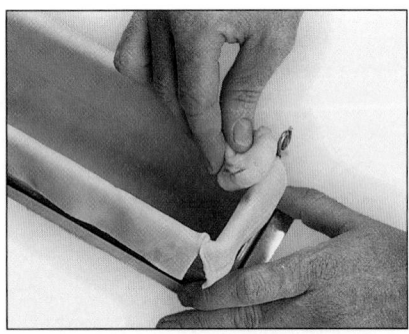

2. Press the dough into the mould with a floured dough ball and your thumbs.

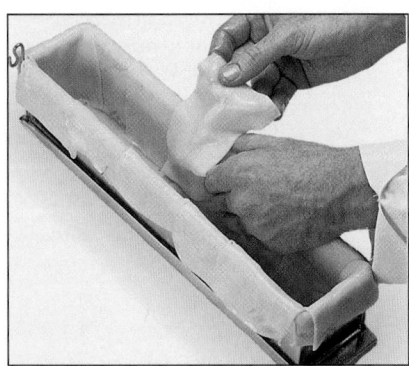

3. Line the mould with thin slices of backfat.

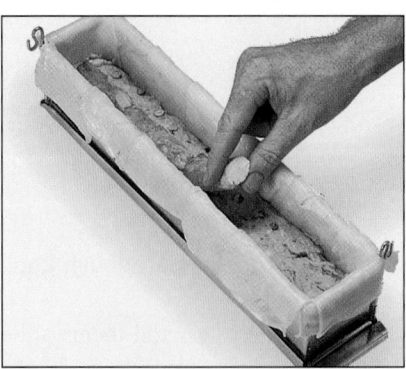

4. Fill the lined mould with the forcemeat and garnish.

5. Use egg wash on the surface and place the top on the pâté.

6. Insert an aluminum chimney in
one of the holes of the baked pâté
and pour aspic jelly into the hole.

7. Slice the pâté with a thin-bladed
knife.

13. Bake the pâté in a preheated 230°C (450°F) oven for 15 minutes. Then
mask the surface of the pâté with aluminum foil. Reduce the heat to
180°C (350°F) and continue baking until the internal temperature reaches
60°C (140°F) for meat pâtés or 55°C (130°F) for fish and vegetable pâtés.

14. Allow the pâté to cool for at least 1 hour or overnight. Using a funnel,
pour cool liquid aspic jelly through the holes to fill the space created
when the pâté shrank during cooling. Allow the pâté en croûte to chill
overnight before slicing.

Basic Procedure for Glazing Pâté Slices with Aspic Jelly

Slices of chilled terrines, pâtés en croûte or galantines (discussed below) may
be garnished and coated with aspic to preserve their colour, prevent drying
and create a more attractive presentation.

1. Stir slowly to cool the clarified
aspic jelly.

2. Brush or spoon the aspic jelly over
slices of chilled pâté arranged on a
cooling rack. Repeat the process
until the coating reaches the
desired thickness.

Galantines

A classic **galantine** is a boned chicken stuffed with a chicken-based forcemeat
to resemble its original shape and then poached. Today, galantines are still
most often prepared from whole ducks or chickens, but they can also be made

--- --- ◆◆◆ --- ---
ORIGINS

Galantine—from Old French *galant*, meaning showy

Ballotine—from the Italian *balla*, meaning ball

Terrine—from the Latin *terra*, meaning earth

Pâté—from the Old French *pasté*, meaning paste

Mousse—French for "froth"

Quenelle—from Alsatian French *knödel*, meaning dumpling

from game, veal, fish or shellfish. When appropriate, the forcemeat is stuffed in the skin, which has been removed in one piece, sometimes with flesh still attached. When the skin is not available or its use is inappropriate or in the case of fish and shellfish where there is no skin, the galantine is made by forming the forcemeat into a cylindrical shape and wrapping it in plastic wrap and foil before poaching. Galantines are almost always served cold and are often displayed on buffets, sliced and glazed with aspic jelly.

A **ballotine** is similar to a galantine. It is made by removing the bones from a poultry leg, filling the cavity with an appropriate forcemeat and poaching or braising the leg with vegetables (it can also be made with fish or game). Ballotines are served hot with a sauce made from the cooking liquid.

Basic Procedure for Preparing a Poultry Galantine

1. Bone the chicken by cutting through the skin along the length of the backbone and then following the natural curvature of the carcass. Keep all the meat attached to the skin. Remove the legs and wings by cutting through the joints when you reach them; leave the legs and wings attached to the skin. Then cut off the wings. Bone the thighs and legs, leaving the skin and meat attached to the rest of the bird. Trim the skin to form a large rectangle.
2. Prepare a forcemeat using the meat from the skinned bird or any other appropriate meat. Reserve a portion of the meat as garnish if desired. Prepare any other garnishes. Refrigerate the forcemeat and garnishes until ready for use.
3. Spread out the skin and meat on plastic wrap or several layers of cheesecloth with the skin side down and the flesh up.
4. Remove the chicken tenderloins and pull the tendon out of each. Butterfly the breasts and tenderloins and cover the entire skin with a thin layer of meat.
5. Arrange the forcemeat and garnishes in a cylindrical shape across the centre of the skin.
6. Tightly roll the skin around the forcemeat and garnishes to form a tight cylinder. (Use the plastic wrap to assist the process.)

1. Butterfly the breasts and tenderloins and place a thin layer of meat over the skin.

2. Arrange the forcemeat and garnishes in a cylindrical shape across the centre of the meat.

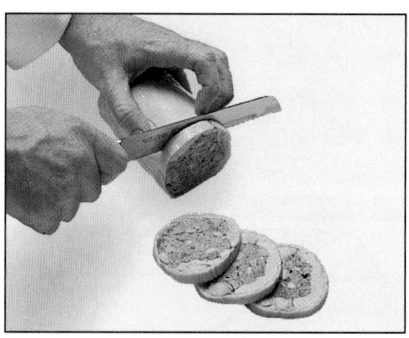

3. Use plastic wrap to roll the galantine into a tight cylinder.

4. Secure the galantine with heavy-duty aluminum foil.

5. Slice the finished product.

7. Tie the ends of the plastic wrap with butcher's twine and secure the galantine at even intervals using strips of cheesecloth. Wrap the galantine with heavy-duty aluminum foil.

8. Poach the galantine in a water bath of 80°C (175°F) to an internal temperature of 60°C (140°F) for meat-based forcemeats or 55°C (130°F) for fish- or vegetable-based forcemeats.

9. Cool the galantine rapidly in its cooking liquid until it can be handled. Use an ice bath. This helps maintain the round shape. Refrigerate overnight.

Sausages

Sausages are forcemeats stuffed into casings. For centuries, sausages consisted of ground meat, usually pork, and seasonings. Today sausages are made not only from pork, but also from game, beef, veal, poultry, fish, shellfish and even vegetables.

There are three main types of sausages:

1. **Fresh sausages** include breakfast sausage links and Italian sausages. They are made with fresh ingredients that have not been cured or smoked.

2. **Smoked** and **cooked sausages** are made with raw meat products treated with chemicals, usually the preservative sodium nitrite. Examples are kielbasa, bologna and hot dogs.

3. **Dried** or **hard sausages** are made with cured meats, then air-dried under controlled conditions. Dry sausages may or may not be smoked or cooked. Dried or hard sausages include salami, pepperoni, Lebanon bologna and landjäger.

Smoked and cooked sausages and dry or hard sausages are rarely prepared in typical food service operations. They are produced by specialty shops and will not be discussed here. We do discuss the ingredients and procedures for a variety of fresh sausages that can be prepared in almost any kitchen.

Sausage Components

Sausage Meats

Sausage meats are forcemeats with particular characteristics and flavourings. Coarse Italian and lamb sausages, for example, are simply a country-style forcemeat without liver and with different seasonings, stuffed into casings and formed into links. Hot dogs, bratwurst and other fine-textured sausages are variations of basic forcemeats stuffed into casings and formed into links.

♦♦♦

TECHNOLOGY

Combitherm ovens have revolutionized the way we cook pâtés, galantines and terrines. With dry and moist heat capabilities, precise temperature settings and automatic probe thermometers, the quality of the final product can be better assured.

FIGURE 20.2   *Sausage nozzles*

Sausage Casings

Although sausage mixtures can be cooked without casings, most sausages are stuffed into casings before cooking. Two types of sausage casings are commonly used in food service operations:

1. **Natural casings** are portions of hog, sheep or cattle intestines. Their diameters are measured in millimetres and they come in several sizes depending upon the animal or portion of the intestine used. Hog casings are the most popular; sheep casings are considered the finest-quality small casings. Both hog and sheep casings are used to make hot dogs and many types of pork sausage. Beef casings are quite large and are used to make sausages such as ring bologna and Polish sausage. Most natural casings are purchased in salt packs. In order to rid them of salt and impurities, the casings must be carefully rinsed in warm water and allowed to soak in cool water for at least one hour or overnight before use.

2. **Collagen casings** are manufactured from collagen extracted from cattle hides. They are generally inferior to natural casings in taste and texture, but they do have advantages: Collagen casings do not require any washing or soaking prior to use and they are uniform in size.

Preparing Sausages

Equipment for Sausage Making

Sausage-stuffing machines are best if you engage in large-scale sausage production. Otherwise, all you need is a grinder with a sausage nozzle attachment such as the ones shown in Figure 20.2. Nozzles are available in several sizes to accommodate the various casing sizes.

Basic Procedure for Making Sausages

1. Prepare a forcemeat.
2. Thoroughly chill all parts of the sausage stuffer that will come in contact with the forcemeat.
3. Rinse and soak the casings if using natural ones. Cut the casings into 1–2 m (4–6 foot) lengths.
4. Put the forcemeat in the sausage stuffer.
5. Slide the casing over the nozzle of the sausage stuffer. Tie the end in a knot and pierce with a skewer to prevent an air pocket.

1. Slide the casing over the nozzle of the sausage stuffer.

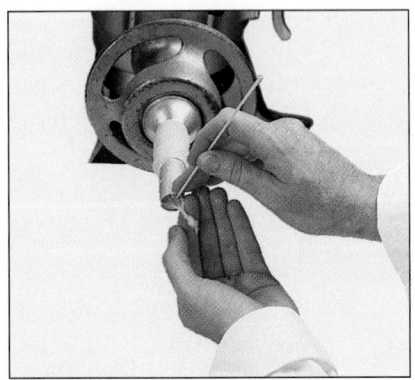

2. Knot and pierce the casing with a skewer.

3. Support and guide the casing off the end of the nozzle as the forcemeat is extruded from the machine into the casing.

4. Twist or tie the sausage into uniform links.

6. Support and guide the casing off the end of the nozzle as the forcemeat is extruded from the nozzle into the casing.

7. After all the forcemeat has been stuffed into the casing, twist or tie the sausage into uniform links of the desired size.

SALT-CURING, BRINING AND SMOKING

Curing, brining and smoking are ancient techniques for preserving food. Today, foods such as hams, corned beef and smoked salmon are salt-cured, brined or smoked primarily for flavour. Cured meats have a characteristic pink colour caused by the reaction of sodium nitrite, which is added during processing, with the naturally occurring myoglobin protein in the meat.

Salt-Curing

Salt-curing is the process of surrounding a food with salt or a mixture of salt, sugar, nitrite-based curing salt, herbs and spices. Salt-curing dehydrates the food, inhibits bacterial growth and adds flavour. It is most often used with pork products and fish. Salt-curing is not a quick procedure—and the time involved adds money to production costs. For example, country-style hams are salt-cured. Proper curing requires approximately 1.5 days per 450 g (1 lb.) of ham, which means three weeks for the average ham.

Some salt-cured hams such as Smithfield and prosciutto are not actually cooked. The curing process preserves the meat and makes it safe to consume raw.

Gravlax is a well-known salmon dish prepared by salt-curing salmon fillets with a mixture of salt, sugar, pepper and dill. A recipe for gravlax (Recipe 20.20) is included at the end of this chapter.

Brining

A brine is actually a very salty marinade. Most brines have approximately 20% salinity, which is equivalent to 450 g (1 lb.) of salt per 4 L (1 gal.) of water. As with dry-salt cures, brines can also contain sugar, nitrites, herbs and spices. Brining is sometimes called pickling.

Today, most cured meats are prepared in large production facilities where the brine is injected into the meat for rapid and uniform distribution. Commercially brined corned beef is cured by this process, as are most common hams. After brining, hams are further processed by smoking.

Smoking

There are two basic methods of smoking foods: cold smoking and hot smoking. The principal difference is that hot smoking actually cooks the food, cold smoking does not.

Both are done in a **smoker** specifically designed for this purpose. Smokers can be gas or electric; they vary greatly in size and operation. But they have several things in common. All consist of a chamber that holds the food being smoked, a means of burning wood to produce smoke and a heating element.

Different types of wood can be used to smoke food. Specific woods are selected to impart specific flavours. Hickory is often used for pork products; alder is excellent for smoked salmon. Maple, chestnut, juniper, mesquite and

---

◆◆◆
TYPES OF SAUSAGE

Andouille—A very spicy smoked pork sausage, popular in Cajun cuisine.

Chorizo—A course, spicy smoked pork sausage flavoured with ground chiles and removed from its casing before cooking; used in Mexican and Spanish cuisines.

Mortadella—An Italian smoked sausage made with ground beef, pork and pork fat, flavoured with coriander and white wine; it is air-dried and has a delicate flavour; also a large American bologna-type pork sausage studded with pork fat and garlic.

Pepperoni—A hard, thin, air-dried Italian sausage seasoned with red and black pepper.

Soppressata—A hard, aged Italian sausage salami, sometimes coated with cracked peppercorns or herbs.

many other woods are also used. Resinous woods such as pine give food a bitter flavour and should be avoided.

Cold smoking is the process of exposing foods to smoke at temperatures of 10°C–29°C (50°F–85°F). Meat, poultry, game, fish, shellfish, cheese, nuts and even vegetables can be cold-smoked successfully. Most cold-smoked meats are generally salt-cured or brined first. Salt-curing or brining adds flavour, allows the nitrites (which give the ham, bacon and other smoked meats their distinctive pink colour) to penetrate the flesh and, most importantly, extracts moisture from the food, allowing the smoke to penetrate more easily. Cold-smoked foods are actually still raw. Some, like smoked salmon (lox), are eaten without further cooking. Others, such as bacon and hams, must be cooked before eating.

Hot smoking is the process of exposing foods to smoke at temperatures of 93°C–121°C (200°F–250°F). As with cold smoking, a great variety of foods can be prepared by hot smoking. Meats, poultry, game, fish and shellfish that are hot-smoked also benefit from salt-curing or brining. Although most hot-smoked foods are fully cooked when removed from the smoker, many are used in other recipes that call for further cooking.

Pan smoking is a process used for smaller or portion cuts. A heavy old roasting pan is heated on an open flame. Wood shavings or tea leaves and rice are placed on foil that is set in the pan. The food to be smoked is placed on a rack and set over the shavings when they begin to smoke. A lid or foil tent is placed over the food to promote even, rapid smoking. The lightly smoked food usually requires further cooking; however, shellfish or thin slices may fully cook with this method. Be careful not to oversmoke or the product will be bitter.

Pork Products

Preparing hams and curing and smoking pork products are a traditional part of charcuterie. Although most bacon and ham is now produced in large commercial facilities, the chef still works with these products and must be able to identify them properly.

Canadian Bacon, Sliced Bacon and Pancetta

Most **bacon** comes from a hog's fatty belly.

Side bacon is produced by brining and cold smoking trimmed pork belly. It is available in slab or sliced form. Sliced bacon is purchased by count (number of slices) per pound; thick-sliced bacon runs 10–14 slices per pound, while thin-sliced bacon may contain as many as 28–32 slices per pound.

Canadian bacon is produced from a boneless pork loin, trimmed so that only a thin layer of fat remains on its surface. It is then brined and smoked.

Pancetta is an Italian pork-belly bacon that is not smoked. It is salt-cured, peppered and often rolled into a cylinder shape. It can be sliced into rounds and fried; it is diced, rendered and combined with sauce to make fettuccine carbonara.

A **fresh ham** is a hog's hind leg; it is a primal cut. Many processed products produced from the primal fresh ham are also called ham.

Ham, in Canada, describes a variety of processed pork products, most of which come from the primal fresh leg. **Boneless** or **formed hams** are produced by separating a primal leg into its basic muscles, defatting the meat, curing it, stuffing the meat into various-sized and -shaped casings and cooking it. Boneless or formed hams are either smoked or liquid smoke flavouring is added during the curing process. The quality of boneless or formed hams varies greatly. The best hams are formed from only one or two large muscles, have low fat content and no added water other than that used during the curing process. Hams of lesser quality are formed from many small pieces of muscle and have a higher fat and water content. Many boneless or formed hams are listed in *The Meat Buyers Guide* and are indexed by the IMPS/NAMP system.

Country ham is a specialty of the southeastern United States. Country hams are dry-cured, smoked and hung to air-dry for a period ranging from several weeks to more than a year. During drying, a mould develops on the ham rind that must be scrubbed off before the ham is cooked. It is best cooked by first soaking, then slow simmering. The most famous country hams are Virginia hams; those from Smithfield, Virginia, are considered the finest. Only hams produced in rural areas can be called country hams; others must be labelled country-style ham.

Prosciutto is Italian for ham. What we call prosciutto in this country is called **Parma** in Italy. It is available raw (*crudo*) or cooked (*cotto*). Parma ham, produced near that Italian city, is made from hogs fed on the whey of cheese processed nearby. The ham is salt-cured and air-dried but not smoked. The curing process makes it safe and wholesome to consume raw. Several domestic varieties of prosciutto are produced (the raw variety is more popular), varying widely in quality. Imported prosciuttos are much larger than the domestic varieties because Italian hogs are larger when butchered.

Westphalian ham is dry-cured, brined and then smoked with beechwood. Authentic Westphalian hams are produced in the Westphalia region of Germany and are quite similar to prosciutto. They are sold bone-in or boneless. Their characteristic flavour is derived from the juniper berries used in the curing process and the beechwood used for smoking.

IMPS No. 501, Ham short shank, cured and smoked.

IMPS No. 510, Ham, boneless, skinless, cured and smoked, fully cooked.

CONCLUSION

The classic art of charcuterie is as popular today as ever. Consumers regularly enjoy high-quality pâtés, sausages, hams and other charcuterie products.

Although production procedures have changed as new technologies and equipment have developed, the basic principles remain the same: Terrines, pâtés and sausages should be produced only from high-quality forcemeats, and temperature control is fundamental to the proper production of forcemeats and other charcuterie products.

Armed with a basic knowledge of the procedures used for charcuterie, you can use your imagination and creativity to produce a variety of charcuterie products.

QUESTIONS FOR DISCUSSION

1. Explain why the art of charcuterie is relevant to the training of modern cooks.
2. Compare the three styles of forcemeat.
3. In what way is a terrine different from a pâté? How does a pâté differ from a pâté en croûte?
4. Describe the differences and the similarities between a ballotine and a galantine.
5. Describe the typical procedure for making sausages. Why is the selection of casings important?
6. Explain the difference between hot smoking and cold smoking. Describe a food typically prepared by each of these methods.

ADDITIONAL CHARCUTERIE RECIPES

RECIPE 20.6

VEGETABLE TERRINE

LA BELLE AUBERGE RESTAURANT, RICHMOND, BC
Chef-Owner Bruno Marti, CCC

Bruno Marti, CCC
Bruno began his career as a 15-year-old apprentice in Switzerland, moving to Canada in his early 20s and beginning his culinary career at the Queen Elizabeth Hotel in Montreal. After working as the Manager of Catering for Canadian Pacific Airlines for 12 years, he became chef and owner of La Belle Auberge. Over the last 25 years, Bruno has contributed to Canada's regional and national culinary teams as Member, Manager and, most recently, Coach. In the 2000 Culinary Olympics, he coached Team Canada to a Grand Gold!

Yield: 1 Terrine mould, 10 x 10 x 30 cm (4 x 4 x 12 inches), with lid
20 servings

Eggplant, cubed	200 g	7 oz.
Garlic clove, chopped	1	1
Olive oil	as needed	as needed
Shallots, chopped fine	75 g	2
Green beans	100 g	3-1/2 oz.
Water	50 mL	2 fl. oz.
Salt and pepper	TT	TT
Butternut squash, peeled, de-seeded, sliced lengthwise, 1 cm (1/2 inch) thick	200 g	7 oz.
Fresh herbs, chopped: oregano, thyme, basil	TT	TT
Celeriac, peeled, sliced lengthwise, 1 cm (1/2 inch) thick	200 g	7 oz.
Shiitake mushrooms, whole, stems removed	100 g	3-1/2 oz.
Leeks, washed and cleaned, left whole (not split)	2 medium	2 medium
Leaf gelatin	10 g	6 sheets
Carrots, peeled, cut into long, thin strips, the length of the carrot	4 large	4 large
Tomatoes, peeled, halved, seeded	200 g	7 oz.

1. Sauté eggplant in half the garlic and oil. Roast in the oven at 190°C (375°F) for 20 minutes, then purée, adding a little water, if needed.

2. Sauté shallots in oil for 1 minute. Add the beans and the water. Season to taste and simmer until cooked, but still crisp. Allow to cool.

3. In a few drops of oil and water, simmer squash in a 200°C (400°F) oven until tender, about 10 minutes. Turn once, and season with herbs.

4. Repeat with celeriac, cover and cook in moderate oven (180–190°C/350–375°F) for 30 minutes.

5. Sauté mushrooms in a little oil and water. Season with salt, pepper and the remaining garlic.

6. Blanch leeks for 10 minutes and carrots for 3 minutes in boiling, salted water. Cool them in ice water.

7. Drain vegetables well.

8. Melt package of gelatin according to manufacturer's instructions.

9. Line the mould with plastic wrap. Add carrot slices, placing them across the mould with excess curving up sides and hanging over edges. Brush with gelatin.

10. Layer tomatoes, celeriac, eggplant, beans (arrange them lengthwise), leeks, mushrooms and squash. Alternate ingredients to give an attractive colour combination. Brush each layer with gelatin. After brushing the final layer, fold the carrots over the gelatin to seal. Fold in plastic wrap. Place weight on top and refrigerate for at least one day before slicing.

RECIPE 20.6

Approximate values per serving:

Calories	46
Total fat	1.3 g
Saturated fat	0.2 g
Cholesterol	0 mg
Sodium	118 mg
Total carbohydrates	7.2 g
Protein	1.3 g

RECIPE 20.7

CARPACCIO OF SEARED BEEF WITH PARMESAN FANS AND PERFUMED MASCARPONE

SOUTHERN ALBERTA INSTITUTE OF TECHNOLOGY, CALGARY, AB
Chef Instructor Fred Malley, CCC

Yield: 10 Servings

Beef tenderloin, centre cut, trimmed and cleaned	600 g	20 oz.
Ground black pepper	TT	TT
Oil	as needed	as needed
Watercress sprigs	60	60
Artichoke hearts, halved, grilled and marinated in olive oil vinaigrette	80 pieces	80 pieces
Parmesan fans (shards, sliced from Parmesan block)	60–90	60–90
Mascarpone, flavoured with 4 roasted mashed garlic cloves	250 g	8 oz.
Espresso coffee beans, ground	pinch	pinch
Garlic chips (crisp deep-fat fried slices)	30	30
Cherry tomatoes, sliced or wedged	30	30

1. Sprinkle the meat with pepper and sear in the hot oil.
2. Wrap in plastic wrap to make a roll or log shape and chill for 2 hours in the freezer.
3. Slice the beef paper thin using an electric slicer, then arrange the slices in a ring on a plate.
4. Place watercress and artichokes in the centre of the meat ring with some of the vinaigrette. Top with the Parmesan fans. Pipe three rosettes of mascarpone on the plate and sprinkle espresso lightly over each. Top with the garlic chips. Place tomato pieces between the mascarpone rosettes.

Fred Malley, CCC
Fred's career includes being an educator, chef, food and beverage manager, caterer and food stylist. He currently instructs aspiring culinarians at S.A.I.T., mentors for professional designation, and is actively involved in curriculum development. His food styling appears internationally for major corporations, and he has ventured into research and development for food companies.

Photo by George Webber, SAIT.

RECIPE 20.7

Approximate values per serving:

Calories	459
Total fat	35 g
Saturated fat	15 g
Cholesterol	94 mg
Sodium	503 mg
Total carbohydrates	11 g
Protein	25 g

RECIPE 20.8

SALMON TARTAR MILLE FEUILLE

NORTHERN ALBERTA INSTITUTE OF TECHNOLOGY, EDMONTON, AB
Chef Instructor Troy Lymburner

Yield: 4 Portions

Fresh salmon, finely diced	225 g	8 oz.
Canola oil	5 mL	1 tsp.
Fresh chives	10 g	1 Tbsp.
Tabasco sauce	TT	TT
Salt	TT	TT
Black pepper, freshly ground	TT	TT
Phyllo pastry	3 sheets	3 sheets
Grain Mustard Sauce:		
Grainy Dijon mustard	50 mL	1-1/2 fl. oz.
Sour cream	50 mL	1-1/2 fl. oz.

Continued

Troy Lymburner
Born and raised in Edmonton, Troy graduated from the Culinary Arts program at N.A.I.T. and immediately set out to train in Switzerland. Upon returning to Canada, he worked at a number of upscale properties honing his culinary creativity. Most recently, Troy helped to coach Student Culinary Team Alberta to a Gold medal at the 2000 International Culinary Olympics.

RECIPE 20.8

Approximate values per serving:

Calories	844
Total fat	80 g
Saturated fat	32 g
Cholesterol	180 mg
Sodium	1020 mg
Total carbohydrates	14 g
Protein	17 g

Chive Oil:		
Fresh chives	125 g	4 oz.
Olive oil	125 mL	4 fl. oz.
Lemon Yogurt:		
Plain yogurt	110 mL	3-1/2 fl. oz.
Lemon juice, freshly squeezed	30 mL	1 fl. oz.
Lemon zest, finely chopped	10 g	2 tsp.
Butter, melted	200 g	7 oz.
Golden whitefish caviar	20 g	3/4 oz.

1. Combine salmon, oil, chives and seasonings in a nonreactive bowl and chill.
2. Brush one sheet of phyllo with melted butter and place second sheet on top. Repeat with third sheet. Divide phyllo into 12 equal squares, cut and place on parchment-lined baking sheet. Bake at 180° (375°F) until golden-brown.
3. Combine mustard and sour cream for mustard sauce.
4. Blanch chives briefly and drain well. Add an equal volume of olive oil and purée in blender.
5. Combine ingredients for lemon yogurt.
6. To assemble on plate, divide 60 g (2 oz.) of salmon mixture in three, place first amount in centre of plate and top with phyllo square. Repeat in three equal layers. Top with a dollop of lemon yogurt and a spoonful of caviar.
7. Garnish plate with drizzle of mustard sauce and chive oil.

Christophe Luzeux, CCC

Christophe comes from Marcq-en-Baroeul in the north of France and is a graduate of Lycée Michel Servet in Lille, France. Afterwards, he honed his skills in several of France's top establishments. His more recent culinary achievements include winning silver in the Individual Competition in the 2000 Culinary Team Canada Competition and functioning as the captain of Team Nova Scotia, when it won silver in both 1998 and 1999.

◆ ◆ ◆

RECIPE 20.9

Foie Gras

WORLD TRADE AND CONVENTION CENTRE, Halifax, NS
Executive Chef Christophe Luzeux, CCC

Yield: 1.5 kg (3-1/2 lb.)   **Method:** Baking

Goose or duck liver	1.8 kg	4 lb.
Salt	150 g	5 oz.
Pepper	40 g	1-1/2 oz.
Nutmeg	20 g	5 tsp.
Port	125 mL	4 fl. oz.
Cognac	125 mL	4 fl. oz.

1. Soak the liver in water overnight.
2. Mix the salt, pepper and nutmeg together.
3. Cut the liver open and remove all the nerves and built-up blood (keep the liver intact as much as possible).
4. Put the liver in a bowl and add the seasonings, port and cognac. Toss the liver carefully and let set, covered, in the fridge for 24 hours.
5. Place the liver in a terrine, press it and cook for 1.5 hours at 75°C (170°F) in a bain marie.
6. Remove the terrine from the bain marie. Let it cool. Remove some of the excess grease (set aside for later use) on top and press the liver with a wood plank wrapped in foil. Put in the fridge for 4 hours. Remove the plank of wood and pour the reserved melted grease on top to protect your foie gras. Return to the fridge to chill for 24 hours before cutting.

RECIPE 20.9

Approximate values per 60 g serving:

Calories	105
Total fat	3.4 g
Saturated fat	1.4 g
Cholesterol	371 mg
Sodium	2428 mg
Total carbohydrates	6.6 g
Protein	12 g

◆◆◆

RECIPE 20.10

SALMON AND SEA BASS TERRINE WITH SPINACH AND BASIL

Yield: 1 Terrine, 30 x 10 x 7.5 cm (12 x 4 x 3 inches)
20 servings

Salmon fillet, boneless, skinless	700 g	1 lb. 8 oz.
Salt	10 g	2 tsp.
Egg whites	3	3
White pepper	TT	TT
Cayenne pepper	TT	TT
Cream, 35%	up to 700 mL	up to 24 fl. oz.
Basil leaves	12	12
Truffle, brunoise (optional)	20 g	3/4 oz.
Spinach leaves, cleaned	175 g	6 oz.
Sea bass fillets	350 g	12 oz.

1. Grind the salmon through the large plate of a well-chilled meat grinder.
2. Place the salmon in the bowl of a food processor with salt and process until smooth and firm.
3. Add the egg whites, one at a time, pulsing the processor to incorporate. Scrape down the bowl and season with white pepper and cayenne pepper.
4. With the machine running, add the cream in a steady stream. Scrape down the bowl again and process the mousseline until it is smooth and well mixed but still firm. You may not use all the cream.
5. Blanch the basil leaves and refresh. Chop them finely.
6. Remove the mousseline from the bowl of the processor. Fold in the basil leaves and truffle and refrigerate.
7. Blanch and refresh the spinach leaves.
8. Spread the spinach leaves on a piece of plastic wrap, completely covering a rectangle approximately the length and width of the terrine mould.
9. Cut the sea bass fillets into strips approximately 2.5 cm (1 inch) wide and place end to end on the spinach leaves. Season with salt and white pepper.
10. Use the plastic wrap to wrap the spinach leaves tightly around the fish fillets.
11. Oil terrine and line it with plastic wrap.
12. Half-fill the lined terrine with salmon mousseline.
13. Carefully unwrap the spinach and sea bass fillets and place them down the centre of the terrine. Fill the terrine with the remaining mousseline.
14. Tap the terrine mould firmly to remove any air pockets, then fold the plastic wrap over the top.
15. Cover and bake the terrine in a water bath at 150°C (300°F) to an internal temperature of 57°C (135°F), approximately 1.5 hours.
16. Cool the terrine well, unmould, slice or decorate and serve as desired.

RECIPE 20.10

Approximate values per serving:

Calories	198
Total fat	16 g
Saturated fat	8.5 g
Cholesterol	75 mg
Sodium	249 mg
Total carbohydrates	1.4 g
Protein	12 g

Marcel Kretz, C.M.

Born, raised and trained in France, Marcel has had an illustrious, award-winning career in Europe and Canada. He is credited with launching the movement to emphasize Quebec products in top Quebec restaurants, and in 1998 became the first chef ever to receive the Order of Canada.

RECIPE 20.11

Approximate values per serving:

Calories	126
Total fat	9.2 g
Saturated fat	3.6 g
Cholesterol	174 mg
Sodium	45 mg
Total carbohydrates	1.7 g
Protein	9.1 g

RECIPE 20.11

CHICKEN LIVER TERRINE

Chef Marcel Kretz, C.M., retired

Yield: 2 Moulds, half-moon shaped, approximately 25 × 10 × 7 cm (10 × 4 × 3 inches); 30 servings

Chicken livers, cleaned and trimmed	1 kg	2 lb.
Milk	500 mL	16 fl. oz.
Salt	TT	TT
Brandy	100 mL	3 fl. oz.
Fresh pork flank or pork cheeks, ground	250 g	8 oz.
Eggs	2	2
Cream, 35%	100 mL	3 fl. oz.
Neutral gelatin (powder)	20 g	3 Tbsp.
Mace	pinch	pinch
Sugar	pinch	pinch
Pepper	pinch	pinch
Curing salt	pinch	pinch
Dry morels, soaked and chopped	15 g	1/2 oz.
Pork backfat, thinly sliced	175 g	6 oz.

1. Soak the chicken livers overnight in the milk, with a pinch of salt added. Drain and rinse carefully for 15 minutes, under running water.
2. Drain thoroughly, place in bowl, then add the brandy and a few grains of salt. Marinate for 10 minutes, then drain again, reserving the brandy marinade.
3. Swiftly blanch 750 g (1-1/2 lb.) of the chicken livers in boiling salted water. Cool rapidly under running water and refrigerate.
4. Purée pork and remaining raw livers in the blender with eggs, cream, gelatin, mace, sugar, marinade, curing salt, salt and pepper. When smooth, add morels, but do not purée them.
5. Line moulds with some of the thinly sliced backfat (reserve the rest for finishing). Line with half the creamy pork and liver farce, then add all the whole chicken livers and cover with remaining farce. Top with more backfat. Wrap in plastic wrap and then cover with foil.
6. Cook in a bain marie in the oven at 250°C (500°F) for 15 minutes, then reduce the heat to 175°C (350°F) and let cook for 30 minutes. The hot water should be three-quarters up the sides of the mould.
7. Remove from oven and put under a press (a foil-covered wooden board the size of the mould). Put some weight on the press and tie it down. Cool for at least 12 hours before unmoulding.

VARIATION: Replace the chicken liver with quail or duck liver.

RECIPE 20.12

ROASTED RED PEPPER MOUSSE

Yield: 700 mL (1-1/2 pt.)

Onion, small dice	100 g	3 oz.
Garlic, chopped	5 g	1 tsp.

Olive oil	30 mL	1 fl. oz.
Red bell pepper, roasted and peeled, small dice	200 g	6 oz.
Salt and pepper	TT	TT
Saffron, ground	1 g	pinch
Tomato paste	30 g	1 oz.
Chicken stock	250 mL	8 fl. oz.
Gelatin	5 leaves	5 leaves
Dry white wine	50 mL	2 fl. oz.
Cream, 35%, whipped	175 mL	6 fl. oz.

1. Sauté the onion and garlic in the olive oil until tender, approximately 2 minutes.

2. Add the bell pepper, salt, pepper, saffron, tomato paste and chicken stock. Bring to a boil, reduce to a simmer and cook until ingredients are tender and liquid is reduced.

3. Soften the gelatin in cold water, squeeze well, then add to the hot pepper mixture with the white wine. Purée the pepper mixture in a blender or food processor and strain through a conical strainer.

4. Place the pepper purée over an ice bath. Stir until cool but do not allow the gelatin to set. Fold in the whipped cream. Pour the mousse into aspic-lined or well-oiled timbales or moulds and refrigerate several hours or overnight.

5. Unmould the mousse and serve as desired.

VARIATIONS: Substitute yellow or green bell peppers for part or all of the red bell peppers. *Broccoli Mousse:* Substitute 225 g (8 oz.) of blanched, chopped broccoli for the red bell peppers and omit tomato paste.

RECIPE 20.12

Approximate values per 35mL serving:

Calories	56
Total fat	4.8 g
Saturated fat	2.3 g
Cholesterol	12 mg
Sodium	77 mg
Total carbohydrates	2.1 g
Protein	1 g

✦✦✦

RECIPE 20.13

SMOKED SALMON MOUSSE

Yield: 900 g (2 lb.)

Smoked salmon, boneless, skinless	300 g	10 oz.
Fish velouté, warm	250 mL	8 fl. oz.
Cream, 35%	250 mL	8 fl. oz.
Granulated gelatin	25 g	3 Tbsp.
Sherry	150 mL	5 fl. oz.
Salt and white pepper	TT	TT
Cayenne pepper	TT	TT

1. Finely chop the salmon and transfer it to the food processor. Add the warm velouté in a steady stream while the machine is running.

2. Whip the cream to soft peaks and reserve.

3. Add the gelatin to the sherry and allow it to soften for 5 minutes. Heat the gelatin mixture to liquefy the gelatin.

4. Transfer the salmon and velouté to a mixing bowl and stir in the gelatin mixture (wine aspic). Season with salt, pepper and cayenne pepper.

5. When the mixture has cooled to near room temperature, fold in the whipped cream with a rubber spatula until just mixed.

6. The mousse is now ready to be formed into timbales, or moulded into various shapes as desired.

RECIPE 20.13

Approximate values per 60 g serving:

Calories	106
Total fat	8.4 g
Saturated fat	4.8 g
Cholesterol	30 mg
Sodium	465 mg
Total carbohydrates	2.1 g
Protein	5.6 g

RECIPE 20.14

RECIPE 20.14

DUCK CONFIT

Yield: 4 Servings

Duck, 1.8 kg (4 lb.), cut into 4 pieces	1	1
Kosher salt	25 g	2 Tbsp.
Black pepper, cracked	3 g	1 tsp.
Bay leaves, crumbled	4	4
Fresh thyme	6 sprigs	6 sprigs
Garlic cloves, crushed	20 g	6
Duck or goose fat, melted	900 g	2 lb.

1. Rub the duck with the salt. Place skin side down in a roasting pan just large enough to hold the pieces in one layer; season with the black pepper, crumbled bay leaves, thyme and garlic. Cover and refrigerate overnight.

2. Bake the duck at 160°C (325°F) until brown, approximately 15–20 minutes. Add enough melted duck or goose fat to cover the pieces completely.

3. Cover the pan and cook in a 150°C (300°F) oven until the duck is very tender, approximately 2 hours.

4. Remove the duck from the fat and place in a narrow, deep hotel pan. Ladle enough of the cooking fat over the pieces to cover them completely. Be careful not to add any of the cooking juices.

5. Cover the pan and refrigerate for 2 days to allow the flavours to mellow.

6. To serve, remove the duck from the fat and scrape off the excess fat. Bake at 180°C (350°F) until the skin is crisp and the meat is hot, approximately 30 minutes.

RECIPE 20.14

Approximate values per serving:

Calories	607
Total fat	51 g
Saturated fat	16 g
Cholesterol	152 mg
Sodium	2558 mg
Total carbohydrates	2.1 g
Protein	35 g

Philippe Wettel

A native Frenchman, Philippe began his career at the prestigious Hôtel Restaurant au Cygne, in France, and soon thereafter trained under the famous French Chef Michel Guérard. Having owned and operated his own restaurant in Alsace, today Philippe is part of Westin Hotels & Resorts' world-renowned team of Executive Chefs.

RECIPE 20.15

Approximate values per serving:

Calories	236
Total fat	6.1 g
Saturated fat	3.4 g
Cholesterol	56 mg
Sodium	426 mg
Total carbohydrates	42 g
Protein	3.2 g

RECIPE 20.15

OLD-FASHIONED GINGERBREAD

THE WESTIN, OTTAWA, ON
Executive Chef Philippe Wettel

An old-fashioned spiced bread to serve with pâté or foie gras.

Yield: 1 Loaf
    20 servings

Sugar	70 g	2-1/2 oz.
Lemon juice	5 mL	1 tsp.
Water	55 mL	2 fl. oz.
Instant coffee	5 mL	1 tsp.
Honey, warm	360 g	13 oz.
Milk, warm	145 mL	5 fl. oz.
Candied orange, fine dice	300 g	11 oz.
Butter	115 g	4 oz.
Salt	5 g	1 tsp.
Eggs, beaten	200 g	7 oz.
Flour	300 g	11 oz.
Baking soda	18 g	5 tsp.
Gingerbread spice	10 g	2 Tbsp.

1. Bring sugar, lemon, water and coffee powder to a boil. Pour over warm honey and stir to dissolve.

2. Mix together milk, orange, butter and salt and combine with honey mixture. Stir in eggs.

3. Sift dry ingredients together and mix into wet ingredients.

4. Place in a greased loaf tin and bake at 160°C (320°F) for 4 minutes, then reduce the temperature to 150°C (280°F) for 1 hour. Do not open oven.

5. Cool bread and slice thinly.

NOTE: Gingerbread spice is 2 parts cinnamon, 1 part ginger and 1 part cloves.

◆◆◆

RECIPE 20.16

DUCK PROSCIUTTO WITH MELON AND FIG SALAD

BISON FOOD SERVICES, SASKATOON, SK
Executive Chef and Owner Peter Phillips

Yield: 225 g (8 oz.)

Duck breasts, boneless, each 175 g (6 oz.)	2	2
Kosher salt	40 g	3 Tbsp.
Brown sugar	15 g	1 Tbsp.
Paprika	3 g	1 tsp.
Soy sauce (Japanese)	as required	as required
Honeydew melon, cubed	1/2	1/2
Black mission figs, preferably fresh, quartered	4	4
Lime Coriander Vinaigrette (recipe follows)	60 mL	2 fl. oz.
Baguette	as required	as required

1. Remove skin from duck breast, retaining 3 mm (1/8 inch) of fat.

2. Combine salt, sugar and paprika.

3. Brush duck breasts with soy sauce, then cover with sugar/salt mixture.

4. Refrigerate uncovered for 24 hours.

5. Wrap duck breasts in cheesecloth and hang in refrigerator for 10–28 days.

6. For service, crisp duck breasts fat side up in a hot pan.

7. Toss cubed melon and quartered figs in Lime Coriander Vinaigrette and arrange with thinly sliced duck prosciutto. Serve with baguette.

LIME CORIANDER VINAIGRETTE

Lime juice and zest	1	1
Coriander seeds, ground	5 mL	1 tsp.
Honey	15 g	2 tsp.
Olive oil	30 mL	1 fl. oz.
White wine vinegar	10 mL	2 tsp.

Mix together all ingredients.

Peter Phillips, CCC
After leaving his home of Nipawin, Saskatchewan, to attend Humber College's Culinary Arts Program, Peter attained top student honours, as well as numerous other awards. After his apprenticeship at a golf and country club in Winnipeg, and an exciting position at a ski resort in Japan, Peter returned to Saskatchewan and soon thereafter began managing Boffins Café. While having a strong interest in and aptitude for the business and management side of the culinary industry, he continues to develop his artistic talents through national and international competitions.

RECIPE 20.16

Approximate values per 55 g serving:

Calories	262
Total fat	10 g
Saturated fat	2 g
Cholesterol	58 mg
Sodium	4145 mg
Total carbohydrates	27 g
Protein	16 g

♦♦♦

RECIPE 20.17

TEX-MEX TURKEY SAUSAGE

Yield: 1.8 kg (4 lb.)

Canola oil	50 mL	4 Tbsp.
Onion, chopped fine	350 g	12 oz.
Garlic, minced	15 g	1 Tbsp.
Jalapeño, chopped	15 g	1 Tbsp.
Turkey breast meat, trimmed of fat	1 kg	2 lb.
Veal, lean	250 g	8 oz.
White wine vinegar	60 mL	2 fl. oz.
Water	250 mL	8 fl. oz.
Fresh cilantro, chopped	100 g	1/2 cup
White pepper	3 g	1 tsp.
Chili powder	3 g	1 tsp.
Cumin, ground	1 g	1/2 tsp.
Salt	5 g	1 tsp.

RECIPE 20.17

Approximate values per 60 g serving:

Calories	81
Total fat	4.2 g
Saturated fat	0.8 g
Cholesterol	28 mg
Sodium	95 mg
Total carbohydrates	1.6 g
Protein	9.3 g

1. Heat the oil and sauté the onion, garlic and jalapeño until the onion is translucent; remove and chill well.
2. Grind the turkey and veal in a cold meat grinder, first through the large plate and then through the medium plate. Working over an ice bath, combine the meats, vinegar, water and seasonings. Add the sautéed vegetables.
3. Blend well, then cook a small portion to test the flavour and texture. Adjust the seasonings.
4. Stuff into casings or portion into 60-g (2-oz.) patties and broil. Serve with papaya salsa.

♦♦♦

RECIPE 20.18

SPICY ITALIAN SAUSAGE

Yield: 2.2 kg (5 lb.)

Pork butt	2.2 kg	5 lb.
Salt	25 g	1-1/2 Tbsp.
Black pepper	4 g	1-1/2 tsp.
Fennel seeds	3 g	1-1/2 tsp.
Paprika	8 g	1 Tbsp.
Red pepper, crushed	3 g	1-1/2 tsp.
Coriander, ground	1.5 g	3/4 tsp.
Ice water	150 mL	5 fl. oz.

RECIPE 20.18

Approximate values per 60 g serving:

Calories	136
Total fat	9.6 g
Saturated fat	3.3 g
Cholesterol	40 mg
Sodium	307 mg
Total carbohydrates	0.3 g
Protein	12 g

1. Cut the meat into 5-cm (2-inch) cubes.
2. Combine the pork with the remaining ingredients except the water.
3. Grind the meat once through the coarse plate of a well-chilled grinder.
4. Add the ice water and mix well.
5. Stuff the sausage into casings.

♦♦♦

RECIPE 20.19

CHORIZO

Yield: 3.4 kg (7 lb. 8 oz.)

Pork, lean	2.2 kg	5 lb.
Backfat	1.1 kg	2 lb. 8 oz.

Red pepper flakes	2 g	1 tsp.
Garlic, chopped	30 g	1 oz.
Cumin	20 g	3 Tbsp.
Cayenne pepper	15 g	2 Tbsp.
Salt	20 g	4 tsp.
Paprika	40 g	5 Tbsp.
Red wine vinegar	90 mL	3 fl. oz.

1. Cut the pork and backfat into 2.5-cm (1-inch) pieces. Grind the pork once using a medium plate. Grind half of the pork a second time together with the backfat through a fine plate.

2. Combine all the ingredients in the bowl of a mixer and mix, using the paddle attachment. The sausage may be used in bulk or formed into links as desired.

◆◆◆

RECIPE 20.20

GRAVLAX ON A WILD RICE FRITTER WITH CARROT PICKLE AND FRESH HERBS

CALGARY, AB
Chef dee Hobsbawn-Smith

This is a luxurious dish that must be started several days in advance. Use salmon, Arctic char or steelhead for the gravlax. Cut two fillets from one fish, preferably from the tail and preferably from opposite sides of the backbone so that they lie together in a perfect fit.

Yield: 12 Portions

Steelhead or salmon fillet in two pieces of equal size and shape	1 kg	2 lb.
White sugar	60 g	1/4 cup
Kosher salt	60 g	1/4 cup
Mustard seed, dry-roasted and ground	20 g	2 Tbsp.
Dillweed, fresh, minced	20 g	2 Tbsp.
Black pepper, freshly cracked	5 g	2 tsp.
Lemon, zest only	1	1
Pickled ginger, minced (available in Japanese markets)	30 g	2 Tbsp.
Pepper-flavoured vodka	60 mL	1/4 cup
Wild Rice Fritters (recipe follows)	1 recipe	1 recipe
Carrot Pickle (recipe follows)	60 mL	1/4 cup
Crème fraîche or sour cream	125 mL	1/2 cup
Dill, fresh, minced	10 g	1 Tbsp.
Fresh chives and chive blossoms	as garnish	as garnish

1. Using tweezers or needle-nose pliers, pull the pinbones out of the salmon. Combine the sugar and salt, then sprinkle it evenly over the fillets. Wrap the pieces, flesh side to flesh side, snugly in plastic wrap and chill for 24–48 hours over a drip pan to catch weeping liquids.

2. Unwrap the fish and brush off any undissolved crystals of salt and sugar. Sprinkle the surface with mustard seed, dillweed, pepper, lemon zest and pickled ginger. Drizzle the vodka over the herbs and spices. Wrap and chill 12–24 hours, then slice thinly on an angle.

3. Prepare the Wild Rice Fritters and the Carrot Pickle.

4. Combine the crème fraîche with the minced dill, then spread a little on each hot fritter. Top with a gently folded slice of gravlax, and garnish with two to three thin slivers of carrot pickle. Add a sprig of chives and pull apart a chive blossom, sprinkling the petals over top.

RECIPE 20.19

Approximate values per 60 g serving:

Calories	245
Total fat	23 g
Saturated fat	8.1 g
Cholesterol	36 mg
Sodium	161 mg
Total carbohydrates	0.9 g
Protein	8.6 g

dee Hobsbawn-Smith

dee—a Calgary-based professional chef, caterer, culinary educator, and author—has been delighting Calgary diners and readers since 1983. She studied cooking at Vancouver Vocational Institute, completed her Red Seal in Calgary and studied with eminent chef and educator Madeleine Kamman in Annecy, France. Since selling her restaurant, Foodsmith, in 1994, dee has turned to food writing and now has three cookbooks and many magazine articles and columns under her belt.

RECIPE 20.20

Approximate values per serving:

Calories	179
Total fat	6 g
Saturated fat	2 g
Cholesterol	58 mg
Sodium	378 mg
Total carbohydrates	7 g
Protein	21 g

WILD RICE FRITTERS

This is an adaptation of "Wild Rice and Lobster Fritters,"
which first appeared in Skinny Feasts *(Whitecap Books, 1997).*

Yield: 24–36 Fritters, depending on size

Wild rice	50 g	1/4 cup
Basmati rice	200 g	1 cup
Eggs, lightly beaten	4	4
Arrowroot powder	45 mL	3 Tbsp.
Fresh dill, thyme or oregano, minced	60 mL	4 Tbsp.
Green onions, minced	1 bunch	1 bunch
Kosher salt and pepper	TT	TT
Canola oil	as needed	as needed

Wild Rice Fritters—Approximate values per fritter:

Calories	38
Total fat	1 g
Saturated fat	0 g
Cholesterol	24 mg
Sodium	30 mg
Total carbohydrates	6 g
Protein	1 g

1. Cook the wild rice in 500 mL (2 cups) water, covered, until the grains split open (35–55 minutes). Add water if needed to prevent sticking. Drain and cool. Bring 500 mL (2 cups) water to the boil. Add the basmati rice and return to the boil. Cover and reduce heat to low and cook for 16 minutes. Cool. Combine all the ingredients except canola oil in a mixing bowl, mixing well.

2. Heat a griddle or large nonstick sauté pan, add a small amount of canola oil and drop the fritter mixture onto the hot surface in spoonfuls. Flatten with the back of a spoon. When brown and crispy, turn and cook the other side. Keep warm in a slow oven or make the fritters in advance and reheat before serving.

CARROT PICKLE

Yield: 1 L (1 qt.)

Carrot, fine julienne	900 g	2 lb.
Garlic, peeled and thinly sliced	1 head	1 head
Ginger root, peeled and thinly sliced	TT	TT
Kalonji* (black onion seed)	8 mL	1-1/2 tsp.
Fenugreek	5 mL	1 tsp.
Anise seed	5 mL	1 tsp.
Coriander seed	3 mL	1/2 tsp.
Cumin seed	2 mL	1/4 tsp.
Mustard seed	5 mL	1 tsp.
Black peppercorns, cracked	3 mL	1/2 tsp.
Lemons, juice and zest	2	2
Apple cider vinegar	110 mL	1/2 cup
Mustard oil	as needed	as needed

Carrot Pickle—Approximate values per 60 mL serving:

Calories	30
Total fat	0 g
Saturated fat	0 g
Cholesterol	0 g
Sodium	18 mg
Total carbohydrates	8 g
Protein	1 g

Mix the carrot, garlic and ginger in a nonreactive bowl. Dry-roast the kalonji, fenugreek, anise, coriander, cumin, mustard and pepper in a small sauté pan over high heat until fragrant and beginning to colour, then add to the carrots, garlic and ginger. Add the lemon juice and zest and the vinegar. Pack into a clean 1 L (1 qt.) jar and fill to the top with mustard oil.

*Kalonji is available in specialty spice stores.

RECIPE 20.21

GINGER MARINATED ATLANTIC SALMON

THE FAIRMONT PALLISER, Calgary, AB
Executive Chef Takashi Ito, CCC

Yield: 1 Serving

Marinade:

Fresh ginger, thinly sliced	5 g	1/2 Tbsp.
Soy sauce	50 mL	4 Tbsp.
Garlic, minced	5 g	1/2 Tbsp.
Black pepper	TT	TT
Canola oil	200 mL	1 cup
Water	100 mL	1/2 cup
Atlantic salmon, cut in slices and marinated, each piece 40 g (1-1/2 oz.)	2 pieces	2 pieces
Spinach, cleaned	25 g	1 cup
Red pepper, julienned	5 g	1 tsp.
Orange Kiwi Dressing (recipe follows)	30–40 mL	1-1/2 fl. oz.

1. Combine the marinade ingredients in a mixing bowl.
2. Place the salmon in the marinade and marinate for at least 3 hours.
3. Remove the salmon from the marinade and grill on a hot grill for about 15 seconds per side.
4. Arrange the spinach on a cold plate, cover with the salmon and red pepper.
5. Drizzle Orange Kiwi Dressing on top.

ORANGE KIWI DRESSING

Yield: 60 mL (1/4 cup)

Mandarin oranges (canned)	3 pieces	3 pieces
White wine vinegar	15 mL	3 tsp.
Olive oil	20 mL	4 tsp.
Canola oil	20 mL	4 tsp.
Kiwi, ripe	1/4	1/4
Salt and black pepper	TT	TT

1. Purée the oranges in a blender.
2. Add the vinegar and oils and blend well. Add the kiwi. Do not overblend; keep the kiwi seeds whole.
3. Adjust the seasoning with salt and pepper.

Takashi Ito

Takashi has been a Certified Chef de Cuisine since 1992, and has won several medals in competition, including the gold at the 1993 Grand Salon Culinaire in Vancouver. He is particularly notable for his skill and creativity in carving ice sculptures, for which he has also won numerous awards.

RECIPE 20.21

Approximate values per serving:

Calories	480
Total fat	40 g
Saturated fat	4 g
Cholesterol	40 mg
Sodium	855 mg
Total carbohydrates	7 g
Protein	23 g

Orange Kiwi Dressing— Approximate values per 30 mL serving:

Calories	178
Total fat	18 g
Saturated fat	2 g
Cholesterol	0 mg
Sodium	119 mg
Total carbohydrates	4 g
Protein	0 g

WEBLINKS

Galloping Goose Sausage Company (B.C.)
www.islandnet.com/~sausage/

Salt Curing Meat in Brine
www.lis.ab.ca/walton/old/brine.html

CHAPTER 21

DEEP-FAT FRYING

LEARNING OUTCOMES

After studying this chapter you will be able to:

+ select and maintain the proper equipment and fats for deep-fat frying
+ use breadings and batters
+ prepare fritters and croquettes

P

roperly prepared, foods that are deep-fat fried can be deliciously tender and juicy—and their contrasting crispy crusts and moist interiors add to eating enjoyment. Deep-fried foods enjoy wide popularity with consumers and form a major component of some food service menu offerings.

Perhaps no other cooking method can be applied to such a wide variety of foods. Meats, poultry, fish and shellfish, vegetables, potatoes and other starches, fruits, pastries and even ice cream can be deep-fat fried successfully. That is why we devote a separate chapter to the process.

This versatile procedure is relatively simple provided a few basic guidelines are followed. This chapter explains those guidelines and provides recipes for breading and batters. Also included are illustrative recipes utilizing deep-fat frying techniques. Other recipes that use deep-fat frying are found in the various chapters on vegetables, fish, starches and quick breads.

Deep-fat frying is a dry-heat cooking method using fat as the cooking medium. Boiling and deep-fat frying are conceptually similar. For both cooking methods, food is placed in a liquid and heat is transferred from the hot liquid (water and fat, respectively) to the food being cooked through conduction (the transfer of heat by direct contact) and convection (the transfer of heat through the currents in a liquid or gas).

The principal difference between boiling and deep-fat frying is the temperature of the cooking medium. The boiling point, 100°C (212°F), is the hottest temperature at which food can be cooked in water. At this temperature, most foods require a long cooking period and surface sugars cannot caramelize. With deep-fat frying, temperatures up to 200°C (400°F) are used. These high temperatures cook food more quickly and allow the food's surface to brown. Even though the food is cooked in a liquid, deep-fat frying is not a moist-heat cooking method because the liquid fat contains no moisture.

SELECTING EQUIPMENT FOR DEEP-FAT FRYING

Unlike most kitchen equipment, a deep-fat fryer has only one purpose: to cook foods in a large amount of hot fat. Fryers are sized by the amount of fat they hold. Most commercial fryers range between 7 and 37 kg (15 and 82 lb.). Fryers can be either gas or electric and are thermostatically controlled for temperatures between 90°C and 200°C (200F° and 400°F).

When choosing a fryer, look for a fry tank with curved, easy-to-clean sloping sides. Some fryers have a cold zone (an area of reduced temperature) at the bottom of the fry tank to trap particles. This prevents them from burning, creating off-flavours and shortening the life of the fryer fat.

Deep-fat fryers usually come with steel wire baskets to hold the food during cooking. Fryer baskets may be lowered into the fat and raised manually, although many models have automatic basket mechanisms controlled by timers.

As with any piece of equipment, read the operator's manual or have an experienced colleague show you how to operate any deep-fat fryer before using or cleaning it.

The most important factor when choosing a deep-fat fryer is **recovery time**. Recovery time is the length of time it takes the fat to return to the desired cooking temperature after food is submerged in it. When food is submerged, heat is immediately transferred to the food from the fat. This heat transfer lowers the fat's temperature. The more food added at one time, the greater the drop in the fat's temperature. If the temperature drops too much or does not return quickly to the proper cooking temperature, the food may absorb excess fat and become greasy.

Deep-fat frying foods in a sauce pot on the stove top is discouraged because it is both difficult and dangerous. Recovery time is usually very slow and temperatures are difficult to control. Also the fat can spill easily, leading to injuries or creating a fire hazard.

SELECTING FATS FOR DEEP-FAT FRYING

Many types of fats can be used for deep-fat frying. (In this chapter, the term *fat* applies to both solid fats and liquid oils.) Although animal fats, such as rendered beef fat, are sometimes used to impart their specific flavours to deep-fried foods, by far the most common fats used for deep-fat frying are vegetable oils such as soybean, safflower and canola oil.

Specially formulated deep-fat frying compounds are also available. These are usually composed of a vegetable oil or oils to which antifoaming agents, antioxidants and preservatives have been added. These additives increase usable life and raise smoke points.

A fat's **smoke point** is the temperature at which it visibly begins to smoke and chemically begins to break down. Animal fats generally have low smoke points of about 180°C (350°F), making them unsuitable for deep-fat frying. Vegetable oils generally have higher smoke points of about 250°C (475°F), thus providing the high temperatures desired for deep-fat frying. (See Chapter 7, Kitchen Staples, for a list of fat smoke points.)

Some frying fats are also hydrogenated. Hydrogenation is a chemical process that adds hydrogen to oils and turns a liquid oil into a solid (margarine is hydrogenated vegetable oil). Hydrogenated fats are more resistant to oxidation and chemical breakdown.

When fats break down, their chemical structure is altered; the triglyceride molecules that make up fat are converted into individual fatty acids. These acids add undesirable flavours to the fat and can ruin the flavour of the food being cooked. When a fat becomes very dark, foams excessively or adds off-flavours to foods, it has broken down and must be changed. (See Table 21.1.)

To choose the right fat, consider flavour, smoke point and resistance to chemical breakdown. High-quality frying fat should have a clean or natural flavour, a high smoke point and, when properly maintained, be resistant to chemical breakdown.

Maintaining Fryer Fat

Properly maintaining fryer fat greatly extends its useful life. To do so:

1. Store the fat in tightly sealed containers away from strong light; cover the fat in the fryer when not in use. Prolonged exposure to air and light turns fat rancid.

2. Skim and remove food particles from the fat's surface during frying. Food particles cause fat to break down; if they are not removed they will accumulate in the fryer and burn.

3. Do not salt food over the fat. Salt causes fat to break down chemically.

4. Prevent excessive water from coming into contact with the fat; pat-dry moist foods as much as possible before cooking and dry the fryer, baskets and utensils well after cleaning. Water, like salt, causes fat to break down.

5. Do not overheat the fat (turn the fryer down or off if not in use). High temperatures break down the fat.

6. Filter the fat each day or after each shift if the fryer is heavily used. Best results are obtained by using a filtering machine designed specifically for this purpose. Many large commercial fryers even have built-in filter systems. Less well equipped operations can simply pour the hot fat through a paper cone filter into a metal container and then transfer the filtered fat into the cleaned fryer tank. Exercise caution and emphasize safety.

7. Ensure proper rinsing of soap residues after washing.

TABLE 21.1

Fryer fat can be damaged by:	Change fryer fat when it:
Salt	Becomes dark
Water	Smokes
Overheating	Foams
Food particles	Develops off-flavours
Oxygen	
Soap	

PROCEDURES FOR DEEP-FAT FRYING

The temperature of the fat is critical to successful deep-fat frying. The fat must be hot enough to quickly seal the surface of the food so it does not become excessively greasy, yet it should not be so hot that the food's surface burns before the interior is cooked.

Nearly all foods that are deep-fat fried are cooked at temperatures between 160°C and 190°C (325°F and 375°F). The fat's temperature can be adjusted within this range to allow the interior of thicker foods or frozen foods to cook before their surfaces become too dark.

Try not to fry delicately flavoured foods in the same fat used for more strongly flavoured ones. For example, do not cook fruit fritters in the same fat used for catfish. If the fritters are fried in the catfish fat, they could develop an odd taste from the residual flavours left from the catfish.

Deep-Fat Frying Methods

There are two distinct deep-fat frying methods for standard electric or gas fryers: the basket method and the swimming method. Which is used depends upon the food being fried.

The **basket method** of deep-fat frying uses a basket to hold foods that are breaded, individually quick frozen or otherwise do not tend to stick together during cooking. The basket is removed from the fryer and filled as much as two-thirds full of product. (Do not fill the basket while it is hanging over the fat as this allows unnecessary crumbs, salt and food particles to fall

1. Basket method of deep-fat frying.

into the fat, shortening its life.) The filled basket is then submerged in the hot fat. When cooking is completed, the basket is used to remove the food from the fat.

A variation on this procedure is the **double-basket method**. This variation is necessitated by the fact that many fried foods float as they cook. This may produce undesirable results because the section of the food not submerged may not cook. To prevent this and to promote even cooking, a second basket is used to keep the foods submerged in the fat.

Most battered foods initially sink to the bottom when placed in hot fat, then rise to the top as they cook. Because they would stick to a basket, the **swimming method** of deep-fat frying is used for these foods. With the swimming method, battered foods are carefully dropped directly into the hot fat. (Baskets are not used.) They will rise to the top as they cook. When the surface that is in contact with the fat is properly browned, the food is turned over with a spider or a pair of tongs so that it can cook evenly on both sides. When done, the product is removed and drained, again using a spider or tongs.

2. Double-basket method of deep-fat frying

Draining and Holding after Deep-Fat Frying

All foods that are deep-fat fried must be drained of excess oil before they are served. When removing foods from the deep-fat fryer, allow excess fat to drain into the fryer. Then transfer the foods to a hotel pan that is either lined with absorbent paper or fitted with a rack.

The foods should then be kept under a heat lamp. Steam tables do not keep these foods hot because very little of the food's crisp surface actually touches the hot surface of the steam table's pan.

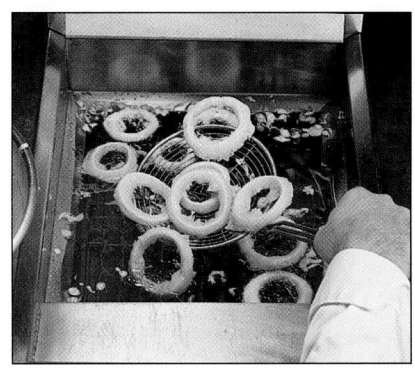

3. Swimming method of deep-fat frying

SELECTING FOODS FOR DEEP-FAT FRYING

Only tender foods should be deep-fat fried. Deep-fat frying cooks foods at relatively high temperatures for short periods of time and does not have a tenderizing effect. Young tender poultry is ideal, as are most types of lean fish and shellfish. Fruits and vegetables can also be deep-fat fried. Probably the most popular food for deep-fat frying is the potato, which is cooked in an endless variety of shapes and forms. (Several of the recipes found in Chapter 23, Potatoes, Grains and Pasta, call for deep-fat frying.) Foods that are deep-fat fried together should be of the same size or thickness so they cook evenly. Slow-cooking vegetables such as broccoli, cauliflower and okra can be blanched first so they cook more quickly.

PREPARING FOODS FOR DEEP-FAT FRYING

With some exceptions (french fries, for example), most foods for deep-fat frying are first breaded or battered. Breading and batter coat the food, keeping it moist and preventing it from becoming excessively greasy during cooking.

Seasoning Foods to Be Deep-Fat Fried

Breaded and battered foods can be seasoned before the breading or batter is applied. Seasonings may also be added to the flour, bread crumbs or batter before the main item is coated.

Food that is deep-fat fried is often salted after being removed from the fat. This should be done immediately after the food is removed from the fryer so the salt will cling more readily.

Breading Foods to Be Deep-Fat Fried

A breaded item is any food that is coated with bread crumbs, cracker meal, cornmeal or other dry meal to protect it during cooking. Breaded foods are generally cooked by deep-fat frying or pan-frying. The breading makes a solid coating that seals during cooking to prevent the fat from coming in direct contact with the food and making it greasy.

Standard Breading Procedure

Whether breading meats, poultry, fish, shellfish or vegetables, a three-step process is typically used. Called the **standard breading procedure**, it gives foods a relatively thick, crisp coating.

1. Pat the food dry and dredge it in seasoned flour. The flour adds seasoning to the food, helps seal it, and allows the egg wash to adhere.
2. Dip the floured food in an egg wash. The egg wash should contain whole eggs whisked together with up to 15 mL (1 Tbsp.) milk or water per egg. The egg wash will cause the crumbs or meal to completely coat the item and form a tight seal when the food is cooked.
3. Coat the food with bread crumbs, cracker crumbs or other dry meal. Shake off the excess crumbs and place the breaded item in a pan. As additional breaded items are added to the pan, align them in a single layer; do not stack them or the breadings will get soggy and the foods will stick together.

Figure 21.1 shows the proper setup for breading foods using the standard breading procedure.

The following procedure helps to bread foods more efficiently:

1. Assemble the mise en place as depicted in Figure 21.1.
2. With your left hand, place the food to be breaded in the flour and coat it evenly. With the same hand, remove the floured item, shake off the excess flour and place it in the egg wash.
3. With your right hand, remove the item from the egg wash and place it in the bread crumbs or meal.
4. With your left hand, cover the item with crumbs or meal and press lightly to make sure the item is completely and evenly coated. Shake off the excess crumbs or meal and place the breaded food in the empty pan for the finished product.

The key is to use one hand for the liquid ingredients and the other hand for the dry ingredients. This prevents your fingers from becoming coated with layer after layer of breading.

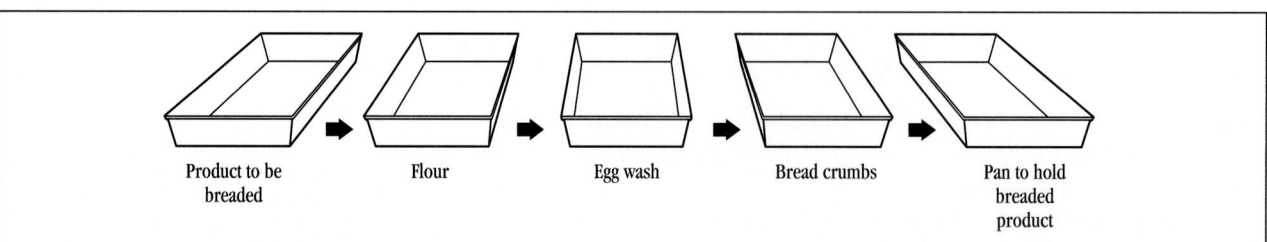

Product to be breaded   Flour   Egg wash   Bread crumbs   Pan to hold breaded product

FIGURE 21.1 *Setup for the Standard Breading Procedure*

Applying the Basics

RECIPE 21.1

DEEP-FRIED CATFISH FILLETS WITH TARTAR SAUCE

Yield: 8 Servings

Catfish fillets, uniform-size pieces	1.5 kg	3 lb.
Salt and pepper	TT	TT
Flour	as needed	as needed
Egg wash	as needed	as needed
White cornmeal	as needed	as needed
Tartar Sauce (Recipe 24.19)	350 mL	12 fl. oz.

1. Season the fillets with salt and pepper.
2. Bread the fillets using the standard breading procedure (the white cornmeal is the final coating).
3. Using the basket method, deep-fat fry the fillets until done. Drain well and serve with the tartar sauce.

RECIPE 21.1

Approximate values per serving:

Calories	75
Total fat	6 g
Saturated fat	1 g
Cholesterol	20 mg
Sodium	114 mg
Total carbohydrates	2 g
Protein	4 g

1. Flour the seasoned fish fillets.

2. Pass the floured fillets through the egg wash.

3. Coat the fillets with white cornmeal.

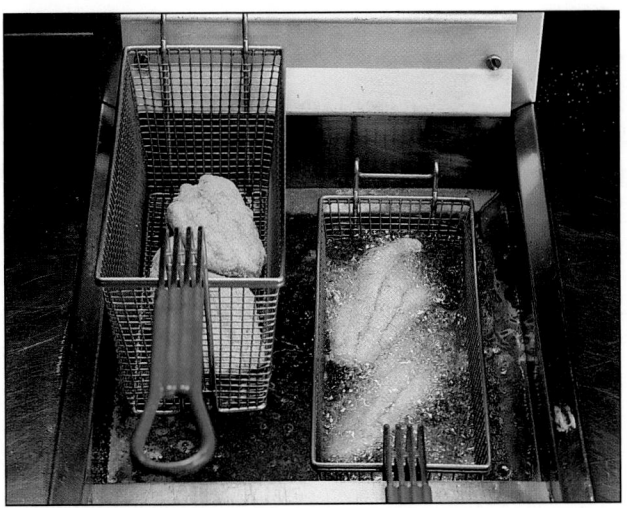

4. Deep-fat fry the fillets using the basket method.

Croquettes

Croquettes are cooked meats, poultry, vegetables, fish or potatoes, usually bound with a heavy béchamel or velouté sauce and seasoned. They are then breaded and deep-fat fried.

Applying the Basics

SALMON CROQUETTES

Yield: 12 Croquettes

Onion, small dice	50 g	2 oz.
Whole butter	90 g	3 oz.
Flour	100 g	3 oz.
Milk	250 mL	8 fl. oz.
Egg yolk	1	1
Salmon, poached and flaked	500 g	1 lb.
Fresh dill, chopped	20 g	2 Tbsp.
Salt and pepper	TT	TT
Lemon juice	15 mL	1 Tbsp.

1. Sweat the onion in the butter until translucent.
2. Add the flour and cook to make a white roux.
3. Add the milk to make a heavy béchamel sauce. Cook the sauce until very thick, approximately 5 minutes.
4. Remove the sauce from the heat and stir in the tempered egg yolk. Transfer it to a mixing bowl. Add the flaked salmon. Season the mixture with dill, salt, pepper and lemon juice and mix well.
5. Spread the mixture in a hotel pan, cover and refrigerate until cold.
6. Portion the mixture using a #20 portion scoop. Form each portion into a cone or other shape. Bread the croquettes using the standard breading procedure.
7. Using the basket method, deep-fat fry the breaded croquettes until done.

RECIPE 21.2

Approximate values
per 2 croquettes:

Calories	314
Total fat	17.6 g
Saturated fat	9.4 g
Cholesterol	130 mg
Sodium	198 mg
Total carbohydrates	16 g
Protein	23.6 g

1. Portion the croquette mixture with a portion scoop.

2. Form the mixture into cones or other shapes.

3. Deep-fat fry the croquettes using the basket method.

Battering Foods to Be Deep-Fat Fried

Batters, like breading, coat the food being cooked, keeping it moist and preventing it from becoming excessively greasy.

Batters consist of a liquid such as water, milk or beer, combined with a starch such as flour or cornstarch. Many batters also contain a chemical leavening agent such as baking powder. Two common batters are beer batter, which uses the beer for leavening as well as for flavour, and tempura batter.

Basic Procedure for Battering Foods

1. Pat the food dry and dredge in flour if desired.
2. Dip the item in the batter and place it directly in hot fat.

Applying the Basics

RECIPE 21.3

BEER-BATTERED ONION RINGS

Yield: 1 L (1 qt.), enough for approx. 1.5 kg (4 lb.) rings

Flour	300 g	10 oz.
Baking powder	7 g	2 tsp.
Salt	10 g	2 tsp.
White pepper	0.5 g	1/4 tsp.
Egg	1	1
Beer	500 mL	16 fl. oz.
Onions, whole	1.5 kg	4 lb.
Flour, for dredging	as needed	as needed

1. Sift the dry ingredients together.
2. Beat the egg in a separate bowl. Add the beer to the beaten egg.
3. Add the egg-and-beer mixture to the dry ingredients; mix until smooth.
4. Peel the onions and cut in 2-cm (1/2-inch) slices.
5. Break the slices into rings and dredge in flour.
6. Dip the rings in the batter a few at a time and fry at 190°C (375°F) until done. Drain on absorbent paper, season with additional salt and white pepper and serve hot.

RECIPE 21.3

Approximate values per 100 g serving:

Calories	255
Total fat	11 g
Saturated fat	3 g
Cholesterol	6 mg
Sodium	510 mg
Total carbohydrates	34 g
Protein	4.5 g

1. Dredge the onion rings in flour.

2. Dip the floured rings in batter.

3. Fry the onion rings using the swimming method.

♦♦♦
TEMPURA

Relatively new to Japanese cuisine, it originates from Portugal. The secret to excellent tempura is ice-cold batter and ice-cold ingredients. The tempura must be served immediately upon removal from the fryer.

Applying the Basics

RECIPE 21.4

TEMPURA SHRIMP AND VEGETABLES WITH DIPPING SAUCE

Yield: 1 L (1 qt.), enough for 1.8 kg (4 lb.) of vegetables or shrimp

Sweet potato	250 g	8 oz.
Dipping Sauce:		
Mirin	50 mL	2 fl. oz.
Soy sauce	100 mL	4 fl. oz.
Rice wine vinegar	50 mL	2 fl. oz.
Lemon juice	15 mL	1 Tbsp.
Wasabi powder	0.5 g	1 tsp.
Tempura Batter:		
Eggs	2	2
Water, ice cold	450 mL	16 fl. oz.
Baking soda	0.5 g	1/4 tsp.
Flour, bread	220 g	6 oz.
Shrimp, 21–25 count, butterflied with tails on	1 kg	2 lb.
Mushrooms, small, whole	450 g	1 lb.
Zucchini, batonnet	250 g	8 oz.

1. Peel the sweet potato and cut in 6-mm (1/4-inch) slices. If the potato is large, cut each slice in half to make semicircles.
2. Combine all ingredients for the dipping sauce. Set aside.
3. To prepare the batter, beat the eggs and cold water until frothy.
4. Add the baking soda and flour to the egg-and-water mixture and mix until it is incorporated. There should still be small lumps in the batter. Overmixing develops gluten, which is undesirable. Keep the batter very cold.
5. Dry the shrimp well and keep them thoroughly chilled. Holding them by the tail, dip them into the batter and drop them into a 190°C (375°F) deep-fat fryer using the swimming method. Cook until done.
6. Drop the vegetables into the batter a few at a time. Remove them from the batter one at a time and drop them into the deep-fat fryer using the swimming method. Cook until batter is a pale, golden colour and crisp.
7. Arrange the tempura shrimp and vegetables on a serving platter and present immediately. Serve the dipping sauce on the side.

RECIPE 21.4

Approximate values per 125 g serving:

Calories	500
Total fat	21 g
Saturated fat	4 g
Cholesterol	229 mg
Sodium	1543 mg
Total carbohydrates	42 g
Protein	29 g

Fritters

Fritters contain diced or chopped fish, shellfish, vegetables or fruits bound together with a thick batter and deep-fat fried. The main ingredient is usually precooked. Fritters are spooned or dropped directly into the hot fat; they form a crust as they cook. Popular examples are clam fritters, corn fritters, artichoke fritters and apple fritters.

Applying the Basics

RECIPE 21.5

APPLE FRITTERS

Yield: 100 5-cm (2-inch) Fritters

Eggs, separated	6	6
Milk	500 mL	16 fl. oz.

Flour, all purpose	500 g	1 lb.
Baking powder	10 g	1 Tbsp.
Salt	5 g	1 tsp.
Sugar	50 g	2 oz.
Cinnamon	1 g	1/2 tsp.
Apples, peeled, cored, medium dice	700 g	1 lb. 8 oz.
Powdered sugar	as needed	as needed

1. Combine the egg yolks and milk.
2. Sift together the flour, baking powder, salt, sugar and cinnamon. Add the dry ingredients to the milk-and-egg mixture; mix until smooth.
3. Allow the batter to rest 1 hour.
4. Stir the apples into the batter.
5. Just before the fritters are to be cooked, whip the egg whites to soft peaks and fold into the batter.
6. With a small scoop drop the fritters into 180°C (350°F) deep fat, using the swimming method. Cook until done.
7. Dust with powdered sugar and serve hot.

RECIPE 21.5

*Approximate values
per 125 g serving:*

Calories	62
Total fat	4.5 g
Saturated fat	1.3 g
Cholesterol	15.7 mg
Sodium	40.7 mg
Total carbohydrates	5.7 g
Protein	1.1 g

1. Add the dry ingredients to the liquids.

2. Fold the egg whites into the batter.

3. Drop the fritters into the deep fat.

4. Dust the fritters with powdered sugar.

DETERMINING DONENESS

When deep-fat frying, it is difficult to determine the doneness of foods, especially breaded or battered ones. The keen sense of timing that develops with experience is a useful tool. Otherwise:

1. Colour is the most commonly used method for determining doneness. Most fried foods should be deep golden-brown when done. However, colour can be deceiving. If the temperature of the fat is too high, the food's surface will darken quickly and appear done while the centre remains raw. Also, fat becomes dark with use; dark fat prematurely darkens food, again allowing foods to appear done before they are. Similarly, foods with high sugar content darken quickly in hot fat.

2. Large items such as fried chicken can be removed from the fat and checked with an instant-read thermometer. The internal temperature should be 74–77°C (165–170°F) for chicken.

3. Fish and shellfish cook quickly and are easily overcooked. If practical, remove a piece and cut it open to determine its doneness. Then rely on timing and colour for the remaining batches.

4. Vegetables should be tender when their surfaces are the proper colour.

5. Potatoes should be attractively browned and cooked to the desired crispness.

Generally, foods must be completely cooked in the deep-fat fryer. It is possible, however, to finish some foods (for example, fried chicken) in the oven after being browned in the fat. However, there is a problem to doing so. As the food cooks in the oven, moisture is released that may cause the breading to become soggy on the bottom. Placing the food on a rack can help alleviate this problem.

CONCLUSION

Deep-fat frying is a useful and versatile dry-heat cooking method. To produce high-quality deep-fried foods it is important to understand what foods respond well to deep-fat frying and how to prepare them for cooking. You must also understand how to prevent deep-fried foods from becoming excessively greasy by properly coating them with batters or breadings and controlling cooking temperatures. Finally, you must understand how to determine doneness. By following the guidelines discussed in this chapter you will be able to consistently produce the desired results.

QUESTIONS FOR DISCUSSION

1. What qualities should be considered when choosing a fat for deep-fat frying?
2. Name and describe two styles of deep-fat frying.
3. List three signs that fryer fat has broken down and should be replaced. What causes fryer fat to break down? What can you do to extend the life of fryer fat?
4. Explain the differences between breading and battering foods for deep-fat frying.
5. Describe the correct mise en place for the standard breading procedure.
6. Explain several similarities and differences between fritters and croquettes.

Additional Deep-Fat Frying Recipe

RECIPE 21.6

Whole Sizzling Catfish with Ginger and Ponzu Sauce

Note: *This dish appears in the Chapter Opening photograph.*

CHINOIS ON MAIN, SANTA MONICA, CA
Chef Wolfgang Puck

Yield: 4 Servings

Catfish, cleaned, 1.3 kg (3 lb.)	1	1
Salt and pepper	TT	TT
Fresh ginger, sliced and blanched	6 pieces	6 pieces
Peanut oil	as needed	as needed
Lemon juice	as needed	as needed
Ponzu Sauce:		
Soy sauce	125 mL	4 fl. oz.
Mirin	125 mL	4 fl. oz.
Rice vinegar	125 mL	4 fl. oz.
Lemon juice	125 mL	4 fl. oz.
Fresh wood ear mushrooms	as needed for garnish	
Fresh cilantro	as needed for garnish	
Green onions	as needed for garnish	

1. Season the catfish with salt and pepper. Make three 5-cm (2-inch) incisions on each side of the fish and stuff each incision with blanched ginger.
2. Deep-fat fry the catfish in peanut oil, being careful to submerge the entire fish. Cook until golden-coloured and crispy.
3. Squeeze fresh lemon juice over top the fish.
4. Make the Ponzu Sauce by combining the listed ingredients.
5. Serve the whole catfish on a platter garnished with wood ear mushrooms, cilantro and green onions. Serve the Ponzu Sauce on the side.

RECIPE 21.6

Approximate values per serving:

Calories	958
Total fat	45 g
Saturated fat	11.5 g
Cholesterol	328 mg
Sodium	2598 mg
Total carbohydrates	58 g
Protein	72.3 g

Weblinks

Learn2 Shop for Cooking Oils
  learn2.com/08/0864/08646.html

Canola Oil Frying Tips
  www.canolainfo.org/html/fry.html

American Council on Science and Health: The Fat Wars (article by Agnes Heinz, Ph.D., discussing public misconceptions about fat consumption)
  www.acsh.org/publications/priorities/0301/fatwars.html

Recipes
  www.cooksrecipes.com/tips/deep-fat-frying-basics.html

Frying
  www.farwestmeats.com/Frying.htm

CHAPTER 22

VEGETABLES

*L*ong overcooked and underrated, vegetables are enjoying a welcome surge in popularity. Gone are the days when a chef included vegetables as an afterthought to the "meat and potatoes" of the meal. Now, properly prepared fresh vegetables are used to add flavour, colour and variety to almost any meal. Many restaurants are featuring vegetarian entrees, an extensive selection of vegetable side dishes or an entire vegetarian menu. This trend reflects the demands of more knowledgeable and health-conscious consumers as well as the increased availability of high-quality fresh produce.

In this chapter we identify many of the vegetables typically used by food service operations. (Potatoes, although vegetables, are discussed in Chapter 23, Potatoes, Grains and Pasta, and salad greens are discussed in Chapter 24, Salads and Salad Dressings.) Here we also discuss how fresh and preserved vegetables are purchased, stored and prepared for service or cooking. Many of the cooking methods analyzed in Chapter 9, Principles of Cooking, are then applied to vegetables.

The term **vegetable** refers to any herbaceous plant that can be partially or wholly eaten. An herbaceous plant has little or no woody tissue. The portions we consume include the leaves, stems, roots, tubers, seeds and flowers. Vegetables contain more starch and less sugar than fruits. Therefore vegetables tend to be savoury, not sweet. Also unlike fruits, vegetables are most often eaten cooked, not raw.

IDENTIFYING VEGETABLES

This book presents fruits and vegetables according to the ways most people view them and use them, rather than by rigid botanical classifications. Although produce such as tomatoes, peppers and eggplants are botanically fruits, they are prepared and served like vegetables and are included here under the category we call "fruit-vegetables." Potatoes, although botanically vegetables, are discussed with other starches in Chapter 23, Potatoes, Grains and Pasta.

We divide vegetables into 11 categories based upon either botanical relationship or edible part. They are: bulb, flower/bud, fungus, leafy, pod, root, legume/pulse, shoot, stalk, tuber and fruit type. Some people recognize more and fewer categories. There is no definitive answer to what a vegetable is. A vegetable may have several names, varying from region to region or on a purveyor's whim. The names given here follow generally accepted custom and usage.

Flowers/Buds

The *Brassica* or cabbage family includes a wide range of vegetables used for their heads, flowers or leaves. They are generally quick-growing, cool-weather crops. Many are ancient plants with unknown origins. They are inexpensive, readily available and easy to prepare.

Bok Choy

Bok choy, also known as pok choy, is a white-stemmed variety of southern Chinese cabbage. The relatively tightly packed leaves are dark green, with long white ribs attached at a bulbous stem. The stalks are crisp and mild with a flavour similar to romaine lettuce. Although bok choy may be eaten raw, it is most often stir-fried or used in soups.

Choose heads with bright white stalks and dark green leaves; avoid those with brown, moist spots. Fresh bok choy is available all year. Jars of pickled and fermented bok choy (known as Korean kim chee) are also available. Baby bok choy is popular with restaurateurs.

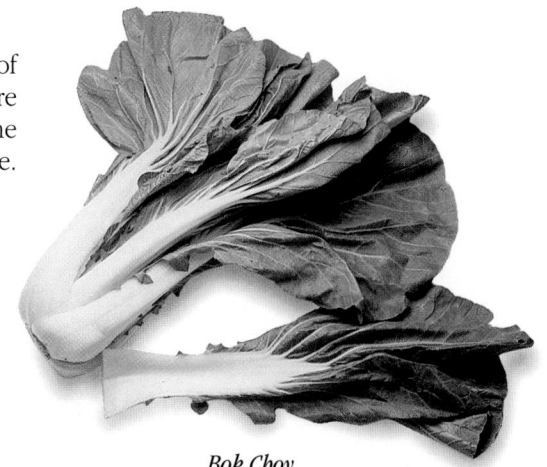

Bok Choy

Broccoli

Broccoli, a type of flower, has a thick central stalk with greyish-green leaves topped with one or more heads of green florets. Broccoli may be eaten raw or steamed, microwaved or sautéed and served warm or cold. Broccoli stalks are extremely firm and benefit from blanching. Stems are often slow-cooked for soups. Generally, broccoli leaves are not eaten.

Choose firm stalks with compact clusters of tightly closed dark green florets. Avoid stalks with yellow flowers. Broccoli is available all year. Rapini or rabé is now widely used.

Broccoli

Basic Procedure for Cutting Broccoli Spears

Cut off the thick, woody portion of the stalk, then cut the florets and stems into spears. Peel the stalk and use in stir-frys.

Brussels Sprouts

Brussels sprouts (Fr. *choux de Bruxelles*) were first cultivated around 1700. The plant produces numerous small heads arranged in neat rows along a thick stalk. The tender young sprouts are similar to baby cabbages and are usually steamed or roasted. Brussels sprouts have a strong, nutty flavour that blends well with game, ham, duck or rich meats.

Brussels Sprouts

Choose small, firm sprouts that are compact and heavy. The best size is 2 to 4 cm (3/4 to 1-1/2 inches) in diameter. They should be bright green and free of blemishes. Their peak season is from September through February.

Cauliflower

Cauliflower (Fr. *chou-fleur*) is the king of the cabbage family. Each stalk produces one flower or head surrounded by large green leaves. The head, composed of creamy white florets, can be cooked whole or cut into separate florets for steaming, blanching or stir-frying.

Cauliflower

Choose firm, compact heads. Any attached leaves should be bright green and crisp. A yellow colour or spreading florets indicate that the vegetable is overly mature. Cauliflower is available all year, especially from the late fall through the spring. A cross of cauliflower and broccoli called broccoflower is available.

Basic Procedure for Cutting Cauliflower Florets

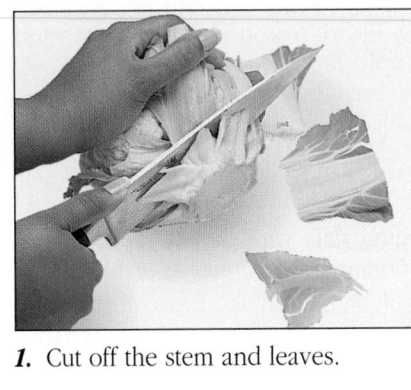

1. Cut off the stem and leaves.

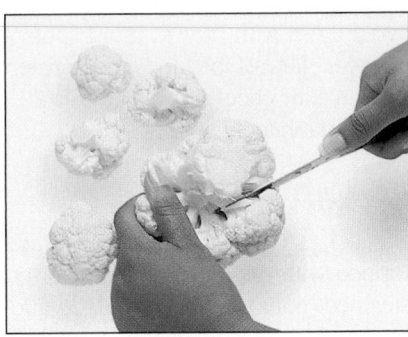

2. Cut the florets off the core.

Green and Red Cabbages

Green and Red Cabbages

Cabbage (Fr. *chou*) has been a staple of northern European cuisine for centuries. The familiar green cabbages have large, firm, round heads with tightly packed pale green leaves, which are actually flower petals. Flat and conical-shaped heads are also available. Red (or purple) cabbages are a different strain and may be tougher than green cabbages. When cooking red cabbage an acid (vinegar) is used to preserve the red colour. Cabbage can be eaten raw (as in coleslaw) or used in soups or stews; it can be braised, steamed or stir-fried. The large, waxy leaves can also be steamed until soft, then wrapped around a filling of seasoned meat.

Choose firm heads without dried cores. Cabbages are available all year.

Kale

Kale has large ruffled, curly or bumpy leaves. Its rather bitter flavour goes well with rich meats such as game, pork or ham. Kale is typically boiled, stuffed or used in soups.

Choose leaves that are crisp, with a greyish-green colour. Kale is available all year, with peak season during the winter months.

Ornamental or flowering kale, sometimes marketed as "savoy," is edible, but its pink, purple, yellow or white-and-green variegated leaves are best used for decoration and garnish.

Kale

Ornamental Kale

Napa Cabbage

Napa cabbage, also known as Chinese cabbage, is widely used in Asian cuisines. It has a stout, elongated head with relatively tightly packed, firm, pale green leaves. It is moister and more tender than common green and red cabbages, with a milder, more delicate flavour. Napa cabbage may be eaten raw but is particularly well suited for stir-frying or steaming.

Choose heads with crisp leaves that are free of blemishes. Napa cabbage is available fresh all year.

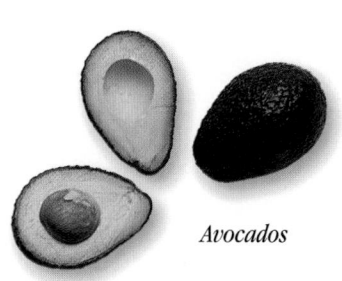

Napa Cabbage

Savoy

Savoy cabbage has curly or ruffled leaves, often in variegated shades of green and purple. (The term "savoyed" is used to refer to any vegetable with bumpy, wavy or wrinkled leaves.) Savoy cabbage tends to be milder and more tender than regular cabbages and can be substituted for them, cooked or uncooked. Savoy leaves also make an attractive garnish.

Choose heads that are loose or tight, depending on the variety, with tender, unblemished leaves. Peak season is from August through the spring.

Savoy

Fruit-Vegetables

Botanists classify avocados, eggplants, peppers, tomatoes, gourds and squashes as fruits because they develop from the ovary of flowering plants and contain one or more seeds. Chefs, however, prepare and serve them like vegetables; therefore, they are discussed here.

Avocados

Avocados include several varieties of pear-shaped fruits with rich, high-fat flesh. This light golden-green flesh surrounds a large, inedible, oval-shaped seed (pit). Some varieties have smooth, green skin; others have pebbly, almost black skin. Avocados should be used at their peak of ripeness, a condition that lasts only briefly. Firm avocados lack the desired flavour and creamy texture. Ripe avocados should be soft to the touch but not mushy. Ripe Haas avocados have almost-black skins; the skins of the other varieties remain green when ripe. Firm avocados can be left at room temperature to ripen, then refrigerated for one or two days. Avocados are most often used raw to garnish salads, mashed or puréed for sauces, sliced for sandwiches or diced for omelettes. Avocado halves are popular containers for chilled meat, fish, shellfish or poultry salads. Because avocado flesh turns brown very quickly once cut, dip avocado halves or slices in lemon juice and keep unused portions tightly covered with plastic wrap.

Choose avocados that are free of blemishes or moist spots. The flesh should be free of dark spots or streaks. Available all year, the peak season for Haas avocados is April through October; for Fuertes avocados it is November through April.

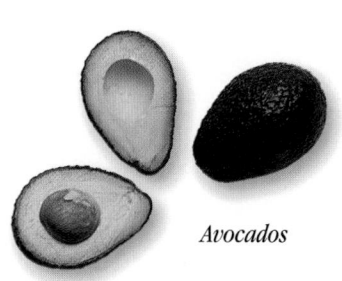

Avocados

Basic Procedure for Cutting and Pitting Avocados

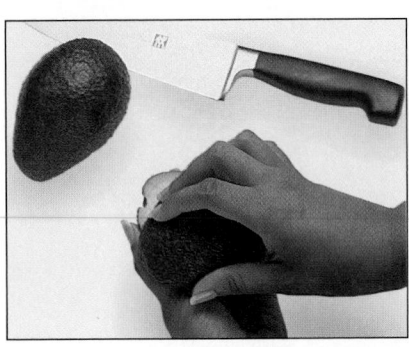

1. Cut the avocado in half lengthwise. Separate the two halves with a twisting motion.

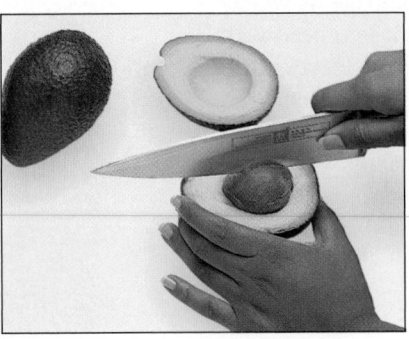

2. Insert a chef's knife into the pit and twist to remove.

3. Scoop the flesh out of the skin with a large spoon.

Western Eggplant

Eggplants

Two types of eggplants (Fr. *aubergine*) are commonly available: Asian and western. Asian varieties are either round or long and thin, with skin colours ranging from creamy white to deep purple. Western eggplants, which are more common in North America, tend to be shaped like a plump pear with shiny lavender to purple-black skin. Both types have a dense, khaki-coloured flesh with a rather bland flavour that absorbs other flavours well during cooking. Eggplants can be grilled, baked, steamed, fried or sautéed. They are commonly used in Mediterranean and East Indian cuisines (especially in vegetarian dishes), but also appear in European and North American dishes. The skin may be left intact or removed before or after cooking, as desired. Sliced eggplants may be salted and left to drain for 30 minutes to remove moisture and bitterness before cooking and to reduce oil absorption.

Asian Eggplants

Choose plump, heavy eggplants with a smooth, shiny skin that is not blemished or wrinkled. Asian varieties tend to be softer than western. Eggplants are available all year, with peak season during the late summer.

Peppers

Members of the *Capsicum* family are native to the Americas. When "discovered" by Christopher Columbus he called them "peppers" because of their sometimes fiery flavour. These peppers, which include sweet peppers and hot peppers (chiles), are unrelated to peppercorns, the East Indian (Asian) spice for which Columbus was actually searching. Interestingly, "New World" peppers were readily accepted in Indian and Asian cuisines, in which they are now considered staples.

Fresh peppers are found in a wide range of colours—green, red, yellow, orange, purple or white—as well as shapes, from tiny teardrops to cones to spheres. They have dense flesh and a hollow central cavity. The flesh is lined with placental ribs (the white internal veins), to which tiny white seeds are attached. A core of seeds is also attached to the stem end of each pepper.

Chile peppers get their heat from capsaicin, which is found not in the flesh or seeds, but in the placental ribs. Thus a pepper's heat can be greatly reduced by carefully removing the ribs and attached seeds. Generally, the smaller the chile, the hotter it is. The amount of heat varies from variety to variety, however, and even from one pepper to another depending on growing conditions. Hot, dry conditions result in hotter peppers than do cool, moist conditions. A pepper's heat can be measured by Scoville Heat Units, a subjective rating in which the sweet bell pepper usually rates 0 units, the jalapeño rates from 2500 to 5000 units, the tabasco rates from 30 000 to 50 000 units and the habanero rates a whopping 100 000 to 300 000 units.

When selecting peppers, choose those that are plump and brilliantly coloured with smooth, unblemished skins. Avoid wrinkled, pitted or blistered peppers. A bright green stem indicates freshness.

Green Bell Pepper

Sweet Peppers

Common sweet peppers, known as bell peppers, are thick-walled fruits available in green, red, yellow, purple, orange and other colours. They are heart-shaped or boxy, with a short stem and crisp flesh. Their flavour is warm, sweet (red peppers tend to be the sweetest) and relatively mild. Raw bell peppers may be sliced or diced and used in salads or sandwiches. Bell peppers may also be stuffed and baked, grilled, fried, sautéed or puréed for soups, sauces or condiments. Green bell peppers are available all year; other types are more readily available during the summer and fall. Many coloured peppers are greenhouse-grown.

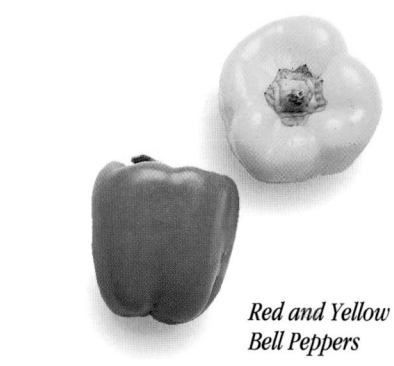

Red and Yellow Bell Peppers

Basic Procedure for Cutting Peppers Julienne

1. Trim off the ends of the pepper; cut away the seeds and core.

2. Cut away the pale ribs, trimming the flesh to the desired thickness.

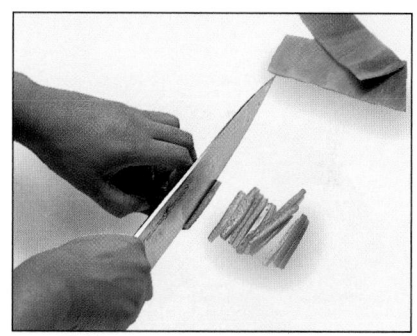

3. Slice the flesh in julienne.

Hot Peppers

Hot peppers, also known as chiles, are also members of the *Capsicum* family. Although a chile's most characteristic attribute is its pungency, each chile actually has a distinctive flavour, from mild and rich to spicy and sweet to fiery hot.

Chiles are commonly used in Asian, Indian, Mexican and Latin American cuisines. The larger (and milder) of the hot peppers, such as Anaheim and poblano, can be stuffed and baked or sautéed as a side dish. Most chiles, however, are used to add flavour and seasoning to sauces and other dishes. Fresh chiles are available all year and are also available canned in a variety of processed forms such as whole or diced roasted, pickled or marinated plus dried forms.

(clockwise from bottom left) Red and Green Serrano; Green and Red Jalapeño; Yellow Hot; Poblano; and Anaheim Chiles.

The popularity of Southwestern cuisine, hot condiments and salsas has brought with it a new appreciation and respect for chiles. Diners, and cooks, may find the names given to the various chiles confusing, however. Most chiles can be used either fresh or dried; drying changes not only the pepper's flavour, but also its name. Regional variations in chile names also add to the confusion. Several of the more frequently encountered chiles are listed here according to the names most commonly used for both their fresh and their dried forms.

Fresh (Fresco)	Dried (Seco)
Anaheim	Mild Red or California
Chilaca	Pasilla or Negro
Jalapeño	Chipotle (smoked)
Mirasol	Guajillo
New Mexico Green	New Mexico Red
New Mexico Red	Chile Colorado
Pimento	Paprika
Poblano	Ancho or Mulato

Dried Chiles

Tomatillos

Procedure for Coring Jalapeños

Cut the jalapeño in half lengthwise. Push the core and seeds out with your thumb. You can avoid burning your fingers by wearing rubber gloves when working with hot chiles.

Dried chiles are widely used in Mexican, Central American and southwestern cuisines. They may be ground to create a powdered spice called chilli or soaked in liquid, then puréed, for sauces or condiments. Drying radically alters the flavour of chiles, making them stronger and more pungent. Dried chiles are often called by names different from those of their fresh versions. For example, the fresh poblano becomes the dried ancho; the fresh jalapeño becomes the dried, smoked chipotle.

Choose dried chiles that are clean and unbroken, with some flexibility. Avoid any with white spots or a stale aroma.

Basic Procedure for Roasting Peppers

1. Roast the pepper over an open flame until completely charred. Place in a tightly covered bowl to steam.

2. Remove the burnt skin and rinse under running water.

Tomatillos

Tomatillos, also known as Mexican or husk tomatoes, grow on small, weedy bushes. They are bright green, about the size of a small tomato, and are covered with a thin, papery husk. They have a tart, lemony flavour and crisp, moist flesh. Although an important ingredient in southwestern and northern Mexican cuisines, tomatillos may not be readily available in other areas. Tomatillos can be used raw in salads, puréed for salsa or cooked in soups, stews or vegetable dishes.

Choose tomatillos whose husks are split but still look fresh. The skin should be plump, shiny and slightly sticky. They are available all year, with peak season during the summer and fall. Wash them after husking.

Tomatoes

Tomatoes (Fr. *tomate* or *pomme d'amour;* It. *pomodoro*) are available in a wide variety of colours and shapes. They vary from green (unripe) to golden yellow to ruby red; from tiny spheres (currant tomatoes) to huge, squat ovals (beefsteak). Some, such as the plum tomato, have lots of meaty flesh with only a few seeds; others, such as the slicing tomato, have lots of seeds and juice, but only a few meaty membranes. All tomatoes have a similar flavour, but the levels of sweetness and acidity vary depending on the species, growing conditions and ripeness at harvest.

Because tomatoes are highly perishable, they are usually harvested when mature but still green (unripe), then shipped to wholesalers who ripen them in temperature- and humidity-controlled rooms. The effect on flavour and texture is unfortunate.

Tomatoes are used widely in salads, soups, sauces and baked dishes. They are most often eaten raw, but can be grilled, pickled, pan-fried, roasted or sautéed as a side dish.

Choose fresh tomatoes that are plump with a smooth, shiny skin. The colour should be uniform and true for the variety. Tomatoes are available all year, with a summer peak season for most varieties. Many canned tomato products are also available (for example, purée, paste, sauce or stewed whole), as are dried tomatoes. Heirloom varieties are now being grown and marketed.

(clockwise from lower right) Pear, Cherry, Plum and Beefsteak Tomatoes

---

♦♦♦
THREE TREASURES
OF THE NEW WORLD

In lieu of many spices, golden treasures and precious gems, early Spanish explorers returned to Spain with items of much greater significance: tomatoes, potatoes and corn. Unfortunately for those who financed the voyagers, the value of this produce was not immediately appreciated.

The Spanish and the Italians hailed the tomato (whose name comes from the Aztec name *tomatl*) as an aphrodisiac—perhaps because of its resemblance to the human heart—when it arrived from the New World during the 16th century. However, even though tomatoes soon became part of Spanish and Italian cuisines, most other Europeans, New World colonists and, later, Americans considered tomatoes poisonous. (There is some truth to this notion: tomato vines and leaves contain tomatine, an alkaloid that can cause health problems.) Thus for many years and in many societies, only the adventurous ate tomatoes. Tomato historians consider September 26, 1820, a red-letter day marking the popular acceptance of the tomato. On that day, the then-well-known eccentric Colonel Robert Gibbon Johnson ate an entire bushel of toma-

toes on the Salem, New Jersey, courthouse steps before a crowd of thousands—and lived. Tomatoes soon became one of the most popular of all vegetables.

Similarly, the potato, first delivered to Europe from its native Peru by Francisco Pizarro in the 16th century, did not win wide acceptance in haute cuisine until Antoine-Augustin Parmentier (1737–1813), a French army pharmacist, induced King Louis XVI of France (reign 1775–1793) to try one. He and his courtiers liked them so much they even began wearing potato blossom boutonnières. Parmentier was ultimately honoured for his starchy contribution to French cuisine by having several potato dishes named for him. Indeed, the French still call potato soup *potage Parmentier* in his honour. Not only did Parmentier lobby for the acceptance of the potato as a food fit for a king, he also prophesied that the potato would make starvation impossible. Potatoes ultimately did become a staple of many diets. However, sadly, the converse of Parmentier's prophecy came true during the Irish Potato Famine of 1846–1848, when a terrible blight destroyed the potato crop.

Nearly 1.5 million people died and an equal number emigrated to North America. They brought with them a cuisine that incorporated potatoes; thus an appreciation of the common potato was reintroduced to its native land.

When returning from his second voyage to the New World, Columbus took corn with him. Called *mahiz* or *maize* by West Indian natives, corn had been a staple of Central American diets for at least 5000 years. Although Europeans did not actively shun corn as they did tomatoes and potatoes, corn never really caught on in most of Europe. (As with another famous New World import, corn's origin was mistakenly attributed by the British, Dutch, Germans and Russians to Turkey. They called corn "Turkish wheat"; the Turks simply called it "foreign grain.") Grown for human consumption mostly in Italy, Spain and southwestern France, corn was and still is usually eaten ground and boiled as polenta. However, despite an unenthusiastic European reception, corn's popularity quickly spread well beyond Europe: Within 50 years of Columbus's journey, corn was being cultivated in lands as distant from the New World as China, India and sub-Saharan Africa.

◆◆◆

TOMATO CONCASSÉE

Traditionally, a concassée is sweated with a small amount of oil and shallots. Current interpretation usually means peeled, seeded and diced tomato flesh. Plum tomatoes have the best yield.

Basic Procedure for Making Tomato Concassée

1. With a paring knife, mark an X on the bottom of the tomato just deep enough to penetrate the skin.

2. Blanch the tomato in boiling water for 20 seconds; refresh in ice water.

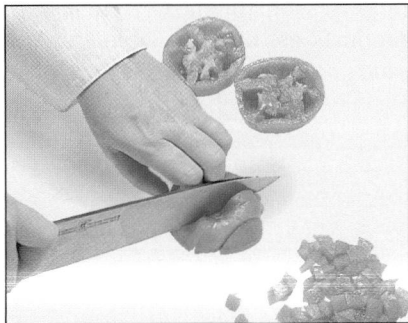

3. Using a paring knife, cut out the core and peel the tomato.

4. Cut the tomato in half horizontally and squeeze out the seeds and juice. A melon baller can be used to ensure that all of the seeds are removed.

5. Chop or dice the tomato as desired for the recipe. Strain juice for further use.

Cucumbers

Cucumbers can be divided into two categories: pickling and slicing. The two types are not interchangeable. Pickling cucumbers include the cornichon, dill and gherkin. They are recognizable by their sharp black or white spines and are quite bitter when raw. Slicing cucumbers include the burpless, the seedless English (or hothouse), the lemon (which is round and yellow) and the common green field cucumber. Most have relatively thin skins and may be marketed with a wax coating to prevent moisture loss and improve appearance. Waxed skins should be peeled. All cucumbers are valued for their refreshing cool taste and astringency. Slicing cucumbers are usually served raw, in salads or mixed with yogurt and dill or mint as a side dish, especially for spicy dishes. Pickling cucumbers are generally served pickled, without any further processing.

Choose cucumbers that are firm but not hard. Avoid those that are limp, yellowed or have soft spots. The common varieties are available all year, although peak season is from April through October.

(from left to right) Pickling, Green and English (Hothouse) Cucumbers

Gourds and Squashes

The *Cucurbitaceae* or gourd family includes almost 750 species; its members are found in warm regions worldwide. Gourds are characterized by large, complex root systems with quick-growing, trailing vines and large leaves. Their flowers are often attractive and edible. Although some members of the gourd family originated in Africa, chayotes and most squashes are native to the Americas.

Chayotes

The chayote, also known as merliton or vegetable pear, is a food staple throughout Central America. The vine bears slightly lumpy, pear-shaped fruits with a smooth, light green skin and a paler green flesh. There is a single white, edible seed in the centre. Chayotes are starchy and very bland and are usually combined with more flavourful ingredients. They may be eaten raw, but their flavour and texture benefit from roasting, steaming, sautéing or grilling.

Choose chayotes that have well-coloured skin with few ridges. Avoid those with very soft spots or bruises. Their peak season is the late fall and winter.

Chayotes

Squashes

Squashes are the fleshy fruits of a large number of plants in the gourd family. Many varieties are available in a range of colours, shapes and sizes. Squashes can be classified as winter or summer based on their peak season and skin type. All squashes have a centre cavity filled with many seeds, although in winter varieties the cavity is more pronounced. Squash blossoms are also edible: They may be added to salads raw, dipped in batter and deep-fat fried or filled with cheese or meat and baked.

Choose squashes with unbroken skins and good colour for the variety. Avoid any squash with soft, moist spots.

Winter squashes include the acorn, banana, butternut, Hubbard, pumpkin and spaghetti varieties. They have hard skins (shells) and seeds. Pumpkin seeds are roasted and eaten. The flesh, which may be removed from the shell before or after cooking, tends to be sweeter and more strongly flavoured than that of summer squash. Winter squashes should not be served raw; they can be baked, steamed or sautéed. Most winter squashes can also be puréed for soups or pie fillings. Their peak season is October through March.

Spaghetti

Banana

Acorn

Pumpkin

Butternut

Zucchini

Summer squashes include the pattypan, yellow crookneck and zucchini (courgette) varieties. They have soft edible skins and seeds that are generally not removed before cooking. Most summer squashes may be eaten raw, but are also suitable for grilling, sautéing, steaming or baking. Although summer squashes are now available all year, their peak season is April through September.

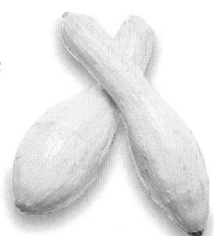

Yellow Crookneck

Leafy Greens

The term *leafy* refers to a variety of leafy green vegetables that may be served raw, but are usually cooked. Greens have long been used in the cuisines of India, Asia and the Mediterranean and are an important part of regional cuisine in the southern United States. Most have strong, spicy flavours. Mustard, sorrel, spinach, Swiss chard, dandelion and turnip greens fall into this category. The milder varieties of greens that are eaten almost always raw include the lettuces discussed in Chapter 24, Salads and Salad Dressings.

Greens have an extremely high water content, which means that cooking causes drastic shrinkage. As a general rule, allow 250 g (8 oz.) per portion before cooking.

Choose young, tender greens with good colour and no limpness. Avoid greens with dry-looking stems or yellow leaves. Most greens are available fresh all year, especially from November through June. The more popular greens are also available canned or frozen.

Mustard

Mustard, a member of the cabbage family, was brought to North America by early European immigrants. Mustard has large, dark green leaves with frilly edges. It is known for its assertive, bitter flavour. Mustard greens can be served raw in salads or used as garnish. Or they can be cooked, often with white wine, vinegar and herbs.

Choose crisp, bright green leaves without discolouration.

Mustard

Sorrel

Sorrel is an abundant and rather ordinary wild member of the buckwheat family. Its tartness and sour flavour are used in soups and sauces and to accent other vegetables. It is particularly good with fatty fish or rich meats. Sorrel leaves naturally acquire the texture of a purée after only a few minutes of moist-heat cooking.

Choose leaves that are fully formed, with no yellow blemishes.

Sorrel

Spinach

Spinach (Fr. *épinard*) is a versatile green that grows rapidly in cool climates. It has smooth, bright green leaves attached to thin stems. Spinach may be eaten raw in salads, cooked by almost any moist-heat method, microwaved or sautéed. It can be used in stuffings, baked or creamed dishes, soups or stews. Spinach grows in sandy soil and must be rinsed repeatedly in cold water to remove all traces of grit from the leaves. It bruises easily and should be handled gently during washing. Stems and large mid-ribs should be removed.

Choose bunches with crisp, tender, deep green leaves; avoid yellow, blemished leaves. Picked, washed spinach leaves are readily available.

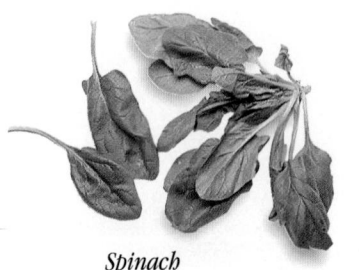

Spinach

Swiss Chard

Chard—the reference to "Swiss" is inexplicable—is a type of beet that does not produce a tuberous root. It is used for its wide, flat, dark green leaves. Chard can be steamed, sautéed or used in soups. Its tart, spinachlike flavour blends well with sweet ingredients such as fruit.

Choose leaves that are crisp, with some curliness or savoying. Ribs should be an unblemished white or red.

Turnip Greens

The leaves of the turnip root have a pleasantly bitter flavour, similar to peppery mustard greens. The dark green leaves are long, slender and deeply indented. Turnip greens are best eaten steamed, sautéed, baked or microwaved.

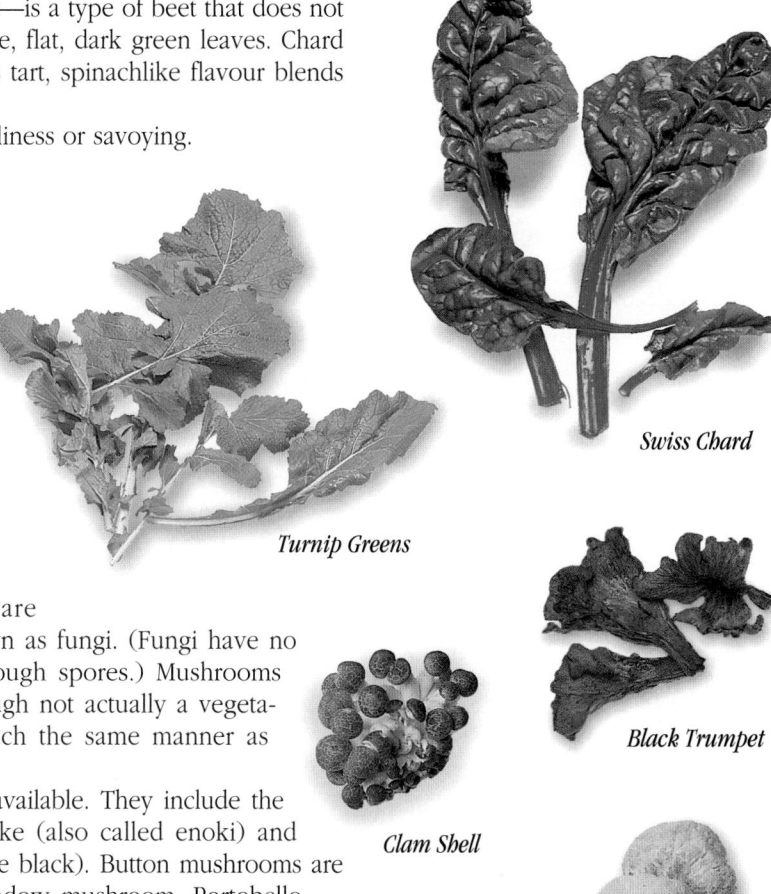

Swiss Chard

Turnip Greens

Fungi

Mushrooms

Mushrooms (Fr. *champignon*; It. *funghi*) are members of a broad category of plants known as fungi. (Fungi have no seeds, stems or flowers; they reproduce through spores.) Mushrooms have a stalk with an umbrellalike top. Although not actually a vegetable, mushrooms are used and served in much the same manner as vegetables.

Several types of cultivated mushroom are available. They include the meadow (or white), shiitake, straw, enokidake (also called enoki) and cloud ear (also known as wood ear or Chinese black). Button mushrooms are the smallest, most immature form of the meadow mushroom. Portobello and crimini are now commonly available, along with chanterelles, lobster, oyster, porcini and morels.

Many wild mushrooms are gathered and sold by specialty purveyors. Because wild mushroom spores are spread around the world by air currents, the same item may be found in several areas, each with a different common name. Wild mushrooms have a stronger earthy or nutty flavour than cultivated mushrooms, and should generally be cooked before eating.

Mushrooms, whether cultivated or gathered from the wild, are available fresh, canned or dried. Because mushrooms are composed of up to 80% water, dried products are often the most economical, even though they may cost hundreds of dollars per kilogram. Dried mushrooms can be stored in a cool, dry place for months. When needed, they are rehydrated by soaking in warm water until soft, approximately 10–20 minutes.

Choose fresh mushrooms that are clean, without soft or moist spots or blemishes. Fresh cultivated mushrooms are generally available all year; fresh wild mushrooms are available seasonally, usually during the summer and fall. Cultivated mushrooms with exposed gills (the ridges on

Black Trumpet

Clam Shell

Pom Pom Blanc

Hen of the Woods

Morel

Porcini (cèpe or cep)

Enokidake

Oyster

Shiitake

White

♦♦♦
MUSHROOM SAFETY

Some mushrooms are deadly; others can cause severe illness. Picking edible mushrooms in the wild is not simply a process of comparing specimens with photographs or illustrations in a guidebook. So, do not gather mushrooms from the wild unless you are accompanied by a well-trained, experienced mycologist or guide. Always purchase wild mushrooms from reputable purveyors.

the underside of the umbrellalike top) are old and should be avoided. Fresh mushrooms can be refrigerated in an open container for up to five days. Normally, it is not necessary to peel mushrooms; if they are dirty, they should be quickly rinsed (not soaked) in cool water just before use.

Truffles

Truffles are actually tubers that grow near the roots of oak or beech trees. They can be cultivated only to the extent that oak groves are planted to encourage truffle growth. The two principal varieties are the Périgord (black) and the Piedmontese (white). Fresh truffles are gathered in the fall and are rarely marketed outside their locale. Truffles, especially white ones, have a strong aroma and flavour, requiring only a small amount to add their special flavour to soups, sauces, pasta and other items. Black truffles are often used as a garnish or to flavour pâtés, terrines or egg dishes. Because fresh imported truffles can cost several hundred dollars per kilogram, most kitchens purchase truffles canned, dried or frozen.

Black Truffles

Bulbs

Onions are strongly flavoured, aromatic members of the lily family and are the most widely known bulb. Most have edible grasslike or tubular leaves. Almost every culture incorporates them into its cuisine as a vegetable and for flavouring.

Bulb Onions

Common or bulb onions (Fr. *oignons*) may be white, yellow (Spanish) or red (Bermuda). Medium-sized yellow and white onions are the most strongly flavoured. Larger onions (Vidalia) tend to be sweeter and milder. Widely used as a flavouring ingredient, onions are indispensable in mirepoix. Onions are also prepared as a side dish by deep-fat frying, roasting, grilling, steaming or boiling.

Pearl onions are small, about 1.25 cm (1/2 inch) in diameter, with yellow, red or white skins. They have a mild flavour and can be grilled, boiled, roasted or sautéed whole as a side dish, or used in soups or stews.

Choose onions that are firm, dry and feel heavy. The outer skins should be dry and brittle. Avoid onions that have begun to sprout. They should be stored in a cool, dry, well-ventilated area. Do not refrigerate onions until they are cut. Onions are available all year.

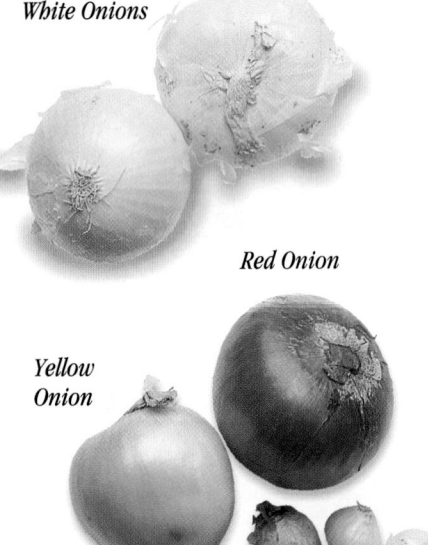

White Onions

Red Onion

Yellow Onion

Shallots   *Pearl Onions*

Fennel

Fennel (Fr. *fenouil*) is a Mediterranean favourite used for thousands of years as a vegetable (the bulb), an herb (the leaves) and a spice (the seeds). The bulb (often incorrectly referred to as sweet anise) has short, tight, overlapping celerylike stalks with feathery leaves. The flavour is similar to anise or licorice, becoming milder when cooked. Fennel bulbs may be eaten raw or grilled, steamed, sautéed, baked or microwaved.

Choose fairly large, bright white bulbs on which the cut edges appear fresh, without dryness or browning. The bulb should be compact, not spreading. Fresh fennel's peak season is September through May.

Fennel

Garlic

Garlic (Fr. *ail*; Sp. *ajo*) is also used in almost all of the world's cuisines. A head of garlic is composed of many small cloves. Each clove is wrapped in a thin husk or peel; the entire head is encased in several thin layers of papery husk. Of the 300 or so types of garlic known, only three are commercially significant. The most common is pure white, with a sharp flavour. A Mexican variety is pale pink and more strongly flavoured. Elephant garlic is apple-sized and particularly mild. Although whole bulbs can be baked or roasted, garlic is most often separated into cloves, peeled, sliced, minced or crushed and used to flavour a wide variety of dishes. When using garlic remember that the more finely the cloves are crushed, the stronger the flavour will be. And, cooking reduces garlic's pungency; the longer it is cooked, the milder it becomes.

Garlic

Choose firm, dry bulbs with tightly closed cloves and smooth skins. Avoid bulbs with green sprouts. Store fresh garlic in a cool, well-ventilated place; do not refrigerate. Fresh garlic is available all year. Jars of processed and pickled garlic products are also available.

Kohlrabi

Although it looks rather like a round root, kohlrabi is actually a bulbous stem vegetable created by cross-breeding cabbages and turnips. When purchased, both the leaves (which are attached directly to the bulbous stem) and roots are generally removed. Depending on the variety, the skin may be light green, purple or green with a hint of red. The interior flesh is white, with a sweet flavour similar to turnips. (Kohlrabies can be substituted for turnips in many recipes.) Younger plants are milder and more tender than large, mature ones. The outer skin must be removed from mature stems; young stems need only to be well scrubbed before cooking. Kohlrabi can be eaten raw, or it can be cooked (whole, sliced or diced) with moist-heat cooking methods such as boiling and steaming. The stems may also be hollowed out and stuffed with meat or vegetable mixtures.

Kohlrabi

Choose small, tender stems with fresh, green leaves. Peak season for kohlrabi is from June through September.

Leeks

Leeks (Fr. *poireaux*) look like large, overgrown scallions with a fat white tip and wide green leaves. Their flavour is sweeter and stronger than scallions, but milder than common bulb onions. Leeks must be carefully washed to remove the sandy soil that gets between the leaves. Leeks can be baked, braised or grilled as a side dish, or used to season stocks, soups or sauces.

Choose leeks that are firm, with stiff roots and stems. Avoid those with dry leaves, soft spots or browning. Leeks are available all year.

Leeks

Scallions

Scallions, also known as green onions or bunch onions, are a variety of onion that does not develop a large bulb. The leaves are bright green with either a long and slender or slightly bulbous white base. Green onions are used in stir-fries, salads and as a flavouring in other dishes. The green tops can also be sliced in small rings and used as a garnish.

Choose scallions with bright green tops and clean white bulbs. Avoid those with limp or slimy leaves. Scallions are available all year, with a peak summer season. Store, wrapped in paper, in plastic bags for better shelf life.

Scallions

Shallots

Shallots (Fr. *échalotes*) are shaped like small bulb onions with one flat side. When peeled, a shallot separates into multiple cloves, similar to garlic. They have a mild yet rich and complex flavour. Shallots are the basis of many classic sauces and meat preparations; they can also be sautéed or baked as a side dish.

Choose shallots that are plump and well shaped. Avoid those that appear dry or have sprouted. They should be stored in a cool, dry, unrefrigerated place. Shallots are available all year.

Pods and Seeds

Pod and seed vegetables include corn, legumes and okra. They are grouped together here because the parts consumed are all the seeds of their respective plants. In some cases only the seeds are eaten; in others, the pod containing the seeds is eaten as well. Seeds are generally higher in protein and carbohydrates (starch and fibre) than other vegetables.

Corn

Yellow and White Corn

Sweet corn (Fr. *maïs*; Sp. *maíz*) is actually a grain, a type of grass. Corn kernels, like peas, are plant seeds. (Dried corn products are discussed in Chapter 23, Potatoes, Grains and Pasta.) The kernels, which may be white or yellow, are attached to a woody, inedible cob. The cob is encased by strands of hairlike fibres called silks and covered in layers of thin leaves called husks. The silks and husks should be shucked prior to cooking, although the husks may be left on for roasting or grilling. Shucked ears can be grilled, boiled, microwaved or steamed. The kernels can be cut off the cob before or after cooking. Corn on the cob is available fresh or frozen; corn kernels are available canned or frozen.

Choose freshly picked ears with firm, small kernels. Avoid those with mould or decay at the tip of the cob or brownish silks. Summer is the peak season for fresh corn. Refrigeration diminishes quality.

Basic Procedure for Cutting Kernels off Ears of Corn

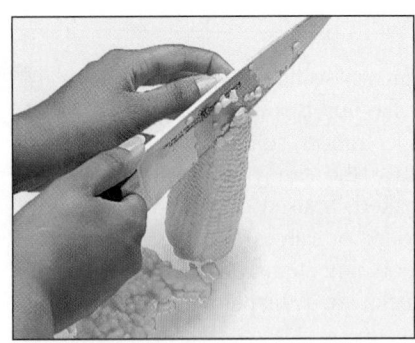

Hold the cob upright and use a chef's knife to slice off the kernels.

Legumes/Pulses

Beans (Fr. *haricots*; It. *fagiolio*) and peas (Fr. *pois*) are members of the legume family, a large group of vegetables with double-seamed pods containing a single row of seeds. Of the hundreds of known varieties of beans, some are used for their edible pods, others for shelling fresh and some only for their dried seeds. Dried beans are actually several varieties of seeds or peas left in the pod until mature, then shelled and dried.

Fresh Beans

Beans used for their edible pods, commonly referred to as green beans, string beans, runner beans or snap beans, are picked when immature. Except for the stem, the entire pod can be eaten. This category includes the green bean, the yellow wax bean and the French haricot vert, a long, slender pod with an intense flavour and tender texture. If there are any strings along the pod's seams, they should be pulled off before cooking. Beans may be left whole, cut lengthwise into thin slivers (referred to as french cut) or cut cross-wise on the diagonal.

Shelling beans are those grown primarily for the edible seeds inside the pod. Common examples are flageolets, lima beans and fava (broad) beans. Their tough pods are not usually eaten.

All beans can be prepared by steaming, microwaving or sautéing. They can be added to soups or stews and they blend well with a variety of flavours, from coconut milk to garlic and olive oil. Cooked beans can be chilled and served as a salad or crudité.

Choose beans that have a bright colour without brown or soft spots. Large pods may be tough or bitter. The peak season for fresh beans is from April through December. Most bean varieties are available frozen or canned, including pickled and seasoned products.

Green Beans

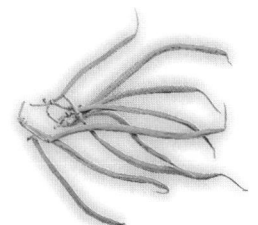

Haricots Verts

Dried Beans

Anthropologists report that for thousands of years cultures worldwide have preserved some members of the legume family by drying. Common dried beans include kidney beans, pinto beans, chickpeas, lentils, black beans, black-eyed peas and split green peas. Shape is the clearest distinction among these products: Beans are oval or kidney-shaped; lentils are small, flat disks; peas are round.

Beans and peas destined for drying are left on the vine until they are fully matured and just beginning to dry. They are then harvested, shelled and quickly dried with warm air currents. Some dried legumes are sold split, which means the skin is removed, causing the seed's two halves to separate.

Most dried beans need to be soaked in water before cooking. Soaking softens and rehydrates the beans, thus reducing cooking time. Lentils and split peas generally do not require soaking, however, and will cook faster than beans. After soaking, beans are most often simmered or baked in a liquid until soft and tender. One type may be substituted for another in most recipes, although variations in colour, starch content and flavour should be considered.

Dried beans and peas are available in bulk or in poly-bags. They should be stored in a cool, dry place, but not refrigerated. Many of these beans are also available fully cooked, then canned or frozen. Some dried beans may be fermented or processed into flour, oil or bean curd.

Dried Black-Eyed Peas

Lentils

Red Kidney Beans

Basic Procedure for Soaking Dried Beans

1. Pick through the dried beans and remove any grit, pebbles or debris.
2. Place the beans in a bowl and cover with cold water; remove any skins or other items that float to the surface.
3. Drain the beans in a colander, then rinse under cold running water.
4. Return the beans to a bowl and cover with fresh cold water. Allow approximately 750 mL (3 cups) of water for each 250 mL (1 cup) of beans.
5. Soak the beans in the cold water for the time specified in the recipe, usually several hours or overnight. Drain through a colander, discarding the water.

Pinto Beans

Great Northern Beans

Basic Procedure for Quick-Soaking Dried Beans

The soaking procedure can be accelerated by the following technique:

1. Rinse and pick through the beans.
2. Place the beans in a saucepan and add enough cool water to cover them by 5 cm (2 inches).
3. Bring to a boil and simmer for 2 minutes.
4. Remove from the heat, cover and soak for 1 hour.
5. Drain and discard the soaking liquid. Proceed with the recipe.

Fresh Shelling Peas

Of the shelling peas that are prepared fresh, the most common are green garden peas (English peas) and the French petit pois. Because they lose flavour rapidly after harvest, most shelling peas are sold frozen or canned. Shelling peas have a delicate, sweet flavour best presented by simply steaming until tender but still al dente. Peas may also be braised with rich meats such as ham or used in soups. Cooked peas are attractive in salads or as garnish.

Choose small fresh pea pods that are plump and moist. Peak season is April and May.

Fresh Shelling Peas

Edible Podded Peas

Snow peas, also known as Chinese pea pods, are a common variety of edible pea pod. They are very flat and have only a few very small green peas. Snow peas have a string along their seams which can be removed by holding the leafy stem and pulling from end to end. The pods can be eaten raw, lightly blanched or steamed, or stir-fried.

Another variety of edible pea pod is the sugar snap pea, a cross between the garden pea and snow pea, which was developed during the late 1970s. They are plump, juicy pods filled with small, tender peas. The entire pod is eaten; do not shell the peas before cooking.

Choose pea pods that are firm, bright green and crisp. Avoid those with brown spots or a shrivelled appearance. Pea pods are available all year, with a peak season in March and April. Asian markets also sell pea sprouts.

Snow Peas

Okra

Okra, a common ingredient in African and Arab cuisines, was brought to the United States by slaves and French settlers. It is now integral to Creole, Cajun, southern and southwestern cuisines. Its mild flavour is similar to asparagus. Okra is not eaten raw; it is best pickled, boiled, steamed, or deep-fat fried. Okra develops a gelatinous texture when cooked for long periods, so it is used to thicken gumbos and stews. To avoid the slimy texture some find objectionable, do not wash okra until ready to cook, then trim the stem end only. Cook okra in stainless steel as other metals cause discolouration.

Choose small to medium pods (3.75–5 cm; 1–2 inches) that are deep green, without soft spots. Pale spears with stiff tips tend to be tough. Okra's peak season is from June through September. Frozen okra is widely available.

Okra

Roots and Tubers

Taproots (more commonly referred to as roots) are single roots that extend deep into the soil to supply the above-ground plant with nutrients. Tubers are fat underground stems. Most roots and tubers can be used interchangeably. All

TOFU

Tofu or bean curd (Fr. *fromage de soja*) is a staple of Japanese and Chinese cuisines and is gaining acceptance in North American kitchens because of its high nutritional value, low cost and flavour adaptability. Tofu is made by processing soybeans into "milk," which is then coagulated (nowadays with calcium sulfate). The curds are then placed in a perforated mould lined with cloth and pressed with a weight to remove the liquid. The result is a soft, creamy-white substance similar to cheese. Tofu is easy to digest, very high in protein, with very little fat and sodium and no cholesterol.

Tofu is an ancient foodstuff, probably created in China during the 2nd century A.D. It was introduced to Japan by Buddhist priests during the 8th century and was "discovered" by Western travellers during the 17th century. Today Japanese tofu is said to be the finest, perhaps because of the superiority of the soybeans grown in the Yamato region, near the city of Kyoto. Japanese cuisine values the natural flavour and texture of tofu and uses it in a tremendous vari-ety of ways. Chinese cuisine uses it as an additive, not as a principal ingredient.

Tofu may be eaten fresh; added to soup, broth or noodle dishes; tossed in cold salads; grilled; deep-fat fried or sautéed. Its flavour is bland, but it readily absorbs flavours from other ingredients.

Two types of tofu are widely available: cotton and silk. Cotton tofu is the most common. Its texture is firm, with an irregular surface caused by the weave of the cotton fabric in which it is wrapped for pressing. Silk tofu has a silky-smooth appearance and texture, and a somewhat more delicate flavour. Unlike cotton tofu, the water has not been pressed out of silk tofu. Consequently, silk tofu should not be cooked at high temperatures or for a long time, as it falls apart easily. The use of either type in most recipes is simply a matter of personal preference.

Fresh tofu is usually packaged in water. It should be refrigerated and kept in water until used. If the water is drained and changed daily, the tofu should last for one week.

Silk Tofu

store well at cool temperatures, without refrigeration. Potatoes, the most popular tuber, are discussed in Chapter 23, Potatoes, Grains and Pasta.

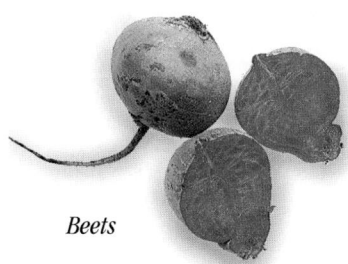

Beets

Beets

Although records suggest that they were first eaten in ancient Greece, beets are most often associated with the colder northern climates, where they grow for most of the year. Beets can be boiled, then peeled and used in salads, soups or baked dishes.

Choose small to medium-sized beets that are firm, with smooth skins. Avoid those with hairy root tips, as they may be tough. Beets are available all year, with a peak season from March to October.

Carrots

Carrots (Fr. *carotte*), among the most versatile of vegetables, are large taproots. Although several kinds exist, the Imperator is the most common. It is long and pointed, with a medium to dark orange colour. It has a mild, sweet flavour. Carrots can be cut into a variety of shapes and eaten raw, used for a mirepoix or prepared by moist-heat cooking methods, grilling, microwaving or roasting. They are also grated and used in baked goods, particularly cakes and muffins.

Choose firm carrots that are smooth and well shaped, with a bright orange colour. If the tops are still attached, they should be fresh-looking and bright green. Carrots are available all year.

Carrots

Celery Root

Celery Root

Celery root, also known as celeriac, is a large, round root, long popular in northern European cuisines. It is a different plant from stalk celery, and its stalks and leaves are not eaten. Celery root has a knobby brown exterior; a creamy white, crunchy flesh and a mild, celerylike flavour. Its thick outer skin must be peeled away; the flesh is then cut as desired. Often eaten raw, celery root can be baked, steamed or boiled. It is used in soups, stews or salads and goes well with game and rich meats. Raw celery root may be placed in acidulated water to prevent browning.

Choose small to medium-sized roots that are firm and relatively clean, with a pungent smell. Their peak season is October through April.

Jicama

Jicama

Jicama is actually a legume that grows underground as a tuber. It is becoming increasingly popular because of its sweet, moist flavour; crisp texture; low calorie content and long shelf life. After its thick brown skin is cut away, the crisp, moist white flesh can be cut as desired. Jicama is often eaten raw in salads, with salsa or as a crudité. It is also used in stir-fried dishes.

Choose firm, well-shaped jicamas that are free of blemishes. Size is not an indication of quality or maturity. They are available all year, with a peak season from January through May.

Parsnips

Parsnips

Parsnips (Fr. *panais*) are white taproots that look and taste like carrots and have the texture of sweet potatoes. Parsnips should be 12.5 to 25 cm (5 to 10 inches) in length, with smooth skins and tapering tips. Parsnips, peeled like carrots, can be eaten raw or cooked by almost any method. When steamed until very soft, they can be mashed like potatoes.

Choose small to medium-sized parsnips that are firm, smooth and well shaped; avoid large, woody ones. Parsnips are available all year, with peak supplies from December through April.

Radishes

Radishes (Fr. *radis*) are used for their peppery flavour and crisp texture. Radishes are available in many colours, including white, black and all shades of red; most have a creamy to pure white interior. Asian radishes, known as daikons, produce roots 5 to 10 cm (2 to 4 inches) in diameter and 15 to 50 cm (6 to 20 inches) long. Radishes can be steamed or stir-fried, but most often are eaten raw, in salads or used as garnish. Radish leaves can be used in salads or cooked as greens.

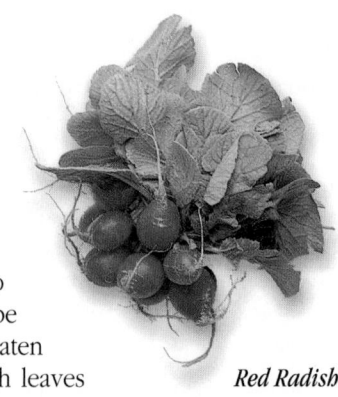

Red Radishes

Choose radishes that are firm, not limp. Their interior should be neither dry nor hollow. Radishes are available all year.

Daikon

Rutabagas

Rutabagas are a root vegetable and a member of the cabbage family. Their skin is purple to yellow and they have yellow flesh with a distinctive starchy, cabbagelike flavour. Rutabagas and turnips are similar in flavour and texture when cooked and may be used interchangeably. Rutabaga leaves are not eaten. Rutabagas should be peeled with a chef's knife, then cut into quarters, slices or cubes. They are often baked, boiled and then puréed, or sliced and sautéed. They are especially flavourful when seasoned with caraway seeds, dill or lemon juice.

Choose small to medium-sized rutabagas that are smooth, firm and feel heavy. Their peak season is January through March.

Rutabagas

Turnips

Also a root vegetable from the cabbage family, turnips have white skin with a rosy-red or purple blush and white interior. Their flavour, similar to that of a radish, can be rather hot. Turnips should be peeled, then diced, sliced or julienned for cooking. They may be baked or cooked with moist-heat cooking methods, and are often puréed like potatoes.

Choose small to medium-sized turnips that have smooth skin and feel heavy. They should be firm, not rubbery or limp. Any attached leaves should be bright green and tender. Spring is their peak season.

Turnips

Stalks and Shoots

Stalk vegetables are plant stems with a high percentage of **cellulose** fibre. These vegetables should be picked while still young and tender. Tough fibres should be trimmed before cooking.

Artichokes

Artichokes (Fr. *artichaut*) are the immature flowers of a thistle plant introduced to America by Italian and Spanish settlers. Young, tender globe artichokes can be cooked whole, but more mature plants need to have the fuzzy centre (known as the choke) removed first. Whole artichokes can be simmered, steamed or microwaved; they are often served with lemon juice, garlic butter or hollandaise sauce. The heart may be cooked separately, then served in salads, puréed as a filling or served as a side dish. Artichoke hearts and bottoms are both available canned.

Choose fresh artichokes with tight, compact heads that feel heavy. Their colour should be solid green to grey-green. Brown spots on the surface caused by frost are harmless. The artichoke's peak season is March through May.

Artichokes

Basic Procedure for Preparing Fresh Artichokes

1. Using kitchen shears or scissors, trim the barbs from the large outer leaves of the artichoke.

2. With a chef's knife, cut away the stem and the top of the artichoke. Steam or boil the artichoke as desired.

Asparagus

Asparagus

Asparagus (Fr. *asperges*), a member of the lily family, generally has bright green shoots with a ruffle of tiny leaves at the tip. Larger spears or shoots tend to be tough and woody, but can be used in soups or for purée. Asparagus are eaten raw or steamed briefly, stir-fried, microwaved or grilled. Fresh spring asparagus is excellent with nothing more than lemon juice or clarified butter; asparagus with hollandaise sauce is a classic preparation.

Choose firm, plump spears with tightly closed tips and a bright green colour running the full length of the spear. Asparagus should be stored, refrigerated at 4°C (40°F), upright in 1.25 cm (1/2 inch) of water or with the ends wrapped in moist paper towelling. They should not be washed until just before use. Canned and frozen asparagus are also available. Peak season is March through June.

White asparagus is sometimes available fresh, or readily available canned. It has a milder flavour and soft, tender texture. It is produced by covering the stalks with soil as they grow; this prevents sunlight from reaching the plant and retards the development of chlorophyll.

Celery

Once a medicinal herb, stalk celery (Fr. *céleri*) is now a common sight in kitchens world-wide. Stalk celery is pale green with stringy curved stalks (ribs). Often eaten raw in salads or as a snack, it can be braised or steamed as a side dish. Celery is also a mirepoix component.

Choose stalks (ribs) that are crisp, without any sign of dryness. Celery is available all year.

Celery

Nopales

Nopales

The pads of a prickly pear cactus can be prepared as a vegetable known as nopales. Cactus pads have a flavour similar to green bell peppers. Their texture tends to be rather gelatinous or mucilaginous, making them good for stews or sauces. To prepare fresh nopales, hold the pad with tongs and cut off the thorns and "eyes" with a sharp knife or vegetable peeler. Trim off the edge all the way around. Slice the pad into julienne strips or cubes. The pieces can be boiled or steamed and served hot, or chilled and added to salads. Nopales can also be sautéed with onions, peppers and seasonings for a side dish or added to southwestern-style casseroles.

Some cultivated varieties have thin, thornless pads. Choose pads that are stiff and heavy without blemishes. They should not be dry or soggy. Fresh cactus pads are available all year, with peak season in the late spring. Canned and pickled nopales are also available.

Baby Vegetables

Many fine restaurants serve baby vegetables: tiny turnips, finger-length squash, miniature carrots and petite heads of cauliflower. First cultivated in Europe but now widely available elsewhere, baby vegetables include both hybrids bred to be true miniatures as well as regular varieties that are picked before maturity. Baby vegetables are often marketed with blossoms or greens still attached. They tend to be easily bruised and are highly perishable. Many baby vegetables can be eaten raw, but they are usually left whole, then steamed or lightly sautéed and attractively presented as an accompaniment to meat, fish or poultry entrees.

Baby Yellow Squash with Blossoms

Baby Globe Carrots

Chiogghi Beets

Baby Zucchini with Blossoms

NUTRITION

Most vegetables are more than 80% water; the remaining portions consist of carbohydrates (primarily starches) as well as small amounts of protein and fat. The relative lack of protein and fat makes most vegetables especially low in calories.

Much of a vegetable's physical structure is provided by generally indigestible substances such as cellulose and lignin, also known as fibre. This fibre produces the characteristic stringy, crisp or fibrous textures associated with vegetables.

✦✦✦

TO BE OR NOT TO BE: VEGETARIAN

In the not too distant past, vegetarianism was linked with aging hippies, musty health food stores and the religiously observant. Not any more. Now most supermarkets stock vegetarian burgers, soy cheeses, tofu and rice milk, while national chains of modern, upscale groceries cater specifically to vegetarian and health-conscious shopper. Even fast-food restaurants now offer foods like vegetarian submarine sandwiches and soy-filled tacos.

So, just how many vegetarians are there in the U.S.? The Vegetarian Resource Group has tried to answer this question. In a 2000 poll, it asked respondents "which of the following foods, if any, [do] you never eat? Meat, Poultry, Fish/

Seafood, Dairy Products, Eggs, Honey." Approximately 2.5 of the sample population responded that they did not eat meat, poultry or fish, while a total of 4.5% indicated they did not eat red meat. In fact, only 72% indicated that they eat items from all of the listed food groups. When the same question was asked in 1994 and again in 1997, only about 1% indicated that they were vegetarian (defined as those who never eat meat, poultry or fish).

Adults aren't the only vegetarians. According to another Vegetarian Resource Group poll in 2000, 2% of children aged 6 to 17 responded that they never eat meat, fish or poultry, while 6% don't eat red meat.

Significantly, nonvegetarians also enjoy meatless dishes from time to time. According to a 1999 poll, approximately 57% of U.S. adults say they "sometimes, often or always" order a vegetarian entree when dining out.

This growing demand for vegetarian food clearly has an impact on restaurants and institutional foodservice operations. When more than half of the population sometimes orders vegetarian cuisine, it is no longer sufficient to offer a one-dish-fits-all vegetarian entree. As with nonvegetarian dishes, flavour, freshness, quality and variety will keep customers satisfied and eager to return.

◆◆◆

ANCIENT PLANTS AND ANCIENT WAYS VANISH

Since the days of Columbus, half of all native American crop varieties have become extinct. If this trend continues, several hundred more will become extinct in our lifetimes. Similarly, ancient farming practices have all but been abandoned. As late as the 1920s, the Tohono O'odham Indians of Arizona still used traditional methods to cultivate more than 10 000 acres without pumping groundwater. Today, only a few scattered floodwater fields remain.

When species disappear we lose an irreplaceable source of genetic diversity—a source of extraordinary genes that could someday improve modern hybrid crops. When native desert crops vanish, so does the ancient tradition of native agriculture, which has selected these crops over millennia to thrive in extreme temperatures, in alkaline soils without millions of gallons of precious water and without expensive, ecologically destructive chemicals.

Today, six highly bred species—wheat, rice, corn, sorghum, potatoes and cassava—supply most of the world's nutrition. As food crops become more and more homogeneous, they often lose their natural ability to tolerate pests, disease and drought. In the past, farmers grew thousands of food crop varieties. These traditional crop varieties contain a storehouse of genetic diversity that enables them to flourish in the most difficult environments. This broad spectrum of genetic variability is a cushion against natural predators and diseases. Wild chiles from the Sierra Madre, for example, are highly disease resistant. Their virus-tolerant genes have been bred into commercial varieties of bell pepper and jalapeños.

Native Seeds/SEARCH, one of the country's first regional seed banks, was founded to keep ancient desert plants and traditional farming methods from disappearing forever. Since 1983 we've ridden mules into remote areas and made more than 1200 collections of desert-adapted crops and wild relatives. We've gathered the seeds of chapalote (a brown popcorn), blue indigo (used for dyes), tepary (a heat- and drought-tolerant bean), teosinte (a wild relative of corn), wild chiles and other plants. These seeds are available to researchers, gardeners, farmers and seed banks. Seeds are offered free to Native Americans.

Each loss of biological and cultural diversity alters and damages the balance of life on earth, often in ways we do not understand. Each loss of leaf, stem and flower diminishes our earth's richness and beauty in ways we often don't appreciate until they're gone.

DR. GARY PAUL NABHAN
NATIVE SEEDS/SEARCH
Tucson, Arizona

Vegetables are also a good source of vitamins and minerals. Care must be taken during preparation to preserve their nutritional content, however. Once peeled or cut, vegetables lose nutrients to the air, or to any liquid in which they are allowed to soak. Vitamins are concentrated just under the skin, so peel vegetables thinly, if at all.

PURCHASING AND STORING FRESH VEGETABLES

Fresh vegetables should be selected according to seasonal availability. Using a vegetable at the peak of its season has several advantages: Price is at its lowest, selection is at its greatest and the vegetable's colour, flavour and texture are at their best.

Grading

The Canadian Food Inspection Agency has developed a grading system for fresh vegetables traded on wholesale markets. The system is based on appearance, condition and other factors affecting waste or eating quality. Grades for all vegetables include, in descending order of quality, Canada Fancy, Canada No. 1, Canada No. 2 and Canada Domestic Grade.

Consumer or retail grading is required for all domestic and imported vegetables. It uses alphabetical listings, with Canada No. 1 being the finest.

Purchasing

Fresh vegetables are sold by weight or count. They are packed in cartons referred to as cases, lugs, bushels, flats or crates. The weight or count packed in each of these containers varies depending on the size and type of vegetable as well as the packer. For example, celery is packed in 25-kg (55-lb.) cartons containing 18 heads depending on the size of each head. Celery hearts, however, are packed in pairs in a cello pack of 12 per case.

Some of the more common fresh vegetables (e.g., onions, carrots, celery and lettuces) can be purchased from wholesalers trimmed, cleaned and cut according to your specifications. Although the unit price will be higher for diced onions than for whole onions, for example, the savings in time, labour, yield loss and storage space can be substantial. Processed vegetables may suffer a loss of nutrients, moisture and flavour, however.

Ripening

Although vegetables do not ripen in the same manner as fruits, they do continue to breathe (respire) after harvesting. The faster the respiration rate, the faster the produce ages or decays. This decay results in wilted leaves and dry, tough or woody stems and stalks. Respiration rates vary according to the vegetable variety, its maturity at harvest and its storage conditions after harvest.

Ripening proceeds more rapidly in the presence of ethylene gas. Ethylene gas is emitted naturally by fruits and vegetables and can be used to encourage further ripening in some produce, especially fruit-vegetables such as tomatoes. Items harvested and shipped when mature but green (unripe) are routinely exposed to ethylene gas to induce colour development (ripening) just before sale.

Storing

Some fresh vegetables are best stored at cool temperatures, between 4°C and 16°C (40°F and 60°F), ideally in a separate produce refrigerator. These include winter squash, potatoes, onions, shallots and garlic. If a produce refrigerator is not available, store these vegetables at room temperature in a dry area with good ventilation. Do not store them in a refrigerator set at conventional temperatures. Colder temperatures convert the starches in these vegetables to sugars, changing their texture and flavour.

Most other vegetables benefit from cold storage at temperatures between 2°C and 4°C (34°F and 40°F) with relatively high levels of humidity. Greens and other delicate vegetables should be stored away from apples, tomatoes, bananas and melons, as the latter give off a great deal of ethylene gas.

PURCHASING AND STORING PRESERVED VEGETABLES

Preservation techniques are designed to extend the shelf life of vegetables. These methods include irradiation, canning, freezing and drying. Except for drying, these techniques do not substantially change the vegetable's texture or flavour. Canning and freezing can also be used to preserve cooked vegetables.

FIGURE 22.1 *Irradiation Symbol (USA)*

Irradiated U.S. Vegetables

Although Canada does not currently allow irradiation of foods, the United States has introduced irradiated foods into their markets. The irradiation process uses ionizing radiation (usually gamma rays of cobalt 60 or cesium 137) to sterilize foods. When foods are subjected to radiation, parasites, insects and bacteria are destroyed, ripening is slowed and sprouting is prevented. Irradiation works without a noticeable increase in temperature; consequently, the flavour and texture of fresh foods are not affected. Some nutrients, however, may be destroyed. Irradiated vegetables do not need to be sprayed with post-harvest pesticides and they have an extended shelf life.

The FDA classifies irradiation as a food additive. Although it is not yet approved for all foods, grains, fruits and vegetables may be treated with low-dose radiation. Irradiated foods must be labelled "Treated with radiation" or "Treated by irradiation." The symbol shown in Figure 22.1 may also be used.

Irradiated produce is purchased, stored and used like fresh produce.

Canned Vegetables

Canned vegetables are an integral part of menu planning for many food service operations. In commercial canning, raw vegetables are cleaned and placed in a sealed container, then subjected to high temperatures for a specific period of time. Heating destroys the microorganisms that cause spoilage, and the sealed environment created by the can eliminates oxidation and retards decomposition. However, the heat required by the canning process also softens the texture of most vegetables and alters their nutritional content; many vitamins and minerals may be lost through the canning process. Green vegetables may also suffer colour loss, becoming a drab olive hue.

Canned vegetables are graded by the Canadian Food Inspection Agency as Canada Fancy, Grade Choice and Grade Substandard. Canada Fancy vegetables must be top quality, tender and free of blemishes. Canada Grade Substandard vegetables may lack uniformity or flavour, but can be used in casseroles or soups if cost is a concern.

Combinations of vegetables as well as vegetables with seasonings and sauces are available canned. For example, corn kernels are available canned in water, in seasonings and sauces, combined with other vegetables or creamed. Canned vegetables are easy to serve because they are essentially fully cooked during the canning process.

Canned vegetables are purchased in cases of standard-sized cans (see Appendix I). Canned vegetables can be stored for extended periods at room temperature. Once a can is opened, any unused contents must be transferred to an appropriate storage container and refrigerated. Cans with bulges or dents must be discarded immediately, without opening.

Frozen Vegetables

The Canadian Food Inspection Agency applies the same grading standards for frozen vegetables as for canned or preserved vegetables. Frozen vegetables are almost as convenient to use as canned. However, they often require some cooking, and expensive freezer space is necessary if an inventory is to be maintained. Regardless, freezing is a highly effective method for preserving vegetables. It severely inhibits the growth of microorganisms that cause spoilage without destroying many nutrients. Generally, green vegetables retain their colour, although the appearance and texture of most vegetables may be somewhat altered because of their high water content: Ice crystals form from the water in the cells and burst the cells' walls.

Some vegetables are available individually quick frozen (IQF). This method employs blasts of cold air, refrigerated plates, liquid nitrogen, liquid air or other techniques to chill the vegetables quickly. By speeding the freezing process, the formation of ice crystals can be greatly reduced.

Combinations of vegetables as well as vegetables with seasonings and sauces are available frozen. Some frozen vegetables are raw when frozen; others are blanched before freezing so final cooking time is reduced. Many others are fully cooked before freezing and only need to be thawed or heated for service. Frozen vegetables generally do not need to be thawed before being heated. Once thawed or cooked, they should be stored in the refrigerator and reheated in the same manner as fresh vegetables. Do not refreeze previously frozen vegetables.

Frozen vegetables are graded in the same manner as canned vegetables. They are usually packed in cases containing 1–2.5 kg (2–5 lb.) boxes or bags. All frozen vegetables should be sealed in moisture-proof wrapping and kept at a constant temperature of –18°C (0°F) or below. Temperature fluctuations can draw moisture from the vegetables, causing poor texture and flavour loss. Adequate packaging also prevents freezer burn, an irreversible change in the colour, texture and flavour of frozen foods.

Dried Vegetables

Except for beans, peas, peppers and tomatoes, few vegetables are commonly preserved by drying. Unlike other preservation methods, drying dramatically alters flavour, texture and appearance. The loss of moisture concentrates flavours and sugars and greatly extends shelf life.

APPLYING VARIOUS COOKING METHODS

Vegetables are cooked in order to break down their cellulose and gelatinize their starches. Cooking gives vegetables a pleasant flavour; creates a softer, more tender texture; and makes them more digestible. Ideally, most vegetables should be cooked as briefly as possible in order to preserve their flavour, nutrients and texture. Unfortunately, sometimes you must choose between emphasizing appearance and maintaining nutrition, because cooking methods that preserve colour and texture often remove nutrients.

Acid/Alkali Reactions

The acid or alkaline content of the cooking liquid affects the texture and colour of many vegetables. (See Table 22.1.) This is of greater concern with moist-heat cooking methods, but it is also a consideration with dry-heat cooking methods, as they often call for blanched or parboiled vegetables.

Texture

The acidity or alkalinity of the vegetable's cooking liquid influences the finished product's texture. If an acid such as lemon juice, vinegar or wine is added to the liquid for flavouring, the vegetable will resist softening and will require a longer cooking time. On the other hand, an alkaline cooking medium will quickly soften the vegetable's texture and may cause it to become mushy. Alkalinity also causes nutrient loss (especially thiamin) and may impart

TABLE 22.1 ACID/ALKALI REACTIONS

Vegetable	Pigment Family	Effect of Acid on:		Effect of Alkali on*:		Cook Covered?
		Colour	Texture	Colour	Texture	
Spinach, Broccoli	chlorophyll	drab olive green	firm	bright green	mushy	no
Carrots, Tomatoes	carotenoid	no change	firm	no change	mushy	no difference
Cauliflower	flavonoid anthoxanthin	white	firm	yellow	mushy	yes
Red cabbage	flavonoid anthocyanins	red	firm	blue	mushy	yes

*Alkalinity always causes a loss of thiamin and other nutrients.

a bitter flavour. Alkalinity can be caused by tap water, detergent residue on utensils or the addition of baking soda (a base) to the cooking liquid. (You could add, for example, 0.25 g (1/8 tsp.) of baking soda per 225 mL (1 cup) of navy beans to speed the softening of the dried beans.)

Colour

The acidity or alkalinity of the liquid also affects the plant's pigments, causing both desirable and undesirable colour changes. There are three principal pigment categories: chlorophyll, carotenoid and flavonoid (which includes anthocyanins and anthoxanthins). A plant's unique colour is the result of a combination of these pigments. Chlorophyll pigments predominate in green vegetables such as spinach, green beans and broccoli. Carotenoid pigments predominate in orange and yellow vegetables such as carrots, tomatoes, red peppers and winter squashes. Anthocyanin and flavonoid pigments predominate in red, purple and white vegetables such as red cabbage, potatoes and cauliflower. Beets contain a pigment called betalain and are best peeled after cooking.

Initially, as vegetables are cooked, their original colours intensify. Exposure to heat makes pigments, especially chlorophyll, appear brighter. Exposure to acids and bases affects both chlorophyll and flavonoid pigments. Acids will gradually turn green vegetables an olive-drab colour, while a slight alkalinity promotes chlorophyll retention. The opposite occurs with vegetables containing flavonoids: They retain desirable colours in a slightly acidic environment while losing colours in an alkaline one. (Carotenoid is not affected by either acidity or alkalinity.) Colour changes alone do not affect flavour; however, the altered appearance can make the product so visually unappealing as to become inedible.

Colours also change as the naturally occurring acids in vegetables are released during cooking. If the cooking pan is kept covered, the acids can concentrate, creating richer flavonoid pigments but destroying chlorophyll pigments.

◆◆◆

METALLIC REACTIONS

Some pigments in vegetables react with metal ions. Anthocyanins (red) will react with tin or iron, turning bluish. Anthoxanthins (white) will darken with iron and turn yellowish with aluminum. Choose cooking pots accordingly.

Guidelines for Vegetable Cookery

The following general guidelines for vegetable cookery should be considered regardless of the cooking method used.

1. Vegetables should be carefully cut into uniform shapes and sizes to promote even cooking and provide an attractive finished product.

2. Cook vegetables for as short a time as possible to preserve texture, colour and nutrients.

3. Cook vegetables as close to service time as possible. Holding vegetables in a steam table continues to cook them.

4. When necessary, vegetables may be blanched in advance, refreshed in ice water and refrigerated. They can then be reheated as needed.

5. White and red vegetables (those with flavonoid pigments) may be cooked with a small amount of acid such as lemon juice, vinegar or white wine to help retain their colour.

6. When preparing an assortment of vegetables, cook each type separately, then combine them. Otherwise some items will be overcooked in the time required to cook others properly.

VEGETABLE SAUNA

"Sweating vegetables" in a little oil over low heat in a covered pot is, in effect, a vegetable sauna. All of the flavors of the vegetables emerge slowly in a juicy tangle, in a much more intense manner than if you simply added them just-cut to a stock. Like roasting garlic, it is a way to enlarge the natural flavors very dramatically.

*—from CHINA MOON COOKBOOK
by* BARBARA TROPP

Determining Doneness

There are so many types of vegetables, with such varied responses to cooking, that no one standard for doneness is appropriate. Each item should be evaluated on a recipe-by-recipe basis. Generally, however, most cooked vegetables are done when they are just tender when pierced with a fork or the tip of a paring knife. Leafy vegetables should be wilted but still have a bright colour.

You can avoid overcooking vegetables by remembering that some carryover cooking will occur through the residual heat contained in the foods. Always rely on objective tests—sight, feel, taste and aroma—rather than the clock.

Dry-Heat Cooking Methods

Broiling and Grilling

Broiling and grilling use high heat to cook vegetables quickly. This preserves their nutritional content and natural flavours. The radiant heat of the broiler or grill caramelizes the vegetables, creating a pleasant flavour that is not generally achieved when vegetables are cooked by other methods.

Selecting and Preparing Vegetables to Broil or Grill

Broiling is often used to cook soft vegetables such as tomatoes or items that might not rest easily on a grill rack. Broiling is also used to warm and brown items just before service. If necessary, the vegetables can be basted to prevent them from drying out under the broiler's direct heat. Sometimes a cooked vegetable is napped with sauce or clarified butter and placed briefly under the broiler as a finishing touch at service time.

A large range of vegetables can be grilled. Carrots, peppers, squashes, eggplants and similar vegetables should be cut into broad, thin slices. They can then be placed on the grill in the same manner as a portion of meat or fish to create attractive crosshatchings. (See Chapter 9, Principles of Cooking.) Smaller vegetables such as mushrooms, cherry tomatoes and pearl onions can be threaded onto skewers for easy handling.

Seasoning Vegetables to Be Broiled or Grilled

Vegetables contain little fat and therefore benefit greatly from added fat when being broiled or grilled. The added fat can be a brushing of clarified butter or a marinade such as one made from olive oil and herbs. Some vegetables may be brushed with butter and crusted with bread crumbs or Parmesan cheese before broiling (gratinée).

Basic Procedure for Broiling or Grilling Vegetables

1. Heat the grill or broiler.
2. Use a wire brush to remove any charred or burnt particles that may be stuck to the broiler or grill grate. The grate may be wiped with a lightly oiled towel to remove any remaining particles and help season it.
3. Prepare the vegetables to be broiled or grilled by cutting them into appropriate shapes and sizes, then seasoning, marinating or otherwise preparing them as desired or directed in the recipe.
4. Place the vegetables on the broiler grate, broiler platter or grill grate and cook to the desired doneness while developing the proper surface colour.

Applying the Basics

RECIPE 22.1

GRILLED VEGETABLE SKEWERS

Yield: 12 Skewers

Marinade:		
Rice wine vinegar	125 mL	4 fl. oz.
Vegetable oil	250 mL	8 fl. oz.
Garlic, chopped	30 g	1 oz.
Dried thyme	3 g	2 tsp.
Salt	15 g	1 Tbsp.
Pepper	0.5 g	1/2 tsp.
Zucchini	175 g	6 oz.
Yellow squash	175 g	6 oz.
Broccoli florets, large	12	12
Cauliflower florets, large	12	12
Onion, large dice	24 pieces	24 pieces
Red bell pepper, large dice	12 pieces	12 pieces
Mushroom caps, medium	12	12

1. Combine all ingredients for the marinade and set aside.
2. Cut the zucchini and yellow squash into 1.25-cm-thick (1/2-inch) semicircles.
3. Blanch and refresh the zucchini, yellow squash, broccoli florets, cauliflower florets, onions and red bell pepper as discussed in the following section, Moist-Heat Cooking Methods.
4. Drain the vegetables well and combine them with the marinade. Add the mushroom caps to the marinade. Marinate the vegetables for 30–45 minutes, remove and drain well.
5. Skewer the vegetables by alternating them on 10-cm (6-inch) bamboo skewers (pre-soaked in water).
6. Place the vegetable skewers on a hot grill and cook until done, turning as needed. The vegetables should brown and char lightly during cooking. Serve hot.

Skewers of grilled marinated vegetables.

RECIPE 22.1

Approximate values per skewer:

Calories	60
Total fat	2.5 g
Saturated fat	0 g
Cholesterol	0 mg
Sodium	534 mg
Total carbohydrates	8 g
Protein	2 g

Roasting and Baking

The terms *roasting* and *baking* are used interchangeably when referring to vegetables. Roasting or baking is used to bring out the natural sweetness of many vegetables while preserving their nutritional values. The procedures are basically the same as those for roasting meats.

Selecting and Preparing Vegetables to Roast or Bake

Hearty vegetables such as winter squash and eggplant are especially well suited for roasting or baking. Vegetables such as onions, carrots and turnips are sometimes cooked alongside roasting meats or poultry. The vegetables add flavour to the finished roast and accompanying sauce, and the fats and juices released from the cooking roast add flavour to the vegetables.

Vegetables can be baked whole or cut into uniform-size pieces. Squash, for example, is usually cut into large pieces. Vegetables may be peeled or left unpeeled, depending on the desired finished product.

Seasoning Vegetables to Be Roasted or Baked

Vegetables may be seasoned with salt and pepper and rubbed with butter or oil before baking, or they may be seasoned afterwards with a wide variety of herbs and spices. Some vegetables, such as winter squashes and sweet potatoes, may be flavoured with brown sugar or honey as well.

Basic Procedure for Roasting or Baking Vegetables

1. Wash the vegetables. Peel, cut and prepare them as desired or directed in the recipe.
2. Season the vegetables and rub with oil or butter if desired.
3. Place the vegetables in a baking dish and bake in a preheated oven until done (tender).

Applying the Basics

RECIPE 22.2

BAKED BUTTERNUT SQUASH

Yield: 4 125-g (4-oz.) Servings

Butternut squash, medium dice	450 g	1 lb.
Salt and pepper	TT	TT
Cinnamon	0.25 g	1/4 tsp.
Cardamom, ground	0.15 g	1/8 tsp.
Brown sugar	25 g	2 Tbsp.
Lemon juice	30 mL	2 Tbsp.
Whole butter, melted	50 g	2 oz.

1. Place the squash in a buttered pan. Season with salt, pepper, cinnamon, cardamom and brown sugar.
2. Drizzle the lemon juice and butter over the top of the squash.
3. Bake, uncovered, in a 180°C (350°F) oven until tender, approximately 50 minutes.

RECIPE 22.2

Approximate values per 125 g (4-oz.) serving:

Calories	160.3
Total fat	10.2 g
Saturated fat	6.3 g
Cholesterol	27.4 mg
Sodium	110.3 mg
Total carbohydrates	18.6 g
Protein	1.2 g

Sautéing or Stir-Frying

Sautéed or stir-fried vegetables should be brightly coloured and slightly crisp when done and show little moisture loss. When sautéing vegetables, all preparation must be complete before cooking begins because timing is important and cooking progresses rapidly. Have all vegetables, herbs, spices, seasonings and sauces ready before you begin.

Selecting and Preparing Vegetables to Sauté

A wide variety of vegetables can be sautéed. Whatever vegetables are used, they should be cut into uniform-size pieces to ensure even cooking.

Quick-cooking vegetables such as summer squashes, onions, greens, stalks, fruit-vegetables and mushrooms can be sautéed without any preparation except washing and cutting. Other vegetables such as Brussels sprouts, green beans, winter squashes, broccoli, cauliflower and most root vegetables are usually first blanched or otherwise partially cooked by baking, steaming or simmering. They are then sautéed to reheat and finish. Carrots, squash and other vegetables are sometimes finished by sautéing in butter and then adding a small amount of honey or maple syrup to glaze them. Some cooked vegetables are reheated by simply "sautéing" them in a small amount of stock or sauce.

Seasoning Vegetables to Be Sautéed

Sautéed vegetables can be seasoned with a great variety of herbs and spices. Seasonings should be added towards the end of the cooking process after all other ingredients have been incorporated in order to evaluate the flavour of the finished dish accurately.

Because sautéing vegetables uses slightly lower temperatures than sautéing meats and poultry, usually whole butter can be used in place of clarified butter. For additional flavours, fats such as bacon fat, olive oil, nut oils or sesame oil can be used in lieu of butter.

Basic Procedure for Sautéing Vegetables

1. Wash and cut the vegetables into uniform shapes and sizes.
2. Heat a sauté pan and add enough fat to just cover the bottom. The pan should be large enough to hold the vegetables without overcrowding.
3. When preparing an assortment of vegetables, add the ingredients according to their cooking times (first add the vegetables that take the longest to cook). Plan carefully so that all vegetables will be done at the same time. Do not overcrowd the pan; maintain high enough heat so the vegetables do not cook in their own juices.
4. Toss the vegetables using the sloped sides of the sauté pan or wok to flip them back on top of themselves. Do not toss more than necessary. The pan should remain in contact with the heat source as much as possible to maintain proper temperatures.
5. Add any sauces or vegetables with high water content, such as tomatoes, last.
6. Season the vegetables as desired with herbs or spices, or add ingredients for a glaze.

Applying the Basics

RECIPE 22.3

RECIPE 22.3

STIR-FRIED ASPARAGUS WITH SHIITAKE MUSHROOMS

Yield: 450 g (1 lb.)

Asparagus	450 g	1 lb.
Shiitake mushrooms, fresh	175 g	6 oz.
Vegetable oil	15 mL	1 Tbsp.
Sesame oil	15 mL	1 Tbsp.
Garlic, chopped	8 g	2 tsp.

*Approximate values
per 90 g serving:*

Calories	105
Total fat	6 g
Saturated fat	1 g
Cholesterol	8 mg
Sodium	848 mg
Total carbohydrates	10 g
Protein	4 g

| Oyster sauce | 125 mL | 4 fl. oz. |
| Crushed red chiles, optional | TT | TT |

Stir-fried mushrooms and asparagus.

1. Wash the asparagus, trim the ends, peel lower stalk and slice on the bias into 2.5- to 5-cm (1- to 2-inch) pieces.
2. Wash the mushrooms, trim off the stems and slice the caps into 1.25-cm (1/2-inch) slices.
3. Heat the oils in a wok or sauté pan.
4. Add the garlic and stir-fry for a few seconds.
5. Add the mushrooms and asparagus and stir-fry for 1 minute.
6. Add the oyster sauce and crushed red chiles (if using) and continue to stir-fry until the asparagus is nearly tender, approximately 3 minutes.

Pan-Frying and Deep-Fat Frying

Pan-frying is not as popular as other techniques for cooking vegetables. Green tomatoes, however, are sometimes seasoned, floured and pan-fried; eggplant slices are seasoned, floured, pan-fried and used for Eggplant Parmesan. When pan-frying vegetables, follow the procedures outlined in Chapter 9, Principles of Cooking.

Deep-fat frying is a popular method of preparing vegetables such as potatoes, squashes and mushrooms. They can be served as hors d'oeuvre, appetizers or accompaniments to a main dish. Starchy vegetables may be deep-fat fried plain. Most other vegetables are first breaded or battered. Vegetables can also be grated or chopped and incorporated into fritters or croquettes. Any deep-fat fried item should have a crisp, golden exterior with a tender, non-greasy centre. See Chapter 21, Deep-Fat Frying, for additional information.

Moist-Heat Cooking Methods

Blanching and Parboiling

Blanching and parboiling are variations on boiling; the difference between them is the length of cooking time. Blanched and parboiled vegetables are often finished by other cooking methods such as sautéing.

Blanching is the partial cooking of foods in a large amount of boiling water for a very short period of time, usually only a few seconds. Besides preparing vegetables for further cooking, blanching is used to remove strong or bitter flavours, soften firm foods, set colours or loosen skins for peeling. Kale, chard, snow peas and tomatoes are examples of vegetables that are sometimes blanched for purposes other than preparation for further cooking.

Parboiling is the same as blanching, but the cooking time is longer, usually several minutes. Parboiling is used to soften vegetables and shorten final cooking times. Parboiling is commonly used for preparing root vegetables, cauliflower, broccoli and winter squashes.

Boiling

Vegetables are often boiled. Boiled vegetables can be served as is, or they can be further prepared by quickly sautéing with other ingredients, puréeing or mashing. Boiled vegetables are also chilled, then used in salads.

Starchy root vegetables are generally not boiled but rather simmered slowly so that the heat penetrates to their interiors and cooks them evenly. Green vegetables should be boiled quickly in a large amount of water in order to retain their colour and flavour.

1. Blanch, parboil or boil the vegetables to the desired doneness.

2. Remove the vegetables from the cooking liquid and submerge them in ice water just until they are cold.

Refreshing

Unless the boiled, blanched or parboiled vegetables will be eaten immediately, they must be quickly chilled in ice water after they are removed from the cooking liquid. This prevents further cooking and preserves (sets) their colours. This process is known as **refreshing** or **shocking** the vegetables. The vegetables are removed from the ice water as soon as they are cold. Never soak or hold the vegetables in the water longer than necessary or valuable nutrients and flavour will be leached away.

Selecting and Preparing Vegetables to Boil

Nearly any type of vegetable can be boiled. Carrots, cabbages, green beans, turnips and red beets are just a few of the most common ones. Vegetables can be large or small, but they should be uniform in size to ensure even cooking. Some vegetables are cooked whole and only require washing before boiling. Others must be washed, peeled and trimmed or cut into smaller or more manageable sizes.

Seasoning Vegetables to Be Boiled

Often vegetables are boiled in nothing more than salted water. Lemon juice, citrus zest, wine and other acidic ingredients are sometimes added to white and red vegetables; if so, they should be added to the liquid before the vegetables. Herbs and spices in a sachet or a bouquet garni are often used to add flavour to boiled vegetables and should be added according to the recipe.

After boiling, vegetables are sometimes finished with herbs, spices, butter, cream or sauces.

Basic Procedure for Boiling Vegetables

1. Wash, peel, trim and cut the vegetables into uniform shapes and sizes.
2. Bring an adequate amount of water, stock, court bouillon or other liquid to a boil. The liquid should cover the vegetables and they should be able to move around freely without overcrowding.
3. Add seasonings if desired or as directed in the recipe.
4. Add the vegetables to the boiling liquid. If more than one vegetable is to be cooked and they have different cooking times, they should be cooked separately to ensure that all are cooked to the proper doneness. The pot may be covered if cooking white, red or yellow vegetables. Do not cover the pot when boiling green vegetables.
5. Cook the vegetables to the desired doneness.
6. Remove the vegetables from the water with a slotted spoon or a spider or drain through a colander.
7. Refresh the vegetables in ice water, drain and refrigerate until needed, or finish the hot boiled vegetables as desired and serve immediately.

RECIPE 22.4

*Approximate values
per 90 g serving:*

Calories 227.9
Total fat   21.2 g
Saturated fat   5.4 g
Cholesterol 18.2 mg
Sodium 472 mg
Total carbohydrates   10.3 g
Protein   3.6 g

Applying the Basics

RECIPE 22.4

BRUSSELS SPROUTS IN PECAN BUTTER

Yield: 6 90-g (3-oz.) Servings

Brussels sprouts	450 g	1 lb.
Whole butter	50 g	2 oz.
Pecans, chopped	125 g	4 oz.
Salt and pepper	TT	TT

1. Trim the Brussels sprouts and mark an X in the bottom of each with a paring knife to promote even cooking.
2. Boil the sprouts in salted water until tender, approximately 10 minutes.
3. Drain and hold the sprouts in a warm place.
4. Heat the butter in a sauté pan until it turns nut brown; this is called **beurre noisette**. Add the pecans and toss to brown them.
5. Add the Brussels sprouts and toss to reheat and blend flavours. Adjust the seasonings and serve.

1. Mark an X in the bottom of each Brussels sprout.

2. Boil the Brussels sprouts in the appropriate amount of water.

3. Toss the Brussels sprouts with the butter and pecans.

Basic Procedure for Cooking Dried Beans

Dried beans are best rehydrated by soaking as discussed earlier and then cooking in a boiling (actually simmering) liquid. After rehydration and cooking, the beans can be served or further cooked in baked, sautéed or puréed dishes.

1. After soaking, place the drained beans in a heavy saucepan and cover with cold water or stock. Allow approximately three times as much liquid as there are beans. Add flavouring ingredients as directed in the recipe, but do not add acids or salt until the beans have reached the desired tenderness. Acids and salt cause the exterior of beans to toughen and resist any further efforts at tenderizing.
2. Slowly bring the liquid to a boil. Boil uncovered for 10 minutes or as directed in the recipe. Use a ladle to remove any scum that rises to the surface.
3. Cover and reduce the heat. Allow the mixture to simmer until the beans are tender. Whole beans generally require 1–2.5 hours, lentils 20–35 minutes and split peas 30–60 minutes. Add additional hot liquid if necessary. Do not stir the beans during cooking.
4. Drain the cooked beans in a colander.

Applying the Basics

RECIPE 22.5

BAKED BEANS

Yield: 2 kg (60 oz.)   **Method:** Baking

Great Northern beans, soaked	500 g	1 lb.
Onion, small dice	125 g	4 oz.
Bacon lardons	125 g	4 oz.

Continued

Anaheim chile, small dice	30 g	1 oz.
Molasses	100 mL	3 fl. oz.
Maple sugar	100 g	3 oz.
Ketchup	250 mL	8 fl. oz.
Dry mustard	2 g	1 tsp.
Cider vinegar	15 mL	1 Tbsp.
Worcestershire sauce	30 mL	2 Tbsp.
Instant coffee powder	2 g	1 Tbsp.
Salt and pepper	TT	TT

RECIPE 22.5

Approximate values per 100 g serving:

Calories	120
Total fat	3 g
Saturated fat	1 g
Cholesterol	5 mg
Sodium	1216 mg
Total carbohydrates	19 g
Protein	4.5 g

1. Simmer the beans in water until almost tender, approximately 45 minutes. Drain well.

2. Combine the remaining ingredients, blending well.

3. Add the sauce to the beans, tossing to coat thoroughly. Adjust the seasonings.

4. Place the beans in a hotel pan or a 2 L (2-qt.) baking dish. Cover and bake in a 180°C (350°F) oven until the beans are completely tender, approximately 30–40 minutes.

Steaming

Vegetables can be steamed in a convection steamer or by suspending them over boiling liquid on a rack set over a wok, saucepan or hotel pan. Vegetables can also be pan-steamed by cooking them in a covered pan with a small amount of liquid. Although the food will be touching the cooking liquid, most of the cooking is done by steam because only a small portion of the food is submerged in the liquid. Steamed vegetables can be eaten plain, partially cooked and sautéed lightly to finish, incorporated into casseroles or puréed. If they are not served immediately, they must be refreshed and refrigerated until used.

Properly steamed vegetables should be moist and tender. They generally retain their shape better than boiled vegetables. Vegetables cook very rapidly in steam and overcooking is a common mistake.

Selecting and Preparing Vegetables to Steam

Nearly any vegetable that can be boiled can also be steamed successfully. All vegetables should be washed, peeled and trimmed if appropriate and cut into uniform-size pieces. Pan-steaming is appropriate for vegetables that are small or cut into fairly small pieces such as peas and beans or broccoli and cauliflower florets.

Seasoning Vegetables to Be Steamed

Steaming produces vegetables with clean, natural flavours. Foods cooked in convection steamers can be seasoned with herbs and spices; but convection steamers use water to produce steam and the foods being cooked do not gain flavour from the cooking liquid. Vegetables steamed over liquids or pan-steamed in small amounts of liquids can be flavoured by using stocks or court bouillon as the cooking liquid. Herbs, spices and aromatic vegetables can be added to any liquid for additional flavour.

Basic Procedure for Steaming Vegetables

1. Wash, peel, trim and cut the vegetables into uniform shapes and sizes.

2. If a convection steamer is not being used, prepare a steaming liquid and bring it to a boil in a covered pan or double boiler.

3. Place the vegetables in a perforated pan in a single layer; do not crowd the pan. Place the pan over the boiling liquid, or add the vegetables to the liquid.

4. Cover the pan and cook to the desired doneness.

5. Remove the vegetables from the steamer and serve, or refresh and refrigerate until needed.

Applying the Basics

RECIPE 22.6

BROCCOLI AMANDINE

Yield: 8 Servings

Broccoli, fresh	1 kg	2 lb.
Salt and pepper	TT	TT
Whole butter	50 g	2 oz.
Almonds, sliced	25 g	1 oz.
Garlic clove, minced	5 g	1
Lemon juice	50 mL	2 fl. oz.

1. Cut the broccoli into uniform spears. Rinse and sprinkle lightly with salt and pepper.

2. Place the broccoli in a single layer in a perforated hotel pan and cook in a convection steamer until tender but slightly crisp, approximately 3 minutes.

3. Melt the butter in a sauté pan. Add the almonds and garlic and cook just until the nuts are lightly browned.

4. Arrange the broccoli on plates for service and sprinkle with the lemon juice. Drizzle the almonds and butter over the broccoli and serve immediately.

1. Place the broccoli spears in a perforated pan for steaming.

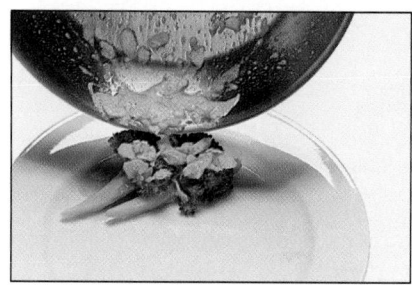

2. Drizzle the browned almonds and butter over the broccoli for service.

RECIPE 22.6

Approximate values per 180 g (6 oz.) serving:

Calories	101
Total fat	7 g
Saturated fat	3.5 g
Cholesterol	15 mg
Sodium	453 mg
Total carbohydrates	8 g
Protein	4.5 g

Combination Cooking Methods

Braising and Stewing

Braised and stewed vegetables are cooked slowly in a small amount of liquid. The liquid, including any given off by the vegetables, is reduced to a light sauce, becoming part of the finished product. Generally, a braised dish is prepared with only one vegetable; a stew is a mixture of several vegetables. The main ingredients are sometimes browned in fat before the liquid is added in order to enhance flavour and colour.

Both braises and stews can be exceptionally flavourful because they are served with all of their cooking liquid. (Boiled vegetables lose some of their flavour to the cooking liquid.) Braised and stewed vegetables generally can be held hot for service longer than vegetables prepared by other cooking methods.

Selecting and Preparing Vegetables to Braise or Stew

Various lettuces, especially romaine and Boston, are often braised. Cabbages, Belgian endive, leeks and many other vegetables are also commonly braised. Stews may contain a wide variety of vegetables such as summer squashes, eggplant, onions, peppers, tomatoes, carrots, celery and garlic. Leafy green vegetables and winter squashes are less commonly braised or stewed.

The vegetables should be washed and peeled or trimmed if appropriate. Vegetables to be braised may be left whole, cut into uniform pieces or shredded, as desired. Lettuces are usually cut into halves or quarters; cabbage is usually shredded.

Seasoning Vegetables to Be Braised or Stewed

Both braises and stews usually include flavouring ingredients such as garlic, herbs, bacon or mirepoix. The liquid may consist of water, wine, stock or tomato juice. Vegetables can even be braised in butter and sugar or honey to create a glazed dish.

Both braises and stews can be seasoned with a variety of herbs and spices. Add the seasonings before covering the pot to finish the cooking process. Strongly flavoured vegetables such as celery root and turnips are usually parboiled first in order to reduce their strong presence.

Basic Procedure for Braising and Stewing Vegetables

1. Wash, peel, trim and cut the vegetables.
2. Sauté or sweat the flavouring ingredients in fat to release their flavours. Or, sauté or sweat the main ingredients in fat.
3. For a braise, add the main ingredient in a single layer. For a stew, add the ingredients according to their cooking times or as directed in the recipe.
4. Add the cooking liquid; it should partially cover the vegetables. Bring the liquid to a boil, reduce to a simmer, cover and cook in the oven or on the stove top until done.
5. If desired, remove the main ingredients from the pan and reduce the sauce or thicken it with beurre manié, cornstarch or arrowroot. Then return the main ingredients to the sauce.

Applying the Basics

RECIPE 22.7

BRAISED CELERY WITH BASIL

Yield: 12 Servings

Celery	3 heads	3 heads
Onion, small dice	250 g	8 oz.
Garlic, minced	10 g	2 tsp.
Whole butter	50 g	2 oz.
Olive oil	40 mL	1 fl. oz.
Fresh thyme	2 g	1 tsp.
Fresh basil, chiffonade	20 leaves	20 leaves
Dry white wine	250 mL	8 fl. oz.
Chicken stock	500 mL	1 pt.
Salt and pepper	TT	TT

RECIPE 22.7

Approximate values per 90 g (3 oz.) serving:

Calories	60
Total fat	4.5 g
Saturated fat	1.5 g
Cholesterol	5 mg
Sodium	170 mg
Total carbohydrates	2 g
Protein	1 g

1. Trim and cut the celery.

2. Add the liquid to the celery.

3. Reduce the sauce.

1. Trim the outer ribs from the celery heads, leaving only the tender hearts. Trim the heads to 15-cm (6-inch) lengths. Trim the root slightly, leaving each head together. Cut each head lengthwise into quarters.
2. Sauté the onions and garlic in the butter and olive oil, without colouring, until tender. Add the celery quarters to the pan and sauté, turning occasionally.
3. Add the thyme, basil, wine and chicken stock. Bring to a boil, reduce to a simmer, cover and braise (étuver) in the oven at 180°C (350°F) until tender, approximately 1 hour.
4. Remove the celery and reserve. Reduce the cooking liquid on the stove top until it thickens. Adjust the liquid's seasonings and return the celery to the pan to reheat. Serve the celery with a portion of the sauce.

Microwaving

Fresh vegetables are among the few foods that can be consistently well prepared in a microwave oven. Often microwave cooking can be accomplished without any additional liquid, thus preserving nutrients. With microwaving, colours and flavours stay true and textures remain crisp.

Microwave cooking is actually a form of steaming. As explained in Chapter 9, Principles of Cooking, microwaves agitate water molecules, thus creating steam. The water may be the moisture found naturally in the food or may be added specifically to create the steam.

Cooking time depends on the type of microwave oven as well as on the freshness, moisture content, maturity and quantity of vegetables being prepared.

Selecting and Preparing Vegetables to Microwave

Any vegetable that can be steamed successfully can be microwaved with good results. Because typical microwave ovens are relatively small, they are impractical for producing large quantities of food. They are most useful for reheating small portions of vegetables that have been blanched or partially cooked using another cooking method.

Seasoning Vegetables to Be Microwaved

Microwaving, like steaming, brings out the natural flavours of food and produces a clean, unadulterated flavour. Herbs and spices can be added to the vegetables before they are microwaved. Or, after microwaving, the vegetables can be tossed with butter, herbs and spices or combined with a sauce.

Basic Procedure for Microwaving Vegetables

1. Wash, peel, trim and cut the vegetables into uniform shapes and sizes.
2. Place the vegetables in a steamer designed for microwave use or arrange the vegetables on a microwavable dish. Cover the vegetables with the lid or plastic wrap. If using plastic wrap, it should be punctured to allow some steam to escape during cooking.
3. Cook the vegetables to the desired doneness, allowing for some carryover cooking. Or reheat the previously cooked vegetables until hot. Stir or turn the vegetables as necessary to promote even cooking.
4. Serve the vegetables or refresh and refrigerate until needed.

Puréeing

Puréeing is a technique often used with vegetables. Cooked vegetable purées can be served as is, stuffed into other vegetables or be used as an ingredient in other preparations such as pumpkin pie, mashed potatoes or vegetable soufflés. Purées can also be bound with eggs, seasoned and used to make vegetable timbales and terrines.

Puréed vegetables are generally first cooked by baking, boiling, steaming or microwaving. White, red and yellow vegetables should be cooked until quite soft. They are more easily puréed when hot or warm; this also helps ensure a smooth finished purée. For most preparations, green vegetables must be refreshed after cooking and puréed while cold or they will overcook and become discoloured.

Seasoning Vegetables to Be Puréed

Vegetables for purées can be seasoned before they are puréed following the guidelines for the cooking procedure used. They can also be seasoned after they are puréed with a wide variety of ingredients such as herbs or spices, cheese, honey or brown sugar.

Finishing Puréed Vegetables

Purées can be finished with stocks, sauces, butter or cream to add richness and flavour. First purée the main ingredient, then add additional liquids to obtain the desired consistency.

Basic Procedure for Puréeing Vegetables

1. Cook the vegetables. White, red and yellow vegetables should be cooked until very soft. Green vegetables should be cooked until tender but not overcooked to the point of being discoloured.
2. Purée the vegetables in a VCM, food processor or blender or by passing them through a food mill.
3. Season or finish the puréed vegetables as desired or directed in the recipe, or use them in another recipe.

Applying the Basics

RECIPE 22.8

PARSNIP PURÉE

Yield: 2.5 kg (5 lb.)

Parsnips	2 kg	4 lb.
Russet potatoes	700 g	1 lb. 8 oz.
Cream, 35%, hot	250 mL	8 fl. oz.
Whole butter, melted	125 g	4 oz.
Salt and white pepper	TT	TT
Nutmeg	TT	TT

1. Peel the parsnips and potatoes and cut into large pieces of approximately the same size.
2. Boil the parsnips and potatoes separately in salted water until tender.
3. Drain the parsnips and potatoes well. Purée them together through a food mill.

RECIPE 22.8

Approximate values per 100 g serving:

Calories	158
Total fat	8 g
Saturated fat	5 g
Cholesterol	24 mg
Sodium	291 mg
Total carbohydrates	21.5 g
Protein	2 g

4. Add the cream and butter and mix to combine. Adjust the consistency by adding cream as desired. Season the mixture with salt, white pepper and nutmeg and serve hot.

VARIATION: Substitute celeriac flavoured with saffron.

CONCLUSION

Vegetables are an essential part of the human diet. They provide the body with vitamins, minerals and fibre. They appeal to the appetite with taste, colour and texture. Increased market availability of fresh, high-quality vegetables as well as new hybrids gives you an ever-increasing variety of vegetables from which to choose. Vegetables are a relatively inexpensive food that can be prepared in limitless ways. They can be served as an entire meal or as an accompaniment to or part of a wide variety of other dishes. And when cooking vegetables, remember what James Beard (1903–1985), the great American food consultant, culinary educator and writer once said: "No vegetable exists which is not better slightly undercooked."

QUESTIONS FOR DISCUSSION

1. Explain how season affects the price, quality and availability of vegetables.
2. List and describe three processing techniques commonly used to extend the shelf life of vegetables.
3. What special concerns exist regarding the storage of fresh vegetables? Explain why some vegetables should not be refrigerated.
4. Why is it important to cut vegetables into a uniform size before cooking?
5. Discuss several techniques used for determining the doneness of vegetables. Is carryover cooking a concern when preparing vegetables? Explain your answer.
6. Discuss the role of acid in a cooking liquid used for preparing vegetables. Which vegetables, if any, benefit from an acidic cooking environment?
7. Describe the necessary mise en place and procedure for refreshing vegetables.

ADDITIONAL VEGETABLE RECIPES

RECIPE 22.9

SUMMER VEGETABLES WITH TARRAGON AIOLI

NOTE: *This dish appears in the Chapter Opening photograph.*

GREENS RESTAURANT, SAN FRANCISCO, CA
Executive Chef Annie Somerville

Yield: 8–10 Servings		Method: Boiling
Baby artichokes	6	6
Carrots	250 g	8 oz.
Yellow or green zucchini	500 g	1 lb.

Continued

Sunburst squash	500 g	1 lb.
Green beans	250 g	8 oz.
Yellow wax beans	250 g	8 oz.
Broccoli florets	500 g	1 lb.
Cauliflower florets	500 g	1 lb.
Red radishes	1 bunch	1 bunch
Cherry tomatoes	175 g	1/2 pt.
Niçoise or Gaeta olives	250 g	8 oz.
Tarragon Aioli (recipe follows)	250 g	8 oz.

1. Trim the artichokes. Steam or boil them until tender; refresh.

2. Cut the carrots, zucchini and squash as desired. Snip the ends from the beans. Parboil all the vegetables except the radishes, tomatoes and olives, one variety at a time, in salted water until nearly tender but still crisp. Refresh each and drain well.

3. Wash the radishes. Trim the root end but leave the green tops attached.

4. Wash the cherry tomatoes and remove the stems.

5. Loosely arrange the vegetables on a platter, leaving room for the aioli unless it is to be served separately in a small bowl.

TARRAGON AIOLI

Yield: 250 mL (1/2 pt.)

Egg yolk, large	1	1
Fresh lemon juice	15 mL	1 Tbsp.
Light olive oil	250 mL	8 fl. oz.
Garlic clove, chopped	5 g	1
Champagne vinegar	5 mL	1 tsp.
Fresh tarragon, chopped	8 g	2 tsp.
Salt	TT	TT

1. Whisk the yolk and 3 mL (1/2 tsp.) of lemon juice together until smooth.

2. Whisk in the oil, very slowly at first, until the aioli begins to emulsify. Add a few drops of lemon juice as necessary to thin the sauce. Continue until all the oil and lemon juice have been incorporated.

3. Season with the garlic, vinegar, tarragon and salt. If the aioli is too thick, thin it with a little warm water.

4. Refrigerate aioli and use within three days.

RECIPE 22.9

Approximate values per serving:

Calories	468
Total fat	34 g
Saturated fat	4.5 g
Cholesterol	30 mg
Sodium	768 mg
Total carbohydrates	30 g
Protein	8 g

◆ ◆ ◆

RECIPE 22.10

SPINACH AU GRATIN

Yield: 8 225-g (8-oz.) Servings as an entree,   **Method:** Gratin
    16 Servings as a side vegetable

Clarified butter	60 mL	2 fl. oz.
Flour	30 g	1 oz.
Cream, 18%, warm	450 mL	1 pt.
Garlic cloves, minced	10 g	2
Spinach, fresh chopped	1.1 kg	2 lb. 8 oz.
Salt, pepper and nutmeg	TT	TT
Cheddar or Swiss cheese, shredded	650 g	1 lb. 8 oz.

1. Heat half the butter in a saucepan. Add the flour and cook to make a blond roux.

2. Add the cream, whisking to remove any lumps of roux. Bring to a simmer and cook for 15 minutes.

3. Sauté the garlic in the remaining clarified butter. Add spinach and cook for 2 minutes. Remove from the heat and drain well.

4. Combine the hot spinach with the cream sauce and adjust the seasonings.

5. Fill 16 150-mL (3/4-cup) gratin dishes with the creamed spinach. Top each with 40 g (1-1/2 oz.) shredded cheese and place under the broiler until the cheese is melted and browned and the spinach is very hot. Serve immediately.

RECIPE 22.10

Approximate values per 225 g (8 oz.) serving:

Calories	457
Total fat	33 g
Saturated fat	21 g
Cholesterol	101 mg
Sodium	782 mg
Total carbohydrates	16 g
Protein	26 g

◆◆◆

RECIPE 22.11

BROILED TOMATO

Yield: 2 Servings   **Method:** Broiling

Tomato, large	1	1
Sugar	10 g	2 tsp.
Garlic butter, melted	15 g	1/2 oz.
Fresh parsley, chopped	10 g	1 Tbsp.
Fresh white bread crumbs	5 g	1 Tbsp.

1. Core and halve the tomato.

2. Sprinkle sugar on top of each half. Place on a broiler platter and broil until tender.

3. Drizzle with garlic butter and garnish with parsley and bread crumbs.

4. Quickly brown crumbs under broiler.

RECIPE 22.11

Approximate values per 1/2 tomato:

Calories	98
Total fat	6.5 g
Saturated fat	4 g
Cholesterol	16 mg
Sodium	92 mg
Total carbohydrates	10 g
Protein	1 g

◆◆◆

RECIPE 22.12

GRILLED PORTOBELLO CAPS

Yield: 3 120-g (4-oz.) Servings   **Method:** Grilling

Olive oil	15 mL	1 Tbsp.
Garlic, chopped	5 g	1 tsp.
Fresh thyme, chopped	2 g	1 tsp.
Portobello mushroom caps	500 g	1 lb.
Salt and pepper	TT	TT

1. Combine the olive oil, garlic and thyme and let infuse.

2. Wipe the mushroom caps clean with a damp towel and brush with infused oil.

3. Season the mushrooms with salt and pepper.

4. Grill or broil the mushrooms until tender, approximately 8 minutes, depending on the size of the caps. Serve with a vegetable risotto as a vegetarian entree.

RECIPE 22.12

Approximate values per 120 g (4 oz.) serving:

Calories	86
Total fat	5 g
Saturated fat	1 g
Cholesterol	0 mg
Sodium	242 mg
Total carbohydrates	8.5 g
Protein	4 g

❖❖❖

RECIPE 22.13

DUXELLE

Yield: 360 g (12 oz.)   **Method:** Sautéing

Mushrooms	500 g	1 lb.
Whole butter	15 g	1 Tbsp.
Shallots, minced	25 g	2 Tbsp.
Garlic, chopped	5 g	1 tsp.
Salt and pepper	TT	TT
Fresh parsley, chopped	10 g	1 Tbsp.

1. Chop the mushrooms very finely.
2. Sauté the shallots and garlic in butter until tender. Add the mushrooms and sauté until dry.
3. Season with salt and pepper and add the parsley. Cool.
4. Use the duxelle as a stuffing for vegetables or as a flavouring ingredient in other recipes.

RECIPE 22.13

Approximate values per 30 g (1 oz.) serving:

Calories	22
Total fat	1 g
Saturated fat	0.5 g
Cholesterol	3 mg
Sodium	208 mg
Total carbohydrates	2.5 g
Protein	1 g

❖❖❖

RECIPE 22.14

SAUTÉED CHICKEN BREAST WITH BLACK MUSHROOMS

HOLIDAY INN SELECT, MONTREAL, QC
Executive Chef Ken Chong

Yield: 2 Servings   **Method:** Stir-frying

Black mushrooms, dried	8	8
Chicken breast, boneless, skinless	225 g	8 oz.
Egg white	30 g	1
Cornstarch	8 g	1 Tbsp.
Canola oil	15 mL	1 Tbsp.
Red pepper, julienned	50 g	1-1/2 oz.
Green pepper, julienned	50 g	1-1/2 oz.
Ginger root, slices	2	2
Green onions, sliced	25 g	2
Sugar	5 g	1 tsp.
Vinegar	3 mL	1/2 tsp.
Pepper	0.5 g	1/3 tsp.

1. Soak black mushrooms for 2 hours in water, rinse and julienne.
2. Cut the chicken into fine strips and coat with the egg white and cornstarch. Let rest for 10 minutes.
3. Heat canola oil in wok until smoking and sauté chicken strips until browned.
4. Add mushrooms, peppers, ginger and green onions. Stir-fry until vegetables soften.
5. Add the sugar, vinegar and pepper. Stir well and serve immediately.

Ken Chong

Ken has been Executive Chef at the Holiday Inn since 1994. He is a multi-award winner, including the prestigious Chef of the Year 2000 from the Quebec Chapter of the CFCC. He has extensive work experience at establishments such as the Hilton Bonaventure, Ritz Carleton Montreal, Sheraton Centre Toronto and Westin Ottawa.

RECIPE 22.14

Approximate values per serving:

Calories	296
Total fat	10 g
Saturated fat	1 g
Cholesterol	84 mg
Sodium	89 mg
Total carbohydrates	14 g
Protein	37.5 g

Note: Based on 2 servings

RECIPE 22.15

Glazed Pearl Onions

Yield: 500 g (1 lb.)   **Method:** Boiling

Pearl onions, peeled	500 g	1 lb.
Whole butter	50 g	1-1/2 oz.
Sugar	20 g	1 Tbsp.
Salt and pepper	TT	TT

1. Place the onions, butter and sugar in a sauté pan and add enough water to barely cover.

2. Boil the onions, allowing the water to evaporate. As the water evaporates, the butter-and-sugar mixture will begin to coat the onions. When the water is nearly gone, test the doneness of the onions. If they are still firm, add a small amount of water and continue to boil until the onions are tender.

3. Sauté the onions in the butter-and-sugar mixture until they are glazed. Season to taste with salt and pepper.

VARIATIONS: Vegetables such as carrots, turnips, zucchini and other squashes can also be glazed using this procedure. They should be cut into appropriate shapes and be large enough so they glaze properly without overcooking. When preparing a mix of glazed vegetables, cook each type separately because each has a different cooking time.

RECIPE 22.15

Approximate values per 60 g (2 oz.) serving:

Calories	78
Total fat	5 g
Saturated fat	3 g
Cholesterol	14 mg
Sodium	337 mg
Total carbohydrates	8 g
Protein	1 g

RECIPE 22.16

Harvard Beets

Yield: 8 120-g (4-oz.) Servings   **Method:** Boiling

Sugar	60 g	2 oz.
Cornstarch	15 g	2 Tbsp.
White wine vinegar	125 mL	4 fl. oz.
Salt and pepper	TT	TT
Beets, boiled, peeled, medium dice	1 kg	2 lb. 8 oz.

1. Combine the sugar, cornstarch, vinegar, salt and pepper in a heavy saucepan. Whisk until the cornstarch and sugar dissolve.

2. Bring to a boil, then cook, stirring constantly, until the mixture is thick and clear.

3. Add the beets, stirring gently to coat. Serve warm.

VARIATIONS: Add 20 g (2 Tbsp.) orange zest or a pinch of cloves.

RECIPE 22.16

Approximate values per 120 g (4 oz.) serving:

Calories	93
Total fat	0 g
Saturated fat	0 g
Cholesterol	0 mg
Sodium	480 mg
Total carbohydrates	22 g
Protein	2 g

RECIPE 22.17

Maple-Glazed Carrots

Yield: 16 120-g (4-oz.) Servings   **Method:** Sautéing

Carrots	2.2 kg	5 lb.
Whole butter	125 g	4 oz.
Salt and pepper	TT	TT
Maple syrup	125 mL	4 fl. oz.
Fresh parsley, chopped	20 g	2 Tbsp.

Continued

RECIPE 22.17

Approximate values per 120 g (4 oz.) serving:

Calories	146
Total fat	7 g
Saturated fat	4 g
Cholesterol	17 mg
Sodium	261 mg
Total carbohydrates	22 g
Protein	2 g

1. Peel the carrots and cut into a shape such as oblique, turned or rondelle.
2. Parboil the carrots in salt water and refresh. The carrots should be firm.
3. Sauté the carrots in butter until nearly tender.
4. Season with salt and pepper and add the maple syrup. Garnish with the parsley.

◆ ◆ ◆

RECIPE 22.18

CREAMED CORN WITH BASIL

Yield: 10 120-g (4-oz.) Servings   **Method:** Sautéing

Corn	12 ears	12 ears
Whole butter	60 g	2 oz.
Onion, small dice	125 g	4 oz.
Cream, 10%	250 mL	8 fl. oz.
Basil leaves, chopped	10 g	2 Tbsp.
Salt and white pepper	TT	TT

1. Cut the kernels from the ears of corn.
2. Sauté the onion in the butter without browning.
3. Add the corn and sauté until hot.
4. Add the cream. Bring to a boil, simmer to reduce slightly. When the corn is tender, add the basil and season with salt and white pepper.

RECIPE 22.18

*Approximate values
per 120 g (4 oz.) serving:*

Calories	211
Total fat	14 g
Saturated fat	8 g
Cholesterol	44 mg
Sodium	277 mg
Total carbohydrates	19 g
Protein	3 g

◆ ◆ ◆

RECIPE 22.19

RATATOUILLE

Yield: 20 100-g (3-oz.) Servings   **Method:** Sautéing

Eggplant, medium dice	350 g	12 oz.
Onion, medium dice	350 g	12 oz.
Garlic, chopped	10 g	1 Tbsp.
Olive oil	125 mL	4 fl. oz.
Green bell pepper, medium dice	200 g	6 oz.
Red bell pepper, medium dice	200 g	6 oz.
Zucchini, medium dice	250 g	8 oz.
Mushrooms, quartered	350 g	12 oz.
Tomato concassée	700 g	24 oz.
Fresh basil, chiffonade	30 g	1 oz.
Salt	30 g	1 oz.
Pepper	TT	TT
Tomato purée	as needed	as needed

1. Lightly salt the diced eggplant and allow to drain for 45 minutes in a colander.
2. Sauté the onion and garlic in the olive oil.
3. Lightly salt the diced eggplant and allow to drain for 45 minutes in a colander.
4. Add the peppers, eggplant, zucchini and mushrooms. Sauté until tender, approximately 10 minutes.
5. Add the tomato, fresh basil and seasonings. Stew for 5 minutes. Adjust the seasonings. If the sauce is too thin, add a small amount of tomato purée to thicken.

NOTE: Fresh herbs such as oregano, thyme or others may also be used.

RECIPE 22.19

*Approximate values
per 100 g (3 oz.) serving:*

Calories	82
Total fat	1 g
Saturated fat	6 g
Cholesterol	0 mg
Sodium	587 mg
Total carbohydrates	7 g
Protein	1 g

◆◆◆

RECIPE 22.20

GARLIC TIMBALES

Yield: 8 60-mL (2-oz.) Timbales   **Method:** Baking

Garlic cloves, peeled	40 g	10
Milk	75 mL	3 fl. oz.
Cream, 35%	250 mL	8 fl. oz.
Eggs, beaten	2	2
Dried thyme	1 g	1 tsp.
Salt and pepper	TT	TT

1. Butter eight small ramekins or timbales.

2. Place the garlic in a small saucepan, add enough water to cover and bring to a boil. Drain. Repeat this blanching procedure two more times.

3. Place the garlic in a blender with the milk and blend until smooth. Add the cream, eggs and thyme; stir until smooth. Season with salt and pepper. Strain.

4. Divide the custard among the timbales and place in a water bath. Bake for 30–45 minutes at 160°C (325°F).

5. Run a paring knife around the rim and unmould onto the serving plate.

VARIATIONS: Broccoli or cauliflower timbales—Place 30 g (1 oz.) of blanched chopped broccoli or cauliflower in 12 buttered timbales. Add 1 more egg to the garlic custard mixture.

◆◆◆

RECIPE 22.21

GARLIC AND VINEGAR BRAISED KALE

CAFÉ BRIO, VICTORIA, BC
Chef Jeff Keenliside

Yield: 4 Servings   **Method:** Braising

Kale, red Russian or Siberian	500 g	1 lb.
Olive oil	25 mL	1 fl. oz.
Garlic, sliced	10 g	3 cloves
Stock, chicken or vegetable	125 mL	4 fl. oz.
Red wine vinegar	60 mL	2 fl. oz.
Salt and pepper	TT	TT

1. Wash and remove large stems from kale.

2. Blanch kale for 30 seconds in boiling salted water. Shock in ice water and drain thoroughly.

3. In a braisier, sweat the garlic in olive oil.

4. Add the kale, toss and add stock. Cover and cook 4–5 minutes or until tender.

5. Finish with vinegar, season with salt and pepper and serve immediately.

RECIPE 22.20

*Approximate values
per 60 mL (2 oz.) serving:*

Calories	136
Total fat	13 g
Saturated fat	7.5 g
Cholesterol	96 mg
Sodium	320 mg
Total carbohydrates	3 g
Protein	3 g

Jeff Keenliside
Though born in Halifax, Jeff was raised on the West Coast. He began his apprenticeship at Aerie Resort and finished it at Café Brio, which specializes in West Coast contemporary food with a Tuscan hint. While working at Brio, Jeff was awarded Apprentice of the Year and was chosen to compete in the Vancouver Island Apprentice Black Box competition.

RECIPE 22.21

Approximate values per serving:

Calories	124
Total fat	7 g
Saturated fat	1 g
Cholesterol	0 mg
Sodium	392 mg
Total carbohydrates	14 g
Protein	5 g

Simon Smotkowicz, CCC

Simon has been a member and a leader of award-winning Canadian culinary teams for many years, most recently managing Team Canada to a world championship in Glasgow in 1997 and 2001. In 1995 he was elected Chef of the Year for the Western Region by his peers in the CFCC.

RECIPE 22.22

*Approximate values
per 45 g (1.5 oz.) serving:*

Calories	462
Total fat	37 g
Saturated fat	5 g
Cholesterol	0 mg
Sodium	305 mg
Total carbohydrates	27 g
Protein	8.5 g

RECIPE 22.23

*Approximate values
per 120 g (4 oz.) serving:*

Calories	174
Total fat	11 g
Saturated fat	4 g
Cholesterol	20 mg
Sodium	540 mg
Total carbohydrates	11.5 g
Protein	8 g

◆◆◆

NOTE

Traditionally, braised red cabbage is thickened with raw grated potato. One medium potato may be added in step 3.

◆◆◆

RECIPE 22.22

SOCCA

SHAW CONFERENCE CENTRE, Edmonton, AB
Executive Chef Simon Smotkowicz, CCC

Yield: 4 Side Dishes/Appetizers   **Method:** Broiling

Chickpea flour	175 g	1-1/2 cups
Extra virgin olive oil	150 mL	2/3 cup
Salt	3 g	1/2 tsp.
Thyme, chopped	0.5 g	1/2 tsp.
Rosemary, chopped	0.5 g	1/2 tsp.
Water	450 mL	16 fl. oz.
Black peppercorns, cracked	TT	TT

1. Combine chickpea flour, 75 mL (2-1/2 fl. oz.) olive oil, salt, herbs and water. Mix and let rest for 1 hour in refrigerator.
2. Preheat a cast-iron frying pan to moderate heat. Preheat broiler/salamander.
3. Ladle batter in pan to coat like a crêpe.
4. Place pan under broiler for 2–3 minutes.
5. Remove pan, sprinkle a little olive oil on crêpe, return to broiler until flat bread is crisp and golden.
6. Sprinkle with pepper, slide onto plate, keep warm and repeat process.
7. Cut Socca into wedges and serve with ratatouille and cheese.

◆◆◆

RECIPE 22.23

BRAISED RED CABBAGE WITH APPLES AND WINE

Yield: 16 125-g (4-oz.) Servings   **Method:** Braising

Red cabbage	1.5 kg	3 lb.
Bacon, medium dice	400 g	12 oz.
Onion, medium dice	250 g	8 oz.
Cider vinegar	75 mL	2 fl. oz.
Red wine	250 mL	8 fl. oz.
Salt and pepper	TT	TT
White stock	250 mL	8 fl. oz.
Cinnamon sticks	2	2
Medium potato, grated (optional)	175 g	1
Apples, tart, cored and shredded	350 g	12 oz.
Brown sugar	30 g	1 oz.
Red currant jelly	100 mL	4 fl. oz.

1. Shred the cabbage.
2. Render the bacon. Add the onion and sweat in the bacon fat until tender.
3. Add the cabbage and moisten with vinegar and wine. Season with salt and pepper. Add the stock, cinnamon sticks and the potato, if using. Cover and braise until the cabbage is almost tender, approximately 30 minutes. Moisten with additional stock if necessary.
4. Add the apples, brown sugar and red currant jelly and mix well.
5. Cover and braise until the apples are tender and dissolved, approximately 5 minutes.

◆◆◆

RECIPE 22.24

SWISS CHARD, POTATO AND CANADIAN BACON GRATIN

STAGE WEST HOTEL, TORONTO, ON
Executive Chef Rudolph Fischbacher

Yield: 10 Portions   **Method:** Gratin

Swiss chard, stemmed, washed	250 g	8 oz.
Butter	25 g	1 oz.
Garlic	5 g	1 clove
Salt	2 g	1/2 tsp.
Pepper	1 g	1/2 tsp.
Baking potato, peeled, sliced 30 mm (1/8 inch)	700 g	1-1/2 lb.
Pepper	TT	TT
Gruyère cheese, grated	125 g	4 oz.
Canadian bacon, sliced thin	250 g	8 oz.
Chicken stock	175 mL	6 fl. oz.

1. Slice the chard into 30-mm (1/8-inch) slices.
2. Melt butter over medium heat, sweat garlic, add chard and stew for 3 minutes or until liquid has evaporated. Season with salt and pepper.
3. In a buttered 20 x 20 cm (8 x 8 inch) gratin dish, layer one-third of the potatoes. Season with pepper.
4. Layer one-third of the cheese, one-half the bacon and all the chard.
5. Layer remaining potatoes and season with pepper.
6. Layer one-third of the cheese and remaining bacon.
7. Sprinkle remaining cheese, add stock and bake in a 200°C (425°F) oven for 30 minutes or until golden-brown.

Rudolph Fischbacher
Rudi trained in his native Austria and worked in Switzerland, Sweden, Spain and Germany before coming to Canada. Currently he is the Executive Chef and Food and Beverage Manager at the Stage West Hotel. He and his staff of 50 provide services for dinner theatre, banquets, the restaurant, lounge, patio and in-room dining.

RECIPE 22.24

Approximate values per serving:

Calories	201
Total fat	8 g
Saturated fat	4 g
Cholesterol	34 mg
Sodium	643 mg
Total carbohydrates	19 g
Protein	12 g

◆◆◆

RECIPE 22.25

BRAISED ROMAINE LETTUCE

Yield: 12 Servings   **Method:** Braising

Romaine lettuce	3 heads	3 heads
Onion, small dice	250 g	8 oz.
Celery, small dice	250 g	8 oz.
Carrot, small dice	250 g	8 oz.
Bacon ends and pieces, small dice	250 g	8 oz.
White stock	600 mL	24 fl. oz.
Salt and pepper	TT	TT

1. Trim the lettuce heads. Blanch them in salted boiling water, refresh and drain well.
2. Combine the onion, celery, carrot, bacon pieces and white stock in a sauce pot and simmer for 10 minutes.
3. Quarter the heads of romaine and trim off most of the core, leaving just enough to hold the leaves together.
4. Place 15 g (1 Tbsp.) of the mirepoix in each portion of lettuce and fold to make a bundle.

RECIPE 22.25

Approximate values per serving:

Calories	171
Total fat	11 g
Saturated fat	4 g
Cholesterol	21 mg
Sodium	534 mg
Total carbohydrates	11.5 g
Protein	8 g

Continued

5. Pour the remaining stock mixture into a hotel pan and arrange the lettuce portions in the pan. Season with salt and pepper.

6. Cover the pan and braise in a 180°C (350°F) oven for approximately 1 hour. Serve each portion with vegetables, bacon and a portion of the cooking liquid.

◆◆◆

RECIPE 22.26

ROASTED VEGETABLE AND BOCCONCINI STACKS ON POLENTA ROUNDS

Chef-Consultant Anne Milne, VANCOUVER, BC

Anne Milne

After 16 years as a successful Vancouver chef, Anne is now a self-employed chef-consultant whose prestigious clients include the Bedford Hotel and the Butchart Gardens in Victoria. Anne is also a food writer for The Vancouver Sun, City Food Magazine, *and* City Palate *of Calgary.*

Yield: 8 Appetizers or 4 Main Course Servings   **Method:** Roasting

Cornmeal	150 g	1 cup
Butter	10 g	2 tsp.
Salt	5 g	1 tsp.
Japanese eggplant, cut into 1-cm (1/2-inch) rounds	2 large	2 large
Roma tomatoes, cut into 1-cm (1/2-inch) rounds	4 large	4 large
Zucchini, cut into 1-cm (1/2-inch) rounds	2 medium	2 medium
Red onions, cut into 1-cm (1/2-inch) rounds	2 medium	2 medium
Shiitake mushrooms	250 g	8 oz.
Salt and fresh cracked pepper	as needed	as needed
Olive oil	15 mL	1 Tbsp.
Balsamic vinegar	10 mL	2 tsp.
Mozzarella (bocconcini balls), fresh	250 g	8 oz.
Fresh basil leaves	4 large	4 large
Rosemary stems, fresh	4 or 8	4 or 8
Marinara sauce	500 mL	16 fl. oz.

1. To make the polenta, boil 1 L (4 cups) water in a heavy-bottomed pot. Whisk in cornmeal in a slow, steady stream. Stir over reduced heat until cooked, approximately 15 minutes. Stir in butter and salt.

2. Pour the polenta into a greased cookie sheet and spread to 1-cm (1/2-inch) thickness. Cool and cut out circles with a cookie cutter. (Large circles are used for main course and smaller circles for appetizers.)

3. Sprinkle vegetables with salt and pepper and drizzle with olive oil. Heat oven to 225°C (450°F) and brush olive oil on two cookie sheets. Spread the vegetables on the sheets and roast in the oven until tender and just starting to brown. (Vegetables may also be grilled.) Remove from oven and sprinkle with balsamic vinegar. Let cool.

4. Arrange the polenta circles on a clean, oiled baking sheet and stack the vegetables and cheese in the following order on top of each polenta round: polenta, bocconcini, one fresh basil leaf, red onion, eggplant, zucchini, tomato and shiitake mushrooms. Secure the stacks by spearing them with a bamboo skewer. Coat tops of stacks with olive oil and bake in a 190°C (375°F) oven for approximately 10 minutes, or just until cheese begins to melt.

5. Remove from the oven and replace the bamboo skewers with a stem of fresh rosemary. Serve stacks on a thin layer of marinara sauce.

RECIPE 22.26

Approximate values per appetizer:

Calories	320
Total fat	9 g
Saturated fat	4 g
Cholesterol	22 mg
Sodium	418 mg
Total carbohydrates	39 g
Protein	15 g

◆◆◆

RECIPE 22.27

WILD RICE AND MUSHROOM STRUDEL

SHERATON WINNIPEG HOTEL, WINNIPEG, MB
Executive Chef Joseph Lindthorst

Yield: 4 Portions

Method: Baking

Butter	25 g	1 oz.
Onion, brunoise	50 g	2 oz.
Garlic, minced	5 g	1 tsp.
Forest mushrooms		
(porcini, crimini, chanterelle), sliced	100 g	3-1/2 oz.
Parsley, chopped	10 g	1 Tbsp.
Oregano	1 g	1/2 tsp.
Wild rice, cooked	100 g	3-1/2 oz.
Chicken or veal velouté	50 mL	2 fl. oz.
Smoked Gruyère, grated	25 g	1 oz.
Salt and pepper	TT	TT
Phyllo dough	3 sheets	3 sheets
Olive oil	50 mL	3 Tbsp.

1. Heat butter in sauté pan and sweat onion and garlic.
2. Add mushrooms and sauté until tender. Remove from heat.
3. Stir in parsley, oregano, wild rice, velouté and cheese. Season to taste.
4. Lay out first sheet of phyllo and brush with olive oil. Repeat with other two sheets.
5. Form a log of filling at one end of sheet. Roll up, tucking in ends to form a compact package. Brush with more olive oil.
6. Bake in a 180°C (360°F) oven until golden. Slice strudel on the bias and place pieces on plate.

VARIATION: Try an herb-infused oil on the phyllo dough.

RECIPE 22.27

Approximate values per serving:

Calories	304
Total fat	23 g
Saturated fat	8 g
Cholesterol	31 mg
Sodium	425 mg
Total carbohydrates	20 g
Protein	7 g

WEBLINKS

Ontario White Bean Producers—Buying, Storing, Soaking and Cooking Beans
www.wwdc.com/whitepeabeans/basics.htm

Vegetable Categories
www.produceoasis.com/Hierarchy_folder/
Vegetables_folder/MainVegetable.html

Vegetarian
recipes.alastra.com/vegetarian/default.html

Exotic Vegetables
www.rain.org/greennet/docs/exoticveggies.html

Asian Fruits and Vegetables
www.agric.nsw.gov.au/Hort/Fmrs/Asian_veg/

National Onion Association
www.onions-usa.org/

Mushrooms: The Mushroom Council
www.mushroomcouncil.com/

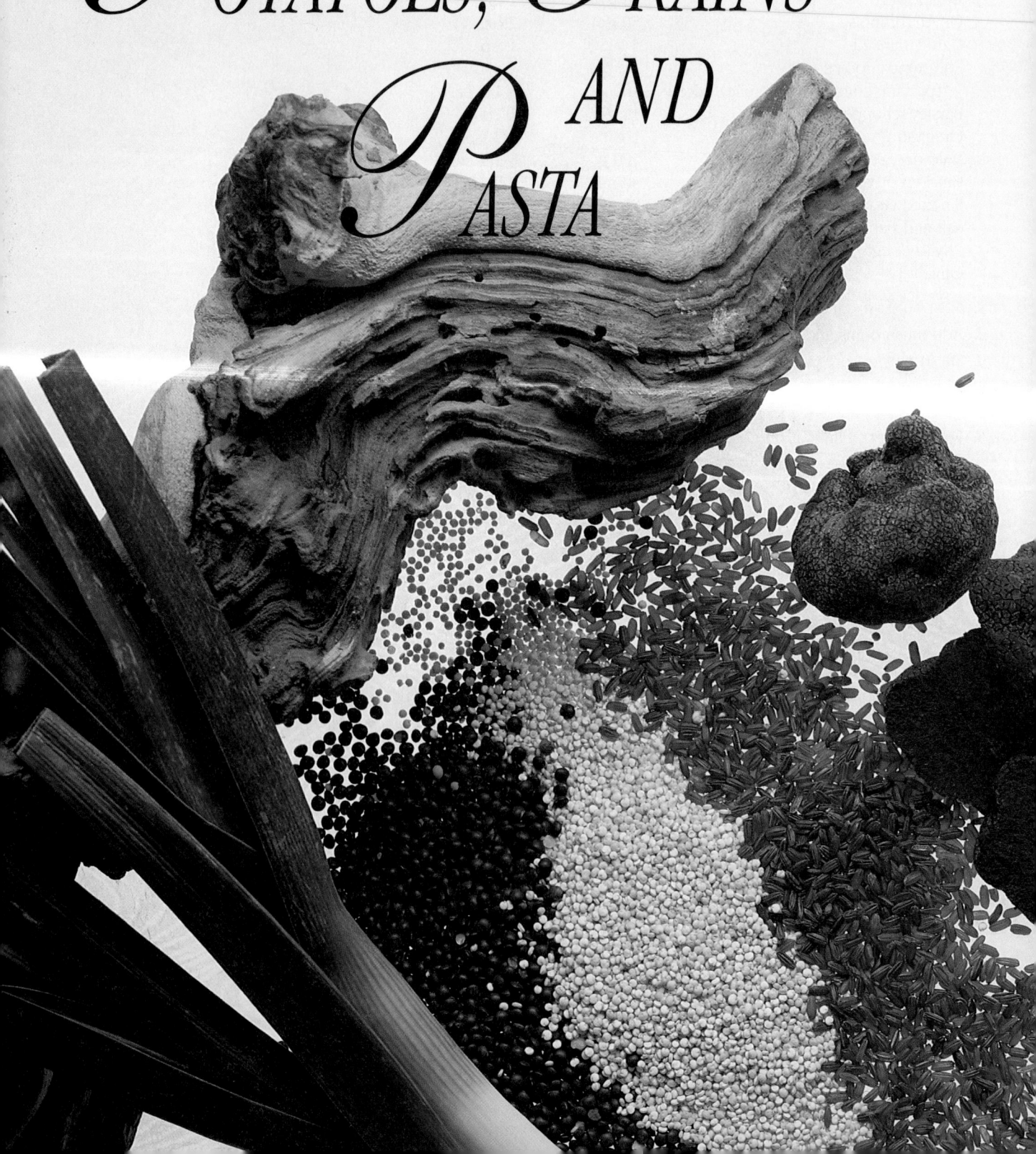

CHAPTER 23

POTATOES, GRAINS AND PASTA

LEARNING OUTCOMES

After studying this chapter you will be able to:

◆ identify a variety of potatoes
◆ apply various cooking methods to potatoes: baking, baking en casserole, sautéing and pan-frying, boiling
◆ identify a variety of grains
◆ apply various cooking methods to grains: simmering, risotto method, pilaf method
◆ identify pasta products
◆ make fresh pasta: rolling and cutting the dough, making ravioli
◆ cook pasta: to order, in advance

*P*otatoes, grains (corn, rice, wheat and others) and pastas are collectively known as starches. Some of these foods are vegetables; others are grasses. Pastas, of course, are prepared products made from grains. Starches are, for the most part, staple foods: foods that define a cuisine and give it substance. All are high in starchy carbohydrates, low in fat and commonly used as part of a well-balanced meal.*

Today's chefs are rediscovering traditional and ethnic dishes that rely on grains seldom used in typical food service operations. Pasta, made from a variety of grains in numerous shapes and flavours and accompanied by countless sauces and garnishes, now regularly appears on many menus alongside the ubiquitous potato prepared in many classic and modern styles.

POTATOES

Potatoes (Fr. *pommes de terre*) are one of the few vegetables native to the New World, probably originating in the South American Andes. Botanically, potatoes are succulent, nonwoody annual plants and members of the nightshade family. The portion we consume is the tuber, the swollen fleshy part of the underground stem. Potatoes are hardy and easy to grow, making them inexpensive and widely available.

Identifying Potatoes

The following are some of the more commonly used types of potatoes. Other varieties are regularly being developed or rediscovered and tested in the marketplace.

Choose potatoes that are heavy and very firm with clean skin and few eyes. Avoid those with many eyes, sprouts, green streaks, soft spots, cracks or cut edges. Most varieties are available all year.

Purple Potatoes

Purple (or blue) potatoes have a deep purple skin. The flesh is bright purple, becoming lighter when cooked. They are mealy, with a flavour and texture similar to russets. The most common varieties are All Blue and Caribe, which were quite popular in the mid-19th century.

Purple Potatoes

Red Potatoes

Red potatoes have a thin red skin and crisp, white, waxy flesh, best suited to boiling or steaming. They do not have the dry, mealy texture successful baking requires. **New potatoes** are small, immature red potatoes usually marketed during the early summer as "creamers."

Red Potatoes

Russet Potatoes

Russet potatoes, also referred to as Idaho potatoes, are the standard baking potato. They are long with rough, reddish-brown skin and mealy flesh. Russets are excellent baked and are the best potatoes for frying. They tend to fall apart when boiled. They are marketed in several size categories and should be purchased in the size most appropriate for their intended use.

White Potatoes

White potatoes are available in round or long varieties. They have a thin, tender skin with a tender, waxy yellow or white flesh. The smaller ones are sometimes marketed as new potatoes (not to be confused with new red potatoes). Round white potatoes are also referred to as all-purpose potatoes. Yukon Gold and White Rose are common varieties. Bintje is an increasingly popular variety; it has a golden skin, creamy flesh and buttery flavour. White potatoes are usually cooked with moist heat or used for sautéing.

Russet Potatoes

White Potatoes

Sweet Potatoes

Sweet potatoes are from a different botanical family than ordinary potatoes, although they are also tubers that originated in the New World. Two types are commonly available. One has yellow flesh and a dry, mealy texture; it is known as a boniato, white or Cuban sweet potato. The other has a darker orange, moister flesh and is high in sugar; it is known as a red sweet potato. Both types have thick skins ranging in colour from light tan to brownish red. (Sometimes dark-skinned sweet potatoes are erroneously labelled *yams*.) Sweet potatoes should be chosen according to the desired degree of sweetness. They are best suited for boiling, baking and puréing, although the less sweet varieties can be deep-fat fried. The cooked flesh can also be used in breads, pies and puddings. Sweet potatoes are available canned, often in a spiced or sugary sauce.

Sweet Potatoes

Yams

Yams are a third type of tuber, botanically different from both sweet and common potatoes. Yams are less sweet than sweet potatoes, but they can be used interchangeably. The flesh of yams ranges from creamy white to deep red. Yams are Asian in origin and are now found in Africa, South America and the southern United States.

Nutrition

Potatoes contain a high percentage of easily digested complex carbohydrates and little or no fat. They are also a good source of many minerals and some vitamins. See Table 23.1.

TABLE 23.1   NUTRITIONAL VALUES OF SELECTED POTATOES

Per 112 g (4 oz.), baked in skin	Kcal	Protein (g)	Carbohydrates (g)	Fibre (g)	Total Fat (g)	Niacin (g)	Phosphorus (mg)	Potassium (mg)
Russet	124	2.6	28.6	0.7	0.1	1.9	64.8	475.5
Sweet potato	93	1.6	21.7	2.4	<0.1	mq	mq	mq
Yam	132	1.7	31.2	mq	0.2	0.4	33	455

The Corinne T. Netzer Encyclopedia of Food Values 1992
mq = measurable quantity, but data are unavailable

Purchasing and Storing Potatoes

Mealy versus Waxy

One of the most important considerations in selecting potatoes is choosing between the mealy and waxy varieties. You should understand the differences and purchase the type best suited to your needs. See Table 23.2.

Mealy potatoes (also known as starchy potatoes) have a high starch content and thick skin. They are best for baking and are often ordered from suppliers simply as "bakers." Their low sugar content also allows them to be deep-fat fried long enough to cook the interior fully without burning the exterior. Mealy potatoes tend to fall apart when boiled, making them a good choice for whipped or puréed potatoes.

Waxy potatoes have a low starch content and thin skin. They are best for boiling. They will not develop the desired fluffy texture when baked. Because of their high moisture content they tend to become limp and soggy when deep-fat fried.

TABLE 23.2 COMPARISON OF MEALY AND WAXY POTATOES

	Content of:			Best to:			
	Starch	Moisture	Sugar	Bake	Boil	Sauté	Deep-fat fry
Mealy: russet, white rose, purple	high	low	low	✓			✓
Waxy: red, new (red), Finnish yellow	low	high	high		✓	✓	

Grading

Potatoes sold in Canada are graded according to size and cleanliness. Canada No. 1 grade potatoes must be "reasonably free from dirt" with "not more than a slight amount of loose dirt or foreign material in the container." Round varieties of potatoes must have a minimum diameter of 57 mm (2-1/4 inches) and a maximum diameter of 89 mm (3-1/2 inches) to be graded as Canada No. 1. Long varieties must have a minimum diameter of 51 mm (2 inches) and a maximum diameter of 70 mm (2-3/4 inches). New potatoes must have a minimum diameter of 48 mm (1-7/8 inches) to be graded Canada No. 1.

Canada No. 2 grade potatoes have an "appreciable amount of dirt adhering to them" and "there is not more than a moderate amount of loose dirt or foreign material in the container" with them. Canada No. 2s must have a minimum diameter of 44 mm (1-3/4 inches) and a maximum diameter of 114 mm (4-1/2 inches).

Purchasing

Potatoes are usually packed in 22-kg (50-lb.) cartons. Counts vary depending on average potato size. For example, in a 100-count carton, each potato would weigh an average of 250 g (8 oz.). Eighty-, 90- and 100-count cartons are the most common. Generally, larger-sized potatoes (i.e., smaller counts) are more expensive. Size does not affect quality, however, and selection should be based on intended use.

Storing

Temperatures between 7°C and 10°C (45°F and 50°F) are best for storing potatoes. Do not store potatoes in the refrigerator. At temperatures below 4°C (40°F) potato starch turns to sugar, making the cooked product too sweet and increasing the risk that the potato will turn grey or streaky when cooked. Potatoes with a high sugar content also burn more easily when fried.

Potatoes should be stored in a dark room, as light promotes chlorophyll production, turning them green and bitter. Any green patches indicate the possible presence of solanine, a toxin harmful if eaten in large amounts, and should be peeled away. Solanine is also present in the eyes and sprouts and they, too, should be removed and discarded before cooking.

Under proper conditions, fresh potatoes should last for two months. Do not wash potatoes until ready to use, as washing promotes spoilage.

Applying Various Cooking Methods

Potatoes have a relatively neutral flavour, making them a perfect accompaniment to many savoury dishes. They can be prepared with almost any dry- or moist-heat cooking method: baking, sautéing, pan-frying, deep-fat frying, boiling or steaming. They can be combined with other ingredients in braises and stews. Potatoes are used in soups (vichyssoise), dumplings (gnocchi), breads, pancakes (latkes), puddings, salads and even vodka.

Many potato dishes, both classic and modern, employ more than one cooking method. For example, lorette potatoes require boiling and deep-fat frying; hash browns require parboiling, then sautéing. Even french fries are best when first blanched in hot oil.

Determining Doneness

Most potatoes are considered done when they are soft and tender or offer little resistance when pierced with a knife tip. Fried potatoes should have a crisp, golden-brown surface; the interior should be moist and tender.

Roasting and Baking

Potatoes may be roasted with meat or poultry, becoming coated with the fat and drippings released from the main item as it cooks. Either mealy or waxy potatoes, peeled or unpeeled, can be roasted successfully.

Mealy potatoes such as russets are ideal for baking. The skin is left intact, although it may be pierced with a fork to allow steam to escape. A true baked potato should not be wrapped in foil or cooked in a microwave; this changes the cooking method to steaming and prevents a crisp skin from forming. A properly baked potato should be white and fluffy, not yellowish or soggy. Once baked, potatoes can be eaten plain (or with butter, sour cream and other garnishes) or used in other recipes.

Basic Procedure for Baking Potatoes

1. Scrub the potatoes well.
2. Using a fork, pierce the potato skins.
3. Rub the potatoes with oil and salt if desired. Do not wrap them in foil.
4. Bake the potatoes until done. A paring knife should penetrate them easily.

RECIPE 23.1

Approximate values per potato:

Calories	271
Total fat	6 g
Saturated fat	0.5 g
Cholesterol	0 mg
Sodium	1227 mg
Total carbohydrates	51 g
Protein	5 g

◆ ◆ ◆

DERIVATIVES FROM BAKED POTATOES

Pommes Macaire—Remove baked potato from skins using a spoon. Mash and mix in butter, season to taste. Using a little flour, mould into 2-cm (1-inch) cakes. Pan-fry.

Stuffed Baked Potato—Cut top off baked potato and scoop out flesh. Mash with sour cream, bacon bits, chives, salt and pepper. Pipe back into shells, sprinkle with grated cheese and bake to heat through.

Applying the Basics

RECIPE 23.1

BAKED POTATOES

Yield: 8 Servings

Russet potatoes	8	8
Vegetable oil	50 mL	3 Tbsp.
Kosher salt	25 g	1 Tbsp.

1. Scrub the potatoes well, but do not peel. Pierce the skin of each potato to allow steam to escape.
2. Rub the potatoes with the oil, then sprinkle with kosher salt.
3. Place the potato on a rack over a sheet pan. Bake in a 200°C (400°F) oven until done, approximately 1 hour. The potatoes should yield to gentle pressure and a paring knife inserted in the thickest part should meet little resistance.
4. Hold uncovered in a warm spot and serve within 1 hour.

Baking in a Casserole

Many classic potato dishes require baking either raw or parboiled potatoes with sauce, cheese, meat or other seasonings in a baking dish or casserole. Well-known examples include scalloped potatoes, which are baked in béchamel sauce, and au gratin, which are topped with cheese and baked. These dishes usually develop a crisp, brown crust, which is part of their appeal.

The casserole should hold its shape when cut; the potatoes should be tender and the sauce should be smooth, not grainy.

Potato casseroles can be fully baked, then held loosely covered in a steam table for service. Portions can be reheated or browned briefly under a broiler or salamander at service time.

Basic Procedure for Baking Potatoes en Casserole

1. Prepare the potatoes by washing, peeling, slicing or partially cooking as desired or as directed in the recipe.
2. Add the potatoes to the baking pan in layers, alternating with the sauce, cream, cheese or other ingredients. Or combine the potatoes with the other ingredients and place in a buttered baking pan.
3. Bake the potatoes until done.

Applying the Basics

RECIPE 23.2

GRATIN DAUPHINOISE

Yield: 1.8–2.2 kg (4–5 lb.)

Potatoes	1.5 kg	3 lb.
Whole butter	as needed	as needed
Salt and white pepper	TT	TT

Gruyère cheese, grated	250 g	8 oz.
Cream, 18%	700 mL	24 fl. oz.
Nutmeg	0.5 g	1/4 tsp.
Egg yolks	3	3

1. Peel the potatoes and cut into very thin slices.
2. Place a single layer of potatoes in a well-buttered, full-size hotel pan.
3. Season with salt and pepper. Sprinkle on a thin layer of cheese.
4. Add another layer of potatoes and cheese and repeat until all the potatoes and about three-quarters of the cheese are used.
5. Heat the cream and nutmeg to a simmer. Whisk the egg yolks together in a bowl, then gradually add the hot cream.
6. Pour the cream-and-egg mixture over the potatoes. Top with the remaining cheese.
7. Bake uncovered at 180°C (350°F) until the potatoes are tender and golden-brown, approximately 50–60 minutes.

RECIPE 23.2

Approximate values per 85 g serving:

Calories	154
Total fat	7 g
Saturated fat	4 g
Cholesterol	48 mg
Sodium	153 mg
Total carbohydrates	17 g
Protein	6 g

Sautéing and Pan-Frying

Waxy potatoes, such as red- and white-skinned varieties, are best for sautéing or pan-frying. Often they are first parboiled or even fully cooked—a convenient way to use leftover boiled potatoes. They are then cooked in fat following the general procedures for sautéing and pan-frying discussed in Chapter 9, Principles of Cooking.

The fat can be clarified butter, oil, bacon fat or lard, depending on the desired flavour of the finished dish. The fat must be hot before the potatoes are added so that they will develop a crust without absorbing too much fat. Sautéed potatoes should have a crisp, well-browned crust and tender interior. They should be neither soggy nor greasy.

Potatoes can be sautéed or pan-fried by two methods: tossing and still-frying. The **tossing method** is used to cook relatively small pieces of potatoes in a small amount of fat. The potatoes are tossed using the pan's sloped sides so that they brown evenly on all sides. The **still-frying method** is used to create a disc-shaped potato product. The shredded or sliced potatoes are added to the pan, usually covering its bottom, and allowed to cook without stirring or flipping until they are well browned on the first side. The entire mass is then turned and cooked on the second side. When the potatoes are done, they can be cut into wedges for service.

Basic Procedure for Sautéing and Pan-Frying Potatoes

1. Wash, trim, peel, cut and/or cook the potatoes as desired or as directed in the recipe.
2. Heat the pan, add and heat the fat. Add the potatoes to the hot fat. Do not overcrowd the pan. Use enough fat to prevent the potatoes from sticking to the pan. Depending on the recipe, use either the tossing method or still-frying method.
3. Add garnishes, seasonings and other ingredients as desired or as directed in the recipe.
4. Cook the potatoes until done.

RECIPE 23.3

*Approximate values
per 120 g serving:*

Calories	170
Total fat	12 g
Saturated fat	7 g
Cholesterol	33 mg
Sodium	650 mg
Total carbohydrates	16 g
Protein	1 g

◆◆◆

MORE THAN A FRENCH FRY

Thanks to the genius of Carême, Escoffier and others, few vegetables have as extensive a classic repertoire as potatoes. Some of these dishes begin with the duchesse potatoes mixture; in this regard, duchesse potatoes can be considered the mother of many classic potato preparations. For example,

Duchesse + Tomato concassée = *Marquis*

Duchesse + Chopped truffles + Almond
   coating + Deep-fat frying = *Berny*

Duchesse + Pâte à choux = *Dauphine*

Dauphine + Grated Parmesan + Piped
   shape + Deep-fat frying = *Lorette*

Duchesse + Shaping + Breading + Deep-fat
   frying = *Croquettes*

Other classic potato preparations not based on duchesse potatoes include:

Anna—thin slices are arranged in several circular layers in a round pan or mould coated with clarified butter; additional butter is brushed on and the potatoes are baked until crisp, then cut into wedges for service.

Boulangère—onions and potatoes are sautéed in butter, then transferred to a baking pan, stock is added and the potatoes are cooked uncovered until done.

Château—turned potatoes are sautéed in clarified butter until golden and soft.

Parisienne—small spheres are cut from raw, peeled potatoes with a parisienne scoop; they are seasoned and sautéed in clarified butter, then tossed with a meat glaze and garnished with chopped parsley.

Rösti—potatoes are shredded, seasoned and pan-fried in the shape of a pie, then cut into wedges for service.

Applying the Basics

RECIPE 23.3

LYONNAISE POTATOES

Yield: 8 120-g (4-oz.) Servings

Potatoes, waxy variety	1 kg	2 lb.
Onion, julienned	250 g	8 oz.
Clarified butter	125 mL	4 fl. oz.
Salt and pepper	TT	TT
Parsley, chopped	10 g	1 Tbsp.

1. Partially cook the potatoes by baking, boiling or steaming. Allow to cool.
2. Peel and cut the potatoes into 1/2-cm-thick (1/4-inch) slices.
3. Sauté the onions in half the butter until tender. Remove the onions from the pan with a slotted spoon and set aside.
4. Add the remaining butter to the pan. Add the potatoes and sauté, tossing as needed, until well browned on all sides.
5. Return the onions to the pan and sauté to combine the flavours. Season to taste with salt and pepper and garnish with parsley.

Deep-Fat Frying

Potato chips and french fries (Fr. *pomme frites*) are extremely popular in a variety of shapes, sizes and seasonings. While a wide range of shapes, sizes and preseasoned frozen products are available, fresh fried potatoes can be a delicious, economical menu item.

Top-quality russet potatoes are recommended for deep-fat frying. The skin may be removed or left attached. If peeled, the potatoes should be soaked in clear, cold water until ready to cut and cook. This keeps them crisp and white by leaching some of the starch that might otherwise make the potatoes gummy or cause smaller cuts to stick together when cooked.

The potatoes are usually blanched in oil ranging in temperature from 120°C to 150°C (250°F to 300°F) until tender and translucent. They are then drained and held for service, at which time they are finished in hotter oil, usually at a temperature between 180°C and 190°C (350°F and 375°F).

Deep-fat frying is also used to finish cooking several classic potato dishes such as croquettes and dauphine, in which fully cooked potatoes are puréed, seasoned, shaped and fried.

Deep-fat fried potatoes should be drained on absorbent paper briefly and served immediately.

In general, the procedures for deep-fat frying found in Chapter 21 also apply here. Specific recipes for several types of deep-fat fried potatoes are given at the end of this chapter.

Boiling

Waxy potatoes are best for all moist-heat cooking methods. Boiled potatoes (which are actually simmered) may be served as is or used in multistep preparations such as purées, salads, soups and baked casseroles. Potatoes are usually boiled in water, although stock may be used or milk added for flavour. Always begin cooking potatoes in cold liquid to ensure even cooking. Unlike other vegetables, potatoes should not be refreshed in cold water; it makes them soggy.

Basic Procedure for Boiling Potatoes

1. Wash, peel or trim the potatoes as desired.

2. Cut the potatoes into uniform-size pieces. The pieces should not be too small or they will absorb a large amount of water as they cook, making the final product soggy.

3. Add the potatoes to enough cool liquid to cover them by several inches. Bring to a boil, reduce to a simmer and cook until done. If a slightly firm finished product is desired, remove and drain the potatoes when they are slightly underdone and allow carryover cooking to finish cooking them.

4. Drain the potatoes in a colander and serve or use for further preparation.

Applying the Basics

RECIPE 23.4

DUCHESSE POTATOES

Yield: 1 kg (2 lb.)

Potatoes, peeled and quartered	1 kg	2 lb.
Whole butter	50 g	2 oz.
Nutmeg	TT	TT
Salt and pepper	TT	TT
Egg yolks	4	4

1. Boil the potatoes in salted water until tender. Drain and immediately turn out onto a sheet pan to allow the moisture to evaporate.

2. While still warm, press the potatoes through a ricer or food mill, or grind through a grinder's medium plate. Blend in the butter and season to taste with nutmeg, salt and pepper.

3. Mix in the egg yolks, blending well.

4. Place the duchesse mixture in a piping bag fitted with a large star tip. Pipe single portion-sized spirals onto a parchment-lined sheet pan. Brush with clarified butter and bake at 190°C (375°F) until the edges are golden-brown, approximately 8–10 minutes. Serve immediately.

USAGE: Duchesse potatoes are often used to decorate platters used for buffets, tableside preparations or to present chateaubriand. To create borders and garnishes, the standard mixture for duchesse potatoes is forced through a piping bag while still very hot and relatively soft.

RECIPE 23.4

Approximate values per 100 g serving:

Calories	168
Total fat	6 g
Saturated fat	3 g
Cholesterol	97 mg
Sodium	261 mg
Total carbohydrates	25 g
Protein	3.5 g

1. Pass boiled potatoes through a food mill.

2. Pipe duchesse potatoes.

3. The finished potatoes.

Grains

Botanically, grains are grasses that bear edible seeds. Corn, rice and wheat are the most significant. Both the fruit (i.e., the seed or kernel) and the plant are called a grain (see Figure 23.1).

Most grain kernels are protected by a **hull** or husk. All kernels are composed of three distinct parts: the **bran**, **endosperm** and **germ**. The bran is the tough outer layer covering the endosperm. Bran is a good source of fibre and B vitamins. The endosperm is the largest part of the kernel and is a source of protein and carbohydrates (starch). It is the part used primarily in milled products such as flour. The germ is the smallest portion of the grain and is the only part that contains fat. It is also rich in thiamin. The bran, endosperm and germ are usually separated by milling.

Identifying Grains

This section presents information on corn, rice and wheat as well as several minor grains that are nutritionally significant and gaining popularity.

Some products are available in a stone-ground form. This means that the grains were ground with a stone mill rather than by the steel blades typically used for **cracking**, **grinding**, **hulling** and **pearling**. Stone grinders are gentler and more precise, so they are less likely to overgrind the grain. Stone-ground products will always be labelled as such and are usually more expensive than steel-ground ones.

Corn

Corn (Sp. *maíz*; It. *granturco*) is the only grain that is also eaten fresh as a vegetable. (Fresh corn is discussed in Chapter 22, Vegetables.) Its use as a dried grain dates back several thousand years in Central America and long preceded its use as a vegetable.

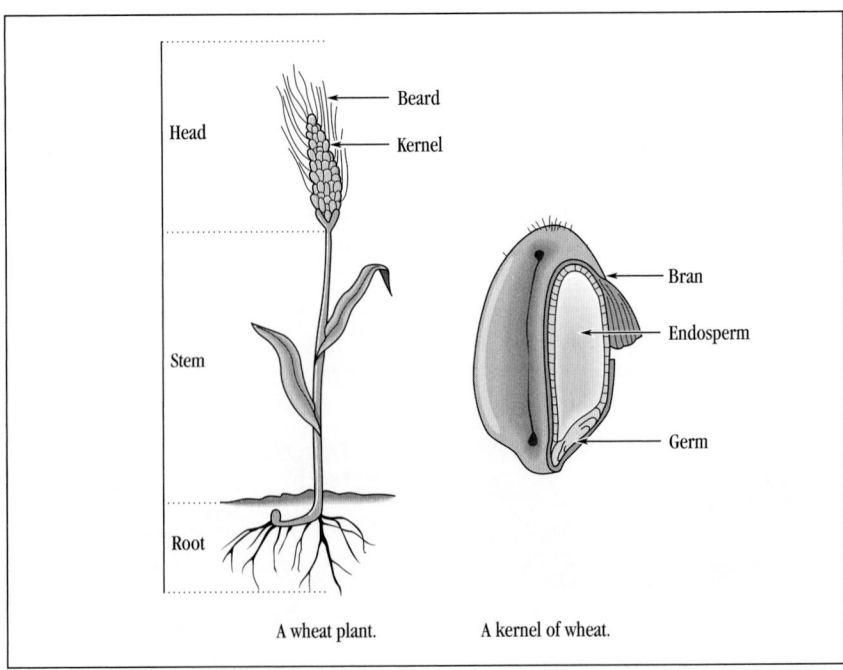

A wheat plant.   A kernel of wheat.

FIGURE 23.1

Cornmeal

Cornmeal is made by drying and grinding a special type of corn known as *dent*, which may be yellow, white or blue. Cornmeal is most often used in breads, as a coating for fried foods or cooked as polenta or mush. Products made with cornmeal have a gritty texture and a sweet but starchy flavour.

Cornmeal

Hominy

Hominy, also known as posole or samp, is dried corn that has been soaked in hydrated lime or lye. This causes the kernels to swell, loosening the hulls. The hulls and germs are removed and the kernels dried. These white or yellow kernels resemble popcorn, but with a soft, chewy texture and smoky-sour flavour. Hominy is available dried or cooked and canned. It may be served as a side dish or used in stews or soups. **Masa harina**, a finely ground flour made from hominy, is used for making breads, tortillas, tamales and other Mexican and southwestern dishes.

Hominy

Grits

Grits are traditionally made by grinding dried hominy. These tiny white granules may be used in baked dishes but are most often served as a hot breakfast cereal, usually topped with butter or cheese. Quick-cooking and instant grits are available.

Rice

Rice (Fr. *riz*; It. *riso*; Sp. *arroz*) is the starchy seed of a semiaquatic grass. Probably originating on the Indian subcontinent or in Southeast Asia, rice is used as a staple by more than half of the world's population.

Rice can be incorporated into almost any cuisine, from Asian to Spanish to classic French. Its flavour adapts to the foods and seasonings with which the rice is cooked or served. Its texture adds an appealing chewiness to meat and poultry dishes, salads, breads and puddings. Rice is not limited to a side dish, but may be used in stews or curries, for stuffing vegetables or game birds, in puddings, salads, beverages (such as *horchata*) and breads.

Rice is divided into three types based on seed size: **long-grain**, **medium-grain** and **short-grain**. Long-grain rice is the most versatile and popular worldwide. The grains remain firm, fluffy and separate when cooked. (Long-grain rice can, however, become sticky if overcooked or stirred frequently during cooking.) Short-grain rice has more starch and becomes quite tender and sticky when cooked. Italian risotto, Japanese sushi and Spanish paella are all traditionally made with short-grain rice. The appearance and starch content of medium-grain rice falls somewhere in between. Medium-grain rice becomes sticky when cool, so it is best eaten freshly made and piping hot.

Long-grain, medium-grain and short-grain rice are available in different processed forms. All rice is originally brown. The grains can be left whole, with the bran attached, for **brown rice**. Or they can be pearled for the more familiar polished **white rice**. Both brown rice and white rice can be processed into converted rice and instant rice.

Converted rice is parboiled to remove the surface starch. This procedure also forces nutrients from the bran into the grain's endosperm. Therefore, converted rice retains more nutrients than regular milled white rice, although the flavour is the same. Converted rice is neither precooked nor instant; in fact, it cooks more slowly than regular milled white rice.

Instant or **quick-cooking rice** is widely available and useful if time is a concern. Instant rice is created by fully cooking then flash-freezing milled rice. Unfortunately, this processing removes some of the nutrients and flavour.

Converted Rice

Arborio Rice

Basmati Rice

Arborio Rice

Arborio is a round, short-grain rice used primarily in Italian dishes such as risotto. It is very sticky, with a white colour and mild flavour.

Basmati Rice

Basmati is one of the finest long-grain rices in the world. It grows in the Himalayan foothills and is preferred in Indian cuisine. It is highly aromatic, with a sweet, delicate flavour and a creamy yellow colour. Basmati rice is usually aged to improve its aromatic qualities and should be washed well before cooking.

Brown Rice

Brown rice is the whole natural grain of rice. Only the husk has been removed. Brown rice has a nutty flavour; its chewy texture is caused by the high-fibre bran. Brown rice absorbs more water and takes longer to cook than white rice.

Brown Rice

Wild Rice

Wild rice is prepared in the same manner as traditional rice, although it is actually the seed of an unrelated reedlike aquatic plant. Wild rice has long, slender grains with a dark brown to black colour. It has a nuttier flavour and chewier texture than traditional rice. Three grades are available: giant (the best quality, with very long grains); fancy (a medium-sized grain, suitable for most purposes); and select (a short grain, suitable for soups, pancakes or baked goods). Cultivated in Saskatchewan, Manitoba and Ontario, it is generally served with game, used as a stuffing for poultry or combined with regular rice for a side dish. Wild rice is expensive, but small quantities are usually sufficient.

Wild Rice

Wild Pecan Rice

Wild pecan rice is neither wild nor made with pecans. It is a unique long-grain rice grown only in the bayou country of southern Louisiana. Wild pecan rice has a nutty flavour and exceptionally rich aroma.

Wild Pecan Rice

Guidelines for Cooking Rice

Rice may be rinsed before cooking to remove dirt and debris, but doing so also removes some nutrients. It is not necessary to rinse most American-grown rice as it is generally clean and free of insects. Rice may also be soaked before cooking. Soaking softens the grains, removes some starch and speeds cooking.

TABLE 23.3 GUIDELINES FOR COOKING RICE

Type of Rice	Ratio Rice : Water (by Volume)	Preparation	Cooking Time (simmering)	Yield from 200 g (1 cup) Raw Rice
Arborio	1 : 2.5–3	Do not rinse or soak	15–20 min.	2.5–3 cups
Basmati	1 : 1.75	Rinse well; soak	15 min.	3 cups
Brown, long-grain	1 : 2.5	Do not rinse; can soak	45–50 min.	3–4 cups
Converted	1 : 2.5	Do not rinse	20–25 min.	3–4 cups
White, long-grain (regular milled)	1 : 2	Do not rinse	15 min.	3 cups
Wild	1 : 3	Rinse	35–60 min., depending on grade	3–4 cups

The standard ratio for cooking rice is 2 parts liquid to 1 part rice. The actual ratio varies, however, depending on the type of rice. Guidelines for cooking rice are found in Table 23.3.

Once cooked, rice is highly perishable. Because of its neutral pH and high protein content, cooked rice is a potentially hazardous food. To avoid the risk of food-borne illnesses, be sure to store cooked rice out of the temperature danger zone.

Wheat

Wheat (Fr. *blé*) is most often milled into the wide range of flours discussed in Chapter 26, Principles of the Bakeshop. But wheat and products derived from it are also used as starchy side dishes or ingredients in soups, salads, ground meat dishes and breads. These products include cracked wheat, bulgur and couscous. When cooked they are slightly chewy with a mild flavour. All should be fluffy; none should be soggy or sticky.

Wheat germ and *wheat bran* are widely available and highly touted for their nutritional values. Bran and germ are not generally used alone, but may be added to bread or other cooked dishes.

Cracked Wheat

Cracked wheat is the whole wheat kernel (known as a **berry**) broken into varying degrees of coarseness. It is not precooked, and the kernel's white interior should be visible. The bran and germ are still intact, so cracked wheat has a great deal of fibre but a short shelf life. Whole wheat berries must be soaked for several hours before cooking. Cracked wheat can be fully cooked by long, gentle simmering.

Bulgur

Bulgur is a wheat berry that has had the bran removed; it is then steam-cooked, dried and ground into varying degrees of coarseness. Bulgur has a nutlike flavour and texture; it is a uniform golden-brown colour (uncooked cracked wheat is not) and requires less cooking time than cracked wheat. Generally, cracked wheat and bulgur cannot be substituted for one another in recipes.

Bulgur only needs to be soaked in water, then drained, for use in salads, or briefly cooked when used in stews or pilafs. Bulgur is good with grilled meats and as an alternative to rice in stuffings and other dishes. The fine grind is most often used in packaged mixes such as tabouli; the medium grind is most often available in bulk.

Couscous

Couscous is made by removing the bran and germ from **durum wheat** berries. The endosperm is then steamed, pressed to form tiny pellets and dried. Couscous is available in varying degrees of coarseness; medium-fine is the most popular. Couscous is prepared by steaming over water or stock in a pot called a couscousier. Couscous, traditionally served with North African stews, can be used or served like rice.

Other Grains

Barley

Barley is one of the oldest culinary grains, used by humans since prehistoric times. Barley is extremely hardy, growing in climates from the tropics to the near-Arctic. Although much of the barley crop is used to make beer or feed

Bulgur

Couscous

Barley

animals, some does find its way into soups, stews and stuffings. The most common type is pearled to produce a small, round white nugget of endosperm. It has a sweet, earthy flavour similar to oats, and goes well with onions, garlic and strong herbs. Barley's texture ranges from chewy to soft, depending on the amount of water in which it is cooked. Its starchiness can be used to thicken soups or stews.

Buckwheat/Kasha

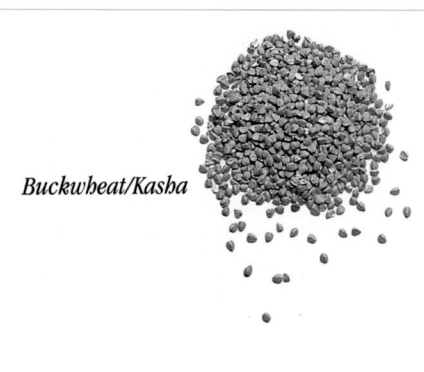

Buckwheat/Kasha

Buckwheat is not a type of wheat; it is not even a grain. Rather, it is the fruit of a plant distantly related to rhubarb. Buckwheat is included here, however, because it is prepared and served in the same manner as grains.

The whole buckwheat kernel is known as a **groat**. The product most often sold as buckwheat is actually kasha, which is a hulled, roasted buckwheat groat. Kasha is reddish brown with a strong, nutty, almost scorched flavour. It is available whole or ground to varying degrees of coarseness. Whole kasha remains in separate grains after cooking; the finer grinds become rather sticky. Kasha can be served as a side dish, usually combined with pasta or vegetables, or it can be chilled and used in salads.

Raw buckwheat groats are ground into flour typically used in pasta, blini and other pancakes. Buckwheat flour contains no gluten-forming proteins and it tends to remain grainy, with a sandy texture. Therefore, it should not be substituted for all of the white or whole wheat flour in breads or baked goods.

Oats

Oats

After rice, oats are probably the most widely accepted whole-grain product in the North American diet. Oats are consumed daily as a hot breakfast cereal (oatmeal) and are used in breads, muffins, cookies and other baked goods.

An oat groat is the whole oat kernel with only the husk removed. It contains both the bran and germ. *Steel-cut oats*, sometimes known as Irish oats, are groats that are toasted then cut into small pieces with steel blades. *Rolled oats*, marketed as "old-fashioned oats," are groats that have been steamed, then rolled into flat flakes. *Quick-cooking oats* are simply rolled oats cut into smaller pieces to reduce cooking time. *Instant oats* are partially cooked and dried before rolling so they need only to be rehydrated in boiling water. Several flavoured versions are also marketed as breakfast cereal. Rolled oats and quick-cooking oats can be used interchangeably, but instant oats should not be substituted in most recipes.

Oat bran is the outer covering of a hulled oat. It is available as a separate product, although rolled and cut oats do contain some oat bran.

The term *oatmeal* is commonly used to refer to both processed groats and the cooked porridge made from them. The processed groats known as oatmeal are a grey-white colour with a starchy texture and sweet flavour. They cook into the soft, thick porridge with a robust flavour called oatmeal.

Nutrition

Grains are an excellent source of vitamins, minerals, proteins and fibre (Table 23.4). The amount of milling or refining and the method of preparation affect their nutritional values, however. Unrefined and less-refined grains are excellent sources of dietary fibre. Rice is also quite nutritious: It is low in sodium and calories and contains all the essential amino acids. Some grains, especially white rice and oats, are usually enriched with calcium, iron and B vitamins.

TABLE 23.4 NUTRITIONAL VALUES OF SELECTED GRAINS

Per 120 g (4 oz.), cooked	Kcal	Protein (g)	Carbohydrates (g)	Fibre (g)	Total Fat (g)	Niacin (g)	Phosphorus (mg)	Potassium (mg)
Barley, pearled	139	2.6	32	0.3	0.5	1.6	42.5	72.5
Bulgur	94	3.5	21.1	0.4	0.3	0.9	36.5	62
Grits	68	1.6	14.7	0.1	0.2	0.8	15	27
Kasha	104	3.8	22.6	0.6	0.7	1.2	80	95
Oats	45	3.6	13	0.4	1	0.2	89	66
Rice, brown, long-grain	126	2.9	26	1.9	1	1.5	81	42
Rice, converted	90	1.5	21.1	mq	0.7	mq	mq	mq
Rice, white, long-grain	146	3.1	31.6	0.1	0.3	1.5	47	40
Wheat germ (toasted)	432	33.2	56.4	14.8	12	6.4	1280	1076

The Corinne T. Netzer Encyclopedia of Food Values 1992

mq = measurable quantity, but data are unavailable

Purchasing and Storing Grains

Purchasing

When buying grains, look for fresh, plump ones with a bright, even colour. Fresh grains should not be shrivelled or crumbly; there should be no sour or musty odours.

Grains are sold by weight. They come in bags or boxes ranging from 450 g to 45 kg (1 to 100 lb.). Units of 4.5, 11 and 22 kg (10, 25 and 50 lb.) are usually available.

Storing

All grains should be stored in air-tight containers placed in a dark, cool, dry place. Air-tight containers prevent dust and insects from entering. Air-tight containers and darkness also reduce nutrient loss caused by oxidation or light. Coolness inhibits insect infestation; dryness prevents mould.

Vacuum-sealed packages will last for extended periods. Whole grains, which contain the oily germ, should be refrigerated to prevent rancidity.

Applying Various Cooking Methods

Three basic cooking methods are used to prepare grains: simmering, risotto and pilaf. Unlike simmered grains, those cooked by either the risotto or pilaf method are first coated with hot fat. The primary distinction between the pilaf and risotto methods is the manner in which the liquid is then added to the grains. When grains are used in puddings, breads, stuffings and baked casseroles, they are almost always first fully cooked by one of these methods.

Determining Doneness

Most grains should be cooked until tender, although some recipes do require a chewier or more al dente product. Doneness can usually be determined by cooking time and the amount of liquid remaining in the pan. Some grains, such as wild rice, are fully cooked when they puff open.

In general, grains will be fully cooked when almost all of the cooking liquid is absorbed. This is indicated by the appearance of tunnel-like holes between the grains. Grains can be cooked until almost all of the liquid is absorbed, then removed from the heat and left to stand, covered, for 5–10 minutes. This allows the cooked grains to absorb the remaining moisture without burning.

Simmering

The most commonly used method for preparing grains is simmering. To do so, simply stir the grains into a measured amount of boiling salted water in a saucepan on the stove top. When the liquid returns to a boil, lower the heat, cover, and simmer until the liquid is absorbed and the grains are tender. The grains are not stirred during cooking.

The grains can be flavoured by using stock as the cooking liquid. Herbs and spices can also be added.

Basic Procedure for Simmering Grains

1. Bring the cooking liquid to a boil.
2. Stir in the grains. Add herbs or spices as desired or as directed in the recipe.
3. Return the mixture to a boil, cover and reduce to a simmer.
4. Simmer the grains until tender and most of the liquid is absorbed.
5. Remove the grains from the heat.
6. Drain if appropriate or keep covered and allow the excess moisture to evaporate, approximately 5 minutes. Fluff the grains with a fork before service.

Applying the Basics

RECIPE 23.5

BASIC SIMMERED RICE

Yield: 750 mL (3 cups)

Water	500 mL	16 fl. oz.
Salt	2 g	1/2 tsp.
White rice	200 g	1 cup (7 oz.)

1. Bring the water and salt to a boil in a heavy saucepan. Slowly add the rice.
2. Cover the pan and reduce the heat so that the liquid simmers gently. Cook until the rice is tender and the water is absorbed, approximately 15–20 minutes.
3. Remove from the heat and transfer to a hotel pan. Do not cover. Allow any excess moisture to evaporate for approximately 5 minutes.
4. Fluff the rice and serve, or refrigerate for use in another recipe.

Risotto Method

Risotto is a classic Northern Italian rice dish in which the grains remain firm but merge with the cooking liquid to become a creamy, almost puddinglike dish. True risotto is made with a short-grain starchy rice such as arborio, but the risotto method can also be used to cook other grains such as barley and oats.

The grains are not rinsed before cooking, as this removes the starches needed to achieve the desired consistency. The grains are coated, but not cooked, in a hot fat such as butter or oil. A hot liquid is then gradually added to the grains so that the mixture is kept at a constant simmer. The cooking liquid should be a rich, flavourful stock. Unlike simmering and the pilaf method, the risotto method requires frequent, sometimes constant, stirring.

When finished, the grains should be creamy and tender, but still al dente in the centre. Grated cheese, 35% cream, cooked meat, poultry, fish, shellfish, herbs and vegetables can be added to create a flavourful side dish or a complete meal.

Basic Procedure for Preparing Grains by the Risotto Method

1. Bring the cooking liquid to a simmer.
2. Heat the fat in a heavy saucepan over moderate heat. Add any onions, garlic or other flavouring ingredients and sauté for 1–2 minutes without browning.
3. Add the grains to the saucepan. Stir well to make sure the grains are well coated with fat. Do not allow the grains to brown.
4. Add any wine and cook until it is fully absorbed.
5. Begin to add the simmering stock 120 mL (4 fl. oz.) at a time, stirring frequently. Wait until each portion of cooking liquid is almost fully absorbed before adding the next.
6. Test for doneness after the grains have cooked for approximately 18–20 minutes. There should be a little crunch remaining.
7. Remove the saucepan from the heat and stir in any butter, grated cheese, herbs or other flavouring ingredients as directed. Serve immediately.

Applying the Basics

RECIPE 23.6

RISOTTO MILANESE

Yield: 24 120-g (4-oz.) Servings

Chicken stock	2.5 L	2-1/2 qt.
Whole butter	125 g	4 oz.
Onion, minced	150 g	5 oz.
Arborio rice	700 g	1 lb. 8 oz.
Dry white wine	250 mL	8 fl. oz.
Saffron threads, crushed	0.5 g	1/2 tsp.
Parmesan cheese, grated	125 g	4 oz.

1. Bring the chicken stock to a simmer.
2. Heat 90 g (3 oz.) of the butter in a large, heavy saucepan. Add the onion and sauté without browning until translucent.
3. Add the rice to the onion and butter. Stir well to coat the grains with butter but do not allow the rice to brown. Add the wine and stir until it is completely absorbed.
4. Add the saffron. Add the simmering stock, 125 mL (4 fl. oz.) at a time, stirring frequently. Wait until the stock is absorbed before adding the next 125-mL (4-fl.-oz.) portion.
5. After approximately 18–20 minutes all of the stock should be incorporated and the rice should be al dente. Remove from the heat and stir in the remaining butter and the grated cheese. Serve immediately.

VARIATIONS: Risotto with Radicchio (*al Radicchio*)—Omit the saffron and Parmesan. Just before the risotto is fully cooked, stir in 125 mL (4 fl. oz.) of 35% cream and 100 g (3 oz.) of finely chopped radicchio leaves.

1. Sauté the rice and onions in butter.

2. Add the stock gradually while stirring frequently.

3. Stir in the remaining butter and grated cheese.

RECIPE 23.6

Approximate values per 120 g (4 oz.) serving:

Calories	120
Total fat	6 g
Saturated fat	3.5 g
Cholesterol	15 mg
Sodium	483 mg
Total carbohydrates	9 g
Protein	7 g

Risotto with Four Cheeses (*al Quattro Formaggi*)—Omit the saffron. When the risotto is fully cooked, remove from the heat and stir in 50 g (2 oz.) each of grated Parmesan, Gorgonzola, fontina and mozzarella cheeses. Garnish with toasted pine nuts and chopped parsley.

Risotto with Smoked Salmon (*al Salmone Affumicato*)—Omit the butter, saffron and Parmesan. Sauté the onion in 100 mL (3 fl. oz.) of corn or safflower oil instead of butter. When the risotto is fully cooked, remove from the heat and stir in 250 mL (8 fl. oz.) of 18% cream, 100 mL (3 fl. oz.) of fresh lemon juice and 250 g (8 oz.) of good-quality smoked salmon. Garnish with chopped fresh parsley and dill. Serve with lemon wedges.

Pilaf Method

With the pilaf method, the raw grains are lightly sautéed in oil or butter, usually with onions or seasonings for additional flavour. Hot liquid, often a stock, is then added. The pan is covered and the mixture left to simmer until the liquid is absorbed.

1. Sauté the bulgur in butter.

2. Add the hot stock to the bulgur.

3. Fluff the finished bulgur.

RECIPE 23.7

*Approximate values
per 125 g (4 oz.) serving:*

Calories	110
Total fat	6 g
Saturated fat	3.5 g
Cholesterol	14 mg
Sodium	468 mg
Total carbohydrates	9 g
Protein	7 g

Basic Procedure for Preparing Grains by the Pilaf Method

1. Bring the cooking liquid (either water or stock) to a boil.
2. Heat the fat in a heavy saucepan over moderate heat. Add any onions, garlic or other flavourings and sauté for 1–2 minutes without browning.
3. Add the grains to the saucepan. Stir well to make sure the grains are well coated with fat. Do not allow the grains to brown.
4. All at once, add the hot cooking liquid to the sautéed grains.
5. Return the liquid to a boil, reduce to a simmer and cover.
6. Allow the mixture to simmer, either in the oven or on the stove top, until the liquid is absorbed.

Applying the Basics

RECIPE 23.7

BULGUR PILAF

Yield: 8 125-g (4-oz.) Servings

Whole butter	50 g	2 oz.
Onion, fine dice	125 g	4 oz.
Bulgur	300 g	10 oz.
Bay leaf	1	1
Chicken stock, hot	1 L	1 qt.
Salt and pepper	TT	TT

1. Melt the butter in a large, heavy saucepan over moderate heat. Add the onion and cook until translucent.
2. Add the bulgur and bay leaf. Sauté until the grains are well coated with butter.
3. Add the hot stock and season to taste with salt and pepper. Reduce the heat until the liquid barely simmers.
4. Cover and continue cooking until all of the liquid is absorbed and the grains are tender, approximately 18–20 minutes.
5. Fluff with a fork and adjust the seasonings before service.

VARIATION: Barley Pilaf—Substitute 500 g (2 cups) of pearled barley for the bulgur. Cooking time may increase by 10–15 minutes.

PASTA

Pasta is made from an unleavened dough of liquid mixed with flour. The liquid is usually egg and/or water. The flour can be from almost any grain: wheat, buckwheat, rice or a combination of grains. The dough can be coloured and flavoured with puréed vegetables, herbs or other ingredients and it can be cut or **extruded** into a wide variety of shapes and sizes.

Pasta can be cooked fresh while the dough is still moist and pliable, or the dough can be allowed to dry completely before cooking. Pasta can be filled or sauced in an endless variety of ways. It can stand alone or be used in salads, desserts, soups or casseroles.

Pasta is widely used in the cuisines of Asia, North America and Europe. In Italy, pasta dishes are usually served as a separate course, referred to as the *minestre*; in other European countries, Asia and North America, pasta dishes may be served as an appetizer, entree or side dish.

Identifying Pastas

The better-known pastas are based on the Italian tradition of kneading wheat flour with water and eggs to form a smooth, resilient dough. This dough is rolled very thin and cut into various shapes before being boiled in water or dried for longer storage.

Commercially prepared dried pasta products are usually made with semolina flour. Semolina flour, ground from hard durum wheat and available from specialty purveyors, has a rich cream colour and produces a very smooth, durable dough. Semolina dough requires a great deal of kneading, however, and bread flour is an acceptable substitute when preparing fresh pasta by hand.

Asian pasta, generally known as noodles, is made from wheat, rice, bean or buckwheat flour. It is available fresh or dried from commercial purveyors and at specialty markets.

✦✦✦
THE MACARONI MYTH

The popular myth holds that noodles were first invented in China and discovered there by the Venetian explorer Marco Polo during the 13th century. He introduced the food to Italy and from there the rest of Europe. While there is little doubt that the Chinese were making noodles by the 1st century A.D., it is now equally clear that they were not alone.

Middle Eastern and Italian cooks were preparing macaroni long before Marco Polo's adventures. A clear reference to boiled noodles appears in the *Jerusalem Talmud* of the 5th century A.D. There, rabbis debate whether noodles violate Jewish dietary laws (they do, but only during Passover). Tenth-century Arabic writings refer to dried noodles purchased from vendors. Literary references establish that dishes called lasagna, macaroni and ravioli were all well known (and costly) in Italy by the mid-13th century.

Pasta's current popularity dates from the 18th century, when mass production by machine began in Naples, Italy. English gentlemen on their Grand Tours of the Continent developed a fondness for pasta; the word *macaroni* became a synonym for a dandy or a vain young man. Macaroni arrived in America with English colonists, who preferred it with cream sauce and cheese or in a sweet custard. Domestic factories soon opened, and by the Civil War (1861–1865) macaroni was available to the working class. Pasta became a staple of the American middle-class diet following the wave of Italian immigrants in the late 19th century.

During the 1980s pasta became ubiquitous. Restaurants began serving it in ways previously unimagined. Corner grocery stores and local supermarkets began offering at least a dozen different shapes, often fresh and sometimes flavoured. Dedicated cooks began to make pasta from scratch, though they sometimes tossed it with bottled sauce. Many also became interested in Asian noodles. Chinese, Japanese, Korean and Thai restaurants expanded their menu offerings to include traditional noodle dishes eagerly ordered by curious consumers. Pasta's popularity continues to grow as chefs discover the versatility of this inexpensive, nutritious food.

Spinach Fettuccine

Lasagna

Fettuccine

Spaghetti

Capellini

Italian-Style Pasta

Although all Italian-style pasta is made from the same type of dough, the finest commercial pastas are those made with pure semolina flour, which gives the dough a rich, yellow colour. Grey or streaked dough probably contains softer flours. Dried pasta should be very hard and break with a clean snap. The surface should be lightly pitted or dull. (A smooth or glossy surface will not hold or absorb sauces as well.)

Dried pasta, both domestic and imported, is available in a wide range of flavours and shapes. In addition to the traditional white (plain), green (spinach) and red (tomato) pastas, manufacturers are now offering such unusual flavour combinations as lemon-peppercorn, whole wheat–basil, jalapeño–black bean and carrot-ginger. Small pieces of herbs or other flavourings are often visible in these products.

There are hundreds of recognized shapes of pasta, but only two or three dozen are generally available in Canada. When experimenting with unusual flavours and shapes, be sure to consider the taste and appearance of the final dish after the sauce and any garnishes are added.

Italian-style pasta can be divided into three groups based on the shape of the final product: ribbons, tubes and shapes. There is no consistent English nomenclature for these pastas; the Italian names are recognized and applied virtually worldwide. (A specific shape or size may be given different names in different regions of Italy, however. These distinctions are beyond the scope of this text.)

Ribbons

Pasta dough can be rolled very thin and cut into strips or ribbons of various widths. All ribbon shapes work well with tomato, fish and shellfish sauces. Thicker ribbons, such as spaghetti and fettuccine, are preferred with cream or cheese sauces. Sheets of fresh pasta dough can be filled and shaped to create ravioli, cappelletti and tortellini. Filled pasta is usually served with a light cream- or tomato-based sauce that complements the filling's flavours.

Tubes

Cylindrical forms or tubes are made by extrusion. The hollow tubes can be curved or straight, fluted or smooth. Tubes are preferred for meat and vegetable sauces and are often used in baked casseroles.

Manicotti

Rigatoni

Ziti

Penne

Spira

Shapes

The extrusion process can also be used to shape pasta dough into forms. The curves and textures produced provide nooks and crevices that hold sauces well.

Conchiglie

Farfalle

Fusilli

Rotelle

Orzo

Shaped pastas, such as conchiglie, farfalle and fusilli, are preferred with meat sauces and oil-based sauces such as pesto. Larger shaped pastas can be cooked, then stuffed with meat or cheese fillings and baked or served as a casserole.

Asian Noodles

Asian noodles are not cut into the same wealth of shapes and sizes as Italian-style pasta, nor are they usually flavoured or coloured with vegetable purées, herbs or other ingredients.

Virtually all Asian noodles are ribbons—some thin, some thick—folded into bundles and packaged. Differences arise because of the flours used for the dough.

Most dried Asian noodles benefit by soaking in hot water for several minutes before further preparation. The water softens the noodle strands; the bundles separate, and the noodles cook more evenly.

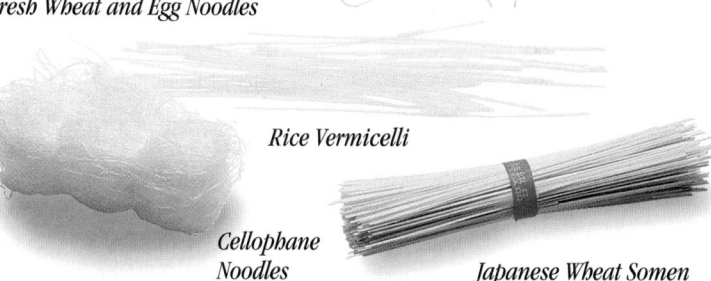

Flour Stick Wheat Noodles (without egg)

Fresh Wheat and Egg Noodles

Rice Vermicelli

Cellophane Noodles

Japanese Wheat Somen

Wheat Noodles

Wheat noodles, also known as egg noodles, are the most popular and widely available of the Asian noodles. They are thin, flat noodles with a springy texture; they are available fresh or dried. Dried egg noodles can be deep-fat fried after boiling to create crisp golden noodles (chow mein) used primarily as a garnish.

Japanese wheat noodles, known as somen (if thick) and udon (if thin), may be round, square or flat. They are eaten in broth or with a dipping sauce.

Rice Noodles

Rice noodles are dried thin noodles made with rice flour. They should be soaked in hot water before cooking and rinsed in cool running water after boiling to remove excess starch and prevent sticking. Rice noodles are often served in soups or sautéed.

Rice vermicelli, which has very fine strands, can be fried in hot oil without presoaking. In only a few seconds the strands will turn white, puff up and become crunchy. Mounds of crunchy rice noodles can be used as a base for sautéed dishes or for presenting hors d'oeuvre.

Bean Starch Noodles

Bean starch noodles are also known as spring rain noodles, bean threads, bean noodles or cellophane noodles. They are thin, transparent noodles made from mung beans. Dried bean noodles can be fried in the same manner as rice

♦♦♦

DUMPLINGS

A **dumpling** is a small mound of dough cooked by steaming or simmering in a flavourful liquid. Dumplings are found in many cuisines: Italian gnocchi, Jewish matzo balls, German spaetzle, Chinese won tons and Polish pierogi. Dumplings can be sweet or savoury, plain or filled.

Plain or **drop dumplings** are made with a breadlike dough, often leavened with yeast or chemical leavening agents. They should be light and tender, but firm enough to hold their shape when cooked. Drop dumplings may be served with stews or broths, or coated with butter or sauce as an appetizer or side dish. Recipes for gnocchi and spaetzle are included at the end of this chapter.

Filled dumplings are made by wrapping noodle dough around seasoned meat, vegetables, cheese or fruit. These parcels are then steamed, fried or baked and served as a snack food, appetizer or side dish. A recipe for deep-fat fried won tons is included in Chapter 33, Appetizers and Sandwiches (Recipe 33.8).

vermicelli. Otherwise, they must be soaked in hot water before using in soups, stir-fries or braised dishes.

Buckwheat Noodles

Buckwheat flour is used in the noodles of Northern Japan and the Tokyo region, known as soba noodles. Soba noodles are available fresh or dried and do not need soaking before cooking. They are traditionally served in broth or with a dipping sauce, but may be substituted for Italian-style pasta if desired.

Nutrition

Pastas are very low in fat and are an excellent source of vitamins, minerals, proteins and carbohydrates. (See Table 23.5.) Also, the processed products are sometimes enriched with additional nutrients.

Purchasing and Storing Pasta Products

Pasta products are purchased by weight, either fresh or dried. Tubes and shapes are not generally available fresh. Dried products, by far the most common, are available in boxes or bags, usually in 500-g, 5- and 20-kg (1-, 10- and 20-lb.) units. They can be stored in a cool, dry place for several months. Fresh pasta can be stored in an air-tight wrapping in the refrigerator for a few days or in the freezer for a few weeks.

Preparing Fresh Pasta

Making Fresh Pasta

Fresh pasta is easy to make, requiring almost no special equipment and only a few staples. The basic form is the **sfoglia**, a thin, flat sheet of dough that is cut into ribbons, circles or squares.

Although pasta dough can be kneaded by hand, stretched and rolled with a rolling pin and cut with a chef's knife, pasta machines make these tasks easier. Pasta machines are either electric or manual. Some electric models mix and knead the dough, then extrude it through a cutting disk. An extrusion machine is most practical in a food service operation regularly serving large quantities of pasta. The pasta machine more often encountered is operated manually with a hand crank. It has two rollers that knead, press and push the dough into a thin, uniform sheet. Adjacent cutting rollers slice the thin dough into various widths for fettuccine, spaghetti, capellini or the like.

TABLE 23.5   NUTRITIONAL VALUES OF SELECTED PASTA

Per 120 g (4 oz.), cooked	Kcal	Protein (g)	Carbohydrates (g)	Fibre (g)	Total Fat (g)	Niacin (g)	Phosphorus (mg)	Potassium (mg)
Noodle, Japanese soba (buckwheat)	113	5.8	24.4	mq	0.1	0.6	29	40
Pasta, wheat, dried	186	9.2	35.9	0.3	0.2	1.2	38	22
Pasta, wheat, spinach and egg, fresh	147	5.7	28.4	mq	1.10	1.2	65	42

The Corinne T. Netzer Encyclopedia of Food Values 1992
mq = measurable quantity, but data are unavailable

Applying the Basics

Basic Pasta Dough

Yield: 1.8 kg (4 lb.)

Eggs	850 g	15
Olive oil	30 mL	1 fl. oz.
Salt	15 g	1 Tbsp.
Bread flour or semolina	1.1 kg	2 lb. 8 oz.

1. Place the eggs, oil and salt in a large mixer bowl. Use the paddle attachment to combine.

2. Add one-third of the flour and stir until the mixture begins to form a soft dough. Remove the paddle attachment and attach the dough hook.

3. Gradually add more flour until the dough is dry and cannot absorb any more flour.

4. Remove the dough from the mixer, wrap it well with plastic wrap and set it aside at room temperature for 20–30 minutes.

5. After the dough has rested, roll it into flat sheets by hand or with a pasta machine. Work with only a small portion at a time, keeping the remainder well covered to prevent it from drying out.

6. While the sheets of dough are pliable, cut them into the desired width with a chef's knife or pasta machine. Sheets can also be used for making ravioli, as illustrated below.

VARIATIONS: Garlic-Herb—Roast 1 head of garlic. Peel and purée the cloves and add to the eggs. Add up to 50 g (2 oz.) of finely chopped assorted fresh herbs just before mixing is complete.

Spinach—Add 250 g (8 oz.) of cooked, puréed and well-drained spinach to the eggs. Increase the amount of flour slightly if necessary.

Tomato—Add 125 g (4 oz.) of tomato paste to the eggs; omit the salt. Increase the amount of flour slightly if necessary.

NOTE: Semolina flour can be substituted in this recipe, although it makes a stronger dough that is more difficult to work with by hand. Try half semolina (durum) and half bread flour.

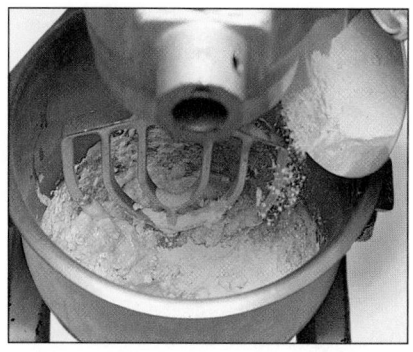

1. Add flour to the mixing bowl and use the paddle until the mixture forms a soft dough.

2. The finished dough.

RECIPE 23.8

Approximate values per 85 g serving:

Calories	232
Total fat	6 g
Saturated fat	1.5 g
Cholesterol	154 mg
Sodium	322 mg
Total carbohydrates	36 g
Protein	11.5 g

Basic Procedure for Rolling and Cutting Pasta Dough

1. Work with a small portion of the dough. Leave the rest covered with plastic wrap to prevent it from drying out.

2. Flatten the dough with the heel of your hand.

3. Set the pasta machine rollers to their widest setting. Insert the dough and turn the handle with one hand while supporting the dough with the other hand. Pass the entire piece of dough through the rollers.

4. Dust the dough with flour, fold it in thirds and pass it through the pasta machine again.

5. Repeat the folding and rolling procedure until the dough is smooth. This may require 4–6 passes.

6. Tighten the rollers one or two marks, then pass the dough through the machine. Without folding it in thirds, pass the dough through the machine repeatedly, tightening the rollers one or two marks each time.

1. Pass the entire piece of dough through the pasta machine.

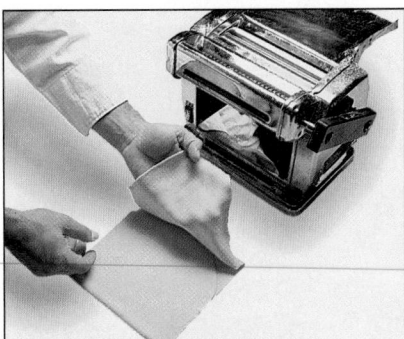

2. Fold the dough in thirds.

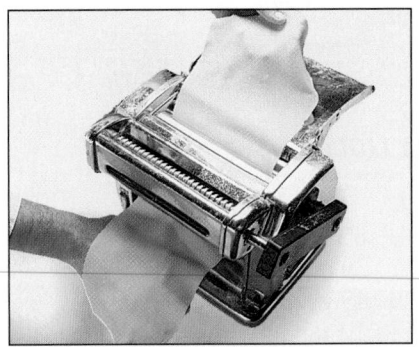

3. Pass the dough through the pasta machine to achieve the desired thickness.

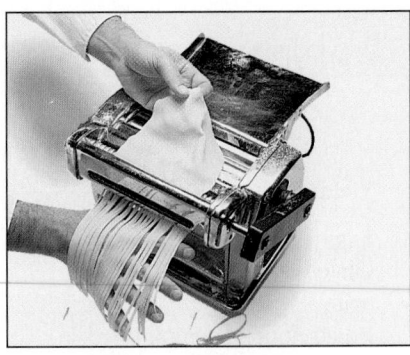

4. Use the pasta machine to cut the pasta into the desired width.

7. When the dough is thin enough to see your hand through, but not so thin that it begins to tear, it is ready to use or cut into ribbons. This sheet is the *sfoglia.*

8. To cut the sfoglia into ribbons, gently feed a manageable length of dough through the desired cutting blades.

9. To dry the pasta, lay it out in a single layer on a sheet pan dusted with flour. Layers of pasta ribbons can be separated with parchment paper.

Filling Pasta

Sheets of raw pasta dough can be filled or folded to create ravioli (squares), tortellini (round "hats" with a brim of dough), lunettes (circles of dough folded into half-moons), agnolotti (squares of dough folded into rectangles), cappelletti (squares of dough folded and shaped into rings) and other shapes. The filled pieces of dough are then cooked in boiling water using the procedure for cooking pasta ribbons discussed later. The filling can include almost anything—cheese, herbs, vegetables, fish, shellfish, meat or poultry. It can be uncooked or precooked. However, any meat filling should be fully cooked before the pasta is assembled, as the time it takes for the dough to cook may not be sufficient to cook the filling.

Cannelloni is a different type of filled pasta: a large square of cooked dough is wrapped around a meat or cheese filling and baked. Popular lasagna dishes are similar. Lasagna pasta, which consists of wide, flat sheets, are cooked then layered with cheese, tomato sauce and meat or vegetables as desired. The finished casserole is baked and cut into portions.

Some of the larger, commercially prepared pasta shapes such as large shells (conchigloni or rigate) or large tubes (manicotti) can be partially cooked in boiling water, then filled, sauced and baked as a casserole.

Asian noodle dough is also made into filled items such as dumplings, won tons, egg rolls (made with egg noodle dough) and spring rolls (made with rice paper). These items are usually steamed, pan-fried or deep-fat fried.

When making filled pasta, consider the flavours and textures of the filling, dough and sauce. Each should complement the others. Combinations can range from traditional unflavoured semolina pasta with herb and ricotta filling in a tomato sauce to an elegant escargot in garlic-and-herb pasta served with a beurre blanc to pork, ginger, soy and scallions in Asian egg noodle dough served with a soy-based dipping sauce.

Basic Procedure for Preparing Ravioli

1. Prepare a basic pasta dough of the desired flavour.

2. Prepare and chill the desired filling.

3. Roll out two thin sheets of dough between the rollers of a pasta machine. Gently lay the dough flat on the work surface.

4. Using a piping bag or a small portion scoop, place small mounds of filling on one of the dough pieces. Space the fillings evenly, allowing approximately 5 cm (2 inches) between each mound.

5. Brush the exposed areas of dough with water.

6. Gently place the second sheet of dough over the mounds and press firmly around each mound to remove air pockets and seal the dough.

7. Cut between the mounds with a chef's knife, pastry wheel or circular cutter.

1. Pipe the filling onto the dough.

2. Press around the mounds of filling to seal the dough and remove any air pockets.

3. Cut around the mounds with a circular cutter.

Cooking Method

Determining Doneness

Italian-style pastas are properly cooked when they are al dente, firm but tender. Cooking times vary depending on the shape and quantity of pasta, the amount of water used, the hardness of the water and even the altitude. Fresh pasta cooks rapidly, sometimes in seconds. Noodles and dried pasta may require several minutes.

Although package or recipe directions offer some guidance, the only way to accurately test doneness is to bite into a piece. When the pasta is slightly firmer than desired, remove it from the stove and drain. It will continue to cook through residual heat.

Unlike Italian pasta, Asian noodles are not served al dente. Rather, they are either boiled until soft or stir-fried until very crisp.

Boiling

All Italian-style pasta and most Asian noodles are cooked by just one method: boiling. The secret to boiling pasta successfully is to use ample water. Allow 4 L (1 gal.) of water for each 500 g (1 lb.) of pasta.

Use a saucepan or stockpot large enough to allow the pasta to move freely in the boiling water, otherwise the starch released by the dough will make the pasta gummy and sticky. The water should be brought to a rapid boil, then all the pasta should be added at once.

Salt should be added to the water. Pasta absorbs water and salt during cooking. Adding salt to the pasta after it is cooked will not provide the same seasoning effect.

Chefs disagree on whether to add oil to the cooking water. Purists argue against adding oil, on the theory that it makes the dough absorb water unevenly. Others think oil should be added to reduce surface foam. Another theory is that oil keeps the pasta from sticking, although this works only when oil is added to cooked, drained pasta.

Asian noodles may be prepared by boiling until fully cooked, or they may be parboiled then stir-fried with other ingredients to finish cooking.

Basic Procedure for Cooking Pasta to Order

1. Bring the appropriate amount of water to a boil over high heat.
2. Add oil to the water if desired.
3. Add the pasta and salt to the rapidly boiling water.
4. Stir the pasta to prevent it from sticking together. Bring the water back to a boil and cook until the pasta is done.
5. When the pasta is properly cooked, immediately drain it through a colander. A small amount of oil may be gently tossed into the pasta if desired to prevent it from sticking together.
6. Serve hot pasta immediately, or refresh in cold water for use in salads or other dishes. (Do not rinse pasta that is to be served hot.)

Basic Procedure for Cooking Dried Pasta in Advance

Fresh pasta is so delicate and cooks so rapidly (sometimes in as little as 15 seconds) that it should be cooked to order. Dried pasta, however, can be cooked in advance for quantity service.

1. Follow the above directions for cooking pasta, but stop the cooking process when the pasta is about two-thirds done.

PASTA SAUCES

Ragus are braised dishes used as a sauce. Usually, several flavouring ingredients and meat or poultry are browned, then a liquid and often a tomato product are added. The liquid can be a combination of stock, wine, water, milk or cream.

Seafood sauces can be white or red. White seafood sauces are most often made with white wine or stock and rarely use cream. They are often flavoured with herbs. Red seafood sauces are tomato-based. Traditionally, these sauces are not garnished with cheese.

Vegetable sauces often use tomatoes as the base and a stock as the liquid. Mirepoix, garlic and red pepper flakes are commonly used for flavourings. Vegetable sauces include the traditional tomato sauce as well as primavera.

Cream sauces are based on milk or cream and are sometimes thickened with roux. Cheese is often included for flavour, richness and thickening.

Garlic-oil sauces (It. *aglio-olio*) consist mainly of garlic and oil; often herbs are added. Garlic-oil sauces can be hot or cold, cooked or uncooked. Pesto is a well-known example of an uncooked, cold garlic-oil sauce.

Uncooked sauces include a variety of dressings such as fresh tomatoes, basil and olive oil; or olive oil, lemon juice, parsley, basil and hot red pepper flakes. Other flavouring ingredients include capers, anchovies, garlic and olives as well as fresh herbs, fresh vegetables, flavoured oils and cubed cheeses.

TABLE 23.6   COMBINING SAUCES, PASTA AND GARNISHES

Sauce	Pasta Shape	Garnish
Ragu	Ribbons, tubes, shapes, filled	Grated cheese
Seafood	Ribbons (fettuccine and capellini)	Fish or shellfish
Vegetable	Ribbons, tubes, filled	Meatballs, sausage, grated cheese
Cream	Thick ribbons (spaghetti and fettuccine), filled	Ham, peas, sausage, mushrooms, smoked salmon, nuts, grated cheese
Garlic-oil	Ribbons, shapes, filled	Grated cheese (if uncooked or cold), herbs
Uncooked	Ribbons, shapes	Cubed or grated cheese, fresh vegetables, herbs

2. Drain the pasta, rinse it lightly and toss it in a small amount of oil.

3. Divide the pasta into appropriate-sized portions. Individual portions can be wrapped in plastic or laid on a sheet pan and covered. Refrigerate until needed.

4. When needed, place a portion in a conical strainer and immerse in boiling water to reheat. Drain, add sauce and serve immediately.

Accompaniments to Pasta

Pasta is widely accepted by consumers and easily incorporated in a variety of cuisines—from Italian and Chinese to Thai and spa. It is used in broths; as a bed for stews, fish, shellfish or meat; or tossed with sauce. Today's creative chefs are constantly developing nontraditional but delicious ways of serving pasta.

Pasta and Broths

Small shapes can be cooked in the broth with which they are served, or cooked separately, then added to the hot liquid at service time. Soups such as cappelletti in brodo and chicken noodle are examples of these techniques.

Pasta Sauces

There are hundreds of Italian pasta sauces as well as sauces for Italian-style pasta, but most can be divided into six categories: ragus, seafood sauces, vegetable sauces, cream sauces, garlic-oil sauces and uncooked sauces. Recipes for a selection of pasta sauces are in Chapter 10, Stocks and Sauces.

Although there are no firm rules governing the combinations of sauces and pasta, Table 23.6 offers some of the more common combinations.

 ONCLUSION

Most meals would seem incomplete without a starch. The most popular starches are potatoes, grains (especially rice) and pasta. All are low in fat and a good source of energy. Most can be prepared with several dry- and moist-heat cooking methods. Starches can be sauced, seasoned or flavoured in limitless ways.

$\mathcal{Q}$UESTIONS FOR $\mathcal{D}$ISCUSSION

1. Explain the differences between mealy and waxy potatoes. Give two examples of each.

2. Describe the two methods of sautéing or pan-frying potatoes.

3. Explain why duchesse potatoes are regarded as the "mother" of many classic potato dishes. Name and describe two such dishes.

4. All grains are composed of three parts. Name and describe each of these parts.

5. Describe and compare the three general cooking methods used to prepare grains.

6. Name the three categories of Italian-style pasta shapes and give an example of each.

7. Why is it necessary to use ample water when cooking pasta? Should pasta be cooked in salted water? Should oil be added to the cooking water? Explain your answers.

8. Discuss the differences between cooking fresh pasta and cooking dried, factory-produced pasta.

$\mathcal{A}$DDITIONAL $\mathcal{S}$TARCH $\mathcal{R}$ECIPES

RECIPE 23.9

QUINOA, RED RICE AND LENTIL SALAD WITH TRUFFLE VINAIGRETTE

Note: *This dish appears in the Chapter Opening photograph.*

THE RITZ CARLTON, Chicago, IL
Executive Chef George Bumbaris

Yield: 4 Servings   **Method:** Simmering

Quinoa (recipe follows)	250 g	8 oz.
Red Rice (recipe follows)	250 g	8 oz.
Beluga Lentils (recipe follows)	250 g	8 oz.
Carrots, brunoise, cooked	50 g	2 oz.
Leeks, brunoise, cooked	50 g	2 oz.
Truffle Vinaigrette (recipe follows)	60 mL	2 fl. oz.
Kosher salt	TT	TT
Pepper	TT	TT
Black truffles	4 slices	4 slices
Herb-infused oil	as needed for garnish	
Truffle Vinaigrette (recipe follows)	as needed for garnish	

RECIPE 23.9

Approximate values per serving:

Calories	307
Total fat	23 g
Saturated fat	3 g
Cholesterol	0 mg
Sodium	585 mg
Total carbohydrates	22 g
Protein	3 g

1. Mix the Quinoa, Red Rice, Beluga Lentils, carrots, leeks, Truffle Vinaigrette, and salt and pepper together.

2. Shape into a ring on each serving plate. Garnish with a truffle slice. Drizzle the herb oil and additional Truffle Vinaigrette around each plate.

QUINOA

Yield: 250 g (1 cup)

Onion, diced	75 g	2-1/2 oz.
Olive oil	30 mL	1 Tbsp.
Quinoa	100 g	1/2 cup
Water or vegetable stock	250 mL	8 fl. oz.
Kosher salt	TT	TT
Pepper	TT	TT

Quinoa—Approximate values per 60 mL (1/4 cup) serving:

Calories	56
Total fat	3 g
Saturated fat	0.5 g
Cholesterol	0 mg
Sodium	182 mg
Total carbohydrates	6 g
Protein	1 g

1. In a small sauce pot, sauté the onion in the olive oil over medium heat.
2. Add the quinoa and allow it to brown slightly.
3. Add the stock and season with salt and pepper. Bring the stock to a full simmer.
4. Remove from the stove and cover the pot. Allow the quinoa to steep until tender, approximately 8 minutes.

RED RICE

Yield: 250 g (1 cup)

Onion, diced	40 g	1 oz.
Olive oil	15 mL	1 Tbsp.
Red rice	100 g	1/2 cup
Water	250 mL	8 fl. oz.
Kosher salt	TT	TT
Pepper	TT	TT

Red Rice—Approximate values per 60 mL (1/4 cup) serving:

Calories	22
Total fat	2 g
Saturated fat	0.5 g
Cholesterol	0 mg
Sodium	288 mg
Total carbohydrates	1 g
Protein	0 g

1. In a small sauce pot, sauté the onion in the olive oil over medium heat.
2. Add the red rice, water, salt and pepper.
3. Cover and simmer until the rice is tender and the liquid has been absorbed, approximately 15 minutes.

BELUGA LENTILS

Yield: 250 g (1 cup)

Olive oil	30 mL	2 Tbsp.
Onion, peeled	1 small	1 small
Clove	1	1
Carrot, peeled and cut in half lengthwise	1 large	1 large
Celery, cut in half	2 ribs	2 ribs
Garlic cloves	4	4
Shallots, minced	75 g	2-1/2 oz.
Bay leaves	2	2
Fresh thyme	2 sprigs	2 sprigs
Kosher salt	TT	TT
Pepper	TT	TT
Beluga lentils, soaked for 1 hour	100 g	1/2 cup
Water or vegetable stock	500 mL	16 fl. oz.

Beluga Lentils—Approximate values per 60 mL (1/4 cup) serving:

Calories	26
Total fat	2 g
Saturated fat	0.5 g
Cholesterol	0 mg
Sodium	123 mg
Total carbohydrates	2 g
Protein	1 g

1. In a large sauce pot, heat the olive oil. Stud the onion with the clove and sweat the carrot, celery and onion in the oil.
2. Add the garlic and shallots. When the shallots are translucent, add the bay leaves, fresh thyme, salt, pepper, lentils and stock.
3. Simmer until tender, approximately 40 minutes. Make sure the lentils are covered with liquid at all times.
4. After the lentils cool, remove the carrot, celery, onion, garlic cloves, bay leaves and thyme.

TRUFFLE VINAIGRETTE

Yield: 400 mL (9 fl. oz.)

Brandy	100 mL	2 fl. oz.
Madeira	100 mL	2 fl. oz.
Port	100 mL	2 fl. oz.
Truffles	75 g	2 oz.
Balsamic vinegar	25 mL	1/2 fl. oz.
Canola oil	25 mL	1/2 fl. oz.
Truffle oil	10 mL	1-1/2 tsp.
Kosher salt	TT	TT
Pepper	TT	TT

Truffle Vinaigrette—Approximate values per 30 mL (1 oz.) serving:

Calories	81
Total fat	2 g
Saturated fat	0 g
Cholesterol	0 mg
Sodium	27 mg
Total carbohydrates	12 g
Protein	0 g

1. Simmer the brandy, madeira and port to remove the alcohol. Remove from the heat and add the truffles. Allow them to steep until the liquid is cool.
2. Place all of the ingredients in a blender and emulsify.

◆ ◆ ◆

RECIPE 23.10

GRILLED POTATO SALAD

GREENS RESTAURANT, SAN FRANCISCO, CA
Executive Chef Annie Somerville

Yield: 4–6 Servings   **Method:** Baking/Grilling

New potatoes	1 kg	2 lb.
Light olive oil	as needed	as needed
Salt and pepper	TT	TT
Cherry tomatoes, sweet one hundreds or pear cherry tomatoes	125 g	4 oz.
Frisée or salad greens (optional)	125 g	4 oz.
Red and yellow bell peppers, roasted, seeded and cut into strips	500 g	1 lb.
Basil Vinaigrette (recipe follows)	125 mL	4 fl. oz.
Champagne vinegar	as needed	as needed
Niçoise or Gaeta olives	12	12

RECIPE 23.10

Approximate values per serving:

Calories	354
Total fat	22 g
Saturated fat	3 g
Cholesterol	0 mg
Sodium	1398 mg
Total carbohydrates	34 g
Protein	4 g

1. Toss the potatoes with the olive oil in a baking dish; sprinkle with a few pinches of salt and pepper.
2. Cover the potatoes and place in a 200°C (400°F) oven. Cook until tender, approximately 35–40 minutes. Set aside to cool.
3. Cut the cooled potatoes in half or quarters if they are large. Thread onto skewers for grilling. (Skewers are not necessary if the grill grating is fine enough.) Grill the potatoes cut side down until they are golden and crisp with defined grill marks.
4. Cut the tomatoes in half or leave whole if small.
5. Prepare, wash and spin-dry the salad greens, if using.
6. To assemble the salad, slide the grilled potatoes from the skewers and toss with the peppers, cherry tomatoes and Basil Vinaigrette. Adjust the seasoning, if necessary, with a splash of champagne vinegar and salt and pepper.
7. Loosely arrange the greens on plates or a platter, spoon the potatoes and other vegetables over the greens and garnish with the olives.

BASIL VINAIGRETTE

Yield: 125 mL (4 fl. oz.)

Champagne vinegar	30 mL	1 fl. oz.
Extra virgin olive oil	90 mL	3 fl. oz.
Fresh basil leaves	9	9
Salt	3 g	1/2 tsp.
Garlic clove, chopped	5 g	1

Combine the ingredients in a blender or food processor until smooth.

Basic Vinaigrette—Approximate values per 30 mL (1 oz.) serving:

Calories	200
Total fat	21 g
Saturated fat	3 g
Cholesterol	0 mg
Sodium	292 mg
Total carbohydrates	1 g
Protein	0 g

◆ ◆ ◆

RECIPE 23.11

CANDIED SWEET POTATOES

Yield: 6 125-g (4-oz.) Servings   **Method:** Baking

Sweet potatoes	1 kg	2 lb.
Brown sugar	150 g	5 oz.
Water	50 mL	2 fl. oz.
Whole butter	50 g	2 oz.
Vanilla extract	5 mL	1 tsp.

1. Wash the sweet potatoes and cut as necessary to promote even cooking.
2. Bake the sweet potatoes on a sheet pan at 180°C (350°F) until cooked but still firm, approximately 30 minutes.
3. Combine the brown sugar, water and butter and bring to a boil. Add the vanilla and remove from the heat.
4. Peel the potatoes and slice or cut as desired. Arrange the potatoes in a baking dish and pour the sugar mixture over them.
5. Sprinkle the potatoes with additional brown sugar if desired and bake for 20 minutes, basting occasionally with the sugar mixture.

RECIPE 23.11

Approximate values per 120 g (4 oz.) serving:

Calories	327
Total fat	7 g
Saturated fat	4 g
Cholesterol	18 mg
Sodium	97 mg
Total carbohydrates	64 g
Protein	3 g

◆ ◆ ◆

RECIPE 23.12

POTATO PANCAKES

Yield: 18 Pancakes   **Method:** Pan-frying

Eggs, whole	2	2
Egg whites	4	4
Milk	350 mL	12 fl. oz.
Onion, grated	150 g	6 oz.
Parsley, chopped	20 g	2 Tbsp.
Garlic clove, minced	5 g	1
Flour	100 g	4 oz.
Sour cream	100 mL	3 fl. oz.
Potatoes, grated	500 g	1 lb.
Bacon, fried, diced	125 g	4 oz.
Canola oil	15 mL	1 Tbsp.
Baking powder	10 g	1 Tbsp.
Salt and pepper	TT	TT
Canola oil	as needed for cooking	

RECIPE 23.12

Approximate values per 120 g (4 oz.) serving:

Calories	130
Total fat	6 g
Saturated fat	2 g
Cholesterol	35 mg
Sodium	186 mg
Total carbohydrates	12 g
Protein	5 g

Continued

1. Separate the whole eggs and put all the egg whites in a bowl.
2. Whip the egg whites until stiff. In a separate bowl, beat the yolks, then blend into whites.
3. Fold in the milk, onion, parsley, garlic, flour, sour cream, grated potatoes, bacon, oil, baking powder, salt and pepper.
4. Heat the oil in a heavy-bottomed pan. Add the potato mixture to the oil in uniform-size pancakes. Pan-fry the pancakes until tender, turning once when well browned on the first side. Remove from the pan and drain well.

◆ ◆ ◆

RECIPE 23.13

PARSNIP, POTATO AND GOAT CHEESE PIE

AUBERGE DU POMMIER, Toronto, ON
Executive Chef Todd Clarmo

CANOE RESTAURANT & BAR, Toronto, ON
Executive Chef Anthony Walsh

Yield: 6–8 Servings   **Method:** Baking

Parsnips, peeled and cut into sticks	300 g	4 large
Olive oil	30 mL	2 Tbsp.
Fresh garlic, minced	5 g	1 tsp.
Salt and pepper, freshly ground	TT	TT
Unsalted butter, softened	15 g	1 Tbsp.
Red onion, minced	150 g	1 medium
Fresh thyme leaves, chopped	10 g	1 Tbsp.
Fresh savory leaves, chopped	10 g	1 Tbsp.
Yukon Gold potatoes, peeled and cut into rounds 3 mm (1/8 inch) thick	700 g	3
Soft goat cheese, crumbled	200–250 g	6–8 oz.
Cream, 35%	250 mL	8 fl. oz.

1. Heat oven to 200°C (400°F).
2. Place the parsnips in a nonreactive bowl; toss them with the olive oil, garlic, salt and pepper. Transfer to baking dish and roast until golden-brown (approximately 20 minutes); remove from oven; reserve.
3. Reduce oven heat to 175°C (350°F).
4. Grease a 20 x 20 cm (8 x 8 inch) ovenproof casserole with softened butter. Layer the bottom with the red onion; sprinkle with thyme and savory. Add half the Yukon Gold potatoes in a layer; season with salt and pepper. Cover potato layer with roasted parsnips. Sprinkle with goat cheese. Pour in 80 mL (1/3 cup) cream. Layer top of pie with remaining potatoes and season with salt and pepper.
5. Pour remaining cream on top; cover casserole with foil. Place in oven and bake for 40 minutes or until tender. Remove foil and bake another 15 minutes until golden-brown.
6. Remove from oven. Cool slightly. When ready to serve, cut into squares for individual portions.

Todd Clarmo and Anthony Walsh
When they worked together at Canoe, Todd and Anthony received rave reviews for their innovative menu offerings. While you can still find Anthony at Canoe, Todd recently moved to Auberge du Pommier—another successful Oliver Bonacini Restaurant. Together, Todd and Anthony continue to bring culinary magic to the Toronto restaurant scene.

RECIPE 23.13

Approximate values per serving:

Calories	385
Total fat	25 g
Saturated fat	8 g
Cholesterol	45 mg
Sodium	204 mg
Total carbohydrates	33 g
Protein	9 g

♦♦♦

RECIPE 23.14

RÖSTI POTATOES

THE FOUR SEASONS, New York, NY
Chef Christian Albin

Yield: 6 Servings   **Method:** Pan-frying

Boiling potatoes, large	1 kg	4
Bacon fat	60 g	2 oz.
Lard	60 g	2 oz.
Kosher salt and pepper	TT	TT
Whole butter	30 g	1 oz.

1. Cook the potatoes in salted water until almost done.

2. Drain and cool the potatoes, then peel and coarsely grate them.

3. Heat the bacon fat and lard in a heavy, shallow 25-cm (10-inch) skillet with sloping sides until quite hot. Spread half the potatoes over the bottom of the pan; sprinkle with salt and pepper. Cover with the remaining potatoes and cook over medium-high heat until the bottom turns brown and crusty, approximately 10 minutes.

4. Turn the potatoes in one piece. This is easiest to do by placing a large plate over the pan and turning both together so the potatoes fall onto the plate. Slip the turned-over potatoes off the plate back into the pan, browned side up. Cook until the bottom is browned.

5. Before serving, smooth the edges of the potatoes with a spatula. Sprinkle with salt and brush the edge of the pan with whole butter. It will melt and run into the potatoes.

Continued

RECIPE 23.14

Approximate values per serving:

Calories	298
Total fat	24 g
Saturated fat	14 g
Cholesterol	30 mg
Sodium	425 mg
Total carbohydrates	20 g
Protein	3 g

Fried Potato Variations

Cottage fries.

Shoestring potatoes.

French fries.

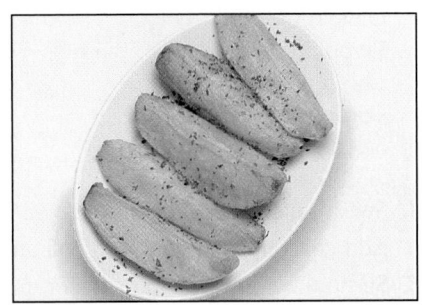

Steak fries.

VARIATION: Cheddar Cheese Rösti Potatoes—Make two thin potato cakes. Top one with a layer of 200 g (7 oz.) sour cream, 60 g (2 oz.) cubed sharp cheddar cheese and 20 g (2 Tbsp.) chopped chives. Top with the other cake. Dot with 15 g (1 Tbsp.) whole butter and bake in a 200°C (400°F) oven for 15 minutes.

◆◆◆

RECIPE 23.15

Approximate values
per 100 g serving:

Calories	216
Total fat	11 g
Saturated fat	6.5 g
Cholesterol	34 mg
Sodium	352 mg
Total carbohydrates	23.5 g
Protein	6 g

Michael Allemeier, CCC
Born in South Africa, Michael started cooking at the age of sixteen at the St. Boniface Golf Club in Winnipeg. He went on to spend six years of his career at the famous Bishop's Restaurant (Vancouver), where he had the honour of preparing dinner for presidents Clinton and Yeltsin. In 2001, he became host of "Cook Like a Chef" (Food Network).

RECIPE 23.16

Approximate values per serving:

Calories	401
Total fat	25 g
Saturated fat	4 g
Cholesterol	0 mg
Sodium	822 mg
Total carbohydrates	35 g
Protein	9 g

RECIPE 23.15

POLENTA

Yield: 800 g (1 lb. 12 oz.)   **Method:** Simmering

Shallots, chopped	10 g	2 tsp.
Whole butter	60 g	2 oz.
Milk, white stock or water	1 L	1 qt.
Cornmeal, yellow or white	180 g	6 oz.
Salt and pepper	TT	TT

1. Sauté the shallots in 15 g (1 Tbsp.) of butter for 30 seconds. Add the liquid and bring to a boil.

2. Slowly add the cornmeal while stirring constantly to prevent lumps, then simmer for 30 minutes. Season with salt and pepper. Stir regularly.

3. Scrape the polenta into a buttered nonaluminum dish; spread to an even thickness with a spatula that has been dipped in water. Refrigerate the polenta until well chilled.

4. To serve, unmould the polenta and cut into shapes following the procedure discussed in Chapter 35, Plate Presentation. Sauté or grill the polenta for service, or sprinkle with grated Parmesan cheese and heat under a broiler or salamander.

◆◆◆

RECIPE 23.16

PUMPKIN WHIPPED SOFT POLENTA

TEATRO RESTAURANT, CALGARY, AB
Executive Chef Michael Allemeier, CCC

Yield: 4 Servings

Onion, diced	75 g	3 oz.
Garlic, fine dice	10 g	3 cloves
Olive oil	100 mL	3 fl. oz.
Pumpkin flesh, diced	150 g	5 oz.
Chicken stock	1 L	1 qt.
Cornmeal	150 g	5 oz.
Salt and pepper	TT	TT

1. Sweat onion and garlic in olive oil with the pumpkin.

2. Add chicken stock, bring to boil and simmer until the pumpkin is tender.

3. Stir in the cornmeal and simmer until no longer gritty. Stir constantly.

4. Season with salt and pepper.

♦ ♦ ♦

RECIPE 23.17

BROWN RICE PILAF WITH PINE NUTS

Yield: 10 90-g (3-oz.) Servings   **Method:** Pilaf

Saffron threads	0.25 g	1/2 tsp.
Chicken stock, hot	500 mL	16 fl. oz.
Sesame oil	15 mL	1 Tbsp.
Vegetable oil	15 mL	1 Tbsp.
Pine nuts	50 g	2 oz.
Onion, medium dice	175 g	6 oz.
Red bell pepper, medium dice	175 g	6 oz.
Garlic, chopped	10 g	2 tsp.
Brown rice	200 g	1 cup
Salt	5 g	1 tsp.
Pepper	TT	TT
Currants, dry	50 g	2 oz.

1. Steep the saffron threads in the hot stock for 5 minutes.
2. Heat the oils and sauté the pine nuts until lightly browned.
3. Add the onion, red pepper and garlic and sauté without browning.
4. Add the rice and stir to coat the rice with the oil.
5. Add the salt and stock to the rice. Season with pepper, bring to a boil, reduce the heat and cover. Cook on the stove top or in the oven until done, approximately 30 minutes.
6. Stir in the currants, cover and allow them to soften for 5 minutes.

RECIPE 23.17

Approximate values per 90 g (3 oz.) serving:

Calories	159
Total fat	6 g
Saturated fat	1 g
Cholesterol	0 mg
Sodium	361 mg
Total carbohydrates	23 g
Protein	4.5 g

♦ ♦ ♦

RECIPE 23.18

WILD RICE AND CRANBERRY STUFFING

Yield: 2.5 L (5 pt.)   **Method:** Simmering

Dried morels	30 g	1 oz.
Wild rice	350 g	12 oz.
Onion, minced	250 g	8 oz.
Poultry seasoning	2 g	1 tsp.
Butter or chicken fat	50 g	2 oz.
Chicken stock, hot	approx. 1 L	approx. 1 qt.
Dried cranberries	175 g	6 oz.
Salt and pepper	TT	TT
Fresh parsley, chopped fine	50 g	4 Tbsp.

1. Soak the dried morels overnight in lightly salted water. Drain, reserving the liquid. Rinse well, drain again and chop coarsely.
2. Rinse the wild rice well in cold water.
3. Sauté the onion and poultry seasoning in the butter or chicken fat until tender. Add the morels and wild rice.
4. Strain the reserved liquid from the morels through several layers of cheesecloth to remove all sand and grit. Add enough chicken stock to make 1.5 L (3 pt.). Add the stock mixture and cranberries to the rice. Cover and simmer until the rice is dry and fluffy, approximately 45 minutes.
5. Season to taste with salt and pepper and stir in the parsley. This rice may be served as a side dish or used for stuffing duck or game hens.

RECIPE 23.18

Approximate values per 150 mL serving:

Calories	130
Total fat	3 g
Saturated fat	2 g
Cholesterol	7 mg
Sodium	235 mg
Total carbohydrates	21 g
Protein	5 g

♦ ♦ ♦

RECIPE 23.19

RICE PILAF

Yield: 10 Servings   **Method:** Pilaf

Butter	30 g	1 oz.
Olive oil	30 mL	1 fl. oz.
Onion, fine dice	100 g	3 oz.
Bay leaf	1	1
Long-grain rice	500 g	1 lb.
Chicken stock, boiling	1 L	32 fl. oz.
Salt	TT	TT

1. Heat the butter and olive oil in a heavy sautoir or sauce pot.
2. Add the onion and bay leaf and sauté until tender, but not brown.
3. Add the rice and stir to coat completely with the hot fat. Do not allow the rice to brown.
4. Pour in the boiling chicken stock and season with salt.
5. Cover the pot tightly and place it in a 175°C (350°F) oven. Bake for 18–20 minutes, until the liquid is absorbed and the rice is fluffy and tender.
6. Transfer the cooked rice to a hotel pan and fluff the rice with a fork. Remove the bay leaf and keep the rice hot for service.

RECIPE 23.19

Approximate values per 180 g (6 oz.) serving:

Calories	248
Total fat	6 g
Saturated fat	2 g
Cholesterol	7 mg
Sodium	712 mg
Total carbohydrates	41 g
Protein	6 g

♦ ♦ ♦

RECIPE 23.20

SAFFRON RICE

Yield: 10 Servings

Basmati rice	500 g	16 oz.
Saffron threads	0.5 g	1 tsp.
Boiling water	1 L	32 fl. oz.
Ghee (or clarified butter)	100 g	3 oz.
Cinnamon stick, 5 cm (2 inches) long	1	1
Cloves, whole	4	4
Onion, fine dice	150 g	5 oz.
Dark brown sugar	15 g	1 Tbsp.
Salt	10 g	2 tsp.
Cardamom, ground	1 g	1/4 tsp.

1. Wash the rice and drain thoroughly.
2. Steep the saffron in 60 mL (2 fl. oz.) of the boiling water.
3. In a saucepan, heat the ghee, add the cinnamon and cloves. Add the onion and stir-fry until it is soft and slightly brown.
4. Add the rice and stir until it is well coated with the ghee and the grains are a light golden colour.
5. Stirring constantly, add the remaining boiling water, brown sugar, salt and cardamom. Bring to a boil and reduce to a simmer.
6. Gently stir in the saffron and its water, cover and simmer until the rice has absorbed all the liquid.
7. Fluff with a fork and serve at once.

RECIPE 23.20

Approximate values per 120 g (4 oz.) serving:

Calories	268
Total fat	8.5 g
Saturated fat	5 g
Cholesterol	22 mg
Sodium	477 mg
Total carbohydrates	43 g
Protein	4 g

✦✦✦

RECIPE 23.21

BUCKWHEAT LINGUINE WITH SMOKED PHEASANT AND WILD MUSHROOMS

TORONTO, ON
Chef David Jones

Yield: 4 Servings

Garlic clove, minced	5 g	1
Butter, unsalted, melted	25 g	1 oz.
Wild mushrooms	125 g	4 oz.
Scallions, sliced thin	50 g	2 oz.
Nutmeg	pinch	pinch
Dry sherry	30 mL	1 fl. oz.
Cream, 35%, reduced by 1/3	300 mL	10 fl. oz.
Meat glaze	30 g	1 oz.
Smoked pheasant, sliced	175 g	6 oz.
Salt and fresh ground white pepper	TT	TT
Buckwheat Pasta (recipe follows), cut into linguini, cooked	500 g	1 lb.

1. Sweat the garlic in the melted butter, then add the mushrooms.
2. Add scallions (reserving some for garnish) and nutmeg. Add the sherry and deglaze, reducing *au sec*.
3. Add reduced cream, meat glaze and smoked pheasant. Reduce to sauce consistency. Season to taste.
4. Blanch buckwheat linguini in slightly salted water, drain well and toss in sauce. Garnish with reserved sliced scallions.

David Jones
David was born in Wales and trained in Canada. His career has been varied, from running hotel kitchens to developing a property in a Cree community on the shores of James Bay, to providing training to the U.S. Navy in Hong Kong, Hawaii and California. David has instructed in the culinary programs at Humber College and is currently with the Toronto District School Board.

RECIPE 23.21

Approximate values per serving:

Calories	761
Total fat	48 g
Saturated fat	24 g
Cholesterol	263 mg
Sodium	660 mg
Total carbohydrates	59 g
Protein	25 g

BUCKWHEAT PASTA

Yield: 8 Servings

Semolina flour	200 g	7 oz.
Buckwheat flour	65 g	2-1/4 oz
Whole eggs	2	2
Olive oil	30 mL	1 fl. oz.
Water	50 mL	2 fl. oz.

1. Combine the flours in a bowl.
2. Combine the eggs and oil in another bowl.
3. Make a mound of the dry ingredients on the table, and make a well in the centre. Pour the egg-oil mixture into the well and incorporate it with the dry ingredients, gradually enlarging the well as you mix in the flour.
4. Add water until the dough is firm enough to knead, then knead well for at least 15 minutes.
5. Cover and let stand at room temperature for at least 30 minutes.
6. Roll out dough as thin as possible.
7. Cut into ribbons or desired shape.

Buckwheat Pasta—
Approximate values per serving:

Calories	170
Total fat	5 g
Saturated fat	1 g
Cholesterol	59 mg
Sodium	21 mg
Total carbohydrates	25 g
Protein	6 g

◆◆◆

RECIPE 23.22

GOAT-CHEESE RAVIOLI IN HERBED CREAM SAUCE

Yield: 72 5-cm (2-inch) Ravioli and 750 mL (1-1/2 pt.) Sauce

Fresh goat cheese	300 g	11 oz.
Cream cheese	250 g	8 oz.
Fresh basil, chopped fine	30 g	3 Tbsp.
Fresh thyme, chopped fine	8 g	2 tsp.
Fresh parsley, chopped	30 g	3 Tbsp.
Pepper	TT	TT
Pasta, fresh	1 kg	2 lb.
Cream, 35%	1 L	32 fl. oz.
Parmesan cheese, grated	50 g	2 oz.
Salt	TT	TT

RECIPE 23.22

Approximate values per serving:

Calories	790
Total fat	64 g
Saturated fat	35 g
Cholesterol	242 mg
Sodium	500 mg
Total carbohydrates	36 g
Protein	18 g

1. To make the cheese filling, combine the goat and cream cheeses with 30 g (2 Tbsp.) basil, 4 g (1 tsp.) thyme and the parsley; season to taste with pepper.
2. Make ravioli using the cheese mixture and pasta.
3. To make the sauce, combine the cream with the remaining herbs and bring to a boil. Reduce by one-third and add the Parmesan cheese. Season with salt and pepper.
4. Boil the ravioli until done. Drain, toss gently with the sauce and serve.

◆◆◆

RECIPE 23.23

FETTUCCINE ALFREDO

Yield: 4 180-g (6-oz.) Servings

Fresh fettuccine	250 g	8 oz.
Whole butter	60 g	2 oz.
Cream, 35%	350 mL	12 fl. oz.
Parmesan cheese, grated	60 g	2 oz.
Salt and white pepper	TT	TT

RECIPE 23.23

Approximate values per 200 g serving:

Calories	546
Total fat	49 g
Saturated fat	30 g
Cholesterol	179 mg
Sodium	437 mg
Total carbohydrates	19 g
Protein	11 g

1. Boil the pasta, keeping it slightly undercooked. Refresh and drain.
2. To make the sauce, combine the butter, cream and cheese in a sauté pan. Bring to a boil and reduce slightly.
3. Add the pasta to the pan and boil the sauce and pasta until the sauce is thick and the pasta is cooked. Adjust the seasonings and serve.

❖❖❖

RECIPE 23.24

GRILLED PACIFIC SHRIMP WITH BAKED GARLIC AND BUTTERNUT SQUASH RISOTTO AND PISTACHIO BROWN BUTTER

WILDWOOD RESTAURANT GROUP, CALGARY, AB
Executive Chef Michael Noble

Yield: 4 Servings　　　　　　　　　　　**Method:** Sautéing

Butter	50 g	3 Tbsp.
Risotto:		
Onion, medium dice	60 g	2 oz.
Arborio rice	200 g	7 oz.
Chicken or prawn stock, hot	300–400 mL	10–15 fl. oz.
Bay leaf, small	1	1
Salt and white pepper	TT	TT
Garlic bulb, roasted whole and mashed	1	1
Squash purée (butternut is best)	50 g	2 oz.
Butternut squash, diced		
and roasted in olive oil	50 g	4 Tbsp.
Parmesan cheese, grated	50 g	2 oz.
Parsley, chopped	20 g	2 Tbsp.
Olive oil	15 mL	1 Tbsp.
Salt and ground black pepper	TT	TT
Black tiger shrimp or similar,		
shelled/deveined	8	8
Pistachio Brown Butter (recipe follows)	as needed	as needed
Tomato concassée	as needed	as needed

1. Heat a pan over medium heat. Add one-third of the butter and heat until the butter is bubbly. Do not burn. Add the diced onion and sauté until translucent. Add the rice and continue stirring until the rice is warm. Add a small amount of the hot stock and the bay leaf. Lower the heat, season the rice a little and continue cooking while stirring constantly. As the rice gets dry, add more stock, a little at a time, and continue cooking until the rice is al dente. Add the mashed, roasted garlic, the squash purée, the roasted, diced squash and a little more stock. When everything has warmed through, add the rest of the butter and the Parmesan and season to taste. Just before serving, remove the bay leaf and add the chopped parsley.

2. Just before the risotto has finished cooking, heat olive oil in a sauté pan over medium heat. Season the shrimp and sauté, turning 2–3 times for 2 minutes or until the shrimp are cooked through. Remove and set aside and make the Pistachio Brown Butter in the same pan.

3. Serve by dividing the risotto into four soup plates and setting the shrimp decoratively on top. Drizzle the Pistachio Brown Butter around the risotto.

4. Garnish with a sprinkle of tomato concassée and an herb sprig.

Continued

Michael Noble
Michael was fated to become a chef after cooking a successful Belgian waffle in a high school economics class! He began his apprenticeship in Vancouver, though he also gained valuable European experience in the early stages of his career. In 1996, Michael opened Vancouver's Diva at the Met and, within a year, it was propelled into the culinary spotlight, winning awards from Gourmet Magazine, Vancouver Magazine, and GQ. One of Canada's leading chefs, Michael achieved Canada's highest standing ever at the Bocuse d'Or World Cuisine championship in Lyons in 1995 and 1997.

RECIPE 23.24

Approximate values per serving:

Calories	420
Total fat	19 g
Saturated fat	9 g
Cholesterol	36 mg
Sodium	555 mg
Total carbohydrates	24 g
Protein	36 g

PISTACHIO BROWN BUTTER

Butter	60 g	4 Tbsp.
Salt and white pepper	TT	TT
Juice from 1/2 lemon		
Worcestershire sauce	dash	dash
Pistachio nuts, peeled and chopped coarse	20 g	4 tsp.

*Pistachio Brown Butter—
Approximate values per serving:*

Calories	542
Total fat	60 g
Saturated fat	32 g
Cholesterol	135 mg
Sodium	806 mg
Total carbohydrates	9 g
Protein	4 g

Melt the butter in a pan over medium-high heat, and season with salt and pepper. Just as the milk solids begin to colour, add the lemon juice, Worcestershire sauce and chopped nuts. Correct the seasoning.

◆ ◆ ◆

RECIPE 23.25

ANGEL HAIR WITH TOMATO VINAIGRETTE

Yield: 4 250-g (8-oz.) Servings

Vinaigrette:		
Tomato concassée	250 g	8 oz.
Fresh basil, thyme or marjoram	30 g	1 oz.
Balsamic vinegar	100 mL	3 fl. oz.
Shallots, minced	25 g	2 Tbsp.
Olive oil	250 mL	8 fl. oz.
Salt and pepper	TT	TT
Angel hair or rice noodle pasta, cooked	500 g	1 lb.

RECIPE 23.25

*Approximate values
per 250 g (8 oz.) serving:*

Calories	224
Total fat	2 g
Saturated fat	0.5 g
Cholesterol	0 mg
Sodium	288 mg
Total carbohydrates	44 g
Protein	7.5 g

1. Combine all vinaigrette ingredients. Season to taste with salt and pepper. Set aside for 20–30 minutes to allow the flavours to blend.
2. Toss the sauce with warm or cold cooked pasta. Adjust the seasonings. Serve immediately or refrigerate and serve chilled.

◆ ◆ ◆

RECIPE 23.26

PESTO SAUCE

Yield: 1 kg (30 oz.)

Olive oil	400 mL	12 fl. oz.
Pine nuts	100 g	3 oz.
Fresh basil leaves	200 g	6 oz.
Garlic, chopped	15 g	4 cloves
Parmesan cheese, grated	125 g	4 oz.
Romano cheese, grated	125 g	4 oz.
Salt and pepper	TT	TT

RECIPE 23.26

*Approximate values
per 50 g serving:*

Calories	243
Total fat	24 g
Saturated fat	5 g
Cholesterol	11 mg
Sodium	192 mg
Total carbohydrates	2 g
Protein	6 g

1. Place one-third of the olive oil in a blender or food processor and add all the remaining ingredients.
2. Blend or process until smooth. Add the remaining olive oil and blend a few seconds to incorporate.

VARIATION: *Walnut Pesto*—Substitute walnuts for pine nuts in the above recipe.

◆◆◆

RECIPE 23.27

CAPPELLETTI IN BRODO

Yield: 10 450-mL (16-fl.-oz.) Servings with 12 cappelletti each

Filling:

Pork, roasted	175 g	6 oz.
Mortadella	125 g	4 oz.
Ricotta cheese	175 g	6 oz.
Parmesan cheese, finely grated	175 g	6 oz.
Egg	1	1
Nutmeg	TT	TT
Basic Pasta Dough (Recipe 23.8)	750 g	1 lb. 8 oz.
Beef Broth (Recipe 11.1)	5 L	5 qt.
Parmesan cheese, shredded	250 g	8 oz.
Fresh parsley, chopped fine	30 g	3 Tbsp.

1. To prepare the cappelletti filling, place the meats and cheeses in a food processor fitted with the metal blade. Process until finely ground. Add the egg and season lightly with nutmeg. Process until blended but not smoothly puréed.

2. Work with one-quarter of the pasta dough at a time, keeping the rest covered to prevent it from drying out. Roll out a portion of the dough until it is very thin. Cut the dough into 5-cm (2-inch) squares using a fluted pasta wheel.

3. Place 5 mL (1 tsp.) of filling in the centre of each square. Fold the dough over the filling to form a rectangle, pinching the edges together to seal. Bring the ends of each rectangle together, overlapping them and pressing to seal.

4. Place the finished cappelletti on a paper-lined sheet pan. Leave them uncovered and turn them over once or twice so that they dry evenly. Continue working until all the filling is used. The cappelletti may be cooked immediately or refrigerated for later use.

5. Heat the beef broth to a gentle boil. Drop the cappelletti in and cook until tender, approximately 3–5 minutes.

6. Portion the broth and cappelletti into warmed soup bowls and garnish with the shredded Parmesan and parsley.

RECIPE 23.27

*Approximate values
per 12 cappelletti:*

Calories	283
Total fat	19 g
Saturated fat	11 g
Cholesterol	79 mg
Sodium	957 mg
Total carbohydrates	4 g
Protein	28 g

◆◆◆

RECIPE 23.28

SOBA NOODLES IN BROTH

Yield: 6 500-mL (16-fl.-oz.) Servings

Soba noodles	500 g	1 lb.
Dashi or chicken broth	1.5 L	1-1/2 qt.
Soy sauce	50 mL	3 Tbsp.
Mirin	15 mL	1 Tbsp.
Sugar	15 g	1 Tbsp.
Green onions, chopped	25 g	4 Tbsp.
White sesame seeds	5 g	1 Tbsp.

Continued

1. Boil the noodles in salted water until tender. Drain, rinse in hot water and drain again. Set aside.

2. Heat the dashi or chicken broth with the soy sauce, mirin and sugar. Add the noodles to the hot broth, simmering just until thoroughly reheated.

3. Portion into warmed bowls and top with the green onions and sesame seeds.

NOTE: Dashi is a stock made with dried bonito flakes and dried kelp. It is used extensively in Japanese cuisine and is available as an instant powder or a concentrate.

❖❖❖

RECIPE 23.29

MACARONI AND CHEESE

Yield: 24 250-g (8-oz.) Servings

Cheddar sauce (see page 206)	2 L	2 qt.
Worcestershire sauce	TT	TT
Hot pepper sauce	TT	TT
Elbow macaroni, boiled and refreshed	1 kg	2 lb.
Cheddar cheese, grated	1 kg	2 lb.
Whole butter	250 g	8 oz.
Bread crumbs	30 g	1 oz.

1. Season the cheese sauce with Worcestershire and hot pepper sauces.

2. Mix the macaroni with the cheese sauce and the grated cheese.

3. Pour into a buttered full-sized hotel pan. Sprinkle with bread crumbs.

4. Bake uncovered at 180°C (350°F) until hot, approximately 30 minutes.

VARIATIONS: Macaroni and Cheese with Ham and Tomato—Stir 1 kg (2 lb.) each diced cooked ham and tomato concassée into the macaroni and cheese before pouring it into the hotel pan.

❖❖❖

RECIPE 23.30

BAKED ZITI WITH TOMATO SAUCE

Yield: 30 Servings

Eggs	6	6
Ricotta cheese	1.75 kg	4 lb.
Fresh thyme	20 g	2 Tbsp.
Fresh oregano	20 g	2 Tbsp.
Fresh basil	20 g	2 Tbsp.
Salt and pepper	TT	TT
Italian sausage links	1.5 kg	3 lb.
Ziti, cooked, refreshed and drained	1.75 kg	4 lb.
Parmesan cheese, grated	250 g	8 oz.
Tomato Sauce (Recipe 10.13)	3 L	3 qt.
Mozzarella cheese, shredded	1 kg	2 lb.

RECIPE 23.28

Approximate values per 500 mL (16 fl. oz.) serving:

Calories	148
Total fat	2 g
Saturated fat	1 g
Cholesterol	0 mg
Sodium	1399 mg
Total carbohydrates	22 g
Protein	10 g

RECIPE 23.29

Approximate values per 240 g (8 oz.) serving:

Calories	453
Total fat	27 g
Saturated fat	17 g
Cholesterol	80 mg
Sodium	290 g
Total carbohydrates	35 g
Protein	17 g

1. Combine the eggs, ricotta cheese, thyme, oregano, basil, salt and pepper. Mix well and reserve.

2. Place the sausage links in a 5-cm-deep (2-inch) full-sized hotel pan; cook in a 180°C (350°F) oven for 20 minutes. Remove and cool. Drain the sausage. Slice the links into rounds and reserve.

3. Place the ziti in the hotel pan that was used to cook the sausage. Top with an even coating of the cheese mixture, sausage slices and Parmesan cheese.

4. Pour the tomato sauce over the top layer and stir slightly to distribute the sauce.

5. Bake at 190°C (375°F) for 1 hour. Sprinkle the mozzarella evenly over the pasta and return to the oven for 10 minutes. Serve.

6. Ziti may also be prepared in individual casseroles. Decrease baking time as necessary.

NOTE: This recipe is best when made with a fresh tomato sauce.

RECIPE 23.30

Approximate values per serving:

Calories	454
Total fat	23 g
Saturated fat	10 g
Cholesterol	141 mg
Sodium	1306 mg
Total carbohydrates	27 g
Protein	36 g

◆◆◆

RECIPE 23.31

SPINACH AND RICOTTA LASAGNA WITH BOLOGNESE SAUCE

Yield: 28 250-g (8-oz.) Servings

Fresh spinach pasta dough, rolled into sheets	1 kg	2 lb.
Spinach, stemmed	1 kg	2 lb.
Whole butter	50 g	2 oz.
Ricotta cheese	500 g	1 lb.
Parmesan cheese, grated	175 g	6 oz.
Eggs	2	2
Salt and pepper	TT	TT
Bolognese sauce (see page 213)	3 L	3 qt.
Béchamel sauce (Recipe 10.7)	1 L	1 qt.

1. Cut the pasta dough into 10-cm (4-inch) strips. Boil in salted water until done and drain well.

2. Sauté the spinach in the butter. Drain well and cool.

3. Combine the spinach with the ricotta cheese, 125 g (4 oz.) of the Parmesan cheese and eggs. Season to taste with salt and pepper.

4. Ladle a small amount of the Bolognese sauce into the bottom of a standard full-sized hotel pan. Cover the sauce with a layer of cooked pasta. Spread a thin layer of the spinach-and-cheese mixture on the pasta. Ladle a portion of the béchamel sauce over the spinach and spread in a thin even layer. Ladle a portion of the Bolognese sauce over the béchamel sauce and spread in an even layer.

5. Add another layer of pasta and repeat the process until all of the ingredients are used, finishing with a layer of béchamel sauce. Sprinkle the remaining Parmesan cheese on top and bake, covered, at 180°C (350°F) until heated through, approximately 40 minutes. Uncover the lasagna for the final 15 minutes so it browns.

VARIATION: Dry cottage cheese may be substituted for ricotta.

RECIPE 23.31

Approximate values per 250 g (8 oz.) serving:

Calories	284
Total fat	9 g
Saturated fat	4 g
Cholesterol	219 mg
Sodium	1138 mg
Total carbohydrates	12.5 g
Protein	37 g

Judson Simpson

Born, raised, and trained in Canada, Judson got his start in a local fishmarket where he learned the basics of cooking that still serve him well. Later, he decided to enrol at Toronto's George Brown College to study cooking in a formal environment. In 1991, Jud and his family moved to the nation's capital where, to this day, he continues to practice and teach his artistically personal brand of Canadian cuisine.

◆ ◆ ◆

RECIPE 23.32

THAI CHICKEN WITH CANTON NOODLE SALAD

PARLIAMENTARY RESTAURANT, HOUSE OF COMMONS, Ottawa, ON
Executive Chef Judson Simpson

Yield: 8 Servings

Lemon grass, chopped very fine	2 g	1/2 tsp.
Green finger hot chile	1/2	1/2
Lime juice, fresh	50 mL	1-1/2 fl. oz.
Sugar	10 g	2 tsp.
Cilantro, chopped	10 g	1 Tbsp.
Light soy sauce	15 mL	1 Tbsp.
Extra virgin olive oil	30 mL	2 Tbsp.
Shallot, chopped fine	25 g	2 Tbsp.
Water	30 mL	2 Tbsp.
Organic chicken breast, boneless, skinless	1.5 kg	3 lb.
Rice noodles	150 g	5 oz.
Canton noodles	250 g	8 oz.
Asparagus, blanched, cut on bias	500 g	1 lb.
Shiitake mushrooms, sliced, sautéed	85 g	3 oz.
Baby corn, cut on bias	200 g	6 oz.
Ginger, chopped	2 g	1/2 tsp.
Garlic, minced	5 g	1 clove
Light soy sauce	30 mL	2 Tbsp.
Teriyaki sauce	30 mL	2 Tbsp.
Olive oil	30 mL	2 Tbsp.
Lime juice, fresh	15 mL	1 Tbsp.
White wine vinegar	10 mL	2 tsp.
Raddichio	1/2 head	1/2 head
Endive	1 head	1 head
Sesame seeds	5 g	1 Tbsp.

1. In a nonreactive bowl, combine lemon grass, chile, lime juice, sugar, cilantro, soy sauce, olive oil, shallot and water to make dressing.

2. Lightly brush chicken breasts with one-half of the dressing and bake at 220°C (425°F) until cooked.

3. Cook the rice and canton noodles separately in boiling salted water. Chill.

4. Prepare salad by combining noodles with asparagus, mushrooms, corn, ginger, garlic, soy and teriyaki sauces, olive oil, lime juice and vinegar.

5. To serve, arrange raddichio and endive on plate. Place noodle salad and arrange sliced chicken breast. Drizzle with remaining dressing and sprinkle with sesame seeds.

RECIPE 23.32

Approximate values per serving:

Calories	590
Total fat	12 g
Saturated fat	2 g
Cholesterol	141 mg
Sodium	626 mg
Total carbohydrates	57 g
Protein	66 g

◆ ◆ ◆

RECIPE 23.33

GNOCCHI

Yield: 1.5 kg (3 lb.)

Boiled potatoes	1 kg	2 lb.
Eggs	2	2
Salt, pepper and nutmeg	TT	TT
Flour, all-purpose	400 g	14 oz.

1. Place boiled potatoes on a tray and place in warm oven to dry slightly, then rice them in a food mill.
2. In mixing bowl, incorporate the potatoes, eggs and seasonings.
3. Add 350 g (12 oz.) of the flour to the ingredients in the bowl, all at once.
4. Mix lightly to form a medium-soft dough.
5. If needed, add more flour to adjust the consistency.
6. Roll the dough out to 1-cm (1/2-inch) thickness on lightly floured table, then let it cool. Cut into 1.5 cm × 1.5 cm (3/4 inch × 3/4 inch) squares. Roll the squares over the back of a table fork to make indents, forming a shell shape.
7. Cook in simmering, salted water for 3–4 minutes, or until they double in size.

RECIPE 23.33	
Approximate values per 125 g serving:	
Calories	205
Total fat	1 g
Saturated fat	0.5 g
Cholesterol	36 mg
Sodium	115 mg
Total carbohydrates	42 g
Protein	6 g

❖❖❖

RECIPE 23.34

SPAETZLE

Yield: 3.5 kg (7-1/2 lb.)

Eggs	30	30
Water	500 mL	16 fl. oz.
Salt	30 g	1 oz.
Nutmeg	TT	TT
Flour, all-purpose	1.5 kg	3 lb. 4 oz.

1. In the bowl of the food mixer, beat the eggs, water, salt and nutmeg together.
2. With paddle attachment and on low speed, mix in the flour until just incorporated, then mix on high speed for 1 minute. Do not overbeat or the dumplings will be tough.
3. Suspend a large-holed colander over a pot of boiling water. In small batches, press the mixture through the colander so that the batter drops into the water.
4. Cook the dumplings until they float to the surface, approximately 2–3 minutes.
5. Remove them from the water with a skimmer and refresh in ice water. Do not leave them to soak.
6. Drain well and reserve in refrigerator, covered.
7. To serve, sauté the spaetzle in butter and finish with chopped parsley.

RECIPE 23.34	
Approximate values per 100 g serving:	
Calories	219
Total fat	5 g
Saturated fat	1.5 g
Cholesterol	184 mg
Sodium	453 mg
Total carbohydrates	33 g
Protein	10 g

 EBLINKS

The Potato Growers of Alberta—Producers of Mother Nature's Vitamins
  www.potatonet.com/
Ancient Grains
  www.cap.mcgill.ca/CPC_9.htm
U.S. Grains Nutrition Information Center
  www.wheatfoods.org/
Wild Rice
  www.mnwildrice.com/recipes.htm
Potato Facts
  www.thehotpotato.com/english/potato_facts.htm
U.S. National Pasta Association: Pasta FAQs and Facts
  www.ilovepasta.org/faqs.html

CHAPTER 24

SALADS AND SALAD DRESSINGS

*T*his chapter discusses all types of salads: the small plate of crisp iceberg lettuce with tomato wedges, cucumber slices and ranch dressing; the dinner plate of sautéed duck breast fanned across bright red grilled radicchio and toothy green arugula, sprayed with a vinaigrette dressing; the scoop of shredded chicken, mango chutney and seasonings, bound with mayonnaise; and the bowl of artichokes and mushrooms marinated in olive oil and lemon juice.

Each of these dishes fits the definition of a salad: a single food or a mix of different foods accompanied or bound by a dressing. A salad can contain meat, grains, fruits, nuts or cheese and absolutely no lettuce. It can be an appetizer, a second course served after the appetizer, an entree (especially at lunch) or served with the main course, a course following the entree or even dessert.

The colour, texture and flavour of each salad ingredient should complement those of the others, and the dressing should complement all of the ingredients. Harmony is critical to a salad's success—no matter what type of salad is being prepared.

This chapter opens with a section identifying greens commonly used in salads. A discussion of salad dressings follows. Finally, techniques for preparing green salads (both tossed and composed), bound salads, vegetable salads and fruit salads are discussed.

SALAD GREENS

Identifying Salad Greens

Salad greens are not necessarily green: Some are red, yellow, white or brown. They are all, however, leafy vegetables. Many are members of the lettuce or chicory families.

Lettuce

Lettuce (Fr. *laitue*; It. *lattuga*) has been consumed for nearly as long as people have kept records of what they and others ate. Archaeologists found that Persian royalty were served lettuce at their banquets more than 2500 years ago. Now grown and served worldwide, lettuces are members of the genus *Lactuca.* The most common types of lettuce are butterleaf, iceberg, leaf and romaine.

Boston

Boston and bibb are two of the most popular butterleaf lettuces. Their soft, pliable, pale green leaves have a buttery texture and flavour. Boston is larger and paler than bibb. Both Boston and bibb lettuce leaves form cups when separated from the heads; these cups make convenient bases for holding other foods on cold plates or providing height and texture as part of the garnish.

Boston

Iceberg

Iceberg lettuce is the most common of all lettuce varieties in Canada and the United States; it outsells all other varieties combined. Its tightly packed spherical head is made up of crisp, pale green leaves with a very mild flavour. Iceberg lettuce remains crisp for a relatively long period of time after being cut or prepared. Select heads that are firm but not hard and leaves that are free of burnt or rusty tips.

Iceberg

Leaf

Leaf lettuce grows in bunches. It has separate, ruffle-edged leaves branching from a stalk. Because it does not grow into a firm head, it is easily damaged during harvest and transport. Both red and green leaf lettuce have bright colours, mild flavours and tender leaves. Good-quality leaf lettuce should have nicely shaped leaves free of bruises, breaks or brown spots.

Red and Green Leaf Lettuces

Romaine

Romaine lettuce, also known as cos, is a loosely packed head lettuce with elongated leaves and thick midribs. Its outer leaves are dark green and although they look coarse, they are crisp, tender and tasty without being bitter. The core leaves are paler and more tender but still crisp. Romaine has enough flavour to stand up to strongly flavoured dressings such as the garlic and Parmesan cheese used in a Caesar salad. A good-quality head of romaine has dark green outer leaves that are free of blemishes or yellowing.

Baby Lettuces

Innovative chefs are always looking for new and different foods to add a twist or flair to their dishes. This has led to the popularity of baby lettuces and other specialty greens. Baby greens have similar but more subtle flavours than their mature versions. They are often less bitter and are always more tender and delicate. Because of their size and variety, they are perfect for composed salads. **Mesclun** is a mixture of several kinds of baby lettuce, herbs and flowers. Field and spring mixes are popular with food service operators.

Romaine

Brune d'hiver

Baby Red Bibb

Red Sails

Baby Green Bibb

Lola Rosa

Baby Red Oak Leaf

Pirate

Baby Red Romaine

Belgian Endive

Curly Endive

Escarole

Radicchio

Arugula

Dandelion

Chicory

Chicories come in a variety of colours, shapes and sizes; most are slightly bitter. Chicories are quite hearty and can also be cooked, usually grilled or braised.

Belgian Endive

Belgian endive (witloof) grows in small, tight heads with pointed leaves. It is actually the shoot of a chicory root. The small sturdy leaves are white at the base with yellow fringes and tips. (A purple-tipped variety is sometimes available.) Whole leaves can be separated, trimmed and filled with soft butters, cheeses or spreads and served as an hors d'oeuvre. Or they can be used for composed salads. The leaves, cut or whole, can also be added to cold salads. Heads of Belgian endive are often braised or grilled and served with meat or poultry. Belgian endive is imported from Belgium or Holland at certain times and is grown in greenhouses locally.

Curly Endive

In this country, curly endive is often called by its family name, chicory, or its French name, frisée. The dark green outer leaves are pointed, sturdy and slightly bitter. The yellow inner leaves are more tender and less bitter. Curly endive has a strong flavour that goes well with strong cheeses, game and citrus. It is often mixed with other greens to add texture and flavour.

Escarole

Escarole, sometimes called broadleaf endive, has thick leaves and a slightly bitter flavour. It has green outer leaves and pale green or yellow centre leaves. Escarole is very sturdy and is often mixed with other greens for added texture. Its strong flavour stands up to full-flavoured dressings. It is a good accompaniment to grilled meats and poultry.

Radicchio

Radicchio resembles a small red cabbage. It retains its bright reddish colour when cooked and is popular braised or grilled and served as a vegetable side dish. Because of its attractive colour, radicchio is popular in cold salads, but it has a very bitter flavour and should be used sparingly and mixed with other greens in a tossed salad. Radicchio is quite expensive and availability is sometimes limited.

Other Salad Greens and Ingredients

Leafy vegetables besides lettuce and chicory, as well as other ingredients, are used to add texture, flavour and colour to salads. A partial listing follows.

Arugula

Arugula, also known as rocket, is a member of the cabbage family. Its individual leaves are similar to dandelion leaves in size and shape. The best are 5 to 10 cm (2 to 4 inches) long. Arugula has a very strong, spicy, peppery flavour—so strong, in fact, that it is rarely served by itself. It is best when used to add zip to salads by combining it with other greens.

Dandelion

Dandelion grows as a weed throughout most of the world. It has long, thin, toothed leaves with a prominent midrib. When purchasing dandelion for salads, look for small leaves. They are more tender and less bitter. Older, tougher leaves can be cooked and served as a vegetable.

Mâche

Mâche or lamb's lettuce is very tender and very delicately flavoured. Its small, cuplike pale to dark green leaves have a slightly nutty flavour. Because its flavour is so delicate, mâche should be combined only with other delicately flavoured greens such as Boston or bibb lettuce and dressed sparingly with a light vinaigrette dressing.

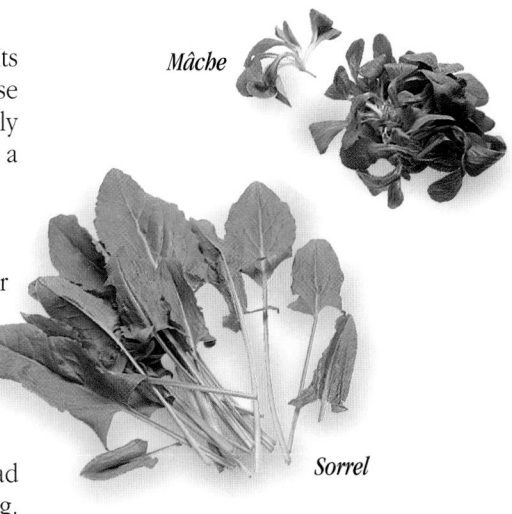

Mâche

Sorrel

Sorrel, sometimes called sourgrass, has leaves similar to spinach in colour and shape. Sorrel has a very tart, lemony flavour that goes well with fish and shellfish. It should be used sparingly and combined with other greens in a salad. Sorrel can also be made into soups, sauces and purées.

Sorrel

Spinach

Like sorrel, spinach can be cooked or used as a salad green. As a salad green, it is popular served wilted and tossed with a hot bacon dressing. Spinach is deep green with a rich flavour and tender texture. Good-quality spinach should be fairly crisp. Avoid wilted or yellowed bunches.

Sprouts

Sprouts are not salad greens but are often used as such in salads and sandwiches. Sprouts are very young alfalfa, daikon, sunflower, radish or mustard plants. Alfalfa sprouts are very mild and sweet. Daikon and mustard sprouts are quite peppery.

Sprouts

Spinach

Watercress

Watercress has tiny, dime-sized leaves and substantial stems. It has a peppery flavour and adds spice to a salad. Good-quality fresh watercress is dark green with no yellowing. To preserve its freshness, watercress must be kept very cold and moist. It is normally packed topped with ice. Individual leaves are plucked from the stems and rinsed just before service.

Watercress

Edible Flowers

Many specialty produce growers offer edible, pesticide-free blossoms. They are used for salads and as garnishes wherever a splash of colour would be appreciated. Some flowers such as nasturtiums, calendulas and pansies are grown and picked specifically for eating. Others, such as yellow cucumber flowers and squash blossoms, are byproducts of the vegetable industry.

Squash blossoms and other very large flowers should be cut in julienne strips before being added to salads. Pick petals from large and medium-sized flowers. Smaller whole flowers can be tossed in a salad or used as a garnish when composing a salad. Very small flowers or petals can be sprinkled on top of a salad so they are not hidden by the greens.

Nasturtiums

Calendulas

Pansies

Fresh Herbs

Basil, thyme, tarragon, oregano, dill, cilantro, marjoram, mint, sage, savory and even rosemary are used to add interesting flavours to otherwise ordinary salads. Because many herbs have strong flavours, use them sparingly so the delicate flavours of the greens are not overpowered. Leafy herbs such as basil and sage can be cut chiffonade. Other herbs can be picked into sprigs or chopped before being tossed with the salad greens. Flowering herbs such as

---

◆◆◆

FLOWER SAFETY

Many flowers and blossoms are toxic, especially those grown from bulbs. Even flowers that would otherwise be edible may contain pesticides that can be harmful if ingested. Use only flowers grown specifically for use as food; purchase edible flowers only from reputable purveyors.

TABLE 24.1   NUTRITIONAL VALUES OF SELECTED SALAD GREENS AND DRESSINGS

Salad greens per 112-g (4-oz.) serving, trimmed; Salad dressings per 28-g (1-oz.) serving	Kcal	Protein (g)	Carbohydrates (g)	Fibre (g)	Total Fat (g)	Vitamin A (I.U.)	Vitamin C (mg)	Calcium (mg)	Iron (mg)
Belgian endive	20	1.6	3.6	1.2	0.4	2052	8	52	0.8
Boston lettuce	16	1.6	2.8	1.2	0.4	816	6.7	mq	0.2
Chicory greens	28	2	5.2	0.8	0.4	14 400	88	360	3.2
Dandelion greens	52	3.2	10.4	2	0.8	mq	mq	mq	mq
Iceberg lettuce	16	1.2	2.4	1.2	0.4	383	5.8	23	0.6
Romaine lettuce	20	2	2.8	2	0.4	2912	28	40	1.2
Blue cheese dressing	143	1.4	2.1	<0.1	14.8	32	<1	12	tr
Mayonnaise	110	0.3	6.8	0	9.5	32	0	2	tr
Vinaigrette	67	<0.1	2.3	mq	6.5	0	0	0	0

The Corinne T. Netzer Encyclopedia of Food Values 1992

mq = measurable quantity, but data are unavailable   tr = trace amounts

chive blossoms are used like other edible flowers to add colour, flavour and aroma. Refer to Chapter 7, Kitchen Staples, for more information on herbs.

Nutrition

Salad greens are an especially healthful food. (Table 24.1 provides a comparison of selected greens.) Greens contain virtually no fat and few calories and are high in vitamins A and C, iron and fibre. But when garnished with meat and cheese and tossed with a dressing (many of which are oil-based), fat and calories are added. In an attempt to maintain the healthful nature of greens, low-fat or fat-free dressings should be available to customers. Due to high nitrate content, greens, as well as broccoli and cauliflower, may be a migraine trigger.

Purchasing and Storing Salad Greens

Purchasing

Lettuces are grown in nearly every part of Canada and the United States, both outdoors and in greenhouses; nearly all types are available year-round. Principal salad greens such as spinach are available all year; many of the specialty greens are seasonal.

Lettuce is generally packed in cases of 24 heads with varying weights. Other salad greens are packed in trays or boxes of various sizes and weights.

Because salad greens are simply washed and eaten, it is extremely important that they be as fresh and blemish-free as possible. Try to purchase salad greens several times per week. All greens should be fresh-looking, with no yellowing. Heads should be heavy, with little or no damage to the outer leaves.

Many types of salad greens are available precut and prewashed. These greens are often modified atmosphere-packed to increase shelf life, although delicate greens are sometimes loosely packaged in 2.5–5-kg (5–10-lb.) boxes. Precut and prewashed greens are relatively expensive, but can reduce labour costs dramatically.

♦♦♦

NITRATES, NITRITES AND MSG

Many vegetables contain these compounds naturally. Spinach, lettuce, broccoli and cauliflower have relatively high nitrate concentrations compared to cured meats. Celery contains high levels of MSG. This is why many labels read "No MSG added" rather than "MSG-free."

Storing

Although some types of salad greens are hearty enough to keep for a week or more under proper conditions, all salad greens are highly perishable. Generally, softer-leaved varieties such as Boston and bibb tend to perish more quickly than the crisper-leaved varieties such as iceberg and romaine.

Greens should be stored in their original protective cartons in a specifically designated refrigerator. Ideally, greens should be stored at temperatures between 1°C and 3°C (34°F and 38°F) (most other vegetables should be stored at warmer temperatures of 4–10°C [40–50°F]). Greens should not be stored with tomatoes, apples or other fruits that emit ethylene gas, which causes greens to wilt and accelerates spoilage.

Do not wash greens until you need them, as excess water causes them to deteriorate quickly.

Preparing Salad Greens

Unless salad greens are purchased precut and prewashed, they will need to undergo some preparation before service, principally tearing, cutting, washing and drying. Do not leave salad greens soaking in water for storage. The nutrients will be leached out.

Tearing and Cutting

Some cooks prefer all salad greens torn by hand. Delicate greens such as butterhead and baby lettuces look nicer and it is less likely they will be bruised if hand-torn. But often it is not practical to hand-tear all greens. It is perfectly acceptable to cut hardy greens with a sharp stainless steel knife.

Basic Procedure for Cutting Romaine Lettuce

1. To cut romaine lettuce, trim the outer leaves and damaged tips with a chef's knife and split the head lengthwise.

2. Make one or two cuts along the length of the head, leaving the root intact, then cut across the width of the head.

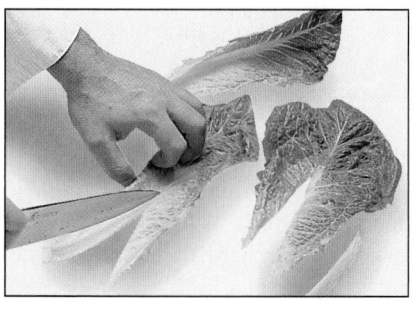

1A. Trim the outer leaves and damaged tips with a chef's knife. Pull the leaves from the core and cut the rib out of each leaf. The leaf can then be cut to the desired size. Yield and therefore food cost are affected by this method— there is more wastage.

Basic Procedure for Coring Iceberg Lettuce

 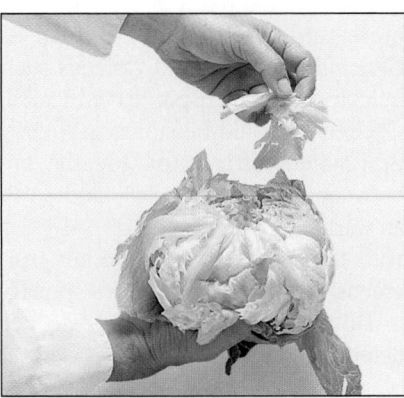

1. Loosen the core by gripping the head and smacking the core firmly on the cutting board.

2. Remove the core and cut the lettuce as desired.

Basic Procedure for Removing the Midrib From Spinach

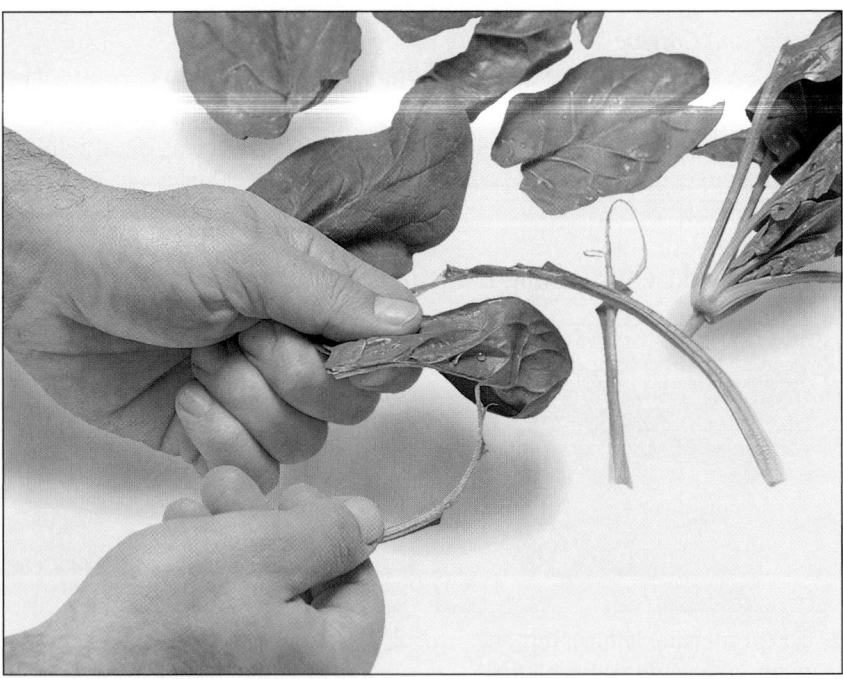

Fold the leaf in half and pull off the stem and midrib. Only the tender leaf should remain.

Washing

All lettuce and other salad greens should be washed before use. Even though they may look clean, greens may harbour hidden insects, sand, soil and pesticides. All greens should be washed after they are torn or cut. Whole heads can be washed by repeatedly dipping them in cold water and allowing them to drain. But washing whole heads is not recommended: It will not remove anything trapped near the head's centre, and water trapped in the leaves can accelerate spoilage.

Basic Procedure for Washing Salad Greens

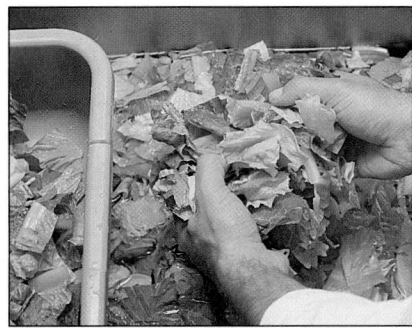

1. Fill a sink with cold water. Place the cut or torn greens in the water.

2. Gently stir the water and greens with your hands and remove the greens. Do not allow the greens to soak. Using fresh water each time, repeat the procedure until no grit can be detected on the bottom of the sink after the greens are removed.

Drying

Salad greens should be dried after washing. Wet greens do not stay as crisp as thoroughly dried ones. Also, wet greens tend to repel oil-based dressings and dilute their flavours. Greens may be dried by draining them well in a colander and blotting them with a clean absorbent paper towel, or, preferably, they can be dried in a salad spinner, which uses centrifugal force to remove the water. Spin for 20 to 30 seconds.

SALAD DRESSINGS

A dressing is a sauce for a salad. Just as sauces for hot foods should complement rather than mask the flavour of the principal food, the sauce (dressing) for a salad should complement rather than mask the flavours of the other ingredients. Although a great many ingredients can be used to make salad dressings, most are based on either a mixture of oil and vinegar, called a vinaigrette, or a mayonnaise or other emulsified product.

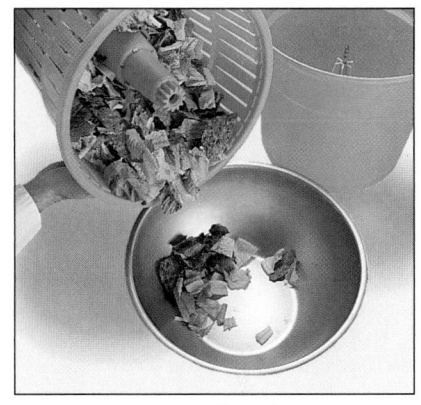

3. Drain greens well and spin if possible to remove excess moisture.

Vinaigrette-style dressings can be made without oil; creamy dressings similar to mayonnaise-based dressings can be made with sour cream, yogurt or buttermilk instead of mayonnaise. Nevertheless, for all practical purposes these dressings are still prepared like vinaigrettes and mayonnaise-based dressings and they are treated that way here.

Vinaigrette Dressings

The simple vinaigrette, also known as **basic French dressing**, is a temporary emulsion of oil and vinegar seasoned with salt, pepper and mustard. The standard ratio is three parts oil to one part vinegar. The ratio can vary, however. When using strongly flavoured oils, less than three parts oil to one part vinegar generally suffices. In some recipes, all or part of the vinegar is replaced with citrus juice, in which case it may take more than one part vinegar and citrus juice to three parts oil to achieve the proper acidity level. The best way to determine the correct ratio of oil to vinegar is to taste the dressing, preferably on the food it will dress.

Oils and vinegars have unique flavours that can be mixed and matched to achieve the correct balance for a particular salad. Olive oil goes well with red wine vinegar; nut oils go well with balsamic or sherry vinegars. Neutral-flavoured oils such as canola, corn or safflower can be mixed with a flavoured vinegar.

Oil and vinegar repel each other and will separate almost immediately when mixed. They should be whisked together immediately before use.

Oils

Many types of oil can be used to make salad dressings. Light, neutral-flavoured oils such as canola, corn, cottonseed, soybean and safflower are relatively low priced and used extensively for this purpose. Other oils can be used to add flavour. Olive oil is very popular; both mild-flavoured pure olive oil and full-flavoured extra virgin olive oil are used. Nut oils such as hazelnut and walnut are expensive but they add unique and interesting flavours. Infused oils are also popular, but great care must be taken in preparing them to avoid botulism.

Vinegars

Many different vinegars can be used to make salad dressings. Red wine vinegar is the most common because it is inexpensive and its flavour blends well with many foods. But other vinegars such as cider, balsamic, white wine and rice are also used. Fruit-flavoured vinegars (particularly raspberry) are extremely popular and widely available, as are herb- and garlic-flavoured ones.

Flavoured vinegars are easy to make. Fruit, herbs or garlic are added to a wine vinegar (either red or white) and left for several days for the flavours to blend. The vinegar is then strained off and used as desired.

Acidic juices such as lemon, orange and lime are sometimes substituted for all or part of the vinegar in a salad dressing.

Other Flavouring Ingredients

Herbs, spices, shallots, garlic, mustard and sweeteners are only a few of the many flavouring ingredients used to enhance a vinaigrette dressing. Items such as herbs, shallots and garlic should be minced or chopped before being added to the dressing. If dried herbs are used, the dressing should rest for at least one hour to allow the flavours to develop. Other ingredients may be added at any time.

Basic Procedure for Preparing a Vinaigrette

1. Choose an oil and vinegar that complement each other as well as the foods they will dress.
2. Combine the vinegar, seasonings and any other flavourings in a bowl.
3. Whisk in the oil.
4. Allow the finished dressing to rest for one hour at room temperature before using so that the flavours can blend.
5. Rewhisk immediately before use. Store in refrigerator. Use in 3 to 4 days.

RECIPE 24.1

Approximate values per 15 mL serving:

Calories	93
Total fat	10.5 g
Saturated fat	1 g
Cholesterol	0 mg
Sodium	38 mg
Total carbohydrates	0 g
Protein	0 g

Applying the Basics

RECIPE 24.1

BASIC VINAIGRETTE DRESSING

Yield: 1 L (1 qt.)

Dry mustard	1.5 g	1 tsp.
Wine vinegar	250 mL	8 fl. oz.
Salt and pepper	TT	TT
Salad oil	750 mL	24 fl. oz.

1. Dissolve the mustard in a little of the vinegar.

2. Combine all ingredients and mix well. Store in refrigerator.

VARIATIONS: Dijon Vinaigrette—Add 125 g (4 oz.) Dijon-style mustard to the vinegar and 100 g (3-1/2 oz.) finely chopped shallots. Proceed with the recipe.

Herbed Vinaigrette—Add 20 g (2 Tbsp.) fresh herbs or 5 g (1 Tbsp.) dried herbs such as basil, tarragon, thyme, marjoram or chives to the vinaigrette.

Mayonnaise

Although most food service operations buy commercially made mayonnaise, every cook should know how it is made to more fully understand how to use it and why it reacts the way it does when used. Knowing how to make mayonnaise also allows you to create a mayonnaise with the exact flavourings you want.

Mayonnaise is an **emulsified sauce**. An emulsified sauce is formed when two liquids that would not ordinarily form a stable mixture are forced together and held in suspension. To make mayonnaise, oil is whisked together with a very small amount of vinegar (it is the water in the vinegar that does not normally mix with oil). As the oil and vinegar are whisked together, the oil breaks into microscopic droplets that are separated from each other by a thin barrier of vinegar. If left alone, the droplets would quickly regroup, forming a large puddle of oil and a small puddle of vinegar. To prevent the oil droplets from regrouping, an emulsifier is added. For mayonnaise, the emulsifier is lecithin, a protein found in egg yolks. Lecithin has the unique ability to combine with both oil and water. It surrounds the oil droplets, binding them together and preventing them from coming in contact with each other and regrouping.

The balance of liquid, oil, lecithin and agitation (whipping) is crucial to achieve a proper emulsion. The higher the proportion of oil to vinegar, the thicker the sauce will be. The higher the proportion of vinegar to oil, the thinner the sauce will be. (For example, the emulsified vinaigrette dressing discussed on page 667 is a thin emulsion.)

There is a limit to how much oil each egg yolk can emulsify, however. One large yolk contains enough lecithin to emulsify approximately 200 mL (7 fl. oz.) of oil. If more than that amount of oil per egg yolk is added, the sauce will break; that is, the oil and vinegar will separate and the mayonnaise will become very thin and curdled.

Ingredients

A neutral-flavoured vegetable oil is most often used for a standard mayonnaise. Other oils are used to contribute their special flavours. For example, olive oil is used to make a special mayonnaise called aïoli.

Rice or wine vinegar is preferable for a standard mayonnaise. Flavoured vinegars such as tarragon vinegar are often used to create unique flavours.

Seasonings vary according to the intended use but typically include dry mustard, salt, pepper and lemon juice.

Standard white or pickling vinegars are generally too acidic to make a mayonnaise with a balanced flavour.

Basic Procedure for Preparing Mayonnaise

1. Gather all ingredients and hold at room temperature. Room-temperature ingredients emulsify more easily than cold ones.

2. By hand or in an electric mixer, whip the egg yolks on high speed until frothy.

1. Whip the egg yolks until frothy.

2. Add the oil very slowly, allowing the emulsion to form.

3. The finished mayonnaise.

RECIPE 24.2

*Approximate values
per 25 mL serving:*

Calories	170
Total fat	19 g
Saturated fat	1.5 g
Cholesterol	22 mg
Sodium	49 mg
Total carbohydrates	0 g
Protein	0 g

3. Add the seasonings to the yolks and whip to combine. Salt and other seasonings will dissolve or blend more easily when added at this point rather than if added to the finished mayonnaise.

4. Add a small amount of the vinegar from the recipe and whip to combine. This helps to promote the formation of an emulsion by setting the yolks slightly for better binding ability.

5. With the mixer on high or whisking vigorously by hand, begin to add the oil very slowly until an emulsion forms.

6. After the emulsion forms, the oil can be added a little more quickly but still in a slow, steady stream. The mayonnaise can now be whipped at a slightly slower speed.

7. The mayonnaise will become very thick as more oil is added. A small amount of liquid can be added if it becomes too thick. Alternate between oil and liquid two or three times until all the oil is added and the correct consistency is reached. *Important:* A large egg yolk has the ability to emulsify up to 200 mL (7 fl. oz.) of oil; adding more oil may cause the mayonnaise to break.

8. Taste the mayonnaise and adjust the seasonings. Refrigerate immediately.

Applying the Basics

RECIPE 24.2

MAYONNAISE

Yield: 1 L (1 qt.)

Egg yolks, large	4	4
Salt	5 g	1 tsp.
White pepper	TT	TT
Dry mustard	1.5 g	1 tsp.
Wine vinegar	50 mL	3 Tbsp.
Salad oil	800 mL	28 fl. oz.
Lemon juice	TT	TT

1. Place the egg yolks in the bowl of a mixer and whip on high speed until frothy. Use pasteurized yolks, if available.

2. Add the dry ingredients and half the vinegar to the yolks; whisk to combine.

3. Begin to add the oil a drop at a time until the mixture begins to thicken and an emulsion begins to form.

4. Add the remaining oil in a slow steady stream, thinning the mayonnaise occasionally by adding a little vinegar. Continue until all oil and vinegar have been incorporated. A little water may be used.

5. Adjust the seasonings and add lemon juice to taste.

6. Store in a covered noncorrosive container. Refrigerate until needed.

Mayonnaise-Based Dressings

Mayonnaise-based salad dressings are sauces that use mayonnaise as a base, with other ingredients added for flavour, colour and texture. These ingredients include dairy products (especially buttermilk and sour cream), vinegar, fruit juice, vegetables (either puréed or minced), tomato paste, garlic, onions, herbs, spices, condiments, capers, anchovies and boiled eggs. Recipes for several mayonnaise-based salad dressings are at the end of this chapter.

Emulsified Vinaigrette Dressings

An emulsified vinaigrette is a standard vinaigrette dressing emulsified with whole eggs, modified starches or vegetable gums. An emulsified vinaigrette dressing is thinner and lighter than a mayonnaise-based dressing and heavier than a basic vinaigrette. Its taste is similar to a basic vinaigrette, but it will not separate and it clings to greens quite easily. Emulsified vinaigrettes are very popular.

Basic Procedure for Preparing an Emulsified Vinaigrette Dressing

1. Gather all ingredients and hold at room temperature. Room-temperature ingredients emulsify more easily than cold ones.
2. Whip the eggs until frothy.
3. Add the dry ingredients and any flavourings such as garlic, shallots and herbs.
4. Add a small amount of the liquid from the recipe and whip to incorporate the ingredients.
5. With the mixer on high or whisking vigorously by hand, begin adding the oil very slowly until the emulsion forms.
6. After the emulsion is formed, the oil can be added a little more quickly, but still in a slow, steady stream.
7. Alternate between oil and liquid two or three times until all the oil is added. The dressing should be much thinner than mayonnaise. If it is too thick it can be thinned with a little water, vinegar or lemon juice. Determine which to use by first tasting the dressing.

Applying the Basics

RECIPE 24.3

EMULSIFIED VINAIGRETTE DRESSING

Yield: 1 L (1 qt.)

Eggs, whole	2	2
Salt	15 g	1 Tbsp.
Black pepper, ground	1 g	1/2 tsp.
Dry mustard	4.5 g	1 Tbsp.
Sugar	15 g	1 Tbsp.
Herbes de Provence	5 g	1 Tbsp.
Cayenne pepper	TT	TT
Wine vinegar or cider vinegar	150 mL	4 fl. oz.
Salad oil	750 mL	24 fl. oz.
Lemon juice	100 mL	3 fl. oz.

1. Place the eggs in the bowl of a mixer and whip at high speed until frothy.
2. Add the dry ingredients and approximately 30 mL (1 fl. oz.) of vinegar to the eggs; whip to combine.
3. While whipping at high speed, begin adding the oil very slowly until an emulsion forms.
4. Add the remaining oil in a slow, steady stream. Occasionally thin the dressing by adding a little vinegar and lemon juice. Continue until all of the oil, vinegar and lemon juice have been incorporated.
5. Adjust the flavour and consistency.
6. Refrigerate until needed.

NOTE: Omit the herbs and add 6 g (1 Tbsp.) paprika and 50 mL (2 fl. oz.) ketchup for an orange-coloured "American French" dressing.

♦♦♦

CONVENIENCE PRODUCTS

A great many prepared and dry-mix salad dressings are available. Although they vary greatly in quality, they can be very economical; they reduce labour costs and sometimes food costs. Some of these products use stabilizers, artificial flavourings and colours; nearly all contain preservatives. When considering the advantages of prepared or dry-mix salad dressings, always keep quality in mind.

RECIPE 24.3

Approximate values per 25 mL serving:

Calories	160
Total fat	18 g
Saturated fat	1 g
Cholesterol	11 mg
Sodium	149 mg
Total carbohydrates	1 g
Protein	0.5 g

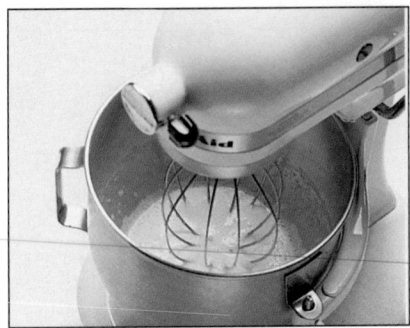

1. Whip the whole eggs.

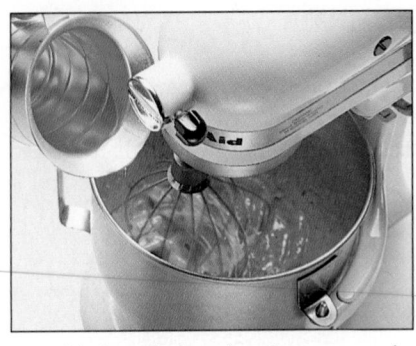

2. Add the oil drop by drop to establish the emulsion.

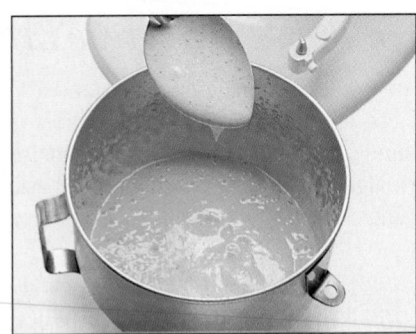

3. The finished emulsified vinaigrette dressing.

◆◆◆
SIMPLE SALADS

Green Salad (Salade verte)—any green lettuce served with vinaigrette.

Potato Salad (Salade de pomme de terre)—cooked potatoes diced or sliced. Mixed with mayonnaise vinaigrette, chopped onion, chives, salt and pepper.

Egg Salad (Salade des oeufs)—chopped hard-boiled eggs, mustard, chives, salt and pepper.

PREPARATION METHODS

There are two types of **green salads**: tossed and composed. The more informal **tossed salad** is prepared by placing the greens, garnishes and dressing in a large bowl and tossing to combine. A **composed salad** usually has a more elegant look. It is prepared by arranging each of the ingredients on plates in an artistic fashion.

Other types of salads include **bound salads**, which are cooked meats, poultry, fish, shellfish, pasta or potatoes bound with a dressing, **vegetable salads** and **fruit salads**.

Traditionally, salads were divided into two categories. Simple salads contain one main featured ingredient. Compound mixed salads contain more than one featured ingredient.

Green Salads

Tossed

Tossed salads are made from leafy vegetables such as lettuce, spinach, watercress, arugula or dandelion greens. They may consist only of greens and dressing or they can be garnished with fruits, vegetables, nuts or cheese. They can be dressed with many different types of dressings, from a light oil and vinegar to a hearty hot bacon. It is important that salad dressings be added at the last possible moment before service. Acidic dressings cause most greens to wilt and become soggy.

Matching Dressings and Salad Greens

There is a simple rule to follow when choosing dressings for salads: The more delicate the texture and flavour of the greens or other ingredients, the lighter and more subtle the dressing should be. Vinaigrette-based dressings are much lighter than mayonnaise-based or similar dressings and should be used with butterleaf lettuces, mâche or other delicate greens. Crisp head lettuce such as iceberg and hardy lettuce such as romaine can stand up to heavier, mayonnaise-based or similar dressings. Bitter greens are balanced with tart dressings. (See Table 24.2.)

Salad Garnishes

It is impossible to make a complete list of the garnishes that can be combined with salad greens for a tossed salad. A partial list includes:

◆ Vegetables—nearly any vegetable—raw, blanched or fully cooked—cut into appropriate sizes and uniform shapes.

TABLE 24.2 MATCHING DRESSINGS AND SALAD GREENS

Dressing	Greens
Vinaigrette dressing made with vegetable oil and red wine vinegar	Any greens: iceberg, romaine, leaf lettuce, butterleaf lettuce, escarole, curly endive, Belgian endive, radicchio, baby lettuces, sorrel, arugula, dandelion
Vinaigrette dressing made with a nut oil and balsamic vinegar	Delicate greens: butterleaf lettuce, bibb lettuce, Belgian endive, radicchio, baby lettuces, arugula, mâche, watercress
Emulsified vinaigrette dressing	Any greens: romaine, leaf lettuce, butterleaf lettuce, escarole, curly endive, Belgian endive, radicchio, baby lettuces, sorrel, arugula, watercress
Mayonnaise-based dressing such as blue cheese or green goddess	Hardy greens: iceberg, romaine, leaf lettuce, escarole, curly endive, sorrel, dandelion

- ◆ Fruits—citrus segments, apples or pears; dried fruits such as raisins, currants or apricots.
- ◆ Meats, poultry, fish and shellfish—cooked meats and poultry sliced or diced neatly and uniformly; poached, grilled or cured fish, diced or flaked; small, whole cooked shellfish such as shrimp and scallops; lobster or crab sliced, diced or chopped.
- ◆ Cheeses—grated hard cheeses such as Parmesan, Romano or Asiago; semi-hard cheese such as cheddar and Swiss, cut julienne or shredded.
- ◆ Nuts—nearly any are appropriate, roasted, candied or smoked.
- ◆ Croutons—assorted breads, seasoned in various ways and toasted.

Basic Procedure for Preparing Tossed Salads

1. Select greens with various colours, textures and flavours.
2. Carefully cut or tear, wash and dry the greens.
3. Prepare the garnishes as directed or desired.
4. Prepare the dressing.
5. Combine the greens, garnishes and dressing by tossing them together. Or toss the greens and garnishes and, using a spray bottle, spray the greens with the dressing.

Applying the Basics

RECIPE 24.4

MESCLUN SALAD WITH RASPBERRY VINAIGRETTE

Yield: 6 Servings

Baby lettuces, assorted	approx. 8 heads	approx. 8 heads
Mâche	125 g	4 oz.
Fresh herbs	20 g	2 Tbsp.
Edible flowers	approx. 12	approx. 12
Raspberry Vinaigrette (Recipe 24.9)	125 mL	4 fl. oz.

Continued

◆◆◆

MORE SIMPLE SALADS

Artichauts—	artichoke !
Aubergine—	eggplant !
Betteraves—	beetroot !
Céleris—	celery ▲
Céleri-rave—	celeriac ▲
Chou-rave—	kohlrabi ▲
Choux vert—	green cabbage ▲
Choux rouges—	red cabbage ▲
Concombres—	cucumber *
Cresson—	watercress *
Endive—	chicory ▲
Pissenlit—	dandelion ▲
Fenouil—	fennel ▲
Laitues—	lettuce ▲
Poireau—	leek !
Haricots verts—	green beans !
Panais—	parsnip !
Tomate—	Tomato *

Note: * Raw only

  ! Cooked only

  ▲ Raw or cooked

Simple salads should be served tossed or bound with an appropriate dressing.

A simple mesclun salad.

RECIPE 24.4

Approximate values per serving:

Calories	155
Total fat	9 g
Saturated fat	1 g
Cholesterol	0 mg
Sodium	189 mg
Total carbohydrates	15 g
Protein	4 g

1. Trim, wash and dry the baby lettuces and mâche.
2. Pick the fresh herbs from their stems. If using leafy herbs such as basil, they may be cut chiffonade or left as whole leaves.
3. Pick the petals from the edible flowers.
4. Place the lettuces and mâche in a bowl and add the herbs. Ladle the dressing over them and toss gently, using two spoons.
5. Transfer the salads to cold plates. Some of the larger leaves may be used as liners if desired.
6. Garnish each salad with flower petals.

Composed

Composed green salads usually use a green as a base and are built by artistically arranging other ingredients on the plate. There are usually four components: the base, body, garnish and dressing.

Mist salads while on a sheet pan and transfer to chilled plates for service.

The **base** is usually salad greens that partially line or anchor the plate on which the salad will be served. Depending upon the desired effect, the leaves can be cup-shaped or flat.

The **body** is the main ingredient. It can be lettuce or other greens, or another salad made from cooked or blended ingredients, such as chicken salad or fruit.

The **garnish** is added to the salad for colour, texture and flavour. It can be as substantial as a grilled, sliced duck breast or as simple as a sprinkling of chopped herbs; it can be warm or cold. The choice is unlimited but whatever is used should always complement and balance the flavour of the body.

The salad **dressing** should complement rather than mask the other flavours in the salad. If the body already contains a dressing, as in a bound salad, additional dressing may not be necessary.

Composed green salads are usually dressed by ladling the dressing over the salad after it is plated. Alternatively, the individual ingredients can be dressed before they are arranged on the plate. A third method that may be limited by the intricacy of the salad but will save precious time during a busy period is to prepare individual salads on a sheet pan. Then, just before service, mist them with dressing using a spray bottle designated for this purpose, then transfer them to chilled plates using a spatula as illustrated. Foam beverage cups work well too.

Basic Procedure for Preparing Composed Salads

1. Gather all ingredients for the salad and wash, trim, cut, cook, chill or otherwise prepare them as necessary or as called for in the recipe.
2. Arrange all ingredients artistically on the plates, dressing each ingredient as desired or as directed in the recipe.
3. At service time, heat or cook any items that are being served hot and add them to the salad.

Applying the Basics

SALAD NIÇOISE

Yield: 6 Servings

Red wine vinegar	125 mL	4 fl. oz.
Salt and pepper	TT	TT
Virgin olive oil	350 mL	12 fl. oz.
Basil leaves, chiffonade	12	12
Belgian endive	1 head	1 head
Tomatoes, peeled	6	6
Waxy potatoes, cooked	700 g	1 lb. 8 oz.
Green beans	350 g	12 oz.
Eggs, hard-boiled	6	6
Artichokes	6	6
Romaine lettuce leaves, washed	12	12
Tuna, fresh, grilled and chilled	750 g	1 lb. 8 oz.
Niçoise olives	125 g	4 oz.
Anchovy fillets	12	12

1. Make a vinaigrette dressing using the red wine vinegar, salt, pepper, olive oil and basil leaves.
2. Wash and dry the endive leaves.
3. Core and cut each tomato into eight wedges.
4. Slice the potatoes and moisten with some of the dressing.
5. Trim and cook the green beans al dente, refresh in ice water.
6. Peel the eggs and cut into wedges.
7. Cook the artichokes. Trim the outer leaves from each artichoke leaving only the heart. Remove the choke from the heart and cut each heart into quarters.
8. Line each cold plate with romaine lettuce leaves and endive spears, then arrange the remaining ingredients artistically. Use the contrasting shapes, colours and textures to create an attractive presentation.
9. At service, whisk the dressing to combine the ingredients and pour approximately 75 mL (2-1/2 fl. oz.) over each salad.

RECIPE 24.5

Approximate values per serving:

Calories	957
Total fat	70 g
Saturated fat	11 g
Cholesterol	241 mg
Sodium	777 mg
Total carbohydrates	34 g
Protein	50 g

Bound Salads

The creative cook can prepare a wide variety of salads by combining cooked meats, poultry, fish, shellfish, potatoes, pasta, grains and/or legumes with a dressing and garnishes. Although the combinations vary greatly, these salads are grouped together here because their ingredients are all bound. That is, each salad consists of one or more ingredients held together in a cohesive mass. The binding agent can be either a vinaigrette or mayonnaise-based or similar dressing. The ingredients should be evenly distributed throughout, and the degree of cohesiveness can range from tightly packed to flaky and easily separated.

The foods that can be used to produce bound salads are so varied that it is impossible to list them all. Generalizing preparation techniques is also very difficult. There are as many ways to prepare a bound salad as there are ingredients, dressings and garnishes.

Bound salads can be used as the body of a composed salad (for instance, a serving of shrimp salad on a bed of greens). Some are used in sandwiches but not ordinarily as side dishes—for example, egg or ham salad. Some are served as side dishes but not in sandwiches, for example, potato, pasta or cucumber salad. Follow specific recipes and traditional uses for each salad until you are confident enough in your skills to let your imagination take over.

Basic Procedure for Preparing Bound Salads

1. Preparing a salad from cooked foods is a good opportunity to use leftovers, but be sure they are fresh and of good quality. The finished salad can be only as good as each of its ingredients.
2. When making a bound salad, choose ingredients whose flavours blend well and complement each other.
3. Choose ingredients for colour; a few colourful ingredients will turn a plain salad into a spectacular one.
4. To improve appearance, generally cut all ingredients the same size and shape. If the main ingredient is diced, then dice the other ingredients. Be cautious combining diced, sliced and julienned foods in the same salad.
5. All ingredients should be cut into pieces that are small enough to be eaten easily with a fork.
6. Be sure all meats, poultry, fish and shellfish are fully cooked before using them. Undercooked foods can cause food-borne illness and spoilage.
7. Always chill cooked ingredients well before using them. Warm ingredients promote bacterial growth, especially in mayonnaise-based salads.
8. Always use dressings sparingly. They should enhance the flavours of the other salad ingredients, not mask them.

Applying the Basics

RECIPE 24.6

TUNA SALAD

Yield: 1.5 kg (3 lb.)

Tuna, drained, flaked	1 kg	2 lb.
Celery, small dice	125 g	4 oz.
Green onion, sliced	50 g	2 oz.
Mayonnaise	250 mL	8 fl. oz.
Lemon juice	50 mL	2 fl. oz.
Salt and pepper	TT	TT

Combine the tuna, celery, green onion, mayonnaise and lemon juice in a bowl; mix well. Season to taste with salt and pepper.

NOTE: Diced chicken, turkey, flaked boneless and skinless salmon, chopped hard-boiled eggs or seafood may be substituted for the tuna. Substitute lemon juice with mustard in the egg salad. Use 200 g (7 oz.) diced pineapple for the chicken salad instead of lemon juice.

RECIPE 24.6

Approximate values per 85 g serving:

Calories	180
Total fat	11 g
Saturated fat	1 g
Cholesterol	19 mg
Sodium	274 mg
Total carbohydrates	1 g
Protein	18 g

Vegetable Salads

Vegetable salads are made from cooked or raw vegetables or a combination of both. They can be served on buffets, as an appetizer or salad course. As with other salads, vegetable salads must successfully combine colour, texture and flavour. Some vegetable salads such as coleslaw and carrot-raisin salad may be made with mayonnaise. Most, however, are made by either marinating the vegetables or combining them in a vinaigrette dressing.

Almost any vegetable can be successfully marinated. The amount of time depends on the vegetables and the marinade, but several hours to overnight is usually sufficient for flavours to blend. Soft vegetables such as mushrooms, zucchini and cucumbers can be added directly to a cold marinade. Hard vegetables such as carrots and cauliflower should be blanched in salted water, refreshed, drained and then added to a cold marinade. Carrots, artichokes, mushrooms, cauliflower, zucchini, pearl onions and the like are sometimes simmered quickly in a marinade flavoured with lemon juice and olive oil, and then served cold. This style is called *à la grecque*.

Many marinated salads will last several days under proper refrigeration. As the salads age in the marinade they will change in appearance and texture. This may or may not be desirable. For example, mushrooms and artichokes become more flavourful, while green vegetables are discoloured by the acids in the marinade. If marinated salads are prepared in advance, check their appearance as well as their seasonings carefully at service time.

Basic Procedure for Preparing Vegetable Salads

1. Gather and wash all vegetables.
2. Trim, cut, shred or otherwise prepare the vegetables as desired or as directed in the recipe.
3. Blanch or cook the vegetables if necessary.
4. Combine the vegetables with the marinade or dressing. Adjust the seasonings.

Applying the Basics

RECIPE 24.7

TOMATO, ORANGE, MOZZARELLA AND BASIL SALAD

Yield: 4 Servings

Mozzarella cheese, fresh (bocconcini)	250 g	8 oz.
Tomatoes, peeled, sliced	4	4
Oranges, peeled, sliced	4	4
Virgin olive oil	60 mL	2 fl. oz.
Balsamic vinegar	15 mL	1 Tbsp.
Basil leaves, chiffonade	8	8
Kosher salt and freshly ground pepper	TT	TT

1. Slice cheese to the same thickness as the tomato and orange slices.
2. Arrange the cheese, tomato and orange slices on plates.
3. Prepare a dressing with the olive oil and vinegar.
4. Sprinkle the slices with the basil and dressing.
5. Season with freshly ground pepper and kosher salt.

RECIPE 24.7

Approximate values per serving:

Calories	373
Total fat	27 g
Saturated fat	9 g
Cholesterol	37 mg
Sodium	312 mg
Total carbohydrates	23 g
Protein	18 g

Fruit Salads

There are so many different fruits with beautiful bright colours and sweet delicious flavours that preparing fruit salads is easy work. Fruit salads are a refreshing addition to buffets and can be served as the first course of a lunch or dinner. A more elaborate fruit salad can be served as a light lunch.

Always prepare fruit salads as close to service time as possible. The flesh of many types of fruit becomes soft and translucent if cut long before service. Other fruits turn brown in a matter of minutes after cutting. Refer to Chapter 25, Fruits, for more information on this browning reaction and for information on specific fruits. Fruit salad recipes are found at the end of that chapter.

If a fruit salad is dressed at all, the dressing is usually sweet and made with honey or yogurt mixed with fruit juices or purées. Melons work well with herbed vinaigrettes when a sweet/sour effect is desired. Alternatively, Grand Marnier, crème de menthe or other liqueurs sprinkled over the salad can serve as a dressing. Fruit salads can be tossed or composed. Either should offer the consumer a pleasing blend of colours, shapes, sizes, flavours and textures.

CONCLUSION

A salad can be a small part of a meal or the entire meal. There are many styles of salads, and a seemingly endless variety of foods can be used to prepare them. Salads are extremely popular, especially with those interested in lighter dining alternatives. You can tempt these diners by determining the appropriate style of the salads and skilfully combining the main ingredients and dressing to achieve a delicious and appealing balance of colours, textures and flavours.

QUESTIONS FOR DISCUSSION

1. Name several factors that will cause salad greens to wilt or deteriorate.
2. Describe the proper procedure for washing and drying lettuce.
3. Explain the difference between a vinaigrette and an emulsified vinaigrette dressing.
4. Describe the procedure for making mayonnaise. How can the flavour of a mayonnaise be altered?
5. Explain what happens to the ingredients when an emulsion "breaks." How can it sometimes be repaired?
6. Describe a typical bound salad. How does a bound salad differ from a dressed salad?
7. List five ways salads can be presented or offered on a menu.

ADDITIONAL SALAD RECIPES

RECIPE 24.8

SEAFOOD SALAD

NOTE: *This dish appears in the Chapter Opening photograph.*

GOTHAM BAR AND GRILL, NEW YORK, NY
Chef/Owner Alfred Portale

Yield: 4 Servings

Lobster, 700 g (1 lb. 8 oz.)	1	1
Court bouillon	4 L	4 qt.

Sea scallops	125 g	4 oz.
Squid, cleaned	100 g	3 oz.
Mussels, debearded	12	12
Avocado	1	1
Frisée	1 head	1 head
Baby red oak	1 head	1 head
Shallot, finely minced	20 g	2 Tbsp.
Fresh basil, chopped	5 g	1 Tbsp.
Fresh chives, finely minced	5 g	1 Tbsp.
Fresh Italian parsley, chopped	5 g	1 Tbsp.
Lemon Vinaigrette (recipe follows)	as needed	as needed
Salt and white pepper	TT	TT

1. Boil the lobster in the court bouillon, then chill it. Remove the meat from the shell; dice it.

2. Poach the sea scallops and squid in the same court bouillon. Cool and thinly slice each of them.

3. Steam the mussels in a portion of the court bouillon. Chill and remove the meat from the shells.

4. Peel, pit, quarter and thinly slice the ripe avocado.

5. Wash and dry the greens.

6. Toss the shellfish with the shallot, herbs and a portion of the vinaigrette. Dress the lettuces and avocado.

7. Season all with salt and white pepper. Arrange the lettuces, shellfish and fanned avocado on four plates.

LEMON VINAIGRETTE

Yield: 400 mL (14 fl. oz.)

Dijon-style mustard	5 mL	1 tsp.
Salt and white pepper	TT	TT
Red wine vinegar	30 mL	1 fl. oz.
Extra virgin olive oil	300 mL	10 fl. oz.
Lemon juice	60 mL	2 fl. oz.
Cayenne pepper	pinch	pinch

1. Whisk together the mustard, salt, white pepper and red wine vinegar. Slowly whisk in the olive oil.

2. Adjust the acidity with the lemon juice and add a pinch of cayenne.

◆ ◆ ◆

RECIPE 24.9

RASPBERRY VINAIGRETTE

Yield: 1 L (1 qt.)

Red wine vinegar	125 mL	4 fl. oz.
Rice wine vinegar	125 mL	4 fl. oz.
Lemon juice	25 mL	1-1/2 fl. oz.
Dried thyme	1 g	1-1/2 tsp.
Salt	15 g	1-1/2 tsp.
Pepper, black ground	7 g	1-1/2 tsp.
Garlic, minced	10 g	1-1/2 tsp.
Honey	60 g	2 oz.

Continued

RECIPE 24.8

Approximate values per serving:

Calories	610
Total fat	20 g
Saturated fat	2.5 g
Cholesterol	241 mg
Sodium	1693 mg
Total carbohydrates	12 g
Protein	62 g

Lemon Vinaigrette—Approximate values per 30 mL (1 oz.) serving:

Calories	180
Total fat	12 g
Saturated fat	1 g
Cholesterol	0 mg
Sodium	174 mg
Total carbohydrates	5 g
Protein	0 g

RECIPE 24.9

Approximate values per 30 mL (1 oz.) serving:

Calories	115
Total fat	11 g
Saturated fat	1 g
Cholesterol	0 mg
Sodium	178 mg
Total carbohydrates	5 g
Protein	0 g

Raspberry preserves, without seeds	125 g	4 oz.
Olive oil	175 mL	6 fl. oz.
Salad oil	225 mL	8 fl. oz.

1. Whisk together the vinegars, lemon juice, thyme, salt, pepper and garlic.
2. Slowly whisk in the honey and raspberry preserves.
3. Whisk in the oils slowly, emulsifying the dressing.

VARIATION: Prepare Basic Vinaigrette using raspberry vinegar.

◆◆◆

RECIPE 24.10

RECIPE 24.10

CHIVE ESSENCE*

HALIFAX, NS
Chef Michael Smith

Yield: 250 mL (8 fl. oz.)

| Chives, chopped | 70 g | 1 cup |
| Canola oil | 250 mL | 8 fl. oz. |

1. Place chives and oil in a high-speed blender and process until very smooth. Pour into a thick-bottomed pot.
2. Bring mixture to a simmer over medium heat. Do not stir. As soon as it boils, remove from heat.
3. Strain through a fine-meshed sieve. Let it drain without squeezing to minimize moisture extraction.
4. Refrigerate until needed. Use within 3 days.

*This oil's brilliant green colour and delicate chive flavour make it an ideal garnish – you may substitute green onions or leek tops for the chives.

Approximate values
per 20 mL serving:

Calories	171
Total fat	19 g
Saturated fat	1.4 g
Cholesterol	0 mg
Sodium	0 mg
Total carbohydrates	0 g
Protein	0 g

Michael Smith

Chef Michael Smith has dedicated his career to furthering the ideals of Canadian cuisine. He hosts Food Network Canada's "Chef at Large" and frequently crisscrosses the country leading cooking classes. His company "Chef Michael's Flavours" brings the flavours of the Maritimes to the world.

◆◆◆

RECIPE 24.11

TOMATO ANCHOVY VINAIGRETTE

HALIFAX, NS
Chef Michael Smith

Yield: 500 mL (16 fl. oz.)

Tomatoes, ripe, chopped	350 g	12 oz.
Anchovies	15 g	1/2 oz.
Lemons, zested and juiced	2	2
Extra virgin olive oil	125 mL	4 fl. oz.
Dijon-style mustard	15 mL	1 Tbsp.
Tabasco sauce	dash	dash

1. Place all ingredients in a high-speed blender and purée until very smooth and aerated.
2. Strain the purée through a fine-meshed sieve to remove seeds and skin bits.
3. Reserve, chilled, until needed.

NOTE: Use only ripe tomatoes. Great with smoked salmon. Warm slightly to accompany grilled fish.

RECIPE 24.11

Approximate values
per 50 mL serving:

Calories	126
Total fat	12 g
Saturated fat	2 g
Cholesterol	5 mg
Sodium	243 mg
Total carbohydrates	4 g
Protein	2.5 g

✦ ✦ ✦

RECIPE 24.12

CAESAR DRESSING

Yield: 1.5 L (1-1/2 qt.)

Dry mustard	2 g	1/2 tsp.
Lemon juice	150 mL	5 fl. oz.
Salt	5 g	1 tsp.
Eggs, whole	5	5
Anchovy paste	30 g	1 oz.
Worcestershire sauce	5 mL	1 tsp.
Garlic cloves, crushed	2	2
Olive oil	1 L	1 qt.
Black pepper, ground	3 g	1 tsp.
Parmesan cheese (optional)	100 g	3 oz.

1. Dissolve the mustard in the lemon juice with the salt.
2. Whisk mixture with the eggs, anchovy paste, Worcestershire sauce and garlic until frothy.
3. Slowly drizzle the olive oil into mixture while whisking.
4. Once the emulsion forms, add remaining oil in a steady stream.
5. Add the remaining ingredients and adjust seasoning.
6. Store covered in a noncorrosive container under refrigeration. Use within 3–4 days.

RECIPE 24.12

Approximate values per 50 mL serving:

Calories	301
Total fat	32 g
Saturated fat	5 g
Cholesterol	39 mg
Sodium	176 mg
Total carbohydrates	1 g
Protein	3 g

✦ ✦ ✦

RECIPE 24.13

CAESAR SALAD

Yield: 4 Servings

Crisp, chilled romaine, chopped into 3–4 cm (1–1-1/2 inch) pieces	1 large	1 large
Garlic clove	1	1
Anchovy fillets, chopped	15 g	1/2 oz.
English dry mustard	1 g	1/2 tsp.
Juice from 1 lemon	1	1
Salt	2 g	1/2 tsp.
Worcestershire sauce	5 mL	1 tsp.
Coddled eggs	2	2
Olive oil	125 mL	4 fl. oz.
Black pepper, fresh ground	TT	TT
Parmesan cheese, grated	125 g	4 oz.
Garlic Croutons (Recipe 24.20)	250 mL (heaping)	1 cup (heaping)

1. The romaine should be chopped, crisp, dry and chilled.
2. Line up all ingredients ready for use at the tableside. Use only the very best brands of condiments.
3. In a small wooden bowl, crush the garlic with a fork and remove the pieces.
4. Mash the anchovies in the bowl.
5. Add the mustard, lemon juice, salt, Worcestershire sauce and coddled eggs. Mix well.
6. Very slowly mix in the oil, creating an emulsion.

RECIPE 24.13

Approximate values per serving:

Calories	451
Total fat	41 g
Saturated fat	11 g
Cholesterol	136 mg
Sodium	962 mg
Total carbohydrates	3 g
Protein	18 g

Continued

=== ◆◆◆ ===

HISTORY OF CAESAR SALAD

Caesar salad originated in Tijuana, Mexico, and was created by Caesar Cardini more than 100 years ago. Today's versions—and there are many—often bear little resemblance to the original. Julia Child documented this salad from memories of Cardini preparing it and input from Rosa, his daughter. The leaves used were the whole centre heart. The dressing was simply 125 mL (4 fl. oz.) olive oil, juice of 1 lemon, 2 coddled eggs (simmer 1 minute), salt, freshly ground pepper and Worcestershire sauce. The salad was garnished with pan-fried garlic croutons and Reggiano Parmesan, and eaten with the fingers.

Modern restaurateurs have added anchovies, far too much raw garlic, bacon bits and even capers and parsley. This may be due in part to the mistaken notion that the salad is Italian in origin. These varations are more aptly referred to as house-style salads, although the recipes here reflect current style.

7. Mix in pepper and half of the Parmesan cheese.

8. Toss romaine in dressing.

9. Sprinkle on remaining Parmesan and croutons.

10. Serve immediately on chilled plates. Finish with a little Parmesan.

=== ◆◆◆ ===

RECIPE 24.14

THOUSAND ISLAND DRESSING

Yield: 1 L (1 qt.)

Red wine vinegar	15 mL	1 Tbsp.
Sugar	15 g	1 Tbsp.
Mayonnaise	400 mL	16 fl. oz.
Ketchup	200 g	7 oz.
Sweet pickle relish	150 g	5 oz.
Hard-cooked eggs, chopped	3	3
Fresh parsley, chopped	30 mL	2 Tbsp.
Green onions, chopped	1	1
Salt and pepper	TT	TT
Worcestershire sauce	TT	TT

RECIPE 24.14

Approximate values per 30 mL (1 oz.) serving:

Calories	104
Total fat	10 g
Saturated fat	1.5 g
Cholesterol	29 mg
Sodium	173 mg
Total carbohydrates	4 g
Protein	1 g

1. Combine the vinegar and sugar; stir to dissolve the sugar.

2. Add the remaining ingredients and mix well.

3. Adjust the seasonings with the salt, pepper and Worcestershire sauce.

=== ◆◆◆ ===

RECIPE 24.15

GREEN GODDESS DRESSING

Yield: 1 L (1 qt.)

Fresh parsley	30 g	1 oz.
Mayonnaise	500 mL	1 pt.
Sour cream	400 mL	12 fl. oz.
Garlic, chopped	15 g	1 Tbsp.
Anchovy fillets, minced	30 g	1 oz.
Fresh chives, chopped	30 g	1 oz.
Fresh tarragon, chopped	10 g	1 Tbsp.

RECIPE 24.15

Approximate values per 30 mL (1 oz.) serving:

Calories	125
Total fat	13 g
Saturated fat	2 g
Cholesterol	14 mg
Sodium	112 mg
Total carbohydrates	1 g
Protein	1 g

Lemon juice	30 mL	1 fl. oz.
White wine vinegar	30 mL	1 fl. oz.
Salt and white pepper	TT	TT
Worcestershire sauce	TT	TT

1. Rinse and chop the parsley but do not dry it or you will remove some of the chlorophyll.

2. Combine all ingredients up to and including vinegar and mix well. Season to taste with salt, white pepper and Worcestershire sauce.

◆◆◆

RECIPE 24.16

CREAMY BLUE CHEESE DRESSING

Yield: 1.5 L (1-1/2 qt.)

Mayonnaise	700 mL	24 fl. oz.
Sour cream	500 mL	16 fl. oz.
Cream, 35%	200 mL	7 fl. oz.
Blue cheese, grated	200 g	7 oz.
Green onion, finely chopped	10 g	1 Tbsp.
Worcestershire sauce	5 mL	1 tsp.
Salt	15 g	1 Tbsp.
Pepper	1 g	1/4 tsp.
Cider vinegar	50 mL	2 fl. oz.
Lemon juice	20 mL	1 fl. oz.

Combine all ingredients.

◆◆◆

RECIPE 24.17

CUCUMBER DRESSING

Yield: 1.6 L (50 fl. oz.)

Mayonnaise	500 mL	16 fl. oz.
Yogurt, plain	500 mL	16 fl. oz.
English cucumber, grated	500 g	1
Vinegar, white wine or rice	125 mL	4 fl. oz.
Salt	10 g	1-1/2 tsp.
Pepper	0.5 g	1/4 tsp.
Sugar	10 g	2 tsp.

Combine all ingredients.

◆◆◆

RECIPE 24.18

RANCH DRESSING

Yield: 3.25 L (3-1/4 qt.)

Sour cream	1 L	32 fl. oz.
Buttermilk	1 L	32 fl. oz.
Mayonnaise	1 L	32 fl. oz.
Cider vinegar	150 mL	5 fl. oz.
Worcestershire sauce	10 mL	2 tsp.

Continued

◆◆◆

ROQUEFORT DRESSING

Classically, this is a vinaigrette dressing made with olive oil, wine vinegar and crumbled Roquefort whisked in to form an emulsion.

RECIPE 24.16

Approximate values per 30 mL (1 oz.) serving:

Calories	319
Total fat	34 g
Saturated fat	16 g
Cholesterol	91 mg
Sodium	267 mg
Total carbohydrates	2 g
Protein	2 g

RECIPE 24.17

Approximate values per 30 mL (1 oz.) serving:

Calories	73
Total fat	7 g
Saturated fat	1 g
Cholesterol	6 mg
Sodium	126 mg
Total carbohydrates	1 g
Protein	1 g

RECIPE 24.18

Approximate values per 30 mL (1 oz.) serving:

Calories	98
Total fat	10 g
Saturated fat	3 g
Cholesterol	17 mg
Sodium	113 mg
Total carbohydrates	1 g
Protein	1 g

Parsley, chopped	10 g	1/4 cup
Green onion, chopped	100 mL	1/2 cup
Salt	15 g	1 Tbsp.
Black pepper, ground	3 g	1 tsp.

1. Combine all ingredients.

2. Adjust seasoning.

VARIATION: Add 100 g (3 oz.) crumbled, cooked bacon.

◆ ◆ ◆

RECIPE 24.19

RECIPE 24.19

TARTAR SAUCE

Yield: 500 mL (20 fl. oz.)

Mayonnaise	400 mL	16 fl. oz.
Capers, chopped	50 g	2 oz.
Sour gherkins, chopped	100 g	3 oz.
Shallot, minced	25 g	2 Tbsp.
Fresh parsley, minced	20 g	2 Tbsp.
Lemon juice	15 mL	1 Tbsp.
Salt	TT	TT
Hard-boiled eggs, chopped	2	2

Stir all of the ingredients together until well blended. Chill thoroughly before serving. For rémoulade add 25 g (2 Tbsp.) chopped anchovies and omit eggs.

◆ ◆ ◆

RECIPE 24.20

GARLIC CROUTONS FOR SALADS

Yield: 600 g (1 lb. 4 oz.)

Whole butter	200 g	6 oz.
Garlic, chopped	10 g	1 Tbsp.
French or sourdough bread cubes	750 g	1 lb. 8 oz.
Parmesan cheese, grated	30 g	1 oz.

1. Melt the butter in a small saucepan and add the garlic. Cook the garlic in the butter for 5 minutes.

2. Place the bread cubes in a bowl and add the Parmesan cheese.

3. Pour the garlic butter over the bread cubes and immediately toss to combine.

4. Spread the bread cubes on a sheet pan in a single layer and bake at 180°C (350°F). Stir the croutons occasionally and cook until dry and lightly browned, approximately 15 minutes.

◆ ◆ ◆

RECIPE 24.21

WILTED SPINACH SALAD WITH ROASTED PEPPERS

Yield: 2 Large or 4 Small Servings

Red or yellow bell pepper, medium	175 g	1
Olive oil	50 mL	2 fl. oz.
Salt and pepper	TT	TT
Red onion, sliced thin	60 g	2 oz.
Baguette, thin slices for croutons	12	12
Spinach	450 g	1 lb.

RECIPE 24.19

*Approximate values
per 30 mL (1 oz.) serving:*

Calories	220
Total fat	23 g
Saturated fat	4 g
Cholesterol	20 mg
Sodium	420 mg
Total carbohydrates	2 g
Protein	0 g

RECIPE 24.20

*Approximate values
per 30 mL (1 oz.) serving:*

Calories	182
Total fat	10 g
Saturated fat	6 g
Cholesterol	23 mg
Sodium	339 mg
Total carbohydrates	20 g
Protein	4 g

Frisée or escarole	1 head	1 head
Balsamic vinegar	45 mL	3 Tbsp.
Niçoise or Gaeta olives, pitted	10	10
Safflower oil	30 mL	1 fl. oz.
Garlic clove, chopped fine	1	1
Parmesan cheese, grated	30 g	1 oz.

1. Roast, peel and cut the pepper into 5-mm (1/4-inch) strips. Toss the pepper strips with 10 mL (1/2 Tbsp.) of olive oil and a few pinches of salt and pepper. Set aside to marinate.

2. Cover the onion slices with cold water to leach the strong onion flavour. Set aside.

3. Place the baguette slices on a baking sheet and brush them lightly with olive oil. Toast in a 190°C (375°F) oven until crisp and lightly browned, approximately 5 minutes.

4. Stem, wash and dry the spinach. Trim the stem end of the frisée or escarole and discard the tough outer leaves. Wash and dry.

5. Drain the onions. In a large bowl, combine the vinegar, 2 mL (1/2 tsp.) salt and a few pinches of pepper. Add the greens, onions, peppers and olives.

6. Heat the safflower oil in a sauté pan with garlic until it is hot. Sauté the spinach quickly. Immediately pour it over the dressing and toss with a pair of metal tongs to coat and wilt the leaves.

7. Plate, sprinkle on the Parmesan cheese and croutons and serve immediately.

❖❖❖

RECIPE 24.22

DANDELION AND SPRING ASPARAGUS SALAD WITH CARAMELIZED QUINCE DRESSING

CLASSICO RESTAURANT, RIMROCK HOTEL, Banff, AB
Restaurant Chef Nigel Robinson, CCC

Yield: 4 Portions

Asparagus, peeled and picked	500 g	1 lb.
Cucumber, peeled, seeded	300 g	10 oz.
Dandelion greens, trimmed and washed	500 g	1 lb.
Belgian endive, julienned	100 g	3 oz.
Tomato concassée	50 g	2 oz.
Chive spears	4	4

1. Blanch the asparagus for 3 minutes, refresh, chill and reserve.
2. Cut the cucumber in long strips.

GARLIC AND CHIVE TUILE

Flour	50 g	2 oz.
Icing sugar	50 g	2 oz.
Butter, melted	50 g	2 oz.
Egg white	50 g	2 oz.
Garlic, roasted, minced	25 g	1 oz.
Chives, finely chopped	25 g	1 oz.

1. Sift flour and icing sugar. Add butter and egg white. Mix until smooth. Fold in garlic and chives. Reserve.
2. Prepare a rectangular template, 3 x 7 cm (1-1/2 x 3 inches).

Continued

RECIPE 24.21

Approximate values per serving:

Calories	692
Total fat	52 g
Saturated fat	9 g
Cholesterol	10 mg
Sodium	1163 mg
Total carbohydrates	38 g
Protein	17 g

Nigel Robinson, CCC
Nigel first entered the culinary arts as an apprentice at The Savoy in London, England. In 1991, he arrived in Canada to work at the Palliser in Calgary and then moved on to Château Whistler in British Columbia. After a brief stint in Australia and the Caribbean, he returned to Canada to become chef at Classico Restaurant, located in Banff's Rimrock Resort Hotel.

RECIPE 24.22

Approximate values per serving:

Calories	102
Total fat	1 g
Saturated fat	0 g
Cholesterol	0 mg
Sodium	106 mg
Total carbohydrates	21 g
Protein	7 g

3. On a parchment-lined baking sheet, use the template to spread four tuile rectangles. Bake for 6 minutes at 185°C (375°F).

4. As soon as they come from the oven, cut a round 2-cm (1-inch) hole in the centre. Lay the tuile over a rolling pin to form an arch. Leave to cool.

CARAMELIZED QUINCE DRESSING

Quince, peeled, diced	100 g	3 oz.
Sugar	50 g	1-1/2 oz.
Water	200 mL	7 fl. oz.
Champagne vinegar	75 mL	2-1/2 fl. oz.
Dijon-style mustard	50 mL	2 fl. oz.
Organic canola oil	250 mL	8 fl. oz.
Salt and pepper	TT	TT
Chives, chopped	10 g	2 Tbsp.

1. Place the quince, sugar and water in a sauce pot and bring to a simmer. Reduce until the sugar turns a light caramel colour. Cool immediately.

2. In a food processor, combine the quince, vinegar and mustard and purée.

3. With the food processor running, slowly pour in the oil to emulsify.

4. Pass mixture through a fine sieve, season and stir in chives.

ASSEMBLY:

1. Coat the asparagus, dandelion greens and endive with dressing.

2. Arrange dressed salad on a plate with an arched tuile.

3. Garnish with tomato concassée and cucumber strips. Place chive spears through hole in tuile.

◆◆◆

RECIPE 24.23

FENNEL AND MUSHROOMS À LA GRECQUE

Yield: 18 100-g (3-oz.) Servings   **Method:** Simmering

Mushrooms, small	500 g	1 lb.
Pearl onions, peeled	125 g	4 oz.
Olive oil	50 mL	2 fl. oz.
White wine	125 mL	4 fl. oz.
White stock	500 mL	16 fl. oz.
Tomato concassée	400 g	12 oz.
Tomato paste	50 g	1 oz.
Lemon juice	25 mL	1 fl. oz.
Coriander, ground	3 g	1 tsp.
Bouquet garni:		
Carrot stick, 10 cm (4 inches)	1	1
Leek, split, 10-cm (4-inch) piece	1	1
Fresh thyme	1 sprig	1 sprig
Bay leaf	2	2
Salt and pepper	TT	TT
Fennel, batonnet	500 g	1 lb.

1. Wash the mushrooms and trim the stems.

2. Sauté the onions in the olive oil, browning lightly. Add the white wine, stock, tomato concassée, tomato paste, lemon juice, coriander and bouquet garni. Season to taste with salt and pepper and bring to a boil.

3. Add the fennel and mushrooms and simmer for 15 minutes.

4. Remove from the heat and allow to cool to room temperature. Remove the bouquet garni. Adjust the seasonings and refrigerate. Serve chilled.

RECIPE 24.24

SALAD OF AHI TUNA SEARED WITH LAVENDER AND PEPPER WITH WHOLE-GRAIN MUSTARD SAUCE

FETZER VINEYARDS, HOPLAND, CA
Culinary Director John Ash

Yield: 8 Servings, each 90 g (3 oz.) tuna
and 30 g (1 oz.) greens

Lavender-pepper coating:		
Coarse sea salt	7 g	1-1/2 tsp.
Whole black peppercorns	8 g	2 tsp.
Whole fennel seeds	10 g	2 tsp.
White peppercorns	4 g	1 tsp.
Dried lavender flowers	3 g	1-1/2 tsp.
Ahi tuna, a solid 7.5-cm (3-inch)		
square piece, well trimmed	700 g	1 lb. 8 oz.
Olive oil	45 mL	3 Tbsp.
Mustard sauce:		
Whole-grain mustard	60 mL	2 fl. oz.
Olive oil	30 mL	1 fl. oz.
Mustard seeds, toasted	5 g	1 tsp.
Rice wine vinegar	5 mL	1 tsp.
Sugar or honey	5 mL	1 tsp.
Baby greens	250 g	8 oz.

1. Using a mortar and pestle or a rolling pin, crush the ingredients for the lavender-pepper coating.
2. Lightly oil the tuna with 10 mL (2 tsp.) of olive oil; coat lightly and evenly with the lavender-pepper mixture. Heat the remaining oil in a skillet to just smoking and quickly sear the tuna on all sides. This should not take more than 2 minutes. Immediately chill the seared tuna.
3. Mix the ingredients for the mustard sauce. Set aside.
4. To serve, thinly slice the tuna into 3–4 medallions per serving. Arrange on a chilled plate with baby greens and a small dollop of the mustard sauce.

RECIPE 24.24

Approximate values per serving:

Calories	184
Total fat	10 g
Saturated fat	1.5 g
Cholesterol	35 mg
Sodium	583 mg
Total carbohydrates	3 g
Protein	21 g

RECIPE 24.25

CHAR-GRILLED CALAMARI WITH WHITE BEAN AND ROASTED VEGETABLE SALAD

MUSTARD GRILLE, MISSISSAUGA, ON
Executive Chef Anthony Borgo

Yield: 4 Servings

White navy beans	350 g	12 oz.
Zucchini	350 g	1 large
Olive oil	as needed	as needed
Kalamata olives, cut in quarters	12 pieces	12 pieces
Lemon zest	5 g	1 Tbsp.
Lemon peel, grated	10 g	1 Tbsp.

Anthony Borgo
Since graduating in 1991, Anthony has gained a wealth of international experience working in Ireland, England, Switzerland, Japan and Canada and has risen through the ranks in the kitchen to the position of Chef.

Continued

Capers	40 g	3 Tbsp.
Basil, julienned	20 g	2 Tbsp.
Chives, finely chopped	20 g	2 Tbsp.
Red peppers, roasted, seeded, skinned and julienned	300 g	2
Lemon Basil Vinaigrette (recipe follows)		
Calamari tubes	12 pieces	12 pieces
Calamari tentacles	12 pieces	12 pieces
Salt and pepper	TT	TT
Olive oil	30 mL	1 fl. oz.
Lemon juice	30 mL	1 fl. oz.

1. Cook white beans until tender. Drain and allow to cool.

2. Slice the zucchini into paysanne cut. Roast the zucchini in a sauté pan with a little olive oil. Allow to cool.

3. In a bowl combine the beans, zucchini, olives, lemon zest and grated lemon peel, capers, basil, chives and red peppers. Reserve a few spoonfuls of the Lemon Basil Vinaigrette, then toss the bean mixture with the remaining vinaigrette. Set aside.

4. Place the calamari tubes and tentacles in a bowl. Season them with salt, pepper, olive oil and lemon juice. Cook the calamari on the grill or broiler for 1 minute or until cooked through.

5. Position equal quantities of the bean salad in the centre of each of the four plates. Place three calamari tubes on top of each salad. Put three tentacles around the rim of each plate. Spoon the reserved Lemon Basil Vinaigrette around the plates to accent the presentation.

LEMON BASIL VINAIGRETTE

Yield: 210 mL (7-1/2 fl. oz.)

Lemon juice, squeezed fresh	30 mL	1 fl. oz.
Lemon oil	30 mL	1 fl. oz.
Olive oil	90 mL	3 fl. oz.
Garlic clove, minced	5 g	1
Basil leaves, julienned	20 g	8 large
Salt and pepper	TT	TT

Combine the lemon juice, lemon oil, olive oil, garlic, basil, salt and pepper in a bowl. Using a whisk, mix until the vinaigrette is emulsified.

◆◆◆

RECIPE 24.26

HEIRLOOM TOMATO SALAD

Yield: 4 Servings

Heirloom tomatoes	500 g	1 lb.
Grape tomatoes	100 g	1/2 pt.
Mixed baby greens	4 heads	4 heads
Kosher salt and black pepper	TT	TT
Cucumber, sliced on bias	1	1
Extra virgin olive oil	50 mL	3 Tbsp.
Balsamic vinegar	30 mL	2 Tbsp.

1. Core the heirloom tomatoes and cut into wedges or thick slices. Pluck the stems from the grape tomatoes; leave whole if small or cut in half if large.

RECIPE 24.25

Approximate values per serving:

Calories	419
Total fat	21 g
Saturated fat	3 g
Cholesterol	256 mg
Sodium	817 mg
Total carbohydrates	34 g
Protein	26 g

Lemon Basil Vinaigrette— Approximate values per 30 mL (1 oz.) serving:

Calories	182
Total fat	20 g
Saturated fat	2 g
Cholesterol	0 mg
Sodium	360 mg
Total carbohydrates	1 g
Protein	0 g

2. Wash the mixed baby greens and dry. Spread the greens on plates or a serving platter and arrange the tomatoes over them. Season the tomatoes with freshly ground salt and pepper.

3. Garnish the salad with cucumber slices.

4. Drizzle on the olive oil; follow with a light drizzle of vinegar.

5. Arrange the grape tomatoes over the salad.

RECIPE 24.26

Approximate values per serving:

Calories	186
Total fat	11 g
Saturated fat	1.5 g
Cholesterol	0 mg
Sodium	677 mg
Total carbohydrates	16 g
Protein	5 g

RECIPE 24.27

COBB SALAD

Yield: 8 Entree Servings

Romaine lettuce	250 g	8 oz.
Green leaf lettuce	125 g	4 oz.
Watercress	125 g	4 oz.
Avocados	4	4
Bacon slices	16	16
Roquefort cheese, crumbled	350 g	12 oz.
Turkey breast, roasted, julienned	350 g	12 oz.
Tomato concassée	500 g	16 oz.
Eggs, hard-boiled, chopped	4	4
Dijon mustard vinaigrette	500 mL	16 fl. oz.

1. Tear, wash and dry the lettuces. Pick over and wash the watercress.

2. Pit, peel and cut the avocados into wedges.

3. Dice the bacon and cook in a sauté pan until crisp. Remove and drain well.

4. Toss the salad greens together and arrange each of the garnishes on top in an artistic fashion.

5. Prepare a simple vinaigrette dressing using Dijon-style mustard; serve on the side.

RECIPE 24.27

Approximate values per serving:

Calories	913
Total fat	79 g
Saturated fat	16 g
Cholesterol	210 mg
Sodium	1590 mg
Total carbohydrates	14 g
Protein	41 g

RECIPE 24.28

GREEK SALAD

Yield: 2.6 kg (5 lb. 8 oz.)

Extra virgin olive oil	125 mL	4 fl. oz.
Lemon juice	25 mL	1 fl. oz.
Red wine vinegar	25 mL	1 fl. oz.
Fresh oregano, chopped	15 g	3 Tbsp.
English cucumbers or field cucumbers	2	2
Feta cheese	350 g	12 oz.
Red and green peppers, diced	500 g	1 lb.
Olives, kalamata or other Greek variety	500 g	1 lb.
Tomatoes, cut into six wedges	500 g	3
Fresh parsley, chopped	30 g	1 oz.
Red onion	250 g	8 oz.
Black pepper, fresh ground	TT	TT
Romaine lettuce	1 head	1 head

1. To make the dressing, whisk together the olive oil, lemon juice, vinegar and oregano.

2. Dice the cucumber. If using field cucumber, peel and slice in half lengthwise. Remove the seeds and cut into medium dice.

RECIPE 24.28

Approximate values per 350 g serving:

Calories	437
Total fat	37 g
Saturated fat	11.5 g
Cholesterol	46 mg
Sodium	1906 mg
Total carbohydrates	19 g
Protein	11 g

Continued

3. Dice or crumble the feta cheese into medium pieces.

4. Dice the peppers into 1-cm (1/2-inch) pieces.

5. Combine the olives, cucumbers, tomatoes, chopped parsley and red onion in a bowl and add the dressing. Toss to combine and season to taste with pepper.

6. Line plates or a platter with the romaine lettuce leaves. Add the salad mixture and sprinkle on the feta cheese. Garnish as desired.

◆ ◆ ◆

RECIPE 24.29

SALAD OF LOBSTER WITH TOMATO TARTARE, HARICOT VERT AND BASIL "CRACKLING"

FOUR SEASONS HOTEL, Toronto, ON
Executive Chef Robert Sulatycky

Robert Sulatycky

Robert's professional training comes from having worked at top, haute cuisine establishments in London and Paris, but he credits the simple cooking methods of his grandmother (now 98), who was an accredited cook all her life, as having inspired his culinary passion. Robert's food stylings have been showcased in the namesake Absolut Vodka print ads, his titled "Absolut Sulatycky" (Fall 1998). In 2000, he not only became the first Canadian Chef to receive the coveted Robert Mondavi Culinary Award of Excellence, but he was also handpicked by the producers of The Great Canadian Food Show for an episode that explored the question "What makes a great chef great?"

Yield: 4 Servings

Lobster, each 450 g (1 lb.)	4	4
Haricots verts	180 g	6 oz.
Plum tomato concassée	180 g	6 oz.
Watercress	1 bunch	1 bunch
Shallots, brunoise	30 g	1 oz.
Chives, brunoise	3 g	1 tsp.
Basil chiffonade	5 g	2 tsp.
Basil oil	40 mL	3 Tbsp.
Sea salt	TT	TT
White pepper	TT	TT
Vegetable oil	as needed	as needed
Banyuls vinegar	10 mL	2 tsp.
Basil leaves, large	8	8
Fleur de sel	TT	TT
Chervil, sprigs	4	4

1. Blanch lobster for 6 minutes in court bouillon, chill and shuck.

2. Blanch haricots verts until tender but still bright green. Refresh.

3. Finely dice the peeled, seeded, vine-ripened plum tomatoes.

4. Wash, pick and remove stems from watercress.

5. Combine tomato concassée, 20 g (2/3 oz.) shallots, chives, basil chiffonade and 10 mL (2 tsp.) basil oil. Season with salt and pepper.

6. Tightly line a microwaveable plate with plastic wrap. Place eight basil leaves on the plastic and put two drops of vegetable oil on each leaf. Microwave on high for 3 minutes or until leaves are perfectly flat and crisp.

7. In a noncorrosive bowl, whisk remaining basil oil with the vinegar and remaining shallots. Season with salt and pepper.

8. Slice the lobster tail into medallions and keep the claws whole.

9. Toss the watercress and haricots verts with 2/3 of the vinaigrette.

10. In the centre of the plates, divide the tomato tartare into four 7.5-cm (3–inch) rings. Remove the rings and place some of the beans on top of the tomato. Place watercress on the beans. Artfully present the lobster medallions and claw on each salad.

11. Drizzle remaining vinaigrette around salad. Top each salad with two basil leaves.

12. Season with fleur de sel and a sprig of chervil.

RECIPE 24.29

Approximate values per serving:

Calories	563
Total fat	13 g
Saturated fat	1 g
Cholesterol	324 mg
Sodium	1954 mg
Total carbohydrates	13 g
Protein	94 g

◆◆◆

RECIPE 24.30

ASPARAGUS AND MINTED NEW POTATO SALAD WITH SUN-DRIED TOMATO MAYONNAISE

SHAW CONFERENCE CENTRE, EDMONTON, AB
Executive Chef Simon Smotkowicz, CCC

Yield: 4 Servings

Asparagus	500 g	1 lb.
Olive oil	75 mL	4 Tbsp.
Raspberry vinegar	25 mL	4 tsp.
Salt and pepper	TT	TT
New potatoes, very small	500 g	1 lb.
Fresh mint, chopped	30 g	3 Tbsp.
Salt	10 g	2 tsp.
Sun-dried tomatoes, finely chopped	15 g	1 Tbsp.
White wine or water	25 mL	2 Tbsp.
Mayonnaise	250 mL	8 fl. oz.
Spinach or pea tops	as needed	as needed
Fresh mint, chopped	10 g	1 Tbsp.

1. To prepare the asparagus, bring a large pot of salted water to a boil. Add the asparagus and cook for 3–5 minutes.
2. Cool at once in a bowl filled with iced water.
3. To prepare the vinaigrette, whisk together the olive oil and raspberry vinegar.
4. In a bowl, toss the asparagus with the vinaigrette. Season with salt and pepper and let sit for 1 hour before serving.
5. To prepare the potato salad, place the potatoes, 7 g (3 Tbsp.) mint and salt in a saucepan. Cover the potatoes with cold water.
6. Bring to a boil and simmer for 15–20 minutes, until done. Drain and let cool.
7. Mix together the sun-dried tomatoes, white wine and mayonnaise.
8. In a bowl, toss the potatoes with the sun-dried tomato mayonnaise.
9. To assemble, lightly cover each plate with springtime greens such as spinach or pea tops.
10. Mound the potato salad on top of the greens, arrange the asparagus on top and sprinkle with 2 g (4 Tbsp.) mint.

◆◆◆

RECIPE 24.31

POTATO SALAD

Yield: 2.5 kg (6 lb. 8 oz.)

Potatoes, waxy, skin on	1.5 kg	4 lb.
Eggs, hard-cooked	5	6
Celery, medium dice	250 g	8 oz.
Green onions, sliced	1 bunch	1 bunch
Mayonnaise	250 mL	10 fl. oz.
Sour cream	150 mL	6 fl. oz.
Red wine or tarragon vinegar	50 mL	2 fl. oz.

Continued

Simon Smotkowicz, CCC
Simon has been a member and a leader of award-winning Canadian culinary teams for many years, most recently managing Team Canada to a world championship in Glasgow in 1997 and 2001. In 1995 he was elected Chef of the Year for the Western Region by his peers in the CFCC.

RECIPE 24.30

Approximate values per serving:

Calories	596
Total fat	56 g
Saturated fat	8 g
Cholesterol	31 mg
Sodium	818 mg
Total carbohydrates	20 g
Protein	6 g

RECIPE 24.31

Approximate values per 85 g serving:

Calories	134
Total fat	9 g
Saturated fat	1.5 g
Cholesterol	47 mg
Sodium	193 mg
Total carbohydrates	11 g
Protein	3 g

Dijon-style mustard	50 mL	2 fl. oz.
Fresh parsley, chopped	30 g	1 oz.
Salt and pepper	TT	TT

1. Boil the potatoes in salted water until nearly cooked. Drain the potatoes, spread them on a sheet pan and refrigerate until cold.
2. Peel and cut the cold potatoes into medium or large dice.
3. Peel and chop the eggs.
4. Combine all ingredients and adjust the seasonings with salt and pepper.

❖ ❖ ❖

RECIPE 24.32

CREAMY COLESLAW

Yield: 1 kg (2 lb.)

Mayonnaise	250 mL	8 fl. oz.
Sour cream or crème fraîche	125 mL	4 fl. oz.
Sugar	50 g	1 oz.
Cider vinegar	50 mL	1 fl. oz.
Green cabbage, shredded	500 g	1 lb.
Celery, julienne	250 g	8 oz.
Carrot, shredded	125 g	4 oz.
Salt and white pepper	TT	TT

1. Combine the mayonnaise, sour cream or crème fraîche, sugar and vinegar in a bowl; whisk together.
2. Add the shredded cabbage, celery and carrot to the dressing and mix well. Season to taste with salt and pepper.

❖ ❖ ❖

RECIPE 24.33

PAN-SEARED STEELHEAD TROUT WITH FLAXSEED BISCUIT RING AND BABY SALAD GREENS IN LEMON GINGER DRESSING

SASKATCHEWAN LEGISLATURE, Regina, SK
Executive Chef/Manager Trent Brears

Yield: 4 Servings

Steelhead trout fillets, each 100 g (3 oz.)	4	4
Sea salt	TT	TT
Canola oil	50 mL	2 fl. oz.
Salad greens	120 g	4 oz.

1. Season trout and sear quickly in hot oil. Cool.

BISCUIT RING

Bread flour	200 g	7 oz.
Baking powder	14 g	4 tsp.
Cream of tartar	0.5 g	1/4 tsp.
Salt	2 g	1/2 tsp.
Sugar	10 g	2 tsp.
Flaxseeds	15 g	4 tsp.

RECIPE 24.32

*Approximate values
per 85 g serving:*

Calories	142
Total fat	13 g
Saturated fat	3 g
Cholesterol	14 mg
Sodium	238 mg
Total carbohydrates	6 g
Protein	1 g

Trent Brears

Born and raised in Saskatchewan, Trent worked in several hotels and convention facilities in Regina before becoming Executive Chef and Manager at the Legislative Building. In 1987 he began participating in culinary competitions and, in the past 13 years, has captured more than 20 gold medals. In 1997, he became captain of the Saskatchewan Culinary Team, which competed in the 2000 World Culinary Olympics.

RECIPE 24.33

Approximate values per serving:

Calories	1000
Total fat	78 g
Saturated fat	21 g
Cholesterol	148.5 mg
Sodium	1132 mg
Total carbohydrates	43 g
Protein	36 g

| Butter, soft | 125 g | 4 oz. |
| Milk | 175 mL | 6 fl. oz. |

1. Sift dry ingredients together and add flaxseeds.
2. Cut in the butter until mixture resembles oatmeal. Add the milk and mix just to combine.
3. Knead the dough lightly on a floured table and roll out to 2-cm (3/4-inch) thickness.
4. Cut into 12.5-cm (5-inch) donuts.
5. Bake at 200°C (425°F) for 10–12 minutes. Cool.

LEMON GINGER DRESSING

Canola oil	125 mL	4 fl. oz.
Rice wine vinegar	30 mL	1 fl. oz.
Ginger, minced	3 g	1 tsp.
Lemon juice	30 mL	1 fl. oz.
Garlic, minced	10 g	1 Tbsp.
Parsley, chopped	10 g	1 Tbsp.
Tabasco sauce	4 drops	4 drops
Salt and pepper	TT	TT

1. Whisk all ingredients together.

ASSEMBLY:
1. Place biscuit ring on plate.
2. Toss greens with enough dressing just to moisten.
3. Place salad in ring.
4. Top with trout fillet and drizzle with more dressing.

Biscuit Ring—
Approximate values per serving:

Calories	442
Total fat	29 g
Saturated fat	17 g
Cholesterol	74.5 mg
Sodium	587 mg
Total carbohydrates	40.5 g
Protein	9 g

Lemon Ginger Dressing—
Approximate values per serving:

Calories	262
Total fat	29 g
Saturated fat	2 g
Cholesterol	0 mg
Sodium	240 mg
Total carbohydrates	2 g
Protein	0 g

◆ ◆ ◆

RECIPE 24.34

TABBOULEH (BULGUR WHEAT) SALAD

Yield: 15 90-g (3-oz.) Servings

Bulgur	300 g	10 oz.
Onions, brunoise	250 g	8 oz.
Green onions, sliced	60 g	2 oz.
Fresh parsley, chopped	200 g	6 oz.
Fresh mint, chopped	50 g	2 oz.
Olive oil	250 mL	8 fl. oz.
Lemon juice	250 mL	8 fl. oz.
Tomato concassée	500 g	1 lb.
Salt and pepper	TT	TT
Pine nuts, toasted	120 g	4 oz.

1. Place the bulgur in a bowl and cover with cold water. Soak the bulgur until tender, approximately 2 hours.
2. Drain the bulgur and squeeze out all of the excess water.
3. Add the onions, green onions, parsley, mint, olive oil and lemon juice. Mix well.
4. Add the tomatoes; mix to combine. Season with salt and pepper.
5. Garnish with the toasted pine nuts.

RECIPE 24.34

Approximate values
per 90 g (3 oz.) serving:

Calories	210
Total fat	16 g
Saturated fat	2 g
Cholesterol	0 mg
Sodium	135 mg
Total Carbohydrates	13 g
Protein	4 g

◆◆◆

RECIPE 24.35

MIXED BEAN SALAD

Yield: 12 90-g (3-oz.) Servings   **Method:** Boiling

Green beans,		
cut in 1.25-cm (1/2-inch) pieces	125 g	4 oz.
White wine vinegar	50 mL	2 fl. oz.
Vegetable oil	100 mL	3 fl. oz.
Lemon juice	25 mL	1 Tbsp.
Lemon peel, grated	3 g	1 tsp.
Garlic cloves, crushed	8 g	2
White sugar	15 g	1 Tbsp.
Dried red chile, chopped fine	1	1
Red kidney beans, soaked and cooked	250 g	8 oz.
Chickpeas, soaked and cooked	250 g	8 oz.
Lima or cannellini beans,		
soaked and cooked	250 g	8 oz.
White onion, sliced	125 g	4 oz.
Red and green peppers, julienned	125 g	4 oz.
Salt and pepper	TT	TT

1. Steam the green beans until tender-crisp, approximately 3–4 minutes. Refresh.

2. To make the dressing, combine the white wine vinegar, oil, lemon juice, lemon peel, garlic, sugar and chile.

3. Mix together all the drained beans and peas and pour the dressing over them. Add the onion and peppers. Season with salt and pepper and toss to combine. Marinate for several hours before serving.

RECIPE 24.35

*Approximate values
per 90 g (3 oz.) serving:*

Calories	171
Total fat	8 g
Saturated fat	1 g
Cholesterol	0 mg
Sodium	200 mg
Total carbohydrates	20 g
Protein	6 g

◆◆◆

RECIPE 24.36

MELON SALAD

Yield: 2.5 L (2-1/2 qt.)

Honeydew, medium	1	1
Cantaloupe, medium	1	1
English cucumber	1	1
Tomatoes	4	4
Parsley, chopped	10 g	1 Tbsp.
Oregano, chopped, fresh	5 g	2 tsp.
Black pepper, cracked	3 g	1 tsp.
Lemon juice, fresh	50 mL	2 fl. oz.
Lemon zest	3 g	1 tsp.
Canola oil	150 mL	6 fl. oz.
White wine vinegar	25 mL	1 Tbsp.

1. Split, seed and use a parisienne scoop to form melon balls.

2. Trim ends and split cucumber lengthwise. Slice 1 cm (1/2 inch) thick.

3. Core and cut the tomatoes into wedges.

4. Combine all ingredients and toss to coat.

5. Refrigerate salad for 1 hour before service.

RECIPE 24.36

Approximate values per serving:

Calories	171
Total fat	12 g
Saturated fat	1 g
Cholesterol	0 mg
Sodium	20 mg
Total carbohydrates	17 g
Protein	2 g

◆ ◆ ◆

RECIPE 24.37

ANTIPASTI VEGETABLES

Yield: 4 L (4 qt.)

Cauliflower florets	350 g	12 oz.
Zucchini, carrot, green beans, daikon—batonettes, each	200 g	7 oz.
Onion, sliced	100 g	3-1/2 oz.
Baby corn cobs	12	12
Celery, bias-cut	200 g	7 oz.
Red and green pepper triangles, each	100 g	3-1/2 oz.
Pickling salt	300 g	11 oz.
Water	1.5 L	1-1/2 qt.
White vinegar	500 mL	1 pt.
Water	500 mL	1 pt.
Sugar	50 g	2 oz.
Garlic cloves	4	4
Dried chiles	4	4
Mustard seed	10 g	2 tsp.
Whole cloves	16	16

1. Layer cut vegetables in a noncorrosive container and sprinkle with pickling salt. Cover with 1.5 L (1-1/2 qt.) water; weigh down vegetables with a plate to ensure submersion. Refrigerate overnight, covered. Drain, rinse well under running water and drain well.

2. Prepare a brine with the remaining ingredients. Bring to a boil, add vegetables and simmer for 3 minutes. Cool pickled vegetables and store in a noncorrosive container in refrigerator.

RECIPE 24.37

Approximate values per 75 g serving:

Calories	43
Total fat	0.5 g
Saturated fat	0 g
Cholesterol	0 mg
Sodium	4837 mg
Total carbohydrates	10 g
Protein	2 g

 EBLINKS

Salad Vegetables
www.produceoasis.com/Hierarchy_folder/Vegetables_folder/L2SVeg_folder/
MainSVeg.html

The Leafy Greens Council
www.leafy-greens.org/

Salad Dressings
www.cs.cmu.edu/~mjw/recipes/salad/salad-dressing/index.html

Flowers
www.garnishclub.com/herbs_salads_edible_flowers.htm

Olive Oil
www.oliveoilsource.com

CHAPTER 25 FRUITS

After studying this chapter you will be able to:

+ identify a variety of fruits
+ purchase fruits appropriate for your needs
+ store fruits properly
+ explain how fruits are preserved
+ prepare fruits for cooking or service: segment and zest citrus fruits, cut citrus peels, peel prickly pears, core apples, pit cherries, pit and cut mangoes, trim and slice pineapples
+ apply various cooking methods to fruits: broil or grill, bake, sauté, poach, simmer, make preserves

otanically, a fruit is an organ that develops from the ovary of a flowering plant and contains one or more seeds. Culinarily, a fruit is the perfect snack food; the basis of a dessert, colourful sauce or soup; or an accompaniment to meat, fish, shellfish or poultry. No food group offers a greater variety of colours, flavours and textures than fruit.

This chapter identifies many of the fruits typically used by food service operations. It then addresses general considerations in purchasing fresh and preserved fruits. A discussion follows about some of the cooking methods presented in Chapter 9, Principles of Cooking, as they apply to fruits. Recipes in which a fruit is the primary ingredient are presented at the end of this chapter.

IDENTIFYING FRUITS

This book presents fruits according to the ways most people view them and use them, rather than by rigid botanical classifications. Fruits are divided here into eight categories: berries, citrus, exotics, grapes, melons, pomes, stone fruits and tropicals, according to either their shape, seed structure or natural habitat. Botanically, tomatoes, beans, eggplant, capsicum peppers and other produce are fruits. But in ordinary thinking they are not; they are vegetables and are discussed in Chapter 22, Vegetables.

A fruit may have several names, varying from region to region or on a purveyor's whim. Botanists are also constantly reclassifying items to fit new findings. The names given here follow generally accepted custom and usage.

Berries

Berries are small, juicy fruits that grow on vines and bushes worldwide. Berries are characterized by thin skins and many tiny seeds that are often so small they go unnoticed. Some of the fruits classified here as berries do not fit the botanical definition (for example, raspberries and strawberries), while fruits that are berries botanically (for example, grapes) are classified elsewhere.

Berries may be eaten plain or used in everything from beer to bread, soup to sorbet. They make especially fine jams and compotes.

Berries must be fully **ripened** on the vine, as they will not ripen further after harvesting. Select berries that are plump and fully coloured. Avoid juice-stained containers and berries with whitish-grey or black spots of mould. All berries should be refrigerated and used promptly. Do not wash berries until you are ready to use them, as washing removes some of their aroma and softens them.

Several varieties of fruits are extremely responsive to selective breeding and cross-breeding and have been toyed with by botanists and growers since at least the time of ancient Rome. Two distinct products are recognized: hybrids and varieties. **Hybrids** result from cross-breeding fruits from different species that are genetically unalike. The result is a unique product. Citrus is particularly responsive to hybridization. **Varieties** result from breeding fruits of the same species that have different qualities or characteristics. Breeding two varieties of apples, for example, produces a third variety with the best qualities of both parents.

Blackberries

Blackberries

Blackberries are similar to raspberries, but are larger and shinier, with a deep purple to black colour. Thorny blackberry vines are readily found in the wild; commercial production is limited. Peak season is mid-June through August. Loganberries, ollalie berries and boysenberries are blackberry hybrids.

Blueberries

Blueberries (Fr. *myrtilles*) are small and firm, with a true blue to almost black skin and a juicy, light grey-blue interior. Cultivated berries (high-bush varieties) tend to be larger than wild (low-bush) ones. Blueberries are native to North America and are grown commercially in almost all provinces of Canada, with the Lac St. Jean region being the most famous. Peak season is short, from mid-June to mid-August.

Blueberries

Cranberries

Cranberries, another native North American food, are tart, firm fruit with a mottled red skin. They grow on low vines in cultivated bogs (swamps) throughout Ontario, British Columbia, Massachusetts, Wisconsin and New Jersey. Rarely eaten raw, they are made into sauce or relish or are used in breads, pies or pastries. Cranberries are readily available frozen, dried (candied) or made into a jelly-type sauce and canned. Although colour does not indicate ripeness, cranberries should be picked over before cooking to remove those that are soft or bruised. Peak harvesting season is from Labour Day through October, leading to the association of cranberries with Thanksgiving dinner.

Cranberries

Currants

Currants are tiny, tart fruits that grow on shrubs in grapelike clusters. The most common are a beautiful, almost translucent red, but black and golden (or white) varieties also exist. All varieties are used for jams, jellies and sauces, and black currants are made into a liqueur, crème de cassis. Fresh North American production is growing. Currants are very popular and widely available in Europe, with a peak season during the late summer. (The dried fruits called currants are not produced from these berries; they are a special variety of dried grapes.)

White Currants

Red Currants

Raspberries

Raspberries (Fr. *framboises*) are perhaps the most delicate of all fruits. They have a tart flavour and velvety texture. Red raspberries are the most common, with black, purple and golden berries available in some markets. When ripe, the berry pulls away easily from its white core, leaving the characteristic hollow centre. Because they can be easily crushed and are susceptible to mould, most of the raspberries grown are marketed frozen. They grow on thorny vines in cool climates from British Columbia to the Maritimes and are imported from New Zealand and South America. The peak domestic season is from late May through November.

Raspberries

Strawberries

Strawberries (Fr. *fraises*) are brilliant red, heart-shaped fruits that grow on vines. Actually a perennial herb, the berry's flesh is covered by tiny tan seeds called achenes, which are the plant's true fruits. Select berries with a good red colour and intact green leafy hull. (The hulls can be easily removed with a paring knife.) Avoid berries with soft or brown spots. Huge berries may be lovely to look at but they often have hollow centres and little flavour or juice. Although available to some extent all year, fresh strawberries are at their peak from April through June.

Strawberries

The tiny wild or Alpine berries, known by their French name *fraises des bois*, have a particularly intense flavour and aroma. They are not widely available commercially in Canada.

Citrus (genus Citrus)

Citrus fruits include lemons, limes, grapefruits, tangerines, kumquats, oranges and several hybrids. They are characterized by a thick rind, most of which is a bitter white pith (albedo) with a thin exterior layer of coloured skin known as the zest. Their flesh is segmented and juicy. Citrus fruits are acidic, with a strong aroma; their flavours vary from bitter to tart to sweet.

Citrus fruits grow on trees and shrubs in tropical and subtropical climates worldwide. All citrus fruits are fully ripened on the tree and will not ripen further after harvesting. They should be refrigerated for longest storage.

Select fruits that feel heavy and have thin, smooth skins. Avoid those with large blemishes or moist spots.

Grapefruits

Grapefruits (Fr. *pamplemousse*) are large and round with a yellow skin, thick rind and tart flesh. They are an 18th-century hybrid of the orange and pummelo (a large, coarse fruit used mostly in Middle and Far Eastern cuisines). Two varieties of grapefruit are widely available all year: white-fleshed and pink- or ruby-fleshed. White grapefruits produce the finest juice, although pink grapefruits are sweeter. Fresh grapefruits are best eaten raw or topped with brown sugar and lightly broiled. Grapefruit segments are available canned in syrup.

White Grapefruits

Ruby Grapefruits

Kumquats

Kumquats

Kumquats are very small, oval-shaped, orange-coloured fruits with a soft, sweet skin and slightly bitter flesh. They can be eaten whole, either raw or preserved in syrup, and may be used in jams and preserves.

Lemons

The most commonly used citrus fruits, lemons (Fr. *citrons*), are oval-shaped, bright yellow fruits available all year. Their strongly acidic flavour makes them unpleasant to eat raw but perfect for flavouring desserts and confections. Lemon juice is also widely used in sauces, especially for fish, shellfish and poultry. Lemon zest is candied or used as garnish. Try grilling wedges or slices.

Lemons

Limes

Limes (Fr. *limons*) are small fruits with thin skins ranging from yellow-green to dark green. Limes are too tart to eat raw and are often substituted for lemons in prepared dishes. They are also juiced or used in cocktails, curries or desserts. Lime zest can be grated and used to give colour and flavour to a variety of dishes. Limes are available all year, with a peak season during the summer.

Limes

Oranges

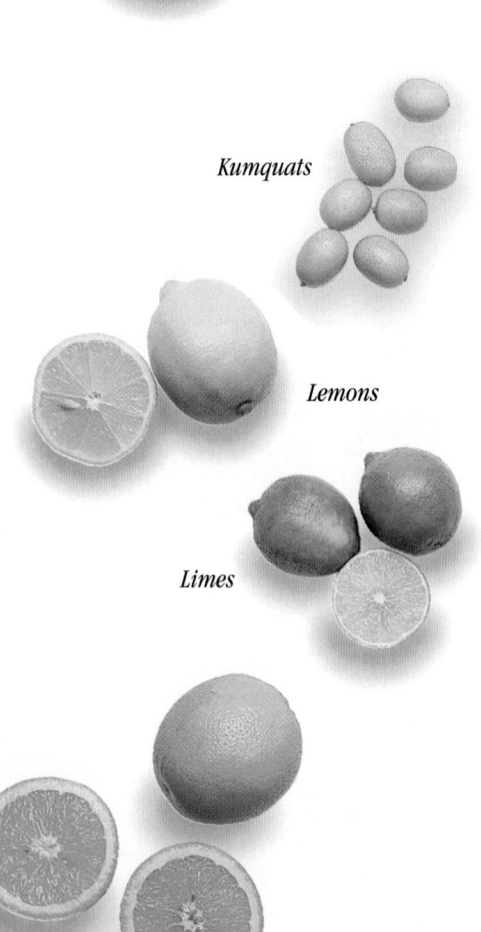

Oranges are round fruits with a juicy, orange-coloured flesh and a thin, orange skin. They can be either sweet or bitter.

Valencia oranges and navel oranges (a seedless variety) are the most popular sweet oranges. They can be juiced for beverages or sauces and the flesh may be eaten raw, added to salads, cooked in desserts or used as a garnish. The zest may be grated or julienned for sauces or garnish. Sweet oranges are available all

Valencia Oranges

year, with peak season from December to April. Blood oranges are also sweet but are small, with a rough, reddish skin. Their flesh is streaked with a blood-red colour. Blood oranges are available primarily during the winter months and are eaten raw, juiced or used in salads or sauces. When selecting sweet oranges, look for fruits that feel plump and heavy, with unblemished skin. The colour of the skin depends on weather conditions; a green rind does not affect the flavour of the flesh.

Bitter oranges include the Seville and bergamot. They are used primarily for the essential oils found in their zest. Oil of bergamot gives Earl Grey tea its distinctive flavour; oil of Seville is essential to curaçao, Grand Marnier and orange flower water. Seville oranges are also used in marmalades and sauces for meats and poultry.

Navel Oranges

Blood Oranges

Tangerines

Tangerines, sometimes referred to as mandarins, are small and dark orange. Their rind is loose and easily removed to reveal sweet, juicy, aromatic segments. Tangerines are most often eaten fresh and uncooked, but are available canned as mandarin oranges.

Tangelos are a hybrid of tangerines and grapefruits. They are the size of a medium orange; they have a bulbous stem end and few to no seeds.

Tangerines

Basic Procedure for Segmenting Citrus Fruits

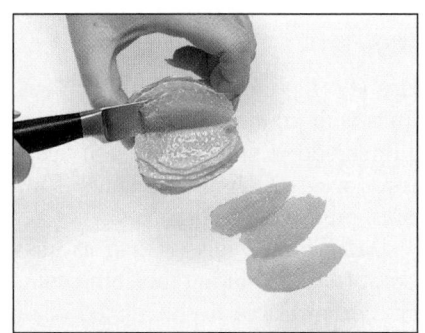

1. Citrus segments, known as fillets or *supremes*, are made by first carefully cutting off the entire peel (including the bitter white pith) in even slices.

2. Individual fillets are then removed by gently cutting alongside each membrane.

Basic Procedure for Zesting Citrus Fruits

A five-hole zester is used to remove paper-thin strips of the coloured rind.

Basic Procedure for Cutting Citrus Peels

Large strips of citrus zest may be used as a garnish or to flavour soups or sauces.

Exotics

Improved transportation has led to the increasing availability (although sporadic in some areas) of exotic or unusual fresh fruits such as figs, persimmons, pomegranates, prickly pears, rhubarb and star fruits. Other exotic fruits, such as breadfruit, lychee, guava, feijoa and loquat, still are available only on a limited basis from specialty purveyors and are not discussed here.

Figs

Figs (Fr. *figues*) are the fruit of ficus trees. They are small, soft, pear-shaped fruits with an intensely sweet flavour and rich, moist texture made crunchy by a multitude of tiny seeds. Fresh figs can be sliced and served in salads or with cured meats such as prosciutto. They can also be baked, poached or used in jams, preserves or compotes.

Dark-skinned figs, known as Mission figs, are a variety planted at Pacific Coast missions during the 18th century. They have a thin skin and small seeds and are available fresh, canned or dried. The white-skinned figs grown commercially include the White Adriatic, used principally for drying and baking, and the all-purpose Kadota. The most important domestic variety, however, is the Calimyrna. These large figs have a rich yellow colour and large nutty seeds. Fresh Calimyrna figs are the finest for eating out of hand; they are also available dried.

For the best flavour, figs should be fully ripened on the tree. Unfortunately, fully ripened figs are very delicate and difficult to transport. Most figs are in season from June through October; fresh Calimyrna figs are available only during June.

Persimmons

Persimmons

Persimmons, sometimes referred to as kaki or Sharon fruits, are a bright orange, acorn-shaped fruit with a glossy skin and a large papery blossom. The flesh is bright orange and jellylike, with a mild but rich flavour similar to honey and plums. Persimmons should be peeled before use; any seeds should be discarded. Select bright orange fruits and refrigerate only after they are completely ripe. When ripe, persimmons will be very soft and the skin will have an almost translucent appearance.

Ripe persimmons are delicious eaten raw; halved and topped with cream or soft cheese; or peeled, sliced and added to fruit salads. Persimmon bread, muffins, cakes and pies are also popular. Underripe persimmons are almost inedible, however. They are strongly tannic with a chalky or cottony texture.

Persimmons are tree fruits grown in subtropical areas worldwide, although the Asian varieties—now grown in California—are the most common. Fresh persimmons are available from October through January.

Pomegranates

An ancient fruit native to Persia (now Iran), pomegranates have long been a subject of poetry and a symbol of fertility. Pomegranates are round, about the size of a large orange, with a pronounced calyx. The skin forms a hard shell with a pinkish-red colour. The interior is filled with hundreds of small, red seeds (which are, botanically, the actual fruits) surrounded by juicy red pulp. An inedible yellow membrane separates the seeds into compartments. Pomegranates are sweet-sour and the seeds are pleasantly crunchy. The bright red seeds make an attractive garnish. Pomegranate juice is a popular beverage in Mediterranean cuisines and grenadine syrup is made from concentrated pomegranate juice.

Pomegranates

Select heavy fruits that are not rock-hard, cracked or heavily bruised. Whole pomegranates can be refrigerated for several weeks. Pomegranates are available from September through December, with peak season in October.

Prickly Pears

Prickly pear fruits, also known as cactus pears and barbary figs, are actually the berries of several varieties of cactus. They are barrel- or pear-shaped, about the size of a large egg. Their thick, firm skin is green or purple with small sharp pins and nearly invisible stinging fibres. Their flesh is spongy, sweet and a brilliant pink-red, dotted with small black seeds. Prickly pears have the aroma of watermelon and the flavour of sugar-water.

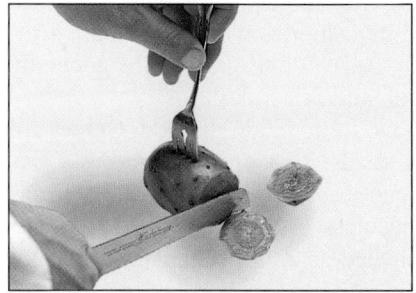

Prickly Pears

Once peeled, prickly pears can be diced and eaten raw, or they can be puréed for making jams, sauces, custards or sorbets, to which they give a vivid pink colour. Prickly pears are especially common in Mexican and southwestern cuisines.

Select fruits that are full-coloured, heavy and tender, but not too soft. Avoid those with mushy or bruised spots. Ripe prickly pears can be refrigerated for a week or more. Prickly pears are grown in Mexico and several states of the southwestern U.S. and are available from September through December.

Basic Procedure for Peeling Prickly Pears

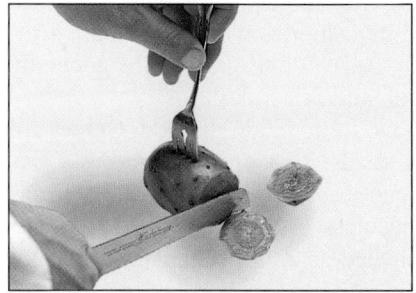

1. To avoid being stung by a prickly pear, hold it steady with a fork, then use a knife to cut off both ends.

2. Cut a lengthwise slit through the skin. Slip the tip of the knife into the cut and peel away the skin by holding it down while rolling the fruit away.

Rhubarb

Rhubarb

Although botanically a vegetable, rhubarb is most often prepared as a fruit. It is a perennial plant that grows well in temperate and cold climates. Only the pinkish-red stems are edible; the leaves contain high amounts of oxalic acid, which is toxic.

Rhubarb stems are extremely acidic, requiring large amounts of sugar to create the desired sweet-sour taste. Cinnamon, ginger, orange and strawberry are particularly compatible with rhubarb. It is excellent for pies, cobblers, preserves or stewing. Young, tender stalks of rhubarb do not need to be peeled. When cooked, rhubarb becomes very soft and turns a beautiful light pink colour.

Fresh rhubarb is sold as whole stalks, with the leaves removed. Select crisp, unblemished stalks. Peak season is during the early spring, from February through May. Frozen rhubarb pieces are readily available and are excellent for pies, tarts or jams. Powdered rhubarb juice is now available. It goes well with fish sauces and fruit coulis.

Star Fruits

Star fruits, also known as carambola, are oval, up to 12.5 cm (5 inches) long, with five prominent ribs or wings running their length. A cross-section cut is shaped like a star. The edible skin is a waxy orange-yellow; it covers a dry, paler yellow flesh. Its flavour is similar to plums, sweet but bland. Star fruits do not need to be peeled or seeded. They are most often sliced and added to fruit salad or used as a garnish. Unripe fruits can be cooked in stews or chutneys.

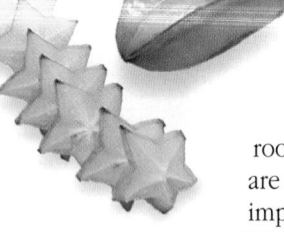

Star Fruit

Colour and aroma are the best indicators of ripeness. The fruits should be a deep golden-yellow and the edge of the ribs should be brown. The aroma should be full and floral. Green fruits can be kept at room temperature to ripen, then refrigerated for up to two weeks. Star fruits are cultivated in Hawaii, Florida, California and Asia, though some are still imported from the Caribbean. Fresh fruits are available from August to February.

Grapes (Vitis vinifera)

Grapes are the single largest fruit crop in the world, due, of course, to their use in wine making. This section, however, discusses only table grapes, those grown for eating. Grapes are berries that grow on vines in large clusters. California is the world's largest producer, with more than a dozen varieties grown for table use. Grapes are classified by colour as white (which are actually green) or black (which are actually red). White grapes are generally blander than black ones, with a thinner skin and firmer flesh.

The grape's colour and most of its flavour are found in the skin. Grapes are usually eaten raw, either alone or in fruit salads. They are also used as a garnish or accompaniment to desserts and cheeses. Dried grapes are known as raisins (usually made from Thompson Seedless or muscat grapes), currants (made from Black Corinth grapes and labelled as Zante currants) or sultanas (made from sultana grapes).

Grapes are available all year because the many varieties have different harvesting schedules. Look for firm, unblemished fruits that are firmly attached to the stem. A surface bloom or dusty appearance is caused by yeasts and indicates recent harvesting. Wrinkled grapes or those with brown spots around the stem are past their prime. All grapes should be rinsed and drained prior to use.

◆◆◆

GRAPES INTO WINE

Virtually all the fine wine made in the world comes from varieties of a single grape species, *Vitis vinifera*. Although a European species, it is also grown in Canada, the United States, South Africa, South America, the Middle East, Australia and wherever fine wine is made. The variety of grapes used in any given wine determines the wine's character, and most wine-producing countries carefully regulate the growing areas and production of grapes.

North American wines are known by their varietal names, whereas European wines are generally known by the vineyard's location. The major varietals of wine grapes and the wines in which they are used are listed below.

Grape Varietal	Wine
Pinot Noir	Red Burgundy and champagne
Chardonnay	White Burgundy, Chablis and champagne
Syrah	Côte Rotie and Hermitage
Cabernet Sauvignon	Bordeaux and red Graves
Sauvignon Blanc	Sauterne, white Graves, Fumé Blanc and Sancerre
Merlot	Saint-Emilion and for blending with Cabernet Sauvignon
Zinfandel	Red and white Zinfandel (California claims a virtual monopoly)
Chenin Blanc	Vouvray

Red Flame Grapes

Red Flame grapes are a seedless California hybrid, second only in importance to the Thompson Seedless. Red Flame grapes are large and round with a slightly tart flavour and variegated red colour.

Red Flame Grapes

Thompson Seedless Grapes

The most commercially important table grapes are a variety known as Thompson Seedless, which are pale green with a crisp texture and sweet flavour. Peak season is from June to November. Many are dried in the hot desert sun of California's San Joaquin Valley to produce dark raisins. For golden raisins, Thompson Seedless grapes are treated with sulphur dioxide to prevent browning, then dried mechanically.

Of the table grapes containing seeds, the most important varieties are the Concord, Ribier and Emperor. They range from light red to deep black in colour, and all three are in season during the autumn. Concord grapes, one of the few grape varieties native to the New World, are especially important for making juices and jellies.

Thompson Seedless Grapes

Melons

Like pumpkins and cucumbers, melons are members of the gourd family (*Cucurbitaceae*). The dozens of melon varieties can be divided into two general types: sweet (or dessert) melons and watermelons. Sweet melons have a tan, green or yellow netted or farrowed rind and dense, fragrant flesh. Watermelon has a thick, dark green rind surrounding crisp, watery flesh.

Melons are almost 90% water, so cooking destroys their texture, quickly turning the flesh to mush. Most are served simply sliced, perhaps with a bit of lemon or lime juice. Melons also blend well in fruit salads or with rich, cured meats such as prosciutto. Melons may be puréed and made into soups or sorbets.

Melons should be vine-ripened. A ripe melon should yield slightly and spring back when pressed at the blossom end (opposite the stem). It should also give off a strong aroma. Avoid melons that are very soft or feel damp at the stem end. Ripe melons may be stored in the refrigerator, although the flavour will be better at room temperature. Slightly underripe melons can be stored at room temperature to allow flavour and aroma to develop.

Cantaloupes

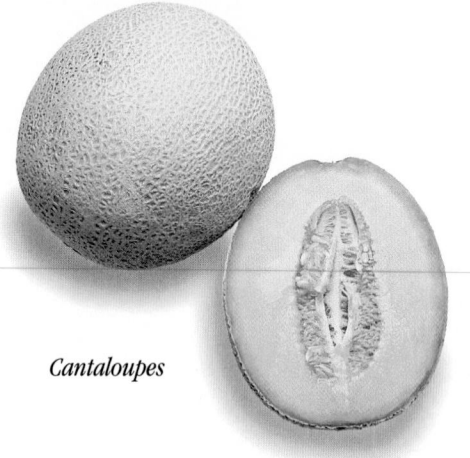

Cantaloupes

North American cantaloupes, which are actually muskmelons, are sweet melons with a thick, yellow-green netted rind, a sweet, moist, orange flesh and a strong aroma. (European cantaloupes, which are not generally available in this country, are more craggy and furrowed in appearance.) As with all sweet melons, the many small seeds are found in a central cavity. Cantaloupes are excellent for eating alone and are especially good with ham or rich meats.

Avoid cantaloupes with the pronounced yellow colour or mouldy aroma that indicates overripeness. Mexican imports ensure a year-round supply, although their peak season is summer.

Casaba Melons

Casaba Melons

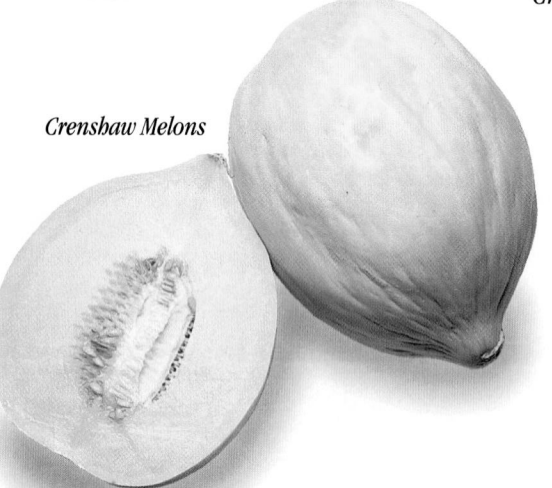

Casaba melons are a teardrop-shaped sweet melon. They have a coarse, yellow skin and a thick, ridged rind; their flesh is creamy white to yellow. Casaba melons are used like cantaloupes. Casaba melons do not have an aroma, so selection must be based on a deep skin colour and the absence of dark or moist patches. Peak season is during September and October.

Crenshaw Melons

Crenshaw Melons

Crenshaw (or cranshaw) melons have a mottled, green-yellow ridged rind and orange-pink flesh. Crenshaws are large and pear-shaped, with a strong aroma. The flesh has a rich, spicy flavour and may be used like cantaloupe. Crenshaws are available from July through October, with peak season during August and September.

Honeydew Melons

Honeydew melons are large oval melons with a smooth rind that ranges from white to pale green. Although the flesh is generally pale green, with a mild, sweet flavour, pink- or gold-fleshed honeydews are also available.

Gold Honeydews

Green Honeydews

Like casaba melons, honeydew melons have no aroma. They are available almost all year, with peak season from June through October.

Santa Claus Melons

Santa Claus or Christmas melons are large, elongated melons with a green-and-yellow-striped, smooth rind. The flesh is creamy white or yellow and tastes like casaba. They are a winter variety, with peak availability during December, which explains the name.

Santa Claus Melons

Watermelons

Watermelons are large (up to 13.5 kg or 30 lb.), round or oval-shaped melons with a thick rind. The skin may be solid green, green-striped or mottled with white. The flesh is crisp and extremely juicy with small, hard, black seeds throughout. Seedless hybrids are available, although they are relatively expensive. Most watermelons have pink to red flesh, although golden-fleshed varieties are becoming more common.

Watermelons are of a different genus from the sweet melons described above. They are native to tropical Africa and are now grown commercially in Texas and several of the southern U.S. states.

Red Seedless Watermelon

Gold Watermelon

Pomes (*family* Rosaceae)

Pomes are tree fruits with thin skin and firm flesh surrounding a central core containing many small seeds called pips or carpels. Pomes include apples, pears and quince. Almonds are in this family as well.

Apples

Apples (Fr. *pommes*), perhaps the most common and commonly appreciated of all fruits, grow on trees in temperate zones worldwide. They are popular because of their convenience, taste, variety and availability.

Rome *Red Delicious*

Granny Smith *Golden Delicious*

McIntosh

Apples can be eaten raw out of hand, or they can be used in a wide variety of cooked or baked dishes. They are equally useful in breads, desserts or vegetable dishes and go well with game, pork and poultry. Classic dishes prepared with apples are often referred to as *à la Normande*. Apple juice (cider) produces alcoholic and nonalcoholic beverages and cider vinegar.

Of the hundreds of known apple varieties, only 20 or so are commercially significant in Canada. Several varieties and their characteristics are noted in Table 25.1. Most have a moist, creamy white flesh with a thin skin of yellow, green or red. They range in flavour from very sweet to very tart, with an equally broad range of textures, from firm and crisp to soft and mealy.

In Europe, apples are divided into distinct cooking and eating varieties. Cooking varieties are those that disintegrate to a purée when cooked. North American varieties are less rigidly classified. Nevertheless, not all apples are appropriate for all types of cooking. Those that retain their shape better during cooking are the best choices where slices or appearance is important. Varieties with a higher malic acid content break down easily, making them more appropriate for applesauce or juicing. Either type may be eaten out of hand, depending on personal preference.

Although not native to North America, apples are now grown commercially in most provinces of Canada, with Ontario, British Columbia and Nova Scotia leading in production. Apples are harvested when still slightly underripe, then stored in a controlled atmosphere (temperature and oxygen are greatly reduced) for extended periods until ready for sale. Modern storage techniques make fresh apples available all year, although peak season is during the autumn. Also, imports ensure a constant supply.

When selecting apples, look for smooth, unbroken skins and firm fruits, without soft spots or bruises. Badly bruised or rotting apples should be discarded immediately. They emit quantities of ethylene gas that speed spoilage of nearby fruits. (Remember the saying about "one bad apple spoils the barrel.") Store apples chilled for up to six weeks. Apple peels (the skin) may be eaten or removed as desired, but in either case, apples should be washed just prior to use to remove pesticides and any wax that was applied to improve appearance. Apple slices may be frozen (often with sugar or citric acid added to slow spoilage) or dried.

Gala Apple

TABLE 25.1	APPLE VARIETIES				
Variety	Skin Colour	Flavour	Texture	Peak Season	Use
Golden Delicious	Glossy, greenish-gold	Sweet	Semifirm	Sept.–Oct.	In tarts; with cheese; in salads
Granny Smith	Bright green	Tart	Firm and crisp	Oct.–Nov.	Eating; in tarts
Jonathan	Brilliant red	Tart to acidic	Tender	Sept.–Oct.	Eating; all-purpose
McIntosh	Red with green background	Tart to acidic	Soft	Fall	Applesauce; in closed pies
Pippin (Newton)	Greenish-yellow	Tart	Semifirm	Fall	In pies; eating; baking
Red Delicious	Deep red	Sweet but bland	Soft to mealy	Sept.–Oct.	Eating
Rome	Red	Sweet-tart	Firm	Oct.–Nov.	Baking; pies; sauces
Winesap	Dark red with yellow streaks	Tangy	Crisp	Oct.–Nov.	Cider; all-purpose

Basic Procedure for Coring Apples

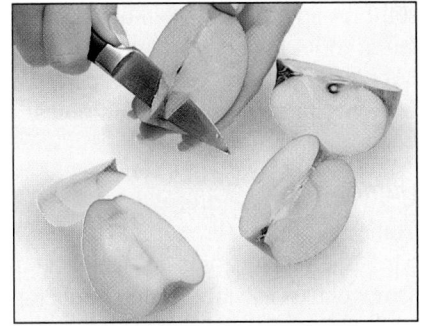

1. Remove the core from a whole apple with an apple corer by inserting the corer from the stem end and pushing out the cylinder containing the core and seeds.

2. Alternatively, first cut an apple into quarters, then use a paring knife to cut away the core and seeds.

Pears

Pears (Fr. *poires*) are an ancient tree fruit grown in temperate areas throughout the world. Most of the pears marketed in this country are grown in British Columbia, California, Washington and Oregon.

Although literally thousands of pear varieties have been identified, only a dozen or so are commercially significant. Several varieties and their characteristics are noted in Table 25.2. Pear varieties vary widely in size, colour and flavour. They are most often eaten out of hand, but can be baked or poached. Pears are delicious with cheese, especially blue cheeses, and can be used in fruit salads, compotes or preserves.

Asian pears, also known as Chinese pears or apple-pears, are of a different species than common pears. They have the moist, sweet flavour of a pear and the round shape and crisp texture of an apple. They are becoming increasingly popular in this country, particularly those known as Twentieth Century or Nijisseiki.

Anjou

Red d'Anjou

Bartlett

Bosc

Asian Pears

TABLE 25.2   PEAR VARIETIES

Variety	Appearance	Flavour	Texture	Peak Season	Use
Anjou (Beurre d'Anjou)	Greenish-yellow skin; egg-shaped with short neck; red variety also available	Sweet and juicy	Firm, keeps well	Oct.–May	Eating; poaching; baking
Bartlett (Williams)	Thin yellow skin; bell-shaped; red variety also available	Very sweet, buttery, juicy	Tender	Aug.–Dec.	Eating; canning; in salads
Bosc	Golden-brown skin; long, tapered neck	Buttery	Dry, holds its shape well	Sept.–May	Poaching; baking
Comice	Yellow-green skin; large and chubby	Sweet, juicy	Smooth	Oct.–Feb.	Eating
Seckel	Tiny; brown to yellow skin	Spicy	Very firm, grainy	Aug.–Dec.	Poaching; pickling

When selecting pears, look for fruits with smooth, unbroken skin and an intact stem. Pears will not ripen properly on the tree, so they are picked while still firm and should be allowed to soften before use. Underripe pears may be left at room temperature to ripen. A properly ripened pear should have a good fragrance and yield to gentle pressure at the stem end. Pears can be prepared or stored in the same way as apples.

Quince

Quince

Common quince (Fr. *coing*) resemble large, lumpy yellow pears. Their flesh is hard, with many pips or seeds, and they have a wonderful fragrance. Too astringent to eat raw, quince develop a sweet flavour and pink colour when cooked with sugar. Quince are used in meat stews, jellies, marmalades and pies. They have a high **pectin** content and may be added to other fruit jams or preserves to encourage gelling.

Fresh quince, usually imported from South America or southeast Europe, are available from October through January. Select firm fruits with a good yellow colour. Small blemishes may be cut away before cooking. Quince will keep for up to a month under refrigeration.

Stone Fruits (genus Prunus)

Stone fruits, also known as drupes, include apricots, cherries, nectarines, peaches and plums. They are characterized by a thin skin, soft flesh and one woody stone or pit. Although most originated in China, the shrubs and trees producing stone fruits are now grown in temperate climates worldwide.

The domestic varieties of stone fruits are in season from late spring through summer. They tend to be fragile fruits, easily bruised, difficult to transport and with a short shelf life. Do not wash them until ready to use, as moisture can cause deterioration. Avoid ingesting the pits—most contain toxic acids. Stone fruits are excellent dried and are often used to make liqueurs or brandies.

Apricots

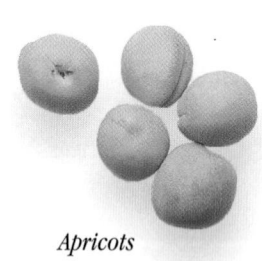

Apricots

Apricots (Fr. *abricots*) are small, round stone fruits with a velvety skin that varies in colour from deep yellow to vivid orange. Their juicy orange flesh surrounds a dark, almond-shaped pit. Apricots can be eaten out of hand, poached, stewed, baked or candied. They are often used in fruit compotes or savoury sauces for meat or poultry, and are also popular in quick breads, fruit tarts or puréed for dessert sauces, jams, custards or mousses.

Apricots enjoy a short season, peaking during June and July, and do not travel well. Select apricots that are well shaped, plump and fairly firm. Avoid those that are greenish-yellow or mushy. Fresh apricots will last for several days under refrigeration, but the flavour is best at room temperature. If fresh fruits are unavailable, canned apricots are usually an acceptable substitute. Dried apricots and apricot juice (known as nectar) are readily available.

Cherries

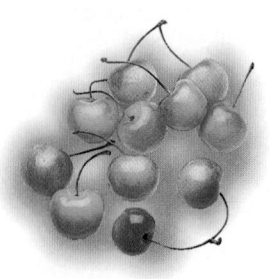

Rainier Cherries

Readily grown in most provinces of Canada are the two most important types of cherry: the sweet cherry and the sour (or tart) cherry.

Sweet cherries (Fr. *cerises*) are round to heart-shaped, about 2.5 cm (1 inch) in diameter, with skin that ranges in colour from yellow to deep red to nearly black. The flesh, which is sweet and juicy, may vary from yellow to dark red.

The most common and popular sweet cherries are the dark red Bings. Yellow-red Royal Ann and Rainier cherries are also available in some areas.

Sweet cherries are often marketed fresh, made into maraschino cherries or candied for use in baked goods. Fresh sweet cherries have a very short season, peaking during June and July. Cherries will not ripen further after harvesting. Select fruits that are firm and plump with a green stem still attached. There should not be any brown spots around the stem. A dry or brown stem indicates that the cherry is less than fresh. Once the stem is removed, the cherry will deteriorate rapidly. Store fresh cherries in the refrigerator and do not wash them until ready to use.

Sour cherries are light to dark red in colour and are so acidic they are rarely eaten uncooked. The most common sour cherries are the Montmorency and Morello. Most sour cherries are canned or frozen, or cooked with sugar and starch (usually cornstarch or tapioca) and sold as prepared pastry and pie fillings.

Both sweet and sour varieties are available dried.

Bing Cherries

Basic Procedure for Pitting Cherries

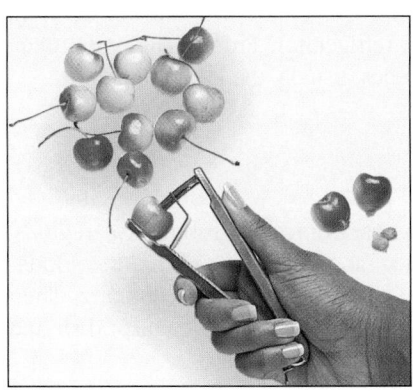

Remove the stem and place the cherry in the pitter with the indentation facing up. Squeeze the handles together to force out the pit.

Peaches and Nectarines

Peaches (Fr. *pêches*) are moderate-sized, round fruits with juicy, sweet flesh. Nectarines are a variety of peach, the main difference between the two being their skin. Peaches have a thin skin covered with fuzz, while nectarines have a thin, smooth skin. The flesh of either fruit ranges from white to pale orange. Although their flavours are somewhat different, they may be substituted for each other in most recipes.

Peaches and nectarines are excellent for eating out of hand or in dessert tarts or pastries. They are also used in jams, chutneys, preserves and savoury relishes, having a particular affinity for Asian and Indian dishes. Although the skin is edible, peaches are generally peeled before being used. (Peaches are easily peeled if blanched first.)

Peaches and nectarines are either freestones or clingstones. With freestones, the flesh separates easily from the stone; freestone fruits are commonly eaten out of hand. The flesh of clingstones adheres firmly to the stone; they hold their shape better when cooked and are the type most often canned.

Select fruits with a good aroma, an overall creamy, yellow or yellow-orange colour and an unwrinkled skin free of blemishes. Red patches are not an indication of ripeness; a green skin indicates that the fruit was picked too early and it will not ripen further. Peaches and nectarines will soften but do not become sweeter after harvesting.

Peaches

Nectarines

The United States, especially California and Georgia, is the world's largest producer of peaches and nectarines. In Canada, Ontario's Niagara Region produces abundant peach crops. Peak season is through the summer months, with July and August producing the best crop. South American peaches are sometimes available from January to May. Canned and frozen peaches are readily available.

Plums

Santa Rosa Plums

Plums (Fr. *prunes*) are round to oval-shaped fruits that grow on trees or bushes. Dozens of plum varieties are known, although only a few are commercially significant. Plums vary in size from very small to 7.5 cm (3 inches) in diameter. Their thin skin can be green, red, yellow or various shades of blue-purple.

Plums are excellent for eating out of hand. Plums can also be used in pies, cobblers or tarts, or be baked or poached; they are often used in jams or preserves, and fresh slices can be used in salads or compotes.

Damson Plums

Fresh plums are widely available from June through October, with a peak season in August and September. When selecting plums, look for plump, smooth fruits with unblemished skin. Generally, they should yield to gentle pressure, although the green and yellow varieties remain quite firm. Avoid plums with moist, brown spots near the stem. Plums may be left at room temperature to ripen, then stored in the refrigerator. Prunes, discussed later, are produced by drying special plum varieties, usually the French Agen.

Tropicals

Tropical fruits are native to the world's hot, tropical or subtropical regions. Most are now readily available throughout Canada thanks to rapid transportation and distribution methods. All can be eaten fresh, without cooking. Their flavours complement each other and go well with rich or spicy meat, fish and poultry dishes.

Bananas

Common Yellow Bananas

Common yellow bananas (Fr. *bananes*) are actually the berries of a large tropical herb. Grown in bunches called hands, they are about 17.5–22.5 cm (7–9 inches) long, with a sticky, soft, sweet flesh. Their inedible yellow skin is easily removed. Red bananas are also available seasonally.

Properly ripened bananas are excellent eaten out of hand or used in salads. Lightly bruised or overripe fruits are best used for breads or muffins. Bananas blend well with other tropical fruits and citrus. Their unique flavour is also complemented by curry, cinnamon, ginger, honey and chocolate.

Fresh bananas are available all year. Bananas are always harvested when still green, because the texture and flavour will be adversely affected if the fruits are allowed to turn yellow on the tree. Unripe bananas are hard, dry and starchy. Because bananas ripen after harvesting, it is acceptable to purchase green bananas if there is sufficient time for final ripening before use. Bananas should be left at room temperature to ripen. A properly ripened banana has a yellow peel with brown flecks. The tip should not have any remaining green colouring. As bananas continue to age, the peel darkens and the starches turn to sugar, giving the fruits a sweeter flavour. Avoid bananas that have large brown bruises or a grey cast (a sign of cold damage).

Plantains

Plantains, also referred to as cooking bananas, are larger but not as sweet as common bananas. They are frequently cooked as a starchy vegetable in tropical cuisines.

Dates

Dates are the fruit of the date palm tree, which has been cultivated since ancient times. Dates are about 2.5–5 cm (1–2 inches) long, with a paper-thin skin and a single grooved seed in the centre. Most are golden to dark brown when ripe.

Medjool Dates

Although dates appear to be dried, they are actually fresh fruits. They have a sticky-sweet, almost candied texture and rich flavour. Dates provide flavour and moisture for breads, muffins, cookies and tarts. They can also be served with fresh or dried fruits, or stuffed with meat or cheese as an appetizer.

Pitted dates are readily available in several packaged forms: whole, chopped or extruded (for use in baking). Whole unpitted dates are available in bulk. Date juice is also available for use as a natural sweetener, especially in baked goods. Although packaged or processed dates are available all year, peak season for fresh domestic dates is from October through December. When selecting dates, look for those that are plump, glossy and moist.

Kiwis

Kiwis, sometimes known as kiwifruits or Chinese gooseberries, are small oval fruits, about the size of a large egg, with a thin, fuzzy brown skin. The flesh is bright green or yellow with a white core surrounded by hundreds of tiny black seeds.

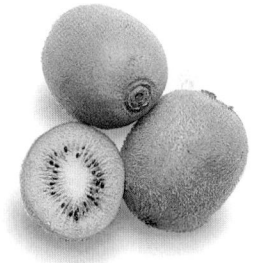

Kiwis

Kiwis are sweet, but somewhat bland. They are best used raw, peeled and eaten out of hand or sliced for fruit salads or garnish. Although kiwis are not recommended for cooking because heat causes them to fall apart, they are a perfect addition to glazed fruit tarts and can be puréed for sorbets, mousses or Bavarians. Kiwis contain an enzyme, similar to that in fresh pineapple or papaya, that has a tenderizing effect on meat and prevents gelling.

♦♦♦

FRIEDA AND THE KIWIFRUIT

How did a fuzzy brown unknown become a media darling and a hugely viable crop? The answer is thanks to Frieda Caplan. In 1962 Frieda, founder of Frieda's Inc., launched her historical worldwide promotion of kiwifruit. Acting on a suggestion that Chinese gooseberries, then grown only in New Zealand, might sell better under the name kiwifruit (the kiwi is the national bird of New Zealand), Frieda unleashed a produce giant. This story of the kiwifruit is studied throughout the world as one of the great successes in food marketing.

In 1980, after 18 years of Freida's continual, creative, aggressive and expensive marketing, the kiwifruit became a North American star when nouvelle cuisine chefs prominently featured it in their mixes of strawberry, banana, melon and pineapples. Since that time, the question asked most commonly of Frieda's Inc. is "What will be the next kiwifruit?"

The answer is that there will never be another kiwifruit. When the kiwifruit was accepted into the world's fruit vernacular, there was an unconditional paradigm shift. Today, new specialty produce does not have to go through the rigorous acceptance process inflicted on the kiwifruit. There can never be another kiwifruit because the marketing climate and consumer palate have shifted in a wonderful, irreversible way. Now when a new fruit like red bananas or yellow seedless watermelon comes onto the market, the consuming public does not react with fear and say "Bananas are supposed to be yellow" or "It really isn't watermelon if there aren't any seeds and it's not red." They respond with positive open minds (much the same as Frieda did when she purchased her first flat of kiwifruit in 1962) and a new-found knowledge that new foods will bring quality and variety, not discord, to their diets.

—KAREN CAPLAN
Frieda's eldest daughter and president of FRIEDA'S, INC.

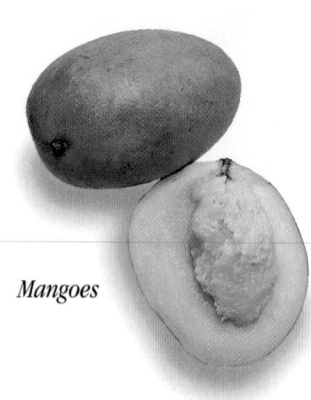

Mangoes

Mangoes

Mangoes are oval or kidney-shaped fruits that normally weigh between 180 and 500 g (6 oz. and 1 lb.). Their skin is smooth and thin but tough, varying in colour from yellow to orange-red, with patches of green, red or purple. As mangoes ripen, the green disappears. The juicy, bright orange flesh clings to a large, flat pit.

A mango's unique flavour is spicy-sweet, with an acidic tang. Mangoes can be puréed for use in drinks or sauces, or the flesh can be sliced or cubed for use in salads, pickles, chutneys or desserts. Mangoes go well with spicy foods such as curry and with barbecued meats.

Although Florida produces some mangoes, most of those available in North America are from Mexico. Peak season is from May through August. Select fruits with good colour that are firm and free of blemishes. Ripe mangoes should have a good aroma, and should not be too soft or shrivelled. Allow mangoes to ripen completely at room temperature, then refrigerate for up to one week.

Basic Procedure for Pitting and Cutting Mangoes

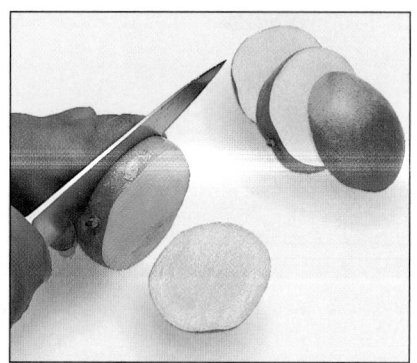

1. Cut along each side of the pit to remove two sections.

2. Each section can then be cubed using the "hedgehog" technique: Make crosswise cuts through the flesh, just to the skin; press up on the skin side of the section, exposing the cubes.

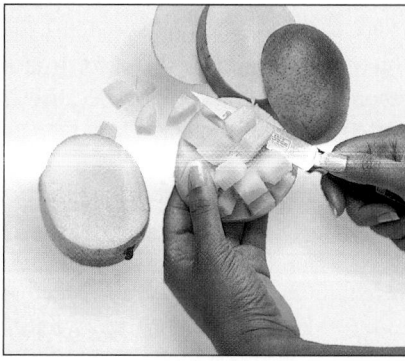

3. The mango may be served like this, or the cubes can be cut off to use in salads or other dishes.

Regular Papayas

Papayas

Papayas, also known as pawpaws, are greenish-yellow fruits shaped rather like large pears and weighing 500–1000 g (1–2 lb.). When halved, they resemble a melon. The flesh is golden to reddish-pink; its centre cavity is filled with round, silver-black seeds resembling caviar. Ripe papayas can be eaten raw, with only a squirt of lemon or lime juice. They can also be puréed for sweet or spicy sauces, chilled soups or sorbets.

Papayas contain **papain**, which breaks down proteins, and therefore papayas are an excellent meat tenderizer. Meats can be marinated with papaya juice or slices before cooking. Papain, however, makes fresh papayas unsuitable for use in gelatins because it inhibits gelling. Unripe (green) papayas are often used in pickles or chutneys, and can be baked or stewed with meat or poultry.

Papaya seeds are edible, with a peppery flavour and slight crunch. They are occasionally used to garnish fruit salads or add flavour to fruit salsas and compotes.

Papayas are grown in tropical and subtropical areas worldwide. Although available year round, peak season is from April through June. Select papayas that are plump, with a smooth, unblemished skin. Colour is a better determinant of ripeness than is softness: The greater the proportion of yellow to green skin colour, the riper the fruit. Papayas may be held at room temperature until completely ripe, then refrigerated for up to one week.

Red Papayas

Passion Fruits

Passion fruits (It. *granadillas*) have a firm, almost shell-like purple skin with orange-yellow pulp surrounding large, black, edible seeds. They are about the size and shape of large hen eggs, with a sweet, rich and unmistakable citrusy flavour. The pulp is used in custards, sauces and ice creams.

Passion Fruits

Select heavy fruits with dark, shrivelled skin and a strong aroma. Allow them to ripen at room temperature, if necessary, then refrigerate. Passion fruits are in season only during February and March. Bottles or frozen packs of purée are readily available, however, and provide a strong, true flavour.

Pineapples

Pineapples (Fr. *ananas*) are the fruit of a shrub with sharp spear-shaped leaves. Each fruit is covered with rough, brown eyes, giving it the appearance of a pine cone. The pale yellow flesh, which is sweet and very juicy, surrounds a cylindrical woody core that is edible but too tough for most uses. Most pineapples weigh approximately 1 kg (2 lb.), but dwarf varieties are also available.

Pineapples are excellent eaten raw, alone or in salads. Slices can be baked or grilled to accompany pork or ham. The cuisines of Southeast Asia incorporate pineapple into various curries, soups and stews. Pineapple juice is a popular beverage, often used in punch or cocktails. Canned or cooked pineapple can be added to gelatin mixtures, but avoid using fresh pineapple, as an enzyme (bromelin) found in fresh pineapple breaks down gelatin.

Pineapples do not ripen after harvesting. They must be left on the stem until completely ripe, at which time they are extremely perishable. The vast majority of pineapples come from Hawaii. Fresh pineapples are available all year, with peak supplies in March through June. Select heavy fruits with a strong, sweet aroma and rich colour. Avoid those with dried leaves or soft spots. Pineapples should be used as soon as possible after purchase. Pineapples are also available canned in slices, spears, cubes or crushed, dried or candied.

Pineapples

Basic Procedure for Trimming and Slicing Pineapples

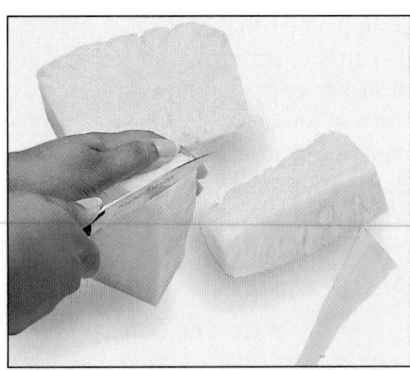

1. Slice off the leaves and stem end. Stand the fruit upright and cut the peel off in vertical strips.

2. Cut the peeled fruit in quarters, then cut away the woody core.

3. The flesh can then be cut as desired.

NUTRITION

Most fruits are quite nutritious. They have a high water content (usually 75% to 95%) and low protein and fat contents, all of which makes them low in calories. They are also an excellent source of fibre, and the sugar content of ripe fruits is a good source of energy. Some fruits, such as citrus, melons and strawberries, contain large amounts of vitamin C (which may be destroyed, however, by cooking or processing). Deep yellow and green fruits, such as apricots, mangoes and kiwis, are high in vitamin A; bananas, raisins and figs are a good source of potassium. (See Table 25.3.)

PURCHASING FRESH FRUITS

Fresh fruits have not been subjected to any processing (such as canning, freezing or drying). Fresh fruits may be ripe or unripe, depending on their condition when harvested or the conditions under which they have been stored. In order to use fresh fruits to their best advantage, it is important to make careful purchasing decisions. The size of each piece of fruit, its grade or quality, its ripeness on delivery and its nutritional content may affect your ability to use the fruit in an appropriate and cost-effective manner.

TABLE 25.3   NUTRITIONAL VALUES OF SELECTED FRUITS

Per serving, fresh, raw and/or as noted	Kcal	Protein (g)	Carbohydrates (g)	Fibre (g)	Total Fat (g)	Vitamin A (I.U.)	Vitamin C (mg)	Phosphorus (mg)	Potassium (mg)
Apple, 1 medium 7 cm (2-3/4 in.) diameter, unpeeled	81	0.3	21.1	3	0.5	74	8	10	159
Banana, peeled 112 g (4 oz.)	104	1.2	26.4	2	0.4	59.4	6.4	14.2	290
Cantaloupe, 1/2 of 12.5 cm (5 in.) diameter melon, approx. 210 g (7 oz.) of flesh	94	2.3	22.3	2.1	0.7	8608	113	45	825
Cherries, Bing, 10 medium, approx. 73 g (2.6 oz.)	49	0.8	11.3	1	0.7	146	5	13	152
Figs, 10 dried, approx. 185 g (6.6 oz.)	477	5.7	122.2	17.4	2.2	248	2	128	1332
Grapes, Thompson Seedless, 20, approx. 98 g (3.5 oz.)	72	0.6	17.8	0.8	0.6	72	10	12	186
Orange, navel, 1/2 medium, approx. 101 g (3.6 oz.)	35.6	0.8	8.9	0.3	<0.1	128	40	13.5	125
Pineapple, trimmed, 112 g (4 oz.)	56	0.4	14	1.2	0.4	25	17	8.5	125
Raisins, seedless, 112 g (4 oz.)	340	3.6	89.6	6	0.4	8	4	108	852
Strawberries, trimmed, 112 g (4 oz.)	36	0.8	8	2.5	0.4	28.7	60	19.8	175

The Corinne T. Netzer Encyclopedia of Food Values 1992

Grading

Fresh fruits traded on the wholesale market may be graded under the standards of the Canadian Food Protection Agency. The grades, based on size and uniformity of shape, colour and texture as well as the absence of defects, are Canada No. 1, Canada No. 2 and Canada Domestic. Most fruits purchased for food service operations are Canada No. 1. Fruits with lower grades are suitable for processing into sauces, jams, jellies or preserves.

Ripening

Several important changes take place in a fruit as it ripens. The fruit reaches its full size; its pulp or flesh becomes soft and tender; its colour changes. In addition, the fruit's acid content declines, making it less tart, and its starch content converts into the sugars, fructose and glucose, that provide the fruit's sweetness, flavour and aroma.

Unfortunately, these changes do not stop when the fruit reaches its peak of ripeness. Rather, they continue, deteriorating the fruit's texture and flavour and eventually causing spoilage.

Depending upon the species, fresh fruits can be purchased either fully ripened or unripened. Figs and pineapples, for example, ripen only on the plant and are harvested at or just before their peak of ripeness then rushed to market. They should not be purchased unripened as they will never attain full flavour or texture after harvesting. On the other hand, some fruits, including bananas and pears, continue to ripen after harvesting and can be purchased unripened.

With most harvested fruits, the ripening time as well as the time during which the fruits remain at their peak of ripeness can be manipulated. For instance, ripening can be delayed by chilling. Chilling slows down the fruit's respiration rate (fruits, like animals, consume oxygen and expel carbon dioxide). The slower the respiration rate, the slower the conversion of starch to sugar. For quicker ripening, fruit can be stored at room temperature.

Ripening is also effected by ethylene gas, a colourless, odourless hydrocarbon gas. Ethylene gas is naturally emitted by ripening fruits and can be used to encourage further ripening in most fruits. Apples, tomatoes, melons and bananas give off the most ethylene and should be stored away from delicate fruits and vegetables, especially greens. Fruits that are picked and shipped unripened can be exposed to ethylene gas to induce ripening just before sale. Conversely, if you want to extend the life of ripe fruits a day or two, isolate them from other fruits and keep them well chilled.

Fresh fruits will not ripen further once they are cooked or processed. The cooking or processing method applied, however, may soften the fruits or add flavour.

Purchasing

Fresh fruits are sold by weight or by count. They are packed in containers referred to as crates, bushels, cartons, cases, lugs or flats. The weight or count packed in each of these containers varies depending on the type of fruit, the purveyor and the place where the fruits were packed. For example, Texas citrus is packed in cartons equal to 7/10 of a bushel; Florida citrus is packed in cartons equal to 4/5 of a bushel. Sometimes size must be specified when ordering fruit. A 13.5-kg (30-lb.) case of lemons, for example, may contain 96, 112 or 144 individual lemons, depending on their size.

Some fresh fruits, especially melons, pineapples, peaches and berries, are available trimmed, cleaned, peeled or cut, and sugar and preservatives are sometimes added. They are sold in bulk containers, sometimes packed in water. These items offer a consistent product with a significant reduction in labour costs. The purchase price may be greater than that for fresh fruits and flavour and freshness and nutritional qualities may suffer somewhat from the processing.

PURCHASING AND STORING PRESERVED FRUITS

Preserving techniques are designed to extend the shelf life of fruits in essentially fresh form. These methods include irradiation, acidulation, canning, freezing and drying. Except for drying, these techniques do not substantially change the fruits' texture or flavour. Canning and freezing can also be used to preserve cooked fruits.

Preserves such as jellies and jams are cooked products and are discussed later in this chapter.

Irradiated Fruits

Some fruits can be subjected to ionizing radiation to destroy parasites, insects and bacteria. The treatment also slows ripening without a noticeable effect on the fruits' flavour and texture. Irradiated fruits must be labelled "treated with radiation," "treated by irradiation" or with a symbol when sold in the United States. Canada currently (2002) does not permit irradiation of food products.

Acidulation

Apples, pears, bananas, peaches and other fruits turn brown when cut. Although this browning is commonly attributed to exposure to oxygen, it is actually caused by the reaction of enzymes.

Enzymatic oxidative browning can be retarded by immersing cut fruits in an acidic solution such as lemon or orange juice. This simple technique is sometimes referred to as **acidulation**. Soaking fruits in water or lemon juice and water (called acidulated water) is not recommended. Unless a sufficient amount of salt or sugar is added to the water, the fruits will just become mushy. But if enough salt or sugar is added, the flavour will be affected.

Canned Fruits

Almost any type of fruit can be canned successfully; pineapple and peaches are the largest sellers. In commercial canning, raw fruits are cleaned and placed in a sealed container, then subjected to high temperatures for a specific amount of time. Heating destroys the microorganisms that cause spoilage, and the sealed environment created by the can eliminates oxidation and retards decomposition. But the heat required by the canning process also softens the texture of most fruits. Canning has little or no effect on vitamins A, B, C and D because oxygen is not present during the heating process. Canning also has no practical effect on proteins, fats or carbohydrates.

In *solid pack* cans, little or no water is added. The only liquid is from the fruits' natural moisture. *Water pack* cans have water or fruit juice added, which must be taken into account when determining costs. *Syrup pack* fruits have a sugar syrup—light, medium or heavy—added. The syrup should also be taken into account when determining food costs, and the additional sweetness should be considered when using syrup-packed fruits. Cooked fruit products such as pie fillings are also available canned.

Canned fruits are purchased in cases of standard-size cans (see Appendix I). Canned fruits can be stored for extended time periods at room temperature. Once a can is opened, any unused contents must be transferred to an appropriate storage container and refrigerated. Cans with bulges must be discarded immediately, without opening. Canned fruits are graded as follows: Canada Fancy (top quality), Canada Choice and Canada Substandard.

Frozen Fruits

Freezing is a highly effective method for preserving fruits. It severely inhibits the growth of microorganisms that cause fruits to spoil. Freezing does not destroy nutrients, although the appearance or texture of most fruits can be affected because of their high water content. This occurs when ice crystals formed from the water in the cells burst the cells' walls.

Many fruits, especially berries and apple and pear slices, are now individually quick frozen (IQF). This method employs blasts of cold air, refrigerated plates, liquid nitrogen, liquid air or other techniques to chill the produce quickly. By speeding the freezing process, known as shock freezing, the formation of ice crystals can be greatly reduced.

Fruits can be trimmed and sliced before freezing and are also available frozen in sugar syrup, which adds flavour and prevents browning. Berries are frozen whole, while stone fruits are usually peeled, pitted and sliced. Fruit purées are also available frozen.

Frozen fruits are graded as Canada Fancy, Canada Choice or Extra Standard, or Canada Substandard. The "Canada" grade indicates that a government inspector has graded the product, but packers may use grade names without an actual inspection if the contents meet the standards of the grade indicated.

Individually quick frozen fruits can be purchased by the case. All frozen fruits should be sealed in moistureproof wrapping and kept at a constant temperature of –18°C (0°F) or below. Temperature fluctuations can cause freezer burn.

Dried Fruits

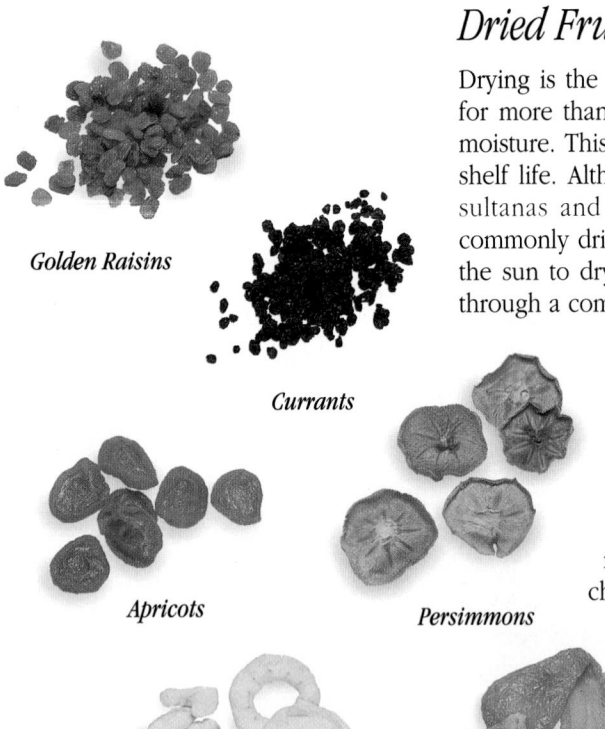

Golden Raisins

Currants

Apricots

Persimmons

Kiwis

Apples

Pears

Drying is the oldest-known technique for preserving fruits, having been used for more than 5000 years. When ripe fruits are dried they lose most of their moisture. This concentrates their flavours and sugars and dramatically extends shelf life. Although most fruits can be dried, plums (prunes), grapes (raisins, sultanas and currants), apricots, cranberries and figs are the fruits most commonly dried. The drying method can be as simple as leaving ripe fruits in the sun to dry naturally or the more cost-efficient technique of passing fruits through a compartment of hot, dry air to quickly extract moisture.

Dried fruits actually retain from 16% to 25% residual moisture, which leaves them moist and soft. They are often treated with sulphur dioxide to prevent browning (oxidation) and to extend shelf life.

Dried fruits may be eaten out of hand; added to cereals or salads; baked in muffins, breads, pies or tarts; stewed for chutneys or compotes; or used as a stuffing for roasted meats or poultry. Before use, dried fruits may be softened by soaking them for a short time in a hot liquid such as water, wine, rum, brandy or other liquor. Some dried fruits should be simmered in a small amount of water before use.

Store dried fruits in airtight containers to prevent further moisture loss; keep in a dry, cool area away from sunlight. Dried fruits may become mouldy if exposed to both air and high humidity.

JUICING

Fruit juice is used as a beverage, alone or mixed with other ingredients, and as the liquid ingredient in other preparations. Juice can be extracted from fruits (and some vegetables) in two ways: pressure and blending.

Pressure is used to extract juice from fruits such as citrus that have a high water content. Pressure is applied by hand-squeezing or with a manual or electric reamer. All reamers work on the same principle: A ribbed cone is pressed against the fruit to break down its flesh and release the juice. Always strain juices to remove seeds, pulp or fibrous pieces.

A blender or an electric juice extractor can be used to liquefy less juicy fruits and vegetables such as apples, carrots, tomatoes, beets and cabbage. The extractor pulverizes the fruit or vegetable, then separates and strains the liquid from the pulp with centrifugal action.

Interesting and delicious beverages can be made by combining the juice of one or more fruits or vegetables: Pineapple with orange, apple with cranberry, strawberry with tangerine and papaya with orange. Colour should be considered when creating mixed-juice beverages, however. Some combinations can cause rather odd colour changes. Although yellow and orange juices are not a problem, those containing red and blue flavonoid pigments (such as Concord grapes, cherries, strawberries, raspberries and blueberries) can create some unappetizing colours. Adding an acid such as lemon juice helps retain the correct red/blue hues.

Applying Various Cooking Methods

Although most fruits are edible raw and typically served that way, some fruits can also be cooked. Commonly used cooking methods are broiling and grilling, baking, sautéing, deep-fat frying, poaching and simmering.

When cooking fruits, proper care and attention are critical. Even minimal cooking can render fruits overly soft or mushy. To combat this irreversible process, sugar can be added. When fruits are cooked with sugar, the sugar will be absorbed slowly into the cells, firming the fruits. Acids (notably lemon juice) also help fruits retain their structure. (Alkalis, such as baking soda, cause the cells to break down more quickly, reducing the fruits to mush.)

Determining Doneness

There are so many different fruits with such varied responses to cooking that no one standard for doneness is appropriate. Each item should be evaluated on a recipe-by-recipe basis. Generally, however, most cooked fruits are done when they are just tender when pierced with a fork or the tip of a paring knife. Simmered fruits, such a compotes, should be softer, cooked just to the point of disintegration.

You can avoid overcooking fruits by remembering that some carryover cooking will occur through the residual heat contained in the foods. Always rely on objective tests—sight, feel, taste and aroma—rather than the clock.

Dry-Heat Cooking Methods

Broiling and Grilling

Fruits are usually broiled or grilled just long enough to caramelize sugars. But cooking must be done quickly in order to avoid breaking down the fruits' structure. Good fruits to broil or grill are pineapples, apples, grapefruits, bananas, persimmons and peaches. The fruits may be cut into slices, chunks or halves as appropriate. A coating of sugar, honey or liqueur adds flavour, as do lemon juice, cinnamon and ginger.

When broiling fruits, use an oiled sheet pan or broiling platter. When grilling fruits, use a clean grill grate or thread the pieces onto skewers. Only thick fruit slices will need to be turned or rotated to heat fully. Broiled or grilled fruits can be served alone, as an accompaniment to meat, fish or poultry or as a topping for ice creams or custards.

Basic Procedure for Broiling or Grilling Fruits

1. Select ripe fruits and peel, core or slice as necessary.
2. Top with sugar or honey to add flavour and aid caramelization.
3. Place the fruits on the broiler platter, sheet pan or grill grate.
4. Broil or grill at a high temperature, turning as necessary to heat the fruits thoroughly but quickly.

Applying the Basics

RECIPE 25.1

BROILED GRAPEFRUIT

Yield: 8 Servings

Ruby grapefruits	4	4
Sweet sherry	30 mL	2 Tbsp.
Brown sugar	50 g	4 Tbsp.

1. Cut each grapefruit in half (perpendicular to the segments), then section with a sharp knife, carefully removing any visible seeds.
2. Sprinkle the grapefruit halves with the sherry and sugar.
3. Arrange on a baking sheet and place under a preheated broiler. Cook briefly, only until well heated and the sugar caramelizes. Serve immediately.

RECIPE 25.1

Approximate values per 1/2 grapefruit:

Calories	70
Total fat	0 g
Saturated fat	0 g
Cholesterol	0 mg
Sodium	0 mg
Total carbohydrates	16 g
Protein	1 g

Baking

After washing, peeling, coring or pitting, most pomes, stone fruits and tropicals can be baked to create hot, flavourful desserts. Fruits with sturdy skins, particularly apples and pears, are excellent for baking alone as their skin (peel) holds in moisture and flavour. They can also be used as edible containers by filling the cavity left by coring with a variety of sweet or savoury mixtures.

Combinations of fruits can also be baked successfully. Try mixing fruits for a balance of sweetness and tartness (for example, strawberries with rhubarb, apples with plums).

Several baked desserts are simply fruits (fresh, frozen or canned) topped with a crust (and called a *cobbler*), streusel (and called a *crumple* or *crisp*) or batter (and called a *buckle*). (See Recipe 29.16, Blackberry Cobbler.) Fruits, sometimes poached first, can also be baked in a wrapper of puff pastry, flaky dough or phyllo dough to produce an elegant dessert.

Basic Procedure for Baking Fruits

1. Select ripe but firm fruits and peel, core, pit or slice as necessary.
2. Add sugar or any flavourings.

3. Wrap the fruits in pastry dough if desired or directed in the recipe.

4. Place the fruits in a baking dish and bake uncovered in a moderate oven until tender or properly browned.

Applying the Basics

BAKED APPLES

Yield: 8 Servings

Apples, Red or Golden Delicious	8	8
Raisins	175 g	6 oz.
Orange zest	15 g	1-1/2 Tbsp.
Brown sugar	125 g	4 oz.

1. Rinse and core each apple. The peels should be scored or partially removed to allow the pulp to expand without bursting the skin during baking.

2. Plump the raisins by soaking them in hot water for 10 minutes. Drain the raisins thoroughly.

3. Combine the raisins, orange zest and brown sugar. Fill the cavity of each apple with this mixture.

4. Stand the apples in a shallow baking dish. Add enough water to measure about 1.25 cm (1/2 inch) deep.

5. Bake the apples at 190°C (375°F) for 15 minutes. Reduce the temperature to 150°C (300°F) and continue baking until the apples are tender but still hold their shape, approximately 1 hour. Occasionally baste the apples with liquid from the baking dish.

RECIPE 25.2

Approximate values per apple:

Calories	220
Total fat	0.5 g
Saturated fat	0 g
Cholesterol	0 mg
Sodium	12 mg
Total carbohydrates	52 g
Protein	1 g

Sautéing

Fruits develop a rich, syrupy flavour when sautéed briefly in butter, sugar and, if desired, spices or liqueur. Cherries, bananas, apples, pears and pineapples are good choices. They should be peeled, cored and seeded as necessary and cut into uniform-size pieces before sautéing.

For dessert, fruits are sautéed with sugar to create a caramelized glaze or syrup. The fruits and syrup can be used to fill crêpes or to top spongecakes or ice creams. Liquor may be added and the mixture flamed (flambéed) in front of diners, as with Bananas Foster (Recipe 25.14).

For savoury mixtures, onions, shallots or garlic are often added.

In both sweet and savoury fruit sautés, the fat used should be the most appropriate for the finished product. Butter and bacon fat are typical choices.

Basic Procedure for Sautéing Fruits

1. Peel, pit and core the fruits as necessary and cut into uniform-size pieces.

2. Melt the fat in a hot sauté pan.

3. Add the fruit pieces and any flavouring ingredients. Do not crowd the pan, as this will cause the fruit to stew in its own juices.

4. Cook quickly over high heat.

Applying the Basics

SAVOURY FRUIT (CHUTNEY)

Yield: 750 mL (24 fl. oz.)

Onion, fine dice	175 g	6 oz.
Garlic, minced	25 g	5 cloves
Butter	30 g	1 oz.
Fruit medley, apples (tart) or peaches, pineapple, etc.	500 g	1 lb.
Raisins	100 g	1/2 cup
Ginger, grated	25 g	2 Tbsp.
Malt vinegar	250 mL	8 fl. oz.
Dry chile, seedless	1	1
Granulated sugar	175 g	6 oz.
Allspice	0.5 g	1/3 tsp.
Salt	5 g	1 tsp.

1. Sweat the onion and garlic in the butter without browning.

2. Slice the fruit into thin, even pieces. Add to the onion and cook for 1–2 minutes. Add the remaining ingredients.

3. Cook, uncovered, over medium heat for 10 minutes or until tender.

4. Serve warm or chilled as an accompaniment.

RECIPE 25.3

Approximate values per 75 mL serving:

Calories	163
Total fat	3 g
Saturated fat	1.5 g
Cholesterol	7 mg
Sodium	222 mg
Total carbohydrates	37 g
Protein	1 g

Deep-Fat Frying

Few fruits are suitable for deep-fat frying. Apples, bananas, pears, pineapples and firm peaches mixed in or coated with batter, however, produce fine results. These fruits should be peeled, cored, seeded and cut into evenly sized slices or chunks. They may also need to be dried with paper towels so that the batter or coating can adhere. The procedures for deep-fat frying are found in Chapter 21, Deep-Fat Frying.

Moist-Heat Cooking Methods

Poaching

One of the more popular cooking methods for fruits is poaching. Poaching softens and tenderizes fruits and infuses them with additional flavours such as spices or wine. Poached fruits can be served hot or cold and used in tarts, pastries or as an accompaniment to meat or poultry dishes.

The poaching liquid can be water, wine, liquor or sugar syrup. (As noted above, sugar helps fruits keep their shape, although it takes longer to tenderize fruits poached in sugar syrup.) The low poaching temperature (85°C/185°F) allows fruits to soften gradually. The agitation created at higher temperatures would damage them.

Cooked fruits should be allowed to cool in the flavoured poaching liquid or syrup. Most poaching liquids can be used repeatedly. If they contain sufficient sugar, they can be reduced to a sauce or glaze to accompany the poached fruits.

Basic Procedure for Poaching Fruits

1. Peel, core and slice the fruits as necessary.
2. In a sufficiently deep, nonreactive saucepan, combine the poaching liquid (usually water or wine) with sugar, spices, citrus zest and other ingredients as desired or as directed in the recipe.
3. Submerge the fruits in the liquid. Place a circle of parchment paper over the fruits to help them stay submerged.
4. Place the saucepan on the stove top over a medium-high flame; bring to a boil.
5. As soon as the liquid boils, reduce the temperature. Simmer gently.
6. Poach until the fruits are tender enough for the tip of a small knife to be easily inserted. Cooking time depends on the type of fruit used, its ripeness and the cooking liquid.
7. Remove the saucepan from the stove top and allow the liquid and fruits to cool.
8. Remove the fruits from the liquid and then refrigerate. The liquid can be returned to the stove top and reduced until thick enough to use as a sauce or glaze or refrigerated for further use.

Applying the Basics

RECIPE 25.4

PEARS POACHED IN RED WINE

NOTE: *This dish appears in the Chapter Opening photograph.*

CULINARY ARTS INSTITUTE, MISSISSIPPI UNIVERSITY FOR WOMEN
Director Sarah Labensky

Yield: 8 Servings

Ripe pears, Anjou or Bartlett	8	8
Zinfandel or Burgundy wine	1.5 L	50 fl. oz.
Whole peppercorns	8–10	8–10
Vanilla bean	1	1
Granulated sugar	350 g	12 oz.
Fresh basil, chopped	30 g	1 oz.
Zest of 1 orange		

1. Peel and core the pears, leaving the stems intact.
2. Combine the remaining ingredients in large nonreactive saucepan. Arrange the pears in the liquid in a single layer.
3. Place the pears on the stove top over medium-high heat. Bring to just below a boil, then immediately reduce the heat and allow the liquid to simmer gently. Cover with a round of parchment paper if necessary to keep the pears submerged.
4. Continue poaching the pears until tender, approximately 1–1.5 hours. Remove the saucepan from the stove and allow the pears to cool in the liquid.
5. Remove the pears from the poaching liquid and return the liquid to the stove top. Reduce until the liquid is thick enough to coat the back of a spoon, then strain.
6. Serve the pears chilled or at room temperature in a pool of the reduced wine syrup.

RECIPE 25.4

Approximate values per serving:

Calories	414
Total fat	1.5 g
Saturated fat	0 g
Cholesterol	0 mg
Sodium	35 mg
Total carbohydrates	92 g
Protein	6 g

Simmering

Simmering techniques are used to make stewed fruits and compotes. Fresh, frozen, canned and dried fruits can be simmered or stewed. As with any moist-heat cooking method, simmering softens and tenderizes fruits. The liquid used may be water, wine or the juices naturally found in the fruits. Sugar, honey and spices may be added as desired. Stewed or simmered fruits can be served hot or cold, as a first course, a dessert or an accompaniment to meat or poultry dishes.

Basic Procedure for Simmering Fruits

1. Peel, core, pit and slice the fruits as necessary.
2. Bring the fruits and cooking liquid, if used, to a simmer. Cook until the fruit is tender.
3. Add sugar or other sweeteners as desired or as directed in the recipe.

Applying the Basics

RECIPE 25.5

DRIED FRUIT COMPOTE

Yield: 1.5 kg (3 lb.)

Dried apricots	150 g	5 oz.
Prunes, pitted	150 g	5 oz.
Dried pears or apples	150 g	5 oz.
Dried peaches	150 g	5 oz.
Hot water or apple juice	750 mL	24 fl. oz.
Cinnamon stick	1	1
Light corn syrup	350 mL	12 fl. oz.
Cointreau	50 mL	2 fl. oz.

1. Coarsely chop the fruits, if desired. Place the pieces in a nonreactive saucepan and add the liquid and cinnamon stick.
2. Bring the mixture to a simmer, cover and cook until tender, approximately 12–15 minutes.
3. Add the corn syrup and Cointreau. Simmer uncovered until thoroughly heated. Serve warm or refrigerate for longer storage.

RECIPE 25.5

Approximate values per 150 g serving:

Calories	188
Total fat	0 g
Saturated fat	0 g
Cholesterol	0 mg
Sodium	52 mg
Total carbohydrates	47 g
Protein	1 g

Preserving

Fresh fruits can be preserved with sugar if the fruit and sugar mixture is concentrated by evaporation to the point that microbial spoilage cannot occur. The added sugar also retards the growth of, but does not destroy, microorganisms.

Pectin, a substance present in varying amounts in all fruits, can cause cooked fruits to form a semisolid mass known as a **gel**. Fruits that are visually unattractive but otherwise of high quality can be made into gels, which are more commonly known as **jams**, **jellies**, **marmalades** and **preserves**.

The essential ingredients of a fruit gel are fruit, pectin, acid (usually lemon juice) and sugar. They must be carefully combined in the correct ratio for the gel to form. For fruits with a low pectin content (such as strawberries) to form gels, pectin must be added, either by adding a fruit with a high pectin content (for example, apples or quinces) or by adding packaged pectin.

Basic Procedure for Making Fruit Preserves

1. Clean, peel, core, pit and cut the fruits as necessary.
2. Firm fruits should be simmered in water or juice until tender.
3. Add sugar and other flavourings to the fruits as desired or as directed in the recipe.
4. Simmer until the mixture thickens.

Applying the Basics

RECIPE 25.6

QUINCE JAM

Yield: 1 L (1 qt.)

Water	1 L	1 qt.
Lemon juice	30 mL	1 fl. oz.
Fresh quince	1.3 kg	3 lb.
Granulated sugar	350 g	12 oz.
Vanilla bean	1/2	1/2

1. Combine the water and 15 mL (1/2 fl. oz.) of lemon juice in a large, non-reactive saucepan.
2. Peel, quarter and core the quince. Cut each quarter into small cubes and add to the water.
3. Bring the water to a boil, reduce the heat, cover and simmer until the quince is tender, approximately 30 minutes.
4. Remove about half the quince with a slotted spoon and set aside. Purée the remaining quince and the cooking liquid.
5. Return the purée and the quince pieces to the saucepan and bring to a simmer. Add the remaining lemon juice, the sugar and the vanilla bean.
6. Simmer uncovered, stirring frequently, until the jam holds its shape, approximately 15 minutes. Remove from the heat and cool over an ice bath.

RECIPE 25.6

Approximate values per 30 mL serving:

Calories	64
Total fat	0 g
Saturated fat	0 g
Cholesterol	0 mg
Sodium	3 mg
Total carbohydrates	17 g
Protein	0 g

CONCLUSION

Fruits, whether fresh, frozen, canned or dried, are one of the most versatile and popular of foods. Fruits can be used uncooked or incorporated into a soup, salad, bread, meat dish or dessert. When selecting fresh fruits it is important to consider seasonal availability, storage conditions and ripeness. It is important that they be at their peak of ripeness for the best flavour, texture, aroma and appearance.

QUESTIONS FOR DISCUSSION

1. Define ripeness and explain why ripe fruits are most desirable. How does the ripening process affect the availability of some fruits?
2. Describe the proper storage conditions for most fruits. Which fruits emit ethylene gas and why is this a consideration when storing fruits?
3. Explain why some apple varieties are preferred for cooking, while other varieties are preferred for eating. Which variety is generally preferred for making applesauce?

4. Which types of fruits are best for dry-heat cooking methods? Explain your answer. Why is sugar usually added when cooking any type of fruit?

5. List and describe three ways to prepare fruits for extended storage.

*A*DDITIONAL *F*RUIT *R*ECIPES

RECIPE 25.7

TROPICAL FRUIT WITH PASSION FRUIT PURÉE

CAMPTON PLACE RESTAURANT, KEMPINSKI HOTELS, SAN FRANCISCO, CA

Yield: 6 Servings

Mangoes	2	2
Papayas	2	2
Brazilian red bananas	2	2
Fresh coconut	1	1
Lime	1	1
Cherimoya (optional)	1	1
Guavas	2	2
Pineapple, medium, trimmed	1/3	1/3
Passion fruit	12	12
Sugar	125 g	4 oz.
Honey	175 g	6 oz.
Berries	as needed for garnish	

RECIPE 25.7

Approximate values per serving:

Calories	560
Total fat	5 g
Saturated fat	4 g
Cholesterol	0 mg
Sodium	26 mg
Total carbohydrates	123 g
Protein	4 g

1. Trim, peel and slice or cut all of the fruit, except the passion fruit, into interesting shapes. Hold in the refrigerator for service.

2. Cut the passion fruit in half and scoop out the seeds and membrane into a nonreactive saucepan. Add any fleshy trimmings from the mango, papaya, guava and pineapple. Add the sugar and honey and cook to a sauce consistency. Strain and cool.

3. Ladle 45 mL (1-1/2 oz.) of the sauce onto a cold plate or bowl. Arrange the sliced fruit attractively on the sauce. Garnish with berries.

❖❖❖

RECIPE 25.8

FIGS WITH BERRIES AND HONEY MOUSSE

GREENS RESTAURANT, SAN FRANCISCO, CA
Executive Chef Annie Somerville

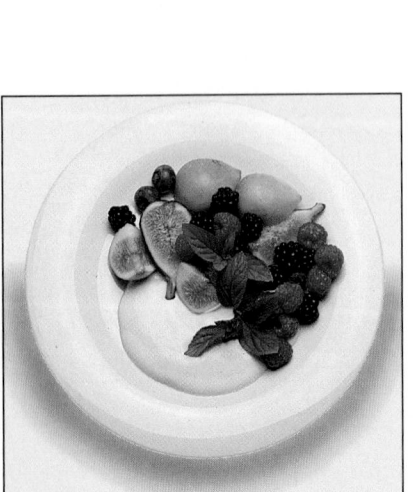

Yield: 4 Servings

Raspberries or blackberries	300 g	10 oz.
Fresh figs such as Black Mission,		
Kadota or Calimyrna	300 g	10 oz.
Honey	175 g	6 oz.
Egg yolks	4	4
Cream, 35%	450 mL	1 pt.

1. Pick through the berries, rinse quickly and drain immediately because water will dilute their flavour.

2. Rinse the figs and cut them in half, leaving the stem attached.

3. To make the mousse, whisk the honey and egg yolks together in a bowl over a pan of barely simmering water. Whisk the mixture continuously for 8 minutes. After 5 minutes, the mousse will begin to thicken and the texture will become creamy. Whisk vigorously until the mousse leaves thick ribbons on its surface when poured over itself. Set aside to cool. The texture of the cooled mousse will be stiff and sticky.

4. Whisk 30 mL (2 Tbsp.) of cream into the mousse, working it until it loosens.

5. Whip the remaining cream until it is firm, fold it into the mousse until it is just incorporated, then whisk the two together. The texture will be light and creamy.

6. Loosely arrange the figs on a platter, sprinkle with the berries and serve with the mousse.

RECIPE 25.8	
Approximate values per serving:	
Calories	689
Total fat	48 g
Saturated fat	28 g
Cholesterol	370 mg
Sodium	214 mg
Total carbohydrates	57 g
Protein	6 g

◆◆◆

RECIPE 25.9

PINEAPPLE PAPAYA SALSA

Yield: 2 L (2 qt.)

Tomatoes	450 g	3
Pineapple, fresh	1	1
Papaya, fresh	1	1
Green onions, sliced	1 bunch	1 bunch
Fresh cilantro, chopped	1 bunch	1 bunch
Jalapeños, seeded, minced	2	2
Lemon juice	50 mL	3 Tbsp.
Garlic, chopped	5 g	1 tsp.
Salt	10 g	2 tsp.

1. Core and dice the tomatoes.
2. Peel and dice the pineapple.
3. Peel, seed and dice the papaya.
4. Combine all ingredients and chill well.

RECIPE 25.9	
Approximate values per 50 mL serving:	
Calories	12
Total fat	0 g
Saturated fat	0 g
Cholesterol	0 mg
Sodium	115 mg
Total carbohydrates	3 g
Protein	0 g

◆◆◆

RECIPE 25.10

TROPICAL FRUIT SALAD WITH YOGURT DRESSING

Yield: 4 Small Salads

Mango, cut into 12-mm (1/2-inch) cubes	175 g	6 oz.
Pineapple, cut into 12-mm (1/2-inch) cubes	175 g	6 oz.
Papaya, cut into 12-mm (1/2-inch) cubes	125 g	4 oz.
Grapefruit segments	16	16
Pineapple or grapefruit juice	50 mL	2 fl. oz.

Continued

Yogurt, plain, nonfat	125 mL	4 fl. oz.
Honey	50 g	2 Tbsp.
Lime juice, fresh	15 mL	1 Tbsp.
Butterleaf lettuce, large leaves, separated and cleaned	4	4
Kiwi, peeled and sliced	1	1
Poppy seeds	3 g	1 tsp.

1. Mix the mango, pineapple, papaya and grapefruit together with the pineapple or grapefruit juice.

2. To make the dressing, whisk the yogurt, honey and lime juice together.

3. Line the plates with the butterleaf lettuce. Arrange the kiwi slices and the fruit salad over the lettuce.

4. Drizzle the dressing over the fruits and top with poppy seeds.

◆◆◆

RECIPE 25.11

GRATIN OF FRESH BERRIES WITH CRÈME FRAÎCHE

Yield: 1 Serving

Assorted fresh berries, such as raspberries, blueberries and blackberries	125 g	4 oz.
Crème fraîche	60 mL	2 fl. oz.
Orange liqueur	5 mL	1 tsp.
Brown sugar	15 g	1 Tbsp.

1. Arrange the berries in an even layer in a shallow, heatproof serving dish.

2. Stir the crème fraîche and orange liqueur together. Spoon this mixture over the berries.

3. Sprinkle the brown sugar over the crème fraîche. Place under a broiler or salamander just until the sugar melts. Serve immediately.

◆◆◆

RECIPE 25.12

APPLE CARPACCIO

STAGE WEST HOTEL, TORONTO, ON
Executive Chef Rudolph Fischbacher

Yield: 6 Portions

Apples: Jonagold, Gala or Golden Delicious	2	2
Walnut oil	50 mL	2 fl. oz.
Flat leaf parsley, chopped	20 g	2 Tbsp.
Lemon juice, fresh	50 mL	2 fl. oz.
Salt and pepper	TT	TT
Toasted walnuts, chopped	100 g	3 oz.
Cocoa bean nibs, roasted, shelled	30 g	1 oz.
Monterey Jack cheese, shaved	125 g	4 oz.

1. Slice apples crosswise with a mandolin, 3 mm (1/8 inch) thick. Arrange on plate in overlapping circles.

2. Mix walnut oil and parsley. Brush over apples.

Rudolph Fischbacher

Rudi trained in his native Austria and worked in Switzerland, Sweden, Spain and Germany before coming to Canada. Currently he is the Executive Chef and Food and Beverage Manager at the Stage West Hotel. He and his staff of 50 provide services for dinner theatre, banquets, the restaurant, lounge, patio and in-room dining.

3. Sprinkle lemon juice over apples.

4. Season and sprinkle with walnuts and cocoa nibs.

5. Shave cheese over apples and serve.

◆◆◆

RECIPE 25.13

CHERRY CONFIT

Yield: 125 g (4 oz.)

Red onion, small dice	25 g	2 Tbsp.
Whole butter	10 g	2 tsp.
Dried cherries	100 g	3 oz.
Brandy	25 mL	1 Tbsp.
Port	25 mL	1 Tbsp.
Sherry vinegar	5 mL	1/2 tsp.

1. Sauté the onion in butter without colouring.

2. Add the cherries. Add the brandy and flambé.

3. Add the port and sherry vinegar; cook until almost dry. Serve warm or at room temperature with charcuterie items, or grilled or roasted meats.

4. The confit can be kept, refrigerated, for up to 1 week.

◆◆◆

RECIPE 25.14

BANANAS FOSTER

BRENNAN'S, NEW ORLEANS, LA
Chef Michael Roussel

Bananas Foster was created in 1951 by Brennan's chef Paul Blangé to promote New Orleans' role as the major port of entry for bananas arriving from Central and South America. The dish was named for Richard Foster, chairman of the New Orleans Crime Commission, a civic group working to clean up the French Quarter. Foster was a good friend to Owen Edward Brennan and a frequent customer at his restaurant. Today Brennan's flambés some 35 000 lb. of bananas each year for this world famous dessert.

Yield: 4 Servings		**Method:** Sautéing
Whole butter	60 g	2 oz.
Brown sugar	225 g	8 oz.
Cinnamon	2 g	1/2 tsp.
Banana liqueur	60 mL	2 fl. oz.
Bananas, cut into quarters	4	4
White rum	60 mL	2 fl. oz.
Vanilla ice cream	4 scoops	4 scoops

1. Combine the butter, sugar and cinnamon in a sauté or flambé pan. Cook over low heat, stirring until the sugar dissolves.

2. Stir in the banana liqueur, then place the bananas in the pan. When the bananas soften and begin to brown, carefully add the rum.

3. Continue to cook until the rum is hot, then tip the pan slightly to ignite the rum. When the flames subside, lift the bananas out of the pan and place four pieces over each portion of ice cream. Spoon the warm sauce over the ice cream and serve immediately.

RECIPE 25.12

Approximate values per serving:

Calories	284
Total fat	24.5 g
Saturated fat	6 g
Cholesterol	18.5 mg
Sodium	308 mg
Total carbohydrates	11 g
Protein	8 g

RECIPE 25.13

Approximate values per 50 mL serving:

Calories	26
Total fat	2 g
Saturated fat	1 g
Cholesterol	6 mg
Sodium	16 mg
Total carbohydrates	2 g
Protein	0 g

RECIPE 25.14

Approximate values per serving:

Calories	555
Total fat	15 g
Saturated fat	9 g
Cholesterol	40 mg
Sodium	161 mg
Total carbohydrates	93 g
Protein	2 g

RECIPE 25.15

Approximate values per serving:

Calories	60
Total fat	1.5 g
Saturated fat	1 g
Cholesterol	10 mg
Sodium	36 mg
Total carbohydrates	11 g
Protein	1 g

Roary MacPherson, CCC

The youngest of 14 children, Roary took turns with his brothers and sisters to help out in the kitchen and knew he was hooked while regularly cooking for a table of 16. He received his Journeyman's Red Seal from the Cabot Institute of Technology and his Chef-de-Cuisine designation from the Southern Alberta Institute of Technology. Roary began his career with Fairmont Hotels & Resorts when he secured a position with The Fairmont Newfoundland.

RECIPE 25.16

Lemon Curd—Approximate values per 50 mL serving:

Calories	232
Total fat	16 g
Saturated fat	9.5 g
Cholesterol	124.5 mg
Sodium	171 mg
Total carbohydrates	22 g
Protein	3 g

◆◆◆

RECIPE 25.15

BANANA FRITTERS

Yield: 40 Fritters

Egg, beaten	1	1
Milk	250 mL	8 fl. oz.
Unsalted butter, melted	50 g	2 oz.
Vanilla extract	5 mL	1 tsp.
Orange zest, finely grated	20 g	2 Tbsp.
Orange juice	50 mL	2 fl. oz.
Ripe banana	1 large	1 large
Pastry flour, sifted	325 g	12 oz.
Granulated sugar	100 g	4 oz.
Baking powder	10 g	1 Tbsp.
Salt	2 g	1/2 tsp.
Confectioner's sugar	as needed for garnish	

1. Whisk together the egg, milk, butter and vanilla. Add the orange zest and juice.

2. Peel and dice the banana (6-mm/1/4-inch size) and add to the egg mixture.

3. Sift together the flour, sugar, baking powder and salt. Gently stir in the banana-egg mixture to form a thick batter.

4. Heat deep-fat fryer oil to 180°C (350°F). Fry 15-g (1-Tbsp.) portions of the batter until the fritters are brown and crisp, approximately 5 minutes.

5. Drain on paper towels, dust with confectioner's sugar and serve hot.

◆◆◆

RECIPE 25.16

LEMON CURD AND SASKATOON BERRY ICE CREAM PROFITEROLES, WHISKY AND MILK CHOCOLATE FONDUE

THE FAIRMONT HOTEL MACDONALD, EDMONTON, AB

Executive Chef Roary MacPherson, CCC

Yield: 1 L (1 qt.)

LEMON CURD

Lemons	8	8
Sugar	350 g	12 oz.
Eggs	8	8
Butter	350 g	12 oz.

1. Juice the lemons and strain.

2. Mix sugar and eggs together, then add lemon juice.

3. Cook on a double boiler, stirring frequently until very thick.

4. Whisk in butter and cool quickly in an ice bath.

OPTION: Zest of four lemons can be included.

SASKATOON BERRY ICE CREAM

Vanilla ice cream	1 L	1 qt.
Lemon curd	500 mL	16 fl. oz.
Saskatoon berries	125 g	4 oz.

Mix all ingredients together and refreeze.

WHISKY AND MILK CHOCOLATE FONDUE

Milk chocolate, melted	200 g	8 oz.
Cream, 35%, hot	50 mL	2 fl. oz.
Canadian whisky	50 mL	2 fl. oz.

Blend chocolate, cream and whisky together. Keep warm.

ASSEMBLY:

1. Slice profiteroles and fill with ice cream. Arrange on plate.
2. Drizzle with fondue and garnish with a few berries and Chantilly cream.

◆◆◆

RECIPE 25.17

BRAISED RHUBARB

Yield: 4.5 kg (10 lb.)

Tart green apples, peeled and cubed	1 kg	2 lb. 8 oz.
Rhubarb, fresh or IQF pieces	3 kg	7 lb.
Unsalted butter	100 g	4 oz.
Sweet white wine	250 mL	8 fl. oz.
Brown sugar	400 g	14 oz.
Vanilla extract	10 mL	2 tsp.
Cinnamon	5 g	1 Tbsp.
Nutmeg	0.5 g	1/4 tsp.
Orange juice	50 mL	2 fl. oz.

1. Sauté the apples and rhubarb in the butter until they begin to soften.
2. Add the wine and reduce by half. Add the remaining ingredients. Simmer until the rhubarb is very tender.
3. Serve at room temperature in prebaked pastry cups, topped with crème chantilly, or serve warm over ice cream.

◆◆◆

RECIPE 25.18

BERRY COMPOTE

Yield: 450 mL (16 fl. oz.)

Berries, fresh or frozen	350 g	12 oz.
Granulated sugar	125 g	4 oz.
Oranges, juice and zest	2	2
Honey	100 g	3 oz.
Cinnamon stick	1	1
Brandy	50 mL	3 Tbsp.

Continued

Saskatoon Berry Ice Cream— Approximate values per 75 mL serving:

Calories	196
Total fat	13 g
Saturated fat	8 g
Cholesterol	155 mg
Sodium	107 mg
Total carbohydrates	19.5 g
Protein	3 g

Whisky and Milk Chocolate Fondue—Approximate values per 15 mL serving:

Calories	61
Total fat	4 g
Saturated fat	2 g
Cholesterol	5 mg
Sodium	2 mg
Total carbohydrates	6 g
Protein	0.5 g

RECIPE 25.17

Approximate values per 50 g serving:

Calories	84
Total fat	3 g
Saturated fat	1 g
Cholesterol	0 mg
Sodium	35 mg
Total carbohydrates	11 g
Protein	0 g

1. Select an assortment of fresh or frozen berries—strawberries, blueberries, raspberries, blackberries and cherries can be used, depending on availability.
2. Place the fruits and sugar in a nonreactive saucepan. Add the juice of two oranges. Bring to a simmer over low heat; cook until the fruits are soft but still intact.
3. Strain the mixture, saving both the fruits and the liquid. Return the liquid to the saucepan. Add the finely grated zest from one orange, the honey, cinnamon and brandy.
4. Bring to a boil and reduce until the mixture thickens enough to coat the back of a spoon. Remove from the heat and cool to room temperature.
5. Gently stir the reserved fruits into the sauce, cover and chill.

◆◆◆

RECIPE 25.19

APPLESAUCE

Yield: 1 L (1 qt.)

McIntosh apples	1.75 kg	4 lb.
Cinnamon sticks	2	2
Granulated sugar	150 g	5 oz.
Lemon juice	15 mL	1 Tbsp.

1. Peel, core and quarter the apples. Place in a saucepan with just enough cold water to cover the bottom of the pan. Add the cinnamon sticks.
2. Bring to a simmer, cover and cook until the apples are tender, approximately 15 minutes.
3. Add the sugar and lemon juice. Simmer 10 minutes more.
4. Remove the cinnamon sticks and press the apples through a food mill.

◆◆◆

RECIPE 25.20

CRANBERRY-ORANGE SAUCE

Yield: 3 L (3 qt.)

Granulated sugar	450 g	1 lb.
Orange juice	125 mL	4 fl. oz.
Water	225 mL	8 fl. oz.
Fresh or frozen cranberries	700 g	1 lb. 8 oz.
Cinnamon stick	1	1
Orange liqueur	50 mL	2 fl. oz.
Orange zest, finely grated	20 g	2 Tbsp.
Oranges, filleted	2	2

1. Combine the sugar, juice and water in a nonreactive saucepan; bring to a boil.
2. Add the cranberries and cinnamon stick and simmer uncovered until the berries begin to burst, approximately 15 minutes. Skim off any foam that rises to the surface.
3. Add the orange liqueur and zest and simmer for another 5 minutes.
4. Remove from the heat and remove the cinnamon stick. Add the orange fillets. Cool and refrigerate.

◆◆◆

RECIPE 25.21

DRIED STRAWBERRY LEAVES

SHAW CONFERENCE CENTRE, EDMONTON, AB
Pastry Chef Clayton Folkers

Yield: 50 Leaves

Red Delicious apples	225 g	2
Lemon juice, fresh	25 mL	1-1/2 Tbsp.
Fresh strawberry purée	600 g	20 oz.
Sugar	100 g	3-1/2 oz.
Orange juice	60 mL	2 fl. oz.

1. Peel and core the apples. Purée with lemon juice until smooth.
2. Continue blending while slowly adding the strawberry purée.
3. Add the sugar and orange juice and blend until smooth.
4. Place template on silicone baking pad and spread the pulp.
5. Dry in a 95°C (200°F) convection oven for 30–35 minutes.
6. Remove leaves from pad while still warm.
7. Store in a warm, dry place.

◆◆◆

RECIPE 25.22

PARSNIP AND RHUBARB SOUP WITH DRIED PEAR CHIPS

WILDWOOD RESTAURANT GROUP, CALGARY, AB
Executive Chef Michael Noble

Yield: 10 Servings

Onion, diced	1	1
Butter, melted	100 g	4 oz.
Parsnip, diced	800 g	2 lb.
Rhubarb stalks, diced	4	4
Celery ribs, diced	2	2
Pear, diced	2	2
Ginger, grated	75 g	3 oz.
Flour	100 g	4 oz.
Chicken stock, hot	2 L	70 fl. oz.
Salt and white pepper	TT	TT
Cream, 35%	500 mL	20 fl. oz.
Pear Chips (recipe follows)	as needed for garnish	

1. Sweat off the onion in the melted butter, over medium heat. Add the parsnip, rhubarb, celery, pear and ginger. Continue sautéing until the vegetables are slightly soft.
2. Sprinkle the flour over the vegetables to make a roux. Add the chicken stock. Bring to a simmer and add a little salt and white pepper. Continue simmering for approximately 40 minutes, adding the cream during the last 10 minutes of cooking.
3. Purée the soup, correct the seasoning and add more cream, if desired. Garnish with pear chips.

Clayton Folkers
Born in Canada, Clayton earned his Commercial Cooking Diploma from the Northern Alberta Institute of Technology, in Edmonton, and was immediately invited by the Four Seasons Hotel to extend his work-study program with them into a permanent position. Looking specifically to enhance his pastry skills, Clayton attended the Privinciaal Hoger Instituut PIVA in Antwerp, Belgium, where he completed a graduate program while gaining experience as a Production Chef in a prominent pastry shop. Returning home to Edmonton, he honed his pastry skills at the Four Seasons Hotel, at La Favorite Pastry Shop, which he co-owned, and at the Shaw Conference Centre, where he has been Pastry Chef since 1989.

RECIPE 25.21

Approximate values per leaf:

Calories	15
Total fat	0 g
Saturated fat	0 g
Cholesterol	0 mg
Sodium	0 mg
Total carbohydrates	4 g
Protein	0 g

Michael Noble
Michael was fated to become a chef after cooking a successful Belgian waffle in a high school economics class! He began his apprenticeship in Vancouver, though he also gained valuable European experience in the early stages of his career. In 1996, Michael opened Vancouver's

continued

Diva at the Met and, within a year, it was propelled into the culinary spotlight, winning awards from Gourmet Magazine, Vancouver Magazine, and GQ. One of Canada's leading chefs, Michael achieved Canada's highest standing ever at the Bocuse d'Or World Cuisine championship in Lyons in 1995 and 1997.

RECIPE 25.22

Approximate values per whole recipe:

Calories	143
Total fat	0 g
Saturated fat	0 g
Cholesterol	0 mg
Sodium	0 mg
Total carbohydrates	37 g
Protein	1 g

PEAR CHIPS

Pear, ripe, but firm	1	1
Icing sugar	to dust	to dust

1. Slice the pear into very thin slices. Lay the slices on a baking pan on silicon paper. Dust the slices with icing sugar and bake in a 165°C (325°F) oven until dry and golden-brown (approximately 15 minutes).
2. Use to garnish the soup as it is being served.

WEBLINKS

Fruit Categories
www.produceoasis.com/Hierarchy_folder/MainFruits_folder/MainFruits.html

Citrus
www.thefruitpages.com/citrus/shtml

Berries
www.receipe2aar.com/search/search.25p?query=berr

Apples
incolour.inetnebr.com/nrolls/a_desc.html

Cranberry Home Page
www.scs.carleton.ca/~palepu/cranberry.html

Pear Pages—Pear Varieties
www2.usapears.com/pears/pbvar.htm

North American Blueberry Council
www.blueberry.org/

U.S. Cherry Marketing Institute: Consumer Information
www.cherrymkt.org/consinfo.html

PART FOUR
BAKING

Like cooking, learning to bake
fresh breads and to prepare both
classic and contemporary pastries
and desserts is not simply a matter
of following written directions. You must understand
the baking process as well as fundamental techniques
and procedures.

In order to provide you with a
thorough introduction to the
skills needed in a bakeshop, we
focus on preparing the types of
breads and desserts usually
found in a small retail shop or restaurant.
Because this book is not designed for large
wholesale or commercial
bakeries, mixes, stabilizers and
mechanical preparation and shaping
skills are not included.

Part Four begins with a chapter on preparation
and ingredients, then presents chapters on quick
breads and yeast breads. We then shift to desserts
with chapters on pies, pastries and cookies
(including classic doughs such as puff pastry
and éclair paste), cakes and frostings (including
brownies), and creams, custards, frozen desserts and dessert sauces. Many of
the recipes found at the end of these chapters are assembled using components
from one or more other chapters.

Throughout this portion of the book, you will see the word formula used in
place of recipe. This is standard terminology in the industry.

CHAPTER 26

PRINCIPLES OF THE BAKESHOP

After studying this chapter you will be able to:

- recognize and select ingredients used in a bakeshop
- control the development of gluten
- cook sugar correctly
- explain how to use sheet gelatin
- control the baking process
- recognize many of the specialized tools and equipment used in the bakeshop

*F*lour, sugar, eggs, milk, butter, flavourings—with this simple list of ingredients you can produce a seemingly endless variety of goods, from breads to sauces to pastries. But to produce consistently good brioche, Bavarians, biscuits or the like, you must pay careful attention to the character and quantity of each ingredient, the way the ingredients are combined and how heat is applied to them. Unlike a cut of meat that can be grilled, roasted, sautéed or braised and still be the same cut of meat, bakeshop products depend on careful, precise preparation for their very identity.*

Accurate measurements are critical in the bakeshop. It is equally important to follow bakeshop formulas carefully and completely. Unlike the rest of the kitchen, mistakes in the bakeshop often cannot be discovered until the product is finished, by which time it is too late to correct them. For example, if you omit the salt when preparing a stew, the mistake can be corrected by adding salt at service time. If you omit the salt from a loaf of bread, however, the mistake cannot be corrected after the bread has baked—and its texture and flavour may be ruined as a result. To follow a written formula, to measure ingredients precisely and to combine them accurately are more important in the bakeshop than anywhere else in the kitchen.

INGREDIENTS

While substituting ingredients may have little or no effect on some dishes (you can use carrots instead of turnips in a stew, for instance), this is not the case with baked goods. Different flours, fats, liquids and sweeteners function differently. Bread flour and cake flour are not the same, nor are shortening and butter. If you substitute one ingredient for another, the results will be different.

Understanding ingredients, why they function the way they do and how to adjust for their differences will make your baking experiences more successful and consistent. This chapter discusses flours, sugar and other sweeteners, fats, thickeners and flavourings such as chocolate, extracts and liquors. Eggs and dairy products, also common in baked goods, are discussed in Chapter 8, Eggs and Dairy Products.

Flours

Wheat Flour

The most frequently used—and therefore the most important—ingredient in the bakeshop is wheat flour (Fr. *farine*). Flour provides bulk and structure to baked goods.

Flour is produced by milling wheat kernels (berries). As discussed in Chapter 23, Potatoes, Grains and Pasta, a wheat kernel has an outer covering called bran. It is composed of several layers that protect the endosperm, which contains starches and proteins. The innermost part is the germ, which contains fat and serves as the wheat seed (see Figure 23.1). During milling, the kernels first pass through metal rollers to crack them, then the bran and germ are removed through repeated stages of sifting and separation. The remaining endosperm is then ground into flour. Flour derived from the portion of the endosperm closest to the germ is finer; flour derived from the portion of the endosperm nearer the bran is coarser and darker.

The character of the wheat determines the character of the flour. Wheats are classified as *soft* or *hard* depending on the kernel's hardness. The harder the wheat kernel, the higher its protein content. Soft wheat yields a soft flour with a low protein content. Soft flour, also called weak flour, is best for tender products such as cakes. Hard wheat yields a hard flour with a high protein content. Hard flour, also known as strong or patent flour, is used for yeast breads.

Various types of flour are created by mixing or blending flours from different sources. **All-purpose flour**, a blend of hard and soft flours, is designed for use in a wide range of foods. It is also referred to in this book because it is readily available in quantities appropriate for small food service operations. Large bakeshops rarely use all-purpose flour; instead, they choose flours specifically milled and blended for industrial uses.

Aging and Bleaching

Any flour develops better baking qualities if allowed to rest for several weeks after milling. Freshly milled flour produces sticky doughs and products with less volume than those made with aged flour. While aging, flour turns white through a natural oxidation process referred to as bleaching.

Natural aging and bleaching are somewhat unpredictable, time-consuming processes, however, so chemicals are now used to do both. Benzoyl peroxide and chlorine dioxide gas rapidly ages flour. Chlorine dioxide and other chemicals bleach flour by removing yellow pigments in order to obtain a uniform white colour. Bleaching destroys small amounts of the flour's naturally occurring vitamin E, which is replaced in fortified or enriched products.

Composition of Flour

Flour is composed primarily of five nutrients: fat, minerals, moisture, starches and proteins. Fat and minerals each generally account for less than 1% of flour's content. The moisture content of flour is also relatively low—when packaged, it cannot exceed 15% under government standards. However, its actual moisture content varies depending on climatic conditions and storage. In damp areas, flour absorbs moisture from the atmosphere.

Starches comprise 63% to 77% of flour, and are necessary for the absorption of moisture during baking. This process, known as **gelatinization**, occurs primarily at temperatures above 60°C (140°F). Starches also provide food for yeast during **fermentation**.

Flour proteins are important because of their gluten-forming potential. **Gluten** is the tough, rubbery substance created when wheat flour is mixed with water. Gluten strands are both plastic (i.e., they change shape under pressure) and elastic (they resume their original shape when that pressure is removed). Gluten is responsible for the volume, texture and appearance of baked goods. It provides structure and enables dough to retain the gases given off by leavening agents. Without gluten, there could be no raised breads: The gases created by yeast fermentation or chemical leaveners would simply escape if there were no network of gluten strands to trap them in the dough.

The higher a flour's protein content, the greater that flour's gluten-forming potential. The proteins responsible for gluten formation are *glutenin* and *gliadin*. Flour does not contain gluten; only a dough or batter can contain gluten. Gluten is produced when glutenin and gliadin are moistened and

TABLE 26.1   PROTEIN CONTENT OF FLOURS

Type of Flour	Percent Protein	Uses
Cake	7–9.5	Tender cakes
Pastry	7.5–10	Biscuits, pie crusts
All-purpose	10–13	General baking
Bread (patent or clear)	12–15	Yeast breads
Whole wheat (straight)	13–14	Breads
High gluten	41–42	To increase protein content of weaker flours for bread making

manipulated, as when they are stirred or kneaded. Generally, the longer a substance is mixed, the more gluten will develop. Products requiring a dough that can be kneaded and shaped, such as French rolls, require a flour with a higher protein content than products meant to be tender, such as cakes or muffins.

Table 26.1 lists the protein content and uses for several common flours. Remember that substitutions will result in a changed and probably less desirable product.

Specialty Flours

Whole Wheat

Whole Wheat Flour

Whole wheat flour, also referred to as graham flour, is made by milling the entire wheat kernel, except the germ. Whole wheat flour has a nutty, sweet flavour and brown, flecked colour. Products made with whole wheat flour will be denser, with less volume than those made with white flour. Whole wheat milled with the germ is not a commercial commodity in Canada because the fat content of the germ may cause rancidity. Whole wheat flour with germ is available in health food stores.

Self-Rising

Self-rising flour is an all-purpose flour to which salt and a chemical leavener, usually baking powder, have been added. It is not recommended for professional use. Chemicals lose their leavening ability over time and may cause inconsistent results. Furthermore, different formulas call for different ratios of salt and leaveners; no commercial blend is appropriate for all purposes.

Nonwheat Flours

Nonwheat flours, also referred to as composite flours, are made from grains, seeds or beans. Corn, soybeans, rice, oats, buckwheat, potatoes and other items provide flours, but none of them contains the gluten-forming proteins of wheat flour. Composite flours are generally blended with a high-protein wheat flour for baking. Substituting a composite flour for wheat flour changes the flavour and texture of the product. Specialized bakeries produce gluten-free products for people with celiac sprue. Combinations of starches are used in addition to other ingredients to produce products with texture. Care must be taken not to contaminate gluten-free products with flours that form gluten.

Rye flour is commonly used in bread baking. It is milled from the rye berry much like wheat flour is milled from the wheat berry. Rye flour comes in four grades or colours: white, medium, dark and pumpernickel. White rye flour is

TABLE 26.2   NUTRITIONAL VALUES OF SELECTED FLOURS

Per 28-g (1-oz.) unit	Kcal	Protein (g)	Carbohydrates (g)	Fibre (g)	Total Fat (g)
All-purpose flour	103	2.9	21.6	0.8	0.3
Bread flour	102	3.4	20.6	mq	0.5
Rye flour, dark	92	4	19.5	mq	0.8
Whole wheat flour	96	3.9	20.6	3.6	0.5

The Corinne T. Netzer Encyclopedia of Food Values 1992
mq = measurable quantity but data are unavailable

Rye Flour

made from only the centre of the rye berry. Medium and dark rye flours are made from the whole rye berry after the bran is removed. Pumpernickel is made by grinding the entire rye berry, including the bran. All rye flours have a warm, pungent flavour similar to caraway and a grey-brown colour. Although rye flour contains proteins, they will not form gluten, so a bread made with 100% rye flour will be dense and flat. Therefore, rye flour is usually blended with a high-protein wheat flour to produce a more acceptable product.

Nutrition

Flours are generally high in carbohydrates and low in fat. (See Table 26.2.) The grains from which they are milled are often rich in vitamins and minerals. Some of these nutrients, however, are lost during milling. In enriched flours, thiamin, riboflavin, niacin and iron are added at levels set by the government.

Purchasing and Storing

Most flours are purchased in 20- and 40-kg (50- and 100-lb.) bags. They should be stored in a well-ventilated room at temperatures no higher than 27°C (80°F). Flour can be stored in a refrigerator or freezer if necessary to prevent the onset of rancidity if the germ is present. Refrigeration may cause the flour to absorb moisture, however, which will limit the flour's ability to absorb additional moisture during actual use.

An open bag of flour should be transferred to a closed container to prevent contamination. Even unopened bags of flour should not be stored near items with strong odours, as flour readily absorbs odours.

Sugar and Sweeteners

Sugar (Fr. *sucre*) and other sweeteners serve several purposes in the bakeshop: They provide flavour and colour, tenderize products by weakening gluten strands, provide food for yeasts, act as a preservative to increase shelf life (keeping qualities) by retaining moisture and act as a creaming or foaming agent to assist with leavening. Sugars also give colour to crusts.

Sugar

Sugars are carbohydrates. They are classified as either (1) single or simple sugars (monosaccharides) such as glucose and fructose, which occur naturally in honey and fruits, or (2) double or complex sugars (disaccharides) which may occur naturally, such as lactose in milk, or in refined sugars.

◆◆◆

SUGAR:
A SWEET AND SORDID PAST

Few foods have so murky an early history as sugar, now one of the most commonplace of foods. Neither botanists nor anthropologists know precisely where sugar cane first grew or when sugar was first extracted from it.

Nevertheless, there are records of a crude sugar being used as a sweetener in India more than 2500 years ago. Sugar cane was being cultivated in the Middle East by the 6th century A.D. and spread from there to North Africa and Spain. Egyptians were manufacturing sugar commercially by the 10th century A.D.

Western Europeans first encountered sugar in the Middle East during the 12th-century Crusades. During the succeeding centuries, sugar remained a rare luxury in Europe. The small amounts available were traded by spice merchants and dispensed by apothecaries. At first sugar was used only as a medicine, a condiment or, occasionally, as a preservative. English cookbooks dating from the late 1300s illustrate an indiscriminate use of sugar as a condiment for meats, fish and vegetables. Like spices, sugar was used to show a person's wealth and position.

When Columbus landed in the West Indies he found an environment perfectly suited for growing sugar cane, so he brought sugar cane cuttings to the New World on his second voyage in 1493. Huge sugar cane plantations soon flourished in the New World, built and worked by enslaved Africans and their descendants.

By the 18th century European and American middle classes were able to afford sugar by the pound. Sugar was now being used principally as a sweetener, particularly in connection with three other imports: coffee, tea and chocolate. Sugar, in fact, had become one of the principal components of a vast and complex trade network involving molasses from the West Indies, distilled rum from New England, finished goods from Europe and slaves from Africa.

Early sugars bore little resemblance to the white granulated substance we use today. Until vacuum pans and centrifuges were invented in the late 19th century, pure sugars were unobtainable. All contained varying amounts of molasses and other impurities. Most of the world's sugar was sold only in large, brown cones. The price of sugar depended on its whiteness and fineness, with the whitest sugar being the most costly.

After two centuries of prosperity, the sugar cane industry began to decline in the 19th century. Several factors contributed to this: abolition of slavery, discovery of alternative sweeteners and falling sugar prices.

If cane sugar was an ancient plant exploited in the New World, then beet sugar is a modern plant fully realized in the Old World. While the ability to refine a crude sweetener from root vegetables had been known for centuries, scientists and chefs mistakenly believed that sugar could be obtained only from plants grown in tropical heat. It was not until 1747 that a German chemist, Andreas Marggraf, proved otherwise. He isolated sucrose—the same substance produced from sugar cane—from white beets. His research, however, did not have a commercial application until cane sugar supplies were threatened. During the Napoleonic Wars, the British blockade of European ports cut off supplies of cane sugar. At Napoleon's urging, research into manufacturing beet sugar progressed. The first beet sugar factory was built in France in 1812. Soon France, Germany and Belgium were virtually self-sufficient in sugar production.

Consumers accepted this new sugar with few complaints; most were totally unaware of any difference. Today about 40% of the world's sugar is manufactured from beets, primarily in Russia, Germany, the United States and Canada.

The sugar most often used in the kitchen is **sucrose**, a refined sugar obtained from both the large tropical grass called sugar cane (*saccharum officinarum*) and the root of the sugar beet (*beta vulgaris*). Sucrose is a disaccharide, composed of one molecule each of glucose and fructose. The chemical composition of beet and cane sugars is identical. The two products taste, look, smell and react the same. Sucrose is available in many forms: white granulated, light or dark brown granulated, molasses or powdered.

Sugar Manufacturing

Common **refined** or **table sugar** is produced from sugar cane or sugar beets. The first step in sugar production is to crush the cane or beet to extract the juice. This juice contains tannins, pigments, proteins and other undesirable components that must be removed through refinement. Refinement begins by dissolving the juice in water, then boiling it in large steam evaporators. The solution is then crystallized in heated vacuum pans. The uncrystallized liquid byproduct, known as **molasses**, is separated out in a centrifuge. The remaining crystallized product, known as **raw sugar**, contains many impurities and is considered unfit for direct use in food.

Raw sugar is washed with steam to remove some of the impurities. This yields a product known as **demerara sugar**. Refining continues as the demerara is heated, liquefied, centrifuged and filtered. Chemicals may be used to bleach and purify the liquid sugar. Finally, the clear liquid sugar is recrystallized in vacuum pans as **granulated white sugar**.

Pure sucrose is sold in granulated and powdered forms and is available in several grades. Because there are no government standards regulating grade labels, various manufacturers' products may differ slightly.

Demerara Sugar

Demerara sugar, sometimes called turbinado sugar, is the closest consumable product to raw sugar. It is partially refined, light brown in colour, with coarse crystals and a caramel flavour. It is sometimes used in beverages and certain baked goods. Because of its high and variable moisture content, demerara sugar is not recommended as a substitute for granulated or brown sugar.

Sanding Sugar

Sanding sugar has a large, coarse crystal structure that prevents it from dissolving easily. It is used almost exclusively for decorating cookies and pastries.

Regular Granulated Sugar

This is the all-purpose sugar used throughout the kitchen. The crystals are a fine, uniform size suitable for a variety of purposes.

Cube Sugar

Sugar cubes are formed by pressing moistened granulated sugar into moulds and allowing it to dry. Cube sugar is most often used for beverage service.

Brown Sugar

Brown sugar is simply regular refined sugar with some of the molasses returned to it. Light brown sugar contains approximately 3.5% molasses; dark brown sugar contains about 6.5%. Molasses adds moisture and a distinctive flavour. Brown sugar can be substituted for refined sugar, measure for measure, in any formula where its flavour is desired. Because of the added moisture, brown sugar tends to lump, trapping air into pockets. It should be measured by weight or if measured by volume it should be packed firmly into the measuring cup in order to remove any air pockets. Always store brown sugar in an airtight container to prevent it from drying and hardening.

Clockwise from top left: Demerara sugar cubes, light brown sugar, icing sugar, sugar cubes, brown sugar crystals, granulated sugar

Superfine or Castor Sugar

Superfine sugar is granulated sugar with a smaller-sized crystal. Also known as castor sugar, it can be produced by processing regular granulated sugar in a food processor for a few moments. Superfine sugar dissolves quickly in liquids and produces light and tender cakes.

Icing or Confectioner's Sugar

Icing sugar (Fr. *sucre en poudre*) is made by grinding granulated sugar crystals through varying degrees of fine screens. Icing sugar cannot be made in a food processor. It is widely available in three degrees of fineness: 10X is the finest and most common; 6X and 4X are progressively coarser. Because of icing sugar's tendency to lump, 3% cornstarch is added to absorb moisture. Icing sugar is most often used in icings and glazes and for decorating baked products.

Liquid Sweeteners

Liquid sweeteners can be used to achieve the same benefits as sugar, except for leavening, in baked goods. Most of these liquids have a distinctive flavour as well as sweetness. Some liquid sweeteners are made from sugar cane; others are derived from other plants, grains or bees.

Corn Syrup

Corn syrup is produced by extracting starch from corn kernels and treating it with acid or an enzyme to develop a sweet syrup. This syrup is extremely thick or viscous and less sweet-tasting than honey or refined sugar. Its viscosity gives foods a thick, chewy texture. Corn syrup is available in light and dark forms; the dark syrup has caramel colour and flavour added. Corn syrup is a **hygroscopic** (water-attracting) sweetener, which means it will attract water from the air on humid days and lose water through evaporation more slowly than granulated sugar. Thus, it keeps products moister and fresher longer.

Honey

Honey

Honey (Fr. *miel*) is a powerful sweetener composed of fructose and glucose. It is created by honey bees from nectar collected from flowers. Its flavour and colour vary depending on the season, the type of flower the nectar came from and its age. Commercial honey is often a blend, prepared to be relatively neutral and consistent. Like corn syrup, honey is highly hygroscopic. Its distinctive flavour is found in several ethnic foods such as baklava and halvah, and beverages such as Drambuie and Benedictine.

Maple Syrup

Maple syrup is made from the sap of sugar maple trees. Sap is collected during the spring, then boiled to evaporate its water content, yielding a sweet brown syrup. One sugar maple tree produces about 48 L (12 gallons) of sap each season; 120 to 160 L (30–40 gallons) of sap will produce about 4 L (1 gallon) of syrup. Pure maple syrup must weigh not less than 1.25 kg per litre; it is graded according to colour, flavour and sugar content. The more desirable products, Canada No. 1, light and medium, have a light amber colour and delicate flavour. Pure maple syrup is expensive, but it does add a distinct flavour to baked goods, frostings and, of course, pancakes and waffles.

Maple-flavoured syrups, often served with pancakes, are usually corn syrups with artificial colourings and flavourings added. Birch tree syrup is a prized product when available.

Molasses

Molasses

As mentioned earlier, molasses (Fr. *mélasse*) is the liquid byproduct of sugar refining. Edible molasses is derived only from cane sugar, as beet molasses has an unpleasant odour and bitter flavour. *Unsulphured molasses* is not a true byproduct of sugar making. It is intentionally produced from pure cane syrup and is preferred because of its lighter colour and milder flavour. *Sulphured molasses* is a byproduct and contains some of the sulphur dioxide used in secondary sugar processing. It is darker and has a strong, bitter flavour.

TABLE 26.3   NUTRITIONAL VALUES OF SELECTED SWEETENERS

Units as Noted	Kcal	Carbohydrates (g)	Sodium (mg)
Corn syrup, light, 30 mL (2 Tbsp.)	120	30	60
Honey, 30 mL (2 Tbsp.)	120	32	na
Molasses, unsulphured, 30 mL (2 Tbsp.)	140	34	56
Sugar, brown, light, 28 g (1 oz.)	106	27	1
Sugar, granulated, 28 g (1 oz.)	109	28	<1
Sugar, powdered, 28 g (1 oz.)	109	28	<1

The Corinne T. Netzer Encyclopedia of Food Values 1992

The final stage of sucrose refinement yields *blackstrap molasses*, which is somewhat popular in the American South. Blackstrap molasses is very dark and thick, with a strong, unique flavour that is unsuitable for most purposes.

Sorghum molasses is produced by cooking down the sweet sap of a brown corn plant, known as sorghum, which is grown for animal feed. The flavour and appearance of sorghum molasses are almost identical to unsulphured sugar cane molasses.

Nutrition

Sweeteners are carbohydrates. They are high in calories and contain no fibre, protein, fat, vitamin A or vitamin C. They contain only trace amounts of thiamin, riboflavin and niacin. (See Table 26.3.)

Cooking Sugar

Sugar can be incorporated into a prepared item in its dry form or first liquefied into a syrup. **Sugar syrups** (not to be confused with liquid sweeteners such as molasses) take two forms: **simple syrups**, which are mixtures of sugar and water, and **cooked syrups**, which are made of melted sugar cooked until it reaches a specific temperature. Be extremely careful when working with hot sugar syrup. Because sugar reaches very high temperatures it can cause severe burns.

Simple Sugar Syrups

Simple or stock syrups are solutions of sugar and water. They are used in the bakeshop to moisten cakes and to make sauces, fruit sorbets, buttercreams and candied fruits.

The syrup's density or concentration is dictated by its intended purpose. Cold water will dissolve up to double its weight in sugar; heating the solution forms denser, more concentrated syrups. A hydrometer, which measures specific gravity and shows degrees of concentration on the Baumé scale, is the most accurate guide to density. See the photo to the right.

Simple syrups can be prepared without the aid of a hydrometer, however. To make a simple sugar syrup, specific amounts of water and sugar are combined in a saucepan and brought to a boil. Once the solution boils, it is important not to stir it, as this may cause recrystallization or lumping. For successful simple sugar syrups, the following formulas must be followed precisely.

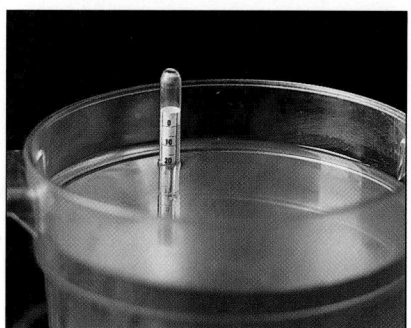

Using a Baumé hydrometer.

◆ *Light syrup*—Boil 2 parts water with 1 part sugar by weight for 1 minute. This concentration would measure 17–20° on the Baumé scale. A light syrup can be used for making sorbet or moistening spongecake.

◆ *Medium syrup*—Boil 1 part sugar with 1.5 parts water by weight for 1 minute. This concentration would measure 21–24° on the Baumé scale. A medium syrup can be used for candying citrus peel.

◆ *Heavy syrup*—Boil equal weights of water and sugar for 1 minute. This concentration would measure 28–30° on the Baumé scale, and the solution should be at 104°C (220°F). Heavy syrup is a basic, all-purpose syrup kept on hand in many bakeshops and diluted as needed.

Cooked Sugars

Caramel sauce, candy and other confections often need liquid sugar that will have a cooked caramel flavour or be firm when cool. For these purposes, sugar needs to be cooked to temperatures far higher than simple syrups. A small amount of water is generally added at the beginning to help the sugar dissolve evenly. As the mixture boils, the water evaporates, the solution's temperature rises and its density increases. The syrup's concentration depends on the amount of water remaining in the final solution: The less water, the harder the syrup will become when cool.

The sugar's temperature indicates its concentration. If there is a great deal of water present, the temperature will not rise much above 100°C (212°F). As water evaporates, however, the temperature will rise until it reaches 160°C (320°F), the point at which all water is evaporated. At temperatures above 160°C (320°F), the pure sugar begins to brown or caramelize. As sugar caramelizes, its sweetening power decreases dramatically. At approximately 190°C (375°F), sugar will burn, developing a bitter flavour. If allowed to continue cooking, sugar will ignite.

Sugar solutions are unstable because of their molecular structure. They can recrystallize because of agitation or uneven heat distribution. Several steps should be taken to prevent recrystallization:

1. Caramelizing sugar.

2. Washing sugar crystals from the side of the pan.

1. Always use a heavy, clean saucepan, preferably copper.

2. Stir the solution to make sure all sugar crystals dissolve before it reaches a boil. Do not stir the solution after it begins boiling, however.

3. An interferent may be added when the solution begins to boil. Cream of tartar, vinegar, glucose (a monosaccharide) and lemon juice are known as **interferents** because they interfere with the formation of sugar crystals. Some formulas specify which interferent to use, although most are used in such small quantities that their taste cannot be detected.

4. Brush down the sides of the pan with cold water to wash off crystals that may be deposited there. These sugar crystals may seed the solution, causing more crystals (lumps) to form if not removed. Instead of using a brush to wash away crystals, you can cover the pan for a few moments as soon as the solution comes to a boil. Steam will condense on the cover and run down the sides of the pan, washing away the crystals.

The concentration of sugar syrup should be determined with a candy thermometer that measures very high temperatures. If a thermometer is not available, use the traditional but less accurate ice-water test: Spoon a few drops of the hot sugar into a bowl of very cold water. Check the hardness of the cooled sugar with your fingertips. Each stage of cooked sugar is named according to its firmness when cool—for example, soft ball or hard crack.

TABLE 26.4	STAGES OF COOKED SUGAR	
Stage	Temperature	Ice-Water Test
Thread	110°C (236°F)	Spins a 5-cm (2-in.) thread when dropped
Soft ball	116°C (240°F)	Forms a soft ball
Firm ball	119°C (246°F)	Forms a firm ball
Hard ball	125°C (260°F)	Forms a hard, compact ball
Soft crack	132°C (270°F)	Separates into a hard, but not brittle, thread
Hard crack	149°C (300°F)	Separates into a hard, brittle sheet
Caramel	170°C (338°F)	Liquid turns brown

  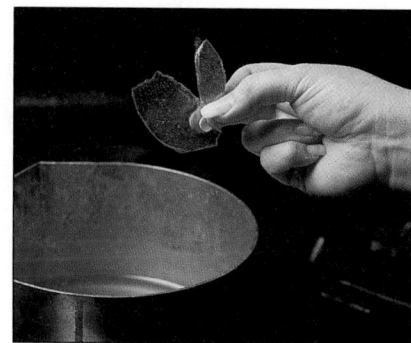

1. Soft ball stage **2.** Hard ball stage **3.** Hard crack stage

Table 26.4 lists the various stages of cooked sugar and the temperature for each. Each stage is also identified by the ice-water test result. Note that even a few degrees makes a difference in the syrup's concentration.

Fats

Fat is the general term for butter, lard, oil and margarine. Shortenings are hydrogenated vegetable oils. Fats provide flavour and colour, add moisture and richness, assist with leavening, help extend a product's shelf life and shorten gluten strands.

The flavour and texture of a baked good depends on the type of fat used and the manner in which it is incorporated with other ingredients. In pastry doughs, solid fat shortens or tenderizes the gluten strands; in bread doughs, fat increases loaf volume and lightness; in cake batters, fat incorporates air bubbles and helps leaven the mixture. Fats should be selected based on their flavour, melting point and ability to form emulsions.

Most bakeshop ingredients combine completely with liquids; fats do not. Fats will not dissolve but will break down into smaller and smaller particles through mixing. With proper mixing, these fat particles are distributed, more or less evenly, throughout the other ingredients.

All-Purpose Shortening

Any fat is a shortening in baking because it shortens gluten strands and tenderizes the product. What is generally referred to as shortening, however, is a type of solid, white, generally tasteless fat, specially formulated for baking. Shortenings are made from animal fats and/or vegetable oils that are solidified through hydrogenation. These products are 100% fat with a relatively high melting point. Solid shortenings are ideal for greasing baking pans because they are tasteless and odourless.

Emulsified Shortening

Emulsifiers may be added to regular shortening to assist with moisture absorption and retention as well as leavening. Emulsified shortenings, also known as high-ratio shortenings, are used in the commercial production of cakes and frostings where the formula contains a large amount of sugar. If a formula calls for an emulsified shortening, use it. If you substitute any other fat, the product's texture suffers.

Lard

Lard (Fr. *saindoux*) is rendered pork fat. It is a solid white product of almost 100% pure fat; it contains only a small amount of water. Lard yields flaky, flavourful pastries, such as pie crusts, but is rarely used commercially because it turns rancid quickly and is not acceptable to some religious beliefs.

Butter and Margarine

Butter is prized in the bakeshop for its flavour; however, it melts at a relatively low temperature of 33°C (93°F) and burns easily. Unsalted butter is preferred for baking because it tends to be fresher, and additional salt might interfere with product formulas. Margarine melts at a slightly higher temperature than butter, making it useful for some rolled-in doughs such as puff pastry or danish. For detailed information on butter and margarine see Chapter 8, Eggs and Dairy Products. Whole butter is approximately 80% fat.

Oil

Unlike butter and other fats, oil blends evenly throughout a mixture. It therefore coats more of the proteins, and the gluten strands produced are much shorter, a desirable result in fine-textured products such as muffins or chiffon cakes. For baking, select a neutral-flavoured oil unless the distinctive taste of olive oil is desired, as in some breads. Never substitute oil in a formula requiring a solid shortening. For detailed information on oil, see Chapter 7, Kitchen Staples.

Nutrition

Fats are high in calories and contain varying levels of saturated fats. Although they have no carbohydrates, a few fats such as butter have trace amounts of protein and minerals. (See Table 26.5.) Butter is also high in Vitamin A.

TABLE 26.5   NUTRITIONAL VALUES OF SELECTED FATS

Per 30 mL (2 Tbsp.)	Kcal	Total Fat (g)	Saturated Fat (g)	Cholesterol (mg)	Sodium (mg)
Butter, unsalted	200	22.8	14.2	62	2
Corn oil	240	27.2	3.4	0	0
Lard	230	25.6	10	24	0
Margarine	200	22	4	0	200
Margarine, diet	100	12	2	0	260
Shortening, all-purpose	226	25.6	6.4	0	0

The Corinne T. Netzer Encyclopedia of Food Values 1992

Thickeners

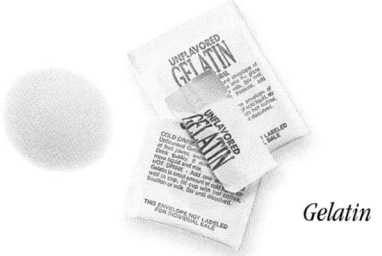

Gelatin

Starches are often used as thickening agents in bakeshop products. Cornstarch, arrowroot, instant starch, waxy maize and flour can be used as thickeners for pastry creams, sauces, custards and fruit fillings. Some of these thickeners are discussed in Chapter 10, Stocks and Sauces.

One of the most commonly used thickeners in the bakeshop is **gelatin**, a natural product derived from the animal protein collagen. It is available in two forms: granulated gelatin and sheet (also called leaf) gelatin. A two-step process is necessary to use either form: The gelatin must first be softened (bloomed) in a cold liquid, then dissolved in a hot liquid.

Granulated gelatin is available in bulk or in 7 g (1/4-oz. or slightly less than 1 Tbsp.) envelopes. One envelope is enough to set 450 mL (1 pt.) of liquid. Granulated gelatin should be softened in a cool liquid for at least 5 minutes, then heated gently to dissolve. The initial softening in a cold liquid is necessary to separate the gelatin molecules so that they will not lump together when the hot liquid is added.

Sheet or leaf gelatin is available in 1-kilogram boxes, sometimes further packaged in 5- or 6-sheet envelopes. The sheets are produced in varying thicknesses and weights. They must be separated and soaked in ice water until very soft, at least 15 minutes. They are then removed from the water, squeezed to remove excess moisture and stirred into a hot liquid to completely dissolve.

♦♦♦

GELATIN BLOOM

Gelatin sheets or powder is dry and must be rehydrated in a cold liquid before melting. "Blooming" the gelatin is an important step and cannot be skipped, otherwise some of the gelatin will lump and not be available to provide thickening.

Basic Procedure for Using Sheet Gelatin

1. Gelatin sheets are submerged in ice water for several minutes to soften.

2. Softened gelatin sheets are then removed from the ice water and incorporated into a hot liquid.

Granulated and sheet gelatin can be substituted weight for weight in any formula. Sheet gelatin, though more expensive, is preferred for its lack of flavour and colour. It also tends to dissolve more readily and evenly and has a longer shelf life than the granulated product.

Once incorporated into a product such as a Bavarian, gelatin can be frozen, or melted and reset once or twice without a loss of thickening ability. Because it scorches easily, gelatin and mixtures containing gelatin should not be allowed to boil; a double boiler or steam jacket is recommended.

♦♦♦

MODIFIED STARCHES

The use of modified corn starches produced from waxy maize is increasing. They are manufactured to provide controlled thickening under various conditions. The best products are pre-cooked and work either hot or cold. Premium products will have acid resistance and a high shear value. Frozen products can be successfully thawed without "breaking," particularly if they were shock-frozen.

Flavourings

Many spices and flavourings are used in the bakeshop. The most popular spices such as cinnamon, cloves, nutmeg and allspice are discussed in Chapter 7, Kitchen Staples. Here we discuss emulsions and extracts, vanilla, chocolate and alcoholic beverages.

Emulsions and Extracts

Emulsions and extracts are liquid flavouring agents derived from various oils.

Emulsions are flavouring oils mixed into water with the aid of emulsifiers. Lemon and orange are the most common emulsions. Emulsions are much stronger than extracts and should be used carefully and sparingly.

Extracts are mixtures of flavouring oils and ethyl alcohol. Vanilla, almond and lemon are frequently used extracts. An extract may be made with pure flavouring oils or with artificial flavours and colours. Contents are regulated and must be clearly labelled.

Emulsions and extracts are highly volatile. They should be stored in sealed containers in a cool area away from direct light.

Vanilla

Vanilla (Fr. *vanille*) is the most frequently used flavouring in the bakeshop. It comes from the pod fruit, called a bean, of a vine in the orchid family. Vanilla beans are purchased whole, individually or by weight. They should be soft and pliable, with a rich brown colour and good aroma. The finest vanilla comes from Tahiti and Madagascar. Mexico is a major producer.

To use a vanilla bean, cut it open lengthwise with a paring knife. Scrape out the moist seeds with the knife's tip and stir them into the mixture being flavoured. The seeds do not dissolve and will remain visible as small black or brown flecks. After all the seeds have been removed, the bean can be stored in a covered container with sugar to create vanilla sugar.

Vanilla beans should be stored in an airtight container in a cool, dark place. During storage, the beans may develop a white coating. This is not mould, but rather crystals of vanilla flavour known as **vanillin**. It should not be removed.

Pure vanilla extract is an easy and less expensive way to give bakeshop products a true vanilla flavour. It is dark brown and aromatic, and comes in several strengths referred to as folds. Each fold requires the extract from 13.35 ounces of vanilla beans per gallon of liquid. A two-fold contains 26.7 ounces per gallon and a four-fold contains 40.5 ounces. Single- or two-fold are the most commonly available; the stronger products are used only in manufacturing. By law, any product labelled vanilla extract must not contain artificial flavourings and must be at least 35% alcohol by volume.

Vanilla extract should be stored at room temperature in a closed, opaque container. It should not be frozen.

Artificial or imitation vanilla flavouring is made with synthetic vanillin. Artificial flavouring is available in a clear form, which is useful for white buttercreams where the dark brown colour of pure vanilla extract would be undesirable. Although inexpensive, artificial vanilla is, at best, weaker and less aromatic than pure extract. It can also impart a chemical or bitter taste to foods.

Scrape seeds from the interior of a vanilla bean.

Chocolate

Chocolate is one of the most—perhaps *the* most—popular flavouring for candies, cookies, cakes and pastries. Chocolate is also served as a beverage and is an ingredient in the traditional spicy Mexican molé sauce. Chocolate is available in a variety of forms and degrees of sweetness.

Chocolate Production

Chocolate (Fr. *chocolat*) begins as yellow fruit pods dangling from the trunk and main branches of the tropical cacao tree. Each pod contains about 40 almond-sized cocoa beans. After the pods ripen, the beans are placed in the

Cocoa

sun for several days to dry and ferment. They are then cleaned, dried, cured and roasted to develop flavour and reduce bitterness. Next the beans are crushed to remove their shells, yielding the prized chocolate **nib**.

Nibs are shipped to manufacturers worldwide where they can be further roasted. They are crushed into a thick (nonalcoholic) paste known as **chocolate liquor** or **chocolate mass**. Chocolate mass contains about 53% fat, known as **cocoa butter**. The chocolate mass is further refined depending on the desired product. If **cocoa powder** is to be produced, virtually all of the cocoa butter is removed. A variety of other products are created by adding

---

◆◆◆

FROM CACAO TO CHOCOLATE CHIPS

To understand the history of chocolate a chef or chocoholic must first understand the fundamental difference between its original use as a beverage and its later transformation into a candy.

The cacao tree (called *theobroma cacao,* meaning "food of the gods") originated in the river valleys of South America and was carried into what is now Mexico by the Mayans before the 7th century A.D. It was cultivated by Mayans, Aztecs and Toltecs not only as a source of food but also as currency. Chocolate was consumed only as a treasured drink. Cacao beans were roasted, crushed to a paste and steeped in water, then thickened with corn flour to create a cold, bitter beverage. Sometimes honey, vanilla or spices, including chiles, were added. The Aztec emperor Montezuma was so enamoured of the beverage that he reportedly consumed 50 cups at each meal.

Columbus brought cacao beans to Spain from his fourth voyage to the New World in 1504. (The common term *cocoa* is actually a western European mispronunciation of the proper term *cacao,* caused by confusion with another New World delicacy, the coconut.) But almost 20 years passed before Spanish conquistadors, led by Cortez, understood the beans' value. With Montezuma's encouragement, Cortez and his soldiers slowly acquired a taste for the bitter beverage, spurred on by the intoxicating effects of caffeine.

Cortez's most important contribution to the history of chocolate was to take beans with him when he left Mexico. He planted them on the islands he passed on his return to Spain: Trinidad, Haiti and Fernando Po, from which the giant African cocoa industry grew. Through Cortez's far-sighted efforts, Spain controlled all

aspects of the cocoa trade until well into the 18th century.

The Spanish began drinking chocolate at home during the 16th century. It was usually mixed with two other expensive imports, sugar and vanilla, and frothed with a carved wooden swizzle stick known as a *molinet.* This thick, cold drink was made from tablets of crushed cocoa beans produced and sold by monks. The Spanish believed that cocoa cured all ills and supplied limitless stamina. In the early 17th century cocoa beverages, now served hot, crept into France via royal marriages.

Cocoa spread through the rest of Europe by different routes. The Dutch, who had poached on Spanish trade routes for many years, eventually realized the value of the unusual beans they found on Spanish ships. Holland soon became the most important cocoa port outside of Spain. From there, a love of cocoa spread to Germany, Scandinavia and Italy. In 1655 England acquired Jamaica and its own cocoa plantations.

Until the Industrial Revolution, cocoa was made by hand using mortar and pestle or stone-grinding disks to crush the cocoa nibs. By the 1700s cocoa factories had opened throughout Europe. James Baker opened the first cocoa factory in the United States in 1765.

Conrad van Houten, a Dutch chemist, patented "chocolate powder" in 1825. His work marked the beginning of a shift from drinking to eating chocolate. It also paved the way for everything we know as chocolate today. Van Houten developed a screw press that removed most of the cocoa butter from the bean, leaving a brown, flaky powder, essentially the same substance as modern cocoa powder.

Eventually it was discovered that the extra cocoa butter resulting from the production of cocoa powder could be added to ground beans to make the paste more malleable, smoother and more tolerant of added sugar. The English firm of Fry and Sons introduced the first eating chocolate in 1847. Their recipe was the same then as today: crushed cocoa beans, cocoa butter and sugar.

In 1876 Swiss chocolatier Daniel Peter invented solid milk chocolate using the new condensed milk created by baby food manufacturer Henri Nestlé. Pennsylvania cocoa manufacturer Milton Hershey introduced his milk chocolate bars in 1894, followed by Hershey's Kisses in 1907. Nestlé Foods introduced the chocolate chip, perfect for cookies, in 1939.

Chocolate Chef, sculpted by Chef Rubin Foster, Arizona Biltmore, Phoenix, AZ.

✦✦✦
MELTING CHOCOLATE

Two important rules for melting chocolate:
1. Chocolate must never exceed 49°C (120°F) or there will be a loss of flavor.
2. Water—even a drop in the form of steam—must never touch the chocolate.

When a droplet of water enters melted chocolate, the chocolate becomes lumpy (a process called *seizing*). There must be a minimum of 15 mL/30 mL (1 Tbsp.) of chocolate to keep this from happening.

If seizing does occur, the addition of fat such as vegetable shortening, clarified butter, or cocoa butter will somewhat restore the chocolate to a workable condition.

For melting chocolate, unlined copper is the traditional "chocolate pot" because it is so responsive to changes in temperature. Aluminum or heatproof glass also works well. Ideally, chocolate should be heated to 49°C (120°F), the point at which all the different fat fractions in the cocoa butter are melted.

When melting chocolate or cocoa butter, temperatures exceeding 49°C (120°F) adversely affect the flavor. There are many acceptable methods for melting dark chocolate. If the heat source does not exceed 49°C (120°F) it is fine to add the dark chocolate in large pieces and leave it to melt unmonitored. When the heat source is capable of bringing the chocolate over 49°C (120°F), however, the chocolate should be finely chopped or grated to ensure uniformity of melting. The chocolate must be carefully watched and stirred to avoid overheating. If using a double boiler, water in the lower container should not exceed 60°C (140°F) and the upper container should not touch the water. The chocolate should be stirred constantly.

Milk and white chocolate must always be stirred frequently while melting because they contain milk solids which seed (lump) if left undisturbed.

Remove chocolate from the heat source when it reaches 46°C (115°F) as the temperature may continue to rise, and stir vigorously to prevent overheating and to distribute the cocoa butter evenly.

Always melt chocolate uncovered as moisture could condense on the lid, drop back in the chocolate, and cause seizing.

—*from THE CAKE BIBLE by ROSE LEVY BERANBAUM*

more cocoa butter, sugar, milk solids and flavourings to the chocolate mass. Most manufacturers of fine chocolates use the Swiss technique of **conching** to increase smoothness. Conching involves stirring large vats of blended chocolate with a heavy roller or paddle to smooth out sugar crystals and improve the flavour by removing acidity from the chocolate, a process that may last from 12 hours to 3 days.

Tasting Chocolates

There are two types of chocolate beans: a very hardy, abundant African variety used as a base bean, and a very flavourful, aromatic variety from Costa Rica used for flavour. Unlike wine or coffee, you cannot taste processed chocolate and tell which beans were used. All chocolates are blends, created by their manufacturer to be unique yet consistent.

Roasting greatly affects the final flavour of chocolate. Generally, German and Spanish manufacturers use a high (or strong) roast; Swiss and American makers use a low (or mild) roast.

Refining is also a matter of national taste. Swiss and German chocolate is the smoothest, followed by English chocolates. American chocolate is noticeably more grainy.

Chocolate quality is actually the product of several factors besides taste. All these factors should be evaluated when selecting chocolates.

1. *Appearance*—colour should be even and glossy, without any discolouration.
2. *Smell*—should be chocolatey with no off-odours or staleness.
3. *Break*—should snap cleanly without crumbling.
4. *Texture*—should melt quickly and evenly on the tongue.

Unsweetened Chocolate

Unsweetened chocolate is pure hardened chocolate liquor without any added sugar or milk solids. It is frequently used in baking and is sometimes referred to as "baking chocolate." Unsweetened chocolate is approximately 53% cocoa butter and 47% cocoa solids. Its flavour is pure and chocolatey, but the absence of sugar makes it virtually inedible as is.

Bittersweet and Semi-sweet Chocolates

Both bittersweet and semi-sweet chocolates contain at least 35% chocolate liquor plus additional cocoa butter, sugar, flavourings and sometimes emulsifiers. Generally, semi-sweet chocolate will be sweeter than bittersweet chocolate, but there are no precise definitions so flavour and sweetness will vary from brand to brand. Both are excellent eating chocolates and can usually be substituted measure for measure in any formula.

Sweet Chocolate

Government standards require that sweet chocolate contain not less than 15% chocolate liquor and varying amounts of sugar, milk solids, flavourings and emulsifiers. As the name implies, sweet chocolate is sweeter, and thus less chocolatey, than semi-sweet chocolate.

Milk Chocolate

The favourite eating chocolate in North America is milk chocolate. It contains sugar, vanilla, perhaps other flavourings and, of course, milk solids. The milk solids that make the chocolate milder and sweeter than other chocolates also make it less suitable for baking purposes. Do not substitute milk chocolate for dark chocolate in any product that must be baked, as the milk solids tend to burn. If melted slowly and carefully, milk chocolate can be used in glazes, mousses or candies.

Cocoa Powder

The brown powder left after the fat (cocoa butter) is removed from cocoa beans is known as cocoa powder. It does not contain any sweeteners or flavourings and is primarily used in baked goods. Alkalized or Dutch-processed cocoa powder has been treated with an alkaline solution, such as potassium carbonate, to raise the powder's pH from 5.5 to 7 or 8. Alkalized powder is darker and milder than nonalkalized powder and has a reduced tendency to lump. Either can be used in baked goods, however.

Cocoa Butter

Chocolate liquor is approximately 53% cocoa butter. Cocoa butter has long been prized for its resistance to rancidity and its use as a cosmetic. Cocoa butter has a very precise melting point, just below body temperature.

Clockwise from lower left: Semi-sweet chips, disks of chocolate liquor, block of bittersweet chocolate, block of milk chocolate, disks of white chocolate, alkalized cocoa powder.

White Chocolate

This ivory-coloured substance is not the product of an albino cocoa bean. It is actually a confectionery product that does not contain any chocolate solids or liquor. (Thus it cannot be labelled "chocolate" in the United States or Canada.) The finest white chocolates contain cocoa butter, sugar, milk solids, vanilla or other flavours. Other products replace all or part of the cocoa butter with partially hydrogenated palm kernel oil. These confectionery products will be less expensive than those containing pure cocoa butter, but their flavour and texture will be noticeably inferior. White chocolate melts at a lower temperature than dark chocolate and burns easily. It is excellent for eating and candy making, but is less-often used in baked goods.

Imitation Chocolate

A less-expensive product substituted in many prepared foods, imitation chocolate is made with partially hydrogenated palm kernel oil instead of cocoa butter. The resulting product melts at a higher temperature. Products containing imitation chocolate should be labelled "chocolate flavoured." Carob is a common ingredient.

Nutrition

Chocolates are high in calories and fat. (See Table 26.6.) They contain minimal amounts of Vitamin A and trace amounts of other vitamins as well as some sodium, phosphorus, potassium and other minerals.

TABLE 26.6   NUTRITIONAL VALUES OF SELECTED CHOCOLATES

Per 28-g (1-oz.) Unit	Kcal	Protein (g)	Carbohydrates (g)	Total Fat (g)	Sodium (mg)
Chocolate, semi-sweet chips (Nestlé's)	150	2	18	8	0
Chocolate, unsweetened (Baker's)	140	3	9	15	0
Cocoa powder (Hershey's)	120	7	13	4	10
Milk chocolate (Hershey's)	150	2	27	12	55
White chocolate (Nestlé's)	160	2	15	10	25

The Corinne T. Netzer Encyclopedia of Food Values 1992

♦♦♦
TO TEMPER OR NOT TO TEMPER

The number-one mystique that surrounds chocolate has to do with tempering. From the dessert maker and pastry chef's point of view, I take a radical position: I do not think it is necessary or practical to temper. But what are we talking about anyway?

Briefly, tempering is a process of slowly raising and lowering the temperature of melted chocolate, stirring constantly, until the complex fat crystals in the cocoa butter stabilize and "behave" in concert with each other. At a cool room temperature, chocolate that has been tempered will dry rapidly to a hard and shiny piece that breaks with a snap. It shrinks slightly as it dries, enabling it to release easily from a mold. A tempered chocolate piece keeps at room temperature for months without losing its luster or snap. Any bar of chocolate that you purchase to eat or to melt has been tempered. Once melted or exposed to heat, however, it loses its temper, though it can be retempered.

Chocolate that is melted but not tempered will dry slowly, at room temperature, to a soft, almost cakey texture. It will stick inside a mold. Untempered chocolate "blooms"—that is, it becomes dull and streaky, or it takes on a mottled appearance—unless it is refrigerated immediately.

Candy makers almost always temper the chocolate they use. But dessert chefs have little need to temper. There is no reason to temper the chocolate used in cake and torte batters, buttercreams, and most ganaches. The same is true for mousses, custards, and creams. Chocolate that will be stored in the refrigerator or consumed quickly need not be tempered. Chocolate glazes, properly handled, do not require tempering to remain shiny for the short life of the dessert.

—from COCOLAT: EXTRAORDINARY
CHOCOLATE DESSERTS
by ALICE MEDRICH

Storing Chocolate

All chocolates should be stored at a cool, consistent temperature, away from strong odours and moisture. Dark chocolate, white chocolate and cocoa powder can be kept for up to one year without loss of flavour. Milk chocolate will not keep as well because it contains milk solids.

Chocolate may develop greyish-white spots during storage. This is called **fatbloom**; it results from the migration of cocoa butter crystals to the surface when temperatures change. Bloom will not affect the flavour or function of chocolate and will disappear when the chocolate is melted.

Alcoholic Beverages

Liquors, **liqueurs**, **wines** and **brandies** are frequently used flavourings in the bakeshop. Rum is a popular flavouring liquor because it blends well with other flavours such as chocolate and coffee. Liqueurs are selected for their specific flavours: for example, kirsch for cherry, amaretto for almond, Kahlúa for coffee, crème de cassis for black currant and crème de cacao for chocolate. They are used to either add or enhance flavours. Wine, both still and sparkling, is used as a flavouring (for example, in sabayon sauce) or as a cooking medium (for example, pears poached in red wine). Brandy, especially the classic orange-flavoured Grand Marnier, is another common bakeshop flavouring. Brandy complements fruits and rounds off the flavour of custards and creams.

When selecting an alcoholic beverage for baking, make quality your first concern. Only high-quality products will enhance the flavour and aroma of your baked goods.

MIXING METHODS

An important step in the production of all baked goods is the mixing of ingredients. The techniques used to mix or combine ingredients affect the baked good's final volume, appearance and texture. There are several mixing methods: **beating**, **blending**, **creaming**, **cutting**, **folding**, **kneading**, **sifting**, **stirring** and **whipping**. These terms are used throughout this part of the text, especially in procedure discussions and formulas. Use the designated mixing method as well as the appropriate equipment or tool to ensure a good-quality finished product.

THE BAKING PROCESS

Baked goods are made from doughs and batters. A **dough** has a low water content. The water-protein complex known as gluten forms the continuous medium into which other ingredients are embedded. A dough is usually prepared by beating, blending, cutting or kneading and is often stiff enough to cut into various shapes.

A **batter** generally contains more fat, sugar and liquids than a dough. Gluten development is minimized and liquid forms the continuous medium in which other ingredients are disbursed. A batter bakes into softer, moister and more crumbly products. A batter is usually prepared by blending, creaming, stirring or whipping and is generally thin enough to pour.

The changes that occur in a dough or batter as it bakes seem mysterious and complex. A pourable liquid becomes a tender, light cake; a sticky mass becomes soft, chewy cookies; a soft, elastic dough becomes firm, crusty French bread. Yet the same physical changes that occur during baking cause all of these results. Namely, gases form and are trapped within the dough or batter; starches, proteins and sugars cook; fats melt; moisture evaporates and staling begins.

By learning to control these changes, you are also learning to control the final product. Control can be exerted in the selection of ingredients and method by which those ingredients are combined as well as the baking temperature and duration.

Gases Form

A baked product's final texture is determined by the amount of leavening or rise that occurs both before and during baking. This rise is caused by the gases present in the dough or batter. These gases are carbon dioxide, air and steam. Air and carbon dioxide are present in doughs and batters before they are heated. Other gases are formed when heat is applied. For example, steam is created as the moisture in a dough is heated; yeast and baking powder rapidly release additional carbon dioxide when placed in a hot oven. These gases then expand and leaven the product. (See Table 26.7.) Additional information on baking powder and baking soda is found in Chapter 27, Quick Breads; additional information on yeast is found in Chapter 28, Yeast Breads.

Gases Are Trapped

The stretchable network of proteins created in a batter or dough either by egg proteins or gluten traps gases in the product. Without an appropriate network of proteins, the gases would just escape without causing the mixture to rise.

TABLE 26.7	LEAVENING AGENTS IN BAKED GOODS
Leavening Agent	Present In
Air	All products, especially those containing whipped eggs or creamed fat
Steam	All products when liquids evaporate or fats melt
Carbon dioxide	Products containing baking soda, baking powder, baking ammonia or yeast

Starches Gelatinize

When starch granules reach a temperature of approximately 60°C (140°F), they absorb additional moisture—up to 10 times their own weight—and expand. This contributes to the baked good's structure.

Proteins Coagulate

Gluten and dairy and egg proteins begin to coagulate (solidify) when the dough or batter reaches a temperature of 71°C (160°F). This process provides most of the baked good's structure.

Proper baking temperatures are important for controlling the point at which proteins coagulate. If the temperature is too high, proteins will solidify before the gases in the product have expanded fully, resulting in a product with poor texture and volume. If the temperature is too low, gases will escape before the proteins coagulate, resulting in a product that may collapse.

Fats Melt

As fats melt, steam is released and fat droplets are dispersed throughout the product. These fat droplets coat the starch (flour) granules, thus moistening and tenderizing the product by keeping the gluten strands short. Shortenings melt at different temperatures. It is important to select a fat with the proper melting point for the product being prepared.

Water Evaporates

Throughout the baking process the water contained in the liquid ingredients will turn to steam and evaporate. This steam is a useful leavener. As steam is released, the dough or batter dries out, starting from the outside, resulting in the formation of a crust.

Sugars Caramelize

As sugars are heated above the boiling point they caramelize, adding flavour and causing the product to darken. Sugars are found in eggs, dairy products and other ingredients, not just in refined sugar and liquid sweeteners.

Carryover Baking

The physical changes in a baked good do not stop when it is removed from the oven. The residual heat contained in a product continues the baking process as the product cools. That is why a cookie or biscuit may seem a bit underbaked when removed from the oven; it will finish baking as it cools.

Staling

Staling is a change in a baked good's texture and aroma caused by both moisture loss and changes in the structure of the starch granules. Stale products have lost their fresh aroma and are firmer, drier and more crumbly than fresh goods.

Staling is not just a general loss of moisture into the atmosphere; it is also a change in the location and distribution of water molecules within the product. This process, known as **starch retrogradation**, occurs as starch molecules cool, becoming more dense and expelling moisture.

In breads, this moisture migrates from the interior to the drier crust, causing the crust to become tough and leathery. If the product is not well wrapped, moisture will escape completely into the surrounding air. In humid conditions, unwrapped bread crusts absorb moisture from the atmosphere, resulting in the same loss of crispness. The flavour and texture of breads can be revived by reheating them to approximately 60°C (140°F), the temperature at which starch gelatinization occurs. Usually, products can be reheated only once without causing additional quality loss.

The retrogradation process is temperature-dependent. It occurs most rapidly at temperatures of approximately 4°C (40°F). Therefore, baked products should not be refrigerated unless they contain perishable components such as cream fillings. It is better to store products frozen or at room temperature.

Products containing fats and sugars, which retain moisture, tend to stay fresh longer. Commercial bakeries usually add chemical emulsifiers or gums to retard staling, but these additives are not practical for small-scale production.

BAKESHOP TOOLS AND EQUIPMENT

As a beginning cook, you may find the tools of the bakeshop a bit complex. Indeed, the tools required for a professional patisserie are quite specialized. A well-equipped cook need not be concerned with possessing every gadget available, but should recognize and be familiar with most of the items shown in the photograph on page 756. Although many of these hand tools will make a task easier, most can be improvised by a creative cook. Several of the items shown, such as the springform pans, tartlet pans and petit four moulds, are used for shaping or holding batters and doughs. The various spatulas and pallet knives are used for spreading icings or fillings. The piping tools and cake comb are used for decorating and finishing baked goods.

When purchasing tools and equipment, look for quality and durability. As your baking skills grow, so will your equipment selection.

Bakeshop ovens may be conventional, convection or steam injection models. Convection ovens can reduce cooking time, but the air currents may damage delicate products such as spongecake or puff pastry. Steam injection ovens use conventional heat flow but allow the baker to add steam automatically to

Clockwise from centre back: Cake turntable, cake pans, flan ring, tartlet pans, cannoli forms, cake comb, offset spatulas, flat cake spatula, blade for slashing breads, flower nail, rectangular tartlet pans, piping bag and tips, metal spatula, dough cutter, rolling pin, springform pan, copper sugar pot (on cooling rack), nest of round cutters

the cooking chamber as needed to produce crisp-crusted breads. Although expensive, steam injection ovens are a necessity for commercial bakeries and most larger restaurant and hotel bakeshops. Baking instructions in the following chapters are based on the use of a conventional oven. If a convection oven is used instead, remember that the temperature and baking time may need to be reduced.

An accurate scale is essential for successful professional baking. Two are generally needed: one for larger weights and one for smaller weights such as spices and herbs.

Conclusion

Of the many stations of the kitchen, the bakeshop often requires the most conscientious attention to detail. The correct use of flour, thickeners, sugar, fat, chocolate and other flavourings is essential. During preparation and baking, doughs and batters go through many physical changes. One of the most important is the development of gluten, the elastic network of wheat proteins created when doughs and batters are prepared, which gives baked goods body and structure. You should understand the changes baked goods undergo and learn to control or adjust them as needed.

QUESTIONS FOR DISCUSSION

1. What is gluten? How is it produced and why is it important in the preparation of baked goods?
2. Discuss four functions of sugar and other sweeteners in baked goods.
3. Describe several steps that can be taken to prevent crystals from forming in sugar solutions.
4. Describe the effect of fat on gluten strands. Why is fat an important ingredient in baked goods?
5. Explain the difference between chocolate liquor and semi-sweet chocolate. Can these two types of chocolate be used interchangeably in most recipes? Explain your answer.
6. List and describe the nine steps in the baking process.
7. Name several specialized hand tools or pans often used in the bakeshop.
8. What are the differences between a steam injection oven, a convection oven and a conventional oven? Why might you select one type of oven over another?

WEBLINKS

American Institute of Baking
  www.aibonline.org/
International School of Baking: Welcome
  www.empnet.com/domocorp/
Bakery Production and Marketing
  www.cahners.com/mainmag/bpm.htm
Bakery-Net
  www.bakery-net.com/rdocs/option12.html

CHAPTER 27

QUICK BREADS

*B*uttermilk biscuits, blueberry muffins, banana-nut bread and currant scones are all quick breads. Although the origin of the name may be a mystery, why they are so named is obvious: They are quick to make and quick to bake. With only a few basic ingredients and no yeast, almost any food service operation can provide its customers with fresh muffins, biscuits, scones and loaf breads.

The variety of ingredients is virtually limitless: cornmeal, whole wheat, fruits, nuts, spices and vegetables all yield popular products. And the use of these products is not limited to breakfast service; they are equally appropriate for lunch, snacks and buffets.

CHEMICAL LEAVENING AGENTS

Quick breads are made with chemical leavening agents, principally baking soda and baking powder. This sets them apart from breads that are made with yeast and require additional time for fermentation and proofing. Understanding how chemical leavening agents operate is essential to successful quick-bread production.

Chemical leavening agents release gases through chemical reactions between acids and bases contained in the formula. These gases form bubbles or air pockets throughout the dough or batter. As the product bakes, the dough or batter sets around these air pockets, thus giving the quick bread its rise and texture.

Baking Soda

Sodium bicarbonate ($NaHCO_3$) is more commonly known as household baking soda. Baking soda is an alkaline compound (a base) that releases carbon dioxide gas (CO_2) if both an acid and moisture are present. Heat is not necessary for this reaction to occur; however, the chemical reaction will be faster at higher temperatures. Therefore, products made with baking soda must be baked at once, before the carbon dioxide has a chance to escape from the batter.

Acids commonly used with baking soda are buttermilk, sour cream, lemon juice, honey, molasses and fresh fruit. Generally, the amount of baking soda used in a formula is only the amount necessary to neutralize the acids present. If more leavening action is needed, baking powder, not more baking soda, should be used. Too much baking soda causes the product to taste soapy or bitter; it may also cause a yellow colour and brown spots to develop.

Baking Powder

Baking powder is a mixture of sodium bicarbonate and one or more acids, generally cream of tartar ($KHC_4H_4O_6$) and/or sodium aluminum sulphate ($Na_2SO_4 \cdot Al_2[SO_4]_3$). Baking powder also contains a starch to prevent lumping and to balance the chemical reactions. Because baking powder contains both the acid and the base necessary for the desired chemical reaction, the formula does not need to contain any acid. Only moisture is necessary to induce the release of gases.

There are two types of baking powder: single-acting and double-acting. An excess of either type produces undesirable flavours, textures and colours in baked products.

Single-acting baking powder requires only the presence of moisture to start releasing gas. This moisture is supplied by the eggs, milk, water or other liquids in the formula. As with baking soda, products using single-acting baking powder must be baked immediately.

Double-acting baking powder is more popular. With double-acting baking powder, there is a small release of gas upon contact with moisture and a second, stronger release of gas when heat is applied. Products made with double-acting baking powder need not be baked immediately, but can sit for a short time without loss of leavening ability. All formulas in this book rely on double-acting baking powder.

Both baking soda and baking powder are sometimes used in one formula. This is because baking soda can release CO_2 only to the extent that there is also an acid present in the formula. If the soda/acid reaction alone is insufficient to leaven the product, baking powder is needed for additional leavening.

Baking Ammonia

Baking ammonia (ammonia bicarbonate or ammonia carbonate) is also used as a leavening agent in some baked goods, primarily cookies and crackers. Baking ammonia releases ammonia and carbon dioxide very rapidly when heated. It is suitable for low-moisture products with large surface areas that are baked at high temperatures, such as crackers. Consequently, it is rarely used in quick breads.

Purchasing and Storing

Purchase chemical leaveners in the smallest unit appropriate for your operation. Although a large can of baking powder may cost less than several small ones, if not used promptly the contents of a larger container can deteriorate, causing waste or unusable baked goods.

Chemical leavening agents should always be kept tightly covered. Not only is there a risk of contamination if left open, but they can also absorb moisture from the air and lose their effectiveness. They should be stored in a cool place, as heat deteriorates them. A properly stored and unopened container of baking powder or baking soda has a shelf life of approximately one year.

MIXING METHODS

Quick breads are generally mixed by either the **biscuit method**, the **muffin method** or the **creaming method**.

Biscuit Method

The biscuit method is used for biscuits and scones and is very similar to the technique used to make flaky pie doughs. The goal is to create a baked good that is light, flaky and tender.

Basic Procedure for Preparing Products with the Biscuit Method

1. Measure all ingredients.
2. Sift the dry ingredients together.
3. Cut in the fat, which should be in a solid form.
4. Combine the liquid ingredients, including any eggs.
5. Add the liquid ingredients to the dry ingredients. Mix just until the ingredients are combined and form a soft dough. Do not overmix, as this causes toughness and inhibits the product's rise.
6. Place the dough on the bench and knead it lightly 10 or 15 times (about 20–30 seconds). The dough should be soft and slightly elastic, but not sticky. Too much kneading toughens the biscuits.
7. The dough is now ready for makeup and baking.

Makeup of Biscuit Method Products

1. Roll out the dough on a floured surface to a thickness of 1.25 to 2 cm (1/2 to 3/4 inches). Be careful to roll it evenly. Biscuits should double in height during baking.
2. Cut into the desired shapes. Cut straight down; do not twist the cutters, as this inhibits rise. Space cuts as close together as possible to minimize scraps.
3. Position the biscuits on a lightly greased or paper-lined sheet pan. If placed with sides nearly touching, the biscuits will rise higher and have softer sides. Place farther apart for crusty sides.
4. Scraps may be rerolled one time without overtoughening the product. To do so, press the dough together gently; do not knead.
5. Tops may be brushed with egg wash before baking or with melted butter after baking. Bake immediately in a hot oven.
6. Cool the finished products on a wire rack.

◆◆◆

BISCUITS AND SCONES: A GENEALOGY

Biscuit is a French word used to describe any dry, flat cake, whether sweet or savoury. It was, perhaps, originally coined to describe twice-baked cakes (*bis* = twice + *cuit* = cooked). Crusader chronicles, for example, mention soldiers eating a "bread called 'bequis' because it is cooked twice" and still, today, the Reims biscuit is returned to the oven for further baking after it is removed from its tin.

Over the centuries the French began to use the term *biscuit* generically and appended modifiers to identify the particular type of dry, flat cake. For example, a *biscuit de guerre* [war] was the very hard, barely risen product of flour and water used from the time of the Crusades to the era of Louis XIV as an army ration; *biscuit de Savoie* is a savoury spongecake; *biscuit de pâtisserie* is a sweet biscuit.

To the British, a biscuit is what North Americans call a cracker or cookie. Yet there appears to be no British quick bread quite comparable to the North American biscuit— the closest relative would be the scone. But because a scone contains eggs and butter, it is much richer than a biscuit.

Elizabeth Alston, in *Biscuits and Scones*, proposes that the biscuit is an American variant of the scone. She theorizes that early British colonists in America brought with them traditional scone recipes. Unable to find or afford the necessary fresh butter and eggs, these practical bakers substituted lard and omitted the eggs. What they created, however, were not mock scones, but rather a new product, different from scones but still delicious. Alston further speculates that French cooks initially called the new American product "biscuit de something" and eventually dropped the "de something."

Applying the Basics

RECIPE 27.1

SCONES

THE FAIRMONT EMPRESS, VICTORIA, BC
Pastry Chef Ken Harper

Afternoon tea at The Empress is a world-renowned tradition.

Yield: 2 Dozen   **Method:** Biscuit

Pastry flour	150 g	5 oz.
Bread flour	150 g	5 oz.
Sugar	120 g	4 oz.
Baking powder	20 g	2 Tbsp.
Butter	75 g	2-1/2 oz.
Cream, 35%	225 mL	8 fl. oz.
Eggs	2	2
Raisins	60 g	2 oz.
Egg wash		

1. Sift the dry ingredients together.
2. Cut in the butter until mealy; do not overmix.
3. Mix cream and eggs together.
4. Add raisins and liquid to dry ingredients; mix until just combined.
5. Knead 2–3 times and roll out 2 cm (3/4 inch) thick. Cut with a floured cutter.
6. Place biscuits on a lined sheet, brush with egg wash (see page 785) and let rest 45 minutes.
7. Bake at 170°C (325°F) for 20–25 minutes until golden-brown.

Ken Harper

Born and raised in Victoria, Ken completed his scholarship in Camosun College's Culinary program and then joined The Fairmont Empress as an apprentice chef. Highlights of his career include joining the culinary teams at the Fairmont Banff Springs Hotel, the Fairmont Château Whistler Resort and the Pan Pacific Hotel. He has been Pastry Chef at the Empress since 1997.

RECIPE 27.1

Approximate values per scone:

Calories	130
Total fat	6.5 g
Saturated fat	4 g
Cholesterol	37 mg
Sodium	96 mg
Total carbohydrates	17 g
Protein	2 g

1. Sift the dry ingredients together.

2. Cut in the fat.

3. Knead the dough.

4. Cut the biscuits.

✦✦✦

BANNOCK: THE "STAFF OF LIFE"

Bannock, a simple quick bread, is found in many Canadian Native cultures. The bread is usually fried in fat or wrapped around a green hardwood stick and baked next to an open fire. The origin of the bread is not Native, however. Bannock is a "borrowed" food that arrived in Canada with the Scottish sailors of the Hudson's Bay Company just over 300 years ago.

RECIPE 27.2

Approximate values per serving:

Calories	295
Total fat	10 g
Saturated fat	2 g
Cholesterol	0 mg
Sodium	671 mg
Total carbohydrates	48.5 g
Protein	4 g

Applying the Basics

RECIPE 27.2 (ABORIGINAL)

CORN FLOUR BANNOCK

Yield: 4 Servings   **Method:** Biscuit

Corn flour	250 g	8 oz.
Baking powder	10 g	1 Tbsp.
Salt	5 g	1 tsp.
Vegetable shortening	30 g	1 oz.
Water	100 mL	3 fl. oz.

1. Lightly grease a heavy cast-iron frying pan or baking sheet. Heat the oven to 230°C (450°F) if using the baking sheet.
2. Combine flour, baking powder and salt in a bowl. Rub in the shortening, then add the water gradually.
3. Work the mixture into a soft, sticky dough.
4. Turn the dough onto a lightly floured surface. Knead it gently 8–10 times. Roll out to 1.25 cm (1/2 inch) thick.
5. Turn the mixture into the frying pan or onto baking sheet. Cook in frying pan on top of stove or on baking sheet in the oven for approximately 12–15 minutes, or until golden-brown. If cooking in the frying pan, turn the bannock over to brown it on both sides.

Applying the Basics

RECIPE 27.3 (ABORIGINAL)

MISSIIAGAAN-PAKWEJIGAN (SUNFLOWER BANNOCK)

Yield: 6 Cakes   **Method:** Biscuit

Sunflower seeds, shelled	100 g	3-1/2 oz.
Salt	TT	TT
Water	150 mL	7 fl. oz.
Corn flour	12 g	1 Tbsp.
Corn oil (for cooking)	35 mL	2 Tbsp.

1. Combine sunflower seeds, salt and water and simmer, covered, for 1.5 hours.
2. Purée seeds into a paste.
3. Add corn flour a little at a time to thicken. Work into a soft, sticky dough.
4. Knead slightly.
5. Form into flat cakes approximately 13 cm (5 inches) in diameter.
6. Heat corn oil and fry cakes until golden-brown and cooked throughout.
7. Drain and serve.

RECIPE 27.3

Approximate values per cake:

Calories	748
Total fat	64 g
Saturated fat	7 g
Cholesterol	0 mg
Sodium	780 mg
Total carbohydrates	33 g
Protein	20 g

Muffin Method

Muffins are any small, cakelike baked good made in a muffin tin (pan). Batters for muffins and loaf quick breads are generally interchangeable. For example, banana muffin batter may be baked in a loaf pan by altering the baking time.

When preparing baked goods by the muffin method, the goal is to produce a tender product with an even shape and an even distribution of fruits, nuts or other ingredients. The most frequent problem with muffin-method products is overmixing. This causes toughness and may cause large holes to form inside the baked product, a condition known as **tunnelling**.

Basic Procedure for Preparing Products with the Muffin Method

1. Measure all ingredients.
2. Sift the dry ingredients together.
3. Combine the liquid ingredients, including melted fat or oil. Melted butter or shortening may resolidify when combined with the other liquids; this is not a cause for concern.
4. Add the liquid ingredients to the dry ingredients and stir just until combined. Do not overmix. The batter may be lumpy.
5. The batter is now ready for makeup and baking.

Makeup of Muffin Method Products

1. Muffin pans and loaf pans should be greased with butter, shortening or a commercial pan grease. Paper liners may be used and will prevent sticking if the batter contains fruits or vegetables. Paper liners, however, inhibit rise.
2. A portion scoop is convenient for ensuring uniform-sized muffins. Be careful not to drip or spill batter onto the edge of the muffin cups; it will burn and cause sticking.
3. Allow muffins and loaf breads to cool for several minutes before attempting to remove them from the pan.
4. Cool the finished products on a wire rack.

Applying the Basics

RECIPE 27.4

BLUEBERRY MUFFINS

Yield: 12 Muffins   **Method:** Muffin

All-purpose flour	250 g	8 oz.
Sugar	150 g	5 oz.
Baking powder	7 g	2 tsp.
Salt	1 g	1/4 tsp.
Egg	1	1
Milk	250 mL	8 fl. oz.
Unsalted butter, melted	60 mL	2 fl. oz.
Vanilla	5 mL	1 tsp.
Blueberries	175 g	6 oz.
Lemon zest	10 g	1 Tbsp.

1. Sift the dry ingredients together.
2. Stir together the liquid ingredients, including the melted butter.
3. Stir the liquid mixture into the dry ingredients. Do not overmix. The batter should be lumpy.
4. Gently fold in the blueberries and lemon zest.
5. Portion into greased or paper-lined muffin cups and bake at 180°C (350°F) until light brown and set in the centre, approximately 18 minutes.
6. Cool the muffins in the pan for several minutes before removing.

1. Combine the liquid ingredients.

2. Fold in the blueberries.

3. Portion the batter.

RECIPE 27.4

Approximate values per muffin:

Calories	188
Total fat	5 g
Saturated fat	3 g
Cholesterol	32 mg
Sodium	93 mg
Total carbohydrates	32 g
Protein	3.5 g

Creaming Method

The creaming method is comparable to the mixing method used for many butter cakes. The final product will be cakelike, with a fine texture. There is less danger of overmixing with this method because the higher fat content shortens gluten strands and tenderizes the batter.

Basic Procedure for Preparing Products with the Creaming Method

1. Measure all ingredients.
2. Sift the dry ingredients together.
3. Combine softened fat and sugar in a mixer bowl. Cream until the colour lightens and the mixture fluffs.
4. Add eggs gradually, mixing well.
5. Add the dry and liquid ingredients to the creamed fat alternately. In other words, a portion of the flour is added to the fat and incorporated, then a portion of the liquid is added and incorporated. These steps are repeated until all the liquid and dry ingredients are incorporated. By adding the liquid and dry ingredients alternately you avoid overmixing the batter and prevent the butter and sugar mixture from curdling.
6. The batter is now ready for makeup and baking.

Makeup of Creaming Method Products

Panning and baking procedures are the same as those for quick breads prepared with the muffin method.

Applying the Basics

RECIPE 27.5

SOUR CREAM MUFFINS

Yield: 15 Muffins   Method: Creaming

Ingredient		
Unsalted butter, room temperature	250 g	8 oz.
Sugar	250 g	8 oz.
Eggs	2	2
Bread flour	200 g	7 oz.
Cake/pastry flour	100 g	3 oz.
Baking powder	3 g	1 tsp.
Baking soda	3 g	1 tsp.
Salt	5 g	1 tsp.
Sour cream	300 g	10 oz.
Vanilla	5 mL	1 tsp.

RECIPE 27.5

Approximate values per muffin:
Calories	292
Total fat	17 g
Saturated fat	10 g
Cholesterol	73 mg
Sodium	218 mg
Total carbohydrates	32 g
Protein	4 g

1. Cream the butter and sugar until light and fluffy. Add the eggs. Beat well.
2. Sift the dry ingredients together.
3. Stir the dry ingredients and sour cream, alternately, into the butter mixture. Stir in the vanilla.
4. Portion and bake at 180°C (350°F) until light brown and set, approximately 20 minutes.
5. Allow the muffins to cool briefly in the pan before removing.

VARIATIONS: Sour cream muffins can be topped with **streusel** (Recipe 27.6) or flavoured with a wide variety of fruits or nuts by adding approximately 125–175 g (4–6 oz. or 1 cup) fresh or frozen drained fruit to the batter. Blueberries, dried cherries, candied fruits, pecans and diced pears yield popular products. By adding 0.25 g (1/2 tsp.) each of cinnamon and nutmeg, basic spice muffins are produced.

1. Cream the butter and sugar.

2. Add the sour cream.

3. Top the muffins with streusel.

Applying the Basics

RECIPE 27.6

STREUSEL TOPPING

Yield: 750 g (1 lb. 8 oz.)

Cake/pastry flour	250 g	8 oz.
Cinnamon	8 g	1/4 oz.
Brown sugar	125 g	4 oz.
Sugar	125 g	4 oz.
Whole butter, cold	250 g	8 oz.

1. Combine all dry ingredients. Cut in the butter until the mixture is coarse and crumbly.

2. Sprinkle on top of muffins or quick breads prior to baking. Streusel topping will keep for several weeks under refrigeration.

RECIPE 27.6

Approximate values per 15 g serving:

Calories	74
Total fat	4 g
Saturated fat	2.5 g
Cholesterol	11 mg
Sodium	42 mg
Total carbohydrates	9 g
Protein	0.5 g

Griddlecakes

Griddlecakes or griddle breads, such as **pancakes** and **waffles**, are actually a type of quick bread. They are usually leavened with baking soda or baking powder and are quickly cooked on a very hot griddle or waffle iron with very little fat. They are described in detail in Chapter 32, Breakfast and Brunch.

TABLE 27.1   TROUBLESHOOTING CHART FOR QUICK BREADS

Problem	Cause	Solution
Soapy or bitter taste	Chemical leaveners not properly mixed into batter	Sift chemicals with dry ingredients
	Too much baking soda	Adjust formula
Elongated holes (tunnelling)	Overmixing	Do not mix until smooth; mix only until moistened
Crust too thick	Too much sugar	Adjust formula
	Oven temperature too low	Adjust oven
Flat top with only a small peak in centre	Oven temperature too low	Adjust oven
Cracked, uneven top	Oven temperature too high	Adjust oven
No rise; dense product	Old batter	Bake promptly
	Damaged leavening agents	Store new chemicals properly
	Overmixing	Do not overmix

CONCLUSION

First you must master the three mixing methods used in producing quick breads (muffin, biscuit and creaming) and understand the interaction between chemical leaveners and other ingredients. Then, with an imaginative use of flavouring ingredients, you can successfully produce a wide array of fresh-baked breads for almost any food service operation. Table 27.1 provides some troubleshooting guidelines should you encounter difficulties.

QUESTIONS FOR DISCUSSION

1. Name two chemical leavening agents and explain how they cause batters and doughs to rise.
2. List three common methods used for mixing quick breads. What is the significance of the type of fat used for each of these mixing methods?
3. What is the most likely explanation for discoloured and bitter-tasting biscuits? What is the solution?
4. Describe the resulting product when muffin batter has been overmixed.

Additional Quick Bread Formulas

RECIPE 27.7

Buttermilk Apple Cake (gluten free)

VALLEY NUTRITION AND FOOD SERVICES, MIDDLETON, NS
Chef/Registered Dietitian Howard Selig, RDT

Howard Selig, RDT
Howard lives in Nova Scotia's bountiful Annapolis Valley, where he provides contract management services for tourism hospitality and continuing care. He worked as a professional cook, chef and kitchen manager for 15 years before undertaking the study of nutrition. Through his company, Valley Nutrition & Food Services (www.flaxflour.com), he explores the functional and therapeutic uses of flaxflour, which he mills from Manitoba flax seeds for wholesale and retail markets.

Yield: 12 Servings **Method:** Biscuit

Brown sugar	85 g	3 oz.
Buttermilk	500 mL	16 fl. oz.
Brown rice flour	150 g	1 cup
Flax flour	125 g	1 cup
Baking powder	3.5 g	1 tsp.
Baking soda	3.5 g	1 tsp.
Cinnamon	3 g	2 tsp.
Salt	2 g	1/2 tsp.
Apples, medium, cored, chopped fine	2	2

1. Lightly grease and flour a 2 L (2 qt.) Bundt pan or 20-cm (8-inch) square baking pan.

2. Beat sugar and buttermilk together.

3. Combine dry ingredients. Add, with apples, to wet ingredients. Mix to just combine.

4. Spread batter evenly in pan.

5. Bake in a 180°C (350°F) oven for 40–45 minutes. Cool in pan before removing.

RECIPE 27.7

Approximate values per serving:

Calories	156
Total fat	4 g
Saturated fat	1 g
Cholesterol	2 mg
Sodium	222 mg
Total carbohydrates	26 g
Protein	4 g

RECIPE 27.8

Basic Berry Muffins

STOUFFER STANFORD COURT HOTEL, SAN FRANCISCO, CA
Former Executive Chef Ercolino Crugnale

Yield: 60 Muffins **Method:** Muffin

Eggs	8	8
Cream, 35%	1 L	1 qt.
Lemon zest, finely grated	20 g	from 2 lemons
Nutmeg	0.5 g	1/4 tsp.
Granulated sugar	600 g	1 lb. 4 oz.
Baking powder	60 g	6 Tbsp.
Cake flour	1.4 kg	3 lb.
Kosher salt	15 g	1 Tbsp.
Berries or nuts	1–1.5 L	1–1-1/2 qt.
Unsalted butter, melted	500 g	1 lb.

1. Whip the eggs, cream and zest together.

2. Sift the dry ingredients together. Add the berries or nuts, tossing to coat them evenly with the flour mixture.

Continued

RECIPE 27.8

Approximate values per muffin:

Calories	254
Total fat	13.5 g
Saturated fat	8 g
Cholesterol	67 mg
Sodium	187 mg
Total carbohydrates	31 g
Protein	3 g

3. Add the dry ingredients to the egg mixture and stir until about two-thirds mixed. Add the melted butter and finish mixing.

4. Portion into greased muffin tins and bake at 190°C (375°F) for approximately 15–18 minutes.

VARIATIONS: Blueberries, blackberries, raspberries, chopped pecans or walnuts may be used, as desired.

◆◆◆

RECIPE 27.9

MORNING GLORY MUFFINS

Yield: 18 Muffins   **Method:** Muffin

All-purpose flour	500 g	1 lb.
Granulated sugar	550 g	18 oz.
Baking soda	15 g	4 tsp.
Cinnamon	10 g	4 tsp.
Carrots, grated	425 g	14 oz.
Raisins	200 g	6 oz.
Pecan pieces	100 g	4 oz.
Coconut, shredded	125 g	4 oz.
Apple, unpeeled, grated	200 g	6 oz.
Eggs	6	6
Canola oil	350 mL	12 fl. oz.
Vanilla extract	20 mL	4 tsp.

1. Sift the dry ingredients together and set aside.
2. Combine the carrots, raisins, pecans, coconut and apple.
3. Combine the eggs, oil and vanilla.
4. Toss the carrot mixture in the dry ingredients. Add the liquid ingredients, stirring just until combined.
5. Bake in well-greased muffin tins at 170°C (350°F) until done, approximately 25 minutes.

RECIPE 27.9

Approximate values per muffin:

Calories	527
Total fat	26 g
Saturated fat	4 g
Cholesterol	72 mg
Sodium	278 mg
Total carbohydrates	70 g
Protein	6 g

◆◆◆

RECIPE 27.10

BRAN MUFFINS

Yield: 4.5 Dozen   **Method:** Muffin

Bran	250 g	9 oz.
Buttermilk	1 L	1 qt.
Brown sugar	250 g	9 oz.
White sugar	225 g	8 oz.
Canola oil	350 mL	12 fl. oz.
Vanilla	8 mL	1-1/2 tsp.
Eggs	6	6
All-purpose flour	600 g	20 oz.
Baking soda	15 g	1/2 oz.
Raisins	250 g	9 oz.

RECIPE 27.10

Approximate values per muffin:

Calories	162
Total fat	7 g
Saturated fat	1 g
Cholesterol	24 mg
Sodium	130 mg
Total carbohydrates	25 g
Protein	3 g

1. In a bowl, soak bran in buttermilk; may be refrigerated overnight.
2. Combine sugars, oil, vanilla and eggs. Beat well.
3. Stir in sifted flour and baking soda.
4. Stir in bran/buttermilk mixture and mix until combined.
5. Fold in raisins.
6. Scoop into greased or paper-lined muffin tins. Bake at 170°C (350°F) until lightly browned and firm in centre, approximately 20 minutes.

RECIPE 27.11

ZUCCHINI BREAD

Yield: 2 24-cm × 12-cm (9-inch × 5-inch) Loaves   **Method:** Muffin

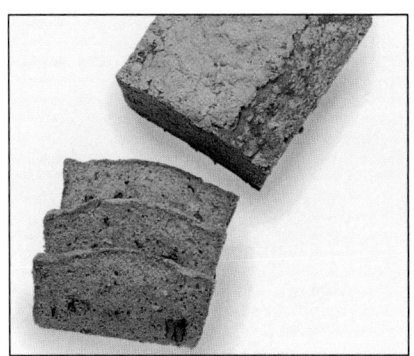

Whole eggs	3	3
Canola oil	250 mL	8 fl. oz.
Sugar	500 g	1 lb. 2 oz.
Vanilla	5 mL	1 tsp.
Cinnamon	5 g	2 tsp.
Salt	5 g	1 tsp.
Baking soda	3.5 g	1 tsp.
Baking powder	1 g	1/2 tsp.
All-purpose flour	450 g	14 oz.
Zucchini, coarsely grated	350 g	11 oz.
Pecans, chopped	125 g	4 oz.

1. Combine all ingredients using the muffin method.
2. Bake in two greased loaf pans at 170°C (350°F), approximately 1 hour.

RECIPE 27.11

Approximate values per slice:

Calories	280
Total fat	14 g
Saturated fat	1 g
Cholesterol	27 mg
Sodium	133 mg
Total carbohydrates	36 g
Protein	3 g

RECIPE 27.12

IRISH SODA BREAD

Yield: 1 20-cm-round (8-inch) Loaf   **Method:** Muffin

Currants	60 g	2 oz.
Irish whisky	45 mL	1-1/2 fl. oz.
All-purpose flour, sifted	360 g	12 oz.
Salt	5 g	1 tsp.
Baking powder	5.25 g	1-1/2 tsp.
Baking soda	3.5 g	1 tsp.
Brown sugar	15 g	1 Tbsp.
Buttermilk	500 mL	16 fl. oz.

1. Soak the currants in the whisky until plump, at least 1 hour.
2. Sift the dry ingredients together. Stir in the currants and whisky.
3. Stir in the buttermilk, making a stiff batter.
4. Spread the batter in a greased 20-cm-round (8-inch) cake pan. Bake at 170°C (350°F) until well browned and firm, approximately 45 minutes.

RECIPE 27.12

Approximate values per slice:

Calories	143
Total fat	1 g
Saturated fat	0 g
Cholesterol	1.5 mg
Sodium	320 mg
Total carbohydrates	27 g
Protein	5 g

◆ ◆ ◆

RECIPE 27.13

CORN MUFFINS

Yield: 2 Dozen   **Method:** Creaming

Butter	125 g	4 oz.
Sugar	50 g	2 oz.
Eggs	2	2
Salt	2 g	1/2 tsp.
Cake flour	350 g	12 oz.
Baking powder	20 g	2 Tbsp.
Cornmeal, coarse	400 g	14 oz.
Milk (approx.)	450 mL	16 fl. oz.
Green pepper, fine dice	120 g	4 oz.
Red pepper, fine dice	120 g	4 oz.
Jalapeño, seeded, fine dice	1	1
Carrot, grated	120 g	4 oz.
Corn, fresh kernels	2 ears	2 ears
Sharp cheddar cheese, grated	50 g	2 oz.

1. Cream butter and sugar; beat in eggs.
2. Combine dry ingredients. Add alternately with milk to make a stiff batter.
3. Toss vegetables and cheese together and fold into batter.
4. Portion into greased muffin tins or divide between two greased springform pans.
5. Bake for 30–35 minutes at 190°C (375°F). The springform pans will take 45 minutes, or until firm and lightly browned.

RECIPE 27.13

Approximate values per muffin:

Calories	201
Total fat	6.5 g
Saturated fat	4 g
Cholesterol	34 mg
Sodium	179 mg
Total carbohydrates	31 g
Protein	5 g

◆ ◆ ◆

RECIPE 27.14

BANANA BREAD

Yield: 4 Loaves   **Method:** Creaming

Bananas, ripe	1.5 kg	3 lb. 8 oz.
Baking soda	50 g	2 oz.
Cake flour	500 g	1 lb. 4 oz.
Bread flour	500 g	1 lb. 4 oz.
Butter	380 g	13 oz.
Brown sugar	850 g	2 lb.
Whole egg	400 g	15 oz.
Dates, chopped	125 g	4 oz.

1. Purée banana and reserve.
2. Combine soda and flours (sifted).
3. Using the paddle, beat butter and sugar on #2 speed until light in colour. Scrape down sides of bowl.
4. Add egg, beat and scrape down sides of bowl.
5. Combine half the flour mixture with the dates and stir into creamed mixture.
6. Add banana and mix thoroughly on #1 speed.
7. Add remaining flour and mix thoroughly, scraping down sides of bowl.
8. Oil four loaf pans and line bottoms with parchment paper.
9. Divide batter among the pans and level it.
10. Bake at 190°C (375°F) for 65–70 minutes or until done (knife comes out clean).

RECIPE 27.14

Approximate values per slice:

Calories	242
Total fat	8 g
Saturated fat	4.5 g
Cholesterol	53 mg
Sodium	367 mg
Total carbohydrates	42 g
Protein	4 g

RECIPE 27.15

Biscotti

Yield: 2-1/2 Dozen

Butter	125 g	4 oz.
Sugar	175 g	6 oz.
Salt	5 g	1 tsp.
Eggs	2	2
Orange zest, grated	5 g	2 tsp.
Orange oil	1 g	5 drops
Pastry flour	300 g	10 oz.
Baking powder	5 g	1-1/2 tsp.
Pistachios, skinned	100 g	3-1/2 oz.
Egg wash	as needed	as needed

1. Cream butter, sugar and salt until light.

2. Beat in eggs until smooth with orange zest and oil.

3. Sift together flour and baking powder and stir into creamed mixture on low speed. When combined, mix on high speed for 5–8 seconds.

4. Fold in pistachios.

5. Form into two logs about 5 cm (2 inches) in diameter. Place on parchment-lined sheet pans. The dough may be a bit sticky. Brush with egg wash.

6. Bake at 160°C (325°F) for about 35 minutes or until lightly browned.

7. Remove from oven and cool slightly.

8. Cut into 5-mm (1/2-inch) bars on the diagonal and lay them flat on pan.

9. Bake again at 135°C (275°F) until lightly toasted, approximately 30 minutes.

VARIATIONS: Substitute almonds and lemon zest for pistachio and orange. Try 5 g (1-1/2 tsp.) espresso (instant) dissolved in 15 mL (1 Tbsp.) coffee and chocolate chips.

RECIPE 27.15

Approximate values per serving (1 biscotti):

Calories	113
Total fat	5.4 g
Saturated fat	2.4 g
Cholesterol	23 mg
Sodium	111 mg
Total carbohydrates	14 g
Protein	2 g

 EBLINKS

Science of Foods, Oregon State University: Quickbreads
www.orst.edu/instruct/nfm236/quickbread/index.html
Tortilla Industry Association: Consumer Information
www.tortilla-info.com/consumer.htm
Flat Breads—A Taste of Ancient Civilizations
www.efn.org/~sundance/FlatBreads.html
Ask the BreadLady™
members.aol.com/BreadLady1/AskBreadLady.html

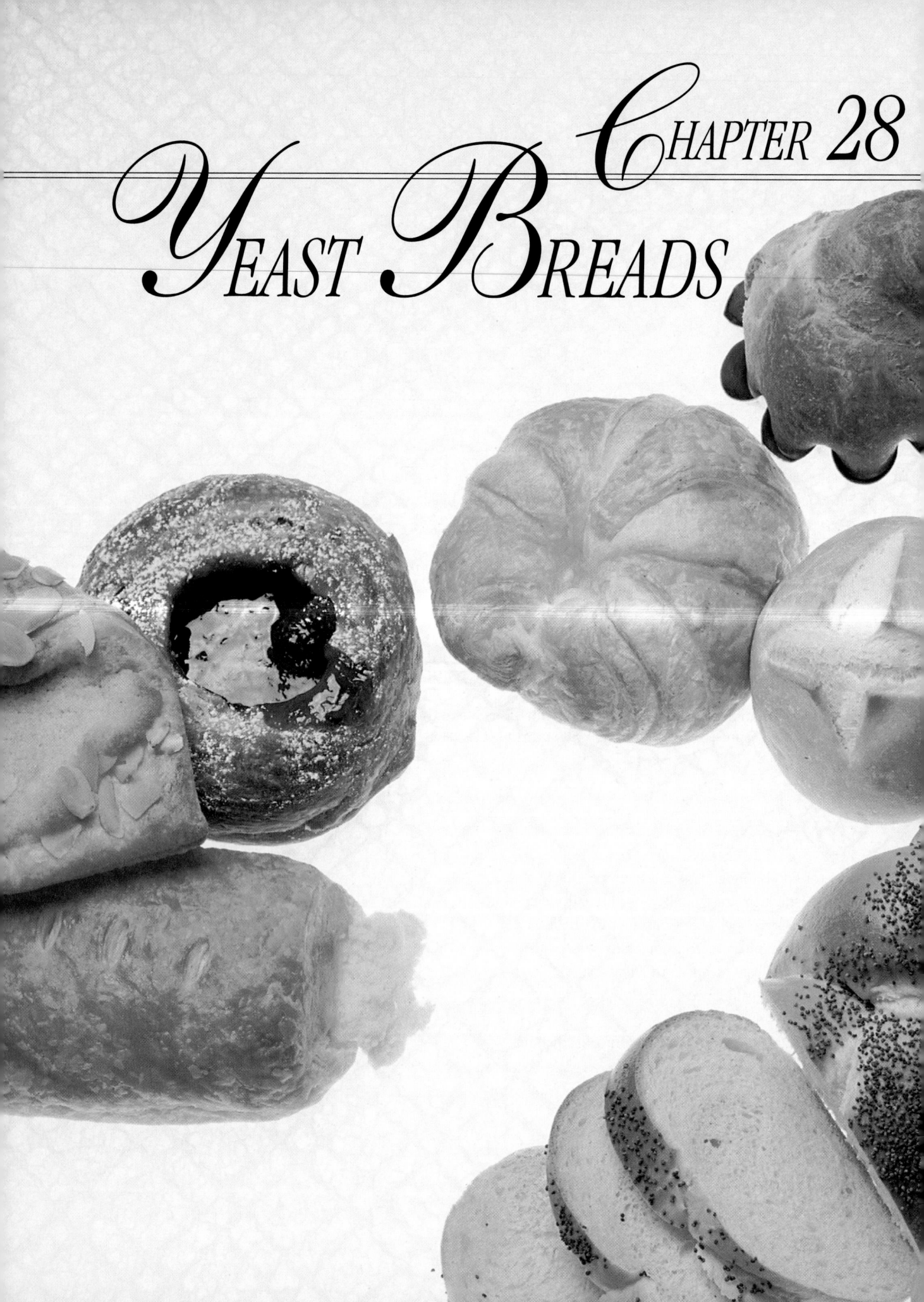

CHAPTER 28
YEAST BREADS

━━━━ ✦✦✦ ━━━━

LEARNING OUTCOMES

After studying this chapter you will be able to:

◆ select and use yeast
◆ perform the 10 steps involved in yeast bread production, including kneading by hand
◆ mix yeast doughs using the straight dough method and sponge method
◆ prepare rolled-in doughs

━━━━━━━━━━━━

*A*lthough few baked goods intimidate novice bakers as much as yeast breads, few baked goods are actually as forgiving or as comforting to prepare as yeast breads. By mastering a few basic procedures and techniques, you can offer your customers delicious, fresh yeast products.

Yeast breads can be divided into two categories: lean doughs and rich doughs. Lean doughs, such as those used for French and Italian breads, contain little or no sugar or fat. Rich doughs, such as brioche and some multigrain breads, contain significantly more sugar and fat. Rolled-in doughs, so-called because the fat is rolled into the dough in layers, are a type of rich dough used for baked goods such as croissants and sweetened danish.

The study of yeast breads could well occupy this entire text and an entire course. The focus here is narrowed to an understanding of fundamental techniques and procedures for making the most common styles of yeast breads for a small retail shop or restaurant. Some of the formulas in this chapter yield only one or two loaves or a few dozen rolls. Although most of these formulas can be increased successfully if necessary, you can best develop proper judgement skills by first preparing small quantities. We discuss hands-on mixing and makeup techniques and also include commercial (i.e., mechanical) bread production.

YEAST

Yeast is a living organism: a one-celled fungus. Various strains of yeast are present virtually everywhere. Yeast feeds on carbohydrates, converting them to carbon dioxide and alcohol in an organic process known as **fermentation**:

Yeast + Carbohydrates = Alcohol + Carbon Dioxide

When yeast produces carbon dioxide gas during bread making, the gas becomes trapped in the dough's gluten network. The trapped gas leavens the bread, providing the desired rise and texture. The small amount of alcohol produced by fermentation evaporates during baking.

As with most living things, yeast is very sensitive to temperature. It prefers temperatures between 21°C and 54°C (70°F and 130°F) depending on the type of yeast. The range used in most bakeries is 32°C to 43°C (90°F to 110°F). At temperatures below 2°C (34°F) it becomes dormant; above 59°C (138°F) it dies. (See Table 28.1.)

Salt is used in bread making because it conditions gluten, making it stronger and more elastic. Salt also affects yeast fermentation. Because salt inhibits the growth of yeast, it helps control the dough's rise. Too little salt and not only will the bread taste bland, but it will also rise too rapidly. Too much salt, however, and the yeast will be destroyed. By learning to control the amount of food for the yeast and the temperatures of fermentation, you can learn to control the texture of your yeast-leavened products.

TABLE 28.1   TEMPERATURES FOR YEAST DEVELOPMENT

Temperature		Yeast Development
2°C	34°F	Inactive
16–21°C	60–70°F	Slow action
21–32°C	70–90°F	Best temperature for growth of fresh yeast
41–46°C	105–115°F	Best temperature for growth of dry yeast
52–54°C	125–130°F	Best temperature for activating instant yeast
59°C	138°F	Yeast dies

The addition of fats or shortenings to a dough will tenderize, moisturize and increase volume, but it will slow down fermentation.

Types of Yeast

Baker's yeast is available in two forms: compressed and active dry. (You may also encounter a product called brewer's yeast; it is a nutritional supplement with no leavening ability.)

Compressed Yeast

Compressed yeast is a mixture of yeast and starch with a moisture content of approximately 70%. Also referred to as **fresh yeast**, compressed yeast must be kept refrigerated. It should be creamy white and crumbly with a fresh, yeasty smell. Do not use compressed yeast that has developed a sour odour, brown colour or slimy film.

Compressed yeast is available in 17-g (0.6-oz.) cubes and 450-g (1-lb.) blocks. Under proper storage conditions, compressed yeast has a shelf life of two to three weeks.

Active Dry Yeast

Active dry yeast differs from compressed yeast in that virtually all of the moisture has been removed by hot air. The absence of moisture renders the organism dormant and allows the yeast to be stored without refrigeration for several months. When preparing doughs, dry yeast is generally rehydrated in a lukewarm (approximately 43°C [110°F]) liquid before being added to the other ingredients.

Dry yeast is available in 7-g (1/4-oz.) packages and 450-g or 1-kg (1- or 2-lb.) vacuum-sealed bags. It should be stored in a cool, dry place and refrigerated after opening.

Instant Yeast

Instant or **quick-rise dry yeast** is also available. It must be blended with the dry ingredients in a bread formula, then activated with hot (approximately 52–54°C [125–130°F]) water. It dramatically speeds the rising process. Instant yeast can be substituted measure for measure for regular dry yeast. Instant yeast is still a living organism and will be destroyed at temperatures above 59°C (138°F).

The flavours of dry and compressed yeasts are virtually indistinguishable, but dry yeast is approximately twice as strong. Because too much yeast can ruin bread, always remember to reduce the specified weight of dry yeast when substituting for compressed yeast in a formula. Likewise, if a formula specifies dry yeast, increase the amount when substituting compressed yeast. In this text, all of the formulas requiring yeast use regular active dry yeast. Generally, 40% dry yeast is used to replace 100% fresh yeast.

Sourdough Starter

Prior to commercial yeast production, bakers relied on starters to leaven their breads. Early starters were simple but magical mixtures of flour and liquid (water, potato broth, milk) left to capture wild yeasts from the air and then ferment. Only a portion of the starter was used at a time. The rest was kept for later use, replenished periodically with additional flour and liquid so the magic could continue.

Today, starters are generally fortified with yeast to provide consistency and reliability; they are prized for the unique, sour flavours they impart. Prepared dry cultures are often used commercially to give bread a "sourdough" flavour without requiring the time and space necessary to develop and maintain an active starter.

Sourdough Starter

RECIPE 28.1	
Approximate values per 225 mL serving:	
Calories	801
Total fat	4 g
Saturated fat	0.5 g
Cholesterol	0 mg
Sodium	5 mg
Total carbohydrates	170 g
Protein	35 g

Applying the Basics

RECIPE 28.1

SOURDOUGH STARTER (FOR WHITE BREADS)

Yield: 1 L (1 qt.)

Active dry yeast	5 g	1 tsp.
Water, warm	120 g	4 oz.
Water, room temperature	400 g	14 oz.
Bread flour	1 kg	2 lb. 3 oz.

1. Combine the yeast and warm water. Let stand until foamy, approximately 10 minutes.
2. Stir in the room-temperature water, then add the flour, 100 g (3 oz.) at a time.
3. Blend by hand or with the paddle attachment of an electric mixer on low speed for 2 minutes.
4. Place the starter in a warmed bowl and cover with plastic wrap. Let stand at room temperature overnight. The starter should triple in volume but still be wet and sticky. Refrigerate until ready to use.
5. Each time a portion of the starter is used, it must be replenished. To replenish the starter, stir in equal amounts by volume of flour and warm water. Then allow the mixture to ferment at room temperature for several hours or overnight before refrigerating.

NOTE: If liquid rises to the top of the starter it should be stirred back into the mixture. If the starter develops a pink or yellow film it has been contaminated and must be discarded.

Production Stages for Yeast Breads

The production of yeast breads can be divided into 10 stages:

1. scaling the ingredients
2. mixing and kneading the dough
3. fermenting the dough
4. punching down the dough
5. portioning the dough
6. rounding the portions
7. shaping the portions
8. proofing the products
9. baking the products
10. cooling and storing the finished products

Stage 1: Scaling the Ingredients

As with any other bakeshop product, it is important to scale or measure ingredients accurately when making a yeast bread. Be sure that all necessary ingredients are available and at the proper temperature before starting.

The amount of flour required in a yeast bread may vary depending upon the humidity level, storage conditions of the flour and the accuracy with which other ingredients are measured. The amount of flour stated in most formulas is to be used as a guide; experience teaches when more or less flour is actually needed. The moisture content of the flour is an important consideration.

Stage 2: Mixing and Kneading the Dough

The way ingredients are combined affects the outcome of the bread. A dough must be mixed properly in order to combine the ingredients uniformly,

---

◆◆◆
THE RISE OF YEAST BREADS

How and when the first yeast-leavened bread came into being no one knows. Perhaps some wild yeasts—the world is full of them—drifted into a dough as it awaited baking. Perhaps some ancient baker substituted fermented ale or beer for water one day. In any case, the resulting bread was different, lighter and more appetizing.

Based on models, images and writings found in excavated tombs, we can be fairly certain that the ancient Egyptians saved a bit of fermented dough from one day's baking to add to the next day's. This use of sourdough starter continues today, enjoying widespread popularity.

Other cultures developed their own leavening methods. The Greeks and Romans prepared a wheat porridge with wine, which caused their doughs to ferment. The Gauls and Iberians added the foamy head from ale to their doughs. Both methods resulted in lighter breads that retained their fresh textures longer.

Since ancient times, bread baking has been one of the first household tasks readily turned over to professionals. The first cooks to work outside homes during the Greek and Roman empires were bakers. The bakery trade flourished during the Middle Ages, with a wide variety of breads being produced. Yeast-leavened breads remained the exception, not the norm, until well into the 17th century, however.

The first real collection of bread recipes is found in Nicolas Bonnefon's *Les Délices de la campagne*, published in 1654. Bonnefon's instructions, meant for those dissatisfied with commercial products of the time, included the use of beer yeast. By the end of the 17th century, published works included recipes for breads leavened with sourdough starter and the yeasts used in breweries.

Louis Pasteur finally identified yeast as a living organism in 1857. Soon after, a process for distilling or manufacturing baker's yeast was developed. By 1868, commercial baking yeast was available in stores.

distribute the yeast and develop the gluten. If the dough is not mixed properly, the bread's texture and shape suffer.

Yeast breads are usually mixed by either the **straight dough method** or the **sponge method**. A third method used for rich, flaky doughs is discussed later in the section on **rolled-in doughs**.

Once ingredients are combined, the dough must be kneaded to develop gluten, the network of proteins that gives a bread its shape and texture. Kneading can be done by hand or by an electric mixer with its dough hook attachment. Dough should be kneaded until it is smooth and moderately elastic. The presence of a few blisterlike air bubbles on the dough's surface also signals that kneading is complete. Because fat and sugar slow gluten development, rich, sweet doughs are generally kneaded longer than lean doughs. Overkneading results in dough that is, at best, difficult to shape and, in extreme cases, sticky and inelastic. Overkneading is rarely a problem, however, except when using a high-speed mixer or food processor.

Basic Procedure for Kneading Dough by Hand

1. First, bring a portion of the dough towards you.

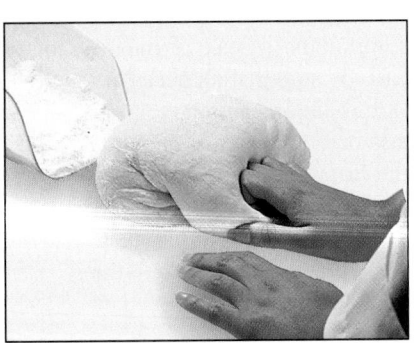

2. Then push the dough away from you with your fist.

3. Repeat until the dough is properly kneaded.

Straight Dough Method

The simplest and most common method for mixing yeast doughs is known as the straight dough method. With this method, all ingredients are simply combined and mixed. The yeast may or may not be combined first with a warm liquid. Be careful that the temperature of the liquid ingredients does not exceed 59°C (138°F) or the yeast will die.

Once the ingredients are combined, the dough is kneaded until it is smooth and elastic. Kneading time varies according to the kneading method used and the type of dough being produced. The straight dough method is illustrated with Recipe 28.2, Soft Yeast Dinner Rolls (see page 786).

Sponge Method

The sponge method of mixing yeast doughs has two stages. During the first stage the yeast, liquid and approximately one-half of the flour are combined to make a thick batter known as a **sponge**. The sponge is allowed to rise until bubbly and doubled in size. During the second stage the fat, salt, sugar and remaining flour are added. The dough is kneaded and allowed to rise again. These two fermentations give sponge method breads a somewhat different flavour and a lighter texture than breads made with the straight dough method.

Do not confuse sponge method breads with sourdough starters. The sponge method is most often used to improve the texture of heavy doughs such as rye. Unlike a sourdough starter, the first-stage sponge is prepared only for the specific formula and is not reserved for later use. The sponge method is illustrated with Recipe 28.3, Medium Sour Rye Bread (see page 788).

Stage 3: Fermenting the Dough

As mentioned earlier, fermentation is the process by which yeast converts sugar into alcohol and carbon dioxide. Fermentation also refers to the time that yeast dough is left to rise—that is, the time it takes for carbon dioxide gas to form and become trapped in the gluten network. Note that **fermentation** refers to the rise given to the entire mass of yeast dough, while **proofing** refers to the rise given to shaped yeast products just prior to baking.

For fermentation, place the kneaded dough into a lightly oiled container large enough to allow the dough to expand. The surface of the dough may be lightly oiled to prevent drying. Cover the dough and place it in a warm place—that is, at temperatures between 24°C and 29°C (75°F and 85°F). It is better to allow the dough to rise slowly in a cool place than to rush fermentation.

Fermentation is complete when the dough has approximately doubled in size and no longer springs back when pressed gently with two fingers. The time necessary varies depending on the type of dough, the temperature of the room and the temperature of the dough.

Stage 4: Punching Down the Dough

After fermentation, the dough is gently folded down to expel excessive gas pockets with a technique known as **punching down**. Punching down dough also helps even out the dough's temperature.

Stage 5: Portioning the Dough

The dough is now ready to be divided into portions. For loaves, the dough is scaled to the desired weight. For individual rolls you can first shape the dough into an even log, then cut off portions with a chef's knife or dough cutter. Weighing the cut dough pieces on a portion scale ensures even-sized portions. When portioning, work quickly and keep the dough covered to prevent it from drying out.

Stage 6: Rounding the Portions

The portions of dough must be shaped into smooth, round balls in a technique known as **rounding**. Rounding stretches the outside layer of gluten into a smooth coating. This helps hold in gases and makes it easier to shape the dough. Unrounded rolls rise unevenly and have a rough, lumpy surface.

Stage 7: Shaping the Portions

Lean doughs and some rich doughs can be shaped into a variety of forms: large loaves, small loaves, free-form or country-style rounds or individual dinner rolls. Table 28.2 identifies common pan sizes and the approximate weight of the dough used to fill them. Some shaping or makeup techniques are shown in Figures 28.1 through 28.5. Other doughs, particularly brioche, croissant and danish, are usually shaped in very specific ways. Those techniques are discussed and illustrated with their specific formulas.

TABLE 28.2	PAN SIZES FOR YEAST BREADS	
Pan	Approximate Size	Weight of Dough*
Sandwich loaf	16 in. × 4 in. × 4-1/2 in.	1800 g (4 lb.)
Pullman	13 in. × 4 in. × 3 in.	1300 g (3 lb.)
Large	9 in. × 5 in. × 3 in.	900 g (2 lb.)
Medium	8 in. × 4 in. × 2 in.	680 g (1 lb. 8 oz.)
Small	7 in. × 3 in. × 2 in.	450 g (1 lb.)
Miniature	5 in. × 3 in. × 2 in.	225 g (8 oz.)

*Weights given are approximate; variations may occur based on the type of dough used as well as the temperature and time of proofing.

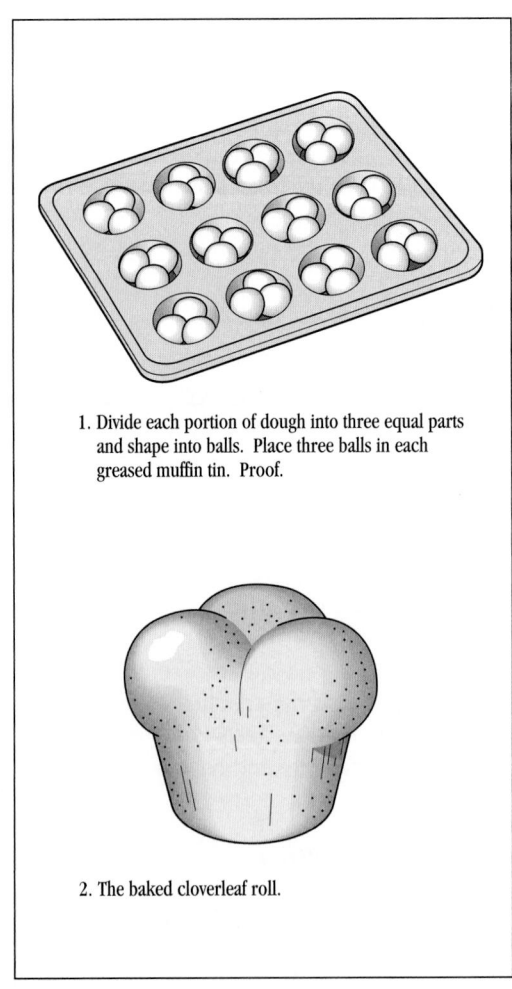

1. Divide each portion of dough into three equal parts and shape into balls. Place three balls in each greased muffin tin. Proof.

2. The baked cloverleaf roll.

FIGURE 28.1   *Cloverleaf Rolls*

1. Roll dough into a thin rectangle. Brush with melted butter and cut into 3.75-cm (1½-inch) wide strips.

2. Stack 6 or 7 strips together, then cut into slices.

3. Place each slice into a greased muffin tin, cut side up. Proof.

4. The baked butterflake roll.

FIGURE 28.2 *Butterflake Rolls*

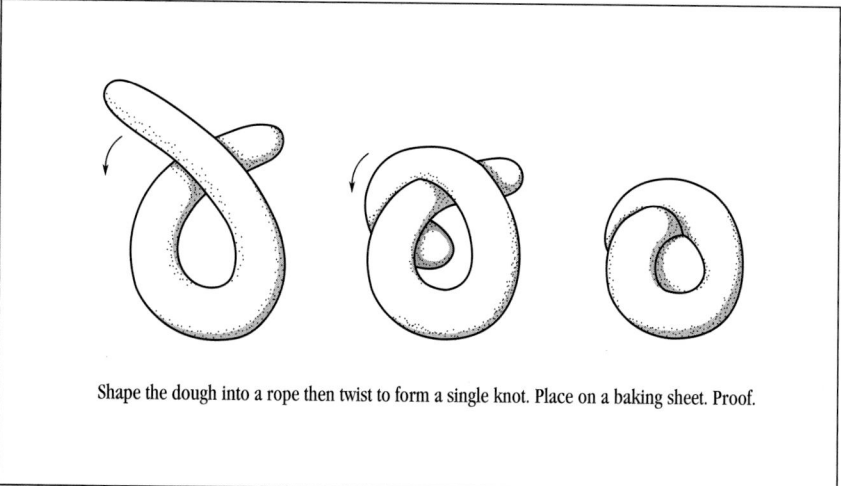

Shape the dough into a rope then twist to form a single knot. Place on a baking sheet. Proof.

FIGURE 28.3 *Bow Knot Rolls*

1. Flatten the dough into a rectangle. Fold over one short edge and press the seam together.

2. Continue to roll the dough, pressing the seam firmly with each turn. Stretch the front corners as necessary to maintain the shape.

3. Place the finished roll of dough in a greased pan, seam side down. Proof.

FIGURE 28.4   *Pan Loaves*

1. Roll the dough into a rectangle then roll up from the long side, jelly-roll fashion. Pinch the seam to seal.

2. Place loaf on a baking sheet, seam side down, and shape ends. Proof.

FIGURE 28.5   *Free-Form Loaves*

Stage 8: Proofing the Products

Proofing is the final rise of shaped or panned yeast products before baking. The temperatures should be between 35°C and 46°C (95°F and 115°F), slightly higher than the temperatures for fermentation. Some humidity is also desirable to prevent the dough from drying or forming a crust. Temperature and humidity can be controlled with a special cabinet known as a **proof box**.

Proofing should continue until the product doubles in size and springs back slowly when lightly touched. Underproofing results in poor volume and texture. Overproofing results in a sour taste, poor volume and a paler colour after baking.

Stage 9: Baking the Products

As yeast breads bake, a variety of chemical and physical changes turn the dough into an edible product. These changes are discussed in Chapter 26, Principles of the Bakeshop.

Because of the expansion of gases, yeast products experience a sudden rise when first placed in a hot oven. This rise is known as **oven spring**. As the dough's temperature increases, the yeast dies, the gluten fibres become firm, the starches gelatinize, the moisture evaporates and, finally, the crust forms and turns brown.

Before baking, products can be washed and then, if desired, slashed.

Washes

The appearance of yeast breads can be altered by applying a glaze or **wash** to the dough before baking. The crust is made shiny or matte, hard or soft, darker or lighter by the proper use of washes. (See Table 28.3.) Washes are also used to attach seeds, wheat germ, oats or other toppings to the dough's surface.

The most commonly used wash is an egg wash, composed of whole egg and water. Yeast products can also be topped with plain water, a mixture of egg and milk, plain milk or richer glazes containing sugar and flavourings. Even a light dusting of white flour can be used to top dough. (This is commonly seen with potato rolls.)

Avoid using too much wash, as it can burn or cause the product to stick to the pan. Puddles or streaks of egg wash on the dough will cause uneven browning.

Washes may be applied before or after proofing. If applied after proofing, be extremely careful not to deflate the product.

Occasionally a formula will specify that melted butter or oil be brushed on the product after baking. Do not, however, apply egg washes to already baked products, as the egg will remain raw and the desired effect will not be achieved.

Slashing

The shape and appearance of some breads can be improved by cutting their tops with a sharp knife or razor just before baking. This is referred to as **slashing**. Hard-crusted breads are usually slashed to allow for continued rising and the escape of gases after the crust has formed. Breads that are not properly slashed will burst or break along the sides. Slashing can also be used to make an attractive design on the product's surface.

Steam Injection

The crisp crust desired for certain breads and rolls is achieved by introducing moisture into the oven during baking. Professional bakers' ovens have built-in steam injection jets to provide moisture as needed. To create steam in any oven you can spray or mist the bread with water several times during baking, place ice cubes on the oven floor to melt or keep a pan of hot water on the oven's lowest rack. Rich doughs, which do not form crisp crusts, are baked without steam.

Determining Doneness

Baking time is determined by a variety of factors: the product's size, the oven thermostat's accuracy and the desired crust colour. Larger items require a

---

◆◆◆
ROPE INFECTION

Caused by the hay bacilli (*bacillus mesentericus*) that live in soil, the spores survive the baking process and germinate in the crumb structure of the product. The infection is not obvious for 12–24 hours. Rope causes the crumb to lose elasticity and become stringy and slimy. There will be an odour of fermenting fruit. Contaminated product is adulterated and cannot be sold. It must be incinerated completely. If consumed, vomiting and diarrhea can occur.

To prevent rope infection from occuring, wash equipment with quaternary ammonium or a vinegar solution. Do not store soil-grown vegetables in a bakery area. Cool baked products rapidly. Bake products thoroughly.

TABLE 28.3	WASHES FOR YEAST PRODUCTS
Wash	**Use**
Whole egg and water	Shine and colour
Whole egg and milk	Shine and colour with a soft crust
Egg white and water	Shine with a firm crust
Water	Crisp crust
Flour	Texture and contrast
Milk or cream	Colour with a soft crust

✦✦✦
FROZEN DOUGHS

There are many frozen dough products on the market today. They come shaped and partially or fully proofed. After flash or shock freezing they are packaged for distribution. The raw product is trayed, allowed to thaw and proof, then baked. Par-baked items are placed directly in a hot oven to finish baking.

longer baking time than smaller ones. Lean dough products bake faster and at higher temperatures than rich dough products.

Bread loaves can be tested for doneness by tapping them on the bottom and listening for a hollow sound. This indicates that air, not moisture, is present inside the loaf. If the bottom is damp or heavy, the loaf probably needs more baking time. The texture and colour of the crust are also a good indication of doneness, particularly with individual rolls. As you bake a variety of yeast products you will develop the experience necessary to determine doneness without strict adherence to elapsed time.

Stage 10: Cooling and Storing the Finished Products

The quality of even the finest yeast products suffers if they are cooled or stored improperly. Yeast products should be cooled at room temperature and away from drafts. Yeast breads and rolls should be removed from their pans for cooling. Allow loaves to cool completely before slicing.

Once cool, yeast products should be stored at room temperature or frozen for longer storage. Do not refrigerate baked goods, as refrigeration promotes staling. Do not wrap Italian or French loaves, as this causes crusts to lose the desired crispness.

Applying the Basics

RECIPE 28.2

SOFT YEAST DINNER ROLLS

Yield: 75 Rolls   **Method:** Straight Dough

Ingredient	Metric	Imperial
Water, warm	600 g	1 lb. 4 oz.
Active dry yeast	60 g	2 oz.
Bread flour	1.2 kg	2 lb. 10 oz.
Salt	30 g	1 oz.
Sugar	120 g	4 oz.
Dried milk powder	60 g	2 oz.
Shortening	60 g	2 oz.
Unsalted butter, softened	60 g	2 oz.
Eggs, whole	120 g	4 oz.
Egg wash	as needed	as needed

1. Combine the water and yeast in a small bowl. Combine the remaining ingredients (except the egg wash) in the bowl of an electric mixer.
2. Add the water-and-yeast mixture to the remaining ingredients; stir to combine.
3. Knead with a dough hook on second speed for 10 minutes.
4. Transfer the dough to a lightly greased bowl, cover and place in a warm spot. Let rise until doubled, approximately 1 hour.
5. Punch down the dough. Let it rest a few minutes to allow the gluten to relax.
6. Divide the dough into 35-g (1-1/4-oz.) portions and round. Shape as desired and arrange on paper-lined sheet pans. Proof until doubled in size.
7. Carefully brush the proofed rolls with egg wash. Bake at 200°C (400°F) until medium brown, approximately 12–15 minutes.

RECIPE 28.2

Approximate values per roll:

Calories	78
Total fat	2 g
Saturated fat	1 g
Cholesterol	9 mg
Sodium	161 mg
Total carbohydrates	13 g
Protein	3 g

1. Mix the soft yeast dough:

    a) Combine the ingredients in a mixer bowl with the dough hook attached.

b) Add the yeast-and-water mixture.

2. Knead the dough.

3. The dough before rising.

4. Punch down the dough:

    a) Press down on the centre of the dough with your fist.

b) Fold the edges of the dough in towards the centre.

5. Scale the dough.

6. Round the rolls.

7. Egg-wash the rolls.

Applying the Basics

MEDIUM SOUR RYE BREAD

Yield: 4.3 kg (9 lb.) (6 Loaves)

Dark rye flour	600 g	1 lb. 8 oz.
Light rye flour	600 g	1 lb. 8 oz.
Bread flour	1.25 kg	2 lb. 12 oz.
Salt	50 g	1-3/4 oz.
Dehydrated sour*	40 g	1-1/4 oz.
Yeast, fresh	75 g	2-1/2 oz.
Water, 21°C (70°F)	1.7 kg	3 lb. 6 oz.

1. Blend the first five ingredients with a hook in mixing bowl for 1 minute on low speed.
2. Dissolve yeast in water and add to the flour.
3. Mix for 2 minutes on low speed and 5 minutes on second speed.
4. Bench for 30 minutes (benching refers to the time the dough rests in its first proofing stage at room temperature).
5. Divide dough into 700 g (1 lb. 8 oz.) rounds and rest 15 minutes.
6. Bake at 220°C (430°F) for 10–15 minutes then turn oven down to 180°C (390°F) to finish baking, approximately 30 minutes.

*Prepared dry culture (see page 78).

RECIPE 28.3

Approximate values per slice:

Calories	70
Total fat	0 g
Saturated fat	0 g
Cholesterol	0 mg
Sodium	165 mg
Total carbohydrates	15 g
Protein	3 g

1. Rye bread starter.

2. Mix the rye dough.

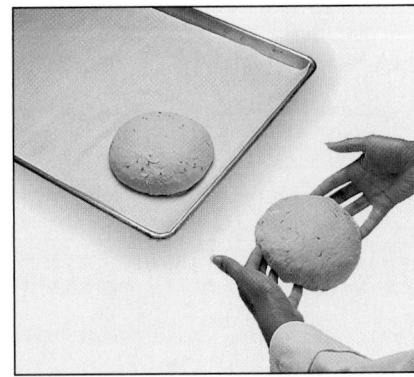

3. Shape the rye loaves.

ROLLED-IN DOUGHS

Baked goods made with rolled-in doughs include croissants, danish pastries and the non-yeast-leavened puff pastry. (Puff pastry is discussed in Chapter 29, Pies, Pastries and Cookies.) The dough is so named because the fat is incorporated through a process of rolling and folding. Products made with a rolled-in dough have a distinctive flaky texture created by the repeated layering of fat and dough. As the dough bakes, moisture is released from the fat in the form of steam. The steam is then trapped between the layers of dough, causing them to rise and separate.

Making Rolled-In Doughs

Rolled-in doughs are made following most of the 10 production stages discussed earlier. The principal differences are (1) the butter is incorporated through a folding process after the dough base is fermented and punched down; (2) rolled-in doughs are portioned somewhat differently than other yeast doughs; and (3) the portions are then shaped without rounding.

Butter is often used for rolled-in products because of its flavour. Unfortunately, butter is hard to work with because it cracks and breaks when cold and becomes too soft to roll at room temperature. Margarine, shortening or specially formulated high-moisture fats can be used, sometimes in combination with butter, in order to reduce costs or to make it easier to work with the dough.

The dough base should not be kneaded too much as gluten will continue to develop during the rolling and folding process. Commercial bakeries, hotels and larger restaurants generally use an electric dough sheeter to roll the dough. This saves time and ensures a more consistent product.

Basic Procedure for Preparing Rolled-In Doughs

1. Mix the dough and allow it to rise.
2. Shape the butter or shortening, then chill it.
3. Roll out the dough evenly, then top with the chilled butter.
4. Fold the dough around the butter, enclosing it completely.
5. Roll out the dough into a rectangle, about 0.6 to 1.25 cm (1/4 to 1/2 inch) thick. Always be sure to roll at right angles; do not roll haphazardly or in a circle as you would pastry doughs.
6. Fold the dough in thirds. Be sure to brush off any excess flour from between the folds. This completes the first turn. Chill the dough for 20 to 30 minutes.
7. Roll out the dough and fold it in the same manner a second and third time, allowing the dough to rest between each turn. After completing the third turn, wrap the dough carefully and allow it to rest for several hours or overnight before shaping and baking.

Applying the Basics

RECIPE 28.4

CROISSANTS

Yield: 60 Rolls   **Method:** Rolled-In

Bread flour	1 kg	2 lb. 3 oz.
Salt	30 g	1 oz.
Sugar	60 g	2 oz.
Milk	650 g	1 lb. 6 oz.
Active dry yeast	30 g	1 oz.
Unsalted butter, soft	720 g	1 lb. 8 oz.
Egg wash	as needed	as needed

1. Stir the flour, salt and sugar together in a mixer bowl fitted with a dough hook.
2. Warm the milk to approximately 32°C (90°F). Stir in the yeast.
3. Add the milk-and-yeast mixture to the dry ingredients. Stir until combined, then knead on second speed for 10 minutes.

Continued

◆◆◆
THE CULTURED CROISSANT

A croissant brings to mind a Parisian sidewalk café and a steaming cup of café au lait. It is, however, a truly international delicacy. Created by bakers in Budapest (Hungary) to celebrate the city's liberation from Turkey in 1686, its shape was derived from the crescent moon of the Turkish flag. The delicacy was soon adopted as a breakfast pastry by both the French and the Italians. The first machine for mass-producing croissants was designed by a Japanese firm and manufactured in Italy. Although croissants became popular in North America only during the last generation or so, millions of croissants are now consumed each year.

RECIPE 28.4

Approximate values per croissant:

Calories	151
Total fat	10 g
Saturated fat	6 g
Cholesterol	38 mg
Sodium	201 mg
Total carbohydrates	13 g
Protein	3 g

4. Place the dough in a large floured bowl, cover and let rise until doubled in size, approximately 1 hour.

5. Prepare the butter while the dough is rising. Place the butter in an even layer between two large pieces of plastic wrap and roll into a flat rectangle, approximately 20 cm × 27 cm (8 inches × 11 inches) and chill.

6. After the dough has risen, punch it down. Roll out the dough into a large rectangle, about 1.25 cm (1/2 inch) thick and large enough to enclose the rectangle of butter. Place the unwrapped butter in the centre of the dough and fold the dough around the butter, enclosing it completely.

7. Roll out the block of dough into a long rectangle, about 2.5 cm (1 inch) thick. Fold the dough in thirds, as if you were folding a letter. This completes the first turn. Wrap the dough in plastic and chill for approximately 20–30 minutes.

8. Repeat the rolling and folding process two more times, chilling the dough between each turn. When finished, wrap the dough well and chill it overnight before shaping and baking.

9. To shape the dough into croissant rolls, cut off one-quarter of the block at a time, wrapping and returning the rest to the refrigerator. Roll each quarter of dough into a large rectangle, about 6 mm (1/4 inch) thick.

10. Cut the dough into uniform triangles. Starting with the large end, roll each triangle into a crescent and place on a paper-lined sheet pan.

11. Brush lightly with egg wash. Proof until doubled, but do not allow the dough to become so warm that the butter melts.

12. Bake at 190°C (375°F) until golden-brown, approximately 12–15 minutes.

1. Roll out the butter between two sheets of plastic wrap.

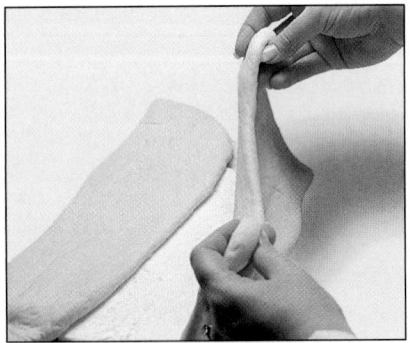

2. After positioning the butter on the rolled-out dough, fold the dough around the butter.

3. Brush the excess flour from the rolled-out dough.

4. Fold the dough in thirds.

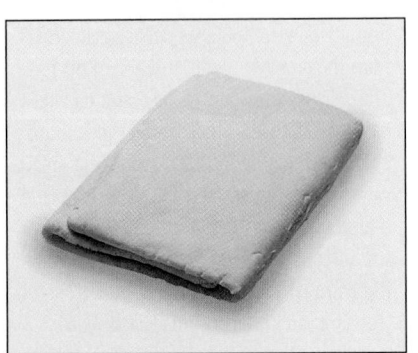

5. The finished croissant dough.

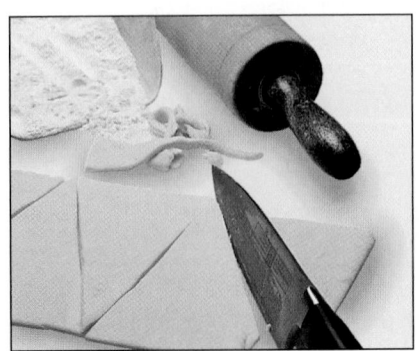

6. Cut the dough into triangles.

7. Baked croissants.

TABLE 28.4 TROUBLESHOOTING CHART FOR YEAST BREADS

Problem	Cause	Solution
Cannonball of dough	Too much flour forced into the dough	Gradually add water; adjust formula
Crust too pale	Oven temperature too low	Adjust oven
	Dough overproofed	Proof only until almost doubled, then bake immediately
Crust too dark	Oven too hot	Adjust oven
	Too much sugar in dough	Adjust formula or measure sugar carefully
Top crust separates from rest of loaf	Dough improperly shaped	Shape dough carefully
	Crust not slashed properly	Slash dough to a depth of 1.25 cm (1/2 inch)
	Dough dried out during proofing	Cover dough during proofing
Sides of loaf are cracked	Bread expanded after crust had formed	Slash top of loaf before baking
Dense texture	Not enough yeast	Adjust formula or measure yeast carefully
	Not enough fermentation time	Let dough rise until doubled or as directed
	Too much salt	Adjust formula or measure salt carefully
Ropes of undercooked dough running through the product	Insufficient kneading	Knead dough until it is smooth and elastic or as directed
	Insufficient rising time	Allow adequate time for rising
	Oven too hot	Adjust oven
Free-form loaf spreads and flattens	Dough too soft	Add flour
Large holes in bread	Too much yeast	Adjust formula or measure yeast carefully
	Overkneaded	Knead only as directed
	Inadequate punch-down	Punch down properly to knead out excess air before shaping
Blisters on crust	Too much liquid	Measure ingredients carefully
	Improper shaping	Knead out excess air before shaping
	Too much steam in oven	Reduce amount of steam or moisture in oven

CONCLUSION

Fresh yeast breads are a popular and inexpensive addition to any menu and are surprisingly easy to prepare. By understanding and appreciating the importance of each of the 10 production stages described in this chapter, you will be able to create and adapt formulas to suit your specific operation and needs. Table 28.4 provides some troubleshooting guidelines should you encounter difficulties.

QUESTIONS FOR DISCUSSION

1. Describe the characteristics of lean and rich doughs and give an example of each.

2. Explain the differences between active dry yeast and compressed yeast. Describe the correct procedures for working with these yeasts.

3. Explain the differences between a sponge and a sourdough starter. How are each of these items used?

4. Describe the straight dough mixing method and give two examples of products made using this procedure.

5. Briefly describe the procedure for making a rolled-in dough and give two examples of products made from rolled-in doughs.

6. List the 10 production stages for yeast breads. Which of these production stages would also apply to quick-bread production? Explain your answer.

*A*DDITIONAL *Y*EAST *B*READ *F*ORMULAS

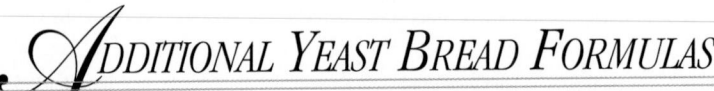

RECIPE 28.5

*B*AGUETTE

Yield: 12.5 kg (25 lb.)

Method: Straight Dough
Dough Temperature 28°C (82°F)

Bread flour	7.5 kg	14 lb.
Salt	150 g	4 oz.
Malt	75 g	2-1/2 oz.
Shortening	75 g	2-1/2 oz.
Format (if available)	60 g	2-1/2 oz.
Yeast, fresh	150 g	5 oz.
Water	4.5 kg	8-1/4 qt.

RECIPE 28.5

Approximate values per serving:

Calories	2521
Total fat	20 g
Saturated fat	4 g
Cholesterol	0 mg
Sodium	5838 mg
Total carbohydrates	518 g
Protein	111 g

1. Place flour, salt, malt, shortening and format (if using) into a mixing bowl.
2. Dissolve the yeast in water and add to mix.
3. Mix with a hook for 1 minute on low speed, then check the dough for consistency and continue mixing for 9–10 minutes at second speed.
4. Bench for 15 minutes at a dough temperature of 28°C (82°F).
5. Divide dough into 600-g (22-oz.) portions and give 10 minutes' intermediate proof.
6. Mould, proof, cut and bake at 215°C (420°F) for 30–35 minutes.

NOTE: Format is a dough conditioner that speeds up fermentation. If unavailable, proceed with the next ingredients but be aware that the proofing will take longer.

❖❖❖

RECIPE 28.6

*W*HITE *P*AN *B*READ

Yield: 18 kg (40 lb.)

Method: Straight Dough
Dough Temperature 28°C (82°F)

Bread flour	10 kg	22 lb.
Sugar	450 g	15-3/4 oz.
Salt	200 g	7 oz.
Milk powder	300 g	10-1/2 oz.
Shortening	400 g	14 oz.
Yeast, fresh	375 g	13 oz.
Water	6–7 L	190–220 fl. oz.

RECIPE 28.6

Approximate values per slice:

Calories	59
Total fat	1 g
Saturated fat	0 g
Cholesterol	0 mg
Sodium	117 mg
Total carbohydrates	11 g
Protein	2.5 g

1. Place all ingredients except yeast and water in a mixing bowl.
2. Dissolve the yeast in water and add to the mix.
3. Mix for 2 minutes on low speed.

4. Check dough for consistency and add more flour or water as needed. Continue mixing for 9–10 minutes on second speed.

5. Divide dough into 540-g (18-oz.) units, shape into rounds and give them 10 minutes' intermediate proof.

6. Mould dough pieces and place in bread pans.

7. Proof.

8. Bake at 200°C (400°F) for about 30 minutes.

9. Cool on wire rack before slicing and bagging.

❖❖❖

RECIPE 28.7

POTATO CHEDDAR CHEESE BREAD

STOUFFER STANFORD COURT, San Francisco, CA
Former Executive Chef Ercolino Crugnale

Yield: 7 600-g (1 lb. 4 oz.) Loaves   **Method:** Straight Dough

Water, heated to 38°C/100°F	250 mL	8 fl. oz.
Active dry yeast	60 g	2 oz.
Bread flour	2.4 kg	5 lb.
Potatoes, boiled, peeled and puréed	1 kg	2 lb.
Kosher salt	45 g	1-1/2 oz.
Cracked pepper	30 g	1 oz.
Unsalted butter, melted	90 g	3 oz.
Cheddar cheese, grated	500 g	1 lb.
Water, room temperature	500 g	1 lb.

1. Dissolve the yeast in the warm water and set aside.

2. Combine the flour, potatoes, salt, pepper, butter and cheese. Blend on low speed for 2–3 minutes.

3. Slowly add the room-temperature water and the yeast mixture. Mix on medium speed for 8–10 minutes.

4. Allow the dough to rise in a warm spot until doubled, approximately 2 hours. Punch down the dough and divide into loaves.

5. Proof until doubled in size, approximately 45 minutes. Bake at 180°C (350°F) until brown, approximately 20–30 minutes.

RECIPE 28.7

Approximate values per 50 g serving:

Calories	163
Total fat	4 g
Saturated fat	2 g
Cholesterol	10 mg
Sodium	295 mg
Total carbohydrates	27 g
Protein	7 g

❖❖❖

RECIPE 28.8

SUN-DRIED TOMATO ROLLS

Yield: 20 Rolls   **Method:** Straight Dough
                                      Dough Temperature 28°C (82°F)

Bread flour	360 g	12 oz.
Semolina flour	60 g	2 oz.
Sun-dried tomatoes, diced fine	30 g	1 oz.
Granulated sugar	30 g	2 Tbsp.
Active dry yeast	6 g	1-1/2 tsp.
Salt	8 g	1-1/2 tsp.
Garlic, minced	7 g	1 tsp.
Whole butter, softened	30 g	1 oz.
Water, warm	300 g	10 oz.

RECIPE 28.8

Approximate values per roll:

Calories	90
Total fat	1.5 g
Saturated fat	0.8 g
Cholesterol	3 mg
Sodium	200 mg
Total carbohydrates	17 g
Protein	3 g

Continued

1. Combine all the ingredients using the straight dough method. Knead until smooth and elastic, approximately 10 minutes.
2. Place the dough in a lightly greased bowl, cover and proof until it doubles.
3. Punch down the dough and proof a second time.
4. Punch down the dough again and divide into 45-g (1-1/2-oz.) portions. Round the dough and shape as desired. Proof until the rolls double in size, approximately 20 minutes.
5. Bake at 200°C (400°F) until golden-brown and done, approximately 18 minutes.

❖❖❖

RECIPE 28.9

60% WHOLE WHEAT BREAD

Yield: 19 kg (42 lb.)   **Method:** Straight Dough
                                             Dough Temperature 28°C (82°F)

Bread flour	4.3 kg	9 lb.
Whole wheat flour	6.3 kg	13 lb.
Sugar	450 g	15-3/4 oz.
Shortening	400 g	14 oz.
Milk powder	300 g	10-1/2 oz.
Salt	200 g	7 oz.
Yeast, fresh	350 g	12-1/4 oz.
Water	7–8 L	190–260 fl. oz.

1. Place flour and all ingredients except yeast and water in mixing bowl.
2. Dissolve yeast in water and add to mix.
3. Mix 2 minutes on low speed.
4. Check dough for proper consistency and add more water or flour as needed. Continue mixing for 9–10 minutes on second speed.
5. Divide dough into 540-g (18-oz.) units, round and give 10 minutes' intermediate proof.
6. Mould dough pieces and place into bread pans.
7. Proof.
8. Bake at 200°C (400°F) for about 30 minutes.
9. Cool on wire rack before slicing and bagging.

RECIPE 28.9

Approximate values per serving:

Calories	1381
Total fat	22 g
Saturated fat	6 g
Cholesterol	10 mg
Sodium	2643 mg
Total carbohydrates	261 g
Protein	48 g

❖❖❖

RECIPE 28.10

MULTIGRAIN DATE BREAD

Yield: 2 Small Loaves   **Method:** Straight Dough

Dates, chopped	250 g	8 oz.
Bread flour	725 g	1 lb. 8 oz.
Active dry yeast	15 g	1/2 oz.
Water, heated to 20°C/70°F	500 g	16 oz.
Honey	125 g	4 oz.
Unsalted butter, melted	60 g	2 oz.
Nonfat dry milk	35 g	1-1/4 oz.
Salt	15 g	1 Tbsp.
Whole wheat flour	175 g	6 oz.
Rye flour	50 g	2 oz.
Wheat germ	50 g	2 oz.

Bran flakes, toasted	50 g	2 oz.
Sesame seeds	10 g	2 Tbsp.
Egg wash	as needed	as needed
Poppy or sesame seeds	10 g	2 Tbsp.

1. In a small bowl, combine the dates with 60 g (2 oz.) of the bread flour; toss to coat and set aside.

2. In a large mixer bowl, dissolve the yeast in the warm water. Add the honey, butter, milk powder, salt and whole wheat flour. Beat at medium speed for 2 minutes.

3. Stir in the rye flour, wheat germ, bran flakes, sesame seeds and date mixture.

4. Slowly add enough of the remaining bread flour to make a soft dough. Knead until smooth and elastic, approximately 5 minutes.

5. Place the dough in a lightly greased bowl and cover. Allow to rise until doubled, approximately 1.5 hours.

6. Punch down the dough and knead for a few seconds.

7. Divide the dough in half. Shape each piece and place in a lightly greased loaf pan. Cover and allow to rise until almost doubled, approximately 45 minutes.

8. Slash the top of the loaves as desired and top with egg wash and poppy or sesame seeds. Bake at 190°C (375°F) until golden-brown and firm, approximately 40 minutes. Loaves should be dry and sound hollow when tapped on the bottom. Remove the loaves from the pans to cool.

◆◆◆

RECIPE 28.11

BREADSTICKS

Yield: 24 Breadsticks   **Method:** Straight Dough

Active dry yeast	15 g	1/2 oz.
Water, heated to 20°C/70°F	300 g	10 oz.
Sugar	30 g	1 oz.
Olive oil	120 mL	4 fl. oz.
Salt	10 g	2 tsp.
Bread flour	500 g	1 lb. 2 oz.
Egg wash	as needed	as needed
Sesame seeds	15 g	1/2 oz.

1. Stir the yeast, water and sugar together in a mixer bowl.

2. Blend in the oil, salt and 250 g (8 oz.) of the flour.

3. Gradually add the remaining flour. Knead the dough until it is smooth and cleans the sides of the bowl, approximately 5 minutes.

4. Remove the dough from the bowl and allow it to rest for a few minutes. Roll the dough into a rectangle, about 0.5 cm (1/4 inch) thick.

5. Cut the dough into 24 even pieces. Roll each piece into a rope and twist; bring the ends together, allowing the sides to curl together. Place on a paper-lined sheet pan.

6. Brush with egg wash and top with sesame seeds. Let the sticks rise until doubled, approximately 20 minutes.

7. Bake at 190°C (375°F) until golden-brown, approximately 12–15 minutes.

VARIATIONS: *Garlic Breadsticks*—Knead 30 g (1 oz.) grated Parmesan cheese and 25 g (2 Tbsp.) minced garlic into the dough. *Herbed Breadsticks*—Knead 30 g (3 Tbsp.) chopped fresh herbs such as basil, parsley, dill and oregano into the dough.

RECIPE 28.10

Approximate values per slice:

Calories	162
Total fat	3 g
Saturated fat	1 g
Cholesterol	4 mg
Sodium	203 mg
Total carbohydrates	32 g
Protein	5.5 g

1. Roll the breadstick dough.

2. Twist the breadstick dough.

RECIPE 28.11

Approximate values per breadstick:

Calories	64
Total fat	5 g
Saturated fat	1 g
Cholesterol	10 mg
Sodium	190 mg
Total carbohydrates	3 g
Protein	1 g

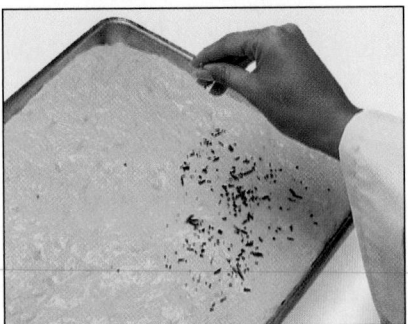

Top the focaccia (flatbread) dough with crushed rosemary.

♦ ♦ ♦

RECIPE 28.12

FOCACCIA

Yield: 1 Sheet Pan, 30 cm × 45 cm   **Method:** Straight Dough
(12 inches × 18 inches)

Sugar	15 g	1 Tbsp.
Active dry yeast	10 g	1 Tbsp.
Water, lukewarm	350 mL	12 fl. oz.
Bread flour	500 g	1 lb. 2 oz.
Kosher salt	10 g	2 tsp.
Onion, chopped fine	90 g	3 oz.
Olive oil	10 mL	2 tsp.
Fresh rosemary, crushed	25 g	2 Tbsp.

1. Combine the sugar, yeast and water. Stir to dissolve the yeast. Stir in the flour 125 g (4 oz.) at a time.

2. Stir in 5 g (1 tsp.) of salt and the onion. Mix well, then knead on a lightly floured board until smooth.

3. Place the dough in an oiled bowl, cover and let rise until doubled.

4. Punch down the dough, then flatten it onto an oiled sheet pan. It should be no more than 2.5 cm (1 inch) thick. Brush the top of the dough with the olive oil. Let the dough proof until doubled, about 15 minutes.

5. Sprinkle the crushed rosemary and remaining salt on top of the dough. Bake at 200°C (400°F) until lightly browned, approximately 20 minutes.

RECIPE 28.12

Approximate values per serving:

Calories	156
Total fat	2 g
Saturated fat	0 g
Cholesterol	0 mg
Sodium	325 mg
Total carbohydrates	32 g
Protein	6 g

♦ ♦ ♦

RECIPE 28.13

PIZZA DOUGH

Yield: 1 Large or 8 Individual Pizzas   **Method:** Straight Dough

Water, heated to 20°C/70°F	60 g	2 oz.
Active dry yeast	10 g	1 Tbsp.
Bread flour	450 g	16 oz.
Water, cool	175 g	6 oz.
Salt	5 g	1 tsp.
Olive oil	45 mL	1-1/2 fl. oz.

1. Stir the yeast into the warm water to dissolve. Add the flour.

2. Stir the cool water, salt and olive oil into the flour mixture. Knead with a dough hook or by hand until smooth and elastic, approximately 5 minutes.

3. Place the dough in a lightly greased bowl and cover. Allow the dough to rise in a warm place for 30 minutes. Punch down the dough and divide into portions. The dough may be wrapped and refrigerated for up to 2 days.

4. On a lightly floured surface, roll the dough into very thin rounds and top as desired. Bake at 200°C (400°F) until crisp and golden-brown, approximately 8–12 minutes.

NOTE: Substitute all-purpose flour for a more tender crust; but reduce water by 2–3%.

RECIPE 28.13

Approximate values per individual serving:

Calories	228
Total fat	6 g
Saturated fat	1 g
Cholesterol	0 mg
Sodium	243 mg
Total carbohydrates	38 g
Protein	8 g

◆◆◆

RECIPE 28.14

BASIC SOURDOUGH BREAD

Yield: 2 Large Loaves   **Method:** Sponge

Active dry yeast	10 g	1 Tbsp.
Water, heated to 20°C/70°F	350 mL	12 fl. oz.
Sourdough Starter (Recipe 28.1)	225 mL	1 cup
Honey	20 g	1 Tbsp.
Bread flour	650 g	1 lb. 6 oz.
Kosher salt	7 g	1-1/2 tsp.
Distilled vinegar	30 mL	1 fl. oz.
Baking soda	1.5 g	1/2 tsp.

RECIPE 28.14	
Approximate values per slice:	
Calories	130
Total fat	0 g
Saturated fat	0 g
Cholesterol	0 mg
Sodium	212 mg
Total carbohydrates	27 g
Protein	4 g

1. Prepare a sponge by mixing the yeast, water, Sourdough Starter and honey. Stir in 125 g (4 oz.) of flour. Beat vigorously by hand or in a mixer on second speed for 3 minutes.

2. Place the sponge in a clean bowl and cover. Set aside until doubled, approximately 1–2 hours.

3. Place the risen sponge into the bowl of a mixer fitted with a dough hook. Add the salt, vinegar and baking soda. Gradually add enough bread flour to make a stiff dough. Knead for 3 minutes on second speed. The dough should clean the bowl, forming a ball around the dough hook.

4. Allow the dough to rest for 5 minutes. Then shape into two round or oval loaves and place on a baking sheet that has been dusted with cornmeal.

5. Cover the dough and set aside to proof until doubled, approximately 45 minutes. Slash the top of the loaf with a razor or sharp knife.

6. Bake the bread for 10 minutes in a 230°C (450°F) oven with steam added. Reduce the oven temperature to 190°C (375°F) and continue baking until golden-brown and firm, approximately 30–40 minutes.

◆◆◆

RECIPE 28.15

CHALLAH

Challah is the traditional bread for Jewish Sabbaths and celebrations. Rich with eggs and flavoured with honey, it is braided into oval loaves and topped with poppy or sesame seeds. Challah is excellent for toast or sandwiches.

Yield: 2 Large Loaves   **Method:** Straight Dough

Honey	180 g	6 oz.
Salt	15 g	1 Tbsp.
Bread flour	800 g	1 lb. 12 oz.
Active dry yeast	15 g	1/2 oz.
Water, warm	400 g	14 oz.
Eggs	225 g	4
Unsalted butter, melted	120 g	4 oz.
Egg wash	as needed	as needed
Sesame or poppy seeds	as needed	as needed

1. Stir together the honey, salt and 250 g (8 oz.) of flour in a mixer bowl. Add the yeast, water, eggs and butter. Stir until smooth.

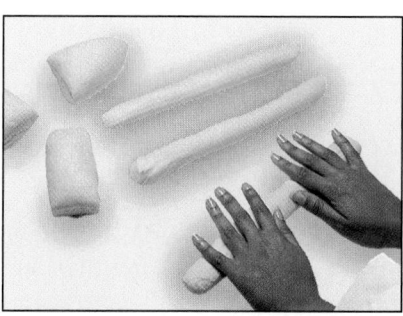

1. Roll the challah dough into ropes.

2. Braid the challah dough.

Continued

2. Using the dough hook, knead the dough on second speed, adding the remaining flour 60 g (2 oz.) at a time until smooth and elastic, approximately 5 minutes.

3. Place the dough in a lightly greased bowl, cover and let rise until doubled, approximately 1–1.5 hours.

4. Punch down the dough and divide into six equal portions. Roll each portion into a long strip, about 2.5 cm (1 inch) in diameter and 30 cm (12 inches) long. Lay three strips side by side and braid. Pinch the ends together and tuck them under the loaf. Place the loaf on a paper-lined sheet pan. Braid the three remaining pieces of dough in the same manner.

5. Brush the loaves with egg wash and sprinkle with sesame or poppy seeds. Proof until doubled, approximately 45 minutes.

6. Bake at 170°C (350°F) until the loaves are golden-brown and sound hollow when thumped, approximately 40 minutes.

❖❖❖

RECIPE 28.16

BRIOCHE

Brioche is a rich, tender bread made with an abundance of eggs and butter. The high ratio of fat makes this dough difficult to work with, but the flavour is well worth the extra effort. Brioche is traditionally made in fluted pans and has a cap or topknot of dough; this shape is known as brioche à tête. The dough may also be baked in a loaf pan, making it perfect for toast or canapés.

Yield: 3 Large Loaves or 60 7.5-cm (3-inch) Rolls   **Method:** Straight Dough

Bread flour	2 kg	4 lb. 7 oz.
Eggs	1.3 kg	24
Salt	20 g	3/4 oz.
Sugar	100 g	3-1/2 oz.
Active dry yeast	40 g	1-1/2 oz.
Water, heated to 20°C/70°F	225 mL	7 fl. oz.
Unsalted butter, room temperature	1.3 kg	3 lb.

1. Place the flour, eggs, salt and sugar into the bowl of a large mixer fitted with the dough hook. Stir the ingredients together.

2. Combine the yeast and water and add to the other ingredients.

3. Knead for 20 minutes on second speed. The dough will be smooth, shiny and moist. It should not form a ball.

4. Slowly add the butter to the dough. Knead only until all the butter is incorporated. Remove the dough from the mixer and place it into a bowl dusted with flour. Cover and let rise at room temperature until doubled.

5. Punch down the dough, cover well and refrigerate overnight.

6. Shape the chilled dough as desired. Place the shaped dough in well-greased pans and proof at room temperature until doubled. Do not proof brioche in a very warm place; the butter may melt out of the dough before proofing is complete.

7. Bake at 190°C (375°F) until the brioche are a dark golden-brown and sound hollow. Baking time will vary depending on the temperature of the dough and the size of the rolls or loaves being baked.

VARIATION: *Raisin Brioche*—Gently warm 90 mL (3 fl. oz.) rum with 180 g (6 oz.) raisins. Set aside until the raisins are plumped. Drain off the remaining rum into the mixture and add the raisins to the dough after the butter is incorporated.

RECIPE 28.15

Approximate values per slice:

Calories	109
Total fat	4 g
Saturated fat	2 g
Cholesterol	31 mg
Sodium	153 mg
Total carbohydrates	18 mg
Protein	4 g

RECIPE 28.16

Approximate values per roll:

Calories	302
Total fat	20 g
Saturated fat	12 g
Cholesterol	141 mg
Sodium	159 mg
Total carbohydrates	25 g
Protein	8 g

1. Combine the ingredients for brioche.

2. Add the yeast-and-water mixture to the dough.

3. Brioche dough after 20 minutes of kneading.

4. Add the butter to the brioche dough.

5. The finished brioche dough ready for fermentation.

6. Shape the brioche à tête.

7. Pan the rolls.

8. A finished loaf of brioche baked in a pullman pan.

❖❖❖

RECIPE 28.17

PECAN STICKY BUNS

Yield: 12–15 Buns

Method: Straight Dough

Active dry yeast	30 g	1 oz.
Sugar	60 g	2 oz.
Milk	15 mL	1 Tbsp.
Buttermilk	175 mL	5-1/2 fl. oz.
Vanilla	5 mL	1 tsp.
Lemon zest, grated	10 g	1 Tbsp.
Lemon juice	5 mL	1 tsp.

Continued

RECIPE 28.17

Approximate values per bun:

Calories	484
Total fat	26 g
Saturated fat	11 g
Cholesterol	79 mg
Sodium	100 mg
Total carbohydrates	55 g
Protein	5 g

Egg yolks	2	2
Bread flour	425 g	14 oz.
Salt	2 g	1/2 tsp.
Unsalted butter, very soft	250 g	8 oz.
Topping:		
Honey	175 g	6 oz.
Brown sugar	175 g	6 oz.
Pecans, chopped	100 g	3 oz.
Filling:		
Cinnamon	5 g	2 tsp.
Pecans, chopped	100 g	3 oz.
Brown sugar	125 g	4 oz.
Unsalted butter, melted	100 g	3 oz.

1. Stir the yeast, sugar, and milk together in a small bowl. Set aside.

2. Stir the buttermilk, vanilla, lemon zest and lemon juice together and add to the yeast mixture.

3. Add the egg yolks, flour, salt and softened butter to the liquid mixture. Turn out onto a lightly floured board and knead until the butter is evenly distributed and the dough is smooth. Cover and let rise until doubled.

4. Prepare the topping and filling mixtures while the dough is rising. To make the topping, cream the honey and sugar together. Stir in the nuts. This mixture will be very stiff. To make the filling, stir the cinnamon, pecans and sugar together.

5. Lightly grease muffin cups, then distribute the topping mixture evenly, about 20 g (1 Tbsp.) per muffin cup. Set the pans aside at room temperature until the dough is ready.

6. Punch down the dough and let it rest 10 minutes. Roll out the dough into a rectangle about 1.25 cm (1/2 inch) thick. Brush with the melted butter and cover evenly with the filling mixture.

7. Starting with either long edge, roll up the dough. Cut into slices about 1.8 to 2.5 cm (3/4 to 1 inch) thick. Place a slice in each muffin cup over the topping.

8. Let the buns proof until doubled, approximately 20 minutes. Bake at 170°C (350°F) until very brown, approximately 25 minutes. Immediately invert the muffin pans onto paper-lined sheet pans to let the buns and their topping slide out.

1. Brush melted butter over the sticky bun dough.

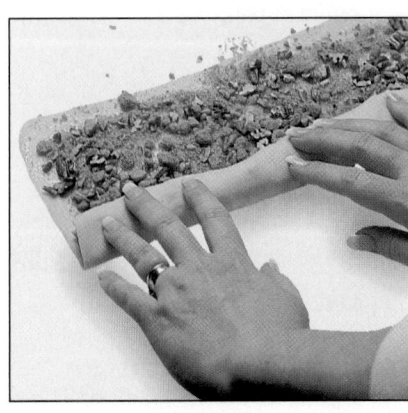

2. Roll up the filling in the sticky bun dough.

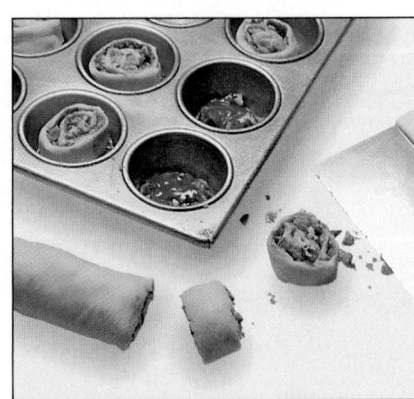

3. Cut and pan the sticky buns.

+ + +

RECIPE 28.18

DANISH PASTRIES

Danish pastry was actually created by a French baker more than 350 years ago. He forgot to knead butter into his bread dough and attempted to cover the mistake by folding in softened butter. This rich, flaky pastry is now popular worldwide for breakfasts, desserts and snacks. The dough may be shaped in a variety of ways and is usually filled with jam, fruit, cream or marzipan.

DOUGH FOR DANISH PASTRIES

Yield: 36 Pastries   **Method:** Rolled-In

Active dry yeast	15 g	1/2 oz.
Bread flour	600 g	1 lb. 4 oz.
Sugar	60 g	2 oz.
Water, cold	125 mL	4 fl. oz.
Milk, cold	125 mL	4 fl. oz.
Eggs, room temperature	2	2
Salt	5 g	1 tsp.
Mace, ground	1.5 g	1/2 tsp.
Unsalted butter, melted	50 g	1-1/2 oz.
Unsalted butter, cold	450 g	1 lb.
Filling (recipes follow)	as needed	as needed
Egg wash	as needed	as needed

1. In a large bowl, stir together the yeast and 350 g (12 oz.) of flour. Add the sugar, water, milk, eggs, salt, mace and melted butter. Stir until well combined.

2. Add the remaining flour gradually, kneading the dough by hand or with a mixer fitted with a dough hook. Knead until the dough is smooth and only slightly tacky to the touch, approximately 2–3 minutes. Do not overmix.

3. Place the dough in a bowl that has been lightly dusted with flour. Cover and refrigerate for 1–1.5 hours.

4. Prepare the remaining butter while the dough is chilling. Soften the butter in a mixer bowl with paddle attachment on low speed.

5. On a lightly floured surface, roll out the dough into a large rectangle about 1.25 cm (1/2 inch) thick. Brush away any excess flour.

6. Spread the butter evenly over two-thirds of the dough. Fold the unbuttered third over the centre, then fold the buttered third over the top. Press the edges together to seal in the butter.

7. Roll the dough into a rectangle about 30 cm × 45 cm (12 inches × 18 inches). Fold the dough in thirds as before. This rolling and folding (called a turn) must be done a total of three times. Chill the dough between turns as necessary. After the final turn, wrap the dough well and refrigerate for at least 4 hours or overnight.

8. Shape and fill the danish dough as desired. Place the shaped pastries on a paper-lined baking sheet and allow to proof for approximately 15–20 minutes.

9. Brush the pastries with egg wash and sprinkle lightly with sugar if desired. Bake at 190°C (375°F) until light brown, approximately 12–15 minutes.

RECIPE 28.18

Approximate values per serving:

Calories	167
Total fat	12 g
Saturated fat	7 g
Cholesterol	43 mg
Sodium	61 mg
Total carbohydrates	13 g
Protein	3 g

1. Spread the butter over the rolled-out dough.

2. Fold the dough in thirds to cover the butter.

3. Roll out the dough.

4. Fold the dough in thirds to complete a turn.

5. Cut rectangles of danish dough.

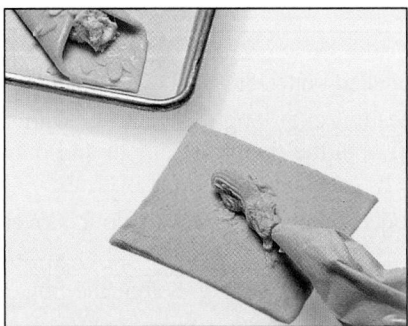

6. Pipe the filling onto the danish dough.

7. Shape snails from danish dough.

FILLINGS FOR DANISH PASTRIES

CREAM CHEESE

Cream cheese	450 g	1 lb.
Sugar	225 g	8 oz.
Salt	1 g	1/4 tsp.
Vanilla	5 mL	1 tsp.
Flour	15 g	2 Tbsp.
Egg yolk	1	1
Lemon extract	5 mL	1 tsp.
Lemon zest	8 g	2 tsp.

Cream Cheese—Approximate values per 30 g (1 oz.) serving:

Calories	103
Total fat	6 g
Saturated fat	4 g
Cholesterol	28 mg
Sodium	71 mg
Total carbohydrates	10 g
Protein	2 g

Beat the cream cheese until light and fluffy. Stir in the remaining ingredients.

ALMOND CREAM

Almond paste	300 g	10 oz.
Unsalted butter, soft	120 g	4 oz.
Salt	1 g	1/4 tsp.
Vanilla	5 mL	1 tsp.
Egg whites	2	2

Blend the almond paste and butter until smooth. Add the salt and vanilla, then the egg whites. Blend well.

Almond Cream—Approximate values per 30 g (1 oz.) serving:

Calories	132
Total fat	11 g
Saturated fat	4 g
Cholesterol	15 mg
Sodium	40 mg
Total carbohydrates	8 g
Protein	3 g

APRICOT

Dried apricots	225 g	8 oz.
Orange juice	450 mL	16 fl. oz.
Sugar	180 g	6 oz.
Salt	1 g	1/4 tsp.
Unsalted butter	60 g	2 oz.

1. Place the apricots and orange juice in a small saucepan. Cover and simmer until the apricots are very tender, approximately 25 minutes. Stir in the sugar and salt. When the sugar is dissolved, add the butter and remove from the heat.

2. Purée the mixture in a blender until smooth. Cool completely before using.

Apricot—Approximate values per 30 g (1 oz.) serving:

Calories	55
Total fat	2 g
Saturated fat	1 g
Cholesterol	4 mg
Sodium	110 mg
Total carbohydrates	6 g
Protein	3 g

 EBLINKS

Fleischmann's Yeast (Canada): Preparing Yeast and Dough
    www.breadworld.com/canada/tips/baking/preparing.html
Fleischmann's Yeast (Canada): Tips: Working with the Dough
    www.breadworld.com/canada/tips/baking/working.html
The Bread Bakers Guild of America
    www.bbga.org/
Breadbaking Secrets
    members.aol.com/BreadLady1/BreadTips.html
Bread Chemistry
    ericir.syr.edu/Projects/Newton/12/Lessons/bread.html

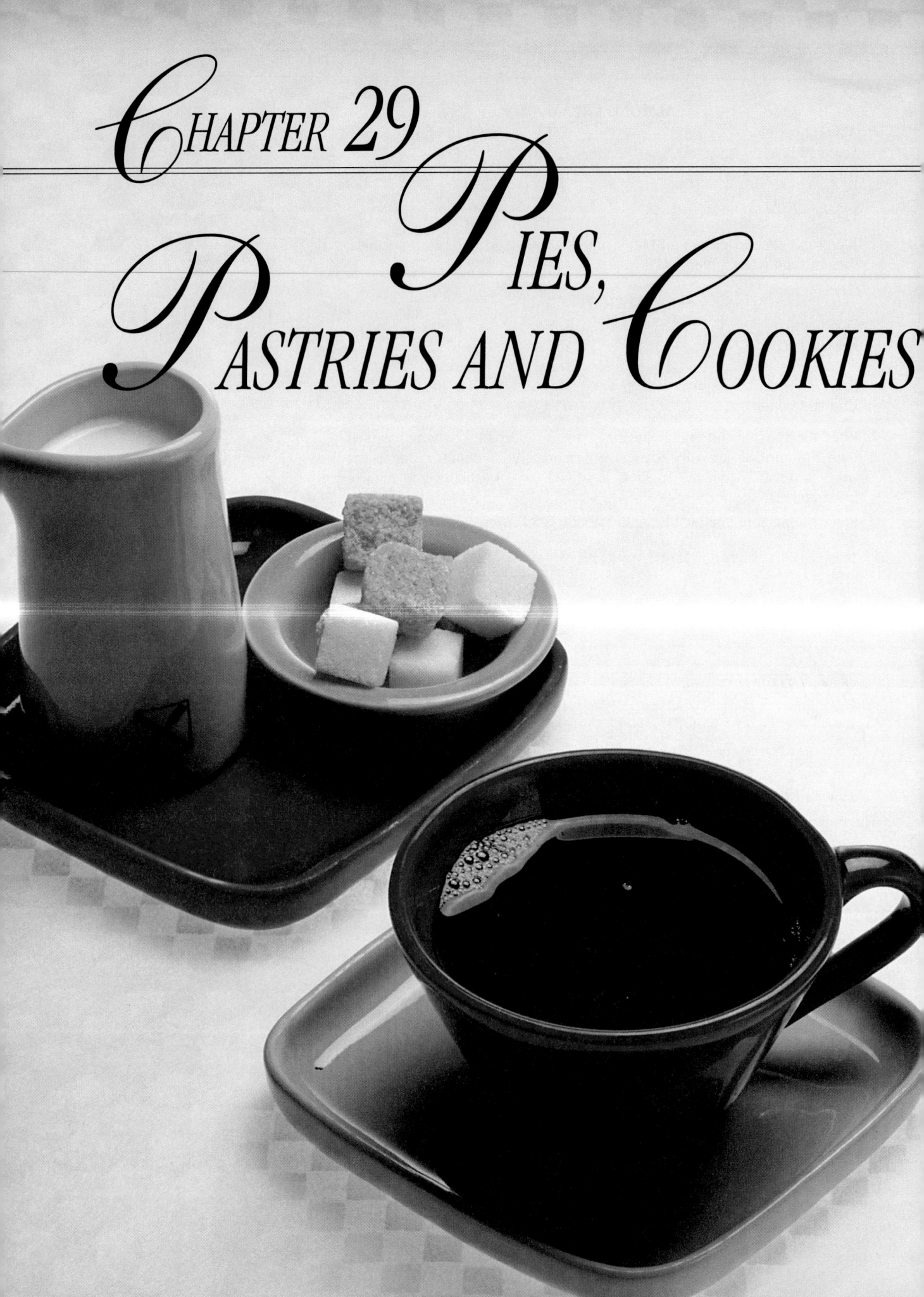

CHAPTER 29 PIES, PASTRIES AND COOKIES

After studying this chapter you will be able to:

- ◆ prepare a variety of pie crusts and fillings, including flaky and mealy doughs and sweet dough/paste
- ◆ prepare a variety of classic pastries, including pie crust and tart shells, tartlet shells, top crust, lattice crust, unfilled crusts, cooked fruit fillings, cooked juice fillings, baked fruit fillings, puff pastry, shape vol-au-vents and bouchées, shape feuilletées, make choux paste
- ◆ prepare a variety of meringues
- ◆ prepare a variety of cookies, including mixing cookie doughs
- ◆ prepare a variety of dessert and pastry items, incorporating components from other chapters

*M*ention pastry to diners and most conjure up images of buttery dough baked to crisp flaky perfection and filled or layered with rich cream, ripe fruit or smooth custard. Mention pastry to novice cooks and most conjure up images of sophisticated, complex and intimidating work. Although the diners are correct, the novice cooks are not. Pastry making is the art of creating containers for a variety of fillings. Taken one step at a time, most pastries are nothing more than selected building blocks or components assembled in a variety of ways to create traditional or unique desserts.

Perhaps the most important (and versatile) building block is the dough. Pastries can be made with flaky dough, mealy dough, sweet dough/paste, puff pastry, choux paste or meringue. See Table 29.1. Because pies, tarts and cookies are constructed from some of these same doughs (principally pie dough and sweet dough), they, as well as pie fillings, are discussed in the section on pies and tarts; puff pastry, choux paste and baked meringue are discussed in the section on classic pastries. The cream, custard and mousse fillings used in some of the recipes at the end of this chapter are discussed in Chapter 31, Custards, Creams, Frozen Desserts and Dessert Sauces. Cakes and frostings are covered in Chapter 30.

PIES AND TARTS

A **pie** is composed of a sweet or savoury filling in a baked crust. It can be open-faced (without a top crust) or, more typically, topped with a full or lattice crust. A pie is generally made in a round, slope-sided pan and cut into wedges for service. A **tart** is similar to a pie except it is made in a shallow, straight-sided pan, often with fluted edges. A tart can be almost any shape; round, square, rectangular and petal shapes are the most common. It is usually open-faced and derives much of its beauty from an attractive arrangement of glazed fruit.

TABLE 29.1	CLASSIFICATION OF PASTRY DOUGHS		
Dough	French Name	Characteristics After Baking	Use
Flaky dough	Pâte brisée	Very flaky; not sweet	Prebaked pie shells; pie top crusts
Mealy dough	Pâte à foncer	Moderately flaky; not sweet	Custard, cream or fruit pie crusts; quiche crusts
Sweet dough	Pâte sucrée (sèche sucrée, sablée)	Very rich; crisp; not flaky	Tart and tartlet shells
Choux paste	Pâte à choux	Hollow with crisp exterior	Cream puffs; éclairs; savoury products
Puff pastry	Pâte feuilletée	Rich but not sweet; hundreds of light, flaky layers	Tart and pastry cases; cookies; layered pastries; savoury products
Meringue	Meringue	Sweet; light; crisp or soft depending on preparation	Topping or icing; baked as a shell or component for layered desserts; cookies

Crusts

Pie crusts and tart shells can be made from several types of doughs or crumbs. **Flaky dough, mealy dough** and **crumbs** are best for pie crusts; **sweet or short paste** is usually used for tart shells. A pie crust or tart shell can be shaped and completely baked before filling (known as **baked blind**) or filled and baked simultaneously with the filling.

Flaky and Mealy Doughs

Flaky and mealy pie doughs are quick, easy and versatile. Flaky dough, sometimes known as pâte brisée, takes its name from its final baked texture. It is best for pie top crusts and lattice coverings and may be used for prebaked shells that will be filled with a cooled filling shortly before service. Mealy dough takes its name from its raw texture. It is used whenever a soggy crust would be a problem (for example, as the bottom crust of a custard or fruit pie) because it resists soaking better than flaky dough. Both flaky and mealy doughs are too delicate for tarts that will be removed from the pan for service. Sweet dough, described below, is better for these types of tarts.

Flaky and mealy doughs contain little or no sugar and can be prepared from the same formula with only a slight variation in mixing method. For both types of dough a cold fat, such as butter or shortening, is cut into the flour. The amount of flakiness in the baked crust depends on the size of the fat particles in the dough. The larger the pieces of fat, the flakier the crust will be. This is because the flakes are actually the sides of fat pockets created during baking by the melting fat and steam. When preparing flaky dough, the fat is left in larger pieces, about the size of peas or peanuts. When preparing mealy dough, the fat is blended in more thoroughly, until the mixture resembles coarse cornmeal. Because the resulting fat pockets are smaller, the crust is less flaky.

The type of fat used affects both the dough's flavour and flakiness. Butter contributes a delicious flavour, but does not produce as flaky a crust as other fats. Butter is also more difficult to work with than other fats because of its lower melting point and its tendency to become brittle when chilled. All-purpose vegetable shortening produces a flaky crust but contributes nothing to its flavour. The flakiest pastry is made with lard, but because some people cannot eat pork products lard is not often used. Some chefs prefer to use a combination of butter with either shortening or lard. Oil is not an appropriate substitute as it disperses too thoroughly through the dough; when baked, the crust is stiff and crisp.

After the fat is cut into the flour, water or milk is added to form a soft dough. Less water is needed for mealy dough because more flour is already in contact with the fat, reducing its ability to absorb liquid. Cold water is normally used for both flaky and mealy doughs. The water should be well chilled to prevent softening the fat or shortening. Milk may be used to increase richness and nutritional value. It will produce a darker, less crisp crust, however. If dry milk powder is used, it should be mixed with the flour.

Hand mixing is best for small to moderate quantities of dough. You retain better control over the procedure when you can feel the fat being incorporated. It is very difficult to make flaky dough with an electric mixer or food processor, as they tend to cut the fat in too thoroughly. Overmixing makes the dough elastic and difficult to use. When an electric mixer must be used for large quantities, use the paddle attachment at the lowest speed and be sure the fat is well chilled, even frozen.

Basic Procedure for Preparing Flaky and Mealy Doughs

1. Sift flour, salt and sugar (if used) together in a large bowl.
2. Cut the fat into the flour.
3. Gradually add a cold liquid, mixing gently until the dough holds together. Do not overmix.
4. Cover the dough with plastic wrap and chill thoroughly before using.

Applying the Basics

RECIPE 29.1

BASIC PIE DOUGH

Yield: 2.7 kg (5 lb.)

Pastry flour	1.5 kg	3 lb.
Milk powder	85 g	3 oz.
Shortening	800 g	26 oz.
Water, cold	425 mL	14 oz.
Salt	40 g	1-1/2 oz.

1. Blend the flour and milk powder in a mixing bowl.
2. Add the shortening and cut it into the flour with a paddle attachment until the fat is pea-size.
3. Dissolve the salt in the water.
4. Add the water all at once to the flour and fat mixture. Blend on No. 1 speed only until the mix comes together.

NOTE: For mealy pie crust, the fat should be crumb size.

RECIPE 29.1

*Approximate values
per 30 g serving:*

Calories	144
Total fat	9 g
Saturated fat	2 g
Cholesterol	0 mg
Sodium	178 mg
Total carbohydrates	14 g
Protein	2 g

1. Cut the fat into the flour coarsely for flaky dough.

2. Cut the fat into the flour finely for mealy dough.

3. The finished dough.

Sweet Paste

Sweet paste or **pâte sucrée** is a rich, nonflaky dough used for sweet tart shells. It is sturdier than flaky or mealy dough because it contains egg yolks and the fat is thoroughly blended in. It is also more cookielike than basic pie dough and has the rich flavour of butter. It creates a crisp but tender crust and is excellent for tartlets as well as for straight-sided tarts that will be removed from their pans before service. Sweet paste crusts may be prebaked then filled, or filled and baked simultaneously with the filling. The raw dough may be kept refrigerated for up to two weeks or frozen for up to three months.

Basic Procedure for Preparing Sweet Paste

1. Cream softened butter. Add sugar and beat until the mixture is light and fluffy.
2. Slowly add eggs, blending well.
3. Slowly add flour, mixing only until incorporated. Overmixing toughens the dough.
4. Cover the dough with plastic wrap and chill thoroughly before using.

Applying the Basics

RECIPE 29.2

SWEET (SHORT) PASTE

Yield: 2.35 kg (5 lb.)

Unsalted butter, softened	700 g	1 lb. 8 oz.
Sugar	425 g	1 lb.
Whole eggs	225 g	8 oz.
Pastry flour	1 kg	2 lb.

1. Cream the butter and sugar in a large mixer bowl using the paddle attachment.
2. Slowly add the eggs to the creamed butter. Mix until smooth and free of lumps, scraping down the sides of the bowl as needed.
3. With the mixer on low speed, slowly add the flour to the butter-and-egg mixture. Mix only until incorporated; do not overmix. The dough should be firm, smooth and not sticky.
4. Dust a half-sheet pan with flour. Pack the dough into the pan evenly. Wrap well in plastic wrap and chill until firm.
5. Work with a small portion of the chilled dough when shaping tart shells or other products.

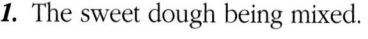

1. The sweet dough being mixed.

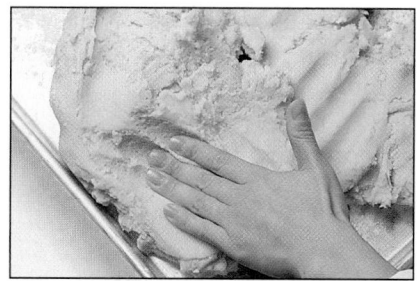

2. The finished sweet dough.

Shaping Crusts

Crusts are shaped by rolling out the dough to fit into a pie pan or tart shell (mould) or to sit on top of fillings. Mealy, flaky and sweet doughs are all easier to roll out and work with if well chilled, as chilling keeps the fat firm and prevents stickiness. When rolling and shaping the dough, work on a clean, flat surface (wood or marble is best). Lightly dust the work surface, rolling pin and dough with bread flour before starting to roll the dough. Also, work only with a manageable amount at a time: usually enough for one pie crust or a standard-sized tart or enough for 10–12 tartlet shells.

◆◆◆

TERMINOLOGY

Pâte à foncer—short pastry with a low (10–12%) sugar content. Powdered sugar is used for this lining paste.

Pâte sèche sucrée—sweet short paste with 40% butter and high egg content.

Pâte sucrée—sweet short paste with 80% butter and low egg content.

Pâte sablée—sweet short paste with 65% butter and 35% powdered sugar.

Sweet pastes are the basis of many cookies and can be flavoured accordingly. The butter percentages are approximate and pastry chefs have their own preferred formulas.

RECIPE 29.2

Approximate values per 30 g serving:

Calories	136
Total fat	8 g
Saturated fat	5 g
Cholesterol	32 mg
Sodium	5 mg
Total carbohydrates	16 g
Protein	1.5 g

Roll out the dough from the centre, working towards the edges. Periodically, lift the dough gently and rotate it. This keeps the dough from sticking and helps produce an even thickness. If the dough sticks to the rolling pin or work surface, dust with a bit more flour. Too much flour, however, makes the crust dry and crumbly and causes grey streaks.

Basic Procedure for Rolling and Shaping Dough for a Pie Crust or Tart Shell

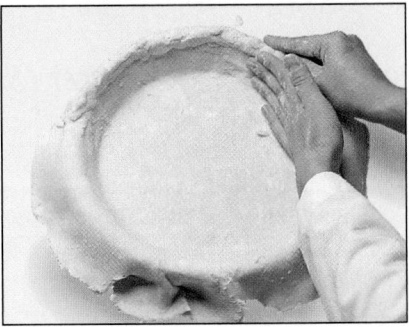

1. A typical pie crust or tart shell should be rolled to a thickness of approximately 3 mm (1/8 inch); it should also be at least 5 cm (2 inches) larger in diameter than the baking pan.

2. Carefully roll the dough up onto a rolling pin. Position the pin over the pie pan or tart shell and unroll the dough, easing it into the pan or shell. Trim the edges as necessary and flute. Bake or fill as desired.

Basic Procedure for Rolling and Shaping Dough for Tartlet Shells

1. A typical crust for tartlets should be approximately 3 mm (1/8 inch) thick.
2. Roll the dough out as described above. Then roll the dough up onto the rolling pin.

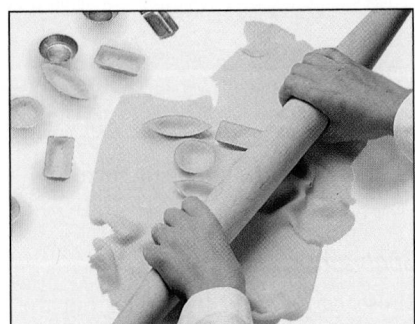

3. Lay out a single layer of tartlet moulds. Unroll the dough over the moulds, pressing the dough gently into each mould.

4. Roll the rolling pin over the top of the tartlet shells. The edge of the moulds will cut the dough. Be sure the dough is pressed against the sides of each mould. Bake or fill as desired.

Basic Procedure for Rolling and Shaping Dough for a Top Crust

1. Roll the dough out as before, making a circle large enough to hang over the pan's edge. The dough may be lifted into place by rolling it onto the rolling pin, as done with the bottom crust. Slits or designs can be cut in the top crust to allow steam to escape.

2. Seal the top crust to the bottom crust with egg wash or water. Crimp as desired.

Basic Procedure for Rolling and Shaping Dough for a Lattice Crust

1. Roll the dough out as described before. Using a ruler as a guide, cut even strips of the desired width, typically 1.25 cm (1/2 inch). A special cutter is available to stamp out the lattice crust on the table top. The crust is then laid over the pie.

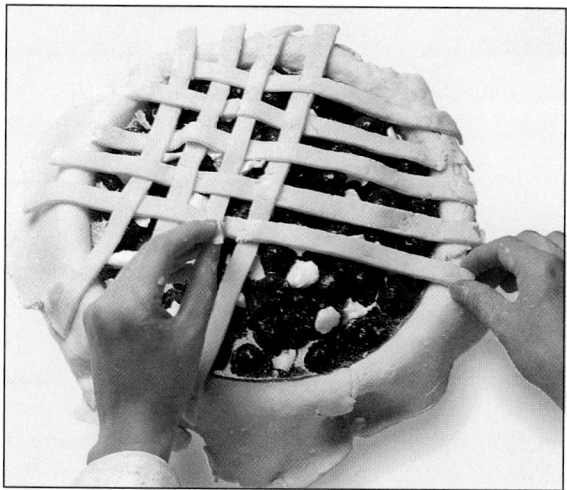

2. Using an over-under-over pattern, weave the strips together on top of the filling. Be sure the strips are evenly spaced for an attractive result. Crimp the lattice strips to the bottom crust to seal.

Streusel topping is also used for some pies, particularly fruit pies. A standard recipe is given in Chapter 27, Quick Breads.

Baking Crusts

Pie crusts can be filled and then baked, or baked and then filled. Unfilled baked crusts can be stored at room temperature for 2–3 days or wrapped in plastic wrap and frozen for as long as 3 months.

Basic Procedure for Baking Unfilled (Baked Blind) Pie Crusts

1. Roll the dough out to the desired thickness and line the pie pan or tart shell. A crimped edge or border can be added.
2. **Dock** the dough with a fork or docking wheel. Cover and allow the dough to rest in the fridge for several hours.
3. Cover the dough with baking parchment or greased aluminum foil. Press the paper or foil against the edge or walls of the shell. Allow a portion of the paper or foil to extend above the pan.
4. Fill the pan with baking weights, dry rice or beans. These will prevent the crust from rising.
5. Bake the weighted crust at 200°C (400°F) for 10–15 minutes.
6. Remove the weights and paper and return the crust to the oven. Bake until golden-brown and fully cooked, approximately 5–8 minutes.
7. Allow to cool, then fill as desired or store.

1. Dock the dough.

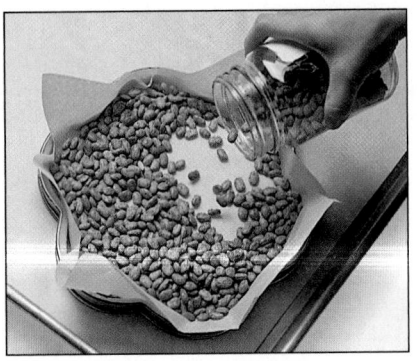

2. Use weights to prevent the crust from rising.

3. Remove weights and paper before returning the crust to the oven for browning.

Crumb Crusts

A quick and tasty bottom crust can be made from finely ground crumbs moistened with melted butter. Crumb crusts can be used for unbaked pies such as those with cream or chiffon fillings, or they can be baked with their fillings, as with cheesecakes.

Chocolate cookies, graham crackers, gingersnaps, vanilla wafers and macaroons are popular choices for crumb crusts. Some breakfast cereals such as corn flakes or bran flakes are also used. Ground nuts and spices can be added for flavour. Whatever cookies or other ingredients are used, be sure they are ground to a fine, even crumb. If packaged crumbs are unavailable, crumbs can be prepared in a food processor or blender or with a rolling pin.

The typical ratio for a crumb crust is one part melted butter, two parts sugar and four parts crumbs. For example, 250 g (8 oz.) graham crackers mixed with 125 g (4 oz.) sugar and 60 mL (2 fl. oz.) melted butter produce enough crust to line one 22- to 25-cm (9- to 10-inch) pan. The amount of sugar may need to be adjusted depending on the type of crumbs used, however; for example, chocolate sandwich cookies need less sugar than graham crackers. If the mixture is too dry to stick together, gradually add more melted butter. Press the mixture into the bottom of the pan and chill or bake it before filling.

Press the crumb mixture into the pan.

Fillings

Fillings make pies and tarts distinctive and flavourful. Four types of fillings are discussed here: **cream**, **fruit**, **custard** and **chiffon**. There is no one correct presentation or filling-and-crust combination. The apples in an apple pie, for example, may be sliced, seasoned and topped with streusel; caramelized, puréed and blended with cream; chopped and covered with a flaky dough lattice; or poached, arranged over pastry cream and brushed with a clear glaze. Only an understanding of the fundamental techniques for making fillings—and some imagination—ensures success.

Cream Fillings

A cream filling is really nothing more than a flavoured pastry cream. Pastry cream is a type of starch-thickened egg custard discussed in Chapter 31, Custards, Creams, Frozen Desserts and Dessert Sauces. When used as a pie filling, pastry cream should be thickened with cornstarch so that it gels and is firm enough to hold its shape when sliced. Popular flavours are chocolate, banana, coconut and lemon.

A cream filling is fully cooked on the stove top, so a prebaked or crumb crust is needed. The crust can be filled while the filling is still warm, or the filling can be chilled and later placed in the crust. A cream pie may be topped with meringue, which is then browned quickly in an oven or under a broiler. Chantilly cream is the most popular topping.

♦♦♦

PASTRY CREAM

The filling for the cream pie is a basic pastry cream. This mixture is used extensively in dessert preparations. Some recipes use a combination of whole eggs and yolks. Pastry cream may be flavoured with fruit compounds. Whipped cream or Italian meringue may be added. Note that no gelatin is used; the resulting gel is solely obtained from the cooked cornstarch.

Applying the Basics

RECIPE 29.3

BASIC CREAM PIE

Yield: Two 22-cm (9-inch) Pies

Pastry Cream:

Granulated sugar	250 g	8 oz.
Milk	1 L	1 qt.
Egg yolks*	10	10
Cornstarch	90 g	3 oz.
Unsalted butter	60 g	2 oz.
Vanilla extract	15 g	1/2 oz.
Pie shells, baked	2	2

1. In a heavy saucepan, dissolve 125 g (4 oz.) of sugar in the milk. Bring just to a boil.
2. Meanwhile, whisk the egg yolks in a large bowl.
3. Sift the cornstarch and remaining sugar (125 g/4 oz.) into the eggs. Whisk until smooth.
4. **Temper** the egg mixture with approximately half of the hot milk. Stir the warmed egg mixture back into the remaining milk and return it to a boil, stirring constantly.
5. Stirring constantly and vigorously, allow the cream to boil until thick, approximately 30 seconds. Remove from the heat and stir in the butter and vanilla. Stir until the butter is melted and incorporated.

Continued

6. Pour the cream into prebaked pie crusts.

7. The pies may be topped with meringue while the filling is still warm. The meringue is then lightly browned in a 210°C (425°F) oven. Chill the pies for service or, when chilled, top with whipped cream.

*Alternatively, 3 whole eggs and 2 yolks may be used.

VARIATIONS: Chocolate—Melt 175 g (6 oz.) bittersweet chocolate. Fold the melted chocolate into the hot cream after adding the butter and vanilla.

Banana—Layer 250 g (8 oz.) sliced bananas (about 2 medium bananas) into the baked shell. The juice of one-half lemon may be added to the bananas to help prevent browning. Fill shell with pastry cream.

Coconut I—Substitute 175 mL (6 fl. oz.) cream of coconut for 175 mL (6 fl. oz.) of milk and 60 g (2 oz.) of sugar. Top the pie with whipped cream and shredded toasted coconut.

Coconut II—Stir 125 g (4 oz.) toasted coconut into the warm cream.

RECIPE 29.3

Approximate values per slice:

Calories	306
Total fat	16 g
Saturated fat	6 g
Cholesterol	151 mg
Sodium	159 mg
Total carbohydrates	35 g
Protein	5 g

1. Fill the pie shell with chocolate pastry cream.

2. Top with meringue.

Fruit Fillings

A fruit filling is a mixture of fruit, fruit juice, spices and sugar thickened with starch. Apple, cherry, blueberry and peach are traditional favourites. The fruit can be fresh, frozen or canned. (See Chapter 25, Fruits, for comments on selecting the best fruits for fillings.) The starch can be cornstarch, tapioca or a packaged commercial instant or pregelatinized starch. The ingredients for a fruit filling are most often combined using one of three methods: **cooked fruit**, **cooked juice** or **baked**.

Cooked Fruit Fillings

The cooked fruit filling method is often used when the fruits need to be softened by cooking (for example, apples, rhubarb or dried fruits). (Poaching fruit, discussed in Chapter 25, Fruits, is a variation of this procedure.) A cooked fruit filling can be used with a prebaked or unbaked crust. If an unbaked raw crust is used, the pie is baked before service.

Basic Procedure for Preparing Cooked Fruit Fillings

1. Combine the fruit, sugar and some juice or liquid in a heavy, nonreactive saucepan and bring to a boil.

2. Dissolve the starch (usually cornstarch) in cold liquid, then add to the boiling fruit.

3. Stirring constantly, cook the fruit-and-starch mixture until the starch is clear and the mixture is thickened.

4. Add any other flavourings and any acidic ingredients such as lemon juice. Stir to blend.

5. Remove from the heat and cool before use.

Applying the Basics

RECIPE 29.4

APPLE-CRANBERRY PIE

Yield: One 22-cm (9-inch) Pie   **Method:** Cooked Fruit Filling

Fresh tart apples such as Granny Smiths, peeled, cored and cut in 2.5-cm (1-inch) cubes	500 g	1 lb.
Brown sugar	125 g	4 oz.
Granulated sugar	125 g	4 oz.
Orange zest	10 g	1 Tbsp.
Ground cinnamon	2 g	1 tsp.
Salt	1 g	1/4 tsp.
Cornstarch	6 g	2 tsp.
Orange juice	90 mL	3 fl. oz.
Fresh cranberries, rinsed	250 g	8 oz.
Partially baked mealy dough pie shell	1	1
Streusel Topping (Recipe 27.6)	125 g	4 oz.

1. Combine the apples, brown sugar, granulated sugar, orange zest, cinnamon and salt in a large, nonreactive saucepan.

2. Dissolve the cornstarch in the orange juice and add it to the apples.

3. Cover and simmer until the apples begin to soften, stirring occasionally. Add the cranberries, cover and continue simmering until the cranberries begin to soften, approximately 2 minutes. Cool the mixture to room temperature.

4. Place the apple-cranberry mixture in the pie shell and cover with the prepared streusel topping. Bake at 200°C (400°F) until the filling is bubbling hot and the topping is lightly browned, approximately 20 minutes.

VARIATION: *Apple-Rhubarb Pie*—Substitute cleaned rhubarb, cut into 2.5-cm (1-inch) chunks, for the cranberries. Add 0.25 g (1/8 tsp.) nutmeg.

RECIPE 29.4

Approximate values per slice:

Calories	298
Total fat	8 g
Saturated fat	2 g
Cholesterol	0 mg
Sodium	177 mg
Total carbohydrates	57 g
Protein	2 g

Cooked Juice Fillings

The cooked juice filling method is recommended for delicate fruits that cannot withstand cooking such as strawberries, pineapple or blueberries and frozen berries. Because only the juice is cooked, the fruit retains its shape, colour and flavour better. A cooked juice filling can be used with a prebaked or unbaked crust.

Basic Procedure for Preparing Cooked Juice Fillings

1. Drain the juice from the fruit. Measure the juice and add water if necessary to create the desired volume.

2. Combine the liquid with sugar in a nonreactive saucepan and bring to a boil.
3. Dissolve the starch in cold water, then add it to the boiling liquid. Cook until the starch is clear and the juice is thickened.
4. Add any other flavouring ingredients.
5. Pour the thickened juice over the fruit and stir gently.
6. Cool the filling before use.

Applying the Basics

BLUEBERRY PIE FILLING

Yield: 3.1 kg (6 lb.) Filling   **Method**: Cooked Juice Filling

Frozen blueberries, unsweetened	2.25 kg	5 lb.
Water	as needed	as needed
Sugar	600 g	1 lb. 4 oz.
Cornstarch	100 g	3 oz.
Water	175 mL	6 fl. oz.
Cinnamon	1 g	1/2 tsp.
Lemon juice	30 mL	1 fl. oz.
Lemon zest, grated fine	10 g	1 Tbsp.

1. Thaw berries and retain juice.
2. Measure the juice and, if necessary, add enough water to provide 400 mL (15 fl. oz.) of liquid. Bring to a boil, add the sugar and stir until dissolved.
3. Dissolve the cornstarch in water.
4. Add the cornstarch to the boiling juice and return to a boil. Cook until the mixture thickens and clears. Remove from the heat.
5. Add the cinnamon, lemon juice, lemon zest and reserved blueberries. Stir gently to coat the fruit with the glaze.
6. Allow the filling to cool, then use it to fill pie shells or other pastry items.

NOTE: A modified starch (waxy maize) (70 g or 2-1/4 oz.) may be used if the pie will be frozen.

Baked Fruit Fillings

The baked fruit filling method is a traditional technique in which the fruit, sugar, flavourings and starch are combined in an unbaked shell. The dough and filling are then baked simultaneously. Almost any type of fruit and starch can be used. The results are not always consistent, however, because thickening is difficult to control.

Basic Procedure for Preparing Baked Fruit Fillings

1. Combine the starch, spices and sugar.
2. Peel, core, cut or drain the fruit as desired or as directed in the recipe.
3. Toss the fruit with the starch mixture, coating well.
4. Add a portion of juice to moisten the fruit. Small lumps of butter are also often added.
5. Fill an unbaked shell with the fruit mixture. Cover with a top crust, lattice or streusel and bake.

RECIPE 29.5

Approximate values per 125 g serving:

Calories	154
Total fat	0.5 g
Saturated fat	0 g
Cholesterol	0 mg
Sodium	2 mg
Total carbohydrates	39 g
Protein	0 g

Applying the Basics

CHERRY PIE

Yield: Two 22-cm (9-inch) Pies   **Method:** Baked Fruit Filling

Tapioca	45 g	1-1/2 oz.
Salt	pinch	pinch
Granulated sugar	450 g	1 lb.
Almond extract	2 mL	1/2 tsp.
Canned pitted cherries, drained		
(reserve the liquid)	1.3 kg	3 lb.
Unbaked pie shells	2	2
Unsalted butter	30 g	1 oz.
Egg wash	as needed	as needed
Sanding sugar	as needed	as needed

1. Stir the tapioca, salt and sugar together. Add the almond extract and cherries.
2. Stir in up to 250 mL (8 fl. oz.) of the liquid drained from the cherries, adding enough liquid to moisten the mixture thoroughly.
3. Allow the filling to stand for 30 minutes. Then stir gently and place the filling in an unbaked pie shell.
4. Cut the butter into small pieces. Dot the filling with the butter.
5. Place a top crust or a lattice crust over the filling; seal and flute the edges. Cut several slits in the top crust to allow steam to escape. Brush with an egg wash and sprinkle with sanding sugar.
6. Place on a preheated sheet pan and bake at 200°C (400°F) for 50–60 minutes.

Approximate values per slice:

Calories	340
Total fat	9 g
Saturated fat	3 g
Cholesterol	5 mg
Sodium	183 mg
Total carbohydrates	63 g
Protein	2 g

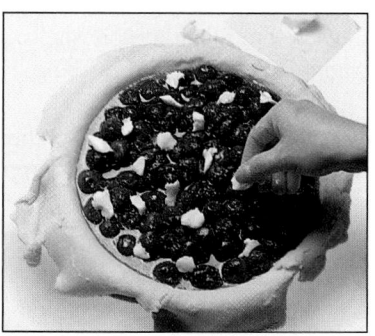

Dot the cherry filling with butter.

Custard Fillings

A custard pie has a soft filling that bakes along with the crust. Popular examples include pumpkin, egg custard and pecan pies. As explained in Chapter 31, Custards, Creams, Frozen Desserts and Dessert Sauces, custards are liquids thickened by coagulated egg proteins. To make a custard pie, a custard sauce containing eggs is poured into a pie shell. When baked, the egg proteins coagulate, firming and setting the filling.

The procedure for making custard pies is simple: combine the ingredients and bake. But there is often a problem: baking the bottom crust completely without overcooking the filling. For the best results, bake the pie in a 200°C (400°F) oven. After 10 minutes, reduce the heat to 160–180°C (325–350°F) to finish cooking the filling slowly.

═══ ◆◆◆ ═══
CONVENIENCE PRODUCTS

Prepared or canned pie fillings are available in a variety of fruit and custard flavours. These products offer convenience and the ability to serve fruit pies out of season. The ratio of fruit to pregelled liquid varies greatly from brand to brand, however. Most commercial fillings are stabilized to permit any additional cooking needed to assemble the final product. Shelf life tends to be extremely long, often without the need for refrigeration. Dry custard mixes are also available, needing only the addition of water or milk. Despite the convenience, most prepared pie fillings are a disappointing substitute for a well-made fresh fruit or custard filling.

RECIPE 29.7

Approximate values per 1/8 pie:

Calories	214
Total fat	10 g
Saturated fat	2.5 g
Cholesterol	30 mg
Sodium	231 mg
Total carbohydrates	26 g
Protein	4 g

To determine the doneness of a custard pie:

1. Shake the pie gently. It is done if it is no longer liquid. The centre should show only a slight movement.
2. Insert a thin knife about 2.5 cm (1 inch) from the centre. The filling is done if the knife comes out clean.

Applying the Basics

RECIPE 29.7

PUMPKIN PIE

Yield: Two 22-cm (9-inch) Pies   **Method:** Baked Custard Filling

Eggs, beaten slightly	225 g	4
Pumpkin purée	600 g	1 lb. 6 oz.
Brown sugar	350 g	12 oz.
Pastry flour	30 g	1 oz.
Salt	2 g	1/2 tsp.
Nutmeg, ground	0.5 g	1/4 tsp.
Cloves, ground	0.5 g	1/4 tsp.
Cinnamon, ground	2 g	1 tsp.
Ginger, ground	1 g	1/2 tsp.
Evaporated milk or cereal cream	600 mL	24 fl. oz.
Mealy dough pie shells	2	2

1. Combine the eggs and pumpkin. Blend in the sugar and pastry flour.
2. Add the salt and spices, then the evaporated milk. Whisk until completely blended and smooth.
3. Allow the filling to rest for 15–20 minutes before filling the pie shells. This allows the starch in the pumpkin to begin absorbing liquid, making it less likely to separate after baking.
4. Pour the filling into unbaked pie shells. Place in the oven on a preheated sheet pan at 220°C (400°F). Bake for 15 minutes. Lower the oven temperature to 180°C (350°F) and bake until a knife inserted near the centre comes out clean, approximately 40–50 minutes.

Chiffon Fillings

A chiffon filling is created by adding gelatin to a stirred custard or a fruit purée. Whipped egg whites are then folded into the mixture. The filling is placed in a prebaked crust and chilled until firm. These preparations are the same as those for chiffons, mousses and Bavarians discussed in Chapter 31, Custards, Creams, Frozen Desserts and Dessert Sauces.

Assembling Pies and Tarts

The various types of pie fillings can be used to fill almost any crust or shell, provided the crust is prebaked as necessary. The filling can then be topped with meringue or whipped cream as desired. Garnishes such as toasted coconut, cookie crumbs and chocolate curls are often added for appearance and flavour. (See Table 29.2.) If you encounter quality issue with pies, Table 29.3 provides troubleshooting information.

TABLE 29.2   SUGGESTIONS FOR ASSEMBLING PIES

Filling	Crust	Topping	Garnish
Vanilla or lemon cream	Prebaked flaky dough or crumb	None, meringue or whipped cream	Crumbs from the crust
Chocolate cream	Prebaked flaky dough or crumb	None, meringue or whipped cream	Crumbs from the crust or shaved chocolate
Banana cream	Prebaked flaky dough	Meringue or whipped cream	Dried banana chips
Coconut cream	Prebaked flaky dough	Meringue or whipped cream	Shredded coconut
Fresh fruit	Unbaked mealy dough or sweet dough if shallow tart	Lattice, full crust or streusel	Sanding sugar or cut-out designs if lattice or top crust is used
Canned or frozen fruit	Unbaked mealy dough	Lattice, full crust or streusel	Sanding sugar or cut-out designs if lattice or top crust is used
Chiffon or mousse	Crumb or prebaked, sweetened flaky dough	None or whipped cream	Crumbs, fruit or shaved chocolate
Custard (e.g., pecan or pumpkin)	Unbaked mealy dough	None	Whipped cream
Vanilla pastry cream	Prebaked sweet dough	Fresh fruit	Glaze

Storing Pies and Tarts

Pies and tarts filled with cream or custard must be kept refrigerated to retard bacterial growth. Baked fruit pies should be held at refrigerator temperature.

Unbaked fruit pies or unbaked pie shells may be frozen for up to two months. Freezing baked fruit pies is not recommended unless waxy maize or modified starch, not regular cornstarch, is used in preparing the filling. Custard, cream and meringue-topped pies should not be frozen as the eggs will separate, making the product runny.

TABLE 29.3   TROUBLESHOOTING CHART FOR PIES

Problem	Cause	Solution
Crust shrinks	Overmixing	Adjust mixing technique
	Overworking dough	Adjust rolling technique
	Not enough fat	Adjust formula
Soggy crust	Wrong dough used	Use mealier dough
	Oven temperature too low	Adjust oven
	Not baked long enough	Adjust baking time
Crumbly crust	Not enough liquid	Adjust formula
	Too much fat	Adjust formula
Tough crust	Not enough fat	Adjust formula
	Overmixing	Adjust mixing technique
Runny filling	Insufficient starch	Adjust formula
	Starch insufficiently cooked	Allow starch to gelatinize completely
Lumpy cream filling	Starch not incorporated properly	Stir filling while cooking
	Filling overcooked	Adjust cooking time
Custard filling weeps or separates	Too many eggs	Reduce egg content or add starch to the filling
	Eggs overcooked	Reduce oven temperature or baking time

CLASSIC PASTRIES

Puff pastry, **choux paste** and **meringue** are classic components of French pastries; they are used to create a wide variety of dessert and pastry items. Many combinations are traditional. Once you master the skills necessary to produce these products, however, you will be free to experiment with other flavours and assembly techniques.

Puff Pastry

Puff pastry is one of the bakeshop's most elegant and sophisticated products. Also known as **pâte feuilletée**, it is a rich, buttery dough that bakes into hundreds of light, crisp layers.

Puff pastry is used for both sweet and savoury preparations. It can be baked and then filled or filled first and then baked. Puff pastry may be used to wrap beef (for beef Wellington), pâté (for pâté en croûte) or almond cream (for an apple tart). It can be shaped into shells or cases known as vol-au-vents or bouchées and filled with shellfish in a cream sauce or berries in a pastry cream. Puff pastry is essential for napoleons, pithiviers and tartes tatin.

Like croissant and danish dough (discussed in Chapter 28, Yeast Breads), puff pastry is a rolled-in dough. But unlike those doughs, puff pastry does not contain any yeast or chemical leavening agents. Fat is rolled into the dough in horizontal layers; when baked, the fat melts, separating the dough into layers. The fat's moisture turns into steam, which causes the dough to rise and the layers to further separate.

Butter is the preferred fat because of its flavour and melt-in-the-mouth quality. But butter is rather difficult to work with as it becomes brittle when cold and melts at a relatively low temperature. Therefore, specially formulated puff pastry shortenings are used to compensate for butter's shortcomings. They do not, however, provide the true flavour of butter. Some bakers use a combination of butter and specially formulated shortening.

Raw, frozen, commercially prepared puff pastry is readily available in sheets or precut in a variety of shapes. Some convenience products, especially those made with butter, provide excellent, consistent results. Their expense may be offset by the savings in time and labour. Keep these frozen doughs well wrapped to prevent drying and freezer burn, and prepare according to package directions.

Making Puff Pastry

The procedure described here for making puff pastry is just one of many. Each chef will have his or her own formula and folding method. All methods, however, depend upon the proper layering of fat and dough through a series of turns or folds to give the pastry its characteristic flakiness and rise.

Some chefs prefer to prepare a dough called **blitz** or *quick puff pastry*. It does not require the extensive rolling and folding procedure used for true puff pastry. Blitz puff pastry is less delicate and flaky but may be perfectly acceptable for some uses. A formula for it is given at the end of this chapter.

◆◆◆

MAKING PUFF PASTRY

English method—fat covers two-thirds of dough and single folds are used to create layers. Either 6 × 3 or 4 × 4 folds (bookfold) can be used.

Blitz method—fat is incorporated as in flaky pie dough, only fat pieces are larger; dough is given two or three single folds.

Basic Procedure for Preparing Puff Pastry

1. Prepare the dough (**détrempe**) by combining the flour, water, salt and a small amount of fat. Do not overmix. Overmixing results in greater gluten formation; too much gluten can make the pastry undesirably tough.

2. Wrap the détrempe and chill for several hours or overnight. This allows the gluten to relax and the flour to absorb the liquid.

3. Shape the butter into a rectangle of even thickness; wrap and chill until ready to use.

4. Allow the détrempe and butter to sit at room temperature until slightly softened and of the same consistency.

5. Roll out the détrempe into a rectangle of even thickness.

6. Place the butter in the centre of the dough. Fold the dough around the butter, enclosing it completely.

7. Roll out the block of dough and butter into a long, even rectangle. Roll only at right angles so that the layered structure is not destroyed.

8. Fold the dough like a business letter: Fold the bottom third up towards the centre so that it covers the centre third, then fold the top third down over the bottom and middle thirds. This completes the first turn.

9. Rotate the block of dough one-quarter turn (90 degrees) on the work surface. Roll out again into a long, even rectangle.

10. Fold the dough in thirds again (single fold). This completes the second turn. Wrap the dough and chill for approximately 20 to 30 minutes. The resting period allows the gluten to relax; the chilling prevents the butter from becoming too soft. Overchilling will harden the butter too much.

11. Repeat the rolling and folding process, chilling between every one or two turns, until the dough has been turned a total of five times.

12. Wrap well and chill overnight. Raw dough may be refrigerated for a few days or frozen for two to three months.

13. Shape and bake as needed. Baked, unfilled puff pastry can be stored at room temperature for two to three days.

✦✦✦
BOOKFOLDS

The process of folding the dough and rolling it out and folding it again is referred to as bookfolds or turns. There are single folds (layering the dough in thirds) as described here and bookfolds, bringing both outside edges to the centre and then folding in half again. The more folds, the more layers of fat and the flakier the pastry becomes—to a point. Too many folds results in the dough becoming too thin to support the structure as it develops during baking.

✦✦✦
ROLL-IN FAT

There are several special pastry shortenings (S.P.S.) on the market. Some are coloured and flavoured to resemble butter. The purposes for using them are cost and ease of handling. For superior taste, however, nothing beats a pure butter puff pastry.

Applying the Basics

RECIPE 29.8

PUFF PASTRY

Yield: 1.3 kg (2 lb.) **Method:** Rolled-In Dough

Shortening	60 g	2 oz.
Bread flour	500 g	1 lb.
Water, cold	300–330 mL	10–11 fl. oz.
S.P.S., softened*	460 g	1 lb.

1. To form the détrempe, cut the shortening into small pieces and then rub the pieces into the flour until the mixture resembles coarse cornmeal.

2. Make a well in the centre of the mixture and add all the water at once. Using a rubber spatula or your fingers, gradually draw the flour into the water. Mix until all of the flour is incorporated.

3. Turn the détrempe out onto a lightly floured surface. Knead the dough a few times by hand, rounding it into a ball. Wrap the dough tightly in plastic and chill overnight.

4. To roll the fat in, first prepare the piece of fat by placing it between two sheets of plastic wrap. Use a rolling pin to roll the softened fat into a rectangle approximately 12.5 cm × 20 cm (5 inches × 8 inches). It is important that the détrempe and butter be of almost equal consistency. If necessary, allow the détrempe to sit at room temperature to soften or chill the butter briefly to harden.

RECIPE 29.8

Approximate values per 50 g serving:

Calories	209
Total fat	17 g
Saturated fat	10 g
Cholesterol	39 mg
Sodium	147 mg
Total carbohydrates	13 g
Protein	3 g

Continued

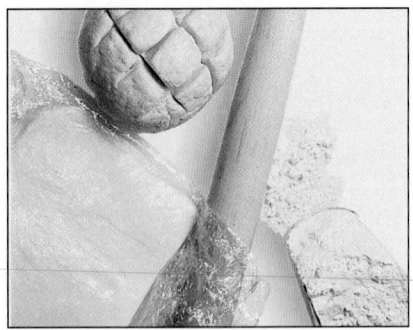

1. Mise en place for puff pastry. The détrempe is shown on the top left.

2. Fold the dough around the butter.

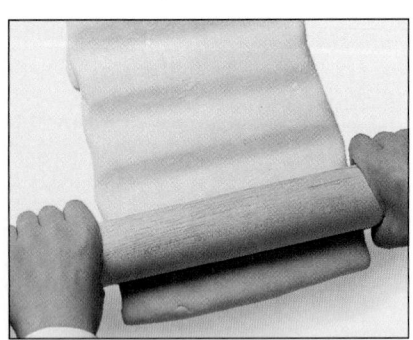

3. Roll out the dough.

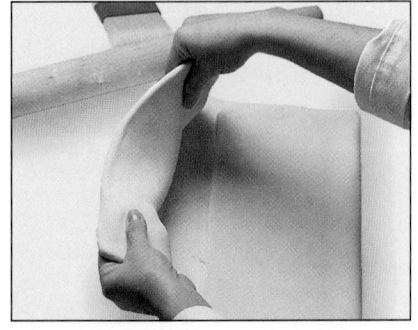

4. Fold the dough in thirds.

5. On a lightly floured board, roll the détrempe into a rectangle approximately 30 cm × 37.5 cm (12 inches × 15 inches). Lift and rotate the dough as necessary to prevent sticking.

6. Use a dry pastry brush to brush away any flour from the dough's surface. Loose flour can cause grey streaks and can prevent the puff pastry from rising properly when baked.

7. Peel one piece of plastic wrap from the fat. Position the fat in the centre of the rectangle and remove the remaining plastic. Fold the four edges of the détrempe over the fat enclosing it completely. Stretch the dough if necessary; it is important that none of the butter be exposed.

8. With the folded side facing up, press the dough several times with a rolling pin. Use a rocking motion to create ridges in the dough. Place the rolling pin in each ridge and slowly roll back and forth to widen the ridge. Repeat until all of the ridges are doubled in size.

9. Using the ridges as a starting point, roll the dough out into a smooth, even rectangle approximately 20 cm × 60 cm (8 inches × 24 inches). Be careful to keep the corners of the dough at right angles.

10. Use a dry pastry brush to remove any loose flour from the dough's surface. Fold the dough in thirds, like a business letter. If one end is damaged or in worse condition, fold it in first; otherwise start at the bottom. This completes the first turn.

11. Rotate the block of dough 90 degrees, so that the folded edge is on your left and the dough faces you like a book. Roll the dough out again, repeating the ridging technique. Once again, the dough should be in a smooth, even rectangle of approximately 20 cm × 60 cm (8 inches × 24 inches).

12. Fold the dough in thirds again, completing the second turn. Cover the dough with plastic wrap and chill for 20–30 minutes.

13. Repeat the rolling and folding technique until the dough has had a total of five turns. Do not perform more than two turns without a resting and chilling period. Cover the dough completely and chill overnight before shaping and baking.

*For a richer dough use 50% butter.

NOTES: The détrempe can be made in a food processor. To do so, combine the flour, salt and pieces of butter in a food processor bowl fitted with the metal blade. Process until a coarse meal is formed. With the processor running, slowly add the water. Turn the machine off as soon as the dough comes together to form a ball. Proceed with the remainder of the recipe.

It is not necessary to work with the entire block of dough when making bouchées, cookies or the like. Cut the block into thirds or quarters and work with one of these portions at a time, keeping the rest chilled until needed.

Shaping Puff Pastry

Once puff pastry dough is prepared, it can be shaped into containers of various sizes and shapes. Classic shapes are bouchées, vol-au-vents and feuilletées. **Bouchées** are small puff pastry shells often used for hors d'oeuvre or appetizers. **Vol-au-vents** are larger, deeper shells, often filled with savoury mixtures for a main course. Although they are most often round or square, special vol-au-vent cutters are available in the shape of fish, hearts or petals.

Feuilletées are square, rectangular or diamond-shaped puff pastry boxes. They can be filled with a sweet or savoury mixture.

When making straight cuts in puff pastry, press the tip of your knife into the dough and cut by pressing down on the handle. Do not drag the knife through the dough or you will crush the layers and deform the pastry.

Basic Procedure for Shaping Vol-au-Vents and Bouchées

1. Roll out the puff pastry dough to a thickness of approximately 6 mm (1/4 inch).

2. Cut the desired shape and size using a vol-au-vent cutter or rings.

3. Place the vol-au-vent or bouchée on a paper-lined sheet pan. If you used rings, place the base on the paper-lined sheet pan, brush lightly with water, then top it with the dough ring; score the edge with the back of a paring knife. Chill for at least 20 minutes to allow the dough to relax before baking.

4. Egg-wash if desired and dock the centre with a fork.

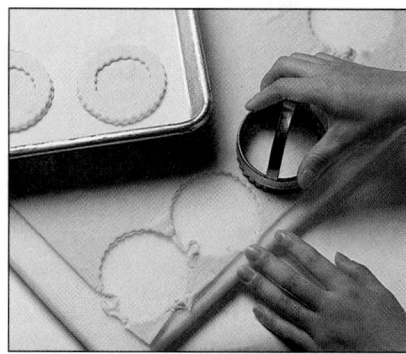

1. A vol-au-vent cutter looks like a double cookie cutter with one cutter about 2.5 cm (1 inch) smaller than the other. To cut the pastry, simply position the cutter and press down.

2. To shape with rings, use two rings, one approximately 2.5 cm (1 inch) smaller in diameter than the other. The larger ring is used to cut two rounds. One will be the base and is set aside. The smaller ring is then used to cut out an interior circle from the second round, leaving a border ring of dough. (The scrap of dough from the dough ring's centre has no further use in making vol-au-vents but may be used to make bouchées or fleurons.)

Basic Procedure for Shaping Feuilletées

1. Roll out the puff pastry dough into an even rectangle approximately 3 to 6 mm (1/8 to 1/4 inch) thick.

2. Using a sharp paring knife or chef's knife, cut squares that are about 5 cm (2 inches) larger than the desired interior of the finished feuilletée.

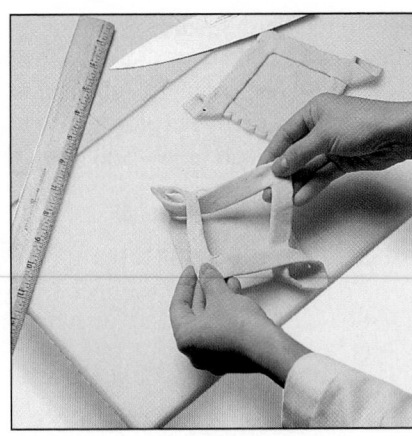

3. Fold each square in half diagonally. Cut through two sides of the dough, about 1.25 cm (1/2 inch) from the edge. Cut a "V," being careful not to cut through the corners at the centre fold.

4. Open the square and lay it flat. Lift opposite sides of the cut border at the cut corners and cross them.

5. Brush water on the edges to seal the dough. Place the feuilletées on a paper-lined sheet pan.

6. Score the edges with the back of a paring knife. Chill for at least 30 minutes to allow the dough to relax before baking.

7. Egg-wash if desired and dock the centre with a fork.

Puff pastry scraps cannot be rerolled and used for products needing a high rise. The additional rolling destroys the layers. Scraps (known as *rognures*), however, can be used for cookies such as palmiers (Recipe 29.24), turnovers, decorative crescents (fleurons), tart shells, napoleons (Recipe 29.23) or any item for which rise is less important than flavour and flakiness.

Most puff pastry products bake best in a hot oven, about 200–220°C (400–425°F).

Choux Paste

Choux paste (**pâte à choux**), sometimes called éclair paste, bakes up into golden-brown, crisp pastries. The inside of these light pastries are mostly air pockets with a bit of moist dough. They can be filled with sweet cream, custard, fruit or even savoury mixtures. The dough is most often piped into rounds for **cream puffs**, fingers for **éclairs** or rings for **Paris-Brest** or gougères. Choux paste may also be piped or spooned into specific shapes and deep-fat fried for doughnut-type products known as **beignets**, **churros** and **crullers**.

Preparing Choux Paste

Choux paste is unique among doughs because the flour is cooked before baking. The cooking occurs when the flour is added to a boiling mixture of water, milk and butter. This process breaks down the starches in the flour, allowing them to absorb the liquid, speeding gelatinization. Eggs are added to the flour mixture for leavening. The paste produced is batterlike with a smooth, firm texture; it does not have the dry, elastic or crumbly texture of other doughs. Without this technique the paste would not puff up and develop the desired large interior air pockets when baked.

Basic Procedure for Preparing Choux Paste

1. Combine liquid ingredients and butter and bring to a boil.
2. Add all of the flour to the saucepan as soon as the water-and-butter mixture comes to a boil. If the liquid is allowed to boil, evaporation occurs; this can create an imbalance in the liquid-to-flour ratio.
3. Stir vigorously until the liquid is absorbed. Continue cooking the dough until it forms a ball that comes away from the sides of the pan, leaving only a thin film of dough in the pan.
4. Transfer the dough to a mixing bowl. Add eggs one at a time, beating well after each addition. This may be done in a mixer with the paddle attachment or by hand. The number of eggs used varies depending on the size of each egg and the moisture content of the flour mixture. Stop adding eggs when the paste just begins to fall away from the beaters or it forms a soft peak.
5. The finished paste should be smooth and pliable enough to pipe through a pastry bag; it should not be runny.
6. Pipe the paste as desired and bake immediately. A high oven temperature is necessary at the start of baking; it is then reduced gradually to finish baking and dry the product. Do not open the oven door during the first half of the baking period.
7. Allow the paste to bake until completely dry. If the products are removed from the oven too soon, they will collapse.
8. Baked choux paste can be stored, unfilled, for several days at room temperature or frozen for several weeks. Once filled, the pastry should be served within two or three hours as it quickly becomes soggy.

◆◆◆
MASTERING CHOUX PASTE

Choux paste requires some experience to achieve the proper consistency. If the paste is too firm, it will not rise properly; if it is too soft, it will not hold its shape when piped. For a crisper baked choux, only water is used; however, a small amount of sugar needs to be added for crust colour.

Applying the Basics

RECIPE 29.9

BASIC CHOUX PASTE

Yield: Approx. 1.7 kg (3-3/4 lb.)

Milk, 2%	400 mL	14. fl. oz.
Water	225 mL	8 fl. oz.
Butter	250 g	9 oz.
Bread flour	375 g	11 oz.
Eggs	625 g	10–11

1. Preheat the oven to 220°C (425°F). Line a sheet pan with parchment. Have a pastry bag with a large plain tip ready.

Continued

1. Heat the butter, milk and water.

2. Add the flour to the hot liquid.

3. Stir the dough to dry it.

4. The finished batter after the eggs have been incorporated.

5. Pipe éclairs or other shapes.

2. Place the milk, water and butter in a saucepan. Bring to a rolling boil. Make sure the butter is fully melted.

3. Remove from the heat and immediately add all the flour. Vigorously beat the dough by hand. Put the pan back on the heat and continue beating the dough until it comes away from the sides of the pan. The dough should look relatively dry.

4. Transfer the dough to a mixing bowl and allow it to cool briefly to a temperature of approximately 54°C (130°F) or lower. Using the mixer's paddle attachment, begin beating in the eggs one at a time on #2 speed and incorporating thoroughly.

5. Continue to add the eggs until the mixture is shiny but firm. It may not be necessary to use all the eggs. The paste should pull away from the sides of the bowl in thick threads; it will not clear the bowl.

6. Put a workable amount of dough into the pastry bag and pipe onto the sheet pan in the desired shapes at once.

7. Bake immediately, beginning at 220°C (425°F) for 10 minutes, then lowering the heat to 190°C (375°F) for another 10 minutes. Continue gradually lowering the oven temperature until the shapes are brown and dry inside. Open the oven door as little as possible to prevent rapid changes in the oven's temperature.

8. Cool completely, then fill as desired. Leftovers can be frozen or stored at room temperature.

RECIPE 29.9

Approximate values per 30 g serving:

Calories	68
Total fat	4 g
Saturated fat	2 g
Cholesterol	50 mg
Sodium	16 mg
Total carbohydrates	5 g
Protein	2 g

Meringues

Meringues are egg whites whipped with sugar. The texture—hard or soft—depends on the ratio of sugar to egg whites.

An equal or lesser sugar content in ratio to the egg whites creates a **soft meringue**. Soft meringues can be folded into a mousse to lighten it or used in a spongecake or soufflé. Meringues with only a small amount of sugar will always be soft; they will not become crisp no matter how they are used.

They can be incorporated into a butter cream or pastry cream or used to top a pie or baked Alaska. These toppings are usually placed briefly under a broiler to caramelize the sugar, creating an attractive brown surface.

Hard meringues are made with twice as much sugar, or more, as egg whites. They can be piped into disks or other shapes and dried in an oven. A low oven temperature evaporates the eggs' moisture, leaving a crisp, sugary, honeycomb-like structure. Disks of baked meringue can be used as layers in a torte or cake.

Cups or shells of baked meringue can be filled with cream, mousse, ice cream or fruit. Often baked meringues also contain ground nuts (and are then known as *japonaise*), cocoa powder or other flavourings.

Making Meringues

There are three methods for making meringues: **common**, **Swiss** and **Italian**. Regardless of which preparation method is used, the final product should be smooth, glossy and moist. A meringue should never be completely dry or spongelike. You should review the procedure for whipping egg whites given in Chapter 8, Eggs and Dairy Products. Table 29.4 provides some troubleshooting guidelines should you encounter quality issues with meringues.

Common Meringues

Common meringues are made by first beating egg whites to a soft foam (soft peaks). Granulated sugar is then added slowly and beaten into the egg whites. The final product may be hard or soft depending on the ratio of sugar to egg whites.

Swiss Meringues

Swiss meringues are made by combining unwhipped egg whites with sugar and warming the mixture over a bain marie to a temperature of approximately 40°C (105°F). The syrupy solution is then whipped until cool and stiff. The final product may be hard or soft depending on the ratio of sugar to egg whites. Swiss meringues are extremely stable but rather difficult to prepare. If the mixture gets too hot it will not whip properly; the result will be syrupy and runny. Swiss meringue is often used as a topping or in buttercream.

Italian Meringues

Italian meringues are made by slowly pouring a hot sugar syrup into whipped egg whites. The heat from the syrup cooks the egg whites, adding stability. Be sure that the sugar syrup reaches the correct temperature and that it is added to the egg whites in a slow, steady stream. Italian meringues are used in buttercream (see Chapter 30, Cakes and Frostings) or folded into pastry cream to produce crème Chiboust. They may be flavoured and used as a cake filling and frosting called boiled icing.

TABLE 29.4 TROUBLESHOOTING CHART FOR MERINGUES

Problem	Cause	Solution
Weeps or beads of sugar syrup are released	Old eggs	Use fresher eggs or add starch or stabilizer
	Egg whites overwhipped	Whip only until stiff peaks form
	Not enough sugar	Increase sugar
	Not baked long enough	Increase baking time
	Browning too rapidly	Do not dust with sugar before baking; reduce oven temperature
	Moisture in the air	Do not refrigerate baked meringue
Fails to attain any volume or stiffness	Fat present	Start over with clean bowls and utensils
	Sugar added too soon	Allow egg whites to reach soft peaks before adding sugar
	Too much sugar added too quickly	Add sugar gradually
Lumps	Not enough sugar	Add additional sugar gradually or start over
	Overwhipping	Whip only until stiff peaks form
Not shiny	Not enough sugar	Add additional sugar gradually or start over
	Overwhipping	Whip only until stiff peaks form

◆◆◆

PHYLLO DOUGH

Phyllo (FEE-low), also spelled filo or fillo, is from the Greek *phyllon* meaning thin sheet or leaf. Although its name is Greek, its origin is unknown. Indians, Turks, Syrians, Yugoslavs and Austrians all claim it as their own. Somewhat blandly-flavoured phyllo sheets are brushed with melted butter or oil, stacked and then used in many Mediterranean, Middle Eastern and Central Asian dishes as a tart crust or a wrapper for various sweet or savoury fillings.

Phyllo dough is made from flour, water, a bit of oil and eggs. The dough must be stretched tissue-paper thin, using techniques that can take years to master. Fortunately, excellent commer-cially prepared phyllo is available in frozen sheets. Sheets of phyllo can stick together if thawed too quickly, so thaw frozen dough slowly for a day or so in the refrigerator. Then temper the package of dough at room temperature for at least one hour before opening. Unused phyllo should not be refrozen; it will keep for several days in the refrigerator if tightly wrapped.

When ready to use, open the package and unfold the stack of leaves. Place them flat on a sheet pan or work surface and cover with a sheet of plastic wrap topped with a damp towel. Remove one leaf at a time from the stack, keeping the remainder well covered to prevent it from drying out. Brush melted butter or oil over the sheet's entire surface. Chopped nuts, sugar, cocoa powder or bread crumbs can be dusted over the butter or oil for additional flavour. Repeat with additional leaves until the desired number of layers have been prepared and stacked together. The number of layers will depend on the thickness of the sheets and their use. Generally, a filled tart or casserole requires more leaves than a folded or wrapped hors d'oeuvre. Cut the stacked phyllo with scissors or a very sharp knife and use as directed in the recipe. Recipes using phyllo dough are found at the end of this chapter and in Chapter 33, Appetizers and Sandwiches.

Applying the Basics

RECIPE 29.10

JAPONAISE MERINGUE

Yield: 2 kg (4 lb.)

Egg whites	500 g	16 oz.
Granulated sugar	500 g	16 oz.
Icing sugar	500 g	16 oz.
Ground hazelnuts	500 g	16 oz.

1. Whip egg whites at medium speed to soft peaks.
2. With the machine still running, add the granulated sugar in small quanti-ties. Whip to a soft peak.
3. Combine icing sugar and nuts, then fold into the meringue.
4. Using a pencil, mark circles on silicone sheets. Turn the sheets over and place on tray.
5. Pipe the japonaise mixture onto the sheets using a plain 12–15 mm (1/2-inch) tube. Using the pencilled circles as a guide, pipe in a spiral.
6. Bake at 120°C (250°F) until crisp, 1.5–2 hours. Use the meringues to make tortes.

RECIPE 29.10

*Approximate values
per 30 g serving:*

Calories	103
Total fat	4 g
Saturated fat	0 g
Cholesterol	0 mg
Sodium	24 mg
Total carbohydrates	15 g
Protein	2 g

Applying the Basics

RECIPE 29.11

ITALIAN MERINGUE

Yield: Approx. 8 L (2 gal.)

Granulated sugar	800 g	28 oz.
Egg whites, room temperature	400 g	14 oz.

1. Place 500 g (18 oz.) of the sugar in a heavy saucepan and add enough water to moisten the sugar thoroughly. Attach a candy thermometer to the pan and bring the sugar to a boil over high heat.
2. Place the egg whites in the bowl of an electric mixer fitted with the whip attachment. As the temperature of the boiling sugar approaches 115°C (238°F) begin whipping the egg whites. When the whites form soft peaks, gradually add the remaining 300 g (10 oz.) of sugar. Lower the mixer speed and continue whipping.

RECIPE 29.11

*Approximate values
per 30 g serving:*

Calories	21
Total fat	0 g
Saturated fat	0 g
Cholesterol	0 mg
Sodium	4 mg
Total carbohydrates	5 g
Protein	0.5 g

3. When the sugar reaches 115°C (238°F) pour it into the whites, with the mixer running. Pour in a steady stream between the side of the bowl and the beater. Continue whipping the whites at medium speed until they are cool.

COOKIES

Cookies are small, flat pastries usually eaten alone (although not singularly) and sometimes used as a component in other desserts. The recent proliferation of cookie shops in malls and office buildings attests to the popularity of freshly baked cookies. They are indeed among the world's best-loved foods.

Part of the pleasure of cookies comes from their versatility. They may be eaten as a midmorning snack or as the elegant end to a formal dinner. Cookies also provide the finishing touch to a serving of ice cream, custard or fruit. Flavours are limited only by the baker's imagination; chocolate, oatmeal, cornmeal, fresh and dried fruit and nuts all find their way into several types of cookies. Several cookie formulas are given at the end of this chapter.

Mixing Methods

Most cookie doughs are mixed by the creaming method used for quick breads and cake batters. (See Chapter 27, Quick Breads, and Chapter 30, Cakes and Frostings.) Because cookie dough contains less liquid than these batters, the liquid and flour need not be added alternately, however. Cookies may be leavened with baking soda, baking powder or just air and steam. Most cookies are high in fat, which contributes taste and tenderness and extends shelf life. Overdevelopment of gluten is usually not a problem with cookies because of their high fat and low moisture contents. Careless mixing can cause the dough to become tough and dense instead of tender and flaky.

Basic Procedure for Mixing Cookie Doughs

1. Cream the fat and sugar together to incorporate air and to blend the ingredients completely.
2. Add the eggs gradually, scraping down the bowl as needed.
3. Stir in the liquid ingredients.
4. Stir in the flour, salt, spices and leaveners.
5. Fold in any nuts, chocolate chips or chunky ingredients by hand or by mixer on low speed.

Makeup Methods

Cookie varieties are usually classified by the way in which the individual cookies are prepared. This section describes six preparation or makeup techniques: **drop**, **icebox**, **bar**, **cut-out** or **rolled**, **pressed** and **wafer**. Some doughs can be made up by more than one method. For example, chocolate chip cookie dough can be (a) baked in sheets and cut into bars, (b) dropped in mounds or (c) rolled into logs, chilled and sliced like icebox cookies. Regardless of the makeup method used, uniformity of size and shape is important for appearance and baking time. Cookies should also be evenly spaced on sheet pans for proper air circulation and crust formation.

Drop Cookies

Drop cookies are made from a soft dough that is spooned or scooped into mounds for baking. Chunky cookies such as chocolate chip, oatmeal raisin and nut jumbles are common examples. Although a uniform appearance is not as

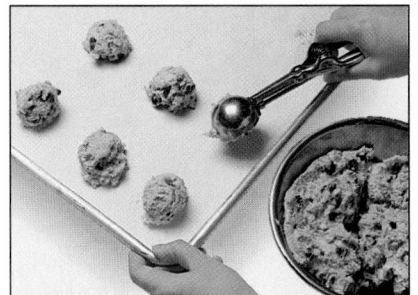

Drop Cookies

important for drop cookies as for other types, uniform size and placement results in uniform baking time. A portion scoop is recommended for portioning the dough. Drop cookies tend to be thick with a soft or chewy texture.

Icebox Cookies

Icebox cookies are made from dough that is shaped into logs or rectangles, chilled thoroughly, then sliced into individual pieces and baked as needed. Icebox cookies can be as simple as a log of chocolate chip dough or as sophisticated as elegant pinwheel and checkerboard cookies assembled with two colours of short dough. This method usually produces uniform, waferlike cookies with a crisp texture.

Icebox Cookies

Bar Cookies

Bar cookie dough is pressed or layered in shallow pans and cut into portions after baking, usually squares or rectangles to avoid waste or scraps. This category, also known as sheet cookies, contains a wide variety of layered or fruit-filled products. Brownies, often considered a bar cookie, are discussed in Chapter 30, Cakes and Frostings.

Bar Cookies

Cut-Out or Rolled Cookies

Cut-out or rolled cookies are made from a firm dough that is rolled out into a sheet and then cut into various shapes before baking. A seemingly infinite selection of cookie cutters is available, or you can use a paring knife or pastry wheel to cut the dough into the desired shapes. Always start cutting cookies from the edge of the dough, working inward. Cut the cookies as close to each other as possible to avoid scraps. Cut-out cookies are usually baked on an ungreased pan to keep the dough from spreading.

Cut-out cookies are often garnished or decorated with nuts, glaze, fruit or candies. Raw cookies should be decorated as soon as they are placed on the pan. If the dough is allowed to stand, the surface will dry out and the garnish will not adhere properly.

Cut-Out or Rolled Cookies

Pressed Cookies

Also referred to as bagged or spritz cookies, these products are made with a soft dough that is forced through a pastry tip or cookie gun. Pressed cookies are usually small, with a distinct, decorative shape. The task of piping out

TABLE 29.5 COOKIE TEXTURES

Desired Texture	Content of					
	Fat	Sugar	Liquid	Flour	Size or Shape	Baking
Crispness	High	High; use granulated sugar	Low	Bread or pastry	Thin dough	Well done; cool on baking sheet
Softness	Low	Low; use hygroscopic sugars	High	Pastry or cake	Thick dough portion	Use parchment-lined pan; underbake
Chewiness	High	High; use hygroscopic sugars	High	Bread or pastry	Not relevant; chilled dough	Underbake; cool on rack
Spread	High	High; use coarse granulated sugar	High; especially from eggs	Pastry or cake	Not relevant; room-temperature dough	Use greased pan; low temperature

dozens of identical cookies may seem daunting, but the skill can be mastered with practice and an understanding of doughs. Doughs for pressed cookies often include eggs as their only liquid. Egg whites, which are a toughener, contribute body and help the cookies retain their shape. The yolks act as a tenderizer. Using too much fat or too-soft flour (i.e., one low in protein) can cause the cookies to spread and lose their shape.

Wafer Cookies

Wafer cookies are extremely thin and delicate. They are made with a thin batter that is poured or spread onto a baking sheet and baked. Then, while still hot, the wafer is moulded into a variety of shapes. The most popular shapes are the tightly rolled cigarette, the curved tuile and the cup-shaped tulip. Wafer batter is sweet and buttery and is often flavoured with citrus zest or ground nuts.

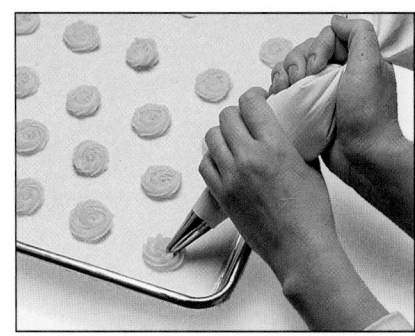

Pressed Cookies

Cookie Textures

The textures associated with cookies—crispness, softness, chewiness or spread—are affected by various factors, including the ratio of ingredients in the dough, the oven's temperature and the pan's coating. Understanding these factors allows you to adjust formulas or techniques to achieve the desired results. See Table 29.5.

Storing Cookies

Most cookies can be stored for up to one week in an airtight container. Do not store crisp cookies and soft cookies in the same container, however. The crisp cookies will absorb moisture from the soft cookies, ruining the texture of both. Do not store strongly flavoured cookies, such as spice, with those that are milder, such as shortbread.

Most cookies freeze well if wrapped air tight to prevent moisture loss or freezer burn. Raw dough can also be frozen, either shaped or unshaped.

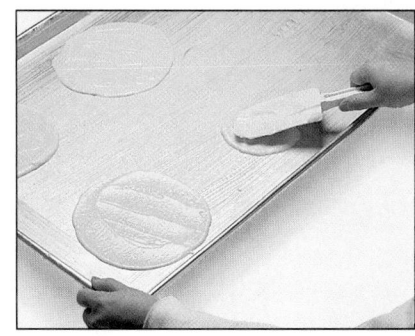

Wafer Cookies

CONCLUSION

Pastry making is the backbone of dessert preparation. A wide variety of pastry doughs can be prepared from flour, fat and a liquid. Proper mixing, rolling and shaping techniques are crucial to the success of the finished product. With a selection of properly prepared doughs and fillings, you can create an endless variety of tempting desserts.

QUESTIONS FOR DISCUSSION

1. How does the type of pie filling influence the selection of a pie crust? What type of crust would be best for a fresh unbaked fruit pie? Explain your answer.
2. How does rolling fat into a dough in layers (as with puff pastry) produce a flaky product? Why isn't sweet dough (which contains a high ratio of butter) flaky?

3. Explain the difference between a cream pie filling and a custard pie filling. Give two examples of each type of filling.

4. List and describe three ways of preparing fruit fillings for pies.

5. Why is it said that choux paste is the only paste that is cooked before it is baked? Why is this step necessary? List three ways for using choux paste in making classic desserts.

6. Explain the differences and similarities between common, Swiss, Italian and japonaise meringues.

7. List and describe four makeup methods for cookie doughs.

$\mathcal{A}$DDITIONAL PIE, PASTRY AND COOKIE FORMULAS

Several of the formulas given below are combinations of the pastry items presented in this chapter and the creams, custards and other dessert products covered in other chapters. For example, the Strawberry Napoleon is made with the puff pastry discussed in this chapter, the pastry cream and crème Chantilly discussed in Chapter 31, Custards, Creams, Frozen Desserts and Dessert Sauces, and the fondant glaze discussed in Chapter 30, Cakes and Frostings.

◆ ◆ ◆

RECIPE 29.12

GÂTEAU ST. HONORÉ

NOTE: *This dish appears in the Chapter Opening photograph.*
Chefs Susan Feniger and Mary Sue Milliken

Yield: 10 Servings

Puff pastry	500 g	1 lb.
Milk	125 mL	4 fl. oz.
Unsalted butter	50 g	1-3/4 oz.
Salt	1/2 g	1/8 tsp.
Bread flour	75 g	2-1/2 oz.
Eggs	2	2
Pastry Cream (Recipe 29.3)	600 g	20 oz.
Sugar	300 g	10 oz.
Water	120 mL	4 fl. oz.
City Chocolate (recipe follows)	as needed	as needed
Cream, 35%, cold	450 mL	1 pt.
Semi-sweet chocolate, melted	90 g	3 oz.

1. Roll out the puff pastry to form a 25-cm (10-inch) square; reserve in the refrigerator.

2. Make the choux paste by combining the milk, butter and salt in a medium-heavy saucepan. Bring to a boil. Add the flour all at once. Mix quickly with a wooden spoon until a ball forms on the spoon and the flour is evenly moistened. Transfer to a bowl, cool mixture to below 54°C (130°F) and add the eggs one at a time, beating well after each addition.

3. Fit a piping bag with a large plain tip; fill it with choux paste. Line a baking sheet with parchment paper. Pipe paste onto the baking sheet to form small cream puffs about the size of quarters. With a finger dipped in cold water, flatten the point on top of each puff. Drop the pan from a height of 5 cm (2 inches) onto the counter to set the puffs.

4. Bake at 230°C (450°F) until uniformly puffed and golden, approximately 10 minutes. Reduce heat to 190°C (375°F) and bake an additional 15–20 minutes. Test for doneness by opening a puff. The inside should be totally dry. Set aside to cool on a rack.

5. Place the puff pastry on a parchment paper–lined baking sheet and, with a 25-cm (10-inch) round cake pan inverted over the dough, trace a circle using a sharp knife. This will be the base for the cake. Prick the circle of puff pastry all over with a fork and set in the refrigerator to rest for 15 minutes.

6. Bake the puff pastry at 220°C (425°F) until puffed and golden, approximately 20 minutes. Reserve at room temperature.

7. Fit a piping bag with a No. 2 tip; fill it with pastry cream. Make a hole in the bottom of each puff using a small paring knife. Fill each puff with pastry cream and reserve.

8. To make the caramel, combine the sugar and water in a saucepan and cook until golden-brown. Immediately remove from heat. Using a fork, dip half of each cream puff into the warm caramel and place on a tray lined with parchment paper. When the caramel has set, turn each puff and dip the uncoated half in the caramel. Immediately arrange the puffs, flat side up, along the edge of the cooled puff pastry to form the wall.

9. Fill the centre of the pastry with an even layer of City Chocolate.

10. Whip the cold cream until soft peaks form. Fold half of this cream into the 90 g (3 oz.) of melted chocolate and set aside.

11. Spoon the remaining whipped cream into a pastry bag fitted with a No. 8 plain tip. Pipe about five rows of Hershey's Kiss–shaped domes (pointy chocolate kiss shapes) over the chocolate filling, leaving even spaces between the rows. Fill the bag with the chocolate-flavoured cream and repeat, filling the spaces between rows. Chill until serving time.

RECIPE 29.12

Approximate values per serving:

Calories	409
Total fat	26 g
Saturated fat	15 g
Cholesterol	115 mg
Sodium	68 mg
Total carbohydrates	41 g
Protein	4 g

CITY CHOCOLATE

Yield: 850 g (1 lb. 12 oz.)

Brandy	25 mL	1-1/2 Tbsp.
Golden raisins	50 g	1-1/2 oz.
Semi-sweet chocolate	275 g	9 oz.
Unsalted butter	225 g	7 oz.
Eggs, separated	5	5

1. Combine the brandy and raisins in a small saucepan and warm over low heat. Reserve.

2. Chop the chocolate into small pieces and melt with butter over a bain marie. Remove from the heat and stir in the raisins and brandy. Whisk in the egg yolks until combined.

3. Whisk the egg whites until soft peaks form. Gently fold the whites into the chocolate mixture in two stages.

City Chocolate—Approximate values per 30 g serving:

Calories	120
Total fat	9 g
Saturated fat	6 g
Cholesterol	55 mg
Sodium	15 mg
Total carbohydrates	7 g
Protein	2 g

Evelyn McManus, Ph.D.

Evelyn holds a Ph.D. in Biochemistry, as well as her Red Seal chef papers and her Patissiere papers. She is a graduate of the Stratford Chef School, where she won the Eckhardt award for outstanding achievement in pastry. Following several successful years as a chef in fine dining establishments, Evelyn is currently self-employed as a chef-consultant-food scientist and is the corporate chef for M&M Meat Shops in Kitchener.

◆◆◆

RECIPE 29.13

CARAMEL FLAN

PAIRDOCS SWEETS, Kitchener, ON
Evelyn McManus, Ph.D.

Yield: One 22-cm (10-inch) Flan

CREAM CHEESE PASTRY

Butter	250 g	8 oz.
Cream cheese	250 g	8 oz.
Salt	pinch	pinch
Lemon zest	10 g	1 Tbsp.
Pastry flour	300 g	10-1/2 oz.

1. Cream butter, cheese, salt and lemon zest until light and fluffy.

2. Add flour all at once and mix just until dough forms a ball. Chill at least 1 hour before using.

3. Line flan with pastry.

4. Bake blind at 175°C (350°F) until golden.

FILLING

Sugar	280 g	10 oz.
Eggs	450 g	8
Butter, unsalted	225 g	8 oz.
Salt	pinch	pinch
Sugar, caramelized	280 g	10 oz.
Hazelnuts, roasted, skinned, chopped	200 g	7 oz.
Dark chocolate ganache	300 g	10–11 oz.

1. Cream sugar, eggs, butter and salt until light and fluffy.

2. Dry cook second sugar to dark caramel colour; remove from heat and set the pot in cold water to stop the cooking process.

3. Stir the creamed mixture into the caramel, return to heat and bring to a boil. Cook until all lumps disappear and the mixture is smooth and glossy (about 10 minutes).

4. Add nuts, remove from heat and pour into cooked shell. Cool.

5. Top with dark chocolate ganache. Chill overnight.

◆◆◆

RECIPE 29.14

LINZER COOKIES

THE FAIRMONT EMPRESS, Victoria, BC
Pastry Chef Ken Harper

Yield: 15 Dozen

Sugar	200 g	6 oz.
Butter, unsalted, soft	250 g	8 oz.
Egg yolks	75 g	3
Bread flour	250 g	8 oz.
Cinnamon, ground	3.5 g	2 tsp.
Cloves, ground	1 g	1/2 tsp.
Hazelnuts, ground	200 g	6 oz.
Orange zest	8 g	2 tsp.

Cream Cheese Pastry—
Approximate values per serving:

Calories	313
Total fat	24 g
Saturated fat	15 g
Cholesterol	67 mg
Sodium	431 mg
Total carbohydrates	20 g
Protein	4 g

Filling—
Approximate values per serving:

Calories	481
Total fat	30 g
Saturated fat	11 g
Cholesterol	203 mg
Sodium	129 mg
Total carbohydrates	50 g
Protein	6.5 g

RECIPE 29.14

Approximate values per cookie:

Calories	29
Total fat	2 g
Saturated fat	1 g
Cholesterol	8 mg
Sodium	0 mg
Total carbohydrates	3 g
Protein	0.5 g

| Apricot jam | 100 g | 3 oz. |
| Icing sugar | as needed | as needed |

1. Combine sugar, butter and yolks in bowl using paddle at low speed.

2. Sift flour with cinnamon and cloves.

3. Add flour mixture, hazelnuts and zest to butter mixture. Mix until incorporated and smooth; overmixing will cause dough to be difficult to work with.

4. Cover dough and refrigerate 4 hours or overnight.

5. Roll dough out to 6-mm (1/4-inch) thickness. Cut cookies with 15-mm (1/2-inch) round cutter.

6. Bake at 175°C (350°F) for 10 minutes or until edges are very lightly browned. Cool.

7. Pipe apricot jam on half the cookies and press the tops on the jam. Dust with icing sugar just before serving. (Raspberry jam is traditional.)

❖❖❖

RECIPE 29.15

LEMON MERINGUE PIE

Yield: Two 22-cm (9-inch) Pies

Granulated sugar	600 g	1 lb. 5 oz.
Cornstarch	90 g	3 oz.
Salt	0.5 g	pinch
Water, cold	750 mL	26 fl. oz.
Egg yolks	225 g	10
Fresh lemon juice	250 mL	8 fl. oz.
Lemon zest, grated	25 g	2 Tbsp.
Butter	60 g	2 Tbsp.
Pie shells, prebaked	2	2
Egg whites	250 g	8 oz.
Granulated sugar	250 g	8 oz.

1. To make the filling, combine the 600 g (1 lb. 5 oz.) of sugar, cornstarch, salt and water in a heavy saucepan. Cook over medium-high heat, stirring constantly, until the mixture becomes thick and almost clear.

2. Remove from the heat and slowly whisk in the egg yolks. Stir until completely blended. Return to the heat and cook, stirring constantly, until thick and smooth.

3. Stir in the lemon juice and zest. When the liquid is completely incorporated, remove the filling from the heat. Add the butter and stir until melted.

4. Set the filling aside to cool briefly. Fill two prebaked pie shells with the lemon filling.

5. To prepare the meringue, whip the egg whites until soft peaks form. Slowly add the 250 g (8 oz.) of sugar while whisking constantly. The meringue should be stiff and glossy, not dry or spongy looking.

6. Mound the meringue over the filling, creating decorative patterns with a spatula. Be sure to spread the meringue to the edge of the crust, so all the filling is covered.

7. Place the pie in a 200°C (400°F) oven until the meringue is golden-brown, approximately 5–8 minutes. Let cool at room temperature, then refrigerate. Serve the same day.

VARIATION: *Key Lime Pie*—Substitute 200 mL (7 fl. oz.) key lime juice for the lemon juice and zest. Pour the filling into two prebaked pie shells and chill. Top with whipped cream. True Key Lime Pie is made with sweetened condensed milk.

Ken Harper

Born and raised in Victoria, Ken completed his scholarship in Camosun College's Culinary program and then joined the Fairmont Empress as an apprentice chef. Highlights of his career include joining the culinary teams at the Fairmont Banff Springs Hotel, the Fairmont Château Whistler Resort and the Pan Pacific Hotel. He has been Pastry Chef at the Empress since 1997.

RECIPE 29.15

*Approximate values
per 1/8 pie:*

Calories	404
Total fat	12 g
Saturated fat	4 g
Cholesterol	135 mg
Sodium	310 mg
Total carbohydrates	68 g
Protein	5 g

♦♦♦

RECIPE 29.16

Blackberry Cobbler

*A **cobbler** is a home-style baked fruit dessert, usually made with a top crust of flaky pie dough, biscuit dough or streusel topping. The finished product will be slightly runny and is often served warm in a bowl or rimmed dish, accompanied by whipped cream or ice cream.*

Yield: 10 Servings

Individually quick-frozen blackberries	2 L	2 qt.
Sugar	250 g	8 oz.
Tapioca	60 g	2 oz.
Water	300 mL	10 fl. oz.
Unsalted butter	60 g	2 oz.
Lemon zest	10 g	1 Tbsp.
Topping (see Step 3)		

1. Combine all ingredients, tossing the berries gently until well coated with the other ingredients.
2. Transfer to a lightly buttered half-size hotel pan, then set aside for at least 30 minutes before baking.
3. The cobbler can be topped with basic pie dough (about 200 g/7 oz.) (Recipe 29.1), scone dough (300–500 g/10–18 oz.) (Recipe 27.1) or streusel topping (300–500 g/10–18 oz.) (Recipe 27.6) before baking.
4. Bake at 180°C (350°F) until the berry mixture bubbles and the crust is appropriately browned, approximately 40–50 minutes.

♦♦♦

RECIPE 29.16

Approximate values per serving:

Calories	210
Total fat	5 g
Saturated fat	3 g
Cholesterol	20 mg
Sodium	10 mg
Total carbohydrates	39 g
Protein	1 g

Albert Liu

Albert began his career as a pâtissier at the Four Seasons Hotel in Vancouver, worked as an Executive Pastry Chef in the Bahamas, and then became the Executive Pastry Chef at the Palliser Hotel in Calgary. Currently he is a Pastry Chef Instructor at SAIT in Calgary.

RECIPE 29.17

Approximate values per 1/12 pie:

Calories	435
Total fat	25 g
Saturated fat	9 g
Cholesterol	140 mg
Sodium	105 mg
Total carbohydrates	52 g
Protein	5.5 g

RECIPE 29.17

Pecan Pie

SOUTHERN ALBERTA INSTITUTE OF TECHNOLOGY, Calgary, AB
Pastry Chef Albert Liu

Yield: One 20-cm (8-inch) Pie

Brown sugar	225 g	8 oz.
Corn syrup	225 g	8 oz.
Butter	50 g	1-1/2 oz.
Whole eggs	275 g	5
Vanilla	2 mL	1/2 tsp.
Pecans, whole	200 g	7 oz.
Sweet Paste (Recipe 29.2)	500 g	1 lb.

1. In a saucepan, heat brown sugar, corn syrup and butter and bring to a boil. Remove from heat.
2. Mix the whole eggs and vanilla, then gradually whisk the hot sauce into the egg mixture.
3. Pour the filling in the prepared pie shell. Sprinkle pecans onto each pie.
4. Bake at 160°C (325°F) from 45 minutes to 1 hour or until set.

◆◆◆

RECIPE 29.18

APPLE CUSTARD FLAN

SOUTHERN ALBERTA INSTITUTE OF TECHNOLOGY, CALGARY, AB
Pastry Chef Albert Liu

Yield: One 20-cm (8-inch) Flan

Sweet Paste (Recipe 29.2)	300 g	10-1/2 oz.
Golden apples	5	5
Whole eggs	110 g	2
Granulated sugar	75 g	2-1/2 oz.
Cornstarch	15 g	1/2 oz.
Milk, 2%	125 g	4 oz.
Cream, 35%	125 g	4 oz.
Vanilla	2 mL	1/2 tsp.
Nutmeg, grated	pinch	pinch

1. Line the flan tin with the sweet paste. Set aside.
2. Peel and slice the apples.
3. Arrange the apples in the flan, overlapping them in a circle.
4. In a bowl, combine the eggs, sugar and cornstarch.
5. Add the milk, cream, vanilla and nutmeg. Whisk to blend.
6. Pour mixture over apples.
7. Bake at 170°C (350°F) until custard is set, about 45 minutes.

Albert Liu
Albert began his career as a pâtissier at the Four Seasons Hotel in Vancouver, worked as an Executive Pastry Chef in the Bahamas, and then became the Executive Pastry Chef at the Palliser Hotel in Calgary. Currently he is a Pastry Chef Instructor at SAIT in Calgary.

RECIPE 29.18

Approximate values per 1/12 flan:

Calories	252
Total fat	13 g
Saturated fat	8 g
Cholesterol	86 mg
Sodium	26 mg
Total carbohydrates	33 g
Protein	3.5 g

◆◆◆

RECIPE 29.19

FRESH BERRY TART

Yield: One 22-cm (9-inch) Tart

Sweet Paste tart shell, fully baked (Recipe 29.2)	1	1
Pastry Cream (Recipe 31.2)	500 mL	1 pt.
Fresh berries (strawberries, blackberries, blueberries or raspberries)	1.5 L	3 pt.
Apricot glaze	as needed	as needed

1. Fill a cool tart shell with pastry cream.
2. Arrange the berries over the pastry cream in an even layer. Be sure to place the berries so the pastry cream is covered.
3. Heat the apricot glaze and brush over the fruit to form a smooth coating.

RECIPE 29.19

Approximate values per 1/6 tart:

Calories	135
Total fat	3 g
Saturated fat	1 g
Cholesterol	2 mg
Sodium	62 g
Total carbohydrates	26 g
Protein	2 g

1. Arrange the fruit over the pastry cream.

2. Brush the apricot glaze over the fruit.

◆◆◆

RECIPE 29.20

QUICK PUFF PASTRY

ADAPTED FROM *Nick Malgieri's Perfect Pastry*
(New York: Macmillan, 1989)

Yield: 550 g (1 lb. 4 oz.)

Unbleached bread flour	175 g	6-1/4 oz.
Cake flour	35 g	1-1/4 oz.
Unsalted butter	225 g	8 oz.
Salt	2 mL	1/2 tsp.
Water, very cold	120 mL	4 fl. oz.

1. To mix the dough, place the bread flour in a 2-L (2-qt.) mixer bowl and sift the cake flour over it. Thoroughly stir the two flours together.

2. Slice 30 g (1 oz.) of the butter into thin pieces and add to the bowl. Rub in the butter by hand, tossing and squeezing in the butter until no visible pieces remain.

3. Cut the remaining butter into 10-mm (1/2-inch) cubes. Add the butter cubes to the flour mixture. Toss with a rubber spatula just to separate and distribute the butter. Do not rub the butter into the flour.

4. Dissolve the salt in the water. Make a well in the flour-butter mixture and add the water. Toss gently with the spatula until the dough is evenly moistened. Add drops of water, if necessary, to complete the moistening. Press and squeeze the dough in a bowl to form a rough cylinder.

5. To turn the dough, first lightly flour the work surface and the dough. Using the palm of your hand, press down on the dough three to four times to shape the dough into a rough rectangle.

6. Press and pound the dough with a rolling pin to form an even rectangle about 10 mm (1/2 inch) thick. Roll the dough back and forth along its length once or twice until it is an even rectangle about 6 mm (1/4 inch) thick. At this stage, pieces of butter are likely to stick to the work surface. If the dough does stick, loosen it with a long spatula or scraper. Clean the surface to minimize further sticking.

7. Fold both ends of the dough in towards the centre, then fold them in towards the centre again to make four layers. The folded package of dough will resemble a book, with a spine on one side and the cover opening opposite it. Position the package of dough so that the spine is on the left.

8. Lightly flour the work surface and the dough and repeat the pressing as before. Roll the dough along its length as before, then roll several times along its width to form a rectangle approximately 15 × 45 cm (6 × 18 inches). Fold the dough, both ends in towards the centre, then over again as before. Repeat the process once more so that the dough will have three double turns.

9. Wrap the dough well in plastic and chill for at least 1 hour before using.

10. The dough can be refrigerated for about 3 days or frozen for up to 1 month. Defrost frozen dough in the refrigerator overnight before using it.

RECIPE 29.20

*Approximate values
per 50 g serving:*

Calories	209
Total fat	17 g
Saturated fat	10 g
Cholesterol	45 mg
Sodium	88 mg
Total carbohydrates	13 g
Protein	2.5 g

♦♦♦

RECIPE 29.21

Saskatoon Almond Tart with Cinnamon Ice Cream and Oatmeal Praline

HARDWARE GRILL, Edmonton, AB
Chef/Owner Larry Stewart, CCC

Yield: 6 Servings

DOUGH

Unsalted butter, cubed	100 g	3 oz.
Egg	1	1
Icing sugar	50 g	1-1/2 oz.
Pastry flour	175 g	6 oz.
Baking powder	7 g	2 tsp.

1. Beat butter and egg with a paddle attachment until the mixture resembles scrambled eggs. Add icing sugar and beat on high speed until mixture is smooth.
2. On low speed, add flour and baking powder. Mix just until mixture comes away from sides of bowl.
3. Form dough into a ball and chill for at least 1 hour. Divide dough into six pieces and roll into 15-cm (6-inch) rounds. Line tart moulds and par-bake at 175°C (350°F) for 10 minutes.

ALMOND STREUSEL

Butter, softened	60 g	2 oz.
Rolled oats	50 g	1-1/2 oz.
Brown sugar	50 g	1-1/2 oz.
Almonds, sliced	50 g	1-1/2 oz.
Flour, pastry	50 g	1-1/2 oz.
Cinnamon	1 g	1/4 tsp.

Combine all ingredients into a crumbly mixture.

SASKATOON ALMOND FILLING

Almond paste	150 g	5-1/2 oz.
Butter, softened	70 g	2-1/2 oz.
Sugar	120 g	4 oz.
Eggs	120 g	2
Lemon zest	10 g	1 Tbsp.
Grand Marnier	15 mL	1/2 fl. oz.
Flour	20 g	2-1/2 Tbsp.
Baking powder	0.25 g	1/2 tsp.
Saskatoon berries, thawed and drained	175 g	6 oz.

1. Mix the almond paste, butter and sugar with paddle. Add eggs, lemon zest and Grand Marnier and mix well.
2. Add sifted flour and baking powder. Mix to blend. Fold in saskatoon berries.
3. Divide almond batter among tart shells and top with streusel.
4. Bake at 160°C (325°F) for approximately 20 minutes.

OATMEAL PRALINE

Butter, melted	60 g	2 oz.
Brown sugar	45 g	1-1/2 oz.

Larry Stewart, CCC
Run by Larry since its opening in 1996, the Hardware Grill restaurant recently received a two-star rating, making it one of only 57 restaurants nationwide to have earned this ranking for food, wine and service. As the owner, Larry is also proud of the fact that his restaurant is listed in Where to Eat in Canada *for the fourth consecutive year.*

Dough—
Approximate values per serving:

Calories	270
Total fat	15 g
Saturated fat	9 g
Cholesterol	72 mg
Sodium	98 mg
Total carbohydrates	31.5 g
Protein	3.5 g

Almond Streusel—
Approximate values per serving:

Calories	214
Total fat	13 g
Saturated fat	6 g
Cholesterol	22 mg
Sodium	87 mg
Total carbohydrates	22 g
Protein	4 g

Saskatoon Almond Filling—
Approximate values per serving:

Calories	329
Total fat	18 g
Saturated fat	7 g
Cholesterol	112 mg
Sodium	128 mg
Total carbohydrates	36 g
Protein	6 g

Continued

Sugar	30 g	1 oz.
Corn syrup	30 g	1 oz.
Rolled oats	115 g	4 oz.

1. Mix all ingredients well.
2. Spread on a small baking sheet.
3. Bake for 8–10 minutes at 175°C (350°F).
4. Cool and break into small pieces.

CINNAMON ICE CREAM

Milk	250 mL	8 fl. oz.
Cream, 35%	250 mL	8 fl. oz.
Honey	125 g	4 oz.
Cinnamon	15 g	3 Tbsp.
Vanilla bean, split	1	1
Egg yolks	16	16
Sugar	250 g	8 oz.

1. Scald milk, cream, honey, cinnamon and vanilla bean. Let steep 1 hour and cool. Remove vanilla bean.
2. Whisk yolks and sugar to ribbon stage.
3. Slowly whisk the scalded mixture into the egg mixture. Return the mixture to a medium flame and whisk constantly until the custard thickens. Strain and cool.
4. Follow the manufacturer's directions for churn freezing.

ASSEMBLY:

Place a warm tart on a plate. Serve with a scoop of ice cream. Sprinkle oatmeal praline over tart and ice cream.

◆ ◆ ◆

RECIPE 29.22

LEMON THYME PEAR TART WITH JASMINE TEA GLAZE

THE FAIRMONT EMPRESS, VICTORIA, BC
Pastry Chef Ken Harper

Yield: 10 Servings

Puff pastry	250 g	8 oz.
Lemon Thyme Almond Cream (recipe follows)	450 g	1 lb.
Poached pear halves, fanned	10	10
Jasmine Tea Glaze (recipe follows)	as needed	as needed

1. Roll out puff pastry into a circle, approximately 22 cm (9 inches) in diameter and 3 mm (1/8 inch) thick. Lay the dough on a sheet pan lined with parchment paper. Dock with a fork.
2. Using a plain tip, pipe 10 teardrops of Lemon Thyme Almond Cream around the ring of puff pastry.
3. Arrange the pear fans over the almond cream, overlapping slightly.
4. Bake at 180°C (375°F) until the dough is golden, approximately 15 minutes.
5. Serve warm, glazed with Jasmine Tea Glaze and accompanied by vanilla ice cream.

Oatmeal Praline—
Approximate values per serving:

Calories	208
Total fat	9 g
Saturated fat	5 g
Cholesterol	22 mg
Sodium	89 mg
Total carbohydrates	29 g
Protein	3 g

Cinnamon Ice Cream—
Approximate values per serving:

Calories	555
Total fat	30 g
Saturated fat	14 g
Cholesterol	634 mg
Sodium	57 mg
Total carbohydrates	65 g
Protein	10 g

Ken Harper
Born and raised in Victoria, Ken completed his scholarship in Camosun College's Culinary program then joined The Fairmont Empress as an apprentice chef. Highlights of his career include joining the culinary teams at the Fairmont Banff Springs Hotel, the Fairmont Château Whistler Resort, and the Pan Pacific Hotel. He has been Pastry Chef at the Empress since 1997.

RECIPE 29.22

Approximate values per serving:

Calories	441
Total fat	27.5 g
Saturated fat	11 g
Cholesterol	146 mg
Sodium	96 mg
Total carbohydrates	43 g
Protein	7 g

LEMON THYME ALMOND CREAM (FRANGIPANE)

Yield: 700 g (1.5 lb.)

Unsalted butter, softened	100 g	3-1/2 oz.
Granulated sugar	125 g	4 oz.
Eggs	125 g	2
All-purpose flour	10 g	4 tsp.
Almonds, ground	175 g	6 oz.
Lemon zest	10 g	1
Lemon thyme	2 g	1 tsp.

1. Cream the butter and sugar. Slowly add the eggs, scraping down the sides of the bowl as necessary.

2. Stir the flour, ground almonds, lemon zest and lemon thyme together, then add to the butter mixture. Blend until no lumps remain.

JASMINE TEA GLAZE

White wine	180 mL	6-1/2 fl. oz.
Jasmine tea	15 mL	1 Tbsp.
Sugar	60 g	2 oz.
Jelly powder	5 g	1-1/2 tsp.
Apricot jam	15 g	1 Tbsp.

1. Bring wine to a boil, add tea and steep for 2 hours. Strain.

2. Bring back to a boil and whisk in sugar, jelly powder and jam.

❖❖❖

RECIPE 29.23

STRAWBERRY NAPOLEON

Yield: 10 Servings

Puff pastry, cut into 10-cm × 37-cm (4-inch × 15-inch) strips, docked and baked	3	3
Pastry Cream (Recipe 31.2)	500 mL	1 pt.
Fresh strawberries, sliced	1 L	1 qt.
Crème Chantilly (Recipe 31.6)	500 mL	1 pt.
Sugar Glaze (Recipe 30.13)	as needed	as needed
Dark chocolate, melted	30 g	1 oz.

1. Allow the puff pastry to cool completely before assembling.

2. Place a strip of puff pastry on a cake cardboard for support. Pipe on a layer of pastry cream, leaving a clean margin of almost 10 mm (1/2 inch) on all four sides.

3. Top the cream with a layer of berries.

4. Spread on a thin layer of crème Chantilly. Repeat the procedure for the second layer of puff pastry.

5. Chill while you prepare the sugar glaze. When ready to glaze, place the third strip of puff pastry on an icing rack, flat side up. Pour the sugar glaze down the length of the pastry and spread evenly with a metal cake spatula. Allow the excess to drip over the sides.

6. Immediately pipe thin lines of chocolate across the glaze. Use a toothpick to pull a spiderweb pattern in the glaze. Chill to set the glaze, then place the top in position on the napoleon.

Lemon Thyme Almond Cream (Frangipane)—Approximate values per 70 g serving:	
Calories	245
Total fat	19 g
Saturated fat	6 g
Cholesterol	76 mg
Sodium	19 mg
Total carbohydrates	17 g
Protein	5 g

Jasmine Tea Glaze— Approximate values per serving:	
Calories	41
Total fat	0 g
Saturated fat	0 g
Cholesterol	0 mg
Sodium	3 mg
Total carbohydrates	7 g
Protein	0.5 g

RECIPE 29.23

Approximate values per serving:

Calories	320
Total fat	20 g
Saturated fat	9 g
Cholesterol	115 mg
Sodium	65 mg
Total carbohydrates	29 g
Protein	4 g

◆◆◆

RECIPE 29.24

PALMIERS

Puff pastry	as needed
Granulated sugar	as needed

1. Roll out the puff pastry into a very thin rectangle. The length is not important but the width should be at least 17.5 cm (7 inches).
2. Sprinkle puff pastry sheet lightly with granulated sugar. Using a rolling pin, gently press the granulated sugar into the dough. Flip over and repeat.
3. Along the long edges of the dough make a 2.5-cm (1-inch) fold towards the centre. Sprinkle on additional sugar.
4. Make another 2.5-cm (1-inch) fold along the long edges towards the centre. The two folds should almost meet in the centre. Sprinkle on additional sugar.
5. Fold one side on top of the other. Press down gently with a rolling pin or your fingers so that the dough adheres. Chill for 1 hour.
6. Cut the log of dough in thin slices. Place the cookies on a paper-lined sheet pan and bake at 200°C (400°F) until the edges are brown, approximately 8–12 minutes.

RECIPE 29.24

Approximate values per 30 g serving:

Calories	130
Total fat	5 g
Saturated fat	1 g
Cholesterol	0 mg
Sodium	35 mg
Total carbohydrates	19 g
Protein	1 g

1. Fold the dough towards the centre from both edges.

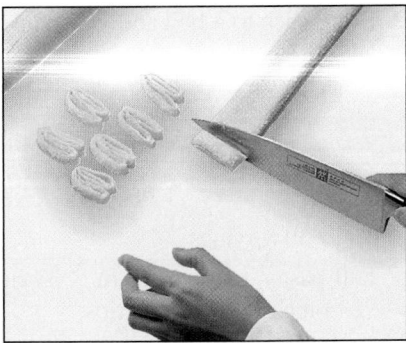

2. Slice the log of dough into individual cookies.

◆◆◆

RECIPE 29.25

CHOCOLATE ÉCLAIRS

Yield: 20 Éclairs

Baked éclair shells, 10 cm (4 inches) long, made from Basic Choux Paste (Recipe 29.9)	20	20
Pastry Cream (Recipe 31.2), chocolate flavoured	1 L	1 qt.
Chocolate glaze:		
Unsweetened chocolate	125 g	4 oz.
Semi-sweet chocolate	125 g	4 oz.
Unsalted butter	125 g	4 oz.
White corn syrup	25 mL	4 tsp.
White chocolate, melted (optional)	as needed	as needed

RECIPE 29.25

Approximate values per serving:

Calories	410
Total fat	31 g
Saturated fat	17 g
Cholesterol	110 mg
Sodium	230 mg
Total carbohydrates	27 g
Protein	5 g

1. Use a paring knife or skewer to cut a small hole into the end of each baked, cooled éclair shell.

2. Pipe the pastry cream into each shell using a piping bag fitted with a small plain tip. Be sure that the cream fills the full length of each shell. Refrigerate the filled éclairs.

3. Prepare the glaze by melting all ingredients together over a bain marie. Remove from the heat and allow to cool, occasionally stirring, until slightly thickened.

4. In a single, smooth stroke, dip the top of each filled éclair through the glaze. Only the very top of each pastry should be coated with chocolate.

5. Melted white chocolate may be piped onto the wet glaze, then pulled into patterns using a toothpick. (See sauce-pulling techniques in Chapter 35, Plate Presentation.) Keep finished éclairs refrigerated and serve within 8–12 hours.

1. Fill the éclairs with pastry cream using a piping bag.

2. Dip the éclairs in chocolate glaze.

♦♦♦

RECIPE 29.26

CHOCOLATE DÉLICE

Yield: One 20-cm (8-inch) Cake

Classic Dacquoise (recipe follows)
Ganache (Recipe 30.15)
Crème Chantilly (Recipe 31.6)
Candied Almonds (recipe follows)

1. Spread an even layer of ganache over two of the dacquoise disks.

2. Top one disk with about 200 g (7 oz.) of crème Chantilly. Place the second disk on top, chocolate side up. Top with another 200 g (7 oz.) of crème Chantilly. Position the third disk on top, flat side up.

3. Spread the remaining crème Chantilly over the top and sides.

4. Sprinkle candied almonds over the top and sides of the cake.

5. Freeze to firm the cream, approximately 1 hour. Remove from freezer and refrigerate for service.

CLASSIC DACQUOISE

Blanched almonds	60 g	2 oz.
Granulated sugar	180 g	6 oz.
Egg whites	90 g	3 oz.

1. Preheat oven to 110°C (225°F). Line a baking sheet with parchment. Draw three 20-cm (8-inch) circles on the parchment.

2. Grind the nuts in a food processor. They should be the consistency of cornmeal and as dry as possible. Combine with 60 g (2 oz.) of the sugar and set aside.

3. Whip the egg whites on medium speed until foamy. Increase the speed and gradually add 30 g (1 oz.) of the sugar.

4. Continue whipping until the egg whites form soft peaks. Gradually add the remaining 90 g (3 oz.) of sugar.

5. Continue whipping until smooth and glossy, about 2 minutes.

6. Sprinkle the almond-sugar mixture over the meringue and fold together by hand using a spatula.

7. Using a pastry bag with a plain tip and the circles on the parchment paper as a guide, pipe the meringue into three 20-cm (8-inch) disks.

8. Bake until firm and crisp but not brown, approximately 60–75 minutes. Cool completely.

RECIPE 29.26

Approximate values per serving:

Calories	490
Total fat	32.5 g
Saturated fat	13 g
Cholesterol	50 mg
Sodium	35 mg
Total carbohydrates	39 g
Protein	10 g

Classic Dacquoise—
Approximate values per serving:

Calories	100
Total fat	2.5 g
Saturated fat	0 g
Cholesterol	0 mg
Sodium	15 mg
Total carbohydrates	16 g
Protein	2 g

CANDIED ALMONDS

Egg whites	2	2
Granulated sugar	60 g	2 oz.
Sliced almonds	250 g	8 oz.

1. Preheat oven to 160°C (325°F).
2. Whisk the egg whites and sugar together. Add the almonds. Toss with a rubber spatula to coat the nuts completely.
3. Spread the nuts in a thin layer on a lightly greased baking sheet. Bake until lightly toasted and dry, approximately 15–20 minutes. Watch closely to prevent burning.
4. Stir the nuts with a metal spatula every 5–7 minutes during baking.
5. Cool completely. Store in an airtight container for up to 10 days.

Candied Almonds—Approximate values per serving:

Calories	160
Total fat	10 g
Saturated fat	1 g
Cholesterol	0 mg
Sodium	10 mg
Total carbohydrates	10 g
Protein	6 g

❖❖❖

RECIPE 29.27

OATMEAL COCONUT COOKIES

Yield: Thirty-Five 85-g (3-oz.) Cookies

Shortening	360 g	13 oz.
Brown sugar	540 g	20 oz.
Salt	10 g	2 tsp.
Baking soda	5 g	1-1/2 tsp.
Whole eggs	90 g	3-1/2 oz.
Milk	50 mL	2 fl. oz.
Oatmeal	225 g	8 oz.
Coconut, fine	180 g	6 oz.
Pastry flour	360 g	13 oz.
Baking powder	10 g	1 Tbsp.

1. Cream the shortening, brown sugar, salt and baking soda until light and fluffy.
2. Beat in eggs and milk, scraping down bowl.
3. Add mixture of oatmeal, coconut, pastry flour and baking powder. Blend together until just well combined.
4. Portion with a scoop, flatten slightly and bake in a 190°C (375°F) oven for 15–20 minutes or until lightly browned on the edges.

RECIPE 29.27

Approximate values per cookie:

Calories	221
Total fat	12 g
Saturated fat	4 g
Cholesterol	11 mg
Sodium	194 mg
Total carbohydrates	26 g
Protein	1.5 g

❖❖❖

RECIPE 29.28

SUGAR COOKIES

Yield: 3 Dozen   **Method:** Cut-out Cookies

Pastry flour	375 g	12 oz.
Baking powder	7 g	2 tsp.
Mace, ground	0.75 g	1/4 tsp.
Unsalted butter, softened	125 g	4 oz.
Granulated sugar	250 g	8 oz.
Vanilla extract	5 mL	1 tsp.
Egg	55 g	1

1. Stir together the flour, baking powder and mace. Set aside.
2. Cream the butter and sugar until light and fluffy. Blend in the vanilla. Add the egg and beat again until fluffy. Gradually add the flour mixture, beating just until well combined.

RECIPE 29.28

Approximate values per cookie:

Calories	92
Total fat	3 g
Saturated fat	2 g
Cholesterol	14 mg
Sodium	17 mg
Total carbohydrates	15 g
Protein	1 g

3. Wrap the dough in plastic wrap and refrigerate until firm, about 1–2 hours.

4. Work with about half the dough at a time, keeping the remainder refrigerated. On a lightly floured board, roll out the dough to a thickness of about 3 mm (1/8 inch). Cut as desired with cookie cutters. Carefully transfer the cookies to lightly greased baking sheets.

5. Bake at 160°C (325°F) until golden brown, approximately 10–12 minutes. Let stand for about 1 minute, then transfer to wire racks to cool.

VARIATION: Ken Harper, Fairmont Empress, recommends flavouring with 15 g (5 Tbsp.) dried, crushed, lavender.

❖❖❖

RECIPE 29.29

SPRITZ PIPED COOKIES

Yield: 5 Dozen   **Method:** Pressed Cookies

Unsalted butter, softened	350 g	12-1/2 oz.
Shortening	160 g	5-3/4 oz.
Bread flour	340 g	12 oz.
Cake flour, sifted	340 g	12 oz.
Vanilla extract	5 mL	1 tsp.
Lemon zest (optional)	TT	TT
Egg whites	110 g	4 oz.
Icing sugar	120 g	4 oz.

1. Cream the butter and shortening until light and fluffy. Add the flours, vanilla and lemon zest (if desired) and beat well for 6–8 minutes until fluffy.

2. Make a stiff meringue from the egg whites and sugar.

3. Blend the flour and meringue mixtures until smooth.

4. Pipe the dough onto an ungreased sheet pan using a piping bag fitted with a medium or large star tip.

5. Bake at 190°C (375°F) until lightly browned around edges, approximately 10 minutes. Transfer to wire racks to cool.

NOTE: May be drizzled with chocolate or the ends may be dipped in chocolate.

RECIPE 29.29

Approximate values per cookie:

Calories	81
Total fat	5 g
Saturated fat	2.5 g
Cholesterol	9 mg
Sodium	3 mg
Total carbohydrates	7 g
Protein	1 g

❖❖❖

RECIPE 29.30

ALMOND TULIP (TUILE) MIX

Yield: Varies according to template

Almond paste	500 g	17-1/2 oz.
Sugar	200 g	7 oz.
Egg whites	275 g	10 oz.
Salt	0.5 g	pinch
Vanilla	1 mL	dash
Cinnamon	0.25 g	pinch
Lemon juice	5 mL	1 tsp.
Cream, 35%	125 mL	4 fl. oz.
Bread flour	300 g	10-1/2 oz.

1. Beat the almond paste, sugar and egg whites until smooth. Add the salt, vanilla, cinnamon, lemon juice and cream and beat until smooth.

RECIPE 29.30

Approximate values per 30 g serving:

Calories	96
Total fat	4 g
Saturated fat	1 g
Cholesterol	4 mg
Sodium	26 mg
Total carbohydrates	13 g
Protein	4 g

Continued

Mark Jorundson

Mark received his Journeyman certification from the Northern Alberta Institute of Technology, earning the title "Canadian Apprentice of the Year." He went on to travel Europe, eventually catering to the rich and famous at the renowned Anton Mossiman's Belfry in London. Upon returning to Canada, Mark joined Canadian Pacific Hotels and offered Canadian cuisine at the Lodge at Kananaskis and the Hotel Macdonald in Edmonton, Alberta.

RECIPE 29.31

Approximate values per horn:

Calories	35
Total fat	2 g
Saturated fat	1 g
Cholesterol	4 mg
Sodium	17 mg
Total carbohydrates	5 g
Protein	0 g

Dean Cole

Dean trained first in Birmingham, England, where he won the "Taste of Britain" competition and Chef of the Year in 1989. He spent three years at the Connaught Hotel in London, specializing in patisserie. Dean moved to Toronto in 1995 and now is the Pastry Chef at the new Winston's in Toronto. He likes to teach demonstration classes in his spare time.

---

2. Add the flour and mix until smooth and free of lumps.

3. Let the batter rest for 1 hour or overnight.

4. Spread the mixture into a template to give it a shape. Bake at 200°C (400°F) until the edges are brown and the dough is dry, approximately 12–18 minutes.

◆◆◆

RECIPE 29.31

BRANDY SNAPS

CHANCE RESTAURANT, EDMONTON, AB
Executive Chef Mark Jorundson

Yield: 100 Horns

Granulated sugar	200 g	8 oz.
Honey	200 g	8 oz.
Butter	200 g	8 oz.
Bread flour	200 g	8 oz.
Brandy	25 mL	1 fl. oz.
Orange zest, grated fine	25 g	2 Tbsp.

1. Cream the sugar, honey and butter together, then add the flour and brandy. Mix at medium speed for about 5 minutes to form a paste.

2. Add the orange zest.

3. Pipe or spoon an amount of mixture no larger than 1 cm (1/2 inch) onto a silicone-sheeted pan. (Mixture will spread to a circle 10–15 cm/4–6 inch in diameter.)

4. Bake at 200°C (400°F) until mixture spreads and is bubbly. Edges should begin to appear crisp.

5. Remove from oven and shape over a cream horn tube, a dowel or rod, or a cup or glass (to form a basket). If desired, shape hot cookies with a cutter to form perfect circles.

◆◆◆

RECIPE 29.32

BANANA BUTTER TART WITH BITTER CHOCOLATE SORBET AND RUM AND RAISIN CRÈME ANGLAISE

WINSTON'S, TORONTO, ON
Pastry Chef Dean Cole

Yield: 12 Servings

Cinnamon Sablée Paste (recipe follows)
Butter Mix (recipe follows)
Bananas (3, sliced); sugar to glaze
Rum and Raisin Crème Anglaise (recipe follows)
Bitter Chocolate Sorbet (recipe follows)
Banana Wafers (recipe follows)
Mint leaves

1. Prepare shells using Cinnamon Sablée Paste.

2. Pour Butter Mix into shells and bake at 120°C (250°F) until set, about 15 minutes. Do not let the filling boil.

3. When filling is cold, layer thin slices of banana on top. Sprinkle with sugar and caramelize.

4. Mirror the centre of a plate with Rum and Raisin Crème Anglaise and place the butter tart in the centre.

5. Top the tart with a rounded scoop of Bitter Chocolate Sorbet.

6. Place one Banana Wafer in the centre of the scoop, pointed side down.

7. Garnish with two mint leaves and serve immediately.

CINNAMON SABLÉE PASTE

Yield: 12 Tart Shells

Flour, pastry	275 g	9 oz.
Cinnamon	7 g	1/4 oz.
Sugar	90 g	3 oz.
Butter	175 g	6 oz.
Egg yolks	2	2

1. Using the blender's paddle attachment at low speed, cut in flour, cinnamon, sugar and butter until fine crumb stage is reached.

2. Add egg yolks and mix just until evenly blended.

3. Place mixture on a floured surface and cream with the palm of the hand until the paste has a soft, smooth consistency.

4. Chill for several hours.

5. Line twelve 9-cm (3-1/2-inch) metal rings with paste and bake at 175°C (350°F) for 7 minutes to set.

BUTTER MIX

Golden brown sugar	400 g	14 oz.
Dark corn syrup	350 g	12 oz.
Salt	3 g	1/2 tsp.
Cinnamon	4 g	2 tsp.
Ginger	1.6 g	1 tsp.
Eggs, whole	225 g	4
Butter, melted	300 g	10 oz.

1. Using the blender's paddle attachment at low speed, mix together brown sugar, corn syrup, salt, cinnamon and ginger until blended.

2. With machine running, add eggs one at a time.

3. Pour melted butter into mixture and mix thoroughly.

RUM AND RAISIN CRÈME ANGLAISE

Raisins	75 g	3 oz.
Rum	50 mL	2 fl. oz.
Egg yolks	5	5
Sugar	50 g	2 oz.
Milk	250 g	8-1/2 oz.
Cream, 35%	175 g	6 oz.
Vanilla bean	1	1
Sugar	50 g	2 oz.

1. Boil raisins in water for 1 minute.

2. Strain and add rum. Set aside.

3. Whisk together egg yolks and sugar until white and thick.

4. Scald milk, cream, vanilla bean and sugar. Infuse vanilla for 5 minutes and scald again.

5. Temper the egg mixture with the infused liquid.

RECIPE 29.32

Approximate values per serving:

Calories	1126
Total fat	68 g
Saturated fat	40 g
Cholesterol	368 mg
Sodium	159 mg
Total carbohydrates	133 g
Protein	14 g

Cinnamon Sablée Paste—
Approximate values per tart shell:

Calories	220
Total fat	13 g
Saturated fat	8 g
Cholesterol	67 mg
Sodium	4 mg
Total carbohydrates	24 g
Protein	2 g

Butter Mix—Approximate values
per 30 g serving:

Calories	109
Total fat	6 g
Saturated fat	3 g
Cholesterol	33 mg
Sodium	62 mg
Total carbohydrates	15 g
Protein	0.5 g

Rum and Raisin Crème Anglaise—
Approximate values
per 30 g serving:

Calories	69
Total fat	4 g
Saturated fat	2 g
Cholesterol	61 mg
Sodium	10 mg
Total carbohydrates	7 g
Protein	1 g

Continued

6. Transfer to a clean saucepan and cook over low heat, stirring constantly until the mixture coats the back of a wooden spoon (rose stage).

7. Strain and chill quickly and thoroughly over ice.

8. Add rum-flavoured raisins.

BITTER CHOCOLATE SORBET

Cocoa powder	60 g	2 oz.
Sugar	280 g	10 oz.
Water	800 g	27 oz.
Dark chocolate, chopped	500 g	1 lb. 2 oz.

Bitter Chocolate Sorbet— Approximate values per 30 g serving:

Calories	66
Total fat	5 g
Saturated fat	3 g
Cholesterol	0 mg
Sodium	2 mg
Total carbohydrates	8 g
Protein	1 g

1. Make a syrup by heating cocoa powder, sugar and water and stirring until the liquid comes to a boil.

2. Add chopped chocolate to the syrup and stir until melted. Chill over an ice bath.

3. Freeze in an ice cream freezer.

BANANA WAFER

Bananas, ripe	2	2
Honey	30 g	1 oz.

Banana Wafer—Approximate values per 30 g serving:

Calories	39
Total fat	0.1 g
Saturated fat	0.1 g
Cholesterol	0 mg
Sodium	0.5 mg
Total carbohydrates	10 g
Protein	0 g

1. Purée banana.

2. Pass the banana purée through a fine sieve and add the honey.

3. Using a template with 12-cm (5-inch) circles, pour the mixture onto parchment paper. Each wafer should be about 2 mm (1/16-inch) thick.

4. Dry in the oven at 82°C (180°F) until golden-brown.

5. Remove one by one and fold in half to form an open-fan shape.

6. If wafers harden, return them to the oven.

7. Store in a sealed container until ready to use.

＋＋＋

RECIPE 29.33

APPLE STRUDEL

SOUTHERN ALBERTA INSTITUTE OF TECHNOLOGY, CALGARY, AB
Master Pâtissier Hermann Greineder

Yield: 4–5 Strudels, each 60 cm (24 inches) long

Hermann Greineder
Currently a Pastry Instructor at SAIT, Hermann received his German Master Certification as "Chef Pâtissier" in 1971. He has 45 years of experience in a wide range of establishments, and has won several medals in competition for his beautiful chocolate showpieces.

STRUDEL DOUGH

Bread flour	1.75 kg	4 lb.
Butter, melted	500 g	17 oz.
Whole eggs	325 g	6
Hot water	750 mL	26 fl. oz.

Combine all ingredients and knead dough until window test is accepted. Let rest for 30 minutes.

FILLING

Bread crumbs	750 g	1-1/2 lb.
Butter	100 g	3-1/2 oz.
Golden Delicious apples, peeled, cored and sliced	40	40
Cinnamon	50–75 g	2–3 oz.
Sugar	500 g	1 lb. 2 oz.

Butter, whole, melted	600 g	1 lb. 5 oz.
Raisins, marinated in rum (optional)	750 g	1-1/2 lb.
Butter, unsalted, melted	500 g	1 lb.
Icing sugar	250 g	8 oz.

1. Combine bread crumbs and butter and toast until fragrant. Reserve.
2. Cover table with a linen cloth dusted with flour.
3. Place one-fifth of the dough on the cloth and roll it into a long strip (60 cm/24 inches).
4. Stretch the dough out using the back of your hands to form a rectangle. The dough should be paper-thin.
5. Sprinkle one-fifth of the toasted crumbs evenly over the dough.
6. Sprinkle one-fifth of the sliced apples evenly over the crumbs.
7. Combine cinnamon and sugar and sprinkle 110 g (4 oz.) over the apples, followed by 110 g (4 oz.) of melted whole butter.
8. Optional: Scatter one-fifth of the marinated raisins over the apple slices.
9. Trim the thick edges off the dough.
10. Using the cloth, roll up the strudel like a jelly roll into a log.
11. Place the strudel on a well-buttered baking sheet. Repeat the process with the remaining dough and filling.
12. Bake strudels at 200°C (400°F) for approximately 30–45 minutes, depending on the thickness of the strudel. They should have an even, golden-brown colour. Remove from oven and brush each strudel with 100 g (3-1/2 oz.) melted unsalted butter. Dust with icing sugar.
13. To serve, slice strudels into portions and plate. Garnish with crème Chantilly or a rum-flavoured vanilla custard sauce (crème Anglaise).

RECIPE 29.33

Approximate values per strudel:

Calories	5956
Total fat	301 g
Saturated fat	177 g
Cholesterol	1024 mg
Sodium	3396 mg
Total carbohydrates	792 g
Protein	86 g

 EBLINKS

The Pie Page
  www.teleport.com/~psyched/pie/pie.html
Baker Boulanger—Pie Crust Primer
  www.betterbaking.com/pieprimermeth.html
Tarts
  www.joyofbaking.com/tarts.html

CHAPTER 30

CAKES AND FROSTINGS

LEARNING OUTCOMES

After studying this chapter you will be able to:

◆ prepare a variety of cakes, including buttercakes, high-ratio cakes, genoise, spongecakes, angel food cakes, chiffon cakes
◆ prepare a variety of frostings, including simple buttercream, Italian buttercream, French buttercream, fudge frosting, glazes, royal icing, ganache
◆ assemble cakes using basic finishing and decorating techniques, including filling a piping bag, piping a buttercream rose

akes are popular in most bakeshops because a wide variety of finished products can be created from only a few basic cake, filling and frosting formulas. Many of these components can be made in advance and assembled into finished desserts as needed. Cakes are also popular because of their versatility: They can be served as unadorned sheets in a high-volume cafeteria or as the elaborate centrepiece of a wedding buffet.

Cake making need not be difficult or intimidating, but it does require an understanding of ingredients and mixing methods. This chapter begins by explaining how typical cake ingredients interact. Each of the traditional mixing methods is then explained and illustrated with a recipe. Information on panning batters, baking temperatures, determining doneness and cooling methods follows. The second portion of this chapter presents mixing methods and formulas for a variety of frostings and icings. The third section covers cake assembly and presents some simple and commonly used cake decorating techniques. A selection of popular cake formulas concludes the chapter.

Chapter 29 covers Pies, Pastries and Cookies; Chapter 31 covers Custards, Creams, Frozen Desserts and Dessert Sauces. Some of the desserts presented in those chapters use cake or frosting formulas presented here.

CAKES

Most cakes are created from liquid batters with high fat and sugar contents. The baker's job is to combine all of the ingredients to create a structure that will support these rich ingredients, yet keep the cake as light and delicate as possible. As with other baked goods, it is impossible to taste a cake until it is fully baked and too late to alter the formula. Therefore, it is extremely important to study any formula before beginning and to follow it with particular care and attention to detail. Accurate scaling of ingredients is essential.

Ingredients

Good cakes begin with high-quality ingredients (see Chapter 26, Principles of the Bakeshop). However, even the finest ingredients must be combined in the proper balance. Too much flour and the cake may be dry; too much egg and the cake will be tough and hard. Changing one ingredient may necessitate a change in one or more of the other ingredients.

Each ingredient performs a specific function and has a specific effect on the final product. Cake ingredients can be classified by function as tougheners, tenderizers, moisteners, driers, leaveners and flavourings. Some ingredients fulfil more than one of these functions. For example, eggs contain water, so they are moisteners, and they contain protein, so they are tougheners. By understanding the function of various ingredients you should be able to understand why cakes are made in particular ways and why a preparation sometimes fails. With additional experience, you should be able to recognize and correct flawed formulas and develop your own cake formulas.

Tougheners

Flour, milk and eggs contain protein. Protein provides structure and toughens the cake. Too little protein and the cake may collapse; too much protein and the cake may be tough and coarse-textured.

Tenderizers

Sugar, fats and egg yolks shorten gluten strands, making the cake tender and soft. These ingredients also improve the cake's keeping qualities.

Moisteners

Liquids such as water, milk, juice and eggs bring moisture to the mixture. Moisture is necessary for gluten formation and starch gelatinization, as well as improving a cake's keeping qualities.

Driers

Flour, starches and milk solids absorb moisture, giving body and structure to the cake. The lower protein content of cake/pastry flour contributes to producing a tender, short crumb.

Leaveners

Cakes rise because gases in the batter expand when heated. Cakes are leavened by the air trapped when fat and sugar are creamed together, by carbon dioxide released from baking powder and baking soda and by air trapped in beaten eggs. All cakes rely on natural leaveners—steam and air—to create the proper texture and rise. Because baking soda and baking powder are also used in some cake formulas, you should review the material on chemical leaveners in Chapter 27, Quick Breads.

Flavourings

Flavourings such as extracts, cocoa, chocolate, spices, salt, sugar and butter provide cakes with the desired flavours. Acidic flavouring ingredients such as sour cream, chocolate and fruit also provide the acid necessary to activate baking soda.

Cake ingredients should be at room temperature, approximately 21°C (70°F), before mixing begins. If one ingredient is too cold or too warm, it may affect the batter's ability to trap and hold the gases necessary for the cake to rise.

Mixing Methods

Even the finest ingredients will be wasted if the cake batter is not mixed correctly. When mixing any cake batter your goals are to combine the ingredients uniformly, incorporate air cells and develop the proper texture.

All mixing methods can be divided into two categories: *high fat*—those that create a structure that relies primarily on **creamed fat** (air) and flour, and *egg foam*—those that create a structure that relies primarily on **whipped eggs** (air) and flour. Within these broad categories are several mixing methods or types of cakes. Creamed-fat cakes include **butter cakes** (also known as **creaming method cakes**) and **high-ratio cakes**. Whipped-egg cakes include **genoise**, **spongecakes**, **angel food cakes** and **chiffon cakes**. See Table 30.1. Although

EGGS

The function of eggs is critical to the success of most bakery products. Eggs perform a variety of functions depending on the formula and the interaction of the various ingredients.

Leavening occurs when the tiny air pockets in beaten eggs expand when heated.

Structure is provided by the proteins coagulating. Together with gluten protein, cakes become stable.

Moisture derives from the high water content of eggs.

Emulsifying properties in yolks allow for fats and liquids to combine. Egg yolks contain lethicin, an emulsifier that contributes to a smooth batter resulting in better volume and texture.

Shortening characteristics result from the fat in the yolks.

Colour is enhanced: yellow from the yolks and better crust colour.

Flavour and nutritional value are enhanced.

TABLE 30.1   CAKES

Category	Mixing Method/Type of Cake	Key Formula Characteristics	Texture
Creamed fat (high fat)	Butter (creaming method)	High-fat formula; chemical leavener used	Fine grain; air cells of uniform size; moist crumb; thin and tender crust
	High-ratio (two-stage)	Emulsified shortening; two-part mixing method	Very fine grain; moist crumb; relatively high rise
Whipped egg (egg foam)	Genoise	Whole eggs are whipped with sugar; no chemical leaveners	Dry and spongy
	Sponge	Egg yolks are mixed with other ingredients, then whipped egg whites are folded in	Moister and more tender than genoise
	Angel food	No fat; large quantity of whipped egg whites; high percentage of sugar	Tall, light and fluffy
	Chiffon	Vegetable oil used; egg yolks mixed with other ingredients, then whipped egg whites folded in; baking powder may be added	Tall, light and fluffy; moister and richer than angel food

certain general procedures are used to prepare each cake type, there are, of course, variations. Follow specific formula instructions precisely. For a selected comparison of nutritional values of cakes, see Table 30.2.

Creamed Fat

Creamed-fat cakes include most of the popular North American–style cakes: poundcakes, layer cakes, coffeecakes and even brownies. All are based on high-fat formulas containing chemical leaveners. A good high-fat cake has a fine grain, cells of uniform size and a crumb that is moist rather than crumbly. Crusts should be thin and tender.

Creamed-fat cakes can be divided into two classes: butter cakes and high-ratio cakes.

Butter Cakes

Butter cakes, also known as creaming method cakes, begin with softened butter or shortening creamed to incorporate air cells. Because of their high fat content, these cakes usually need the assistance of a chemical leavener to achieve the proper rise.

TABLE 30.2   NUTRITIONAL VALUES OF SELECTED CAKES

Per 1/12 Portion of a 22.5-cm (9-inch) Cake, Unfrosted	Kcal	Protein (g)	Carbohydrates (g)	Total Fat (g)	Saturated Fat (g)	Sodium (mg)
Angel food	130	3	30	0	0	170
Butter cake	260	3	37	11	6	350
Chiffon, lemon	200	4	36	5	mq	200
Devil's food	260	4	35	12	3	450
Sponge (5-cm/2-inch square)	80	1	11	3	1	125

All cakes are prepared from a typical mix according to package directions.
The Corinne T. Netzer Encyclopedia of Food Values 1992
mq = measurable quantity but data are unavailable

Modern-day butter cakes—the classic layer cakes, popular for birthdays and special occasions—are made with the creaming method. These cakes are tender yet sturdy enough to handle rich buttercreams or fillings. High-fat cakes are too soft and delicate, however, to use for roll cakes or to slice into extremely thin layers.

When making butter cakes, the fat should be creamed at low to moderate speeds to prevent raising its temperature. An increased temperature could cause a loss of air cells.

Basic Procedure for Preparing Butter (Creaming Method) Cakes

1. Preheat the oven and prepare the pans.
2. Sift the dry ingredients together and set aside.
3. Add the butter and sugar and cream the mixture until it is light and fluffy. Add the sugar and cream until the mixture is fluffy and smooth.
4. Add the eggs slowly, beating well after each addition.
5. Add the dry and liquid ingredients alternately. Start with flour and finish with flour.
6. Divide the batter into prepared pans and bake immediately.

Applying the Basics

RECIPE 30.1

CLASSIC POUNDCAKE

Yield: 2 30 × 10-cm (12 × 4-inch) Loaves   **Method:** Creaming

Cake flour	500 g	1 lb.
Baking powder	7 g	2 tsp.
Salt	2 g	1/2 tsp.
Unsalted butter, softened	500 g	1 lb.
Granulated sugar	350 g	12 oz.
Eggs	500 g	16 oz.
Vanilla extract	5 mL	1 tsp.
Lemon extract	5 mL	1 tsp.

1. Sift the cake flour, baking powder and salt together; set aside.
2. Cream the butter and sugar until light and fluffy. Add the eggs one at a time, beating well after each addition. Stir in the extracts.
3. Fold in the dry ingredients by hand. Divide the batter into greased loaf pans.
4. Bake at 160°C (325°F) until golden-brown and springy to the touch, approximately 1 hour and 10 minutes. *Continued*

RECIPE 30.1

Approximate values per 1/12 cake:

Calories	250
Total fat	15 g
Saturated fat	9 g
Cholesterol	108 mg
Sodium	66 mg
Total carbohydrates	25 g
Protein	4 g

1. Cream the butter.

2. Fold in the flour.

3. Pan the batter.

VARIATION: *French-Style Fruitcake*—Add 175 g (6 oz.) finely diced nuts, raisins and candied fruit to the batter. Substitute vanilla extract for the lemon extract and add 50 mL (3 Tbsp.) rum to the batter. After baking, brush the warm cake with additional rum.

High-Ratio Cakes

Commercial bakers often use a special two-stage mixing method to prepare large quantities of a very liquid cake batter. These formulas require emulsified shortenings and are known as two-stage cakes because the liquids are added in two stages or portions. If emulsified shortenings are not available, do not substitute all-purpose shortening or butter as they cannot absorb the large amounts of sugar and liquid in the formula.

Because they contain a high ratio of sugar and liquid to flour, these cakes are often known as high-ratio cakes. They have a very fine, moist crumb and relatively high rise. High-ratio cakes are almost indistinguishable from modern butter cakes and may be used interchangeably.

Basic Procedure for Preparing High-Ratio Cakes

1. Preheat the oven and prepare the pans.
2. Place all the dry ingredients and emulsified shortening into a mixer bowl. Blend on low speed for several minutes.
3. Add approximately one-half of the liquid and blend.
4. Scrape down the mixer bowl and add the remaining liquid ingredients. Blend into a smooth batter, scraping down the bowl as necessary.
5. Pour the batter into prepared pans using liquid measurements to ensure uniform division.

Applying the Basics

RECIPE 30.2

HIGH-RATIO YELLOW CAKE

Yield: 3–4 Sheet Pans   **Method:** High-Ratio

Cake flour	2.2 kg	5 lb.
Granulated sugar	2.3 kg	5 lb. 4 oz.
Emulsified shortening	1.1 kg	2 lb. 8 oz.
Salt	60 g	2 oz.
Baking powder	120 g	4 oz.
Powdered milk	225 g	8 oz.
Light corn syrup	340 g	12 oz.
Water, cold	1 L	1 qt.
Eggs	1.1 kg	2 lb. 8 oz.
Water, cold	2.25 L	2-1/4 qt.
Lemon extract	30 mL	1 fl oz.

1. Combine the flour, sugar, shortening, salt, baking powder, powdered milk, corn syrup and 1 L (1 qt.) cold water in a large bowl of a mixer fitted with the paddle attachment. Beat for 5 minutes on low speed.
2. Combine the remaining ingredients in a separate bowl. Add these liquid ingredients to the creamed-fat mixture in three additions. Scrape down the sides of the bowl after each addition.
3. Beat for 2 minutes on low speed.

RECIPE 30.2

Approximate values per serving:

Calories	314
Total fat	13 g
Saturated fat	4 g
Cholesterol	50 mg
Sodium	367 mg
Total carbohydrates	46 g
Protein	4 g

4. Divide the batter into greased and floured pans. Pans should be filled only halfway. Four litres (4 qt.) of batter is sufficient for a 45- × 60- × 5-cm (18- × 24- × 2-inch) sheet pan. Bake at 170°C (340°F) until a cake tester comes out clean and the cake springs back when lightly touched, approximately 12–18 minutes.

Whipped Egg

Cakes based on whipped egg foams include European-style genoise as well as spongecakes, angel food cakes and chiffon cakes. Some formulas contain chemical leaveners, but the air whipped into the eggs (whether whole or separated) is the primary leavening agent. Egg-foam cakes contain little or no fat.

Genoise

Genoise is the classic European-style cake. It is based on whole eggs whipped with sugar until very light and fluffy. Chemical leaveners are not used. A small amount of oil or melted butter is sometimes added for flavour and moisture. Genoise is often baked in a thin sheet and layered with buttercream, puréed fruit, jam or chocolate filling to create multilayered specialty desserts. Because genoise is rather dry, it is usually soaked with a flavoured sugar syrup (see Chapter 26, Principles of the Bakeshop) or liquor for additional flavour and moisture.

1. Whip the eggs.

2. Fold in the flour.

3. Add the melted butter.

Basic Procedure for Preparing Genoise

1. Preheat the oven and prepare the pans.
2. Sift the flour with any additional dry ingredients.
3. Combine the whole eggs and sugar in a large bowl and warm over a double boiler to a temperature of 40°C (104°F).
4. Whip the egg-and-sugar mixture until very light and tripled in volume.
5. Fold the sifted flour into the whipped eggs carefully but quickly.
6. Fold in oil or melted butter if desired.
7. Divide into pans and bake immediately.

Applying the Basics

RECIPE 30.3

CLASSIC GENOISE

Yield: 3 Full Sheet Pans

Method: Whipped Egg

Cake flour	750 g	1 lb. 8 oz.
Eggs	1.25 kg	2 lb. 12 oz.
Granulated sugar	750 g	1 lb. 8 oz.
Unsalted butter, melted (optional)	125 g	4 oz.

1. Sift the flour and set aside.
2. Whisk the eggs and sugar together in a large mixer bowl. Place the bowl over a bain marie and warm the eggs to about 40°C (104°F). Stir frequently to avoid cooking the eggs.
3. When the eggs are warm, remove the bowl from the bain marie and attach to a mixer fitted with a whip attachment. Whip the egg-and-sugar mixture at medium speed until tripled in volume.

4. Pan the batter.

RECIPE 30.3

Approximate values per serving:

Calories	174
Total fat	5 g
Saturated fat	2 g
Cholesterol	118 mg
Sodium	34 mg
Total carbohydrates	28 g
Protein	5 g

Continued

4. Quickly fold the flour into the egg mixture by hand. Be careful not to deflate the batter.

5. Pour the melted, cooled butter around the edges of the batter and fold in quickly.

6. Divide the batter immediately into parchment-lined pans. Bake at 180°C (350°F) until light brown and springy to the touch, approximately 8 minutes.

VARIATION: *Chocolate Genoise*—Sift 100 g (3-1/2 oz.) of cocoa powder with the flour. Reduce flour by 100 g (3-1/2 oz.).

Spongecakes

Spongecakes (Fr. *biscuits*) are made with whole separated eggs. A batter is prepared with the egg yolks and other ingredients, then the egg whites are whipped to firm peaks with a portion of the sugar (common meringue method) and folded into the batter. Spongecakes are primarily leavened with air, but baking powder may be included in the formula. As with genoise, oil or melted butter may be added if desired.

Spongecakes are extremely versatile. They can be soaked with sugar syrup or a liquor and assembled with buttercream as a traditional layer cake. Or they can be sliced thinly and layered, like genoise, with jam, custard, chocolate or cream filling.

Basic Procedure for Preparing Spongecakes

1. Preheat the oven and prepare the pans.
2. Separate the eggs. Whip the egg whites with a portion of the sugar.
3. Sift the dry ingredients together and combine with liquid ingredients, including the egg yolks, as directed.
4. Carefully fold the whipped egg whites into the batter.
5. Pour the batter into the pans and bake immediately.

Applying the Basics

RECIPE 30.4

CLASSIC SPONGECAKE

Yield: Two 22-cm (9-inch) Rounds   **Method:** Whipped Egg

Cake flour, sifted	180 g	6 oz.
Granulated sugar	300 g	11 oz.
Eggs	10 large	10 large
Vanilla extract	7 mL	1-1/2 tsp.
Cream of tartar	7 mL	1-1/2 tsp.

1. Line the bottom of two springform pans with parchment. Do not grease the sides of the pans.

2. Sift the flour and 180 g (6 oz.) of the sugar together and set aside.

3. Separate the eggs, placing the yolks and the whites in separate mixing bowls. Whip the yolks on high speed for 3–5 minutes, until thick, pale and at least doubled in volume. Whip in the vanilla extract. The yolks should be whipped "to ribbon," that is, until they fall from the beater in thick ribbons that slowly disappear into the batter's surface.

4. Place the bowl of egg whites on the mixer and, using a clean whip attachment, beat until foamy. Add the cream of tartar and 30 g (2 Tbsp.) of sugar. Whip at medium speed until the whites are glossy and stiff but not dry.

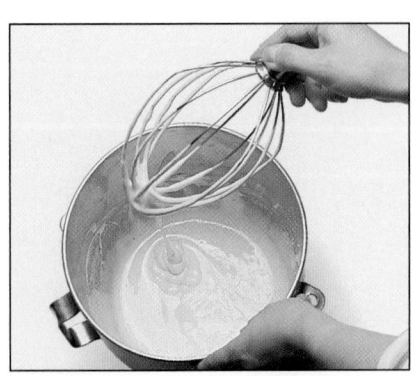

Whip the egg yolks to ribbon stage.

5. Remove the bowl from the mixer. Pour the egg yolks onto the whipped whites. Quickly fold the two mixtures together by hand. Sprinkle the remaining sugar (90 g/3 oz.) over the mixture and fold in lightly.

6. Sprinkle one-third of the sifted flour over the batter and fold in. Repeat the procedure until all of the flour is incorporated. Do not overmix; fold just until incorporated.

7. Pour the batter into the prepared pans, smoothing the surface as needed. Bake immediately at 190°C (375°F) until the cake is golden-brown and spongy, approximately 30 minutes. A toothpick inserted in the centre will be completely clean.

8. Invert the cake, remove from pan; run a thin metal spatula around the edge of the pan to remove the cakes if they stick. Plate on racks or parchment paper. Sprinkle with granulated sugar, then let cool.

9. When the cake is completely cool it can be frosted or wrapped in plastic wrap and frozen for 2–3 months.

Applying the Basics

EMULSIFIED SPONGECAKE

Yield: Six 20-cm (8-inch) Cakes

Milk powder	70 g	2-1/2 oz.
Sugar	750 g	1 lb. 11 oz.
Baking powder	10 g	1/3 oz.
Cake flour, sifted	650 g	1 lb. 6 oz.
Cold water	300 mL	12 fl. oz.
Whole eggs, chilled	650 g	1 lb. 6 oz.
K-68 emulsifier, chilled	20 g	1 oz.
Melted butter	120 g	4-1/4 oz.

1. Place all the dry ingredients into the mixer bowl. Blend together on slow speed, using a whip attachment.

2. Add water, eggs and emulsifier to the dry ingredients. Blend on slow speed, scraping down the bowl, then whip on high speed for 3 minutes exactly.

3. Fold in the melted butter by spatula.

4. Scale 350 g (12 oz.) of batter per cake tin and bake at 190°C (380°F) for 20–30 minutes.

NOTE: This recipe is adjusted for an altitude of 1000 metres. For chocolate spongecake, add 60 g (2 oz.) cocoa sifted with the flour.

Angel Food Cakes

Angel food cakes are tall, light cakes made without fat and leavened with a large quantity of whipped egg whites. Angel food cakes are traditionally baked in ungreased tube pans, but large loaf pans can also be used. The pans are left ungreased so that the batter can cling to the sides as it rises. The cakes should be inverted as soon as they are removed from the oven and left in the pan to cool. This technique allows gravity to keep the cakes from collapsing or sinking as they cool.

Although they contain no fat, angel food cakes are not low in calories as they contain a high percentage of sugar. The classic angel food cake is pure white, but flavourings, ground nuts or cocoa powder may be added for variety.

RECIPE 30.4

Approximate values per 1/16 cake:

Calories	122
Total fat	2.5 g
Saturated fat	1 g
Cholesterol	105 mg
Sodium	31 mg
Total carbohydrates	22 g
Protein	3 g

RECIPE 30.5

RECIPE 30.5

Approximate values per 1/12 cake:

Calories	103
Total fat	3 g
Saturated fat	1.5 g
Cholesterol	44 mg
Sodium	39 mg
Total carbohydrates	18 g
Protein	2 g

Although angel food cakes are rarely frosted, they may be topped with a fruit-flavoured or chocolate glaze. They are often served with fresh fruit, a fruit compote or whipped cream.

Basic Procedure for Preparing Angel Food Cakes

1. Preheat the oven.
2. Sift the dry ingredients together.
3. Whip the egg whites with a portion of the sugar until stiff and glossy.
4. Gently fold the dry ingredients into the egg whites.
5. Spoon the batter into an ungreased pan and bake immediately.
6. Allow the cake to cool inverted in its pan.

Applying the Basics

RECIPE 30.6

RECIPE 30.6

CHOCOLATE ANGEL FOOD CAKE

Yield: One 25-cm (10-inch) Tube Cake   **Method:** Whipped Egg

Cocoa powder, alkalized	30 g	1 oz.
Water, warm	60 g	2 oz.
Vanilla extract	10 mL	2 tsp.
Granulated sugar	340 g	12 oz.
Cake flour, sifted	100 g	3-1/2 oz.
Salt	1 g	1/4 tsp.
Egg whites (large eggs)	480 g	16
Cream of tartar	7 g	2 tsp.

1. Combine the cocoa powder and water in a bowl. Add the vanilla and set aside.
2. In another bowl, combine 150 g (5 oz.) of the sugar with the flour and salt.
3. Whip the egg whites until foamy, add the cream of tartar and beat to soft peaks. Gradually beat in the remaining sugar. Continue beating until the egg whites are stiff but not dry.
4. Whisk approximately 250 g (1 cup) of the whipped egg whites into the cocoa mixture. Fold this into the remaining egg whites.
5. Sift the dry ingredients over the whites and fold in quickly but gently.
6. Pour the batter into an ungreased tube pan and smooth the top with a spatula. Bake immediately at 180°C (350°F) until the cake springs back when lightly touched and a cake tester comes out clean, approximately 40–50 minutes. The cake's surface will have deep cracks.

Approximate values per 1/16 cake:

Calories	125
Total fat	0.2 g
Saturated fat	0 g
Cholesterol	0 mg
Sodium	89 mg
Total carbohydrates	28 g
Protein	4 g

1. Fold the cocoa mixture into the whipped egg whites.

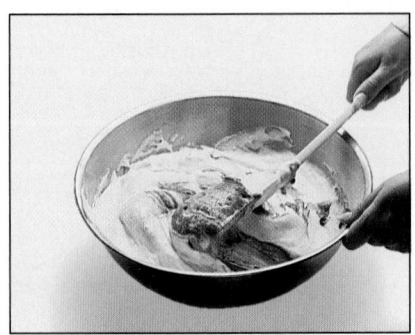

2. Fold in the flour.

3. Cool the cake upside down in its pan.

4. Remove the cake from the pan.

7. Remove the cake from the oven and immediately invert the pan onto the neck of a bottle. Allow the cake to rest upside down until completely cool.

8. To remove the cake from the pan, run a thin knife or spatula around the edge of the pan and the edge of the interior tube. If a two-piece tube pan was used, the cake and tube portion are lifted out of the pan. Use a knife or spatula to loosen the bottom of the cake, then invert it onto a cake board or serving platter.

Chiffon Cakes

Although chiffon cakes are similar to angel food cakes in appearance and texture, the addition of egg yolks and vegetable oil makes them moister and richer. Chiffon cakes are usually leavened with whipped egg whites but may contain baking powder as well. Like angel food cakes, chiffon cakes are baked in an ungreased pan to allow the batter to cling to the pan as it rises. Chiffon cakes can be frosted with a light buttercream or whipped cream or topped with a glaze. Lemon and orange chiffon cakes are the most popular, but formulas containing chocolate, nuts or other flavourings are also common.

Basic Procedure for Preparing Chiffon Cakes

1. Preheat the oven.
2. Whip the egg whites with a portion of the sugar until almost stiff. Set aside.
3. Sift the dry ingredients together. Add the liquid ingredients, including oil.
4. Fold the whipped egg whites into the batter.
5. Spoon the batter into an ungreased pan and bake immediately.
6. Allow the cake to cool inverted in its pan.

Applying the Basics

RECIPE 30.7

ORANGE CHIFFON CAKE

Yield: One 25-cm (10-inch) Tube Cake   **Method:** Whipped Egg

Cake flour, sifted	250 g	8 oz.
Sugar	375 g	12 oz.
Baking powder	10 g	1 Tbsp.
Salt	5 g	1 tsp.
Vegetable oil	125 mL	4 fl. oz.
Egg yolks (large eggs)	130 g	6
Water, cool	60 mL	2 fl. oz.
Orange juice	125 mL	4 fl. oz.
Orange zest	10 g	1 Tbsp.
Vanilla extract	15 mL	1 Tbsp.
Egg whites	250 g	8 oz.

1. Sift together the flour, 175 g (6 oz.) of sugar, the baking powder and salt.
2. In a separate bowl mix the oil, yolks, water, juice, zest and vanilla. Add the liquid mixture to the dry ingredients.
3. In a clean bowl beat the egg whites until foamy. Slowly beat in the remaining sugar. Continue beating until the egg whites are stiff but not dry.
4. Stir one-third of the egg whites into the batter to lighten it. Fold in the remaining egg whites.

Continued

♦♦♦

A BAKER CREATED CHIFFON CAKES

Chiffon cake is one of the few desserts whose history can be traced with absolute certainty. According to Gerry Schremp in her book *Kitchen Culture: Fifty Years of Food Fads*, a new type of cake was invented by Henry Baker, a California insurance salesman, in 1927. Dubbed *chiffon*, it was as light as angel food and as rich as poundcake. For years he kept the formula a secret, earning fame and fortune by selling his cakes to Hollywood restaurants. The cake's secret ingredient—vegetable oil—became public knowledge in 1947 when Baker sold the formula to General Mills, which promoted it on packages of cake flour. Chiffon cakes, in a variety of flavours, became extremely popular nationwide.

RECIPE 30.7

Approximate values per 1/16 cake:

Calories	255
Total fat	10 g
Saturated fat	1 g
Cholesterol	106 mg
Sodium	197 mg
Total carbohydrates	37 g
Protein	4 g

5. Pour the batter into an ungreased 25-cm (10-inch) tube pan. Bake at 160°C (325°F) until a toothpick inserted in the centre comes out clean, approximately 1 hour.

6. Immediately invert the pan over the neck of a bottle. Allow the cake to cool upside down, then remove from the pan.

ORANGE GLAZE

Powdered sugar	90 g	3 oz.
Orange juice	30 mL	2 Tbsp.
Orange zest	8 g	2 tsp.

1. Sift the sugar, then stir in the juice and zest.
2. Drizzle the glaze over the top of the cooled cake.

VARIATION: *Lemon Chiffon Cake*—Substitute 60 mL (2 fl. oz.) fresh lemon juice and 60 mL (2 fl. oz.) water for the orange juice. Substitute lemon zest for the orange zest. Top with Basic Sugar Glaze, Recipe 30.13.

Panning, Baking and Cooling

Preparing Pans

To prevent cakes from sticking, most baking pans are coated with fat or a nonstick baking parchment. (See Table 30.3.) Pans should be prepared before the batter is mixed, so that they may be filled and the cakes baked as soon as the batter is finished. If the batter stands while the pans are prepared, air cells within the batter will deflate and volume may be lost.

Solid shortening is better than butter for coating pans because it does not contain any water; butter and margarine do contain water and this may cause the cake to stick in places. Solid shortening is also less expensive, tasteless and odourless. Finally, solid shortening does not burn as easily as butter and it holds a dusting of flour better.

Pan-release sprays are useful but must be applied carefully and completely. Although relatively expensive, sprays save time and are particularly effective when used with parchment pan liners.

In kitchens where a great deal of baking is done, it may be more convenient to prepare quantities of pan coating to be kept available for use as needed. Pan coating is a mixture of equal parts oil, shortening and flour, creamed together, that can be applied to cake pans with a pastry brush. It is used whenever pans need to be greased and floured. Pan coating will not leave a white residue on the cake's crust as a dusting of flour often does.

◆◆◆ CONVENIENCE PRODUCTS

Packaged cake mixes are a tremendous time saver for commercial food service operations. Almost any operation can serve a variety of cakes made by relatively unskilled employees using prepared mixes. The results are consistent and the texture and flavour are acceptable to most consumers. Indeed, a well-prepared packaged mix cake is preferable to a poorly prepared cake made from scratch. Most packaged cake mixes can be adapted to include flavourings, nuts, spices or fruits, which can improve the product's overall quality. Frostings, fillings and attractive decorations complete these items.

The convenience of mixes is not without cost, however. Packaged cake mixes are often more expensive than the ingredients needed for an equal number of cakes made from scratch. Cakes made from mixes are also softer and more cottony than scratch cakes, and their flavour tends to be more artificial.

TABLE 30.3   PAN PREPARATIONS

Pan Preparation	Used For
Ungreased	Angel food and chiffon cakes
Ungreased sides; paper on bottom	Genoise layers
Greased and papered	High-fat cakes, sponge sheets
Greased and coated with flour	High-fat cakes, chocolate cakes, anything in a bundt or shaped pan
Greased, floured and lined with paper	Cakes containing melted chocolate, fruit chunks or fruit or vegetable purées

Applying the Basics

RECIPE 30.8

PAN COATING

Yield: 1.5 kg (3 lb.)

Vegetable oil	500 g	1 lb.
All-purpose shortening	500 g	1 lb.
Bread flour	500 g	1 lb.

1. Combine all ingredients in a mixer fitted with the paddle attachment. Blend on low speed for 5 minutes or until smooth.
2. Store in an airtight container at room temperature for up to 2 months.
3. Apply to baking pans in a thin, even layer using a pastry brush.

RECIPE 30.8

Approximate values per 3 g serving:

Calories	21
Total fat	2 g
Saturated fat	0.3 g
Cholesterol	0 mg
Sodium	0 mg
Total carbohydrates	0.7 g
Protein	0.1 g

Pan coating is not appropriate for all cakes, however. Those containing chocolate, raisins or fruit should still be baked in pans lined with parchment paper to prevent sticking.

Angel food and chiffon cakes are baked in ungreased, unlined pans because these fragile cakes need to cling to the sides of the pan as they rise. Spongecakes and genoise are often baked in pans with a paper liner on the bottom and ungreased sides. While the ungreased sides give the batter a surface to cling to, the paper liner makes removing the cake from the pan easier.

Filling Pans

Pans should be filled no more than one-half to two-thirds full. This allows the batter to rise during baking without spilling over the edges.

Pans should be filled to uniform depths. High-fat and egg-foam cake batters can be ladled into each pan according to weight. High-ratio cake batter is so liquid that it can be measured by volume and poured into each pan. Filling the pans uniformly prevents both uneven layers and over- or underfilled pans. If you are baking three 20-cm (8-inch) layers to be stacked for one presentation and the amount of batter is different in each pan, the baking times will vary and the final product will suffer.

The cake batter should always be spread evenly in the pan. Use an offset spatula. Do not work the batter too much, however, as this destroys air cells and prevents the cake from rising properly.

❖❖❖

BROWNIES

Where do you draw the line between cakes and brownies? The decision must be a matter of texture and personal preference, for the preparation methods are nearly identical. Brownies are generally chewy and fudgy, sweeter and denser than even the richest of butter cakes.

Brownies are a relatively inexpensive and easy way for a food service operation to offer its customers a fresh-baked dessert. Although not as sophisticated as an elaborate gâteau, a well-made brownie can always be served with pride (and a scoop of ice cream).

Brownies are prepared using the same procedures as those for high-fat cakes. Good brownies are achieved with a proper balance of ingredients: A high percentage of butter to flour produces a dense, fudgy brownie; less butter produces a more cakelike brownie. Likewise, the higher the ratio of sugar, the gooier the finished brownie. In some formulas, the fat is creamed to incorporate air, as with butter cakes. In others, the fat is first melted and combined with other liquid ingredients. Brownies are rarely made with whipped egg whites, however, as this makes their texture too light and cakelike.

Each customer and cook has his or her own idea of the quintessential brownie. Some are cloyingly sweet, with a creamy texture and an abundance of chocolate; others are bitter and crisp. Baked brownies can be frozen for 2–3 months if well wrapped.

Baking

Temperatures

Always preheat the oven before preparing your batter. If the finished batter must wait while the oven reaches the correct temperature, valuable leavening will be lost and the cake will not rise properly.

Most cakes are baked at temperatures between 160°C and 190°C (325°F and 375°F). The temperature must be high enough to create steam within the batter and cause that steam and other gases in the batter to expand and rise quickly. If the temperature is too high, however, the cake may rise unevenly and the crust may burn before the interior is completely baked. The temperature must also be low enough that the batter can set completely and evenly without drying out. If the temperature is too low, however, the cake will not rise sufficiently and may dry out before baking completely.

If no temperature is given in a formula or you are altering the dimensions of the baking pan from those specified, use common sense in setting the oven temperature. Usually, the larger the surface area, the higher the temperature can be. Tall cakes, such as bundt or tube cakes, should be baked at a lower temperature than thin layer or sheet cakes. Tube or loaf cakes take longer to bake than thin sheet cakes; butter cakes, because they contain more liquid, take longer to bake than genoise or spongecakes.

Altitude Adjustments

As you learned in Chapter 9, Principles of Cooking, altitude affects the temperatures at which foods cook. The decreased atmospheric pressure at altitudes above 900 m (3000 feet) affects the creation of steam and the expansion of hot air in cake batters. These factors must be considered when making cakes. Because gases expand more easily at higher altitudes, your cake may rise so much that its structure cannot support it and the cake can collapse.

Therefore, the amount of leavening should be decreased at higher altitudes. (See Figure 30.1.) Chemical leaveners should usually be reduced by 20% at 1050 m (3500 feet) and by 40% at altitudes over 1500 m (5000 feet). Eggs should be underwhipped to avoid incorporating too much air, and the volume should be increased by approximately 10%. An additional 10% of liquid may be required. In general, oven temperatures should also be increased by 4°C (25°F) at altitudes over 1050 m (3500 feet) to help the cake's structure to set rapidly.

Because the boiling point decreases at higher altitudes, more moisture will evaporate from your cake during baking. This may cause dryness and an excessive proportion of sugar, which shows up as white spots on the cake's surface. Correct this by reducing every 225 g (8 oz.) of sugar by 15 g (1/2 oz.) at 900 m (3000 feet) and by 45 g (1-1/2 oz.) at 2100 m (7000 feet).

Attempting to adjust typical (i.e., sea level) formulas for high altitudes is somewhat risky, especially in a commercial operation. Try to find and use formulas developed especially for your area.

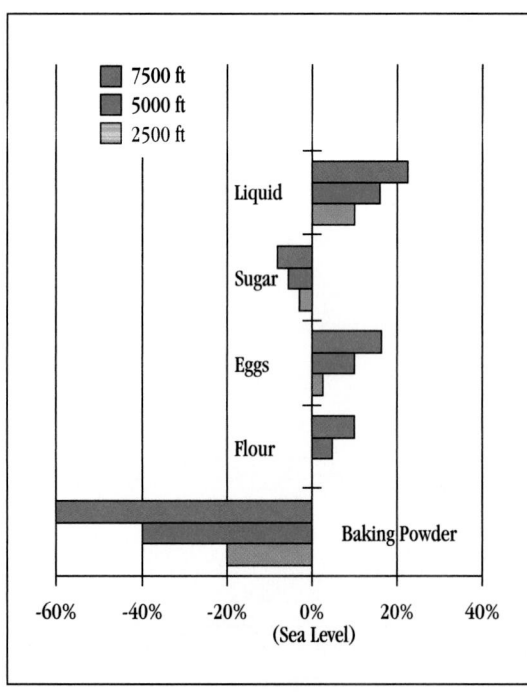

FIGURE 30.1 *Altitude Adjustments*
Source: Andreas Schwarzer, SAIT.

Determining Doneness

In addition to following the baking time suggested in a formula, several simple tests can be used to determine doneness. Whichever test or tests are used, avoid opening the oven door to check the cake's progress. Cold air or a drop in oven temperature can cause the cake to fall. Use a timer to note the minimum suggested baking time. Then, and only then, should you use the following tests to evaluate the cake's doneness:

+ *Appearance*—The cake's surface should be a light to golden-brown. Unless noted otherwise in the formula, the edges should just begin to pull away from the pan. The cake should not jiggle or move beneath its surface.
+ *Touch*—Touch the cake *lightly* with your finger. It should spring back quickly without feeling soggy or leaving an indentation.
+ *Cake tester*—If appearance and touch indicate that the cake is done, test the interior by inserting a toothpick, bamboo skewer or metal cake tester into the cake's centre. With most cakes, the tester should come out clean. If wet crumbs cling to the tester the cake probably needs to bake a bit longer.

If a formula provides particular doneness guidelines, they should be followed. For example, some flourless cakes are fully baked even though a cake tester will not come out clean.

Cooling

Generally, a cake is allowed to cool for 10–15 minutes in its pan after being removed from the oven. This helps prevent the cake from cracking or breaking after it is removed from its pan.

To remove the partially cooled cake from its pan, run a thin knife or spatula blade between the pan and the cake to loosen it. Place a wire rack, cake board or sheet pan over the cake and invert. Then remove the pan. The cake can be left upside down to cool completely or inverted again to cool top side up. Wire racks are preferred for cooling cakes because they allow air to circulate, speeding the cooling process and preventing steam from making the cake soggy.

Angel food and chiffon cakes should be turned upside down immediately after they are removed from the oven. They are left to cool completely in their pans to prevent the cake from collapsing or shrinking. The top of the pan should not touch the countertop so that air can circulate under the inverted pan.

All cakes should be left to cool away from drafts or air currents that might cause them to collapse. Cakes should not be refrigerated to speed the cooling process, as rapid cooling can cause cracking. Prolonged refrigeration also causes cakes to dry out. (See Table 30.4 for troubleshooting tips should you encounter problems with cakes.)

FROSTINGS

Frosting, also known as **icing**, is a sweet decorative coating used as a filling between the layers or as a coating over the top and sides of a cake. It is used to add flavour and to improve the cake's appearance. Frosting can also extend a cake's shelf life by forming a protective coating.

There are seven general types of frosting: **buttercream**, **foam**, **fudge**, **fondant**, **glaze**, **royal icing** and **ganache**. (See Table 30.5.) Each type can be produced with a number of formulas and in a range of flavourings.

Because frosting is integral to the flavour and appearance of many cakes, it should be made carefully using high-quality ingredients and natural flavours and colours. A good frosting is smooth; it is never grainy or lumpy. (Table 30.6 provides some troubleshooting guidelines for frostings.) It should complement the flavour and texture of the cake without overpowering it.

TABLE 30.4   TROUBLESHOOTING CHART FOR CAKES

Problem	Cause	Solution
Batter curdles during mixing	Ingredients too warm or too cold	Eggs must be room temperature and added slowly
	Incorrect fat used	Use correct ingredients
	Fat inadequately creamed before liquid was added	Add a portion of the flour, then continue adding the liquid
	Too much liquid was added	Add a portion of the flour, then continue adding the liquid
Cake lacks volume	Flour too strong	Use a weaker flour
	Old chemical leavener	Replace with fresh leavener
	Egg foam underwhipped	Use correct mixing method, do not deflate eggs during folding
	Oven too hot	Adjust oven temperature
Crust burst or cracked	Too much flour or too little liquid	Adjust formula
	Oven too hot	Adjust oven temperature
Cake shrinks after baking	Weak internal structure	Adjust formula
	Too much sugar or fat for the batter to support	Adjust formula
	Cake not fully baked	Test cake for doneness before removing from oven
	Cake cooled too rapidly	Cool away from drafts
Texture is dense or heavy	Too little leavening	Adjust formula
	Too much fat or liquid	Cream fat or whip eggs properly
	Oven too cool	Adjust oven temperature
Texture is coarse with an open grain	Overmixing	Alter mixing method
	Oven too cool	Adjust oven temperature
Poor flavour	Poor ingredients	Check flavour and aroma of all ingredients
	Unclean pans	Do not grease pans with rancid fats
Uneven shape	Butter not incorporated evenly	Incorporate fats completely
	Batter spread unevenly	Spread batter evenly
	Oven rack not level	Adjust oven racks
	Uneven oven temperature	Adjust oven temperature

TABLE 30.5   FROSTINGS

Frosting	Preparation	Texture/Taste
Buttercream	Mixture of sugar and fat (usually butter); can contain egg yolks or egg whites	Rich but light; smooth, fluffy
Foam	Meringue made with hot sugar syrup	Light, fluffy; very sweet
Fudge	Cooked mixture of sugar, butter and water or milk; applied warm	Heavy, rich and candylike
Fondant	Cooked mixture of sugar and water; applied warm	Thick; opaque; sweet
Glaze	Confectioner's sugar with liquid	Thin
Royal icing	Uncooked mixture of confectioner's sugar and egg whites	Hard and brittle when dry
Ganache	Blend of melted chocolate and cream	Rich, smooth, intense flavour

TABLE 30.6 TROUBLESHOOTING CHART FOR FROSTINGS

Problem	Cause	Solution
Frosting breaks or curdles	Fat added too slowly or eggs too hot when fat was added	Add shortening or sifted confectioner's sugar
Frosting is lumpy	Confectioner's sugar not sifted	Sift dry ingredients
	Ingredients not blended	Use softened fat
	Sugar syrup lumps in frosting	Add sugar syrups carefully
Frosting is gritty	Granulated sugar not dissolved	Cook sugar syrups properly; cook fudge frostings as directed
Frosting is too stiff	Not enough liquid	Adjust formula; add small amount of water or milk to thin frosting
	Too cold	Bring frosting to room temperature
Frosting will not adhere to cake	Cake too hot	Cool cake completely
	Frosting too thin	Adjust frosting formula

Buttercream

A buttercream is a light, smooth, fluffy mixture of sugar and fat (butter, margarine or shortening). It may also contain egg yolks for richness or whipped egg whites for lightness. A good buttercream will be sweet, but not heavy; buttery, but not greasy.

Buttercreams are popular and useful for most types of cakes and may be flavoured or coloured as desired. They may be stored, covered, in the refrigerator for several days but must be softened before use and creamed again.

Although there are many types of buttercream and many formula variations, we discuss the three most popular styles: **simple**, **Italian** and **French**.

Simple Buttercream

Simple buttercream is made by creaming butter and powdered sugar together until the mixture is light and smooth. Cream, eggs, preferably pasteurized (whole, yolks or whites) and flavourings may be added as desired. Simple buttercream is quick and easy to prepare.

If cost is a consideration, high-ratio or emulsified shortening can be substituted for a portion of the butter, but the flavour and mouth-feel will be different. Buttercream made with shortening tends to taste greasier and heavier because shortening does not melt on the tongue like butter. It will be more stable than buttercream made only with butter, however, and is useful for products that will be on display.

Basic Procedure for Preparing Simple Buttercream

1. Cream softened butter or shortening until the mixture is light and fluffy.
2. Beat in egg, if desired.
3. Beat in sifted powdered sugar, scraping down the sides of the bowl as needed.
4. Beat in the flavouring ingredients.

RECIPE 30.9

*Approximate values
per 30 g serving:*

Calories	142
Total fat	8 g
Saturated fat	5 g
Cholesterol	25 mg
Sodium	79 mg
Total carbohydrates	19 g
Protein	0 g

Applying the Basics

RECIPE 30.9

SIMPLE BUTTERCREAM

Yield: 1.5 kg (3 lb.)

Lightly salted butter, softened	450 g	1 lb.
Egg (optional)	1	1
Powdered sugar, sifted	900 g	2 lb.
Vanilla extract	10 mL	2 tsp.

1. Using a mixer fitted with the paddle attachment, cream the butter until light and fluffy.
2. Beat in the egg, if using. Gradually add the sugar, frequently scraping down the sides of the bowl.
3. Add the vanilla and continue beating until the frosting is smooth and light.

VARIATIONS: *Light Chocolate*—Dissolve 30 g (1 oz.) sifted cocoa powder in 60 mL (2 fl. oz.) cool water. Add to the buttercream along with the vanilla.

Lemon—Decrease the vanilla extract to 5 mL (1 tsp.). Add 5 mL (1 tsp.) lemon extract and the finely grated zest of one lemon.

Italian Buttercream

Italian buttercream, also known as **meringue buttercream**, is based on an Italian meringue, that is, whipped egg whites enriched with hot sugar syrup. (See Chapter 29, Pies, Pastries and Cookies.) Softened butter is then whipped into the cooled meringue and the mixture is flavoured as desired. This type of buttercream is extremely soft and light. It can be used on most types of cakes and is particularly popular for multilayered genoise and spongecakes.

Basic Procedure for Preparing Italian Buttercream

1. Whip the egg whites until soft peaks form.
2. Beat granulated sugar into the egg whites and whip until firm and glossy.
3. Meanwhile, combine additional sugar with water and cook to soft ball stage (115°C/238°F).
4. With the mixer on medium speed, pour the sugar syrup into the whipped egg whites. Pour slowly and carefully to avoid splatters.
5. Continue whipping the egg-white-and-sugar mixture until completely cool.
6. Whip softened, but not melted, butter into the cooled egg-white-and-sugar mixture.
7. Add flavouring ingredients as desired.

1. Add the sugar syrup to the whipped egg whites.

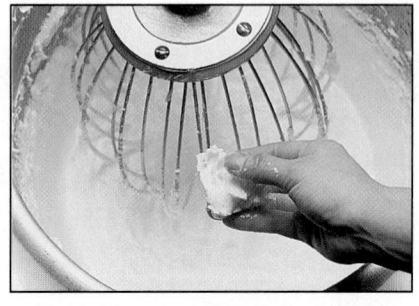

2. Add the softened butter to the cooled Italian meringue.

3. Finished Italian buttercream.

Applying the Basics

ITALIAN BUTTERCREAM

Yield: 2.2 kg (5 lb.)

Egg whites	200 g	7 oz.
Sugar	50 g	2 oz.
Sugar	450 g	1 lb.
Water	125 mL	4 fl. oz.
Lightly salted butter, softened but not melted	1.2 kg	2 lb. 10 oz.

1. All ingredients should be at room temperature before beginning.
2. Place the egg whites in a mixer bowl. Have 50 g (2 oz.) of sugar nearby.
3. Place 450 g (1 lb.) of sugar and water in a heavy saucepan. Bring to a boil over high heat.
4. As the sugar syrup's temperature approaches a soft ball stage (115°C/238°F), begin whipping the egg whites. Watch the sugar closely so that the temperature does not exceed 115°C (238°F).
5. When soft peaks form in the egg whites, gradually add the 50 g (2 oz.) of sugar to them.
6. When the sugar syrup reaches soft ball stage, immediately pour it into the whites while the mixer is running. Pour the syrup in a steady stream between the side of the bowl and the beater. If the syrup hits the beater it will splatter and cause lumps. Continue beating at medium speed until the meringue is cool and forms stiff peaks.
7. Gradually add the softened butter to the Italian meringue, blending it well. When all of the butter is incorporated, turn to medium speed and beat until fluffy. Add flavouring ingredients as desired.

VARIATION: *Chocolate*—Add 15 mL (1 Tbsp.) vanilla extract and 300 g (10 oz.) melted and cooled bittersweet chocolate.

RECIPE 30.10

Approximate values per 30 g serving:

Calories	166
Total fat	15 g
Saturated fat	9.5 g
Cholesterol	41 mg
Sodium	160 mg
Total carbohydrates	8 g
Protein	0.5 g

French Buttercream

French buttercream, also known as **mousseline buttercream**, is similar to Italian buttercream except that the hot sugar syrup is whipped into beaten egg yolks (not egg whites). Softened butter and flavourings are added when the sweetened egg yolks are fluffy and cool. An Italian meringue such as the one created in the above formula is *sometimes* folded in for additional body and lightness. French buttercream is perhaps the most difficult type of buttercream to master, but it has the richest flavour and smoothest texture. Like a meringue buttercream, mousseline buttercream may be used on almost any type of cake.

Basic Procedure for Preparing French Buttercream

1. Prepare a sugar syrup and cook to soft ball stage (115°C/238°F).
2. Beat egg yolks to a thin ribbon.
3. Slowly beat the hot sugar syrup into the egg yolks.
4. Continue beating until the yolks are pale, stiff and completely cool.
5. Gradually add softened butter to the cooled yolks.
6. Fold in Italian meringue (optional).
7. Stir in flavouring ingredients.

RECIPE 30.11

Approximate values
per 30 g serving:

Calories	152
Total fat	11 g
Saturated fat	7 g
Cholesterol	77 mg
Sodium	105 mg
Total carbohydrates	13 g
Protein	1 g

Applying the Basics

RECIPE 30.11

FRENCH BUTTERCREAM

Yield: 1.5 kg (3.3 lb.)

Glucose	100 g	3-1/2 oz.
Granulated sugar	500 g	17-1/2 oz.
Water	200 g	7 oz.
Egg yolks	185 g	8 large
Butter, softened	600 g	21 oz.
Flavouring to taste	50 g	2 oz.

1. Combine the glucose, sugar and water in a small saucepan and bring to a boil. Continue boiling until the syrup reaches 115°C (238°F).
2. Meanwhile, beat the egg yolks in a mixer fitted with a wire whisk on medium speed. When the sugar syrup reaches 115°C (238°F), pour it slowly into the egg yolks, gradually increasing the speed at which they are whipped. Continue beating at medium-high speed until the mixture is very pale, stiff and cool.
3. Gradually add the softened butter to the egg mixture, frequently scraping down the sides of the bowl.
4. Stir in flavouring extracts as desired.

VARIATION: One litre (1 qt.) Italian meringue may be folded in for a lighter buttercream.

Foam Frosting

Foam frosting, sometimes known as **boiled icing**, is simply a meringue made with hot sugar syrup. Foam frosting is light and fluffy but very sweet. It may be flavoured with extract, liqueur or melted chocolate.

Foam frosting is rather unstable. It should be used immediately and served the day it is prepared. Refrigeration often makes the foam weep beads of sugar. Freezing causes it to separate or melt.

An easy foam frosting can be made by following the formula for Italian Buttercream (Recipe 30.10). As soon as the meringue has cooled to room temperature it can be flavoured with extracts as desired.

Fudge Frosting

A fudge frosting is a warmed mixture of sugar, butter and water or milk. It is heavy, rich and candylike. It is also stable and holds up well. A fudge frosting should be applied warm and allowed to dry on the cake or pastry. When dry, it will have a thin crust and a moist interior. A fudge frosting can be vanilla- or chocolate-based and is used on cupcakes, layer cakes and sheet cakes.

Basic Procedure for Preparing Fudge Frostings

1. Blend sifted powdered sugar with corn syrup, beating until the sugar is dissolved and the mixture is smooth.
2. Blend in warm melted shortening and/or butter.
3. Blend in hot liquids. Add extracts or flavourings.
4. Use fudge frosting while still warm.

Cocoa fudge frosting.

Applying the Basics

RECIPE 30.12

BASIC FUDGE FROSTING

Yield: 2 kg (4 lb.)

Icing sugar, sifted	1.5 kg	3 lb.
Salt	1 g	1/4 tsp.
Light corn syrup	60 mL	2 fl. oz.
Shortening, melted	120 g	4 oz.
Water, hot (60°C/140°F)	300 mL	10 fl. oz.
Vanilla extract	30 mL	2 Tbsp.

1. Blend the sugar, salt and corn syrup. Beat until smooth.
2. Add the melted shortening and blend well.
3. Add the hot water and vanilla and blend well. If the fudge is too stiff it may be thinned with a simple sugar syrup. Use before the icing cools.

VARIATION: *Cocoa Fudge Frosting*—Sift 125 g (4 oz.) cocoa powder with the powdered sugar. Add 60 mL (2 fl. oz.) melted unsalted butter with the shortening.

RECIPE 30.12

Approximate values per 30 g serving:

Calories	136
Total fat	2.5 g
Saturated fat	0.5 g
Cholesterol	0 mg
Sodium	17 mg
Total carbohydrates	29 g
Protein	0 g

Fondant

Fondant is a thick, opaque sugar paste commonly used for glazing napoleons, petit fours and other pastries as well as some cakes. It is a cooked mixture of sugar and water, with **glucose** or corn syrup added to encourage the correct type of sugar crystallization. Poured over the surface being coated, fondant quickly dries to a shiny, nonsticky coating. It is naturally pure white and can be tinted with food colouring. Fondant can also be flavoured with melted chocolate.

Fondant is rather difficult to make, so it is almost always purchased prepared. To use, warm fondant to 38°C (100°F) over medium heat, stirring constantly to prevent overheating. If necessary, thin fondant with water or simple syrup after warming up the fondant. Commercially prepared fondant will keep for several months at room temperature in an airtight container. The surface of the fondant should be coated with simple syrup, however, to prevent a crust from forming.

♦♦♦

ROLLED FONDANT

Rolled fondant is a very stiff doughlike type of fondant that is used for covering cakes and for making flowers and other decorations. As the name implies, it is rolled out to the desired thickness, then draped over a cake or torte to create a very smooth, flat coating. After the fondant dries, the cake may be decorated with royal icing or buttercream. Rolled fondant is available in a ready-to-use form. It can be flavoured or coloured if desired. Be sure to keep the fondant tightly wrapped in plastic and stored in an airtight container to prevent if from drying out and cracking.

Glaze

A glaze is a thin coating meant to be poured or dripped onto a cake or pastry. A glaze is usually too thin to apply with a knife or spatula. It is used to add moisture and flavour to cakes on which a heavy frosting would be undesirable—for example, a chiffon or angel food cake.

Flat icing or **water icing** is a specific type of glaze used on danish pastries and coffeecakes. It is pure white and dries to a firm gloss.

Basic Procedure for Preparing Glazes

1. Blend sifted powdered sugar with a small amount of liquid and flavourings.
2. Use immediately.

RECIPE 30.13

*Approximate values
per 10 g serving:*

Calories	32
Total fat	0 g
Saturated fat	0 g
Cholesterol	0 mg
Sodium	0 mg
Total carbohydrates	8 g
Protein	0 g

Applying the Basics

RECIPE 30.13

BASIC SUGAR GLAZE

Yield: 300 g (13 oz.)

Icing sugar, sifted	225 g	9-1/2 oz.
Water, warm	50 mL	2 fl. oz.
Glucose or corn syrup	25 g	1 oz.
Vanilla extract	5 mL	2 tsp.

1. Stir the ingredients together in a small bowl until smooth.
2. Adjust the consistency by adding more water to thin the glaze if necessary.
3. Adjust the flavour as necessary.
4. Use immediately, before the glaze begins to dry.

VARIATION: Another extract, such as lemon or almond, may be used if desired.

Royal Icing

Royal icing, also known as **decorator's icing**, is similar to flat icing except it is much stiffer and becomes hard and brittle when dry. It is an uncooked mixture of icing sugar and egg whites. It may be dyed with food colouring pastes.

Royal icing is used for making decorations, particularly intricate flowers or lace patterns. Prepare royal icing in small quantities and always keep any unused portion covered with a damp towel to prevent hardening.

Basic Procedure for Preparing Royal Icing

1. Combine egg white and lemon juice, if used.
2. Beat in sifted icing sugar until the correct consistency is reached.
3. Beat until very smooth and firm enough to hold a stiff peak.
4. Colour as desired with paste food colourings.
5. Store covered with a damp cloth and plastic wrap.

◆◆◆

CONVENIENCE PRODUCTS

A wide selection of prepared icings, glazes and toppings is available. Often, chocolate and vanilla fudge icing bases are purchased, then flavoured or coloured as needed. Foam frostings can be purchased in powder form, to which you add water and then whip. Even prepared "buttercreams" are available, although they contain little or no real butter.

Prepared icings are often exceedingly sweet and overpowered by artificial flavours and chemical preservatives. These products save time but often cost more than their counterparts made from scratch. They should be used only after balancing the disadvantages against the benefits for your particular operation.

Applying the Basics

RECIPE 30.14

ROYAL ICING

Yield: 200 g (7 oz.)

Icing sugar	180 g	6 oz.
Egg white, room temperature	1	1
Lemon juice	1 mL	1/4 tsp.

1. Sift the sugar and set aside.
2. Place the egg white and lemon juice in a stainless steel bowl.
3. Add 125 g (4 oz.) of sugar and beat with an electric mixer or metal spoon until blended. The mixture should fall from a spoon in heavy globs. If it pours, it is too thin and will need the remaining 55 g (2 oz.) of sugar.

RECIPE 30.14

*Approximate values
per 30 g serving:*

Calories	120
Total fat	0 g
Saturated fat	0 g
Cholesterol	0 mg
Sodium	9 mg
Total carbohydrates	30 g
Protein	1 g

4. Once the consistency is correct, continue beating for 3–4 minutes. The icing should be white, smooth and thick enough to hold a stiff peak. Food colouring paste can be added at this time if desired.

5. Cover the icing with a damp towel and plastic wrap to prevent it from hardening.

Ganache

Ganache is a blend of chocolate and cream. It may also include butter, liquor or other flavourings. Any bittersweet, semi-sweet or dark chocolate may be used; the choice depends on personal preference and cost considerations.

Depending on its consistency, ganache may be used as a filling, frosting or glaze-type coating on cakes or pastries. The ratio of chocolate to cream determines how thick the cooled ganache will be. Equal parts chocolate and cream generally are best for frostings and fillings. Increasing the percentage of chocolate produces a thicker ganache. Warm ganache can be poured over a cake or pastry and allowed to harden as a thin glaze, or the ganache may be cooled and whipped to create a rich, smooth frosting. If it becomes too firm, ganache can be remelted over a bain marie.

1. Pour the hot cream over the chopped chocolate.

Basic Procedure for Preparing Ganache

1. Melt finely chopped chocolate with cream in a double boiler. Or,
2. Bring cream just to a boil. Then pour it over finely chopped chocolate and allow the cream's heat to gently melt the chocolate.
3. Whichever method is used, cool the cream and chocolate mixture over an ice bath.

Do not attempt to melt chocolate and then add cool cream. This will cause the chocolate to resolidify and lump.

2. Cool, firm ganache.

Applying the Basics

RECIPE 30.15

CHOCOLATE GANACHE

Yield: 1.1 kg (2 lb. 5 oz.)

Bittersweet chocolate	500 g	1 lb.
Cream, 35%	500 g	1 lb.
Liqueur	50 mL	2 fl. oz.
Butter, softened	100 g	3 oz.

1. Chop the chocolate into small pieces and place in a large metal bowl.
2. Bring the cream just to a boil, then immediately pour it over the chocolate, whisking to blend until the mixture is smooth.
3. Stir in the liqueur, followed by the softened butter.
4. Allow to cool, stirring frequently until the desired consistency is achieved. An ice bath may be used to speed the cooling process.

RECIPE 30.15

Approximate values per serving:

Calories	130
Total fat	10 g
Saturated fat	6 g
Cholesterol	15 mg
Sodium	0 mg
Total carbohydrates	10 g
Protein	1 g

ASSEMBLING AND DECORATING CAKES

Much of a cake's initial appeal lies in its appearance. This is true whether the finished cake is a simple sheet cake topped with swirls of buttercream or an elaborate wedding cake with intricate garlands and bouquets of royal icing roses. Any cake assembled and decorated with care and attention to detail is preferable to a carelessly assembled or garishly overdecorated one.

Thousands of decorating styles or designs are possible, of course. This section describes a few simple options that can be prepared by beginning pastry cooks using a minimum of specialized tools. In planning your cake's design consider the flavour, texture and colour of the components used as well as the number of guests or portions that must be served. Consider who will be cutting and eating the cake and how long the dessert must stand before service.

Assembling Cakes

Before a cake can be decorated, it must be assembled and coated with frosting. Most cakes can be assembled in a variety of shapes and sizes: sheet cakes, round layer cakes and rectangular layer cakes are the most common. When assembling any cake, the goal is to fill and stack the cake layers evenly and to apply an even coating of frosting that is smooth and free of crumbs.

Most of the photographs used in this section show the assembly and decoration of a wedding cake. The finished cake is shown in the photograph that introduces this chapter. The complete formula is found in Recipe 30.16.

◆◆◆

ADVANCED PÂTISSERIE

Sugar can be used to create a number of doughs, pastes and syrups used for artistic and decorative work. Mastering even some of these products takes years of experience and practice. Although formulas and preparation methods are beyond the scope of this book, it is important that all pastry cooks be able to recognize and identify certain decorative sugar products.

Blown sugar—a boiled mixture of sucrose, glucose and tartaric acid that is coloured and shaped (in a manner very similar to glass blowing) using an air pump. It is used for making pieces of fruit and containers such as bowls and vases.

Gum paste—a smooth dough made of sugar and gelatin; it dries relatively slowly, becoming very firm and hard. The paste can be coloured and rolled out, cut and shaped, or moulded. It is used for making flowers, leaves and small figures.

Marzipan—a mixture of almond paste and sugar that may be coloured and used like modelling clay for sculpting small fruits, flowers or other objects. Marzipan may also be rolled out and cut into various shapes or used to cover cakes or pastries.

Nougat—a candy made of caramelized sugar and almonds that can be moulded into shapes or containers. Unlike other sugar decorations, nougat remains deliciously edible.

Pastillage—a paste made with sugar, cornstarch and gelatin. It can be rolled into sheets, then cut into shapes. It dries in a very firm and sturdy form, like plaster. Naturally pure white, it can be painted with cocoa or food colourings. Pastillage is used for showpieces and large decorative items.

Pulled sugar—a doughlike mixture of sucrose, glucose and tartaric acid that is coloured, then shaped by hand. Pulled sugar is used for making birds, flowers, leaves, bows and other items.

Spun sugar—made by flicking dark caramelized sugar rapidly over a dowel to create long, fine, hairlike threads. Mounds or wreaths of these threads are used to decorate ice cream desserts, croquembouche and gâteaux.

Basic Procedure for Assembling Cakes

1. Begin by levelling the cake and trimming the edges as needed with a serrated knife.

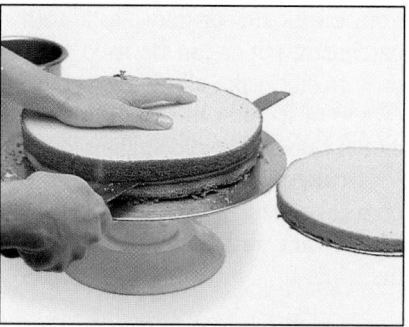

2. Split the cake horizontally into thin layers if desired. Use cake boards to support each layer as it is removed. Brush away any loose crumbs with a dry pastry brush.

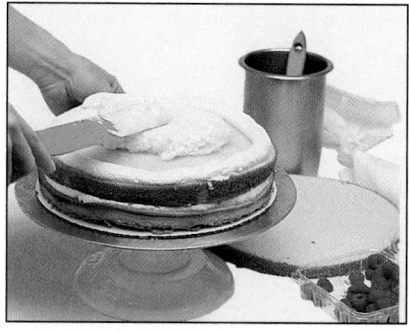

3. Position the bottom layer on a cake board. Place the layer on a revolving cake stand, brush cake with a flavoured simple syrup. Top the layer with a mound of frosting or filling, then use a cake spatula to spread it evenly to the edges.

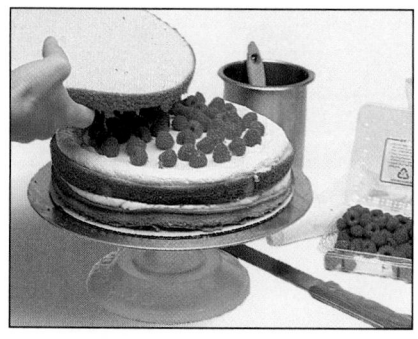

4. Position the next cake layer over the filling and continue layering and filling the cake as desired.

5. Place a mound of frosting in the centre of the cake top. Push it to the edge of the cake with a cake spatula. Do not drag the frosting back and forth or lift the spatula off the frosting, as these actions tend to pick up crumbs.

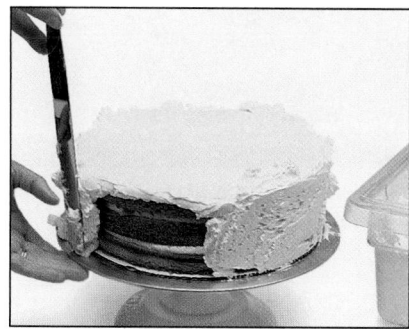

6. Cover the sides with excess frosting from the top, adding more as necessary. Hold the spatula upright against the side of the cake and, pressing gently, turn the cake stand slowly. This smooths and evens the sides. When the sides and top are smooth, the cake is ready to be decorated as desired.

Simple Decorating Techniques

An extremely simple yet effective way to decorate a frosted cake is with a garnish of chopped nuts, fruit, toasted coconut, shaved chocolate or other foods arranged in patterns or sprinkled over the cake. Be sure to use a garnish that complements the cake and frosting flavours or reflects one of the cake's ingredients. For example, finely chopped pecans would be an appropriate garnish for a carrot cake that contains pecans; shaved chocolate would not.

Side masking is the technique of coating only the sides of a cake with garnish. The top may be left plain or decorated with icing designs or a message. Be sure to apply the garnish while the frosting is still damp enough for it to adhere.

Stencils can be used to apply patterns of finely chopped garnishes, confectioner's sugar or cocoa powder to the top of a cake. A design can be cut from cardboard, or thin plastic forms can be purchased. Even simple strips of parchment paper can be used to create an attractive pattern. If using a stencil on a frosted cake allow the frosting to set somewhat before laying the stencil on top of it. After the garnishes have been sprinkled over the stencil, carefully lift the stencil to avoid spilling the excess garnish and messing the pattern.

A **cake** or **baker's comb** or a serrated knife can be used to create patterns on a cake iced with buttercream, fudge or ganache. Hold the comb against the frosted cake and rotate the cake slowly and evenly to create horizontal lines in the icing.

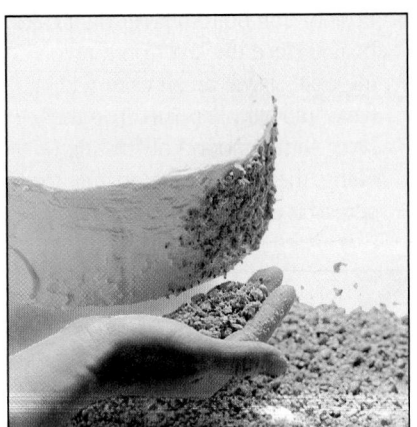

Side masking—coating the sides of a carrot cake with chopped pecans.

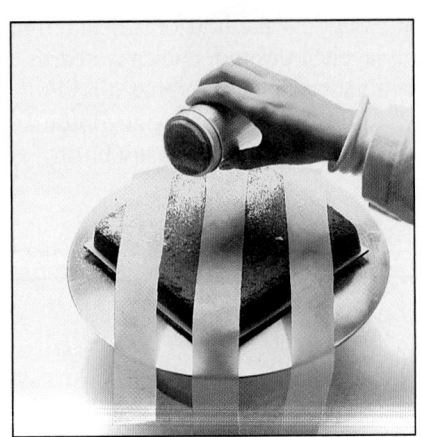

Stencils—creating a design with confectioner's sugar and strips of parchment paper.

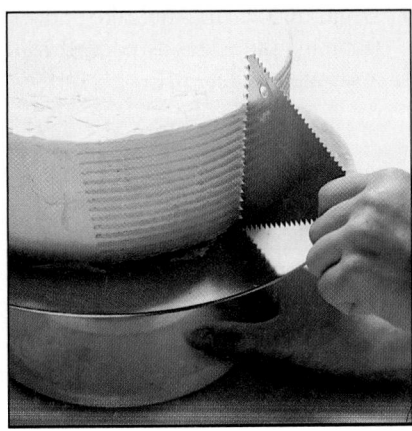

Cake comb—creating a pattern on a frosted cake.

Piping Techniques

More elaborate and difficult decorations can be produced with the aid of a piping bag and an assortment of pastry tips. With these tools, frosting or royal icing can be used to create borders, flowers and messages. Before applying any decoration, however, plan a design or pattern that is appropriate for the size and shape of the item being decorated.

When used properly, coloured frostings can bring cake decorations to life. Buttercream, royal icing and fondant are easily tinted using paste food colouring. Liquid food colourings are not recommended as they may thin the frosting too much. Always add colouring gradually with a toothpick. Frosting colours tend to darken as they sit. It is easy to add more later to darken the colour if necessary, but it is difficult to lighten the colour if too much is added.

Piping bags made from plastic, nylon or plastic-coated canvas are available in a range of sizes. A disposable piping cone can also be made from parchment paper.

Most decorations and designs are made by using a piping bag fitted with a pastry tip. Pastry tips are available with dozens of different openings and are referred to by standardized numbers. Some commonly used tips are shown on page 877. You can produce a variety of borders and designs by changing the pressure, the angle of the bag and the distance between the tip and the cake surface.

Basic Procedure for Filling a Piping Bag

1. Select the proper size piping bag for your task. Insert the desired tip.

2. Fold down the top of the bag, then fill approximately half full with frosting. Do not overfill the bag.

3. Be sure to close the open end tightly before you start piping. Hold the bag firmly in your palm and squeeze from the top. Do not squeeze from the bottom or you may force the contents out the wrong end. Use the fingers of your other hand to guide the bag as you work.

Piped-On Decorating Techniques

Instead of leaving the sides of a frosted cake smooth or coating them with chopped nuts or crumbs, you can pipe on frosting designs and patterns. A simple but elegant design is the basket weave, shown on page 878.

Leaf—#67

Basket Weave—#48

Drop Flower—#2D

Rosettes—#32

Bead Border—#8

Shell Border—#32

Tip Patterns

Normally a border pattern will be piped around the base of the cake and along the top edge. Borders should be piped on after nuts or any other garnishes are applied.

Each slice or serving of cake can be marked with its own decoration. For example, a rosette of frosting or a whole nut or piece of fruit could be used as shown below. This makes it easier to portion the cake evenly.

Delicate flowers such as roses can be piped, allowed to harden, then placed on the cake in attractive arrangements. Royal icing is particularly useful for making decorations in advance because it dries very hard and lasts indefinitely.

Applying a basket weave pattern to the sides of the wedding cake.

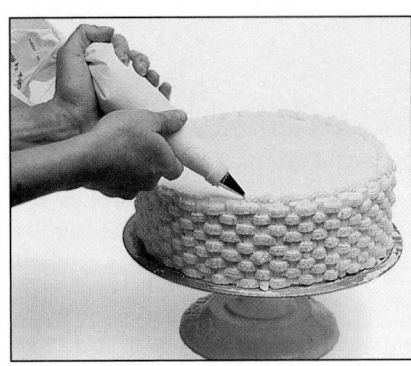

Applying a shell border to the wedding cake.

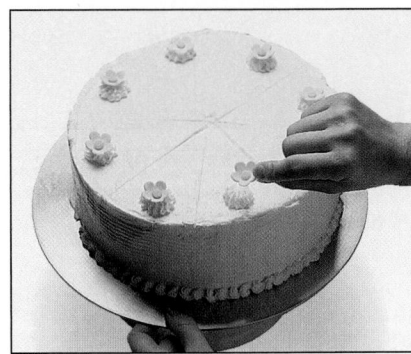

Placing royal icing flowers onto cake portions.

Basic Procedure for Piping a Buttercream Rose

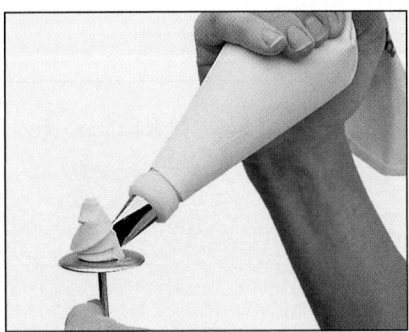

1. Using a #104 tip, pipe a mound of icing onto a rose nail.

2. Pipe a curve of icing around the mound to create the centre of the rose.

3. Pipe 3 overlapping petals around the centre.

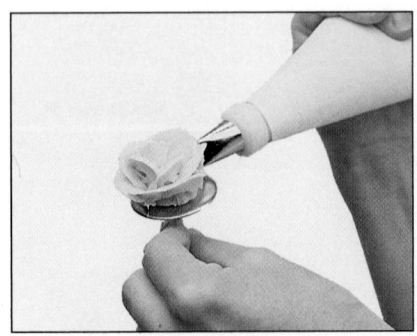

4. Pipe 5 more overlapping petals around the first 3 petals.

5. The finished rose is placed on the cake.

◆◆◆

MAKING A PARCHMENT-PAPER CONE

A disposable piping bag or cone is easily made from parchment paper. Begin with an equilateral triangle of uncreased paper. Shape it into a cone as shown, folding the top edges together to hold the shape. The point of the cone can be cut as desired. Paper cones are especially useful for writing messages or piping melted chocolate.

1. Wrap opposite ends of the parchment triangle.

2. Fold the ends together to seal.

3. Cut the tip of the filled parchment cone.

The key to success with a piping bag is practice, practice, practice. Use plain all-purpose shortening piped onto parchment paper to practise and experiment with piping techniques. Once you are comfortable using a piping bag, you can apply these newfound skills directly to cakes and pastry decorating. Piping skills are also used in other areas of food preparation.

Storing Cakes

Unfrosted cake layers or sheets can be stored at room temperature for two or three days if well covered. Frosted or filled cakes are usually refrigerated to prevent spoilage. Simple buttercreams or sugar glazes, however, can be left at room temperature for one or two days. Any cake containing custard filling or whipped cream, as well as cakes finished with buttercream containing eggs, must be refrigerated. Cakes made with foam-type frosting should be eaten the day they are prepared.

Cakes can usually be frozen with great success; this makes them ideal for baking in advance. Unfrosted layers or sheets should be well covered with plastic wrap and frozen at –18°C (0°F) or lower. High-fat cakes will keep for up to six months; egg foam cakes begin to deteriorate after two or three months.

Frostings and fillings do not freeze particularly well, often losing flavour or changing texture when frozen. Buttercreams made with egg whites or sugar syrups tend to develop crystals and graininess. Foam frostings weep, expelling beads of sugar and becoming sticky. Fondant will absorb moisture and separate from the cake. If you must freeze a filled or frosted cake, it is best to freeze it unwrapped first, until the frosting is firm. The cake can then be covered with plastic wrap without damaging the frosting design. Leave the cake wrapped until completely thawed. It is best to thaw cakes in the refrigerator if time permits. Do not refreeze thawed cakes.

CONCLUSION

The ability to produce good cakes and frostings depends on using the right balance of high-quality ingredients and combining them with the proper techniques. When preparing cakes and frostings, always combine flavours and textures with care; apply frostings, garnishes and decorations with care also. Avoid overly rich, cloyingly sweet or garishly decorated products. With study and practice, you can learn the mixing techniques and assembly skills necessary for producing good cakes. Additional practice will develop the decorating and garnishing skills of a fine pastry chef.

QUESTIONS FOR DISCUSSION

1. Raw cake ingredients can be classified by function into six categories. List them and give an example of each.
2. What is the primary leavening agent in cakes made with the foaming method? How is this similar to or different from cakes made with the creaming method?
3. What is the difference between a spongecake and a classic genoise?
4. Describe the procedures for making three types of frosting or icing as discussed in this chapter.
5. List the steps employed in assembling and frosting a three-layer cake.

ADDITIONAL CAKE AND FROSTING FORMULAS

RECIPE 30.16

VANILLA RASPBERRY LAYER CAKE WITH WHITE CHOCOLATE BUTTERCREAM

NOTE: *This dish appears in the Chapter Opening photograph.*

HYATT REGENCY SCOTTSDALE AT GAINEY RANCH, SCOTTSDALE, AZ
Executive Pastry Chef Judy Doherty

VANILLA CAKES

Yield: One 20-cm (8-inch), One 25-cm (10-inch) and One 35-cm (14-inch) tier for Wedding Cake   **Method:** Two-Stage

Cake flour	850 g	1 lb. 14 oz.
Granulated sugar	1.25 kg	2 lb. 8 oz.
Baking powder	70 g	2-1/2 oz.
Eggs	1.4 kg	48 oz.
Salt	30 g	1 oz.
Fluid Flex	570 g	1 lb. 4 oz.
Milk	450 mL	1 pt.

1. Prepare the pans by spraying with pan release and lining with parchment paper.
2. Combine the flour, sugar, baking powder, eggs and salt in a large mixer bowl. Whip on high speed for 8 minutes.

RECIPE 30.16

Approximate values per serving:

Calories	600
Total fat	28 g
Saturated fat	7 g
Cholesterol	240 mg
Sodium	520 mg
Total carbohydrates	75 g
Protein	10 g

3. Add Fluid Flex (an emulsifier for spongecakes) and milk. Mix for 8 more minutes at medium speed.

4. Divide the batter among one 20-cm (8-inch), one 25-cm (10-inch) and one 35-cm (14-inch) cake pan. Fill each pan halfway.

5. Bake at 180°C (350°F) for 35–60 minutes, depending on tier size. The cake is done when it springs back when lightly touched in the centre. Allow to cool, then remove from the pans and freeze.

RASPBERRY SYRUP

Granulated sugar	500 g	1 lb.
Water	500 mL	16 fl. oz.
Raspberry liqueur	60 mL	2 fl. oz.

Bring the sugar and water to a boil, then cool to room temperature. Add the raspberry liqueur.

DIPLOMAT CREAM FILLING

Pastry cream, chilled	4 L	1 gal.
Raspberry liqueur	125 mL	4 fl. oz.
Gelatin	45 g	1-1/2 oz.
Water	175 mL	6 fl. oz.
Whipped cream	1 L	1 qt.

1. Place the pastry cream in a large mixer bowl and whip on high speed until smooth. Add the raspberry liqueur.

2. Soften the gelatin in the water, then place over a low flame and heat to dissolve.

3. Add 500 mL (1 pt.) of the raspberry-flavoured pastry cream to the gelatin. Place over a low flame and whip by hand until smooth and the gelatin is incorporated. Add this mixture to the remainder of the pastry cream.

4. Fold in the whipped cream.

Diplomat Cream Filling— Approximate values per 30 g serving:

Calories	40
Total fat	2 g
Saturated fat	1 g
Cholesterol	30 mg
Sodium	10 mg
Total carbohydrates	5 g
Protein	1 g

WHITE CHOCOLATE BUTTERCREAM

Sugar	2.5 kg	5 lb. 8 oz.
Water	625 mL	1 lb. 6 oz.
Egg whites	800 g	1 lb. 12 oz.
Unsalted butter, softened	3.15 kg	7 lb.
White crème de cacao	250 mL	9 fl. oz.
White chocolate, melted	675 g	1 lb. 8 oz.

1. Cook the sugar and water to 117°C (242°F), then pour into a measuring container with a handle for easier pouring.

2. Start whipping the egg whites when the sugar reaches 113°C (235°F).

3. When the whites are whipped to firm peaks, add the hot sugar syrup slowly while continuing to whip at low speed. Whip until completely cool.

4. Add the butter and whip until smooth.

5. Add the crème de cacao to the white chocolate. Whip until smooth, then add to the buttercream.

White Chocolate Buttercream— Approximate values per 30 g serving:

Calories	140
Total fat	11 g
Saturated fat	7 g
Cholesterol	25 mg
Sodium	10 mg
Total carbohydrates	10 g
Protein	1 g

ASSEMBLY: Each cake tier is sliced horizontally into three layers. The layers are brushed with the raspberry syrup, then filled with diplomat cream and fresh raspberries. The top and sides of each tier are coated with the white chocolate buttercream; the sides are coated with a basket weave design; and the tiers are decorated with pulled sugar and royal icing roses. The assembly is illustrated in the photographs appearing throughout this chapter.

◆◆◆

RECIPE 30.17

CARROT CAKE WITH CREAM CHEESE FROSTING

Yield: One Sheet Cake or Four 22.5-cm (9-inch) Rounds   **Method:** Creaming

Vegetable oil	650 g	1 lb. 8 oz.
Brown sugar	900 g	2 lb.
Eggs	450 g	8
Vanilla	5 mL	1 tsp.
Carrots, shredded	900 g	2 lb.
Crushed pineapple, with juice	900 g	2 lb.
Baking soda	25 g	1 oz.
Cinnamon	3 g	2 tsp.
Salt	2 g	1/4 tsp.
Bread flour	1 kg	2 lb. 3 oz.
Hazelnut, ground	450 g	1 lb.

1. Blend the oil and sugar in a large mixer bowl fitted with the paddle attachment. Add the eggs and vanilla and incorporate.

2. Blend in the carrots and pineapple.

3. Sift the dry ingredients together, then add them to the batter.

4. Divide the batter into four greased and floured pans.

5. Bake at 175°C (350°F) until springy to the touch and a cake tester comes out almost clean.

CREAM CHEESE FROSTING

Unsalted butter, softened	125 g	4 oz.
Cream cheese, softened	350 g	12 oz.
Icing sugar, sifted	125 g	4 oz.
Lemon, zest and juice	1	1

1. Cream the butter and cream cheese until smooth. Add the icing sugar and beat well, scraping down the side of the bowl.

2. Beat in the lemon juice and finely grated zest.

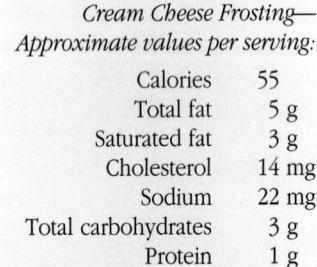

RECIPE 30.17

Approximate values per serving:

Calories	352
Total fat	21 g
Saturated fat	2 g
Cholesterol	36 mg
Sodium	184 mg
Total carbohydrates	38 g
Protein	5 g

Cream Cheese Frosting—
Approximate values per serving:

Calories	55
Total fat	5 g
Saturated fat	3 g
Cholesterol	14 mg
Sodium	22 mg
Total carbohydrates	3 g
Protein	1 g

◆◆◆

RECIPE 30.18

SACHER TORTE

SOUTHERN ALBERTA INSTITUTE OF TECHNOLOGY, CALGARY, AB
Pastry Chef Andreas Schwarzer

Yield: Six 22-cm (9-inch) Cakes

Butter	500 g	1 lb.
Sugar	500 g	1 lb.
Sweet chocolate, melted	625 g	1 lb. 6 oz.
Egg yolks	500 g	1 lb.
Vanilla	15 mL	1/2 fl. oz.
Egg whites	750 g	1 lb. 10 oz.
Salt	4 g	1/8 oz.
Sugar	375 g	13 oz.
Cake flour, sifted	500 g	1 lb.

Andreas Schwarzer
Andreas worked in pastry shops and bakeries in Germany before coming to Canada. He has won several medals for his pastries and showpieces, and has worked on banquets for such celebrities as Clint Eastwood, Arnold Schwarzenegger, Margaret Thatcher and Prince Philip.

Apricot jam	as needed	as needed
Chocolate icing	as needed	as needed
Chocolate glaze	as needed	as needed

1. Grease the sides of six 22-cm (9-inch) springform pans with some butter and line the bottoms with parchment circles.

2. Cream the butter until light and add 500 g (1 lb.) sugar, beating until fluffy.

3. Beat in melted chocolate until smooth.

4. Add egg yolks in five stages, beating well after each addition.

5. Beat in vanilla.

6. Whip egg whites and salt to soft peaks.

7. Gradually whisk in 375 g (13 oz.) sugar to form soft meringue.

8. Add flour in stages. Fold in meringue last for maximum aeration.

9. Pan batter. Bake at 180°C (375°F) for 45–60 minutes.

10. Cool cakes for 5 minutes and depan. Cool completely, then cut each cake horizontally into two layers. Spread apricot jam between layers and stack to make six cakes.

11. Ice cakes with chocolate icing and refrigerate.

12. Pour chocolate glaze over each cake to form a complete, smooth, glossy coating.

NOTE: This recipe has been adjusted for preparation at an altitude of 1200 metres.

RECIPE 30.18

Approximate values per 1/12 torte:

Calories	276
Total fat	15 g
Saturated fat	8 g
Cholesterol	128 mg
Sodium	92 mg
Total carbohydrates	34 g
Protein	5 g

❖❖❖

RECIPE 30.19

ZUPPA ROMANA

SOUTHERN ALBERTA INSTITUTE OF TECHNOLOGY, CALGARY, AB
Master Pâtissier Hermann Greineder

Yield: 12–16 Servings

White sponge cake, 22 cm (9 inches)	1	1
Simple syrup	300 mL	10 fl. oz.
Brandy	50 mL	2 fl. oz.
Rum	50 mL	2 fl. oz.
Pastry Cream Filling:		
Pastry cream	200 g	7 oz.
Cream, 35%, whipped	1 L	1 qt.
Fruit Filling:		
Cherry pie filling	150 g	5 oz.
Mandarin sections	75 g	2-1/2 oz.
Fresh strawberries	75 g	2-1/2 oz.
Lemon, juice and grated rind	1	1
Cream, 35%, whipped	1 L	1 qt.

Hermann Greineder
Currently a Pastry Instructor at SAIT, Hermann received his German Master Certification as "Chef Pâtissier" in 1971. He has 45 years of experience in a wide range of establishments, and has won several medals in competition for his beautiful chocolate showpieces.

RECIPE 30.19

Approximate values per serving:

Calories	562
Total fat	29 g
Saturated fat	17 g
Cholesterol	225 mg
Sodium	172 mg
Total carbohydrates	64 g
Protein	7 g

1. Slice sponge cake into three 6-mm-thick (1/4-inch) layers. Place first sponge layer in appropriate dish (a silver platter, for example). Soak the cake well with about a third of the simple syrup, flavoured with brandy and rum.

2. Make the pastry cream filling by mixing the pastry cream and whipped cream together. Prepare the fruit filling by mixing the cherry pie filling, mandarin sections, strawberries and lemon juice and rind.

Continued

3. Spread pastry cream filling 3-mm (1/8-inch) thick on the bottom layer. Place all the fruit filling on top of the pastry cream. Add the next sponge layer, another third of the syrup and a layer of pastry cream. Place final sponge layer on top of filling and soak it very well with the remaining syrup. Ice with whipped cream and decorate.

♦♦♦

RECIPE 30.20

DEVIL'S FOOD CAKE

Yield: 1 Sheet Pan or   **Method:** High-Ratio (two-stage method)
Six 20-cm (8-inch) Rounds

Cake flour	500 g	1 lb.
Granulated sugar	600 g	1 lb. 3 oz.
Emulsified shortening	300 g	9-1/2 oz.
Cocoa powder	100 g	3-1/4 oz.
Salt	25 g	1/2 oz.
Baking powder	20 g	5 Tbsp.
Baking soda	10 g	2-1/2 Tbsp.
Nonfat dry milk powder	55 g	2 oz.
Vanilla extract	15 mL	1 Tbsp.
Corn syrup	100 g	3 oz.
Water, cold	450 mL	14-1/2 fl. oz.
Eggs	400 g	12-1/2 oz.

1. Mix the cake flour, sugar and emulsified shortening in a large mixer bowl on low speed for 5 minutes.
2. Add the cocoa powder, salt, baking powder, baking soda, milk powder, vanilla, corn syrup and 200 mL (7 fl. oz.) of the cold water. Blend well, then scrape down the bowl.
3. Combine the eggs with the remaining cold water and add to the batter in three equal parts, blending well and scraping down the bowl after each addition.
4. After all ingredients are incorporated, blend on low speed for 2 minutes.
5. Divide into greased and floured pans, scaling 450 g (1 lb.) for each 20-cm (8-inch) round layer.
6. Bake at 170°C (340°F) until springy and a toothpick inserted in the centre comes out clean.

RECIPE 30.20

Approximate values per serving:

Calories	169
Total fat	7 g
Saturated fat	2 g
Cholesterol	36 mg
Sodium	308 mg
Total carbohydrates	24 g
Protein	3 g

♦♦♦

RECIPE 30.21

BÛCHE DE NOËL

Yield: 10–12 Servings

Genoise (Recipe 30.3), freshly baked	one-half sheet	one-half sheet
Simple syrup	as needed	as needed
Buttercream		
(coffee, chocolate or vanilla)	1 L	1 qt.

1. Roll up the genoise in a spiral, starting with the long side. Wrap in parchment paper and cool.
2. Carefully unroll the cake. Brush the interior with simple syrup and coat with buttercream, leaving a 2.5-cm (1-inch) unfrosted rim around each edge.

RECIPE 30.21

Approximate values per serving:

Calories	650
Total fat	21 g
Saturated fat	6 g
Cholesterol	0 mg
Sodium	330 mg
Total carbohydrates	115 g
Protein	2 g

1. Roll the cake filled with buttercream.

2. Attach the cut end to the log.

3. Pipe on the buttercream.

3. Reroll the cake tightly and position it with the seam down on a cake cardboard.

4. Cut one end from the cake on a diagonal. Place the cut piece on top of the log, securing with skewers until iced in place.

5. Pipe additional buttercream onto the cake log using a large star tip. Remove skewers. Pipe the buttercream onto the ends in a spiral pattern. Decorate as desired with buttercream flowers, baked meringue mushrooms or marzipan figures.

◆◆◆

RECIPE 30.22

ALMOND CHOCOLATE SHEET SPONGE

RITZ CARLTON, NEW ORLEANS, LA

Assistant Pastry Chef Pierre St. Pierre

Yield: 4 Sheet Pans

Butter	675 g	1 lb. 8 oz.
Icing sugar	575 g	1 lb. 4 oz.
Eggs	375 g	14 oz.
Egg yolks	625 g	1 lb. 6 oz.
Dark chocolate, melted	940 g	2 lb.
Egg whites	675 g	1 lb. 8 oz.
Icing sugar	225 g	8 oz.
Bread flour	285 g	10 oz.
Almond flour	680 g	1 lb. 8 oz.

1. Cream butter and icing sugar (575 g/1 lb. 4 oz.). Slowly add eggs and yolks, scraping sides of bowl.

2. Add melted chocolate.

3. Make a common meringue of egg whites and icing sugar (225 g/8 oz.).

4. Fold meringue into chocolate mixture.

5. Sift bread and almond flour together and fold into batter.

6. Divide batter evenly among four lined sheet pans and spread evenly and thinly.

7. Bake at 190°C (375°F) for approximately 5 minutes.

NOTE: This sponge is an excellent base for individual mousses or opera-style entremets.

Pierre St. Pierre

Pierre trained at George Brown College and later received his journeyman certification and Interprovincial Red Seal. He began his career as Food and Beverage Host with Walt Disney World Company's Epcot Centre, in Florida, and went on to work in pastries at Jasper Park Lodge, the Ritz-Carlton Buckhead (in Atlanta, Georgia) and the Ritz-Carlton Huntington (in Pasadena, California). Highlights of his career include being the Grand Prize Winner in the 1999 Southern Pastry Classic, in Atlanta, Georgia, and creating a chocolate Inukshuk showpiece that was displayed for the 1998 International Olympic Committee.

RECIPE 30.22

Approximate values per piece:

Calories	103
Total fat	7 g
Saturated fat	4 g
Cholesterol	58 mg
Sodium	40 mg
Total carbohydrates	8 g
Protein	3 g

◆◆◆

RECIPE 30.23

FLOURLESS ORANGE ALMOND CAKE

Chef Alexander Herbert

Yield: Two 23-cm (9-inch) Flans

Oranges, seeded, chopped	3	3
Baking powder	5 g	1-1/2 tsp.
Ground almonds	375 g	14 oz.
Eggs	385 g	7
Sugar	325 g	11-1/2 oz.

RECIPE 30.23

Approximate values per slice:

Calories	122
Total fat	4 g
Saturated fat	1 g
Cholesterol	52 mg
Sodium	30 mg
Total carbohydrates	15.5 g
Protein	7 g

1. Simmer oranges for 1 hour in just enough water to cover. Purée, cool and strain.
2. Combine baking powder with ground almonds.
3. Beat the eggs and sugar to a ribbon stage. Fold in orange purée and almond mixture.
4. Divide between two 23-cm (9-inch) rings.
5. Bake at 180°C (350°F) for approximately 1 hour.

◆◆◆

BISCUIT JOCONDE

Traditional Joconde sponge is mostly eggs and egg whites with lesser amounts of nut flour, icing sugar and cake flour enriched with butter. The ribbon is created with a stencil paste made of equal weights of butter, icing sugar, egg whites and cake flour. Colour with powder or paste food colours. For chocolate, substitute 20% cocoa for flour.

Albert Kurylo

Albert was trained in pastry in Poland and worked in Banff before joining the Southern Alberta Institute of Technology. He combines classical and contemporary offerings equally well and is quality driven.

RECIPE 30.24

Approximate values per piece:

Calories	68
Total fat	4 g
Saturated fat	1 g
Cholesterol	47 mg
Sodium	21 mg
Total carbohydrates	6 g
Protein	2 g

◆◆◆

RECIPE 30.24

RIBBON SPONGE

SOUTHERN ALBERTA INSTITUTE OF TECHNOLOGY, CALGARY, AB
Pastry Chef Albert Kurylo

Yield: 1 Full Sheet Pan

Eggs	250 g	8 oz.
Egg yolks	80 g	3 oz.
Sugar	100 g	3-1/2 oz.
Almonds, fine ground	200 g	7 oz.
Bread flour	55 g	2 oz.
Egg whites	120 g	4-1/4 oz.
Sugar	100 g	3-1/2 oz.
Butter, melted	55 g	2 oz.

1. Place eggs, egg yolks and sugar (100 g/3-1/2 oz.) in a bowl. Heat over a bain marie, stirring constantly, to a temperature of 49°C (120°F). Remove from heat and whip at high speed for 1 minute.
2. Thoroughly combine ground almonds and flour.
3. Whip egg whites and sugar (100 g/3-1/2 oz.) until mixture has the appearance of snow (thick and foaming, but will not hold a peak).
4. Stir the almond mixture into the whole egg mixture.
5. Stir in the melted butter.
6. Gradually fold in the egg-white mixture.
7. Colour a small portion of the paste and apply in a pattern on a silicone mat.
8. Spread the remaining paste 5 mm (1/4 inch) thick on a silicone mat and bake at 200°C (400°F) until set.

◆◆◆

RECIPE 30.25

Applesauce Brownies

Yield: 1 Sheet Pan

Unsweetened chocolate	125 g	4 oz.
Cake flour, sifted	500 g	1 lb.
Cocoa powder	275 g	9 oz.
Salt	10 g	2 tsp.
Egg whites	12	12
Whole eggs	8	8
Granulated sugar	1 kg	2 lb. 2 oz.
Light corn syrup	1 kg	2 lb.
Unsweetened applesauce	750 mL	1-1/2 pt.
Canola oil	225 mL	7 fl. oz.
Vanilla extract	30 mL	2 Tbsp.

1. Coat a sheet pan with pan-release spray.
2. Melt the chocolate over a bain marie and set aside.
3. Sift the flour, cocoa powder and salt together and set aside.
4. Whisk the egg whites and whole eggs together. Add the sugar, corn syrup, applesauce, oil and vanilla. Whisk in the chocolate.
5. Fold the flour mixture into the egg mixture. Pour into the prepared pan and bake at 180°C (350°F) until a cake tester comes out clean, approximately 25 minutes.

RECIPE 30.25

Approximate values per 1/48 sheet:

Calories	265
Total fat	7 g
Saturated fat	2 g
Cholesterol	36 mg
Sodium	132 mg
Total carbohydrates	51 g
Protein	4 g

◆◆◆

RECIPE 30.26

Tiramisu Torte

BISON FOOD SERVICES, Saskatoon, SK
Executive Chef-Owner Peter Phillips, CCC

Yield: One 22.5-cm (9-inch) Torte

Gelatin leaves	4	4
Water, cold	30 mL	1 fl. oz.
Egg yolks	125 g	6
Mascarpone	500 g	18 oz.
Egg whites	180 g	6
Sugar	90 g	3 oz.
Espresso	125 mL	4 fl. oz.
Ladyfingers and Cake (recipe follows)		
Cocoa powder, dutched	TT	TT

1. Soak gelatin in cold water until soft, approximately 10 minutes. Heat gently to melt the gelatin.
2. At medium speed, whisk the egg yolks until light and fluffy.
3. Add the gelatin to the egg yolks in small quantities and continue mixing until well blended.
4. Add the mascarpone and mix well.
5. In a separate bowl, whip the egg whites until foamy. Continue to whip while gradually adding sugar, until soft peaks form.

Peter Phillips, CCC
Leaving his home of Nipawin, Saskatchewan, to attend Humber College's Culinary Arts Program, Peter attained top student honours, as well as numerous other awards. After his apprenticeship at a golf and country club in Winnipeg and an exciting position at a ski resort in Japan, Peter returned to Saskatchewan and soon thereafter began managing Boffins Café. While having a strong interest in and aptitude for the business and management side of the culinary industry, he continues to develop his artistic talents through national and international competitions.

Continued

6. Fold egg-white mixture into cheese mixture in three stages, mixing well.

7. Place the 22.5-cm (9-inch) cake layer in a 22.5-cm (9-inch) cake ring on a 30-cm (12-inch) cake board and brush lightly with espresso.

8. Cut each ladyfinger in half and place upright around the inside of the cake ring.

9. Pour in half the cheese mixture.

10. Place the remaining cake layer on top of the mixture and brush well with espresso.

11. Pour in the remaining cheese mixture.

12. Refrigerate for 2–3 hours.

13. Dust with cocoa powder.

RECIPE 30.26

Approximate values per slice:

Calories	472
Total fat	24 g
Saturated fat	13 g
Cholesterol	308 mg
Sodium	274 mg
Total carbohydrates	51 g
Protein	16 g

LADYFINGERS AND CAKE

Yield: 20 Ladyfingers, One 22.5-cm (9-inch) Layer and One 17.5-cm (7-inch) Layer

Egg yolks	6	6
Vanilla	5 mL	1 tsp.
Sugar	180 g	6-1/2 oz.
Egg whites	6	6
Bread flour, sifted	140 g	5 oz.
Cornstarch	30 g	1 oz.

1. At medium speed, whisk the egg yolks, vanilla and 30 g (1 oz.) of sugar until light and fluffy.

2. In a separate bowl, whip the egg whites until foamy. Continue to whip while gradually adding the remaining sugar, until soft peaks form.

3. Fold approximately one-third of the egg whites into the whipped yolks to lighten them; fold in another third and then the remaining third.

4. Sift together flour and cornstarch, and fold into the egg mixture.

5. Place batter in a piping bag fitted with a plain No. 8 tip.

6. To make the ladyfingers, pipe twenty 10-cm-long (4-inch) cookies onto paper-lined sheet pans. Allow for some spreading during baking.

7. To make the base and centre layers of cake, draw one 22.5-cm (9-inch) circle and one 17.5-cm (7-inch) circle on parchment paper to make a template and turn over onto a sheet pan (allow for some spreading during baking). Pipe batter onto the circles.

8. Sprinkle both trays with sugar and bake at 220°C (425°F) until golden-brown, 8–10 minutes.

*Ladyfingers and Cake—
Approximate values
per 30 g serving:*

Calories	77
Total fat	1 g
Saturated fat	0.5 g
Cholesterol	53 mg
Sodium	35 mg
Total carbohydrates	14 g
Protein	2 g

◆◆◆

RECIPE 30.27

Savarin (Baba)

Yield: Two 20-cm (8-inch) moulds

DOUGH

Eggs	6	6
Sugar	30 g	1 oz.
Salt	10 g	2 tsp.
Butter	175 g	6 oz.
Water or milk, warm	375 mL	12 fl. oz.
Bread flour	500 g	1 lb. 2 oz.
Yeast	25 g	1 oz.

1. Beat eggs, sugar and salt together until pale and light.

2. Stir in softened butter.

3. Mix in warm water of milk (45°C/110°F).

4. Stir in flour and yeast to make a soft dough.

5. Cover dough and allow to proof in a warm place for 15 minutes.

6. Grease moulds with butter.

7. Fill moulds half full of dough.

8. Proof until dough reaches top of moulds.

9. Bake at 190°C (375°F) until golden. Turn onto rack to cool.

SYRUP

Sugar	225 g	8 oz.
Water	375 mL	12 fl. oz.
White wine	175 mL	6 fl. oz.
Rum	150 mL	5 fl. oz.

1. Simmer sugar, water and wine for 6 minutes.

2. Stir in rum and cool slightly.

ASSEMBLY: Soak savarin in hot syrup to moisten. Brush savarin with warm apricot glaze. Plate with Chantilly cream and fresh or candied fruit.

VARIATION: Add 300 g of rum-soaked raisins to the dough.

RECIPE 30.27	
Approximate values per serving:	
Calories	278
Total fat	10 g
Saturated fat	5.5 g
Cholesterol	93 mg
Sodium	304 mg
Total carbohydrates	35 g
Protein	6 g

WEBLINKS

American Cake Decorating Magazine
   www.cakemag.com/
Wedding Cake Decorating
   www.pastrywiz.com/season/wedding.htm
Cakes
   www.joyofbaking.com/cakes.html

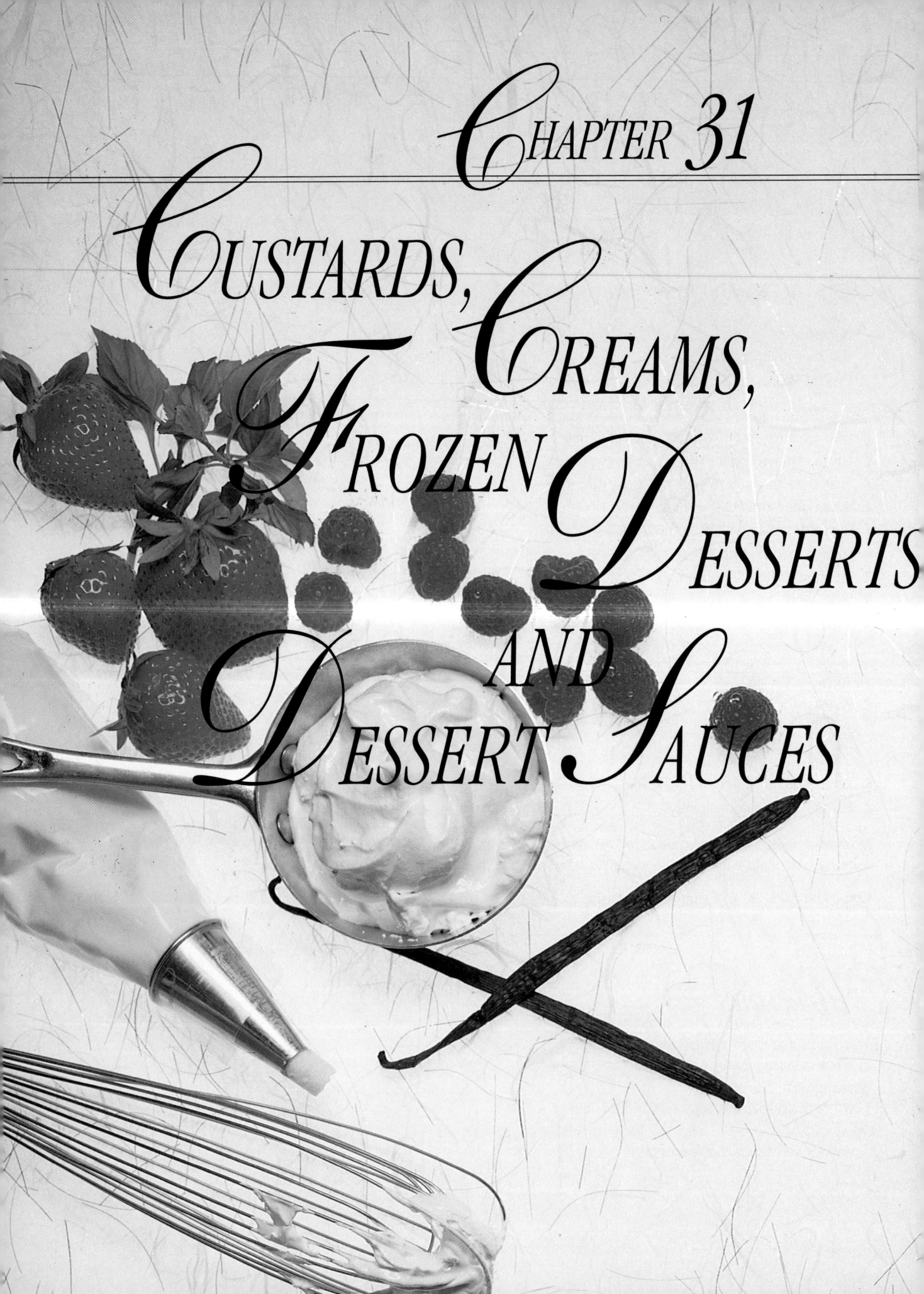

CHAPTER 31

CUSTARDS, CREAMS, FROZEN DESSERTS AND DESSERT SAUCES

After studying this chapter you will be able to:

◆ prepare a variety of custards and creams, including vanilla custard sauce and pastry cream, sabayon, baked soufflés, Bavarian creams, chiffons and mousses

◆ salvage curdled vanilla custard sauce

◆ prepare a variety of ice creams, sorbets and frozen dessert items

◆ prepare a variety of dessert sauces

◆ use these products in preparing and serving other pastry and dessert items

◆ plan and prepare assembled desserts

The bakeshop is responsible for more than just quick breads, yeast breads, pies, pastries, cookies and cakes. It also produces many delightfully sweet concoctions that are not baked and often not even cooked. These include sweet custards, creams, frozen desserts and dessert sauces. Sweet custards are cooked mixtures of eggs, sugar and milk; starch may be added. Sweet custards can be flavoured in a variety of ways and eaten hot or cold. Some are served alone as a dessert or used as a filling, topping or accompaniment for pies, pastries or cakes. Creams include whipped cream and mixtures lightened with whipped cream such as Bavarians, chiffons and mousses. Frozen desserts include ice cream and sorbet as well as the still-frozen mousses called semifreddi.

Sauces for these desserts, including fruit purées, caramel sauces and chocolate syrup, are also made in the bakeshop and are discussed in this chapter. Indeed, many of the items presented in this chapter are components, meant to be combined with pastries (Chapter 29) or cakes (Chapter 30) to form complete desserts. Guidelines for assembling desserts are given at this chapter's end.

CUSTARDS

A **custard** is any liquid thickened by the coagulation of egg proteins. A custard's consistency depends on the ratio of eggs to liquid and the type of liquid used. The more eggs used, the thicker and richer the final product will be. The richer the liquid (cream versus milk, for example), the thicker the final product. Most custards, with the notable exception of pastry creams, are not thickened by starch.

A custard can be stirred or baked. A **stirred custard** tends to be soft, rich and creamy. A **baked custard**, typically cooked in a bain marie, is usually firm enough to unmould and slice.

Stirred Custards

A stirred custard is cooked on the stove top either directly in a saucepan or over a double boiler. It must be stirred throughout the cooking process to prevent curdling (overcooking).

A stirred custard can be used as a dessert sauce, incorporated into a complex dessert or eaten alone. The stirred custards most commonly used in food service operations are **vanilla custard sauce** and **pastry cream**. Other popular stirred custards are **lemon curd** (Recipe 25.16) and **sabayon** (Recipe 31.3).

Vanilla Custard Sauce/Crème Anglaise

A custard sauce is made with egg yolks, sugar and milk or cereal cream. Usually flavoured with vanilla bean or pure vanilla extract, a custard sauce can also be flavoured with liquor, chocolate, ground nuts or other extracts.

It is prepared on the stove top over direct heat. When making custard sauce, be extremely careful to stir the mixture continually and not allow it to boil, or it will curdle. A properly made custard sauce should be smooth and thick enough to coat the back of a spoon. It should not contain any noticeable bits of cooked egg.

Vanilla custard sauce (Fr. *crème anglaise*) is served with cakes, pastries, fruits and soufflés and is often used for decorating dessert plates. It may be served hot or cold. It is also used as the base for many ice creams.

A very thick version of custard sauce can be made using 35% cream and additional egg yolks. Its consistency is more like a pudding than a sauce. This custard is often served over fruit, or in a small ramekin or other container and then topped with caramelized sugar for a dessert known as **crème brûlée** (burnt cream). See Recipe 31.15.

Pastry Cream

Pastry cream (Fr. *crème pâtissière*) is a stirred custard made with egg yolks, sugar and milk and thickened with cornstarch. Because starch protects the egg yolks from curdling, pastry cream can be boiled. In fact, it must be boiled to fully gelatinize the starch and eliminate the taste of raw starch.

Pastry cream can be flavoured with chocolate, liquors, extracts or fruits. (Pudding is nothing more than flavoured pastry cream.) It is used for filling éclairs, cream puffs, napoleons, fruit tarts and other pastries. Pastry cream is also the filling for cream pies (see Chapter 29, Pies, Pastries and Cookies). Pastry cream is thick enough to hold its shape without making pastry doughs soggy.

Pastry cream can be rather heavy. It can be lightened by folding in whipped cream to produce a **mousseline**, or Italian meringue can be folded in to produce a **crème Chiboust**.

Basic Procedure for Preparing Vanilla Custard Sauce and Pastry Cream

1. Place milk and/or cream in a heavy, nonreactive saucepan; add scraped vanilla bean if desired.
2. In a mixing bowl, whisk together the egg yolks, sugar and starch (if used). Do not use an electric mixer as it incorporates too much air.
3. Bring the liquid just to a boil. **Temper** the egg mixture with approximately one-third of the hot liquid.
4. Pour the tempered eggs into the remaining hot liquid and return the mixture to the heat. The stove's temperature can be as hot as you dare: The lower the temperature, the longer the custard will take to thicken; the higher the temperature, the greater the risk of curdling. The thickening agent for custard sauce is eggs. The thickener for pastry cream is cornstarch.
5. Cook, stirring constantly, until thickened. Custard sauce should reach a temperature of 85°C (185°F). Pastry cream should be allowed to boil for a few moments.
6. Immediately remove the cooked custard from the hot saucepan to avoid overcooking. Butter or other flavourings can be added at this time.
7. Cool over an ice bath. Store in a clean, shallow container, cover and refrigerate.

Basic Procedure for Salvaging Curdled Vanilla Custard Sauce

1. Strain the sauce into a bowl. Place the bowl over an ice bath and whisk vigorously.
2. If this does not smooth out the overcooked sauce, place the sauce in a blender and process for a few moments.

EGGS AND SANITATION

Eggs are high-protein foods that are easily contaminated by bacteria such as salmonella that cause food-borne illnesses. Because custards cannot be heated to temperatures high enough to destroy these bacteria without first curdling the eggs, it is especially important that sanitary guidelines be followed in preparing the egg products discussed in this chapter.

1. Cleanliness is important: Wash your hands thoroughly before beginning; be sure to use clean, sanitized bowls, utensils and storage containers.
2. When breaking or separating eggs, minimize contact between the egg shell and raw egg.
3. Heat the milk to just below a boil before combining it with the eggs. This reduces the final cooking time.
4. Chill the finished product quickly in an ice bath and refrigerate immediately.
5. Do not use your fingers to taste the custard.
6. Do not store any custard mixture, cooked or uncooked, at room temperature.
7. Purchase pasteurized egg products if possible.

*Approximate values
per 50 mL serving:*

Calories	132
Total fat	8 g
Saturated fat	4 g
Cholesterol	162 mg
Sodium	23 mg
Total carbohydrates	12.5 g
Protein	3 g

Applying the Basics

VANILLA CUSTARD SAUCE (CRÈME ANGLAISE)

Yield: 1.2 L (40 fl. oz.)

Cereal cream	1 L	1 qt.
Vanilla bean, split*	1	1
Egg yolks, large	275 g	12
Granulated sugar	250 g	8 oz.

1. Using a heavy, nonreactive saucepan, bring the cream and vanilla bean just to a boil.
2. Whisk the egg yolks and sugar together in a mixing bowl. Temper the egg mixture with approximately one-third of the hot cream, then return the entire mixture to the saucepan with the remaining cream.
3. Cook the sauce over medium heat, stirring constantly, until it is thick enough to coat the back of a spoon. Do not allow the sauce to boil.
4. As soon as the sauce thickens, remove it from the heat and pour it through a fine mesh strainer into a clean bowl. Chill the sauce over an ice bath, then cover and keep refrigerated. Use the sauce within 2 days.

*If vanilla bean is not available, stir in 30 mL (1 fl. oz.) of vanilla extract when sauce is removed from heat.

VARIATIONS: *Chocolate*—Stir 180 g (6 oz.) of finely chopped dark chocolate into the strained custard while it is still warm. The heat of the custard will melt the chocolate.

Coffee—Add 30 mL (2 Tbsp.) of coffee (café) extract or compound to the warm custard.

Frangelico—Omit the vanilla bean. Stir in 2 mL (1/2 tsp.) vanilla and 30–45 mL (2–3 Tbsp.) of Frangelico, to taste.

Pistachio—Omit the vanilla bean. Place 120 g (4 ounces) of finely chopped pistachio nuts in the saucepan with the barely boiling half-and-half. Remove from the heat, cover and steep for up to 1 hour. Uncover the mixture, reheat and continue preparing the sauce as directed. The ground nuts will be strained out in step 4.

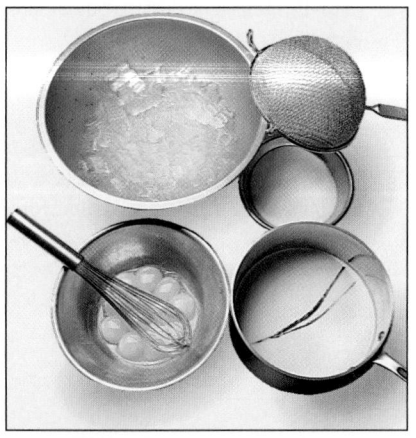

1. Mise en place for vanilla sauce.

2. Temper the eggs.

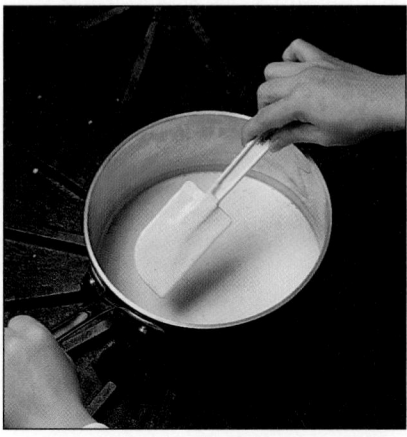

3. The properly cooked sauce.

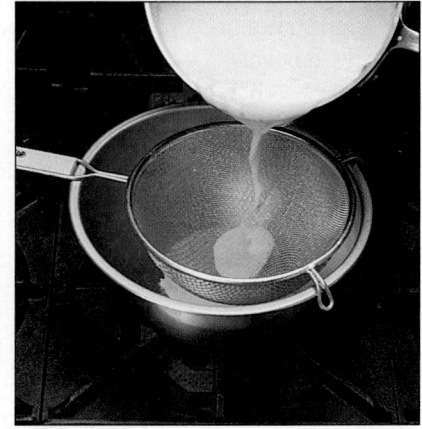

4. Strain the sauce into a bowl.

Applying the Basics

PASTRY CREAM

Yield: 1.5 L (1-1/2 qt.)

Cornstarch	90 g	3 oz.
Sugar	250 g	8-1/2 oz.
Milk	1 L	32 fl. oz.
Egg yolks	2	2
Whole eggs	170 g	3
Butter	60 g	2 oz.
Vanilla	5 mL	1 tsp.

1. Dilute the cornstarch and half the sugar with 250 mL (8 fl. oz.) of cold milk, egg yolks and whole eggs. Whisk until very smooth.
2. Bring the remaining milk and sugar to a boil.
3. Blend the two mixtures together gradually, stirring constantly.
4. Place back on the heat and cook for a few minutes, stirring constantly, until thickened.
5. Remove the pan from the heat and stir in butter and vanilla. Transfer mixture to a clean bowl.
6. Cover with plastic film and cool over ice bath. Store in refrigerator.

RECIPE 31.2

Approximate values per 50 mL serving:

Calories	92
Total fat	4 g
Saturated fat	2 g
Cholesterol	48 mg
Sodium	41 mg
Total carbohydrates	13 g
Protein	2 g

1. Stir the pastry cream as it comes to a boil.

2. Fold butter and vanilla into the cooked pastry cream.

Sabayon

Sabayon (It. *zabaglione*) is a foamy, stirred custard sauce made by whisking eggs, sugar and wine over low heat. The egg proteins coagulate, thickening the mixture, while the whisking incorporates air to make it light and fluffy. Usually a sweet wine is used; marsala and champagne are the most popular choices.

The mixture can be served warm, or it can be chilled. Sabayon may be served alone or as a sauce or topping with fruit or pastries such as spongecake or ladyfingers.

Basic Procedure for Preparing Sabayon

1. Combine egg yolks, sugar and wine in the top of a double boiler.
2. Place the double boiler over low heat and whisk constantly until the sauce is foamy and thick enough to form a ribbon when the whisk is lifted.
3. Remove from the heat and serve immediately, or whisk over an ice bath until cool. If allowed to sit, the hot mixture may separate.

The thickened sabayon.

RECIPE 31.3

Approximate values per serving:

Calories	252
Total fat	16 g
Saturated fat	8 g
Cholesterol	256 mg
Sodium	20.5 mg
Total carbohydrates	21 g
Protein	3.5 g

Applying the Basics

RECIPE 31.3

CHAMPAGNE SABAYON

Yield: 1 L (1 qt.)

Egg yolks	8	8
Granulated sugar	150 g	5-1/4 oz.
Dry champagne	180 mL	6 fl. oz.
Lemon or orange juice	30 mL	1 fl. oz.
Cream, 35% (optional; see Variation)	250 mL	8 fl. oz.

1. Combine the egg yolks and sugar in a stainless steel bowl.

2. Add champagne and juice to the egg mixture.

3. Place the bowl over a pan of barely simmering water. Whisk vigorously until the sauce is thick and pale yellow, approximately 10 minutes. Serve immediately.

VARIATION: To prepare a Sabayon Mousseline, place the bowl of sabayon over an ice bath and continue whisking until completely cold. Whip the cream to soft peaks and fold it into the cold sabayon. For Sabayon Sauce, increase the wine to 200 mL (7 fl. oz.) and flavour with 125 mL (4 fl. oz.) liqueur.

Baked Custards

A baked custard is based on the same principle as a stirred custard: A liquid thickens by the coagulation of egg proteins. However, with a baked custard, the thickening occurs in an oven. The container of custard is usually placed in a water bath (bain marie) to protect the eggs from curdling. Even though the water bath's temperature will not exceed 100°C (212°F), care must be taken not to bake the custards for too long or at too high a temperature. An over-baked custard will be watery or curdled; a properly baked custard should be smooth-textured and firm enough to slice.

Baked custards include simple mixtures of egg yolks, sugar and milk such as **crème caramel** as well as custard mixtures in which other ingredients are suspended, for example, **cheesecake**, rice pudding, **bread pudding** and quiche.

Crème Caramel

Crème caramel, crème renversée and flan all refer to an egg custard baked over a layer of caramelized sugar and inverted for service. The caramelized sugar produces a golden-brown surface on the inverted custard and a thin caramel sauce.

Applying the Basics

RECIPE 31.4

TOFFEE CARAMEL FLAN

Yield: Ten 180-mL (6-fl.-oz.) Ramekins

Granulated sugar	350 g	12-1/2 oz.
Lemon juice	20 mL	1/2 fl. oz.
Water	60 mL	2 fl. oz.
Milk	700 mL	25 fl. oz.

Cream, 35%	500 mL	18 fl. oz.
Cinnamon sticks	2	2
Vanilla bean, split	1	1
Whole eggs	450 g	8
Egg yolks	4	4
Brown sugar	200 g	7 oz.
Molasses	15 g	1/2 oz.
Amaretto liqueur	30 mL	1 fl. oz.

Fill the ramekins for flans.

1. Combine the granulated sugar, lemon juice and water in a small, heavy saucepan; bring to a boil. Cook until the sugar reaches a deep golden-brown. Set the pot into cold water to stop the cooking. Immediately divide the caramel sugar into each of the lightly buttered ramekins. Arrange the ramekins in a 5-cm-deep (2-inch) hotel pan and set aside.

2. Combine the milk, cream, cinnamon sticks and vanilla bean in a large saucepan. Bring just to a boil, cover and remove from the heat. Allow this mixture to **steep** for about 30 minutes.

3. Whisk the eggs, egg yolks, brown sugar, molasses and amaretto together in a large bowl.

4. Uncover the milk mixture and return it to the stove top. Bring just to a boil. Temper the egg-and-sugar mixture with approximately one-third of the hot milk. Whisk in the remaining hot milk.

5. Strain the custard through a fine mesh strainer. Pour into the caramel-lined ramekins, filling to just below the rim.

6. Pour enough warm water into the hotel pan to reach halfway up the sides of the ramekins. Bake at 160°C (325°F) for approximately 30–40 minutes. The custards should be almost set, but still slightly soft in the centre.

7. Completely chill the baked custards before serving. To unmould, run a small knife around the edge of the custard, invert onto the serving plate and give the ramekin a firm sideways shake. Garnish with fresh fruit or caramelized almonds and a rosette of Chantilly cream.

RECIPE 31.4

Approximate values per ramekin:

Calories	529
Total fat	27 g
Saturated fat	14.5 g
Cholesterol	355 mg
Sodium	122 mg
Total carbohydrates	63 g
Protein	10 g

Cheesecake

Cheesecakes, which are almost as old as western civilization, have undergone many changes and variations since the ancient Greeks devised the first known recipe. Americans revolutionized the dessert with the development of cream cheese in 1872.

Cheesecake is a baked custard that contains a smooth cheese, usually a soft, fresh cheese such as cream, ricotta, cottage or farmer cheese. A cheesecake may be prepared without a crust or it may have a base or sides of short dough, cookie crumbs, ground nuts or spongecake. The filling can be dense and rich (New York style) or light and fluffy (Italian style). Fruit, nuts and flavourings may also be included in the filling. Cheesecakes are often topped with fruit or sour cream glaze. Recipes for both dense and light cheesecakes are at the end of this chapter.

Some cheesecakes are unbaked and rely on gelatin for thickening; others are frozen. These are not really custards, however, but are more similar to the chiffons or mousses discussed later.

Bread Pudding

Bread pudding is a home-style dessert in which chunks of bread, flavourings and raisins or other fruit are mixed with an egg custard and baked. The result is somewhat of a cross between a cake and a pudding. It is often served with custard sauce, ice cream, whipped cream or a whisky-flavoured butter sauce. Bread pudding is a delicious way to use stale or leftover bread or overripe fruit. A recipe for Chocolate, Cherry and Croissant Pudding (Recipe 31.20) appears at the end of this chapter.

Soufflés

A soufflé is made with a custard base that is lightened with whipped egg whites and then baked. The air in the egg whites expands to create a light, fluffy texture and tall rise. A soufflé is not as stable as a cake or other pastry item, however, and will collapse very quickly when removed from the oven.

Soufflés can be prepared in a wide variety of sweet and savoury flavours. The flavourings may be incorporated into the custard, as in the following recipe. Alternatively, an unflavoured pastry cream can be used as the base; the liqueur, fruit or chocolate are then added to each portion separately.

When making a soufflé, the custard base and egg whites should be at room temperature. First, the egg whites will whip to a better volume, and second, if the base is approximately the same temperature as the egg whites, the two mixtures can be more easily incorporated. The egg whites are whipped to stiff peaks with a portion of the sugar for stability. The whipped egg whites are then gently folded into the base immediately before baking.

A soufflé is baked in a straight-sided mould or individual ramekin. The finished soufflé should be puffy with a lightly browned top. It should rise well above the rim of the baking dish. A soufflé must be served immediately, before it collapses. A warm custard sauce (crème anglaise) is often served as an accompaniment to a sweet soufflé.

A frozen soufflé is not a true soufflé. Rather, it is a creamy custard mixture thickened with gelatin, lightened with whipped egg whites or whipped cream and placed in a soufflé dish wrapped with a tall paper collar. When the paper is removed, the mixture looks as if it has risen above the mould like a hot soufflé.

Basic Procedure for Preparing Baked Soufflés

1. Butter the mould or ramekins and dust with granulated sugar. Preheat the oven to approximately 220°C (425°F).
2. Prepare the custard base. Add flavourings as desired.
3. Whip the egg whites and sugar to stiff peaks. Fold the whipped egg whites into the base.
4. Pour the mixture into the prepared mould or ramekins and bake immediately.

Applying the Basics

RECIPE 31.5

CHOCOLATE SOUFFLÉS

Yield: 8 Servings

Orange juice	450 mL	1 pt.
Sugar	120 g	4 oz.
Butter	50 g	2 oz.
Bread flour	90 g	3 oz.
Bittersweet chocolate, chopped fine	150 g	5-1/2 oz.

RECIPE 31.5

Approximate values per serving:

Calories	350
Total fat	15 g
Saturated fat	8 g
Cholesterol	210 mg
Sodium	65 mg
Total carbohydrates	48 g
Protein	10 g

Eggs, separated	8	8
Orange liqueur	50 mL	2 fl. oz.
Butter, melted	as needed	as needed
Granulated sugar	as needed	as needed

1. Fold the whipped egg whites into the chocolate base.

1. To prepare the base, heat the orange juice and 90 g (3 oz.) sugar and whisk in a paste made from the butter and flour. Bring to a boil and simmer 5–10 minutes while stirring constantly to cook out the flour taste.

2. Add the chocolate and stir until smooth.

3. Cool mixture to below 60°C (140°F).

4. Incorporate the egg yolks and liqueur. This base mixture may be refrigerated but must be brought to room temperature for use.

5. To prepare the soufflés, brush individual-serving-sized ramekins with melted butter and dust with granulated sugar.

6. Preheat the oven to 220°C (425°F). Place a sheet pan in the oven, onto which you will place the soufflés for baking. (This makes it easier to remove the hot soufflé cups from the oven.)

7. Whip the egg whites to soft peaks with the remaining 30 g (1 oz.) of sugar. Fold the meringue into the chocolate base and spoon the mixture into the prepared ramekins. The ramekins should be filled to within 6 mm (1/4 inch) of the rim. Smooth the top of each soufflé with a spatula and bake immediately.

8. Bake for approximately 20–30 minutes. The soufflés are done when well risen, golden-brown on top and the edges appear dry. Do not touch a soufflé to test doneness.

9. Sprinkle the soufflés with powdered sugar if desired and serve immediately with a sabayon sauce.

2. Fill the ramekins.

3. The finished soufflé, ready for service.

CREAMS

Creams (Fr. *crèmes*) include light, fluffy or creamy-textured dessert items made with whipped egg whites or cream. Some, such as **Bavarian creams** and **chiffons**, are thickened with gelatin. Others, such as **mousses** and **Chantilly cream**, are softer and lighter. Table 31.1 provides a summary. The success of all, however, depends on the proper whipping and incorporation of egg whites or heavy cream.

You should review the material on whipping cream found in Chapter 8, Eggs and Dairy Products. Note that whipping cream has a butterfat content of 30–40%. When preparing any whipped cream be sure that the cream, the mixing

TABLE 31.1   CREAM (CRÈME) COMPONENTS

For a:	Begin with a Base of:	Thicken with:	Then Fold in:
Bavarian	Custard	Gelatin	Whipped cream
Chiffon	Custard or starch-thickened fruit	Gelatin	Whipped egg whites
Mousse	Melted chocolate, puréed fruit or custard	Nothing or gelatin	Whipped cream, whipped egg whites or both

bowl and all utensils are well chilled and clean. A warm bowl can melt the butterfat, destroying the texture of the cream. Properly whipped cream should increase two to three times in volume.

Chantilly Cream/Crème Chantilly

Properly whipped crème Chantilly

Crème Chantilly is simply heavy cream whipped to soft peaks and flavoured with sugar and vanilla. It can be used for garnishing pastry or dessert items, or it can be folded into cooled custard or pastry cream and used as a component in a pastry.

When making crème Chantilly, the vanilla extract and sugar should be added after the cream begins to thicken. Either granulated or icing sugar may be used; there are advantages and disadvantages to both. Granulated sugar assists in forming a better foam than icing sugar, but it may cause the cream to feel gritty. Icing sugar dissolves more quickly and completely than granulated sugar, but does nothing to assist with foaming. Whichever sugar is used, it should be added just before the whipping is complete to avoid interfering with the cream's volume and stability.

Applying the Basics

RECIPE 31.6

CRÈME CHANTILLY

Yield: 2–2.5 L (2–2-1/2 qt.)

Cream, 35%, chilled	1 L	1 qt.
Icing sugar	90 g	3 oz.
Vanilla extract	10 mL	2 tsp.

1. Place the cream in a chilled mixing bowl. Using a balloon whisk, whisk the cream until slightly thickened.

2. Add the sugar and vanilla and continue whisking to the desired consistency. The cream should be smooth and light, not grainy. Do not overwhip.

3. Crème Chantilly may be stored in the refrigerator for several hours. If the cream begins to soften, gently rewhip as necessary.

RECIPE 31.6

Approximate values
per 30 g serving:

Calories	100
Total fat	10 g
Saturated fat	6 g
Cholesterol	35 mg
Sodium	10 mg
Total carbohydrates	3 g
Protein	1 g

Bavarian Cream

A Bavarian cream (Fr. *bavarois*) is prepared by first thickening custard sauce with gelatin, then folding in whipped cream. The final product is poured into a mould and chilled until firm enough to unmould and slice. Although a Bavarian cream can be moulded into individual servings, it is most often poured into a round mould lined with jellyroll slices or ladyfingers to create the classic desserts known as **charlotte royale** and **charlotte russe**.

Bavarians may be flavoured by adding chocolate, puréed fruit, chopped nuts, extracts or liquors to the custard sauce base. Layers of fruit or liquor-soaked spongecake may also be added for flavour and texture.

When thickening a dessert cream with gelatin, it is important to use the correct amount of gelatin. If not enough gelatin is used or it is not incorporated completely the cream will not become firm enough to unmould. If too much gelatin is used, the cream will be tough and rubbery. The recipes given here use sheet gelatin, although an equal amount by weight of granulated gelatin can be substituted. Refer to Chapter 26, Principles of the Bakeshop, for information on using gelatin.

Basic Procedure for Preparing Bavarian Creams

1. Prepare a custard sauce of the desired flavour.
2. While the custard sauce is still quite warm, stir in softened gelatin. Make sure the gelatin is completely incorporated.
3. Chill the custard until almost thickened, then fold in the whipped cream.
4. Pour the Bavarian into a mould or charlotte form. Chill until set.

Applying the Basics

RECIPE 31.7

BAVARIAN CREAM/CRÈME BAVAROISE

Yield: 1.5 L (1-1/2 qt.)

Egg yolks	8	8
Sugar	150 g	5-1/2 oz.
Milk	500 mL	16 fl. oz.
Vanilla or flavouring	TT	TT
Gelatin sheets, softened	9	9
Cream, 35%	400 mL	14 fl. oz.

1. Lightly spray the bottom of moulds with pan release spray.
2. Prepare a vanilla custard sauce using the yolks, sugar, milk and vanilla. Remove from the saucepan when it reaches 80–85°C (175–180°F).
3. Add softened, squeezed gelatin sheets to the hot custard. Chill until thick, but do not allow the custard to set.
4. Whip the cream until stiff and fold it into the chilled and thickened custard. Fill the ramekins with the Bavarian cream. Chill until completely set, approximately 2 hours.
5. Unmould onto a serving dish. Garnish the top with fruit and whipped cream as desired.

NOTE: Gelatin may separate in the freezer, so quick chilling is not recommended. Products made with gelatin keep well for 1–2 days but stiffen with age.

VARIATION: *Charlotte*—Line a 1- to 1.5-L (1- to 1-1/2-qt.) charlotte mould with ladyfingers (Recipe 30.26) before filling with layers of fruit and Bavarian. Invert onto a serving platter when firm and garnish with whipped cream.

1. Add gelatin to the custard base.

2. Fold in the whipped cream.

Chiffon

A chiffon is similar to a Bavarian except that whipped egg whites instead of whipped cream are folded into the thickened base. The base may be a custard or a fruit mixture thickened with cornstarch. Although a chiffon may be moulded like a Bavarian, it is most often used as a pie or tart filling.

CHARLOTTE, SWEET CHARLOTTE

The original charlotte was created during the 18th century and named for the wife of King George III of England. It consisted of an apple compote baked in a round mould lined with toast slices. A few decades later, the great French chef Carême adopted the name but altered the concept in response to a kitchen disaster. When preparing a grand banquet for King Louis XVIII, he found that his gelatin supply was insufficient for the Bavarian creams he was making, so Carême steadied the sides of his sagging desserts with ladyfingers. The result became known as charlotte russe, probably due to the reigning fad for anything Russian. A fancier version, known as charlotte royale, is made with pinwheels or layers of spongecake and jam instead of ladyfingers. The filling for either should be a classic Bavarian cream.

RECIPE 31.7

Approximate values per 90 g serving:

Calories	169
Total fat	12 g
Saturated fat	7 g
Cholesterol	144 mg
Sodium	28.5 mg
Total carbohydrates	12 g
Protein	3 g

Basic Procedure for Preparing Chiffons

1. Prepare the base, which is usually a custard or a fruit mixture thickened with cornstarch.
2. Add gelatin to the warm base.
3. Fold in whipped egg whites.
4. Pour into a mould or pie shell and chill.

Applying the Basics

RECIPE 31.8

LIME CHIFFON

Yield: One 25-cm (10-inch) Pie or 8 Servings

Granulated gelatin	7 g	1/4 oz.
Water	150 mL	5 fl. oz.
Granulated sugar	200 g	7 oz.
Fresh lime juice	90 mL	3 fl. oz.
Lime zest	10 g	1 Tbsp.
Eggs, separated	4	4

1. Soften the gelatin in 30 mL (1 fl. oz.) of the water.
2. Combine 120 g (4 oz.) of the sugar, the remaining water, lime juice, zest and egg yolks in a bowl over a pan of simmering water.
3. Whisk the egg-and-lime mixture together vigorously until it begins to thicken. Add the softened gelatin and continue whipping until very thick and foamy.
4. Remove from the heat, cover and refrigerate until cool and as thick as whipping cream.
5. Meanwhile, whip the egg whites to soft peaks. Whip in the remaining sugar and continue whipping until stiff but not dry.
6. Fold the meringue into the egg-and-lime mixture. Pour into a prepared pie crust or serving dishes and chill for several hours, until firm.

VARIATIONS: *Lemon Chiffon*—Substitute lemon juice and lemon zest for the lime juice and zest.

Orange Chiffon—Substitute orange juice for the lime juice and for 120 mL (4 fl. oz.) of the water. Substitute orange zest for the lime zest. Reduce the amount of sugar in the egg yolk mixture to 30 g (1 oz.).

RECIPE 31.8

Approximate values per serving:

Calories	139
Total fat	2.5 g
Saturated fat	1 g
Cholesterol	10 mg
Sodium	35 mg
Total carbohydrates	26 g
Protein	4 g

Mousse

The term *mousse* applies to an assortment of dessert creams not easily classified elsewhere. A mousse is similar to a Bavarian or chiffon in that it is lightened with whipped cream, whipped egg whites or both. A mousse is generally softer than these other products, however, and only occasionally contains a small amount of gelatin. A mousse is generally too soft to mould.

A mousse may be served alone as a dessert or used as a filling in cakes or pastry items. Sweet mousses may be based on a custard sauce, melted chocolate or puréed fruit.

Basic Procedure for Preparing Mousses

1. Prepare the base, which is usually a custard sauce, melted chocolate or puréed fruit.

2. If gelatin is used, soften it first, then dissolve it in the warm base.

3. Fold in whipped egg whites, if used. If the base is slightly warm when the egg whites are added their proteins will coagulate, making the mousse firmer and more stable.

4. Allow the mixture to cool completely, then fold in whipped cream, if used.

NOTE: The egg whites are folded in before any whipped cream. Although the egg whites may deflate somewhat during folding, if the cream is added first it may become overwhipped when the egg whites are added, creating a grainy or coarse product.

Applying the Basics

RECIPE 31.9

CLASSIC CHOCOLATE MOUSSE

SOUTHERN ALBERTA INSTITUTE OF TECHNOLOGY, CALGARY, AB
Pastry Chef Andreas Schwarzer

Yield: 2.65 kg (5 lb. 10 oz.)

Couverture	850 g	30 oz.
Cream, 35%	1.2 L	40 fl. oz.
Egg yolks	280 g	10 oz.
Granulated sugar	250 g	9 oz.
Water	75 mL	2-1/2 fl. oz.

1. Melt the couverture in a double boiler to not more than 40°C (104°F).

2. Whip the cream to soft peaks, being careful not to overwhip.

3. In a bowl, start mixing the yolks on slow speed.

4. At the same time, make the syrup by mixing the sugar and water and bringing to a boil—125°C (256°F).

5. Add the syrup in a steady stream to the egg yolks while mixing at a medium speed.

6. Add the melted couverture to the cool, whipped egg yolk mixture.

7. Fold in the whipped cream, carefully.

NOTE: The temperature of the sugar syrup will determine the thickness of the mousse. If you like a softer chocolate mousse, cook the syrup to only 115°C (240°F). A good couverture (a fine grade of chocolate with a high cocoa butter content) gives the mousse a pure chocolate taste, which chocolate lovers will appreciate. Chocolate coating will not give as rich and tasteful a chocolate mousse. The mousse will be soft and weaker in flavour.

FROZEN DESSERTS

Frozen desserts include **ice cream** and **gelato** and desserts assembled with ice cream such as baked Alaska, bombes and parfaits. Frozen fruit purées, known as **sorbets** and **sherbets**, are also included in this category. Still-frozen desserts,

---

◆◆◆
CONVENIENCE PRODUCTS

Commercially prepared powders and mixes can be used to make a wide assortment of puddings, custards, mousses, gelatin desserts and creams. Although these mixes are not recommended for fine dining facilities, pastry cooks in institutions such as schools and hospitals base much of their dessert preparation on them. The advantages are speed, cost, quality control and the ability to use semiskilled assistants. Packaged mixes are simply prepared according to the directions provided by the manufacturer, then portioned for service. The pastry cook can often improve on the final product by adding whipped cream, fruit or an appropriate garnish. As with other convenience products, quality varies from merely adequate to very good. Sample and experiment with several brands to select the best for your operation.

Andreas Schwarzer
Andreas worked in pastry shops and bakeries in Germany before coming to Canada. He has won several medals for his pastries and showpieces, and has worked on banquets for such celebrities as Clint Eastwood, Arnold Schwarzenegger, Margaret Thatcher and Prince Philip.

RECIPE 31.9

Approximate values per 75 g serving:

Calories	270
Total fat	22.5 g
Saturated fat	13 g
Cholesterol	140 mg
Sodium	15 mg
Total carbohydrates	17.5 g
Protein	2.5 g

known as **semifreddi**, are made from custards or mousses that are frozen without churning.

When making any frozen mixture, remember that cold dulls flavours. Although perfect at room temperature, flavours seem weaker when the mixture is cold. Thus, it may be necessary to oversweeten or overflavour creams or custards that will be frozen for service. Although liquors and liqueurs are common flavouring ingredients, alcohol drastically lowers a liquid mixture's freezing point. Too much alcohol as well as too much sugar will prevent the mixture from freezing; thus any liqueurs or liquors and sugar must be used in moderation.

Ice Cream and Gelato

Ice cream and gelato are custards that are churned during freezing. They can be flavoured with a seemingly endless variety of fruits, nuts, extracts, liqueurs and the like. Gelato is an Italian-style ice cream. It is denser than American-style products because less air is incorporated during churning.

The Canadian Food Inspection Agency requires that products labelled "ice cream" contain not less than 10% milk fat and 20% milk solids, and have no more than 50% **overrun**. "Ice milk" refers to products that do not meet the standards for ice cream. Low-fat products made without cream or egg yolks are also available for the health conscious. Frozen yogurt uses yogurt as its base. Although touted as a nutritious substitute for ice cream, frozen yogurt may have whole milk or cream added for richness and smoothness.

One hallmark of good ice cream and gelato is smoothness. The ice crystals that would normally form during freezing can be avoided by constant stirring or churning. Churning, usually accomplished mechanically, also incorporates air into the product. The air causes the mixture to expand. Gelato has little

◆◆◆

ICE CREAM:
FROM ANCIENT CHINA TO DOUBLE FUDGE BROWNIE CHOCOLATE CHIP
WITH COOKIE DOUGH AND TOASTED ALMOND SLIVERS

Despite claims to the contrary, it is impossible to identify any one country as having invented ice cream. More likely, it was invented in several places around the world at various times.

Early ancestors of today's ice creams were flavoured water ices, which have been popular in China since prehistoric times. They have also been popular in the Mediterranean and Middle East since the Golden Age of Greece. In fact, Alexander the Great had a penchant for wine-flavoured ices, made with ice brought down from the mountains by runners. The Roman Emperor Nero served his guests mixtures of fruit crushed with snow and honey. The Saracens brought their knowledge of making flavoured ices with them when they migrated to Sicily in the 9th century. And 12th-century Crusaders returned to western Europe with memories of Middle Eastern sherbets.

The Italians are said to have developed gelato from a recipe brought back from China by Marco Polo in the 13th century. Somehow the dish spread to England by the 15th century, where it was recorded that King Henry V served it at his coronation banquet. Catherine de Medici brought the recipe with her when she married the future king of France in 1533. A different flavour was served during each of the 34 days of their marriage festivities.

Ice cream was first served to the public in Paris during the late 17th century. It was available at fashionable cafés serving another new treat: coffee. French chefs quickly developed many elaborate desserts using ice creams including bombes, coupes and parfaits.

Many of the founders of the United States —Thomas Jefferson, Alexander Hamilton, James and Dolly Madison—were confirmed ice cream addicts. George Washington spent over $200, a very princely sum, for ice cream during the summer of 1790.

The mechanized ice cream freezer was invented in 1846, setting the stage for mass production and wide availability. By the late 19th century ice cream parlours were popular gathering places. (Many of today's ice cream parlours take their décor from "Gay Nineties" motifs.)

Despite the disappearance of most ice cream wagons, soda fountains and lunch counters, all of which were popular ice cream purveyors for much of the 20th century, ice cream sales have never waned. Today, more than 80% of all ice cream is sold in supermarkets or convenience stores. The public's demand for high-fat, homemade-style "super-premium" ice creams with rich and often-elaborate flavour combinations shows no sign of declining.

incorporated air. Good-quality ice creams and sorbets have enough air to make them light; inferior products often contain overrun. The difference becomes obvious when equal volumes are weighed.

Many food service operations use ice cream makers that have internal freezing units to chill the mixture while churning it. Most commercial machines are suitable for churning either ice cream or sorbet. Follow the manufacturer's directions for using and cleaning any ice cream maker.

Basic Procedure for Preparing Ice Creams

1. Place the milk and/or cream in a heavy saucepan. If vanilla bean is being used it may be added at this time.
2. Whisk the egg yolks and sugar together in a mixing bowl.
3. Bring the liquid just to a boil. Temper the egg mixture with approximately one-third of the hot liquid.
4. Pour the tempered eggs into the remaining hot liquid and return the mixture to the heat.
5. Cook, stirring constantly, until warm (84°C/183°F).
6. Remove the cooked custard sauce from the hot saucepan immediately. If left in the hot saucepan, it will overcook. Flavourings may be added at this time.
7. Cool the cooked custard sauce over an ice bath. Store covered and refrigerated until ready to process.
8. Process according to the machine manufacturer's directions.

Applying the Basics

RECIPE 31.10

ICE CREAM BASE

Yield: 2.5 L (2-1/2 qt.)

Whole milk	1.5 L	1-1/2 qt.
Cream, 35%	500 mL	1 pt.
Vanilla bean (optional)	1	1
Egg yolks	325 g	16
Granulated sugar	600 g	20 oz.

1. Combine the milk and cream in a heavy saucepan and bring to a boil. Add the split and scraped vanilla bean, if desired.
2. Whisk the egg yolks and sugar together in a mixing bowl.
3. Temper the eggs with one-third of the hot milk. Return the egg mixture to the saucepan.
4. Cook over medium heat until slightly thickened. Pour through a fine mesh strainer into a clean bowl.
5. Chill the cooked custard sauce completely before processing.
6. Allow the finished ice cream to ripen overnight in the freezer to fully develop the flavours and texture.

VARIATIONS: *Chocolate*—Add approximately 200 g (7 oz.) of finely chopped bittersweet chocolate per litre (quart) of ice cream base. Add the chocolate to the hot mixture after it is strained. Stir until completely melted.

RECIPE 31.10

Approximate values per 85 mL serving:

Calories	209
Total fat	11 g
Saturated fat	6 g
Cholesterol	175 mg
Sodium	37 mg
Total carbohydrates	24 g
Protein	4 g

Continued

Cappuccino—Steep the hot milk and cream with the vanilla bean and 2–3 cinnamon sticks. After the ice cream base is made, stir in 30 mL (2 Tbsp.) coffee extract.

Brandied Cherry—Drain the liquid from one 500-g (16-oz.) can of tart, pitted cherries. Soak the cherries in 50 mL (2 fl. oz.) brandy. Prepare the ice cream base as directed, omitting the vanilla bean. Add the brandy-soaked cherries to the cooled custard before processing.

Sherbets/Sorbets and Granité

Sherbet and sorbet are frozen mixtures of fruit juice or fruit purée. Sherbet or sorbet may contain milk and/or egg yolks for creaminess.

Sorbet can be prepared in a wide variety of fruit, herb and some vegetable flavours; it is often flavoured with an alcoholic beverage. It is served as a first course, a palate refresher between courses or a dessert. Sorbets with milk content tend to be richer, so are generally reserved for dessert. The French style contains no milk or egg yolks.

For wine sorbets, use 1 L (1 qt.) each wine and base mixture adjusted with water to 15° Baumé and add 50 g (2 oz.) Italian meringue. For liqueur sorbets, use 250 mL (8 fl. oz.) liqueur to 1 L (1 qt.) base and adjust to 16° Baumé. Add 50 g (2 oz.) Italian meringue.

Granité is still or churn frozen and has a grainy texture. The flavoured syrup has a density of 14° Baumé.

Applying the Basics

RECIPE 31.11

SORBET

Yield: Approximately 2 kg (4-1/2 lb.)

Water	400 mL	16 fl. oz.
Sugar	400 g	1 lb.
Glucose	80 g	3 oz.
Juice or purée	1 L	32 fl. oz.
Lemon juice	30 mL	1 fl. oz.
Water	as needed	as needed

1. Boil water, sugar and glucose for 2 minutes. Cool. It should be approximately 30° Baumé (base mixture).
2. Add fruit juice or purée and lemon juice and enough water to adjust the density to 17° Baumé. Strain.
3. Pour the syrup into an ice cream machine, filling it half full, and churn freeze for approximately 7–10 minutes or until set.

RECIPE 31.11

Approximate values per 60 g serving:

Calories	31
Total fat	0 g
Saturated fat	0 g
Cholesterol	0 mg
Sodium	1 mg
Total carbohydrates	18 g
Protein	0 g

Serving Suggestions for Ice Creams and Sorbets

Ice creams and sorbets are usually served by the scoop, often in cookie cones. Or they can be served as **sundaes**. More formal presentations include **baked Alaska**, **bombes**, **coupes** and **parfaits**.

Still-Frozen Desserts

Still-frozen desserts (It. *semifreddi*) are made with frozen mousse, custard or cream. Layers of spongecake and/or fruit may be added for flavour and texture.

Because these mixtures are frozen without churning, air must be incorporated by folding in relatively large amounts of whipped cream or meringue. The air helps keep the mixture smooth and prevents it from becoming too hard. Still-frozen desserts develop ice crystals quicker than churned products, so they tend to have a shorter shelf life than ice creams or sorbets.

Still-frozen products include frozen soufflés, **marquise**, mousses and **neapolitans**. No gelatin is used for a still-frozen dessert.

DESSERT SAUCES

Pastries and desserts are often accompanied by sweet sauces. Dessert sauces provide flavour and texture and enhance plate presentation. Vanilla sauce (Recipe 31.1) is the principal dessert sauce. It can be flavoured and coloured with chocolate, coffee extract, liquor or fruit compound as desired. Other dessert sauces include fruit purées, caramel sauces and chocolate syrups. Techniques for decorating plates with sauces are discussed in Chapter 35, Plate Presentation.

Fruit Purées

Many types of fruit can be puréed for dessert sauces: Strawberries, raspberries, blackberries, apricots, mangoes and papayas are popular choices. They produce thick sauces with strong flavours and colours. Fresh or individually quick frozen (IQF) fruits are recommended.

Puréed fruit sauces, known as **coulis**, are uncooked. Fruit sauce generally denotes a cooked product. Cooking thickens sauces by reduction and allows the starch thickener to gelatinize. Fruit sauces cooked and thickened with waxy maize or modified starches tend to have a better shine than cornstarch achieves. Glucose contributes to a better consistency, particularly for coulis. They can also be sweetened with granulated sugar or a sugar syrup. The amount of sweetener will vary depending upon the fruit's natural sweetness.

Raspberry Coulis

Applying the Basics

RECIPE 31.12

RASPBERRY COULIS

Yield: 1 L (1 qt.)

Raspberries, fresh or IQF	1 kg	2 lb.
Granulated sugar	500 g	1 lb.
Lemon juice	30 mL	1 fl. oz.

1. Purée the berries and strain through a fine etâmine.

2. Stir in the sugar and lemon juice. Adjust the flavour with additional sugar if necessary.

NOTE: A small amount of modified cornstarch may be blended in to make a thicker coulis. If the coulis is too thick, thin with simple syrup.

RECIPE 31.12	
Approximate values per 25 mL serving:	
Calories	61
Total fat	0 g
Saturated fat	0 g
Cholesterol	0 mg
Sodium	0 mg
Total carbohydrates	155 g
Protein	0 g

Caramel Sauce

Caramel sauce is a mixture of caramelized sugar and heavy cream. A liqueur or citrus juice may be used for added flavour. Review the material on caramelizing sugar in Chapter 26, Principles of the Bakeshop, before making caramel sauce.

Caramel Sauce

RECIPE 31.13

Approximate values per 25 mL serving:

Calories	96
Total fat	5 g
Saturated fat	3 g
Cholesterol	18 mg
Sodium	5 mg
Total carbohydrates	13 g
Protein	0.5 g

Applying the Basics

RECIPE 31.13

CARAMEL SAUCE

Yield: 1 L (1 qt.)

Granulated sugar	500 g	1 lb. 2 oz.
Lemon juice	15 mL	1/2 fl. oz.
Water	125 mL	4 fl. oz.
Cream, 35%, room temperature	500 mL	16 fl. oz.
Unsalted butter, cut into pieces	40 g	1 oz.

1. Combine the sugar, lemon juice and water in a large, heavy saucepan. Stir to moisten the sugar completely. Place the saucepan on the stove top over high heat and bring to a boil. Brush down the sides of the pan with water to remove any sugar granules.
2. Do not stir the sugar. Continue boiling until the sugar caramelizes, turning a dark golden-brown and producing a rich aroma.
3. Remove the saucepan from the heat. Gradually add the cream. Be extremely careful, as the hot caramel may splatter. Whisk in the cream to blend.
4. Add the pieces of butter. Stir until the butter melts completely. If necessary, return the sauce to the stove to reheat enough to melt the butter.
5. Strain the sauce and cool completely at room temperature. The sauce may be stored for several weeks under refrigeration. Stir before using.

Chocolate Syrup

Chocolate syrup or sauce can be prepared by adding finely chopped chocolate to warm vanilla custard sauce. A darker syrup can also be made with unsweetened chocolate or cocoa powder. Fudge-type sauces are essentially variations on ganache, discussed in Chapter 30, Cakes and Frostings.

Dark Chocolate Sauce

RECIPE 31.14

Approximate values per 25 mL serving serving:

Calories	89
Total fat	9 g
Saturated fat	5.5 g
Cholesterol	5.5 mg
Sodium	3 mg
Total carbohydrates	5 g
Protein	2 g

Applying the Basics

RECIPE 31.14

DARK CHOCOLATE SAUCE

Yield: 500 mL (1 pt.)

Cocoa powder	50 g	2 oz.
Water	300 mL	10-1/2 fl. oz.
Chocolate, dark, fine chopped	250 g	9 oz.
Unsalted butter	50 g	2 oz.

1. Mix the cocoa powder with just enough water to make a smooth paste.
2. Bring the remaining water to a boil in a small, heavy saucepan. Immediately add the cocoa paste, whisking until smooth.
3. Pour over the fine-chopped chocolate and bring back to a simmer, stirring constantly, then remove from the heat.
4. Stir the butter into the warm cocoa mixture. Serve warm or at room temperature.

NOTE: The consistency of the sauce can be adjusted with either simple syrup or glucose.

ASSEMBLING DESSERTS

As noted previously, many pastries and other desserts are assembled from the baked doughs discussed in Chapter 29, Pies, Pastries and Cookies; the cakes, icings and glazes discussed in Chapter 30, Cakes and Frostings; and the creams, custards and other products discussed in this chapter. Many of these desserts are classic presentations requiring the precise arrangement of specific components. Formulas for some of these desserts are found at the end of the chapters in this part. But once you begin to master the basic skills presented in these chapters, you can use your creativity, taste and judgement to combine these components into a wide selection of new, unique and tempting desserts.

Assembled pastries and other desserts generally consist of three principal components: the base, the filling and the garnish. The **base** is the dough, crust or cake product that provides structure and forms the foundation for the final product. The **filling** refers to whatever is used to add flavour, texture and body to the final product. The **garnish** is any glaze, fruit, sauce or accompaniment used to complete the dish.

Basic Guidelines for Assembling Desserts

1. There should be a proper blend of complementary and contrasting flavours. For example, pears, red wine and blue cheese go well together, as do chocolate and raspberries. Do not combine flavours simply for the sake of originality, however.
2. There should be a proper blend of complementary and contrasting textures. For example, crisp puff pastry, soft pastry cream and tender strawberries are combined for a strawberry napoleon.
3. There should be a proper blend of complementary and contrasting colours. For example, a garnish of red raspberries and green mint looks great.
4. Garnishes should not be overly fussy or garish.
5. The base should be strong enough to hold the filling and garnish without collapsing, yet thin or tender enough to cut easily with a fork.
6. The filling or garnish may cause the base to become soft or even soggy. This may or may not be desirable. If you want a crisp base, assemble the product very close to service. If you want this softening to occur, assemble the product in advance of service.
7. Consider the various storage and keeping qualities of the individual components. It may be best to assemble or finish some products at service time.
8. The final construction should not be so elaborate or fragile that it cannot be portioned or served easily or attractively.
9. Consider whether the product would be better prepared as individual portions or as one large item. This may depend on the desired plate presentation and the ease and speed with which a large product can be cut and portioned for service.

◆◆◆

PLATING DESSERTS

There are four different ways to plate and present desserts.
1. The dessert by itself.
2. The dessert with fruit, sugar or chocolate garnish.
3. The dessert and sauce painting.
4. The complex presentation: two or more desserts on one plate. One or more sauces, garnishes or both may also be included.

CONCLUSION

If pastry doughs are the backbone of dessert preparations, then custards, creams, mousses and the like are the heart. The skills and techniques presented in this chapter are essential to successful pastry production. Many of these skills, such as whipping cream or preparing custards, will be useful in other areas of the kitchen as well. Once you have mastered these skills as well as those discussed in Chapter 29, Pies, Pastries and Cookies, and Chapter 30, Cakes and Frostings, you will be able to prepare a wide variety of tempting desserts.

QUESTIONS FOR DISCUSSION

1. Eggs and dairy products are susceptible to bacterial contamination. What precautions should be taken to avoid food-borne illnesses when preparing custards?
2. Explain why pastry cream should be boiled and why custard sauce should not be boiled.
3. Identify three desserts that are based on a baked custard.
4. Compare a classically prepared Bavarian, chiffon, mousse and soufflé. How are they similar? How are they different?
5. Describe the procedure for making a typical still-frozen dessert. What is the purpose of including whipped cream or whipped egg whites?
6. Explain three ways in which sweet sauces can be used in preparing or presenting a dessert.

ADDITIONAL CUSTARD, CREAM, FROZEN DESSERT AND DESSERT SAUCE FORMULAS

Robert Bourassa

Born and raised in Montreal, Robert began working in the food industry at the age of 16, as an apprentice charcutier for his family's business, La Belle Fermière. He is a graduate of the Institut du Tourisme et de l'Hôtellerie du Québec and also holds a Bachelor of Business Administration degree from Loyola University. Having gained extensive experience in Canada and abroad, in 1982 Robert fulfilled a life-long ambition to own his own restaurant and purchased Café Henry Burger, which celebrates its 80th anniversary in 2002.

RECIPE 31.15

Approximate values per ramekin:

Calories	470
Total fat	33 g
Saturated fat	19 g
Cholesterol	308 mg
Sodium	37 mg
Total carbohydrates	40 g
Protein	4 g

RECIPE 31.15

CRÈME BRÛLÉE

CAFÉ HENRY BURGER, HULL, QC
Chef/Owner Robert Bourassa

Yield: 6–8 Ramekins

Cream, 35%	650 mL	24 fl. oz.
Vanilla bean	1/2	1/2
Egg yolks	125 g	6
Granulated sugar	100 g	3-1/2 oz.
Vanilla extract	3 mL	1/2 tsp.
Granulated sugar	200 g	7 oz.

1. Place the cream and the vanilla bean in a large, heavy saucepan. Heat just to a boil.
2. Whisk the egg yolks and sugar together until smooth and well blended.
3. Temper the eggs with one-third of the hot cream, return the egg mixture to the saucepan and cook, stirring constantly, until very thick. Do not allow the custard to boil.

4. Strain into a clean bowl and pour into small ramekins.

5. Set ramekins in a bain marie and add warm water halfway up. Bake at 150°C (300°F) for 45–60 minutes. Cool overnight.

6. Sprinkle approximately 25–30 g (1 oz.) granulated sugar over the top of the custard in each ramekin and caramelize with a propane torch. Serve immediately with fresh fruit.

❖❖❖

RECIPE 31.16

Crème Chiboust

CONA SUCRE D'ART, Nanaimo, BC
Pâtissier Confiseur George Wagner

Yield: 2 L (2 qt.)

Egg yolks	200 g	7 oz.
Sugar	150 g	5 oz.
Lemon juice	150 mL	5 fl. oz.
Cream, 35%	300 mL	10 fl. oz.
Cornstarch	10 g	1 Tbsp.
Gelatin leaves (soaked in cold water)	6	6
Egg whites	350 g	12-1/4 oz.
Sugar	250 g	8 oz.

1. Whisk egg yolks, 150 g (5 oz.) of sugar and lemon juice in a double boiler until warm and foamy.

2. Blend cream and cornstarch in a heavy-bottomed saucepan.

3. Add yolk mixture to cream mixture and bring to a boil for 4 minutes.

4. Squeeze excess moisture from gelatin leaves and add to hot mixture. Stir until dissolved.

5. Whip egg whites and remaining sugar to form soft meringue.

6. Gently fold meringue into hot sauce.

❖❖❖

RECIPE 31.17

Chocolate and Cinnamon Pots de Crème

RITZ CARLTON, New Orleans, LA
Assistant Pasty Chef Pierre St. Pierre

Yield: 8 120-mL (4-fl.-oz.) Servings

Milk	250 mL	9 fl. oz.
Cream, 35%	750 mL	26 fl. oz.
Granulated sugar	110 g	4 oz.
Cinnamon sticks	6	6
Vanilla bean, scraped	1	1
Egg yolks	170 g	8
Dark chocolate, chopped	140 g	5 oz.
Cocoa powder	30 g	1 oz.

Continued

George Wagner
Born and raised in France, George was apprenticed at the age of 14 and later specialized in pâtisserie. He came to Canada in 1966 and was Pastry Instructor at Malaspina University College from 1978 to 1994. George now owns his own school, where he instructs students in the art of sugar and chocolate confections.

RECIPE 31.16

Approximate values per 125 mL serving:

Calories	220
Total fat	10.5 g
Saturated fat	5 g
Cholesterol	187 mg
Sodium	48 mg
Total carbohydrates	27 g
Protein	5 g

Pierre St. Pierre
Pierre trained at George Brown College and later received his journeyman certification and Interprovincial Red Seal. He began his career as Food and Beverage Host with Walt Disney World Company's Epcot Centre, in Florida, and went on to work in pastries at Jasper Park Lodge, the Ritz-Carlton Buckhead (in Atlanta, Georgia), and the Ritz-Carlton Huntington (in Pasadena, California). Highlights of his career include being the Grand Prize Winner in the 1999 Southern Pastry Classic, in Atlanta, Georgia, and creating a chocolate Inukshuk showpiece that was displayed for the 1998 International Olympic Committee.

RECIPE 31.17

*Approximate values
per 120 mL serving:*

Calories	549
Total fat	49 g
Saturated fat	28 g
Cholesterol	195 mg
Sodium	401 mg
Total carbohydrates	26.5 g
Protein	9.5 g

1. Heat the milk, cream, sugar, cinnamon sticks and vanilla bean to a boil.
2. Whisk the egg yolks together, temper with some hot cream and then strain over the chocolate and cocoa powder. Stir until smooth.
3. Pour into ramekins. Pass a torch over top to remove any air bubbles. Place the ramekins in a hotel pan and add enough hot water to reach halfway up the sides of the ramekins.
4. Bake at 150°C (300°F) until custards are almost set in the centre, approximately 30–40 minutes. Remove from the water bath and refrigerate until thoroughly chilled. Serve garnished with whipped cream and chocolate shavings.

George Wagner

Born and raised in France, George was apprenticed at the age of 14 and later specialized in pâtisserie. He came to Canada in 1966 and was Pastry Instructor at Malaspina University College from 1978 to 1994. George now owns his own school, where he instructs students in the art of sugar and chocolate confections.

◆◆◆

RECIPE 31.18

PEAR TART CHIBOUST

CONA SUCRE D'ART, NANAIMO, BC
Pâtissier Confiseur George Wagner

Yield: 1 Torte/Cake (6 Servings)

Puff Pastry (Recipe 29.8)	120 g	4 oz.
Crème Chiboust (Recipe 31.16)	1 L	32 fl. oz.
Pears, freshly poached or canned, thinly sliced	3–4	3–4
Sugar	75 g	2-1/2 oz.
Caramel Sauce (Recipe 31.13), flavoured with pear liqueur	300 mL	10 fl. oz.

1. Cut a circle of puff pastry 20 cm (8 inches) in diameter.
2. Spread a thin layer of Crème Chiboust on it.
3. Arrange pear slices so they overlap on top of Crème Chiboust.
4. Bake at 200°C (400°F) for approximately 15–20 minutes.
5. Place a 20-cm (8-inch) cake ring over the tart and fill with Crème Chiboust to a height of 3.75 cm (1-1/2 inches). Let cool.
6. When firm, sprinkle sugar on top. Using a torch, caramelize the top and let set for a few minutes.
7. Remove the ring and serve with Caramel Sauce.

RECIPE 31.18

Approximate values per 1/6 cake:

Calories	545
Total fat	28 g
Saturated fat	15.5 g
Cholesterol	239 mg
Sodium	117 mg
Total carbohydrates	71 g
Protein	8 g

◆◆◆

RECIPE 31.19

NEW YORK-STYLE CHEESECAKE

Yield: Two 25-cm (10-inch) Cakes
(12–16 Servings per Cake)

Cream cheese, softened	1.6 kg	3 lb. 6 oz.
Cake flour	60 g	2 oz.
Granulated sugar	540 g	18 oz.
Eggs	450 g	8
Cream, 35%	150 mL	5 fl. oz.
Vanilla extract	15 mL	1 Tbsp.
Lemon zest, minced	3 g	1 tsp.
Orange zest, minced	10 g	1 Tbsp.

RECIPE 31.19

Approximate values per 1/10 cake:

Calories	455
Total fat	33 g
Saturated fat	20 g
Cholesterol	194 mg
Sodium	268 mg
Total carbohydrates	32 g
Protein	9 g

1. Cream the cheese at low speed until smooth. Incorporate the flour and sugar.

2. Blend in the eggs slowly, then add the cream, vanilla and lemon and orange zests.

3. Pour the batter into well-buttered springform pans. Bake at 150°C (300°F) until set, approximately 1–1.5 hours.

4. Cool completely before removing the sides of each pan.

NOTE: Pans may be lined with a crumb or short paste crust.

◆◆◆

RECIPE 31.20

CHOCOLATE, CHERRY AND CROISSANT PUDDING

VANCOUVER COMMUNITY COLLEGE, Vancouver, BC
Chef Instructor Glen O'Flaherty

Yield: 20–25 Portions

Whipping cream	1 L	32 fl. oz.
Dark couverture, chopped into small pieces	1 kg	2 lb.
Eggs	450 g	8
Granulated sugar	180 g	6 oz.
Vanilla Sauce (recipe follows)	700 mL	25 fl. oz.
Croissants, day old, 1.5-cm (1/2-inch) cubes	20 pieces	20 pieces
Bing cherries, pitted	1.14 kg	40 oz.
Apricot glaze, melted	200 g	7 oz.

1. Scald cream and pour over chocolate chunks. Continue mixing until a smooth ganache is made.

2. Whisk together eggs, sugar and vanilla sauce, then mix with chocolate ganache. Add croissant cubes and cherries and continue folding until all ingredients come together.

3. Press into a buttered hotel pan 5 cm (2 inches) deep and bake in an oven at 150°C (300°F) in a bain marie for approximately 75 minutes.

4. Cool. Brush with apricot glaze. Refrigerate to completely set.

5. Cut and serve as required.

VANILLA SAUCE

Whipping cream	500 mL	16 fl. oz.
Vanilla bean	1/2	1/2
Egg yolks	125 g	6
Granulated sugar	80 g	3 oz.

1. In a saucepan combine cream and vanilla bean and bring to a boil.

2. Combine egg yolks and sugar, mixing thoroughly. When the cream has come to a boil add a small amount to the egg mixture (temper).

3. Combine egg and sugar mixture with hot cream and cook until thickened.

4. Remove from the heat and set aside to cool.

Glen O'Flaherty

Glen was a 15-year-old dishwasher when the Chef at the Pillar and Post Restaurant Inn called him in and offered him the position of prep cook! Over the following three-and-a-half years, Glen apprenticed and attended culinary classes at both George Brown College, in Toronto, and Niagara College, in Niagara Falls. He held positions at the Muskoka Sands Inn, in northern Ontario, and at two hotels in Nova Scotia before moving to B.C. and becoming Executive Chef at the Newlands Golf and Country Club. Currently, he is a chef instructor at Vancouver Community College.

RECIPE 31.20

Approximate values per serving:

Calories	771
Total fat	69 g
Saturated fat	41 g
Cholesterol	313 mg
Sodium	125 mg
Total carbohydrates	45 g
Protein	12 g

Vanilla Sauce—Approximate values per 25 mL serving:

Calories	203
Total fat	19.5 g
Saturated fat	12 g
Cholesterol	146 mg
Sodium	21 mg
Total carbohydrates	6 g
Protein	2 g

Vinod Varshey

After graduating with a Bachelor of Science degree, Vinod's interests in the food and hospitality industry led him to join the Institute of Hotel Management. He completed his apprenticeship in New Delhi and in Germany, where he worked as a Commis Patissier. After coming to Canada, he worked at prestigious hotels and lodges before joining the culinary team at NAIT, where he has been for the last 10 years.

RECIPE 31.21

Nougat Mousse—
Approximate values per serving:

Calories	131
Total fat	12 g
Saturated fat	5 g
Cholesterol	68.5 mg
Sodium	12 mg
Total carbohydrates	6 g
Protein	2 g

Mango Mousse—
Approximate values per serving:

Calories	116
Total fat	9 g
Saturated fat	5 g
Cholesterol	72 mg
Sodium	20 mg
Total carbohydrates	8 g
Protein	2 g

Cherry Compote—
Approximate values per serving:

Calories	100
Total fat	1 g
Saturated fat	0 g
Cholesterol	0 mg
Sodium	2 mg
Total carbohydrates	22 g
Protein	1 g

◆◆◆

RECIPE 31.21

DUO OF NOUGAT AND MANGO MOUSSE WITH WARM PITTED CHERRY COMPOTE

NORTHERN ALBERTA INSTITUTE OF TECHNOLOGY, EDMONTON, AB
Baking Coordinator Vinod Varshey

Yield: 8–10 Ramekins

NOUGAT MOUSSE

Gelatin leaves	3	3
Egg yolks	2	2
Sugar	40 g	1-1/2 oz.
Milk	200 mL	7 fl. oz.
Hazelnut paste	50 g	1-3/4 oz.
Cream, 35%, whipped	200 mL	7 fl. oz.

1. Soak the gelatin leaves in cold water.
2. Whisk the yolks and sugar over double boiler until ribbon stage.
3. Boil the milk and add to the sugar mixture.
4. Cook until slightly thickened.
5. Add the softened gelatin to the hot sauce and stir until dissolved.
6. Mix in hazelnut paste.
7. Cool to body temperature and fold in the whipped cream.
8. Pour into ramekin half full. Chill.

MANGO MOUSSE

Gelatin leaves	4	4
Egg yolks	2	2
Sugar	50 g	1-3/4 oz.
Milk	200 mL	7 fl. oz.
Mango purée	50 mL	1-3/4 fl. oz.
Mango, small dice	10 g	1 Tbsp.
Cream, 35%, whipped	200 mL	7 fl. oz.

1. Soak the gelatin leaves in cold water.
2. Whisk the yolks and sugar over double boiler until ribbon stage.
3. Boil the milk and add to the sugar mixture.
4. Cook until slightly thickened.
5. Add the softened gelatin and stir until dissolved.
6. Mix in mango purée and pieces.
7. Cool to body temperature and fold in the whipped cream.
8. Pour on top of nougat mousse to fill ramekin.

CHERRY COMPOTE

Cherry juice	80 mL	3 fl. oz.
Sherry	100 mL	3-1/2 fl. oz.
Lemon juice and zest	1	1
Orange juice and zest	1	1
Sugar	90 g	3 oz.
Freshly ground black peppercorn	10 g	4 tsp.
Cinnamon stick	1	1
Dark, pitted cherries	500 g	1 lb. 2 oz.

Whipped cream, fresh fruits and raspberry–passion fruit coulis
 to taste and for presentation

Combine all ingredients except the cherries in a saucepan. Bring to a boil. Add the cherries. Reduce to desired consistency. Remove from heat and serve warm.

ASSEMBLY: Unmould the mousse and place in the centre of a plate. Place the cherry compote on the side of the plate. Drizzle the mousse with coulis and garnish with whipped cream and fresh fruit.

◆◆◆

RECIPE 31.22

MAPLE SYRUP MOUSSE WITH STRAWBERRY COULIS

SOUTHERN ALBERTA INSTITUTE OF TECHNOLOGY, CALGARY, AB
Master Pâtissier Hermann Greineder

Yield: 4–6 Portions

Hermann Greineder

Currently a Pastry Instructor at SAIT, Hermann received his German Master Certification as "Chef Pâtissier" in 1971. He has 45 years of experience in a wide range of establishments, and has won several medals in competition for his beautiful chocolate showpieces.

Egg yolks	4	4
Maple syrup	100 mL	3-1/2 fl. oz.
Cream, 35%, cold	300 mL	10 fl. oz.
Pure white gelatin powder	7 g	1/4 oz.
Strawberry Coulis (recipe follows)		
Almond Tulip Mix (Recipe 29.30)	as needed	as needed

1. Whip the egg yolks and maple syrup in a bowl over boiling water until the mixture thickens to ribbon stage. It should not get too hot, or the egg yolks will curdle. The mixture should have a nice creamy texture.
2. Whip the cold cream.
3. Dissolve gelatin in a few drops of water, let it bloom, then melt over heat.
4. Pour it into syrup mixture. Add whipped cream and mix well, but slowly.
5. Divide the mousse between 4–6 ramekins. Refrigerate.
6. To serve, dip ramekins into hot water to loosen mousse. Turn upside down on a dessert plate. Pour the Strawberry Coulis around the mousse and garnish with Almond Tulip shards to represent a teepee.

STRAWBERRY COULIS

Strawberries	as needed	as needed
Sugar	TT	TT

Blend fresh or frozen strawberries with sugar, to taste, in a blender.

RECIPE 31.22

Approximate values per serving:

Calories	521
Total fat	37 g
Saturated fat	20 g
Cholesterol	230 mg
Sodium	63 mg
Total carbohydrates	41 g
Protein	9 g

Strawberry Coulis—
Approximate values per serving:

Calories	16
Total fat	0 g
Saturated fat	0 g
Cholesterol	0 mg
Sodium	0 mg
Total carbohydrates	4 g
Protein	0 g

◆◆◆

RECIPE 31.23

STICKY TOFFEE PUDDING

COUNTRY CLUB OF THE HAMPTONS, CALGARY, AB
Executive Chef and Manager of Culinary Services John Walker, CCC

Yield: 8 Portions

Sauce:

Butter	225 g	8 oz.
Brown sugar	170 g	6 oz.
Cream, 35%	225 mL	8 fl. oz.
Lemon juice	30 mL	1 fl. oz.

Continued

John Walker, CCC

John spent 22 years as Executive Chef for the Calgary Chamber of Commerce and 15 years at the 400 Club. He apprenticed at the Southern Alberta Institute of Technology and has been a member of the Calgary Academy of Chefs for 36 years.

RECIPE 31.23

Approximate values per serving:

Calories	807
Total fat	51 g
Saturated fat	31 g
Cholesterol	260 mg
Sodium	610 mg
Total carbohydrates	86 g
Protein	7 g

RECIPE 31.24

Approximate values per 100 mL serving:

Calories	158
Total fat	9 g
Saturated fat	5.5 g
Cholesterol	32 mg
Sodium	20 mg
Total carbohydrates	19 g
Protein	2 g

Dates, chopped	225 g	8 oz.
Water, boiling	125 mL	4 fl. oz.
Butter	150 g	5-1/2 oz.
Sugar	225 g	8 oz.
Eggs	225 g	4
Lemon rind, grated	10 g	1 Tbsp.
Pastry flour	150 g	5 oz.
Baking powder	7 g	2 tsp.
Baking soda	3 g	1 tsp.

1. Prepare sauce by combining all ingredients and bring to a boil. Reserve.
2. Cover dates with boiling water.
3. Meanwhile, cream butter and sugar, beat in eggs and lemon rind.
4. Combine flour, baking powder and soda.
5. Mix half the flour mixture with the dates and half into the creamed mixture. Fold the two together.
6. Line a bowl with plastic wrap and pour in half the sauce. Place batter on top and cover with plastic wrap and secure. Steam for 2.5 hours in a convection steamer (or double boiler).
7. Portion and pour remaining sauce on top.

◆◆◆

RECIPE 31.24

RASPBERRY MOUSSE

Yield: 1 L (1 qt.)

Gelatin	6 sheets	6 sheets
Raspberries, puréed	350 g	12 oz.
Granulated sugar	100 g	3 oz.
Raspberry brandy	30 mL	2 Tbsp.
Cream, 35%	250 mL	8 fl. oz.

1. Soften the gelatin in ice water and set aside.
2. Place the raspberry purée, sugar and brandy in a nonreactive saucepan and warm just to dissolve the sugar. Remove from the heat and strain through a fine etâmine.
3. Add the softened gelatin, stirring until it is dissolved. Chill the mixture until thick but not set.
4. Whip the cream to soft peaks and fold it into the raspberry mixture.

◆◆◆

RECIPE 31.25

PARNASSIENNE DE MOUSSE AU CHOCOLAT (CHOCOLATE TOWER)

CHRISTOPHER'S AND CHRISTOPHER'S BISTRO, PHOENIX, AZ
Chef/Owner Christopher Gross

Yield: 8 Servings

Parchment paper moulds	8	8
Dark chocolate, chopped	150 g	5-1/2 oz.

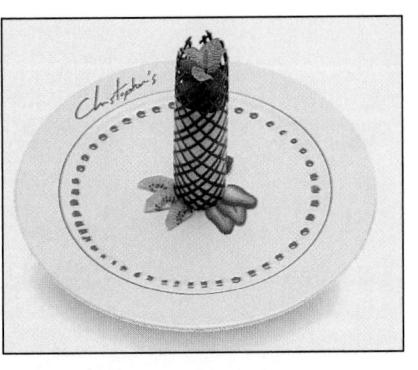

Unsalted butter	45 g	3 Tbsp.
Cream, 35%	50 mL	2 fl. oz.
Egg whites	300 g	10
Superfine sugar	50 g	4 Tbsp.
Dark chocolate, bakers' glaze, melted	60 g	2 oz.
White chocolate, bakers' glaze, melted	150 g	5 oz.
Espresso Sauce (recipe follows)	as needed	as needed
Fresh berries	as needed	as needed

1. To make the moulds, cut parchment paper into 16 strips, each 8.75 cm (3-1/2 inches) high and 12.5 cm (5 inches) long. Roll eight of these strips into tubes and tape closed. Stand the tubes upright on a parchment-lined sheet pan. Reserve the remaining strips for the tower coating.
2. To make the mousse, melt the 150 g (5-1/2 oz.) of chocolate and the butter in a medium bowl over a bain marie.
3. Whip the cream to stiff peaks and refrigerate.
4. Whip the egg whites and the superfine sugar to stiff peaks.
5. Fold the egg whites into the melted chocolate, then fold in the whipped cream.
6. Using a large piping bag fitted with a plain tip, pipe the mousse into the eight parchment paper tubes. Freeze until completely solid, several hours or overnight.
7. To make the tower coating, pipe a pattern of melted dark chocolate onto the eight remaining strips of parchment paper. When the dark chocolate hardens, coat the same side of the parchment with the melted white chocolate. Immediately remove a tube of mousse from the freezer. Remove the paper wrapping and wrap the chocolate-coated parchment strip around the frozen mousse, placing the chocolate side next to the mousse. Refreeze for 5 minutes, then carefully peel the paper off the tower. The dark and white chocolate coating will remain wrapped around the mousse.
8. Repeat the procedure for wrapping the frozen mousse with chocolate-coated paper for the remaining pieces.
9. For service, ladle Espresso Sauce onto eight plates, place a mousse tower in the centre of each plate and garnish with fresh berries.

RECIPE 31.25

Approximate values per serving:

Calories	452
Total fat	35 g
Saturated fat	21 g
Cholesterol	186 mg
Sodium	173 mg
Total carbohydrates	34 g
Protein	12 g

ESPRESSO SAUCE

Yield: 700 mL (1-1/2 pt.)

Egg yolks	175 g	8
Granulated sugar	100 g	3-1/2 oz.
Cream, 18%	450 mL	1 pt.
Espresso beans	85 g	3 oz.
Vanilla bean, scraped	1/2	1/2

1. Whisk the egg yolks and sugar together in a medium bowl.
2. Bring the cream, espresso beans and vanilla bean to a simmer in a heavy saucepan.
3. Temper the egg yolks with a portion of the hot cream, then return the mixture to the saucepan. Cook over low heat, stirring constantly, until the sauce is thick enough to coat the back of a spoon. Strain and cool over an ice bath.

Espresso Sauce—
Approximate values
per 50 mL serving serving:

Calories	127
Total fat	7 g
Saturated fat	3 g
Cholesterol	173 mg
Sodium	21 mg
Total carbohydrates	11 g
Protein	4 g

George Wagner
Born and raised in France, George was apprenticed at the age of 14 and later specialized in pâtisserie. He came to Canada in 1966 and was Pastry Instructor at Malaspina University College from 1978 to 1994. George now owns his own school, where he instructs students in the art of sugar and chocolate confections.

RECIPE 31.26

*Approximate values
per 270 g serving:*

Calories	519
Total fat	31 g
Saturated fat	18 g
Cholesterol	291 mg
Sodium	129 mg
Total carbohydrates	53 g
Protein	8 g

Clayton Folkers
Born in Canada, Clayton earned his Commercial Cooking Diploma from the Northern Alberta Institute of Technology, in Edmonton, and was immediately invited by the Four Seasons Hotel to extend his work-study program with them into a permanent position. Looking specifically to enhance his pastry skills, Clayton attended the Privinciaal Hoger Instituut PIVA in Antwerp, Belgium, where he completed a graduate program while gaining experience as a Production Chef in a prominent pastry shop. Returning home to Edmonton, he honed his pastry skills at the Four Seasons Hotel, at La Favorite Pastry Shop, which he co-owned, and at the Shaw Conference Centre, where he has been Pastry Chef since 1989.

RECIPE 31.27

*Iced Soufflé—
Approximate values per serving:*

Calories	189
Total fat	12 g
Saturated fat	7 g
Cholesterol	88 mg
Sodium	16 mg
Total carbohydrates	19 g
Protein	1.5 g

RECIPE 31.26

BANANA GALETTE WITH NUTMEG ICE CREAM

CONA SUCRE D'ART, NANAIMO, BC
Pâtissier Confiseur George Wagner

Yield: 12 Portions

Phyllo pastry	6 sheets	6 sheets
Melted butter	as needed	as needed
Sugar	30 g	1/8 cup
Cake crumbs	30 g	1/8 cup
Pastry Cream (Recipe 31.2)	1.3 L	48 fl. oz.
Banana slices, thin	as needed	as needed
Sugar	45 g	1-1/2 oz.
Nutmeg Ice Cream	12 scoops	12 scoops
Crème Anglaise		

1. Brush one layer of phyllo pastry with the melted butter. Mix the 30 g (1/8 cup) sugar and cake crumbs together and sprinkle a fifth of it evenly over the phyllo.

2. Place a second sheet of phyllo pastry on the first one and repeat the first step four more times.

3. Cut the phyllo in 7.5 × 7.5-cm (3 × 3-inch) squares and bake at 185°C (375°F) for about 20 minutes.

4. When the squares are baked and cooled pipe 60 mL (2 fl. oz.) of Pastry Cream on each one. Arrange the banana slices on top and sprinkle with 45 g (1-1/2 oz.) of sugar. Use a torch to caramelize. Transfer the towers to individual plates.

5. Add 1 scoop of Nutmeg Ice Cream to each and drizzle Crème Anglaise on plate. Serve immediately.

RECIPE 31.27

STRAWBERRY ICED SOUFFLÉ

SHAW CONFERENCE CENTRE, EDMONTON, AB
Pastry Chef Clayton Folkers

Yield: 110 Servings as part of a composite plate or 25 Individual Soufflés

ICED SOUFFLÉ

Egg yolks	440 g	20
Granulated sugar	675 g	24 oz.
Cream, 35%, whipped	3 L	3 qt.
White chocolate, melted	450 g	1 lb.
Strawberry purée, fresh	900 g	2 lb.
Strawberry concentrate	75 g	2-1/2 oz.
Liquid Filling (recipe follows)		

1. Warm the egg yolks and sugar to 40°C (105°F), stirring constantly, and whip until cold. Fold in one-third of the whipping cream and mix together with the chocolate.

2. Fold in the remaining cream, strawberry purée and concentrate.

3. Fill cone-shaped moulds three-quarters full. Insert a second cone to form an interior cavity and freeze.

4. When frozen, remove the interior cone and fill the centre with Liquid Filling. Return to freezer.

5. Seal the bottom with the remaining soufflé filling and freeze.

LIQUID CENTRE

Water	500 mL	16 fl. oz.
Granulated sugar	850 g	1 lb. 14 oz.
Corn syrup	70 g	2.5 oz.
Passion fruit concentrate	180 g	6 oz.
Grand Marnier	60 mL	2 fl. oz.

1. Combine the water, sugar and corn syrup. Bring to a boil.

2. Cool the liquid, then add the concentrate and Grand Marnier.

Liquid Centre—	
Approximate values per serving:	
Calories	36
Total fat	0 g
Saturated fat	0 g
Cholesterol	0 mg
Sodium	1 mg
Total carbohydrates	9 g
Protein	0 g

❖❖❖

RECIPE 31.28

MARINATED FIELD BERRIES WITH LEMON COOKIES AND ICE WINE SABAYON

WILDWOOD RESTAURANT GROUP, CALGARY, AB

Executive Chef Michael Noble

Yield: 4 Servings

Eggs, separated	5	5
Lemon zest	5 mL	1 tsp.
Sugar	150 g	5-1/2 oz.
Flour, cake	100 g	3-1/2 oz.
Icing sugar	to dust	to dust
Marinated Field Berries (recipe follows)		
Ice Wine Sabayon (recipe follows)		

1. To make the cookies, in a stainless steel mixing bowl, place the egg yolks, lemon zest and sugar. Using a small fine whisk, whip the mixture until it becomes light, fluffy and rather stiff.

2. In a separate bowl, whip the egg whites until they form stiff peaks. Fold the egg whites into the yolk mixture and then fold the flour in to form a batter-like consistency.

3. Using a pastry bag with a straight tube, immediately pipe the batter into round shapes, approximately 7 cm (2-3/4 inches) in diameter, by piping in a spiral motion.

4. When the shapes are piped, dust them lightly with icing sugar and place immediately into a 170°C (340°F) oven; bake for approximately 7 minutes, or until golden-brown. Remove from the oven and let cool.

5. On a dessert plate, place one of the cookies. Spoon some of the berry mixture over it with some of the juice from the marinade. Set another cookie on top and repeat the procedure. Generously spoon some sabayon over it until it completely covers the cookies and berries, flowing over them. Using a small torch, burn the surface until it is a light golden-brown all over. Garnish with a mint sprig and serve.

MARINATED FIELD BERRIES

Strawberries, cut into wedge-like quarters	250 g	8 oz.
Blueberries	250 g	8 oz.
Granulated sugar	40 g	2-1/2 Tbsp.
Lemon juice	1 lemon	1 lemon
Ice wine	60 mL	2 fl. oz.

Place the berries in a nonreactive bowl with the sugar, lemon juice and ice wine. Let marinate in the refrigerator, covered, for 3 hours.

Michael Noble

Michael was fated to become a chef after cooking a successful Belgian waffle in a high school economics class! He began his apprenticeship in Vancouver, though he also gained valuable European experience in the early stages of his career. In 1996, Michael opened Vancouver's Diva at the Met and, within a year, it was propelled into the culinary spotlight, winning awards from Gourmet Magazine, Vancouver Magazine, *and* GQ. *One of Canada's leading chefs, Michael achieved Canada's highest standing ever at the Bocuse d'Or World Cuisine championship in Lyons in 1995 and 1997.*

RECIPE 31.28

Approximate values per serving:

Calories	634
Total fat	12 g
Saturated fat	4 g
Cholesterol	482 mg
Sodium	123 mg
Total carbohydrates	109 g
Protein	15 g

Marinated Field Berries—
Approximate values per serving:

Calories	18
Total fat	0 g
Saturated fat	0 g
Cholesterol	0 mg
Sodium	1 mg
Total carbohydrates	4 g
Protein	0 g

ICE WINE SABAYON

Whole eggs	2	2
Egg yolks	2	2
Sugar	60 g	2 oz.
Ice wine, reduced by half	150 mL	5 fl. oz.
Ice wine, not reduced	60 mL	2 fl. oz.

Place the whole eggs, egg yolks, sugar and ice wines in a stainless-steel mixing bowl. Using a balloon whisk, whip the mixture over a simmering pot of water, taking care to remove the bowl from the water occasionally to keep the eggs from curdling or scrambling. Continue whisking until the sabayon is warm and holds its shape slightly after falling from the whisk.

◆◆◆

RECIPE 31.29

BLACKCURRANT MOUSSE

HRT ALLIANCE, HUMBER COLLEGE, Toronto, ON
Chef Michéal McFadden

Michéal McFadden

Michéal has been helping turn out new chefs at Humber College for the past 15 years. Prior to that, he was the executive Pastry Chef at the former Harbour Castle Hilton. His love of cooking emerged early in life, as he helped his mother around the house in his native Ireland.

Yield: 1.5 L (1-1/2 qt.)

Granulated sugar	300 g	10-1/2 oz.
Water	100 mL	3-1/2 fl. oz.
Egg whites	110 g	5
Icing sugar	50 g	2 oz.
Gelatin leaves	6	6
Blackcurrants, puréed	500 g	17-1/2 oz.
Cream, 35%	1 L	35 fl. oz.
Whipped cream	TT	TT
Blackcurrants, fresh	TT	TT

1. Bring granulated sugar and water to 118°C (244°F) to make a syrup.
2. Whip egg whites and icing sugar together to make a soft meringue.
3. Pour hot syrup into the meringue and whip until cold.
4. Soak gelatin in ice water until soft and then dissolve over a warm-water bath.
5. Add gelatin to the blackcurrant purée and mix well.
6. Whip cream until it forms soft peaks.
7. Add blackcurrant mixture to the cool meringue.
8. Fold in cream and transfer to a stainless steel bowl.
9. Cover with plastic wrap and refrigerate for approximately 2 hours.
10. Using a piping bag with a #10 star tip, pipe mixture into glasses and decorate with whipped cream and fresh blackcurrants.

❖❖❖

RECIPE 31.30

TRUFFLES

CHOCOLATERIE BERNARD CALLEBAUT®, CALGARY, AB
Owner Bernard Callebaut

Yield: 1.5 kg (3 lb.)

Semi-sweet or bittersweet chocolate	1 kg	2.2 lb.
Whipping cream	500 mL	16 fl. oz.
Flavouring compound (optional)	TT	TT
Cocoa powder and icing sugar	as needed	as needed

1. Melt chocolate over a double boiler to 48–55°C (118–130°F).

2. Warm the whipping cream to 50°C (120°F).

3. Add the melted chocolate to the cream while stirring.

4. Add flavouring if you wish, such as orange or coffee.

5. Pour mixture in baking trays and spread to 2.5 cm (1 inch) thick.

6. Cool in fridge until the mixture is hard.

7. Scoop small pieces with a melon baller or coffee spoon.

8. Roll pieces by hand into round or oval shapes.

9. Roll truffles in cocoa powder, icing sugar or anything light.

Bernard Callebaut

Bernard arrived in Canada from Belgium in 1982. His family owned the Callebaut Chocolate Factory in Wieze, Belgium, from 1911 until 1980, when it was purchased by the Suchard Toblerone group. Having achieved renown as an innovative creator of unique fillings for chocolates, Bernard manufactures what is considered to be the highest quality line of Canadian-made chocolates and chocolate-related products, including sauces, bars and ice cream.

RECIPE 31.30

*Approximate values
per 15 g serving:*

Calories	67
Total fat	5 g
Saturated fat	3 g
Cholesterol	8 mg
Sodium	3 mg
Total carbohydrates	7 g
Protein	0.5 g

❖❖❖

CHOCOLATE TRUFFLES

Chocolate truffles are suprisingly simple to make. Fine chocolate is melted with cream and perhaps butter. The mixture is flavoured as desired with liqueur, extracts, fruit or coffee and allowed to harden. Once firm, the ganache is scooped into balls and rolled in cocoa powder, confectioner's sugar or melted chocolate. The classic French truffle is a small, irregularly shaped ball of bittersweet chocolate dusted with cocoa powder. Canadians, however, seem to prefer larger candies, coated with melted chocolate and decorated with nuts or additional chocolate. Recipe 31.30 can be prepared in either style.

Shaping chocolate truffles.

Bernard Callebaut

Bernard arrived in Canada from Belgium in 1982. His family owned the Callebaut Chocolate Factory in Wieze, Belgium, from 1911 until 1980, when it was purchased by the Suchard Toblerone group. Having achieved renown as an innovative creator of unique fillings for chocolates, Bernard manufactures what is considered to be the highest quality line of Canadian-made chocolates and chocolate-related products, including sauces, bars and ice cream.

RECIPE 31.31

Approximate values per 15 g serving:

Calories	86
Total fat	7.5 g
Saturated fat	5 g
Cholesterol	15 mg
Sodium	2 mg
Total carbohydrates	6 g
Protein	0.5 g

♦♦♦

RECIPE 31.31

CHOCOLATE BUTTER CREAM

CHOCOLATERIE BERNARD CALLEBAUT®, CALGARY, AB
Owner Bernard Callebaut

Semi-sweet chocolate	350 g	12 oz.
Unsalted butter, cubed	225 g	8 oz.

1. Melt chocolate over a double boiler.
2. Place butter in a metal bowl and let warm to room temperature.
3. Add the chocolate, which is approximately 30°C (86°F), and mix quickly with a whisk or the chocolate will solidify on the cold metal and the filling will become chunky.
4. Fill a pastry bag and pipe shapes on waxed paper.
5. Put in cooler for 30 minutes so the mixture can harden.

*W*EBLINKS

Ice Cream
   www.foodsci.uoguelph.ca/dairyedu/icecream.html
The Ice Cream Parlor: Frozen Desserts
   www.dsuper.net/~zaz/icecream/frame.html
Tiramisu
   www.geocities.com/NapaValley/2490/
Sweet Soufflés
   www.cs.cmu.edu/~mjw/recipes/souffle/sweet/index.html
Cheesecakes
   SOAR.Berkeley.edu/recipes/baked-goods/desserts/cheesecakes/

PART FIVE

MEAL SERVICE AND PRESENTATION

Part Five begins with a chapter on Breakfast and Brunch and another on Appetizers and Sandwiches. In each, we discuss the preparation and presentation of foods typically associated with these categories. This information is designed to synthesize many of the skills presented earlier in the book.

We then present material on several international cuisines. We emphasize each cuisine's distinguishing flavours and cooking procedures; we do not attempt to provide an array of representative recipes.

Part Five concludes with a chapter on plate presentation in which we demonstrate simple yet effective techniques for making foods visually appealing.

CHAPTER 32
BREAKFAST AND BRUNCH

LEARNING OUTCOMES

After studying this chapter you will be able to:

◆ prepare eggs using a variety of cooking methods: shirred, quiches, scrambled, omelettes, frittatas, pan-fried, soft-boiled and hard-boiled, poached
◆ prepare pancakes and other griddlecakes, such as crepes and French toast
◆ prepare a variety of cereals
◆ identify a variety of breakfast meats
◆ offer your customers a variety of breakfast foods

om always said breakfast was the most important meal of the day, and she was probably right. Breakfast (from the expression "to break fast") gives you the energy to get going after a night's sleep. It should provide at least one-fourth of the calories and nutrients consumed during the day.

Breakfast is often an on-the-go, rushed experience, hence the popularity of breakfast sandwiches, jumbo muffins and take-out coffee. Brunch, on the other hand, is a leisurely experience, combining breakfast and lunch into a social occasion. Brunch menus include traditional breakfast foods along with almost anything else. Unlike breakfast, brunch is often accompanied by champagne or other alcoholic beverages and concludes with a pastry or dessert.

Food service operations must offer a variety of breakfast options to appeal to a wide range of consumers. Hotels and resorts may offer a complimentary continental-style breakfast of coffee, juice and simple rolls; a full-service à la carte dining room; a room service menu and a casual snack bar. The grand hotel Sunday and holiday brunch buffet is an institution for celebrations and special occasions.

Office, retail and commercial complexes are peppered with small shops selling coffee, muffins, bagels and sweet rolls. Coffee houses offering a variety of coffee blends and drinks, pastries, breads and quiche are also popular. Even fast-food facilities have expanded their menus and hours of operation to meet the needs of early-morning diners.

The foods served at breakfast include most of the foods served at other times during the day. A diner's perception of the proper breakfast depends on his or her cultural, ethnic, economic and geographic background as well as sleep patterns and work schedule.

Breakfast menus typically include:

◆ Coffee, tea or other hot beverages
◆ Fruits or fruit juices
◆ Eggs
◆ Breads, including sweet breads
◆ Cereals and grains
◆ Potatoes
◆ Pancakes, waffles and French toast
◆ Meats or fish
◆ Dairy products, including milk, cheese and yogurt

Although few people could sit down to a breakfast including all of these components even occasionally, most food service operations find it necessary to offer some items from each category in order to meet their customers' expectations.

This chapter discusses cooking methods used for eggs, breakfast meats, pancakes and other griddlecakes and cereals. Other foods typically served at breakfast are noted on the following pages and discussed in more detail elsewhere in this text.

BEVERAGES

Few breakfast menus would be complete without offering coffee, tea or other hot beverages. Whether it's black tea in St. Petersburg or café au lait in Paris, cinnamon-spiced chocolate in Mexico City or a cup of fresh-brewed Colombian in Vancouver, people everywhere enjoy starting their day with hot, aromatic, caffeine-laced beverages. Coffees and teas are identified and discussed in Chapter 7, Kitchen Staples.

FRUITS

Fruits are popular breakfast foods because they are light and flavourful, require little or no preparation and provide vitamins and natural sugars for energy. Citrus fruits, melons, berries and bananas are breakfast staples. Fruits, whether raw or cooked, fresh, canned, frozen or dried, can be served alone, with a topping of cream or yogurt or as a garnish for cereals, pancakes or French toast. Fresh seasonal fruits can be served at the beginning of the meal, as garnish with the main course, as a light brunch dessert or as juice. Fruits are identified and discussed in Chapter 25, Fruits.

BREADS

Breads, usually rich, sweet and loaded with fruits and nuts, are a staple of many breakfast menus. Sticky pecan buns, glazed cinnamon rolls, fruit-filled muffins, danish pastries and buttery croissants, which seem too rich later in the day, somehow seem perfect in the morning. Even a humble slice of toast rounds out a breakfast menu, especially if topped with butter and jam. Breakfast breads can be served as an accompaniment to eggs, fruits or other dishes or they can be the complete meal. Chapter 27, Quick Breads; Chapter 28, Yeast Breads; and Chapter 29, Pies, Pastries and Cookies, include several recipes for breakfast breads and pastries.

POTATOES

Potatoes are often served at breakfast and brunch, usually sautéed or pan-fried as hash browns, cottage fries or lyonnaise. Potatoes may be served as a side dish or incorporated into hash or egg casseroles. Unlike breads or fruits, which may be the entire breakfast, potatoes are usually just part of a hearty breakfast, especially one that includes meat and eggs. Potatoes are identified and discussed in Chapter 23, Potatoes, Grains and Pasta.

DAIRY PRODUCTS

Some dairy products are indispensable at breakfast: milk, cream and yogurt, for example. Other dairy products such as crème fraîche and cheese are less commonly served but just as appropriate. Like milk, yogurt and crème fraîche can be used to top cold cereals or fruit. Cheeses are commonly used in omelettes and frittatas, blintzes and danish pastries; an assortment of mild cheeses offered with crusty bread and fresh fruit is a delicious breakfast or brunch alternative. Dairy products are identified and discussed in Chapter 8, Eggs and Dairy Products.

EGGS

No other breakfast food is as popular or as versatile as the egg. Eggs can be cooked by almost any method and served with a wide array of seasonings, accompaniments and garnishes. Whatever cooking method is selected, be sure to prepare the eggs carefully: Overcooked eggs and those cooked at too high a temperature will be tough and rubbery. Eggs are described in Chapter 8, Eggs and Dairy Products.

The following cooking methods are those most often used for egg-based breakfast dishes. They include dry-heat cooking methods (baking, sautéing and pan-frying) and moist-heat cooking methods (in-shell cooking and poaching).

Dry-Heat Cooking Methods

Baking

Shirred Eggs

Baked eggs, also referred to as shirred eggs, are normally prepared in individual ramekins or baking dishes. The ramekins can be lined or partially filled with ingredients such as bread, ham, creamed spinach or artichokes. The eggs are often topped with grated cheese, fresh herbs or a sauce. When properly cooked, the egg whites should be set and the yolks should be soft and creamy. They are not often seen on modern menus although skillet meals are sometimes available.

1. Add the eggs to the ramekin on top of the ham.

2. The finished shirred eggs with ham.

Basic Procedure for Preparing Shirred Eggs

1. Coat each ramekin with melted butter. Add flavouring ingredients as desired.
2. Break one or two eggs into each ramekin. Do not break the yolks. Season with salt and pepper.
3. Bake the eggs until the white is firm, approximately 12–15 minutes. Approximately 3–5 minutes before the eggs are done, add cream or top the eggs with grated cheese, diced ham, fresh herbs or other ingredients as desired.

Applying the Basics

RECIPE 32.1

SHIRRED EGGS WITH HAM

Yield: 1 Serving

Whole butter, melted	as needed	as needed
Baked ham, sliced thin	15 g	1/2 oz.
Eggs	2	2
Salt and pepper	TT	TT
Cream, 35%, hot	15 mL	1 Tbsp.
Swiss cheese, grated	10 g	1 Tbsp.

1. Brush the interior of a 180-mL (6-fl. oz.) ramekin with melted butter. Line the ramekin with the ham.
2. Break the eggs into a cup and pour them carefully into the ramekin on top of the ham. Season with salt and pepper.
3. Bake at 160°C (325°F) until the eggs begin to set, approximately 8–10 minutes. Remove from the oven, add the cream and grated cheese. Return to the oven until the eggs are cooked and the cheese is melted. Serve immediately.

RECIPE 32.1

Approximate values per serving:

Calories	280
Total fat	10 g
Saturated fat	10 g
Cholesterol	470 mg
Sodium	300 mg
Total carbohydrates	2 g
Protein	17 g

Quiche

Quiche is a classic breakfast and brunch entree. It consists of an egg custard (eggs, cream or milk and seasonings) and fillings baked in a crust.

The filling usually includes at least one type of cheese, and can also include any number of other ingredients such as cooked, diced meats (for example, sausage, crumbled bacon, ham, fish or shellfish) or blanched vegetables (for example, mushrooms, sautéed onions, asparagus or broccoli). The flavour and texture of these ingredients should complement each other without overpowering the delicate egg custard. Quiche is a good way of using leftovers, but the ingredients should still be fresh and of good quality.

The crust may be made with whole wheat flour, cornmeal or other grains for added flavour and texture.

Basic Procedure for Preparing Quiche

1. Prepare and parbake a pie shell.
2. Prepare the garnishes and flavouring ingredients and add them to the pie shell.
3. Prepare a custard and add it to the pie shell. Ratios of eggs to milk or heavy cream vary depending on the specific recipe, but 6–8 eggs to 1 L (1 qt.) of liquid is usually sufficient to bind the custard.
4. Bake the quiche until set; allow it to cool slightly before cutting.

Applying the Basics

RECIPE 32.2

QUICHE LORRAINE

Yield: One 20-cm (8-inch) Tart

Short crust pastry (savoury)	300 g	10-1/2 oz.
Bacon, diced	100 g	3-1/2 oz.
Onion, small dice	100 g	3-1/2 oz.
Gruyère cheese, grated	300 g	10-1/2 oz.
Flour	50 g	2 oz.
Milk	175 mL	6 fl. oz.
Cream, 35%	50 mL	2 fl. oz.
Egg yolks	2	2
Egg whites, beaten to soft peak	2	2

1. Line the tart tin with the pastry.
2. Sauté the bacon and onion until the onion is translucent, 2–3 minutes, then cool.
3. Spread the cooled bacon and onion evenly in the shell.
4. Distribute the cheese over the bacon mix.
5. Mix the flour, milk, cream and egg yolks together until smooth.
6. Fold in the beaten egg whites and pour over the cheese. Distribute evenly over the entire pie to cover it completely. The egg white foam makes the top crust.
7. Bake at 175°C (350°F) for about 25 minutes or until a knife inserted about 3 cm (1 inch) from the edge comes out clean.

RECIPE 32.2

Approximate values per 1/8 tart:

Calories	354
Total fat	25 g
Saturated fat	13 g
Cholesterol	161 mg
Sodium	293 mg
Total carbohydrates	16 g
Protein	17 g

Sautéing

Scrambled Eggs

Scrambled eggs are eggs whisked with seasonings and then sautéed. They are stirred nearly constantly during cooking. The finished eggs should be light and fluffy with a tender, creamy texture. A small amount of milk or cream may be added to the eggs near the end of cooking to provide a more delicate finished product. Overcooking or cooking at too high a temperature causes the eggs to become tough and rubbery.

Scrambled eggs are often flavoured by sautéing other foods (for example, onions, mushrooms or diced ham) in the pan before adding the eggs or by adding other foods (for example, grated cheeses or herbs) to the eggs just before cooking is complete. Suggested additions include finely diced bell peppers, onions, mushrooms, zucchini or tomatoes; cottage cheese or any variety of shredded firm cheese; crumbled bacon; diced ham, turkey or beef; bits of smoked salmon, cooked shrimp or cooked sausage; and fresh herbs.

1. Stirring the scrambled eggs.

2. The properly cooked eggs.

Basic Procedure for Preparing Scrambled Eggs

1. Break the eggs into a mixing bowl. Season lightly with salt and pepper.
2. Heat a sauté pan, add clarified butter or oil and heat until the fat begins to sizzle.
3. Sauté any additional ingredients in the hot fat.
4. Pour the eggs into the pan all at once. As the eggs begin to set, stir and shake them with a wooden spoon. When they are half-cooked you may add 12 mL (1 scant Tbsp.) of milk or cream per egg and whisk everything together.
5. Sprinkle on additional ingredients such as cheese or herbs.
6. Cook just until the eggs are set, but still shiny and moist. Remove from the pan and serve immediately.

Applying the Basics

RECIPE 32.3

COUNTRY-STYLE SCRAMBLED EGGS

Yield: 1 Serving

Eggs	2	2
Cream, 35%	10 mL	2 tsp.
Salt and pepper	TT	TT
Chilli powder	pinch	pinch
Green onion, fine dice	10 g	1 Tbsp.
Clarified butter	20 g	1/2 oz.
Ham, diced	25 g	1 oz.
Cheddar cheese, grated	25 g	1 oz.

1. Combine the eggs, cream, salt and pepper and chilli powder in a mixing bowl. Whisk until well blended.
2. Sauté the onion in the butter until translucent but not brown.
3. Pour the egg mixture into the pan and cook, stirring frequently, for approximately 1 minute.
4. Add the ham to the eggs and continue cooking. Just before the eggs are fully cooked, sprinkle on the cheese.
5. Spoon the cooked egg mixture onto serving plate. Serve immediately.

RECIPE 32.3

Approximate values per serving:

Calories	463
Total fat	39 g
Saturated fat	21 g
Cholesterol	526 mg
Sodium	1050 mg
Total carbohydrates	3 g
Protein	24 g

Omelettes

Omelettes are needlessly intimidating egg creations that begin as scrambled eggs. They are usually prepared as individual servings using two or three eggs. The cooked eggs are then folded around a warm filling. Fillings may be cooked into the omelette or a plain omelette may be cut and the filling placed inside.

The filling may contain vegetables, cheeses or meats. Any filling ingredient that needs cooking should be cooked before being added to the omelette. Because the eggs cook relatively quickly, raw fillings would not be properly cooked until the eggs were overcooked. Traditionally, omelettes are formed into a cigar shape.

1. Lift the edge of the eggs to allow them to cook evenly.

Basic Procedure for Preparing Folded Omelettes

1. Fully cook any meats and blanch or otherwise cook any vegetables that will be incorporated into the omelette.
2. Heat an omelette pan over moderately high heat and add clarified butter.
3. Whisk the eggs together in a small bowl. Season with salt and pepper if desired.
4. Pour the eggs into the pan and stir until they begin to set, approximately 10 seconds.
5. Pull cooked egg from the sides of the pan towards the centre, allowing raw egg to run underneath. Continue doing so for 20–30 seconds.
6. Spoon any fillings on top of the eggs or add any other garnishes.
7. When cooked as desired, flip one side of the omelette towards the centre with a spatula or a shake of the pan. Slide the omelette onto the serving plate so that it lands folded in thirds with the seam underneath.
8. Spoon any sauce or additional filling on top, garnish as desired and serve immediately.
9. The inside of the omelette should be very soft; some would call it "undercooked."

2. Add the filling to the eggs.

3. Fold the eggs.

Applying the Basics

RECIPE 32.4

SHRIMP AND AVOCADO OMELETTE

Yield: 1 Serving

Shrimp, peeled, deveined and cut into pieces	50 g	2 oz.
Green onion, sliced	10 g	1 Tbsp.
Clarified butter	30 g	1 oz.
Eggs	3	3
Salt and pepper	TT	TT
Avocado, peeled and diced	1/4	1/4
Cilantro, chopped	5 g	2 tsp.

1. Sauté the shrimp and onion in half of the butter for 1 minute. Remove from the heat and set aside.
2. Heat an omelette pan and add the remaining butter.
3. Whisk the eggs together in a small bowl, season with salt and pepper and pour into the omelette pan.
4. Stir the eggs as they cook. Stop when they begin to set. Lift the edges as the omelette cooks to allow the raw eggs to run underneath.
5. When the eggs are nearly set, add the shrimp filling, avocado and cilantro. Fold one-third of the eggs over and roll the omelette onto a plate.

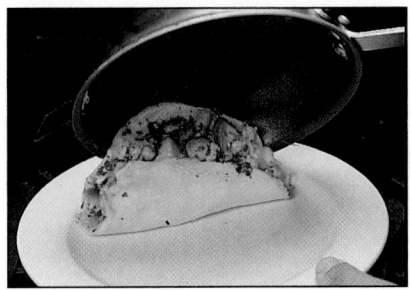

4. Roll the omelette onto the plate. Ensure the seam is on the bottom.

RECIPE 32.4

Approximate values per serving:

Calories	576
Total fat	48 g
Saturated fat	21 g
Cholesterol	788 mg
Sodium	753 mg
Total carbohydrates	7 g
Protein	30 g

Alternate filling method.

1. Slice the shaped omelette.

2. Spoon in the filling.

RECIPE 32.5

Approximate values per serving:

Calories	1045
Total fat	71 g
Saturated fat	39 g
Cholesterol	764 mg
Sodium	646 mg
Total carbohydrates	12 g
Protein	89 g

Frittatas

Frittatas are essentially open-faced omelettes of Spanish-Italian heritage. They may be cooked in small pans as individual portions or in large pans, then cut into wedges for service. A relatively large amount of hearty ingredients are mixed directly into the eggs. The eggs are first cooked on the stove top, then the pan is transferred to an oven or placed under a salamander or broiler to finish cooking.

Basic Procedure for Preparing Frittatas

1. Fully cook any meats and blanch or otherwise prepare any vegetables that will be incorporated into the frittata.

2. Heat a sauté pan and add clarified butter.

3. Whisk the eggs, flavourings and any other ingredients together; pour into the pan.

4. Stir gently until the eggs start to set. Gently lift the cooked eggs at the edge of the frittata so that the raw eggs can run underneath. Continue cooking until the eggs are almost set.

5. Place the pan in a hot oven or underneath a salamander or broiler to finish cooking and lightly brown the top.

6. Slide the finished frittata out of the pan onto a serving platter.

Applying the Basics

RECIPE 32.5

TEX-MEX FRITTATA

Yield: 1 Serving

Chicken breast, 120 g (4 oz.), boneless, skinless	1	1
Garlic, chopped	5 g	1 tsp.
Cumin	TT	TT
Salt and pepper	TT	TT
Mushrooms, sliced	50 g	2 oz.
Unsalted butter	50 g	3 Tbsp.
Jalapeño, seeded, minced	3 g	1 tsp.
Red bell pepper, roasted, seeded, peeled, julienned	60 g	2 oz.
Green onions, sliced	30 g	1 oz.
Cilantro	5 g	2 tsp.
Eggs, beaten	2	2
Monterey Jack or cheddar cheese	50 g	2 oz.

1. Rub the chicken breast with the garlic, cumin, salt and pepper. Grill or broil the chicken until done. Allow it to rest briefly, then cut into strips.

2. In a well-seasoned 23-cm (9-inch) sauté pan, sauté the mushrooms in the butter until tender. Add the jalapeño and sauté for 30 seconds. Add the chicken, roasted pepper, green onions and cilantro and sauté until hot.

3. Add the eggs and season with salt and pepper. Cook the mixture, stirring and lifting the eggs to help them cook evenly, until they begin to set.

4. Sprinkle the cheese over the eggs and place under a salamander or broiler to melt the cheese and finish cooking the eggs. Slide the frittata onto a plate or cut into wedges for smaller portions.

Pan-Frying

Pan-fried eggs are commonly referred to as sunny-side-up or over-easy, over-medium or over-hard. These are visibly different products produced with proper timing and technique. Very fresh eggs are best for pan-frying as the yolk holds its shape better and the white spreads less.

Sunny-side-up eggs are not turned during cooking; their yellow yolks remain visible. They should be cooked over medium-low heat long enough to firm the whites and partially firm the yolks: approximately 4 minutes if cooked on a 120°C (250°F) cooking surface.

For "over" eggs, the egg is partially cooked on one side, then gently flipped and cooked on the other side until done. The egg white should be firm and its edges should not be brown. The yolk should never be broken regardless of the degree of doneness. Not only is a broken yolk unattractive, the spilled yolk will coagulate on contact with the hot pan, making it difficult to serve.

For over-easy eggs, the yolk should remain very runny; on a 120°C (250°F) cooking surface, the egg should cook for about 3 minutes on the first side and 2 minutes on the other. Eggs fried over-medium should be cooked slightly longer, until the yolk is partially set. For over-hard eggs, the yolk should be completely cooked.

Most establishments prepare this style of egg on a griddle.

Over-Easy Eggs

1. Pouring the eggs into the sauté pan.

2. Flipping the eggs.

3. Sliding the eggs onto a plate for service.

Basic Procedure for Preparing Pan-Fried Eggs

1. Select a sauté pan just large enough to accommodate the number of eggs being cooked. (A 20-cm-diameter [8-inch] pan is appropriate for up to three eggs.)
2. Add a small amount of clarified butter and heat until the fat just begins to sizzle.
3. Carefully break the eggs into the pan.
4. Continue cooking over medium-low heat until the eggs reach the appropriate degree of firmness. Sunny-side-up eggs are not flipped during cooking; "over" eggs are flipped once during cooking.
5. When done, gently flip the "over" eggs once again so that the first side is up, then gently slide the cooked eggs out of the pan onto the serving plate. Use a lifter to move the eggs. Blot the lifter on a clean towel before placing the eggs on a plate. Serve immediately.

Basted eggs are a variation of sunny-side-up eggs. Basted eggs are cooked over low heat with the hot butter from the pan spooned over them as they cook. Another version of basted eggs is made by adding 5–10 mL (1–2 tsp.) of water to the sauté pan and then covering the pan. The steam cooks the top of the eggs.

Moist-Heat Cooking Methods

In-Shell Cooking (Simmering)

The difference between **soft-boiled eggs** (also called soft-cooked) and **hard-boiled eggs** (also called hard-cooked) is time. Both styles refer to eggs cooked in their shell in hot water. Despite the word "boiled" in their names, eggs cooked in the shell should never be boiled. Boiling toughens eggs and causes discolouration. Instead, eggs should be simmered. Soft-boiled eggs are usually simmered for 3–5 minutes; hard-boiled eggs may be simmered for as long as 12–15 minutes depending on customer preference and the altitude where you are.

Sometimes it is difficult to remove the shell from very fresh eggs. Eggs that are a few days old are better for cooking in the shell and peeling.

Basic Procedure for Preparing Soft-Boiled Eggs

1. Fill a saucepan or stockpot with sufficient water to cover the eggs. Bring the water to a simmer. Add salt.
2. Carefully lower each egg into the simmering water. Simmer uncovered for 3–5 minutes, depending on the firmness desired and the altitude.
3. Lift each egg out of the water with a slotted spoon or spider. Crack the large end of the shell carefully and serve immediately.

Basic Procedure for Preparing Hard-Boiled Eggs

1. Follow steps 1 and 2 for soft-boiled eggs, simmering the eggs for 12–15 minutes depending on the altitude and the size of the eggs.
2. Lift each egg out of the water with a slotted spoon or spider and place in an ice bath.
3. When the eggs are cool enough to handle, peel them and use as desired or cover and refrigerate for up to 5 days.

Poaching

Eggs that are to be poached should always be very fresh. They should also be kept very cold until used. Cold egg whites stay together better when dropped into hot water. Poached eggs should be soft and moist; the whites should be firm enough to encase the yolk completely, but the yolk should still be runny.

Some chefs add salt to the poaching water for flavour; others feel the salt causes the egg whites to separate. To help the egg whites cling together, add 30 mL (2 Tbsp.) of white vinegar per 1 L (1 qt.) of water.

Basic Procedure for Preparing Poached Eggs

1. Fill a saucepan or stockpot with at least 7.5 cm (3 inches) of water. Add salt and vinegar if desired. Bring the water to a simmer and hold at a temperature of approximately 90°C (200°F).
2. One at a time, crack the eggs into a small ramekin or cup. If a piece of shell falls into the egg, it can be removed; if the yolk breaks, the egg can be set aside for some other use.
3. Gently slide each egg into the simmering water and cook for 3–5 minutes.
4. Lift the poached egg out of the water with a slotted spoon. Trim any ragged edges with a paring knife. Serve immediately.

For quantity service, eggs can be poached in advance and held for up to one day. To do so, cook the eggs as described above. As each egg is removed from the hot water, set it in a hotel pan filled with ice water. This stops the cooking process. The eggs can be stored in the ice water until needed. For banquet-style service, all of the eggs can be reheated at once by placing the entire pan on the stove top. Or, the eggs can be reheated one or two at a time by placing them in a pan of barely simmering water until they are hot.

Applying the Basics

POACHED EGGS

Yield: 1 Serving

Water	1 L	1 qt.
Salt	5 g	1 tsp.
Vinegar	30 mL	2 Tbsp.
Eggs	2	2

1. Bring the water to a simmer; add the salt and vinegar.

2. Crack 1 egg into a cup and carefully add it to the water. Repeat with the other egg.

3. Cook the eggs to the desired doneness, approximately 3–5 minutes. Remove them from the water with a slotted spoon and serve as desired or carefully lower them into ice water and refrigerate for later use.

RECIPE 32.6

Approximate values per serving:

Calories	140
Total fat	10 g
Saturated fat	3 g
Cholesterol	425 mg
Sodium	280 mg
Total carbohydrates	1 g
Protein	12 g

1. Add eggs to a pot of simmering water.

2. Lower the eggs into ice water to cool them for future use.

BREAKFAST MEATS

At other meals, meat is typically the principal food, but at breakfast it is usually an accompaniment. Breakfast meats tend to be spicy or highly flavoured. A hearty breakfast menu may include a small beef steak (usually sirloin and often pan-fried) or pork chop. Corned beef, roast beef or roast turkey can be diced or shredded, then sautéed with potatoes and other ingredients for a breakfast hash. Fish, particularly smoked products, are also served at breakfast.

But the most popular breakfast meats are bacon, ham and sausages. They are all discussed in Chapter 20, Charcuterie. Bacon can be cooked on a flat griddle, in a heavy skillet or baked on a sheet pan. Regardless of the method used, the cooked bacon should be drained on absorbent paper towels to remove excess fat. Canadian back bacon is very lean and requires little cooking, although slices are usually sautéed briefly before serving. The round slices may be served like ham and are essential for eggs Benedict. A ham steak is simply a thick slice ideal for breakfast. Fully cooked ham needs only to be heated briefly on a griddle or in a sauté pan before service. The most popular breakfast sausages are made from uncured, uncooked meats. They can be mild to spicy, slightly sweet or strongly seasoned with sage. Recipes for country-style and other sausages are included in Chapter 20. Breakfast sausage is available in bulk, links or preformed patties. Link sausage is often steamed, then browned by sautéing at service time. It should be drained on absorbent paper towels to remove excess fat before service.

GRIDDLECAKES AND FRENCH TOAST

Griddlecakes

Pancakes and **waffles** are types of griddlecakes or griddle breads. They are usually leavened with baking soda or baking powder and are quickly cooked on a very hot griddle or waffle iron with very little fat. Griddlecakes should be more than just an excuse for eating butter and maple syrup, however. They should have a rich flavour and a light, tender, moist interior.

Pancake and waffle batters may be flavoured with tangy buckwheat flour, flaxseed, fruits, whole grains or nuts. Both pancakes and waffles are usually served with plain or flavoured butter and fruit compote or syrup.

Waffles must be cooked in a special waffle iron. This gives the cakes a distinctive gridlike pattern and crisp texture. Electric waffle irons are available with square, round and even heart-shaped moulds. The grids should be seasoned well, then never washed. (Follow the manufacturer's directions for seasoning.) Crispy Belgian waffles are made in a waffle iron with extra deep grids. They are served for breakfast or as a dessert, topped with fresh fruit, whipped cream or ice cream.

Basic Procedure for Preparing Pancakes

1. Prepare the batter.
2. Heat a flat griddle or thick big-bottomed flat pan over moderately high heat. Lightly coat with vegetable oil.
3. Portion the pancake batter onto the hot griddle using a portion scoop, ladle or adjustable batter dispenser. Pour the portioned batter in one spot; it should spread into an even circle. Pour the batter so that no two pancakes will touch after the batter spreads.
4. Cook until bubbles appear on the surface and the bottom of the cake is set and golden-brown. Flip the pancake using an offset spatula.
5. Cook the pancake until the second side is golden-brown. Avoid flipping the pancake more than once as this causes it to deflate.

Applying the Basics

RECIPE 32.7

BUTTERMILK PANCAKES

Yield: 24 Pancakes

All-purpose flour	450 g	1 lb.
Granulated sugar	60 g	4 Tbsp.
Baking powder	15 g	4 tsp.
Baking soda	8 g	2 tsp.
Salt	5 g	1-1/2 tsp.
Buttermilk	1 L	32 fl. oz.
Unsalted butter, melted	125 g	4 oz.
Eggs, beaten	4	4

RECIPE 32.7

Approximate values per pancake:

Calories	136
Total fat	5 g
Saturated fat	3 g
Cholesterol	47 mg
Sodium	359 mg
Total carbohydrates	18 g
Protein	4 g

1. Sift the flour, sugar, baking powder, baking soda and salt together.
2. Combine the liquid ingredients and add them to the dry ingredients. Mix just until the ingredients are combined.
3. If the griddle is not well seasoned, coat it lightly with vegetable oil. Once its temperature reaches 190°C (375°F), drop the batter onto it in 60-g (2-oz.) portions using a ladle, portion scoop or batter portioner. If the batter is too thick and does not spread enough, thin with a little water.
4. When bubbles appear on the pancake's surface and the bottom is browned, flip the pancake to finish cooking.

Crepes and Blintzes

Crepes are thin, delicate, unleavened pancakes. They are made with a very liquid batter cooked in a small, very hot sauté pan. Crepe batter can be flavoured with buckwheat flour, cornmeal or other grains. Crepes are not eaten as is, but are usually filled and garnished with sautéed fruits, scrambled eggs, cheese or vegetables. Crepes can be prepared in advance, then filled and reheated in the oven.

Blintzes are crepes that are cooked on only one side, then filled with cheese, browned in butter and served with sour cream, fruit compote or preserves. A recipe for cheese blintzes is provided at the end of this chapter.

1. Coat the bottom of the pan evenly with the batter.

Basic Procedure for Preparing Crepes

1. Prepare the batter.
2. Heat a well-seasoned crepe pan over moderately high heat. Add a small amount of clarified butter.
3. Ladle a small amount of batter into the pan. Tilt the pan so that the batter spreads to coat the bottom evenly.
4. Cook until the crepe is set and the bottom begins to brown, approximately 1 minute. Flip the crepe over with a quick flick of the wrist or by lifting it carefully with a spatula.
5. Cook for an additional 30 seconds. Slide the finished crepe from the pan. Crepes can be stacked between layers of parchment paper for storage.

2. Flip the crepe. Notice the proper light brown colour.

Applying the Basics

RECIPE 32.8

SWEET CREPES

Yield: Thirty 15-cm (6-inch) Crepes

Whole eggs	6	6
Egg yolks	6	6
Water	350 mL	12 fl. oz.
Milk	500 mL	18 fl. oz.
Granulated sugar	175 g	6 oz.
Salt	5 g	1 tsp.
Flour	400 g	14 oz.
Unsalted butter, melted	150 g	5 oz.
Clarified butter	as needed	as needed

Continued

RECIPE 32.8

Approximate values per crepe:

Calories	144
Total fat	7 g
Saturated fat	3.5 g
Cholesterol	99.5 mg
Sodium	88 mg
Total carbohydrates	17 g
Protein	4 g

1. Whisk together all liquid ingredients except the melted butter. Add the sugar, salt and flour; whisk together. Stir in the melted butter. Cover and set aside to rest for at least 1 hour before cooking.
2. Heat a small sauté or crepe pan; brush lightly with clarified butter. Pour in 30–45 mL (1–1-1/2 fl. oz.) of batter; swirl to coat the bottom of the pan evenly.
3. Cook the crepe until set and light brown, approximately 30 seconds. Flip it over and cook a few seconds longer. Remove from the pan.
4. Cooked crepes may be used immediately or covered and held briefly in a warm oven. Crepes can also be wrapped well in plastic wrap and refrigerated for 2–3 days or frozen for several weeks.

French Toast

Like a pancake, French toast is sautéed on a griddle and served with butter and syrup. Unlike a pancake, French toast begins with slices of day-old bread. (It is known in France as *pain perdu*, meaning "lost bread," probably because it provided a way to use bread that would otherwise have been discarded.) French bread, sourdough, raisin bread, challah, whole wheat, even stale croissants can be used. The bread is dipped into a batter of eggs, sugar, milk or cream and flavourings, then sautéed in butter. French toast should be served very hot. It may be topped with powdered sugar, fresh fruit, fruit compote or maple syrup as desired.

Basic Procedure for Preparing French Toast

1. Prepare the batter. Store the batter in a hotel pan that is large enough to accommodate the bread slices. Keep the batter refrigerated until ready to use.
2. Slice the bread as desired. Dip each slice of bread into the batter. Allow the bread to absorb the batter through to the centre. Turn the bread so that both sides are coated.
3. Heat a griddle or sauté pan and add clarified butter.
4. Place the batter-dipped bread onto the hot griddle. Cook until the bottom is set and golden-brown. The cooking time will be determined by the thickness of the bread.
5. Flip the bread with an offset spatula and cook the toast on the other side. The toast is done when it is not runny in the middle; however, it should not be dry. Remove and serve immediately.

Applying the Basics

RECIPE 32.9

CINNAMON FRENCH TOAST

Yield: 6 Servings

Eggs, beaten	10	10
Cream, 35%	125 mL	4 fl. oz.
Salt	TT	TT
Cinnamon, ground	TT	TT
Thick-sliced bread such as sourdough, cinnamon, banana or brioche	12 slices	12 slices
Unsalted butter	as needed	as needed
Powdered sugar	as needed	as needed

1. Whisk together the eggs, cream, salt and cinnamon.
2. Place the egg mixture in a shallow pan. Place the slices of bread in the egg mixture and let soak for 2–3 minutes, turning them over after the first minute or so.
3. Cook the slices of French toast in a lightly buttered, preheated sauté pan or griddle set at 180°C (350°F) until well browned. Turn the slices and cook on the second side until done.
4. Cut each slice of bread into two triangles.
5. Arrange four triangles on each plate and dust with powdered sugar.

RECIPE 32.9

Approximate values per serving:

Calories	320
Total fat	17 g
Saturated fat	7 g
Cholesterol	380 mg
Sodium	420 mg
Total carbohydrates	28 g
Protein	15 g

CEREALS AND GRAINS

Oats, rice, corn and wheat are perhaps the most widely eaten breakfast foods. Processed breakfast cereals are ready-to-eat products made from these grains. Most consumers now think of breakfast cereal as a cold food, but not so long ago only hot grains were breakfast staples. Oatmeal served as a hot porridge is still popular, especially with toppings such as cream, brown sugar, fresh or dried fruit or fruit preserves. Oats and oatmeal, grits and other grains are discussed in Chapter 23, Potatoes, Grains and Pasta.

Ready-to-eat (cold) cereal is usually topped with milk or light cream and sugar. Fresh or dried fruits may be added. Many products are enriched or fortified with vitamins and minerals to compensate for the nutrients lost during processing. Creative cooks can avoid overly sweet, artificially flavoured commercial products by making their own ready-to-eat breakfast cereals such as granola, a toasted blend of whole grains, nuts and dried fruits. The results are less expensive, more nutritious and far more interesting.

◆◆◆

FROM HEALTH FOOD TO SUGAR SNACK

The century-old, multibillion-dollar-a-year North American breakfast cereal industry, unlike any other in the world, is rooted in health foods. During the 1890s, Dr. John Harvey Kellogg directed a sanitarium in Battle Creek, Michigan. Among the healthful foods prescribed for his patients was his special mixture of whole grains called "granula." John, along with his brother Will, next created and began marketing wheat flakes as a nutritious breakfast food. They were not an immediate success, however; people found a cold breakfast unappealing. Undeterred, Will continued toying with cold cereals, eventually creating flakes made from toasted corn and malt. Thanks to a massive advertising campaign, the American public finally embraced corn flakes and a financial empire was born.

Charles W. Post was a patient of Dr. Kellogg's Battle Creek Sanitarium in 1891. He adopted the principles of healthful eating espoused by the Kellogg brothers and soon opened his own spa, complete with a factory producing his "Post Toasties" and grape nuts. He promoted them as a cure for appendicitis, consumption and malaria.

Soon Battle Creek became a boomtown, home to more than 40 breakfast cereal companies. Unfortunately for the consumer, not all manufacturers—then and now—were as concerned about health as John, Will and C.W. The addition of sugar, sometimes totalling more than half the cereal's weight, makes some of today's breakfast products more sugary than candy bars. Even some of the granola cereals touted as a healthier alternative to other breakfast cereals and snacks contain 20% or more sugar. But at least they no longer claim to cure malaria.

Applying the Basics

CRUNCHY GRANOLA

Yield: 3 L (12 cups)

Brown sugar	250 g	8 oz.
Water, hot	125 mL	4 fl. oz.
Canola oil	175 mL	6 fl. oz.
Old-fashioned oats	500 g	18 oz.
Wheat germ	125 g	4 oz.
Coconut, shredded	75 g	2-1/2 oz.
Salt (optional)	15 g	1 Tbsp.
Whole wheat flour	60 g	2 oz.
Amaranth flour	60 g	2 oz.
Unbleached all-purpose flour	60 g	2 oz.
Yellow cornmeal	60 g	2 oz.
Pecans, chopped	125 g	4 oz.

1. Dissolve the brown sugar in the hot water. Add the oil.

2. Combine the dry ingredients in a large bowl. Mix thoroughly by hand.

3. Add the brown-sugar-and-oil mixture to the dry ingredients; toss to combine.

4. Spread out the granola in a thin layer on a sheet pan. Bake at 90°C (200°F) until crisp, approximately 1.5–2 hours. Toss lightly with a metal spatula every 30 minutes.

5. Let the baked granola cool completely at room temperature, then store in an airtight container. Chopped dried fruits, additional nuts or fresh fruits can be added at service time.

RECIPE 32.10

Approximate values per 30 g (1 oz.) serving:

Calories	118
Total fat	7 g
Saturated fat	1 g
Cholesterol	15 mg
Sodium	120 mg
Total carbohydrates	15 g
Protein	3 g

TABLE 32.1   NUTRITIONAL VALUES OF SELECTED BREAKFAST FOODS

Per Portion as Noted	Kcal	Protein (g)	Carbohydrates (g)	Total Fat (g)	Saturated Fat (g)	Cholesterol (mg)	Sodium (mg)
Coffee, brewed, 180 mL (6 fl. oz.)	4	0.1	0.8	0	0	0	4
Cream, light, 30 mL (1 fl. oz.)	55	0.8	1	5.5	3.4	19	11
Sugar, granulated, 15 mL (1 Tbsp.)	46	0	11.9	0	0	0	tr
Orange juice, fresh, 180 mL (6 fl. oz.)	83	1.3	19.3	0.4	<0.1	0	2
Egg, hard-cooked, 1 large	77	6.3	0.6	5.3	1.6	213	62
Egg, pan-fried in margarine, 1 large	91	6.2	0.6	6.9	1.9	211	162
Bacon, cooked, 3 slices (20 slices per 500 g [1 lb.])	109	5.8	0.1	9.4	3.3	16	303
English muffin, 1	130	4.3	25.4	1.3	na	0	206
Corn flakes, 28 g (1 oz.)	100	2	24	0	0	0	250
Milk, 240 mL (8 fl. oz.)	88	7.2	11.2	1.6	0.8	8	240

The Corrine T. Netzer Encyclopedia of Food Values 1992
na = not available   tr = trace

Nutrition

Most nutritionists agree that you and your customers should start the day with a nutritious breakfast. Depending upon what is eaten, a breakfast can supply a good percentage of the day's proteins, carbohydrates, fats, vitamins and minerals. (See Table 32.1.)

Conclusion

Breakfast is an important meal for consumers and food service operations alike. Breakfast menus may offer a variety of items, including fruits, cereals, eggs, pancakes and cured meats, or they can be devoted to one or two specialty items such as coffee and cinnamon rolls. Whatever is served should be prepared and served with care.

Questions for Discussion

1. Explain the differences between a typical breakfast and a typical brunch. Create a sample menu for each of these meals.
2. Explain the difference between an omelette and a frittata.
3. Describe four different types of fried eggs and explain how each is prepared.
4. What is the difference between a soft-boiled egg and a hard-boiled egg? Why are these eggs simmered instead of boiled?
5. List three types of griddlecakes and explain how they are prepared.
6. What problems might be encountered when preparing French toast with very thick slices of bread? How can you avoid these problems?
7. Should meats be fully cooked before being incorporated into egg dishes such as omelettes and quiches? Explain your answer.

Additional Breakfast Recipes

RECIPE 32.11

Campton Place Bagels with Smoked Trout Cream Cheese

Note: *This dish appears in the Chapter Opening photograph.*

CAMPTON PLACE RESTAURANT, KEMPINSKI HOTELS, San Francisco, CA
Chef Jan Birnbaum

Yield: 24 Bagels; 825 g (33 oz.) Spread

Dry yeast	10 g	1 Tbsp.
Water (35°C/95°F)	250 mL	8 fl. oz.
Granulated sugar	50 g	3 Tbsp.
Malt	50 mL	3 Tbsp.

Continued

Flour	500 g	1 lb.
Salt	15 g	1 Tbsp.
Vegetable oil	30 mL	2 Tbsp.
Egg wash	as needed	as needed
Cream cheese	525 g	20 oz.
Crème fraîche or sour cream	150 mL	8 fl. oz.
Pepper, cracked	1 g	1/2 tsp.
Chives, cut	25 g	4 Tbsp.
Smoked trout	500 g	20 oz.
Eggs, poached or basted	24	24

1. To make the bagels, dissolve the yeast in the water.
2. Thoroughly combine the sugar, malt, flour and salt.
3. Add the oil to the yeast solution, then add the liquid ingredients to the dry ingredients. Mix thoroughly and knead the dough until hands and board come clean. Cover with a moist towel and allow to proof in a warm place (21–29°C/70–85°F) until doubled.
4. Punch down and cut into 30-g (1-oz.) pieces. Roll into doughnut shapes. Proof the bagels for 15 minutes.
5. Blanch the bagels in simmering water for 4 minutes, turning once. Remove and place on a sheet pan lined with parchment paper.
6. Brush with egg wash and bake at 180°C (350°F) until golden, approximately 20 minutes.
7. To make the cream cheese with smoked trout, beat the cream cheese in an electric mixer with the paddle attachment for approximately 5 minutes to incorporate air.
8. Add the crème fraîche and whisk for 2–3 minutes.
9. Add the pepper and chives and mix until incorporated, approximately 30 seconds.
10. Fold in 125 g (4 oz.) of small diced trout by hand.
11. To assemble, spread 50 g (2 oz.) of smoked trout spread on one half of each bagel. Top with 2–3 thin slices of smoked trout.
12. Place a poached or basted egg on the other half of the bagel.
13. Garnish the plate with fresh tomatoes and baby greens. Serve immediately.

RECIPE 32.11

Approximate values per serving:

Calories	352
Total fat	9 g
Saturated fat	5 g
Cholesterol	33 mg
Sodium	522 mg
Total carbohydrates	55 g
Protein	11 g

◆◆◆

RECIPE 32.12

SPICED CIDER

Yield: 2 L (64 fl. oz.)

Apple cider	1 L	32 fl. oz.
Orange or cranberry juice	1 L	32 fl. oz.
Brown sugar	50 g	2 oz.
Cinnamon sticks	2	2
Cloves, whole	5	5
Allspice, whole	5	5

1. Combine all ingredients in a nonreactive saucepan over medium-low heat.
2. Bring the mixture to a simmer, cover and remove from the heat. Let steep for 10–15 minutes. Strain and serve garnished with sliced lemon or a cinnamon stick.

RECIPE 32.12

Approximate values per 175 mL serving:

Calories	110
Total fat	0 g
Saturated fat	0 g
Cholesterol	0 mg
Sodium	3.5 mg
Total carbohydrates	29 g
Protein	1 g

✦✦✦

RECIPE 32.13

ARTICHOKE FRITTATA

THE INN OF THE WHITE SALMON, WHITE SALMON, WA

Yield: One 22-cm-round (9-inch) Frittata

Artichoke hearts, cooked, fresh or canned	250 g	8 oz.
Unsalted butter	25 g	1 oz.
Parmesan cheese, grated	50 g	2 oz.
Eggs	10	10
Cream, 18%	175 mL	6 fl. oz.
Monterey Jack cheese, grated	125 g	4 oz.

1. Quarter the artichoke hearts.

2. Melt the butter in a sauté pan. Add the artichokes and sauté until heated through but not browned.

3. Distribute the artichokes in an even layer on the bottom of a 22-cm-round (9-inch) nonstick pan. Sprinkle with half of the Parmesan cheese.

4. In a small mixing bowl, whisk the eggs together with the cream. Pour over the artichokes.

5. Sprinkle the Monterey Jack cheese over the entire pan.

6. Bake for 30 minutes at 180°C (350°F). Remove from the oven and sprinkle the remaining Parmesan cheese over the frittata. Return to the oven until the cheese is melted and light brown, approximately 5 minutes.

✦✦✦

RECIPE 32.14

CAJUN CRABCAKE WITH TOMATO CORIANDER SAUCE

CAFÉ HENRY BURGER, HULL, QC
Chef/Owner Robert Bourassa

Yield: 6–8 Portions

Snow crab meat	500 g	1 lb.
Cooked cod, flaked	250 g	8 oz.
Duchesse potatoes	250 g	8 oz.
Eggs, beaten	2	2
Green onions, chopped	3	3
Garlic, chopped	10 g	2 cloves
Asian chile sauce	30 mL	2 Tbsp.
Salt	TT	TT
Cream, 35%	125 mL	4 fl. oz.
Bread crumbs	as needed	as needed
Olive oil	as needed	as needed
Tomato Coulis (recipe follows)		

1. Thaw crab meat and squeeze out excess juice.

2. Combine crab with cod, potato, eggs, green onion, garlic, chile sauce, salt and cream.

3. Form into patties, roll in bread crumbs and pan-fry in olive oil. Serve with Tomato Coulis.

Continued

RECIPE 32.13

Approximate values per 1/4 pie:

Calories	500
Total fat	36 g
Saturated fat	18 g
Cholesterol	600 mg
Sodium	640 mg
Total carbohydrates	10 g
Protein	32 g

Robert Bourassa

Born and raised in Montreal, Robert began working in the food industry at the age of 16, as an apprentice charcutier for his family's business, La Belle Fermière. He is a graduate of the Institut du Tourisme et de l'Hôtellerie du Québec and also holds a Bachelor of Business Administration degree from Loyola University. Having gained extensive experience in Canada and abroad, in 1982 Robert fulfilled a life-long ambition to own his own restaurant and purchased Café Henry Burger, which celebrates its 80th anniversary in 2002.

RECIPE 32.14

Approximate values per serving:

Calories	328
Total fat	13 g
Saturated fat	6 g
Cholesterol	178 mg
Sodium	1084 mg
Total carbohydrates	16 g
Protein	34 g

TOMATO COULIS

Fresh tomatoes	350 g	12 oz.
Cilantro, chopped	75 g	1/2 cup
Green onions, chopped	3	3
Salt and pepper	TT	TT

1. Peel and seed tomatoes.
2. Place all ingredients in blender and purée until smooth.

Tomato Coulis
—*Approximate values per serving:*

Calories	17
Total fat	0 g
Saturated fat	0 g
Cholesterol	0 mg
Sodium	243 mg
Total carbohydrates	4 g
Protein	1 g

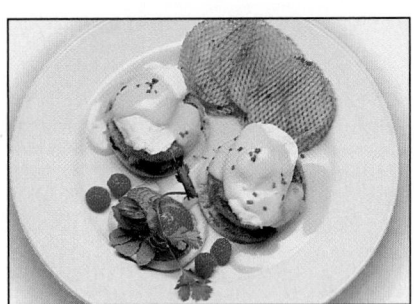

Crabcake Eggs Benedict

RECIPE 32.15

Eggs Benedict

Yield: 1 Serving

English muffin, split	1	1
Canadian back bacon slices, 5 mm (1/4 inch) thick	2	2
Eggs, poached	2	2
Hollandaise sauce (Recipe 10.14)	100 mL	3 fl. oz.
Truffle slices or black olive halves	2	2

1. Toast the English muffin.
2. Sauté or griddle the bacon slices until hot.
3. Remove eggs from poaching liquid. Drain well and dress.
4. Place the muffins on a plate and top with the bacon slices. Place an egg on each slice of bacon and cover with the hollandaise sauce. Gratinée until golden.
5. Garnish each egg with a truffle slice or black olive half and serve.

VARIATIONS: *Poached Eggs Sardou*—poached eggs and creamed spinach on an artichoke bottom with hollandaise sauce.

Poached Eggs Princess Style—poached eggs on an English muffin with asparagus tips and hollandaise sauce.

Try "Bennys" with smoked salmon slices or crab cakes.

RECIPE 32.15

Approximate values per serving:

Calories	466
Total fat	27 g
Saturated fat	10.5 g
Cholesterol	462 mg
Sodium	1596 mg
Total carbohydrates	33 g
Protein	23 g

RECIPE 32.16

Apple Pancakes

Yield: 24 Pancakes

Lemon juice	30 mL	1 fl. oz.
Apples, peeled, cored and chopped fine	3	3
All-purpose flour	150 g	5 oz.
Salt	2 g	1/2 tsp.
Granulated sugar	15 g	1 Tbsp.
Eggs	4	4
Milk	350 mL	12 fl. oz.
Butter, melted	60 mL	2 fl. oz.
Powdered sugar	as needed	as needed
Cinnamon, ground	as needed	as needed

1. Sprinkle the lemon juice over the apples to prevent browning, then set aside.
2. Sift the flour, salt and sugar into a bowl. Beat the eggs with the milk.

RECIPE 32.16

Approximate values per pancake:

Calories	65
Total fat	3 g
Saturated fat	1 g
Cholesterol	41 mg
Sodium	43 mg
Total carbohydrates	8 g
Protein	2 g

3. Stir the egg mixture into the flour mixture, blending well. Fold in the apples.

4. Heat the butter in a sauté pan over medium-high heat. Spoon the batter into the pan, in 60-g (2-oz.) portions. Cook the pancakes, turning once, until golden-brown on both sides. Dust with powdered sugar and cinnamon and serve immediately.

◆◆◆

RECIPE 32.17

YOGURT PANCAKES

Yield: 10–12 Pancakes

Eggs, large	4	4
Plain yogurt	250 mL	8 fl. oz.
Water	50 mL	2 fl. oz.
Rice flour	175 g	3/4 cup
Potato starch flour	15 g	1-1/2 Tbsp.
Baking soda	3 g	3/4 tsp.
Salt	2 g	1/2 tsp.

1. Beat eggs until light and lemon coloured.

2. Blend in yogurt and water.

3. Sift dry ingredients together and add to liquid ingredients. Beat until smooth.

4. Cook 50–60 mL (1-3/4–2 fl. oz.) portions of batter on a lightly greased griddle. Turn when puffy, bubbly and browned on one side. Brown other side.

NOTE: This recipe meets the needs of both celiac sprue and diabetic diets. The pancakes are wonderful with fruit compote and do not taste like a modified diet product. Use for breakfast or as a dessert.

RECIPE 32.17

Approximate values per pancake:

Calories	101
Total fat	2 g
Saturated fat	0.5 g
Cholesterol	45 mg
Sodium	191 mg
Total carbohydrates	17 g
Protein	4 g

◆◆◆

RECIPE 32.18

CHEESE BLINTZES

Yield: 16 Blintzes

Eggs	3	3
Milk	250 mL	8 fl. oz.
Vegetable oil	30 mL	1 fl. oz.
Salt	2 g	1/2 tsp.
Flour	125 g	4 oz.
Clarified butter	as needed	as needed
Ricotta cheese	350 g	12 oz.
Egg yolk	1	1
Salt	1 g	1/4 tsp.
Lemon juice	5 mL	1 tsp.
Vanilla extract	5 mL	1 tsp.
Butter	60 g	2 oz.

1. To make the batter, whisk together the eggs, milk and oil. Add the salt. Stir in the flour and mix until smooth. Allow the batter to rest for 30 minutes.

2. Heat a crepe pan and add a small amount of clarified butter.

RECIPE 32.18

Approximate values per serving:

Calories	110
Total fat	7 g
Saturated fat	3.5 g
Cholesterol	65 mg
Sodium	170 mg
Total carbohydrates	7 g
Protein	5 g

Continued

Patrick Gérôme

Patrick earned his culinary diploma at the École de Paris in France. Having gained experience at a variety of notable restaurants in Quebec and in France, he is currently president of a local chapter of the Société des Chefs, Cuisiniers et Pâtissiers du Québec and has acted as a judge in regional culinary Olympiads.

RECIPE 32.19

Buckwheat Crepes—Approximate values per crepe:

Calories	106.5
Total fat	3.5 g
Saturated fat	0.1 g
Cholesterol	3.5 mg
Sodium	172 mg
Total carbohydrates	17 g
Protein	3 g

Blueberry Compote —Approximate values per serving:

Calories	135
Total fat	0 g
Saturated fat	0 g
Cholesterol	0 mg
Sodium	2.5 mg
Total carbohydrates	36.5 g
Protein	0 g

Blueberry Honey Bavarian —Approximate values per serving:

Calories	122
Total fat	10 g
Saturated fat	6 g
Cholesterol	116 mg
Sodium	21 mg
Total carbohydrates	6 g
Protein	2 g

---

3. Add 30 g (1 oz.) of the batter to the pan. Tip the pan so the batter coats the entire surface in a thin layer.

4. Cook the pancake until lightly browned on the bottom. Remove it from the pan and reserve. Do not stack the pancakes.

5. To make the filling, drain the cheese in a conical strainer. Combine the remaining ingredients (except the butter) with the cheese and mix well.

6. To assemble, place a pancake on the work surface with the uncooked side down. Place 30 g (1 oz.) of the filling in the centre of the pancake. Fold the opposite ends in and then roll up to form a small package.

7. Sauté each blintz in butter until hot. Serve with sour cream or fruit compote as desired.

◆◆◆

RECIPE 32.19

BLUEBERRY HONEY BAVARIAN IN BUCKWHEAT CREPES WITH BLUEBERRIES

LE BALUCHON, ST. PAULIN, QC
Chef Patrick Gérôme

Yield: 12–16 Portions

BUCKWHEAT CREPES

Blueberry honey	45 g	2 Tbsp.
Milk	300 mL	10 fl. oz.
Oil	30 mL	2 Tbsp.
Buckwheat flour	100 g	3/4 cup
All-purpose flour	100 g	3/4 cup
Baking powder	10 g	1 Tbsp.
Salt	3 g	1/2 tsp.

1. Combine all wet ingredients.

2. Combine all dry ingredients and add to wet.

3. Mix until smooth and rest for 30 minutes.

4. Cook crepes in a large crepe pan. Reserve.

BLUEBERRY COMPOTE

Wild blueberries	175 g	1-1/2 cups
Blueberry honey	50 g	2-1/2 Tbsp.

Simmer ingredients until almost all liquid has evaporated.

BLUEBERRY HONEY BAVARIAN

Vanilla bean	1/4	1/4
Milk, hot	250 mL	8 fl. oz.
Blueberry honey	60 g	2 oz.
Gelatin sheets	8 g	4 sheets
Egg yolks	80 g	4
Cream, 35%	250 mL	8 fl. oz.

1. Infuse vanilla in hot milk and honey.

2. Soften gelatin sheets in cold water.

3. Temper egg yolks with some of the hot milk and add to remainder, stirring constantly. Do not let temperature of custard exceed 85°C (185°F).

4. Squeeze gelatin sheets dry and add to hot custard. Combine and cool mixture.

5. Whip cream to soft peaks and fold into cool custard.

MIROIR OF BLUEBERRY

Blueberry purée	50 g	2 oz.
Lemon juice	10 mL	2 tsp.
Sugar	25 g	1 oz.
Gelatin sheet, softened	1	1

1. Heat blueberry purée, lemon juice and sugar.

2. Dissolve gelatin in sauce.

ASSEMBLY:

1. In a springform pan, lay a crepe on the bottom. Spread one-third of the compote and one-third of the Bavarian.

2. Repeat twice and chill to set.

3. Spread warm miroir on top and chill.

4. Unmould and portion.

♦♦♦

RECIPE 32.20

BANANA FRENCH TOAST WITH LEMON CURD

*Inspired by Executive Chef Roary MacPherson, CCC,
at the Fairmont MacDonald, Edmonton, AB*

Yield: 1 Serving

Banana bread, sliced (Recipe 27.14)	3 slices	3 slices
Whole egg, beaten	as needed	as needed
Clarified butter	15 g	1/2 oz.
Lemon curd (Recipe 25.16)	30 mL	1 fl. oz.
Macedoine of strawberries	30 g	1 oz.
Chantilly cream	as needed	as needed
Maple syrup, warm	as needed	as needed

1. Dip slices of banana bread quickly in egg. Sauté in butter until golden.

2. Arrange banana bread, lemon curd and strawberry macedoine attractively on plate. Pipe a rosette of Chantilly cream.

3. Serve warm maple syrup on the side.

♦♦♦

RECIPE 32.21

CORNED BEEF HASH

Yield: 5–6 Servings   **Method:** Sautéing

Onion, diced fine	125 g	4 oz.
Vegetable oil	30 mL	2 Tbsp.
Corned beef, cooked and diced finely	500 g	1 lb.
Potatoes, cooked, diced	250 g	8 oz.
Tomato paste	25 g	1 oz.
Tomato concassé	250 g	1 lb.
Parsley, chopped fine	15 g	1/2 oz.
Salt and pepper	TT	TT

Continued

Miroir of Blueberry	
—Approximate values per serving:	
Calories	12
Total fat	0 g
Saturated fat	0 g
Cholesterol	0 mg
Sodium	0 mg
Total carbohydrates	3 g
Protein	0 g

Roary MacPherson, CCC

The youngest of 14 children, Roary took turns with his brothers and sisters to help out in the kitchen and knew he was hooked while regularly cooking for a table of 16. He received his Journeyman's Red Seal from the Cabot Institute of Technology and his Chef-de-Cuisine designation from the Southern Alberta Institute of Technology. Roary began his career with Fairmont Hotels & Resorts when he secured a position with the Fairmont Newfoundland.

RECIPE 32.20	
Approximate values per serving:	
Calories	633
Total fat	35 g
Saturated fat	20.5 g
Cholesterol	378 mg
Sodium	663 mg
Total carbohydrates	71 g
Protein	13 g

RECIPE 32.21

Approximate values per serving:

Calories	247
Total fat	14 g
Saturated fat	3 g
Cholesterol	82 mg
Sodium	1218 mg
Total carbohydrates	14 g
Protein	17 g

1. Sauté onion in oil until clear.

2. Add the corned beef and sauté until meat is heated through.

3. Add potatoes and sauté mixture until it is lightly browned. Stir periodically.

4. Add tomato paste and concassée. Simmer until liquid is reduced by two-thirds.

5. Add chopped parsley and adjust seasoning with salt and pepper.

6. Cool the mixture and refrigerate until needed.

7. To serve, preheat the skillet and lubricate it with a small amount of oil. Place a portion of the hash in the skillet and sauté until lightly browned, stirring constantly.

8. Shape and transfer to plate.

9. Serve with fried or poached eggs.

ALTERNATIVE METHOD: Reheat and brown mixture in a sauté pan and shape like a cigar.

❖❖❖

RECIPE 32.22

CHEESE SOUFFLÉ

Yield: 12 Individual Servings

Butter	as needed	as needed
Bread crumbs	as needed	as needed
Base Mixture (recipe follows)	600 mL	20 fl. oz.
Sharp cheddar, grated	150 g	5 oz.
Ermite, grated	25 g	1 oz.
Dry mustard	0.5 g	1 tsp.
Salt and pepper	TT	TT
Egg whites	12	12

1. Butter ramekins and lightly coat the interior with bread crumbs.

2. Mix together the base mixture, grated cheeses, mustard, salt and pepper. Blend evenly.

3. Whisk egg whites to soft peaks.

4. Fold one-third of the egg whites into the cheese mixture. Fold in the remaining egg whites in two stages.

5. Spoon the batter into the ramekins to within 10 mm (1/2 inch) of the top. Wipe the rims clean. Tap the ramekins gently to settle the batter.

6. Place the soufflés on a baking sheet and bake in a 210°C (420°F) oven for 15–18 minutes. Do not disturb. Serve immediately.

RECIPE 32.22

Approximate values per serving:

Calories	247
Total fat	18 g
Saturated fat	9 g
Cholesterol	304 mg
Sodium	722 mg
Total carbohydrates	9 g
Protein	14 g

BASE MIXTURE

Yield: 600 mL (20 fl. oz.)

Milk	725 mL	24 fl. oz.
Bay leaf	1	1
Clove, whole	1	1
Butter	60 g	2 oz.
Flour	70 g	2-1/2 oz.
Egg yolks	15	15
Salt and pepper	TT	TT

1. Heat milk with bay leaf and clove to infuse.
2. Prepare a white roux from the butter and flour.
3. Strain the milk and add to the roux to make a béchamel.
4. Simmer approximately 15 minutes, stirring constantly.
5. Temper the egg yolks with some of the béchamel.
6. Incorporate tempered egg yolks into remaining sauce and bring to a simmer for 3–4 minutes. Do not boil. Stir constantly.
7. Adjust seasoning with salt and pepper and reserve. Chill if being used later.

Base Mixture—	
Approximate values per serving:	
Calories	170
Total fat	13 g
Saturated fat	6 g
Cholesterol	289 mg
Sodium	316 mg
Total carbohydrates	8 g
Protein	6 g

WEBLINKS

American Egg Board: Breakfast and Brunch Recipes
www.aeb.org/recipes/breakfast/index.html

Breakfast
www.efn.org/~sundance/Breakfast.html

Creole/Cajun: Breakfast and Breads
www.gumbopages.com/breakfast-home.html

Recipes
soar.berkeley.edu/recipes/breakfast

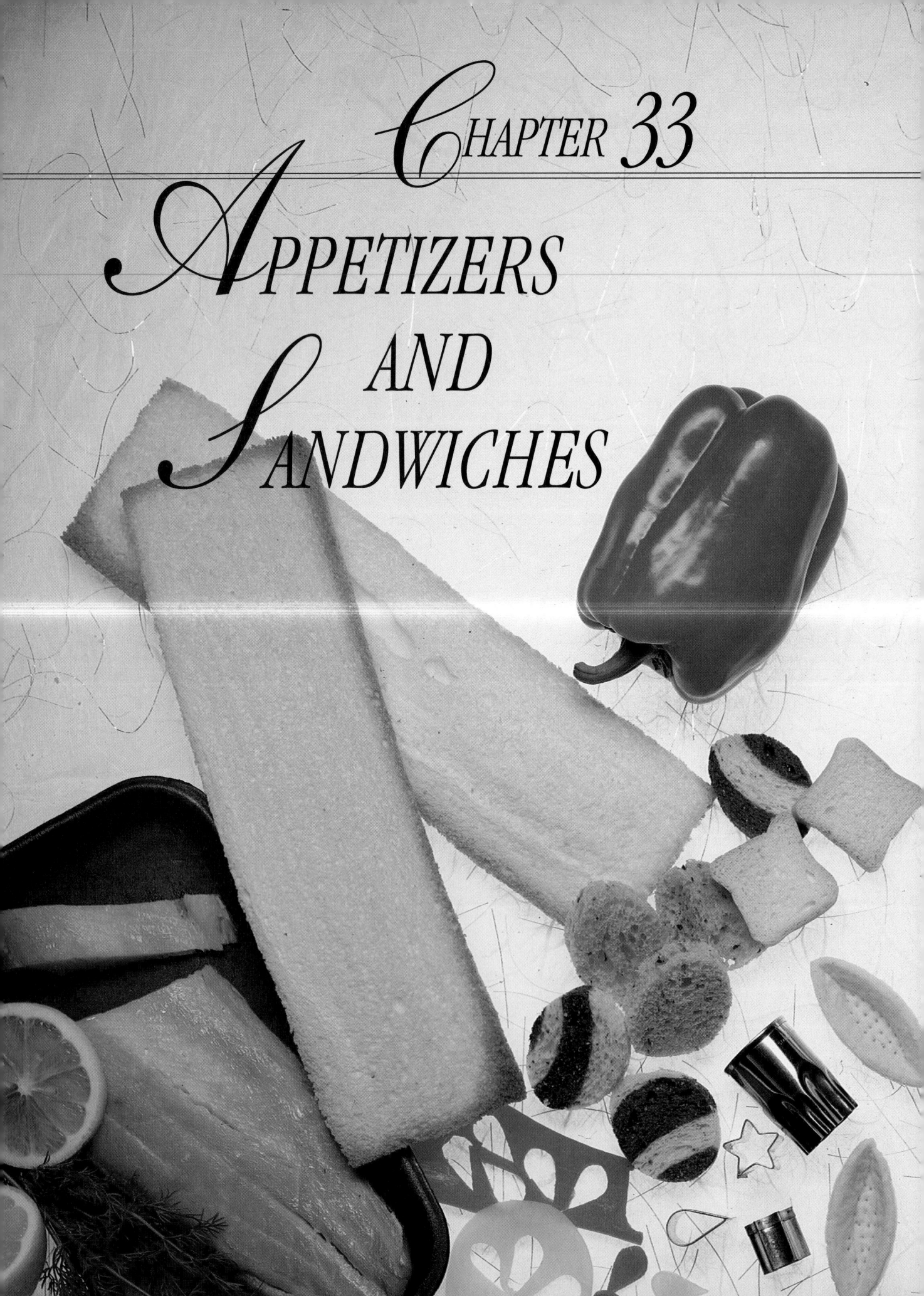

CHAPTER 33
APPETIZERS AND SANDWICHES

After studying this chapter you will be able to:

- prepare and serve a variety of cold and hot hors d'oeuvre
- prepare a variety of appetizers
- choose hors d'oeuvre and appetizers that are appropriate for the meal or event
- select high-quality sandwich ingredients
- identify different types and styles of sandwiches
- prepare sandwiches to order

*H*ors d'oeuvre and canapés, whether hot or cold, are very small portions of foods served before or at the beginning of the meal to stimulate the appetite or at a reception as the accompaniment to liquid refreshments. Hors d'oeuvre can be passed elegantly by waiters or displayed on buffets. Appetizers, whether hot or cold, are generally the first course or introduction to a meal; they are more typically served with dinner than with lunch. Sometimes there is very little difference between an hors d'oeuvre and an appetizer.

Sandwiches, which are usually quick and easy to assemble, also lend themselves to a cook's creativity. Fancy sandwiches can become sensational menu additions in even the most formal restaurants, and amazing sandwiches can keep lunch customers visiting regularly.

The preparation of hors d'oeuvre and sandwiches uses skills from almost every work station. Because they can consist of meat, poultry, fish, shellfish, vegetables, potatoes, grains, pasta, fruits, baked goods and sauces, they require a detailed knowledge of these foods and how they are prepared.

Although hors d'oeuvre and sandwiches can be divided into hot and cold varieties, it is difficult (and unnecessary) to categorize them further because of the vast variety possible and the absence of any one dominant food type or style.

HORS D'OEUVRE

The French term *hors d'oeuvre* translates as "outside the work" although we generally use it to mean appetizer. Its usage was correct under the classic kitchen brigade system, for it was the service staff's responsibility to prepare small tidbits for guests to enjoy while the kitchen prepared the meal. Today, however, the kitchen staff prepares the hors d'oeuvre as well as the meals. Cold hors d'oeuvre are usually prepared by the *garde-manger*; hot ones are prepared in the main kitchen.

There are really only two limitations on the type of food and manner of preparation that can be used for hors d'oeuvre: the cook's imagination and the foods at his or her disposal. There are, however, a few guidelines.

UN ARTISTE DE L'HORS D'OEUVRE

"Well may it be said that a good hors d'oeuvre artist is a man to be prized in any kitchen, for, although his duties do not by any means rank first in importance, they nevertheless demand of the chef the possession of such qualities as are rarely found united in one person, reliable and experienced taste, originality, keen artistic sense, and professional knowledge."

AUGUSTE ESCOFFIER,
LE GUIDE CULINAIRE

Basic Guidelines for Preparing Hors d'Oeuvre

1. They should be small, one to two bites.
2. They should be flavourful and well seasoned without being overpowering.
3. They should be visually attractive.
4. They should complement the foods to follow without duplicating their flavours.

Cold Hors d'Oeuvre

Cold hors d'oeuvre are divided here into five broad categories based upon preparation method, principal ingredient or presentation style. They are canapés, caviars, crudités, dips and sushi. These categories may vary somewhat from classical teachings, but they are completely appropriate for modern menus and food service operations.

Salmon Rosette Canapés

Canapés

Canapés are, essentially, tiny, open-faced sandwiches. They are constructed from a base, a spread and one or more garnishes.

The most common **canapé base** is a thin slice of bread cut into an interesting shape and toasted. Although most any variety of bread can be used, spiced, herbed or otherwise flavoured breads may be inappropriate for some spreads or garnishes. Melba toasts, crackers, or slices of firm vegetables such as cucumbers or zucchini or meat slices are also popular canapé bases. The base must be strong enough to support the weight of the spread and garnish without falling apart when handled.

Salami Cornet Canapés

The **canapé spread** provides much of the canapé's flavour. Spreads are usually flavoured butters, cream cheese or a combination of the two. Examples of spreads are listed in Table 33.1. Each of the spreads is made by adding the desired amount of the main ingredient (chopped or puréed as appropriate) and seasonings to softened butter or cream cheese and mixing until combined. Quantities and proportions vary according to individual tastes. Other canapé spreads include bound salads (for example, tuna or egg), finely chopped shrimp or liver mousse. Any of a number of ingredients can be combined for spreads, provided the following guidelines are followed.

Shrimp and Caviar Canapés

Basic Guidelines for Preparing Canapé Spreads

1. The spread's texture should be smooth enough to produce attractive designs if piped through a pastry bag fitted with a decorative tip.
2. The spread's consistency should be firm enough to hold its shape when piped onto the base, yet soft enough to stick to the base and hold the garnishes in place.
3. The spread's flavour should complement the garnishes and be flavourful enough to stimulate the appetite without being overpowering.

A spread may be a substantial portion of the canapé as well as its distinguishing characteristic. Or it can be applied sparingly and used more as a means of gluing the garnish to the base than as a principal ingredient.

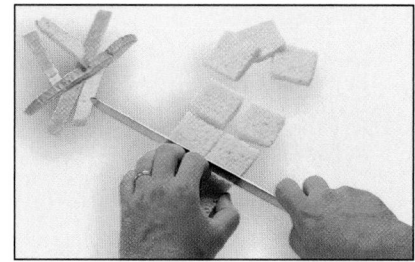

1. Slicing bread into the desired shapes.

2. Applying the spread to the base with a palette knife.

3. Piping the spread onto the base.

4. Coating the entire slice of toasted bread with a spread before cutting it into canapés.

5. Garnishing the canapés.

6. Spraying the finished canapés with aspic.

TABLE 33.1 A SELECTION OF CANAPÉ SPREADS AND SUGGESTED GARNISHES

Spread	Suggested Garnishes
Anchovy butter	Hard-cooked eggs, capers, green or black olive slices
Blue cheese	Grape half, walnuts, roast beef roulade, pear slice, currants, watercress
Caviar butter	Caviar, lemon, egg slice, chives
Devilled ham	Cornichons, mustard butter, sliced radish
Horseradish butter	Smoked salmon, roast beef, smoked trout, marinated herring, capers, parsley
Lemon butter	Shrimp, crab, caviar, salmon, chives, parsley, black olive slices
Liver pâté	Truffle slice, cornichon
Mustard butter	Smoked meats, pâté, dry salami coronet, cornichon
Pimiento cream cheese	Smoked oyster, sardine, pimiento, parsley
Shrimp butter	Poached bay scallops, shrimp, caviar, parsley
Tuna salad	Capers, cornichons, sliced radish

Canapés with bread bases tend to become soggy quickly from both the moisture in the spread and the moisture in the refrigerator where they are stored. Using a spread made with butter will help keep the bread bases crispier, as will buttering the base with a thin coat of softened plain butter before piping on the spread. The best way to ensure a crisp base is to make the canapés as close to service time as possible.

The variety of **canapé garnishes** is vast. The garnish can dominate or complement the spread, or it can be a simple herb sprig intended to provide visual appeal but little flavour. Although several ingredients can be used to garnish the same canapé, remember the limitations imposed by the canapé's size and purpose.

Basic Procedure for Preparing Canapés

This procedure can be adapted and used with a variety of ingredients to produce a variety of canapés. If the canapé base is a bread crouton, begin with step 1. If some other product is used as the base, prepare that base and begin with step 4.

1. Trim the crust from an unsliced loaf of bread. Slice the bread lengthwise approximately 8 mm (1/3 inch) thick.
2. Cut the bread slices into the desired shapes using a serrated bread knife or canapé cutter.
3. Brush the bread shapes with melted butter or olive oil and bake in a 180°C (350°F) oven until they are toasted and dry. Remove and cool.
4. If desired, spread each base with a thin layer of softened plain butter.
5. Apply the spread to the base. If a thin layer is desired, use a palette knife. If a thicker or more decorative layer is desired, pipe the spread onto the base using a pastry bag and decorative tip.
6. Garnish the canapé as desired.
7. If desired, glaze each canapé with a thin coating of aspic jelly. The aspic jelly can be applied with a small spoon or a spray bottle designated for that purpose.

Barquettes, Tartlets and Profiteroles

Barquettes, tartlets and profiteroles are all adaptations of the basic canapé. A **barquette** is a tiny boat-shaped shell made from a savoury dough such as pâte brisée. A **tartlet** is simply a round version of a barquette. A **profiterole** is a small puff made from pâte à choux. These three items can be prepared like canapés by filling them with flavoured spreads and garnishing as desired.

Other Types of Canapés

Vegetables such as cherry tomatoes, blanched snow peas, mushroom caps and Belgian endive leaves are sometimes used as canapé bases. They are filled and garnished in the same manner as barquettes, tartlets and profiteroles. Buffet platters can be garnished with canapés.

Caviar

Caviar, considered by many to be the ultimate hors d'oeuvre, is the salted roe (eggs) of the sturgeon fish. In Canada, only sturgeon roe can be labelled as simply "caviar." Roe from other fish must be qualified as such on the label (e.g., salmon caviar or lumpfish caviar).

Most of the world's caviar comes from sturgeon harvested in the Caspian Sea and imported from Russia and Iran. Imported sturgeon caviar, classified according to the sturgeon species and the roe's size and colour, includes **beluga**, **osetra** and **sevruga** as well as **pressed caviar**. Belugia is the most expensive caviar; it comes from the largest species (the sturgeon can weigh up to 800 kg/1750 lb.); the dark grey and well-separated eggs are the largest and most fragile kind. Osetra is considered by some connoisseurs to be the best caviar; the eggs are medium-sized, golden yellow to brown in colour and quite oily. Sevruga is harvested from small sturgeon; the eggs are quite small and light to dark grey in colour. Pressed caviar is a processed caviar from osetra and sevruga roes. The eggs are cleaned, packed in linen bags and hung to drain; as salt and moisture drain away, the natural shape of the eggs is destroyed and the eggs are pressed together. Approximately 1.3 kg (3 lb.) of roe produce only 450 g (1 lb.) of pressed caviar; pressed caviar has a spreadable, jamlike consistency. Most of the caviar consumed in North America, however, comes from either domestic sturgeon or other fish and is labelled **American sturgeon caviar**, **golden whitefish caviar**, **lumpfish caviar** or **salmon caviar**. American sturgeon caviar is not considered of the same quality as Russian or Iranian caviars; nevertheless, roe from sturgeon harvested in the coastal waters of the American northwest and the Tennessee River is becoming increasingly popular, due in part to its relatively low price. Golden whitefish caviar is a small and very crisp roe; the roe is a natural golden colour and comes from whitefish native to the northern Great Lakes. Lumpfish caviar is readily available and reasonably priced; it is produced from lumpfish harvested in the North Atlantic. The small and very crisp eggs are dyed black, red or gold; the food colouring is not stable, however, and when used to garnish foods, coloured lumpfish caviar has a tendency to bleed. Salmon caviar is the eggs of the chum and silver salmon and is a very popular garnish. The eggs are large with a good flavour and natural orange colour. Tobiko or flying fish roe is widely used.

Beluga Caviar

Sevruga Caviar

Osetra Caviar

Purchasing and Storing Caviars

Although all caviar is processed with salt, the best caviar is labelled **malassol**, which means "little salt." Caviar should smell fresh, with no off-odours. The eggs should be whole, not broken, and they should be crisp and pop when pressed with the tongue. Excessive oiliness may be caused by a large number of broken eggs. The best way to test a caviar's quality is to taste it. Remember, price alone does not necessarily indicate quality.

American Salmon Roe

Most caviar can be purchased fresh or pasteurized in tins or jars ranging from 28 g (1 oz.) to over 2 kg (4 lb.). Some caviars are also available frozen. (Frozen caviar should be used only as a garnish and should not be served by itself.) In order to ensure the freshest possible product, always purchase caviar in small quantities as often as necessary based on your needs.

Fresh caviar should be stored at 0°C (32°F). Because most refrigerators are considerably warmer than that, store the caviar on ice in the coldest part of the refrigerator and change the ice often. If properly handled, fresh caviar will last one to two weeks before opening and several days after opening. Pasteurized caviar does not require refrigeration until it is opened and will last several days in the refrigerator after opening.

Serving Caviars

Fine caviar should be served in its original container or a nonmetal bowl on a bed of crushed ice, accompanied only by lightly buttered toasts or blinis and sour cream. Connoisseurs prefer china, bone or other nonmetal utensils for serving caviar because metal reacts with the caviar, producing off-flavours.

Lesser-quality caviars are often served on ice, accompanied by minced onion, chopped hard-cooked egg whites and yolks (separately), lemon, sour cream and buttered toasts.

Lumpfish and other nonsturgeon caviars are usually not served by themselves. Rather, they are used as ingredients in or garnishes for other dishes.

Crudités

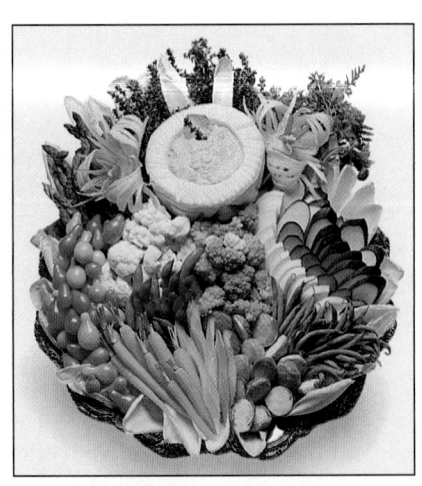

An artful array of crudités and dip.

Crudité, a French word meaning "raw thing," generally refers to raw or slightly blanched vegetables served as an hors d'oeuvre. Although almost any vegetable will do, the most commonly used are broccoli, cauliflower, carrots, celery, asparagus and green beans, all of which are often blanched, and cucumbers, zucchini, yellow squash, radishes, green onions, cherry tomatoes, Belgian endive leaves, mushrooms, peppers and jicama, which are served raw.

When preparing crudités, use only the freshest and best-looking produce available. Because crudités are displayed and eaten raw, blemishes and imperfections cannot be disguised. Vegetables, both blanched and raw, should be cut into attractive shapes. Crudités are usually served with one or more dips.

Dips

Dips can be served hot or cold and as an accompaniment to crudités, crackers, chips, toasts, breads or other foods.

Cold dips often use mayonnaise, sour cream or cream cheese as a base. The methods for preparing mayonnaise- and sour-cream-based dips are identical to those for making mayonnaise-based salad dressings discussed in Chapter 24, Salads and Salad Dressings. The principal difference is that dips are normally thicker than dressings.

To use cream cheese as a base, first soften it by mixing it in an electric mixer with a paddle attachment. Then add the flavouring ingredients such as chopped cooked vegetables, chopped cooked fish or shellfish, herbs, spices, garlic or onions. Adjust the consistency of the dip by adding milk, buttermilk, cream, sour cream or other appropriate liquid.

Some cold dips such as guacamole and hummus use purées of fruits, vegetables or beans as the base.

Hot dips often use a béchamel, cream sauce or cheese sauce as a base and usually contain a dominant flavouring ingredient such as chopped spinach or shellfish. The traditional Italian bagna cauda is an example of a hot, oil-based dip. It is made with olive oil, garlic and anchovies and is kept hot over a small burner while guests dip raw vegetables in it.

Dips can be served in small bowls or hollowed-out cabbages, squash, pumpkins or other vegetables. Hot dips are often served in **chafing dishes**.

The combinations of ingredients and seasonings that can be used to make dips as well as the foods that are dipped in them are limited only by the chef's imagination.

Applying the Basics

RECIPE 33.1

CLAM DIP

Yield: 1.5 L (3 pt.)

Cream cheese	450 g	1 lb.
Worcestershire sauce	30 mL	1 fl. oz.
Dijon-style mustard	15 mL	1 Tbsp.
Sour cream	450 mL	1 lb.
Canned clams, drained	450 g	1 lb.
Lemon juice	30 mL	1 fl. oz.
Salt and pepper	TT	TT
Tabasco sauce	TT	TT
Green onions, sliced	60 g	2 oz.

1. Soften the cream cheese in the bowl of an electric mixer, using the paddle attachment.
2. Add the Worcestershire sauce, Dijon-style mustard and sour cream; mix until smooth.
3. Add the clams and lemon juice and season with salt, pepper and Tabasco sauce.
4. Add the green onions and mix well.

RECIPE 33.1

Approximate values per 25 mL serving:

Calories	48
Total fat	4 g
Saturated fat	2 g
Cholesterol	16 mg
Sodium	280 mg
Total carbohydrates	1 g
Protein	3 g

Sushi

Generally, **sushi** refers to cooked or raw fish and shellfish rolled in or served on seasoned rice. **Sashimi** is raw fish eaten without rice. In Japan, the word sushi (or **zushi**) refers only to the flavoured rice. Each combination of rice and another ingredient or ingredients has a specific name. These include: *nigiri zushi* (rice with raw fish), *norimaki zushi* (rice rolled in seaweed), *fukusa zushi* (rice wrapped in omelette), *inari zushi* (rice in fried bean curd) and *chirashi zushi* (rice with fish, shellfish and vegetables). Although a Japanese sushi master spends years perfecting style and technique, many types of sushi can be produced in any professional kitchen with very little specialized equipment.

Ingredients

Fish—The key to good sushi and sashimi is the freshness of the fish. All fish must be of the highest quality and absolutely fresh, preferably no more than one day out of the water. Ahi and yellowfin tuna, salmon, flounder and sea bass are typically used for sushi. Cooked shrimp and eel are also popular.

Rice—Sushi rice is prepared by adding seasonings such as vinegar, sugar, salt and rice wine (sake or mirin) to steamed short-grain rice. The consistency of the rice is very important. It must be sticky enough to stay together when formed into finger-shaped oblongs, but not too soft.

◆◆◆
SUSHI SEASONINGS

Shoyu—Japanese soy sauce, which is lighter and more delicate than the Chinese variety.

Wasabi—A strong aromatic root, purchased as a green powder. It is sometimes called green horseradish although it is not actually related to the common horseradish.

Pickled ginger—fresh ginger pickled in vinegar, which gives it a pink colour.

Nori—a dried seaweed purchased in sheets; it adds flavour and is sometimes used to contain the rolled rice and other ingredients.

RECIPE 33.2

Approximate values per 35 g serving:

Calories	61
Total fat	0 g
Saturated fat	0 g
Cholesterol	0 mg
Sodium	167 mg
Total carbohydrates	14 g
Protein	1 g

Applying the Basics

RECIPE 33.2

ZUSHI (SUSHI RICE)

Yield: 1 kg (2 lb.)

Short-grain sushi rice	425 g	1 lb.
Water	550 mL	20 fl. oz.
Sugar	45 g	3 Tbsp.
Salt	12 g	2-1/2 tsp.
Rice vinegar	60 mL	2 fl. oz.

1. Wash the rice until the water runs clear. Leave to soak in water for 30 minutes and then allow it to drain for 30 minutes.
2. Combine the rice and water in a saucepan with a tight-fitting lid. Bring to a boil for 2 minutes on high, 5 minutes on medium and about 15 minutes on low. A hissing sound will indicate the rice is done. Remove from heat, remove lid and cover with a clean cloth for 10 minutes.
3. Disolve the sugar and salt in some warmed rice vinegar. Add the remaining rice vinegar and cool.
4. Spread the rice in a shallow bowl or tray.
5. Plough the rice with a paddle (*shamoji*). Go up and down, then across, again and again to separate the grains. As you toss and plough the rice, sprinkle it with the sushi-zu. Fan the rice at the same time. It will take 10–15 minutes to cool down. The finished rice should be glossy and just stick together.
6. Keep cooled mixture covered with a damp cloth. Use immediately.

1. Form a finger-shaped rice mound.

2. Press the fish onto the rice.

RECIPE 33.3

Approximate values per serving:

Calories	80
Total fat	2 g
Saturated fat	0 g
Cholesterol	10 mg
Sodium	310 mg
Total carbohydrates	11 g
Protein	5 g

Applying the Basics

RECIPE 33.3

NIGIRI ZUSHI

Yield: 24 Pieces

Sushi-quality fish fillets such as ahi tuna, salmon, flounder or sea bass	450 g	1 lb.
Wasabi powder	30 g	1 oz.
Water	30 mL	1 fl. oz.
Zushi (Recipe 33.2)	900 g	2 lb.
Pickled ginger, sliced	60 g	2 oz.
Shoyu	90 mL	3 fl. oz.

1. Trim the fish fillets of any skin, bone, imperfections or blemishes. Cut the fillets into 24 thin slices approximately 5 cm long by 2.5 cm wide (2 inches × 1 inch).
2. Mix the wasabi powder and water to form a paste.
3. With your hands, form a 50-g (1-1/2-oz.) portion of rice into a finger-shaped mound.
4. Rub a small amount of wasabi on one side of a slice of fish.
5. Holding the rice mound in one hand, press the fish, wasabi side down, onto the rice with the fingers of the other hand.
6. Serve with additional wasabi, pickled ginger and shoyu.

Applying the Basics

RECIPE 33.4

NORIMAKI ZUSHI

RECIPE 33.4

Approximate values per serving:

Calories	40
Total fat	0 g
Saturated fat	0 g
Cholesterol	5 mg
Sodium	220 mg
Total carbohydrates	6 g
Protein	2 g

Yield: 36 Pieces

Dried shiitake mushrooms	4	4
Shoyu	125 mL	4 fl. oz.
Brown sugar	15 g	1 Tbsp.
Cucumber	1/2	1/2
Sushi-quality fish fillets such as ahi tuna, salmon, flounder or sea bass	150 g	5 oz.
Nori	3 sheets	3 sheets
Zushi (Recipe 33.2)	500 g	18 oz.
Wasabi paste	60 mL	2 fl. oz.
Pickled ginger	60 g	2 oz.

1. Soak the mushrooms in hot water for 20 minutes. Remove the mushrooms and reserve 125 mL (4 fl. oz.) of the liquid. Trim off the mushroom stems.

2. Julienne the mushroom caps. Combine the reserved soaking liquid with 30 mL (2 Tbsp.) of the shoyu and the brown sugar. Simmer the caps in this liquid and reduce *au sec.* Remove from the heat and refrigerate.

3. Peel and seed the cucumber; cut it into strips the size of pencils, approximately 15 cm (6 inches) long.

4. Trim the fish fillets of any skin, bone, imperfections or blemishes. Cut the fillets into strips the same size as the cucumbers.

5. Cut the sheets of nori in half and place one half sheet on a napkin or bamboo rolling mat. Divide the rice into six equal portions; spread one portion over each half sheet of nori, leaving a 12 mm (1/2 inch) border of nori exposed.

6. Spread 5 mL (1 tsp.) of wasabi evenly on the rice.

7. Lay one-sixth of the mushrooms, cucumber and fish strips in a row down the middle of the rice.

8. Use the napkin or bamboo mat to roll the nori tightly around the rice and garnishes.

9. Slice each roll into six pieces and serve with the remaining shoyu, pickled ginger and remaining wasabi.

1. Prepare the garnishes for the sushi roll.

2. Spread the rice over the nori.

3. Add the garnishes in a row down the middle of the rice.

4. With the mat roll the nori around the rice and garnishes.

5. Slice the roll into six pieces.

Hot Hors d'Oeuvre

To provide a comprehensive list of hot hors d'oeuvre would be virtually impossible; therefore we discuss just a few of the more commonly encountered ones that can be easily made in most any kitchen.

Filled Pastry Shells

Because savoury (unsweetened) barquettes and tartlets, choux puffs (profiteroles) and bouchées can hold a small amount of liquid, they are often baked then filled with warm meat, poultry or fish purées, ragouts or salpicons, garnished and served hot. They become soggy quickly, however, and must be prepared at the last possible minute before service.

Brochettes or Kebabs

Hors d'oeuvre brochettes are small skewers holding a combination of meat, poultry, game, fish, shellfish or vegetables. They are normally baked, grilled or broiled and are often served with a dipping sauce. Brochettes or kebabs can be small pieces of boneless chicken breast marinated in white wine and grilled; beef cubes glazed with teriyaki sauce; lamb or chicken satay (saté) with peanut sauce or rabbit and shiitake mushrooms skewered on a sprig of fresh rosemary.

In order to increase visual appeal, the main ingredients should be carefully cut and consistently sized and shaped. The ingredients are normally diced, but strips of meat and poultry can also be threaded onto the skewers. Often, ingredients are first marinated.

As hors d'oeuvre, the skewers should be very small, slightly larger than a toothpick. Bamboo skewers work well, but remember to soak them in water for 20 minutes to prevent splintering of the wood. When assembling brochettes, leave enough exposed skewer so diners can pick them up easily. Wooden skewers have a tendency to burn during cooking. Soaking them in water before using them helps reduce the risk of burning.

Applying the Basics

RECIPE 33.5

RABBIT AND SHIITAKE SKEWERS

Yield: 12 Skewers

Rabbit	1	1
Shiitake mushrooms, stemmed	6–8	6–8
Rosemary sprigs	12	12
Salt and pepper	TT	TT
Olive oil	60 mL	2 fl. oz.
Mushroom ragout (optional)	600 g	22 oz.

1. Bone the rabbit and cut the pieces into 1.25-cm (1/2-inch) cubes. One rabbit should produce 36 cubes.
2. Wash the mushrooms. Trim and discard the stems.
3. Cut enough of the mushrooms into 1.25-cm (1/2-inch) dice to produce 24 pieces.
4. Skewer three pieces of rabbit and two pieces of mushroom alternately onto each rosemary sprig.

RECIPE 33.5

Approximate values per serving:

Calories	160
Total fat	8 g
Saturated fat	1.5 g
Cholesterol	31 mg
Sodium	20 mg
Total carbohydrates	11 g
Protein	12 g

5. Season the skewers with salt and pepper and brush with olive oil. Grill the skewers over medium heat, being careful not to burn the rosemary sprigs.

6. Heat the mushroom ragout. Arrange a portion of ragout and two rabbit skewers on each plate.

Meatballs

Meatballs made from ground beef, veal, pork or poultry and served in a sauce buffet-style are a popular hot hors d'oeuvre. One of the best known is the Swedish meatball. It is made from ground beef, veal and pork bound with eggs and bread crumbs and served in a velouté or cream sauce seasoned with dill. Other sauces that can be used in the same manner are mushroom sauce, red wine sauce or any style of tomato sauce.

Applying the Basics

RECIPE 33.6

SWEDISH MEATBALLS

Yield: 2 kg (4 lb. 8 oz.)

Onions, small dice	250 g	8 oz.
Whole butter	50 g	2 oz.
Ground beef	1 kg	2 lb.
Ground pork	1 kg	2 lb.
Bread crumbs, fresh	125 g	4 oz.
Eggs	3	3
Salt	15 g	1 Tbsp.
Pepper	TT	TT
Nutmeg	TT	TT
Allspice	TT	TT
Lemon zest, grated	3 g	1 tsp.
Demi-glace, hot	1 L	1 qt.
Cream, 35%, hot	250 mL	8 fl. oz.
Fresh dill, chopped	20 g	2 Tbsp.

1. Sauté the onions in butter without colouring. Remove and cool.

2. Combine the onions with all the ingredients except the demi-glace, cream and dill. Mix well.

3. Portion the meat with a #20 scoop; form into balls with your hands and place on a sheet pan.

4. Bake the meatballs at 200°C (400°F) until firm, approximately 15 minutes. Remove the meatballs from the pan with a slotted spoon, draining well, and place in a hotel pan.

5. Combine the demi-glace, cream and dill; pour over the meatballs.

6. Cover the meatballs and bake at 180°C (350°F) until done, approximately 20 minutes. Skim off the grease from the surface and serve.

RECIPE 33.6

Approximate values per 50 g serving:

Calories	188
Total fat	12.5 g
Saturated fat	5.5 g
Cholesterol	72 mg
Sodium	224 mg
Total carbohydrates	3 g
Protein	15 g

Rumaki

Traditionally, rumaki were made by wrapping chicken livers in bacon and broiling or baking them. Today, however, many other foods prepared in the same fashion are called rumaki. For example, blanched bacon can be wrapped around olives, pickled watermelon rind, water chestnuts, pineapple, dates or scallops. These morsels are then broiled, baked or fried and served piping hot.

Applying the Basics

DATE AND CHORIZO RUMAKI

Yield: 32 Pieces

Bacon, thin-cut slices	16	16
Chorizo (Recipe 20.19)	250 g	8 oz.
Cream cheese	125 g	4 oz.
Whole dates, pitted	32	32

1. Partially cook the bacon on a sheet pan in a 180°C (350°F) oven, approximately 5 minutes.
2. Cook the chorizo to render the excess fat. If the chorizo is in links, remove the meat from the casings before cooking.
3. Remove the cooked chorizo from the pan and drain in a mesh strainer or conical strainer to remove excess fat. Then blend the cream cheese into the meat.
4. Cut the dates open, butterfly style. Stuff each date with a portion of the chorizo mixture.
5. Wrap each date with a half slice of bacon, securing with a toothpick.
6. Arrange the rumaki on a rack placed over a sheet pan. Bake at 180°C (350°F) until the bacon is crisp and the dates are hot, approximately 15–20 minutes.

RECIPE 33.7

Approximate values per serving:

Calories	90
Total fat	5 g
Saturated fat	3 g
Cholesterol	15 mg
Sodium	150 mg
Total carbohydrates	7 g
Protein	3 g

Stuffed Won Ton Skins

Won ton skins are an Asian noodle dough used to produce a wide variety of hors d'oeuvre such as a miniature version of the traditional egg roll or a puff filled with a mixture of seasoned cream cheese and crab. Or they can be stuffed with a wide variety of pork, chicken, shellfish and vegetables before cooking. As hors d'oeuvre, stuffed won ton skins can be steamed, but they are more often pan-fried or deep-fat fried.

Applying the Basics

STUFFED WON TONS

Yield: 40 Pieces

Shiitake mushrooms, stemmed, finely chopped	75 g	6
Green onions, finely chopped	4	4
Ground pork	250 g	8 oz.
Shrimp, deveined, chopped	125 g	4 oz.
Salt	8 g	1-1/2 tsp.
Soy sauce	15 mL	1 Tbsp.
Sesame oil	5 mL	1 tsp.
Wraps, thawed	450 g	1 lb.

1. Combine all ingredients, except wraps, and mix well to bind.
2. Lay a few wraps at a time on a table and keep remainder covered with plastic to prevent drying.

RECIPE 33.8

Approximate values per won ton:

Calories	57
Total fat	2 g
Saturated fat	0.5 g
Cholesterol	13 mg
Sodium	180 mg
Total carbohydrates	7 g
Protein	3 g

3. Place a 12 g (1 Tbsp.) portion of filling in the centre of each wrap. Wet two adjacent sides of wrap lightly with water. Fold the wrap in half to form a triangle. Seal the edges well.

4. If the won ton are to be deep-fried as hors d'oeuvre, leave in triangle shapes. For won ton soup, moisten one bottom corner of won ton and press the other point on top of it. The shape should resemble a tortellini.

Other Hot Hors d'Oeuvre

Other types of hot hors d'oeuvre include layers of phyllo dough wrapped around various fillings; vegetables such as mushrooms that are stuffed and baked; tiny red potatoes filled with sour cream and caviar or Roquefort cheese and walnuts; tiny artichoke or clam fritters or any of the hundreds of varieties of chicken wings that are seasoned or marinated, baked, fried, broiled or grilled and served with a cool and soothing or outrageously spicy sauce.

The secret is to let your imagination be your guide, to keep the ingredients harmonious and, if the hors d'oeuvre are to precede dinner, not to allow them to duplicate the foods to be served or overpower them with excessively spicy flavours.

Serving Hors d'Oeuvre

Hors d'oeuvre are not only served as a precursor to dinner. At many events the only food served may be butlered hors d'oeuvre, an hors d'oeuvre buffet or a combination of the two. Whether the hors d'oeuvre are being served before dinner or as dinner, butler style or buffet style, they must always be attractively prepared and displayed.

All events have themes and varying degrees of formality. Long buffets with overflowing baskets of crudités and sweet potato chips with dips presented in hollowed squashes and cabbages may be appropriate for one event, while elegant silver trays of carefully prepared canapés passed among guests by white-gloved, tuxedoed service staff may be appropriate for another. When preparing and serving hors d'oeuvre, always keep the event's theme in mind and plan accordingly.

When choosing hors d'oeuvre, select an assortment that contrasts flavours, textures and styles. There are no limits to the variety of hors d'oeuvre that can be served, but three to four cold and three to four hot selections are sufficient for most occasions. Generally, calculating three hors d'oeuvre per person per hour is sufficient when determining how many to prepare. If no other food will be available, four or five pieces may be appropriate. One must also consider whether they are a meal replacement, in which case larger quantities may be needed.

Butler Service

Butler service hors d'oeuvre or "passed" hors d'oeuvre are presented to guests on trays by the service staff. The hors d'oeuvre can be hot or cold and should be very small to make it easier for the guests to eat them without the aid of a knife or fork. Hot and cold hors d'oeuvre should be passed separately so that they can be kept at the correct temperatures. For a one-hour cocktail reception before a dinner, three to five hors d'oeuvre per person is usually sufficient. Four to five pieces per person, per hour may be needed if hors d'oeuvre are the only food being served.

Buffet Service

An hors d'oeuvre buffet should be beautiful and appetizing. It may consist of a single table to serve a small group of people or several huge multilevel displays designed to feed thousands. Colours, flavours and textures must all be taken into account when planning the menu.

Both hot and cold hors d'oeuvre may be served on buffets. Hot hors d'oeuvre are often kept hot by holding them in chafing dishes. Alternatively, hot hors d'oeuvre can be displayed on trays or platters; the trays and platters, however, must be replaced frequently to ensure that the food stays hot. Cold hors d'oeuvre can be displayed on trays, mirrors, platters, baskets, leaves, papers or other serving pieces to create the desired look.

Arranging Buffet Platters

When displaying hors d'oeuvre and other foods on mirrors, trays or platters, the foods should be displayed in a pattern that is pleasing to the eye and flows towards the guest or from one side to the other. An easy and attractive method for accomplishing this is to arrange the items on a mirror or tray with an attractive centrepiece. The food can be placed in parallel diagonal lines, alternating the various styles and shapes. Be careful not to make the tray or mirror too fussy or cluttered, however; often the best approach is to keep it simple. The diagrams in Figure 33.1 may be used as guides for arranging canapés and other foods on trays.

APPETIZERS OR FIRST COURSES

Because eating habits have changed over the years, the types of foods chefs prepare have also changed. Today, only the most elaborate banquets include hors d'oeuvre, soup, salad, entree and dessert and perhaps separate fish and

FIGURE 33.1 *Simple patterns that can be used to effectively display canapés and other foods on trays or mirrors.*

cheese courses. A more likely progression may be soup (which serves as the appetizer), salad, entree and dessert, or a salad with a small portion of grilled meat or fish that doubles as both appetizer and salad, followed by an entree and dessert. Because of these changes the term **first course** may be more fitting than appetizer.

Generally, appetizers and first courses are small portions of foods intended to whet the appetite in anticipation of more substantial courses to follow. Some appetizers may contain a combination of protein, vegetable and starch. More often, appetizers consist only of the main item accompanied by a sauce and/or garnish. Appetizers do not need to contain any meat, poultry, fish or shellfish, however. Soups, salads, charcuterie items, vegetables, pizzas, pastas and other starch dishes may be served as appetizers. Because they are very rich, some foods such as foie gras and escargots are traditionally served as appetizers. These foods are generally consumed in small amounts and are rarely served as entrees.

Basic Guidelines for Preparing Appetizers

1. The first course should be small. Remember, there are other, more substantial courses to follow. As the name implies, an appetizer should stimulate the appetite rather than satisfy it. Remember that rich cream-based sauces tend to satisfy appetites quickly, even when the portions are small. Sixty to 90 g (2–3 oz.) of pasta and 60 g (2 oz.) of sauce is an ample appetizer portion. Many recipes can be prepared as an appetizer by simply serving smaller portions.
2. Avoid very spicy foods that may deaden the palate and detract from any more delicate flavours that follow.
3. The first course should harmonize with the rest of the meal with respect to the types of foods as well as the style. For example, an appetizer of a roasted Anaheim chile stuffed with grilled corn and goat cheese followed by an entree of paupiettes of sole vin blanc would be a poor combination: The strong spices and flavours of the chile would overpower the delicate flavours of the sole; the chile has strong southwestern ties, the sole is a classic French dish.
4. Avoid duplication of foods within the meal. If fish or shellfish is served as the first course, try not to serve fish or shellfish as the main course.
5. For more variety, use several methods of preparation within the meal. If the entree will be grilled or roasted, serve a first course that is poached or sautéed.
6. A first course should always be attractively presented. Remember that often it is the first food the customer sees. It should set the standard for the rest of the meal.

SANDWICHES

A sandwich is often the first meal a person learns to prepare. Even those who claim to be unable to cook often make delicious hot and cold sandwiches without considering it cooking. Mastering a grilled cheese sandwich or assembling the quintessential BLT may not require a degree in culinary arts, but it does require the ability to select and use ingredients wisely.

Sandwiches offer food service operations economical opportunities for using leftovers and offer customers, especially those with smaller budgets or appetites, meals to eat out of hand. Thus, the ability to correctly prepare hot and cold sandwiches to order is a fundamental skill in many food service operations.

Ingredients for Sandwiches

Sandwiches are constructed from bread, a spread and one or more fillings. These components should be selected and combined carefully so that the finished sandwich is flavourful and visually appealing.

Bread

Bread provides more than a convenient means for handling a sandwich. It holds or contains the spread and fillings and gives the sandwich its shape. Bread also adds flavour, texture, nutrition and colour, and often determines the overall look of the finished product.

Health consciousness and consumer willingness to try new and unusual foods give today's cooks the freedom to create sandwiches without relying on two slices of white bread. Virtually any bread can be used in sandwich-making: rolls, biscuits, bagels, croissants, fruit and nut breads, whole grain breads and savoury breads, as well as flatbreads such as naan, lavosh and tortillas, pocket breads such as pitas and flavourful breads such as focaccia and Swedish limpa.

Whatever bread is used and whether its flavour is mild or intense, the bread should complement the fillings and not overpower them. The bread should be fresh (although day-old bread is easier to slice and is excellent toasted) and its texture should be able to withstand moisture from the spread and fillings without becoming soggy or pasty. An overly hard or crusty bread, however, may make the sandwich difficult to eat.

Spread

A spread is used to add flavour, moisture and richness to the sandwich and, sometimes, it helps hold or bind it together. Some spreads, especially plain or flavoured butters, also act as a barrier to prevent the moisture in the filling from soaking into the bread.

There are three principal spreads:

Butter—One of the most common spreads, plain butter adds flavour and richness; it is also an excellent moisture barrier. Flavoured or compound butters, discussed in Chapter 10, Stocks and Sauces, make excellent sandwich spreads, adding flavour dimensions to the finished product. For example, try caper butter on a Cajun-style blackened beef sandwich or a red chile honey butter on a smoked turkey sandwich. Any butter spread should be softened or whipped so that it will spread easily without tearing the bread.

Mayonnaise—Perhaps the most popular sandwich spread, mayonnaise adds moisture, richness and flavour and complements most meat, poultry, fish, shellfish, vegetable, egg and cheese fillings. Like butter, mayonnaise can be made more exciting by adding flavouring ingredients. Condiments (for example, coarse-grained mustard or grated horseradish), herbs, spices and spice blends (for example, curry or chilli powder) and other ingredients such as sun-dried tomatoes and pesto sauce can be stirred into fresh or commercially prepared mayonnaise. Fresh mayonnaise can also be prepared with flavoured oils, such as olive oil, walnut oil or chile oil. See Chapter 24, Salads and Salad Dressings, for recipes and additional information on mayonnaise.

Vegetable purées—Puréed vegetables are often used as sandwich spreads; after all, lunch boxes everywhere would be incomplete without a purée of roasted peanuts (more commonly known as peanut butter) and fruit jelly. More sophisticated examples include finely chopped black olives flavoured with fresh thyme, oregano and a few drops of olive oil (tapenade) for a sandwich of Italian meats and cheeses, or a well-seasoned chickpea purée with lemon and tahini paste for a vegetarian sandwich. Unlike butter, vegetable purées usually will not provide a moisture barrier between the bread and the fillings.

Filling

The filling is the body of the sandwich, providing most of its flavour. A sandwich often contains more than one filling. For example, the filling in a Reuben sandwich is corned beef, Swiss cheese and sauerkraut and in a BLT it is bacon, lettuce and tomato. Most fillings for cold sandwiches must be precooked and properly chilled, although some hot sandwich fillings may be cooked to order.

When choosing fillings, be sure that the flavours complement each other. Their textures may be similar or contrasting. If an ingredient, such as lettuce, is supposed to be crisp, it should be very crisp, not limp. If an ingredient is supposed to be tender and moist, make sure it is so. Improperly prepared, poor quality or mishandled filling ingredients can ruin an otherwise wonderful sandwich.

Popular fillings include:

Beef—Although the classic hot beef sandwich is the hamburger, other hot or cold beef products are commonly used. For example, hot or cold small steaks, slices of larger cuts such as the tenderloin, thin slices of roast beef, and so on, make excellent fillings. Also popular are hot or cold slices of cured beef products, including corned beef, pastrami and tongue as well as beef sausages such as salami, bologna and hot dogs.

Pork—Various ham and bacon products, served either hot or cold, are extremely popular. In addition, pork loin and tenderloin are light, white meats that adapt well to various flavour combinations and cooking methods. Barbecued pork, pork sausages and pork hot dogs are also popular.

Poultry—Sliced turkey breast, either roasted or smoked, and processed turkey are often used in hot or cold sandwiches. Moreover, food substitutes such as turkey bologna, pastrami, hot dogs and ham are becoming increasingly popular because they generally have a lower fat content than the beef or pork original. Boneless chicken breast, either sliced or whole, is also quite popular as it can be prepared by a variety of methods; it complements a broad range of flavours and it has a relatively low fat content.

Fish and shellfish—Although fried fish fillets are an old standard, grilled fish sandwiches are gaining in popularity. Canned fish products, particularly tuna and salmon, are also widely used. Often fish and shellfish, especially tuna, shrimp and crab, are used for mayonnaise-based bound salads. Sardines and anchovies are less popular than other fish, but are sometimes mixed into bound salads or arranged on open-faced sandwiches.

Vegetables—Vegetables add texture, moisture, flavour and nutrition to most any sandwich. Fresh vegetables such as lettuce, onions and tomatoes are commonly used in combination with meat, cheese and other fillings. Vegetables, however, can stand on their own as sandwich fillings. Marinated, grilled vegetables can be used in hot or cold sandwiches and a combination of sliced, fresh vegetables and a flavourful dressing wrapped in soft lavosh or a tortilla becomes a portable salad.

Eggs—Hard-boiled eggs are most often used as an ingredient in a mayonnaise-based salad, where they are chopped and combined with pickle relish and seasonings. Hard-boiled eggs can also be sliced thin and used as an attractive garnish on open-faced sandwiches. Fried or scrambled eggs can be layered between pieces of bread or rolled in a tortilla for a breakfast sandwich.

Cheese—Cheese is available in such a variety of textures, flavours, colours and styles that it is a welcome addition to nearly any sandwich. Sliced cheese can be used as a filling in hot or cold sandwiches and melted cheese or a cheese sauce makes an excellent topping for hot open-faced sandwiches. Flavoured cream cheese is also used as a spread or filling, particularly with bagels and fruit or nut breads.

Bound Salads—Protein salads bound with mayonnaise or salad dressing are popular sandwich fillings. Examples include chicken, tuna, egg and ham salads. Bound salads are discussed in Chapter 24, Salads and Salad Dressings.

Types of Sandwiches

Sandwiches can be hot or cold, closed or open-faced, depending on the way in which the ingredients are assembled and presented.

Hot Sandwiches

Hot closed sandwiches include those in which the filling ingredients are served hot, such as a hamburger or hot dog, and those where the entire sandwich is heated for service, such as a grilled cheese or Monte Cristo. Hot closed sandwiches can be categorized as basic, grilled or deep-fat fried.

Basic hot closed sandwiches are generally those in which the principal filling is served hot between two pieces of bread. These sandwiches may also include fillings that are not hot, such as tomato slices and lettuce leaves. Variations of the basic hot closed sandwich include tacos, quesadillas, burros (or burritos) and wraps, in which the hot and/or cold fillings are folded or wrapped in a tortilla or other supple flatbread.

Basic Procedure for Preparing Wrap Sandwiches

1. Top the tortilla with a spread or dressing.

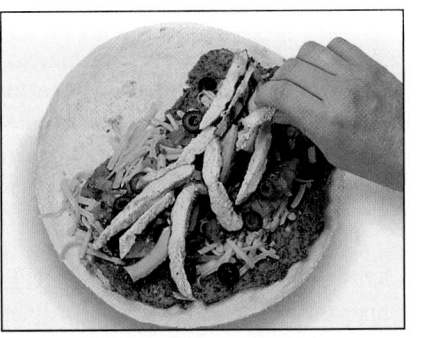

2. Place vegetables and meat, fish or poultry items in a mound across the tortilla.

3. Roll the tortilla tightly around the filling.

Grilled cheese sandwiches

Grilled sandwiches are those in which the filling is placed between two pieces of bread, which are buttered on the outside and then browned on a griddle or in a sauté pan. The filling will be warmed during this procedure but will not cook. Therefore, filings such as bacon or sliced meat should be fully cooked before the sandwich is assembled and grilled.

Deep-fat fried sandwiches are made by dipping a closed sandwich in egg batter or bread crumbs and then deep-fat frying it. The most common example is the Monte Cristo: white bread filled with sliced ham, turkey, Swiss cheese and Dijon mustard.

The hot open-faced turkey or steak sandwich proved long ago that sandwiches do not need to be eaten out of hand. In the typical **hot open-faced sandwich**, bread (grilled, toasted or fresh) is placed on a serving plate, covered with hot meat or other filling and topped with an appropriate gravy, sauce or cheese. (Figure 33.2 illustrates a suggested service style.) The completed dish

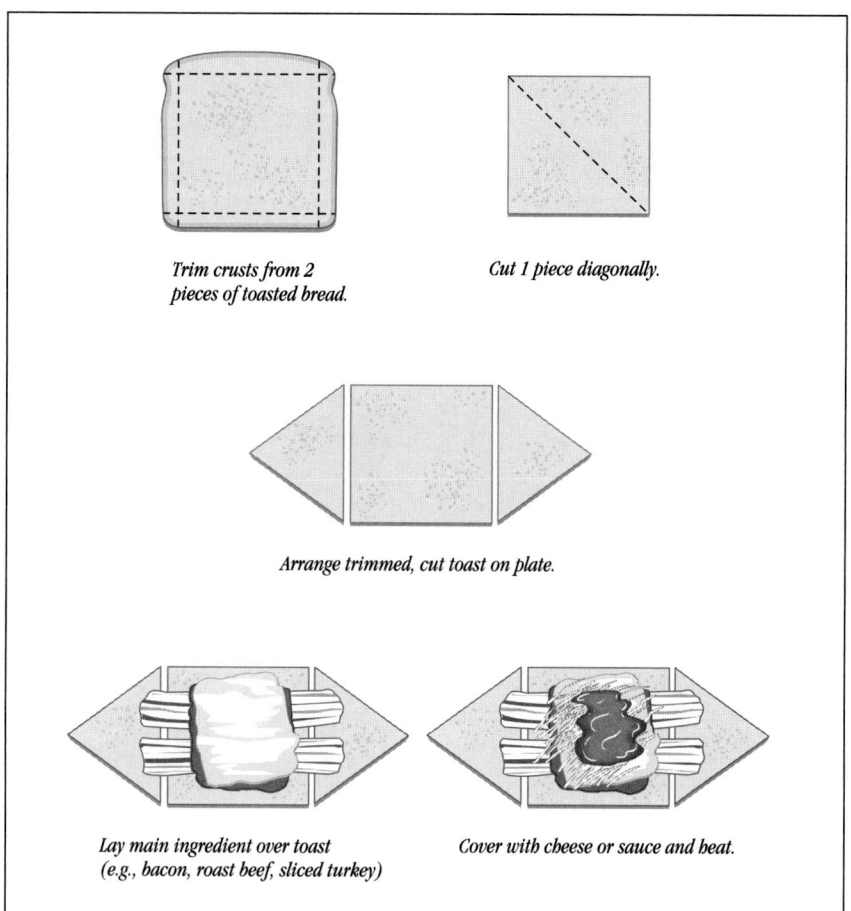

Trim crusts from 2 pieces of toasted bread.

Cut 1 piece diagonally.

Arrange trimmed, cut toast on plate.

Lay main ingredient over toast (e.g., bacon, roast beef, sliced turkey)

Cover with cheese or sauce and heat.

FIGURE 33.2   *The arrangement of a hot open-faced sandwich.*

is often browned under a broiler before service. Condiments and garnishes are usually served on the side.

Perhaps the ultimate hot open-faced sandwich is the pizza. Bread dough is topped with sauce, cheese, meat and vegetables, then baked. Small personal-sized pizzas are a popular menu item even in upscale restaurants.

Cold Sandwiches

Cold sandwiches are simply sandwiches that are eaten cold. They are made with raw ingredients that are not intended to be cooked, such as vegetables and cheese, or with meat, poultry, fish or shellfish that is precooked then chilled before use as a filling. As with hot sandwiches, cold sandwiches may be closed or open-faced.

Cold closed sandwiches are those that contain two or more pieces of bread with one or more fillings and one or more spreads. Cold closed sandwiches are usually eaten with the hands and come in three styles: basic, multi-decker and tea.

Basic cold sandwiches are made with two pieces of bread or one split roll, one spread and one or more fillings. A tuna salad sandwich or an Italian-style submarine are both examples of basic cold closed sandwiches. A variation of the basic cold sandwich is a wrap with cold fillings, for example, a herb-flavoured tortilla spread with peanut sauce and wrapped around spinach leaves, diced grilled chicken and cold cooked rice.

One of the earliest recorded references to foods eaten between two pieces of bread tells of Rabbi Hillel, a great Jewish teacher who lived sometime between 70 B.C. and A.D. 70. He created the Passover custom of eating haroseth (chopped nuts and apples) and mohror (bitter herbs) between two slices of matzo (unleavened bread). This "sandwich" was intended to represent the mortar used by the Jews to build the Egyptians' pyramids and the bitter sadness of their internment away from the land of Israel.

The term *sandwich* came into use approximately 200 years ago. The Fourth Earl of Sandwich, Sir John Montague (1718–1792), is credited with popularizing the concept of eating meats and cheeses between two slices of bread. Apparently the earl, not wanting to leave the gaming tables that he loved so much, would demand that his servants bring him meat and bread. He combined the two and ate them with one hand, allowing him a free hand to continue playing at the tables. Some historians argue that a more likely scenario is that, as the head of defence, the earl was kept busy planning British strategy for the Revolutionary War underway in the American colonies. Whichever the case, the name stuck.

Sandwiches became more popular in North America when soft white bread became common in the early 20th century. Today sandwiches are found on breakfast, lunch and dinner menus and are served by every type of food service operation, from the most casual diner to the fanciest four-star dining room.

Multi-decker cold sandwiches are made with three or more pieces of bread, one or more spreads and two or more fillings. The clubhouse sandwich, in which sliced turkey, bacon, lettuce and tomato are layered with three slices of toasted bread, is a classic example of a multi-decker sandwich, although it is actually served warm.

Basic Procedure for Preparing Cold Multi-Decker Sandwiches

1. Spread butter or mayonnaise on the first slice of toasted bread and top with meat and vegetables.

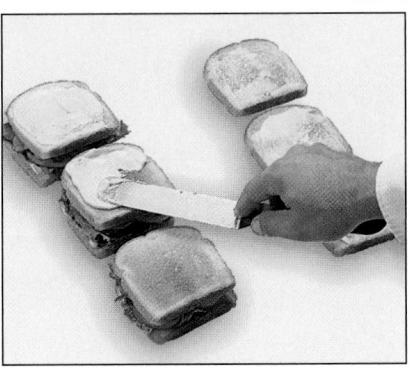

2. Add the second slice of bread and spread with mayonnaise.

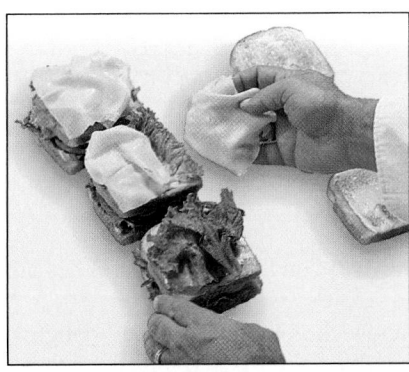

3. Add a second layer of vegetables and meat.

4. Cut the finished sandwich into quarters for service.

Tea sandwiches are small, fancy constructions made with light, soft, trimmed breads and delicate fillings and spreads. They are usually cut or rolled into shapes such as diamonds, circles or pinwheels and served as a finger food at parties and receptions.

Cold open-faced sandwiches are simply larger versions of canapés, discussed earlier in this chapter. The most popular style is the open-faced Danish sandwich known as smørbrød. As with canapés, much emphasis is placed on visual appeal. A single slice of bread is coated with a spread, a small lettuce leaf may be used, then covered with thin slices of meat, poultry or fish, or a portion of a bound salad. Carefully cut and arranged garnishes such as hard-boiled eggs, fresh herbs, pickles, onions and radishes are used to complete the presentation. (See Figure 33.3 for serving suggestions.) A simpler version of an open-faced cold sandwich is a delicatessen classic—a bagel with lox and cream cheese.

FIGURE 33.3   *Cold open-faced sandwiches.*

Preparing Sandwiches

Sandwiches are generally prepared to order and their preparation usually requires a great deal of handwork. Therefore, the goal is to assemble all ingredients and equipment so that your motions will be as quick and efficient as possible at the time of final assembly. Because each menu and food service operation has its own requirements, there is no one correct station setup, but there are a few basic guidelines.

1. *Prepare ingredients.* All sandwich ingredients should be cooked, mixed, sliced and prepared ahead of service to facilitate quick, efficient assembly at service time. So, before service, slice the meats, cheeses and vegetables, blend the flavoured spreads, mix the bound salads, and so on.

2. *Arrange and store ingredients.* Arrange all sandwich ingredients within easy reach of the work area. Cold items must be properly refrigerated at all times. A sandwich bar, similar to a steam table but with refrigerated compartments, is frequently used for this purpose (see Figure 33.4). Under-counter refrigeration can be used for backup supplies and less frequently used ingredients. Sliced meats, cheeses and vegetables must be well covered to prevent dehydration or contamination. Many ingredients can be preportioned, either by weight or count, then wrapped in individual portions for storage.

FIGURE 33.4   *A typical sandwich bar.*

◆◆◆

SANDWICH SANITATION

Sandwiches, whether hot or cold, present a particularly dangerous environment for the spread of food-borne illnesses. The use of pre-cooked, high protein foods, the combination of hot and cold ingredients and the presence of uncooked eggs in spreads such as mayonnaise offer bacteria attractive homes. Cross-contamination can be an especially common problem because of the repeated use of spatulas, spreaders, scales, knives, cutting boards and, deadliest of all, human hands. Take extra care to wash hands frequently and to clean work surfaces and tools with a sanitizer often during service. Latex gloves provide false security. They often cause more problems than they solve. The cardinal rule for proper food handling applies as well: *Keep hot foods hot, keep cold foods cold.* Please review Chapter 2, Food Safety and Sanitation for further information.

3. *Select and arrange equipment.* The heavy equipment needed for making sandwiches can include preparation equipment such as meat slicers, griddles, grills, fryers and broilers as well as storage equipment such as refrigerated sandwich bars for cold ingredients and steam tables for hot ingredients. Even the simplest sandwich menu requires the use of basic hand tools such as spatulas, spreaders, portion scoops, knives and cutting boards. Be sure that the supply of such items is adequate to permit quick handwork and to avoid delays at service time.

Presenting and Garnishing Sandwiches

Sandwiches, especially cold closed sandwiches, are usually cut into halves, thirds or quarters for service. See Figure 33.5 for examples. Cutting makes a sandwich easier for the customer to handle and allows for a more attractive presentation: the sandwich wedges can be arranged to add height to the plate and to expose the fillings' colours and textures. Hot closed sandwiches such as hamburgers are often presented open-faced. Condiments, such as mustard and mayonnaise, and garnishes, such as sliced tomatoes, onions, relish and lettuce leaves, are served on the side or on one of the open bun halves. This tends to be a more attractive presentation and it allows the customer to assemble and add ingredients to the sandwich as desired.

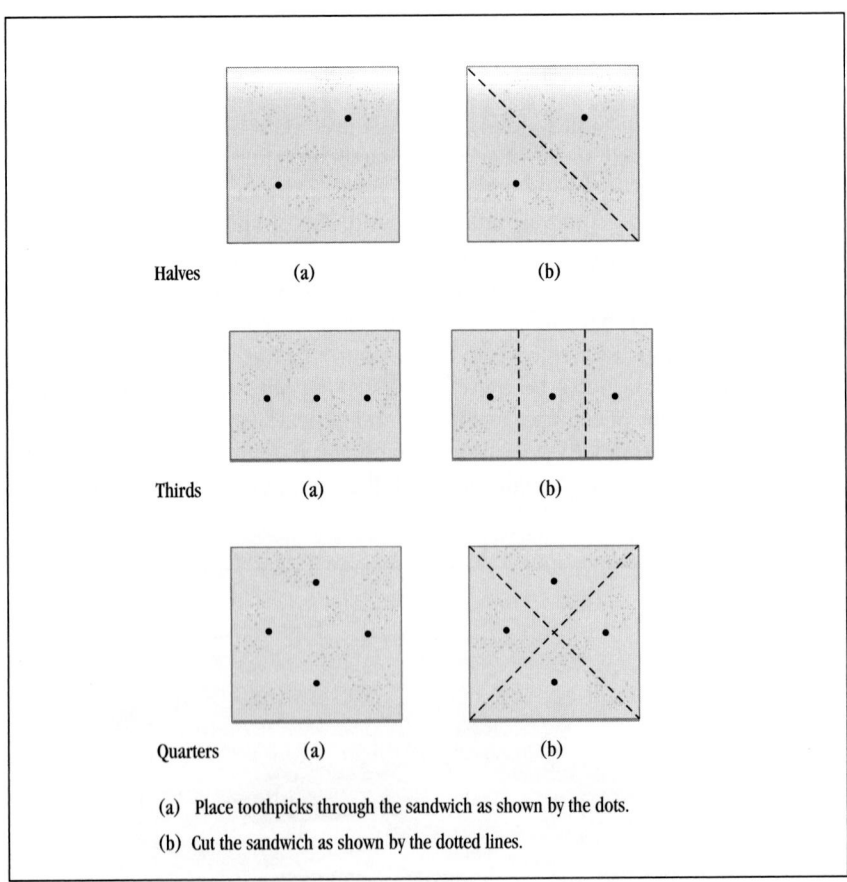

Halves   (a)   (b)

Thirds   (a)   (b)

Quarters   (a)   (b)

(a) Place toothpicks through the sandwich as shown by the dots.

(b) Cut the sandwich as shown by the dotted lines.

FIGURE 33.5   *Cutting sandwiches.*

Although a sandwich can be a meal unto itself, it may be served with a salad or starch accompaniment. Potato chips or french-fried potatoes are, of course, standard fare, perhaps because they also are finger foods and they provide a crunchy texture. Bound salads, such as potato and macaroni, are also common starch accompaniments. Plated sandwiches have long been served with cole slaw, fruit salad or a small mixed green salad as side dishes. Even the standard soup-and-sandwich combo—half of a sandwich with a cup of soup—remains a popular lunch selection.

CONCLUSION

The preparation of hors d'oeuvre and sandwiches provides an opportunity for the cook to demonstrate his or her creativity, knowledge of food and skills in presentation and garnishing. Because hors d'oeuvre and canapés often serve as the guests' introduction to the foods you serve, it is especially important that these foods be properly prepared and of the highest quality.

Quality is equally important for sandwiches, which should be made from fresh, carefully prepared ingredients, presented in an appetizing and appealing manner. Flavours, colours and textures of the bread, spread and filling should be appropriate and complementary. Breads should be fresh, never stale and appropriate for the finished sandwich. Spreads should be carefully chosen to add extra flavours and moisture to the sandwich but should not be used to cover or mask dry or poor-quality fillings or breads. Fillings provide the dominant flavour and are usually the source of the sandwich's name; they should be flavourful and properly prepared. The appearance of even the most basic sandwich can be improved by careful assembly and precise trimming and cutting.

QUESTIONS FOR DISCUSSION

1. Discuss four guidelines that should be followed when preparing hors d'oeuvre.
2. Identify and describe the three parts of a canapé.
3. Describe the differences between beluga, osetra and sevruga caviars and explain how these foods differ from domestic caviars.
4. Create an hors d'oeuvre menu for a small cocktail party. Include three hot and three cold items and explain the reasons for your selections.
5. List and explain five guidelines that should be followed when preparing appetizers or first courses.
6. List examples for each of the three primary sandwich components.
7. Explain the differences between a hot open-faced and a hot closed sandwich.
8. List several hand tools used in sandwich production and explain the need for an ample supply of these tools.
9. Why is cross-contamination a concern when preparing sandwiches? What simple steps can be taken to avoid the spread of pathogenic microorganisms?

ADDITIONAL APPETIZER AND SANDWICH RECIPES

RECIPE 33.9

STUFFED SQUASH BLOSSOMS AND BUCKWHEAT BLINIS WITH SMOKED SALMON AND CAVIAR

Yield: 24 Servings

Chèvre cheese	250 g	8 oz.
Cream cheese	125 g	4 oz.
Assorted fresh herbs, chopped	10 g	2 tsp.
Garlic cloves, minced	2	2
Black pepper	TT	TT
Baby squash with blossoms	24	24
Tempura Batter (Recipe 21.4)	700 g	24 oz.
Bell peppers, red, yellow and green, julienned	350 g	12 oz.
Olive oil	15 mL	1 Tbsp.
Salt	TT	TT
Buckwheat Blinis (recipe follows)	24	24
Blackberry preserves	100 g	3 oz.
Smoked salmon, sliced	500 g	1 lb.
Caviar	50 g	2 oz.
Fresh basil sprigs	24	24

1. Blend the chèvre cheese and cream cheese in the bowl of an electric mixer until smooth. Fold in the herbs and garlic and season with black pepper.
2. Using a pastry bag fitted with a round tip, fill each of the squash blossoms with the cheese mixture and pinch the flowers shut.
3. Dip each of the squash in tempura batter and deep-fat fry until lightly browned, approximately 1 minute. Remove and drain well.
4. Sauté the peppers in olive oil until tender. Season with salt and pepper.
5. Carefully split each squash and blossom in half. Arrange two squash halves on each plate and garnish with the julienned peppers.
6. Spread each blini with blackberry preserves. Form rosettes out of the salmon slices and place one on each blini.
7. Place a blini on the plate with the squash and peppers and garnish with two dollops of caviar and a sprig of basil.

BUCKWHEAT BLINIS

Yield: 24 Blinis

Granulated sugar	10 g	2 tsp.
Dry yeast	7 g	1/4 oz.
Milk, lukewarm	400 mL	14 fl. oz.
Buckwheat flour	125 g	4 oz.
All-purpose flour	100 g	3 oz.
Salt	2 g	1/2 tsp.
Unsalted butter, melted	50 g	3 Tbsp.

RECIPE 33.9

Approximate values per serving:

Calories	190
Total fat	7 g
Saturated fat	4 g
Cholesterol	49 mg
Sodium	416 mg
Total carbohydrates	22 g
Protein	10 g

Vegetable oil	30 mL	2 Tbsp.
Egg yolks	3	3
Egg whites	2	2

1. Stir the sugar and yeast into the warmed milk and let stand until foamy, approximately 5 minutes.

2. Whisk in the flours, salt, butter, oil and egg yolks. Beat until smooth.

3. Cover the batter and allow it to rise in a warm place until doubled, approximately 1 hour.

4. Beat the egg whites to stiff peaks, then fold them into the risen batter.

5. Lightly oil and preheat a large sauté pan. Drop 30 mL (2 Tbsp.) of batter into the sauté pan, spacing the blini at least 2.5 cm (1 inch) apart. Cook until the bottom of each blini is golden, approximately 1 minute. Turn the blini and cook an additional 30 seconds. Remove from the pan and keep warm for service.

◆ ◆ ◆

RECIPE 33.10

HUMMUS

Yield: 1 L (1 qt.)

Chickpeas, cooked	500 g	1 lb.
Tahini paste	250 g	8 oz.
Garlic, chopped	10 g	2 tsp.
Cumin	1 g	1/2 tsp.
Lemon juice	150 mL	5 fl. oz.
Olive oil	100 mL	3 fl. oz.
Salt	5 g	1 tsp.
Cayenne pepper	TT	TT
Fresh parsley, chopped	10 g	2 tsp.

1. Combine the chickpeas, tahini, garlic, cumin, lemon juice and olive oil in a food processor; process until smooth. Season with salt and cayenne.

2. Spoon the hummus onto a serving platter and smooth the surface. Drizzle a little olive oil over the hummus and garnish with the chopped parsley. Serve with warm pita bread that has been cut into quarters.

◆ ◆ ◆

RECIPE 33.11

GUACAMOLE

Yield: 1 L (1 qt.)

Avocados	6	6
Lemon juice	75 mL	2-1/2 fl. oz.
Green onion, sliced	30 g	4 Tbsp.
Cilantro, chopped	30 g	3 Tbsp.
Tomatoes, seeded, diced	50 g	3 Tbsp.
Garlic, chopped	5 g	1 tsp.
Jalapeños, seeded, chopped	1	1
Salt	TT	TT

1. Cut each avocado in half. Remove the seed and scoop out the pulp.

2. Add the lemon juice to the avocado pulp and mix well, mashing the avocado pulp.

3. Add the remaining ingredients. Season with salt and mix well.

Buckwheat Blinis—
Approximate values per serving:

Calories	43
Total fat	1 g
Saturated fat	0.5 g
Cholesterol	2 mg
Sodium	90 mg
Total carbohydrates	8 g
Protein	2 g

RECIPE 33.10

Approximate values per 85 mL serving:

Calories	267
Total fat	19 g
Saturated fat	3 g
Cholesterol	0 mg
Sodium	20 mg
Total carbohydrates	19 g
Protein	8 g

RECIPE 33.11

Approximate values per 50 mL serving:

Calories	100
Total fat	9 g
Saturated fat	1.5 g
Cholesterol	0 mg
Sodium	243 mg
Total carbohydrates	5 g
Protein	1 g

◆◆◆

RECIPE 33.12

SUN-DRIED TOMATO AND BASIL AIOLI

Yield: 1 L (1 qt.)

Garlic cloves, mashed to a paste	4	4
Egg yolks	4	4
Lemon juice	30 mL	2 Tbsp.
Olive oil	700 mL	1-1/2 pt.
Sun-dried tomatoes, packed in olive oil	125 g	4 oz.
Fresh basil, chopped	30 g	4 Tbsp.
Salt	5 g	1 tsp.
Pepper	2 g	1/2 tsp.

RECIPE 33.12

Approximate values per 15 mL serving:

Calories	95
Total fat	10 g
Saturated fat	1.4 g
Cholesterol	13 mg
Sodium	70 mg
Total carbohydrates	1 g
Protein	0.5 g

1. Combine the garlic, egg yolks and a few drops of the lemon juice in a bowl and whip until frothy.
2. While whipping the egg yolk mixture, slowly add the olive oil until an emulsion begins to form. Continue adding the oil while whipping until all of the oil is incorporated. A few drops of lemon juice may be added from time to time to thin the sauce.
3. Finely chop the sun-dried tomatoes. Add them, a portion of the olive oil in which they were packed, and the basil to the aioli.
4. Season with salt, pepper and lemon juice.

◆◆◆

RECIPE 33.13

SATAY WITH PEANUT SAUCE, SINGAPORE STYLE

Yield: 16 Skewers

Chicken breast, beef inside round, pork fillet or lamb leg	500 g	1 lb.
Lemon zest	10 g	2 tsp.
Onion, chopped	200 g	7 oz.
Vegetable oil	25 mL	2 Tbsp.
Light soy sauce	15 mL	1 Tbsp.
Coriander, ground	3 g	2 tsp.
Cumin, ground	3 g	1 tsp.
Turmeric, ground	3 g	1 tsp.
Cinnamon, ground	0.25 g	1/4 tsp.
Salt	5 g	1 tsp.
Sugar	5 g	1 tsp.
Peanut Sauce (recipe follows)		

RECIPE 33.13

Approximate values per skewer and 10 mL sauce:

Calories	100
Total fat	5 g
Saturated fat	1 g
Cholesterol	27 mg
Sodium	248 mg
Total carbohydrates	4 g
Protein	10 g

1. Cut the meat into 1-cm (1/2-inch) cubes.
2. Blend remaining ingredients until smooth, coat meat and marinate for at least 1 hour.
3. Soak bamboo skewers in water for 1 hour before threading five to six pieces of meat on top half of skewer.
4. Grill or broil just until meat is cooked.
5. Serve with Peanut Sauce.

PEANUT SAUCE

Vegetable oil	50 mL	4 Tbsp.
Lemon grass, sliced	1 stalk	1 stalk
Onion, finely chopped	100 g	3 oz.
Garlic, finely chopped	10 g	3 cloves
Dried shrimp paste (blacan)	5 g	2 tsp.
Roasted peanuts, skinless	185 g	6 oz.
Dried tamarind	25 mL	1-1/2 Tbsp.
Hot water	250 mL	8 fl. oz.
Sambal olek	5 g	1 tsp.
Ginger powder	3 g	1-1/2 tsp.
Sugar	30 g	1 oz.
Salt	5 g	1 tsp.
Soy sauce	50 mL	3 Tbsp.

1. In a blender place one-half oil, lemon grass, onion, garlic and shrimp paste. Blend to a paste.
2. Scrape out blender and add peanuts. Crush finely.
3. Soak tamarind in hot water, squeeze to dissolve pulp and strain. Reserve liquid.
4. Place remaining oil in a hot wok and cook purée mixture over medium heat for a few minutes to cook it out.
5. Add remaining ingredients and simmer until gravy thickens, about 7–8 minutes.

NOTE: 100 g (3 oz.) peanut butter may be substituted for the peanuts. Lemon juice can be used for tamarind. A little coconut milk may be added for additional flavour.

Peanut Sauce—Approximate values per 10 mL serving:

Calories	34
Total fat	3 g
Saturated fat	0.5 g
Cholesterol	0 mg
Sodium	95 mg
Total carbohydrates	2 g
Protein	1 g

❖❖❖

RECIPE 33.14

SPANAKOPITA

Yield: 90 Triangles

Onion, small dice	125 g	4 oz.
Unsalted butter, melted	175 g	6 oz.
Fresh spinach, cooked and cooled, or frozen spinach, thawed	700 g	24 oz.
Fresh mint, chopped	10 g	1 Tbsp.
Feta cheese, crumbled	450 g	1 lb.
Eggs, beaten	3	3
Salt and pepper	TT	TT
Phyllo dough	450 g	1 lb.

1. Sauté the onion in 15 g (1 Tbsp.) of melted butter until tender. Remove and cool.
2. Squeeze the water from the spinach. Combine the cooled onion, spinach, mint, feta cheese and beaten eggs. Season with salt and pepper and mix well.
3. Spread one sheet of phyllo dough on the work surface; brush with melted butter. Place another sheet of phyllo on top of the first; brush it with butter. Place a third sheet of phyllo on top of the second and brush it with butter as well.

RECIPE 33.14

Approximate values per serving:

Calories	45
Total fat	3 g
Saturated fat	2 g
Cholesterol	15 mg
Sodium	105 mg
Total carbohydrates	3 g
Protein	2 g

Continued

4. Cut the dough into 5-cm-wide (2-inch) strips.
5. Place 15 g (1 Tbsp.) of the filling on the end of each strip of phyllo.
6. Starting at the end with the filling, fold one corner of the dough over the spinach to the opposite side of the strip to form a triangle. Continue folding the dough, keeping it in a triangular shape, like point-folding a flag (see photograph below).
7. Place the phyllo triangles on a sheet pan and brush with melted butter. Bake at 190°C (375°F) until brown and crispy, approximately 20 minutes.

1. Brush and stack the layers of phyllo pastry with butter.

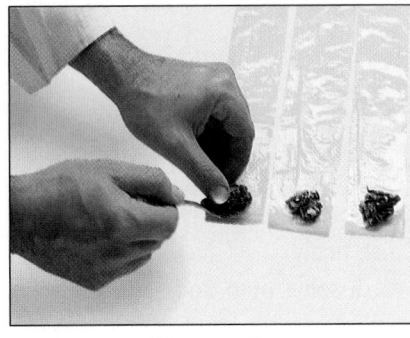

2. Place the filling on the pastry.

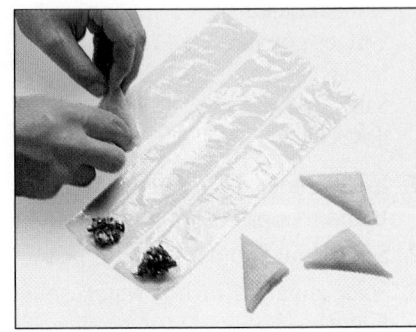

3. Fold the pastry and filling into triangles.

◆◆◆

RECIPE 33.15

KALAMATA OLIVE AND ASIAGO CHEESE CROSTINI

Yield: 12 Pieces

French baguette	1/2 loaf	1/2 loaf
Olive oil	60 mL	2 fl. oz.
Basil leaves, chopped	10 g	50
Tomato concassée	125 g	4 oz.
Garlic, chopped	8 g	2 tsp.
Kalamata olives, pitted, chopped	15	15
Asiago cheese, grated	60 g	2 oz.

1. Slice the bread 6 mm (1/4 inch) thick.
2. Brush bread slices with olive oil and bake until golden and crisp.
3. Combine the remaining ingredients and mix well.
4. Spread 20 g (1 Tbsp.) of the mixture on each slice of bread. Place under the broiler or salamander until hot and the cheese is melted, approximately 2 minutes.

RECIPE 33.15

Approximate values per serving:

Calories	93
Total fat	8 g
Saturated fat	4 g
Cholesterol	15 mg
Sodium	181 mg
Total carbohydrates	4 g
Protein	2 g

◆◆◆

RECIPE 33.16

RED POTATOES WITH WALNUTS AND GORGONZOLA CHEESE

Yield: 80 Pieces

New red potatoes	40	40
Salt and pepper	TT	TT

Fresh thyme leaves	5 g	2 tsp.
Olive oil	60 mL	2 fl. oz.
Cream cheese	250 g	8 oz.
Gorgonzola cheese	100 g	3 oz.
Bacon, small dice, cooked	30 g	1 oz.
Sour cream	125 mL	4 fl. oz.
Walnuts, chopped coarse	50 g	1-1/2 oz.
Worcestershire sauce	TT	TT
Tabasco sauce	TT	TT
Chives, minced	25 g	3 Tbsp.

1. Cut the new potatoes in half and scoop out a portion of the inside with a parisienne scoop.

2. Toss the potatoes with the salt, pepper, thyme and olive oil. Arrange the potatoes on a sheet pan with their flat surfaces down and bake at 200°C (400°F) until brown and cooked through, approximately 15 minutes.

3. Soften the cream cheese in the bowl of an electric mixer. Add the Gorgonzola cheese, bacon bits, sour cream and walnuts. Mix until smooth. Season with the Worcestershire and Tabasco sauces.

4. Using a pastry bag and plain tip, fill each hot potato half with the cold cheese mixture and sprinkle with minced chives.

VARIATION: Fill the cooked potatoes with crème fraîche, top with caviar and sprinkle with chopped chives instead of using the bacon-and-cheese mixture.

RECIPE 33.16

Approximate values per serving:

Calories	38
Total fat	3 g
Saturated fat	1 g
Cholesterol	5 mg
Sodium	61 mg
Total carbohydrates	2 g
Protein	3 g

◆ ◆ ◆

RECIPE 33.17

SPICY FISH RÖSTI

RESTAURANT ST. MORITZ, DORVAL, QC

Chef Proprietor Anton Koch, CCC

Yield: 24 Cakes

Waxy potatoes	350 g	12 oz.
Salmon or lake trout, skinless, boneless	350 g	12 oz.
Green onions, finely chopped	4	4
Fresh ginger, grated	5 g	1 tsp.
Fresh coriander, chopped	20 g	2 Tbsp.
Lemon juice	10 mL	2 tsp.
Salt and cayenne	TT	TT
Sunflower oil	30–45 mL	2–3 Tbsp.
Coriander sprigs and lemon wedges	garnish	garnish

1. Cook potatoes for 10 minutes in boiling water with the skins on. Drain and leave to cool for a few minutes.

2. Finely chop the fish and combine in a bowl with the green onion, ginger, coriander, lemon juice, salt and cayenne.

3. Peel and grate the potatoes and toss with the fish mixture.

4. Form into 24 cakes, pressing to hold together but leaving the edges rough.

5. Heat oil in a large frying pan and fry the fish cakes in batches until golden-brown and crisp. Drain on absorbent paper. Serve garnished with coriander sprigs and lemon wedges.

Anton Koch, CCC

Anton, a Swiss-trained chef, arrived in Montreal to work for Hilton International and later moved to the Swiss restaurant William Tell, where he functioned as Executive Chef and, subsequently, as Manager. He enjoys participating in various culinary exhibitions, notably the Grand Culinary Salon in Montreal and the New York Philanthropic Culinary Salon, where he won Gold in show plates and sugar art. He has been Chef Proprietor at the Restaurant St. Moritz since 1994.

RECIPE 33.17

Approximate values per cake:

Calories	56
Total fat	3 g
Saturated fat	0.5 g
Cholesterol	9 mg
Sodium	246 mg
Total carbohydrates	3.5 g
Protein	4 g

Francisco Rivera
Francisco trained in Toronto and has worked there for most of his career, gravitating towards Italian cuisine. He is a member of the Canadian Federation of Chefs and Cooks and the Escoffier Society of Toronto.

RECIPE 33.18

Approximate values per serving:

Calories	181
Total fat	12 g
Saturated fat	4 g
Cholesterol	17 mg
Sodium	428 mg
Total carbohydrates	16 g
Protein	4 g

✦✦✦

RECIPE 33.18

POACHED PEAR APPETIZER

GALILEO RISTORANTE, TORONTO, ON
Executive Chef Francisco Rivera

Yield: 4 Portions

Bosc pears, peeled and halved	4 whole	4 whole
Amaretto	30 mL	1 fl. oz.
Brandy	30 mL	1 fl. oz.
Cinnamon stick	1	1
Rosemary, fresh	1 pinch	1 pinch
Cashews, chopped	50 g	1-1/2 oz.
Sun-dried tomatoes, julienned	30 g	2 pieces
Pancetta (or smoked goose)	50 g	1-1/2 oz.
Olive oil	15 mL	1 Tbsp.
Butter	30 g	1 oz.
Shiitake mushrooms, julienned	125 g	4 oz.
Plum, halved, sliced thinly	1 whole	1 whole
Salt and pepper	TT	TT
Nutmeg, grated	TT	TT
Cream, 18%	30 mL	2 Tbsp.
Veal stock	150 mL	1/3 pt.

1. Remove core and seeds from pear halves. Keep stems attached.
2. Simmer pear halves in enough water to cover along with amaretto, brandy, cinnamon, rosemary, 15 g (1/2 oz.) cashews and one sun-dried tomato piece.
3. Remove pear halves when tender. Sauté pancetta in olive oil until browned. Remove excess oil and add butter. Add mushrooms, remaining sun-dried tomato piece, remaining cashews and plum.
4. Season to taste with salt and pepper and nutmeg.
5. Add cream and veal stock. Simmer until slightly thickened.
6. Add drained pears.
7. To serve, fill pear halves with mushroom mixture.
8. Coat pears with remaining sauce. Serve warm.

✦✦✦

RECIPE 33.19

GRILLED SHRIMP WITH PROSCIUTTO AND BASIL

Yield: 12 Pieces

Shrimp, 16–20 count, peeled and deveined, tails removed	12	12
Dry white wine	50 mL	2 fl. oz.
Rice wine vinegar	30 mL	1 fl. oz.
Thyme, fresh	5 g	2 tsp.
Onion, minced	25 g	1 oz.
Cumin, ground	5 g	1 Tbsp.
Salt and pepper	TT	TT
Vegetable oil	100 mL	3 fl. oz.

Dried basil	2 g	2 tsp.
Garlic cloves, chopped	2	2
Prosciutto slices	3	3
Fresh basil leaves	6	6

1. Combine all of the ingredients except the prosciutto and fresh basil in a stainless-steel bowl. Marinate for 30 minutes.

2. Remove the shrimps from the marinade and drain them well.

3. Cut each slice of prosciutto into quarters.

4. Wrap each shrimp first with one-half leaf of basil, then a piece of prosciutto; secure with a toothpick.

5. Grill for 1–1.5 minutes per side. Be careful not to overcook. Remove the toothpick and serve hot or cold.

✦✦✦

RECIPE 33.20

SMOKED SALMON ROULADE

THE FOUR SEASONS, NEW YORK, NY
Chef Christian Albin

Yield: 4 Servings

Smoked salmon, sliced	300 g	10 oz.
Wasabi powder	2 g	1 tsp.
Celery root (or celery), small dice	250 g	8 oz.
Sour cream	100 mL	3 fl. oz.
Chives, blanched and refreshed	1 bunch	1 bunch
Black caviar	125 g	4 oz.
Radish, cut into strips		
(placed in ice water to crisp)	4	4
Cucumber, cut in rounds		
(placed in ice water to crisp)	1/2	1/2

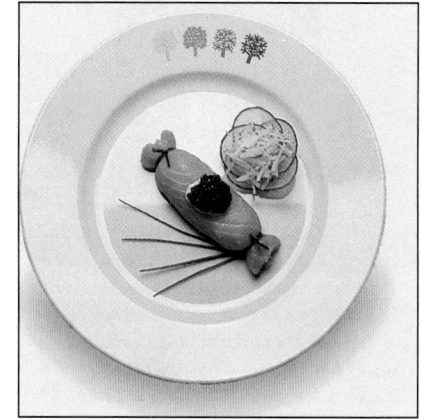

1. Form the slices of smoked salmon into four rectangles. Reserve any salmon trimmings for the stuffing.

2. To make the stuffing, dilute the wasabi powder with 10 mL (2 tsp.) of water. Mix the celery root with the sour cream, diluted wasabi and smoked salmon trimmings.

3. To make the roulades, place an equal portion of stuffing on each smoked salmon rectangle. Roll up each piece of salmon, neatly locking the stuffing in place.

4. Tie each roulade with a chive "string" at each end. Trim the strings.

5. Place each roulade on a plate. Garnish with caviar, radish strips and cucumber rounds.

✦✦✦

RECIPE 33.21

ESCARGOT IN GARLIC BUTTER

Yield: Six 8-Piece Servings

| Snails, canned | 48 | 48 |
| Butter, softened | 500 g | 1 lb. |

Continued

dee Hobsbawn-Smith

dee—a Calgary-based professional chef, caterer, culinary educator, and author—has been delighting Calgary diners and readers since 1983. She studied cooking at Vancouver Vocational Institute, completed her Red Seal in Calgary, and studied with eminent chef and educator Madeleine Kamman in Annecy, France. Since selling her restaurant, Foodsmith, in 1994, dee has turned to food writing and now has three cookbooks and many magazine articles and columns under her belt.

Shallots, minced	20 g	2 Tbsp.
Garlic, chopped	10 g	2 tsp.
Fine bread crumbs	20 g	2 Tbsp.
Brandy	15 mL	1 Tbsp.
Parsley, chopped	20 g	3 Tbsp.
Salt and pepper	TT	TT
Nutmeg	pinch	pinch
Mushroom caps, medium	48	48

1. Drain and rinse the snails.
2. Combine the butter, shallots, garlic, bread crumbs, brandy, parsley, salt, pepper and nutmeg in a mixer or food processor and mix or process until well blended.
3. Sauté the mushroom caps in a small amount of the butter mixture until cooked but still firm. Remove from the heat and place six caps in each of eight shallow ramekins.
4. Place a snail in each cap and top with a generous amount of the garlic butter.
5. Bake the mushrooms and snails at 230°C (450°F) for 5–7 minutes and serve hot.

VARIATIONS:

1. If snail shells are available, place a small amount of the butter in each shell. Push a snail into the buttered shell and add more butter to completely cover the snail. Place the shells in a specially designed escargot dish or a shallow ramekin with 10 mm (1/2 inch) of rock salt to hold them in place and cook as above.
2. Prepare 48 small bouchées from puff pastry or brioche. Sauté the snails in a generous amount of the garlic butter and place one snail in each bouchée. Drizzle the snail with the garlic butter and serve as a hot hors d'oeuvre.

◆◆◆

RECIPE 33.22

SALT-CURED FOIE GRAS WITH MANGO PINEAPPLE SALSA ON BRIOCHE

Chef/Food Writer dee Hobsbawn-Smith, Calgary, AB

Yield: 350–400 g (12–14 oz.)

Foie gras	1 lobe	1 lobe
Kosher salt	as needed	as needed
Mango Pineapple Salsa (recipe follows)		

1. Remove any connective tissue and veins. Wrap in cheesecloth and tie securely.
2. Place in a bowl lined with kosher salt and completely cover with more salt. Chill for at least 24 hours.
3. Remove any fat and the cheesecloth.
4. Slice thinly. Serve on warm brioche with Mango Pineapple Salsa.

MANGO PINEAPPLE SALSA

Mango, diced	1	1
Pineapple, diced	1/2	1/2
Oranges, diced, filleted	4	4

Combine all ingredients gently and chill.

♦♦♦

RECIPE 33.23

MALPEQUE OYSTERS DRESSED IN FENNEL CITRUS WITH CARROT GAZPACHO

CHEF'S BY DESIGN, HALIFAX, NS
Chef Stephan Czapalay

Yield: 10 Servings

CARROT GAZPACHO

Carrot juice	500 mL	17 fl. oz.
Cucumber, peeled, seeded	1	1
Golden tomatoes	2	2
Ginger, chopped	8 g	2 tsp.
Celery heart	450 g	1 lb.
Carrots, sliced	500 g	8
Onion, sliced	350 g	1
Water	2 L	2 qt.
Orange juice	125 mL	4 fl. oz.
Fennel seeds	4	4

1. Purée carrot juice, cucumber, tomatoes, ginger and celery heart, pass through a fine sieve and reserve, chilled.
2. Cook remaining ingredients until tender. Purée and pass through a fine sieve.
3. Combine raw and cooked purées and pass through a sieve again.
4. Chill well.

FENNEL CITRUS SALAD

Fennel, shredded	350 g	12 oz.
Orange juice	30 mL	2 Tbsp.
Lemon juice	15 mL	1 Tbsp.
Olive oil	50 mL	3 Tbsp.

Mix all ingredients together and chill.

ASSEMBLY:

Malpeque oysters, shucked	40	40
Fresh dill	40 sprigs	40 sprigs

1. Ladle 150 mL (5 fl. oz.) of Carrot Gazpacho into a chilled soup cup or ice bowl.
2. Place 10 g (1 Tbsp.) Fennel Citrus Salad on each oyster shell and set oyster on top. Garnish with a dill sprig.
3. On a doily-lined plate, place soup and arrange oysters.

Stephan Czapalay

Stephan began his cooking career in 1984, in Wolfville, Nova Scotia, and worked in a variety of prestigious restaurants in P.E.I., Nova Scotia, Québec, France, Italy and Switzerland in the years that followed. Between 1997 and 2001, he functioned as the proud chef-owner of Seasons in Thyme Restaurant in Summerside, P.E.I., which was awarded a three-star rating from Where to Eat in Canada *and a four-diamond rating by AAA. He regularly upgrades his skills and knowledge with courses and private study, has instructed at the Canadian Culinary Institute in Charlottetown and regularly competes in national and regional competitions, most often placing in the top three.*

RECIPE 33.23

Approximate values per serving:

Calories	134
Total fat	3 g
Saturated fat	1 g
Cholesterol	30 mg
Sodium	202 mg
Total carbohydrates	21 g
Protein	6 g

♦♦♦

RECIPE 33.24

SNOW CRAB FLAN WITH HERBS

L'ORÉE DU BOIS, GATINEAU PARK, OLD CHELSEA, QC
Chef Guy Blain

Yield: 6 Servings

Cream, 18%	250 mL	8 fl. oz.
Eggs	4	4

Continued

Guy Blain

Snow crabmeat	150 g	5 oz.
Shallots, chopped	50 g	1-1/2 oz.
Chopped fresh herbs: chive, parsley, tarragon	30 g	1 oz.
Garlic, minced	5 g	2 cloves
Salt and pepper	TT	TT

1. Mix all ingredients.
2. Divide among six buttered ramekins.
3. Cook in a bain marie at 175°C (350°F) for 20 minutes. Reduce heat to 150°C (300°F) and cook for 20 minutes more.
4. Cool. Unmould and serve with an herb mayonnaise.

◆◆◆

RECIPE 33.25

ARTICHOKE, CHICKEN AND SUN-DRIED TOMATO PIZZA

Yield: One 37-cm (15-inch) or Two 22-cm (9-inch) Pizzas

Pizza Dough (Recipe 28.13)	500 g	1 lb.
Extra virgin olive oil	30 mL	1 fl. oz.
Tomato Sauce (Recipe 10.13)	125 mL	4 fl. oz.
Grilled chicken breast, sliced	175 g	6 oz.
Sun-dried tomatoes, oil packed, diced	5	5
Smoked Gruyère, grated	125 g	4 oz.
Mozzarella cheese, grated	50 g	2 oz.
Marinated artichoke hearts, sliced	50 g	2 oz.
Fresh basil	12 leaves	12 leaves

1. Preheat the oven to 260°C (500°F). Roll out the dough and place it on a lightly oiled pizza pan or well-floured wooden peel; brush it lightly with the olive oil. Spread the tomato sauce.
2. Lay the chicken and sun-dried tomatoes on top. Toss the Gruyère and mozzarella cheeses together and sprinkle onto the pizza.
3. Sprinkle the artichoke pieces and basil leaves on pizza.
4. Bake the pizza until the crust is golden and crisp, approximately 8–12 minutes.

◆◆◆

RECIPE 33.26

SPRING ROLLS

Yield: 24 Rolls

Shiitake mushrooms, diced	8	8
Peanut oil	50 mL	2 fl. oz.
Sesame oil	15 mL	1 Tbsp.
Garlic, chopped	5 g	1 tsp.
Fresh ginger, grated	2 g	1/2 tsp.
Pork, ground	250 g	8 oz.
Raw shrimp, deveined, chopped	250 g	8 oz.

RECIPE 33.24

Approximate values per serving:

Calories	138
Total fat	8 g
Saturated fat	4 g
Cholesterol	175 mg
Sodium	472 mg
Total carbohydrates	4 g
Protein	12 g

RECIPE 33.25

Approximate values per roll:

Calories	761
Total fat	48.5 g
Saturated fat	18 g
Cholesterol	158.5 mg
Sodium	601 mg
Total carbohydrates	29 g
Protein	57 g

Daikon, shredded	175 g	6 oz.
Napa cabbage, julienned	175 g	6 oz.
Bean sprouts	125 g	4 oz.
Water chestnuts, chopped	175 g	12
Bamboo shoots, chopped	175 g	6 oz.
Green onion, finely chopped	6	6
Light soy sauce	15 mL	1 Tbsp.
Oyster sauce	15 mL	1 Tbsp.
Salt and pepper	TT	TT
Cornstarch	10 g	1 Tbsp.
Spring roll wrappers	24	24

RECIPE 33.26

Approximate values per serving:

Calories	144
Total fat	9 g
Saturated fat	1.5 g
Cholesterol	26 mg
Sodium	332 mg
Total carbohydrates	8 g
Protein	6.5 g

1. Remove stems from mushrooms. If dry mushrooms are used, rehydrate.

2. Heat the oils and sauté the garlic and ginger for 5 seconds.

3. Add the pork; sauté for 30 seconds and then add shrimp and stir-fry until cooked. Reserve in refrigerator.

4. Add the prepared vegetables, sauces, salt and pepper. Cook for 30 seconds more. Tilt pan and add cornstarch, dissolved in a little water. Boil and mix thoroughly.

5. Remove from the heat, cool and refrigerate.

6. Combine both mixtures. Place 50 g (2 oz.) of filling at one end of wrap, start to roll, fold the sides over towards the middle and roll up into a cigar shape. Brush the edge with water and press to seal.

7. Deep-fat fry the spring rolls at 180°C (350°F) until hot and crispy, approximately 45 seconds.

RECIPE 33.27

MARINATED SIR LAURIER D'ARTHABASKA CHEESE

BISTRO DU LAPIN AGILE, SUTTON, QC
Executive Chef Carol Paradis

Yield: 4 Servings

Sir Laurier d'Arthabaska	1	1
Lemon juice	15 mL	1 Tbsp.
White wine vinegar	15 mL	1 Tbsp.
Green pepper, diced	30 g	1 oz.
Yellow pepper, diced	30 g	1 oz.
Plum tomatoes, diced	60 g	2 oz.
Garlic, minced	1 clove	1 clove
Fresh parsley, chopped	25 g	1/4 cup
Dijon-style mustard	20 g	1 Tbsp.
Black pepper	TT	TT

1. Place cheese in a ramekin large enough to hold the cheese and marinade.

2. With a fork, poke small holes all over the cheese.

3. Combine remaining ingredients and cover cheese. Cover with plastic wrap and refrigerate 8–12 hours.

4. Unwrap ramekin and bake in a 175°C (350°F) oven for 12–15 minutes.

5. Serve warm as a dip.

Carol Paradis
Born in Mont Joli, Quebec, Carol began his culinary career doing research on Canadian cooking for a Quebec culinary museum. Having taught at the Wolfgang Puck Cooking School and the French Culinary Institute in New York, Carol spent the last two years as Chef-Proprietor of Bistro du Lapin Agile, in Sutton, Quebec. Currently, he works as a chef-consultant doing things like functioning as the Executive Chef at the 2001 Tennis Masters Series and the 2001 International Meeting of Airports.

RECIPE 33.27

Approximate values per serving:

Calories	166
Total fat	13 g
Saturated fat	8 g
Cholesterol	45 mg
Sodium	351 mg
Total carbohydrates	3 g
Protein	10 g

◆◆◆

RECIPE 33.28

GROUPER SANDWICH WITH LEMON RÉMOULADE

PHOENIX BREWING CO., ATLANTA, GA
Executive Chef Kevin Fonzo

Yield: 6 Sandwiches

Olive oil	30 mL	2 Tbsp.
Grouper fillets, each 150 g (5 oz.)	6	6
Salt and pepper	TT	TT
Lemon Rémoulade (recipe follows)	90 mL	6 Tbsp.
Kaiser rolls, sliced, toasted	6	6
Mixed greens	350 g	12 oz.
Tomato slices	6	6

1. Heat the olive oil in a large sauté pan. Season the grouper fillets with salt and pepper and then sauté the fish until golden-brown and cooked through.
2. To assemble each sandwich, spread 15 mL (1 Tbsp.) of the lemon rémoulade on the bottom half of each roll, then top with 60 g (2 oz.) of mixed greens, a tomato slice and the cooked fish. Cover with remaining half of the roll and serve.

LEMON RÉMOULADE

Yield: 600 mL (20 fl. oz.)

Mayonnaise	500 mL	16 fl. oz.
Sweet pickle relish	100 g	3 oz.
Onion, chopped fine	20 g	2 Tbsp.
Parsley, chopped	20 g	2 Tbsp.
Fresh lemon juice	30 mL	2 Tbsp.
Salt and black pepper	TT	TT
Worcestershire sauce	TT	TT
Tabasco	TT	TT

Mix all of the ingredients together until thoroughly blended.

◆◆◆

RECIPE 33.29

HAMBURGER

Yield: 1 Sandwich

Ground round or chuck	125–175 g	4–6 oz.
Salt and pepper	TT	TT
Hamburger bun or an appropriate bread	1	1
Garnishes	as desired	as desired

1. Form the ground round or chuck into a patty, handling the beef as little as possible.
2. Season the patty with salt and pepper and broil or grill to the desired doneness, turning once. While the patty is cooking, toast the bun or bread if desired.

3. Remove the patty from the broiler or grill, place on one-half of the bun or on one slice of bread and garnish the other half with a lettuce leaf, a slice of onion, a slice of tomato and/or pickles. Serve with condiments such as ketchup and mustard.

NOTE: It is recommended that ground beef products be cooked to an internal temperature of 74°C (165°F).

VARIATIONS: *Cheeseburger*—Place 25 g (1 oz.) cheddar, Swiss or other cheese on the cooking patty approximately 1 minute before it is done.

Bacon cheeseburger—Prepare a cheeseburger and place two slices of crisp bacon on top of the cheese when the patty is done.

Mushroom burger—Sauté 50 g (2 oz.) of sliced mushrooms in 5 mL (1 tsp.) of butter. Top the cooked hamburger or cheeseburger with the cooked mushrooms.

California burger—Grill a boneless, skinless chicken breast and serve on a whole wheat bun accompanied by 50 g (2 oz.) of guacamole, 25 g (1 oz.) of alfalfa sprouts, two slices of ripe tomato and one thin slice of red onion.

❖❖❖

RECIPE 33.30

Seared Weathervane Scallops with Pickled Daikon, Pumpkin Seed, Sea Lettuce and Lamanaria Salad

SOOKE HARBOUR HOUSE RESTAURANT, SOOKE, BC
Melissa Craig, 2001 BC Apprentice Winner

Yield: 4 Portions

Melissa Craig
Melissa completed the Cook Apprenticeship Program with Chef Edward Tuson at Sooke Harbour House Restaurant and Camosun Community College, in Victoria, BC. Hard work and dedication have won her top honours: she is the CFCC 2001 Junior Cook Champion.

Pickle Marinade:

Pear cider vinegar	50 mL	2 fl. oz.
Sugar	50 g	2 oz.
Sea salt	5 g	1 tsp.
Ginger, minced	4 g	1 tsp.
Water	125 mL	4 fl. oz.
Daikon radish, julienned	50 g	1/4 cup
Sea lettuce	50 g	1/4 cup
Pumpkinseed oil	30 mL	1 fl. oz.
Shallots, minced	20 g	1 Tbsp.
Garlic, minced	2 g	1/2 tsp.
Salt and pepper	TT	TT
Lamanaria	50 g	1/4 cup
Weathervane scallops	12	12
Leek strips, blanched	4	4
Vegetable oil	as needed	as needed
Pumpkinseeds, toasted	25 g	2 Tbsp.
Arugula flowers	TT	TT
Mustard flowers	TT	TT
Sea salt	TT	TT

RECIPE 33.30

Approximate values per serving:

Calories	204
Total fat	6 g
Saturated fat	0.5 g
Cholesterol	15 mg
Sodium	811 mg
Total carbohydrates	30 g
Protein	10.5 g

1. Combine pickle marinade ingredients, bring to a boil and cool.
2. Add daikon to pickle marinade.

Continued

3. Rinse sea lettuce thoroughly and slice into thin strips.

4. In a bowl, combine pumpkinseed oil, shallots, garlic, salt and pepper. Drain daikon and add to dressing along with sea lettuce and lamanaria.

5. Tie scallops together in bunches of three with the leek strips.

6. Sear scallops in vegetable oil in a hot pan for approximately 2 minutes per side.

7. Meanwhile, toss pumpkinseeds and flowers with salad. Assemble on plates and place scallop bundles on top. Garnish with wasabi mayonnaise.

VARIATION: Wrap scallops individually and set on Asian soup spoons.

◆◆◆

RECIPE 33.31

BLACKENED STEAK SANDWICH

Yield: 2 Sandwiches

Strip loin steak, 280 g (10 oz.)	1	1
Blackened Steak Seasoning (recipe follows)	as needed	as needed
Clarified butter	30 mL	1 fl. oz.
Capers	10 g	1 Tbsp.
Whole butter, softened	30 g	1 oz.
French bread, cut on the bias	2 slices	2 slices
Baby lettuce, cleaned	125 g	4 oz.
Roma tomatoes, sliced	2	2
Red onions, sliced	30 g	1 oz.

1. Heat a cast-iron skillet over high heat for 10 minutes. Pat the steak dry with paper towelling. Coat the steak in the blackened steak seasoning.

2. Carefully place the steak into the hot skillet and ladle 15 mL (1/2 fl. oz.) of clarified butter over the steak. Be very careful, as the butter may flare up. There will be intense smoke and the steak will form a dark crust. Cook the steak for approximately 2 minutes. Do not burn the spice crust.

3. Turn the steak, ladle the remaining clarified butter over it and allow it to cook to the desired degree of doneness. Finish in oven for medium-well and well done. Remove the steak from the pan and hold in a warm place.

4. Chop the capers and combine them with the softened butter. Spread each slice of bread with half of the caper butter.

5. Slice the steak on the bias.

6. To assemble each sandwich, place one-half of the warm steak on a slice of buttered bread, arrange half of the lettuce, tomatoes and onions attractively on the plate and serve.

VARIATION: To serve this sandwich cold, allow the steak to cool after cooking, then refrigerate it until completely cold. Proceed with the recipe.

BLACKENED STEAK SEASONING

Yield: 50 g (6 Tbsp.)

Paprika	12 g	2 Tbsp.
Salt	20 g	4 tsp.
Onion powder	4 g	2 tsp.
Garlic powder	3.5 g	2 tsp.

◆◆◆

BLACKENED DOES NOT MEAN BURNT!

There is a popular misconception that foods cooked by this method must be charred. Not so! Burning imparts a bitter taste and is not palatable. Whether "blackening" beef, fish or chicken, the spice coating should be a deep mahogany colour with the red evident. If thicker pieces of meat are cooked to a more well-done state, it may be necessary to finish the items in the oven.

RECIPE 33.31

Approximate values per sandwich:

Calories	610
Total fat	38 g
Saturated fat	20 g
Cholesterol	180 mg
Sodium	650 mg
Total carbohydrates	21 g
Protein	44 g

Cayenne pepper	4 g	2 tsp.
White pepper	3 g	1 tsp.
Black pepper	2 g	1 tsp.
Dried thyme	1 g	1 tsp.

Combine all ingredients and mix well.

◆◆◆

RECIPE 33.32

REUBEN SANDWICH

Yield: 1 Sandwich

Dark rye bread	2 slices	2 slices
Thousand Island Dressing		
(Recipe 24.14)	30 mL	1 fl. oz.
Cooked corned beef, hot,		
sliced very thinly	125 g	4 oz.
Sauerkraut, hot, drained well	50 g	2 oz.
Swiss cheese	30 g	2 slices
Whole butter, softened	as needed	as needed

1. Spread each slice of bread with half of the Thousand Island dressing.
2. Place the hot corned beef, hot sauerkraut and Swiss cheese on one slice of bread. Top with the second slice of bread, keeping the dressing side down.
3. Butter the top slice of bread and place the sandwich on a hot griddle, top down. Carefully butter the second slice of bread.
4. Fry the sandwich, turning once when the first side is well browned. The sandwich is done when both sides are well browned, the fillings are very hot and the cheese is melted.
5. Cut the sandwich in half diagonally and arrange as desired for service.

RECIPE 33.32

Approximate values per sandwich:

Calories	556
Total fat	27 g
Saturated fat	10 g
Cholesterol	85 mg
Sodium	2150 mg
Total carbohydrates	39 g
Protein	39 g

◆◆◆

RECIPE 33.33

MONTE CRISTO SANDWICH

Yield: 1 Sandwich

Cooked turkey breast, sliced thinly	30 g	1 oz.
Swiss cheese	20 g	2 slices
White bread	3 slices	3 slices
Ham, sliced thinly	30 g	1 oz.
Egg	1	1
Milk	30 mL	1 fl. oz.
Oil	as needed	as needed

1. Arrange the turkey breast and one slice of cheese on top of the first slice of bread.
2. Place the second slice of bread on top of the turkey, then place the ham and second slice of cheese. Place the third slice of bread.
3. Beat the egg and milk together. Dip the sandwich in the egg batter and allow the batter to soak into the bread.
4. Pan-fry the sandwich in oil until it is evenly browned. Remove from the oil and drain well. Cut the sandwich into four pieces and arrange as desired.

VARIATION: Wedge the sandwich before dipping and soaking. Originally this sandwich was deep-fried.

RECIPE 33.33

Approximate values per sandwich:

Calories	627
Total fat	19 g
Saturated fat	7 g
Cholesterol	279 mg
Sodium	932 mg
Total carbohydrates	74 g
Protein	37 g

◆◆◆

RECIPE 33.34

FALAFEL

Yield: 12 Sandwiches

Chickpeas, dry	500 g	1 lb.
Garlic cloves, minced	6	6
Parsley, chopped	15 g	1/2 oz.
Chives, minced	15 g	1/2 oz.
Cumin, ground	10 g	1 Tbsp.
Coriander, ground	8 g	2 tsp.
Cayenne pepper	TT	TT
Eggs	3	3
Salt	TT	TT
Flour	150 g	5 oz.
Plain yogurt	175 mL	6 fl. oz.
Lemon juice	50 mL	2 fl. oz.
Pita bread	12	12
Iceberg lettuce, shredded	175 g	6 oz.
Tomatoes, diced	175 g	6 oz.

1. To make the falafel, soak the chickpeas following the procedures for dried beans outlined in Chapter 22, Vegetables. Drain the chickpeas, place them in a pot and cover with cool water. Simmer until tender, approximately 2–3 hours, remove from the heat and drain well.

2. Process the chickpeas in a food processor or a food chopper until coarsely chopped. Add the garlic, parsley, chives, cumin, coriander and cayenne pepper and process for a few seconds.

3. Add the eggs, salt and flour and process briefly. Remove the falafel from the machine and chill in the refrigerator for 1 hour.

4. Combine the yogurt and lemon juice and mix well. Set aside.

5. Portion the falafel using a #50 scoop (there should be approximately 60 balls) and deep-fat fry the balls at 190°C (375°F) until crisp and hot. Drain well and hold in a warm place.

6. To assemble each sandwich, cut a pita in half or open it to form a pocket, stuff with several balls of falafel and 30 g (1 oz.) of the shredded lettuce and diced tomatoes, and dress with the yogurt sauce. Arrange the sandwiches as desired and serve hot.

RECIPE 33.34

Approximate values per sandwich:

Calories	294
Total fat	3 g
Saturated fat	0.5 g
Cholesterol	55 mg
Sodium	471 mg
Total carbohydrates	56 g
Protein	12 g

◆◆◆

RECIPE 33.35

HOT TURKEY SANDWICH

Yield: 6 Sandwiches

Cream, 35%, hot	175 mL	6 fl. oz.
Romano, grated	175 g	6 oz.
Velouté sauce, hot	1 L	1 qt.
Dry sherry	30 mL	1 fl. oz.
Multigrain toast, crust removed	6 slices	6 slices
Turkey breast, sliced	720 g	1 lb. 8 oz.
Parmesan, grated	50 g	2 oz.
Tomato wedges	12	12
Bacon, lean, cooked crisp	12 slices	12 slices

RECIPE 33.35

Approximate values per sandwich:

Calories	270
Total fat	34 g
Saturated fat	17 g
Cholesterol	185 mg
Sodium	2180 mg
Total carbohydrates	45 g
Protein	59 g

1. To make the sauce, add the cream and the Romano to the velouté sauce and bring to a simmer. Simmer for 1 minute, then strain the sauce through a conical strainer. Stir in the sherry. Hold in a warm place for service.

2. Cut the toast diagonally into triangles.

3. To assemble each sandwich, arrange two toast triangles in a gratin dish and top with 125 g (4 oz.) of turkey and 120 mL (4 fl. oz.) of sauce. Bake at 175°C (350°F) until brown, approximately 15 minutes.

4. Top each sandwich with Parmesan, two tomato wedges and two strips of bacon and serve very hot.

◆◆◆

RECIPE 33.36

ROAST BEEF AND EGG SALAD SANDWICH

Yield: 4 Sandwiches

Butter	120 g	4 oz.
White sourdough bread slices	8	8
Egg salad	180 g	6 oz.
Roast beef, rare, cold, sliced thinly	440 g	1 lb.
Red onion, sliced thinly	60 g	2 oz.
Tomato slices	12	12
Romaine lettuce	4 leaves	4 leaves

To assemble one sandwich, spread 15 g (1 Tbsp.) of butter on a slice of bread and top with 45 g (1-1/2 oz.) of egg salad. Then place 110 g (3-1/2 oz.) of the roast beef on top of the egg salad and cover with the 15 g (1/2 oz.) of red onion, three tomato slices, one leaf of romaine lettuce and a slice of buttered bread.

NOTE: This makes a great open-faced sandwich. Garnish with fried onion rings.

RECIPE 33.36

Approximate values per sandwich:

Calories	702
Total fat	39 g
Saturated fat	20 g
Cholesterol	334 mg
Sodium	794 mg
Total carbohydrates	40 g
Protein	46 g

◆◆◆

RECIPE 33.37

NEW ORLEANS–STYLE MUFFALETTA SANDWICH

Yield: 1 Sandwich, 4–6 Servings

Red bell pepper, roasted, chopped	1	1
Niçoise or Gaeta olives, pitted, chopped	125 g	4 oz.
Olives, green, pitted, chopped	125 g	4 oz.
Virgin olive oil	125 mL	4 fl. oz.
Italian parsley, chopped	20 g	2 Tbsp.
Anchovy fillets, mashed	2	2
Dried oregano	1 g	1 tsp.
Lemon juice	15 mL	1 Tbsp.
Round Italian bread/Focaccia, 18-cm (8-inch) diameter	1	1
Arugula or curly endive, chiffonade	45 g	1-1/2 oz.
Tomato concassée	175 g	6 oz.
Mortadella, sliced thinly	175 g	6 oz.
Soppressata, sliced thinly (see page 527)	125 g	4 oz.
Provolone or fontina, sliced thinly	125 g	4 oz.
Pepper	TT	TT

Continued

RECIPE 33.37

Approximate values per serving:

Calories	670
Total fat	57 g
Saturated fat	14 g
Cholesterol	60 mg
Sodium	2201 mg
Total carbohydrates	16 g
Protein	24 g

1. To make the olive salad, combine the red pepper, olives, olive oil, parsley, anchovies, oregano and lemon juice and marinate for several hours.

2. Cut the loaf of bread in half horizontally. Remove some of the soft interior of the bread to create a slight hollow area.

3. Drain the olive salad, reserving the oil. Brush the interior of the bread with the reserved oil, using it all.

4. Arrange the olive salad, greens, tomato, mortadella, soppressata and cheese in layers on the bottom portion of the loaf of bread, finishing with a thick layer of olive salad. Season the layers with pepper as desired.

5. Place the top on the sandwich and wrap tightly with plastic wrap. Refrigerate the sandwich for several hours so that the layers will remain in place when the sandwich is cut.

6. Cut the sandwich into four to six wedges and arrange as desired for service.

✦✦✦

RECIPE 33.38

SOUTHWESTERN GRILLED CHICKEN WRAP

Yield: 12 Sandwiches

Chicken breast, boneless, skinless	1.4 kg	3 lb.
Salt and pepper	TT	TT
Avocados	3	3
Red bell peppers	300 g	2
Red onion	350 g	1
Tomatoes	350 g	2
Tortillas, 24 cm (10 inches)	12	12
Black Bean Spread (recipe follows)	1.3 kg	3 lb.
Black olives, sliced	175 g	6 oz.
Cilantro, chopped	2 bunches	2 bunches
Cheddar cheese, grated	750 g	1 lb. 8 oz.
Jalapeños, minced	2	2

1. Season the chicken breast with salt and pepper and grill or broil until done. Chill and cut into strips.

2. Peel the avocados and cut each into 12 slices. Clean the bell peppers and cut into strips. Slice the onion thinly. Dice the tomatoes.

3. To make each sandwich, place one tortilla on a cutting board and spread with approximately 120 g (4 oz.) of Black Bean Spread.

4. Sprinkle one-twelfth of the pepper, onions, tomatoes, olives, cilantro, cheese and jalapeños over the bean spread.

5. Top with one-twelfth of the chicken.

6. Roll the tortilla around the ingredients tightly enough so the sandwich will hold its shape. Cut the sandwich as desired for service.

RECIPE 33.38

Approximate values per sandwich:

Calories	642
Total fat	37 g
Saturated fat	16 g
Cholesterol	118 mg
Sodium	695 mg
Total carbohydrates	37 g
Protein	41 g

BLACK BEAN SPREAD

Yield: 1.3 kg (3 lb.)

Black beans, soaked and drained	750 g	1 lb. 8 oz.
Water	4 L	4 qt.
Onion, diced	125 g	4 oz.
Tomatoes, diced	175 g	6 oz.
Cilantro, chopped	20 g	2 Tbsp.

Salt and pepper	TT	TT
Cumin	3 g	1 tsp.
Chili powder	3 g	1 tsp.

1. Combine the beans and the water, bring to a boil, reduce to a simmer and cook until tender, approximately 1–1.5 hours.
2. Add the remaining ingredients and simmer for 10 minutes.
3. Drain the beans, reserving the cooking liquid. Chill the beans and the liquid.
4. Purée the beans in a food processor, adding enough of the cooking liquid to make a soft, spreadable purée.

Black Bean Spread—Approximate values per 60 g (2 oz.) serving:

Calories	100
Total fat	0.5 g
Saturated fat	0 g
Cholesterol	0 mg
Sodium	51 mg
Total carbohydrates	37 g
Protein	12 g

◆◆◆

RECIPE 33.39

VEGGIE WRAP

Yield: 1 Sandwich

Spinach-flavoured tortilla	1	1
Garlic Yogurt Dressing (recipe follows)	30 mL	2 Tbsp.
Jasmine rice, cooked	90 g	3 oz.
Roma tomato, diced	30 g	2 Tbsp.
Cucumber, julienned	30 g	1 oz.
Alfalfa sprouts	as needed	as needed
Broccoli florets	30 g	1 oz.
Red onion, sliced thinly	30 g	1 oz.
Capers	10 g	1 Tbsp.

1. Spread the tortilla with half of the Garlic Yogurt Dressing.
2. Arrange the rice in a mound across the centre of the tortilla. Top the rice with the vegetables and capers.
3. Drizzle the remaining Garlic Yogurt Dressing over the vegetables.
4. Using a piece of parchment paper as a wrapper, roll the tortilla tightly around the filling, then chill and serve.

RECIPE 33.39

Approximate values per serving:

Calories	460
Total fat	3 g
Saturated fat	0.5 g
Cholesterol	0 mg
Sodium	296 mg
Total carbohydrates	94 g
Protein	12 g

GARLIC YOGURT DRESSING

Yield: 500 mL (1 pt.)

Nonfat yogurt, plain	500 mL	1 pt.
Parsley, minced	10 g	1 Tbsp.
Garlic, minced	25 g	2 Tbsp.
Dijon-style mustard	30 g	2 Tbsp.
Black pepper	1 g	1/4 tsp.
Tabasco sauce	TT	TT

Combine all of the ingredients and chill until ready to use.

Garlic Yogurt Dressing— Approximate values per 30 mL (1 oz.) serving:

Calories	19
Total fat	0 g
Saturated fat	0 g
Cholesterol	1 mg
Sodium	46 mg
Total carbohydrates	3 g
Protein	2 g

◆◆◆

RECIPE 33.40

CLUBHOUSE SANDWICH

Yield: 1 Sandwich

Bread, toasted	3 slices	3 slices
Mayonnaise	as needed	as needed

Continued

Lettuce leaves	2	2
Tomato	3 slices	3 slices
Bacon, cooked crisp	3 slices	3 slices
Salt and pepper	TT	TT
Cooked turkey breast, sliced thinly	90 g	3 oz.

1. Spread one side of each slice of toasted bread with mayonnaise.
2. Arrange the lettuce, tomato and bacon on one slice of toast. Season with salt and pepper.
3. Place another slice of toast on top of the bacon.
4. Arrange the turkey breast on top of the second slice of toast.
5. Place the third slice of toast on top of the turkey breast, mayonnaise side down.
6. Place four frilled toothpicks in the sandwich, one on each side, approximately 2.5 cm (1 inch) in from the edge. Cut the sandwich diagonally into quarters and arrange as desired for service.

◆◆◆

RECIPE 33.41

DUNGENESS CRAB AND EGGPLANT CANNELLONI WITH RED PEPPER BISQUE

BISHOP'S RESTAURANT, Vancouver, BC
Executive Chef Dennis Green

Dennis Green

Dennis was raised in Vancouver and started cooking when he was 17. He served his apprenticeship at a small bistro named the Avenue Grill near his high school. He joined Bishop's in 1993 and has been the Executive Chef there since 1997.

Yield: 12 Cannelloni

Eggplant, large	1	1
Salt and pepper	TT	TT
Oil	as needed	as needed
Shallots, diced	100 g	3 oz.
Garlic, minced	3 g	1 tsp.
Butter	30 g	1 oz.
Mascarpone	125 g	4 oz.
Fresh parsley, chopped	20 g	2 Tbsp.
Fresh crabmeat	500 g	1 lb.
Red Pepper Bisque (recipe follows)		

1. Cut eggplant in half lengthwise and cut 12 3-mm (1/8-inch) slices from the centre. Sprinkle with salt and place on paper towel to drain. Dice the remaining eggplant into 5-mm (1/4-inch) cubes, salt and place in strainer to drain.
2. After 30 minutes, rinse excess salt from diced eggplant and reserve.
3. Dry eggplant slices, lightly brush with oil and grill until tender. Cool slices.
4. Sauté shallots, garlic and diced eggplant in butter until softened.
5. Stir in mascarpone, allow to melt and remove from heat. Stir in parsley and crabmeat and adjust seasoning. Cool.
6. Lay out two slices of eggplant, overlapping slightly.
7. Portion 60 g (2 oz.) of filling on one end of eggplant and roll up in cannelloni shape. Repeat with remaining eggplant and filling.
8. Place on parchment paper on a baking sheet and bake for 10 minutes at 200°C (400°F).
9. Serve on a pool of Red Pepper Bisque.

RED PEPPER BISQUE

Red peppers, sliced	350 g	2
Red onion, sliced	175 g	6 oz.
Olive oil	15 mL	1 Tbsp.
Dry sherry	125 mL	4 fl. oz.
Roma tomatoes, sliced	400 g	4
Crab or lobster stock	250 mL	8 fl. oz.
Cream, 35%	125 mL	4 fl. oz.
Salt and pepper	TT	TT

Sauté peppers and onion in olive oil until softened. Add sherry and tomatoes and simmer for 10 minutes. Add crab stock and simmer for 20 minutes. Add cream and simmer for 10 minutes. Purée or pass through a food mill.

Red Pepper Bisque—	
Approximate values per serving:	
Calories	84
Total fat	5 g
Saturated fat	2.5 g
Cholesterol	13.5 mg
Sodium	313 mg
Total carbohydrates	6 g
Protein	1.5 g

 EBLINKS

Enormous Appetizer Collection
  www.cs.cmu.edu/~mjw/recipes/appetizers/enorm-appetizer-coll.html
A Sushi Glossary
  www.cis.unisa.edu.au/~cisjpm/Sushi/Full/glossary.html
Dim Sum
  www.cris.com/~lkarper/dim_sum.html
Sandwiches
  recipes.alastra.com/sandwiches/default.html

INTERNATIONAL FLAVOUR PRINCIPLES

LEARNING OUTCOMES

After studying this chapter you will be able to:

♦ describe the flavour principles of several cuisines
♦ prepare chicken and starch dishes incorporating the flavour principles and representative cooking methods of each of these cuisines

*P*eople worldwide share a love of food. But the ingredients, flavourings, seasonings and cooking methods they use are not the same. Whether defined by geography, history, ethnicity, politics or religion, various societies eat different foods seasoned and prepared in distinctive manners. These differences shape and define their particular cuisine.

Because this book is a guide to understanding the hows and whys of cooking and is not simply a collection of recipes, we will neither explore here all of the world's cuisines nor provide a comprehensive selection of recipes illustrating the cuisines discussed. Instead, we delve into the flavour principles that distinguish several important cuisines from European and North American traditions.

Once you understand these principles, you should be able to prepare a variety of dishes that reflect a particular cuisine's flavour principles and cooking methods. To illustrate this point, and because most societies eat chicken, we include a chicken and starch recipe from each of the cuisines discussed.

♦♦♦
RECIPES FOR
ETHNIC CUISINES

In *Ethnic Cuisine: The Flavor Principle Cookbook*, Elisabeth Rozin writes: "Every culture tends to combine a small number of flavoring ingredients so frequently and so consistently that they become definitive of that particular cuisine" (p. xiv). She calls these defining flavours "flavor principles" and notes that they are "designed to abstract what is absolutely fundamental about a cuisine and, thus, to serve as a guide in cooking and developing new recipes" (p. xvii). She identifies the following flavour principles for European cuisines:

Greek:
Tomato, cinnamon *or* olive oil, lemon, oregano

Italian:
Generally—olive oil, garlic, basil
Northern Italy—wine vinegar, garlic
Southern Italy—olive oil, garlic, parsley and/or anchovy plus tomato as a variation

French:
Generally—olive oil, garlic, basil *or* wine, herb *or* butter and/or cream and/or cheese plus wine and/or stock
Southern France—olive oil, garlic, parsley and/or anchovy plus tomato as a variation
Provence—olive oil, thyme, rosemary, marjoram, sage plus tomato as a variation
Normandy—apple, cider, Calvados

Spanish:
Olive oil, garlic, nut *or* olive oil, onion, pepper, tomato

Hungarian:
Onion, lard, paprika

Eastern European Jewish:
Onion, chicken fat

Eastern and Northern European:
Sour cream, dill *or* paprika *or* allspice *or* caraway

CHINESE CUISINES

China, a large, geographically diverse country, nurtures several distinctive regional cuisines, the most prominent of which are called here Northern, Southern, Western and Eastern. All Chinese cuisines emphasize a sophisticated contrast and harmony of flavours (sweet, sour, bitter, spicy and salty) and textures (crisp, crunchy, chunky, chewy, smooth and liquid) and rely on the quick cooking of attractively cut, bite-sized pieces of food. Reducing all foods to bite-sized pieces promotes the quick infusion of flavourings. Most cooking is done in a wok that can be used for stir-frying, deep-fat frying and steaming. Anthropologists suggest that the reliance on quick cooking methods was the result of chronic fuel shortages. Although these quick cooking methods can produce fully cooked foods in minutes, the careful cutting and preparation techniques often require far more time.

Staples include several varieties of rice, noodles (made from rice, beans and wheat) and soy beans (eaten as seeds, beans, sprouts and curd, and used for oil and sauce). Pork, poultry (particularly chicken and duck), fish (particularly pike, carp and bass) and shellfish are regularly consumed, as are a large assortment of vegetables (including varieties of mushrooms, several cabbages, bamboo shoots, water chestnuts and snow peas) and fruits (including lychee, pears, plums and various citrus fruits).

Common spices are star anise, cinnamon, cloves, fennel and Szechuan peppercorns (these are sometimes blended for five spice powder), lemon balm, tangerine peel, coriander, sesame seeds and oil, lotus nut paste, lotus root and hot chiles (a New World import). Commonly used sauces include plum, oyster, hoisin and both light and dark soy.

Chinese—(clockwise from top left) chicken in black bean sauce, white rice, rolls of moo shu chicken, plum sauce, moo shu chicken

Northern China

Northern China includes Beijing, the capital. Some consider this region's cuisine to be the most aristocratic of the regional cuisines; indeed, it is sometimes referred to as Mandarin cuisine, named for the centuries-old Chinese aristocratic and bureaucratic classes.

Northern Chinese dishes are generally lightly spiced and contain little residual oil. Because northern China is relatively dry, rice is not a regional staple, as rice needs an abundance of water to grow. Instead, wheat and millet, eaten as noodles, dumplings and pancakes, are popular. *Chow mein* is a dish of thin wheat noodles stir-fried with other ingredients. Freshwater fish are regularly consumed, as is lamb, a meat rarely eaten elsewhere in China. Meats and poultry are most often roasted or barbecued; Peking duck is a well-known example. Mongol influence still exists in the form of the Mongolian hot pot: a simmering broth into which each diner submerges bits of meat, poultry, vegetables or bean curd.

A classic Northern Chinese dish is Moo Shu Chicken: The wood ears (mushrooms) and bamboo shoots provide contrasting textures, the duck sauce (also known as plum sauce) is a delicate condiment and the pancakes are classically Mandarin. The dish is best enjoyed by spreading 3 mL (1/2 tsp.) of the duck sauce on each pancake, then topping with green onions and 30–45 mL (2–3 Tbsp.) of the moo shu. The pancake is then rolled up with the ends folded in.

Applying the Basics

RECIPE 34.1

MOO SHU CHICKEN

Yield: 4 Servings

Chicken breast, boneless, skinless	250 g	8 oz.
Marinade:		
Chinese rice wine	5 mL	1 tsp.
Salt	TT	TT
Egg white, beaten	1	1
Soy sauce	3 mL	1/2 tsp.
Wood ear mushrooms, dried	5	5
Eggs	3	3
Vegetable oil	125 mL	4 fl. oz.
Garlic, chopped	5 g	1 tsp.
Hoisin sauce	50 mL	2 fl. oz.
Bamboo shoots, shredded	100 g	3 oz.
Bok choy, shredded	100 g	3 oz.
Carrot, shredded	100 g	3 oz.
Salt	5 g	1 tsp.
Chicken stock	50 mL	2 fl. oz.
Green onions, shredded	30 g	1 oz.

1. Slice the chicken into thin strips, approximately 4 cm × 6 mm (1-1/2 inches × 1/4 inch), and marinate in the rice wine, salt, egg white and soy sauce for 15 minutes.

2. Soak the wood ears in hot water until soft. Break off the hard stems and shred the mushrooms.

3. Beat the eggs. Heat 15 mL (1 Tbsp.) of the oil in a wok and cook the eggs. Do not let them brown. Remove the eggs, shred and set aside.

4. Stir-fry the garlic in 50 mL (2 fl. oz.) of oil until golden. Add the chicken and stir-fry until the chicken is very lightly browned. Remove the chicken, drain and set aside.

5. Add the hoisin sauce and 30 mL (2 Tbsp.) of oil to the wok; quickly stir-fry the sauce. Add the bamboo shoots, bok choy, carrot and shredded mushrooms and cook for 5 minutes.

6. Add the chicken, salt, chicken stock and shredded eggs. Stir-fry over high heat for 1 minute.

7. Serve hot, garnished with green onions.

RECIPE 34.1

Approximate values per serving:

Calories	435
Total fat	33 g
Saturated fat	3 g
Cholesterol	194 mg
Sodium	891 mg
Total carbohydrates	15 g
Protein	21 g

Applying the Basics
RECIPE 34.2

DUCK SAUCE

Yield: 120 mL (4 fl. oz.)

Sweet bean sauce	50 mL	3 Tbsp.
Hoisin sauce	50 mL	3 Tbsp.
Sugar	5 g	1 tsp.
Sesame oil	15 mL	1 Tbsp.

Combine and stir all the ingredients until smooth. Serve at room temperature.

RECIPE 34.2

Approximate values per 20 mL serving:

Calories	68
Total fat	4 g
Saturated fat	1 g
Cholesterol	0 mg
Sodium	293 mg
Total carbohydrates	7 g
Protein	1 g

Applying the Basics
RECIPE 34.3

MANDARIN PANCAKES

Yield: 16 15-cm (7-inch) Pancakes

All-purpose flour	250 g	8 oz.
Boiling water	200 mL	6 fl. oz.
Sesame oil	15 mL	1 Tbsp.

1. Place the flour in a bowl. Add the boiling water and mix with a spoon to make a soft dough. Let dough cool a bit.

2. On a lightly floured surface, knead the dough for 8–10 minutes until smooth. Cover with a plastic wrap and let rest for 30 minutes.

3. Shape the dough into a cylinder about 2.5 cm (1 inch) in diameter, adding more flour if necessary. Slice the log into 16 equal pieces; roll each piece into a ball and then flatten each to make a disk.

4. Using a rolling pin, flatten each pair of disks into a 12.5-cm (5-inch) circle. Brush the tops of eight disks with the sesame oil. Then place an unoiled disk on top of each oiled disk. Cover the pancakes with plastic wrap and roll out to 15 cm (7 inches).

5. Heat an ungreased 20-cm (8-inch) skillet over high heat for 30 seconds to 1 minute. Reduce the heat to medium.

6. Place one pancake pair into the skillet. When it puffs and bubbles appear on its surface, turn it over and cook the other side until it is speckled brown, approximately 1 minute. Then turn the pancake and cook the first side until it too is speckled brown, approximately 30 seconds. Remove the pancake to a plate and cover with plastic.

7. Repeat until each pancake pair is cooked.

8. Just before service, separate each pancake pair by gently pulling apart at the edges. Serve warm.

RECIPE 34.3

Approximate values per pancake:

Calories	65
Total fat	1 g
Saturated fat	0 g
Cholesterol	0 mg
Sodium	1 mg
Total carbohydrates	12 g
Protein	2 g

Southern China

Southern Chinese cuisine is centred in Canton, a fertile area rich with rice paddies, vegetable farms and fruit orchards. All these ingredients are found in the cuisine, along with an abundance of saltwater and freshwater fish and shellfish as well as more exotic ingredients such as abalone, sea urchin, snake, shark fins, turtle, snails and eel. Both rice and wheat noodle dishes are very popular.

Southern Chinese cuisine emphasizes the freshness of its local ingredients; therefore stir-frying is a popular cooking method. When stir-frying, most of the spices and nonliquid flavouring ingredients are added at the start. Their flavours are released by quickly sautéing them in hot oil. The liquid flavouring ingredients are usually mixed with a thickening agent (often cornstarch) and added towards the end of cooking. This mixture then boils and thickens, coating the foods with the flavouring sauce.

Applying the Basics

RECIPE 34.4

CHICKEN AND SNOW PEAS IN BLACK BEAN SAUCE

Yield: 6 Servings

Chicken breasts, boneless, skinless	1 kg	2 lb.
Egg white	1	1
Chinese rice wine	200 mL	6 fl. oz.
Cornstarch	20 g	2 Tbsp.
Soy sauce	60 mL	2 fl. oz.
Granulated sugar	10 g	2 tsp.
Onions, small	150 g	2
Peanut oil	125 mL	4 fl. oz.
Garlic, minced	10 g	1 Tbsp.
Fresh ginger, minced	5 g	2 tsp.
Fermented black beans, mashed	50 g	3 Tbsp.
Snow peas, fresh	125 g	4 oz.

1. Slice the chicken into thin strips, approximately 4 cm × 6 mm (1-1/2 inches × 1/4 inch).
2. Combine the egg white, one-third of the wine and 10 g (1 Tbsp.) of the cornstarch. Add the chicken and refrigerate for 2 hours.
3. For the sauce, mix the soy sauce, sugar and the remaining wine and cornstarch.
4. Quarter the onions and separate the layers.
5. Stir-fry the chicken in 90 mL (3 fl. oz.) of oil. Remove and set aside.
6. If necessary, add all the remaining oil and stir-fry the garlic and ginger for 30 seconds. Add the onions and mashed beans and stir-fry for 30 seconds. Add the snow peas and cook for 1 minute.
7. Return the chicken to the wok, add the sauce mixture and stir-fry until hot and the sauce has thickened.
8. Serve immediately with short-grain white rice.

VARIATION: Add 60 g (2 oz.) sliced mushrooms and reduce the amount of snow peas by half.

RECIPE 34.4

Approximate values per serving:

Calories	727
Total fat	28 g
Saturated fat	7 g
Cholesterol	188 mg
Sodium	1559 mg
Total carbohydrates	26 g
Protein	78 g

Western China

Encompassing the cookery of both Szechuan and Hunan provinces, Western Chinese cuisine is distinguished by its spiciness. Favourite seasonings include ginger, vinegar, garlic, sesame oil, green onions and hot chiles. Szechuan recipes usually incorporate chiles in paste form, while Hunan dishes use fresh chiles. Hunan cuisine is typically more sweet and sour than Szechuan cuisine. Both, however, include countless dishes that offer diners several competing spices. After the first fiery sensation passes, these multiple flavours should be recognizable and savoured.

Both rice and wheat are grown in western China. Fresh and dried freshwater fish, pork, beef and poultry are common ingredients, as are several types of mushrooms. Often the meats are subjected to several preparations for one dish.

Applying the Basics

RECIPE 34.5

JAR GAI
(SZECHUAN-STYLE FRIED CHICKEN)

Yield: 4 Servings

Chicken breasts, boneless, skinless	500 g	1 lb.
Cornstarch	50 g	5 Tbsp.
Salt	5 g	1 tsp.
Five spice powder	2.5 g	3/4 tsp.
Chicken stock	250 mL	8 fl. oz.
Granulated sugar	10 g	2 tsp.
Light soy sauce	15 mL	1 Tbsp.
Sesame oil	3 mL	1/2 tsp.
Rice wine vinegar	5 mL	1 tsp.
Chinese rice wine	10 mL	2 tsp.
Black pepper, ground	0.5 g	1/4 tsp.
Cold water	15 mL	1 Tbsp.
Canola or corn oil	125 mL	4 fl. oz.
Red chiles, dried and seeded	10–15	10–15
Garlic, chopped fine	8 g	2 tsp.
Fresh ginger, peeled and chopped fine	8 g	2 tsp.
Green onions, trimmed and cut into 5-cm (2-inch) lengths	4	4

1. Slice the chicken into thin strips, approximately 4 cm × 6 mm (1-1/2 inches × 1/4 inch).
2. Combine 40 g (4 Tbsp.) of the cornstarch, the salt and 2 g (1/2 tsp.) of the five spice powder. Toss the chicken pieces in the mixture; dust off any excess cornstarch.
3. Mix 125 mL (4 fl. oz.) of the stock with the sugar, soy sauce, sesame oil, vinegar, wine, pepper and the remaining five spice powder.
4. In a separate bowl, mix the water and remaining cornstarch.
5. Heat the oil and stir-fry the chicken in small batches.
6. Degrease the pan, reserving 30 mL (2 Tbsp.) of the oil. Add the chiles, garlic and ginger; stir-fry until the garlic and ginger are golden and the chiles turn dark.

RECIPE 34.5

Approximate values per serving:

Calories	617
Total fat	39 g
Saturated fat	5 g
Cholesterol	94 mg
Sodium	918 mg
Total carbohydrates	28 g
Protein	38 g

Continued

◆◆◆

A CHINESE MEAL

In traditional Chinese culture, little separates philosophy, religion and food, and certain rituals are associated with all meals. Meals are also full of symbolism: Braised turtle, for instance, signifies long life; round foods are consumed on holidays dedicated to the full moon.

Just as each dish should provide contrasting flavours and textures, an entire meal should be composed of several complementary and contrasting dishes. A festive Chinese dinner often starts with a cold dish, followed by several hot dishes, then a light soup, usually clear with a few uncooked or undercooked garnishes. Normally, no one hot dish is meant as the main course, and each should offer a different dominant flavour or texture. Rice, noodles or pancakes are served as an accompaniment; tea is the principal beverage and fresh or crystallized fruit constitutes dessert.

North American and European eating habits have given rise to a first course of small, usually hot appetizers such as steamed or fried pork dumplings (*chiao-tzu*), steamed yeast-risen wheat buns with various fillings (*bao*) or spring rolls. (Traditionally, all manner of stuffed dumplings and other small dishes, known collectively as *dim sum*—Cantonese for "heart's delight"—are served as a midmorning meal.) The appetizers are then followed by soup. Fortune cookies are an American invention; moon cakes (*yue bing*), pastries with various sweet fillings made of bean pastes, nuts or fruits surrounding a piece of salted duck egg yolk, are a more traditional sweet served as dessert.

Although the Chinese knew of forks for centuries, they viewed their use at the table as barbaric, preferring the more delicate chopsticks.

RECIPE 34.6

Approximate values per serving:

Calories	494
Total fat	8 g
Saturated fat	2 g
Cholesterol	255 mg
Sodium	3258 mg
Total carbohydrates	10 g
Protein	89 g

---

7. Add the green onions and toss for a few seconds. Add the stock mixture and bring to a boil.

8. Thicken the sauce with the remaining cornstarch-and-water mixture.

9. Return the chicken to the pan and toss to heat thoroughly. Adjust consistency with additional chicken stock.

10. Serve immediately with short-grain white rice.

Eastern China

Shanghai, a large city on China's east coast, has been the principal point of contact between foreigners and Chinese since the 19th century. Its cuisine reflects this contact. For example, dairy products, which rarely appear in Chinese cuisine, are sometimes used in Eastern Chinese recipes. Similarly, meats are often subjected to slow cooking methods more typical of Europe, such as red-cooking, a form of simmering named for the rich, red-brown sauce that results from cooking the meat in soy sauce. Wine, soy sauces, vinegars (especially an aged vinegar known as Chinkiang) and sugar are the predominant flavourings.

Eastern Chinese cuisine also reflects the fertile area's year-round growing season, many rivers and long shoreline. While most other regional Chinese cuisines incorporate only one or two vegetables in a dish, Shanghai chefs will blend six or more, often cutting them into different shapes.

Applying the Basics

RECIPE 34.6

SEE YO GAI
(RED-COOKED CHICKEN)

Yield: 6–8 Servings

Roasting chicken, 1.3–1.8 kg (3–4 lb.)	1	1
Cold water	350 mL	12 fl. oz.
Dark soy sauce	350 mL	12 fl. oz.
Chinese rice wine	60 mL	2 fl. oz.
Fresh ginger, peeled and sliced thin	60 g	2 oz.
Garlic, chopped	3 g	1 tsp.
Star anise	10	10
Granulated sugar	20 g	1-1/2 Tbsp.
Sesame oil	10 mL	2 tsp.

1. Place the washed chicken, breast side down, in a covered saucepan small enough so that the liquid ingredients will cover the chicken completely.

2. Add all other ingredients except the sesame oil and slowly bring to a boil. Reduce the heat and simmer for 15 minutes. Turn the chicken and simmer for 20 minutes, basting the bird every 5 minutes.

3. Remove the pot from the heat and leave covered until cool.

4. Remove the chicken and brush it with the sesame oil. The chicken can be carved in joints or, in the traditional Chinese manner, split lengthwise and chopped into strips 4 cm (1-1/2 inches) wide.

5. Serve the chicken at room temperature with the leftover sauce for dipping and a noodle dish as an accompaniment.

NOTE: Allowing cooked chicken to cool in this manner and then serving it at room temperature is not consistent with sound food-handling procedures; it is, however, an authentic practice.

JAPANESE CUISINE

As with their arts, the Japanese strive for a cuisine that reflects *sappari*: clarity, lightness, simplicity and order. Small portions of subtly combined ingredients, flavours and textures beautifully presented on dishes that complement the food are its hallmarks.

Rice, both sweet and savoury, is the staple of the Japanese diet; indeed, *gohan*, a Japanese word for rice, also refers to a meal. Rice is served steamed, pressed into cakes or made into noodles. Other staples are soybean products including bean curd (tofu), bean paste (miso), sprouts, seeds and sauce. Japanese cuisine also relies on a variety of noodles, including ones made from wheat (the thin ramen, the thicker somen and the very thick udon), buckwheat (soba) and mung beans.

Fish and shellfish play important roles in Japanese cuisine for two reasons. First, Japan is a nation of mountainous islands that depends on the sea as the source for much of its protein. And, second, until the 19th century much of the Japanese population followed Buddhist teachings that prescribed a vegetarian diet supplemented with fish and shellfish. During this century, however, there has been a marked increase in the consumption of meat (especially beef) and poultry (especially chicken).

Typical seasonings—used, for the most part, quite judiciously—include rice wine vinegar, wasabi (a pungent green root erroneously called green horseradish), daikon (a white radish), pepper, sesame oil and seeds, ginger, soy sauce (known as *shoyu*, generally lighter and more delicate than Chinese soy sauce), rice wine (mirin, which is light and sweet and used only for cooking, and sake, a finer product used for cooking and drinking), tamari sauce, seaweed and pressed algae products (from the delicate to the very fishy), dried fish and

Japanese—(clockwise from top left) sake, white rice, chicken yakitori with dipping sauce, ebi sushi

shellfish and a variety of pickled foods (collectively known as *zuke*) as well as fresh herbs. Many dishes are marinated before cooking.

Yakitori, a classic Japanese flavouring combination of soy sauce, rice wine and sugar, is often used for broiled or grilled dishes.

Applying the Basics

RECIPE 34.7

CHICKEN YAKITORI

Yield: 8 Servings

Soy sauce	250 mL	8 fl. oz.
Sake	250 mL	8 fl. oz.
Granulated sugar	60 g	2 oz.
Chicken breasts, boneless	1 kg	2 lb.
Cornstarch	10 g	1 Tbsp.
Sesame seeds	5 g	1 Tbsp.

1. Combine the soy sauce, sake and sugar. Reserve 250 mL (8 fl. oz.) of the mixture.
2. Brush the chicken with a portion of the reserved soy sauce mixture and grill over hot charcoal until done, basting regularly.
3. To make the sauce, combine 60 mL (2 fl. oz.) of the soy sauce mixture with the cornstarch. Bring the remainder to a boil in a small saucepan and stir in the cornstarch slurry. Stirring constantly, continue boiling until the sauce thickens. Simmer 1 minute.
4. Serve with short-grain white rice and garnish with sesame seeds.

RECIPE 34.7

Approximate values per serving:

Calories	677
Total fat	21 g
Saturated fat	5 g
Cholesterol	188 mg
Sodium	5499 mg
Total carbohydrates	27 g
Protein	75 g

Japanese cooking generally relies on quick cooking of bite-sized pieces of food. Foods can be grilled (called *yakimono*; if done tableside, as is typical, they are referred to as *nabemon*), steamed (*mushimono*), simmered in an aromatic broth (these liquid-based dishes often start with *dashi*, a fish-flavoured stock made from kelp and bonito; the cooking process is referred to as *nimono*) or deep-fat fried (*agemono*). The deep-fat frying technique and batter

◆◆◆

ASIAN FLAVOURS
IN AN AMERICAN KITCHEN

Asian flavours now play an increasingly important role in Western food preparations. Whether called "East-West," "Pan-Asian," or "Pacific Style" food, this type of cooking ranges from ideas as simple as swirling butter into a classic Chinese black bean sauce for a more velvet texture to drizzling an Asian sauce across the top of barbecued salmon to brushing butter infused with ginger, garlic, and cilantro on sourdough baguettes.

Several trends have led to this merging of cuisines. During the late 1960s the environmental movement and the rising popularity of

health foods caused many Americans to reevaluate their diet and move away from meals based heavily on fats, sugar, and starches. Within a few years, starting in the 1970s, the growing interest in a healthier diet resulted in a new type of French cooking, *nouvelle cuisine*, which included experimentation with Asian seasonings. At about the same time, Richard Nixon's 1972 trip to China caused an enormous surge in the popularity of Chinese food in America. Chinese and other Asian seasonings became commonplace in supermarkets.

While many of us were travelling through

Asia, fascinated with these new flavours, a huge Asian emigration to America began. Thai, Vietnamese, Korean, Japanese, and Filipino restaurants now proliferate. The new dishes offered in these restaurants, the "exotic" condiments and fresh herbs available in local Asian markets, and a flood of Asian cookbooks reinforce this ongoing trend. Examples of Asian and Pacific Style food appear on the menus of many of America's top young chefs. The fresh tastes of the Pacific are becoming a common part of contemporary cuisine.

—from CHOPSTIX *by* HUGH CARPENTER

known as tempura are actually derived from cooking techniques and recipes Portuguese Jesuits introduced to the Japanese during the late 16th century.

Japanese cuisine also offers a variety of raw foods, collectively known as *namamono*. Sashimi, small slices of fresh fish served with a soy sauce spiked with mustard and wasabi, is popular; as are *nigiri zushi* (small balls of sushi—vinegar-flavoured rice—topped with a slice of raw fish or shellfish) and *maki zushi* (raw fish or shellfish rolled in sushi and crisp seaweed). Recipes and techniques for these are given in Chapter 33, Appetizers and Sandwiches.

INDIAN CUISINES

Indian cuisine offers more than curry. The Indian subcontinent is home to many peoples, including Hindus, Buddhists and Muslims; each has a distinctive cuisine, and each cuisine has influenced the others, giving rise to several regional cuisines. Kashmir in the far north is famous for its meat and chickpeas, while the northern areas of Delhi and Bengal are famous for their tandoori and intensely sweet desserts, respectively. The western seaport of Bombay is known for its pork and vinegar, while vegetarian dishes made with tamarind, semolina and coconut are popular in the southern seaport of Madras.

The heart of Indian cookery is the masala, the combination of spices that gives each dish its distinctive taste. A masala's preparation, subtlety and sophistication are the tests by which chefs are often judged. The timing of its incorporation into the dish is critical. Common spices for masalas are turmeric, cumin seeds, coriander seeds, fenugreek, saffron, fennel seeds, mace, nutmeg, cardamom, clove, cinnamon, mustard seeds, sesame seeds, and black, red and white peppercorns. Garlic, onions and chiles are also popular flavourings, as are several herbs including coriander leaves, mint leaves and sweet basil. Souring agents include vinegar, lemon juice and imli (water with extract of tamarind). Curry powder is really nothing more than a commercial masala typically containing fenugreek, coriander, cumin, turmeric, ginger, celery seeds, mace and pepper. The word *curry* is probably derived from the Tamil word *kari*, meaning sauce or combination of seasonings; the product is considered an inferior British invention never used in true Indian cooking.

> ◆◆◆
> When discussing foreign—that is, not French—foods, Escoffier opined that "if only for the sake of novelty or variety, it is occasionally permissible to poach upon the preserves of foreign nations."

Applying the Basics

RECIPE 34.8

MASALA

Yield: 67 g (10 Tbsp.)

Coriander seeds	20 g	4 Tbsp.
Cumin seeds	6 g	2 Tbsp.
Black peppercorns, whole	7 g	1 Tbsp.
Cardamom seeds (measure after		
removing pods)	2 g	2 tsp.
Cinnamon, 7.5-cm (3-inch) sticks	20 g	4
Cloves, whole	2 g	1 tsp.
Nutmeg, whole	10 g	1

1. In a small saucepan, separately dry-roast the coriander seeds, cumin seeds, peppercorns, cardamom seeds, cinnamon and cloves. As each begins to smell fragrant, remove from the pan to cool. After dry-roasting the cardamom, peel it, remove the seeds and discard the pods.

RECIPE 34.8

Approximate values per 30 g (1 oz.) serving:

Calories	92
Total fat	4 g
Saturated fat	0 g
Cholesterol	0 mg
Sodium	19 mg
Total carbohydrates	16 g
Protein	3 g

Continued

2. With a mortar and pestle or spice grinder, blend all the roasted spices to a fine powder.

3. Finely grate the nutmeg and mix it in with the other spices.

4. Store tightly covered and away from light.

The staples of Indian cuisine are rice, dals and bread. The rice is usually long-grain and served steamed and mixed with flavourings and garnishes. For special occasions, aromatic rices such as basmati are eaten. Dals are pulses such as lentils, beans and peas; nearly 60 varieties of protein-rich pulses are used in Indian cookery. These include the small, sweet yellow *chana dal*, *moong dal* (mung beans) and the salmon-coloured split pea called *masoor dal*. Breads, called *roti*, include *capitis* (flat, unleavened rounds made of whole wheat flour), *naan* (one of the few leavened breads), *paratha* (a flaky bread fried on a pan called a *tava*) and *poori* (a deep-fat-fried puffy bread). Many pan-fried breads are stuffed with savoury mixtures or dusted with flavourings. Rice and lentil flours are also used for breads.

Devout Muslims do not eat pork; devout Hindus do not eat beef and devout Buddhists do not eat any meat, poultry, fish, shellfish or dairy product.

For those who do eat meat and poultry, the most commonly eaten are mutton and chicken, prepared in a variety of ways: stewed with spices; marinated and grilled; braised in yogurt or cream (called *kormas*); sautéed and baked (called *bhoona*) or formed into meatballs (called *koftas*). A wide variety of freshwater and saltwater fish and shellfish are also consumed. Dairy products include a mild white fresh cheese known as *paneer*.

The long tradition of vegetarianism and the variety of vegetables and spices available have made for a vegetarian cuisine rich in flavours and textures. Vegetables are usually fried with spices and served without any sauce. These pungent dishes are known as *foogath* in the South and *bhujia* in the North. Vegetables can be puréed and delicately spiced (called *bharta*); or mashed, shaped into balls and fried.

Indian—(clockwise from top) naan, chicken tandoor, mango chutney, saffron rice

Chutneys are relishes made from fruits, vegetables and herbs. Sometimes their flavours are tempered by marinating or cooking, although most fresh chutneys are nothing more than a mixture of raw foods, ground or finely cut and blended with seasonings. Chutneys are used to add contrast to the highly spiced dishes that dominate Indian cuisines.

Clarified butter made from water buffalo milk, known as *ghee*, is an important cooking medium, although ghee's expense has made a hydrogenated vegetable fat called *vanaspati* more popular. Usually, only meat is cooked in ghee; vegetable oils are used for vegetables.

The *degchi* is a commonly used cooking vessel. Traditionally made of brass but now also made of aluminum, it is a tall, straight-sided, flat-rimmed pot used for boiling, stewing, braising or steaming. When lidded, it can be used as an oven by placing coals below the pot as well as on the lid.

Northern India

The cuisine of Northern India reflects the strong Muslim presence found in northern and central India since the 16th-century Mogul invasions. This presence has given rise to a regional cuisine using meat. The area's geography favours wheat, not rice, so capitis is a dietary staple. Generally, Northern Indian cuisine produces dryer foods with thick sauces. A typical Northern masala calls for cumin, fenugreek, ginger and garlic. After the spices are ground and mixed, they are added to the dish without further preparation.

One of the best-known Northern Indian dishes is tandoori chicken. The tandoor is a jar-shaped clay oven usually buried in the earth and heated by placing hot coals inside. The meat or poultry is threaded on skewers and placed inside the oven to cook. The finished product has a wonderfully dry, crusty surface. Although it is difficult to reproduce the surface in a conventional oven, it is possible to reproduce the flavours.

Applying the Basics

RECIPE 34.9

TANDOORI MURGH (CHICKEN TANDOOR)

Yield: 4 Servings

Roasting chicken, 1.3 kg (3 lb.)	1	1
Saffron strands	0.25 g	1/2 tsp.
Boiling water	15 mL	1 Tbsp.
Garlic, chopped	25 g	2 Tbsp.
Fresh ginger, peeled and minced	10 g	1 Tbsp.
Lemon juice	30 mL	2 Tbsp.
Chilli powder	3 g	1 tsp.
Paprika	5 g	1-1/2 tsp.
Masala (Recipe 34.8)	8 g	2 tsp.
Salt	5 g	1 tsp.
Ghee (or clarified butter or canola oil)	45 g	3 Tbsp.
Lemons, wedged	2	2

1. Quarter and skin the chicken, making slits in the drumsticks, thighs and breasts to allow the spices to penetrate.

RECIPE 34.9

Approximate values per serving:

Calories	898
Total fat	55 g
Saturated fat	19 g
Cholesterol	311 mg
Sodium	757 mg
Total carbohydrates	7 g
Protein	90 g

Continued

2. Steep the saffron in boiling water for 10 minutes. Then combine it with the garlic, ginger, lemon juice, chilli powder, paprika, masala and salt; blend until smooth.

3. Season the chicken with the spice mixture, covering the entire surface, especially the slits. Cover and marinate, under refrigeration, for at least 2 hours or overnight.

4. Roast the chicken on a rack at 200°C (400°F), basting periodically with ghee, until done, approximately 35–40 minutes.

5. Serve hot, garnished with lemon wedges and accompanied by naan.

Southern India

The cuisine of Southern India is heavily influenced by Hindus. It offers a wide range of meatless dishes with rich, spicy sauces. Rice is the principal crop and it is eaten with almost every meal, as plain or flavoured rice or as rice-flour breads such as *idli* and *dosa*. Southern Indian cuisine uses more fresh herbs than Northern Indian cuisine and its masalas are wet; that is, the ground spices are mixed into a paste with vinegar, water or coconut milk. (Wet masalas must be used immediately.) Typical spices used in Southern Indian masalas include mustard seed, tamarind and asafetida (a fennel-like resin). Chiles are more popular in the south than in the north, as is garlic.

Applying the Basics

RECIPE 34.10

MURGHI KARI (CHICKEN CURRY)

Yield: 4 Servings

Onion, small dice	250 g	8 oz.
Garlic, crushed	10 g	2 tsp.
Ghee (or clarified butter)	30 mL	2 Tbsp.
Fresh ginger, fine dice	60 g	2 oz.
Turmeric	3 g	1-1/2 tsp.
Coriander seeds, ground	2.25 g	1-1/2 tsp.
Cumin seeds, ground	1.6 g	1 tsp.
Cayenne pepper	2 g	1 tsp.
Fenugreek, ground	1 g	1/2 tsp.
Coconut milk	600 mL	20 fl. oz.
Roasting chicken, 1.3 kg (3 lb.), cut into 8 pieces	1	1
Salt	5 g	1 tsp.
Green chiles, slit lengthwise	3	3
Lemon juice	30 mL	1 fl. oz.

1. Stir-fry the onion and garlic in the ghee until the onion is golden-brown.

2. To make the wet masala, mix the ginger, turmeric, coriander, cumin, cayenne pepper and fenugreek; add just enough of the coconut milk to form a paste.

3. Add the wet masala to the onion and stir-fry for 8 minutes.

RECIPE 34.10

Approximate values per serving:

Calories	1198
Total fat	83 g
Saturated fat	44 g
Cholesterol	303 mg
Sodium	781 mg
Total carbohydrates	22 g
Protein	95 g

4. Add the chicken pieces and cook, turning them frequently, for 6–8 minutes.

5. Add the remaining coconut milk, salt and chiles. Bring to a boil, cover and reduce to a simmer. Cook until the chicken is done, approximately 45 minutes.

6. Just before service, stir in the lemon juice and adjust the seasonings. Serve with saffron rice and a chutney.

Applying the Basics

RECIPE 34.11

KESAR CHAVAL (SAFFRON RICE)

Yield: 6 Servings

Basmati rice	400 g	14 oz.
Saffron threads	0.5 g	1 tsp.
Boiling water	900 mL	32 fl. oz.
Ghee (or clarified butter)	90 g	3 oz.
Cinnamon, 5-cm (2-inch) sticks	5 g	1
Cloves, whole	4	4
Onion, fine dice	150 g	5 oz.
Dark brown sugar	15 g	1 Tbsp.
Salt	10 g	2 tsp.
Cardamom seeds	0.25 g	1/4 tsp.

1. Wash the rice and drain thoroughly.

2. Steep the saffron in 60 mL (2 fl. oz.) of the boiling water.

3. In a saucepan, heat the ghee, add the cinnamon and cloves. Add the onion and stir-fry until it is soft and slightly brown.

4. Add the rice and stir until it is well coated with the ghee and the grains are a light golden colour.

5. Stirring constantly, add the remaining boiling water, brown sugar, salt and cardamom seeds. Bring to a boil and reduce to a simmer.

6. Gently stir in the saffron and its water, cover and simmer until the rice has absorbed all the liquid.

7. Fluff with a fork and serve at once.

Throughout India, many foods are eaten in the form of savoury snacks (collectively known as *chat*), which are served as appetizers or at teatime. Examples include *chanachur* (made from split peas, peanuts, lemon, peppers and lentil flour, all the ingredients being fried separately), *samosas* (deep-fat fried turnovers, stuffed with meat, potatoes or vegetables), *pakoras* (vegetables or other foods dipped in chickpea flour and deep-fat fried), spiced fish balls and eggplant fritters served with chutney.

Sweet snacks (collectively known as *meethai*) are also an integral part of Indian cuisines. Many are made from milk that is condensed into a thick mass called *mawa*. *Mawa* is then cooked with sugar and flavourings such as coconut, almond, pistachio or kewra (a perfumed flower essence). *Jelebis* are pretzel-like sweets made from a batter of wheat and chickpea flour, oil and curds that is deep-fat fried and then dipped into a sugar syrup.

✦✦✦
AN INDIAN MEAL

A typical main meal of the day consists of two or three vegetable dishes (one of which is a dal), bread or rice, and a meat or fish dish if the family is not vegetarian. To offset the many highly spiced dishes, chutneys and *raytas* (yogurts mixed with vegetables) are served as accompaniments. A sweet is also often included and is eaten along with the savoury dishes, not afterward. All foods are served at once. Each diner eats off a large, round tray called a *thali*, which holds several small matching bowls called *katoris*. Each bowl holds a small serving of the various dishes. Rice is placed in the centre. Indians traditionally eat with their fingers (right hand only). Rice and bread are used to move sauced foods from katori to mouth. Meals end with *paan*: a digestive and breath freshener made of lime paste spread on a betel (areca) leaf; the leaf is wrapped around chopped betel nut and spices and folded into a little triangle.

RECIPE 34.11

Approximate values per serving:

Calories	374
Total fat	16 g
Saturated fat	9 g
Cholesterol	38 mg
Sodium	659 mg
Total carbohydrates	54 g
Protein	5 g

NORTH AFRICAN
AND MIDDLE EASTERN CUISINES

Stretching from Morocco at the northwest tip of Africa, along the southern and eastern portions of the Mediterranean Sea and north to Lebanon, is a land primarily populated by Arabs. It is rich in religious and culinary traditions and offers a range of national cuisines. These various cuisines can be divided into two main groups: North African and Middle Eastern.

All of the cuisines, however, share certain staples, seasonings and a fondness for sweets. Wheat in various forms is eaten throughout the area. Legumes, including lentils, beans and peas, provide starch. Pork is virtually nonexistent for religious reasons; lamb is the principal meat, chicken the principal poultry. Fish from the Mediterranean is also popular. Garlic, onions, peppers, tomatoes and citrus are commonly used flavouring ingredients. Spices include cumin, ginger and peppercorns; herbs include mint, coriander and parsley. Eggplants, cucumbers, squash, okra, tomatoes, quinces, dates, figs, melons, pomegranates, mangoes and bananas are popular. A consistent theme among the various cuisines is a combination of fruits and nuts cooked with savoury meat dishes.

North African

The cuisines of North Africa include those of Morocco, Algeria and Tunisia as well as those of the more nomadic Bedouin tribes. This area, often referred to as the Maghreb, was once the granary for Imperial Rome. More recently, France was the dominant foreign influence. North African cuisine is based on

North African and Middle Eastern—(clockwise from top left) baklava, medjool dates, pita bread, harissa, Tangier couscous

cereals, vegetables, dried fruits and grilled meats. The national cuisines differ to a degree: Foods are more highly seasoned in Algeria and Tunisia and more subtly spiced in Morocco.

A principal spice mixture (known as *ras al hanout* in Morocco) consists of cinnamon, cumin, coriander, ginger and turmeric. Other North African seasonings and flavouring ingredients include garlic, onions, tomatoes, olives, fresh coriander leaves, fresh mint leaves, parsley and dried limes or lemons.

Many North African meat dishes include fruit or other sweet foods. For example, *tajine*, a type of slow-cooked ragout, may be made with mutton or rabbit with prunes and accompanied by fennel with lemon; chicken is cooked with cinnamon, kumquats and onions, and mutton is cooked with quinces and honey. Meats, often reduced to bite-sized chunks or ground balls, are often grilled or spit-roasted as kebabs. Fish can be grilled or fried. Vegetables are cooked in a sauce and frequently served with scrambled eggs, marinated and served in a salad or stuffed with sweet and savoury foods. Soups are always highly aromatic and often associated with religious festivities. The soups often combine dried vegetables or cereals (lentils, beans, chickpeas, unripe wheat) with meat (diced mutton or chicken) or fish.

Wheat is the principal grain and it is used to make one of the better-known North African dishes: couscous. Couscous refers to both the starch and the completed dish. The starch is made of semolina flour produced from hard durum wheat. It is steamed over a watery stew of lamb, chicken, beef (usually in the form of meatballs), fish or tripe and vegetables in a couscousier. A couscousier consists of two bulbous pots. The bottom one sits on the heat and holds the watery stew. The second sits on top of the first; it has a perforated bottom and holds the couscous. As the stew simmers, steam rising from it gently cooks the couscous and infuses flavours. The dish can be flavoured with saffron (Morocco), tomato purée (Algeria) or ginger and pepper (Tunisia). Traditionally mixed with smeun fat, a sort of rancid butter, the couscous and stew are more typically served with harissa, a hot and pungent sauce (see Recipe 11.14). Couscous is eaten by taking a small amount of the couscous along with a morsel of meat or vegetable, rolling it into a ball and popping it into the mouth. This entire action should be accomplished with only the first three fingers of the right hand.

◆◆◆
A MOROCCAN MEAL

A classic Moroccan meal starts with a *b'stilla* (a semolina dough pie stuffed with layers of ground pigeon meat, spices and sugar and then deep-fat fried) followed by a couscous. Dessert would be a sweet pudding such as one made with raisins, almonds and currants cooked in milk and thickened with semolina, *rghaifs* (pancakes fried in butter and topped with honey or stuffed with almonds) or *criouch* (cakes covered with honey and sesame seeds). Minted tea (which is far more mint than tea) is a typical beverage.

Applying the Basics

RECIPE 34.12

SEKSU TANJAOUI
(TANGIER COUSCOUS)

Yield: 4 Servings

Roaster chicken, quartered with giblets, 1.3–1.8 kg (3–4 lb.)	1	1
Salt	10 g	2 tsp.
Pepper	8 g	1 Tbsp.
Ginger, ground	6 g	2-1/2 tsp.
Saffron, pulverized and mixed with turmeric	1.5 g	1/2 tsp.
Cayenne pepper	pinch	pinch
Onions, medium, quartered	450 g	3
Bouquet garni:		
Fresh coriander	4 sprigs	4 sprigs
Fresh parsley	4 sprigs	4 sprigs

Continued

Whole butter	250 g	8 oz.
Water	2.5 L	2-1/2 qt.
Couscous	700 g	1 lb. 8 oz.
Onion, large, julienned	200 g	1
Raisins	100 g	3 oz.
Chicken stock	as needed	as needed

1. Place the chicken, salt, pepper, ginger, saffron, cayenne, onion quarters, bouquet garni and half the butter in the bottom of the couscousier. Melt the butter and stir the ingredients to coat them with the melted butter. Add 2.5 L (2-1/2 qt.) of water; bring to a boil, reduce to a simmer and cook 1 hour.

2. Combine the couscous with 3 L (3 qt.) of cold water; mix and drain. Gently break apart any lumps.

3. After the stew has simmered for 1 hour, place the couscous in the top pot or a metal colander suspended over the pot, lower the heat and steam for 20 minutes. Do not cover the couscous while it steams.

4. Remove the colander and add the sliced onions and raisins to the stew; adjust its consistency with water or chicken stock if necessary. Replace the colander and steam for 15 minutes. Dot the couscous with the remaining butter and steam for 5 minutes. Fluff the couscous with a fork to distribute the melted butter.

5. Serve the couscous with the stew and harissa (see Recipe 11.14).

RECIPE 34.12

Approximate values per serving:

Calories	392
Total fat	25 g
Saturated fat	11 g
Cholesterol	115 mg
Sodium	399 mg
Total carbohydrates	14 g
Protein	28 g

Middle Eastern

The cuisines of the Middle East include those of Egypt, Jordan, Syria and Lebanon. This is the southern portion of the Levant, an area that stretches from Egypt through Israel, north to Turkey and east through Greece. Now predominantly Arab, the area has been ruled by the Egyptians, Romans, Turks, British and French, to name a few. Each nationality has left its mark.

Generally, rice and wheat (wheat for bread flour and bulgur) are the principal staples, as are legumes, especially chickpeas. Chickpeas are used in many dishes, most notably *hummus*, in which they are mashed with sesame seed paste, and *ful medames*, an ancient Egyptian dish in which the beans are flavoured with garlic and dressed with lemon juice and oil. Important spices include cinnamon, cumin, ginger, coriander, allspice and hot peppers, as well as some more unusual spices such as *mahlab* (ground black-cherry pits, which gives food a slightly fruity flavour), *zatar* (a variety of thyme that tastes like a cross between thyme and oregano) and *sumac* (which gives meats a woody taste). Dried whole limes and verjuice are also used for flavourings.

Yogurt is used as a beverage, pudding and flavouring ingredient. Olive oil is a typical cooking medium as well as a dressing and a basic ingredient in many of the vegetable dishes called *yakhni*. Sesame seed oil is also used, especially in Lebanese dishes. Tahini is a popular paste made from crushed sesame seeds. Produce of importance includes garlic, okra, cucumbers, eggplants and lemons as well as tomatoes and peppers (New World imports).

Several varieties of freshwater and saltwater fish are enjoyed grilled, baked or poached. Little beef is consumed, although camel is eaten (hump meat is the choicest). Lamb, however, dominates Middle Eastern cuisine. It can be grilled, roasted, braised, stewed with vegetables or made into a variety of meatballs (called *kofta*) and kebabs. It is also the basic ingredient in the Lebanese and Syrian dish known as *kibbeh*. For kibbeh, ground lamb is mixed with onion-flavoured bulgur, parsley and pine nuts. It is then shaped into cakes and grilled, deep-fat fried or baked, or stuffed with savoury ingredients and deep-fat fried. Chicken is also popular, whether spit-roasted, marinated in oil and citrus or stuffed with rice and pine nuts and baked in an earthenware casserole.

Applying the Basics

RECIPE 34.13

DAJAJ MAHSHY
(CHICKEN STUFFED WITH RICE, CURRANTS AND PINE NUTS)

Yield: 4 Servings

Long-grain white rice	200 g	6 oz.
Whole butter	125 g	4 oz.
Onion, fine dice	100 g	3 oz.
Fryer chicken, 1.3 to 1.5 kg (3 to 3-1/2 lb.), including coarsely chopped giblets	1	1
Pine nuts	30 g	3 Tbsp.
Water	500 mL	16 fl. oz.
Dried currants	20 g	2 Tbsp.
Salt	30 g	2 Tbsp.
Pepper	TT	TT
Yogurt	60 mL	2 fl. oz.

1. Wash the rice and set aside.
2. Sauté the onion in half of the butter until transparent.
3. Add the coarsely chopped giblets and pine nuts and sauté until the pine nuts are browned.
4. Stir in the rice and cook until the grains are coated with butter.
5. Add the water, currants, 15 g (1 Tbsp.) of the salt and pepper to taste; cover and cook until the rice is done.
6. Remove from the heat and mix in the remaining butter.
7. Stuff the chicken's cavity with the rice mixture and truss.
8. Season the yogurt with the remaining salt and pepper. Brush half of the mixture over the chicken. Roast the chicken at 180°C (350°F), basting periodically with the yogurt mixture until done, approximately 1 hour.
9. Carve the chicken and serve it with the rice.

Middle Eastern sweets are very sweet; they include *ataif* (pancakes drenched with syrup and topped with chopped nuts and thick clotted cream), *muhallabia* (a milk pudding flavoured with orange flower water) and *ma'amoul* (pastries stuffed with dates or nuts and coated with powdered sugar or served in cream) as well as the more familiar halva, candied dates, baklava and Turkish delight.

MEXICAN CUISINE

Mexican cuisine is rooted in its pre-Columbian past and nurtured by centuries of Spanish influence. For thousands of years before Columbus's arrival, the people of Mexico lived on a diet of squash, corn (maize) and beans supplemented with fresh vegetables (avocados, peppers, tomatoes), fruit (manioc and bananas) and occasionally fish, shellfish, game and wild poultry. The population relied on steaming and slow cooking methods such as wrapping meats,

♦♦♦
A LEBANESE MEAL

A classic Lebanese meal would feature one or more appetizers known as *mazza* (or *meze*) such as hummus, lambs' tongues, lambs' brains, chopped kidneys, puff pastry cases filled with spinach or minced meats, *babaghannou* (puréed eggplant with sesame oil) or stuffed vine leaves. Kibbeh would be served along with *tabbouleh*, a mixture of bulgur, mint, spices and tomatoes dressed with oil and lemon. Dessert may be baklava, a classic pastry of chopped nuts baked between layers of thin, flaky dough and drenched in honey or a cinnamon and lemon juice flavoured syrup.

Drinks include water flavoured with orange flower or rose waters, unfermented sugar cane juice, yogurt drinks (*ayran*), herb teas and mint teas. Thick boiled coffee is also enjoyed.

RECIPE 34.13

Approximate values per serving:

Calories	1327
Total fat	79 g
Saturated fat	30 g
Cholesterol	376 mg
Sodium	3208 mg
Total carbohydrates	49 g
Protein	103 g

Mexican—(clockwise from top left) poblano rice, poblano chile, coconut candies, chicken mole on corn tortillas, hibiscus water

poultry and fish in leaves and slow-roasting them over hot embers or stewing foods with little liquid in tightly lidded earthenware pots.

In the wake of Cortez's conquest of Mexico in 1521 came pigs, cattle and dairy products, chicken, wheat, rice, sesame seeds, citrus and almonds. The Spanish also brought with them a new manner of cooking: rendering fat from meat and using the rendered fat and vegetable oils to fry foods. All of these foods, to one degree or another, were soon integrated into the local cuisines; sautéing and pan-frying became standard cooking methods. (Although the people of Mexico quickly adopted European foods and cooking methods, Europeans waited centuries before adopting Mexican foods and appreciating Mexican cuisine.)

Mexico has given rise to several regional cuisines of note. Unfortunately, many consumers in this country erroneously believe that Mexican cuisine starts and ends with tacos and refried beans.

The most characteristic feature of Mexican cookery is the widespread use of chiles. There are about 100 varieties, many of which have a hot, pungent taste. (Unlike English, Mexican Spanish differentiates between the word *hot* as applied to a food's temperature—*caliente*—and *hot* as applied to its degree of spiciness—*chiloso*.) Fresh chiles can be served raw; stuffed and baked; stewed; chopped with tomatoes, herbs and oil for a salsa; or minced and used as a seasoning. Or they can be dried and used whole or ground as a seasoning. Other seasonings include garlic, cinnamon, cumin, oregano, onion, achiote seeds, basil, peppercorns, cilantro and other fresh herbs.

Fresh vegetable salsas accompany many dishes. Guacamole, for example, is an ancient dish made from avocados and flavourings such as onions and tomatoes. The numerous fresh salsas are usually categorized as either red or green. Red salsa, called *salsa roja*, is made from chiles (usually dried), onions and tomato. Green salsa, called *salsa verde*, is made from chiles (usually fresh), onions and tomatillos.

Corn flour is used to make a dough called *masa*. Popular throughout Mexico, smooth masa is pressed (traditionally by hand) into flat rounds and quickly cooked on a griddle to make tortillas. Tortillas are eaten like bread, filled with savoury mixtures for burritos, fried crisp and topped for tostadas, folded around savoury mixtures and fried for tacos, or used for turnovers (quesadillas, empañadas and enchiladas). Tamales are made from a coarser masa dough that is stuffed with a savoury mixture of beans, meats or poultry, encased in corn husks and steamed. Many of these masa-based dishes are considered snack foods known as *antojitos*, the traditional portable snacks of the Mexican marketplace.

Wheat flour is also used for tortillas (especially in north Mexico) as well as for a variety of leavened breads. Rice, although not indigenous, is also a staple of Mexican diets.

As they were during pre-Columbian times, beans are still a staple. They are usually dried, then reconstituted in water and served in a soupy fashion, or mashed and fried in lard or oil to make a smooth paste called *frijoles refritos* (refried beans).

Chicken is popular throughout the country. Meat is used somewhat sparingly in most Mexican regional cuisines. Beef and dairy products are more widely consumed in the north, while goat and goat cheese are more typical of the country's central regions. Fish and shellfish are eaten along both coasts.

The ancient manner of slow cooking is still used for meats, poultry and fish; there is a great variety of stews and soups. The ancient cooking method known as *pibil*, in which meats were wrapped in maguey or banana leaves and cooked in a pit lined with hot coals, is often replaced today by steaming banana-leaf-wrapped meats. Some meats and vegetables are also grilled (called *al carbon*) or seared and roasted. A popular meat marinade known as *adobado* combines chiles, garlic and herbs.

Sauce making is very different from European traditions and includes a step known as "frying the sauce." Most sauces start with dried peppers that are soaked, seeded and ground to a paste and then mixed with herbs, spices and vegetables. The mixture, sometimes thickened with ground toasted pumpkin seeds or nuts, is then puréed and fried in oil or lard. This sauce is added to partially cooked and drained meat or poultry and the dish is then simmered to blend the flavours.

Moles are dishes made with a classic cooking method that incorporates this sauce-making technique. The meat or poultry is cooked and then steeped or simmered in a sauce made from chiles and other ingredients.

♦♦♦
A MEXICAN MEAL

A typical Mexican meal may start with a hearty soup such as *pozole rojo* (pork and hominy soup with red chile and fresh garnishes) followed by a meat-and-sauce dish served with beans, rice and tortillas. Dessert would be flan. Popular beverages include *horchata* (cinnamon-infused milk with ground rice), *agua de jamaica* (usually served before a meal; a sweetened, hibiscus-flower-infused water), *agua de tamarindo* (a sweetened, tamarind-infused water) and *cerveza* (beer).

Applying the Basics

RECIPE 34.14

MOLE ROJO CON POLLO
(RICH RED MOLE WITH CHICKEN)

Yield: 4 Servings

Chiles, dried, stemmed, seeded and deveined:

Chiles anchos	60 g	2 oz.
Chiles mulatos	30 g	1 oz.
Chiles pasillas	10 g	1/3 oz.
Vegetable oil	90 mL	3 fl. oz.

Continued

Tomato, medium, roasted, cored, peeled and diced	1	1
Medium tomatillos, husked, washed and simmered until tender	3	3
Mexican chocolate, chopped	30 g	1 oz.
Oregano, dried	0.25 g	1/2 tsp.
Thyme, dried	0.25 g	1/4 tsp.
Bay leaf	1	1
Peppercorns	8	8
Cloves	3	3
Cinnamon stick	2.5 cm	1 inch
Sesame seeds	10 g	2 Tbsp.
Raisins	25 g	2 Tbsp.
Garlic, chopped	5 g	1 tsp.
Onion, thickly sliced	60 g	2 oz.
Peanuts	30 g	1 oz.
Plantain, small, peeled and diced (optional)	125 g	4 oz.
Corn tortilla, stale	1/2	1/2
White bread slice, stale	1	1
Chicken stock	900 mL	1 qt.
Chicken, 1.6 kg (3-1/2 lb.), quartered	1	1
Salt	5 g	1 tsp.
Granulated sugar	15 g	1 Tbsp.

1. Sauté the chiles in 45 mL (3 Tbsp.) of oil until nutty brown. Remove, reserving the oil. Cover the chiles with boiling water and soak for 1 hour. Drain and set aside.

2. Combine the tomato, tomatillos, chocolate, oregano and thyme in a large bowl. Pulverize the bay leaf, peppercorns, cloves and cinnamon and combine with the tomato mixture.

3. Toast the sesame seeds and add them to the tomato mixture.

4. Sauté the raisins in the reserved chile oil until they puff; add them to the tomato mixture.

5. In the same oil, sauté the garlic, onion and peanuts until they are well browned; add to the tomato mixture.

6. Sauté the plantain until golden-brown; add to the tomato mixture.

7. Sauté the tortilla until brown; shred it and add to the tomato mixture.

8. Lay the bread in the pan and quickly flip it to coat both sides with the fat; then brown it on both sides. Tear it into pieces and add to the tomato mixture.

9. Stir the tomato mixture well. Purée it with 175 mL (6 fl. oz.) of chicken stock and strain through a conical strainer.

10. Purée the reconstituted chiles with 60 mL (2 fl. oz.) of chicken stock; strain through a conical strainer in a separate bowl and set aside.

11. Sauté the chicken in remaining oil. Remove and degrease the pan. In the same pan, sauté the chile purée until it is thick and dark. Add the tomato purée and cook until thick.

12. Add 700 mL (1-1/2 pt.) of chicken stock. Simmer the sauce 45 minutes. Season with salt and sugar. If the sauce is thicker than whipping cream, dilute it with additional chicken stock.

13. Add the chicken to the pan and braise until done.

14. Degrease the sauce. Garnish the chicken with sesame seeds and serve with the sauce and Arroz a la Poblana (see Recipe 34.15).

RECIPE 34.14

Approximate values per serving:

Calories	840
Total fat	53 g
Saturated fat	12 g
Cholesterol	132 mg
Sodium	1468 mg
Total carbohydrates	42 g
Protein	52 g

Applying the Basics

ARROZ A LA POBLANA
(RICE WITH POBLANO CHILES)

Yield: 4 Servings

Onion, small dice	150 g	5 oz.
Vegetable oil	25 mL	1-1/2 Tbsp.
Long- or medium-grain rice	200 g	6 oz.
Chicken stock, hot	400 mL	14 fl. oz.
Salt	TT	TT
Chiles poblanos, fresh, roasted and peeled, seeded, julienned	3	3
Fresh corn kernels	175 g	6 oz.
Mexican queso fresco (or feta or farmer's cheese), crumbled	150 g	5 oz.
Parsley or cilantro sprigs	as needed	as needed

1. Sauté the onion in oil until translucent. Add the rice and sauté without colouring.
2. Add the hot stock, salt, chiles and corn to the rice mixture; bring to a boil, reduce to a simmer, cover and cook until all liquid has evaporated.
3. Add the crumbled cheese to the rice and toss to combine.
4. Serve as a side dish garnished with parsley or cilantro sprigs.

RECIPE 34.15

Approximate values per serving:

Calories	333
Total fat	11 g
Saturated fat	6 g
Cholesterol	33 mg
Sodium	629 mg
Total carbohydrates	48 g
Protein	11 g

Sweets, especially candies, candied fruits and hard cookies or cakes, are popular throughout Mexico. The more commonly encountered desserts such as flans and caramels are derived from the Spanish tradition.

Mexico is a country rich in regional cuisines. A few observations about them follow.

Central (Mexico City)

Blended with tomatoes, the fiery hot *guajillos* or smoky chipotles are the principal chiles used for sauces. Also popular are the common black chile and the pasilla. A great variety of beans are used, but the purplish *flor de mayo* and the tan *bayo* are the most popular. Cooking methods include mole. A typical meat dish would be lamb wrapped in maguey or banana leaves cooked in brick pits and served with a sauce of fermented maguey juice and pasilla.

West Central (Guadalajara)

The defining sauce is made with a purée of the very hot *de arbol* chiles, sometimes thickened with tomatillos. De arbol also come bottled, pickled with vinegar. A great variety of beans are used, but as with Central Mexican cuisine, flor de mayo and bayo are the most popular. A typical meat dish would be kid (young goat) marinated in chiles and slow-cooked in a sealed container. From the west coast also comes seviche, a dish of finely chopped fish and shellfish marinated in lime juice, cilantro, tomato chunks and herbs.

Central East Coast (Veracruz)

Although still used in abundance, chiles play a less prominent role. Herbs (especially cilantro, basil, bay leaves, parsley and oregano) and spices (peppercorns and cinnamon) are a vital part of the cuisine. The area is known for its fish and shellfish cooked in a chunky broth of olives, herbs and chiles (usually jalapeños). The basic bean is black and usually cooked with a sprig of epazote.

Northern (Sonora, Chihuahua)

As in West Central Mexico, the defining sauce is made with a purée of the very hot de arbol chiles, sometimes thickened with tomatillos. This region is known for its wheat and beef, which is sometimes dried and called *carne seca*. A typical pork dish is the simmered *carne con chile colorado*. Popular beans are pintos and the yellowish-tan *piruano*.

Southeastern (Yucatan)

This regional cuisine is unique, using achiote seeds as the principal seasoning. Fresh chiles are usually ground with salt and lime or purchased in a bottled form. A vinegary orange-red and a green sauce made with the local *habañero* chiles are especially popular. Seasonings are added to most dishes in the form of a paste that can be brick red (made from achiote seeds ground with oregano, black pepper, cloves and cumin mixed with garlic and vinegar), olive-amber (a mild blend of garlic, allspice, cinnamon and other spices) or coal black (made from burnt chiles, achiote, spices and garlic). A typical pork dish is flavoured with achiote and wrapped in banana leaves, then slowly steamed or roasted. The most commonly used bean is black and usually cooked with a sprig of epazote.

Southern (Oaxaca)

A wide range of dried peppers are used in many different stews and sauces, some of which combine sweeter spices such as cloves and cinnamon with savoury foods. A typical meat or poultry dish would be kid or chicken marinated in chiles, then wrapped in avocado leaves and steamed. Some consider this region to produce the finest *chorizo*, a pork sausage made with herbs, spices, a touch of vinegar and deep red chiles. The basic black bean is also regularly used throughout the south.

*C*ONCLUSION

Although the foods and flavourings may differ from the cuisine of one culture to the cuisine of another, the fundamentals of cookery do not: Quality ingredients need to be prepared, seasoned and cooked, then presented in an attractive and appropriate manner. With a good purveyor, a little practice and an understanding of the principles discussed throughout this book, a world of great cooking and eating is available to you and your customers.

QUESTIONS FOR DISCUSSION

1. Which of the cuisines discussed rely on slow-cooking methods for meats? Which rely on quick-cooking methods?

2. Identify the flavour principle for each of the cuisines discussed.

3. Which New World product plays an important role in some Asian cuisines?

4. Compare and contrast the cuisines of Japan and North Africa.

5. Compare and contrast one of the cuisines of India and one of the cuisines of China.

6. Explain why there may be several cuisines within a single country.

WEBLINKS

Ethnic Foods and Customs
www.eatethnic.com

Web Resources for Japanese Food
www.bento.com/morefood.html

Moroccan Recipes
www.Maghreb.Net/countries/morocco/recipes.html

Cuisine of India
www.incore.com/india/cuisine.html

Chinascape: Chinese Food and Tea
www.chinascape.org/china/culture/food/index.html

Jewish Food Recipe Archives
www.eskimo.com/~jefffree/recipes/

Hungarian Cuisine
www.fsz.bme.hu/hungary/cuisine/cuisine.html

◆◆◆

LEARNING OUTCOMES

After studying this chapter you will be able to:

◆ apply the basic principles of plate presentation: cut polenta, cut gratin or scalloped potatoes, mould grains and vegetables

◆ use a variety of techniques to add visual appeal to plated foods: arrange foods on a plate, dust dessert plates, paint a design with sauces, paint a spider web design

While food preparation is very much a science, food presentation is an art. Good plate presentation results from careful attention to the colours, shapes, textures and arrangements of the foods. Great plate presentation requires experience and style.

In this chapter we describe several methods of presenting foods. We realize that for every guideline we suggest, there are exceptions. Nor are our examples meant to take the place of more traditional techniques. They are intended only to spark your imagination. As you gain experience, you will undoubtedly develop your own style.

The final step in food preparation is to justify the hours of hard work spent cooking the food by presenting and serving it properly.

Service is the process of delivering the selected foods to diners in the proper fashion. Hot foods should be served very hot and on heated plates; cold foods should be served very cold and on chilled plates. Foods should be cooked to the proper degree of doneness: A roast rack of lamb ordered medium rare should be medium rare—not medium, not rare. Pasta should be served al dente—slightly chewy, not mushy. Bread should be fresh, not stale. Portion sizes should be appropriate. First courses and appetizers should be small enough so that the diner can still appreciate the courses that follow. Rich foods should be served in smaller portions than other foods.

Presentation is the process of offering the selected foods to diners in a fashion that is visually pleasing. When presenting foods, always bear in mind that diners eat first with their eyes and then with their mouths. The foods must be pleasantly and appropriately coloured and shaped. And the colours, textures, shapes and flavours of all foods must work together to form a pleasing composition on the plate. Any decorative touches such as sauce placement or the addition of garnishes should be done thoughtfully. Most importantly, plates should be neat and clean. Inspect all plates before they leave the kitchen; wipe drops of sauce, specks of food and fingerprints from plate rims with a clean towel.

Presentation techniques are divided here into two broad categories: Those applied to specific foods and those applied to the plate as a whole. The techniques described here can be applied to some foods or recipes that appear elsewhere in the text.

THE FOOD

The appearance of food is contingent on the skilful application of techniques: fabrication, cooking, carving, shaping, placement and garnishing. Coupled with the procurement of the best-quality ingredients, the integrity of the food will be preserved and the diner's enjoyment enhanced.

A sirloin steak grilled medium rare should be pink inside; its surface should glisten and be branded with well-defined and neatly executed crosshatch marks. When serving asparagus with hollandaise the stalks should be bright green and tender-crisp; the hollandaise sauce should be smooth and shiny, not grainy or separated. A lemon meringue pie should be attractively browned on

♦♦♦

GARNISHES
(AN ADMITTEDLY CRANKY ADMONITION)

I am a strong believer in the simple, edible garnish that has a close flavor kinship to the dish. In my world, dyed daikon flamingos, writhing carrot dragons, and blinking Christmas lights in the empty eye sockets of a stir-fried lobster—all garnishes of the Hong Kong sort—are out. So, too, are radish flowers, tomato rosettes, and vegetable pellets sculpted to look like suppositories. I find all of this loathsome.

In my own rather minimalist style, the fanciest I get is an occasional scallion brush. Otherwise, a leggy piece of coriander or a flourish of scallion rings are all that our already colorful dishes require. Or, if the dish is green, a confetti of finely diced red bell pepper will do the job.

The issue is a visible one, but it needs to make sense on your tongue. A garnish is primarily designed to tickle the eye, but it also should meld seamlessly with the other flavors on the plate or contrast with them in a meaningful way.

Garnishing the rims of plates—a current feature of trendy restaurants in the 90s—is something I find very peculiar. I spill and splatter my own food quite nicely, thank you, and don't want the kitchen to do it for me.

Ditto the rage for a whole chive aloft each appetizer or a cage of spun sugar looming above a dessert. It is admittedly wonderful to give a little height to a dish: One can arrange cold shrimp, for example, in a lively tumble with just a touch or two. But the unrelated vertical garnish is often absurd, a bit of Dr. Seuss on the plate.

I sound cranky, and perhaps I am! Restaurant cooks frequently spend too much time decorating their food, and too little time paying attention to its taste. This, I think, is sad.

—from CHINA MOON COOKBOOK
by BARBARA TROPP

top; the filling should be a true lemony yellow and the crust golden-brown and without cracks.

Whether a recipe calls for browning foods under a salamander before service, poaching a galantine of chicken wrapped in cheesecloth to maintain its shape or adding vinegar when braising red cabbage, proper cooking procedures can enhance the texture, shape and colour of many cooked foods. Throughout this text we have discussed the proper cooking procedures for many, many foods. Use them.

Cutting Foods

The careful cutting of foods often increases their visual appeal and reflects the chef's attention to detail. Here we distinguish between cutting foods to decorate the plate and cutting the foods to be consumed. Decorative garnishes such as tomato and radish roses, frizzed scallions, watermelon boats and the like fall within the former category. Cutting foods into beautiful garnishes is an art unto itself, requiring skill and practice. While beyond the scope of this text, books on creating food garnishes are listed in References and Recommended Reading.

The latter category includes the meats, poultry, fish, vegetables and starches that are the meal. Each should be carefully shaped. Vegetables can be cut into uniform shapes and sizes such as julienne, batonnet or turned. If serving sliced meats or poultry, the slices should be of even thickness; fish can be cut into fillets. Individual stew ingredients and soup or salad garnishes should be of uniform sizes. All of these techniques are simple, fundamental and effective.

Some foods take the shape of the pan in which they are cooked. Polenta and gratin or scalloped potatoes, for example, can be presented attractively when baked in and removed from individual casseroles, or they can be baked in a hotel pan and then cut into various shapes.

Basic Procedure for Cutting Polenta

1. Cook the polenta according to the recipe. When it is done, pour it onto a well-oiled or buttered half sheet pan. Then chill it in the refrigerator until firm.

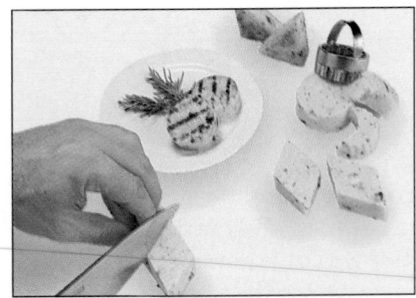

Cutting polenta into various shapes.

Cutting potatoes with a circular cutter.

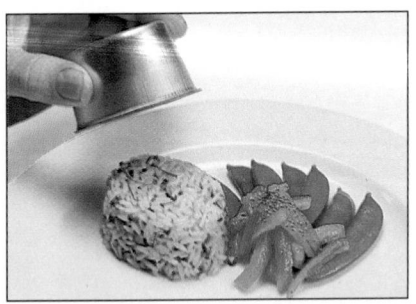

Unmoulding a timbale of rice.

2. Once the polenta is firm, flip the pan over onto a work table. Lift off the pan; the polenta will come out easily. Using a chef's knife or circular cutters, cut the polenta into the desired shape. The polenta can be sautéed or grilled for service.

Basic Procedure for Cutting Gratin or Scalloped Potatoes

1. Select a recipe that produces a firm finished product so that the finished dish will hold its shape after cutting.
2. Bake the potatoes in a well-greased hotel pan and refrigerate until cold and firm. Then cut the potatoes into various shapes with a chef's knife or circular cutters and remove them to a clean pan with a spatula.
3. For service, reheat the potatoes in a 160°C (325°F) oven until hot.

Moulding Foods

Some foods, particularly grains or vegetables bound by sauces, can be moulded into attractive, hard-edged shapes by using metal rings, cutters or timbales. These moulded forms create height and keep the plate neat and clean.

Basic Procedure for Moulding Grains

1. Fill a timbale, soup cup or other mould of the appropriate size and shape with the hot grains, firmly pressing them together.
2. For à la carte service, immediately unmould the grains onto the serving plate by placing the mould upside down on the plate and tapping its rim.
3. For banquet service, place the filled moulds in a hotel pan and refrigerate until needed. Shortly before service, fill the hotel pan with hot water to a point about two-thirds up the side of the moulds. Be careful not to splash any water onto the grains. Cover the pan with foil and place in the oven. Heat until the grains are hot, then plate as desired.

Basic Procedure for Moulding Vegetables

1. Position a ring mould on the plate and fill it with the vegetables. Press the foods into the ring to help them hold the shape. Level the top.

2. Carefully lift off the ring.

THE PLATE

Properly cooked, carefully cut and appropriately moulded foods should not be haphazardly slapped onto a plate. Rather, you should choose and position the foods carefully to achieve a plate presentation with a balanced, harmonious composition.

The composition can be further enhanced by decorating the plate with garnishes or sauces. Some of these techniques (for example, decorating the plate with powdered sugar) do not substantially affect the flavours of the foods, they only make the completed presentation more attractive. Other techniques (for example, garnishing a dessert with finely chopped nuts or painting a plate with two sauces) add flavour and texture to the finished dish.

Choosing Plates

Restaurant china is available in many different shapes, sizes, colours and patterns. It is often the chef's responsibility to choose the appropriate piece of china for a particular dish. Some recipes are by tradition served in a particular dish, for example, a gratin or paella. For most others practicality is the first consideration. The chef's imagination and design abilities can then be showcased. Very few restaurants purchase specific china for every dish featured on the menu. Most often you will be working with existing tableware that is purchased to be cross-functional—appropriate for both dining-room and banquet service. While most food is more attractive when presented on larger plates with appropriate and strategic amounts of white space, that option will not always be available. Careful planning, shaping and placement of the food is critical to providing the diner with a visual treat.

White and cream are by far the most common colours for restaurant china. Almost any food looks good on these neutral colours.

Coloured and patterned plates can be used quite effectively to accent food, however. The obvious choice is to contrast dark plates with bright- or light-coloured foods and light plates with dark-coloured foods.

The food should always be the focal point of any plate. Be careful in selecting restaurant china with intricate designs and brightly coloured patterns that can conflict or compete with the colours, shapes and arrangements of the foods. The colours and shapes in the pattern should blend well and harmonize with the foods served. The swirling patterns of blues, greys, pinks and yellows along the plate rim shown to the right, for example, harmonize well with the colours of the smoked salmon, squash blossoms and accompaniments.

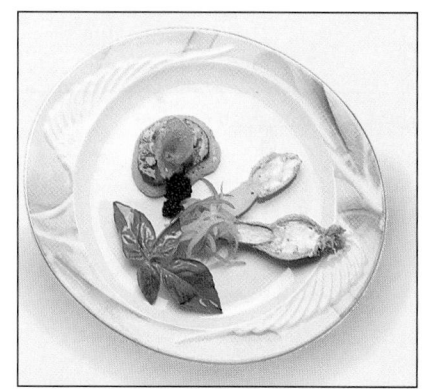

Stuffed Squash Blossoms, Blini and Smoked Salmon

Arranging Foods on Plates

You should strive for a well-balanced plate composition. This can be achieved by carefully considering colours, textures, shapes and arrangements.

Colours

Foods come in a rainbow of colours and, to the extent appropriate, foods of different colours should be presented together. Generally, the colours should provide balance and contrast. But no matter how well prepared or planned, some dishes simply have dull, boring or similar colours. If so, try adding another ingredient or garnish for a splash of colour. The vivid red lobster claws and the shiny black mussel shells shown here add striking colour notes to a paella dish that would otherwise be dominated by yellow rice, tan chicken, brown sausages and grey clam shells.

Paella

Cassoulet

Lamb Loin with Rösti Potatoes

Grilled Duck with Roasted Vegetables

Textures

Visual texture refers to how smooth or rough, coarse or fine a food looks. Mashed potatoes and carrot purée both look smooth and soft. Salmon mousseline and spinach soufflé both have slightly grainy surfaces. Rösti potatoes and meatloaf both appear coarse. The flavours of each food in these pairs differ; their visual textures do not.

Typically, foods with similar textures look boring together; foods with different textures look more exciting. Serve carrots cut julienne with the mashed potatoes to achieve a balance of hard and soft textures; steamed leaf spinach with the salmon mousseline for a combination of smooth and grainy textures; and a baked potato with the meatloaf for pairing fluffy and coarse textures. These pairs generally maintain the same range of flavours as the first set of pairs while providing different visual textures.

The cassoulet shown to the left harmoniously combines several textures in one dish: the pebbly beans, the slices of smooth slab bacon and coarse sausage and the bumpy skin of the duck leg. Indeed, the variation in textures is so dramatic and appealing that many diners may not even notice that all the principal ingredients are essentially the same colour.

Shapes

For a more dramatic presentation, combine foods with different shapes on one plate. The plate shown to the left is an excellent example of simple shapes artfully combined: ovals of evenly sliced lamb loin with cleanly cut triangles of crisp potatoes and long, thin spears of asparagus. The three very different shapes lend contrast and character to the dish.

Arrangements

Having decided on the colours, textures and shapes of the foods that will go on the plate, you must next decide where to place each individual item to achieve a balanced and unified composition. Mostly this takes judgement and style, but there are a few general guidelines.

Basic Guidelines for Arranging Foods on a Plate

1. Strike a balance between overcrowding the plate and leaving large gaps of space. Foods should not touch the plate rim nor necessarily be confined to the very centre.
2. Choose a focal point for the plate—that is, the point to which the eye is drawn. This is usually the highest point on the plate. Design the plate with the highest point to the rear or centre. Avoid placing foods of equal heights around the edge of the plate leaving a hole in the centre—the eye will naturally be drawn to that gap.
3. The plate's composition should flow naturally. For example, make the highest point the back of the plate and have the rest of the food become gradually shorter towards the front of the plate. Slicing and fanning foods can attract the eye and help establish a flow. The customer should be able to access all elements of the plate without tearing it apart.

The grilled duck with roasted vegetables shown here elegantly illustrates these principles. Height is established by a structure composed of the duck leg and thigh, sliced turnips and baby carrots. The structure sits towards the back of the plate. Its height, placement and striking appearance make it the focal point. The neatly sliced duck breast is then fanned across the plate in front of this focal point, drawing the viewer's attention into the plate.

Decorating Plates

The colours, textures, shapes and arrangements of foods on a plate can be improved or highlighted by decorating a plate with herbs, spices and other garnishes, baked hippen masse dough and sauces. If any of these are to be applied after the principal food is placed on the plate, be prepared to do so quickly so that the food is served at its proper temperature.

Plate Dusting

An attractive method for decorating dessert plates is to cover part of the plate with a dusting of powdered sugar, cocoa powder or both before placing the dessert on the plate. Use sugar on dark-coloured plates and cocoa on light-coloured plates. These items can be dusted onto the plate with a shaker can or sifter in a free-form fashion or into any desired pattern by using a template. The template can be a doily or a stencil placed over the plate before it is dusted. Leave sufficient rim clear to facilitate service without smudges.

Basic Procedure for Dusting Dessert Plates

1. Place a template over the plate. Dust the sugar or cocoa over the template.

2. Carefully remove the template.

Provided they complement the food, very finely chopped nuts can also be used to decorate plates for sweet or savoury foods. See, for example, the plate of French toast garnished with chopped macadamia nuts shown here. Plates for savoury foods can be decorated in a similar fashion by sprinkling them with finely chopped herbs such as thyme or diced vegetables such as a combination of brightly coloured peppers.

Garnishing Plates with Herbs

Using fresh herbs is one of the easiest ways to add colour, texture and flow to a plate. Whether the herb is an ingredient in the dish or merely a decoration, it should always complement the foods and be consistent with their seasonings. A sprig of fresh rosemary garnishing a beautifully roasted rack of lamb, or tiny

Banana Brioche French Toast

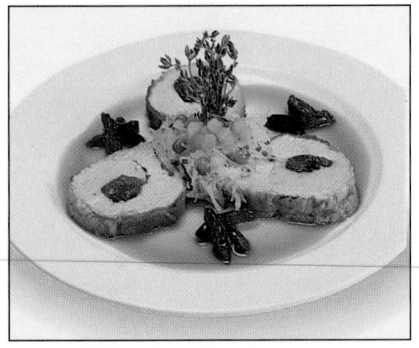

Using herbs to garnish a plate.

leaves of chervil garnishing delicately poached fillets of sole are natural combinations. Sprigs of fresh green mint (often with a fresh berry or two or a strawberry cut in a fan) are often the perfect decoration for a dessert plate.

Garnishing Plates with Hippen Masse and Tuiles

An increasingly popular presentation technique is to pipe batters into intricate designs and then bake them to form crisp, rigid, cookielike garnishes. These garnishes are then used to create height and add texture.

Applying the Basics

RECIPE 35.1

SAVOURY HIPPEN MASSE

ARIZONA BILTMORE, PHOENIX, AZ

Yield: 450 g (1 lb.)

Egg whites, room temperature	250 g	8 oz.
Bread flour	125 g	4 oz.
Cream, 35%	90 mL	3 fl. oz.
Granulated sugar	30 g	1 oz.
Salt and white pepper	TT	TT
Dried thyme, crushed	0.5 g	1 tsp.

1. Stir the egg whites together to blend. Stir in all of the flour at once.
2. Blend in the cream, then add the remaining ingredients.
3. Strain the batter through a conical strainer and allow to rest for 30 minutes.
4. Lightly oil the back of a very flat sheet pan. Pipe the hippen masse onto the pan using a plastic squeeze bottle. Pipe the batter into decorative patterns appropriate for the desired plate presentation.
5. Bake at 190°C (375°F) until set and lightly browned. Remove from the oven, then remove the decorations from the sheet pan while still slightly warm.

RECIPE 35.1

*Approximate values
per 25 g serving:*

Calories	52
Total fat	2 g
Saturated fat	1 g
Cholesterol	6.5 mg
Sodium	260 mg
Total carbohydrates	7 g
Protein	2.5 g

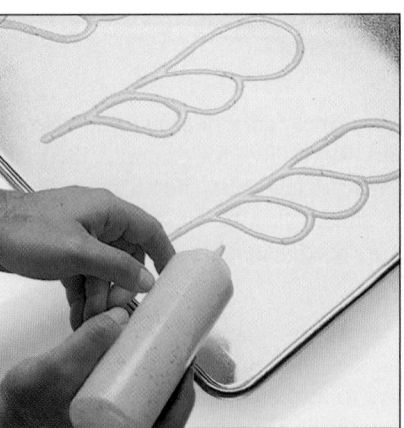

1. Pipe the batter onto an oiled sheet pan.

2. The baked batter as a component of the finished design.

Applying the Basics

RECIPE 35.2

POTATO TUILES

CAMOSUN COLLEGE, VICTORIA, BC
Chef Instructor Gilbert Noussitou, CCC

Yield: 36 7.5 cm (3 inch) Tuiles/Pieces

Duchesse potatoes	50 g	1-3/4 oz.
Egg white, slightly beaten	35 g	1
All-purpose flour	20 g	8 tsp.
Butter, melted	50 g	1-3/4 oz.

1. Combine cool duchesse potatoes with egg white.

2. Add flour and mix to a smooth paste.

3. Stir in the butter.

4. On a parchment-lined baking sheet, brush batter into template.

5. Bake in 200°C (400°F) oven until golden-brown and crisp.

Gilbert Noussitou, CCC
A graduate of École Hôtelière des Pyrénées, in Toulouse, France, Gilbert has been practising his trade for 28 years in some of the finest establishments of France, England and Canada. His varied experience includes owning a restaurant, a catering company and a consulting firm, as well as winning many national and international awards. He currently teaches the Cook Apprenticeship Program at Camosun.

RECIPE 35.2

Approximate values per tuile:

Calories	14
Total fat	1 g
Saturated fat	0.5 g
Cholesterol	3 mg
Sodium	13 mg
Total carbohydrates	1 g
Protein	0 g

Decorating Plates with Sauces

The sauce is an integral part of most any dish: It adds flavour and moisture; it also adds colour, texture and flow to the plate. A rich, glossy bordelaise or Madeira sauce pooled beneath sautéed tournedos of beef is a classic example. A chunky salsa of tomatoes, papaya and pineapple beside a juicy piece of grilled salmon is a more contemporary approach.

Sauces are also used in other, less traditional ways to add visual appeal. For example, if using a vinaigrette dressing for grilled foods, let the oil and vinegar separate and pool on the plate, creating the interesting effect illustrated here.

One or more coloured sauces can also be used to paint plates. One technique is simply to drizzle or splatter the sauce onto the plate.

Alternatively, one or more coloured sauces can be applied to a plate using squirt bottles to create abstract patterns or representational designs. Painting plates with different-coloured sauces also facilitates flow and adds colour. Although this technique can be used with hot sauces, it is more often used with cold sauces (such as vanilla, caramel, chocolate and fruit-flavoured ones) for dessert presentations. The sauces must be thick enough to hold the pattern once it is created and they should all be of the same viscosity.

Grilled Quail with Balsamic Raspberries

Basic Procedure for Painting a Design with Sauces

1. Apply the sauces to the plate in parallel lines of alternating colours.

2. Carefully pull a toothpick through the sauces, perpendicular to the parallel lines in the sauces.

Basic Procedure for Painting a Spider Web Design

 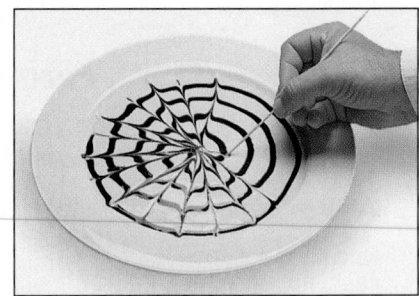

1. Pool one sauce evenly across the entire base of the plate, then apply a contrasting sauce onto the base sauce in a spiral.

2. Draw a thin-bladed knife or a toothpick through the sauces from the centre point towards the edge. Then, leaving a 1.2-cm (1/2-inch) space along the edge, draw a knife blade or toothpick from the edge to the centre.

Other patterns can be produced by squirting the sauces onto the plate in different patterns or by pulling the knife or toothpick through the sauces in different directions. As shown to the left, a circle of chocolate-sauce dots in a pool of vanilla sauce is pulled to create a leaf wreath.

*C*ONCLUSION

Although the techniques described in this chapter—as well as many other ones—can be used to create a variety of effects, often the most elegant plates are those with the simplest designs. Thoughtful presentation improves the appeal and appearance of any food as well as the completed plate, but it cannot mask poor-quality, poorly prepared or bland-tasting foods.

QUESTIONS FOR DISCUSSION

1. Explain why proper service and presentation are important in food service operations.
2. Distinguish between cutting and moulding foods for visual appeal and creating garnishes out of foods.
3. How can the selection of service ware such as bowls and platters affect the visual appeal of the foods served?
4. List and describe four techniques for garnishing plates.
5. Describe how colour, texture, shape and arrangement can be used to create a well-balanced plate composition.

WEBLINKS

Learn2 Set a Table—Intro
  learn2.com/06/0608/0608.html
Garnishing Tools & Gadgets
  www.chef-harvey.com/tools/toolink.htm
Napkin Folding Tips
  www.ywh.com/Tips/Napkin/napkins.html
Presentation
  www.amazon.com/exec/obidos/tg/feature/-/31216/104-7588097-1174306
Flowers
  www.garnishclub.com/edible_flowers.htm

MEASUREMENT AND CONVERSION CHARTS

MEASUREMENT CONVERSION CHART

Formulas for Exact Measures				Rounded Measures for Quick Reference		
	When you know:	Multiply by:	To find:			
Mass	ounces	28.35	grams	1 oz.		= 30 g
(Weight)	pounds	0.45	kilograms	4 oz.		= 120 g
	grams	0.035	ounces	8 oz.		= 225 g
	kilograms	2.2	pounds	16 oz.	= 1 lb.	= 450 g
				32 oz.	= 2 lb.	= 900 g
				36 oz.	= 2-1/4 lb.	= 1000 g (1 kg)
Volume	teaspoons	5.0	millilitres	1/4 tsp.	= 1/24 oz.	= 1 ml
(Capacity)	tablespoons	15.0	millilitres	1/2 tsp.	= 1/12 oz.	= 2 ml
	fluid ounces	29.57	millilitres	1 tsp.	= 1/6 oz.	= 5 ml
	cups	0.24	litres	1 Tbsp.	= 1/2 oz.	= 15 ml
	pints	0.47	litres	1 c.	= 8 oz.	= 250 ml
	quarts	0.95	litres	2 c. (1 pt.)	= 16 oz.	= 500 ml
	gallons	3.785	litres	4 c. (1 qt.)	= 32 oz.	= 1 lt
	millilitres	0.034	fluid ounces	4 qt. (1 gal.)	= 128 oz.	= 3-3/4 lt
Temperature	Fahrenheit	5/9 (after subtracting 32)	Celsius	32°F	= 0°C	
	Celsius	9/5 (then add 32)	Fahrenheit	122°F	= 50°C	
				212°F	= 100°C	

CONVERSION GUIDELINES

1 gallon	=	4 quarts
		8 pints
		16 cups (8 ounces)
		128 ounces
1 fifth bottle	=	approximately 1-1/2 pints or exactly 26.5 ounces
1 measuring cup	=	8 ounces (a coffee cup is generally 6 ounces)
1 large egg white	=	1 ounce (average)
1 lemon	=	1 to 1-1/4 ounces of juice
1 orange	=	3 to 3-1/2 ounces of juice

SCOOP SIZES

Scoop Measure	Level Measure
6	2/3 cup
8	1/2 cup
10	2/5 cup
12	1/3 cup
16	1/4 cup
20	3-1/5 tablespoons
24	2-2/3 tablespoons
30	2-1/5 tablespoons
40	1-3/5 tablespoons

The number scoop determines the number of servings in each quart of a mixture, for example, with a No. 16 scoop, one quart of mixture will yield 16 servings.

LADLE SIZES

Size	Portion of a Cup	Number per Quart	Number per Litre
1 oz.	1/8	32	34
2 oz.	1/4	16	17
2-2/3 oz.	1/3	12	13
4 oz.	1/2	8	8.6
6 oz.	3/4	5-1/3	5.7

CANNED GOOD SIZES

Size	No. of Cans per Case	Average Weight	Average No. Cups per Can
No. 1/2	8	8 oz.	1
No. 1 tall (also known as 303)	2 & 4 doz.	16 oz.	2
No. 2	2 doz.	20 oz.	2-1/2
No. 2-1/2	2 doz.	28 oz.	3-1/2
No. 3	2 doz.	33 oz.	4
No. 3 cylinder	1 doz.	51 oz.	5-2/3
No. 5	1 doz.	3 lb. 8 oz.	5-1/2
No. 10	6	6 lb. 10 oz.	13

REFERENCES AND RECOMMENDED READING

GENERAL INTEREST

Bickel, Walter, ed. and trans. *Hering's Dictionary of Classical and Modern Cookery*. 12th Eng. ed. London: Virtue & Company Limited, 1991.

Culinary Institute of America. *The New Professional Chef*. 5th ed. New York: Van Nostrand Reinhold, 1991.

Dawson, Hannelore. *Great Food for Great Numbers*. New York: Van Nostrand Reinhold, 1991.

Escoffier, Auguste. *Le Guide culinaire*. (Translation entitled *The Escoffier Cookbook and Guide to the Fine Art of Cookery for Connoisseurs, Chefs, Epicures*). New York: Crown Publishers, 1969.

Gisslen, Wayne. *Professional Baking*. New York: John Wiley & Sons, Inc., 1985.

———. *Professional Cooking*. 2nd ed. New York: John Wiley & Sons, Inc., 1989.

The Grand Masters of the French Cuisine. Selected and adapted by Celine Vence and Robert Courtine. New York: G.P. Putnam & Sons, 1978.

Haines, Robert G. *Food Preparation*. Homewood, Ill.: American Technical Publishers, Inc., 1988.

Lang, Jennifer Harvey, ed. *Larousse Gastronomique*. American ed. New York: Crown Publishers, Inc., 1988.

Leith, Prue. *The Cook's Handbook*. New York: A & W Publishers, Inc., 1981.

Pauli, Eugen, *Classical Cooking the Modern Way*. 2nd ed. New York: Van Nostrand Reinhold, 1989.

Pepin, Jacques. *The Art of Cooking*. New York: Alfred A. Knopf, 1987.

———. *La Technique*. New York: Wallaby/Pocket Books, 1976.

Rombauer, Irma von Starkloff and Marion Rombauer Becker. *Joy of Cooking*. New York: The Bobbs-Merrill Co., Inc., Macmillan, 1975.

Shugart, Grace and Mary Molt. *Food for Fifty*. 9th ed. New York: Macmillan, 1993.

Willan, Anne. *La Varenne Pratique*. New York: Crown Publishers, 1989.

FOOD HISTORY

Clair, Colin. *Kitchen & Table: A Bedside History of Eating in the Western World*. New York: Abelard-Schuman Limited, 1965.

Fussell, Betty. *The Story of Corn*. New York: Borzoi Books, Alfred A. Knopf, Inc., 1992.

Hale, William Harlan, and The Editors of Horizon Magazine. *The Horizon Cookbook and Illustrated History of Eating and Drinking Through the Ages*. New York: American Heritage Publishing Co., Inc., 1968.

Mintz, Sidney W. *Sweetness and Power: The Place of Sugar in Modern History*. New York: Penguin Books, 1985.

Montagné, P., and Dr. Gottschalk. *Larousse Gastronomique*. Eds. Nina Froud and Charlotte Turgeon. London: The Hamlyn Publishing Group Ltd., 1974.

Norman, Barbara. *Tales of the Table: A History of Western Cuisine*. Englewood Cliffs, N.J.: Prentice-Hall, 1972.

Revel, Jean-François. *Culture and Cuisine*. (Trans. of *Un Festin en paroles*.) New York: Da Capo Press, Inc., 1982.

Rupp, Rececca. *Blue Corn and Square Tomatoes*. Pownal, Vt.: Garden Way Publishing, 1987.

Schremp, Gerry. *Kitchen Culture: Fifty Years of Food Fads*. New York: Pharos Books, A Scripps Howard Co., 1991.

Shapiro, Laura. *Perfection Salad: Women and Cooking at the Turn of the Century*. New York: Farrar, Straus and Giroux, 1986.

Tannahill, Reay. *Food in History*. New York: Crown Publishers, Inc., 1988.

Toussaint-Samat, Maguelonne. *A History of Food.* Translated by Anthea Bell. Cambridge, Mass.: Blackwell Publishers, 1992.

Wheaton, Barbara Ketcham. *Savoring the Past.* Philadelphia: The University of Pennsylvania Press, 1983.

Willan, Anne. *Great Cooks and Their Recipes: From Taillevent to Escoffier.* Boston: Little, Brown and Co., A Bulfinch Press Book, 1992.

SANITATION AND SAFETY

Canadian Restaurant and Food Services Association publications.

———. *ServSafe: Serving Safe Food.* Workbooks and videos. Distributed in Canada by Kostuch Publications Ltd., Toronto. The Educational Foundation of the National Restaurant Association. *Applied Foodservice Sanitation: A Foundation Textbook.* 4th ed. John Wiley & Sons, Inc., 1992.

Guthrie, Rufus K. *Food Sanitation.* 3d ed. New York: Van Nostrand Reinhold, 1988.

National Assessment Institute. *Handbook for Safe Food Service Management.* Englewood Cliffs, N.J.: Regents/Prentice Hall, 1994.

Southern Alberta Institute of Technology and Calgary Regional Health Authority. *Food Safety and Sanitation Modules.* SAIT, 1998.

NUTRITION

Brody, Jane E. *Jane Brody's Nutrition Book.* New York: Bantam Books, Inc., 1982.

Freyberg, Nicholas, and Willis A. Gortner. *The Food Additives Book.* New York: Bantam Books, Inc., 1982.

Hamilton, Eva Mae Nunnelley, Eleanor Noss Whitney, and Frances Sienkiewicz Sizer. *Nutrition: Concepts and Controversies.* 4th ed. St. Paul, Minn.: West Publishing Co., 1988.

Netzer, Corinne T. *The Corinne T. Netzer Encyclopedia of Food Values.* New York: Dell Publishing, 1992.

Spiller, Gene. *The Super Pyramid Eating Program: Introducing the Revolutionary Five New Food Groups.* New York: Times Books, Random House, Inc., 1993.

FOOD COSTING AND MENU PRICING

Coltman, Michael M. *Financial Control for Your Foodservice Operation.* New York: Van Nostrand Reinhold, 1991.

Keister, Douglas C. *Food and Beverage Control.* 2nd ed. Englewood Cliffs, N.J.: Prentice Hall, 1990.

McVety, Paul J., and Bradley J. Ware. *Fundamentals of Menu Planning.* New York: Van Nostrand Reinhold, 1989.

Miller, Jack E. *Menu Pricing and Strategy.* 2nd ed. New York: Van Nostrand Reinhold, 1987.

Schmidt, Arno. *Chef's Book of Formulas, Yields, and Sizes.* New York: Van Nostrand Reinhold, 1990.

TOOLS

Bridge, Fred, and Jean F. Tibbetts. *The Well-Tooled Kitchen.* New York: William Morrow and Co., 1991.

GENERAL INGREDIENTS

DeMers, John. *The Community Kitchens Complete Guide to Gourmet Coffee.* New York: Simon & Schuster, 1986.

Dowell, Philip, and Adrian Bailey. *Cook's Ingredients.* New York: William Morrow and Co., 1980.

Jordan, Michele Anna. *The Good Cook's Book of Oil & Vinegar.* Reading, Mass.: Addison-Wesley, 1992.

Norman, Jill. *The Complete Book of Spices.* American ed. New York: Viking Studio Books, 1991.

Ortiz, Elisabeth Lambert. *The Encyclopedia of Herbs, Spices and Flavorings.* 1st American ed. New York: Dorling Kindersley, Inc., 1992.

Schapira, Joel, and Karl Schapira. *The Book of Coffee and Tea.* New York: St. Martin's Press, 1975.

Schuler, Stanley, ed. *Simon & Schuster's Guide to Herbs and Spices.* New York: Fireside and Simon & Schuster, 1990.

Stobart, Tom. *Herbs, Spices and Flavorings.* Woodstock, N.Y.: The Overland Press, 1982.

EGGS, DAIRY AND CHEESE

Dairy Farmers of Canada. *Fundamentals of Canadian Cheeses and Their Use in Fine Cuisine.* Montreal: Les Éditions de la Chenelière Inc., 1992.

Eggcyclopedia. 2nd ed. Park Ridge, Ill.: American Egg Board, revised 1989.

Jones, Evan. *The World of Cheese.* New York: Alfred A. Knopf, 1984.

Marquis, Vivienne, and Patricia Haskell. *The Cheese Book.* New York: Simon & Schuster, 1985.

FOOD SCIENCE

Freeland-Graves, H., and Gladys C. Peckham. *Foundations of Food Preparation.* 5th ed. New York: Macmillan, 1987.

McGee, Harold. *On Food and Cooking.* New York: Charles Scribner's Sons, 1984.

McWilliams, Margaret. *Food Fundamentals.* 4th ed. New York: Macmillan, 1985.

Potter, Norman N. *Food Science.* 4th ed. Westport, Conn.: The AVI Publishing Co. Inc., 1986.

STOCKS, SAUCES AND SOUPS

Clayton, Bernard. *The Complete Book of Soups and Stews.* New York: Simon & Schuster, 1984.

Davis, Deidre. *A Fresh Look at Saucing Foods.* Reading, Mass.: Addison-Wesley, 1993.

Larousse, David Paul. *The Sauce Bible: Guide to the Saucier's Craft.* New York: John Wiley & Sons, Inc., 1993.

Peterson, James. *Sauces: Classical and Contemporary Sauce Making.* New York: Van Nostrand Reinhold, 1991.

Sokolov, Raymond A. *The Saucier's Apprentice.* New York: Alfred A. Knopf, 1976.

MEAT

Libby, James A. *Meat Hygiene.* Philadelphia: Lea & Febiger, 1975.

The Meat Buyers Guide. Reston, Va.: National Association of Meat Purveyors, 1990.

Thomas, John R., and P. Thomas Ziegler. *The Meat We Eat.* Danville, Ill.: Interstate Printers & Publishers, Inc., 1985.

The Editors of Time-Life Books. *The Good Cook: Lamb.* London: Time Life International (Nederland) B.V., 1981.

The Editors of Time-Life Books. *The Good Cook: Beef and Veal.* London: Time Life International (Nederland) B.V., 1978.

POULTRY

The Editors of Time-Life Books. *The Good Cook: Poultry.* London: Time Life International (Nederland) B.V., 1978.

GAME

Cameron, Angus, and Judith Jones. *The L.L. Bean Game and Fish Cookbook.* New York: Random House, 1983.

Little, Carolyn. *The Game Cookbook.* Wiltshire, England: The Crowood Press, 1988.

Marrone, Teresa. *Dressing and Cooking Wild Game.* New York: Prentice Hall Press, 1987.

FISH AND SHELLFISH

Cronin, Isaac, Jay Harlow, and Paul Johnson. *The California Seafood Cookbook.* Berkeley, Calif.: Harris Publishing Co., Inc. (Aris Books), 1983.

The Fish List: FDA Guide to Acceptable Market Names for Food Fish Sold in Interstate Commerce. Washington, D.C.: U.S. Government Printing Office, 1988.

Howarth, A. Jan. *The Complete Fish Cookbook.* New York: St. Martin's Press, 1983.

King, Shirley. *Fish, The Basics.* New York: Simon & Schuster, 1990.

———. *Saucing the Fish.* New York: Simon & Schuster, 1976.

Loomis, Susan Herrmann. *The Great American Seafood Cookbook.* New York: Workman Publishing, 1988.

McClane, A. J. *The Encyclopedia of Fish Cookery.* New York: Holt, Rinehart and Winston, 1977.

The Seafood Handbook: Seafood Standards. Rockland, Maine: Seafood Business Magazine, 1991.

CHARCUTERIE

Ehlert, Friedrich W., et al. *Pâtés and Terrines.* Reprint. London: Hearst Books, 1990.

Grigson, Jane. *The Art of Charcuterie.* Reprint. New York: The Echo Press, 1991.

Sonnenschmidt and Nicolas. *The Art of Garde Manger.* 4th ed. New York: Van Nostrand Reinhold, 1988.

The Editors of Time-Life Books. *The Good Cook: Terrines, Pâtés and Galantines.* London: Time Life International (Nederland) B.V., 1981.

VEGETABLES AND FRUITS

Andrews, Jean. *Peppers: The Domesticated Capsicums.* Austin, Tex.: University of Texas Press, 1984.

Bauer, Cathy, and Juel Andersen. *The Tofu Cookbook.* Emmaus, Pa.: Rodale Press, 1979.

Beck, Bruce. *Produce: A Fruit and Vegetable Lovers' Guide.* New York: Friendly Press, 1984.

Brennan, Georgeanne, Isaac Cronin, and Charlotte Glenn. *The New American Vegetable Cookbook.* Berkeley, Calif.: Harris Publishing Co., 1985.

Brown, Marlene. *International Produce Cookbook and Guide.* Los Angeles: HP Books, 1989.

Davidson, Alan. *Fruit: A Connoisseur's Guide and Cookbook.* New York: Simon & Schuster, 1991.

DeWitt, Dave, and Nancy Gerlach. *The Whole Chile Pepper Book.* Boston: Little, Brown and Co., 1990.

Holthaus, Fusako. *Tofu Cookery.* Tokyo: Kodansha International, 1992.

Miller, Mark, with John Harrisson. *The Great Chile Book.* Berkeley, Calif.: Ten Speed Press, 1991.

Murdich, Jack. *Buying Produce.* New York: William Morrow and Co., 1986.

Payne, Rolce Redard, and Dorrit Speyer Senior. *Cooking With Fruit.* New York: Crown Publishers, Inc., 1992.

Schmidt, Jimmy. *Cooking For All Seasons.* New York: Macmillan, 1991.

Schneider, Elizabeth. *Uncommon Fruits and Vegetables: A Commonsense Guide.* New York: Harper & Row, 1986.

GRAINS AND PASTA

Bugialli, Giuliano. *On Pasta.* New York: Simon & Schuster, 1988.

Della Croce, Julia. *Pasta Classica.* San Francisco: Chronicle Books, 1987.

Gelles, Carol. *The Complete Whole Grain Cookbook.* New York: Donald I. Fine, Inc., 1989.

Greene, Bert. *The Grains Cookbook.* New York: Workman Publishing, 1988.

Kummer, Corby. "Pasta." *The Atlantic,* 258, no. 1 (July 1986): 35–47.

Leblang, Bonnie Tandy, and Joanne Lamb Hayes. *Rice.* New York: Harmony Books, 1991.

Scott, Marisa Luisa, and Jack Denton Scott. *Rice*. New York: Times Books, 1985.

Spier, Carol. *Food Essentials: Grains and Pasta*. New York: Crescent Books, 1993.

SALADS AND SALAD DRESSINGS

Blair, Eulalia. C. *Salads for Foodservice Menu Planning*. New York: Van Nostrand Reinhold, 1988.

Idone, Christopher. *Christopher Idone's Salad Days*. New York: Random House, 1989.

Muller, Veronika. *Salads*. New York: Van Nostrand Reinhold, 1989.

Nathan, Amy. *Salad*. San Francisco: Chronicle Books, 1985.

BREADS

Albright, Barbara, and Leslie Weiner. *Mostly Muffins*. New York: St. Martin's Press, 1984.

Alston, Elizabeth. *Biscuits and Scones*. New York: Clarkson N. Potter, Inc., 1988.

Amendola, Joseph. *The Bakers' Manual*. 4th ed. New York: Van Nostrand Reinhold, 1993.

Clayton, Bernard. *Bernard Clayton's New Complete Book of Breads*. Rev. ed. New York: Simon & Schuster, 1987.

Cunningham, Marion. *The Fannie Farmer Baking Book*. New York: Alfred A. Knopf, 1984.

David, Elizabeth. *English Bread and Yeast Cookery*. Notes by Karen Hess. American ed. New York: The Viking Press, 1980.

Jones, Judith, and Evan Jones. *The Book of Bread*. New York: Harper & Row, 1982.

Ortiz, Joe. *The Village Baker: Classic Regional Breads from Europe and America*. Berkeley, Calif.: Ten Speed Press, 1993.

Weiner, Leslie, and Barbara Albright. *Simply Scones*. New York: St. Martin's Press, 1988.

PASTRIES AND DESSERTS

Bernachon, Maurice, and Jean-Jacques Bernachon. *A Passion for Chocolate*. Translated and adapted for the American kitchen by Rose Levy Beranbaum. New York: William Morrow and Co., Inc., 1989.

Braker, Flo. *The Simple Art of Perfect Baking*. Shelburne, Vt.: Chapters Publishing, Ltd., 1992.

Fletcher, Helen S. *The New Pastry Cook*. New York: William Morrow and Co., Inc., 1986.

Friberg, Bo. *The Professional Pastry Chef*. 2nd ed. New York: Van Nostrand Reinhold, 1990.

Healy, Bruce, and Paul Bugat. *Mastering the Art of French Pastry*. Woodbury, N.Y.: Barron's, 1984.

Hyman, Philip, and Mary Hyman, trans. *The Best of Gaston Lenotre's Desserts*. Woodbury, N.Y.: Barron's, 1983.

London, Sheryl, and Mel London. *Fresh Fruit Desserts: Classic and Contemporary*. New York: Prentice Hall Press, 1990.

Purdy, Susan G. *A Piece of Cake*. New York: Macmillan, 1989.

Roux, Michel, and Albert Roux. *The Roux Brothers on Pâtisserie*. New York: Prentice Hall Press, 1986.

Silverton, Nancy. *Desserts by Nancy Silverton*. New York: Harper & Row, 1986.

Sultan, William J. *The Pastry Chef*. New York: Van Nostrand Reinhold, 1983.

Sultan, William J. *Practical Baking*. 5th ed. New York: Van Nostrand Reinhold, 1990.

MEAL SERVICE

Alston, Elizabeth. *Breakfast with Friends: Seasonal Menus to Celebrate the Morning*. New York: McGraw-Hill, 1989.

Bristow, Linda Kay. *Bread and Breakfast*. San Ramon, Calif.: 101 Productions, 1985.

Janericco, Terence. *The Book of Great Hors d'Oeuvre*. New York: Van Nostrand Reinhold, 1990.

Kolpas, Norman. *Breakfast and Brunch Book*. Los Angeles: HP Books, 1988.

Kotschevar, Lendal H. *Short Order Cooking*. New York: Van Nostrand Reinhold, 1990.

INTERNATIONAL CUISINES

Bayless, Rick, with Deann Groen Bayless. *Authentic Mexican: Regional Cooking from the Heart of Mexico*. New York: William Morrow and Co., Inc., 1987.

Bugialli, Giuliano. *The Fine Art of Italian Cooking*. New York: Random House, 1990.

Casas, Penelope. *The Foods and Wines of Spain*. New York: Alfred A. Knopf, 1991.

Curnonsky [Maurice Edmond Sailland]. *Traditional French Cooking*. Translation of *Cuisine et vins de France*, English ed. Jeni Wright. New York: Doubleday, 1989.

Devi, Yamuna. *The Art of Indian Vegetarian Cooking*. New York: E.P. Dutton, 1987.

Downer, Lesley. *At the Japanese Table*. San Francisco: Chronicle Books, 1993.

Efrain, Martinez. *Classic Spanish Cooking with Chef Ef*. Los Angeles: Lowell House, 1993.

Field, Carol. *Celebrating Italy*. New York: William Morrow & Co., Inc., 1990.

Gin, Maggie. *Regional Cooking of China*. San Francisco: 101 Productions, 1984.

Grigson, Jane. *Jane Grigson's Book of European Cookery*. New York: Atheneum, 1983.

Hazan, Marcella. *Essentials of Classic Italian Cooking*. New York: Alfred A. Knopf, 1993.

Jaffrey, Madhur. *An Invitation to Indian Cooking*. New York: Vintage Books, 1973.

———. *A Taste of India.* New York: Atheneum, 1986.

Kasper, Lynn Rossetto. *The Splendid Table: Recipes from Emilia-Romagna the Heartland of Northern Italian Food.* New York: William Morrow & Co., Inc., 1992.

Kennedy, Diana. *The Cuisines of Mexico.* Rev. ed. New York: Harper & Row, 1986.

Lo, Kenneth. *The Encyclopedia of Chinese Cooking.* New York: Bristol Books, 1979.

McDermott, Nancie. *Real Thai: The Best of Thailand's Regional Cooking.* San Francisco: Chronicle Books, 1992.

Olaore, Ola. *Traditional African Cooking.* London: Foulsham & Company Ltd., 1990.

Randelman, Mary Urrutia, and Joan Schwartz. *Memories of a Cuban Kitchen.* New York: Macmillan, 1992.

Richie, Donald. *A Taste of Japan.* New York: Kodansha, 1985.

Roden, Claudia. *A Book of Middle Eastern Food.* New York: Vintage Books, 1972.

Rojas-Lombardi, Felipe. *The Art of South American Cooking.* New York: HarperCollins, 1991.

Rose, Evelyn. *The New Complete International Jewish Cookbook.* New York: Carroll & Graf Publishers, Inc., 1992.

Routhier, Nicole. *The Foods of Vietnam.* New York: Stewart, Tabori & Chang, 1989.

Rozin, Elisabeth. *Ethnic Cuisine: The Flavor-Principle Cookbook.* Lexington, Mass.: S. Green Press, 1983. Reprint. New York: Penguin Books USA Inc., Viking Penguin, 1992.

Sandler, Bea. *The African Cookbook.* New York: World Publishing, 1970.

Scharfenberg, Horst. *The Cuisines of Germany: Regional Specialties and Traditional Home Cooking.* New York: Poseidon Press, 1980.

Solomon, Charmaine. *The Complete Asian Cookbook.* New York: McGraw-Hill, 1976.

———. *Charmaine Solomon's Thai Cookbook.* Rutland, Vt.: Charles E. Tuttle Co., 1991.

Toomre, Joyce. *Classic Russian Cooking: Elena Molokhovets' A Gift to Young Housewives.* Translated, introduced, and annotated by Joyce Toomre. Bloomington, Ind.: Indiana University Press, 1992.

Volokh, Anne, with Mavis Manus. *The Art of Russian Cuisine.* New York: Collier Books, 1983.

Von Bremzen, Anya, and John Welchman. *Please To The Table: The Russian Cookbook.* New York: Workman Publishing Co., 1990.

Wolfert, Paula. *Couscous and Other Good Food from Morocco.* New York: Harper & Row, 1973.

PRESENTATION AND GARNISHING

Budgen, June. *The Book of Garnishes.* Los Angeles: HP Books, 1986.

Grotz, Peter. *Successful Cold Buffets.* New York: Van Nostrand Reinhold, 1990.

Haydock, Robert, and Yukiko Haydock. *Japanese Garnishes.* New York: Holt, Rinehart and Winston, 1980.

Larousse, David Paul. *Edible Art: Forty-Eight Garnishes for the Professional.* New York: Van Nostrand Reinhold, 1987.

Lynch, Francis Talyn. *Garnishing: A Feast for Your Eyes.* Los Angeles: HP Books, 1987.

BOOKS BY CONTRIBUTING CHEFS

Ash, John, and Sid Goldstein. *American Game Cooking.* Reading, Mass.: Addison-Wesley (Aris Books), 1991.

Beranbaum, Rose Levy. *The Cake Bible.* New York: William Morrow and Co., Inc., 1988.

Carpenter, Hugh, and Teri Sandison. *Chopstix: Quick Cooking with Pacific Flavors.* New York: Stewart, Tabori & Chang, 1990.

Golden, Harris. *Golden's Kitchen: The Artistry of Cooking and Dining on the Light Side.* Rev. 2nd ed. Phoenix, Ariz.: Quail Run Books, 1989.

Kerr, Graham. *Graham Kerr's Minimax Cookbook.* New York: Doubleday, 1992.

Malgieri, Nick. *Nick Malgieri's Perfect Pastry.* New York: Macmillan, 1989.

Medrich, Alice. *Cocolat.* New York: Warner Books, 1990.

Milliken, Mary Sue, and Susan Feniger. *City Cuisine.* New York: William Morris and Co., Inc., 1989.

Miller, Mark. *Coyote Cafe.* Berkeley, Calif.: Ten Speed Press, 1989.

Puck, Wolfgang. *Adventures in the Kitchen: 175 New Recipes from Spago, Chinois on Main, Postrio and Eureka.* New York: Random House, 1991.

———. *The Wolfgang Puck Cookbook.* New York: Random House, 1986.

Richard, Michel. *Michel Richard's Home Cooking with a French Accent.* New York: William Morrow and Co., Inc., 1993.

Roberts, Michael. *Secret Ingredients.* New York: Bantam Books, 1988.

Somerville, Annie. *Fields of Greens: New Vegetarian Recipes from the Celebrated Greens Restaurant.* New York: Bantam Books, 1993.

Tropp, Barbara. *China Moon Cookbook.* New York: Workman Publishing Co., 1992.

GLOSSARY

Acid—foods such as citrus juice, vinegar and wine that have a sour or sharp flavour (most foods are slightly acidic); acids have a pH of less than 7.

Acidulation—the process of adding an acid (citrus, acetic or ascorbic) to a liquid. Retards browning of fruit and vegetables, firms proteins and cellulose.

Additives—substances added to foods to prevent spoilage or to improve appearance, texture, taste or nutritional value.

Aerobes—bacteria that thrive on oxygen.

Aging—(1) the period of time during which freshly killed meat is allowed to rest so the effects of rigor mortis dissipate; (2) the period during which freshly milled flour is allowed to rest so it will whiten and produce less sticky doughs; the aging of flour can be chemically accelerated.

Airline breast—a boneless chicken breast with the first wing bone attached.

À la carte—(1) a menu on which each food and beverage is listed and priced separately; (2) foods cooked to order as opposed to foods cooked in advance and held for later service.

Albumen—the principal protein found in egg whites.

Al dente—(ahl den-tay) cooked foods (usually vegetables and pasta) that are prepared firm to the bite, not soft or mushy.

Alkali—also known as a base, any substance with a pH higher than 7; baking soda is one of the few alkaline foods.

Alkaloid—a number of bitter organic substances with alkaline properties; found most often in plants and sometimes used in drugs.

Allemande—(ah-luh-mahnd) a sauce made by adding lemon juice and a liaison to a velouté made from veal or chicken stock; used to make several derivative sauces of the velouté family.

Allumette—(al-u-met) (1) a matchstick cut 3 mm × 3 mm × 5–6 cm (1/8 inch × 1/8 inch × 2–2-1/2 inches) long; usually used for potatoes; (2) a strip of puff pastry with a sweet or savoury filling.

American service—restaurant service where the waiter takes the orders and brings the food to the table; the food is placed on dishes (plated) in the kitchen, making it a relatively fast method for seated service.

Amino acid—the basic molecular component of proteins; each of the approximately two dozen amino acids contain oxygen, hydrogen, carbon and nitrogen atoms.

Anaerobes—bacteria that are able to live and grow without the presence of oxygen.

Animal husbandry—the business, science and practice of raising domesticated animals.

Anterior—at or towards the front of an object or place; opposite of *posterior*.

Appetizers—also known as first courses, usually small portions of hot or cold foods intended to whet the appetite in anticipation of the more substantial courses to follow.

Aquafarming—also known as aquaculture, the business, science and practice of raising large quantities of fish and shellfish in tanks, ponds or ocean pens.

Aromatic—a food added to a preparation to enhance flavour and aroma; includes herbs and spices as well as some vegetables.

Aspic or aspic jelly—a clear jelly usually made from a clarified stock thickened with gelatin; used to coat foods, especially charcuterie items, and for garnish.

As-purchased (A.P.)—the condition or cost of an item as it is purchased or received from the supplier.

Au gratin—(ah graw-ton) foods with a browned or crusted top; often made by browning a food with a bread crumb, cheese and/or sauce topping under a broiler or salamander.

Au jus—(ah zhew) roasted meats, poultry or game served with their natural, unthickened juices.

Au sec—(ah sec) cooked until nearly dry.

Backfat—fresh pork fat from the back of the pig, used primarily for barding.

Bacteria—single-celled microorganisms, some of which can cause diseases, including food-borne diseases.

Bain marie—(bane mah-ree) (1) a hot water bath used to gently cook food or keep cooked food hot; (2) a container for holding food in a hot water bath.

Baking—a dry-heat cooking method in which foods are surrounded by hot, dry air in a closed environment; similar to roasting, the term *baking* is usually applied to breads, pastries, vegetables and fish.

Baking powder—a mixture of sodium bicarbonate and one or more acids, generally cream of tartar and/or sodium aluminum sulphate, used to leaven baked goods; it releases carbon dioxide gas if moisture is present in a formula. *Single-acting baking powder* releases carbon dioxide gas in the presence of moisture only; *double-acting baking powder* releases some carbon dioxide gas upon contact with moisture, more gas is released when heat is applied.

Baking soda—sodium bicarbonate, an alkaline compound that releases carbon dioxide gas when combined with an acid and moisture; used to leaven baked goods.

Ballotine—(bahl-lo-teen) similar to a galantine, it is usually made by stuffing a deboned poultry leg with forcemeat; it is then poached or braised and normally served hot.

Barbecue—(1) to cook foods over dry heat created by the burning of hardwood or hardwood charcoals; (2) a tangy tomato- or vinegar-based sauce used for grilled foods; (3) foods cooked by this method and/or with this sauce.

Barding—tying thin slices of fat, such as bacon or pork backfat, over meats or poultry that have little to no natural fat covering in order to protect and moisten them during roasting.

Basic sauces—also known as mother or leading sauces; the foundation for the entire classic repertoire of hot sauces; the five leading sauces (béchamel, velouté, espagnole [also known as brown], tomato and hollandaise) are distinguished by the liquids and thickeners used to make them. They can be seasoned and garnished to create a wide variety of derivative sauces.

Basting—moistening foods during cooking (usually roasting, broiling or grilling) with melted fat, pan drippings, sauce or other liquids to prevent drying and to add flavour.

Batonnet—(bah-toh-nah) foods cut into matchstick shapes of 6 mm × 6 mm × 5–6 cm (1/4 inch × 1/4 inch × 2–2-1/2 inches).

Batter—(1) a semiliquid mixture containing flour or other starch used to make cakes and breads. The gluten development is minimized and the liquid forms the continuous medium in which other ingredients are disbursed; generally contains more fat, sugar and liquids than a dough; (2) a semiliquid mixture of liquid and starch used to coat foods for deep-fat frying.

Baumé scale—(boh-may) see **Hydrometer**.

Bavarian cream—a sweet dessert mixture made by thickening custard sauce with gelatin and then folding in whipped cream; the final product is poured into a mold and chilled until firm.

Beard—a clump of dark threads found on a mussel.

Béarnaise—(bare-naze) a sauce made of butter and egg yolks and flavoured with a reduction of vinegar, shallots, tarragon and peppercorns.

Beating—a mixing method in which foods are vigorously agitated to incorporate air or develop gluten; a spoon or electric mixer with its paddle attachment is used.

Béchamel—(bay-shah-mell) a leading sauce made by thickening milk with a white roux and adding seasonings.

Beef—the meat of domesticated cattle.

Beefalo—the product of crossbreeding a bison (North American buffalo) and a domestic beef animal.

Berry—(1) the kernel of certain grains such as wheat; (2) a small, juicy fruit that grows on vines and bushes.

Beurre blanc—(burr blanhk) (Fr. for white butter) an emulsified butter sauce made from shallots, white wine and butter.

Beurre composé—(burr kom-poz-a) see **Compound butter**.

Beurre manié—(burr man-yay) a combination of equal amounts by weight of flour and soft, whole butter; it is whisked into a simmering sauce at the end of the cooking process for quick thickening and added sheen and flavour.

Beurre noir—(burr nwar) (Fr. for black butter) whole butter heated until dark brown; sometimes flavoured with vinegar.

Beurre noisette—(burr nwah-zett) whole butter heated until it turns light brown, giving off a nutty aroma.

Beurre rouge—(burr rooge) (Fr. for red butter) an emulsified butter sauce made from shallots, red wine and butter.

Bilateral—symmetrical halves arranged along a central axis.

Biological hazard—a danger to the safety of food from disease-causing microorganisms such as bacteria, molds, yeasts, viruses or fungi.

Biscuit method—a mixing method used to make biscuits, scones and flaky doughs; it involves cutting cold fat into the flour and other dry ingredients before any liquid is added.

Bisque—(bisk) a soup made from shellfish; classic versions are thickened with rice.

Bivalves—mollusks such as clams, oysters and mussels that have two bilateral shells attached at a central hinge.

Blanching—very briefly and partially cooking a food in boiling water or hot fat; usually used to assist preparation (for example, to loosen peels from vegetables), as part of a combination cooking method, to remove undesirable flavours or to prepare a food for freezing.

Blanquette—(blang-kett) a white stew made of a white sauce and meat or poultry that is simmered without first browning.

Blending—a mixing method in which two or more ingredients are combined just until they are evenly distributed; a spoon, rubber spatula, whisk or electric mixer with its paddle attachment is used.

Blown sugar—a boiled mixture of sucrose, glucose and tartaric acid coloured and shaped using an air pump; used to make fruits and containers.

Boiling—a moist-heat cooking method that uses convection to transfer heat from a hot (approximately 100°C/212°F) liquid to the food submerged in it; the turbulent waters and higher temperatures cook foods more quickly than do poaching or simmering.

Bordelaise—(bor-da-lays) a brown sauce flavoured with a reduction of red wine, shallots, pepper and herbs and garnished with marrow.

Bouchées—(boo-shays) small puff pastry shells often filled with a savoury mixture and used for hors d'oeuvre.

Bound salad—a salad composed of cooked meats, poultry, fish, shellfish, pasta or potatoes combined with a dressing.

Bouquet garni—(boo-kay gar-nee) a selection of herbs (usually fresh) and vegetables tied into a bundle with twine and used to flavour stocks, sauces, soups and stews.

Bouquetière—(buk-a-tyer) a garnish (bouquet) of carefully cut and arranged fresh vegetables.

Braising—a combination cooking method in which foods are first browned in hot fat, then covered and slowly cooked in a small amount of liquid over low heat; braising uses a combination of simmering and steaming to transfer heat from the liquid (conduction) and the air (convection) to the foods.

Bran—the tough outer layer of a cereal grain and the part highest in fibre.

Brandy—an alcoholic beverage made by distilling the fermented mash of grapes or other fruits.

Brawn—also called an *aspic terrine*, made from simmered meats packed into a terrine and covered with aspic.

Brazier or **brasier**—a pan designed for braising; usually round with two handles and a tight-fitting lid.

Breading—(1) a coating of bread or cracker crumbs, cornmeal or other dry meal applied to foods that will typically be deep-fat fried or pan-fried; (2) the process of applying this coating.

Brigade—also known as the kitchen brigade, a system of staffing a kitchen so that each worker is assigned a set of specific tasks; these tasks are often related by cooking method, equipment or the type of foods being produced.

Brine—a mixture of salt, water and seasonings used to preserve foods.

Brioche—(bree-yohsh) a rich yeast bread containing large amounts of eggs and butter.

Brochettes—(bro-shetts) skewers, either small hors d'oeuvre or large entree size, threaded with meat, poultry, fish, shellfish and/or vegetables and grilled, broiled or baked; sometimes served with a dipping sauce.

Broiling—a dry-heat cooking method in which foods are cooked by heat radiating from an overhead source.

Broth—a flavourful liquid obtained from the long simmering of meats and/or vegetables.

Browning—see **Caramelization**.

Brown sauce—see **Espagnole**.

Brown stew—a stew in which the meat is first browned in hot fat.

Brown stock—a richly coloured stock made of chicken, veal, beef or game bones and vegetables, all of which are caramelized before they are simmered in water with seasonings.

Brunch—a late morning to early afternoon meal that takes the place of both breakfast and lunch; a brunch menu often offers breakfast foods as well as almost anything else.

Brunoise—(broo-nwah) (1) foods cut into cubes of 1–2 mm × 1–2 mm × 1–2 mm (1/16 inch × 1/16 inch × 1/16 inch); (2) foods garnished with vegetables cut in this manner.

Buffet service—diners generally serve themselves foods arranged on a counter or table or are served by workers assigned to specific areas of the buffet. Usually buffet service–style restaurants charge by the meal; restaurants offering

buffet service that charge by the dish are known as cafeterias.

Butcher—(1) to slaughter and dress or fabricate animals for consumption; (2) the person who slaughters and fabricates animals.

Butler service—the use of servers to pass foods (typically hors d'oeuvre) or drinks arranged on trays.

Buttercream—a light, smooth, fluffy frosting of sugar, fat and flavourings; egg yolks or whipped egg whites are sometimes added. There are three principal kinds: simple, Italian and French.

Butterflying—slicing boneless meat, fish or shrimp nearly in half lengthwise so they spread open like a book; used to increase surface area and speed cooking.

Cafeteria—see **Buffet service**.

Caffeine—an alkaloid found in coffee beans, tea leaves and cocoa beans that acts as a stimulant.

Cake—in North American usage, refers to a broad range of pastries including layer cakes, coffeecakes and gâteaux; can refer to almost anything that is baked, tender, sweet and sometimes frosted.

Calf—a young cow or bull.

Calorie—the unit of energy measured by the amount of heat required to raise 1000 grams of water one degree Celsius; it is also written as kilocalorie or kcal and is used as a measure of food energy.

Canada's Food Guide to Healthy Eating—a dietary guide published by Health Canada that prioritizes and proportions food choices among food groups and promotes nutritious eating.

Canapé—(kahn-ah-pay) tiny open-faced sandwich served as an hors d'oeuvre; usually composed of a small piece of bread or toast topped with a savoury spread and garnish.

Canning—a preservation method in which the food is sealed in a glass or metal container and subjected to high temperatures for a specific period of time in order to destroy microorganisms that cause spoilage; the sealed environment eliminates oxidation and retards decomposition.

Capon—(kay-pahn) the class of surgically castrated male chickens; they have well-flavoured meat and soft, smooth skin.

Capsaicin—(kap-say-ih-sin) an alkaloid found in a chile pepper's placental ribs that provides the pepper's heat.

Caramelization—the process of cooking sugars; the browning of sugar enhances the flavour and appearance of foods.

Carbohydrates—a group of compounds composed of oxygen, hydrogen and carbon that supply the body with energy (4 calories per gram); carbohydrates are classified as *simple* (including certain sugars) and *complex* (including starches and fibre).

Carotenoid—a naturally occurring pigment that predominates in red and yellow vegetables such as carrots and red peppers.

Carryover cooking—the cooking that occurs after a food is removed from a heat source; it is accomplished by the residual heat in the food.

Cartilage—also known as *gristle*, a tough, whitish elastic connective tissue that helps give structure to an animal's body.

Carve—to cut cooked meat or poultry into portions.

Casings—membranes used to hold forcemeat for sausages; they can be natural animal intestines or manufactured from collagen extracted from cattle hides.

Casserole—(1) a heavy dish, usually ceramic, for baking foods; (2) foods baked in a casserole dish.

Caul fat—a fatty membrane from pig or sheep intestines; it resembles fine netting and is used to bard roasts and pâtés and to encase forcemeat for sausages.

Cellulose—a complex carbohydrate found in the cell wall of plants; it is edible but indigestible by humans.

Cephalopods—mollusks with a single, thin internal shell called a pen or cuttlebone, well-developed eyes, a number of arms that attach to the head and a saclike fin-bearing mantle; include squid and octopus.

Chafing dish—a metal dish with a heating unit (flame or electric) used to keep foods warm at tableside or during buffet service.

Chalazae cords—thick, twisted strands of egg white that anchor the yolk in place.

Charcuterie—the production of pâtés, terrines, galantines, sausages and similar foods.

Cheesecloth—a light, fine mesh gauze used to strain liquids and make sachets.

Chef de cuisine—also known simply as *chef*, the person responsible for all kitchen operations, developing menu items and setting the kitchen's tone and tempo.

Chef de partie—also known as *station chef*, produces the menu items under the direct supervision of the chef or sous-chef.

Chef's knife—an all-purpose knife used for chopping, slicing and mincing; its tapering blade is 20–35 cm long.

Chemical hazard—a danger to the safety of food caused by chemical substances, especially cleaning agents, pesticides and toxic metals.

Chemical leavening agents—see **Baking powder** and **Baking soda**; through chemical reactions between acids and bases, these products release gases used to leaven baked goods.

Chèvre—(shev-ruh) (Fr. for goat) generally refers to a cheese made from goat's milk.

Chiffonade—(cheh-fon-nahd) (1) to finely slice or shred leafy vegetables or herbs; (2) the finely cut leafy vegetables or herbs often used as a garnish or bedding.

Chile—pepper; a member of the *capsicum* plant family.

Chili—(1) the stewlike dish containing chiles; (2) a commercial spice powder containing a blend of seasonings.

Chilled—a food that has been refrigerated.

Chlorophyll—a naturally occurring pigment that predominates in green vegetables such as cabbage.

Cholesterol—a fatty substance found in foods derived from animal products and in the human body; it has been linked to heart disease.

Chop—(1) a cut of meat including part of the rib; (2) to cut an item into small pieces where uniformity of size and shape is neither feasible nor necessary.

Choux paste—also known as *éclair paste*, a soft dough that produces hollow baked products with crisp exteriors; used for making éclairs, cream puffs and savoury products.

Chowder—a hearty soup made from fish, shellfish and/or vegetables, usually containing milk and potatoes and often thickened with roux.

Chutney—a sweet-and-sour condiment made of fruits and/or vegetables cooked in vinegar with sugar and spices; some chutneys are reduced to a purée, while others retain recognizable pieces of their ingredients.

Cider—mildly fermented apple juice; nonalcoholic apple juice may also be labelled cider.

Citrus—fruits characterized by a thick rind, most of which is a bitter white pith (albedo) with a thin exterior layer of coloured skin (zest); their flesh is segmented, juicy and varies from bitter to tart to sweet.

Clarification—(1) the process of transforming a broth into a clear consommé by trapping impurities with a clearmeat consisting of the egg white protein albumen, ground meat, an acidic product, mirepoix and other ingredients; (2) the clearmeat used to clarify a broth.

Clarified butter—purified butterfat; the butter is melted and the water and milk solids are removed.

Classes—the subdivisions of poultry kinds based on the bird's age and tenderness.

Classic cuisine—a late 19th- and early 20th-century refinement and simplification of French *grande cuisine*. Classic (or classical) cuisine relies upon the thorough exploration of culinary principles and techniques and emphasizes the refined preparation and presentation of superb ingredients.

Clean—to remove visible dirt and soil.

Clearmeat—see **Clarification**.

Clear soups—unthickened soups including broths, consommés and broth-based soups.

Coagulation—the irreversible transformation of proteins from a liquid or semiliquid state to a drier, solid state; usually accomplished through the application of heat.

Cocoa butter—the fat found in cocoa beans and used in fine chocolates.

Coddled egg—whole shell egg immersed in hot water for 1 minute. When cracked the white will just show traces of setting.

Colander—a perforated bowl, with or without a base or legs, used to strain foods.

Collagen—a protein found in nearly all connective tissues; when cooked with moisture, it dissolves and changes into a soluble protein called gelatin.

Combination cooking methods—cooking methods, principally braising and stewing, that employ both dry-heat and moist-heat procedures.

Composed salad—a salad prepared by arranging each of the ingredients (the base, body, garnish and dressing) on individual plates in an artistic fashion.

Compound butter—also known as a *beurre composé*, a mixture of softened whole butter and flavourings used as a sauce or to flavour and colour other sauces.

Compound sauces—see **Derivative sauces**.

Concasser—(kon-kaas-say) to pound or chop coarsely; usually used for tomatoes or parsley.

Condiment—traditionally, any item added to a dish for flavour, including herbs, spices and vinegars; now also refers to cooked or prepared flavourings such as prepared mustards, relishes, bottled sauces or pickles.

Conduction—the transfer of heat from one item to another through direct contact.

Confit—meat or poultry (often lightly salt-cured) slowly cooked and preserved in its own fat and served hot.

Conical strainer—a cone-shaped strainer made of perforated metal.

Connective tissues—tissues found throughout an animal's body that hold together and support other tissues such as muscles.

Consommé—a rich stock or broth that has been clarified with clearmeat to remove impurities.

Contaminants—biological, chemical or physical substances that can be harmful when consumed in sufficient quantities.

Contamination—the presence, generally unintentional, of harmful organisms or substances.

Convection—the transfer of heat caused by the natural movement of molecules in a fluid (whether air, water or fat) from a warmer area to a cooler one. **Mechanical convection** is the movement of molecules caused by stirring.

Cookery—the art, practice or work of cooking.

Cookies—small, sweet, flat pastries; usually classified by preparation or makeup techniques as drop, icebox, bar, cutout, pressed and wafer.

Cooking—the transfer of energy from a heat source to a food; this energy alters the food's molecular structure, changing its texture, flavour, aroma and appearance.

Cooking medium—the air, fat, water or steam in which a food is cooked.

Coring—the process of removing the seeds or pit from a fruit or fruit-vegetable.

Cost of goods sold—the total cost of food items sold during a given period; calculated as beginning inventory plus purchases minus ending inventory.

Cost per portion—the cost of one serving; calculated as the total recipe cost divided by the number of portions produced from that recipe.

Coulis—(koo-lees) a sauce made from a purée of vegetables or fruit; may be hot or cold.

Count—the number of individual items in a given measure of weight or volume.

Court bouillon—(cort boo-yon) water simmered with vegetables, seasonings and an acidic product such as vinegar or wine; used for simmering or poaching fish, shellfish or vegetables.

Couscoussier—two bulbous pots, the top one has a perforated bottom and sits snugly on the bottom pot; used to cook couscous.

Cows—female cattle after their first calving, principally raised for milk and calf production.

Cream filling—a pie filling made of flavoured pastry cream thickened with cornstarch.

Creaming—a mixing method in which softened fat and sugar are vigorously combined to incorporate air; used for making some quick breads, cookies and high-fat cakes.

Creams—also known as crèmes, include light, fluffy or creamy-textured dessert foods made with whipped cream or whipped egg whites, such as Bavarian creams, chiffons, mousses and crème Chantilly.

Cream soup—a soup made from vegetables cooked in a liquid that is thickened with a starch and puréed; cream is then incorporated to add richness and flavour.

Crème anglaise—(crem ahn-glas) or *crème a l'anglaise*; see **Vanilla custard sauce**.

Crème caramel—(crem cah-rah-mel) like crème renversée and flan, a custard baked over a layer of caramelized sugar and inverted for service.

Crème Chantilly—(crem shan-tee) heavy cream whipped to soft peaks and flavoured with sugar and vanilla; used to garnish pastries or desserts or folded into cooled custard or pastry cream for fillings.

Crème Chiboust—(crem chee-boos) a pastry cream lightened by folding in Italian meringue.

Crème pâtissière—(crem pah-tees-syehr) see **Pastry cream**.

Crepe—(krayp) a thin, delicate unleavened griddlecake made with a very thin egg batter cooked in a very hot sauté pan; used in sweet and savoury preparations.

Critical control point—under the HACCP system, it is any step during the processing of a food when a mistake can result in the transmission, growth or survival of pathogenic bacteria.

Croissant—(krwah-san) a crescent-shaped roll made from a rich, rolled-in yeast dough.

Croquette—(crow-kett) a food that has been puréed or bound with a thick sauce (usually béchamel or velouté), made into small shapes, then breaded and deep-fat fried.

Cross-contamination—the transfer of bacteria or other contaminants from one food, work surface or equipment to another.

Croûte, en—(awn croot) a food encased in a bread or pastry crust.

Crouton—a bread or pastry garnish, usually toasted or sautéed until crisp.

Crudités—(croo-dee-tays) generally refers to raw or blanched vegetables served as an hors d'oeuvre and often accompanied by a dip.

Crustaceans—shellfish characterized by a hard outer skeleton or shell and jointed appendages; include lobsters, crabs and shrimp.

Cuisine—the ingredients, seasonings, cooking procedures and styles attributable to a particular group of people; the group can be defined by geography, history, ethnicity, politics, culture or religion.

Cuisson—(kwee-zon) the liquid used for shallow poaching.

Curdle—the separation of milk or egg mixtures into solid and liquid components; caused by overcooking, high heat or the presence of acids.

Curing salt—a mixture of salt and sodium nitrite that inhibits bacterial growth; used as a preservative, often for charcuterie items.

Custard—any liquid thickened by the coagulation of egg proteins; its consistency depends on the ratio of eggs to liquid and the type of liquid used. Custards can be baked in the oven or cooked in a bain marie or on the stove top.

Cutlet—a relatively thick boneless slice of meat.

Cutting—(1) reducing a food to smaller pieces; (2) a mixing method in which solid fat is incorporated into dry ingredients until only lumps of the desired size remain.

Cutting loss—the unavoidable and unrecoverable loss of food during fabrication; the loss is usually the result of food particles sticking to the cutting board or the evaporation of liquids.

Cuttlebone—also known as the pen, the single, thin internal shell of cephalopods.

Cycle menu—a menu that changes every day for a certain period and then repeats the same daily items in the same order (i.e., on a seven-day cycle, the same menu is used every Monday).

Dairy products—include cow's milk and foods produced from cow's milk such as butter, yogurt, sour cream and cheese.

Decline phase—a period during which bacteria die at an accelerated rate, also known as the *negative growth phase*.

Decoction—(1) boiling a food until its flavour is removed; (2) a procedure used for brewing coffee.

Decorator's icing—see **Royal icing**.

Deep-fat frying—a dry-heat cooking method using convection to transfer heat to a food submerged in hot fat; foods to be deep-fat fried are usually first coated in batter or breading.

Deglaze—to swirl or stir a liquid (usually wine or stock) in a sauté pan or other pan to dissolve cooked food particles remaining on the bottom; the resulting mixture often becomes the base for a sauce or jus.

Degrease—to skim the fat from the top of a liquid such as a sauce or stock.

Demi-glace—(deh-me glass) (Fr. for half-glaze) a mixture of half brown stock and half brown sauce reduced by half.

Derivative sauces—also known as compound or small sauces, they are made by adding one or more ingredients to a basic sauce and are grouped together into families based on their basic sauce. Some derivative sauces have a variety of uses; others are traditional accompaniments for specific foods.

Detrempe—(day-trup-eh) a paste made with flour and water during the first stage of preparing a pastry dough, especially rolled-in doughs.

Deveining—the process of removing a shrimp's digestive tract.

Devilled—meat, poultry or other food seasoned with mustard, vinegar and other spicy seasonings.

Diagonals—elongated or oval-shaped slices of cylindrical vegetables or fruits.

Dice—(1) to cut foods into cubes: 3 mm (1/8 inch) for small, 6 mm (1/4 inch) for medium and 12 mm (1/2 inch) for large; (2) the cubes of cut food.

Dietary fibre—see **Fibre**.

Dip—a thick, creamy sauce, served hot or cold, to accompany crudités, crackers, chips or other foods, especially as an hors d'oeuvre; dips are often based on sour cream, mayonnaise or cream cheese.

Direct contamination—the contamination of raw foods in their natural setting or habitat.

Docking—pricking small holes in an unbaked dough or crust to allow steam to escape and prevent the dough from rising when baked.

Dough—a mixture of flour and other ingredients used in baking; has a low moisture content and gluten forms the continuous medium into which other ingredients are embedded; it is often stiff enough to cut into shapes.

Drawn—a market form for fish in which the viscera is removed.

Dredging—coating a food with flour or finely ground crumbs; usually done prior to sautéing or frying or as the first step of the standardized breading procedure.

Dressed—(1) an animal carcass trimmed or otherwise prepared for consumption; (2) a market form for fish in which the viscera, gills, fins and scales are removed.

Drupes—see **Stone fruits**.

Dry-heat cooking methods—cooking methods, principally broiling, grilling, roasting and baking, sautéing, pan-frying and deep-fat frying, that use air or fat to transfer heat through conduction and convection; dry-heat cooking methods allow surface sugars to caramelize.

Drying—a preservation method in which the food's moisture content is dramatically reduced; drying changes the food's texture, flavour and appearance.

Duchesse potatoes—(duh-shees) a purée of cooked potatoes, butter and egg yolks, seasoned with salt, pepper and nutmeg; can be eaten as is or used to prepare several classic potato dishes.

Dumpling—any of a variety of small starchy products made from doughs or batters that are simmered or steamed; can be plain or filled.

Durum—a type of hard wheat milled into semolina flour, which is used for making pasta.

Duxelles—(duke-sell) a coarse paste made of finely chopped mushrooms sautéed with shallots in butter.

Edible portion (E.P.)—the amount of a food item available for consumption after trimming or fabrication.

Egg wash—a mixture of beaten eggs (whole eggs, yolks or whites) and a liquid, usually milk or water, used to coat doughs before baking to add sheen.

Elastin—a protein found in connective tissues, particularly ligaments and tendons, it often appears as the silver covering on meats known as *silverskin*; elastin does not dissolve when cooked.

Émincé—(eh-manss) a small, thin boneless piece of meat.

Emulsification—the process by which generally unmixable liquids, such as oil and water, are forced into a uniform distribution.

Emulsion—(1) a uniform mixture of two unmixable liquids; (2) flavouring oils such as orange and lemon, mixed into water with the aid of emulsifiers.

Endosperm—the largest part of a cereal grain and a source of protein and carbohydrates (starch); it is the part used primarily in milled products.

Entree—(ahn-tray) the main dish of a Canadian or American meal, usually meat, poultry, fish or shellfish accompanied by a vegetable and starch; in France it is the first course, served before the fish and meat courses.

Enzymatic browning—see **Acidulation**.

Enzyme—a protein that aids specific chemical reactions in plants and animals.

Escallop—(Fr. escalope) a thin, boneless slice of meat.

Espagnole—(ess-spah-nyol) also known as *brown sauce*, a basic sauce made of brown stock, mirepoix and tomatoes thickened with brown roux; often used to produce demi-glace.

Essential nutrients—nutrients that must be provided by food because the body cannot or does not produce them in sufficient quantities.

Etâmine—a conical strainer made of fine mesh, used for straining and puréeing foods.

Ethnic cuisine—generally, the cuisine of a group of people having a common cultural heritage, as opposed to the cuisine of a group of people bound together by geography or political factors.

Ethylene gas—a colourless, odourless hydrocarbon gas naturally emitted from fruits and fruit-vegetables that encourages ripening.

Evaporation—the process by which heated water molecules move faster and faster until the water turns to a gas (steam) and vaporizes; evaporation is responsible for the drying of foods during cooking.

Extracts—concentrated mixtures of ethyl alcohol and flavouring oils such as vanilla, almond and lemon.

Extrusion—the process of forcing pasta dough through perforated plates to create various shapes; pasta dough that is not extruded must be rolled and cut.

Fabricate—to cut a large item into smaller portions; often refers to the butchering of fish or shellfish.

Fabricated cuts—individual portions of meat cut from a subprimal.

Facultative bacteria—those that can adapt and will survive with or without oxygen.

Fancy—(1) fish that has been previously frozen; (2) a quality grade for fruits, especially canned or frozen.

Fatbloom—(1) a white, powdery layer that sometimes appears on chocolate if the cocoa butter separates.

Fats—(1) a group of compounds composed of oxygen, hydrogen and carbon atoms that supply the body with energy (9 calories per gram); fats are classified as saturated, monounsaturated or polyunsaturated; (2) the general term for butter, lard, shortening, oil and margarine used as cooking media or ingredients.

Fermentation—(1) the process by which yeast converts sugar into alcohol and carbon dioxide; (2) the period of time that yeast bread dough is left to rise.

Feuillettes—(fuh-yuh-lyeth) square, rectangular or diamond-shaped puff pastry boxes that can be filled with a sweet or savoury mixture.

Fibre—also known as *dietary fibre*, indigestible carbohydrates found in grains, fruits, and vegetables; fibre aids digestion.

FIFO (First In, First Out)—an inventory storage and utilization process in which the oldest product is always used first.

Filé—(fee-lay) a seasoning and thickening agent made from dried, ground sassafras leaves.

Filet, fillet—(fee-lay) (1) filet: the boneless tenderloin of meat; (2) fillet: the side of a fish removed intact, boneless or semi-boneless, with or without skin; (3) to cut such a piece.

Fish scaler—an inflexible, rasplike tool used to remove scales from fish.

Fish velouté—a velouté sauce made from fish stock.

Flambé—(flahm-bay) food served flaming; produced by igniting brandy, rum or other liquor.

Flash-frozen—food that has been frozen very rapidly using metal plates, extremely low temperatures or chemical solutions.

Flatfish—fish with asymmetrical, compressed bodies that swim in a horizontal position and have both eyes on the top of the head; include sole, flounder and halibut.

Flat icing—a white, glossy glaze used on danish pastries. Also called *water icing*.

Flavonoid—a naturally occurring pigment that predominates in red, purple and white vegetables such as cauliflower and red cabbage.

Flavouring—an item that adds a new taste to a food and alters its natural flavours; flavourings include herbs, spices, vinegars and condiments.

Fleuron—(floor-ahn) a crescent-shaped piece of puff pastry used as a garnish.

Flour—a powdery substance of varying degrees of fineness made by milling grains such as wheat, corn or rye.

Foie gras—(fwah grah) liver of specially fattened geese or ducks.

Fold—a measurement of the strength of vanilla extract.

Folding—a mixing method used to gently incorporate light, airy products into heavier ingredients (for example, mixing dry ingredients with whipped eggs).

Fond—(fahn) (1) Fr. for stock or base; (2) the concentrated juices, drippings and bits of food left in pans after foods are roasted or sautéed; used to flavour sauces made directly in the pans in which the foods were cooked.

Fondant—(fahn-dant) a sweet, thick opaque sugar paste commonly used for glazing pastries such as napoleons or making candies.

Fond lié—(fahn lee-ay) See **Jus lié**.

Food cost—the cost of the materials that go directly into the production of menu items.

Food cost percentage—the ratio of the cost of foods served to the food sales dollars during a given period.

Food danger zone—the temperature range of approximately 4–60°C (40–140°F), which is most favourable for bacterial growth.

Forcemeat—stuffing, often a preparation made from uncooked ground meats, poultry, fish or shellfish, seasoned and emulsified with fat; commonly prepared as country-style, basic and mousseline and used for pâtés, sausages and other charcuterie items.

Formula—a recipe; the term is most often used in the bakeshop.

Formula-fed veal—also known as milk-fed veal, it is the meat of calves fed only a nutrient-rich liquid and kept tethered in pens; this meat is whiter and more mildly flavoured than that of free-range calves.

Frangipane—(fran-juh-pahn) a sweet almond and egg filling cooked inside pastry.

Free-range chickens—chickens allowed to move freely and forage for food, as opposed to chickens raised in coops.

Free-range veal—the meat of calves that are allowed to roam freely and eat grasses and other natural foods; this

meat is pinker and more strongly flavoured than that of formula-fed calves.

Freezer burn—the surface dehydration and discoloration of food that results from moisture loss at below-freezing temperatures.

French service—restaurant service where one waiter (a captain) takes the order, does the tableside cooking and brings the drinks and food, the secondary or back waiter serves bread and water, clears each course, crumbs the table and serves the coffee.

Fresh—a food that is not and has never been frozen.

Fresh-frozen—a food that has been frozen while still fresh.

Fricassee—(frick-a-see) a white stew in which the meat is cooked in fat without browning before the liquid is added.

Frittata—(free-tah-ta) an open-faced omelette of Spanish-Italian heritage.

Frosting—also known as *icing*, a sweet decorative coating used as a filling between the layers or as a coating over the top and sides of a cake.

Fruit—refers to the edible organ that develops from the ovary of a flowering plant and contains one or more seeds (pips or pits).

Fruit-vegetables—foods such as avocados, eggplants, chile peppers and tomatoes that are botanically fruits but are most often prepared and served like vegetables.

Frying—a dry-heat cooking method in which foods are cooked in hot fat; includes sautéing and stir-frying, pan-frying and deep-fat frying.

Fumet—(foo-may) a stock made from fish bones or crustacean shells and vegetables simmered in a liquid with flavourings.

Fungi—a large group of plants ranging from single-celled organisms to giant mushrooms; the most common are molds and yeasts.

Galantine—similar to a ballotine, it is a charcuterie item made from a forcemeat of poultry, game or suckling pig; usually wrapped in the skin of the bird or animal and poached in an appropriate stock; often served cold, usually in aspic.

Game—birds and animals hunted for sport or food; many game birds and animals are now ranch-raised and commercially available.

Game hen—the class of young or immature progeny of Cornish chickens or of a Cornish chicken and White Rock chicken; they are small and very flavourful.

Ganache—(ga-nosh) a rich blend of chocolate and heavy cream and, optionally, flavourings, used as a pastry or candy filling or frosting.

Garde-manger—(gar mawn-zhay) (1) also known as the *pantry chef*, the cook in charge of cold food production, including salads and salad dressings, charcuterie items, cold appetizers and buffet items; (2) the work area where these foods are prepared.

Garnish—(1) food used as an attractive decoration; (2) a subsidiary food used to add flavour or character to the main ingredient in a dish (for example, noodles in chicken noodle soup).

Gastronomy—the art and science of eating well.

Gâteau—(ga-toe) (1) in North American usage, refers to any cake-type dessert; (2) in French usage, refers to various pastry items made with puff pastry, choux paste, short dough or sweet dough.

Gaufrette—a thin lattice or waffle-textured slice of vegetable cut on a mandoline or with a zigzag knife.

Gelatin—a tasteless, odourless protein extracted from bones, connective tissues and other animal parts; when dissolved in a hot liquid and then cooled, it forms a jellylike substance used as a thickener and stabilizer.

Gelatinization—the process by which starch granules are cooked. They absorb moisture when placed in a liquid and heated; as the moisture is absorbed, the product swells, softens and clarifies slightly.

Gelato—(jah-laht-to) an Italian-style ice cream that is denser than North American–style ice cream.

Genoise—(zhen-waahz) (1) a form of whipped-egg cake that uses whole eggs whipped with sugar; (2) a French sponge cake.

Germ—the smallest portion of a cereal grain and the only part that contains fat.

Giblets—the collective term for edible poultry viscera including gizzards, hearts, livers and necks.

Gizzard—a bird's second stomach.

Glaçage—browning or glazing a food, usually under a salamander or broiler.

Glace de poisson—(glahss duh pwah-sawng) a syrupy glaze made by reducing a fish stock.

Glace de viande—(glahss duh vee-awnd) a dark, syrupy meat glaze made by reducing a brown stock.

Glace de volaille—(glahss duh vo-lahy) a light brown, syrupy glaze made by reducing a chicken stock.

Glaze—(1) any shiny coating applied to food or created by browning; (2) the dramatic reduction and concentration of a stock; (3) a thin, flavoured coating poured or dripped onto a cake or pastry.

Gliaden—see **Gluten**.

Glucose—an important energy source for the body; also known as blood sugar.

Gluten—a tough elastic substance created when flour is moistened and mixed; it gives structure and strength to baked goods and is responsible for their volume, texture and appearance. The proteins necessary for gluten formation are glutenin and gliaden.

Glutenin—see **Gluten**.

Grading—a designation given by the Canadian Food Inspection Agency (CFIA) to indicate a food's overall quality; grade has no effect on nutritional value.

Grains—(1) grasses that bear edible seeds, including corn, rice and wheat; (2) the fruit (i.e., seed or kernel) of such grasses.

Gram—the basic unit of weight in the metric system; equal to approximately one-thirtieth of an ounce.

Grande cuisine—the rich, intricate and elaborate cuisine of the 18th- and 19th-century French aristocracy and upper classes. It is based upon the rational identification, development and adoption of strict culinary principles.

Grate—to cut a food into small, thin shreds by rubbing it against a serrated metal plate known as a grater.

Green meats—freshly slaughtered meats that have not had sufficient time to age and develop tenderness and flavour.

Gremolada—(greh-moa-lah-dah) an aromatic garnish of chopped parsley, garlic and lemon zest used for osso buco.

Grilling—a dry-heat cooking method in which foods are cooked by heat radiating from a source located below

the cooking surface; the heat can be generated by electricity or by burning gas, hardwood or hardwood charcoals.

Grind—to pulverize or reduce food to small particles using a mechanical grinder or food processor.

Grinding—a milling process in which grains are reduced to a powder; the powder can be of differing degrees of fineness or coarseness.

Gristle—see **Cartilage**.

Gum paste—a smooth dough of sugar and gelatin that can be coloured and used to make decorations, especially for pastries.

HACCP—see **Hazard Analysis Critical Control Points**.

Hanging—the practice of allowing eviscerated (drawn or gutted) game to age in a dry, well-ventilated place; hanging helps tenderize the flesh and strengthen its flavour.

Hazard Analysis Critical Control Points (HACCP)—a rigorous system of self-inspection used to manage and maintain sanitary conditions in all types of food service operations; it focuses on the flow of food through the food service facility to identify any point or step in preparation (known as a critical control point) where some action must be taken to prevent or minimize a risk or hazard.

Heifers—young cows; cows before their first calving.

Heimlich manoeuvre—the first-aid procedure for victims of choking in which sudden upward pressure is applied to the upper abdomen in order to force any foreign object from the windpipe.

Herbs—any of a large group of aromatic plants whose leaves, stems or flowers are used to add flavours to other foods.

High-ratio cake—a form of creamed-fat cake that uses emulsified shortening and has a two-stage mixing method.

Hollandaise—(holl-uhn-daze) an emulsified sauce made of butter, egg yolks and flavourings (especially lemon juice).

Homogenization—the process by which milk fat is prevented from separating out of milk products.

Hors d'oeuvre—(ohr durvs) very small portions of hot or cold foods served before the meal to stimulate the appetite.

Hotel pan—a rectangular, stainless steel pan with a lip allowing it to rest in a storage shelf or steam table; available in several standard sizes.

Hull—also known as the husk, the outer covering of a fruit, seed or grain.

Hybrid—the result of crossbreeding different species that are genetically not alike; it is often a unique product.

Hybrid menu—a menu combining features of a static menu with a cycle menu or a market menu of specials.

Hydrogenation—the process used to harden oils: Hydrogen atoms are added to unsaturated fat molecules, making them partially or completely saturated and thus solid at room temperature.

Hydrometer—a device used to measure specific gravity; it shows degrees of concentration on the Baumé scale.

Hygroscopic—the characteristic of a food to readily absorb moisture from the air.

Icing—see **Frosting**.

IMPS/NAMP/CMC—see **NAMP**.

Induction cooking—a cooking method that uses a special coil placed below the stove top's surface in combination with specially designed cookware to generate heat rapidly with an alternating magnetic field.

Infection—in the food safety context, a disease caused by the ingestion of live pathogenic bacteria that continue their life processes in the consumer's intestinal tract.

Infrared cooking—a heating method that uses an electric or ceramic element heated to such a high temperature that it gives off waves of radiant heat that cook the food.

Infusion—(1) the extraction of flavours from a food at a temperature below boiling; (2) a group of coffee-brewing techniques including steeping, filtering and dripping; (3) the liquid resulting from this process.

Instant-read thermometer—a thermometer used to measure the internal temperature of foods; the stem is inserted in the food, producing an instant temperature readout.

Intoxication—in the food safety context, a disease caused by the toxins that bacteria produce during their life processes.

Inventory—the listing and counting of all foods in the kitchen, storerooms and refrigerators.

IQF (Individually Quick Frozen)—the technique of rapidly freezing each individual item of food such as slices of fruit, berries or pieces of fish before packaging; IQF foods are not packaged with syrup or sauce.

Irradiation—a preservation method used in the United States and other countries for certain fruits, vegetables and grains in which ionizing radiation sterilizes the food, slows ripening and prevents sprouting; irradiation has little effect on the food's texture, flavour or appearance; Canada does not currently allow irradiation foods. Labelling is not required in Canada.

Jam—a fruit gel made from fruit pulp and sugar.

Jelly—a fruit gel made from fruit juice and sugar.

Juice—the liquid extracted from any fruit or vegetable.

Julienne—(ju-lee-en) (1) to cut foods into stick-shaped pieces, approximately 1–2 mm × 1–2 mm × 2.5–4 cm (1/16 inch × 1/16 inch × 1–2 inches); (2) the stick-shaped pieces of cut food.

Jus lié—(zhew lee-ay) also known as *fond lié*, a sauce made by thickening brown stock with cornstarch or similar starch; often used like a demi-glace, especially to produce derivative sauces.

Kinds—the nine categories of poultry recognized by Agriculture Canada: chicken, duck, goose, pheasant, quail, ostrich, guinea, pigeon and turkey. See also **Classes**.

Kitchen brigade—see **Brigade**.

Kneading—working a dough to develop gluten.

Kosher—prepared in accordance with Jewish dietary laws.

Lag phase—a period, usually following transfer from one place to another, during which bacteria do not experience much growth.

Lamb—the meat of sheep slaughtered under the age of one year.

Lard—the rendered fat of hogs.

Larding—inserting thin slices of fat, such as pork backfat, into low-fat meats in order to add moisture.

Lardon—bacon cut into 6 mm × 6 mm × 5 cm (1/4 inch x 1/4 inch x 2 inch) strips; used to moisten braised dishes and stews.

Leading sauces—see **Basic sauces**.

Lean doughs—yeast doughs that contain little or no sugar or fat; used for French or Italian breads.

Leavener—an ingredient or process that produces or incorporates gases in a baked product in order to increase volume, provide structure and give texture.

Lecithin—a natural emulsifier found in egg yolks.

Legumes—(lay-gyooms) (1) Fr. for vegetables; (2) a large group of vegetables with double-seamed seed pods; depending on the variety, the seeds, pod and seeds together, or the dried seeds are eaten.

Liaison—(lee-yeh-zon) a mixture of egg yolks and heavy cream used to thicken and enrich sauces.

Liqueur—a strong, sweet, syrupy alcoholic beverage made by mixing or redistilling neutral spirits with fruits, flowers, herbs, spices or other flavourings; also known as a *cordial*.

Liquor—an alcoholic beverage made by distilling grains, vegetables or other foods; includes rum, whisky and vodka.

Litre—the basic unit of volume in the metric system, equal to slightly more than a quart.

Log phase—a period of accelerated growth for bacteria.

Macaroni—(1) any dried pasta made with wheat flour and water; (2) in North American usage, an elbow-shaped pasta tube.

Macerate—to soak foods in a liquid, usually alcoholic, to soften them.

Macronutrients—the nutrients needed in large quantities: carbohydrates, proteins, fats and water.

Madeira—a Portuguese fortified wine heated during aging to give it a distinctive flavour and brown colour.

Maître d'hotel (maître d')—(may-tr doh-tel) (1) the leader of the dining room brigade, also known as the dining room manager, he oversees the dining room or "front of the house" staff; (2) a compound butter flavoured with chopped parsley and lemon juice.

Mandoline—a stainless steel, hand-operated slicing device with adjustable blades.

Marbling—whitish streaks of inter- and intramuscular fat.

Marinade—the liquid used to marinate foods; it generally contains herbs, spices and other flavouring ingredients as well as an acidic product such as wine, vinegar or lemon juice.

Marinate—to soak a food in a seasoned liquid in order to tenderize the food and add flavour to it.

Market menu—a menu based upon product availability during a specific time period; it is written to use foods when they are in peak season or readily available.

Marmalade—a citrus jelly that also contains unpeeled slices of citrus fruit.

Marsala—a flavourful fortified sweet-to-semidry Sicilian wine.

Marzipan—a paste of ground almonds, sugar and egg whites used to fill and decorate pastries.

Matzo—thin, crisp unleavened bread made only with flour and water; can be ground into meal that is used for matzo balls and pancakes.

Mayonnaise—a thick, creamy sauce consisting of oil and vinegar emulsified with egg yolks, usually used as a salad dressing.

Mealy potatoes—also known as *starchy potatoes*, those with a high starch content and thick skin; they are best for baking.

Medallion—a small, round, relatively thick slice of meat.

Melt—the process by which certain foods, especially those high in fat, gradually soften then liquefy when heated.

Menu—a list of foods and beverages available for purchase.

Meringue—(muh-reng) a foam made of beaten egg whites and sugar.

Metabolism—all of the chemical reactions and physical processes that continually occur in living cells and organisms.

Metre—the basic unit of length in the metric system, equal to slightly more than one yard.

Mezzaluna—a two-handled knife with one or more thick, crescent-shaped blades used to chop and mince herbs and vegetables.

Micronutrients—the nutrients needed only in small amounts: vitamins and minerals.

Microorganisms—single-celled organisms as well as tiny plants and animals that can be seen only through a microscope.

Microwave cooking—a heating method that uses radiation generated by a special oven to penetrate the food. It agitates water molecules, creating friction and heat; this energy then spreads throughout the food by conduction (and by convection in liquids).

Mignonette—a medallion of meat.

Milling—the process by which grain is ground into flour or meal.

Mince—to cut a food item into very small pieces.

Mineral—inorganic micronutrients necessary for regulating body functions and proper bone and teeth structures.

Mirepoix—(meer-pwa) a mixture of coarsely chopped onions, carrots and celery used to flavour stocks, stews and other foods; generally, a mixture of 50% onions, 25% carrots and 25% celery, by weight, is used.

Mirepoix bordelaise—a mirepoix with diced bacon or ham added. Often used with game or poultry.

Mise en place—(meez on plahs) (Fr. for putting in place) refers to the preparation and assembly of all necessary ingredients and equipment.

Mix—to combine ingredients in such a way that they are evenly dispersed.

Moist-heat cooking methods—cooking methods, principally simmering, poaching, boiling and steaming, that use water or steam to transfer heat through convection; moist-heat cooking methods are used to emphasize the natural flavours of foods.

Molding—the process of shaping foods, particularly grains and vegetables bound by sauces, into attractive, hard-edged shapes by using metal rings, circular cutters or other forms.

Molds—(1) algaelike fungi that form long filaments or strands; for the most part, molds affect only food appearance and flavour; (2) containers used for shaping foods.

Mollusks—shellfish characterized by a soft, unsegmented body, no internal skeleton and a hard outer shell.

Monounsaturated fats—see **Unsaturated fats**.

Monter au beurre—(mohn-tay ah burr) to finish a sauce by swirling or whisking in butter (raw or compound) until it is melted; used to give sauces shine, flavour and richness.

Mortar and pestle—a hard bowl (the mortar) in which foods such as spices are ground or pounded into a powder with a club-shaped tool (the pestle).

Mother sauces—(Fr. *sauce mère*) see **Basic sauces**.

Mousse—(moose) a soft, creamy food, either sweet or savoury, lightened by adding whipped cream, beaten egg whites or both.

Mousseline—(moose-uh-leen) (1) a delicately flavoured forcemeat based on white meat, fish or shellfish lightened with cream and egg whites; (2) a sauce or cream lightened by folding in whipped cream.

Muffin method—a mixing method used to make quick bread batters; it involves combining liquid fat with other liquid ingredients before adding them to the dry ingredients.

Muscles—animal tissues consisting of bundles of cells or fibres that can contract and expand; they are the portions of a carcass usually consumed.

Mushrooms—members of a broad category of plants known as fungi; they are often used and served like vegetables.

Mutton—the meat of sheep slaughtered after they reach the age of one year.

NAMP/IMPS/CMC—the United States Department of Agriculture publishes Institutional Meat Purchasing Specifications (IMPS); the IMPS are illustrated and described in *The Meat Buyers Guide* published by the National Association of Meat Purveyors (NAMP); the Canadian Meat Council (CMC) also publishes full-colour manuals that name and number cuts of meat.

Nappé—(nap) (1) the consistency of a liquid, usually a sauce, that will coat the back of a spoon; (2) to coat a food with sauce.

National cuisine—the characteristic cuisine of a nation.

Nectar—the diluted, sweetened juice of peaches, apricots, guavas, black currants or other fruits, the juice of which would be too thick or too tart to drink straight.

Noisette—(nwah-zet) (1) a small, usually round, portion of meat cut from the rib or loin; (2) Fr. for hazelnut.

Noodles—flat strips of pasta-type dough that contains eggs; may be fresh or dried.

Nouvelle cuisine—(Fr. for new cooking) a mid-20th-century movement away from many classic cuisine principles and towards a lighter cuisine based on natural flavours, shortened cooking times and innovative combinations.

Nut—(1) the edible single-seed kernel of a fruit surrounded by a hard shell; (2) generally refers to any seed or fruit with an edible kernel in a hard shell.

Nutrients—the chemical substances found in food that nourish the body by promoting growth, facilitating body functions and providing energy; there are six categories of nutrients: proteins, carbohydrates, fats, water, minerals and vitamins.

Nutrition—the science that studies nutrients.

Oblique cuts—also known as *roll cuts*; small pieces of food, usually vegetables, with two angle-cut sides.

Offal—also called *variety meats*; the edible entrails (for example, the heart, kidneys, liver, sweetbreads and tongue) and extremities (for example, oxtail and pig's feet) of an animal.

Oignon piqué—(ohn-nawng pee-kay) (Fr. for pricked onion) a bay leaf tacked with a clove to a peeled onion; used to flavour sauces and soups.

Oil—a type of fat that remains liquid at room temperature.

Onion brûlée—(ohn-nawng brew-lay) (Fr. for burnt onion) charred onion halves; used to flavour and colour stocks and sauces.

Organic farming—a method of farming that does not rely on synthetic pesticides, fungicides, herbicides or fertilizers.

Oven spring—the rapid rise of yeast goods in a hot oven, resulting from the production and expansion of trapped gases.

Paillard—(pahy-lahrd) a thin slice of meat pounded until thin; it is usually grilled.

Panada or **panade**—(1) something other than fat added to a forcemeat to enhance smoothness, aid emulsification or both; it is often béchamel, rice or crustless white bread soaked in milk; (2) a mixture for binding stuffings and dumplings, notably quenelles, often choux pastry, bread crumbs, frangipane, puréed potatoes or rice.

Pan-dressed—a market form for fish in which the viscera, gills and scales are removed and the fins and tail are trimmed.

Pan-frying—a dry-heat cooking method in which food is placed in a moderate amount of hot fat.

Pan gravy—a sauce made by deglazing pan drippings from roast meat or poultry and combining them with a roux or other starch and stock.

Papillote, en—(awn poppy-yote) a cooking method in which food is wrapped in paper or foil and then heated so that the food steams in its own moisture.

Parboiling—partially cooking a food in a boiling or simmering liquid; similar to blanching but the cooking time is longer.

Parchment (paper)—heat-resistant paper used throughout the kitchen for tasks such as lining baking pans, wrapping foods to be cooked en papillote and covering foods during shallow poaching.

Parcooking—partially cooking a food by any cooking method.

Paring knife—a short knife used for detail work, especially cutting fruits and vegetables; it has a rigid blade approximately 5–10 cm (2–4 inches) long.

Parstock or par—the amount of stock necessary to cover operating needs between deliveries.

Pasta—(1) an unleavened paste or dough made from wheat flour (often semolina), water and eggs; the dough can be coloured and flavoured with a wide variety of herbs, spices or other ingredients and cut or extruded into a wide variety of shapes and sizes; it can be fresh or dried and is boiled for service; (2) general term for any macaroni product or egg noodle.

Pasteurization—the process of heating a liquid to a prescribed temperature for a specific period of time in order to destroy pathogenic bacteria.

Pastillage—a paste made of sugar, cornstarch and gelatin; it may be cut or molded into decorative shapes.

Pastry cream—also known as *crème pâtissière*, a stirred custard made with egg yolks, sugar and milk and thickened with starch; used for pastry and pie fillings.

Pâte—(paht) Fr. for dough.

Pâté—(pah-tay) traditionally, a fine savoury meat filling wrapped in pastry, baked and served hot or cold as opposed to a terrine, which was a coarsely ground and highly seasoned

meat mixture baked in an earthenware mold and served cold; today the words pâté and terrine are generally used interchangeably.

Pâte au pâté—(paht ah pah-tay) a specially formulated pastry dough used for wrapping pâté when making pâté en croûte.

Pâte brisée—(paht bree-zay) a dough that produces a very flaky baked product containing little or no sugar; flaky dough is used for prebaked pie shells or pie top crusts; mealy dough is a less flaky product used for custard, cream or fruit pie crusts.

Pâte en croûte—(pah-tay awn croot) a pâté baked in pastry dough such as pâte au pâté.

Pâte feuilletée—see **Puff pastry**.

Pâte sucrée—(paht sew-kra) a dough containing sugar that produces a very rich, crisp (not flaky) baked product; also known as sweet dough, it is used for tart shells.

Pathogen—any organism that causes disease; usually refers to bacteria.

Pâtissier—(pah-tees-sir-yair) a pastry chef, the person responsible for all baked items, including breads, pastries and desserts.

Paupiette—(po-pee-et) thin slices of meat, poultry or fish spread with a savoury stuffing and rolled, then braised or poached.

Paysanne—(pahy-sahn) foods cut into flat squares of 12 mm × 12 mm × 3 mm (1/2 inch × 1/2 inch × 1/8 inch).

Pearling—a milling process in which all or part of the hull, bran and germ are removed from the grain.

Pectin—a gelatinlike carbohydrate obtained from certain fruits, used to thicken jams and jellies.

Persillade—(payr-se-yad) (1) a food served with or containing parsley; (2) a mixture of bread crumbs, parsley and garlic used to coat meats, usually lamb.

pH—a symbol for the level of acidity or alkalinity of a solution; expressed on a scale of 0 to 14.0, 7.0 is considered neutral or balanced; the lower the pH value, the more acidic the substance, the higher the pH value, the more alkaline the substance.

Phyllo—(fee-low) pastry dough made with very thin sheets of a flour and water mixture; several sheets are often layered with melted butter and used in sweet or savoury preparations.

Physical hazard—a danger to the safety of food caused by particles such as chips, metal shavings, bits of wood or other foreign matter.

Picked—refers to the crab or lobster meat removed from the shell with a fine, needle-like tool called a pick.

Pigment—any substance that gives colour to an item.

Pilaf—a cooking method for grains in which the grains are lightly sautéed in hot fat and then a hot liquid is added; the mixture is simmered without stirring until the liquid is absorbed.

Poaching—a moist-heat cooking method that uses convection to transfer heat from a hot (approximately 71–82°C/160–180°F) liquid to the food submerged in it.

Polyunsaturated fats—see **Unsaturated fats**.

Pomes—members of the Rosaceae family, they are tree fruits with a thin skin and firm flesh surrounding a central core containing many small seeds (called pips or carpels); include apples, pears and quince.

Pork—the meat of hogs usually slaughtered under the age of one year.

Posterior—at or towards the rear of an object or place; opposite of *anterior*.

Potentially hazardous foods—foods on which bacteria thrive.

Poultry—the collective term for domesticated birds bred for eating; they include chickens, ducks, geese, guineas, pigeons and turkeys.

Preserve—(1) a fruit gel that contains large pieces or whole fruits; (2) to extend the shelf life of a food by subjecting it to a process such as irradiation, canning, vacuum-packing, drying or freezing and/or by adding preservatives.

Primal cuts—the primary divisions of muscle, bone and connective tissue produced by the initial butchering of the carcass; primals are further broken down into smaller, more manageable cuts.

Prime cost—the combination of food costs and direct labour.

Prix fixe—(pree feks) (Fr. for fixed price) refers to a menu offering a complete meal for a set price, also known as *table d'hôte*.

Professional cooking—a system of cooking based upon the application of procedures to maintain the integrity of ingredients while providing wholesome and safe food.

Profiterole—(pro-feet-uh-roll) small round pastry made from choux paste filled with a savoury filling and served as an hors d'oeuvre or filled with ice cream and served as a dessert.

Proofing—the rise given shaped yeast products just prior to baking.

Proteins—a group of compounds composed of oxygen, hydrogen, carbon and nitrogen atoms necessary for manufacturing, maintaining and repairing body tissues and as an alternative source of energy (4 calories per gram); protein chains are constructed of various combinations of amino acids.

Puff pastry—also known as *pâte feuilletée*, it is a rolled-in dough used for pastries, cookies and savoury products; it produces a rich and buttery but not sweet baked product with hundreds of light, flaky layers.

Pulled sugar—a doughlike mixture of sucrose, glucose and tartaric acid that can be coloured and shaped by hand.

Pulses—dried seeds from a variety of legumes.

Pumpernickel—(1) coarsely ground rye flour; (2) bread made with this flour.

Purée—(pur-ray) (1) to process food to achieve a smooth pulp; (2) food that is processed by mashing, straining or fine chopping to achieve a smooth pulp.

Purée soup—a soup usually made from starchy vegetables or legumes; after the main ingredient is simmered in a liquid, the mixture, or a portion of it, is puréed.

Putrefactives—bacteria that spoil food without rendering it unfit for human consumption.

Quenelle—(cuh-nell) a small, dumpling-shaped portion of a mousseline forcemeat poached in an appropriately flavoured stock; it is shaped by using two spoons.

Quiche—a savoury tart or pie consisting of a custard baked in a pastry shell with a variety of flavourings and garnishes.

Quick bread—a bread, including loaves and muffins, leavened by chemical leaveners or steam rather than yeast.

Quinoa—an ancient staple grain with a high protein content, bead-like shape and delicate, almost bland flavour.

Radiation cooking—a heating process that does not require physical contact between the heat source and the food being cooked; instead, energy is transferred by waves of heat or light striking the food. Two kinds of radiant heat used in the kitchen are *infrared* and *microwave*.

Raft—formed during the clarification process from the clearmeat and impurities from the stock; it rises to the top of the simmering stock and releases additional flavours.

Ragout—(rah-goo) (1) traditionally, a well-seasoned, rich stew containing meat, vegetables and wine; (2) any stewed mixture.

Ramekin—a small, ovenproof dish, usually ceramic.

Rancidity—a chemical change in fats caused by exposure to air, light or heat that results in objectionable flavours and odours.

Recipe—a set of written instructions for producing a specific food or beverage; also known as a *formula*.

Recommended Daily Intake (RDI)—a standard for the daily intake of various nutrients established by Health Canada.

Recovery time—the length of time it takes hot fat to return to the desired cooking temperature after food is submerged in it.

Reduce—to cook a liquid mixture, often a sauce, until its quantity decreases because of evaporation; typically done to concentrate flavours and thicken liquids.

Refreshing—submerging a food in cold water to quickly cool it and prevent further cooking, also known as *shocking*; usually used for vegetables.

Regional cuisine—a set of recipes based on local ingredients, traditions and practices; within a larger geographical, political, cultural or social unit, regional cuisines are often variations of each other that blend together to create a national cuisine.

Relishes—cooked or pickled sauces usually made with vegetables or fruits and often used as a condiment.

Remouillage—(Fr. for rewetting) a stock produced by reusing the bones from another stock.

Render—(1) to melt and clarify fat; (2) to cook meats in order to remove the fat.

Ricer—a sieve-like utensil with small holes through which soft food is forced; it produces particles about the size of a grain of rice.

Rich doughs—yeast doughs such as those used for brioche and some multigrain breads that contain a significant amount of sugar and fat.

Rillette—(ree-yet) meat or poultry slowly cooked, mashed and preserved in its own fat and served cold and usually spread on toast.

Ripe—(1) fully grown and developed fruit; the fruit's flavour, texture and appearance are at their peak and the fruit is ready to eat; (2) an unpleasant odour indicating that a food, especially meat, poultry, fish or shellfish, may be past its prime.

Risotto—(re-zot-toe) (1) a cooking method for grains in which the grains are lightly sautéed in butter and then a liquid is gradually added; the mixture is simmered with near-constant stirring until the still-firm grains merge with the cooking liquid; (2) a Northern Italian rice dish prepared this way.

Roasting—a dry-heat cooking method that heats food by surrounding it with hot, dry air in a closed environment or on a spit over an open fire; similar to baking, the term roasting is usually applied to meats, poultry, game and vegetables.

Roe—(roh) fish eggs.

Roll cuts—see **Oblique cuts**.

Rolled-in dough—a dough in which a fat is incorporated in many layers by using a rolling and folding procedure; it is used for flaky baked goods such as croissants, puff pastry and danish.

Rondeau—(ron-doe) a shallow, wide, straight-sided pot with two loop handles.

Rondelles—(ron-dells) or rounds, disk-shaped slices of cylindrical vegetables or fruits.

Rotisserie—cooking equipment that slowly rotates meat or other foods in front of a heating element.

Roulade—(roo-lahd) (1) a slice of meat, poultry or fish rolled around a stuffing; (2) a filled and rolled spongecake.

Round fish—fish with round, oval or compressed bodies that swim in a vertical position and have eyes on both sides of their heads; include salmon, swordfish and cod.

Rounding—the process of shaping dough into smooth, round balls; used to stretch the outside layer of gluten into a smooth coating.

Roux—(roo) a cooked mixture of equal parts flour and fat, by weight, used as a thickener for sauces and other dishes; cooking the flour in fat coats the starch granules with the fat and prevents them from lumping together or forming lumps when introduced into a liquid.

Royal icing—also known as *decorator's icing*, an uncooked mixture of confectioner's sugar and egg whites that becomes hard and brittle when dry; used for making intricate cake decorations.

Russian service—restaurant service in which the entrée, vegetables and starches are served from a platter onto the diner's plate by a waiter.

Sabayon—(sa-by-on) also known as *zabaglione*, a foamy, stirred custard sauce made by whisking eggs, sugar and wine over low heat.

Sachet d'épices or **sachet**—(sah-shay day-pea-say) (Fr. for bag of spices) aromatic ingredients tied in a cheesecloth bag and used to flavour stocks and other foods; a standard sachet contains parsley stems, cracked peppercorns, dried thyme, bay leaf, cloves and, optionally, garlic.

Salad—a single food or a mix of different foods accompanied or bound by a dressing.

Salad dressing—a sauce for a salad; most are based on a vinaigrette, mayonnaise or other emulsified product.

Salad greens—a variety of leafy vegetables that are usually eaten raw.

Salamander—a small broiler used primarily for browning or glazing the tops of foods.

Salsa—(sahl-sah) (Sp. for sauce) (1) generally, a cold chunky mixture of fresh herbs, spices, fruits and/or vegetables used as a sauce for meat, poultry, fish or shellfish; (2) in Italian usage, a general term for pasta sauces.

Salt curing—the process of surrounding a food with salt or a mixture of salt, sugar, nitrite-based curing salt, herbs and spices; salt curing dehydrates the food, inhibits bacterial growth and adds flavour.

Sanitation—the creation and maintenance of conditions that will prevent food contamination or food-borne illness.

Sanitize—to reduce pathogenic organisms to safe levels, usually with heat or chemical disinfectants.

Sashimi—(sah-shee-mee) raw fish eaten without rice; usually served as the first course of a Japanese meal.

Saturated fats—fats found mainly in animal products and tropical oils; they are usually solid at room temperature, the body has more difficulty breaking down saturated fats than either mono-unsaturated or polyunsaturated fats.

Sauce—generally, a thickened liquid used to flavour and enhance other foods.

Sausage—a seasoned forcemeat usually stuffed into a casing; a sausage can be fresh, smoked and cooked, dried or hard.

Sautéing—(saw-tay-ing) a dry-heat cooking method that uses conduction to transfer heat from a hot pan to food with the aid of a small amount of hot fat; cooking is usually done quickly over high temperatures.

Sauteuse—(saw-toose) the basic sauté pan with sloping sides and a single long handle.

Sautoir—(saw-twahr) a sauté pan with straight sides and a single long handle.

Savoury—(1) spiced or seasoned, as opposed to sweet, foods; (2) a highly seasoned last course of a traditional English dinner.

Scald—to heat a liquid, usually milk, to just below the boiling point.

Score—to cut shallow gashes across the surface of a food before cooking.

Scoville Heat Units—a subjective rating for measuring a chile's heat; the sweet bell pepper usually rates 0, the Tabasco rates from 30 000 to 50 000 and the habañera rates from 100 000 to 300 000 units.

Seafood—an inconsistently used term encompassing some or all of the following: saltwater fish, freshwater fish, saltwater shellfish, freshwater shellfish, other edible marine life.

Sear—to brown food quickly over high heat; usually done as a preparatory step for combination cooking methods.

Season—(1) traditionally, to enhance flavour by adding salt; (2) more commonly, to enhance flavour by adding salt and/or pepper as well as herbs and spices; (3) to mature and bring a food (usually beef or game) to a proper condition by aging or special preparation; (4) to prepare a pot, pan or other cooking surface to prevent sticking.

Seasoning—traditionally, an item added to enhance the natural flavours of a food without dramatically changing its taste; salt is the most common seasoning although all herbs and spices are often referred to as seasonings.

Semi à la carte—a menu on which some foods (usually appetizers and desserts) and beverages are priced and ordered separately, while the entrée is accompanied by and priced to include other dishes such as a salad, starch or vegetable.

Semifreddi—(seh-mee-frayd-dee) also known as *still-frozen desserts*, made with frozen mousse, custard or cream into which large amounts of whipped cream or meringue are folded in order to incorporate air; layers of spongecake and/or fruits may be added for flavour and texture; includes frozen soufflés, marquis, mousses and neapolitans.

Semolina—see **Durum**.

Sfoglia—(sfo-glee-ah) a thin, flat sheet of pasta dough that can be cut into ribbons, circles, squares or other shapes.

Shallow poaching—a moist-heat cooking method that combines poaching and steaming; the food (usually fish) is placed on a vegetable bed and partially covered with a liquid (cuisson) and simmered.

Shellfish—aquatic invertebrates with shells or carapaces.

Sherbet—a frozen mixture of fruit juice or fruit purée and syrup that in the U.S. contains milk and/or egg yolks for creaminess.

Shocking—see **Refreshing**.

Shortening—(1) a white, flavourless, solid fat formulated for baking or deep-fat frying; (2) any fat used in baking to tenderize the product by shortening gluten strands.

Shred—to cut into thin but irregular strips.

Shuck—(1) a shell, pod or husk; (2) to remove the edible portion of a food (e.g., clam meat, pea and ear of corn) from its shell, pod or husk.

Side masking—the technique of coating only the sides of a cake with garnish.

Sift—(1) to shake a dry, powdered substance through a sieve or sifter to remove lumps and incorporate air; (2) to mix together powdery substances by sifting.

Silverskin—the tough connective tissue that surrounds certain muscles; see **Elastin**.

Simmering—(1) a moist-heat cooking method that uses convection to transfer

heat from a hot (approximately 85–96°C/185–205°F) liquid to the food submerged in it; (2) maintaining the temperature of a liquid just below the boiling point.

Skim—to remove fat and impurities from the surface of a liquid during cooking.

Slashing—cutting the top of a bread with a sharp knife to improve appearance and allow for continued rising and the escape of gases after the crust has formed.

Slice—to cut an item into relatively broad, thin pieces.

Slurry—a mixture of raw starch and cold liquid used for thickening.

Small sauces—see **Derivative sauces**.

Smoke point—the temperature at which a fat begins to break down and emit smoke.

Smoking—any of several methods for preserving and flavouring foods by exposing them to smoke, includes cold smoking (in which the foods are not fully cooked) and hot smoking (in which the foods are cooked). Pan smoking is used for smaller cuts.

Solid pack—canned fruits or vegetables with little or no water added.

Sorbet—(sore-bay) a frozen mixture of fruit juice or fruit purée and a light syrup or wine.

Soufflé—(soo-flay) either a sweet or savoury fluffy dish made with a custard base lightened with whipped egg whites and then baked; the whipped egg whites cause the dish to puff when baked.

Sous-chef—(soo-shef) a cook who supervises food production and who reports to the executive chef; he or she is second in command of a kitchen.

Specifications or specs—standard requirements to be followed in procuring items from suppliers.

Spices—any of a group of strongly flavoured or aromatic portions of plants (other than leaves) used as flavourings, condiments or aromatics.

Springform pan—a circular baking pan with a separate bottom and a side wall held together with a clamp that is released to free the baked product.

Spring lamb—the meat of sheep slaughtered before they have fed on grass or grains.

Spun sugar—a decoration made by flicking dark caramelized sugar rapidly

over a dowel to create long, fine, hairlike threads.

Squab—the class of young pigeon used in food service operations.

Staling—also known as *starch retrogradation*, a change in the distribution and location of water molecules within baked products; stale products are firmer, drier and more crumbly than fresh baked goods.

Standard breading procedure—the procedure for coating foods with crumbs or meal by passing the food through flour, then an egg wash and then the crumbs; it gives foods a relatively thick, crisp coating when deep-fat fried or pan-fried.

Standardized recipe—a recipe producing a known quality and quantity of food for a specific operation.

Staples—(1) certain foods regularly used throughout the kitchen; (2) certain foods, usually starches, that help form the basis for a regional or national cuisine and are principal components in the diet.

Starch—(1) complex carbohydrates from plants that are edible and either digestible or indigestible (fibre); (2) a rice, grain, pasta or potato accompaniment to a meal.

Starch retrogradation—see **Staling**.

Starchy potatoes—see **Mealy potatoes**.

Static menu—a menu offering patrons the same foods every day.

Station chef—the cook in charge of a particular department in a kitchen.

Steak—(1) a cross-section slice of a round fish with a small section of the bone attached; (2) a cut of meat, either with or without the bone.

Steamer—(1) a set of stacked pots with perforations in the bottom of each pot, they fit over a larger pot filled with boiling or simmering water and are used to steam foods; (2) a perforated insert made of metal or bamboo placed in a pot and used to steam foods; (3) a type of soft-shell clam from the east coast; (4) a piece of gas or electric equipment in which foods are steamed in a sealed chamber.

Steaming—a moist-heat cooking method in which heat is transferred from steam to the food being cooked by direct contact; the food to be steamed is placed in a basket or rack above a boiling liquid in a covered pan.

Steel—a tool, usually made of steel, used to hone or straighten knife blades.

Steep—to soak a food in a hot liquid in order to extract its flavour or impurities or to soften its texture.

Steers—male cattle castrated prior to maturity and principally raised for beef.

Sterilize—to destroy all living microorganisms.

Stewing—a combination cooking method similar to braising but generally involving smaller pieces of meat that are first blanched or browned, then cooked in a small amount of liquid that is served as a sauce.

Stir-frying—a dry-heat cooking method similar to sautéing in which foods are cooked over very high heat using little fat while stirring constantly and briskly; often done in a wok.

Stirring—a mixing method in which ingredients are gently mixed by hand until blended, usually with a spoon, whisk or rubber spatula.

Stock—(Fr. *fond*) a clear, unthickened liquid flavoured by soluble substances extracted from meat, poultry or fish and their bones as well as from a mirepoix, other vegetables and seasonings.

Stone fruits—members of the genus *Prunus* and also known as drupes, they are tree or shrub fruits with a thin skin, soft flesh and one woody stone or pit; include apricots, cherries, nectarines, peaches and plums.

Straight dough method—a mixing method for yeast breads in which all ingredients are simply combined and mixed.

Strain—to pour foods through a sieve, mesh strainer or cheesecloth to separate or remove the liquid component.

Streusel—(stroo-zel) a crumbly mixture of fat, flour, sugar and sometimes nuts and spices; used to top baked goods.

Subcutaneous fat—also known as *exterior fat*; the fat layer between the hide and muscles.

Submersion poaching—a poaching method in which the food is completely covered with the poaching liquid.

Subprimal cuts—the basic cuts produced from each primal.

Sucrose—the chemical name for refined or table sugar, it is refined from the raw sugars found in the large tropical grass called sugar cane and the root of the sugar beet; it is available as white or

brown granules, molasses or powdered sugar.

Sugar—a carbohydrate that provides the body with energy and gives a sweet taste to foods.

Sugar syrups—either simple syrups (thin mixtures of sugar and water) or cooked syrups (melted sugar cooked until it reaches a specific temperature).

Suprême—(su-prem) (1) a sauce made by adding cream to a velouté made from chicken stock; it is used to make several derivative sauces of the velouté family; (2) a boneless, skinless chicken breast with the first wing segment attached.

Sushi—(szu-she) cooked or raw fish or shellfish rolled in or served on seasoned rice.

Sweating—cooking a food (typically vegetables) in a small amount of fat, usually covered, over low heat without browning until the food softens and releases moisture; sweating allows the food to release its flavour more quickly when cooked with other foods.

Sweetbreads—the thymus glands of a calf or lamb.

Sweet dough—see **Pâte sucrée**.

Syrup—sugar that is dissolved in liquid, usually water, and often flavoured with spices or citrus zest.

Syrup pack—cans of fruits with a light, medium or heavy syrup added.

Table d'hôte—(tab-bluh dote) see **Prix fixe**.

Tang—the portion of a knife's blade that extends inside the handle.

Taproots—more commonly referred to as *roots*, includes edible single roots that extend deep into the ground to provide the above-ground plant with nutrients.

Tart—a sweet or savoury filling in a baked crust made in a shallow, straight-sided pan without a top crust.

Tartlet—a small, single-serving tart.

Temperature danger zone—the broad range of temperatures between 4°C and 60°C (40°F and 140°F) at which bacteria multiply rapidly.

Tempering—(1) heating gently and gradually; (2) refers to the process of slowly adding a hot liquid to eggs or other foods to raise their temperature without causing them to curdle; (3) refers to a process for melting chocolate.

Terrine—(1) traditionally, a loaf of coarse forcemeat cooked in a covered earthenware mold and without a crust; today, the word is used interchangeably

with pâté; (2) the mold used to cook such items, usually a rectangle or oval shape and made of ceramic.

Thickening agents—ingredients used to thicken sauces, include starches (flour, cornstarch and arrowroot), gelatin and liaisons.

Timbale—(tim-bull) (1) a small pail-shaped mold used to shape foods; (2) a preparation made in such a mold.

Tisanes—(teh-zahns) beverages made from herbal infusions that do not contain any tea.

Tomato concasser—peeled, seeded and diced tomato.

Tomato sauce—a basic sauce made from tomatoes, vegetables, seasonings and white stock; it may or may not be thickened with roux.

Toque—(toke) the tall white hat worn by chefs.

Torte—in Central and Eastern European usage, refers to a rich cake in which all or part of the flour is replaced with finely chopped nuts or bread crumbs.

Tossed salad—a salad prepared by placing the greens, garnishes and salad dressing in a large bowl and tossing to combine.

Tourner—(toor-nay) (Fr. for to turn), to cut foods, usually vegetables, into football-shaped pieces with seven equal sides and blunt ends.

Toxins—byproducts of living bacteria that can cause illness if consumed in sufficient quantities.

Tranche—(tranch) an angled slice cut from fish fillets.

Trim loss—the amount of a food item removed when preparing it for consumption.

Tripe—the edible lining of a cow's stomach.

Truffles—(1) flavourful tubers that grow near the roots of oak or beech trees; (2) rich chocolate candies made with ganache.

Truss—to tie poultry with butcher's twine into a compact shape for cooking.

Tube pan—a deep round baking pan with a hollow tube in the centre.

Tuber—the fleshy root, stem or rhizome of a plant from which a new plant will grow; some, such as potatoes, are eaten as vegetables.

Tunnelling—the holes that may form in baked goods as the result of overmixing.

Unit cost or **price**—the price paid to acquire one specified unit.

Univalves—single-shelled mollusks with a single muscular foot, such as abalone.

Unsaturated fats—fats that are normally liquid (oils) at room temperature; they may be *monounsaturated* (from plants such as olives and avocados) or *polyunsaturated* (from grains and seeds such as corn, soybeans and safflower as well as from fish).

Vanilla custard sauce—also known as *crème anglaise*, a stirred custard made with egg yolks, sugar and milk or half-and-half and flavoured with vanilla; served with or used in dessert preparations.

Vanillin—(1) whitish crystals of vanilla flavour that often develop on vanilla beans during storage; (2) synthetic vanilla flavouring.

Variety—the result of breeding plants of the same species that have different qualities or characteristics; the new plant often combines features from both parents.

Variety meats—see **Offal**.

Veal—Meat of bovine animals weighing under 160 kg hide off.

Vegetable—refers to any herbaceous plant (one with little or no woody tissue) that can be partially or wholly eaten; vegetables can be classified as cabbages, fruit-vegetables, gourds and squashes, greens, mushrooms and truffles, onions, pods and seeds, roots and tubers, and stalks.

Velouté—(veh-loo-tay) a basic sauce made by thickening a white stock (either fish, veal or chicken) with roux.

Venison—meat from any member of the deer family including elk, moose, reindeer, red-tailed deer, white-tailed deer and mule deer; it is typically a lean, dark red meat with a mild aroma.

Vent—(1) to allow circulation or escape of a liquid or gas; (2) to cool a pot of hot liquid by setting the pot on blocks in a cold water bath and allowing cold water to circulate around it.

Vinaigrette—(vin-nay-greht) a temporary emulsion of oil and vinegar (usually three parts oil to one part vinegar) seasoned with herbs, salt and pepper; used as a salad dressing or sauce. Also known as *basic French dressing*.

Vinegar—a thin, sour liquid used as a preservative, cooking ingredient and cleaning solution.

Viruses—the smallest known form of life; they invade the living cells of a host and take over those cells' genetic material, causing the cells to produce more viruses; some viruses can enter a host through the ingestion of food contaminated with those viruses.

Viscera—internal organs.

Vitamins—compounds present in foods in very small quantities; they do not provide energy but are essential for regulating body functions.

Vol-au-vent—(vul-oh-van) a large, deep puff pastry shell often filled with a savoury mixture for a main course.

Volume—the space occupied by a substance; volume measurements are commonly expressed as litres, tea-spoons, tablespoons, cups, pints and gallons.

Wash—a glaze applied to dough before baking; a commonly used wash is made with whole egg and water.

Water bath—see **Bain marie**.

Water pack—canned fruits with water or fruit juice added.

Waxy potatoes—those with a low starch content and thin skin; they are best for boiling.

Weight—the mass or heaviness of a substance; weight measurements are commonly expressed as kilograms, grams, ounces and pounds.

Wheel—(1) a large boneless piece of fish (such as swordfish or tuna) from which steaks are cut, also known as a centre cut; (2) a cylindrical-shaped cheese.

Whetstone—a dense, grained stone used to sharpen or hone a knife blade.

Whipping—a mixing method in which foods are vigorously beaten in order to incorporate air; a whisk or an electric mixer with its whip attachment is used.

White stew—see **Fricassee** and **Blanquette**.

White stock—a light-coloured stock made from chicken, veal, beef or fish bones simmered in water with vegetables and seasonings.

Whitewash—a thin mixture or slurry of flour and cold water used like cornstarch for thickening.

Wine—an alcoholic beverage made from the fermented juice of grapes; may be sparkling (effervescent) or still (noneffervescent) or fortified with additional alcohol.

Work section—see **Work station**.

Work station—a work area in the kitchen dedicated to a particular task, such as broiling or salad making; work stations using the same or similar equipment for related tasks are grouped together into *work sections*.

Yeasts—microscopic fungi whose metabolic processes are responsible for fermentation; they are used for leavening bread and in cheese, beer, and wine making.

Yield—(1) the total amount of a food item created or remaining after trimming or fabrication; (2) the total amount of a product made from a specific recipe.

Yield factor or percentage—the ratio of the edible portion to the amount purchased.

Zest—the thin, coloured part of a citrus peel.

Zushi—(zhoo-she) the seasoned rice used for sushi.

_I_NDEX

PHOTO CREDITS